Follow these steps to get the most out of reading and studying from *The American Promise*.

FOCUS WHILE YOU READ

Answer the review question after you read each major section.

Pay attention to section headings as you read.

Get the most out of the illustrations. Connect the photos, maps, and tables to what you're reading.

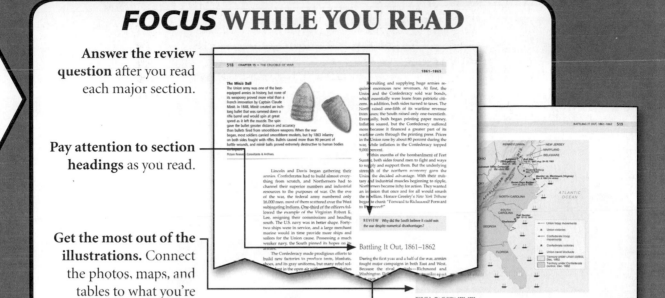

REVIEW AFTER YOU READ

Place the specifics in the big picture. History is not merely a list of facts and dates. Answer the **Review Questions** and **Making Connections** questions and see if you can refer to specific examples or supporting evidence from the chapter. This is a great way to practice for the test!

Review the list of Key Terms. Can you explain their significance? If not, flip back to the page number indicated and skim to refresh your memory.

Review the Timeline. Make sure you understand the relationships among events and their sequence. You should understand which major developments led to other major developments and why.

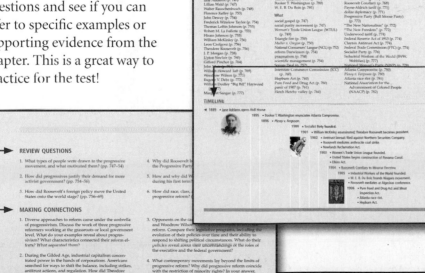

HENRY INMAN (1801–1846), *SEQUOYAH, NATIVE AMERICAN STATESMAN,* CA. 1830, OIL ON CANVAS

National Portrait Gallery, Smithsonian Institution, Washington, D.C., U.S.A. National Portrait Gallery, Smithsonian Institution/Art Resource, NY.

The American Promise

A HISTORY OF THE UNITED STATES

Fourth Edition

Volume I: To 1877

James L. Roark
Emory University

Michael P. Johnson
Johns Hopkins University

Patricia Cline Cohen
University of California, Santa Barbara

Sarah Stage
Arizona State University

Alan Lawson
Boston College

Susan M. Hartmann
The Ohio State University

BEDFORD/ST. MARTIN'S
Boston ◆ New York

FOR BEDFORD/ST. MARTIN'S

Publisher for History: Mary Dougherty
Director of Development for History: Jane Knetzger
Developmental Editor: Laura Arcari
Senior Production Editor: Rosemary R. Jaffe
Senior Production Supervisor: Joe Ford
Executive Marketing Manager: Jenna Bookin Barry
Editorial Assistants: Daniel Cole, Marissa Zanetti
Production Assistants: David Ayers, Katherine Caruana, Lidia MacDonald-Carr, Nicholas McCarthy
Copyeditor: Barbara Jatkola
Text Design: Wanda Kossak, Joan O'Connor
Page Layout: DeNee Reiton Skipper
Photo Research: Pembroke Hebert/Sandi Rygiel, Picture Research Consultants & Archives, Inc.
Indexer: Lois Oster
Cover Design: Billy Boardman
Cover Art: Henry Inman (1801–1846), *Sequoyah, Native American Statesman,* ca. 1830, oil on canvas.
    National Portrait Gallery, Smithsonian Institution, Washington, D.C., U.S.A. National
    Portrait Gallery, Smithsonian Institution/Art Resource, NY.
Cartography: Mapping Specialists Limited
Composition: Aptara
Printing and Binding: R.R. Donnelley & Sons Company

President: Joan E. Feinberg
Editorial Director: Denise B. Wydra
Director of Marketing: Karen Melton Soeltz
Director of Editing, Design, and Production: Marcia Cohen
Assistant Director of Editing, Design, and Production: Elise S. Kaiser
Managing Editor: Elizabeth M. Schaaf

Library of Congress Control Number: 2007927233

Manufactured in the United States of America.

1 0 9 8
f   e   d   c   b

For information, write: Bedford/St. Martin's, 75 Arlington Street, Boston, MA 02116 (617-399-4000)

ISBN–10: 0–312–45291–8   ISBN–13: 978–0–312–45291–9 (combined edition)
ISBN–10: 0–312–45292–6   ISBN–13: 978–0–312–45292–6 (Vol. I)
ISBN–10: 0–312–45293–4   ISBN–13: 978–0–312–45293–3 (Vol. II)
ISBN–10: 0–312–46999–3   ISBN–13: 978–0–312–46999–3 (Vol. A)
ISBN–10: 0–312–47000–2   ISBN–13: 978–0–312–47000–5 (Vol. B)
ISBN–10: 0–312–47001–0   ISBN–13: 978–0–312–47001–2 (Vol. C)

BRIEF CONTENTS

1   Ancient America: Before 1492   *3*

2   Europeans Encounter the New World, 1492–1600   *35*

3   The Southern Colonies in the Seventeenth Century, 1601–1700   *69*

4   The Northern Colonies in the Seventeenth Century, 1601–1700   *103*

5   Colonial America in the Eighteenth Century, 1701–1770   *137*

6   The British Empire and the Colonial Crisis, 1754–1775   *175*

7   The War for America, 1775–1783   *213*

8   Building a Republic, 1775–1789   *251*

9   The New Nation Takes Form, 1789–1800   *287*

10   Republicans in Power, 1800–1824   *321*

11   The Expanding Republic, 1815–1840   *357*

12   The New West and Free North, 1840–1860   *395*

13   The Slave South, 1820–1860   *435*

14   The House Divided, 1846–1861   *475*

15   The Crucible of War, 1861–1865   *511*

16   Reconstruction, 1863–1877   *553*

Appendices   *A-1*

Glossary of Historical Vocabulary   *G-1*

Spot Artifact Credits   *CR*

Index   *I-1*

Atlas of the Territorial Growth of the United States   *M-1*

CONTENTS

Maps, Figures, and Tables   xvii

Special Features   xx

Preface   xxii

About the Authors   xxx

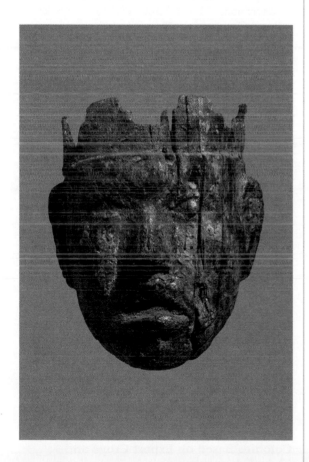

CHAPTER 1

Ancient America: Before 1492   3

OPENING VIGNETTE: *Archaeological discovery proves that humans have inhabited America for more than 10,000 years*   3

Archaeology and History   4

The First Americans   5
African and Asian Origins *6* •
Paleo-Indian Hunters *10*

BEYOND AMERICA'S BORDERS: *Nature's Immigrants*   8

Archaic Hunters and Gatherers   11
Great Plains Bison Hunters *12* • Great Basin Cultures *13* • Pacific Coast Cultures *13* •
Eastern Woodland Cultures *16*

HISTORICAL QUESTION: *Who Were the First Americans?*   14

Agricultural Settlements and Chiefdoms   17
Southwestern Cultures *18* • Woodland Burial Mounds and Chiefdoms *20*

Native Americans in the 1490s   22

THE PROMISE OF TECHNOLOGY: *Ancient American Weaving*   26

The Mexica: A Meso-American Culture   28

Conclusion: The World of Ancient Americans   30

Selected Bibliography   30

REVIEWING THE CHAPTER   32

CHAPTER 2
Europeans Encounter the New World, 1492–1600 · 35

OPENING VIGNETTE: *Queen Isabella of Spain supports Christopher Columbus's risky plan to sail west across the Atlantic* 35

Europe in the Age of Exploration 37
Mediterranean Trade and European Expansion *37* • A Century of Portuguese Exploration *39*

A Surprising New World in the Western Atlantic 40
The Explorations of Columbus *41* • The Geographic Revolution and the Columbian Exchange *42*

Spanish Exploration and Conquest 46
The Conquest of Mexico *46* • The Search for Other Mexicos *48* • New Spain in the Sixteenth Century *52* • The Toll of Spanish Conquest and Colonization *60* • Spanish Outposts in Florida and New Mexico *60*

HISTORICAL QUESTION: *Why Did Cortés Win?* 50

DOCUMENTING THE AMERICAN PROMISE: *Justifying Conquest* 54

SEEKING THE AMERICAN PROMISE: *Spreading Christianity in New Spain* 58

The New World and Sixteenth-Century Europe 62
The Protestant Reformation and the European Order *62* • New World Treasure and Spanish Ambitions *62* • Europe and the Spanish Example *63*

Conclusion: The Promise of the New World for Europeans 64

Selected Bibliography 65

REVIEWING THE CHAPTER 66

CHAPTER 3
The Southern Colonies in the Seventeenth Century, 1601–1700 · 69

OPENING VIGNETTE: *Pocahontas "rescues" John Smith* 69

An English Colony on the Chesapeake 71
The Fragile Jamestown Settlement *72* • Cooperation and Conflict between Natives and Newcomers *73* • From Private Company to Royal Government *75*

A Tobacco Society 77
Tobacco Agriculture *77* • A Servant Labor System *78* • Cultivating Land and Faith *86*

BEYOND AMERICA'S BORDERS: *American Tobacco and European Consumers* 80

DOCUMENTING THE AMERICAN PROMISE: *Virginia Laws Governing Servants and Slaves* 84

The Evolution of Chesapeake Society 87
Social and Economic Polarization *87* • Government Policies and Political Conflict *90* • Bacon's Rebellion *90*

HISTORICAL QUESTION: *Why Did English Colonists Consider Themselves Superior to Indians and Africans?* 88

Religion and Revolt in the Spanish Borderland 92

Toward a Slave Labor System 94
The West Indies: Sugar and Slavery *94* • Carolina: A West Indian Frontier *95* • Slave Labor Emerges in the Chesapeake *97*

GLOBAL COMPARISON: *Migration to the New World from Europe and Africa, 1492–1700* 96

Conclusion: The Growth of English Colonies Based on Export Crops and Slave Labor 98

Selected Bibliography 98

REVIEWING THE CHAPTER 100

CHAPTER 4
The Northern Colonies in the Seventeenth Century, 1601–1700 103

OPENING VIGNETTE: *Roger Williams is banished from Puritan Massachusetts* 103

Puritan Origins: The English Reformation 105

Puritans and the Settlement of New England 107
The Pilgrims and Plymouth Colony *107* • The Founding of Massachusetts Bay Colony *108*

DOCUMENTING THE AMERICAN PROMISE:
King Philip Considers Christianity 110

The Evolution of New England Society 112
Church, Covenant, and Conformity *113* • Government by Puritans for Puritanism *115* • The Splintering of Puritanism *116* • Religious Controversies and Economic Changes *117*

HISTORICAL QUESTION: *Why Were Some New Englanders Accused of Being Witches?* 122

The Founding of the Middle Colonies 120
From New Netherland to New York *120* • New Jersey and Pennsylvania *124* • Toleration and Diversity in Pennsylvania *124*

The Colonies and the English Empire 126
Royal Regulation of Colonial Trade *127* • King Philip's War and the Consolidation of Royal Authority *127*

BEYOND AMERICA'S BORDERS: *New France and the Indians: The British Colonies' Northern Borderlands* 130

Conclusion: An English Model of Colonization in North America 132

Selected Bibliography 132

REVIEWING THE CHAPTER 134

CHAPTER 5
Colonial America in the Eighteenth Century, 1701–1770 137

OPENING VIGNETTE: *The Robin Johns experience horrific turns of fortune in the Atlantic slave trade* 137

A Growing Population and Expanding Economy in British North America 138

New England: From Puritan Settlers to Yankee Traders 140
Natural Increase and Land Distribution *140* • Farms, Fish, and Atlantic Trade *141*

The Middle Colonies: Immigrants, Wheat, and Work 142
German and Scots-Irish Immigrants *143* • Pennsylvania: "The Best Poor [White] Man's Country" *147*

SEEKING THE AMERICAN PROMISE:
A Sailor's Life in the Eighteenth-Century Atlantic World 144

The Southern Colonies: Land of Slavery 151
The Atlantic Slave Trade and the Growth of Slavery *151* • Slave Labor and African American Culture *155* • Tobacco, Rice, and Prosperity *156*

Unifying Experiences 158
Commerce and Consumption *158* • Religion, Enlightenment, and Revival *158* • Borderlands and Colonial Politics in the British Empire *163*

THE PROMISE OF TECHNOLOGY: *Newspapers: "The Spring of Knowledge"* 160

GLOBAL COMPARISON: *Large Warships in European Navies, 1660–1760* 164

DOCUMENTING THE AMERICAN PROMISE:
Missionaries Report on California Missions 168

Conclusion: The Dual Identity of British North American Colonists 170

Selected Bibliography 170

REVIEWING THE CHAPTER 172

CHAPTER 6

The British Empire and the Colonial Crisis, 1754–1775   175

OPENING VIGNETTE: *Loyalist governor Thomas Hutchinson stands his ground in radical Massachusetts*   175

The Seven Years' War, 1754–1763   176
French-British Rivalry in the Ohio Country *177* • The Albany Congress and Intercolonial Defense *179* • The War and Its Consequences *180* • British Leadership, Pontiac's Uprising, and the Proclamation of 1763 *182*

HISTORICAL QUESTION: *How Long Did the Seven Years' War Last in Indian Country?*   184

The Sugar and Stamp Acts, 1763–1765   186
Grenville's Sugar Act *186* • The Stamp Act *187* • Resistance Strategies and Crowd Politics *187* • Liberty and Property *192*

SEEKING THE AMERICAN PROMISE:
Pursuing Liberty, Protesting Tyranny   190

The Townshend Acts and Economic Retaliation, 1767–1770   193
The Townshend Duties *193* • Nonconsumption and the Daughters of Liberty *194* • Military Occupation and "Massacre" in Boston *196*

The Tea Party and the Coercive Acts, 1770–1774   197
The Calm before the Storm *197* • Tea in Boston Harbor *198* • The Coercive Acts *199* • Beyond Boston: Rural Massachusetts *200* • The First Continental Congress *201*

DOCUMENTING THE AMERICAN PROMISE:
How News of the Powder Alarm Traveled   202

Domestic Insurrections, 1774–1775   204
Lexington and Concord *204* • Rebelling against Slavery *206*

Conclusion: How Far Does Liberty Go?   207

Selected Bibliography   208

REVIEWING THE CHAPTER   210

CHAPTER 7

The War for America, 1775–1783   213

OPENING VIGNETTE: *Deborah Sampson masquerades as a man to join the Continental army*   213

The Second Continental Congress   215
Assuming Political and Military Authority *215* • Pursuing Both War and Peace *218* • Thomas Paine, Abigail Adams, and the Case for Independence *220* • The Declaration of Independence *221*

THE PROMISE OF TECHNOLOGY: *Arming the Soldiers: Muskets and Rifles*   216

The First Year of War, 1775–1776   222
The American Military Forces *223* • The British Strategy *225* • Quebec, New York, and New Jersey *225*

GLOBAL COMPARISON: *How Tall Were Eighteenth-Century Men on Average?*   224

The Home Front   228
Patriotism at the Local Level *228* • The Loyalists *229* • Who Is a Traitor? *233* • Financial Instability and Corruption *236*

BEYOND AMERICA'S BORDERS: *Prisoners of War in the Eighteenth Century*   230

DOCUMENTING THE AMERICAN PROMISE: *Families Divide over the Revolution*   234

The Campaigns of 1777–1779: The North and West   236
Burgoyne's Army and the Battle of Saratoga *236* • The War in the West: Indian Country *239* • The French Alliance *240*

The Southern Strategy and the End of the War   241
Georgia and South Carolina *241* • The Other Southern War: Guerrillas *242* • Surrender at Yorktown *243* • The Losers and the Winners *244*

Conclusion: Why the British Lost   246

Selected Bibliography   247

REVIEWING THE CHAPTER   248

CHAPTER 8

Building a Republic,
1775–1789   251

OPENING VIGNETTE: *James Madison comes of age
in the midst of revolution*   251

The Articles of Confederation   252
Congress, Confederation, and the Problem
of Western Lands 253 • Running the New
Government 255

The Sovereign States   255
The State Constitutions 255 • Who Are "the
People"? 256 • Equality and Slavery 258 •
Legal Changes to Slavery, 1777–1804 259

SEEKING THE AMERICAN PROMISE: *A Slave
Sues for Her Freedom*   260

The Confederation's Problems   262
Financial Chaos and Paper Money 263 • The
Treaty of Fort Stanwix 264 • Land Ordinances
and the Northwest Territory 265 • Shays's
Rebellion, 1786–1787 269

The United States Constitution   271
From Annapolis to Philadelphia 271 • The
Virginia and New Jersey Plans 274 •
Democracy versus Republicanism 275

Ratification of the Constitution   275
The Federalists 276 • The Antifederalists
277 • The Big Holdouts: Virginia and New
York 278

HISTORICAL QUESTION: *Was the New United States
a Christian Country?*   280

**Conclusion: The "Republican
Remedy"**   282

Selected Bibliography   282

REVIEWING THE CHAPTER   284

CHAPTER 9

The New Nation Takes Form,
1789–1800   287

OPENING VIGNETTE: *Brilliant and brash,
Alexander Hamilton becomes a polarizing figure
in the 1790s*   287

The Search for Stability   289
Washington Inaugurates the Government 289 •
The Bill of Rights 290 • The Republican
Wife and Mother 291

BEYOND AMERICA'S BORDERS: *France, Britain,
and Woman's Rights in the 1790s*   292

Hamilton's Economic Policies   294
Agriculture, Transportation, and Banking
294 • The Public Debt and Taxes 295 • The
First Bank of the United States and the *Report
on Manufactures* 298 • The Whiskey
Rebellion 299

GLOBAL COMPARISON: *National Census Taking
Worldwide*   297

HISTORICAL QUESTION: *How Did Washington, D.C.,
Become the Federal Capital?*   300

Conflicts West, East, and South   302
To the West: The Indians 302 • Across the
Atlantic: France and Britain 306 • To the
South: The Haitian Revolution 309

Federalists and Republicans   310
The Election of 1796 310 • The XYZ Affair
311 • The Alien and Sedition Acts 312

DOCUMENTING THE AMERICAN PROMISE:
The Crisis of 1798: Sedition   314

Conclusion: Parties Nonetheless   316

Selected Bibliography   316

REVIEWING THE CHAPTER   318

CHAPTER 10
Republicans in Power, 1800–1824   321

OPENING VIGNETTE: *The Shawnee chief Tecumseh attempts to forge a pan-Indian confederacy*   321

Jefferson's Presidency   322
Turbulent Times: Election and Rebellion *323* • The Jeffersonian Vision of Republican Simplicity *326* • The Judiciary and the Midnight Judges *327* • The Promise of the West: The Louisiana Purchase and the Lewis and Clark Expedition *328* • Challenges Overseas: The Barbary Wars *330* • More Transatlantic Troubles: Impressment and Embargo *331*

HISTORICAL QUESTION: *How Could a Vice President Get Away with Murder?*   324

The Madisons in the White House   331
Women in Washington City *332* • Indian Troubles in the West *333* • The War of 1812 *333* • Washington City Burns: The British Offensive *335*

Women's Status in the Early Republic   337
Women and the Law *337* • Women and Church Governance *340* • Female Education *340*

THE PROMISE OF TECHNOLOGY: *Stoves Transform Cooking*   338

SEEKING THE AMERICAN PROMISE: *One Woman's Quest to Provide Higher Education for Women*   342

Monroe and Adams   344
From Property to Democracy *345* • The Missouri Compromise *346* • The Monroe Doctrine *348* • The Election of 1824 *349* • The Adams Administration *351*

Conclusion: Republican Simplicity Becomes Complex   352

Selected Bibliography   352

REVIEWING THE CHAPTER   354

CHAPTER 11
The Expanding Republic, 1815–1840   357

OPENING VIGNETTE: *The rise of Andrew Jackson, symbol of a self-confident and expanding nation*   357

The Market Revolution   358
Improvements in Transportation *359* • Factories, Workingwomen, and Wage Labor *361* • Bankers and Lawyers *365* • Booms and Busts *365*

THE PROMISE OF TECHNOLOGY: *Early Steamboats*   362

The Spread of Democracy   366
Popular Politics and Partisan Identity *367* • The Election of 1828 and the Character Issue *367* • Jackson's Democratic Agenda *368*

Jackson Defines the Democratic Party   369
Indian Policy and the Trail of Tears *369* • The Tariff of Abominations and Nullification *373* • The Bank War and Economic Boom *373*

Cultural Shifts, Religion, and Reform   375
The Family and Separate Spheres *376* • The Education and Training of Youths *378* • The Second Great Awakening *379* • The Temperance Movement and the Campaign for Moral Reform *380* • Organizing against Slavery *381*

GLOBAL COMPARISON: *Changing Trends in Age at First Marriage for Women*   377

BEYOND AMERICA'S BORDERS: *Transatlantic Abolition*   382

Van Buren's One-Term Presidency   385
The Politics of Slavery *385* • The Election of 1836 *386* • Two Panics and the Election of 1840 *386*

SEEKING THE AMERICAN PROMISE: Going Ahead *or* Gone to Smash: *An Entrepreneur Struggles in the 1830s*   388

Conclusion: The Age of Jackson or the Era of Reform?   390

Selected Bibliography   391

REVIEWING THE CHAPTER   392

CHAPTER 12
The New West and Free North, 1840–1860   395

OPENING VIGNETTE: *With the support of his wife, Abraham Lincoln struggles to survive in antebellum America*   395

Economic and Industrial Evolution   397
Agriculture and Land Policy *397* • Manufacturing and Mechanization *398* • Railroads: Breaking the Bonds of Nature *399*

THE PROMISE OF TECHNOLOGY: *The Telegraph: The "Wonder Working Wire"*   402

Free Labor: Promise and Reality   402
The Free-Labor Ideal: Freedom plus Labor *402* • Economic Inequality *405* • Immigrants and the Free-Labor Ladder *405*

GLOBAL COMPARISON: *Nineteenth Century School Enrollment and Literacy Rates*   404

The Westward Movement   407
Manifest Destiny *407* • Oregon and the Overland Trail *408* • The Mormon Exodus *411* • The Mexican Borderlands *412*

Expansion and the Mexican-American War   414
The Politics of Expansion *414* • The Mexican-American War, 1846–1848 *416* • Victory in Mexico *419* • Golden California *420*

HISTORICAL QUESTION: *Who Rushed for California Gold?*   422

Reforming Self and Society   424
The Pursuit of Perfection: Transcendentalists and Utopians *424* • Woman's Rights Activists *425* • Abolitionists and the American Ideal *426*

BEYOND AMERICA'S BORDERS: *Back to Africa: The United States in Liberia*   428

Conclusion: Free Labor, Free Men   430

Selected Bibliography   430

REVIEWING THE CHAPTER   432

CHAPTER 13
The Slave South, 1820–1860   435

OPENING VIGNETTE: *Slave Nat Turner leads a revolt to end slavery*   435

The Growing Distinctiveness of the South   436
Cotton Kingdom, Slave Empire *437* • The South in Black and White *437* • The Plantation Economy *442*

DOCUMENTING THE AMERICAN PROMISE: *Defending Slavery*   440

BEYOND AMERICA'S BORDERS: *White Gold: The International Empire of Cotton*   444

Masters, Mistresses, and the Big House   448
Plantation Masters *448* • Plantation Mistresses *450*

HISTORICAL QUESTION: *How Often Were Slaves Whipped?*   452

Slaves and the Quarter   456
Work *456* • Family, Religion, and Community *457* • Resistance and Rebellion *459*

Black and Free: On the Middle Ground   461
Precarious Freedom *461* • Achievement despite Restrictions *462*

The Plain Folk   462
Plantation Belt Yeomen *463* • Upcountry Yeomen *463* • Poor Whites *464* • The Culture of the Plain Folk *466*

The Politics of Slavery   466
The Democratization of the Political Arena *467* • Planter Power *468*

Conclusion: A Slave Society   469

Selected Bibliography   470

REVIEWING THE CHAPTER   472

CHAPTER 14
The House Divided, 1846–1861   475

OPENING VIGNETTE: *Abolitionist John Brown takes his war against slavery to Harpers Ferry, Virginia*   475

The Bitter Fruits of War   476
The Wilmot Proviso and the Expansion of Slavery *476* • The Election of 1848 *479* • Debate and Compromise *479*

The Sectional Balance Undone   481
The Fugitive Slave Act *481* • *Uncle Tom's Cabin 484* • The Kansas-Nebraska Act *485*

THE PROMISE OF TECHNOLOGY: *Daguerreotypes: The "Sunbeam Art"*   482

Realignment of the Party System   487
The Old Parties: Whigs and Democrats *487* • The New Parties: Know-Nothings and Republicans *490* • The Election of 1856 *493*

BEYOND AMERICA'S BORDERS: *Filibusters: The Underside of Manifest Destiny*   488

SEEKING THE AMERICAN PROMISE: *"A Purse of Her Own": Petitioning for the Right to Own Property*   494

Freedom under Siege   496
"Bleeding Kansas" *496* • The *Dred Scott* Decision *497* • Prairie Republican: Abraham Lincoln *499* • The Lincoln-Douglas Debates *500*

The Union Collapses   501
The Aftermath of John Brown's Raid *501* • Republican Victory in 1860 *502* • Secession Winter *504*

Conclusion: Slavery, Free Labor, and the Failure of Political Compromise   506

Selected Bibliography   506

REVIEWING THE CHAPTER   508

CHAPTER 15
The Crucible of War, 1861–1865   511

OPENING VIGNETTE: *Runaway slave William Gould enlists in the U.S. navy*   511

"And the War Came"   513
Attack on Fort Sumter *513* • The Upper South Chooses Sides *514*

The Combatants   515
How They Expected to Win *515* • Lincoln and Davis Mobilize *517*

Battling It Out, 1861–1862   518
Stalemate in the Eastern Theater *518* • Union Victories in the Western Theater *522* • The Atlantic Theater *523* • International Diplomacy *524*

Union *and* Freedom   524
From Slaves to Contraband *525* • From Contraband to Free People *528* • War of Black Liberation *529*

GLOBAL COMPARISON: *European Cotton Imports, 1860–1870*   525

THE PROMISE OF TECHNOLOGY: *CSS* H. L. Hunley: *The World's First Successful Submarine*   526

The South at War   530
Revolution from Above *531* • Hardship Below *534* • The Disintegration of Slavery *535*

SEEKING THE AMERICAN PROMISE: *The Right to Fight: Black Soldiers in the Civil War*   532

The North at War   536
The Government and the Economy *537* • Women and Work on the Home Front *537* • Politics and Dissent *538*

Grinding Out Victory, 1863–1865   539
Vicksburg and Gettysburg *539* • Grant Takes Command *540* • The Election of 1864 *545* • The Confederacy Collapses *546*

HISTORICAL QUESTION: *Why Did So Many Soldiers Die?*   542

Conclusion: The Second American Revolution   547

Selected Bibliography   548

REVIEWING THE CHAPTER   550

CHAPTER 16
Reconstruction, 1863–1877   553

OPENING VIGNETTE: *James T. Rapier emerges in the early 1870s as Alabama's most prominent black leader*   553

Wartime Reconstruction   555
"To Bind Up the Nation's Wounds" *555* • Land and Labor *556* • The African American Quest for Autonomy *557*

DOCUMENTING THE AMERICAN PROMISE: *The Meaning of Freedom*   558

Presidential Reconstruction   561
Johnson's Program of Reconciliation *561* • White Southern Resistance and Black Codes *562* • Expansion of Federal Authority and Black Rights *564*

Congressional Reconstruction   565
The Fourteenth Amendment and Escalating Violence *565* • Radical Reconstruction and Military Rule *568* • Impeaching a President *570* • The Fifteenth Amendment and Women's Demands *571*

THE PROMISE OF TECHNOLOGY: *Filling the "Empty Sleeve": Artificial Limbs*   566

The Struggle in the South   572
Freedmen, Yankees, and Yeomen *572* • Republican Rule *573* • White Landlords, Black Sharecroppers *578*

HISTORICAL QUESTION: *What Did the Ku Klux Klan Really Want?*   574

Reconstruction Collapses   579
Grant's Troubled Presidency *580* • Northern Resolve Withers *582* • White Supremacy Triumphs *583* • An Election and a Compromise *585*

Conclusion: "A Revolution But Half Accomplished"   586

Selected Bibliography   587

REVIEWING THE CHAPTER   588

APPENDICES
I. Documents   A-1

The Declaration of Independence   A-1

The Articles of Confederation and Perpetual Union   A-3

The Constitution of the United States   A-7

Amendments to the Constitution with Annotations (including the six unratified amendments)   A-12

The Constitution of the Confederate States of America   A-25

II. Facts and Figures: Government, Economy, and Demographics   A-33

U.S. POLITICS AND GOVERNMENT   A-33

Presidential Elections   A-33

Presidents, Vice Presidents, and Secretaries of State   A-36

Admission of States to the Union   A-38

Supreme Court Justices   A-39

Significant Supreme Court Cases   A-40

THE AMERICAN ECONOMY   A-46

Main Sectors of the U.S. Economy: 1849, 1899, 1950, 1990, 2001   A-46

Federal Spending and the Economy, 1790–2005   A-47

A DEMOGRAPHIC PROFILE OF THE UNITED STATES AND ITS PEOPLE   A-48

Population Growth, 1630–2000   A-48

Birthrate, 1820–2000   A-49

Death Rate, 1900–2000   A-49

Life Expectancy, 1900–2000   A-49

Migration and Immigration   A-50

(continued)

III. Research Resources in U.S. History   A-53

Bibliographies and Indexes   A-53
General Overviews   A-53
Specialized Information   A-53
Primary Resources   A-54
Internet Resources   A-54

Glossary of Historical Vocabulary   G-1

Spot Artifact Credits   CR

Index   I-1

Atlas of the Territorial Growth of the United States   M-1

MAPS, FIGURES, AND TABLES

Maps

CHAPTER 1

MAP 1.1 Continental Drift 6

SPOT MAP: Beringia 7

SPOT MAP: Meteor Impact in North America, 65 Million Years Ago 8

MAP 1.2 Native North American Cultures 12

SPOT MAP: Ancient California Peoples 16

SPOT MAP: Southwestern Cultures 18

SPOT MAP: Major Mississippian Mounds, AD 800–1500 20

MAP 1.3 Native North Americans about 1500 24

CHAPTER 2

MAP 2.1 European Trade Routes and Portuguese Exploration in the Fifteenth Century 38

SPOT MAP: Columbus's First Voyage to the New World, 1492–1493 41

MAP 2.2 European Exploration in Sixteenth-Century America 43

SPOT MAP: Cortés's Invasion of Tenochtitlán, 1519–1521 47

MAP 2.3 New Spain in the Sixteenth Century 52

SPOT MAP: Roanoke Settlement, 1585–1590 64

CHAPTER 3

MAP 3.1 Chesapeake Colonies in the Seventeenth Century 78

SPOT MAP: Settlement Patterns along the James River 86

MAP 3.2 The West Indies and Carolina in the Seventeenth Century 95

CHAPTER 4

MAP 4.1 New England Colonies in the Seventeenth Century 109

MAP 4.2 Middle Colonies in the Seventeenth Century 120

MAP 4.3 American Colonies at the End of the Seventeenth Century 126

SPOT MAP: King Philip's War, 1675 127

CHAPTER 5

MAP 5.1 Europeans and Africans in the Eighteenth Century 140

MAP 5.2 Atlantic Trade in the Eighteenth Century 143

SPOT MAP: Patterns of Settlement, 1700–1770 148

MAP 5.3 The Atlantic Slave Trade 152

MAP 5.4 Zones of Empire in Eastern North America 165

SPOT MAP: Spanish Missions in California 166

CHAPTER 6

SPOT MAP: Ohio River Valley, 1753 177

MAP 6.1 European Areas of Influence and the Seven Years' War, 1754–1763 178

MAP 6.2 North America after the Seven Years' War 181

SPOT MAP: Pontiac's Uprising, 1763 183

MAP 6.3 Lexington and Concord, April 1775 205

CHAPTER 7

SPOT MAP: Battle of Bunker Hill, 1775 218

MAP 7.1 The War in the North, 1775–1778 226

MAP 7.2 Loyalist Strength and Rebel Support 232

SPOT MAP: Battle of Saratoga, 1777 238

MAP 7.3 The Indian War in the West, 1777–1782 240

MAP 7.4 The War in the South, 1780–1781 242

SPOT MAP: Siege of Yorktown, 1781 244

CHAPTER 8

MAP 8.1 Cession of Western Lands,
1782–1802   254

SPOT MAP: Legal Changes to Slavery,
1777–1804   259

SPOT MAP: Treaty of Fort Stanwix   265

MAP 8.2 The Northwest Territory and
Ordinance of 1785   266

SPOT MAP: Shays's Rebellion, 1786–1787   269

MAP 8.3 Ratification of the Constitution,
1788–1790   276

CHAPTER 9

SPOT MAP: Major Roads in the 1790s   294

MAP 9.1 Travel Times from New York City
in 1800   295

MAP 9.2 Western Expansion and
Indian Land Cessions to 1810   304

SPOT MAP: Haitian Revolution, 1791–1804   309

CHAPTER 10

MAP 10.1 The Election of 1800   323

MAP 10.2 The Louisiana Purchase and
the Lewis and Clark Expedition   329

SPOT MAP: The Chesapeake Incident,
June 22, 1807   331

MAP 10.3 Indian Lands Ceded
by Treaties in the Northwest
Territory, 1795–1809   334

SPOT MAP: Battle of Tippecanoe, 1811   334

MAP 10.4 The War of 1812   335

MAP 10.5 The Missouri Compromise,
1820   348

MAP 10.6 The Election of 1824   351

CHAPTER 11

MAP 11.1 Routes of Transportation
in 1840   359

SPOT MAP: Cotton Textile Industry, 1839   361

MAP 11.2 The Election of 1828   369

MAP 11.3 Indian Removal and
the Trail of Tears   372

CHAPTER 12

MAP 12.1 Railroads in 1860   400

SPOT MAP: Plains Indians and Trails West
in the 1840s and 1850s   409

MAP 12.2 Major Trails West   409

MAP 12.3 Texas and Mexico in the 1830s   412

SPOT MAP: Texas War for
Independence, 1836   414

MAP 12.4 The Mexican-American War,
1846–1848   416

MAP 12.5 Territorial Expansion by 1860 420

SPOT MAP: Contemporary Liberia   429

CHAPTER 13

SPOT MAP: The Upper and Lower South   437

MAP 13.1 Cotton Kingdom, Slave Empire:
1820 and 1860   438

MAP 13.2 The Agricultural Economy
of the South, 1860   443

SPOT MAP: Immigrants as a Percentage
of State Populations, 1860   447

MAP 13.3 Major Cities in 1860   447

SPOT MAP: The Cotton Belt   463

SPOT MAP: Upcountry of the South   464

CHAPTER 14

SPOT MAP: Mexican Cession, 1848   477

MAP 14.1 The Election of 1848   479

MAP 14.2 The Compromise of 1850   481

SPOT MAP: Gadsden Purchase, 1853   486

MAP 14.3 The Kansas-Nebraska Act,
1854   487

MAP 14.4 Political Realignment,
1848–1860   491

SPOT MAP: "Bleeding Kansas," 1850s   496

MAP 14.5 The Election of 1860   504

SPOT MAP: Secession of the Lower South,
December 1860–February 1861   504

CHAPTER 15

MAP 15.1 Secession, 1860–1861   514

MAP 15.2 The Civil War, 1861–1862   519

SPOT MAP: Peninsula Campaign, 1862   521

SPOT MAP: Battle of Glorieta Pass, 1862   523

SPOT MAP: Vicksburg Campaign, 1863   540

SPOT MAP: Battle of Gettysburg,
July 1–3, 1863   540

MAP 15.3 The Civil War, 1863–1865   541

MAP 15.4 The Election of 1864   544

CHAPTER 16

SPOT MAP: Reconstruction Military
Districts, 1867   568

MAP 16.1 A Southern Plantation
in 1860 and 1881   580

MAP 16.2 The Election of 1868   581

SPOT MAP: Grant's Proposed Annexation
    of Santo Domingo   582

MAP 16.3 The Reconstruction
    of the South   584

MAP 16.4 The Election of 1876   585

Figures and Tables

FIGURE 1.1 Human Habitation of the
    World and the Western Hemisphere   7

FIGURE 1.2 Native American Population
    in North America about 1492
    (Estimated)   23

FIGURE 2.1 New World Gold and Silver
    Imported into Spain during the
    Sixteenth Century, in Pesos   56

THEMATIC CHRONOLOGY English
    Monarchy and the Protestant
    Reformation   105

FIGURE 4.1 Population of the English
    North American Colonies in the
    Seventeenth Century   118

TABLE 5.1 Slave Imports, 1451–1870   152

FIGURE 5.1 Colonial Exports, 1768–1772   159

THEMATIC CHRONOLOGY The Seven
    Years' War   182

TABLE 11.1 The Growth of Newspapers,
    1820–1840   367

FIGURE 11.1 Western Land Sales,
    1810–1860   375

FIGURE 12.1 Antebellum Immigration,
    1820–1860   406

FIGURE 13.1 Black and White
    Populations in the South, 1860   439

FIGURE 13.2 A Southern Plantation   449

TABLE 13.1 Percent of Slaveholders
    and Planters in Southern
    Legislatures, 1860   468

THEMATIC CHRONOLOGY The
    Realignment of Political Parties   490

FIGURE 14.1 Changing Political
    Landscape, 1848–1860   492

FIGURE 15.1 Resources of the
    Union and Confederacy   516

THEMATIC CHRONOLOGY Major Battles
    of the Civil War, 1861–1862   523

THEMATIC CHRONOLOGY Major Battles
    of the Civil War, 1863–1865   539

FIGURE 15.2 Civil War Deaths   542

THEMATIC CHRONOLOGY Major
    Reconstruction Legislation,
    1865–1875   571

FIGURE 16.1 Southern Congressional
    Delegations, 1865–1877   576

SPECIAL FEATURES

BEYOND AMERICA'S BORDERS

Nature's Immigrants	8
American Tobacco and European Consumers	80
New France and the Indians: The English Colonies' Northern Borderlands	130
Prisoners of War in the Eighteenth Century	230
France, Britain, and Women's Rights in the 1790s	292
Transatlantic Abolition	382
Back to Africa: The United States in Liberia	428
White Gold: The International Empire of Cotton	444
Filibusters: The Underside of Manifest Destiny	488

DOCUMENTING THE AMERICAN PROMISE

Justifying Conquest	54
Virginia Laws Governing Servants and Slaves	84
King Philip Considers Christianity	110
Missionaries Report on California Missions	168
How News of the Powder Alarm Traveled	202
Families Divide over the Revolution	234
The Crisis of 1798: Sedition	314
Defending Slavery	440
The Meaning of Freedom	558

GLOBAL COMPARISON

Migration to the New World from Europe and Africa, 1492–1700	96
Large Warships in European Navies, 1660–1760	164
How Tall Were Eighteenth-Century Men on Average?	224
National Census Taking Worldwide	297
Changing Trends in Age at First Marriage for Women	377
Nineteenth-Century School Enrollment and Literacy Rates	404
European Cotton Imports, 1860–1870	525

HISTORICAL QUESTION

Who Were the First Americans?	14
Why Did Cortés Win?	50
Why Did English Colonists Consider Themselves Superior to Indians and Africans?	88
Why Were Some New Englanders Accused of Being Witches?	122
How Long Did the Seven Years' War Last in Indian Country?	184
Was the New United States a Christian Country?	280
How Did Washington, D.C., Become the Federal Capital?	300
How Could a Vice President Get Away with Murder?	324
Who Rushed for California Gold?	422
How Often Were Slaves Whipped?	452
Why Did So Many Soldiers Die?	542
What Did the Ku Klux Klan Really Want?	574

SPECIAL FEATURES

THE PROMISE OF TECHNOLOGY

Ancient American Weaving 26

Newspapers: "The Spring
of Knowledge" 160

Arming the Soldiers: Muskets
and Rifles 216

Stoves Transform Cooking 338

Early Steamboats 362

The Telegraph: The "Wonder
Working Wire" 402

Daguerreotypes: The "Sunbeam Art" 482

CSS H. L. *Hunley:* The World's
First Successful Submarine 526

Filling the "Empty Sleeve":
Artificial Limbs 566

SEEKING THE AMERICAN PROMISE

Spreading Christianity in New Spain 58

A Sailor's Life in the Eighteenth-Century
Atlantic World 144

Pursuing Liberty, Protesting Tyranny 190

A Slave Sues for Her Freedom 260

One Woman's Quest to Provide Higher
Education for Women 342

Going Ahead or *Gone to Smash:*
An Entrepreneur Struggles
in the 1830s 388

"A Purse of Her Own": Petitioning for
the Right to Own Property 494

The Right to Fight: Black Soldiers
in the Civil War 532

PREFACE

AS AUTHORS, WE ARE deeply gratified that *The American Promise* has become one of the most widely adopted texts for the U.S. history survey. This fourth edition has caused us to reflect on the evolution of the book over the years. It rests solidly on our original goals and premises, but it also has changed significantly, in large part because of the crucial suggestions made by adopters who cared enough to help us make the book better. From edition to edition, our revisions have consistently conformed to our goal to make this book the most teachable and readable introductory American history textbook available. In developing the new edition, we were gratified to learn how actively instructors teach from this book, and in response we sought in our revisions to provide instructors with even more flexibility in the classroom. Thus, for example, we've provided a greater array of special features—including new features on America's role in the world and a new biographical feature—from which teachers can construct effective classroom experiences. To engage students more fully in the American story, we've created a more vivid and compelling art program, increased the "voices" of real Americans actively shaping history, and found new ways to position American history in the global world in which students live. Finally, in our quest to make this book even easier to study from, we've created a host of imaginative pedagogical aids that provide students with greater guidance in reading, understanding, and remembering American history. Like America itself over the centuries, the fourth edition of *The American Promise* is both recognizable and new.

From the beginning, *The American Promise* has been shaped by our firsthand knowledge that the survey course is the most difficult to teach and the most difficult to take. Collectively, we have logged considerably more than a century in introductory American history classrooms in institutions that range from small community colleges to large research institutions. Our experience as teachers informs every aspect of our text, beginning with its framework. In our classrooms, we have found that students need **both** the structure a political narrative provides **and** the insights gained from examining social and cultural experience. To write a comprehensive, balanced account of American history, we focused on the public arena—the place where politics intersects social and cultural developments—to show how Americans confronted the major issues of their day and created far-reaching historical change.

We also thought hard about the concerns most frequently voiced by instructors: that students often find history boring, unfocused, and difficult and their textbooks lifeless and overwhelming. Getting students to open the book is one of the biggest hurdles instructors face. We asked ourselves how our text could address these concerns and engage students in ways that would help them understand and remember the main developments in American history. To make the political, social, economic, and cultural changes vivid and memorable and to portray fully the diversity of the American experience, we stitched into our narrative the voices of hundreds of contemporaries—from presidents to pipefitters, sharecroppers to suffragists—whose ideas and actions shaped their times and whose efforts still affect our lives. By incorporating a rich selection of authentic American voices, we seek to capture history as it happened and to create a compelling narrative that captures students' interests and sparks their historical imagination.

Our title, *The American Promise*, reflects our emphasis on human agency and our conviction that American history is an unfinished story. For millions, the nation has held out the promise of a better life, unfettered worship, representative government, democratic politics, and other freedoms seldom found elsewhere. But none of these promises has come with guarantees. As we see it, much of American history is a continuing struggle over the definition and realization of the nation's promise. Abraham Lincoln, in the midst of what he termed the "fiery trial" of the Civil War, pronounced the nation "the last best hope of Earth." Kept alive by countless sacrifices, that hope has been marred by compromises, disappointments, and denials, but it lives still. We believe that *The American Promise*, Fourth Edition, with its increased attention to making history come alive, will help students become aware of the legacy of hope bequeathed to them by previous generations of Americans stretching back nearly four centuries, a legacy that is theirs to preserve and build on.

Features

From the beginning, readers have proclaimed this textbook a visual feast, richly illustrated in ways that extend and reinforce the narrative. The fourth edition offers more than 775 contemporaneous **illustrations**. In our effort to make history tangible, we include over 300 **artifacts**—from boots and political buttons to guns and sewing machines—that emphasize the importance of material culture in the study of the past and enrich the historical account. **Comprehensive captions** for the illustrations in the book entice students to delve deeper into the text itself, and two **new visual activities** per chapter encourage students to assess visual evidence.

Our highly regarded **map program**, with over 170 maps in all, rests on the old truth that "History is not intelligible without geography." Each chapter offers, on average, four **full-size maps** showing major developments in the narrative and two to three **spot maps** embedded in the narrative that emphasize an area of detail from the discussion. To help students think critically about the role of geography in American history, we include **two critical-thinking map exercises** per chapter. New maps in the fourth edition highlight such topics as the Treaty of Fort Stanwix, Zululand and Cape Colony in 1878, worldwide oil reserves in 1980, and the recent conflict in Iraq. Another unique feature is our brief **Atlas of the Territorial Growth of the United States**, a series of full-color maps at the end of each volume that reveal the changing cartography of the nation.

As part of our ongoing efforts to make this the most teachable and readable survey text available, we paid renewed attention to imaginative and effective pedagogy. Thus, this fourth edition has increased its reach, lending greater in-text help to all levels of students. Chapters are constructed to preview, reinforce, and review the narrative in the most memorable and engaging means possible. To prepare students for the reading to come, each chapter begins with a **chapter outline** to accompany the colorful **opening vignette** that invites students into the narrative with lively accounts of individuals or groups who embody the central themes of the chapter. New vignettes in this edition include, among others, Queen Isabella supporting Columbus's expedition to the New World, the Robin Johns' experiences in the Atlantic slave trade, Deborah Sampson masquerading as a man to join the Continental army, Alexander Hamilton as a polarizing figure, James T. Rapier emerging in the early 1870s as Alabama's most prominent black leader, Frances Willard participating in the creation of the Populist Party in 1892, and Congresswoman Helen Gahagan Douglas during the cold war. Each vignette ends with a **narrative overview** of all of the chapter's main topics. Major sections within each chapter have **introductory paragraphs** that preview the subsections that follow and conclude with **new review questions** to help students check their comprehension of main ideas. **Two-tiered runningheads** with dates and topical headings remind students of chronology, and **call-outs** draw attention to interesting quotes. In addition, **thematic chronologies** reinforce points in the narrative, and **Glossary terms**, set in boldface type at first use, make historical terms accessible. At the end of each chapter, a **conclusion** reexamines central ideas and provides a bridge to the next chapter, and a **Selected Bibliography** lists important books to jump-start student research.

Perhaps the most notable new way this edition reaches out to students is through a substantial **new Reviewing the Chapter** section at the end of each chapter that provides step-by-step study plans to ensure student success. These two-page chapter review guides start with clear **study instructions** for reviewing the chapter. Lists of **Key Terms** highlight important people, events, and concepts, while illustrated chapter **Timelines** give clear chronological overviews of key events. Two sets of questions prompt students to think critically and make use of the facts they have mastered: **Review Questions** repeated from within the narrative and **Making Connections** questions that prompt students to think about broad developments. **Online Study Guide cross-references** at the end of the review section point students to free self-assessment quizzes and other study aids.

An enriched array of special features reinforces the narrative and offers teachers more points of departure for assignments and discussion. We've developed two additional options for this edition. To support our increased emphasis on the global context of U.S. history, we include sixteen **new Global Comparison figures** that showcase data visually with an emphasis on global connections. These figures introduce students to both the methods of quantitative analysis and the interesting stories behind the numbers. Features are focused on a wide range of topics, from comparing "Nineteenth-Century School Enrollment and Literacy Rates" worldwide to "Energy Consumption per Capita" in 1980. In addition, we've added seven new **Beyond America's Borders** features. These essays seek to widen students' perspectives and help students see that this country did not develop in isolation. New essays as varied as "Prisoners of War in the Eighteenth Century" and "Imperialism, Colonialism, and the Treatment of the Sioux and the Zulu" consider the reciprocal connections between the United States and the wider world and challenge students to think about the effects of transnational connections over time.

This edition also introduces fifteen **new Seeking the American Promise essays**. Each essay explores a different promise of America—from the promise of home ownership to the promise of higher education, for example—while recognizing that the promises fulfilled for some have meant promises denied to others. Biographical in nature, these features seek to inform students about how ordinary Americans have striven over the centuries to create better, richer, and happier lives for themselves. Students connect to the broader themes through the stories of Americans such as Ebenezer Mackintosh, a little-known Boston shoemaker who pursued liberty during the colonial crisis, and paraplegic Beverly Jones, who sued for access under the American with Disabilities Act in her home state of Tennessee.

Fresh topics in our three enduring special features further enrich this edition. Each **Documenting the American Promise** feature juxtaposes three or four primary documents to dramatize the human dimension of major events and show varying perspectives on a topic or issue. Feature introductions and document headnotes contextualize the sources, and Questions for Analysis and Debate promote critical thinking about primary sources. New topics in this edition include "Virginia Laws Governing Servants and Slaves," "How News of the Powder Alarm Traveled," "Defending Slavery," and "The Final Push for Woman Suffrage." **Historical Questions** essays pose and interpret specific questions of continuing interest so as to demonstrate the depth and variety of possible answers, thereby countering the belief of many beginning students that historians simply gather facts and string them together in a chronological narrative. Students recognize that history is an interpretive enterprise by joining in the questioning, arguing about, and wrestling with the past. New questions in this edition include "Who Were the First Americans?" and "Was There a Sexual Revolution in the 1920s?" The **Promise of Technology** essays examine the ramifications—positive and negative—of technological developments in American society and culture. New topics in this edition include "Electrifying America: The War of the Currents," "Household Appliances: Laborsaving Devices for Women?" and "The Pill."

Textual Changes

Because students live in an increasingly global world and need help making connections with the world outside the United States, we have substantially increased our attention to the global context of American history in the fourth edition. In addition to the two global features—Beyond America's Borders and Global Comparison figures—the transnational context of American history has been integrated throughout the narrative as appropriate, including a new section on international diplomacy during the Civil War and a comparison of the welfare state in the United States and Europe during the cold war. These additions contribute to a broader notion of American history and help students understand more fully the complex development of their nation's history and help prepare them to live in the twenty-first century.

In our ongoing effort to offer a comprehensive text that braids all Americans into the national narrative, we have increased our attention to woman's history in the fourth edition. In addition to enhancing our coverage of women in the narrative—including a new section on women's education in the early republic and more on woman's suffrage—we've added thirteen new features and vignettes focused around women. Features such as a new Promise of Technology essay on laborsaving devices for women and a new Global Comparison figure on the average age of marriage in the nineteenth century place women firmly in the national narrative. Other features introduce students in more depth to many of the women who've contributed to this nation's story. Some of the extraordinary women profiled in this edition include Queen Liliuokalani in a Beyond America's Borders feature on regime change in Hawaii, Ernestine Rose in a new Seeking the American Promise feature on married women's rights to own property, and Frances Willard and Helen Gahagan Douglas in new chapter-opening vignettes.

To strengthen coverage and increase clarity and accessibility, we reorganized certain chapters. In particular, reorganization in Chapter 11, "The Expanding Republic, 1815–1840," and Chapter 12, "The New West and Free North, 1840–1860," provides clearer themes with smoother transitions. Chapter 17—newly titled "The Contested West, 1870–1900"—has also been reorganized to incorporate the latest scholarship on the colonization of the West and to accommodate an expanded treatment of the struggles of Native Americans.

Staying abreast of current scholarship is a primary concern of ours, and this edition reflects that keen interest. We incorporated a wealth of new scholarship into the fourth edition in myriad ways to benefit students. Readers will note that we made good use of the latest works on a number of topics, such as the French and Indian borderlands, the education of women in the early republic, the Barbary Wars, Denmark Vesey, black soldiers in the Civil War, the colonization of the West and the struggles of Native Americans in response to it, and American imperialism in Hawaii, as well as providing up-to-date coverage of the George W. Bush administration, the Middle East, Hurricane Katrina, and the war on terrorism.

Supplements

Developed with our guidance and thoroughly revised to reflect the changes in the fourth edition, the comprehensive collection of free and premium resources accompanying the textbook provides a host of practical learning and teaching aids. Again, we learned much from the book's community of adopters, and we broadened the scope of the supplements to create a learning package that responds to the real needs of instructors and students. Many of the new media options can not only save you and your students time and money but also add sound to the voices, movement to the images, and interactivity to the documents that help bring history to life. Cross-references in the textbook to the Online Study Guide and to the primary source reader signal the tight integration of the core text with the supplements.

For Students

Print Resources

***Reading the American Past: Selected Historical Documents*, Fourth Edition.** Edited by Michael P. Johnson (Johns Hopkins University), one of the authors of *The American Promise*, and designed to complement the textbook, *Reading the American Past* provides a broad selection of over 150 primary source documents, as well as editorial apparatus to help students understand the sources. Emphasizing the important social, political, and economic themes of U.S. history courses, thirty-two new documents (at least one per chapter) were added to provide a multiplicity of perspectives on environmental, western, ethnic, and gender history and to bring a global dimension to the anthology. Available free when packaged with the text and now available as an e-book (see below).

Maps in Context: A Workbook for American History. Written by historical cartography expert Gerald A. Danzer (University of Illinois, Chicago), this skill-building workbook helps students comprehend essential connections between geographic literacy and historical understanding. Organized to correspond to the typical U.S. history survey course, *Maps in Context* presents a wealth of map-centered projects and convenient pop quizzes that give students hands-on experience working with maps. Available free when packaged with the text.

Student Guide for *Shaping America: U.S. History to 1877* and *Transforming America: U.S. History since 1877*. This guide by Kenneth G.

Alfers (Dallas County Community College District) is designed for students using *The American Promise* in conjunction with the Dallas TeleLearning telecourse *Shaping America* and *Transforming America*. Lesson overviews, assignments, objectives, and focus points provide structure for distance learners, while enrichment ideas, suggested readings, and brief primary sources extend the unit lessons. Practice tests help students evaluate their mastery of the material.

NEW Trade Books. Titles published by sister companies Farrar, Straus and Giroux; Henry Holt and Company; Hill and Wang; Picador; and St. Martin's Press are available at a 50 percent discount when packaged with Bedford/St. Martin's textbooks. For more information, visit **bedfordstmartins.com/tradeup.**

NEW *The Bedford Glossary for U.S. History*. This handy supplement for the survey course gives students clear, concise definitions of the political, economic, social, and cultural terms used by historians and contemporary media alike. The terms are historically contextualized to aid comprehension. Available free when packaged with the text.

***History Matters: A Student Guide to U.S. History Online*.** This resource, written by Alan Gevinson, Kelly Schrum, and Roy Rosenzweig (all of George Mason University), provides an illustrated and annotated guide to 250 of the most useful Web sites for student research in U.S. history as well as advice on evaluating and using Internet sources. This essential guide is based on the acclaimed "History Matters" Web site developed by the American History Social Project and the Center for History and New Media. Available free when packaged with the text.

Bedford Series in History and Culture. Over one hundred titles in this highly praised series combine first-rate scholarship, historical narrative, and important primary documents for undergraduate courses. Each book is brief, inexpensive, and focused on a specific topic or period. Package discounts are available.

Historians at Work Series. Brief enough for a single assignment yet meaty enough to provoke thoughtful discussion, each volume in this series examines a single historical question by combining unabridged selections by distinguished historians, each with a different perspective on the issue, with helpful learning aids. Package discounts are available.

New Media Resources

NEW e-Book integrating *The American Promise* with its companion sourcebook and Online Study Guide. Not your usual e-book, this one-of-a-kind online resource integrates the text of *The American Promise*, with the 150 additional written sources of the companion sourcebook, *Reading the American Past*, and the self-testing and activities of the Online Study Guide into one easy-to-use e-book. With search functions stronger than in any competing text, this e-book is an ideal study and reference tool for students. Instructors can easily add documents, images, and other material to customize the text, making this e-book perfect for instructors who wish to build dynamic online courses or use electronic texts and documents. **Can be packaged FREE with the print text or purchased stand-alone for about half the price.**

Online Study Guide at bedfordstmartins.com/ roark. The popular Online Study Guide for *The American Promise* is a free and uniquely personalized learning tool to help students master themes and information presented in the textbook and improve their historical skills. Assessment quizzes let students evaluate their comprehension and provide them with customized plans for further study through a variety of activities. Instructors can monitor students' progress through the online Quiz Gradebook or receive e-mail updates.

NEW Audio Reviews for *The American Promise*, Fourth Edition, at bedfordstmartins.com/roark. Audio Reviews are a new tool that fits easily into students' lifestyles and provides a practical new way for them to study. These twenty-five-to thirty-minute summaries of each chapter in *The American Promise* highlight the major themes of the text and help reinforce student learning.

Online Bibliography at bedfordstmartins .com/roark. Organized by book chapter and topic, the online bibliography provides an authoritative and comprehensive list of references to jump-start student research.

A Student's Online Guide to History Reference Sources at bedfordstmartins.com/roark. This Web site provides links to history-related databases, indexes, and journals, plus contact information for state, provincial, local, and professional history organizations.

The Bedford Research Room at bedfordstmartins .com/roark. The Research Room, drawn from Mike Palmquist's *The Bedford Researcher*, offers a wealth of resources—including interactive tutorials, research activities, student writing samples, and links to hundreds of other places online—to support students in courses across the disciplines. The site also offers instructors a library of helpful instructional tools.

The Bedford Bibliographer at bedfordstmartins .com/roark. *The Bedford Bibliographer*, a simple but powerful Web-based tool, assists students with the process of collecting sources and generates bibliographies in four commonly used documentation styles.

Research and Documentation Online at bedfordstmartins.com/roark. This Web site provides clear advice on how to integrate primary and secondary sources into research papers, how to cite sources correctly, and how to format in MLA, APA, *Chicago*, or CBE style

The St. Martin's Tutorial on Avoiding Plagiarism at bedfordstmartins.com/roark. This online tutorial reviews the consequences of plagiarism and explains what sources to acknowledge, how to keep good notes, how to organize research, and how to integrate sources appropriately. The tutorial includes exercises to help students practice integrating sources and recognize acceptable summaries.

Critical Thinking Modules at bedfordstmartins .com/roark. This Web site offers over two dozen online modules for interpreting maps, audio, visual, and textual sources, centered on events covered in the U.S. history survey.

For Instructors

Print Resources

Instructor's Resource Manual. This popular manual by Sarah E. Gardner (Mercer University) and Catherine A. Jones (Johns Hopkins University) offers both experienced and first-time instructors tools for presenting textbook material in exciting and engaging ways—learning objectives, annotated chapter outlines, lecture strategies, tips for helping students with common misconceptions and difficult topics, and suggestions for in-class activities, including using film and video, ways to start discussions, topics for debate, and analyzing primary sources. The new edition includes model answers for the questions in the book as well as a chapter-by-chapter guide to all of the supplements available with *The American Promise*. An extensive guide for first-time teaching assistants and sample syllabi are also included.

Transparencies. This set of over 160 full-color acetate transparencies includes all full-size maps and many other images from the textbook to help instructors present lectures and teach students important map-reading skills.

Using the Bedford Series in History and Culture in the U.S. History Survey at bedfordstmartins .com/usingseries. This online guide helps instructors integrate volumes from the highly regarded Bedford Series in History and Culture into their U.S. history survey course. The guide not only correlates themes from each series book with the survey course but also provides ideas for classroom discussions.

New Media Resources

NEW HistoryClass. Bedford/St. Martin's course management system for the history classroom provides a complete online learning solution by integrating our e-books and the rich content of our book companion sites.

Instructor's Resource CD-ROM. This disc provides instructors with ready-made and customizable PowerPoint multimedia presentations built around chapter outlines, maps, figures, and selected images from the textbook, plus jpeg versions of all maps, figures, and selected images.

Computerized Test Bank. Written by Bradford Wood (Eastern Kentucky University), Peter Lau (University of Rhode Island), and Sondra Cosgrove (Community College of Northern Nevada), the test bank provides over eighty exercises per chapter, including multiple-choice, fill-in-the-blank, map analysis, short essay, and full-length essay questions. Instructors can customize quizzes, add or edit both questions and answers, and export questions and answers to a variety of formats, including WebCT and Blackboard. The disc includes correct answers and essay outlines as well as separate test banks for the associated telecourses *Shaping America* and *Transforming America*.

Book Companion Site at bedfordstmartins .com/roark. The companion Web site gathers all the electronic resources for *The American Promise*, including the Online Study Guide and related Quiz Gradebook, at a single Web address, providing convenient links to lecture, assignment, and research materials such as PowerPoint chapter outlines and the digital libraries at Make History.

Make History at bedfordstmartins.com/roark. Comprising the content of our five acclaimed online libraries—Map Central, the Bedford History Image Library, DocLinks, HistoryLinks, and PlaceLinks—Make History provides one-stop access to relevant digital content, including maps, images, documents, and Web links. Students and instructors alike can search this free, easy-to-use database by keyword, topic, date, or specific chapter of *The American Promise* and download the content they find. Instructors can also create entire collections of content and store them online for later use or post their collections to the Web to share with students.

Content for Course Management Systems. A variety of student and instructor resources developed for this textbook is ready for use in course management systems such as Blackboard, WebCT, and other platforms. This e-content includes nearly all of the offerings from the book's Online Study Guide as well as the book's test bank and the test banks from the associated telecourses *Shaping America* and *Transforming America*.

NEW Reel Teaching. A valuable tool for enhancing media-rich lectures, short segments in VHS and DVD format are available to qualified adopters from the award-winning telecourses *Shaping America* and *Transforming America* by Dallas TeleLearning at the LeCroy Center for Educational Telecommunications.

The American Promise **via Telecourse.** We are pleased to announce that *The American Promise* has been selected as the textbook for the award-winning U.S. history telecourses *Shaping America: U.S. History to 1877* and *Transforming America: U.S. History since 1877* by Dallas TeleLearning at the LeCroy Center for Educational Telecommunications, Dallas County Community College District. Guides for students and instructors fully integrate the narrative of *The American Promise* into each telecourse. For more information on these distance-learning opportunities, visit the Dallas TeleLearning Web site at http://telelearning .dcccd.edu, e-mail tlearn@dcccd.edu, or call 972-669-6650.

Videos and Multimedia. A wide assortment of videos and multimedia CD-ROMs on various topics in American history is available to qualified adopters.

Acknowledgments

We gratefully acknowledge all of the helpful suggestions from those who have read and taught from the previous editions of *The American Promise*, and we hope that our many classroom collaborators will be pleased to see their influence in the fourth edition. In particular, we wish to thank the talented scholars and teachers who gave generously of their time and knowledge to review this book; their critiques and suggestions contributed greatly to the published work: Kathryn Abbot, *Western Kentucky University;* Carol Anderson, *University of Missouri, Columbia;* Melissa Anyiwo, *University of Tennessee, Chattanooga;* Janis Appier, *University of Tennessee;* Marjorie Berman, *Red Rocks Community College;* Bill Bush, *University of Nevada, Las Vegas;* Charles Byler, *Carroll College;* Dominic Carrillo, *Grossmont College;* Stephanie Cole, *University of Texas, Arlington;* Barak Cook, *University of Missouri;* Sheri David, *North Virginia Community College, Manassas;* Tracy Davis, *Victor Valley College;* Thomas Dicke, *Missouri State University;* Don Doyle, *University of South Carolina;* Bill G. Dykes, *Temple Baptist College;* John Elder, *University of Central Oklahoma;* Karen Enloe, *Glendale Community College;* Amy Essington, *California State University, Long Beach;*

Dana Frank, *University of California, Santa Cruz;* Hal Friedman, *Henry Ford Community College;* Steven Gargo, *Appleton Area Schools;* Michael Garcia, *Arapahoe Community College;* David Gerleman, *George Mason University;* Gina Estep Gompert, *Sierra College;* Larry Grubbs, *University of Georgia;* Allen Hamilton, *St. Phillips College;* Paul Hudson, *Georgia Perimeter College;* Jeffrey Irvin, *Monroe County Community College;* Frances M. Jacobson, *Tidewater Community College;* Jeanette Keith, *Bloomsburg University;* Daniel P. Kotzin, *Kutztown University;* Lou LaGrande, *St. Petersburg College;* Brad Lookingbill, *Columbia College;* Robert Martin, *University of Northern Iowa;* Suzanne Summers McFadden, *Austin Community College;* Rebecca Mead, *Northern Michigan University;* Warren Metcalf, *University of Oklahoma;* Carlos Mujal, *De Anza College;* William Murphy, *SUNY Oswego;* Cassandra Newby-Alexander, *Old Dominion;* Cynthia Clark Northrup, *University of Texas, Arlington;* Carla Pestana, *Miami University;* Caroline Pruden, *North Carolina State;* Kimber Quinney, *California State San Marcos;* Akin Reinhardt, *Towson University;* Rob Risko, *Trinity Valley Community College;* Jere Roberson, *University of Central Oklahoma;* Horacia Salinas Jr., *Laredo Community College;* Sharon Salinger, *University of California, Irvine;* Ken Shafer, *Cerritos College;* Donald R. Shaffer, *University of Northern Colorado;* John Simpson, *Pierce College;* Tiwanna Simpson, *Louisiana State University;* Sherry Smith, *Southern Methodist University;* Melissa Soto-Schwartz, *Cuyahoga Community College;* Mark Stephens, *Los Positus College;* Thomas Summerhill, *Michigan State University;* Wesley Swanson, *San Joaquin Delta College;* Stacy L. Tanner, *Georgia Southern University;* Pat Thompson, *University of Texas, San Antonio;* Stephen Tootle, *University of Northern Colorado;* Kenneth Townsend, *Coastal University;* David White, *McHenry Community College;* LeeAnn Whites, *University of Missouri, Columbia;* and Rosemary Zagarri, *George Mason University.*

A project as complex as this requires the talents of many individuals. First, we would like to acknowledge our families for their support, forbearance, and toleration of our textbook responsibilities. Pembroke Herbert and Sandi Rygiel of Picture Research Consultants, Inc., contributed their unparalleled knowledge, soaring imagination, and diligent research to make possible the extraordinary illustration program.

We would also like to thank the many people at Bedford/St. Martin's who have been crucial to this project. No one contributed more than developmental editor Laura Arcari, who managed the entire revision and oversaw the development of each chapter. The results of her dedication to excellence and commitment to creating the best textbook imaginable are evident on every page. We greatly appreciate the acute intelligence and indomitable good humor that Laura brought to this revision. We thank freelance editors Jan Fitter, Michelle McSweeney, and Terri Wise for their help with the manuscript. Thanks also go to editorial assistant Daniel Cole for his assistance managing the reviews and associate editor Marissa Zanetti, who provided unflagging assistance and who coordinated the supplements. We are also grateful to Jane Knetzger, director of development for history, and Mary Dougherty, publisher for history, for their support and guidance. For their imaginative and tireless efforts to promote the book, we want to thank Jenna Bookin Barry, executive marketing manager; John Hunger, senior history specialist; and Amanda Byrnes, senior marketing associate. With great skill and professionalism, Rosemary Jaffe, senior production editor, pulled together the many pieces related to copyediting, design, and typesetting, with the able assistance of David Ayers, Katherine Caruana, Lidia MacDonald-Carr, and Nicholas McCarthy and the guidance of managing editor Elizabeth Schaaf and assistant managing editor John Amburg. Senior production supervisor Joe Ford oversaw the manufacturing of the book. Designers Wanda Kossak and Joan O'Connor and page makeup artist DeNee Reiton Skipper, copyeditor Barbara Jatkola, and proofreaders Linda McLatchie and Stella Gelboin attended to the myriad details that help make the book shine. Lois Oster provided an outstanding index. The book's gorgeous covers were designed by Billy Boardman. Editor Danielle Slevens and associate editor Marissa Zanetti made sure that *The American Promise* remains at the forefront of technological support for students and instructors. Editorial director Denise Wydra provided helpful advice throughout the course of the project. Finally, Charles H. Christensen, former president, took a personal interest in *The American Promise* from the start, and Joan E. Feinberg, president, guided all editions through every stage of development.

JAMES L. ROARK

Born in Eunice, Louisiana, and raised in the West, James L. Roark received his B.A. from the University of California, Davis, in 1963 and his Ph.D. from Stanford University in 1973. His dissertation won the Allan Nevins Prize. He has taught at the University of Nigeria, Nsukka; the University of Nairobi, Kenya; the University of Missouri, St. Louis; and, since 1983, Emory University, where he is Samuel Candler Dobbs Professor of American History. In 1993, he received the Emory Williams Distinguished Teaching Award, and in 2001–2002 he was Pitt Professor of American Institutions at Cambridge University. He has written *Masters without Slaves: Southern Planters in the Civil War and Reconstruction* (1977). With Michael P. Johnson, he is author of *Black Masters: A Free Family of Color in the Old South* (1984) and editor of *No Chariot Let Down: Charleston's Free People of Color on the Eve of the Civil War* (1984). He has received research assistance from the American Philosophical Society, the National Endowment for the Humanities, and the Gilder Lehrman Institute of American History. Active in the Organization of American Historians and the Southern Historical Association, he is also a fellow of the Society of American Historians.

MICHAEL P. JOHNSON

Born and raised in Ponca City, Oklahoma, Michael P. Johnson studied at Knox College in Galesburg, Illinois, where he received a B.A. in 1963, and at Stanford University in Palo Alto, California, earning a Ph.D. in 1973. He is currently professor of history at Johns Hopkins University in Baltimore, having previously taught at the University of California, Irvine; San Jose State University; and LeMoyne (now LeMoyne-Owen) College in Memphis. His publications include *Toward a Patriarchal Republic: The Secession of Georgia* (1977); with James L. Roark, *Black Masters: A Free Family of Color in the Old South* (1984) and *No Chariot Let Down:*

Charleston's Free People of Color on the Eve of the Civil War (1984); *Abraham Lincoln, Slavery, and the Civil War: Selected Speeches and Writings* (2001); *Reading the American Past: Selected Historical Documents*, the documents reader for *The American Promise*; and articles that have appeared in the *William and Mary Quarterly*, the *Journal of Southern History, Labor History*, the *New York Review of Books*, the *New Republic*, the *Nation*, and other journals. Johnson has been awarded research fellowships by the American Council of Learned Societies, the National Endowment for the Humanities, the Center for Advanced Study in the Behavioral Sciences and Stanford University, and the Times Mirror Foundation Distinguished Research Fellowship at the Huntington Library. He has directed a National Endowment for the Humanities Summer Seminar for College Teachers and has been honored with the University of California, Irvine, Academic Senate Distinguished Teaching Award and the University of California, Irvine, Alumni Association Outstanding Teaching Award. He won the *William and Mary Quarterly* award for best article in 2002 and the Organization of American Historians ABC-CLIO *America: History and Life* Award for best American history article in 2002. He is an active member of the American Historical Association, the Organization of American Historians, and the Southern Historical Association.

PATRICIA CLINE COHEN

Born in Ann Arbor, Michigan, and raised in Palo Alto, California, Patricia Cline Cohen earned a B.A. at the University of Chicago in 1968 and a Ph.D. at the University of California, Berkeley, in 1977. In 1976, she joined the history faculty at the University of California, Santa Barbara. In 2005–2006, she received the university's Distinguished Teaching Award. Cohen has written *A Calculating People: The Spread of Numeracy in Early America* (1982; reissued 1999) and *The Murder of Helen Jewett: The Life and Death of a*

Prostitute in Nineteenth-Century New York (1998). She has also published articles on quantitative literacy, mathematics education, prostitution, and murder in journals including the *Journal of Women's History, Radical History Review,* the *William and Mary Quarterly,* and the *NWSA Journal.* Her scholarly work has received support from the National Endowment for the Humanities, the National Humanities Center, the University of California President's Fellowship in the Humanities, the Mellon Foundation, the American Antiquarian Society, the Schlesinger Library, and the Newberry Library. She is an active associate of the Omohundro Institute of Early American History and Culture, sits on the advisory council of the Society for the History of the Early American Republic, and is past president of the Western Association of Women Historians. She has served as chair of the history department, as chair of the Women's Studies Program, and as acting dean of the humanities and fine arts at the University of California at Santa Barbara. In 2001–2002, she was the Distinguished Senior Mellon Fellow at the American Antiquarian Society. Currently she is working on a book about women's health advocate Mary Gove Nichols.

Sarah Stage

Sarah Stage was born in Davenport, Iowa, and received a B.A. from the University of Iowa in 1966 and a Ph.D. in American studies from Yale University in 1975. She has taught U.S. history for more than twenty-five years at Williams College and the University of California, Riverside. Currently she is professor of Women's Studies at Arizona State University at the West campus in Phoenix. Her books include *Female Complaints: Lydia Pinkham and the Business of Women's Medicine* (1979) and *Rethinking Home Economics: Women and the History of a Profession* (1997), which has been translated for a Japanese edition. Among the fellowships she has received are the Rockefeller Foundation Humanities Fellowship, the American Association of University Women dissertation fellowship, a fellowship from the Charles Warren Center for the Study of History at Harvard University, and the University of California President's Fellowship in the Humanities. She is at work on a book entitled *Women and the Progressive Impulse in American Politics, 1890–1914.*

Alan Lawson

Born in Providence, Rhode Island, Alan Lawson received his B.A. from Brown University in 1955 and his M.A. from the University of Wisconsin in 1956. After Army service and experience as a high school teacher, he earned his Ph.D. from the University of Michigan in 1967. Since winning the Allan Nevins Prize for his dissertation, Lawson has served on the faculties of the University of California, Irvine; Smith College; and, currently, Boston College. He has written *The Failure of Independent Liberalism* (1971) and coedited *From Revolution to Republic* (1976). While completing the forthcoming *Ideas in Crisis: The New Deal and the Mobilization of Progressive Experience,* he has published book chapters and essays on political economy, the cultural legacy of the New Deal, multiculturalism, and the arts in public life. He has served as editor of the *Review of Education* and the *Intellectual History Newsletter* and contributed articles to those journals as well as to the *History of Education Quarterly.* He has been active in the field of American studies as director of the Boston College American studies program and as a contributor to the *American Quarterly.* Under the auspices of the United States Information Agency, Lawson has been coordinator and lecturer for programs to instruct faculty from foreign nations in the state of American historical scholarship and teaching.

Susan M. Hartmann

Professor of history at Ohio State University, Susan M. Hartmann received her B.A. from Washington University and her Ph.D. from the University of Missouri. After specializing in the political economy of the post–World War II period and publishing *Truman and the 80th Congress* (1971), she expanded her interests to the field of women's history, publishing many articles and three books: *The Home Front and Beyond: American Women in the 1940s* (1982); *From Margin to Mainstream: American Women and Politics since 1960* (1989); and *The Other Feminists: Activists in the Liberal Establishment* (1998). Her work has been supported by the Truman Library Institute, the Rockefeller Foundation, the National Endowment for the Humanities, and the American Council of

Learned Societies. At Ohio State, she has served as director of women's studies, and in 1995 she won the Exemplary Faculty Award in the College of Humanities. Hartmann has taught at the University of Missouri, St. Louis, and Boston University, and she has lectured on American history in Australia, Austria, France, Germany, Greece, Japan, Nepal, and New Zealand. She is a fellow of the Society of American Historians; has served on award committees of the American Historical Association, the Organization of American Historians, the American Studies Association, and the National Women's Studies Association; and currently is on the Board of Directors at the Truman Library Institute. Her current research is on gender and the transformation of politics since 1945.

The
American
Promise

A HISTORY OF THE UNITED STATES

Fourth Edition

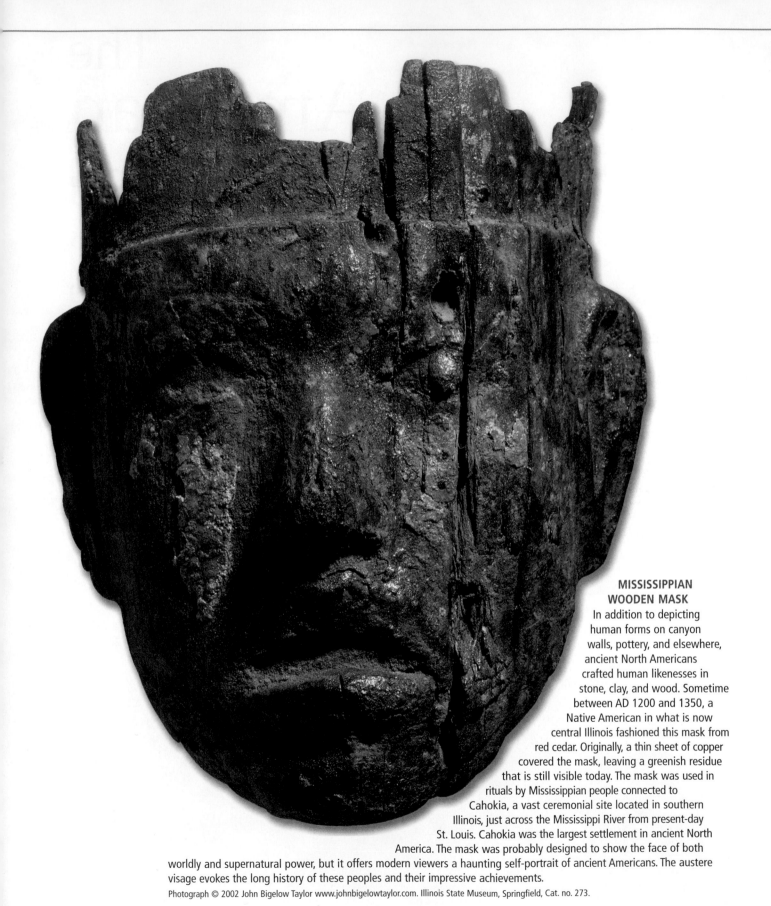

MISSISSIPPIAN WOODEN MASK

In addition to depicting human forms on canyon walls, pottery, and elsewhere, ancient North Americans crafted human likenesses in stone, clay, and wood. Sometime between AD 1200 and 1350, a Native American in what is now central Illinois fashioned this mask from red cedar. Originally, a thin sheet of copper covered the mask, leaving a greenish residue that is still visible today. The mask was used in rituals by Mississippian people connected to Cahokia, a vast ceremonial site located in southern Illinois, just across the Mississippi River from present-day St. Louis. Cahokia was the largest settlement in ancient North America. The mask was probably designed to show the face of both worldly and supernatural power, but it offers modern viewers a haunting self-portrait of ancient Americans. The austere visage evokes the long history of these peoples and their impressive achievements.

Ancient America

Before 1492

■ **Archaeology and History** 4

■ **The First Americans** 5
African and Asian Origins 6
Paleo-Indian Hunters 10

■ **Archaic Hunters
and Gatherers** 11
Great Plains Bison Hunters 12
Great Basin Cultures 13
Pacific Coast Cultures 13
Eastern Woodland Cultures 16

■ **Agricultural Settlements
and Chiefdoms** 17
Southwestern Cultures 18
Woodland Burial Mounds
and Chiefdoms 20

■ **Native Americans
in the 1490s** 22

■ **The Mexica: A Meso-American
Culture** 28

■ **Conclusion: The World
of Ancient Americans** 30

EORGE McJUNKIN, the manager of the Crowfoot Ranch near Folsom, New Mexico, rode out to mend fences and to look for missing cattle after a violent rainstorm in August 1908. An American of African descent, McJunkin had been born a slave in Texas and had been riding horses since he was a boy. After he became free at the end of the Civil War in 1865, McJunkin worked as a cowboy in Colorado and New Mexico before becoming the Crowfoot manager in 1891. Now, as he rode across the ranch land he knew so well to survey damage caused by the recent storm, McJunkin noticed that floodwater had washed away the bank of a gulch called Wild Horse Arroyo and exposed a deposit of stark white bones. Curious, he dismounted and chipped away at the deposit until he uncovered an entire fossilized bone. The bone was much larger than the parched skeletons of range cattle and buffalo that McJunkin often saw, so he saved it, hoping someday to identify it.

Four years later, in 1912, McJunkin met Carl Schwachheim, a white man in Raton, New Mexico. Schwachheim, a blacksmith, shared McJunkin's curiosity about fossils, and the two men became friends. McJunkin told Schwachheim about the fossil deposit he had discovered. Ten years later, a few months after McJunkin's death, Schwachheim finally drove out to Wild Horse Arroyo and dug out several bones. But, like McJunkin, he could not identify any animal that had such big bones.

In 1926, Schwachheim delivered cattle to the stockyards in Denver, and he took some of the fossilized bones to the Denver Museum of Natural History and showed them to J. D. Figgins, a paleontologist who was an expert on fossils of ancient animals. Figgins immediately recognized the significance of the bones and a few months later began an excavation of the Folsom site that revolutionized knowledge about the first Americans.

When Figgins began his dig at Folsom, archaeologists (individuals who examine **artifacts** left by long-vanished peoples as part of the study of **archaeology**) believed that Native Americans had arrived relatively recently in the Western Hemisphere, probably no more than three or four thousand years earlier, when, experts assumed, they had paddled small boats across the icy waters of the Bering Strait from what is now Siberia. At Folsom, Figgins learned that the bones McJunkin had first spotted belonged to twenty-three giant bison, a species known to have been extinct for at least 10,000 years. More startling, Figgins found nineteen flint spear points among the bones (Folsom points, they have since been called). Since no random natural process could have produced the finely crafted Folsom points, they seemed to prove

George McJunkin

This photo shows McJunkin a few years after he discovered the Folsom site but about fifteen years before anyone understood the significance of his find. He appears here in his work clothes on horseback, as he probably was when he made the discovery. The fossilized bones he discovered belonged to an extinct bison species that was much larger than modern bison; the horns of the ancient animal often spanned six feet, wide enough for McJunkin's horse to have stood sideways between them.

Eastern New Mexico University, Blackwater Draw Site, Portales, New Mexico 88130.

their descendants who built southwestern pueblos, eastern burial mounds, and much else. Most of the artifacts made by ancient Americans have been lost, destroyed by animals or natural deterioration, or they still lie buried under geological deposits that accumulated for millennia. But by careful study of the rare ancient artifacts that have survived and been discovered, archaeologists have pieced together an account of the long, complex history of ancient Americans. The story is necessarily incomplete and controversial because so much of what we would like to know about ancient Americans is simply unknowable. Evidence that would resolve uncertainties and settle disputes either no longer exists or awaits discovery. But archaeologists have learned enough in the last eighty years to understand where ancient Americans came from and many basic features of the complex **cultures** they created and passed along to their descendants, some of whom stood on the beach of a small island in the Caribbean in 1492 and watched Christopher Columbus and his men row ashore.

Archaeology and History

Archaeologists and historians share the desire to learn about people who lived in the past, but they usually employ different methods to obtain information. Both archaeologists and historians study artifacts as clues to the activities and ideas of the humans who created them. They concentrate, however, on different kinds of artifacts. Archaeologists tend to focus on physical objects such as bones, spear points, pots, baskets, jewelry, textiles, clothing, graves, and buildings. Historians direct their attention mostly to writings, including personal and private jottings such as letters and diary entries, official and public pronouncements such as laws and speeches, and an enormous variety of other documents, such as newspapers, business ledgers, and court cases. Although historians are interested in other artifacts and archaeologists do not neglect written sources if they exist, the characteristic concentration of historians on writings and archaeologists on other physical objects denotes a rough cultural and chronological boundary between the human beings studied by the two groups of scholars, a boundary marked by the use of writing.

that human beings had been alive at the same time as the giant bison. Skeptics worried that erosion, floods, earthquakes, or other geological events might have accidentally brought the old bones into proximity with possibly much younger Folsom points. But one spear point proved conclusively that the giant bison, the spear points, and the human beings who made them were contemporaries. One Folsom point remained stuck between two ribs of a giant bison, where a Stone Age hunter had plunged it more than 10,000 years earlier. No longer could anyone doubt that human beings had inhabited North America for at least ten millennia.

The Folsom discovery sparked other major finds of ancient artifacts that continue to this day. Since the 1930s, archaeologists have revolutionized our knowledge about ancient Americans. They have learned a great deal about the Folsom-era hunters who killed giant bison with flint-tipped spears, as well as about their ancestors who first arrived in North America and

Mexican Stone Tablet

In 2006, Mexican archaeologists announced the discovery of this stone tablet inscribed with the earliest evidence of writing in the Western Hemisphere. About 3,000 years ago, somebody in what is now the Mexican state of Veracruz incised this stone with sixty-two characters, barely visible in this photograph. Experts have not yet deciphered the writing, but the repetition of certain characters has caused some experts to speculate that it records poetry.

© Michael D. Coe.

Writing is defined as a system of symbols that record spoken language. Writing originated among ancient peoples in China, Egypt, and Central America about 8,000 years ago, within the most recent 2 percent of the 400 millennia that modern human beings (*Homo sapiens*) have existed. Writing came into use even later in most other places in the world. The ancient Americans who inhabited North America in 1492, for example, possessed many forms of symbolic representation, but not writing.

The people who lived during the millennia before writing were biologically nearly identical to us. Their DNA was the template for ours. But unlike us, they did not use writing to communicate across space and time. They invented hundreds of spoken languages; they moved across the face of the globe, learning to survive in almost every natural environment; they chose and honored leaders; they traded, warred, and worshipped; and, above all, they learned from and taught each other. Much of what we would like to know about their experiences remains unknown because it took place before writing existed. The absence of writing forever muffles their words and obscures their history.

Archaeologists specialize in learning about people who did not document their history in writing. They study the millions of artifacts these people created. They also scrutinize soil, geological strata, pollen, climate, and other environmental features to reconstruct as much as possible about the world ancient peoples inhabited. Although no documents chronicle ancient Americans' births and deaths, pleasures and pains, or victories and defeats, archaeologists have learned to make artifacts, along with their natural and human context, tell a great deal about the people who used them.

This chapter relies on studies by archaeologists to sketch a brief overview of ancient America, the long first phase of the history of the United States. Ancient Americans and their descendants resided in North America for thousands of years before Europeans arrived. They did not consider their lives a prelude to a future that included entirely unimaginable creations such as the United States or the twenty-first-century Americans who read this book. For their own reasons and in their own ways, they created societies and cultures of remarkable diversity and complexity. Because they did not use written records, their history cannot be reconstructed with the detail and certainty made possible by writing. But it is better to abbreviate and oversimplify ancient Americans' history than to ignore it.

> **REVIEW**   Why do historians rely on the work of archaeologists to write the history of ancient America?

The First Americans

The first human beings to arrive in the Western Hemisphere emigrated from Asia. They brought with them hunting skills, weapon- and tool-making techniques, and a full range of other forms of human knowledge developed millennia earlier in Africa, Europe, and Asia. These first Americans hunted large mammals, such as the mammoths they had learned in Europe and Asia to kill, butcher, and process for food, clothing,

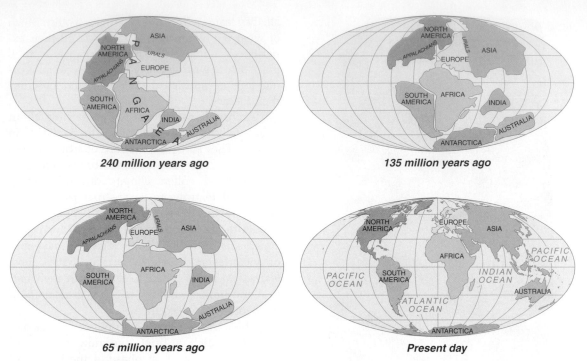

240 million years ago

135 million years ago

65 million years ago

Present day

MAP 1.1   Continental Drift
Massive geological forces separated North and South America from other continents eons before human beings evolved in Africa in the past 1.5 million years.

READING THE MAP: Which continents separated from Pangaea earliest? Which ones separated from each other last? Which are still closely connected to each other?

CONNECTIONS: How does continental drift explain why human life developed elsewhere on the planet for hundreds of thousands of years before the first person entered the Western Hemisphere during the past 15,000 years?

FOR MORE HELP ANALYZING THIS MAP, see the map activity for this chapter in the Online Study Guide at **bedfordstmartins.com/roark.**

building materials, and many other purposes. Most likely, these first Americans wandered into the Western Hemisphere more or less accidentally, hungry and in pursuit of their prey.

African and Asian Origins

Human beings lived elsewhere in the world for hundreds of thousands of years before they reached the Western Hemisphere. Humans lacked a way to travel to the Western Hemisphere because millions of years before humans existed anywhere on the globe, North and South America became detached from the gigantic common landmass scientists now call Pangaea. About 240 million years ago, powerful forces deep within the earth fractured Pangaea and slowly pushed the continents apart to approximately their present positions (Map 1.1). This process of continental drift encircled the land of the Western Hemisphere with large

oceans that isolated it from the other continents, long before early human beings (*Homo erectus*) first appeared in Africa about 2 million years ago. (Hereafter in this chapter, the abbreviation *BP*—archaeologists' notation for "years before the present"—is used to indicate dates earlier than 2,000 years ago. Dates more recent than 2,000 years ago are indicated with the common and familiar notation *AD*—for example, AD 1492.)

More than a million and a half years after *Homo erectus* appeared, or about 400,000 BP, modern humans (*Homo sapiens*) evolved in Africa. All human beings throughout the world today are descendants of these ancient Africans. Slowly, over many millennia, *Homo sapiens* migrated out of Africa and into Europe and Asia. Unlike North and South America, Europe and Asia retained land connections to Africa, making this migration possible for *Homo sapiens*. These ancient humans traveled mostly on foot, although sometimes they navigated rivers and lakes in small boats that could not survive battering by the oceans' winds and waves. The enormous oceans isolating North and South America from the Eurasian landmass kept human beings away for roughly 97 percent of the time *Homo sapiens* have been on earth.

Two major developments made it possible for human beings to migrate to the Western Hemisphere. First, humans successfully adapted to the frigid environment near the Arctic Circle. Second, changes in the earth's climate reconnected North America to Asia.

By about 25,000 BP, *Homo sapiens* had spread from Africa throughout Europe and Asia. People, probably women, had learned to use bone needles to sew animal skins into warm clothing that permitted them to become permanent residents of extremely cold regions such as northeastern Siberia. A few of these ancient Siberians clothed in animal hides walked to North America on land that now lies submerged beneath sixty miles of water that currently separates easternmost Siberia from westernmost Alaska. During the last global cold spell—the Wisconsin glaciation, which endured from about 25,000–14,000 BP to 10,000 BP—snow piled up in glaciers, causing the sea level to drop

as much as 350 feet below its current level. The falling sea level exposed what experts refer to as a land bridge between Asian Siberia and American Alaska. This land bridge, which scientists call Beringia, opened up a pathway hundreds of miles wide between the Eastern and Western Hemispheres.

Siberian hunters presumably roamed Beringia for centuries in search of game animals. (See "Beyond America's Borders," page 8.) Grasses and small shrubs that covered Beringia supported herds of mammoths, bison, and numerous smaller animals. As the hunters ventured farther and farther east, they eventually became pioneers of human life in the Western Hemisphere. Their migrations probably had very little influence on their own lives, which continued more or less in the age-old ways they had learned from their Siberian ancestors. Although they did not know it, their migrations revolutionized the history of the world.

Archaeologists refer to these first migrants and their descendants for the next few millennia

Beringia

FIGURE 1.1   Human Habitation of the World and the Western Hemisphere

These clock faces illustrate the long global history of modern humans (left) and of human history in the Western Hemisphere since the arrival of the first ancient Americans (right). If the total period of human life on earth is considered, American history since the arrival of Columbus in 1492 comprises less than one minute (or one-tenth of 1 percent) of modern human existence. And if the total period of human life in the New World is converted from millennia to a 12-hour clock, ancient American history makes up the first 11½ hours, and all history since the arrival of the Europeans in 1492 occupies only the last half hour.

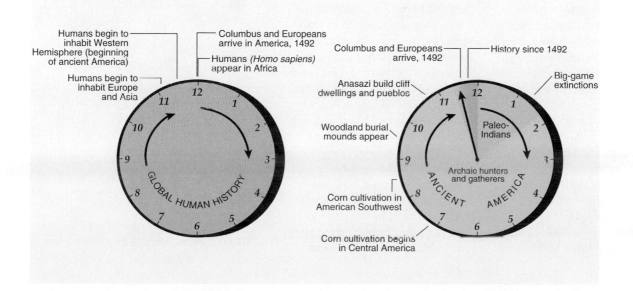

Nature's Immigrants

Like the first human beings who came to the New World, most of the large animals in ancient America were descendants of migrants from elsewhere around the globe. Mammoths, the signature prey of the Clovis hunters of ancient America, illustrate the persistent immigration of animals from Asia to North America. The ancestors of the mammoths that Clovis hunters stalked about 12,000 years ago had emigrated from Asia about 1.7 million years earlier. The first mammoth migrants from Asia followed in the tracks of hundreds of other animal species that had made their way across Beringia to North America for more than 60 million years. These immigrants and their descendants populated the natural environment of America that ancient Americans first encountered. Clearly, America was a land of immigrants long before the first humans arrived.

An extraterrestrial event created the basic precondition for these animal migrations. Scientists have discovered convincing evidence that about 65 million years ago, a meteorite about six miles in diameter slammed into the Yucatán peninsula in Mexico. Experts estimate that the meteorite sped toward the Yucatán at about 54,000 miles an hour and cratered into the earth with an explosion equivalent to trillions of atomic bombs. Coming in at a low angle to the curvature of the earth from the direction of the Southern Hemisphere, the meteorite incinerated almost all the exposed animals and plants in North America with a blast of heat a thousand times hotter than that reaching the earth from the sun. The plume of dust and smoke propelled into the atmosphere by the impact of the meteorite darkened skies, reduced or eliminated photosynthesis, and showered the earth with sulfuric acid. These catastrophic changes in the global environment caused the extinction of many animals worldwide, including dinosaurs that had ruled the earth for more than 100 million years. But outside the fiery blast zone that extended thousands of miles north from ground zero in the Yucatán, many animals survived the mass extinction and became the ancestors of animals that eventually migrated to North America.

Among the animals that survived the great extinction were small ratlike creatures, the ancestors of mammals that began to multiply and remultiply, ultimately filling many of the environmental niches previously occupied by dinosaurs and other extinct species. For example, a tiny hoofed mammal now called *Procerberus* made the trek across Beringia from Asia to North America and within about 4 million years spawned dozens of new species of hoofed mammals in the New World, the largest the size of a small pony. *Procerberus* became the ancient ancestor of both horses and camels, species that evolved first in North America.

In the millions of years that followed the ancestor species' initial migration from Asia, distinctive North American descendants evolved, just as horses and camels did. The ancestor of North American cats migrated from Asia about 17 million years ago, but within a few million years, North America had evolved distinctive cat species, including lions roughly twice as large as the largest male African lions today. Similarly, nature's migrants from Asia developed into distinctive North American elephants (including mammoths), rhinoceroses, and pigs, as well as many smaller creatures such as beavers, skunks, and weasels. Although the migration of ancient birds is less well known because of the scarcity of fossil remains, the ancestor of today's common raven made the colossal journey to North America over millions of years by flying through Asia from its starting point in Australia.

Some animals that evolved in North America eventually migrated back to Asia and beyond. Horses and camels illustrate this two-way traffic on the Beringian land bridge. Horses evolved in North America for about 20 million years before they first wandered across the land bridge

Meteor Impact in North America, 65 Million Years Ago

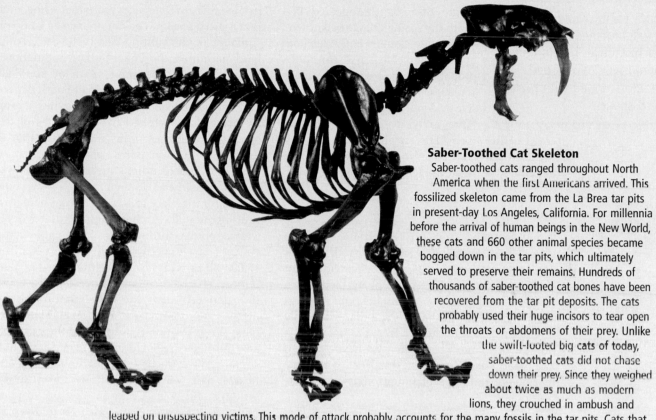

Saber-Toothed Cat Skeleton
Saber-toothed cats ranged throughout North America when the first Americans arrived. This fossilized skeleton came from the La Brea tar pits in present-day Los Angeles, California. For millennia before the arrival of human beings in the New World, these cats and 660 other animal species became bogged down in the tar pits, which ultimately served to preserve their remains. Hundreds of thousands of saber-toothed cat bones have been recovered from the tar pit deposits. The cats probably used their huge incisors to tear open the throats or abdomens of their prey. Unlike the swift-footed big cats of today, saber-toothed cats did not chase down their prey. Since they weighed about twice as much as modern lions, they crouched in ambush and leaped on unsuspecting victims. This mode of attack probably accounts for the many fossils in the tar pits. Cats that attacked prey mired in the sticky tar probably became trapped themselves sometimes. Like many other big mammals that inhabited North America during the Paleo-Indian era, the saber-toothed cat became extinct about 11,000 BP. George C. Page Museum.

to Asia. They didn't stop there. Modern-day zebras on the plains of Africa are the descendants of those ancient American migrant horses. Camels were much more recent out-migrants, wending their way from North America to Asia only about 4 million years ago. Dogs, evidently one of the few native North American mammals, also migrated to Asia, along with other distinctive species. But the dominant stream of nature's migrants was in the other direction, from Asia to North America. The greater variety of well-established species in the larger Asian landmass made it difficult for

many North American species to get a foothold there. Conversely, migrants from Asia more readily carved out an environmental niche for themselves in the New World.

On the eve of the arrival of ancient Americans in the New World, the large mammals they would prey upon—and in some cases compete with for prey—were the descendants of migrants that had preceded the first Americans millions of years earlier. The giant bison that roamed the plains—and whose fossilized remains George McJunkin excavated early in the twentieth century—descended from Asian migrants. So did

the giant sloths that measured eighteen feet from nose to tail and weighed three tons. So did the massive short-faced bear that ran down its prey despite weighing the better part of a ton. So did the saber-toothed cat that, fossil deposits prove, feasted on young mammoths. And so did the mammoths themselves. The human beings who first set foot in the New World were pioneers of human migration to North America, but they were only the latest of latecomers among the thousands of nature's migrants from Asia that had been pioneering in North America for more than 60 million years.

as Paleo-Indians. They speculate that these Siberian hunters traveled in small bands of no more than twenty-five people. How many such bands arrived in North America before Beringia disappeared beneath the sea will never be known. When they came is hotly debated by experts. The first migrants probably arrived sometime after 15,000 BP. Scattered and inconclusive evidence suggests that they may have arrived several thousand years earlier. (See "Historical Question," page 14). Certainly, humans who originated in Asia inhabited the Western Hemisphere by 13,500 BP.

> North, Central, and South America teemed with wildlife that had never before confronted wily two-legged predators armed with razor-sharp spears.

Paleo-Indian Hunters

When humans first arrived in the Western Hemisphere, massive glaciers covered most of present-day Canada. A narrow corridor not entirely obstructed by ice ran along the eastern side of Canada's Rocky Mountains, and most archaeologists believe that Paleo-Indians probably migrated through the ice-free passageway in pursuit of game. They may also have traveled along the Pacific coast in small boats, hunting marine life and hopscotching from one desirable

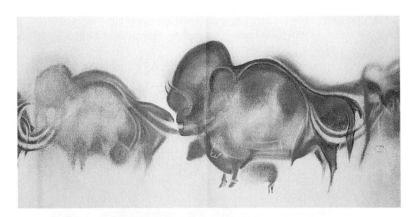

Mammoth Cave Painting
Like Clovis peoples in ancient America, human beings elsewhere in the world hunted mammoths. An ancient artist painted this portrait of mammoths on the wall of a cave in southern France about 16,000 BP. The painting conveys the artist's close observation of mammoths. It is easy to understand why the artist and hunters throughout the world paid respectful attention to mammoths. North American mammoths hunted by Clovis Paleo-Indians stood about fourteen feet tall at the shoulder and weighed eight to ten tons. Their tusks stretched to sixteen feet in length. Each of their four teeth was about the size of a shoebox. Although mammoths were vegetarians, they presumably knew how to throw their weight around against puny humans. Hunters armed with stone-tipped wooden spears needed to study such formidable prey to identify their vulnerabilities.
Musée de l'Homme.

landing spot to another. At the southern edge of the glaciers, Paleo-Indians entered a hunters' paradise. North, Central, and South America teemed with wildlife that had never before confronted wily two-legged predators armed with razor-sharp spears. The abundance of game presumably made hunting relatively easy. Ample food permitted the Paleo-Indian population to grow. Within a thousand years or so, Paleo-Indians had migrated to the tip of South America and virtually everywhere else in the Western Hemisphere, as proved by discoveries of their spear points in numerous excavations that followed George McJunkin's Folsom find.

Early Paleo-Indians used a distinctively shaped spearhead known as a Clovis point, named for the place in New Mexico where it was first excavated. Archaeologists' discovery of Clovis points throughout North and Central America in sites occupied between 13,500 BP and 13,000 BP provides evidence that these nomadic hunters shared a common ancestry and way of life. Paleo-Indians hunted mammoths and bison—judging from the artifacts and bones that have survived from this era—but they probably also hunted smaller animals. They also likely scavenged the carcasses of mammoths and other beasts that became mired in the abundant swamps and bogs. Concentration on large animals, when possible, made sense because just one mammoth kill supplied hunters with meat for weeks or, if dried, for months. Some Paleo-Indians even refrigerated mammoth meat for later use by filling the intestines with stones and sinking the carcass to the bottom of an icy lake. In addition to food, mammoth kills provided hides and bones for clothing, shelter, tools, and much more.

About 11,000 BP, Paleo-Indians confronted a major crisis. The mammoths and other large mammals they hunted became extinct. The extinction was gradual, stretching over several hundred years. Scientists are not completely certain why it occurred, although environmental change probably contributed to it. About this time, the earth's climate warmed, glaciers melted, and sea levels rose. Mammoths and other large mammals probably had difficulty adapting to the warmer climate. Many archaeologists also believe, however, that Paleo-Indians probably contributed to the extinctions in the Western Hemisphere by killing large animals more rapidly than they could reproduce. Although this overkill hypothesis is disputed by some experts, similar environmental changes

Clovis Spear Straightener

Clovis hunters used this bone spear straightener about 11,000 BP at a campsite in Arizona where archaeologists discovered it lying among the butchered remains of two mammoth carcasses and thirteen ancient bison. Similar objects often appear in ancient sites in Eurasia, but this is the only bone artifact yet discovered in a Clovis-era site in North America. Presumably Clovis hunters stuck their spear shafts through the opening and then grasped the handle of the straightener and moved it back and forth along the length of the shaft to remove imperfections and make the spear a more effective weapon.

Arizona State Museum, University of Arizona.

had occurred for millions of years without triggering the large mammal extinctions that followed the arrival of Paleo-Indian hunters. Whatever the causes, Paleo-Indian hunters faced a radical change in the natural environment within just a few thousand years of their arrival in the Western Hemisphere—namely, the extinction of large mammals that had existed for millions of years and whose presence had initially drawn Siberian hunters east across Beringia. After the extinction, Paleo-Indians literally inhabited a new world.

Paleo-Indians adapted to the drastic environmental change of the big-game extinction by making at least two important changes in their way of life. First, hunters began to prey more intensively on smaller animals. Second, Paleo-Indians devoted more energy to foraging—that is, to collecting wild plant foods such as roots, seeds, nuts, berries, and fruits. When Paleo-Indians made these changes, they replaced the apparent uniformity of the big-game-oriented Clovis culture with great cultural diversity. This diversity arose because ancient Americans adapted to the many natural environments throughout the hemisphere, ranging from icy tundra to steamy jungles.

Post-Clovis adaptations to local environments resulted in the astounding variety of Native American cultures that existed when Europeans arrived in AD 1492. By then, more than three hundred major tribes and hundreds of lesser groups inhabited North America alone. Hundreds more lived in Central and South America. These peoples spoke different languages, practiced different religions, lived in different dwellings, followed different subsistence strategies, and observed different rules of kinship and inheritance. Hundreds of other ancient American cultures had disappeared or transformed themselves as their people constantly adapted to environmental change and other challenges.

> **REVIEW** Why were humans able to migrate into North America after 15,000 BP?

Archaic Hunters and Gatherers

Archaeologists use the term **Archaic** to describe both the many different hunting and gathering cultures that descended from Paleo-Indians and the long period of time when those cultures dominated the history of ancient America, roughly from 10,000 BP to somewhere between 4000 BP and 3000 BP. The term usefully describes the era in the history of ancient America that followed the Paleo-Indian big-game hunters and preceded the development of agriculture. It denotes a hunter-gatherer way of life that persisted in North America long after European colonization.

Like their Paleo-Indian ancestors, Archaic Indians hunted with spears; but they also took smaller game with traps, nets, and hooks. Unlike their Paleo-Indian predecessors, most Archaic peoples used a variety of stone tools to prepare food from wild plants. A characteristic Archaic artifact is a grinding stone used to pulverize seeds into edible form. Most Archaic Indians migrated from place to place to harvest plants and hunt animals. They usually did not establish permanent villages, although they often returned to the same river valley

> About 11,000 BP, Paleo-Indians confronted a major crisis. The mammoths and other large mammals they hunted became extinct.

or fertile meadow from year to year. In certain regions with especially rich resources—such as present-day California and the Pacific Northwest—they developed permanent settlements. Many groups became highly proficient basket makers in order to collect and store plant food. But the food they harvested came from wild plants and animals, rather than from agriculture. Archaic peoples followed these practices in distinctive ways in the different environmental regions of North America (Map 1.2, page 12).

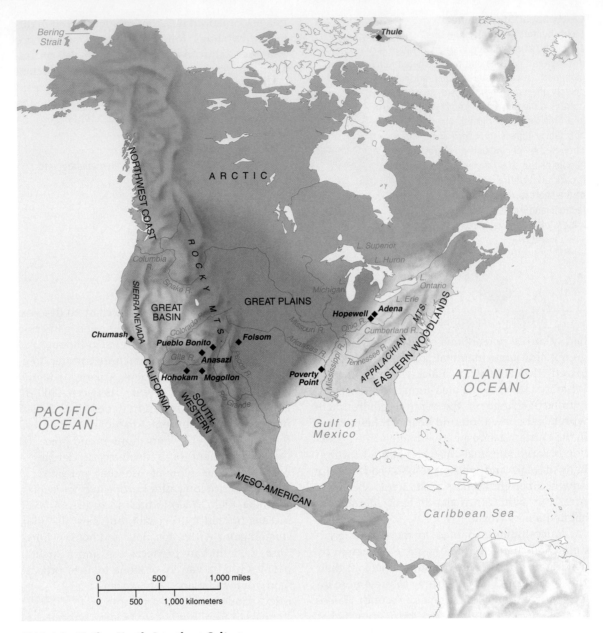

MAP 1.2   Native North American Cultures
Environmental conditions defined the boundaries of the broad zones of cultural similarity among ancient North Americans.

READING THE MAP: What crucial environmental features set the boundaries of each cultural region? (The topography indicated on Map 1.3, "Native North Americans about 1500," may be helpful.)
CONNECTIONS: How did environmental factors and variations affect the development of different groups of Native American cultures? Why do you think historians and archaeologists group cultures together by their regional positions?

FOR MORE HELP ANALYZING THIS MAP, see the map activity for this chapter in the Online Study Guide at bedfordstmartins.com/roark.

Great Plains Bison Hunters

After the extinction of large game animals, some hunters began to concentrate on bison in the huge herds that grazed the grassy, arid plains stretching for hundreds of miles east of the Rocky Mountains. For almost a thousand years after the big-game extinctions, Archaic Indians hunted bison with Folsom points like those found at the site discovered by George McJunkin.

Like their nomadic predecessors, Folsom hunters moved constantly to maintain contact with their prey. Often two or three hunters from a band of several families would single out a few bison from a herd and creep up close enough to spear them. Great Plains hunters also developed trapping techniques that made it easier to kill large numbers of animals. At the original Folsom site, careful study of the bones McJunkin found suggests that early one winter hunters drove bison into the narrow gulch and speared twenty-three of them. At other sites, Great Plains hunters stampeded bison herds over cliffs, then slaughtered the animals that plunged to their deaths.

Bows and arrows reached Great Plains hunters from the north about AD 500. They largely replaced spears, which had been the hunters' weapons of choice for millennia. Bows permitted hunters to wound an animal from farther away, arrows made it possible to shoot repeatedly, and arrowheads were easier to make and therefore less costly to lose than the larger, heavier spear points. But these new weapons did not otherwise alter age-old techniques of bison hunting on the Great Plains. Although we tend to imagine ancient Great Plains bison hunters on horseback, in fact they hunted on foot, like their Paleo-Indian ancestors. Horses that had existed in North America millions of years earlier had long since become extinct. (See "Beyond America's Borders," page 8.) Horses did not return to the Great Plains until Europeans imported them in the decades after 1492. Native American bison hunters acquired them soon thereafter and quickly became expert riders.

Great Basin Cultures

Archaic peoples in the Great Basin between the Rocky Mountains and the Sierra Nevada inhabited a region of great environmental diversity. Some Great Basin Indians lived along the shores of large marshes and lakes that formed during rainy periods. They ate fish of every available size and type, catching them with bone hooks and nets. Other cultures survived in the foothills of mountains between the blistering heat on the desert floor and the cold, treeless mountain heights. Hunters killed deer, antelope, and sometimes bison, as well as smaller game such as rabbits, rodents, and snakes. These broadly defined zones of habitation changed constantly, depending largely on the amount of rain.

Despite the variety and occasional abundance of animals, Great Basin peoples relied on plants for their most important food source. Unlike meat and fish, plant food could be collected and stored for long periods to protect against shortages caused by the fickle rainfall. Many Great Basin peoples gathered ample supplies of piñon nuts as a dietary staple. By diversifying their food sources and migrating to favorable locations to collect and store them, Great Basin peoples adapted to the severe environmental challenges of the region and maintained their Archaic hunter-gatherer way of life for centuries after Europeans arrived in AD 1492.

Pacific Coast Cultures

The richness of the natural environment made present-day California the most densely settled area in all of ancient North America. The land and ocean offered such ample food that

Folsom Point at Wild Horse Arroyo
In 1927, paleontologist J. D. Figgins found this spear point (subsequently named a Folsom point) at the site discovered by George McJunkin. Embedded between the fossilized ribs of a bison that had been extinct for 10,000 years, this point proved that ancient Americans had inhabited the hemisphere at least that long. The importance of this find led one paleontologist to hold up several Folsom points and proclaim, "In my hand I hold the answer to the antiquity of man in America." Although he exaggerated (Folsom was only part of the answer), this discovery in Wild Horse Arroyo stimulated archaeologists to rethink the history of ancient Americans and to uncover fresh evidence of their many cultures.

Who Were the First Americans?

To learn where the first humans who migrated to the Western Hemisphere came from and when they arrived requires following a trail that has grown very cold during the past 15,000 or more years. After millennia of erosion and environmental change, much of the land they walked, hunted, and camped on is now submerged and inaccessible, not only beneath the Bering Sea but also along the Atlantic and Pacific coasts of North America, where rising sea levels have flooded wide, previously exposed coastal plains. Archaeologists have located numerous Paleo-Indian sites, but many of them (such as the Folsom site) date to hundreds of centuries after the first migrants arrived. Kill sites often yield spear points and large animal bones, but Paleo-Indian human skeletal remains are very rare. And yet evidence that Paleo-Indians inhabited the Western Hemisphere is overwhelming and indisputable. Human craftsmanship is the only plausible explanation for Clovis points, and carbon dating establishes that the oldest Clovis sites are about 13,500 years old.

Scattered and controversial evidence suggests, however, that Clovis peoples were not the first arrivals. The Monte Verde excavation in Chile has persuaded many archaeologists that the first Americans resided in South America sometime between 14,750 and 14,000 BP. This site and a few other likely pre-Clovis sites in North America, most notably Meadowcroft in Pennsylvania, contain no Clovis-era artifacts, suggesting that their inhabitants arrived

earlier and differed from the later Clovis peoples. But if the first Americans already lived in Chile and Pennsylvania 14,000 or more years ago, when did they first arrive and from where?

Some experts hypothesize that pre-Clovis peoples sailed or floated across the Pacific from Australia, which had human inhabitants by at least 35,000 BP. Another speculation posits ancient Australians sailing first to Antarctica and then up the west coast of South America. These proposals of ancient Australians or Southeast Asians as the first Americans strike most scholars as far-fetched. The Pacific is too wide and tempestuous for these ancient peoples and their small boats to have survived a long transoceanic trip. The Polynesian islands lie much closer to Australia than does the Western Hemisphere, and human beings did not make that shorter journey until about 3,500 years ago.

Ancient Siberians had the means (hunting skills and adaptation to the frigid climate), motive (pursuit of game animals), and opportunity (the Beringian land bridge) to become the first humans to arrive in America, and most archaeologists believe they did just that. But when they came is difficult to determine, since the Beringian land bridge existed for thousands of years. The extreme rarity of the earliest archaeological sites in North America also makes it difficult to estimate with confidence when pre-Clovis hunters arrived. A rough guess is 15,000 BP, although it might have been considerably earlier. The

scarcity of pre-Clovis sites discovered so far strongly suggests that these ancient Americans were few in number (compared to the much more numerous Clovis-era Paleo-Indians), very widely scattered, and ultimately unsuccessful in establishing permanent residence in the hemisphere. Although they and their descendants may have survived in America for a millennium or more, pre-Clovis peoples appear to have died out. The sparse archaeological evidence discovered to date does not suggest that they evolved into Clovis peoples.

Exactly how Clovis culture emerged remains a mystery. Close counterparts of Clovis points— the signature artifacts of North American Clovis sites—have not been found in Siberia or elsewhere outside America. Clovis culture, according to the archaeological evidence, appears to have arisen, flourished, and spread rapidly, as if it were an improvisation by newly arrived immigrants—an improvisation that perhaps never occurred among the people the immigrants left behind. Although Clovis peoples evidently were not the first humans to arrive in the Western Hemisphere, they may well represent the first Paleo-Indians to establish a permanent American presence.

To investigate where the mysterious first Americans came from, experts have supplemented archaeological evidence with careful study of modern-day Native Americans. Although many millennia separate today's Native Americans from those ancient hunters, most scholars agree that telltale clues to the identity of the first Americans can be gleaned from dental, linguistic, and genetic evidence collected from their descendants who still live throughout the hemisphere.

Detailed scientific analyses of the teeth of thousands of ancient and modern Native Americans have identified distinctive dental shapes—such as incisors with a scooped-out inner surface—commonly found among ancient Siberians, ancient Americans, and modern Native Americans, but rare elsewhere. This dental evidence strongly supports the Asian origins and Beringian migration route of the first Americans with descendants among contemporary Native Americans.

Linguistic analysis of more than a thousand modern Native American languages suggests that they cluster into three principal groups that appear to result from three separate ancient migrations. Aleut, spoken from Alaska across northern Canada to Greenland, seems to have been brought by the most recent migrants, who arrived about 4000 BP. Na-Dené, restricted to western Canada, appears to have arrived with migrants who came about 5,000 years earlier. Amerind is by far the most common group of Native American languages. Some form of Amerind is spoken by Native Americans throughout the hemisphere, the consequence (presumably) of its arrival with the earliest wave of ancient migrants around 13,000 BP. This migration chronology and linguistic analysis remains controversial among experts, but it is consistent with geological evidence of the Beringian land bridge and archaeological evidence of Clovis peoples. Taken together, the evidence suggests that Clovis peoples spoke some ancient form of Amerind.

Genetic research into the mutation rate of DNA inside mitochondria (tiny, intracellular structures that carry out metabolic functions and are believed to mutate at a predictable rate) demonstrates that many modern Native Americans share

Clovis Artifacts
These Clovis-era artifacts were excavated from five mammoth kill sites in the United States. All the stone points show the signature Clovis shape with the distinctive flaking along the edges. The smaller points display a notched indentation at the bottom for tying the points to spear shafts. The largest stone implements in the photograph probably served as knives for butchering game or scrapers for cleaning hides. The bone object with a hole in one end was used to straighten spear shafts by scraping away imperfections. The slender bone rod is precisely inscribed with orderly serrations; its purpose is unknown. Experts speculate that it may have been used to flake chips to make spear points or attached to the end of a spear shaft to strengthen the connection between the shaft and the point. These artifacts illustrate the variety of Clovis objects found throughout the Western Hemisphere and their underlying similarity. Archaeologists believe that the commonalities in Clovis artifacts document a widely shared Clovis culture brought into being by ancient Americans who spread it across thousands of miles and many human generations.
© Peter A. Bostrom.

genetic characteristics commonly found in Asians. Calculating the evolutionary time estimated to account for the subtle differences between Asian and Native American strains of mitochondrial DNA suggests a much earlier migration from Asia, possibly around 25,000 BP or before. But like the other high-tech evidence, this genetic evidence is sharply disputed by experts.

Fascinating as the genetic, linguistic, and dental studies are, they are unlikely to win widespread support among experts until they can be firmly corroborated by archaeological

evidence that, so far, has not been found. As a recent U.S. government study of the earliest Americans concluded, "How far back in time initial colonization [of America] occurred, how many separate migrations took place, whether all these migrations were successful, and the geographical and biological affinities of these founding populations remain ambiguous, and are subjects currently under intensive investigation by archaeologists."

Who were the first Americans? Thus far, no conclusive answer to this historical question has been found.

California peoples remained hunters and gatherers for hundreds of years after AD 1492. The diversity of California's environment also encouraged corresponding diversity among native peoples. The mosaic of Archaic settlements in California included about five hundred separate tribes speaking some ninety languages, each with local dialects. No other region of comparable size in North America exhibited such cultural variety.

The Chumash, one of the many California cultures, emerged in the region surrounding what is now Santa Barbara about 5000 BP. Comparatively plentiful food resources—especially acorns—permitted Chumash people to establish relatively permanent villages. Conflict, evidently caused by competition for valuable acorn-gathering territory, frequently broke out among the villages, as documented by Chumash skeletons that display signs of violent deaths. Although few other California cultures achieved the population density and village settlements of the Chumash, all shared the hunter-gatherer way of life and reliance on acorns as a major food source.

Another rich natural environment lay along the Pacific Northwest coast. Like the Chumash, Northwest peoples built more or less permanent villages. After about 5500 BP, they concentrated on catching whales and large quantities of salmon, halibut, and other fish, which they dried to last throughout the year. They also traded with people who lived hundreds of miles from the coast. Fishing freed Northwest peoples to develop sophisticated woodworking skills. They fashioned elaborate wood carvings that denoted wealth and status, as well as huge canoes for fishing, hunting, and conducting warfare against neighboring tribes. Much of the warfare among Archaic northwesterners grew out of attempts to defend or gain access to prime fishing sites.

Chumash Necklace
Long before the arrival of Europeans, ancient Chumash people in southern California made this elegant necklace of abalone shell. The carefully formed, polished, and assembled pieces of shell illustrate the artistry of the Chumash and their access to the rich and diverse marine life of the Pacific coast. Since living abalone cling stubbornly to submerged rocks along the coast, Chumash divers presumably pried abalone from their rocky perches to obtain their delicious flesh; then one or more Chumash artisans recycled the inedible shell to make this necklace. Its iridescent splendor demonstrates that Chumash people wore beautiful as well as useful adornments.
Natural History Museum of Los Angeles County.

Ancient California Peoples

Tolowa
Yurok Karok Shasta
Wiyot Hupa Achomawi
Chimariko Wintun Atsugewi
Nomlaki Yana Yani Maidu
Yuki
Pomo Konkow
Wappo Patwin
Costano Miwok
NORTH AMERICA
Esselen Mono
Salina Yokut
Chumash Tubatulabal Kitanemuk
Serrano
Fernandeno
Gabrielino
Juaneno Cahuilla
Luiseno Cupeno
Diegueno
Kamia
Akwa'ala
PACIFIC OCEAN
Nakipa Kiliwa
Cochimi
Ignacieno
Waicura
Pericu

0   125   250 miles
0 125 250 kilometers

Eastern Woodland Cultures

East of the Mississippi River, Archaic peoples adapted to a forest environment that included many local variants, such as the major river valleys of the Mississippi, Ohio, Tennessee, and Cumberland; the Great Lakes region; and the Atlantic coast (see Map 1.2). Throughout these diverse locales, Archaic peoples followed similar survival strategies.

Woodland hunters stalked deer as their most important prey. Deer supplied Woodland peoples with food as well as hides and bones that they crafted into clothing, weapons, needles, and many other tools. Like Archaic peoples elsewhere, Woodland Indians gathered edible plants, seeds, and nuts, especially hickory nuts, pecans, walnuts, and acorns. About 6000 BP, some Woodland groups established more or less permanent settlements of 25 to 150 people, usually near a river or lake that offered a wide variety of

Ozette Whale Effigy
This carving of a whale fin decorated with hundreds of sea otter teeth was discovered along with thousands of other artifacts of daily life at Ozette, an ancient village on the tip of the Olympic Peninsula in present-day Washington that was inundated by a catastrophic mud slide about five hundred years ago. The fin illustrates the importance of whale hunting to the residents of Ozette, who set out in canoes, each carrying eight men armed with harpoons to catch and kill animals weighing twenty to thirty tons.
Richard Alexander Cooke III.

plant and animal resources. The existence of such settlements has permitted archaeologists to locate numerous Archaic burial sites that suggest Woodland people had a life expectancy of about eighteen years. Imagine what such a short life expectancy (by modern standards) meant for Archaic Woodland people who needed to learn all the skills necessary to survive, reproduce, and adapt to change.

Around 4000 BP, Woodland cultures added two important features to their basic hunter-gatherer lifestyles: agriculture and pottery. Gourds and pumpkins that were first cultivated thousands of years earlier in Mexico spread north to Woodland peoples through trade and migration. Woodland peoples also began to cultivate local species such as sunflowers, as well as small quantities of tobacco, another import from South America. Corn was the most important plant food carried to North America by traders and migrants from Mexico, and it became a significant Woodland food crop around 2500 BP. Most likely, women learned how to plant, grow, and harvest these crops as an outgrowth of their work gathering edible wild plants. Cultivated crops added to the quantity, variety, and predictability of Woodland food sources, but they did not alter Woodland peoples' dependence on gathering wild plants, seeds, and nuts.

Like agriculture, pottery also probably originated in Mexico. Traders and migrants probably brought pots into North America along with Central and South American seeds. Pots were more durable than baskets for cooking and storage of food and water, but they were also much heavier, and therefore were shunned by nomadic peoples. The permanent settlements of Woodland peoples made the heavy weight of pots much less important than their advantages compared to leaky and fragile baskets. While pottery and agriculture introduced changes in Woodland cultures, ancient Woodland Americans retained the other basic features of their Archaic hunter-gatherer lifestyle, which persisted in most areas to 1492 and beyond.

REVIEW Why did Archaic Native Americans shift from big-game hunting to foraging and smaller-game hunting?

Agricultural Settlements and Chiefdoms

Among Eastern Woodland peoples and most other Archaic cultures, agriculture supplemented, but did not replace, hunter-gatherer subsistence strategies. Reliance on wild animals and plants required most Archaic groups to remain small and mobile. But beginning about 4000 BP, distinctive southwestern cultures slowly began to depend on agriculture

Ceramic Jar
This handsome jar, crafted about 2000 BP by a Woodland potter (probably a woman), illustrates the usefulness of ceramic pots for storage and cooking and exhibits the human delight in decorative artistry.
Gilcrease Museum, Tulsa, Oklahoma.

Ancient Agriculture
Dropping seeds into holes punched in cleared ground by a pointed stick, known as a "dibble," this ancient American farmer sows a new crop while previously planted seeds—including the corn and beans immediately opposite him—bear fruit for harvest. Created by a sixteenth-century European artist, the drawing misrepresents who did the agricultural work in many ancient American cultures—namely, women rather than men. However, the three-foot dibble would have been used as shown here.
The Pierpont Morgan Library/Art Resource, NY; Jerry Jacka Photography.

READING THE IMAGE: In what ways has this ancient farmer modified and taken advantage of the natural environment?
CONNECTIONS: What were the advantages and disadvantages of agriculture compared to hunting and gathering?

FOR MORE HELP ANALYZING THIS IMAGE, see the visual activity for this chapter in the Online Study Guide at bedfordstmartins.com/roark.

and to build permanent settlements. Later, around 2500 BP, Woodland peoples in the vast Mississippi valley began to construct burial mounds and other earthworks that suggest the existence of social and political hierarchies that archaeologists term chiefdoms. Although the hunter-gatherer lifestyle never entirely disappeared, the development of agricultural settlements and chiefdoms represented important innovations to the Archaic way of life.

Southwestern Cultures

Ancient Americans in present-day Arizona, New Mexico, and southern portions of Utah and Colorado developed cultures characterized by agriculture and multiunit dwellings called pueblos. All southwestern peoples confronted the challenge of a dry climate and unpredictable fluctuations in rainfall that made the supply of wild plant food

> In the Southwest, the demands of corn cultivation encouraged hunter-gatherers to restrict their migratory habits in order to tend the crop.

Southwestern Cultures

very unreliable. These ancient Americans probably adopted agriculture in response to this basic environmental condition.

About 3500 BP, southwestern hunters and gatherers began to cultivate corn, their signature food crop. Corn had been grown in Central and South America since about 7000 BP, and it slowly traveled up to North America with migrants and traders. In the centuries after 3500 BP, corn eventually became the most important cultivated crop for ancient Americans throughout North America. In the Southwest, the demands of corn cultivation encouraged hunter-gatherers to restrict their migratory habits in order to tend the crop. A vital consideration was access to water. Southwestern Indians became irrigation experts, conserving water from streams, springs, and rainfall and distributing it to thirsty crops.

About AD 200, small farming settlements began to appear throughout southern New Mexico, marking the emergence of the Mogollon culture. Typically, a Mogollon settlement included a dozen pit houses, made by digging out a rounded pit about fifteen feet in diameter and a foot or two deep and then erecting poles to support a roof of branches or dirt. Larger villages usually had one or two bigger pit houses that may have been the predecessors of the circular *kivas*, the ceremonial rooms that became a characteristic of nearly all southwestern settlements. About AD 900, Mogollon culture began to decline, for reasons that remain obscure. Its descendants included the Mimbres people in southwestern New Mexico, who crafted spectacular pottery adorned with human and animal designs. By about AD 1250, the Mimbres culture disappeared, for reasons unknown.

Around AD 500, while the Mogollon culture prevailed in New Mexico, other ancient people migrated from Mexico to southern Arizona and established the distinctive Hohokam culture. Hohokam settlements used sophisticated grids of irrigation canals to plant and harvest crops twice a year. Hohokam settlements reflected the continuing influence of Mexican cultural practices that migrants brought with them as they traveled north. Hohokam people built sizable

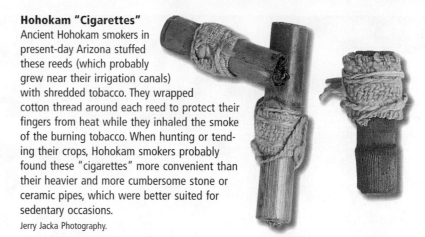

Hohokam "Cigarettes"
Ancient Hohokam smokers in present-day Arizona stuffed these reeds (which probably grew near their irrigation canals) with shredded tobacco. They wrapped cotton thread around each reed to protect their fingers from heat while they inhaled the smoke of the burning tobacco. When hunting or tending their crops, Hohokam smokers probably found these "cigarettes" more convenient than their heavier and more cumbersome stone or ceramic pipes, which were better suited for sedentary occasions.
Jerry Jacka Photography.

platform mounds and ball courts characteristic of many Mexican cultures. About AD 1400, Hohokam culture declined for reasons that remain a mystery, although the rising salinity of the soil caused by centuries of irrigation probably caused declining crop yields and growing food shortages.

North of the Hohokam and Mogollon cultures, in a region that encompassed southern Utah and Colorado and northern Arizona and New Mexico, the Anasazi culture began to flourish about AD 100. The early Anasazi built pit houses on mesa tops and used irrigation much like their neighbors to the south. Beginning around AD 1000 (again, it is not known why), some Anasazi began to move to large, multistory cliff dwellings whose spectacular ruins still exist at Mesa Verde, Colorado, and elsewhere. Other Anasazi communities—like the one whose impressive ruins can be visited at Chaco Canyon, New Mexico—erected huge, stone-

Mexican Ball Court Model
The Mexica and other ancient Central American peoples commonly built special courts (or playing fields) for their intensely competitive ball games. This rare model of a ball court, made in Mexico sometime between 2200 BP and AD 250, shows a game in progress, complete with players and spectators. Players wore padded belts and used their hips to hit the hard rubber ball through the goal. Spectators watched intently, not only to admire the skills of the players but also because a lot was at stake. Spectators bet on the games, and losing players were often killed. A few ball courts have been excavated in North America, providing compelling evidence of one of the many connections between ancient Mexicans and North Americans.
Yale University Art Gallery. Stephen Carlton Clark, B.A. 1903, Fund.

Pueblo Bonito, Chaco Canyon, New Mexico
About AD 1000, Pueblo Bonito stood at the center of Chacoan culture, which extended over more than 20,000 square miles in the region at the intersection of present-day Utah, Colorado, Arizona, and New Mexico. The numerous circular kivas show the significance of ceremonies and rituals to the people of Chaco Canyon. Major buildings appear to have been aligned to mark the spring and winter solstices and the phases of the lunar cycle, suggesting that the ceremonies at Chaco Canyon may have symbolized the potent connections between earth and sky, between humans and the omnipotent celestial ruler.
Richard Alexander Cooke III.

READING THE IMAGE: How do the scale and magnificence of the buildings at Chaco Canyon suggest that the Anasazi were engaged in far more than simple subsistence?
CONNECTIONS: What changes in ancient American culture made the development of the complex structures at Chaco Canyon possible?

FOR MORE HELP ANALYZING THIS IMAGE, see the visual activity for this chapter in the Online Study Guide at bedfordstmartins.com/roark.

---

walled pueblos with enough rooms to house everyone in the settlement. Pueblo Bonito at Chaco Canyon, for example, contained more than eight hundred rooms. Anasazi pueblos and cliff dwellings typically included one or more kivas used for secret ceremonies, restricted to men, that sought to communicate with the supernatural world. The alignment of buildings at Chaco with solar and lunar events (such as the spring and winter solstices) suggests that the site may have been a ceremonial center similar to sites in Mexican cultures to the south that symbolized the connections between earth and the heavens, between human beings and supernatural celestial powers.

Drought began to plague the region about AD 1130, and it lasted for more than half a century, triggering the disappearance

Major Mississippian Mounds, AD 800–1500

of Anasazi culture. By AD 1200, the large Anasazi pueblos had been abandoned. The prolonged drought probably intensified conflict among pueblos and made it impossible to depend on the techniques of irrigated agriculture that had worked for centuries. Some Anasazi migrated toward regions with more reliable rainfall and settled in Hopi, Zuñi, and Acoma pueblos that their descendants in Arizona and New Mexico have occupied ever since.

Woodland Burial Mounds and Chiefdoms

No other ancient Americans created dwellings similar to pueblos, but around 2500 BP, Woodland cultures throughout the vast area drained by the Mississippi River began to build burial mounds. The size of the mounds, the labor and organization required to erect them, and differences in the artifacts buried with certain individuals suggest the existence of a social and political hierarchy that archaeologists term a chiefdom. Experts do not know the name of a single chief, nor do they know the organizational structure a chief headed. But the only way archaeologists can account for the complex and labor-intensive burial mounds and artifacts found in them is to assume that one person—whom scholars term a chief—commanded the labor and obedience of very large numbers of other people, who made up the chief's chiefdom.

Between 2500 BP and 2100 BP, Adena people built hundreds of burial mounds radiating from central Ohio. In the mounds, the Adena usually accompanied burials with grave goods, that included spear points and stone pipes as well as thin sheets of mica (a glasslike mineral) crafted into shapes of birds, beasts, and human hands. Over the body and grave goods Adena people piled dirt into a mound. Sometimes burial mounds were constructed all at once, but often they were built up slowly over many years.

About 2100 BP, Adena culture evolved into the more elaborate Hopewell culture, which lasted about 500 years. Centered in Ohio, Hopewell culture extended throughout the enormous drainage of the Ohio and Mississippi rivers. Hopewell people built larger mounds than their Adena predecessors and filled them with more magnificent grave goods.

Burial was probably reserved for the most important members of Hopewell groups. Most people were cremated. Burial rituals appear to have brought many people together to honor the dead person and to help build the mound. Hopewell mounds were often one hundred feet in diameter and thirty feet high. Skeletons excavated from one mound suggest the high status of hunters; men in important graves showed signs of stress to the elbow joint caused by repetitive spear-throwing. Grave goods at Hopewell sites testify to the high quality of Hopewell crafts and to a thriving trade network that ranged from Wyoming to Florida. Archaeologists believe that Hopewell chiefs probably played an important role in this sprawling interregional trade.

Hopewell culture declined about AD 400 for reasons that are obscure. Archaeologists speculate that bows and arrows, along with increasing reliance on agriculture, made small settlements more self-sufficient and, therefore, less dependent on the central authority of the Hopewell chiefs who were responsible for the burial mounds.

Four hundred years later, another mound-building culture flourished. The Mississippian culture emerged in the floodplains of the major southeastern river systems about AD 800 and lasted until about AD 1500. Major Mississippian sites included huge mounds with platforms on top for ceremonies and for the residences of great chiefs. Most likely, the ceremonial mounds and ritual practices derived from Mexican cultural expressions that were carried north by traders and migrants. The largest Mississippian site was Cahokia, whose remnants can be seen in Illinois near the confluence of the Mississippi and Missouri rivers.

Cahokia Tablet

This stone tablet excavated from the largest mound at Cahokia depicts a bird-man whose sweeping wings and facial features—especially the nose and mouth—resemble those of a bird. Crafted around AD 1100, the tablet probably played some role in rituals enacted on the mound by Cahokian people. Similar birdlike human forms have been found among other Mississippian cultures.
© Peter A. Bostrom.

At Cahokia, more than one hundred mounds were grouped around large open plazas. Monk's Mound, the largest, covered sixteen acres at its base and was one hundred feet tall. Dwellings may have housed as many as thirty thousand inhabitants, easily qualifying Cahokia as the largest settlement in ancient North America. At Cahokia and other Mississippian sites, people evidently worshipped a sun god; the mounds probably elevated elites nearer to the sun's supernatural power. One Cahokia burial mound suggests the authority a great chief exercised. One man—presumably the chief—was buried with the bodies of more than sixty people who had been killed at the time of burial, including fifty young women who had been strangled. Such a mass sacrifice illustrates the coercive power of a Cahokia chief.

Cahokia and other Mississippian cultures dwindled by AD 1500. When Europeans arrived, most of the descendants of Mississippian cultures, like those of the Hopewell culture, lived in small dispersed villages supported by hunting and gathering supplemented by agriculture. Clearly, the conditions that caused large chiefdoms to emerge—whatever they were—had changed, and chiefs no longer commanded the sweeping powers they had once enjoyed.

> **Dwellings may have housed as many as thirty thousand inhabitants, easily qualifying Cahokia as the largest settlement in ancient North America.**

REVIEW How did the availability of food influence the distribution of Native American population across the continent?

Native Americans in the 1490s

About thirteen millennia after Paleo-Indians first migrated to the Western Hemisphere, a new migration—this time from Europe—began in 1492 with the journey of Christopher Columbus. In the decades before 1492, Native Americans continued to employ their ancestors' time-tested survival strategies of hunting, gathering, and agriculture. Those strategies succeeded in both populating and shaping the new world Europeans encountered.

By the 1490s, Native Americans lived throughout North America, but their total population is a subject of spirited debate among scholars. Some experts claim Native Americans numbered 18 million to 20 million, while others place the population at no more than a million. A prudent estimate is about 4 million. On the eve of European colonization, the small island nation of England had about the same number of people as all of North America. The vastness of North America meant the population density was low, just 60 people per hundred square miles, compared to more than 8,000 in England. Compared to England and elsewhere in Europe, Native Americans were spread thin across the land because of their survival strategies of hunting, gathering, and agriculture.

Regions in North America with abundant resources had relatively high population. About one-fifth of Native Americans lived along the West Coast in food-rich California and the Pacific Northwest, where the population density was, respectively, six times greater and four times greater than the average for the whole continent (Figure 1.2). The food-scarce vastness of the Great Plains, Great Basin, and Arctic regions held about one-quarter of Native Americans, but the population density was extremely low, roughly one-tenth the continental average. About a quarter of Native Americans resided in the arid Southwest, where irrigation and intensive agriculture permitted a population density about twice the continental average. But even in California, the most densely inhabited region of North America, population density was just one-twentieth of England's.

The enormous Woodland region east of the Mississippi River was home to about one-third of Native Americans, whose population density approximated the continental average. Eastern Woodland peoples clustered into three broad linguistic and cultural groups: Algonquian, Iroquoian, and Muskogean.

Algonquian tribes inhabited the Atlantic seaboard, the Great Lakes region, and much of the upper Midwest (Map 1.3, page 24). The relatively mild climate along the Atlantic permitted the coastal Algonquians to grow corn and other crops as well as to hunt and fish. Around the Great Lakes and in northern New England, however, cool summers and severe winters made agriculture impractical. Instead, the Abenaki, Penobscot, Chippewa, and other tribes concentrated on hunting and fishing, using canoes both for transportation and for gathering wild rice.

Inland from the Algonquian region, Iroquoian tribes occupied territories centered in Pennsylvania and upstate New York, as well as the hilly upland regions of the Carolinas and Georgia. Three features distinguished Iroquoian tribes from their neighbors. First, their success in cultivating corn and other crops allowed them to build permanent settlements, usually consisting of several bark-covered longhouses up to one hundred feet long and housing five to ten families. Second, Iroquoian societies adhered to matrilineal rules of descent. Property of all sorts belonged to women. Women headed family clans and even selected the chiefs (normally men) who governed the tribes. Third, for purposes of war and diplomacy, an Iroquoian confederation—including the Seneca, Onondaga, Mohawk, Oneida, and Cayuga tribes—formed the League of Five Nations, which remained powerful well into the eighteenth century.

Muskogean peoples spread throughout the woodlands of the Southeast, south of the Ohio River and east of the Mississippi. Including the

---

FIGURE 1.2   Native American Population in North America about 1492 (Estimated)
On the eve of the arrival of Europeans, about a fifth of all native North Americans lived along the Pacific coast—in California and the Northwest—where rich marine resources supported hunter-gatherers in much higher population densities than elsewhere in North America. About a quarter of native North Americans resided in the Southwest, where they depended on agriculture, unlike the Pacific coast peoples. Since sparse rainfall made the southwestern environment less bountiful than that of the Pacific coast, the population density in the Southwest was roughly half that on the West Coast. Woodland peoples east of the Mississippi River—in the Northeast and Southeast—accounted for almost a third of native North Americans. Woodland deer and plants supplemented by agriculture supported a lower population density than in the Southwest or on the West Coast. The population density on the enormous expanses of the Great Plains, Great Basin, and Arctic regions was very low, although in total about a quarter of all native North Americans resided in these areas. Overall, the population density in North America was less than 1 percent of the population density of England, which helps explain why European colonists tended to view North America as a comparatively empty wilderness.

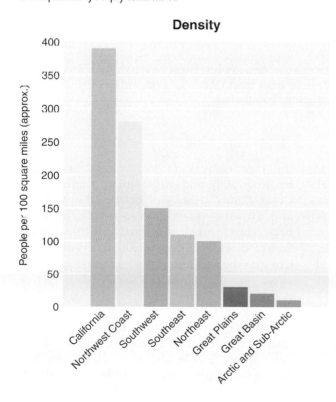

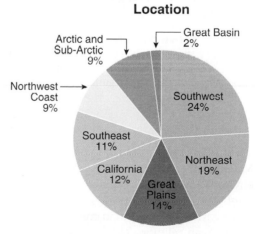

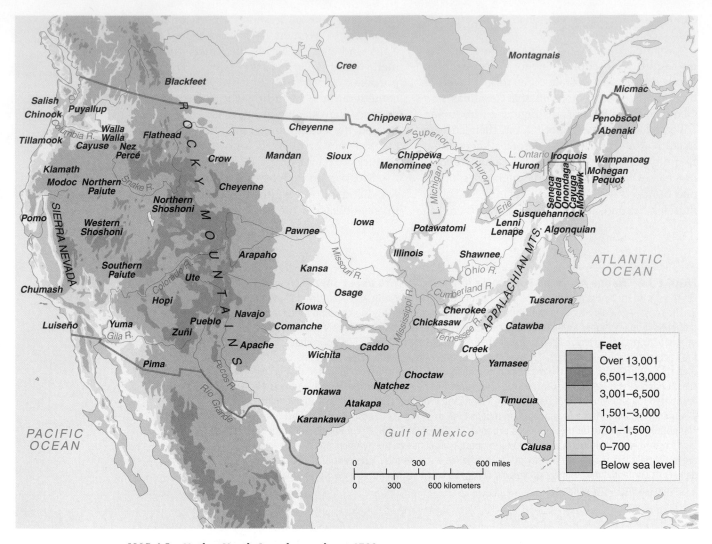

MAP 1.3   Native North Americans about 1500
Distinctive Native American peoples resided throughout the area that, centuries later, would become the United States. This map indicates the approximate location of some of the larger tribes about 1500. In the interest of legibility, many other peoples who inhabited North America at the time are omitted from the map.

Creek, Choctaw, Chickasaw, and Natchez tribes, Muskogeans inhabited a bountiful natural environment that provided abundant food from hunting, gathering, and agriculture. Remnants of the earlier Mississippian culture still existed in Muskogean religion. The Natchez, for example, worshipped the sun and built temple mounds modeled after those of their Mississippian ancestors.

Great Plains peoples accounted for about one out of seven Native Americans. Inhabiting the huge region west of the Eastern Woodland people and east of the Rocky Mountains, many tribes had migrated to the Great Plains within

the past century or two, forced westward by Iroquoian and Algonquian tribes. Some Great Plains tribes—especially the Mandan and Pawnee—farmed successfully, growing both corn and sunflowers. But the Teton Sioux, Blackfeet, Comanche, Cheyenne, and Crow on the northern plains and the Apache and other nomadic tribes on the southern plains depended on buffalo (American bison) for their subsistence.

Southwestern cultures included about a quarter of all native North Americans. These descendants of the Mogollon, Hohokam, and Anasazi cultures lived in settled agricultural communities, many of them pueblos. They continued to grow corn, beans, and squash using methods they had refined for centuries. However, their communities came under attack by a large number of warlike Athapascan tribes who invaded the Southwest beginning around AD 1300. The Athapascans—principally Apache and Navajo—were skillful warriors who preyed on the sedentary pueblo Indians, reaping the fruits of agriculture without the work of farming.

About a fifth of all native North Americans resided along the Pacific coast. In California, abundant acorns and nutritious marine life continued to support high population densities, but they retarded the development of agriculture. Similar dependence on hunting and gathering persisted along the Northwest coast, where fishing reigned supreme. Salmon was so abundant that at The Dalles, a prime fishing site on the Columbia River on the border of present-day Oregon and Washington, Northwest peoples caught millions of pounds of salmon every summer and traded it as far away as California and the Great Plains. Although important trading centers existed throughout North America, particularly in the Southwest, it is likely that The Dalles was the largest Native American trading center in North America.

While trading was common, all native North Americans in the 1490s still depended on hunting and gathering for a major portion of their food. Most of them also practiced agriculture. Some used agriculture to supplement hunting and gathering; for others, the balance was reversed. People throughout North America used bows, arrows, and other weapons for hunting and warfare. None of them employed writing, expressing themselves instead in many other ways: drawings sketched on stones, wood, and animal skins; patterns woven in baskets and textiles (see "The Promise of Technology," page 26); designs painted on pottery, crafted into beadwork, or carved into effigies; and songs, dances, religious ceremonies, and burial rites.

These rich and varied cultural resources of Native Americans did not include features of life common in Europe during the 1490s. Native Americans did not use wheels; sailing ships were unknown to them; they had no large domesticated animals such as horses, cows, or oxen; their use of metals was restricted to copper. However, the absence of these European conveniences mattered less to native North Americans than their own cultural adaptations to the natural environment local to each tribe and to the social environment among neighboring peoples. That great similarity—adaptation to natural and social environments—underlay all the cultural diversity among native North Americans.

It would be a mistake, however, to conclude that native North Americans lived in blissful harmony with nature and each other. Archaeological sites provide ample evidence of violent conflict among Native Americans. Skeletons bear the marks of wounds as well as of ritualistic human sacrifice and even cannibalism. Religious, ethnic, economic, and familial conflicts must have occurred, but they remain in obscurity because they left few archaeological traces. In general, fear and anxiety must have been at least as common among Native Americans as feelings of peace and security.

Native Americans not only adapted to the natural environment; they also changed it in many ways. They built thousands of structures, from small dwellings to massive pueblos and enormous mounds, permanently altering the landscape. Their gathering techniques selected productive and nutritious varieties of plants, thereby shifting the balance of local plants toward useful varieties. The first stages of North American agriculture, for example, probably resulted from Native Americans gathering wild seeds and then sowing them in a meadow for later harvest. It is almost certain that fertile and hardy varieties of corn were developed in this way, first in Mexico and later in North America. To clear land for planting corn, Native Americans set fires that burned off thousands of acres of forest.

Native Americans also used fires for hunting. Great Plains hunters often started fires to force buffalo together and make them easy to slaughter. Eastern Woodland, Southwest, and Pacific coast Indians also set fires to hunt deer and other valuable prey. Hunters crouched downwind from a brushy area while their companions set a fire upwind; as animals raced out of the burning underbrush, hunters killed them.

> The absence of European conveniences mattered less to native North Americans than their own cultural adaptations to the natural environment.

Ancient American Weaving

Weaving—like other ancient American activities such as cooking, hunting, and worship—required the transmission of knowledge from person to person. The workbasket of a master weaver shown here illustrates the technology of ancient American textile production. Found in the Andes in a woman's grave dating from 1,000 years ago, the workbasket contains tools for every stage of textile production.

Most likely, the ancient American woman who owned this workbasket taught her skills to her daughters and other kinswomen. Novices learned by watching, by copying, and by listening to advice about what they did wrong. Since ancient Americans had no instruction manuals for weaving or anything else, all technological knowledge had to be remembered and passed from one person to another. Over time, details of knowledge accumulated into sophisticated technologies that produced marvels of human artistry such as the weaving shown here.

Mastery of the technology of weaving took many years of training and experience. Imagine that you were handed this workbasket and asked to make the weaving pictured here. First of all, you would need to know how to use the various tools in the workbasket. You would need to take fiber from cotton plants or animal wool (such as llama or alpaca) and spin it into thread. To make colored threads, you would dye the fibers before spinning, using different vegetable and mineral concoctions. The pointed sticks wrapped with thread (left center) are spindles for transforming the colored fibers into thread. You would use the small ceramic cup to hold one end of the spindle while you twisted the fiber through your fingers to create strong, thin thread. The two pieces of chalk (to the right of the ceramic cup) served to make a powder that lubricated your fingers to allow the thread to wind smoothly onto the spindle. Skeins of finished thread removed from their spindles are just to the left of the ceramic cup. This small workbasket contained more than 150 spindles for the many varieties of thread required. The beadlike objects at the center are whorls for placing on spindles to anchor the thread and provide decoration. On the right, above the ceramic cup, are bobbins used to pass the thread through the weaving, a bone pick to press down on the threads to tighten the weave, and a long spine needle with a tiny hole to use for sewing and embroidery.

This simple example demonstrates that technology involves more than just physical objects—tools. Human beings must learn how to use the tools. The tools themselves embody the results of human learning that took place over many centuries. Presumably, a woman once discovered that it was easier to twist thread by holding the end of the spindle in a small cup. She probably taught the technique to friends. Eventually, this piece of information became common knowledge among weaving women, and they acquired a cup like the one in this workbasket.

An Ancient American Weaver's Workbasket
Museum of Fine Arts, Boston. Gift of Charles H. White, 02.680.

Chances are, however, even if trained to use the tools in the weaver's workbasket, you could never weave fabrics like the one shown here. Weavers had to learn how to combine color, texture, and shape into a specific design or pattern. Designs were learned and passed from one person to another. Patterns such as those depicted on the weaving shown here required the weaver to learn, express, and transmit knowledge about much more than textile production. To weave an appropriate pattern, the weaver needed to know, for example, how to represent gods, omens, powerful leaders, or sacred places. She had to be familiar with the culture of the people she lived among—their religion, politics, economy, and social organization. Even in the unlikely event that you could copy this weaving, you could not possibly design other fabrics like an ancient American weaver without knowing and understanding her culture as she did. Although weavers possessed specialized training and skill, their technological knowledge had to be used within the specific cultural contours of the people they lived among. A design for a commoner was not fit for a chief, nor was a woman's outfit suitable for a warrior.

The technologies of weaving, pottery-making, cooking, hunting, agriculture, and much more fit into distinctive cultural patterns among the thousands of diverse ancient American societies. Archaeologists use these cultural patterns to distinguish one group of ancient Americans from another. The enormous diversity of these patterns over the millennia of human occupation of the Western Hemisphere and throughout the vast geography of North, Central, and South America

Ancient Weaving

This tunic for Peruvian royalty illustrates the artistry a master weaver could achieve. Woven with wool and cotton sometime between AD 250 and AD 550, the tunic incorporates complex images denoting religious and political authority. In order to know what images to use and how to portray them, the weaver had to be as familiar with Peruvian culture as with the techniques of weaving.

Private Collection.

reflects a basic fact about ancient American technology. Technological developments—such as weaving—occurred when and where they did partly because of subsistence needs and challenges posed by the natural environment. But the technology of weaving, like other technologies, depended above all on human knowledge passed from one person to another in cycle after cycle of teaching and learning.

Over time, technological knowledge accumulated, and achievements—such as this weaving—could reach masterful levels of artistry. But the cycle of teaching and learning was fragile. A weaver's knowledge could die with her if it

had not been taught to somebody else. Wars, famines, droughts, epidemics, and other disasters could extinguish technological knowledge along with its possessors. The fragility of the transmission of human knowledge helps explain the tremendous diversity among ancient American cultures. When the cycle of teaching and learning was broken, technologies and cultures died. Fresh and often distinctive technological knowledge had to be created anew, accumulated, and passed on. The technology of weaving practiced by the owner of this workbasket was developed by the women she learned from and passed on to the women she taught.

Throughout North America, Indians started fires along the edges of woods to burn off shrubby undergrowth and encroaching tree seedlings. These burns encouraged the growth of tender young plants that attracted deer and other game animals, bringing them within convenient range of hunters' weapons. The burns also encouraged the growth of sun-loving food plants that Indians relished, such as blackberries, strawberries, and raspberries.

Because fires set by Native Americans usually burned until they ran out of fuel or were extinguished by rain or wind, enormous regions of North America were burned over. In the long run, fires created and maintained light-dappled meadows for hunting and agriculture, cleared entangling underbrush from forests, and promoted a diverse and productive natural environment. Fires, like other activities of Native Americans, shaped the landscape of North America long before Europeans arrived in 1492.

REVIEW   Why did some Native Americans set fire to the land?

The Mexica: A Meso-American Culture

The indigenous population of the New World (the Western Hemisphere) numbered roughly 80 million in the 1490s, about the same as the population of Europe. Almost all these people lived in Mexico and Central and South America. Like their much less numerous North American counterparts, they too lived in a natural environment of tremendous diversity. They too developed hundreds of cultures, far too numerous to catalog here. But among all these cultures, the Mexica stood out. (Europeans often called these people Aztecs, a name the Mexica did not use.) Their empire stretched from coast to coast across central Mexico, encompassing between 8 million and 25 million people (experts disagree about the total population). We know more about the Mexica than about any other Native American society of the time, principally because of their massive monuments and their Spanish conquerors' well-documented interest in subduing them. Their significance in the history of the New World after 1492 dictates a brief discussion of their culture and society.

Mexican Human Sacrifice

This graphic portrait of human sacrifice was drawn by a Mexican artist in the sixteenth century, after the Spanish conquest. It shows the typical routine of human sacrifice practiced by the Mexica for centuries before Europeans arrived. The victim climbed the temple steps, then was stretched over a stone pillar (notice the priest's helper holding the victim's legs) to make it easier for the priest to plunge a stone knife into the victim's chest, cut out the still-beating heart, and offer it to the bloodthirsty gods. The body of the previous victim has already been pushed down from the temple heights and is about to be dragged away. The Mexica's blood-caked priests and temples repulsed the Spanish conquerors, who considered human sacrifice barbaric. The intent watchfulness among the people portrayed at the base of the temple suggests their keen interest in the gory spectacle as a way of obtaining favors from supernatural powers.

Scala/Art Resource, NY; Biblioteca Nazionale, Florence, Italy.

The Mexica began their rise to prominence about 1325, when small bands settled on a marshy island in Lake Texcoco, the site of the future city of Tenochtitlán, the capital of the Mexican empire. Resourceful, courageous, and cold-blooded warriors, the Mexica often hired out as mercenaries for richer, more settled tribes. By 1430, the Mexica succeeded in asserting their dominance over their former allies and leading their own military campaigns in an ever-widening arc of empire building. Despite pockets of resistance, by the 1490s the Mexica ruled an empire that covered more land than Spain and Portugal combined and contained almost three times as many people.

The empire exemplified the central values of Mexican society. The Mexica worshipped the war god Huitzilopochtli. Warriors held the most exalted positions in the Mexican social hierarchy, even above the priests who performed the sacred ceremonies that won Huitzilopochtli's favor. In the almost constant battles necessary to defend and to extend the empire, young Mexican men exhibited the courage and daring that would allow them to rise in the carefully graduated ranks of warriors. The Mexica considered capturing prisoners the ultimate act of bravery. Warriors usually turned over the captives to Mexican priests, who sacrificed them to Huitzilopochtli by cutting out their hearts. The Mexica believed that human sacrifice fed the sun's craving for blood, which kept the sun aflame and prevented the fatal descent of everlasting darkness and chaos.

The empire contributed far more to Mexican society than victims for sacrifice. At the most basic level, the empire functioned as a military and political system that collected tribute from subject peoples. The Mexica forced conquered tribes to pay tribute in goods, not money. Tribute redistributed to the Mexica as much as one-third of the goods produced by conquered tribes. It included everything from candidates for human sacrifice to textiles and basic food products such as corn and beans, as well as exotic luxury items such as gold, turquoise, and rare bird feathers.

Tribute reflected the fundamental relations of power and wealth that pervaded the Mexican empire. The relatively small nobility of Mexican warriors, supported by a still smaller priesthood, possessed the military and religious power to command the obedience of thousands of non-noble Mexicans and of millions of other non-Mexicans in subjugated provinces. The Mexican elite exercised their power to obtain tribute and thereby to redistribute wealth from the conquered to the conquerors, from the commoners to the nobility, from the poor to the rich. This redistribution of wealth made possible the achievements of Mexican society that eventually amazed the Spaniards: the huge cities, fabulous temples, teeming markets, and luxuriant gardens, not to mention the storehouses stuffed with gold and other treasures.

On the whole, the Mexica did not interfere much with the

> Despite pockets of resistance, by the 1490s the Mexica ruled an empire that covered more land than Spain and Portugal combined and contained almost three times as many people.

Salado Ritual Figure
About AD 1350—more than a century before Columbus arrived in the Western Hemisphere— this figure was carefully wrapped in a reed mat with other items and stored in a cave in a mountainous region of New Mexico by people of the Salado culture, descendants of the Mimbres, who had flourished three centuries earlier. The face of this figure is as close to a self-portrait of ancient Americans on the eve of their encounter with Europeans as we are ever likely to have. Adorned with vivid pigments, cotton string, bright feathers, and stones, the effigy testifies to the human complexity of all ancient Americans, a complexity visible in artifacts that survived the millennia before the arrival of Europeans.
Photography © 2000 The Art Institute of Chicago.

internal government of conquered regions. Instead, they usually permitted the traditional ruling elite to stay in power—so long as they paid tribute. The conquered provinces received very little in return from the Mexica, except immunity from punitive raids. Subjugated communities felt exploited by the constant payment of tribute to the Mexica. By depending on military conquest and constant collection of tribute, the Mexica failed to create among their subjects a belief that Mexican domination was, at some level, legitimate and equitable. The high level of discontent among subject peoples constituted the soft, vulnerable underbelly of the Mexican empire, a fact Spanish intruders exploited after AD 1492 to conquer the Mexica.

REVIEW   How did the payment of tribute influence the Mexican empire?

Conclusion: The World of Ancient Americans

Ancient Americans shaped the history of human beings in the New World for more than twelve thousand years. They established continuous human habitation in the Western Hemisphere from the time the first big-game hunters crossed Beringia until 1492 and beyond. Much of their history remains irretrievably lost because they relied on oral rather than written communication. But much can be pieced together from artifacts they left behind, like the Folsom points among the bones discovered by George McJunkin. Ancient Americans achieved their success through resourceful adaptation to the hemisphere's many and ever-changing natural environments. They also adapted to social and cultural changes caused by human beings—such as marriages, deaths, political struggles, and warfare—but the sparse evidence that has survived renders those adaptations almost entirely unknowable. Their creativity and artistry are unmistakably documented in the artifacts they left at kill sites, camps, and burial mounds. Those artifacts sketch the only likenesses of ancient Americans we will ever have—blurred, shadowy images that are indisputably human but forever silent.

In the five centuries after 1492—just 4 percent of the time human beings have inhabited the Western Hemisphere—Europeans and their descendants began to shape and eventually to dominate American history. Native American peoples continued to influence major developments of American history for centuries after 1492. But the new wave of strangers that at first trickled and then flooded into the New World from Europe and Africa forever transformed the peoples and places of ancient America.

Selected Bibliography

General Works

Robson Bonnichsen and Karen L. Turnmire, *Ice Age Peoples of North America* (1999).
Karen Olsen Bruhns and Karen R. Stothert, *Women in Ancient America* (1999).
Colin G. Calloway, *One Vast Winter Count: The Native American West before Lewis and Clark* (2003).
Thomas D. Dillehay, *The Settlement of the Americas: A New Prehistory* (2000).
Tim Flannery, *The Eternal Frontier: An Ecological History of North America and Its Peoples* (2001).
Richard Fortey, *Earth: An Intimate History* (2005).
Charles C. Mann, *1491: New Revelations of the Americas before Columbus* (2006).
Steven Mithen, *After the Ice: A Global Human History, 20,000–5000 BC* (2003).
David Hurst Thomas, *Skull Wars: Kennewick Man, Archaeology, and the Battle for Native American Identity* (2000).
Nicholas Wade, *Before the Dawn: Recovering the Lost History of Our Ancestors* (2006).

North American Cultures

Mary J. Adair, *Prehistoric Agriculture in the Central Plains* (1988).
Kenneth M. Ames and Herbert D. G. Maschner, *Peoples of the Northwest Coast: Their Archaeology and Prehistory* (1999).
Sally A. Kitt Chappell, *Cahokia: Mirror of the Cosmos* (2002).
Linda S. Cordell, *Prehistory of the Southwest* (1984).
Richard J. Dent Jr., *Chesapeake Prehistory: Old Traditions, New Directions* (1995).
E. James Dixon, *Bones, Boats, and Bison: Archeology and the First Colonization of Western North America* (1999).
Thomas E. Emerson et al., eds., *Late Woodland Societies: Tradition and Transformation across the Midcontinent* (2000).

Kendrick Frazier, *People of Chaco: A Canyon and Its Cultures* (1986).

George C. Frison, *Prehistoric Hunters of the High Plains* (2nd ed., 1991).

Sarah A. Kerr, *Beyond Chaco: Great Kiva Communities on the Mogollon Rim Frontier* (2001).

J. C. H. King, *First People, First Contacts: Native Peoples of North America* (1999).

Steven A. LeBlanc, *Prehistoric Warfare in the American Southwest* (1999).

Stephen H. Lekson, *The Chaco Meridian: Centers of Political Power in the Ancient Southwest* (1999).

Jerald T. Milanich, *Archaeology of Precolumbian Florida* (1994).

Timothy R. Pauketat and Thomas E. Emerson, eds., *Cahokia: Domination and Ideology in the Mississippian World* (2000).

Jefferson Reid and Stephanie Whittlesley, *The Archaeology of Ancient Arizona* (1997).

Karl H. Schlesier, *Plains Indians, A.D. 500–1500: The Archaeological Past of Historic Groups* (1994).

Lynne Sebastian, *The Chaco Anasazi: Sociopolitical Evolution in the Prehistoric Southwest* (1992).

Lynda Shaffer, *Native Americans before 1492: The Mound-building Centers of the Eastern Woodlands* (1992).

Marvin T. Smith, *Coosa: The Rise and Fall of a Southeastern Mississippian Chiefdom* (2000).

Biloine Whiting Young and Melvin L. Fowler, *Cahokia: The Great Native American Metropolis* (1999).

The Mexica

David Carrasco, *City of Sacrifice: The Aztec Empire and the Role of Violence in Civilization* (1999).

Michael D. Coe and Rex Koontz, *Mexico: From the Olmecs to the Aztecs* (5th ed., 2002).

Inga Clendinnen, *Aztecs: An Interpretation* (1991).

Eduardo Matos Moctezuma and Felipe Solis Olguin, *Aztecs* (2002).

▶ **For more books about topics in this chapter,** see the Online Bibliography at bedfordstmartins.com/roark.

▶ **For additional firsthand accounts of this period,** see Chapter 1 in Michael Johnson, ed., *Reading the American Past,* Fourth Edition.

▶ **For Web sites, images, and documents related to topics and places in this chapter,** visit bedfordstmartins.com/makehistory.

REVIEWING THE CHAPTER

Follow these steps to review and strengthen your understanding of the chapter.

STEP 1: *Study the **Key Terms** and **Timeline** to identify the significance of each item listed.*

STEP 2: *Answer the **Review Questions**, drawing on key terms and dates to support your answers.*

STEP 3: *Drawing on the Key Terms, Timeline, and Review Questions, answer the broader **Making Connections** questions.*

KEY TERMS

Who

George McJunkin (p. 3)
Paleo-Indians (p. 10)
Folsom hunters (p. 13)
Archaic Indians (p. 13)
Great Basin peoples (p. 13)
Clovis peoples (p. 14)
California peoples (p. 16)
Chumash (p. 16)
Northwest peoples (p. 16)
Woodland peoples (p. 16)
Southwestern peoples (p. 18)
Mogollon (p. 19)
Hohokam (p. 19)
Anasazi (p. 19)
Adena peoples (p. 21)
Hopewell peoples (p. 21)

Mississippian peoples (p. 21)
Algonquian peoples (p. 22)
Iroquoian peoples (p. 23)
Muskogean peoples (p. 23)
Great Plains peoples (p. 24)
Mexica (p. 28)

What

artifacts (p. 3)
archaeology (p. 3)
Folsom points (p. 3)
Pangaea (p. 6)
continental drift (p. 6)
Homo erectus (p. 6)
Homo sapiens (p. 6)
Wisconsin glaciation (p. 7)
Beringia (p. 7)

Clovis points (p. 14)
hunter-gatherer (p. 11)
pottery (p. 17)
agricultural settlements (p. 17)
pueblo (p. 20)
kiva (p. 20)
burial mounds (p. 20)
chiefdoms (p. 20)
Cahokia (p. 21)
matrilineal rules of descent (p. 23)
League of Five Nations (p. 23)
The Dalles (p. 25)
Tenochtitlán (p. 29)
Mexican empire (p. 29)
Huitzilopochtli (p. 29)
tribute (p. 29)

TIMELINE

NOTE: Major events are depicted below in chronological order, but the time scale between events varies from millennia to centuries.

(*BP* is an abbreviation used by archaeologists for "years before the present.")

◀ c. 400,000 BP • Modern humans (*Homo sapiens*) evolve in Africa.

c. 75,000–45,000 BP and c. 25,000–14,000 BP • Wisconsin glaciation exposes Beringia, land bridge between Siberia and Alaska.

c. 15,000 BP • First humans arrive in North America.

c. 13,500–13,000 BP • Paleo-Indians in North and Central America use Clovis points to hunt big game.

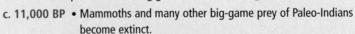

c. 11,000 BP • Mammoths and many other big-game prey of Paleo-Indians become extinct.

c. 10,000–3000 BP • Archaic hunter-gatherer cultures dominate ancient America.

c. 7000 BP • Corn cultivation begins in Central and South America.

c. 4000 BP • Some Eastern Woodland peoples grow gourds and pumpkins and begin making pottery.

c. 3500 BP • Southwestern cultures begin corn cultivation.

c. 2500 BP • Eastern Woodland cultures start to build burial mounds.

REVIEW QUESTIONS

1. Why do historians rely on the work of archaeologists to write the history of ancient America? (pp. 4–5)

2. Why were humans able to migrate into North America after 15,000 BP? (pp. 5–11)

3. Why did Archaic Native Americans shift from big-game hunting to foraging and smaller-game hunting? (pp. 11–17)

4. How did the availability of food influence the distribution of the Native American population across the continent? (pp. 17–22)

5. Why did some Native Americans set fire to the land? (pp. 22–28)

6. How did the payment of tribute influence the Mexican empire? (pp. 28–30)

MAKING CONNECTIONS

1. Explain the different approaches historians and archaeologists bring to studying people in the past. How do the different sources they draw on shape their accounts of the human past? In your answer, cite specific examples from the history of ancient America.

2. Discuss Native Americans' strategies for surviving in the varied climates of North America. How did their different approaches to survival contribute to the diversity of Native American cultures?

3. For more than twelve thousand years, Native Americans both adapted to environmental change in North America and produced significant changes in the environments around them. Discuss specific examples of Native Americans' adaptation to environmental change and the changes they caused in the North American landscape.

4. Rich archaeological and manuscript sources have enabled historians to develop a detailed portrait of the Mexica on the eve of European contact. How did the Mexica establish and maintain their expansive empire?

▶ For practice quizzes, a customized study plan, and other study tools, see the Online Study Guide at bedfordstmartins.com/roark.

---

c. 2500 BP • Some Eastern Woodland peoples begin to cultivate corn.

c. 2500–2100 BP • Adena culture develops in Ohio.

c. 2100 BP–AD 400 • Hopewell culture emerges in Ohio and Mississippi valleys.

c. AD 200–900 • Mogollon culture develops in New Mexico.

c. AD 500 • Bows and arrows appear in North America south of Arctic.

c. AD 500–1400 • Hohokam culture develops in Arizona.

c. AD 800–1500 • Mississippian culture flourishes in Southeast.

c. AD 1000–1200 • Anasazi peoples build cliff dwellings at Mesa Verde and pueblos at Chaco Canyon.

c. AD 1325–1500 • Mexica conquer neighboring peoples and establish Mexican empire.

AD 1492 • Christopher Columbus arrives in New World, beginning European colonization.

SPANISH SWORD

In the hands of a strong Spaniard mounted on horseback, this sixteenth-century sword was a fearsome weapon that could slice through cloth, leather, flesh, bone, and even some metals with deadly effect. Ancient Americans did not possess the Spaniards' highly developed technology of metallurgy, which created strong, relatively lightweight swords honed to a razor-sharp edge. When Christopher Columbus showed swords to the Native Americans he initially encountered, "they took them by the edge and through ignorance cut themselves," he noted in his journal. Swords proved to be indispensable weapons in the Spaniards' military and political conquest of Native Americans during the sixteenth century. Few battle swords and scabbards displayed the elaborate decoration seen here. The decorative motif derives from the artistic traditions of the centuries-long Muslim presence on the Iberian Peninsula, which Spanish warriors and monarchs such as Queen Isabella finally ended in 1492. Such magnificent decoration communicated the ironfisted power of important government officials who might never have wielded a sword in combat. Both ceremonial swords and battle swords were crucial instruments in the Spaniards' creation of the first European empire in the New World.

Museo del Ejercito — Colección/Archivo Oronoz.

Europeans Encounter the New World

1492–1600

- **Europe in the Age of Exploration** 37
  Mediterranean Trade and European Expansion 37
  A Century of Portuguese Exploration 39

- **A Surprising New World in the Western Atlantic** 40
  The Explorations of Columbus 41
  The Geographic Revolution and the Columbian Exchange 42

- **Spanish Exploration and Conquest** 46
  The Conquest of Mexico 46
  The Search for Other Mexicos 48
  New Spain in the Sixteenth Century 52
  The Toll of Spanish Conquest and Colonization 60
  Spanish Outposts in Florida and New Mexico 60

- **The New World and Sixteenth-Century Europe** 62
  The Protestant Reformation and the European Order 62
  New World Treasure and Spanish Ambitions 62
  Europe and the Spanish Example 63

- **Conclusion: The Promise of the New World for Europeans** 64

T WO BABIES WERE BORN in southern Europe in 1451, separated by about seven hundred miles and a chasm of social, economic, and political power. The baby girl, Isabella, was born in a king's castle in what is now Spain. The baby boy, Christopher, was born in the humble dwelling of a weaver near Genoa in what is now Italy. Forty-one years later, the lives and aspirations of these two people intersected in southern Spain and permanently changed the history of the world.

Isabella was named for her mother, the Portuguese second wife of King John II of Castile, whose monarchy encompassed the large central region of present-day Spain. Isabella grew up amid the swirling countercurrents of dynastic rivalries and political conflict. Her father died when she was three, and her half-brother, Henry, assumed the throne. Henry proved an ineffective ruler who made many enemies among the nobility and the clergy. When Isabella was fourteen, Henry's rivals launched a campaign to overthrow him and replace him with her brother, Alfonso.

By then, Isabella had received an excellent education from private tutors who were bishops in the Catholic Church. Her learning helped her become a strong, resolute woman whom Henry tried to control by bringing her to his court where he could watch her. When Alfonso died in 1468, Henry's enemies shifted their support to Isabella, and the king plotted to undermine her independence by arranging her marriage to one of several eligible sons of European monarchs. Isabella refused to accept Henry's choices for her husband and likewise refused to cooperate with Henry's enemies by rebelling and seeking to overthrow him. Instead, she maneuvered to obtain Henry's consent that she would succeed him as monarch, and then she selected Ferdinand, a man she had never met, to be her husband. A year younger than Isabella, Ferdinand was the king of Aragon, a region encompassing a triangular slice of northeastern Spain bordering France and the Mediterranean Sea. The couple married in 1469, and Isabella became queen when Henry died in 1474.

As monarchs, Isabella and Ferdinand fought to defeat other claimants to Isabella's throne, to unite the monarchies of Spain under their rule, to complete the long campaign (known as the Reconquest) to eliminate Muslim strongholds on the Iberian Peninsula, and to purify Christianity. A pious woman, Isabella encouraged the creation of the Inquisition in 1478 to identify and punish heretics, especially Jewish converts. Catholic Church officials believed that many of these converts were "false Christians" who openly embraced Christianity but secretly remained faithful to Judaism.

In the intense, decades-long campaign to defend Christianity, persecute Jews, and defeat the Muslims, Isabella and Ferdinand traveled throughout their realm, staying a month or two in one place after another, meeting local notables, hearing appeals and complaints, and impressing all with their regal splendor. Equally at home on horseback and on the throne, Isabella enjoyed the trappings of royal luxury. Her large entourage, for example, often included a choir of twenty-five or more singers. Although Isabella understood the importance of displaying the magnificence of her royal court, she was a serious, sober ruler who supported the circulation of knowledge in the newfangled technology of print. She read Latin and had a personal library of some four hundred books, a rarity among fifteenth-century monarchs.

Tagging along in the royal cavalcade of mounted lancers, bishops, advisers, clerks, servants, and assorted hangers-on that moved around Spain in 1485 was Christopher Columbus, a deeply religious man obsessed with obtaining support for his scheme to sail west across the Atlantic Ocean to reach China and Japan. An experienced sailor, Columbus became convinced that it was possible to reach the riches of the East by sailing west. Columbus pitched his idea to the king of Portugal in 1484. The king's geography experts declared Columbus's proposal impossible: The globe was too big, the ocean between Europe and China was too wide, and no sailors or ships could possibly withstand such a long voyage.

Rejected in Portugal, Columbus made his way to the court of Isabella and Ferdinand in 1485 and joined their entourage until he finally won an audience with the monarchs in January 1486. They too rejected his plan. Columbus returned to Portugal and once again tried to interest the Portuguese king, without success. Doggedly, he went back to Spain in 1489 and managed to meet privately with Isabella, who told him to see her again as soon as her army had captured the last major Muslim stronghold at Granada. When Granada surrendered early in 1492, Isabella and Ferdinand once again asked their experts to consider Columbus's plan, and again they rejected it. But Isabella soon changed her mind. In hopes of expanding the wealth and influence of the monarchy, she summoned Columbus and in mid-April 1492 agreed to support his risky scheme.

Columbus hurriedly organized his expedition, and just before sunrise on August 3, 1492, three ships under his command caught the tide out of a harbor in southern Spain and sailed

Spanish Tapestry

This detail from a lavish sixteenth-century tapestry depicts Columbus (kneeling) receiving a box of jewels from Queen Isabella (her husband, King Ferdinand, stands slightly behind her) in appreciation for his voyages to the New World. These gifts and others signified the monarchs' elation about the immense promise of the lands and peoples that Columbus encountered. The exact nature of that promise did not become clear until after the deaths of both Columbus and Isabella, when Cortés invaded and eventually conquered Mexico between 1519 and 1521.

© Julio Conoso/Corbis Sygma.

west. Barely two months later, in the predawn moonlight of October 12, 1492, Columbus glimpsed an island on the western horizon. At daybreak, he rowed ashore, and as the curious islanders crowded around, he claimed possession of the land for Isabella and Ferdinand of Spain.

Columbus's encounters in 1492 with Isabella and those islanders transformed the history of the world and unexpectedly made Spain the most important European power in the Western Hemisphere for more than a century. Long before 1492, other Europeans had restlessly expanded the limits of the world known to them, and their efforts helped make possible Columbus's voyage. But without Isabella's sponsorship, it is doubtful that Columbus could have made his voyage. With her support and his own unflagging determination, Columbus blazed a watery trail to a world that neither he nor anyone else in Europe knew existed. As Isabella, Ferdinand, and subsequent Spanish monarchs sought to reap the rewards of what they considered their emerging empire in the West, they created a distinctively Spanish colonial society that conquered and killed Native Americans, built new institutions, and extracted great wealth that enriched the Spanish monarchy and made Spain the envy of other Europeans.

Europe in the Age of Exploration

Historically, the East—not the West—attracted Europeans. Around the year 1000, Norsemen ventured west across the North Atlantic and founded a small fishing village at L'Anse aux Meadows on the tip of Newfoundland that lasted only a decade or so. After the world's climate cooled, choking the North Atlantic with ice, the Norse left. Viking sagas memorialized the Norse "discovery," but it had virtually no other impact in the New World or in Europe. Instead, wealthy Europeans developed a taste for luxury goods from Asia and Africa, and merchants competed to satisfy that taste. As Europeans traded with the East and with one another, they acquired new information about the world they inhabited. A few people—sailors, merchants, and aristocrats—took the risks of exploring beyond the

limits of the world known to Europeans. Those risks were genuine and could be deadly. But sometimes they paid off in new information, new opportunities, and eventually in the discovery of a world entirely new to Europeans.

Mediterranean Trade and European Expansion

From the twelfth through the fifteenth centuries, spices, silk, carpets, ivory, gold, and other exotic goods traveled overland from Persia, Asia Minor, India, and Africa and then were funneled into continental Europe through Mediterranean trade routes (Map 2.1, page 38). Dominated primarily by the Italian cities of Venice, Genoa, and Pisa, this lucrative trade enriched Italian merchants and bankers, who fiercely defended their near **monopoly** of access to Eastern goods. The vitality of the Mediterranean trade offered few incentives to look for alternatives. New routes to the East and the discovery of new lands were the stuff of fantasy.

Preconditions for turning fantasy into reality developed in fifteenth-century Europe. In the mid-fourteenth century, Europeans suffered a catastrophic epidemic of bubonic plague. The Black Death, as it was called, killed about a third of the European population. This devastating pestilence had major long-term consequences. By drastically reducing the population, it made Europe's limited supply of food more plentiful for survivors. Many survivors inherited property from plague victims, giving them new chances for advancement. The turmoil caused by the plague also prompted many peasants to move away from their homes and seek opportunities elsewhere.

Understandably, most Europeans perceived the world as a place of alarming risks where the delicate balance of health, harvests, and peace could quickly be tipped toward disaster by epidemics, famine, and violence. Most people protected themselves from the constant threat of calamity by worshipping the supernatural, by living amid kinfolk and friends, and by maintaining good relations with the rich and powerful. But the insecurity and uncertainty of fifteenth-century European life also encouraged a few people to take greater risks, such as embarking

> The insecurity and uncertainty of fifteenth-century European life encouraged a few people to take greater risks, such as embarking on dangerous sea voyages through uncharted waters to points unknown.

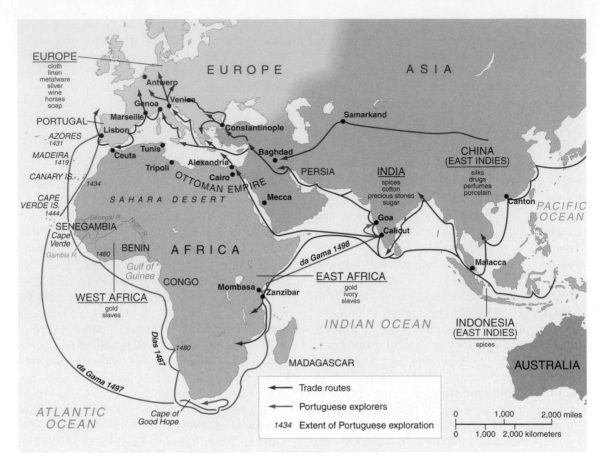

MAP 2.1   European Trade Routes and Portuguese Exploration in the Fifteenth Century
The strategic geographic position of Italian cities as a conduit for overland trade from Asia was slowly undermined during the fifteenth century by Portuguese explorers who hopscotched along the coast of Africa and eventually found a sea route that opened the rich trade of the East to Portuguese merchants.

on dangerous sea voyages through uncharted waters to points unknown.

Exploration promised fame and fortune in European societies to those who succeeded, whether they were kings or commoners. Monarchs such as Isabella who hoped to enlarge their realms and enrich their dynasties also had reasons to sponsor journeys of exploration. More territory meant more subjects who could pay more taxes, provide more soldiers, and participate in more commerce, magnifying the monarch's power and prestige. Voyages of exploration also could stabilize the monarch's regime by diverting unruly noblemen toward distant lands. Some explorers, such as Columbus, were commoners who hoped to be elevated to the aristocracy as a reward for their daring achievements.

Scientific and technological advances also helped set the stage for exploration. The inven-

tion of movable type by Johannes Gutenberg around 1450 in Germany made printing easier and cheaper, stimulating the diffusion of information, including news of discoveries, among literate Europeans. By 1400, crucial navigational aids employed by maritime explorers such as Columbus were already available: compasses; hourglasses, which allowed for the calculation of elapsed time, useful in estimating speed; and the astrolabe and quadrant, which were devices for determining latitude. Detailed sailing maps called *portulanos* illustrated shoreline topography and also noted compass headings for sailing from one port to another. Many people throughout fifteenth-century Europe knew about these and other technological advances. The Portuguese were the first to use them in a campaign to sail beyond the limits of the world known to Europeans.

Ivory Saltcellar

This exquisitely carved sixteenth-century ivory saltcellar combines African materials, craftsmanship, and imagery in an artifact for Portuguese tables. Designed to hold table salt in the central globe, the saltcellar portrays a victim about to be beheaded by the armed man who has already beheaded five others. To Portuguese eyes, the saltcellar dramatized African brutality and quietly suggested the superiority of Portuguese virtues and their beneficial influence in Africa.

Archivio Fotografico del Museo Preistorico Etnografico L. Pigorini, Roma.

A Century of Portuguese Exploration

Portugal had less than 2 percent of the population of Christian Europe, but it devoted far more energy and wealth to the geographical exploration of the world between 1415 and 1460 than all the other countries of Europe combined. Facing the Atlantic on the Iberian Peninsula, the Portuguese lived on the fringes of the thriving Mediterranean trade. As a Christian kingdom, Portugal cooperated with Spain in the Reconquest, the centuries-long drive to expel the Muslims from the Iberian Peninsula. The religious zeal that propelled the Reconquest also justified expansion into what the Portuguese considered heathen lands. A key victory came in 1415 when Portuguese forces conquered Ceuta, the Muslim bastion at the mouth of the Strait of Gibraltar that had blocked Portugal's access to the Atlantic coast of Africa.

The most influential advocate of Portuguese exploration was Prince Henry the Navigator, son of the Portuguese king (and great-uncle of Queen Isabella of Spain). From 1415 until his death in 1460, Henry collected the latest information about sailing techniques and geography, supported new crusades against the Muslims, encouraged fresh sources of trade to fatten Portuguese pocketbooks, and pushed explorers to go farther still. Both the Portuguese king and the Christian pope supported Henry's efforts to extend the Reconquest down the African coast. African expeditions also promised to wrest wheat fields from their Moroccan owners and to obtain gold, the currency of European trade. Gold was scarce in Europe because the quickening pace of commerce increased the need for currency while purchases in the East drained gold away from European markets.

Neither the Portuguese nor anybody else in Europe knew the immensity of Africa or the length or shape of its coastline, which, in reality, fronted the Atlantic for more than seven thousand miles—about five times the considerable distance from Genoa, Columbus's hometown, to Lisbon, the Portuguese capital. At first, Portuguese mariners cautiously hugged the west coast of Africa, seldom venturing beyond sight of land. By 1434, they had reached the northern edge of the Sahara Desert, where strong westerly currents swept them out to sea. They soon learned to ride those currents far away from the coast before catching favorable winds that turned them back toward land, a technique that

Spanish Drummer of African Descent
This drawing of a man of African descent living in Spain, dressed in Spanish clothing and beating a drum while astride a horse (presumably to accompany a procession of important Spaniards), documents the presence of Africans in Spain in the early sixteenth century. The Portuguese traded with peoples along the African coast during the last two-thirds of the fifteenth century. This trade brought both enslaved and free Africans to the Iberian Peninsula for decades before Columbus's 1492 voyage.
Biblioteca Nacional, Madrid.

ivory. Powerful African kingdoms welcomed Portuguese trading ships loaded with iron goods, weapons, textiles, and ornamental shells. Portuguese merchants learned that establishing relatively peaceful trading posts on the coast was far more profitable than attempting the violent conquest and **colonization** of inland regions. In the 1460s, the Portuguese used African slaves to develop sugar plantations on the Cape Verde Islands, inaugurating an association between enslaved Africans and plantation labor that would be transplanted to the New World in the centuries to come.

About 1480, Portuguese explorers began a conscious search for a sea route to Asia. In 1488, Bartolomeu Dias sailed around the Cape of Good Hope at the southern tip of Africa and hurried back to Lisbon with the exciting news that it appeared to be possible to sail on to India and China. In 1498, after ten years of careful preparation, Vasco da Gama commanded the first Portuguese fleet to sail to India. Portugal quickly capitalized on the commercial potential of da Gama's new sea route. By the early sixteenth century, the Portuguese controlled a far-flung commercial empire in India, Indonesia, and China (collectively referred to as the East Indies). Their new sea route to the East eliminated overland travel and allowed Portuguese merchants to charge much lower prices for the Eastern goods they imported and still make handsome profits.

Portugal's African explorations during the fifteenth century broke the monopoly of the old Mediterranean trade with the East, dramatically expanded the world known to Europeans, established a network of Portuguese outposts in Africa and Asia, and developed methods of sailing the high seas that Columbus employed on his revolutionary voyage west.

> **REVIEW** Why did European exploration expand dramatically in the fifteenth century?

allowed them to reach Cape Verde by 1444 (see Map 2.1). To stow the supplies necessary for long periods at sea and to withstand the battering of waves in the open ocean, the Portuguese developed the caravel, a sturdy ship that became explorers' vessel of choice. In caravels, Portuguese mariners sailed into and around the Gulf of Guinea and as far south as the Congo by 1480.

Fierce African resistance confined Portuguese expeditions to coastal trading posts, where they bartered successfully for gold, slaves, and

A Surprising New World in the Western Atlantic

In retrospect, the Portuguese seemed ideally qualified to venture across the Atlantic. They had pioneered the **frontiers** of seafaring, exploration, and geography for almost a century. However, Portuguese and most other experts believed that sailing west across the Atlantic to

Asia was literally impossible. The European discovery of America required someone bold enough to believe that the experts were wrong and the risks were surmountable. That person was Christopher Columbus. His explorations inaugurated a geographical revolution that forever altered Europeans' understanding of the world and its peoples, including themselves. Columbus's landfall in the Caribbean originated a thriving exchange between the people, ideas, **cultures**, and institutions of the Old and New Worlds that continues to this day.

The Explorations of Columbus

Columbus went to sea when he was about fourteen, and he eventually made his way to Lisbon, where he married Felipa Moniz. Felipa's father had been raised in the household of Prince Henry the Navigator, and her family retained close ties to the prince. Through Felipa, Columbus gained access to explorers' maps and papers crammed with information about the tricky currents and winds encountered in sailing the Atlantic. Columbus himself ventured into the Atlantic frequently and at least twice sailed to the central coast of Africa.

Like other educated Europeans, Columbus believed that the earth was a sphere and that theoretically it was possible to reach the East Indies by sailing west. With flawed calculations, he estimated that Asia was only about 2,500 miles from the westernmost boundary of the known world, a shorter distance than Portuguese ships routinely sailed between Lisbon and the Congo. In fact, the shortest distance to Japan from Europe's jumping-off point was nearly 11,000 miles. Convinced by his erroneous calculations, Columbus became obsessed with a scheme to prove he was right.

In 1492, after years of unsuccessful lobbying in Portugal and Spain, plus overtures to England and France, Columbus finally won financing for his journey from the Spanish monarchs, Isabella and Ferdinand. They saw

Columbus's venture as an inexpensive gamble: The potential loss was small, but the potential gain was huge. They gave Columbus a letter of introduction to China's Grand Khan, the ruler they hoped he would meet on the other side of the Atlantic.

After scarcely three months of frantic preparation, Columbus and his small fleet—the *Niña* and *Pinta*, both caravels, and the *Santa María*, a larger merchant vessel—headed west. Six weeks after leaving the Canary Islands, where he stopped for supplies, Columbus landed on a tiny Caribbean island about three hundred miles north of the eastern tip of Cuba.

Columbus claimed possession of the island for Isabella and Ferdinand and named it San Salvador, in honor of the Savior, Jesus Christ. He called the islanders "Indians," assuming that they inhabited the East Indies somewhere near Japan or China. The islanders called themselves Tainos, which in their language means "good" or "noble." The Tainos inhabited most of the Caribbean islands Columbus visited on his first voyage, as had their ancestors for more than two centuries. An agricultural people, the Tainos grew cassava, corn, cotton, tobacco, and other crops. Instead of dressing in the finery Columbus had expected to find in the East Indies, the Tainos "all . . . go around as naked as their mothers bore them," Columbus wrote. Although Columbus concluded that the Tainos "had no religion," in reality they

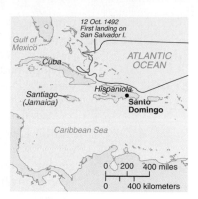

Columbus's First Voyage to the New World, 1492–1493

Taino Zemi Basket

This basket is an example of the effigies Tainos made to represent *zemis*, or deities. The effigy illustrates the artistry of the basket maker, almost certainly a Taino woman. Crafted sometime between 1492 and about 1520, the effigy demonstrates that the Tainos readily incorporated goods obtained through contacts with Europeans into their own traditional beliefs and practices. The basket maker used African ivory and European mirrors as well as Native American fibers, dyes, and designs.

Archivio Fotografico del Museo Preistorico Etnografico L. Pigorini, Roma.

worshipped gods they called *zemis*, ancestral spirits who inhabited natural objects such as trees and stones. The Tainos mined a little gold, but they had no riches. "It seemed to me that they were a people very poor in everything," Columbus wrote.

What the Tainos thought about Columbus and his sailors we can only surmise, since they left no written documents. At first, Columbus got the impression that the Tainos believed the Spaniards came from heaven. But after six weeks of encounters, Columbus decided that "the people of these lands do not understand me nor do I, nor anyone else that I have with me, [understand] them. And many times I understand one thing said by these Indians . . . for another, its contrary." The confused communication between the Spaniards and the Tainos suggests how strange each group seemed to the other. Columbus's perceptions of the Tainos were shaped by European attitudes, ideas, and expectations, just as the Tainos' perceptions of the Europeans were no doubt colored by their own culture.

Columbus and his men understood that they had made a momentous discovery, but they found it frustrating. Although the Tainos proved friendly, they did not have the riches Columbus expected to find in the East. For three months, Columbus cruised from island to island, looking for the king of Japan and the Grand Khan of China. In mid-January 1493, he started back to Spain, taking seven Tainos with him. Queen Isabella and King Ferdinand were overjoyed by his news. With a voyage that had lasted barely eight months, Columbus appeared to have catapulted Spain from the position of an also-ran in the race for a sea route to Asia into that of a serious challenger to Portugal, whose explorers had not yet sailed to India or China. Columbus and his Taino companions became the toast of the royal court. The Spanish monarchs elevated Columbus to the nobility and awarded him the title "Admiral of the Ocean Sea." The seven Tainos were baptized as Christians, and King Ferdinand became their godfather.

Soon after Columbus returned to Spain, the Spanish monarchs rushed to obtain the pope's support for their claim to the new lands in the West. When the pope, a Spaniard, complied, the Portuguese feared their own claims to recently discovered territories were in jeopardy. To protect their claims, the Portuguese and Spanish monarchs negotiated the Treaty of Tordesillas in 1494. The treaty drew an imaginary line eleven hundred miles west of the Canary Islands (Map 2.2).

Land discovered west of the line (namely, the islands that Columbus discovered and any additional land that might be located) belonged to Spain; Portugal claimed land to the east (namely, its African and East Indian trading empire).

Isabella and Ferdinand moved quickly to realize the promise of their new claims. In the fall of 1493, they dispatched Columbus once again, this time with a fleet of seventeen ships and more than a thousand men who planned to locate the Asian mainland, find gold, and get rich. When Columbus returned to the island where he had left behind thirty-nine of his sailors because of a shipwreck near the end of his first voyage, he received disturbing news. In Columbus's absence, his sailors had terrorized the Tainos, kidnapping and sexually abusing their women. In retaliation, the Taino chiefs had killed all the sailors. This small episode prefigured much of what was to happen in encounters between Native Americans and Europeans in the years ahead.

Before Columbus died in 1506, he returned to the New World two more times (in 1498 and 1502) without relinquishing his belief that the East Indies were there, someplace. Other explorers continued to search for a passage to the East or some other source of profit. Before long, however, prospects of beating the Portuguese to Asia began to dim along with the hope of finding vast hoards of gold. Nonetheless, Columbus's discoveries forced sixteenth-century Europeans to think about the world in new ways. He proved that it was possible to sail from Europe to the western rim of the Atlantic and return to Europe. Most important, Columbus made clear that beyond the western shores of the Atlantic lay lands entirely unknown to Europeans.

The Geographic Revolution and the Columbian Exchange

Within thirty years of Columbus's initial discovery, Europeans' understanding of world geography underwent a revolution. An elite of perhaps twenty thousand people with access to Europe's royal courts and trading centers learned the exciting news about global geography. But it took a generation of additional exploration before they could comprehend the larger contours of Columbus's discoveries.

European monarchs hurried to stake their claims to the newly discovered lands. In 1497, King Henry VII of England, who had spurned Columbus a decade earlier, sent John Cabot to

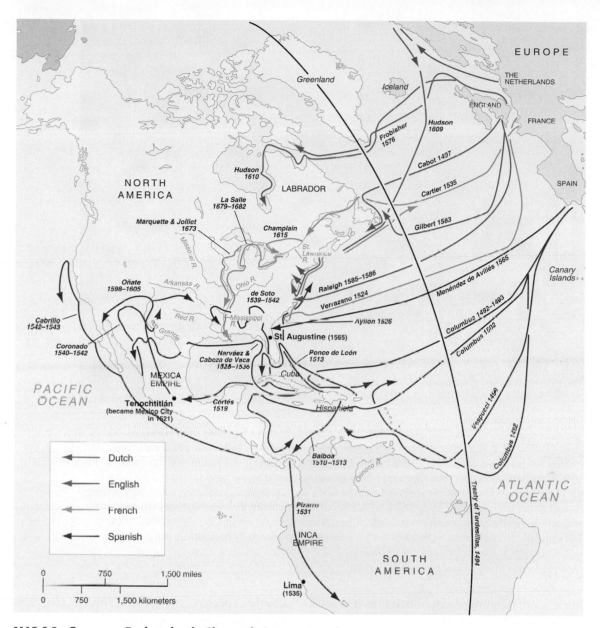

MAP 2.2   European Exploration in Sixteenth-Century America

This map illustrates the approximate routes of early European explorations of the New World.

READING THE MAP: Which countries were most actively exploring the New World? Which countries were exploring later than others?

CONNECTIONS: What were the motivations behind the explorations? What were the motivations for colonization?

FOR MORE HELP ANALYZING THIS MAP, see the map activity for this chapter in the Online Study Guide at bedfordstmartins.com/roark.

look for a "Northwest Passage" to the Indies across the North Atlantic (see Map 2.2). Cabot reached the tip of Newfoundland, which he believed was part of Asia, and hurried back to England, where he assembled a small fleet and sailed west again in 1498. But he was never heard from again.

Three thousand miles to the south, a Spanish expedition landed on the northern coast of South America in 1499 accompanied by Amerigo Vespucci, an Italian businessman. In 1500, Pedro Álvars Cabral commanded a Portuguese fleet bound for the Indian Ocean that accidentally

European Intellectuals

This elaborate painting illustrates men and women in a richly appointed European study poring over geographic information, astronomical instruments, books, and sundry artifacts. Noblemen, prosperous ladies, and scholars are portrayed integrating their knowledge of European paintings and statues (on the walls and the table in the background) with new discoveries from abroad, suggested by the fresh air flooding the room from the wide-open window. Many members of European elites, such as those pictured here, considered keeping abreast of the latest learning highly fashionable, even trendy. But notice that the brightest light seems to originate within the room, vividly illuminating the two standing gentlemen and the objects they examine. This suggests the confidence of the artist and his subjects in the superiority of European enlightenment.

By permission of the Trustees of the National Gallery, London.

made landfall on the coast of Brazil as it looped westward into the Atlantic.

By 1500, European experts knew that several large chunks of land cluttered the western Atlantic. A few cartographers speculated that these chunks were connected to one another in a landmass that was not Asia. In 1507, Martin Waldseemüller, a German cartographer, published the first map that showed the New World separate from Asia; he named the land America, in honor of Amerigo Vespucci.

Two additional discoveries confirmed Waldseemüller's speculation. In 1513, Vasco Núñez de Balboa crossed the Isthmus of Panama and reached the Pacific Ocean. Clearly, more water lay between the New World and Asia. How much water Ferdinand Magellan discovered when he led an expedition to circumnavigate the globe in 1519. Sponsored by King Charles I of Spain, Magellan's voyage took him first to the New World, around the southern tip of South America, and into the Pacific late in November 1520. Crossing the Pacific took almost four months. By the time he reached the Philippines, his crew had been decimated by extreme hunger and thirst. Magellan himself was killed by Philippine tribesmen. A remnant of his expedition continued on to the Indian Ocean and managed to transport a cargo of spices back to Spain in 1522.

In most ways, Magellan's voyage was a disaster. One ship and 18 men crawled back from an expedition that had begun with five ships and more than 250 men. But the geographic information it provided left no doubt that America was a continent separated from Asia by the enormous Pacific Ocean. Magellan's voyage made clear that Columbus was dead wrong about the iden-

Columbian Exchange

The arrival of Columbus in the New World started an ongoing transatlantic exchange of goods, people, and ideas. The Spaniards brought domesticated animals from the Old World, including horses, cattle, goats, chickens, cats, and sheep. The novelty of such animals is demonstrated by the Nahuatl words the Mexican people initially used to refer to these strange new beasts. For a horse, they used the Nahuatl word for deer; a cat was a "little cougar"; a sheep was referred to with the word for cotton, linking the animal with its fibrous woolen coat. The Spaniards brought many other alien items, such as cannons, which the Mexica at first termed "fat fire trumpets," and guitars, which the Mexica called "rope drums." The Spaniards also carried Old World microorganisms that caused devastating epidemics of smallpox, measles, and other diseases (center). Ancient American people, goods, and ideas made the return trip across the Atlantic. In 1493, Columbus told Isabella and Ferdinand about an amazingly productive New World plant he called *maize*, his version of the Taino word *mahiz*, which means "life-giver." This maize (or corn) goddess (left) crafted in Peru about a thousand years before Columbus arrived in the New World suggests ancient Americans' worship of corn. Within a generation after 1493, corn had been carried across the Atlantic and was growing in Europe, the Middle East, Africa, India, and China. Smoking tobacco, like the cigar puffed by an ancient Mayan lord (right), became such a fashion in Europe that some came to believe, as a print of two men relaxing with their pipes was captioned, "Life Is Smoke." The strangeness of New World peoples and cultures also reinforced Europeans' notions of their own superiority. Although the Columbian exchange went in both directions, it was not a relationship of equality. Europeans seized and retained the upper hand.

Bildarchiv Preussischer Kulturbesitz/Art Resource, NY; Arxiu Mas; Collection of Dr. Francis Robicsek.

tity of what he had discovered. It was possible to sail west to reach the East Indies, but that was a terrible way to go. After Magellan, most Europeans who sailed west set their sights on the New World, not on Asia.

Columbus's arrival in the Caribbean anchored the western end of what might be imagined as a sea bridge that spanned the Atlantic, connecting the Western Hemisphere to Europe. Somewhat like the Beringian land bridge tra-

versed by the first Americans millennia earlier, the new sea bridge reestablished a connection between the Eastern and Western Hemispheres. The Atlantic Ocean, which had previously isolated America from Europe, became an aquatic highway, thanks to sailing technology, intrepid seamen, and their European sponsors. This new sea bridge launched the **Columbian exchange**, a transatlantic trade of goods, people, and ideas that has continued ever since.

Spaniards brought novelties to the New World that were commonplace in Europe, including Christianity, iron technology, sailing ships, firearms, wheeled vehicles, horses and other domesticated animals, and much else. Unknowingly, they also smuggled along many Old World microorganisms that caused devastating epidemics of smallpox, measles, and other diseases that would kill the vast majority of Indians during the sixteenth century and continue to decimate survivors in later centuries. European diseases made the Columbian exchange catastrophic for Native Americans. In the long term, these diseases were decisive in transforming the dominant peoples of the New World from descendants of Asians, who had inhabited the hemisphere for millennia, to descendants of Europeans and Africans, the recent arrivals from the Old World by way of the newly formed sea bridge.

Ancient American goods, people, and ideas made the return trip across the Atlantic. Europeans were introduced to New World foods such as corn and potatoes that became important staples in European diets, especially for poor people. Columbus's sailors became infected with syphilis in sexual encounters with New World women and then unwittingly carried the deadly parasite back to Europe, where it may already have had a foothold. New World tobacco created a European fashion for smoking that ignited quickly and has yet to be extinguished. But for almost a generation after 1492, this Columbian exchange did not reward the Spaniards with the riches they yearned to find.

> **REVIEW**   How did Columbus's landfall in the Caribbean help revolutionize Europeans' understanding of world geography?

Spanish Exploration and Conquest

During the sixteenth century, the New World helped Spain become the most powerful monarchy in both Europe and the Americas. Initially, Spanish expeditions reconnoitered the Caribbean, scouted stretches of the Atlantic coast, and established settlements on the large islands of Hispaniola, Puerto Rico, Jamaica, and Cuba. Spaniards enslaved Caribbean tribes and put them to work growing crops and mining gold.

But the profits from these early ventures barely covered the costs of maintaining the settlers. After almost thirty years of exploration, the promise of Columbus's discovery seemed illusory.

In 1519, however, that promise was fulfilled, spectacularly, by Hernán Cortés's march into Mexico. By about 1545, Spanish conquests extended from northern Mexico to southern Chile, and New World riches filled Spanish treasure chests. Cortés's expedition served as the model for Spaniards' and other Europeans' expectations that the New World could yield bonanza profits for its conquerors.

The Conquest of Mexico

Hernán Cortés, who became the richest and most famous conquistador (conqueror), arrived in the New World in 1504, an obscure nineteen-year-old Spaniard seeking adventure and the chance to make a name for himself. He fought in the conquest of Cuba and elsewhere in the Caribbean. In 1519, the governor of Cuba authorized Cortés to organize an expedition to investigate rumors of a fabulously wealthy kingdom somewhere in the interior of the mainland. A charming, charismatic leader, Cortés quickly assembled a force of about six hundred men, loaded his ragtag army aboard eleven ships, and set out.

Cortés's confidence that he could talk his way out of most situations and fight his way out of the rest fortified the small band of Spaniards. But Cortés could not speak any Native American language. Landing first on the Yucatán peninsula, he had the good fortune to receive a gift from a chief of the Tobasco people. Among about twenty other women given to Cortés was a fourteen-year-old girl named Malinali who spoke several native languages, including Mayan and Nahuatl, the language of the Mexica, the most powerful people in what is now Mexico and Central America (see chapter 1). Malinali had acquired her linguistic fluency painfully. Born into a family of the Mexican nobility, she learned Nahuatl as a young child. After her father died and her mother remarried and had a son, Malinali's stepfather sold her as a slave to Mayan-speaking Indians, who subsequently gave the slave girl to the Tobascans. Malinali, whom the Spaniards called Marina, soon learned Spanish and became Cortés's interpreter. She also became one of Cortés's several mistresses and bore him a son. (Several years later, after Cortés's wife arrived in New Spain, Cortés cast Marina aside, and she married one of his soldiers.) Although no word uttered by Marina survives in historical documents, her words were the Spaniards' essential conduit of communication with the Indians. "Without her help," wrote one of the Spaniards who accompanied Cortés, "we would not have understood the language of New Spain and Mexico." With her help, Cortés talked and fought with Indians along the Gulf coast of Mexico, trying to discover the location of the fabled kingdom. By the time Marina died at age twenty-four, the people she had grown up among—the people who had taught her languages, enslaved her, and given her to Cortés—had been conquered by the Spaniards with her help.

In the capital of the Mexican empire, Tenochtitlán, the emperor Montezuma heard rumors about some strange creatures sighted along the coast. (Montezuma and his people are often called Aztecs, but they called themselves Mexica.) He feared that the strangers were led by the god Quetzalcoatl, returning to Tenochtitlán as predicted by the Mexican religion. Montezuma sent representatives to meet with the strangers and bring them gifts fit for gods. Marina had told Cortés about Quetzalcoatl, and when Montezuma's messengers arrived, Cortés donned the regalia they had brought, almost certain proof to the Mexica that he was indeed the god they feared. The Spaniards astounded the messengers by blasting their cannons and displaying their swords.

The messengers hurried back to Montezuma with their amazing news. The emperor arranged for large quantities of food to be sent to the coast to welcome the strangers and perhaps to postpone Quetzalcoatl's dreaded arrival in the capital. Before the Mexican messengers served food to the Spaniards, they sacrificed several hostages and soaked the food in their blood. This fare disgusted the Spaniards and might have been enough to turn them back to Cuba. But along with the food, the Mexica also brought the Spaniards another gift, a "disk in the shape of a sun, as big as a cartwheel and made of very fine gold," as one of the Mexica recalled. Here was conclusive evidence that the rumors of fabulous riches heard by Cortés had some basis in fact.

Cortés Arrives in Tenochtitlán

This portrayal of the arrival of Cortés and his army in the Mexican capital illustrates the importance of Malinali, who stands at the front of the Spaniards' procession, serving as their translator and intermediary with Montezuma (not pictured), who has come out to greet the invaders. Painted by a Mexican artist after the conquest, the work contrasts Cortés—dressed as a Spanish gentleman, respectfully doffing his hat to Montezuma, and accompanied by his horse and African groom—with his soldiers, who are armed and ready for battle. The painting displays the choices confronted by the Mexica: accept the pacific overtures of Cortés or face the lances, swords, and battle-axes of the Spanish soldiers. Also notable is the importance of the Indian porters who carried the Spaniards' food and other supplies. What do you think was the significance of the winged image on the flag? *Bibliothèque Nationale de France.*

Cortés's Invasion of Tenochtitlán, 1519–1521

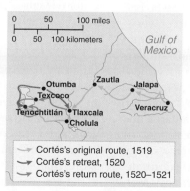

0   50   100 miles
0   50   100 kilometers

Gulf of Mexico

Otumba Zautla Jalapa
Texcoco
Tenochtitlán Tlaxcala Veracruz
Cholula

→ Cortés's original route, 1519
→ Cortés's retreat, 1520
→ Cortés's return route, 1520–1521

In August 1519, Cortés marched inland to find Montezuma. Leading about 350 men armed with swords, lances, and muskets and supported by ten cannons, four smaller guns, and sixteen horses, Cortés had to live off the land, establishing peaceful relations with indigenous tribes when he could and killing them when he thought necessary. On November 8, 1519, Cortés reached Tenochtitlán. Montezuma came out to welcome the Spaniards. After presenting Cortés with gifts, Montezuma ushered the Spaniards to the royal palace and showered them with lavish hospitality. Quickly, Cortés took Montezuma hostage and held him under house arrest, hoping to make him a puppet through which the Spaniards could rule the Mexican empire. This uneasy peace existed

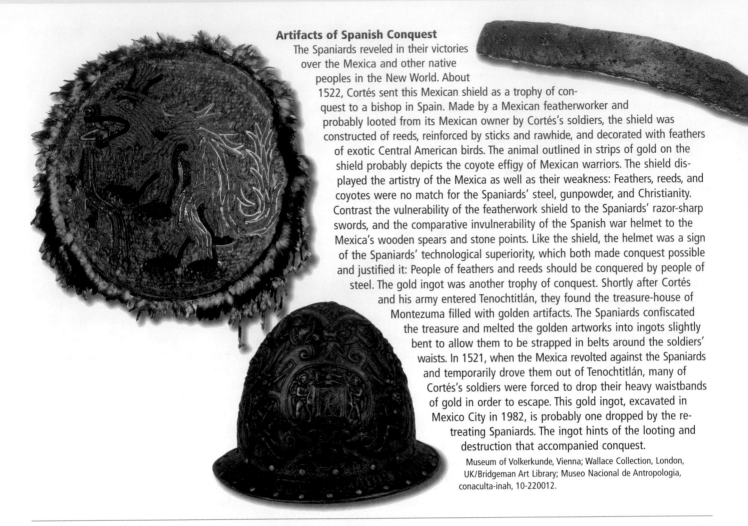

Artifacts of Spanish Conquest
The Spaniards reveled in their victories over the Mexica and other native peoples in the New World. About 1522, Cortés sent this Mexican shield as a trophy of conquest to a bishop in Spain. Made by a Mexican featherworker and probably looted from its Mexican owner by Cortés's soldiers, the shield was constructed of reeds, reinforced by sticks and rawhide, and decorated with feathers of exotic Central American birds. The animal outlined in strips of gold on the shield probably depicts the coyote effigy of Mexican warriors. The shield displayed the artistry of the Mexica as well as their weakness: Feathers, reeds, and coyotes were no match for the Spaniards' steel, gunpowder, and Christianity. Contrast the vulnerability of the featherwork shield to the Spaniards' razor-sharp swords, and the comparative invulnerability of the Spanish war helmet to the Mexica's wooden spears and stone points. Like the shield, the helmet was a sign of the Spaniards' technological superiority, which both made conquest possible and justified it: People of feathers and reeds should be conquered by people of steel. The gold ingot was another trophy of conquest. Shortly after Cortés and his army entered Tenochtitlán, they found the treasure-house of Montezuma filled with golden artifacts. The Spaniards confiscated the treasure and melted the golden artworks into ingots slightly bent to allow them to be strapped in belts around the soldiers' waists. In 1521, when the Mexica revolted against the Spaniards and temporarily drove them out of Tenochtitlán, many of Cortés's soldiers were forced to drop their heavy waistbands of gold in order to escape. This gold ingot, excavated in Mexico City in 1982, is probably one dropped by the retreating Spaniards. The ingot hints of the looting and destruction that accompanied conquest.
Museum of Volkerkunde, Vienna; Wallace Collection, London, UK/Bridgeman Art Library; Museo Nacional de Antropologia, conaculta-inah, 10-220012.

for several months until one of Cortés's men led a brutal massacre of many Mexican nobles, causing the people of Tenochtitlán to revolt. They murdered Montezuma, who seemed to them a Spanish puppet, and they mounted a ferocious assault on the Spaniards. On June 30, 1520, Cortés and about a hundred other Spaniards fought their way out of Tenochtitlán and retreated about one hundred miles to Tlaxcala, a stronghold of bitter enemies of the Mexica. The friendly Tlaxcalans—who had long resented Mexican power—allowed Cortés to regroup, obtain reinforcements, and plan a strategy to conquer Tenochtitlán.

> The great capital of the Mexican empire "looked as if it had been ploughed up," one of Cortés's soldiers remembered.

In the spring of 1521, Cortés mounted a complex campaign against the Mexican capital. The Spaniards and tens of thousands of Indian allies laid siege to the city. With a relentless, scorched-earth strategy, Cortés finally defeated the last Mexican defenders on August 13, 1521. (See "Historical Question," page 50.) The great capital of the Mexican empire "looked as if it had been ploughed up," one of Cortés's soldiers remembered. A few years later, one of the Mexica lamented:

> Broken spears lie in the roads;
> we have torn our hair in grief.
> The houses are roofless now, and their walls
> are red with blood. . . .
> We have pounded our hands in despair
> against the adobe walls,
> for our inheritance, our city, is lost and dead.

The Search for Other Mexicos

Lured by their insatiable appetite for gold, conquistadors quickly fanned out from Tenochtitlán in search of other sources of treasure. The most spectacular prize fell to Francisco Pizarro, who conquered the Incan empire in Peru. The Incas controlled a vast, complex region that contained more than nine million people and stretched along the western coast of South America for more than two thousand miles. In 1532, Pizarro and his army of fewer than two hundred men captured the Incan emperor Atahualpa and held him hostage. As ransom, the Incas gave Pizarro the largest treasure yet produced by the conquests: gold and silver equivalent to half a century's worth of precious-metal production in Europe. With the ransom safely in their hands, the Spaniards executed Atahualpa. The Incan treasure proved that at least one other Mexico did indeed exist, and it spurred the search for others.

Juan Ponce de León had sailed along the Florida coast in 1513. Encouraged by Cortés's success, he went back to Florida in 1521 to find riches, only to be killed in battle with Calusa Indians. A few years later, Lucas Vázquez de Ayllón explored the Atlantic coast north of Florida to present-day South Carolina. In 1526, he established a small settlement on the Georgia coast that he named San Miguel de Gualdape, the first Spanish attempt to establish a foothold in what is now the United States. This settlement was soon swept away by sickness and hostile Indians. Pánfilo de Narváez surveyed the Gulf coast from Florida to Texas in 1528. The Narváez expedition ended disastrously with a shipwreck on the Texas coast near present-day Galveston.

In 1539, Hernando de Soto, a seasoned conquistador who had taken part in the conquest of Peru, set out with nine ships and more than six hundred men to find another Peru in North America. Landing in Florida, de Soto literally slashed his way through much of southeastern North America for three years, searching for the rich, majestic civilizations he believed were there. After the brutal slaughter of many Native Americans and much hardship, de Soto died in 1542. His men buried him in the Mississippi River before turning back to Mexico, disappointed.

Tales of the fabulous wealth of the mythical Seven Cities of Cíbola also lured Francisco Vásquez de Coronado to search the Southwest and Great Plains of North America. In 1540, Coronado left northern Mexico with more than three hundred Spaniards, a thousand Indians, fifteen hundred horses, and a priest who claimed to know the way to what he called "the greatest and best of the discoveries." Cíbola turned out to be a small Zuñi pueblo of about a hundred families. When the Zuñi shot arrows at the Spaniards,

Coronado attacked the pueblo and routed the defenders after a hard battle. Convinced that the rich cities must lie somewhere over the horizon, Coronado kept moving all the way to central Kansas before deciding in 1542 that the rumors he had pursued were just that.

Juan Rodríguez Cabrillo led a maritime expedition in 1542 that sailed along the coast of California. Cabrillo died on Santa Catalina Island, offshore from present-day Los Angeles, but his men sailed on to Oregon, where a ferocious storm forced them to turn back toward Mexico.

These probes into North America by de Soto, Coronado, and Cabrillo persuaded other Spaniards that although enormous territories stretched northward, their inhabitants had little to loot or exploit. After a generation of vigorous exploration, the Spaniards concluded that there was only one Mexico and one Peru.

Zuñi Defend Pueblo against Coronado
This sixteenth-century drawing by a Mexican artist shows Zuñi bowmen fighting back against the arrows of Coronado's men and the entreaties of Christian missionaries. Intended to document the support some Mexican Indians gave to Spanish efforts to extend the conquest into North America, the drawing depicts the Zuñi defender at the bottom of the pueblo aiming his arrow at a Mexican missionary armed only with religious weaponry: a crucifix, a rosary, and a book (presumably the Bible).
Hunterian Museum Library, University of Glasgow. Glasgow University Library, Department of Special Collections.

Why Did Cortés Win?

By conquering Mexico, Hernán Cortés demonstrated that Columbus had in fact discovered a New World of enormous value to the Old. But how did a few hundred Spaniards so far away from home defeat millions of Indians fighting on their home turf?

First, several military factors favored the Spaniards. They possessed superior military technology, which partially offset the Mexica's numerical superiority. They fought with weapons of iron and steel against the Mexica's stone, wood, and copper. They charged on horseback against Mexican warriors on foot. They ignited gunpowder to fire cannons and muskets toward attacking Mexica, whose only source of power was human muscle. But the Mexica's immense numerical superiority could overpower the Spaniards' weaponry.

The Spaniards also possessed superior military organization, although they were far from a highly disciplined, professional fighting force. Cortés's army was composed of soldiers of fortune, young men who hoped to fight for God and king and get rich. The unsteady discipline among the Spaniards is suggested by Cortés's decision to beach and dismantle the ships that had brought his small army to the Mexican mainland. After that, his men had no choice but to go forward.

The Spaniards were a well-oiled military machine compared with the Mexica, who tended to attack from ambush or in waves of frontal assaults, showing great courage but little organization or discipline. The Mexica seldom sustained attacks, even when they had the Spaniards on the run. In the siege of Tenoch-

titlán, for example, the Mexica often paused to sacrifice Spanish soldiers they had captured, taking time to skin "their faces," one Spaniard recalled, "which they afterward prepared like leather gloves, with their beards on." Spanish leaders, in contrast, concentrated their soldiers to magnify the effect of their firepower and to maintain communication during the thick of battle.

But perhaps the Spaniards' most fundamental military advantage was their concept of war. The Mexican concept was shaped by the nature of the empire. The Mexica fought to impose their tribute system on others and to take captives for sacrifice. They believed that war would make their adversaries realize the high cost of continuing to fight and would give them a big incentive to surrender and pay tribute. To the Spaniards, war meant destroying the enemy's ability to fight. In short, the Spaniards sought total victory; the Mexica sought surrender. All these military factors weakened the Mexica's resistance but were insufficient to explain Cortés's victory.

Disease played a major part in the Mexica's defeat. When the Mexica confronted Cortés, they were not at full strength. An epidemic of smallpox and measles had struck the Caribbean in 1519, arrived in Mexico with Cortés and his men, and lasted through 1522. Thousands of Indians died, and many others became too sick to fight. When the Spaniards were regrouping in Tlaxcala after their disastrous evacuation of Tenochtitlán, a great plague broke out in the Mexican capital. As one Mexica explained to a Spaniard shortly after the conquest, the plague lasted for

seventy days, "striking everywhere in the city and killing a vast number of our people. Sores erupted on our faces, our breasts, our bellies. . . . The illness was so dreadful that no one could walk or move. . . . They could not get up to search for food, and everybody else was too sick to care for them, so they starved to death in their beds."

The sickness was not confined to Tenochtitlán. It also killed and weakened people in the areas surrounding the city, spreading back along the network of trade and tribute that fed the city, reducing its food supply and further weakening the survivors. While the Mexica were decimated by their first exposure to smallpox and measles, the Spaniards were for all practical purposes immune, having previously been exposed to the diseases. European viruses probably played at least as large a role in the conquest as weapons and military tactics.

Religion also contributed to the Mexica's defeat. Mexican religious doctrine led Montezuma to be hesitant and uncertain in confronting the Spaniards during the months when they were most vulnerable. While Cortés marched toward Tenochtitlán, the Indians thought that the Spaniards and their horses were immortal deities. Cortés worked hard to maintain the illusion, hiding Spaniards who died. But by the time Cortés retreated from Tenochtitlán, the Mexica knew that the Spaniards could be killed, and their resistance stiffened accordingly.

While the Mexica's religion reduced their initial resistance to the conquistadors, Christianity strengthened the Spaniards. The Spaniards' Christianity was a confident and militant faith that commanded its followers to destroy idolatry, root out heresy, slay infidels, and subjugate nonbelievers. Their religious zeal had been honed for centuries in the battles of the Reconquest. Christianity was as much a part of the conquistadors' armory as swords and gunpowder.

Mexican military commanders often turned to their priests for military guidance. The Spaniards routinely celebrated mass and prayed before battles, but Cortés and his subordinates—tough, wily, practical men—made the military and diplomatic decisions. When the Spaniards suffered defeats, they did not worry that God had abandoned them. However, when the Mexica lost battles advised by their priests, they confronted the distressing fear that their gods no longer seemed to listen to them. The deadly sickness sweeping through the countryside also seemed to show that their gods had abandoned them. "Cut us loose," one Mexica pleaded, "because the gods have died."

Finally, political factors proved decisive in the Mexica's defeat. Cortés shrewdly exploited the tensions between the Mexica and the people they ruled in their empire. Cortés's small army was reinforced by thousands of Indians who were eager to seek revenge against the Mexica. With skillful diplomacy, Cortés obtained cooperation from thousands of Indian porters and food suppliers. Besides fighting alongside Cortés, the Spaniards' Indian allies provided the invaders with a fairly secure base from which to maneuver against the Mexican stronghold. Hundreds of thousands of Indians helped the Spaniards by not contributing to the Mexica's defense. These passive allies of the Spaniards prevented the Mexica from fully capitalizing on their overwhelming numerical superiority. In the end, although many factors contributed to the conquest, Cortés won because the Mexican empire was the source not only of the Mexica's impressive wealth and power but also of their crippling weakness.

Mexican Warrior
Warriors held the most exalted status in Mexican society. This sixteenth-century Mexican painting of a warrior in full battle regalia illustrates the Mexica's careful attention to their magnificent, awe-inspiring costumes. The elaborate clothing and decorative adornments (notice the ornamental stone plug in the warrior's lower lip) expressed the warriors' high status; they also were intended to intimidate enemies who dared oppose the fearsome Mexica. Spanish soldiers developed a healthy respect for the military skills of the Mexica but were not intimidated by the warriors' costumes. They did not understand the meaning the costumes had for the Mexica— for example, the costumes' evocation of supernatural support. In addition, although Mexican wooden swords lined with sharp stones could inflict deadly wounds, they proved no match for Spanish body armor, steel swords, horses, and guns.
Bibliothèque Nationale de France.

New Spain in the Sixteenth Century

For all practical purposes, Spain was the dominant European power in the Western Hemisphere during the sixteenth century (Map 2.3). Portugal claimed the giant territory of Brazil under the Tordesillas treaty but was far more concerned with exploiting its hard-won trade with the East Indies than in colonizing the New World. England and France were absorbed by domestic and diplomatic concerns in Europe and largely lost interest in America until late in the century. In the decades after 1519, the Spaniards created the distinctive colonial society of New Spain that showed other Europeans how the New World could be made to serve the purposes of the Old.

The Spanish monarchy claimed ownership of most of the land in the Western Hemisphere and gave the conquistadors permission to explore and plunder. (See "Documenting the American Promise," page 54.) The crown took one-fifth, called the "royal fifth," of any loot confiscated and allowed the conquerors to divide the rest. In the end, most conquistadors received very little after the plunder was divided among leaders such as Cortés and his favorite officers. To compensate his disappointed, battle-hardened soldiers, Cortés gave them towns the Spaniards had subdued.

The distribution of conquered towns institutionalized the system of *encomienda*, which empowered the conquistadors to rule the Indians and the lands in and around their towns. The

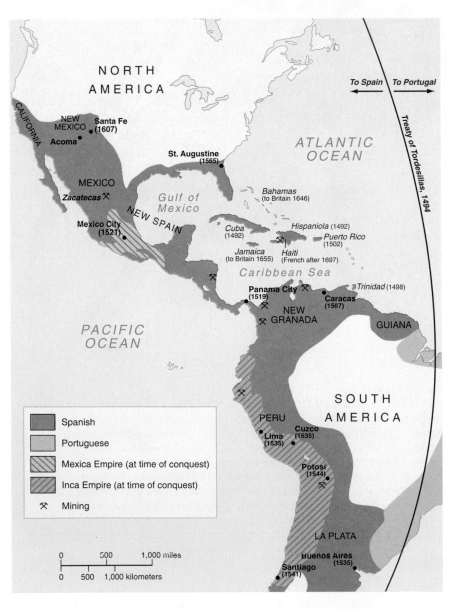

MAP 2.3 New Spain in the Sixteenth Century
Spanish control spread throughout Central and South America during the sixteenth century, with the important exception of Portuguese Brazil. North America, though claimed by Spain under the Treaty of Tordesillas, remained peripheral to Spain's New World empire.

READING THE MAP: Track Spain's efforts at colonization by date. How did political holdings, the physical layout of the land, and natural resources influence where the Spaniards directed their energies?

CONNECTIONS: What was the purpose of the Treaty of Tordesillas? How might the location of silver and gold mines have affected Spain's desire to assert its claims over regions still held by Portugal after 1494, and Spain's interest in California, New Mexico, and Florida?

FOR MORE HELP ANALYZING THIS MAP, see the map activity for this chapter in the Online Study Guide at bedfordstmartins.com/roark.

Testerian Catechism

After the conquest, Catholic missionaries tried to teach the Mexica the basic doctrines of Christianity by using pictures (pictographs) that resembled the symbols in preconquest Mexican codices (books composed of pictographs). The missionaries hoped to appeal to the Mexica's respect for the authority of the ancient texts. These Testerian catechisms demonstrate the missionaries' awareness that the Mexica often retained their faith in their preconquest gods. The catechism shown here incorporates symbols of both Christian and Mexican belief. Try to puzzle out the identity of the various figures and the meanings Catholic missionaries intended them to convey to the Mexica.
Trustees of the British Museum.

concept of encomienda was familiar to the Spaniards, who had used it to govern regions recaptured from the Muslims during the Reconquest. In New Spain, encomienda transferred to the Spanish *encomendero* (the man who "owned" the town) the tribute that the town had previously paid to the Mexican empire.

In theory, encomienda involved a reciprocal relationship between the encomendero and "his" Indians. In return for the tribute and labor of the Indians, the encomendero was supposed to be responsible for their material well-being, to guarantee order and justice in the town, and to encourage the Indians to convert to Christianity. Catholic missionaries labored earnestly to convert the Indians to Christianity. Missionaries fervently believed that God expected them to save the Indians' souls by convincing them to abandon their old, sinful beliefs and to embrace the one true Christian faith. (See "Seeking the American Promise," page 58.) After baptizing tens of thousands of Indians, the missionaries learned that many Indians continued to worship their own gods along with the Christian God. Most friars came to believe that the Indians were lesser beings inherently incapable of fully understanding the Christian faith.

In practice, encomenderos were far more interested in what the Indians could do for them than in what they or the missionaries could do

Justifying Conquest

The immense riches Spain reaped from its New World empire came largely at the expense of the Indians. A few individual Spaniards raised their voices against the brutal exploitation of the Indians. Their criticisms prompted the Spanish monarchy to formulate an official justification of conquest that, in effect, blamed the Indians for resisting Spanish dominion.

DOCUMENT 1
Montecino's 1511 Sermon

In 1511, a Dominican friar named Antón Montecino delivered a blistering sermon that astonished the Spaniards gathered in the church in Santo Domingo, headquarters of the Spanish Caribbean.

Your greed for gold is blind. Your pride, your lust, your anger, your envy, your sloth, all blind. . . . You are in mortal sin. And you are heading for damnation. . . . For you are destroying an innocent people. For they are God's people, these innocents, whom you destroyed. By what right do you make them die? Mining gold for you in your mines or working for you in your fields, by what right do you unleash enslaving wars upon them? They have lived in peace in this land before you came, in peace in their own homes. They did nothing to harm you to cause you to slaughter them wholesale. . . . Are you not under God's command to love them as you love yourselves? Are you out of your souls, out of your minds? Yes. And that will bring you to damnation.

SOURCE: Zvi Dor-Ner, *Columbus and the Age of Discovery* (New York: William Morrow, 1991), 220–21.

DOCUMENT 2
The Requerimiento

Montecino returned to Spain to bring the Indians' plight to the king's attention. In 1512 and 1513, King Ferdinand met with philosophers, theologians, and other advisers and concluded that the holy duty to spread the Christian faith justified conquest. To buttress this claim, the king had his advisers prepare the Requerimiento. According to the Requerimiento, Indians who failed to welcome Spanish conquest and all its blessings deserved to die. Conquistadors were commanded to read the Requerimiento to the Indians before any act of conquest. Beginning in 1514, they routinely did so, speaking in Spanish while other Spaniards brandishing unsheathed swords stood nearby.

On the part of the King . . . [and] queen of [Spain], subduers of the barbarous nations, we their servants notify and make known to you, as best we can, that the Lord our God, living and eternal, created the heaven and the earth, and one man and one woman, of whom you and we, and all the men of the world, were and are descendants. . . .

God our lord gave charge to one man called St. Peter, that he should be lord and superior to all the men in the world, that all should obey him, and that he should be the head of the whole human race, wherever men should live . . . and he gave him the world for his kingdom and jurisdiction.

And he commanded him to place his seat in Rome, as the spot most fitting to rule the world from. . . . This man was called Pope, as if to say, Admirable Great Father and Governor of men. The men who lived in that time obeyed that St. Peter and took him for lord, king, and superior of the universe. So also they have regarded the others who after him have been elected to the pontificate, and so has it been continued even till now, and will continue till the end of the world.

One of these pontiffs, who succeeded that St. Peter as lord of the world . . . made donation of these islands and mainland to the aforesaid king and queen [of Spain] and to their successors. . . .

for the Indians. Encomenderos subjected the Indians to chronic overwork, mistreatment, and abuse. As one Spaniard remarked, "Everything [the Indians] do is slowly done and by compulsion. They are malicious, lying, [and] thievish." Economically, however, encomienda recognized a fundamental reality of New Spain: The most important treasure the Spaniards could plunder from the New World was not gold but uncompensated Indian labor. To exploit that labor, New Spain's richest natural resource, encomienda gave encomenderos the right to force Indians to work when, where, and how the Spaniards pleased.

Encomienda engendered two groups of influential critics. A few of the missionaries were horrified at the brutal mistreatment of the Indians. The cruelty of the encomenderos made it difficult for priests to persuade the Indians of

So their highnesses are kings and lords of these islands and mainland by virtue of this donation; and . . . almost all those to whom this has been notified, have received and served their highnesses, as lords and kings, in the way that subjects ought to do, with good will, without any resistance, immediately, without delay, when they were informed of the aforesaid facts. And also they received and obeyed the priests whom their highnesses sent to preach to them and to teach them our holy faith; and all these, of their own free will, without any reward or condition have become Christians, and are so, and the highnesses have joyfully and graciously received them, and they have also commanded them to be treated as their subjects and vassals; and you too are held and obliged to do the same. Wherefore, as best we can, we ask and require that you consider what we have said to you, and that you take the time that shall be necessary to understand and deliberate upon it, and that you acknowledge the Church as the ruler and superior of the whole world, and the high priest called Pope, and in his name the king and queen [of Spain] our lords, in his place, as superiors and lords and kings of these islands and this mainland by virtue of the said donation, and that you consent and permit that these religious fathers declare and preach to you. . . .

If you do so . . . we . . . shall receive you in all love and charity, and shall leave you your wives and your children and your lands free without servitude, that you may do with them and with yourselves freely what you like and think best, and they shall not compel you to turn to Christians unless you yourselves, when informed of the truth, should wish to be converted to our holy Catholic faith. . . . And besides this, their highnesses award you many privileges and exemptions and will grant you many benefits.

But if you do not do this or if you maliciously delay in doing it, I certify to you that with the help of God we shall forcefully enter into your country and shall make war against you in all ways and manners that we can, and shall subject you to the yoke and obedience of the Church and of their highnesses; we shall take you and your wives and your children and shall make slaves of them, and as such shall sell and dispose of them as their highnesses may command; and we shall take away your goods and shall do to you all the harm and damage that we can, as to vassals who do not obey and refuse to receive their lord and resist and contradict him; and we protest that the deaths and losses which shall accrue from this are your fault, and not that of their highnesses, or ours, or of these soldiers who come with us.

The Indians who heard the Requerimiento could not understand Spanish, of course. No native documents survive to record the Indians' thoughts upon hearing the Spaniards' official justification for conquest, even when it was translated into a language they recognized. But one conquistador reported that when the Requerimiento was translated for two chiefs in Colombia, they responded that if the pope gave the king so much territory that belonged to other people, "the Pope must have been drunk."

Source: Adapted from A. Helps and M. Oppenheim, eds., *The Spanish Conquest in America and Its Relation to the History of Slavery and to the Government of the Colonies*, 4 vols. (London and New York, 1900–1904), 1:264–67.

Questions for Analysis and Debate

1. How did the Requerimiento answer the criticisms of Montecino? According to the Requerimiento, why was conquest justified? What was the source of the Indians' resistance to conquest?

2. What arguments might a critic like Montecino have used to respond to the Requerimiento's justification of conquest? What arguments might the Mexican leader Montezuma have made against those of the Requerimiento?

3. Was the Requerimiento a faithful expression or a cynical violation of the Spaniards' Christian faith?

the tender mercies of the Spaniards' God. "What will [the Indians] think about the God of the Christians," Fray Bartolomé de Las Casas asked, when they see their friends "with their heads split, their hands amputated, their intestines torn open? . . . Would they want to come to Christ's sheepfold after their homes had been destroyed, their children imprisoned, their wives raped, their cities devastated, their maidens deflowered, and their provinces laid waste?" Las Casas and other outspoken missionaries softened few hearts among the encomenderos, but they did win some sympathy for the Indians from the Spanish monarchy and royal bureaucracy. Royal officials interpreted encomenderos' brutal treatment of the Indians as part of the larger general problem of the

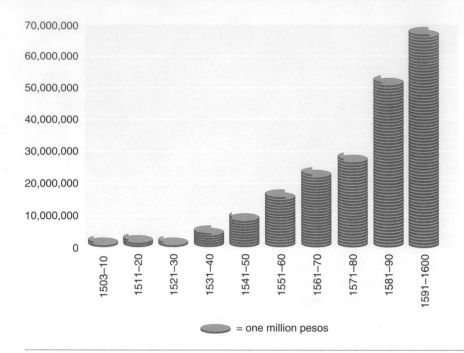

FIGURE 2.1   New World Gold and Silver Imported into Spain during the Sixteenth Century, in Pesos
Spain imported more gold than silver during the first three decades of the sixteenth century, but the total value of this treasure was quickly eclipsed during the 1530s and 1540s, when rich silver mines were developed. Silver accounted for most of the enormous growth in Spain's precious-metal imports from the New World.

troublesome autonomy of encomenderos. The Spanish monarchy moved to abolish encomienda in an effort to replace swashbuckling old conquistadors with royal bureaucrats as the rulers of New Spain.

One of the most important blows to encomienda was the imposition in 1549 of a reform called the *repartimiento*, which limited the labor an encomendero could command from his Indians to forty-five days per year from each adult male. The repartimiento, however, did not challenge the principle of forced labor, nor did it prevent encomenderos from continuing to cheat, mistreat, and overwork their Indians. Slowly, as the old encomenderos died, repartimiento replaced encomienda as the basic system of exploiting Indian labor.

The practice of coerced labor in New Spain grew directly out of the Spaniards' assumption that they were superior to the Indians. As one missionary put it, the Indians "are incapable of learning. . . . The Indians are more stupid than asses and refuse to improve in anything." Therefore, most Spaniards assumed, Indians' labor should be organized by and for their conquerors. The Spaniards seldom hesitated to use violence to punish and intimidate recalcitrant Indians.

From the viewpoint of Spain, the single most important economic activity in New Spain after 1540 was silver mining. Spain imported more

> One colonist wrote to his brother in Spain, "Don't hesitate [to come]. . . . This land [New Spain] is as good as ours [in Spain], for God has given us more here than there, and we shall be better off."

New World gold than silver in the early decades of the century, but that changed with the discovery of major silver deposits at Potosí, Bolivia, in 1545 and Zacatecas, Mexico, in 1546. As these and other mines swung into large-scale production, an ever-growing stream of silver flowed from New Spain to Spain (Figure 2.1). Overall, exports of precious metals from New Spain during the sixteenth century were worth about twenty-five times more than hides, the next most important export. The mines required large capital investments and many miners. Typically, a few Spaniards supervised large groups of Indian miners, who were supplemented by African slaves later in the sixteenth century.

For the Spaniards, life in New Spain was relatively easy. Only a few thousand Spaniards actually fought during the conquests. Although the riches they won fell far short of their expectations, the benefits of encomienda gave them a comfortable, leisurely life that was the envy of many Spaniards back in Europe. As one colonist wrote to his brother in Spain, "Don't hesitate [to come]. . . . This land [New Spain] is as good as ours [in Spain], for God has given us more here than there, and we shall be better off."

During the century after 1492, about 225,000 Spaniards settled in the colonies. Virtually all of them were poor young men of common (non-noble) lineage who came directly from Spain. Laborers and **artisans** made up the largest proportion, but soldiers and sailors were also numerous. Throughout the sixteenth century, men vastly outnumbered women, although the proportion of women grew from about one in twenty before 1519 to nearly one in three by the 1580s.

The gender and number of Spanish settlers shaped two fundamental features of the society of New Spain. First, Europeans never made up more than 1 or 2 percent of the total population. Although the Spaniards ruled New Spain, the population was almost wholly Indian. Second, the shortage of Spanish women meant that Spanish men frequently married Indian women or used them as concubines. For the most part, the relatively few women from Spain married Spanish men, contributing to a tiny elite defined by European origins.

The small number of Spaniards, the masses of Indians, and the frequency of intermarriage created a steep social hierarchy defined by perceptions of national origin and race. Natives of Spain—*peninsulares* (people born on the Iberian Peninsula)—enjoyed the highest social status in New Spain. Below them but still within the white elite were *creoles*, the children born in the New World to Spanish men and women. Together, peninsulares and creoles made up barely 1 or 2 percent of the population. Below them on the social pyramid was a larger group of *mestizos*, the

Mixed Races

The residents of New Spain maintained a lively interest in each person's racial lineage. These eighteenth-century paintings illustrate forms of racial mixture common in the sixteenth century. In the first painting, a Spanish man and an Indian woman have a mestizo son; in the fourth, a Spanish man and a woman of African descent have a mulatto son; in the fifth, a Spanish woman and a mulatto man have a *morisco* daughter. The many racial permutations led the residents of New Spain to develop an elaborate vocabulary of ancestry. The child of a morisco and a Spaniard was a *chino*; the child of a chino and an Indian was a *salta abas*; the child of a salta abas and a mulatto was a *lobo*; and so on. Can you detect hints of some of the meanings of racial categories in the clothing depicted in these paintings?

Bob Schalkwijk / INAH.

READING THE IMAGE: What do these paintings reveal about social status in New Spain?

CONNECTIONS: How do the mixed-race paintings illustrate the power the Spaniards exercised in their New World colonies? What were some other aspects of colonial society that demonstrated Spanish domination?

FOR MORE HELP ANALYZING THIS IMAGE, see the visual activity for this chapter in the Online Study Guide at bedfordstmartins.com/roark.

Spreading Christianity in New Spain

Spanish officials aspired to accompany the military and political conquest of the New World with spiritual conquest. Queen Isabella and her successors gave top priority to a campaign to convert the Indians to Christianity. With royal support, priests flocked to New Spain to harvest the millions of souls unexpectedly disclosed by the voyages of Columbus. In 1529, a young priest named Bernardino de Sahagún sailed to New Spain along with other missionaries and several members of the Mexican nobility whom Cortés had brought to Spain, including a son of Montezuma. Sahagún spent the remaining sixty-one years of his life in Mexico seeking to realize the promise of spreading Christianity to people who had never heard of it.

Sahagún believed that preaching the gospel in the New World was a heaven-sent opportunity to revitalize global Christianity. In Asia, he wrote, "there are nothing but Turks and Moors"; in Africa, "there are no longer any Christians"; in Germany, "there are nothing but heretics"; and in Europe, "in most places there is no obedience to the Church." Now, Sahagún wrote, "Our Lord" ordained "the Spanish people to traverse the Ocean Sea to make discoveries in the West" and to "bring into the embrace of the Church that multitude of peoples, kingdoms, and nations." In pursuit of his goal to rescue Christianity by converting the New World Indians, Sahagún compiled the most important collection of information in existence about the lives and beliefs of sixteenth-century Mexicans—information that church officials and the Spanish monarchy tried to suppress.

Sahagún and other Spaniards considered Christianity the one true faith. When Cortés and his men marched into Mexico a decade before Sahagún arrived, for example, they went out of their way to destroy effigies of Mexican gods and to replace them with crosses, the icons of Christianity. The Spaniards believed that smashing the Mexicans' idols advanced the ultimate reign of Christianity in the New World. "It was necessary," Sahagún wrote, "to destroy the idolatrous things, and all the idolatrous buildings, and even the customs of the [Mexicans'] republic that were intertwined with idolatrous rites and accompanied by idolatrous ceremonies. . . . It was necessary to dismantle it all and . . . [to leave] no trace of idolatrous practices."

What Sahagún considered idolatry was rooted in individual Mexicans' belief in what he called their own "innumerable insanities and gods without number." Sahagún and other priests set out to persuade the Indians to reject belief in traditional deities and to have faith instead in the divinity of Jesus Christ and in the Catholic Church as Christ's representative on earth.

At first, the conversion campaign seemed amazingly successful. One priest claimed that more than nine million Mexicans had been baptized by 1539. But after a few years, Sahagún and other priests realized that many Indians simply accepted "Jesus Christ as one among their many gods." According to Sahagún, baptized Mexicans "took as yet another god the God of the Spaniards without . . . relinquishing their ancient gods." Adopting some of the outward rituals of Christianity while maintaining belief in what Spaniards considered pagan idols was a "twisted perversity," Sahagún wrote, one that caused the New World church "to be founded on falsehood."

Unlike many other Spaniards, Sahagún believed that in order to purge "idolatrous rites, superstitions, and omens," church leaders needed to become "familiar with" the Mexicans' traditional religious ideas. Only by a thorough knowledge of "idolatrous rites" could priests tell whether the Indians had experienced authentic conversions to Christianity or remained tainted by "twisted perversity." Sahagún likened priests to "physicians for the soul," who needed to understand the Mexicans' "spiritual illnesses" in order to recognize and treat them. To diagnose these "illnesses," Sahagún set out to record everything he could learn about the Indians' beliefs.

As a first step, Sahagún learned Nahuatl, the Mexicans' unwritten language. Next, he and other priests started schools to teach Latin and eventually Spanish to young Indian students, usually drawn from elite families. These "trilinguals," as Sahagún called them, could translate religious texts written in Latin into Nahuatl, which the priests could use in their missionary efforts. The trilinguals also could translate spoken Nahuatl into Latin and Spanish.

Beginning in 1558, Sahagún used his trilinguals to undertake a systematic investigation of every facet of Mexican life. Sahagún and his assistants interviewed Mexican elders, asking them not only about gods and religious ceremonies but also about farming, family life, education, poetry, songs, and even their conquest by the Spaniards. Sahagún developed great admiration for both the Mexicans and their language. "They are quick to learn," he wrote, and were experts "in trades such as tailor, shoemaker, silkmaker, printer, scribe, reader, accountant, singer . . . , flute player, . . . trumpeter, [and] organist . . . [as well as in knowing] grammar, logic, rhetoric, astrology, and theology. . . . There is no art for which they do not have the talent to learn and use it." In fact, Sahagún declared, the Mexicans "are held to be barbarians and a people of little worth, yet in truth, in matters of culture, they are a step ahead of many nations that presume to be civilized."

For years, Sahagún edited and organized this massive treasure trove of information about Mexican life and beliefs, all in the hope that it would ultimately help priests make converts to Christianity. In 1575, he and his assistants began to compile the information into Sahagún's magnum opus—twelve large volumes written in Spanish on one side of each page and in Nahuatl on the other side, along with more than eighteen hundred illustrations drawn by Mexican artists in the style of their traditional pictographs.

When church officials heard about Sahagún's great work, they obtained a royal order in 1577 to collect all copies and send them immediately to Spain for destruction. The monarch's order declared that it was "inappropriate" and dangerous for Sahagún's work to "be printed or . . . in any way disseminated," and that officials in New Spain "must not consent to absolutely any person writing about things that deal with superstitions and the ways of the life that the Indians had in any language." The Spanish monarchy and most church officials wanted to stamp out the

Mexicans' beliefs, not preserve them. Sahagún dutifully sent his volumes to Spain, but he was still working on a final copy, which he later gave to a priest friend, who saved it.

Sahagún stayed in Mexico and continued to collect and translate information about the Indians' way of life until he died in 1590. Unbeknownst to him, Sahagún's masterwork ended up in an archive in Florence, Italy, and eventually became known as the Florentine Codex. It is the single most important source of information about sixteenth-century Mexicans in existence today.

Sahagún's disciplined commitment to cultural understanding contributed to the conversion of many Mexicans to Christianity, although their belief in traditional deities continued, despite his efforts. Like other priests and Spanish officials, Sahagún participated in the conquest of the Mexicans. In addition, however, Sahagún's efforts to spread Christianity in the New World by learning about Mexican culture preserved for posterity an unrivaled account of the hearts and souls of sixteenth-century Mexicans in their own words.

Montezuma Receiving Tribute
This drawing from Sahagún's Florentine Codex portrays Montezuma (seated at left) receiving a rich array of featherwork, ritualistic costumes, textiles, battle shields, and other luxuries from one of his subjects. Made by a Mexican artist in the mid-sixteenth century, the drawing adapts preconquest symbols to illustrate the enormous power and respect commanded by Montezuma. By the time the drawing was made, Montezuma had been dead for about forty years, and the Spaniards, not Montezuma's descendants, collected tribute (mostly in the form of labor) from the Indians. The artist who made this drawing probably had never personally experienced the tribute system under Montezuma. The drawing conveys an optimistic view of social harmony and abundance in the Mexican empire before the Spanish conquest, and it fails to suggest the bitter resentments among many Native Americans who were forced to pay tribute to Montezuma.
Bridgeman Art Library Ltd.

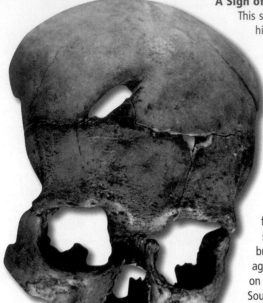

A Sign of Conquest
This skull of an Indian man in his fifties was excavated from the site of a Native American village in southwestern Georgia visited by de Soto's expedition in 1540. The skull shows that the man suffered a fatal sword wound above his right eye. Combined with slashed and severed arm and leg bones from the same site, the skull demonstrates the brutality de Soto employed against indigenous peoples on his journey through the Southeast. No native weapons could have inflicted the wounds left on this skull and the other bones.
Robert L. Blakely.

offspring of Spanish men and Indian women, who accounted for 4 or 5 percent of the population. So many of the mestizos were illegitimate that the term *mestizo* (after the Spanish word for "mixed") became almost synonymous with *bastard* in the sixteenth century. Some mestizos worked as artisans and labor overseers and lived well, and a few rose into the ranks of the elite, especially if their Indian ancestry was not obvious from their skin color. Most mestizos, however, were lumped with the Indians, the enormous bottom slab of the social pyramid.

The society of New Spain established the precedent for what would become a pronounced pattern in the European colonies of the New World: a society stratified sharply by social origin and race. All Europeans of whatever social origin considered themselves superior to Native Americans; in New Spain, they were a dominant minority in both power and status.

The Toll of Spanish Conquest and Colonization

By 1560, the major centers of Indian civilization had been conquered, their leaders overthrown, their religion held in contempt, and their people forced to work for the Spaniards. Profound demoralization pervaded Indian society. As a Mexican poet wrote:

Nothing but flowers and songs of sorrow
are left in Mexico . . .
where once we saw warriors and wise men. . . .
We are crushed to the ground;
we lie in ruins.
There is nothing but grief and suffering
in Mexico.

Adding to the culture shock of conquest and colonization was the deadly toll of European diseases. As conquest spread, the Indians succumbed to virulent epidemics of measles, smallpox, and respiratory illnesses. They had no immunity to these diseases because they had not been exposed to them before the arrival of Europeans. The isolation of the Western Hemisphere before 1492 had protected ancient Americans from the contagious diseases that had raged throughout Eurasia for millennia. The new post-1492 sea bridge eliminated that isolation, and by 1570, the Indian population of New Spain had fallen about 90 percent from what it was when Columbus arrived. The destruction of the Indians was a catastrophe unequaled in human history. A Mayan Indian recalled that when sickness struck his village, "great was the stench of the dead. . . . The dogs and vultures devoured the bodies. The mortality was terrible. . . . So it was that we became orphans. . . . We were born to die!" For most Indians, New Spain was a graveyard.

For the Spaniards, Indian deaths meant that the most valuable resource of New Spain—Indian labor—dwindled rapidly. By the last quarter of the sixteenth century, Spanish colonists felt the pinch of a labor shortage. To help supply the need for laborers, the colonists began to import African slaves. Some Africans had come to Mexico with the conquistadors; one Mexica recalled that among Cortés's men were "some black-skinned one[s] with kink[y] hair." In the years before 1550, while Indian labor was still adequate, only 15,000 slaves were imported from Africa. Even after Indian labor began to decline, the relatively high cost of African slaves kept imports low, approximately 36,000 from 1550 to the end of the century. During the sixteenth century, New Spain continued to rely primarily on a shrinking number of Indians.

Spanish Outposts in Florida and New Mexico

After the explorations of de Soto, Coronado, and Cabrillo, officials in New Spain lost interest in North America. The monarchy claimed that

Indian Silver Miners

This sixteenth-century drawing suggests the hellish conditions endured by Indians forced to labor in the fabulously rich silver mines at Potosí in what is now Bolivia. The backbreaking, dangerous work injured and killed many miners, making it all the more important for the greedy Spaniards to coerce more Indians and African slaves into the mines. Contrast the dark, satanic interior of the mine, symbolizing the Spaniards' brutal exploitation of the naked miners, with the bright, peaceful environment outside the mine, optimistically symbolizing a benign, harmonious natural world unencumbered by Spanish oppression. The drawing conveys the anti-Spanish and anti-Catholic viewpoint of a staunchly Protestant artist who had never set foot in the New World.

Granger Collection.

Spain owned North America and insisted that a few North American settlements be established to give some tangible reality to its claims. Settlements in Florida would have the additional benefit of protecting Spanish ships from pirates and privateers who lurked along the southeastern coast, waiting for the Spanish treasure fleet sailing toward Spain.

In 1565, the Spanish king sent Pedro Menéndez de Avilés to create settlements along the Atlantic coast of North America. In early September, Menéndez founded St. Augustine in Florida, the first permanent European settlement within what became the United States. By 1600, St. Augustine had a population of about five hundred, the only remaining Spanish beachhead on the vast Atlantic shoreline of North America.

More than sixteen hundred miles west of St. Augustine, the Spaniards founded another outpost in 1598. Juan de Oñate led an expedition of about five hundred people to settle northern Mexico, now called New Mexico, and claim the booty rumored to exist there. Oñate had impeccable credentials for both conquest and mining. His father had helped to discover the bonanza silver mines of Zacatecas, and his wife was Isabel Tolosa Cortés Montezuma—the granddaughter of Cortés, the conqueror of Mexico, and the great-granddaughter of Montezuma, the emperor of Mexico before conquest.

After a two-month journey from Mexico, Oñate and his companions reached pueblos near present-day Albuquerque and Santa Fe. He solemnly convened the pueblos' leaders and received their oath of loyalty to the Spanish king and to the Christian God. Oñate sent out scouting parties to find the legendary treasures of the region and to locate the ocean, which he believed must be nearby. Meanwhile, many of his soldiers planned to mutiny, and relations with the Indians deteriorated. When Indians in the Acoma pueblo revolted against the Spaniards, Oñate ruthlessly suppressed the uprising, killing eight hundred men, women, and children. Although Oñate reconfirmed the Spaniards' military superiority, he did not bring peace or stability to the region. After another pueblo revolt occurred in 1599, many of Oñate's settlers returned to Mexico, leaving New Mexico as a small, dusty assertion of Spanish claims to the North American Southwest.

REVIEW Why did New Spain develop a society highly stratified by race and national origin?

The New World and Sixteenth-Century Europe

The riches of New Spain helped make the sixteenth century the Golden Age of Spain. After the deaths of Queen Isabella and King Ferdinand, their sixteen-year-old grandson became King Charles I of Spain in 1516. Three years later, just as Cortés ventured into Mexico, Charles I used judicious bribes to secure his selection as Holy Roman Emperor Charles V. His empire encompassed more than that of any other European monarch. He used the wealth of New Spain to protect his sprawling empire and promote his interests in the fierce dynastic battles of sixteenth-century Europe. He also sought to defend orthodox Christianity from the insurgent heresy of the **Protestant Reformation**. The power of the Spanish monarchy spread the clear message throughout sixteenth-century Europe that a New World empire could bankroll Old World ambitions.

> Luther hoped his ideas would reform the Catholic Church, but instead they ruptured forever the unity of Christianity in western Europe.

The Protestant Reformation and the European Order

In 1517, Martin Luther, an obscure Catholic priest in central Germany, initiated the Protestant Reformation by publicizing his criticisms of the Catholic Church. Luther's ideas won the sympathy of many Catholics, but they were considered extremely dangerous by church officials and monarchs such as Charles V who believed with total conviction that just as the church spoke for God, they ruled for God.

Luther preached a doctrine known as *justification by faith*: Individual Christians could obtain salvation and life everlasting only by having faith that God would save them. Giving offerings to the church, following the orders of priests, or participating in church rituals would not put believers one step closer to heaven. Also, the only true source of information about God's will was the Bible, not the church. By reading the Bible, any Christian could learn as much about God's commandments as any priest. Indeed, Luther called for a "priesthood of all believers."

In effect, Luther charged that the Catholic Church was in many respects fraudulent. Luther insisted that priests were unnecessary for salvation and that they encouraged Christians to violate God's will by promoting religious practices not specifically commanded by the Bible. The church, Luther declared, had neglected its true purpose of helping individual Christians understand the spiritual realm revealed in the Bible and had wasted its resources in worldly conflicts of politics and wars. Luther hoped his ideas would reform the Catholic Church, but instead they ruptured forever the unity of Christianity in western Europe.

Charles V pledged to exterminate Luther's **Protestant** heresies. The wealth pouring into Spain from the New World fueled his efforts to defend orthodox Catholic faith against Protestants, as well as against Muslims in eastern Europe and against any nation bold or foolhardy enough to contest Spain's supremacy. As the wealthiest and most powerful monarch in Europe, Charles V, followed by his son and successor, Philip II, assumed responsibility for upholding the existing order of sixteenth-century Europe.

New World Treasure and Spanish Ambitions

Both Charles V and Philip II fought wars throughout the world during the sixteenth century. Mexican silver funneled through the royal treasury into the hands of military suppliers, soldiers, and sailors wherever in the world Spain's forces fought. New World treasure was dissipated in military adventures that served the goals of the monarchy but did little to benefit most Spaniards.

In a sense, American wealth made the Spanish monarchy too rich and too powerful among the states of Europe since it fueled grandiose Spanish ambitions. The ambitions of Charles V and Philip II were so great that the expenses of constant warfare far outstripped the revenues arriving from New Spain. To help meet military expenditures, both kings raised taxes in Spain more than fivefold during the sixteenth century. Since the nobility, by far the wealthiest class, was exempt from taxation, the burdensome new taxes fell mostly on poor peasants. The ambitions of the monarchy impoverished the vast majority of Spain's population and brought the nation to the brink of bankruptcy. When taxes failed to produce enough revenue to fight its wars, the monarchy borrowed heavily from European bankers. By the end of the sixteenth century, interest payments on royal debts swallowed two-thirds of the crown's annual revenues. In retrospect, the riches from New Spain proved a short-term blessing but a long-term curse.

Algonquian Ceremonial Dance

When the English artist John White visited the coast of present-day North Carolina in 1585 as part of Raleigh's expedition, he painted this watercolor portrait of an Algonquian ceremonial dance. This and White's other portraits are the only surviving likenesses of sixteenth-century North American Indians that were drawn from direct observation in the New World. White's portrait captures the individuality of these Indians' appearances and gestures while depicting a ceremony that must have appeared bizarre and alien to a sixteenth-century Englishman. The significance of this ceremonial dance is still a mystery, although the portrait's obvious signs of order, organization, and collective understanding show that the dancing Indians knew what it meant.

Copyright © The British Museum.

READING THE IMAGE: What values and attitudes seem to be expressed by the ceremonial dancers?
CONNECTIONS: How does this ceremonial dance compare with religious rituals and military ceremonies performed by sixteenth-century Spaniards?

FOR MORE HELP ANALYZING THIS IMAGE, see the visual activity for this chapter in the Online Study Guide at bedfordstmartins.com/roark.

But sixteenth-century Spaniards did not see it that way. As they looked at their accomplishments in the New World, they saw unmistakable signs of progress. They had added enormously to their knowledge and wealth. They had built mines, cities, Catholic churches, and even universities on the other side of the Atlantic. Their military, religious, and economic achievements gave them great pride and confidence.

Europe and the Spanish Example

The lessons of sixteenth-century Spain were not lost on Spain's European rivals. Spain proudly displayed the fruits of its New World conquests. In 1520, for example, Charles V exhibited some of the gifts Montezuma had given to Cortés. The objects astonished the German artist Albrecht Dürer, who wrote in his diary that he "marveled over the subtle ingenuity of the men in these distant lands" who created such "things which were brought to the King . . . [such as] a sun entirely of gold, a whole fathom [six feet] broad." But the most exciting news about "the men in these distant lands" was that they could serve the interests of Europeans as Spain had shown. With a few notable exceptions, Europeans saw the New World as a place for the expansion of European influence, a place where, as one Spaniard wrote, Europeans could "give to those strange lands the form of our own."

France and England tried to follow Spain's example. Both nations warred with Spain in Europe, preyed on Spanish treasure fleets, and ventured to the New World, where they too hoped to find an undiscovered passageway to the East Indies or another Mexico or Peru.

In 1524, France sent Giovanni da Verrazano to scout the Atlantic coast of North America from North Carolina to Canada, looking for a Northwest Passage (see Map 2.2). Eleven years later, France probed farther north with Jacques Cartier's voyage up the St. Lawrence River. Encouraged, Cartier returned to the region with a group of settlers in 1541, but the colony they established—like the search for a Northwest Passage—came to nothing.

English attempts to follow Spain's lead were slower but equally ill fated. Not until 1576, almost eighty years after John Cabot's voyages, did the English try again to find a Northwest Passage. This time Martin Frobisher sailed into the frigid waters of northern Canada (see Map 2.2). His sponsor was the Cathay Company, which hoped to open trade with China. Like many other explorers who preceded and followed him, Frobisher was mesmerized by the Spanish example and was sure he had found gold. But the tons of "ore" he hauled back to England proved worthless, the Cathay Company collapsed, and English interests shifted southward to the giant region on the northern margins of New Spain.

English explorers' attempts to establish North American settlements were no more fruitful than their search for a northern route to China. Sir Humphrey Gilbert led expeditions in 1578 and 1583 that made feeble efforts to found colonies in Newfoundland until Gilbert vanished at sea. Sir Walter Raleigh organized an expedition in 1585 to settle Roanoke Island off the coast of present-day North Carolina. The first group of explorers left no colonists on the island, but two years later Raleigh sent a contingent of more than one hundred settlers to Roanoke under John White's leadership. White went back to England for supplies, and when he returned to Roanoke in 1590, the colonists had disappeared, leaving only the word *Croatoan* (whose meaning is unknown) carved in a tree. The Roanoke colonists most likely died from a combination of natural causes and unfriendly Indians. By the end of the century, England had failed to secure a New World beachhead.

REVIEW   How did Spain's conquests in the New World shape Spanish influence in Europe?

Conclusion: The Promise of the New World for Europeans

The sixteenth century in the New World belonged to the Spaniards who employed Columbus and to the Indians who greeted him as he stepped ashore. Isabella of Spain helped initiate the Columbian exchange between the New World and the Old that massively benefited first Spain and later other Europeans and that continues to this day. The exchange also subjected Native Americans to the ravages of European diseases and Spanish conquest. Spanish explorers, conquistadors, and colonists forced the Indians to serve the interests of Spanish settlers and the Spanish monarchy. The exchange illustrated one of the most important lessons of the sixteenth century: After millions of years, the Atlantic no longer was an impermeable barrier separating the Eastern and Western Hemispheres. After the voyages of Columbus, European sailing ships regularly bridged the Atlantic and carried people, products, diseases, and ideas from one shore to the other.

No European monarch could forget the seductive lesson taught by Spain's example: The New World could vastly enrich the Old. Spain remained a New World power for almost four centuries, and its language, religion, culture, and institutions left a permanent imprint. By the end

Roanoke Settlement, 1585–1590

NORTH CAROLINA

Roanoke R.

Albemarle Sound

Roanoke Island

Cape Hatteras

ATLANTIC OCEAN

0   50   100 miles
0   100 kilometers

of the sixteenth century, however, other European monarchies had begun to contest Spain's dominion in Europe and to make forays into the northern fringes of Spain's New World preserve. To reap the benefits the Spaniards enjoyed from their New World domain, the others had to learn a difficult lesson: how to deviate from Spain's example. That discovery lay ahead.

Selected Bibliography

General Works

J. H. Elliott, *Empires of the Atlantic World: Britain and Spain in America, 1491–1830* (2006).

Jonathan Locke Hart, *Representing the New World: The English and French Uses of the Example of Spain* (2001).

Jonathan Locke Hart, *Columbus, Shakespeare, and the Interpretation of the New World* (2003).

John L. Kessell, *Spain in the Southwest: A Narrative History of Colonial New Mexico, Arizona, Texas, and California* (2002).

Kenneth F. Kiple and Stephen V. Beck, eds., *Biological Consequences of European Expansion, 1450–1800* (1997).

Diarmaid MacCulloch, *The Reformation: A History* (2004).

William D. Phillips and Carla Rahn Phillips, *The Worlds of Christopher Columbus* (1992).

David J. Weber, *The Spanish Frontier in North America* (1992).

Explorers and Empires

Henry Arthur Francis Kamen, *Spain's Road to Empire: The Making of a World Power, 1492–1763* (2002).

Karen Ordahl Kupperman, *Roanoke: The Abandoned Colony* (1984).

John Lynch, *Spain, 1516–1598: From Nation State to World Empire* (1992).

Francesco Relaño, *The Shaping of Africa: Cosmographic Discourse and Cartographic Science in Late Medieval and Early Modern Europe* (2002).

A. J. R. Russell-Wood, *The Portuguese Empire, 1415–1808: A World on the Move* (1998).

Hugh Thomas, *Rivers of Gold: The Rise of the Spanish Empire from Columbus to Magellan* (2004).

Europeans Encounter the New World

Philip P. Boucher, *Cannibal Encounters: Europeans and Island Caribs, 1492–1763* (1992).

Rebecca Catz, *Christopher Columbus and the Portuguese, 1476–1498* (1993).

Noble David Cook, *Born to Die: Disease and New World Conquest, 1492–1650* (1998).

Alfred W. Crosby, *Ecological Imperialism: The Biological Expansion of Europe, 900–1900* (1986).

Valerie J. Flint, *The Imaginative Landscape of Christopher Columbus* (1992).

Anthony Pagden, *Lords of All the World: Ideologies of Empire in Spain, Britain, and France, 1500–1800* (1995).

Irving Rouse, *The Tainos: Rise and Decline of the People Who Greeted Columbus* (1992).

Conquest and New Spain

Herman L. Bennett, *Africans in Colonial Mexico: Absolutism, Christianity, and Afro-Creole Consciousness, 1570–1640* (2003).

Louise M. Burkhart, *The Slippery Earth: Nahua-Christian Moral Dialogue in Sixteenth-Century Mexico* (1989).

David Ewing Duncan, *Hernando de Soto: A Savage Quest in the Americas* (1995).

Richard Flint and Shirley Cushing Flint, *The Coronado Expedition* (2003).

Serge Gruzinski, *The Conquest of Mexico: The Incorporation of Indian Societies into the Western World, Sixteenth–Eighteenth Centuries* (1993).

Ramón A. Gutiérrez, *When Jesus Came, the Corn Mothers Went Away: Marriage, Sexuality, and Power in New Mexico, 1500–1846* (1991).

Robert H. Jackson, *Race, Caste, and Status: Indians in Colonial Spanish America* (1999).

Andrew L. Knaut, *The Pueblo Revolt of 1680: Conquest and Resistance in Seventeenth-Century New Mexico* (1995).

Miguel León-Portilla, *Bernardino de Sahagún: First Anthropologist* (2002).

James Lockhart, *The Nahuas after Conquest: A Social and Cultural History of the Indians of Central Mexico, Sixteenth through Eighteenth Centuries* (1992).

Jerald T. Milanich, *Laboring in the Fields of the Lord: Spanish Missions and Southwestern Indians* (1999).

Carroll L. Riley, *The Kachina and the Cross: Indians and Spaniards in the Early Southwest* (1999).

Charles A. Truxillo, *By the Sword and the Cross: The Historical Evolution of the Catholic World Monarchy in Spain and the New World, 1492–1825* (2001).

Stephanie Gail Wood, *Transcending Conquest: Nahua Views of Spanish Colonial Mexico* (2003).

▶ **For more books about topics in this chapter,** see the Online Bibliography at bedfordstmartins.com/roark.

▶ **For additional firsthand accounts of this period,** see Chapter 2 in Michael Johnson, ed., *Reading the American Past,* Fourth Edition.

▶ **For Web sites, images, and documents related to topics and places in this chapter,** visit bedfordstmartins.com/makehistory.

REVIEWING THE CHAPTER

Follow these steps to review and strengthen your understanding of the chapter.

Step 1: *Study the* **Key Terms** *and* **Timeline** *to identify the significance of each item listed.*

Step 2: *Answer the* **Review Questions**, *drawing on key terms and dates to support your answers.*

Step 3: *Drawing on the Key Terms, Timeline, and Review Questions, answer the broader* **Making Connections** *questions.*

KEY TERMS

Who

Queen Isabella (p. 35)
King Ferdinand (p. 35)
Christopher Columbus (p. 35)
Prince Henry the Navigator (p. 39)
Tainos (p. 41)
John Cabot (p. 42)
Amerigo Vespucci (p. 43)
Martin Waldseemüller (p. 44)
Ferdinand Magellan (p. 44)
Hernán Cortés (p. 46)
Malinali (p. 46)
Montezuma (p. 47)
Mexica (p. 47)
Tlaxcalans (p. 48)
Francisco Pizarro (p. 48)
Atahualpa (p. 49)
Hernando de Soto (p. 49)

Francisco Vásquez de Coronado (p. 49)
Juan Rodríguez Cabrillo (p. 49)
Bartolomé de Las Casas (p. 55)
Juan de Oñate (p. 61)
Holy Roman Emperor Charles V
    (King Charles I of Spain) (p. 62)
Martin Luther (p. 62)
Philip II (p. 62)
Jacques Cartier (p. 64)
Martin Frobisher (p. 64)

What

bubonic plague (p. 37)
the Reconquest (p. 39)
caravel (p. 40)
Treaty of Tordesillas (p. 42)
Northwest Passage (p. 43)
Columbian exchange (p. 45)
conquistador (p. 46)

Tenochtitlán (p. 47)
Incan empire (p. 48)
San Miguel de Gualdape (p. 49)
Seven Cities of Cíbola (p. 49)
New Spain (p. 52)
royal fifth (p. 52)
encomienda (p. 52)
repartimiento (p. 56)
Potosí, Bolivia (p. 56)
Zacatecas, Mexico (p. 56)
peninsulares (p. 57)
creoles (p. 57)
mestizos (p. 57)
Acoma pueblo revolt (p. 61)
Protestant Reformation (p. 62)
justification by faith (p. 62)
Roanoke (p. 64)

TIMELINE

NOTE: Events are depicted chronologically, but the passage of time is not to exact scale.

◄ **1480** • Portuguese ships reach Congo.

1488 • Bartolomeu Dias rounds Cape of Good Hope.

1492 • Christopher Columbus lands on Caribbean island that he names San Salvador.

1493 • Columbus makes second voyage to New World.

1494 • Portugal and Spain negotiate Treaty of Tordesillas.

1497 • John Cabot searches for Northwest Passage.

1498 • Vasco da Gama sails to India.

1513 • Vasco Núñez de Balboa crosses Isthmus of Panama.

1517 • Protestant Reformation begins in Germany.

1519 • Hernán Cortés leads expedition to find wealth in Mexico.
        • Ferdinand Magellan sets out to sail around the world.

1520 • Mexica in Tenochtitlán revolt against Spaniards.

1521 • Cortés conquers Mexica at Tenochtitlán.

REVIEW QUESTIONS

1. Why did European exploration expand dramatically in the fifteenth century? (pp. 37–40)

2. How did Columbus's landfall in the Caribbean help revolutionize Europeans' understanding of world geography? (pp. 40–46)

3. Why did New Spain develop a society highly stratified by race and national origin? (pp. 46–61)

4. How did Spain's conquests in the New World shape Spanish influence in Europe? (pp. 62–64)

MAKING CONNECTIONS

1. The Columbian exchange exposed people on both sides of the Atlantic to surprising new people and goods. It also produced dramatic demographic and political transformations in the Old World and the New. How did the Columbian exchange lead to redistributions of power and population? Discuss these changes, being sure to cite examples from both contexts.

2. Despite inferior numbers, the Spaniards were able to conquer the Mexica and maintain control of the colonial hierarchy that followed. Why did the Spanish conquest of the Mexica succeed, and how did the Spaniards govern the conquered territory to maintain their dominance?

3. Spanish conquest in North America brought new peoples into constant contact. How did the Spaniards' and Indians' perceptions of each other shape their interactions? In your answer, cite specific examples and consider how perceptions changed over time.

4. How did the astonishing wealth generated for the Spanish crown by its conquest of the New World influence European colonial exploration throughout the sixteenth century? In your answer, discuss the ways in which it both encouraged and limited interest in exploration.

▶ FOR PRACTICE QUIZZES, A CUSTOMIZED STUDY PLAN, AND OTHER STUDY TOOLS, see the Online Study Guide at bedfordstmartins.com/roark.

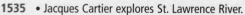

1532 • Francisco Pizarro begins conquest of Peru.

1535 • Jacques Cartier explores St. Lawrence River.

1539 • Hernando de Soto explores southeastern North America.

1540 • Francisco Vásquez de Coronado starts to explore Southwest and Great Plains.

1542 • Juan Rodriguez Cabrillo explores California coast.

1549 • *Repartimiento* reforms begin to replace *encomienda*.

1565 • St. Augustine, Florida, settled.

1576 • Martin Frobisher explores northern Canadian waters.

1587 • English settle Roanoke Island.

1598 • Juan de Oñate explores New Mexico.

1599 • Pueblos revolt against Oñate.

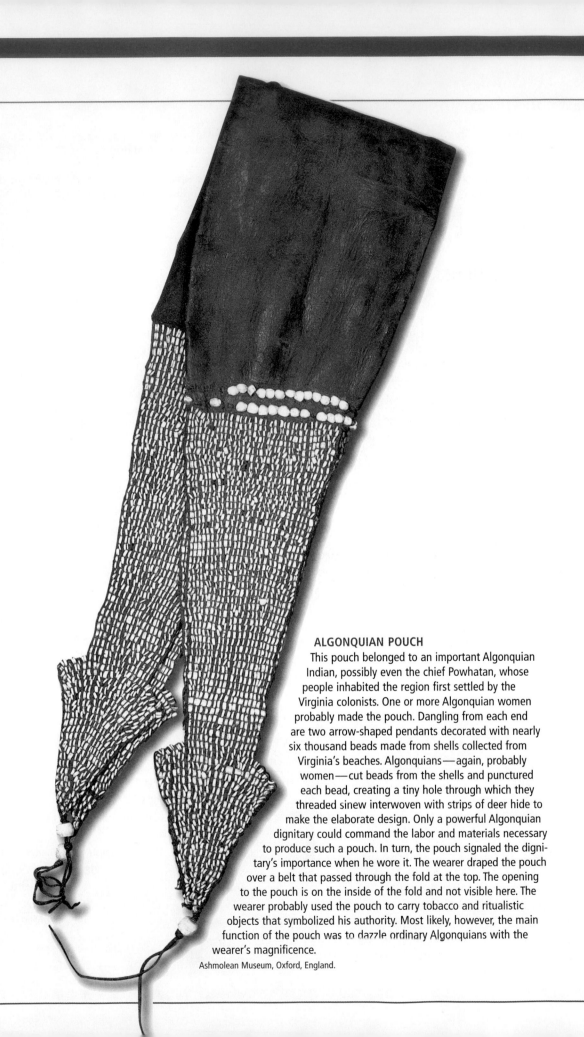

ALGONQUIAN POUCH

This pouch belonged to an important Algonquian
Indian, possibly even the chief Powhatan, whose
people inhabited the region first settled by the
Virginia colonists. One or more Algonquian women
probably made the pouch. Dangling from each end
are two arrow-shaped pendants decorated with nearly
six thousand beads made from shells collected from
Virginia's beaches. Algonquians—again, probably
women—cut beads from the shells and punctured
each bead, creating a tiny hole through which they
threaded sinew interwoven with strips of deer hide to
make the elaborate design. Only a powerful Algonquian
dignitary could command the labor and materials necessary
to produce such a pouch. In turn, the pouch signaled the dignitary's importance when he wore it. The wearer draped the pouch
over a belt that passed through the fold at the top. The opening
to the pouch is on the inside of the fold and not visible here. The
wearer probably used the pouch to carry tobacco and ritualistic
objects that symbolized his authority. Most likely, however, the main
function of the pouch was to dazzle ordinary Algonquians with the
wearer's magnificence.

Ashmolean Museum, Oxford, England.

The Southern Colonies in the Seventeenth Century

1601–1700

■ **An English Colony on the Chesapeake** 71
The Fragile Jamestown Settlement 72
Cooperation and Conflict between Natives and Newcomers 73
From Private Company to Royal Government 75

■ **A Tobacco Society** 77
Tobacco Agriculture 77
A Servant Labor System 78
Cultivating Land and Faith 86

■ **The Evolution of Chesapeake Society** 87
Social and Economic Polarization 87
Government Policies and Political Conflict 90
Bacon's Rebellion 90

■ **Religion and Revolt in the Spanish Borderland** 92

■ **Toward a Slave Labor System** 94
The West Indies: Sugar and Slavery 94
Carolina: A West Indian Frontier 95
Slave Labor Emerges in the Chesapeake 97

■ **Conclusion: The Growth of English Colonies Based on Export Crops and Slave Labor** 98

IN DECEMBER 1607, barely six months after arriving at Jamestown with the first English colonists, Captain John Smith was captured by warriors of Powhatan, the supreme chief of about fourteen thousand Algonquian people who inhabited the coastal plain of present-day Virginia, near the Chesapeake Bay. According to Smith, Powhatan "feasted him after their best barbarous manner." Then, Smith recalled, "two great stones were brought before Powhatan: then as many [Indians] as could layd hands on [Smith], dragged him to [the stones], and thereon laid his head, and being ready with their clubs, to beate out his braines." At that moment, Pocahontas, Powhatan's eleven-year-old daughter, rushed forward and "got [Smith's] head in her armes, and laid her owne upon his to save him from death." Pocahontas, Smith wrote, "hazarded the beating out of her owne braines to save mine, and . . . so prevailed with her father, that I was safely conducted [back] to James towne."

This romantic story of an Indian maiden rescuing a white soldier and saving Jamestown—and ultimately English **colonization** of North America—has been enshrined in the writing of American history since 1624, when Smith published his *Generall Historie of Virginia*. Historians believe that this episode happened more or less as Smith described it. But Smith did not understand why Pocahontas acted as she did. Many commentators have claimed that her love for Smith caused her to rebel against her father's authority. Pocahontas herself left no document that explains her motives; most likely, she could not write. Everything known about her comes from the pen of Smith or other Englishmen. When their writings are considered in the context of what is known about the Algonquian society Pocahontas was born into, her actions appear in an entirely different light.

Most likely, when Pocahontas intervened to save Smith, she was a knowing participant in an Algonquian ceremony that expressed Powhatan's supremacy and his ritualistic adoption of Smith as a subordinate chief, or *werowance*. What Smith interpreted as Pocahontas's saving him from certain death was instead a ceremonial enactment of Powhatan's willingness to incorporate Smith and the white strangers at Jamestown into Powhatan's empire. The ceremony displayed Powhatan's power of life or death and his willingness to give protection to those who acknowledged his supremacy—in this case, the interlopers at Jamestown. By appearing to save Smith, Pocahontas was probably acting out Smith's new status as an adopted member of Powhatan's extended family. Rather than a rebellious, love-struck girl, Pocahontas was almost certainly a dutiful daughter playing the part prescribed for her by her father and her **culture**.

Smith went back to England about two years after the adoption ritual. In the meantime, Pocahontas frequently visited the English settlement and often brought gifts of food from her father. Powhatan routinely attached his sons and daughters to subordinate tribes as an expression of his protection and his dominance. It appears that Pocahontas's attachment to the English colonists grew out of Powhatan's attempt to treat the tribe of white strangers at Jamestown as he did other tribes in his empire—an attempt that failed.

In 1613, after relations between Powhatan and the English colonists had deteriorated into bloody raids by both parties, the colonists captured Pocahontas and held her hostage at Jamestown. Within a year, she converted to Christianity and married one of the colonists, a widower named John Rolfe. After giving birth to a son named Thomas, Pocahontas, her husband, and the new baby sailed for England in the spring of 1616. There, promoters of the Virginia colony dressed her as a proper Englishwoman and even arranged for her to go to a ball attended by the king and queen.

When John Smith heard that Pocahontas was in London, he went to see her. According to Smith, Pocahontas said, "You did promise Powhatan what was yours should bee his, and he the like to you; you called him father, being in his land a stranger, and by the same reason so must I doe you." It seems likely that Pocahontas believed her incorporation into English society was a counterpart of the adoption ritual Powhatan had staged for John Smith in Virginia back in 1607.

Pocahontas died in England in 1617. Her son, Thomas, ultimately returned to Virginia, and by the time of the American Revolution, his descendants numbered in the hundreds. But the world Thomas Rolfe and his descendants inhabited was shaped by a reversal of the power ritualized when his mother "saved" John Smith. By the end of the seventeenth century, Native Americans no longer dominated the newcomers who arrived in the Chesapeake with John Smith.

During the seventeenth century, English colonists learned how to deviate from the example of New Spain (see chapter 2) by growing tobacco, a crop Native Americans had cultivated in small quantities for centuries. The new settlers,

Ætatis suæ 21. A°. 1616.

Matoaks als Rebecka daughter to the mighty Prince Powhatan Emperour of Attanoughkomouck als Virginia converted and baptized in the Christian faith, and Wife to the wor.ll Mr. Tho: Rolff.

Pocahontas in England

Shortly after Pocahontas and her husband, John Rolfe, arrived in England in 1616, she posed for this portrait dressed in English clothing suitable for a princess. The portrait captures the dual novelty of England for Pocahontas and of Pocahontas for the English. Ornate, courtly clothing probably signified to English observers that Pocahontas was royalty and to Pocahontas that the English were accepting her as befitted the "Emperour" Powhatan's daughter. The mutability of Pocahontas's identity is displayed in the identification of her as "Matoaks" or "Rebecka."

National Portrait Gallery, Smithsonian Institution/Art Resource, NY.

however, grew enormous quantities of tobacco, far more than they could chew, smoke, or sniff themselves, and they exported most of it to England. Instead of incorporating Powhatan's people into their new society, the settlers encroached on Indian land and built new societies on the foundation of tobacco agriculture and transatlantic trade.

Producing large crop surpluses for export required hard labor and people who were willing—or could be forced—to do it. For the most part, the Native Americans refused to be conscripted into the colonists' fields. Instead, the settlers depended on the labor of family members, **indentured servants**, and, by the last third of the seventeenth century, African slaves. By the end of the century, the southern colonies had become sharply different both from the world dominated by Powhatan when the Jamestown settlers first arrived and from contemporary English society. In ways unimaginable to Powhatan, Pocahontas, and John Smith, the colonists paid homage to the international market and the English monarch by working mightily to make a good living growing crops for sale to the Old World.

An English Colony on the Chesapeake

When James I became king of England in 1603, he eyed North America as a possible location for English colonies that could be as profitable as the Spanish colonies. Although Spain claimed all of North America under the 1494 Treaty of Tordesillas (see chapter 2), King James believed that England could encroach on the outskirts of Spain's New World empire. In 1588, England had succcessfully defended itself from the Spanish Armada, a large fleet of warships launched to invade England and bring it under Spanish rule. Now England's success in defending itself suggested that it might flex its muscles overseas and build new colonies in North America in the areas Spain could not defend.

In 1606, London investors—including, as they called themselves, "knightes, gentlemen, merchauntes, and other adventurers"—organized the Virginia Company, a joint stock company. English merchants had pooled their capital and shared risks for many years by using joint stock companies for trading voyages to Europe, Asia, and Africa. The Virginia Company, however, had larger ambitions: to establish a colony in North America that might somehow benefit England as Spain's New World empire had rewarded Spain. King James granted the company more than six million acres in North America. In effect, the king's **land grant** was a royal license to poach on both Spanish claims and Powhatan's chiefdom.

The Virginia Company investors hoped to found an empire that would strengthen England both overseas and at home. Richard Hakluyt, a strong proponent of colonization, claimed that a colony would provide work for swarms of poor "valiant youths rusting and hurtfull by lack of employment" in England. Colonists could buy English goods and supply products that England now had to import from other nations. More trade and more jobs would benefit many people in England, but the Virginia Company investors risked their capital because they fervently hoped to reap quick profits from the new colony.

Secotan Village

This engraving, published in 1612, was copied from an original drawing John White made in 1585 when he visited the village of Secotan on the coast of North Carolina. The drawing provides a schematic view of daily life in the village, which may have resembled one of Powhatan's settlements. White noted on the original that the fire burning behind the line of crouching men was "the place of solemne prayer." The large building in the lower left was a tomb where the bodies of important leaders were kept. Dwellings similar to those illustrated on John Smith's map of Virginia (see page 72) lined a central space, where men and women ate. Corn is growing in the fields along the right side of the village. The engraver included hunters shooting deer at the upper left. Hunting was probably never so convenient—no such hunters or deer appear in White's original drawing. This drawing conveys the message that Secotan was orderly, settled, religious, harmonious, and peaceful (notice the absence of fortifications), and very different from English villages.

Princeton University Libraries, Department of Rare Books and Special Collections.

READING THE IMAGE: What does this image say about Indian life in Secotan?
CONNECTIONS: How did Indian society differ from the English tobacco society that emerged later?

FOR MORE HELP ANALYZING THIS IMAGE, see the visual activity for this chapter in the Online Study Guide at bedfordstmartins.com/roark.

Enthusiastic reports from the Roanoke voyages twenty years earlier (see chapter 2) claimed that in Virginia, "the earth bringeth foorth all things in aboundance...without toile or labour." Even if these reports were exaggerated, investors reasoned, maybe some valuable exotic crop could be grown profitably in this Eden. Maybe rich lodes of gold and silver awaited discovery, as they had in New Spain. Or maybe quick and easy profits could be grabbed in an occasional raid on the gold and silver stashed in the holds of Spanish ships that cruised up the Atlantic coast on their way to Spain. Such hopes failed to address the difficulties of adapting European desires and expectations to the New World already inhabited by Native Americans. The Jamestown settlement struggled to survive for nearly two decades, until the royal government replaced the private Virginia Company, which never earned a penny for its investors.

The Fragile Jamestown Settlement

In December 1606, the ships *Susan Constant*, *Discovery*, and *Godspeed* carried 144 Englishmen toward Virginia. They arrived at the mouth of the Chesapeake Bay on April 26, 1607. That night while the colonists rested on shore, one of them later recalled, a band of Indians "creeping upon all foure, from the Hills like Beares, with their Bowes in their mouthes," attacked and dangerously wounded two men. The attack gave the colonists an early warning that the North American wilderness was not quite the paradise described by the Virginia Company's publications in England. A few weeks later, they went ashore on a small peninsula in the midst of Powhatan's chiefdom. With the memory of their first night in America fresh in their minds, they quickly built a fort, the first building in the settlement they named Jamestown.

The Jamestown fort showed the colonists' awareness that they needed to protect themselves from Indians and Spaniards. Spain employed spies to stay informed about the new English colony. Spain planned to wipe out Jamestown when the time was ripe, but that time never came.

John Smith's Map of Virginia

In 1612, John Smith published a detailed map that showed not only geographic features of early Virginia but also the limits of exploration (indicated by small crosses), the locations of the houses of the Indian "kings" (indicated by red boxes), and "ordinary houses" of indigenous people (indicated by dots). The map shows the early settlers' intense interest in knowing where the Indians were—and were not. Notice the location of Jamestown (upriver from Point Comfort) and of Powhatan's residence at the falls (just to the right of the large *P* outside the hut on the upper left side). The drawing of Powhatan surrounded by some of his many wives was almost certainly made by an English artist who had never been to Virginia or seen Powhatan but tried to imagine the scene as described by John Smith.

Powhatan's people defended Virginia as their own. For weeks, the settlers and Powhatan's warriors skirmished repeatedly. English muskets and cannons repelled Indian attacks on Jamestown, but the Indians' superior numbers and knowledge of the Virginia wilderness made it risky for the settlers to venture far beyond the peninsula. Late in June 1607, Powhatan sensed a stalemate and made peace overtures.

The settlers soon confronted dangerous, invisible threats: disease and starvation. During the summer, many of the Englishmen lay "night and day groaning in every corner of the Fort most pittiful to heare," wrote George Percy, one of the settlers. By September, fifty of the colonists had died. The colonists increased their misery by bickering among themselves, leaving crops unplanted and food supplies shrinking. "For the most part [the settlers] died of meere famine," Percy wrote; "there were never Englishmen left in a forreigne Countrey in such miserie as wee were in this new discovered Virginia."

Powhatan's people came to the rescue of the weakened and demoralized Englishmen. Early in September 1607, they began to bring corn to the colony for barter. Accustomed to eating food derived from wheat, the settlers at first did not like corn. An English botanist expressed the common prejudice against corn as a food "of the barbarous Indians which know no better . . . a more convenient food for swine than for man." The famished Jamestown colonists soon overcame their prejudice against corn. Captain John Smith recalled that the settlers were so hungry "they would have sould their soules" for half a basket of Powhatan's corn. When the many baskets of corn from Powhatan's people proved insufficient to keep the colonists fed, the settlers sent Smith to trade (and plunder) for corn with Indians living upriver from Jamestown. His efforts managed to keep 38 of the original settlers alive until a fresh supply of food and 120 more colonists arrived from England in January 1608.

It is difficult to exaggerate the fragility of the early Jamestown settlement. Although the Virginia Company sent hundreds of new settlers to Jamestown each year, each of them eager to find the paradise promised by the company, few survived. During the "starving time" winter of 1609–10, food became so short that one or two famished settlers resorted to eating their recently deceased neighbors. When a new group of colonists arrived in 1610, they found only 60 of the 500 previous settlers still alive. When told they might be taken back to England, the sur-

vivors responded with "a general acclamation, and shoutte of joy," an observer wrote. The Virginia Company continued to pour people into the colony, promising in a 1609 pamphlet that "the place will make them rich." But most settlers went instead to an early grave.

Cooperation and Conflict between Natives and Newcomers

Powhatan's people stayed in contact with the English settlers but maintained their distance. The Virginia Company boasted that the settlers bought from the Indians "the pearles of earth [corn] and [sold] to them the pearles of heaven [Christianity]." In fact, few Indians converted to Christianity, and the English devoted scant effort to proselytizing. Marriage between Indian women and English men also was rare, despite the acute shortage of English women in Virginia in the early years. Few settlers other than John Smith troubled to learn the Indians' language.

> "For the most part [the settlers] died of meere famine," Percy wrote; "there were never Englishmen left in a forreigne Countrey in such miserie as wee were in this new discovered Virginia."

Powhatan's people regarded the English with suspicion, for good reason. Although the settlers often made friendly overtures to the Indians, they did not hesitate to use their guns and swords to enforce English notions of proper Indian behavior. More than once, the Indians refused to trade their corn to the settlers, evidently hoping to starve them out. Each time, the English broke the boycott by attacking the uncooperative Indians, pillaging their villages, and confiscating their corn.

The Indians retaliated against English violence, but for fifteen years they did not organize an all-out assault on the European intruders, probably for several reasons. Although Christianity held few attractions for the Indians, the power of the settlers' God impressed them. One chief told John Smith that "he did believe that our [English] God as much exceeded theirs as our guns did their bows and arrows." Powhatan probably concluded that these powerful strangers would make better allies than enemies. As allies, the English strengthened Powhatan's dominance over the tribes in the region. They also traded with his people, usually exchanging European goods for corn. Native Virginians had some copper weapons and tools before the English arrived, but they quickly recognized the superiority of the intruders' iron

Becaufe many doe defire to know the manner of their Language, I haue inferted thefe few words.

KA katorawincs yowo. What call you this.

Nemarough, a man.

Crenepo, a woman.

Marowancheffo, a boy.

Yehawkans, Houfes.

Matchcores, Skins, or garments.

Mockafins, Shooes.

Tuffan, Beds. *Pokatawer,* Fire.

Attawp, A bow. *Attonce,* Arrowes.

Monacookes, Swords.

Aumouhhowgh, A Target.

Paweuffacks, Gunnes.

Tomahacks, Axes.

Tockahacks, Pickaxes.

Pamefacks, Kniues.

Accowprets, Sheares.

Pawpecones, Pipes. *Mattaffin,* Copper

Vffawaffin, Iron, Braffe, Silver, or any white mettall. *Muffes,* Woods.

Attaffkuff, Leaues, weeds, or graffe.

Chepfin, Land. *Shacquohocan.* A flone.

Wepenter, A cookold.

Suckahanna, Water. *Noughmaff,* Fifh.

Copotone, Sturgeon.

Weghfhaughes, Flefh.

Sawwehone, Bloud.

Netoppew, Friends.

Marrapough, Enemics.

Maskapow, the worft of the enemies.

Mawchick chammay, The beft of friends

Cafacunnakack, peya quagh acquintan vttafantafough, In how many daies will there come hither any more Englifh Ships.

Their Numbers.

Necut, 1. *Ningh,* 2. *Nuff,* 3. *Yowgh,* 4.

Paranske, 5. *Comotinch,* 6. *Toppawoff,* 7

Nuffwafh, 8. *Kekatawgh,* 9. *Kaskeke* 10

They count no more but by tennes as followeth.

Cafe, how many.

Ninghfapooeksku, 20.

Nuffapooeksku, 30.

Yowghapooeksku, 40.

Parankeftaffapoockfku, 50.

Comatinchtaffapoekfku, 60.

Nuffwafhtaffapoekfku, 70.

Kekatanghtaffapoekfku, 90.

Necuttoughtyfinough, 100.

Necuttwevnquaough, 1000.

Rawcofowghs, Dayes.

Kefkowghes, Sunnes:

Toppquough. Nights.

Nepawwefhowghs, Moones.

Pawpaxfoughes, Yeares.

Pummahumps, Starres.

Ofies, Heavens.

Okees, Gods.

Quiyoughcofoughs, Pettie Gods, and their affinities.

Righcomoughes, Deaths.

Kekughes, Liues.

Mowchick woyawgh tawgh noeragh kaquere mecher, I am very hungry? what fhall I eate?

Tawnor nehiegh Powhatan, Where dwels Powhatan.

Mache, nehiegh yourowgh, Orapaks. Now he dwels a great way hence at Orapaks.

Vittapitchewayne anpechitchs nehawper Werowacomoco, You lie, he ftaid ever at Werowacomoco.

Kator nehiegh mattagh neer vttapitchewayne, Truely he is there I doe not lie.

Spaughtynere keragh werowance mawmarinough kekatĕ wawgh peyaquaugh. Run you then to the King Mawmarynough and bid him come hither.

Vtteke, e peya weyack wighwhip, Get you gone, & come againe quickly.

Kekaten Pokahontas patiaquagh ningh tanks manotyens neer mowchick rawrenock audowgh, Bid Pokahontas bring hither two little Baskets, and I will giue her white Beads to make her a Chaine. *FINIS.*

John Smith's Dictionary of Powhatan's Language
In 1612, John Smith published this list of the English equivalents of words used by Powhatan's people, almost the only record of the coastal Algonquian language that exists. Smith probably compiled this list by pointing and listening carefully.
Princeton University Libraries, Department of Rare Books and Special Collections.

READING THE IMAGE: Can you find any of Powhatan's words that made their way into common English usage?
CONNECTIONS: What do the words in the list suggest about Smith's encounters with Powhatan's people? What interested Smith? What compelled the interest of his informants?

FOR MORE HELP ANALYZING THIS IMAGE, see the visual activity for this chapter in the Online Study Guide at bedfordstmartins.com/roark.

decade? First, as the staggering death rate suggests, many settlers were too sick to be productive members of the colony. Second, very few farmers came to Virginia in the early years. Instead, most of the newcomers were gentlemen and their servants. In John Smith's words, these men "never did know what a day's work was." The proportion of gentlemen in Virginia in the early years was six times greater than in England, a reflection of the Virginia Company's urgent need for investors and settlers. The company explained in a 1610 pamphlet that nobody should think that the colony "excludeth Gentlemen . . . for though they cannot digge, use the square, nor practise the axe and chizell, yet [they know] . . . how to employ the force of knowledge, the exercise of counsel, the operation and power of their best breeding and qualities." In Virginia, English gentlemen's breeding and quality proved worthless for growing corn, catching fish, or even hunting deer. John Smith declared repeatedly that in Virginia "there is no country to pillage [as in New Spain]. . . . All you can expect from [Virginia] must be by labor." For years, however, colonists clung to English notions that gentlemen should not work with their hands and tradesmen should work only in trades for which they had been trained. These ideas made more sense in labor-rich England than in labor-poor Virginia. In the meantime, the colonists depended on the Indians' corn for food.

The persistence of the Virginia colony created difficulties for Powhatan's chiefdom. Steady contact between natives and newcomers spread European diseases among the Indians, who suffered deadly epidemics in 1608 and between 1617 and 1619.

and steel knives, axes, and pots, and they traded eagerly to obtain them.

The trade that supplied the Indians with European conveniences provided the English settlers with a necessity: food. But why were the settlers unable to feed themselves for more than a

Trade Goods

These objects excavated from the site of early Jamestown illustrate the trade that linked Powhatan's people, the settlers, and the larger transatlantic world. The broken jug (top right) was made in Italy, probably purchased by Dutch merchants who sold it in England, where it eventually found its way into the baggage of a Jamestown settler, perhaps to hold an alcoholic beverage. Drink alone could not sustain the colonists. They needed the Indians' corn, and to trade for it, they needed something the Algonquians desired. The Indians wanted firearms, but the struggling colonists could ill afford to boost the Indians' military strength. Instead, the colonists appealed to the Indians' interest in items for decoration and display. Jamestown residents often traded cheap glass beads (bottom center) made in Venice, Italy, with sophisticated glassmaking techniques unknown to the Algonquians. The Indians readily adopted glass beads as attractive substitutes for the shell beads they had laboriously made for centuries. Jamestown residents learned that the Algonquians used copper, but the Indians' supplies were limited and difficult to obtain. The colonists cut their own sheets of copper into shapes desired by the Indians for jewelry, such as the triangular copper ornament shown here, conveniently pierced for easy attachment (bottom right). As the colonists learned more about the Indians' fashions, they began to craft items such as the bone pendant shown here (bottom left). To our eyes, it appears as if it might have been made by an Indian craftsperson, but iron file marks along the edges are strong evidence that an English settler made the pendant, using materials and designs familiar to the Indians. In modern language, the pendant reflects the results of the Jamestown settlers' market research about what the Algonquians would accept in exchange for corn.

Courtesy of The Association for the Preservation of Virginia Antiquities.

The settlers' insatiable appetite for corn introduced other tensions within Powhatan's villages. To produce enough corn for their own survival and for trade with the English required the Indians to spend more time and effort growing crops. Since Native American women did most of the agricultural work, their burden increased along with the cultural significance of their chief crop. The corn surplus grown by Indian women was bartered for desirable English goods such as iron pots, which replaced the baskets and ceramic jugs Native Americans had used for millennia. Growing enough corn to feed the English boosted the workload of Indian women and altered age-old patterns of village life. But from the Indians' viewpoint, the most important fact about the always-hungry English colonists was that they were not going away.

Powhatan died in 1618, and his brother Opechancanough replaced him as supreme chief. In 1622, Opechancanough organized an all-out assault on the English settlers. As an English colonist observed, "When the day appointed for the massacre arrived [March 22], a number of savages visited many of our people in their dwellings, and while partaking with them of their meal[,] the savages, at a given signal, drew their weapons and fell upon us murdering and killing everybody they could reach[,] sparing neither women nor children, as well inside as outside the dwellings." In all, the Indians killed 347 colonists, nearly a third of the English population. But the attack failed to dislodge the colonists. In the aftermath, the settlers unleashed a murderous campaign of Indian extermination that in a few years pushed the Indians beyond the small circumference of white settlement. Before 1622, the settlers knew that the Indians, though dangerous, were necessary to keep the colony alive. After 1622, most colonists considered the Indians their perpetual enemies.

From Private Company to Royal Government

The 1622 uprising came close to achieving Opechancanough's goal of pushing the colonists back into the Atlantic—so close that it prompted a royal investigation of affairs in Virginia. The investigators discovered that the appalling mortality

Advertisement for Jamestown Settlers
Virginia imported thousands of indentured servants to labor in the tobacco fields, but the colony also advertised in 1631 for settlers like those pictured here. The notice features men and women equally, although men heavily outnumbered women in the Chesapeake region. How would the English experiences of the individuals portrayed in the advertisement have been useful in Virginia? Why would such individuals have wanted to leave England and go to Virginia? If indentured servants had been pictured, how might they have differed in appearance from these people?
Harvard Map Collection, Pusey Library, Harvard University.

among the colonists was caused more by disease and mismanagement than by Indian raids. In 1624, King James revoked the charter of the Virginia Company and made Virginia a royal colony, subject to the direction of the royal government rather than to the company's private investors, an arrangement that lasted until 1776.

The king now appointed the governor of Virginia and his council, but most other features of local government established under the Virginia Company remained intact. In 1619, for example, the company had inaugurated the House of Burgesses, an assembly of representatives (called burgesses) elected by the colony's inhabitants. (Historians do not know exactly which settlers were considered inhabitants and were thus qualified to vote.) Under the new royal government, laws passed by the burgesses had to be approved by the king's bureaucrats in England rather than by the company. Otherwise, the House of Burgesses continued as before, acquiring distinction as the oldest representative legislative assembly in the English colonies. Under the new royal government, all free adult men in Virginia could vote for the House of Burgesses, giving it a far broader and more representative constituency than the English House of Commons.

The demise of the Virginia Company marked the end of the first phase of colonization of the Chesapeake region. From the first 105 adventurers in 1607, the population had grown to about 1,200 by 1624. Despite mortality rates higher than during the worst epidemics in London, new settlers still came. Their arrival and King James's willingness to take over the struggling colony reflected a fundamental change in Virginia. After years of fruitless experimentation, it was becoming clear that English settlers could make a fortune in Virginia by growing tobacco.

REVIEW Why did Powhatan pursue largely peaceful relations with the Jamestown settlement?

A Tobacco Society

Tobacco grew wild in the New World, and Native Americans used it for thousands of years before Europeans arrived. Columbus observed Indians smoking tobacco on his first voyage to the New World. Many other sixteenth-century European explorers noticed the Indians' habit of "drinking smoke." During the sixteenth century, Spanish colonists in the New World sent tobacco to Europe, where it was an expensive luxury used sparingly by a few. During the next century, English colonists in North America sent so much tobacco to European markets that it became an affordable indulgence used often by many people. (See "Beyond America's Borders," page 80.)

Initially, the Virginia Company had no plans to grow and sell tobacco. "As for tobacco," John Smith wrote, "we never then dreamt of it." John Rolfe—Pocahontas's husband-to-be—planted West Indian tobacco seeds in 1612 and learned that they flourished in Virginia. By 1617, the colonists had grown enough tobacco to send the first commercial shipment to England, where it sold for a high price. After that, Virginia pivoted from a colony of rather aimless adventurers who had difficulty growing enough corn to feed themselves into a society of dedicated **planters** who grew as much tobacco as possible.

Dedicated they were. By 1700, nearly 100,000 colonists lived in the Chesapeake region, encompassing Virginia, Maryland, and northern North Carolina (Map 3.1, page 78). They exported more than 35 million pounds of tobacco, a fivefold increase in per capita production since 1620. Clearly, Chesapeake colonists mastered the demands of tobacco agriculture, and the "Stinkinge Weede" (a seventeenth-century Marylander's term for tobacco) also mastered the colonists. Settlers lived by the rhythms of tobacco agriculture, and their endless need for labor attracted droves of English indentured servants to work in the tobacco fields.

Tobacco Agriculture

A demanding crop, tobacco required close attention and a great deal of hand labor year-round. Primitive tools and methods made this intensive cycle of labor taxing. Like the Indians, the colonists "cleared" fields by cutting a ring of bark from each tree (a procedure known as *girdling*), thereby killing the tree. Girdling brought sunlight to clearings but left fields studded with tree stumps, making the use of plows impractical. Instead, colonists used heavy hoes to till their

Tobacco Wrapper
This wrapper labeled a container of "Virginia Planters Best Tobacco." It shows a colonial planter supervising slaves, who hold hoes they used to chop weeds that robbed the leafy tobacco plants of nutrients and moisture. The planter enjoys a pipe in the shade of an umbrella held by a slave. After the tobacco was harvested and dried, it was pressed tightly into barrels, like those shown here, for shipment overseas. How does this illustration indicate the differences between the planter and the slaves?
Colonial Williamsburg Foundation.

tobacco fields. To plant, a visitor observed, they "just make holes [with a stick] into which they drop the seeds," much as the Indians did. Growing tobacco with such methods left little time for idleness, but the colonists enjoyed the fruits of their labor. "Everyone smokes while working or idling," one traveler reported, including "men, women, girls, and boys, from the age of seven years."

The English settlers worked hard because their labor promised greater rewards in the Chesapeake region than in England. One colonist proclaimed that "the dirt of this Province affords as great a profit to the general Inhabitant, as the Gold of Peru doth to . . . the Spaniard." Although he exaggerated, it was true that a hired man could expect to earn two or three times more in Virginia's tobacco fields than in England. Better still, in Virginia land was so abundant that it was extremely cheap, compared to land in England.

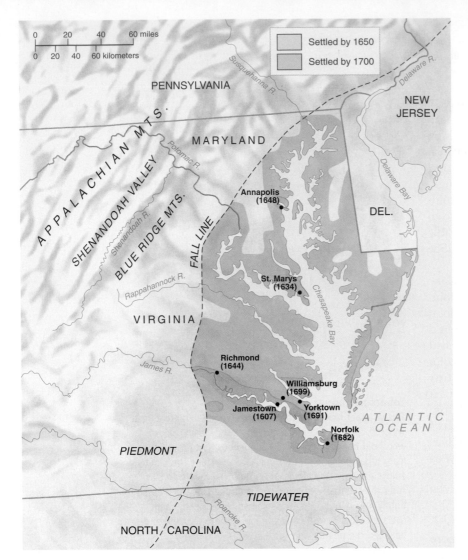

MAP 3.1   Chesapeake Colonies in the Seventeenth Century

The intimate association between land and water in the settlement of the Chesapeake in the seventeenth century is illustrated by this map. The fall line indicates the limit of navigable water, where rapids and falls prevented farther upstream travel. Although Delaware had excellent access to navigable water, it was claimed and defended by the Dutch colony at New Amsterdam (discussed in chapter 4) rather than by the English settlements in Virginia and Maryland shown on this map.

READING THE MAP: Using the notations on the map, create a chronology of the establishment of towns and settlements. What physical features correspond to the earliest habitation by English settlers?

CONNECTIONS: Why was access to navigable water so important? Given the settlers' need for defense against native tribes, what explains the distance between settlements?

FOR MORE HELP ANALYZING THIS MAP, see the map activity for this chapter in the Online Study Guide at bedfordstmartins.com/roark.

By the mid-seventeenth century, common laborers could buy a hundred acres for less than their annual wages—an impossibility in England. New settlers who paid their own transportation to the Chesapeake received a grant of fifty acres of free land (termed a *headright*). The Virginia Company initiated headrights to encourage settlement, and the royal government continued them for the same reason.

A Servant Labor System

Headrights, cheap land, and high wages gave poor English folk powerful incentives to immigrate to the New World. Yet many potential immigrants could not scrape together the money to pay for a trip across the Atlantic. Their poverty and the colonists' crying need for labor formed the basic context for the creation of a servant labor system.

About 80 percent of the immigrants to the Chesapeake during the seventeenth century were indentured servants. Twenty Africans arrived in Virginia in 1619, and they probably were enslaved, although scanty records make it uncertain. Until the 1670s, however, only a small number of slaves labored in Chesapeake tobacco fields. (Large numbers of slaves came in the eighteenth century, as chapter 5 explains.) A few indentured servants of African descent served out their terms of servitude and became free. A few slaves purchased their way out of bondage and lived as free people, even owning land and using the local courts to resolve disputes, much as freed white servants did. A small number of Native Americans also became servants. But the overwhelming majority of indentured servants were white immigrants from England. Instead of a slave society, the seventeenth-century Chesapeake region was fundamentally a society of white servants and ex-servants.

To buy passage aboard a ship bound for the Chesapeake, an English immigrant had to come up with about £5, roughly a year's wages for an English servant or laborer. Earning wages at all was difficult in England since job opportunities were shrinking. Many country landowners needed fewer farmhands because they shifted from growing crops to raising sheep in newly enclosed fields. Unemployed people drifted into seaports such as Bristol, Liverpool, and London, where they learned about the plentiful jobs in North America.

Unable to pay for their trip across the Atlantic, poor immigrants agreed to a contract

Smithfield Market

This portrait of the London livestock market illustrates the consequences of agricultural change in rural England. When English farmers shifted from growing crops to raising livestock—especially the thousands of sheep shown here—they needed many fewer agricultural laborers. In seventeenth-century England, displaced laborers wandered from place to place looking for work. Many came to places such as Smithfield Market, hoping to find someone—such as the men pictured here—to hire them. Those who failed to find work often signed indentures to work in Chesapeake tobacco fields. In this way, the English livestock market was related to the market in indentured servants. Can you spot clues in this picture about how these markets operated? For example, what does the picture suggest about why so many farmers brought their sheep to the market?
Courtesy of the Trustees of the British Library.

American Tobacco and European Consumers

English colonies in the Chesapeake were "wholly built upon smoke," King Charles I remarked. The king's shrewd comment highlighted the fundamental reason the seventeenth-century Chesapeake colonies prospered by growing ever-increasing crops of tobacco: because people on the eastern side of the Atlantic were willing to buy ever-increasing quantities of tobacco to smoke—and to sniff, chew, drink, and even use for enemas. Europeans' desire for tobacco was the only reason it had commercial value. If Europeans had considered tobacco undesirable, the history of both the English North American colonies and the rest of the world would have been very different.

Even so, some Europeans hated tobacco, most notably England's King James I. In *A Counterblaste to Tobacco*, a pamphlet published in 1611, James declared that smoking was "A custome lothsome to the eye, hatefull to the Nose, harmefull to the braine, dangerous to the Lungs, and in the blacke stinking fume thereof, neerest resembling the horrible ... smoke of the pit that is bottomelesse." James pulled out all the stops in attacking smoking. "What honour or policie can moove us to imitate the barbarous and beastly manners of the wilde, godlesse, and slavish Indians, especially in so vile and stinking a custome?" he asked. "Why doe we not as well imitate them in walking naked as they doe? in preferring glasses, feathers, and such toyes, to golde and precious stones, as they do? yea why do we not denie God and adore the Devill, as they doe?"

James reviled the "filthy smoke," the "stinking Suffumigation," the "spitting," the "lust," the "shameful imbecilitie," and the "sin" of tobacco. James's fulminations acknowledged that "the generall use of Tobacco" was "daily practiced ... by all sorts and complexions of people." He noted, "The publike use [of tobacco], at all times, and in all places, hath now so farre prevailed that a man cannot heartily welcome his friend now, but straight they must bee in hand with Tobacco.... It is become ... a point of good fellowship, and he that will refuse to take a pipe of Tobacco among his fellows ... is accounted peevish and no good company." Clearly, James championed a lost cause.

When the Spaniards first brought tobacco to Europe during the sixteenth century, physicians praised it as a wonder drug. One proclaimed that "to seek to tell the virtues and greatness of this holy herb, the ailments which can be cured by it, and have been, the evils from which it has saved thousands would be to go on to infinity.... This precious herb is so general a human need [that it is] not only for the sick but for the healthy." Such strong recommendations from learned men were reinforced by everyday experiences of commoners. Sailors returning from the New World "suck in as much smoke as they can," one Spaniard observed, "[and] in this way they say that their hunger and thirst are allayed, their strength is restored and their spirits are refreshed; [and] ... their brains are lulled by a joyous intoxication." That joyous intoxication—"a bewitching quality," King James called it — made tobacco irresistible to most Europeans. And, as we know all too well today, the bewitching intoxication of tobacco was highly addictive.

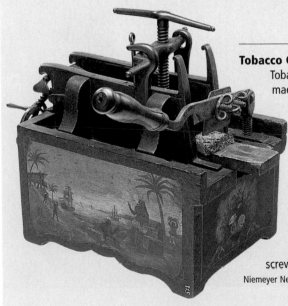

Tobacco Cutter

Tobacconists in Europe used this machine to chop tobacco leaves into small pieces. Then they often flavored the chopped tobacco with oils, herbs, and spices much as coffeehouse baristas today add hazelnut, mocha, or vanilla flavors to lattes and cappuccinos. The picture on the side of the cutter refers to the Native American origins of the tobacco processed by the cutter's screws, clamps, and blades.

Niemeyer Nederlands Tabacologisch Museum.

Feeding that habit was expensive at the beginning of the seventeenth century because tobacco was scarce. In 1603, for example, England imported only about 25,000 pounds of tobacco, all from New Spain. By 1700, England imported nearly 40 million pounds of tobacco, almost all from the Chesapeake colonies. The huge increase in the tobacco supply caused prices to plummet. A quantity of tobacco that sold for a dollar in 1600 cost less than two and a half cents by 1700.

The low prices made possible by bumper crops harvested by planters in the Chesapeake transformed tobacco consumption in England and elsewhere in Europe. Per capita tobacco use in England grew over 200-fold during the seventeenth century, from less than a fifth of an ounce in the 1620s to 2.3 pounds by 1700. American tobacco became the first colonial product of mass consumption by Europeans, blazing a trail followed by New World sugar, coffee, and chocolate.

Tobacco altered European culture. It spawned new industries, new habits, and new forms of social life. Smoking was the most common form of tobacco consumption in the seventeenth century, and smokers needed far more than tobacco to light up. They needed pipes, and hundreds of pipe makers supplied them with millions of ceramic pipes. They needed boxes or tins to hold their tobacco and a container to hold the embers they used to light the tobacco, or a flint and steel to strike sparks; they needed pipe cleaners; they needed spittoons if they were smoking in a respectable place that disapproved of spitting on the floor. European merchants and manufacturers supplied all these needs, along with the tobacco itself, which had to be graded, chopped, flavored,

Smoking Club
In Europe, tobacco smokers congregated in clubs to enjoy the intoxicating weed. This seventeenth-century print satirizes smokers' promiscuous gatherings of fashionable men, women, and children who indulged their taste for tobacco. Emblems of the tobacco trade adorn the wall; pipes, spittoons, and other smoking implements are close at hand; and the dog cleans up after those who cannot hold their smoke.
Koninklijke Bibliotheek, The Hague.

packaged, stored, advertised, and sold. Men and women smoked in taverns, in smoking clubs, around dinner tables, and in bed. A visitor to London noted that tobacco was not only in "frequent use . . . at every hour of the day but even at night [smokers] keep the pipe and steel at their pillows and gratify their longings."

The somewhat cumbersome paraphernalia of smoking caused many tobacco users to shift to snuff, which became common in the eighteenth century. Snuff use eliminated smoke, fire, and spitting with the more refined arts of taking a pinch of powdered, flavored tobacco from a snuffbox and sniffing it into one or both nostrils, which produced a fash-

ionable sneeze followed by a genteel wipe with a dainty handkerchief. Sneezing induced by snuff was considered not only fashionable but healthful. One snuff taker explained that "by its gently pricking and stimulating the membranes, [snuff] causes Sneezing or Contractions, whereby the Glands like so many squeezed Sponges, dismiss their Seriosities and Filth."

Whether consumed by smoking, by sniffing, or in other ways, tobacco profoundly changed European habits, economies, and societies. It is no exaggeration to conclude that planters, servants, and eventually slaves in the Chesapeake colonies made it possible for Europeans to become hooked on tobacco.

called an *indenture*, which functioned as a form of credit. By signing an indenture, an immigrant borrowed the cost of transportation to the Chesapeake from a merchant or ship captain in England. To repay this loan, the indentured person agreed to work as a servant for four to seven years in North America. Once the indentured person arrived in the colonies, the merchant or ship captain sold his right to the immigrant's labor to a local tobacco planter. To obtain the servant's labor, the planter paid about twice the cost of transportation and agreed to provide the servant with food and shelter during the term of the indenture. When the indenture expired, the planter owed the former servant "freedom dues," usually a few barrels of corn and a suit of clothes.

Ideally, indentures allowed poor immigrants to trade their most valuable assets—their freedom and their ability to work—for a trip to the New World and a period of servitude followed by freedom in a land of opportunity. Planters reaped more immediate benefits. Servants meant more hands to grow more tobacco. A planter expected a servant to grow enough tobacco in one year to cover the price the planter paid for the

> One Virginian declared, "Our principall wealth . . . consisteth in servants."

Tobacco Plantation
This print illustrates the processing of tobacco on a seventeenth-century plantation. Workers cut the mature plants and put the leaves in piles to wilt (left foreground and center background). After the leaves dried somewhat, they were suspended from poles in a drying barn (right foreground), where they were seasoned before being packed in casks for shipping. Sometimes, tobacco leaves were left to dry in the fields (center background). The print suggests the labor demands of tobacco by showing twenty-two individuals, all but two of them actively at work with the crop. The one woman, hand in hand with a man in the left foreground, may be on her way to work on the harvested leaves, but it is more likely that she and the man are overseeing the labor of their servants or employees.
From "About Tobacco," Lehman Brothers.

indenture. Servants' labor during the remaining three to six years of the indenture promised a handsome profit for the planter. No wonder one Virginian declared, "Our principall wealth... consisteth in servants." But roughly half of all servants became sick and died before serving out their indentures, reducing planters' gains and destroying servants' hopes. Planters still profited, however, since they received a headright of fifty acres of land from the colonial government for every newly purchased servant.

About three out of four servants were men between the ages of fifteen and twenty-five when they arrived in the Chesapeake. Typically, they shared the desperation of sixteen-year-old Francis Haires, who indentured himself for seven years because, according to his contract, "his father and mother and All friends [are] dead and he [is] a miserable wandering boy." Like Francis, most servants had no special training or skills, although the majority had some experience with agricultural work. "Hunger and fear of prisons bring to us onely such servants as have been brought up to no Art or Trade," one Virginia planter complained. A skilled craftsman could obtain a shorter indenture, but few risked coming to the colonies since their prospects were better in England.

Women were almost as rare as skilled craftsmen in the Chesapeake and more ardently desired. In the early days of the tobacco boom, the Virginia Company shipped young single women servants to the colony as prospective wives for male settlers willing to pay "120 weight [pounds] of the best leaf tobacco for each of them," in effect getting both a wife and a servant. The company reasoned that, as one official wrote in 1622, "the plantation can never flourish till families be planted, and the respect of wives and children fix the people on the soil." The company's efforts as a marriage broker proved no more successful than its other ventures. Women remained a small minority of the Chesapeake population until late in the seventeenth century.

The servant labor system perpetuated the gender imbalance. Although female servants cost about the same as males and generally served for the same length of time, only about one servant in four was a woman. Planters preferred male servants for fieldwork, although many servant women hoed and harvested tobacco fields. Most women servants also did household chores such as cooking, washing, cleaning, gardening, and milking.

Servants—whether men or women, whites or blacks, English or Africans—tended to work together and socialize together. During the first half century of settlement, racial intermingling occurred, although the small number of blacks made it infrequent. Courts punished sexual relations between blacks and whites, but the number of court cases shows that sexual desire readily crossed the color line. In general, the commonalities of servitude caused servants—regardless of their race and gender—to consider themselves apart from free people, whose ranks they longed to join eventually.

Servant life was harsh by the standards of seventeenth-century England and even by the **frontier** standards of the Chesapeake. Unlike servants in England, Chesapeake servants had no control over who purchased their labor—and thus them—for the period of their indenture. Many servants were bought and sold several times before their indenture expired. A Virginia servant protested in 1623 that his master "hath sold me for £150 sterling like a damnd slave." A ship captain reported in 1625 that "servants were sold here [in Virginia] upp and downe like horses." But tobacco planters' need for labor muffled such complaints about treating servants as property.

> A Virginia servant protested in 1623 that his master "hath sold me for £150 sterling like a damnd slave."

For servants, the promise of indentured servitude that loomed large in their decision to leave England and immigrate to the Chesapeake often withered when they confronted the rigors of labor in the tobacco fields. James Revel, an eighteen-year-old thief punished by being indentured to a Virginia tobacco planter, chronicled what happened when he arrived at his new master's plantation:

> My Europian clothes were took from me,
> Which never after I again could see.
> A canvas shirt and trowsers then they gave,
> With a hop-sack frock in which I was to slave:
> No shoes nor stockings had I for to wear,
> Nor hat, nor cap, both head and feet were bare.
> Thus dress'd into the Field I next must go,
> Amongst tobacco plants all day to hoe,
> At day break in the morn our work began,
> And so held to the setting of the Sun.

Severe laws aimed to keep servants in their place. (See "Documenting the American Promise," p. 84.) Punishments for petty crimes stretched servitude far beyond the original terms of indenture.

Virginia Laws Governing Servants and Slaves

Servants and slaves often chafed at the terms of their servitude. Masters usually punished unruly servants and slaves privately. But the Virginia legislature also enacted numerous laws to reinforce masters' rule over servants and slaves. The following selections from seventeenth-century Virginia laws illustrate the emerging legal distinctions between servants, slaves, and free people, as well as between English settlers, Africans, and Native Americans.

DOCUMENT 1
Law Punishing Runaway Servants, 1661

Runaway servants—both white and black—plagued masters. The enactment of this law suggests that by the 1660s, masters sought government help to punish runaways.

Whereas there are diverse loitering runaways in this country who very often absent themselves from their masters service and sometimes in a long time cannot be found, that losse of the time and the charge in the seeking them often exceeding the value of their labor: Bee it therefore enacted that all runaways that shall absent themselves from their said masters service shalbe lyable to make satisfaction by service after the times by custome or indenture is expired (vizt.) double their times of service soe neglected, and if the time of their running away was in the crop or the charge of recovering

them extraordinary[,] the court shall lymitt a longer time of service proportionable to the damage the master shall make appear he hath susteyned.... And in case any English servant shall run away in the company of any negroes who are incapable of making satisfaction by addition of a time, it is enacted that the English soe running away in the company with them shall[,] at the time of service to their owne masters [is] expired, serve the masters of the said negroes for their absence soe long as they should have done by this act if that had not beene slaves, every christian in company serving his proportion; and if the negroes be lost or dye in such time of their being run away, the christian servants in company with them shall by proportion among them, either pay fower thousand five hundred pounds of tobacco...or fower years service for every negroe soe lost or dead.

SOURCE: William Waller Hening, ed., *The Statutes at Large; Being a Collection of All the Laws of Virginia*, 18 vols. (1809–1823), 2:116–17.

DOCUMENT 2
Law Making Slave Status Inherited from Mother, 1662

In 1662, Virginia lawmakers specified that the children of slave mothers inherited their mothers' slave status. This law overturned the precedent of English law, which provided that children inherited their fathers' status. In practice,

the Virginia law meant that if a white man had a child with a female slave, the child was a slave. However, if a male slave had a child with a white woman, the child was free. The law also punished all sexual relations across the color line.

Whereas some doubts have arisen whether children got by any Englishman upon a negro woman should be slave or ffree, Be it therefore enacted and declared...that all children borne in this country shalbe held bond or free only according to the condition of the mother. And that if any christian shall commit fornication with a negro man or woman, hee or shee soe offending shall pay double the ffines imposed by the former act.

SOURCE: William Waller Hening, ed., *The Statutes at Large; Being a Collection of All the Laws of Virginia*, 18 vols. (1809–1823), 2:170.

DOCUMENT 3
Law Specifies That Baptism Does Not Free Slaves, 1667

Virginia legislators declared in 1668 that slaves who converted to Christianity did not thereby become free. Lawmakers officially assured masters that slavery and Christianity were legally compatible, permitting Christianity to be taught to slaves without jeopardizing their slave status.

Whereas some doubts have arisen whether children that are slaves by birth, and by the charity and piety of their owners made pertakers of the blessed sacrament of baptisms, should by vertue of their baptisme be made ffree; It is enacted and declared...that the conferring of baptisme doth not alter the condition of the person as to his bondage or ffreedome; that diverse masters, ffreed from this doubt, may more carefully endeavour the propagation of christianity by permitting children, though slaves, or those of greater growth if capable to be admitted to that sacrament.

SOURCE: William Waller Hening, ed., *The Statutes at Large; Being a Collection of All the Laws of Virginia,* 18 vols. (1809–1823), 2:170.

DOCUMENT 4
Law Makes Killing a Slave Legal, 1669

If a servant assaulted a master, the master could legally extend the servants' period of servitude as punishment. A master had no similar legal remedy to inflict on an obstreperous slave, since a slave was already enslaved for life. In 1669, the Virginia legislature gave masters a green light to use any force they deemed necessary, including death, to control unruly slaves. Lawmakers declared that killing a slave was not murder, but instead was justifiable and legal.

Whereas the only law in force for the punishment of refractory servants resisting their master, mistris or overseer cannot be inflicted upon negroes, nor the obstinacy of many of them by other then violent meanes supprest, Be it enacted and declared ... [that] if any slave resist his master (or other by his masters order correcting him) and by the extremity of the correction should chance to die, that his death shall not be accompted a ffelony, but the master (or that other person appointed by the master to punish him) be acquit from molestation, since it cannot be presumed that prepensed malice (which alone makes murther ffelony) should induce any man to destroy his owne estate.

SOURCE: William Waller Hening, ed., *The Statutes at Large; Being a Collection of All the Laws of Virginia,* 18 vols. (1809–1823), 2:270.

DOCUMENT 5
Law Authorizes Force to Suppress Rebellious Slaves, Indians, and Servants, 1672

In 1672, the Virginia legislature authorized all white colonists to use any necessary force to suppress rebellious slaves, Indians, and servants. In effect, the law deputized white colonists to use deadly force against runaways. Lawmakers also encouraged Indians to help apprehend runaways, providing a reward for any fugitives turned over to white authorities.

Forasmuch as it hath beene manifested to this grand assembly that many negroes have lately beene, and now are out in rebellion in sundry parts of this country, and that noe meanes have yet beene found for the apprehension and suppression of them from whome many mischiefs of a very dangerous consequence may arise to the country if either other negroes, Indians or servants should happen to fly forth and joyne with them; for the prevention of which, be it enacted ... that if any negroe, molatto, Indian slave, or servant for life, runaway and shalbe persued ..., it shall and may be lawful for any person who shall endeavour to take them, upon the resistance of such negroe, molatto, Indian slave, or servant for life, to kill or wound him or them soe resisting.... And if it happen that such negroe, molatto, Indian slave, or servant for life doe dye of any wound in such their resistance ... the master or owner of such shall receive satisfaction from the publique for [value of the slave].... And it is further enacted that the neighbouring Indians doe and hereby are required and enjoyned to seize and apprehend all runaways whatsoever that shall happen to come amongst them, and to bring them before some justice of the peace who ... shall pay unto the said Indians ... a recompence.

SOURCE: William Waller Hening, ed., *The Statutes at Large; Being a Collection of All the Laws of Virginia,* 18 vols. (1809–1823), 2:299–300.

QUESTIONS FOR ANALYSIS AND DEBATE

1. According to these laws, how did slaves differ from servants? What boundaries did these laws draw among the various peoples in servitude?

2. According to these laws, what characterized colonists from England? What terms did the laws use to refer to English colonists? How did those terms differ from the words used to describe slaves?

3. In what ways did these laws reflect important developments that occurred in the southern colonies in the 1660s and 1670s? In what ways do the laws document an emerging hierarchy of race and class?

Christopher Adams, for example, had to serve three extra years for running away for six months. Richard Higby received six extra years of servitude for killing three hogs. After midcentury, the Virginia legislature added three or more years to the indentures of most servants by requiring them to serve until they were twenty-four years old.

Women servants were subject to special restrictions and risks. They were prohibited from marrying until their servitude had expired. A servant woman, the law assumed, could not serve two masters at the same time: one who owned her indentured labor and another who was her husband. However, the predominance of men in the Chesapeake population inevitably pressured women to engage in sexual relations. About a third of immigrant women were pregnant when they married. Pregnancy and childbirth sapped a woman's strength, and a new child diverted her attention, reducing her usefulness as a servant. As a rule, if a woman servant gave birth to a child, she had to serve two extra years and pay a fine. However, for some servant women, premarital pregnancy was a path out of servitude: The father of an unborn child sometimes purchased the indenture of the servant mother-to-be, then freed and married her.

Harsh punishments reflected four fundamental realities of the servant labor system. First, planters' hunger for labor caused them to demand as much labor as they could get from their servants, including devising legal ways to extend the period of servitude. Second, servants hoped to survive their servitude and use their freedom to obtain land and start a family. Third, servants' hopes frequently conflicted with planters' demands. Since servants saw themselves as free people in a temporary status of servitude, they often made grudging, halfhearted workers. Finally, planters put up with this contentious arrangement because the alternatives were less desirable.

Planters could not easily hire free men and women because land was readily available and free people preferred to work on their own land, for themselves. Nor could planters depend on much labor from family members. The preponderance of men in the population meant that families were few, were started late, and thus had few children. And, until the 1680s and 1690s, slaves were expensive and hard to come by. Before then, masters who wanted to expand their labor force and grow more tobacco had few alternatives to buying indentured servants.

Cultivating Land and Faith

Villages and small towns dotted the rural landscape of seventeenth-century England, but in the Chesapeake, acres of wilderness were interrupted here and there by tobacco farms. Tobacco was such a labor-intensive crop that one field worker could tend only about two acres of the plants in a year (an acre is slightly smaller than a football field), plus a few more acres for food crops. A successful farmer needed a great deal more land, however, because tobacco quickly exhausted the fertility of the soil. Since each farmer cultivated only 5 or 10 percent of his land at any one time, a "settled" area comprised swatches of cultivated land surrounded by forest. Arrangements for marketing tobacco also contributed to the dispersion of settlements. Tobacco planters sought land that fronted a navigable river in order to minimize the work of transporting the heavy barrels of tobacco onto ships. A settled region thus resembled a lacework of farms stitched around waterways.

Most Chesapeake colonists were nominally **Protestants**. Attendance at Sunday services and conformity to the doctrines of the Church of England were required of all English men and women. Few clergymen migrated to the Chesapeake, however, and too few of those who did were models of righteousness and piety. Certainly, some colonists took their religion seriously. Church courts punished fornicators, censured blasphemers, and served notice on parishioners who spent Sundays "goeing a fishing." But on the whole, religion did not awaken the zeal of Chesapeake settlers, certainly not as it did the zeal of New England settlers in these same years (see chapter 4). What quickened the pulse of most Chesapeake folk was a close horse race, a bloody cockfight, or—most of all—an exceptionally fine tobacco crop. The religion of the Chesapeake colonists was Anglican, but

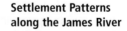

Settlement Patterns along the James River

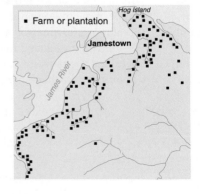

- ■ Farm or plantation

Hog Island

Jamestown

James River

their faith lay in the turbulent, competitive, high-stakes gamble of survival as tobacco planters.

The situation was similar in the Catholic colony of Maryland. In 1632, England's King Charles I granted his Catholic friend Lord Baltimore about six and a half million acres in the northern Chesapeake region. In return, the king specified that Lord Baltimore pay him the token rent of "two Indian arrowheads" a year. Lord Baltimore intended to create a refuge for Catholics, who suffered severe discrimination in England. He fitted out two ships, the *Ark* and the *Dove*, gathered about 150 settlers, and sent them to the new colony, where they arrived on March 25, 1634. However, Maryland failed to live up to Baltimore's hopes. The colony's population grew very slowly for twenty years, and most settlers were Protestants rather than Catholics. The religious turmoil of the **Puritan** Revolution in England (discussed in chapter 4) spilled across the Atlantic, creating conflict between Maryland's few Catholics— most of them wealthy and prominent—and the Protestant majority, most of them neither wealthy nor prominent. During the 1660s, Maryland began to attract settlers as readily as Virginia, mostly Protestants. Although Catholics and the Catholic faith continued to exert influence in Maryland, the colony's society, economy, politics, and culture became nearly indistinguishable from Virginia's. Both colonies shared a devotion to tobacco, the true faith of the Chesapeake.

REVIEW Why did the vast majority of European immigrants to the Chesapeake come as indentured servants?

The Evolution of Chesapeake Society

The system of indentured servitude sharpened inequality in Chesapeake society by the mid-seventeenth century, propelling social and political polarization that culminated in 1676 with Bacon's Rebellion. The rebellion prompted reforms that stabilized relations between elite planters and their lesser neighbors and paved the way for a social hierarchy that muted differences of landholding and wealth and amplified racial differences. (See "Historical Question," page 88.) Amid this social and political evolution, one thing did not change: Chesapeake colonists' dedication to growing tobacco.

Social and Economic Polarization

The first half of the seventeenth century in the Chesapeake was the era of the **yeoman**—a farmer who owned a small plot of land sufficient to support a family and tilled largely by servants and a few family members. A small number of elite planters had larger estates and commanded ten or more servants. But for the first several decades, few men lived long enough to accumulate a fortune sufficient to set them much apart from their neighbors. Until midcentury, the principal division in Chesapeake society was less between rich and poor planters than between free farmers and unfree servants. Although these two groups contrasted sharply in their legal and economic status, their daily lives had many similarities. Servants looked forward to the time when their indentures would expire and they would become free and eventually own land. On the whole, a rough, frontier equality characterized free families in the Chesapeake until about 1650.

Three major developments splintered that equality during the third quarter of the century. First, as planters grew more and more tobacco, the ample supply depressed tobacco prices in European markets. Cheap tobacco reduced planters' profits and made it more difficult for freed servants to save enough to become landowners. Second, because the mortality rate in the Chesapeake colonies declined, more and more servants survived their indentures, and landless freemen became more numerous and grew more discontented. Third, declining mortality also encouraged the formation of a planter elite. By living longer, the most successful planters compounded their success. The wealthiest planters also began to serve as merchants, marketing crops for their less successful neighbors, importing English goods for sale, and giving credit to hard-pressed customers.

By the 1670s, the society of the Chesapeake had become polarized. Landowners—the planter elite and the more numerous yeoman planters—clustered around one pole. Landless colonists, mainly freed servants, gathered at the other. Each group eyed the other with suspicion and mistrust. For the most part, planters saw

Why Did English Colonists Consider Themselves Superior to Indians and Africans?

Were seeds of the racial prejudice that has been such a powerful force in American history planted in the seventeenth-century Chesapeake? To answer that question, historians have paid close attention to the language colonists used to describe Indians, Africans, and themselves.

In the mid-1500s, the English adopted the words *Indian* and *Negro* from Spanish, where they had come to mean, respectively, an aboriginal inhabitant of the New World and a black person of African ancestry. Both terms were generic, homogenizing an enormous diversity of tribal affiliations, languages, and cultures. Neither term originated with the people to whom it referred. The New England minister Roger Williams, who published a book on Indian languages in 1643, reported, "They have often asked mee, why we call them Indians," a poignant question that reveals the European origins of the term.

After *Indians*, the word the settlers used most frequently to describe Native Americans was *savages*. The Indians were savages in the colonists' eyes because they lacked the traits of English civilization. As one Englishman put it in 1625, the natives of Virginia were "so bad a people, having little of humanitie but shape, ignorant of Civilitie, of Arts, of Religion; more brutish than

the beasts they hunt, more wild and unmanly than that unmanned wild countrey, which they range rather than inhabite; captivated also to Satans tyranny in foolish pieties, mad impieties, wicked idlenesse, busie and bloudy wickednesse." Some English colonists counterbalanced this harsh indictment with admiration for certain features of Indian behavior. They praised Indians' calm dignity and poise, their tender love and care for family members, and their simple, independent way of life in apparent harmony with nature.

Color was not a feature of the Indians' savagery. During the seventeenth century, colonists never referred to Indians as "red." Instead, they saw Indians' skin color as tawny or tanned, the "Sun's livery," as one settler wrote. Many settlers held the view that Indians were innately white like the English but in other ways woefully un-English.

Despite their savagery in English eyes, Indians controlled two things colonists desperately wanted: land and peace. Early in the seventeenth century, when English settlements were small and weak, peace with the Indians was a higher priority than land. In this period, English comments on Indian savagery noted the obvious differences between settlers and Indians, but the colonists' need for peace kept them attuned to ways to coexist with the

Indians. By the middle of the seventeenth century, as colonial settlements grew and the desire for land increased, violent conflict with Indians erupted repeatedly. The violence convinced settlers that the only way to achieve both land and peace was to eliminate the Indians, by either killing them or pushing them far away from colonial settlements. Colonists' convictions about the Indians' savagery became the justification for chronic violence against the Indians. English assumptions of their superiority to savage Indians gave a gloss of respectability to the colonists' relentless grab of Indian land.

The colonists identified Africans quite differently. Only a few Africans lived in the Chesapeake early in the seventeenth century. The first recorded arrival of Africans occurred in 1619, when a Dutch man-of-war brought to Virginia "20. and odd Negroes," as John Rolfe wrote. Rolfe's usage illustrates the colonists' most common term for Africans: *Negroes*. But the other word the colonists frequently used to refer to Africans was not *savage* or *heathen* but *black*. What struck English colonists most forcefully about Africans was not their un-English ways but their un-English skin color.

Black was not a neutral color to the colonists. According to the *Oxford English Dictionary* (which catalogs the changing meaning of words), black meant to the English people who settled the Chesapeake "deeply stained with dirt; soiled, dirty, foul . . . having dark or deadly purposes, malignant; pertaining to or involving death, deadly; baneful, disastrous, sinister . . . foul, iniquitous, atrocious, horrible, wicked." Black was the opposite of white, which connoted purity, beauty, and goodness—attributes the colonists identified with themselves. By the middle of the seventeenth century, the colonists referred to themselves not only as English but also as free, implying that people who were not English were not free. After about 1680, colonists often stated that implication in racial terms by referring to themselves as white. By the end of the seventeenth century, blacks were triply cursed in English eyes: un-English, un-white, and un-free.

Virginians did not legally define slavery as permanent, lifelong, inherited bondage until 1660. The sparse surviving evidence demonstrates, however, that colonists practiced slavery long before that. Although there is no way to be certain, it is likely that the "Negroes" who arrived in 1619 were slaves. And the punishments handed out to blacks who broke the law usually took for granted that their servitude could not be extended, presumably because they were already in bondage for life.

The debasements of slavery strengthened the colonists' prejudice toward blacks, while racial prejudices buttressed slavery. A Virginia law of 1662, for instance, provided that "any christian [who] shall commit fornication with a negro man or woman" had to pay a double fine. The law also demonstrates that, despite racial prejudices, sexual relations between white and black settlers were prevalent enough to attract the attention of the legislature. (See "Documenting the American Promise," p. 84.)

For most of the seventeenth century, possession of a black skin did not automatically and necessarily condemn a person to the status of slave in the eyes of whites. Some Africans in the Chesapeake served for limited periods of time like white servants, became free like white servants, and even acquired land, reared families, and participated in local affairs like former white servants. In fact, white colonists' prejudice against blacks echoed wealthy colonists' attitudes toward servants and other poor white people. Masters often considered white servants, like blacks, "the vile and brutish part of mankind."

Colonists' attitudes toward Indians and Africans exaggerated and hardened English notions about social hierarchy, about superiority and inferiority. Colonists' convictions of their own superiority to Indians and Africans justified, they believed, their exploitation of Indians' land and Africans' labor. Those justifications planted the seeds of pernicious racial prejudices that flourished in America for centuries.

European Attitudes toward Africans
This lavish portrait of two seventeenth-century aristocratic ladies illustrates common European attitudes toward Africans. Both ladies appear completely at ease with the black servant boy. One casually drapes her arm over his shoulder; the other daintily plucks fruit from the bowl he holds. While the two ladies gaze confidently at the viewer, the boy stares at the black lapdog, whose color and protruding eyes he shares, along with an ornamental collar. The portrait suggests that the ladies consider the African boy akin to the dog—an exotic pet vastly inferior to them but safely domesticated and fit to be a plaything or ornament decked out in clothing displaying their magnificence. What does the portrait suggest about the attitude of the boy toward the ladies? What does the portrait suggest about white Europeans' attitudes about themselves?
Réunion des Musées Nationaux/Art Resource, NY.

Governor William Berkeley

This portrait illustrates the distance that separated Governor Berkeley and the other Chesapeake grandees from poor planters, landless freemen, servants, and slaves. Berkeley's clothing suited the genteel homes of Jamestown, not the rustic dwellings of lesser Virginians. His haughty, satisfied demeanor suggests his lack of sympathy for poor Virginians, who, he was certain, deserved their lot.

Courtesy of Berkeley Castle Charitable Trust, Gloucestershire.

landless freemen as a dangerous rabble rather than as fellow colonists with legitimate grievances. Governor William Berkeley feared the political threat to the governing elite posed by "six parts in seven [of Virginia colonists who] ... are poor, indebted, discontented, and armed."

Government Policies and Political Conflict

In general, government and politics strengthened the distinctions in Chesapeake society. The most vital distinction separated servants and masters, and the colonial government enforced it with an iron fist. Poor men such as William Tyler complained that "nether the Governor nor Counsell could or would doe any poore men right, but that they would shew favor to great men and wronge the poore." Most Chesapeake colonists, like most Europeans, assumed that "great men" should bear the responsibilities of government. Until 1670, all freemen could vote,

and they routinely elected prosperous planters to the legislature. No former servant served in either the governor's council or the House of Burgesses after 1640. Yet Tyler and other poor Virginians believed that the "great men" used their government offices to promote their selfish personal interests, rather than governing impartially.

As discontent mounted among the poor during the 1660s and 1670s, colonial officials tried to keep political power in safe hands. Beginning in 1661, for example, Governor Berkeley did not call an election for the House of Burgesses for fifteen years. In 1670, the House of Burgesses outlawed voting by poor men, permitting only men who headed a household and were landowners to vote.

The king also began to tighten the royal government's control of trade and to collect substantial revenue from the Chesapeake. A series of navigation acts funneled the colonial trade exclusively into the hands of English merchants and shippers. The Navigation Acts of 1650 and 1651 specified that colonial goods had to be transported in English ships with predominantly English crews. A 1660 act required colonial products to be sent only to English ports, and a 1663 law stipulated further that all goods sent to the colonies must pass through English ports and be carried in English ships manned by English sailors. Taken together, these navigation acts reflected the English government's **mercantilist** assumptions about the colonies: What was good for England should determine colonial policy.

Assumptions about mercantilism also underlay the import duty on tobacco inaugurated by the Navigation Act of 1660. The law assessed an import tax of two pence on every pound of colonial tobacco brought into England, about the price a Chesapeake tobacco farmer received. The tax gave the king a major financial interest in the size of the tobacco crop. During the 1660s, these tobacco import taxes yielded about a quarter of all English customs revenues, an impressive sign of the growing importance of the Chesapeake colonies in England's Atlantic empire.

Bacon's Rebellion

Colonists, like residents of European monarchies, accepted social hierarchy and inequality as long as they believed that government officials ruled for the general good. When rulers violated that precept, ordinary people felt justified in rebelling. In 1676, Bacon's Rebellion erupted as a dispute over Virginia's Indian policy. Before it was over, the rebellion convulsed Chesapeake politics and society, leaving in its wake death, destruction, and a legacy of hostility between the great planters and their poorer neighbors.

Opechancanough, the Algonquian chief who had led the Indian uprising of 1622 in Virginia, mounted another surprise attack in 1644 and killed about five hundred Virginia colonists in two days. During the next two years of bitter fighting, the colonists eventually gained the upper hand, capturing and murdering the old chief. The treaty that concluded the war established policies toward the Indians that the government tried to maintain for the next thirty years. The Indians relinquished all claims to land already settled by the English. Wilderness land beyond the fringe of English settlement was supposed to be reserved exclusively for Indian use. The colonial government hoped to minimize contact between settlers and Indians and thereby maintain the peace.

If the Chesapeake population had not grown, the policy might have worked. But the number of land-hungry colonists, especially poor, recently freed servants, continued to multiply. In their quest for land, they pushed beyond the treaty limits of English settlement and encroached steadily on Indian land. During the 1660s and 1670s, violence between colonists and Indians repeatedly flared along the advancing frontier. The government, headquartered in the tidewater region near the coast, far from the danger of Indian raids, took steps to calm the disputes and reestablish the peace. Frontier settlers thirsted for revenge against what their leader, Nathaniel Bacon, termed "the protected and Darling Indians." Bacon proclaimed his "Design not only to ruine and extirpate all Indians in Generall but all Manner of Trade and Commerce with them." Indians were not the only enemies Bacon and his men singled out. Bacon also urged the colonists to "see what spounges have suckt up the Publique Treasure." He charged that "Grandees," or elite planters, operated the government for their private gain, a charge that made sense to many colonists. Bacon crystallized the grievances of the small planters and poor farmers against both the Indians and the colonial rulers in Jamestown.

Hoping to maintain the fragile peace on the frontier in 1676, Governor Berkeley pronounced Bacon a rebel, threatened to punish him for treason,

Inside a Poor Planter's House
The houses of seventeenth-century Chesapeake settlers were typically "earth-fast": The structural timbers that framed the house were simply placed in holes in the ground, and the floor was packed dirt. No seventeenth-century house was substantial enough to survive until today. This photo shows a carefully documented reconstruction of the interior of a poor planter's house at Historic St. Mary's City, Maryland. The wall of this one-room dwelling with a loft features a window with a shutter but no glass. When the shutter was closed, the only source of light was a candle or a fire. Notice the rustic, unfinished bench, table, and walls. These meager furnishings were usually accompanied by a storage chest and some bedding but not a bed. If and when planters became more prosperous, a bed was likely to be their first acquisition, suggesting that the lack of a good night's sleep was one of their major discomforts.
Image courtesy of Historic St. Mary's City.

and called for new elections of burgesses who, Berkeley believed, would endorse his get-tough policy. To Berkeley's surprise, the elections backfired. Almost all the old burgesses were voted out of office, and they were replaced by local leaders, including Bacon. The legislature was now in the hands of minor grandees who, like Bacon, chafed at the rule of the elite planters.

In June 1676, the new legislature passed a series of reform measures known as Bacon's Laws. Among other changes, the laws gave local settlers a voice in setting tax levies, forbade officeholders from demanding bribes or other extra fees for carrying out their duties, placed limits on holding multiple offices, and restored the vote to all freemen. Under pressure, Berkeley pardoned Bacon and authorized his campaign of Indian warfare. But elite planters soon convinced Berkeley that Bacon and his men were a greater threat than Indians.

When Bacon learned that Berkeley had once again branded him a traitor, he declared war against Berkeley and the other grandees. For three months, Bacon's forces fought the Indians, sacked the grandees' plantations, and attacked Jamestown. Berkeley's loyalists retaliated by plundering the homes of Bacon's supporters. The fighting continued until late October, when Bacon unexpectedly died, most likely from dysentery, and several English ships arrived to bolster Berkeley's strength. With the rebellion crushed, Berkeley hanged several of Bacon's allies and destroyed farms that belonged to Bacon's supporters.

The rebellion did nothing to dislodge the grandees from their positions of power. If anything, it strengthened them. When the king learned of the turmoil in the Chesapeake and its devastating effect on tobacco exports and customs duties, he ordered an investigation. Royal officials replaced Berkeley with a governor more attentive to the king's interests, nullified Bacon's Laws, and instituted an export tax on every hogshead of tobacco as a way of paying the expenses of government without having to obtain the consent of the tightfisted House of Burgesses.

In the aftermath of Bacon's Rebellion, tensions between great planters and small farmers gradually lessened. Bacon's Rebellion showed, a governor of Virginia said, that it was necessary "to steer between . . . either an Indian or a civil war." The ruling elite concluded that it was safer for the colonists to fight the Indians than to fight each other, and the government made little effort to restrict settlers' encroachment on Indian land. Tax cuts also were welcomed by all freemen. The export duty on tobacco imposed by the king allowed the colonial government to reduce taxes by 75 percent between 1660 and 1700. In the long run, however, the most important contribution to political stability was the declining importance of the servant labor system. During the 1680s and 1690s, fewer servants arrived in the Chesapeake, partly because of improving economic conditions in England. Accordingly, the number of poor, newly freed servants also declined, reducing the size of the lowest stratum of free society. In 1700, as many as one-third of the free colonists still worked as tenants on land owned by others, but the social and political distance between them and the great planters did not seem as important as it had been in 1660. The main reason was that by 1700, the Chesapeake was in the midst of transition to a slave labor system that minimized the differences between poor farmers and rich planters and magnified the differences between whites and blacks.

> **REVIEW** Why did Chesapeake colonial society become increasingly polarized between 1650 and 1670?

Religion and Revolt in the Spanish Borderland

While English colonies in the Chesapeake grew and prospered with the tobacco trade, the northern outposts of the Spanish empire in New Mexico and Florida stagnated. Instead of attracting settlers and growing crops for export, New Mexico and Florida appealed to Spanish missionaries seeking to harvest Indian souls. The missionaries baptized thousands of Indians in Spanish North America during the seventeenth century, but they also planted the seeds of Indian uprisings against Spanish rule.

Few Spaniards came to New Spain's northern borderland during the seventeenth century. Only about fifteen hundred Spaniards lived in Florida, and roughly twice as many inhabited New Mexico. One royal governor complained that "no [Spaniard] comes . . . to plow and sow [crops], but only to eat and loaf." In both colonies, Indians outnumbered Spaniards ten or twenty to one.

Spanish Stirrup
This seventeenth-century stirrup used by Spaniards on the northern frontier of New Spain illustrates the use of elaborate ornamentation and display to convey a sense of Spanish power. It is no accident that the stirrup is in the shape of a Christian cross, a vivid symbol of the Spaniards' belief in the divine source of their authority.
© George H. H. Huey.

Royal officials seriously considered eliminating both colonies because their costs greatly exceeded their benefits. Every three years, a caravan from Mexico brought wagons full of goods to outposts in New Mexico. Florida required even larger subsidies because it housed a garrison of soldiers as well as missionaries, who persuaded the Spanish government that instead of being losing propositions, the colonies represented golden opportunities to convert heathen Indians to Christianity. Stirrups adorned with Christian crosses on soldiers' saddles proclaimed the faith behind the Spaniards' swords, and vice versa. Royal officials hoped that the missionaries' efforts would pacify the Indians and be a relatively cheap way to preserve Spanish footholds in North America.

Dozens of missionaries came to Florida and New Mexico, as one announced, to free the Indians "from the miserable slavery of the demon and from the obscure darkness of their idolatry." The missionaries believed that the Indians' religious beliefs and rituals were idolatrous devil worship and that their way of life was barbaric. The missionaries followed royal instructions that Indians should be taught "to live in a civilized manner, clothed and wearing shoes... [and] given the use of... bread, linen, horses, cattle, tools, and weapons, and all the rest that Spain has had." In effect, the missionaries sought to convert the Indians not just into Christians but also into surrogate Spaniards.

The missionaries supervised the building of scores of Catholic churches across Florida and New Mexico. Typically, they conscripted Indian women and men to do the construction. Adopting practices common elsewhere in New Spain, the missionaries forced the Indians both to work and to pay tribute in the form of food, blankets, and other goods. Although the missionaries congratulated themselves on the many Indians they converted, their coercive methods subverted their goals. A missionary reported that an Indian in New Mexico asked him, "If we [missionaries] who are Christians caused so much harm and violence [to Indians], why should they become Christians?"

The Indians retaliated repeatedly against Spanish exploitation, but the Spaniards suppressed the violent uprisings by taking advantage of the disunity among the Indians, much as Cortés did in the conquest of Mexico (see chapter 2). In 1680, however, Pueblo Indians organized a unified revolt under the leadership of Popé, who ordered his followers, as one recounted, to "break up and burn the images of the holy Christ, the Virgin Mary, and the other saints, the crosses, and everything pertaining to Christianity." During the Pueblo Revolt, the Indians desecrated churches, killed two-thirds of the Spanish missionaries, and drove the Spaniards out of New Mexico to present-day El Paso, Texas. The Spaniards managed to return to New Mexico by the end of the seventeenth century, but only by curtailing the missionaries and reducing labor exploitation. Florida Indians never mounted a unified attack on Spanish rule, but they too organized sporadic uprisings and resisted conversion, causing a Spanish official to report by the end of the seventeenth century that "the law of God and the preaching of the Holy Gospel have now ceased."

> Dozens of missionaries came to Florida and New Mexico, as one announced, to free the Indians "from the miserable slavery of the demon and from the obscure darkness of their idolatry."

REVIEW Why did the Pueblo Indians revolt against Spanish missionaries in 1680?

Toward a Slave Labor System

During the sixteenth century, Spaniards and Portuguese in the New World supplemented Indian laborers with enslaved Africans. On this foundation, European colonizers built African slavery into the most important form of coerced labor in the New World. During the seventeenth century, English colonies in the West Indies followed the Spanish and Portuguese examples and developed sugar plantations with slave labor. In the English North American colonies, however, a slave labor system did not emerge until the last quarter of the seventeenth century. During the 1670s, settlers from Barbados brought slavery to the new English mainland colony of Carolina, where the imprint of the West Indies remained strong for decades. In Chesapeake tobacco fields at about the same time, slave labor began to replace servant labor, marking the transition toward a society of freedom for whites and slavery for Africans.

The West Indies: Sugar and Slavery

The most profitable part of the English New World empire in the seventeenth century lay in the Caribbean (Map 3.2). The tiny island of Barbados, colonized in the 1630s, was the jewel of the English West Indies. During the 1640s, Barbadian planters began to grow sugarcane with such success that a colonial official proclaimed Barbados "the most flourishing Island in all those American parts, and I verily believe in all the world for the production of sugar." Sugar commanded high prices in England, and planters rushed to grow as much as they could. By mid-century, annual sugar exports from the English Caribbean totaled about 150,000 pounds; by 1700, exports reached nearly 50 million pounds.

Sugar transformed Barbados and other West Indian islands. Poor farmers could not afford the expensive machinery that extracted and refined sugarcane juice. Planters with the necessary capital to grow sugar got rich. By 1680, the wealthiest Barbadian sugar planters were, on average, four times richer than tobacco grandees in the Chesapeake. The sugar grandees differed from

Sugar Plantation
This portrait of a Brazilian sugar plantation shows the house of the Brazilian owners, attended by numerous slaves. Cartloads of sugarcane are being hauled to the mill, which is powered by a waterwheel (far right), where the cane will be squeezed between rollers to extract the sugary juice. The juice will then be distilled over a fire tended by the slaves (at the left end of the mill) until it has the desired consistency and purity. Notice that all of the working people are of African descent, and probably all of them are slaves. How did the artist differentiate slaves from their owners?
Courtesy of the John Carter Brown Library at Brown University.

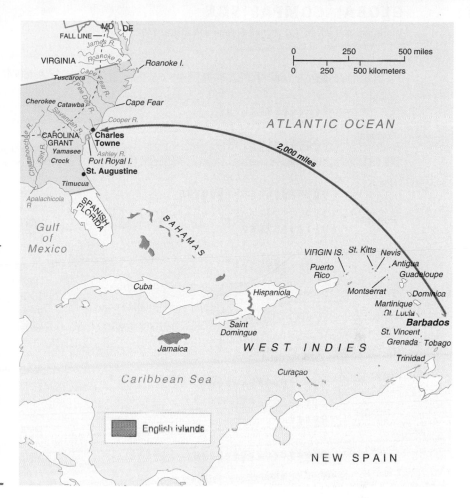

MAP 3.2   The West Indies and Carolina in the Seventeenth Century

Although Carolina was geographically close to the Chesapeake colonies, it was culturally closer to the West Indies in the seventeenth century because its early settlers—both blacks and whites—came from Barbados. South Carolina maintained strong ties to the West Indies for more than a century, long after the arrival of many later settlers from England, Ireland, France, and elsewhere.

READING THE MAP: Locate English colonies in America and English holdings in the Caribbean. Which European country controlled most of the mainland bordering the Caribbean? Where was the closest mainland English territory?

CONNECTIONS: Why were colonists in Carolina so interested in Barbados? What goods did they export? Describe the relationship between Carolina and Barbados in 1700.

FOR MORE HELP ANALYZING THIS MAP, see the map activity for this chapter in the Online Study Guide at bedfordstmartins.com/roark.

their Chesapeake counterparts in another crucial way: The average sugar baron in Barbados owned 115 slaves in 1680.

African slaves planted, cultivated, and harvested the sugarcane that made West Indian planters wealthy. (See "Global Comparison," page 96.) Beginning in the 1640s, Barbadian planters purchased thousands of slaves to work their plantations, and the African population on the island mushroomed. During the 1650s, when blacks made up only 3 percent of the Chesapeake population, they had already become the majority on Barbados. By 1700, slaves constituted more than three-fourths of the island's population.

For slaves, work on a sugar plantation was a life sentence to brutal, unremitting labor. Slaves suffered high death rates. Since slave men outnumbered slave women two to one, few slaves could form families and have children. These grim realities meant that in Barbados and elsewhere in the West Indies, the slave population did not grow by natural reproduction. Instead, planters

continually purchased enslaved Africans. Although sugar plantations did not gain a foothold in North America in the seventeenth century, the West Indies nonetheless exerted a powerful influence on the development of slavery in the mainland colonies.

Carolina: A West Indian Frontier

The early settlers of what became South Carolina were immigrants from Barbados. In 1663, a Barbadian planter named John Colleton and a group of seven other men obtained a charter from England's King Charles II to establish a colony south of the Chesapeake and north of the Spanish territories in Florida. The men, known as "proprietors," hoped to siphon settlers from Barbados and other colonies and encourage them to develop a profitable export crop comparable to West Indian sugar and Chesapeake tobacco. Following the Chesapeake example, the proprietors offered headrights of up to 150 acres

Migration to the New World from Europe and Africa, 1492–1700

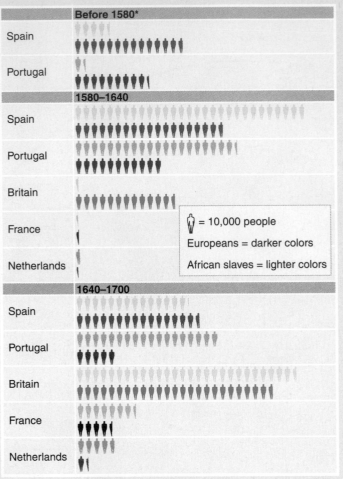

Before 1580*

Spain

Portugal

1580–1640

Spain

Portugal

Britain

France

Netherlands

= 10,000 people

Europeans = darker colors

African slaves = lighter colors

1640–1700

Spain

Portugal

Britain

France

Netherlands

*Note: Before 1580, migration from Britain, France, and the Netherlands was negligible.

Before 1640, Spain and Portugal reaped the rewards of their sixteenth-century voyages of discovery by sending four out of five European migrants to the New World, virtually all of them bound for New Spain or Brazil. But from 1640 to 1700, more migrants came from England than from any other European nation and nearly as many as from all other European nations combined, a measure of the growing significance of England's colonies in both the Caribbean and North America during the seventeenth century. While few enslaved Africans were carried across the Atlantic before 1580, after 1580 more enslaved Africans than Europeans arrived in New World colonies, an outgrowth of the enormous expansion of slave labor in the European colonies. Between 1580 and 1640, Spanish and Portuguese colonies pioneered in the use of large numbers of slaves, especially in sugar-cane fields, and other nations quickly followed suit. Only a comparatively few enslaved Africans were carried to English North American tobacco and rice fields before 1700 (not shown separately in this figure). Overall, from the voyages of Columbus to 1700, more Africans than Europeans crossed the Atlantic to the New World, and virtually all of them were slaves. Of the total number of Africans, roughly what fraction were taken to the colonies of each nation during each of the three periods? What might explain the shifts in the destinations of enslaved Africans? Were those shifts comparable to shifts among European immigrants?

of land for each settler. In 1670, they established the colony's first permanent English settlement, Charles Towne (later spelled Charleston) (see Map 3.2).

As the proprietors had planned, most of the early settlers were from Barbados. In fact, Carolina was the only seventeenth-century English colony to be settled principally by colonists from other colonies rather than from England. The Barbadian immigrants brought their slaves with them. More than a fourth of the early settlers were slaves, and as the colony continued to attract settlers from Barbados, the black population multiplied. By 1700, slaves made up about half the popu-

> The new colony's close association with Barbados caused English officials to refer routinely to "Carolina in ye West Indies."

lation of Carolina. The new colony's close association with Barbados caused English officials to refer routinely to "Carolina in ye West Indies."

The Carolinians experimented unsuccessfully to match their semitropical climate with profitable export crops of tobacco, cotton, indigo, and olives. In the mid-1690s, colonists identified a hardy strain of rice and took advantage of the knowledge of rice cultivation among their many African slaves to build rice plantations. Settlers also sold livestock and timber to the West Indies, as well as another "natural resource": They captured and enslaved several thousand local Indians and sold them to Caribbean planters. Both economically and socially, seventeenth-century Carolina was a frontier outpost of the West Indian sugar economy.

Slave Labor Emerges in the Chesapeake

By 1700, more than eight out of ten people in the southern colonies of English North America lived in the Chesapeake. Until the 1670s, almost all Chesapeake colonists were white people from England. By 1700, however, one out of eight people in the region was a black person from Africa. A few black people had lived in the Chesapeake since the 1620s, but the black population grew fivefold between 1670 and 1700 as hundreds of tobacco planters made the transition from servant to slave labor.

For planters, slaves had several obvious advantages over servants. Although slaves cost three to five times more than servants, slaves never became free. Since the mortality rate had declined by the 1680s, planters could reasonably expect slaves to live longer than a servant's period of indenture. Slaves also promised to be a perpetual labor force, since children of slave mothers inherited the status of slavery.

Slaves had another important advantage over servants: They could be controlled politically. Bacon's Rebellion had demonstrated how disruptive former servants could be when their expectations were not met. A slave labor system promised to avoid the political problems caused by the servant labor system. Slavery kept discontented laborers in permanent servitude, and their color was a badge of their bondage.

The slave labor system polarized Chesapeake society along lines of race and status: All slaves were black, and nearly all blacks were slaves; almost all free people were white, and all whites were free or only temporarily bound in indentured servitude. Unlike Barbados, however, the Chesapeake retained a vast white majority. Among whites, huge differences of wealth and status still existed. By 1700, more than three-quarters of white families had neither servants nor slaves. Nonetheless, poor white farmers enjoyed the privileges of free status. They could own property, get married, have families, and bequeath their property and their freedom to their descendants; they could move when and where they wanted; they could associate freely with other people; they could serve on juries, vote, and hold political office; and they could work, loaf, and sleep as they chose. These privileges of freedom—none of them possessed by slaves—made lesser white folk feel they had a genuine stake in the existence of slavery, even if

they did not own a single slave. By emphasizing the privileges of freedom shared by all white people, the slave labor system reduced the tensions between poor folk and grandees that had plagued the Chesapeake region in the 1670s.

In contrast to slaves in Barbados, most slaves in the seventeenth-century Chesapeake colonies had frequent and close contact with white people. Slaves and white servants performed the same tasks on tobacco plantations,

African Musicians
An Italian missionary in seventeenth-century Angola drew this portrait of three African musicians playing local wind, percussion, and stringed instruments. The textiles worn around their waists probably came from Europe and were traded for African goods that most likely included slaves. The small white cross on the chest of the man in the middle may be a symbol of conversion to Christianity, a mark of the missionary artist's efforts.
Private Collection.

often working side by side in the fields. Slaves took advantage of every opportunity to slip away from white supervision and seek out the company of other slaves. Planters often feared that slaves would turn such seemingly innocent social pleasures to political ends, either to run away or to conspire to strike against their masters. Slaves often did run away, but they were usually captured or returned after a brief absence. Despite planters' nightmares, slave insurrections did not occur.

Although slavery resolved the political unrest caused by the servant labor system, it created new political problems. By 1700, the bedrock political issue in the southern colonies was keeping slaves in their place, at the end of a hoe. The slave labor system in the southern colonies stood roughly midway between the sugar plantations and black majority of Barbados to the south and the small farms and homogeneous villages that developed in seventeenth-century New England to the north (see chapter 4).

> **REVIEW**   Why had slave labor largely displaced indentured servant labor by 1700 in Chesapeake tobacco production?

Conclusion: The Growth of English Colonies Based on Export Crops and Slave Labor

By 1700, the colonies of Virginia, Maryland, and Carolina were firmly established. The staple crops they grew for export provided a livelihood for many, a fortune for a few, and valuable revenues for shippers, merchants, and the English monarchy. Their societies differed markedly from English society in most respects, yet the colonists considered themselves English people who happened to live in North America. They claimed the same rights and privileges as English men and women, while they denied those rights and privileges to Native Americans and African slaves.

The English colonies also differed from the example of New Spain. Settlers and servants flocked to English colonies, in contrast to Spaniards who trickled into New Spain. Few English missionaries sought to convert Indians

to Protestant Christianity, unlike the numerous Catholic missionaries in the Spanish settlements in New Mexico and Florida. Large quantities of gold and silver never materialized in English North America. English colonists never adopted the system of *encomienda* (see chapter 2) because the Indians in these areas were too few and too hostile and their communities too small and decentralized compared with those of the Mexica. Yet some forms of coerced labor and racial distinction that developed in New Spain had North American counterparts, as English colonists employed servants and slaves and defined themselves as superior to Indians and Africans.

By 1700, the remnants of Powhatan's people still survived. As English settlement pushed north, west, and south of the Chesapeake Bay, the Indians faced the new colonial world that Powhatan and Pocahontas had encountered when John Smith and the first colonists had arrived at Jamestown. By 1700, the many descendants of Pocahontas's son, Thomas, as well as other colonists and Native Americans, understood that the English had come to stay.

Selected Bibliography

General Works

Ira Berlin, *Many Thousands Gone: The First Two Centuries of Slavery in North America* (1998).
Alison Games, *Migration and the Origins of the English Atlantic World* (1999).
Stephen J. Hornsby, *British Atlantic, American Frontier: Spaces of Power in Early Modern British America* (2005).
Cathy Matson, ed., *The Economy of Early America: Historical Perspective and New Directions* (2006).
Edmund S. Morgan, *American Slavery, American Freedom: The Ordeal of Colonial Virginia* (1975).
Mary Beth Norton, *Founding Mothers and Fathers: Gendered Power and the Forming of American Society* (1996).
Steven Sarson, *British America, 1500–1800: Creating Colonies, Imagining an Empire* (2005).

Indians

Alan Gallay, *The Indian Slave Trade: The Rise of the English Empire in the American South, 1670–1717* (2002).
Karen Ordahl Kupperman, *Indians and English: Facing Off in Early America* (2000).
James H. Merrell, *The Indians' New World: Catawbas and Their Neighbors from European Contact through the Era of Removal* (1989).
Michael Leroy Oberg, *Dominion and Civility: English Imperialism and Native America, 1585–1685* (1999).

Helen C. Rountree, *Pocahontas, Powhatan, Opechancanough: Three Indian Lives Changed by Jamestown* (2005).

Jayme A. Sokolow, *The Great Encounter: Native Peoples and European Settlers in the Americas, 1492–1800* (2003).

Chesapeake Society

Robert Applebaum and John Wood Sweet, eds., *Envisioning an English Empire: Jamestown and the Making of the North Atlantic World* (2005).

Edward L. Bond, *Damned Souls in a Tobacco Colony: Religion in Seventeenth-Century Virginia* (2000).

Kathleen Brown, *Good Wives, Nasty Wenches, and Anxious Patriarchs: Gender, Race, and Power in Colonial Virginia* (1996).

Lois Green Carr et al., *Robert Cole's World: Agriculture and Society in Early Maryland* (1991).

April Hatfield, *Atlantic Virginia: Intercolonial Relations in the Seventeenth Century* (2003).

Russell R. Menard, *Migrants, Servants and Slaves: Unfree Labor in Colonial British America* (2001).

Debra Meyers, *Common Whores, Vertuous Women, and Loveing Wives: Free Will Christian Women in Colonial Maryland* (2003).

John Ruston Pagan, *Anne Orthwood's Bastard: Sex and Law in Early Virginia* (2003).

Terri L. Snyder, *Brabbling Women: Disorderly Speech and the Law in Early Virginia* (2003).

Linda L. Sturtz, *Within Her Power: Propertied Women in Colonial Virginia* (2002).

Margaret Holmes Williamson, *Powhatan Lords of Life and Death: Command and Consent in Seventeenth-Century Virginia* (2003).

Spanish Borderlands

James F. Brooks, *Captives and Cousins: Slavery, Kinship, and Community in the Southwest Borderlands* (2002).

Ramón A. Gutiérrez, *When Jesus Came, the Corn Mothers Went Away: Marriage, Sexuality, and Power in New Mexico, 1500–1846* (1991).

Jerald T. Milanich, *Laboring in the Fields of the Lord: Spanish Missions and Southeastern Indians* (1999).

Robert W. Preucel, *Archaeologies of the Pueblo Revolt: Identity, Meaning, and Renewal in the Pueblo World* (2002).

Carolina Society and West Indies

Cara Anzilotti, *In the Affairs of the World: Women, Patriarchy, and Power in Colonial South Carolina* (2002).

S. Max Edelson, *Plantation Enterprise in Colonial South Carolina* (2006).

Kirsten Fischer, *Suspect Relations: Sex, Race, and Resistance in Colonial North Carolina* (2002).

Lorri Glover, *All Our Relations: Blood Ties and Emotional Bonds among the Early South Carolina Gentry* (2000).

Russell K. Menard, *Sweet Negotiations: Sugar, Slavery, and Plantation Agriculture in Early Barbados* (2006).

Jennifer L. Morgan, *Laboring Women: Reproduction and Gender in New World Slavery* (2004).

Peter H. Wood, *Black Majority: Negroes in Colonial South Carolina from 1670 through the Stono Rebellion* (1974).

▶ **FOR MORE BOOKS ABOUT TOPICS IN THIS CHAPTER**, see the Online Bibliography at bedfordstmartins.com/roark.

▶ **FOR ADDITIONAL FIRSTHAND ACCOUNTS OF THIS PERIOD**, see Chapter 3 in Michael Johnson, ed., *Reading the American Past*, Fourth Edition.

▶ **FOR WEB SITES, IMAGES, AND DOCUMENTS RELATED TO TOPICS AND PLACES IN THIS CHAPTER**, visit bedfordstmartins.com/makehistory.

REVIEWING THE CHAPTER

Follow these steps to review and strengthen your understanding of the chapter.

STEP 1: *Study the* **Key Terms** *and* **Timeline** *to identify the significance of each item listed.*

STEP 2: *Answer the* **Review Questions**, *drawing on key terms and dates to support your answers.*

STEP 3: *Drawing on the Key Terms, Timeline, and Review Questions, answer the broader* **Making Connections** *questions.*

KEY TERMS

Who

Captain John Smith (p. 69)
Algonquian Indians (p. 69)
Powhatan (p. 69)
Pocahontas (p. 69)
John Rolfe (p. 70)
James I (p. 71)
Opechancanough (p. 75)
Charles I (p. 80)
Lord Baltimore (p. 87)
William Berkeley (p. 90)

Nathaniel Bacon (p. 91)
Pueblo Indians (p. 93)
Popé (p. 93)
Charles II (p. 95)

What

Virginia Company (p. 71)
colonization (p. 74)
Jamestown (p. 70)
royal colony (p. 76)
House of Burgesses (p. 76)

tobacco (p. 77)
headright (p. 78)
indentured servants (p. 78)
yeoman (p. 87)
Navigation Acts (p. 90)
mercantilism (p. 90)
Bacon's Rebellion (p. 90)
grandees (p. 94)
Barbados (p. 94)

TIMELINE

NOTE: Events are depicted chronologically, but the passage of time is not to exact scale.

◄ **1588** • England defeats Spanish Armada.

1606 • Virginia Company receives royal charter.

1607 • English colonists found Jamestown settlement;
Pocahontas "rescues" John Smith.

1607–10 • Starvation plagues Jamestown.

 1612 • John Rolfe begins to plant tobacco in Virginia.

1617 • First commercial tobacco shipment
leaves Virginia for England.
• Pocahontas dies in England.

1618 • Powhatan dies; Opechancanough becomes
chief of the Algonquians.

1619 • First Africans arrive in Virginia.
• House of Burgesses begins to meet in Virginia.

1622 • Opechancanough leads
first Indian uprising
against Virginia colonists.

1624 • Virginia becomes
royal colony.

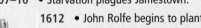

REVIEW QUESTIONS

1. Why did Powhatan pursue largely peaceful relations with the Jamestown settlement? (pp. 71–76)

2. Why did the vast majority of European immigrants to the Chesapeake come as indentured servants? (pp. 77–87)

3. Why did Chesapeake colonial society become increasingly polarized between 1650 and 1670? (pp. 87–92)

4. Why did the Pueblo Indians revolt against Spanish missionaries in 1680? (pp. 92–93)

5. Why had slave labor largely displaced indentured servant labor by 1700 in Chesapeake tobacco production? (pp. 94–98)

MAKING CONNECTIONS

1. Given the extraordinary vulnerability of the Jamestown settlement in its first two decades, why did its sponsors and settlers not abandon it? In your answer, discuss the challenges the settlement faced and the benefits different participants in England and the New World hoped to derive from their efforts.

2. Tobacco dominated European settlement in the seventeenth-century Chesapeake. How did tobacco agriculture shape the region's development? In your answer, be sure to address the demographic and geographic features of the colony.

3. Bacon's Rebellion highlighted significant tensions within Chesapeake society. What provoked the rebellion, and what did it accomplish? In your answer, be sure to consider causes and results in the colonies and in England.

4. In addition to making crucial contributions to the economic success of seventeenth-century English colonies, Native Americans and enslaved Africans influenced colonial politics. Describe how European colonists' relations with these populations contributed to political friction and harmony within the colony.

► For practice quizzes, a customized study plan, and other study tools, see the Online Study Guide at bedfordstmartins.com/roark.

1632 • King Charles I grants Lord Baltimore land for colony of Maryland.

   1634 • Colonists begin to arrive in Maryland.

      1640s • Barbados colonists begin to grow sugarcane with labor of African slaves.

        1644 • Opechancanough leads second Indian uprising against Virginia colonists.

          1660 • Navigation Act requires colonial tobacco to be shipped to English ports.

           1663 • Royal charter is granted for Carolina colony.

             1670 • Charles Towne, South Carolina, founded.

               1670–1700 • Slave labor system emerges in Carolina and Chesapeake colonies.

                 1676 • Bacon's Rebellion.

                   1680 • Pueblo Revolt.

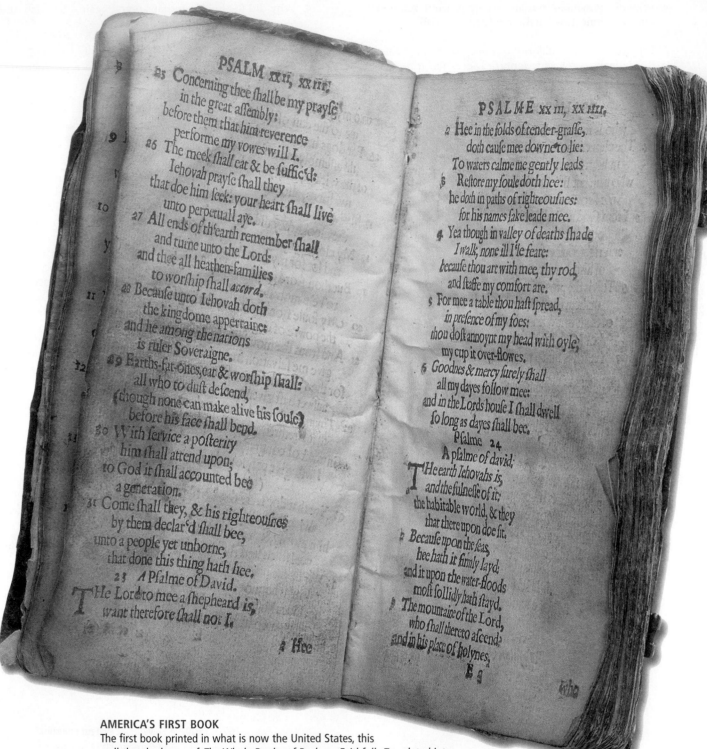

AMERICA'S FIRST BOOK

The first book printed in what is now the United States, this well-thumbed copy of *The Whole Booke of Psalmes Faithfully Translated into English Metre* was published in Cambridge, Massachusetts, in 1640. Puritan services banned musical instruments and other diversions from God's holy Word. Worshippers used this book and others to sing psalms, celebrating with a chorus of voices the wonders of God's Truth. The famous Twenty-third Psalm begins near the bottom of the left-hand page and concludes on the facing page. Read the psalm aloud to re-create the experience of seventeenth-century New England Puritan congregations.

The Northern Colonies in the Seventeenth Century

1601–1700

- **Puritan Origins: The English Reformation** 105

- **Puritans and the Settlement of New England** 107
  The Pilgrims and Plymouth Colony 107
  The Founding of Massachusetts Bay Colony 108

- **The Evolution of New England Society** 112
  Church, Covenant, and Conformity 113
  Government by Puritans for Puritanism 115
  The Splintering of Puritanism 116
  Religious Controversies and Economic Changes 117

- **The Founding of the Middle Colonies** 120
  From New Netherland to New York 120
  New Jersey and Pennsylvania 124
  Toleration and Diversity in Pennsylvania 124

- **The Colonies and the English Empire** 126
  Royal Regulation of Colonial Trade 127
  King Philip's War and the Consolidation of Royal Authority 127

- **Conclusion: An English Model of Colonization in North America** 132

ROGER WILLIAMS AND HIS WIFE, MARY, arrived in Massachusetts in February 1631. Fresh from a superb education at Cambridge University, the twenty-eight-year-old Williams was "a godly [Puritan] minister," noted Governor John Winthrop. Winthrop's Boston church asked Williams to become its minister, but he refused because the church had not openly rejected the corrupt Church of England. New England's premier Puritan church was not pure enough for Williams.

Williams and his wife moved to Plymouth colony for two years. While there, he spent a great deal of time among the Narragansett Indians. "My soul's desire was to do the natives good," he said. Williams believed that "Nature knows no difference between Europeans and [Native] Americans in blood, birth, [or] bodies . . . God having made of one blood all mankind." He sought to learn about the Indians' language, religion, and **culture**, without trying to convert them to Christianity. Williams insisted that the colonists respect the Indians' religion and culture since all human beings—Christians and non-Christians alike—should live according to their consciences as revealed to them by God.

Williams condemned English colonists for their "sin of unjust usurpation" of Indian land. He believed that their claims were legally, morally, and spiritually invalid. In contrast, Massachusetts officials defended colonists' settlement on Indian land. If land "lies common, and hath never been replenished or subdued, [it] is free to any that possess or improve it," Governor Winthrop explained. Besides, he said, "if we leave [the Indians] sufficient [land] for their use, we may lawfully take the rest, there being more than enough for them and us." Winthrop's arguments prevailed, but Williams refused to knuckle under. "God Land," he said, "[is] as great a God with us English as God Gold was with the Spaniards." Although New Englanders claimed to worship the one true God in heaven, Williams declared, "the truth is the great Gods of this world are God-belly, God-peace, God-wealth, God-honour, [and] God-pleasure."

The governor of Plymouth colony, William Bradford, praised Williams as "a man godly and zealous, having many precious parts" and also "some strange opinions." Most New England leaders considered Williams a bit much. One minister censured him for his "self-conceited, and unquiet, and unlamblike frame of . . . Spirit." Williams, however, continued to proclaim his opinions and to refuse to submit lamblike to New England orthodoxy.

In 1633, Williams became the minister of the church in Salem, Massachusetts. Like other New England Puritans, the members of the Salem church had solemnly agreed to "**Covenant** with the Lord and one with another; and doe bynd our selves in the presence of God, to walke together in all his waies, according as he is pleased to reveale himself unto us in his Blessed word of truth [the Bible]." Most New England Puritans believed that churches and governments should enforce both godly belief and behavior according to biblical rules. They claimed that "the Word of God is . . . clear." In contrast, Williams believed that the Bible shrouded the Word of God in "mist and fog." Williams pointed out that devout and pious Christians could and did differ about what the Bible said and what God expected. That observation led him to denounce the emerging New England order as impure, ungodly, and tyrannical.

Williams also disagreed with the New England government's requirement that everyone attend church services. He argued that forcing people who were not Christians to attend church was wrong in four major ways. First, Williams preached, it was akin to requiring "a dead child to suck the breast, or a dead man [to] feast." The only way for any person to become a true Christian was by God's gift of faith revealed to the person's conscience. Second, churches should be reserved exclusively for those already converted, separating "holy from unholy . . . [and] godly from ungodly." He said requiring everybody to attend church was "False Worshipping" that promoted "spiritual drunkenness and whoredom, a soul sleep and a soul sickness." Third, the government had no business ruling on spiritual matters. Williams termed New England's regulation of religious behavior "spiritual rape" that inevitably would lead governments to use coercion and violence to enforce the government's misguided ways. Finally, Williams believed that governments should tolerate all religious beliefs because only God knows the Truth; no person and no religion can understand God with absolute certainty. "I commend that man," Williams wrote, "whether Jew, or Turk, or Papist, or whoever, that steers no otherwise than his conscience dares." In Williams's view, toleration of religious belief and liberty of conscience were the only paths to religious purity and political harmony.

New England's leaders denounced Williams's arguments. One minister wrote that Williams sought "liberty to enfranchise all false Religions," which was "the greatest impiety in the World." Genuine **liberty**, he said, was "to contend earnestly for the Truth; to preserve unity of Spirit, Faith, ordinances, to be all like minded, of one accord." Like-minded New Englanders banished Williams for his "extreme and dangerous" opinions. He escaped from an attempt to ship him back to England and in the winter of 1636 spent fourteen weeks walking south to Narragansett Bay, "exposed to the mercy of an howling Wilderness in Frost and Snow." There he founded the colony of Rhode Island, which enshrined "Liberty of Conscience" as a fundamental ideal and became a refuge for other dissenters.

Although New England's leaders expelled Williams from their holy commonwealth, his dissenting ideas arose from orthodox Puritan doctrines. By urging believers to search for evidence of God's grace, **Puritanism** encouraged the faithful to listen for God's whisper of Truth and faith. Puritanism combined rigid insistence on conformity to God's law and aching uncertainty about how to identify and act upon it. Despite the best efforts of New England's leaders to define their way as God's Way, Puritanism inspired believers such as Roger Williams to draw their own conclusions and stick to them.

During the seventeenth century, New England's Puritan zeal—exemplified by Roger Williams and his persecutors—cooled. The goal of founding a holy New England faded. Late in the century, new "middle" colonies—New York, New Jersey, and Pennsylvania—featuring greater religious and ethnic diversity than New England were founded. Religion remained important throughout all the colonies, but it competed with the growing faith that the promise of a better life required less focus on salvation and more attention to worldly concerns of family, work, and trade.

As settler populations increased throughout the English mainland colonies, settlements encroached on Indian land, causing violent conflict to flare up repeatedly. Political conflict also arose among colonists, particularly in response to major political upheavals in England. By the end of the seventeenth century, the English monarchy exerted greater control over North America and the rest of its Atlantic empire. The lifeblood of the empire, however, remained the continual flow of products, people, and ideas that pulsed between England and the colonies, energizing both.

Puritan Origins: The English Reformation

The religious roots of the Puritans who founded New England reached back to the Protestant Reformation, which arose in Germany in 1517 (see chapter 2). The **Reformation** spread quickly to other countries, but the English church initially remained within the Catholic fold and continued its allegiance to the pope in Rome. King Henry VIII, who reigned from 1509 to 1547, understood that the Reformation offered him an opportunity to break with Rome and take control of the church in England. In 1534, Henry formally initiated the English Reformation. At his insistence, Parliament passed the Act of Supremacy, which outlawed the Catholic Church and proclaimed the king "the only supreme head on earth of the Church of England." Henry seized the vast properties of the Catholic Church in England as well as the privilege of appointing bishops and others in the church hierarchy.

In the short run, the English Reformation allowed Henry VIII to achieve his political goal of controlling the church. In the long run, however, the Reformation brought to England the political and religious turmoil that Henry had hoped to avoid. Henry himself sought no more than a halfway Reformation. Protestant doctrines held no attraction for Henry; in almost all matters of religious belief and practice, he remained an orthodox Catholic. Many English Catholics wanted to revoke the English Reformation; they hoped to return the Church of England to the pope and to restore Catholic doctrines and ceremonies. But many other English people insisted on a genuine, thoroughgoing Reformation; these people came to be called Puritans.

During the sixteenth century, Puritanism was less an organized movement than a set of ideas and religious principles that appealed strongly to many dissenting members of the Church of England. They sought to purify the Church of England by eliminating what they considered the offensive features of Catholicism. For example, they demanded that the church hierarchy be abolished and that ordinary Christians be given greater control over religious life. They wanted to do away with the rituals of

English Monarchy and the Protestant Reformation

1509–1547	Henry VIII	Leads the English Reformation, outlawing the Catholic Church in England and establishing the English monarch as supreme head of the Church of England.
1547–1553	Edward VI	Moves religious reform in a Protestant direction.
1553–1558	Mary I	Outlaws Protestantism and strives to reestablish the Catholic Church in England.
1558–1603	Elizabeth I	Reaffirms the English Reformation and tries to position the Church of England between extremes of Catholicism and Protestantism.
1603–1625	James I	Authorizes a new, Protestant translation of the Bible but is unsympathetic to Puritan reformers.
1625–1649	Charles I	Continues James I's move away from the ideas of Puritan reformers. Puritan-dominated Parliament orders his beheading during the Puritan Revolution.
1642		Puritan Revolution (English Civil War) begins.
1644–1660	Oliver Cromwell	Leads Puritan side to victory in the English Civil War. Parliament proclaims England a Puritan republic (1649) and declares Cromwell the nation's "Lord Protector" (1653).
1660–1685	Charles II	Restored to the monarchy by Parliament and attempts to enforce religious toleration of Catholics and Protestant dissenters from the Church of England.
1685–1688	James II	Mounts aggressive campaign to appoint Catholics to government posts, then flees to France when English Protestants in Parliament offer the throne to his Dutch son-in-law, William. The peaceful accession of William and his wife (the daughter of James II) as corulers is called the "Glorious Revolution" (1688).
1689–1694	William III and Mary II	Reassert Protestant influence in England and its empire.

Queen Elizabeth's Funeral Procession
The death of Elizabeth I in 1603 created uncertainty about the balance of Protestantism and Catholicism in England. Since Elizabeth had no children, James, the son of the staunch Catholic queen Mary II, assumed the throne and soon cracked down on Protestants, especially Puritans. This contemporary painting shows Elizabeth's casket, with a gilded effigy of her on the lid, pulled by four steeds and shaded by a black canopy held aloft by knights. The knights are surrounded by courtiers carrying flags emblazoned with royal insignia. The funeral procession combined mourning with an opulent display of royal magnificence, reminding viewers that the splendor of the monarchy would survive the death of the queen.
Courtesy of the Trustees of the British Library.

Catholic worship and instead emphasize an individual's relationship with God developed through Bible study, prayer, and introspection. Although there were many varieties and degrees of Puritanism, all Puritans shared a desire to make the English church thoroughly Protestant.

The fate of **Protestantism** waxed and waned under the monarchs who succeeded Henry VIII. When he died in 1547, the advisers of the new king, Edward VI—the nine-year-old son of Henry and his third wife, Jane Seymour—initiated religious reforms that moved in a Protestant direction. The tide of reform reversed in 1553 when Edward died and was succeeded by Mary I, the daughter of Henry and Catherine of Aragon, his first wife. Mary was a steadfast Catholic, and shortly after becoming queen, she married Philip II of Spain, Europe's most powerful guardian of Catholicism. Mary attempted to restore the pre-Reformation Catholic Church. She outlawed Protestantism in England and persecuted those who refused to conform, sentencing almost three hundred to burn at the stake.

The tide turned again in 1558 when Mary died and was succeeded by Elizabeth I, the daughter of Henry and his second wife, Anne Boleyn. During her long reign, Elizabeth reaffirmed the English Reformation and tried to position the English church between the extremes of Catholicism and Puritanism. Like her father, she was less concerned with theology than with politics. Above all, she desired a church that would strengthen the monarchy and the nation. By the time Elizabeth died in 1603, many people in England looked on Protestantism as a defining feature of national identity.

When Elizabeth's successor, James I, became king, English Puritans petitioned for further reform of the Church of England. James authorized a new translation of the Bible, known ever since as the King James version. However, neither James I nor his son Charles I, who became king in 1625, was receptive to the ideas of Puritan reformers. James and Charles moved the Church of England away from Puritanism. They enforced conformity to the Church of England and punished dissenters, both ordinary Christians and ministers. In 1629, Charles I dissolved Parliament—where Puritans were well represented—and initiated aggressive anti-Puritan policies. Many Puritans despaired about continuing to defend their faith in England and began to make plans to emigrate. Some left for Europe, others for the West Indies. The largest number set out for America.

REVIEW Why did Henry VIII initiate the English Reformation?

Puritans and the Settlement of New England

Puritans who emigrated aspired to escape the turmoil and persecution of England and to build a new, orderly, Puritan version of England. Puritans established the first small settlement in New England in 1620, followed a few years later by additional settlements by the Massachusetts Bay Company. Allowed self-government through royal charter, these Puritans were in a unique position to direct the new colonies according to their faith. Their faith shaped the colonies they established in almost every way. Although many New England colonists were not Puritans, Puritanism remained a paramount influence in New England's religion, politics, and community life during the seventeenth century.

The Pilgrims and Plymouth Colony

One of the first Protestant groups to emigrate, later known as Pilgrims, espoused a heresy known as separatism. These Separatists sought to withdraw—or separate—from the Church of England, which they considered hopelessly corrupt. In 1608, they moved to Holland; by 1620, they realized that they could not live and worship there as they had hoped. William Bradford, a leader of the group, recalled that "many of their children, by . . . the great licentiousness of youth in [Holland], and the manifold temptations of the place, were drawn away by evil examples." Bradford and other Separatists believed that America promised to better protect their children's piety and preserve their community. Separatists obtained permission to settle in the extensive territory granted to the Virginia Company (see chapter 3). To finance their journey, they formed a joint stock company with English investors. The investors provided the capital; the Separatists provided their labor and lives and received a share of the profits for seven years. In August 1620, the Pilgrim families boarded the *Mayflower*, and after eleven weeks at sea, all but one of the 102 immigrants arrived at the outermost tip of Cape Cod, in present-day Massachusetts.

The Pilgrims realized immediately that they had landed far north of the Virginia grants and had no legal authority to settle in the area. To provide order and security as well as a claim to legitimacy, they drew up the Mayflower Compact on the day they arrived. They pledged to "covenant and combine ourselves together into a civil Body Politick, for our better Ordering and Preservation." The signers (all men) agreed to enact and obey necessary and just laws.

The Pilgrims settled at Plymouth and elected William Bradford their governor. That first winter "was most sad and lamentable," Bradford wrote later. "In two or three months' time half of [our] company died . . . being the depth of winter, and wanting houses and other comforts [and] being infected with scurvy and other diseases."

In the spring, Wampanoag Indians rescued the floundering Plymouth settlement. First Samoset, then Squanto befriended the settlers. Both of them had learned English from previous contacts with sailors and fishermen who had visited the coast to dry fish and make repairs years before the Plymouth settlers arrived. Samoset arranged for the Pilgrims to meet and establish good relations with Massasoit, the Wampanoag chief whose territory included Plymouth. Squanto, Bradford recalled, "was a special instrument sent of God for their [the Pilgrims'] good. . . . He directed them how to set their corn, where to take fish, and to procure other commodities, and was also their pilot to bring them to unknown places." With the Indians' guidance, the Pilgrims managed to harvest enough food to guarantee their survival through the coming winter, an occasion they celebrated in the fall of 1621 with a feast of thanksgiving attended by Massasoit and other Wampanoags.

Still, the Plymouth colony remained precarious. Only seven dwellings were erected that first year; half the original colonists died; and a new group of threadbare, sickly settlers arrived in November 1621, requiring the colony to adopt stringent food rationing. The colonists quarreled with their London investors, who became frustrated when Plymouth failed to produce the expected profits. These struggles to survive constantly frustrated the London investors, but the Pilgrims persisted, living simply and coexisting in relative peace with the Indians. They paid the Wampanoags when settlers gradually encroached on Indian land. By 1630, Plymouth had become a small permanent settlement, but it failed to attract many other English Puritans.

> That first winter "was most sad and lamentable," Bradford wrote later. "In two or three months' time half of [our] company died . . . being the depth of winter, and wanting houses and other comforts [and] being infected with scurvy and other diseases."

The Founding of Massachusetts Bay Colony

In 1629, shortly before Charles I dissolved Parliament, a group of Puritan merchants and country gentlemen obtained a royal charter for the Massachusetts Bay Company. The charter provided the usual privileges granted to joint stock companies, including land for **colonization** that spanned present-day Massachusetts, New Hampshire, Vermont, Maine, and upstate New York. In addition, a unique provision of the charter permitted the government of the Massachusetts Bay Company to be located in the colony rather than in England. This provision allowed Puritans to exchange their status as a harassed minority in England for self-government in Massachusetts.

To lead the emigrants, the stockholders of the Massachusetts Bay Company elected John Winthrop, a prosperous lawyer and landowner, to serve as governor. In March 1630, eleven ships crammed with seven hundred passengers sailed for Massachusetts; six more ships and another five hundred emigrants followed a few months later. Winthrop's fleet arrived in Massachusetts Bay in early June. Unlike the Separatists, Winthrop's Puritans aspired to reform the corrupt Church of England (rather than separate from it) by setting an example of godliness in the New World. Winthrop and a small group chose to settle on the peninsula that became Boston, and other settlers clustered at promising locations nearby (Map 4.1).

In a sermon to his companions aboard the *Arbella* while they were still at sea—probably the most famous sermon in American history—Winthrop proclaimed the cosmic significance of their journey. The Puritans had "entered into a covenant" with God to "work out our salvation under the power and purity of his holy ordinances," Winthrop declared. This sanctified agreement with God meant that the Puritans had to make "extraordinary" efforts to "bring into familiar and constant practice" religious principles that most people in England merely preached. To achieve their pious goals, the Puritans had to subordinate their individual interests to the common good. "We must be knit together in this work as one man," Winthrop preached. "We must delight in each other, make others' conditions our own, rejoice together, mourn together, labor and suffer together." The stakes could not be higher, Winthrop told his listeners: "We must consider that we shall be as a city upon a hill. The eyes of all people are upon us."

That belief shaped seventeenth-century New England as profoundly as tobacco shaped the Chesapeake. Winthrop's vision of a city on a hill fired the Puritans' fierce determination to keep their covenant and live according to God's laws, unlike the backsliders and compromisers who accommodated to the Church of England. Their determination to adhere strictly to God's plan charged nearly every feature of life in seventeenth-century New England with a distinctive, high-voltage piety.

Seal of Massachusetts Bay Colony

In 1629, the Massachusetts Bay Company designed this seal depicting an Indian man inviting English settlers to "come over and help us." Of course, such an invitation was never issued. The seal was an attempt to lend an aura of altruism to the Massachusetts Bay Company's colonization efforts. In English eyes, the Indian man obviously needed help. The only signs that he was more civilized than the pine trees flanking him are his girdle of leaves, his bow and arrow, and his miraculous use of English. In reality, colonists in Massachusetts and elsewhere were far less interested in helping Indians than in helping themselves. For the most part, that suited the Indians, who wanted no "help" from the colonists. Courtesy of Massachusetts Archives.

READING THE IMAGE: What does the seal demonstrate regarding the English view of the Indians?

CONNECTIONS: How did the viewpoint represented by the seal affect colonization in the Americas? What were the English expecting to find when they traveled to America, and in what ways were those expectations not met?

FOR MORE HELP ANALYZING THIS IMAGE, see the visual activity for this chapter in the Online Study Guide at bedfordstmartins.com/roark.

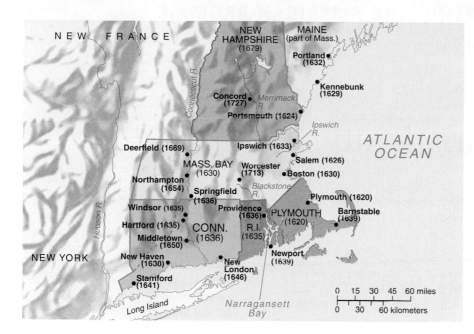

MAP 4.1   New England Colonies in the Seventeenth Century
New Englanders spread across the landscape town by town during the seventeenth century. (For the sake of legibility, only a few of the more important towns are shown on the map.)

READING THE MAP: Using the dates on the map, create a chronology of the establishment of towns in New England. What physical features correspond to the earliest habitation by English settlers?

CONNECTIONS: Why were towns so much more a feature of seventeenth-century New England than of the Chesapeake (see also chapter 3)? How did Puritan dissent influence the settlement of New England colonies?

FOR MORE HELP ANALYZING THIS MAP, see the map activity for this chapter in the Online Study Guide at bedfordstmartins.com/roark.

The new colonists, as Winthrop's son John wrote later, had "all things to do, as in the beginning of the world." Unlike the early Chesapeake settlers, the first Massachusetts Bay colonists encountered few Indians because the local population had been almost entirely exterminated by an epidemic probably caused by contact with Europeans more than a decade earlier. Still, as in the Chesapeake, the colonists fell victim to deadly ailments. More than two hundred settlers died during the first year, including one of Winthrop's sons and eleven of his servants. About the same number returned to England on the first outbound ship in the spring of 1631. But Winthrop maintained a confidence that proved infectious. He wrote to his wife, "I like so well to be heer as I do not repent my comminge. . . . I would not have altered my course, though I had foreseene all these Afflictions." And each year from 1630 to 1640, ship after ship followed in the wake of Winthrop's fleet. In all, more than twenty thousand new settlers came, their eyes focused on the Puritans' city on a hill.

Often, when the Church of England cracked down on a Puritan minister in England, he and many of his followers moved together to New England. Smaller groups of English Puritans moved to the Chesapeake, Barbados, and elsewhere in the New World, including New Amsterdam (present-day New York). By 1640, New England had one of the highest ratios of preachers to population in all of Christendom. A few ministers sought to carry the message of Christianity to the Indians, accompanied by instructions replacing what missionary John Eliot termed the Indians' "unfixed, confused, and ungoverned . . . life, uncivilized and unsubdued to labor and order." (See "Documenting the American Promise," page 110.) For the most part, however, the colonists focused less on saving Indians' souls than on saving their own.

The occupations of New England immigrants reflected the social origins of English Puritans. On the whole, the immigrants came from the middle ranks of English society. The vast majority of immigrants were either farmers or tradesmen, including carpenters, tailors, and textile workers. Indentured servants, whose numbers dominated the Chesapeake settlers, accounted for only about a fifth of those headed for New England. Most New England immigrants paid their way to Massachusetts, even though the journey often took their life savings. They were encouraged by the promise of bounty in New England reported in Winthrop's letter to his son: "Here is as good land as I have seen there [in England]. . . . Here can be no want of anything to those who bring means to raise [it] out of the earth and sea."

In contrast to Chesapeake newcomers, New England immigrants usually arrived as families. In fact, more Puritans came with family members than did any other group of immigrants in all of American history. A ship that left Weymouth, England, in 1635, for example, carried 106 passengers, 98 of whom belonged to one of 14 families typically comprising a husband, a wife, children, and sometimes a servant. Unlike immigrants to the Chesapeake, women and children made up a solid majority in New England.

King Philip Considers Christianity

Beginning in 1646, the Puritan minister John Eliot served as a missionary to New England's Indians, trying to teach the doctrines of Christianity and proper English behavior. During his half-century tenure as leader of the Puritan congregation in Roxbury, Massachusetts, Eliot studied the languages, customs, and beliefs of Native Americans, hoping to help them along the path to Christian piety and to strengthen them against the colonists' unscrupulous encroachment on their land. The efforts of Eliot and other missionaries convinced some Indians to leave their own communities and settle in "praying towns" populated by Native Americans who had agreed to live in conformity with English ways. Most Indians, however, did not move into praying towns or adopt the faith or manners of the colonists.

In Indian Dialogues, a book published in 1671, Eliot illustrated the challenge he and other missionaries confronted as they tried to convince Native Americans of the errors of their ways. Based on decades of missionary experience, Eliot created imaginary conversations between converted Indians and those who resisted Christianity. Eliot's invented conversations echoed arguments that he and other missionaries had encountered repeatedly. The following selection from an imaginary dialogue between two praying Indians, Anthony and William, and King Philip (or Metacomet), the chief (or sachem) of the powerful Wampanoags, documents Eliot's perception of the attractions of Christianity and one Indian leader's doubts about it— doubts that ultimately prevailed when

King Philip led the Wampanoags in an all-out attack against the settlers in 1675.

Anthony: Sachem, we salute you in the Lord, and we declare unto you, that we are sent by the church, in the name of our Lord Jesus Christ, to call you, and beseech you to turn from your vain conversation unto God, to pray unto God, and to believe in Jesus Christ for the pardon of your sins, and for the salvation of your soul. . . . So we are come this day unto you, in the name of Jesus Christ, to call you to come unto the Lord, and serve him. . . . We hear that many of your people do desire to pray to God, only they depend on you. We pray you to consider that your love to your people should oblige you to do them all the good you can. . . . You will not only yourself turn from sin unto God . . . , but all your people will turn to God with you, so that you may say unto the Lord, oh Lord Jesus, behold here am I, and all the people which thou hast given me. We all come unto thy service, and promise to pray unto God so long as we live. . . . Oh how happy will all your people be. . . . It will be a joy to all the English magistrates, and ministers, and churches, and good people of the land, to hear that Philip and all his people are turned to God, and become praying Indians. . . .

Philip: Often have I heard of this great matter of praying unto God,

and hitherto I have refused. . . . Mr. Eliot himself did come unto me. He was in this town, and did persuade me. But we were then in our sports, wherein I have much delighted, and in that temptation, I confess, I did neglect and despise the offer, and lost that opportunity. Since that time God hath afflicted and chastised me, and my heart doth begin to break. And I have some serious thoughts of accepting the offer, and turning to God, to become a praying Indian, I myself and all my people. But I have some great objections, which I cannot tell how to get over, which are still like great rocks in my way, over which I cannot climb. And if I should, I fear I shall fall down the precipice on the further side, and be spoiled and undone. By venturing to climb, I shall catch a deadly fall to me and my posterity.

The first objection that I have is this, because you praying Indians do reject your sachems, and refuse to pay them tribute, in so much that if any of my people turn to pray unto God, I do reckon that I have lost him. He will no longer own me for his sachem, nor pay me any tribute. And hence it will come to pass, that if I should pray to God, and all my people with me, I must become as a common man among them, and so lose all my power and authority over them. This is such a temptation as . . . I, nor any of the other great sachems, can tell how to get over. Were this temptation removed, the way would be more easy and open for me to turn praying Indian.

I begin to have some good likance of the way, but I am loth to buy it at so dear a rate.

William: . . . I say, if any of the praying Indians should be disobedient (in lawful things) and refuse to pay tribute unto their sachems, it is not their religion and praying to God that teaches them so to do, but their corruptions. . . . I am sure the word of God commandeth all to be subject to the higher powers, and pay them tribute. . . . And therefore, beloved sachem, let not your heart fear that praying to God will alienate your people from you . . . for the more beneficent you are unto them, the more obligation you lay upon them. And what greater beneficence can you do unto them than to further them in religion, whereby they may be converted, pardoned, sanctified, and saved? . . .

Philip: I have another objection stronger than this, and that is, if I pray to God, then all my men that are willing to pray to God will (as you say) stick to me, and be true to me. But all such as love not and care not to pray to God, especially such as hate praying to God, all these will forsake me, yea will go and adjoin themselves unto other sachems that pray not to God. And so it will come to pass, that if I be a praying sachem, I shall be a poor and weak one, and easily trod upon by others, who are like to be more potent and numerous. And by this means my tribute will be small, and my people few, and I

shall be a great loser by praying to God. In the way I am now, I am full and potent, but if I change my way and pray to God, I shall be empty and weak. . . .

William: . . . Suppose all your subjects that hate praying to God should leave you. What shall you lose by it? You are rid of such as by their sins vitiate others, and multiply transgression, and provoke the wrath of God against you and yours. But consider what you shall gain by praying to God. . . . All the praying Indians will rejoice at it, and be your friends, and they are not a few. . . . [And] you shall gain a more intimate love of the Governor, and Magistrates. . . . They will more honor, respect, and love you, than ever they did. . . . The Governor and Magistrates of the Massachusetts will own you, and be fatherly and friendly to you. . . . Yea more, the King of England, and the great peers who . . . yearly send over means to encourage and promote our praying to God, they will take notice of you.

Philip: I perceive that in your praying to God, and in your churches, all are brought to an equality. Sachems and people they are all fellow brethren in your churches. Poor and rich are equally privileged. The vote of the lowest of the people hath as much weight as the vote of the sachem. Now I doubt [worry] that this way will lift up the heart of the poor to too much boldness, and debase the rulers to[o] low. This bringing all to

an equality will bring all to a confusion. . . . There is yet another thing that I am much afraid of, and that is your church admonitions and excommunications. I hear that your sachems are under that yoke. I am a sinful man as well as others, but if I must be admonished by the church, who are my subjects, I know not how I shall like that. I doubt [worry] it will be a bitter pill, too hard for me to get down and swallow. . . . I feel your words sink into my heart and stick there. You speak arrows. . . . I desire to ponder and consider of these things. . . . I am willing they should still lie soaking in my heart and mind.

SOURCE: John Eliot, *Indian Dialogues* (Cambridge, 1671), in Henry W. Bowden and James P. Ronda, eds., *John Eliot's Indian Dialogues: A Study in Cultural Interaction*, 120–31. Copyright © 1980. Reproduced with permission of Greenwood Publishing Group, Inc., Westport, CT.

QUESTIONS FOR ANALYSIS AND DEBATE

1. To what degree is Eliot's dialogue a reliable guide to Philip's doubts about the wisdom of becoming a praying Indian?

2. According to Eliot, was Philip's religion a stumbling block to his acceptance of Christianity? What made Philip fear that he would "fall down the precipice"?

3. If Philip had written a dialogue proposing that Eliot convert to the Wampanoag way of life, what arguments might he have made?

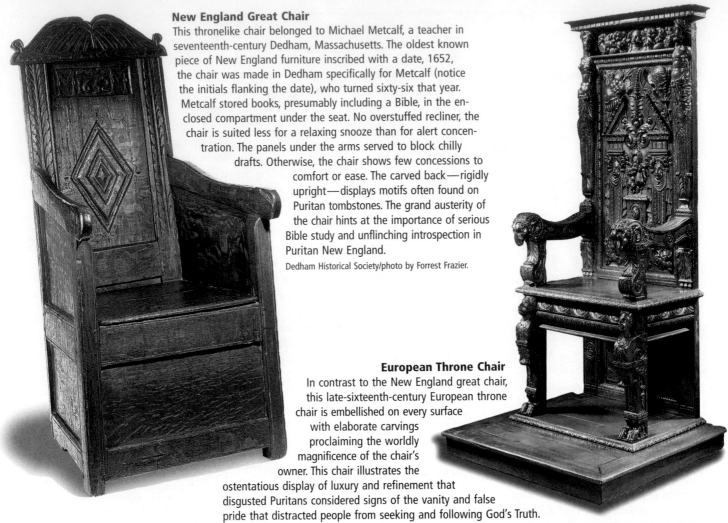

New England Great Chair

This thronelike chair belonged to Michael Metcalf, a teacher in seventeenth-century Dedham, Massachusetts. The oldest known piece of New England furniture inscribed with a date, 1652, the chair was made in Dedham specifically for Metcalf (notice the initials flanking the date), who turned sixty-six that year. Metcalf stored books, presumably including a Bible, in the enclosed compartment under the seat. No overstuffed recliner, the chair is suited less for a relaxing snooze than for alert concentration. The panels under the arms served to block chilly drafts. Otherwise, the chair shows few concessions to comfort or ease. The carved back—rigidly upright—displays motifs often found on Puritan tombstones. The grand austerity of the chair hints at the importance of serious Bible study and unflinching introspection in Puritan New England.

Dedham Historical Society/photo by Forrest Frazier.

European Throne Chair

In contrast to the New England great chair, this late-sixteenth-century European throne chair is embellished on every surface with elaborate carvings proclaiming the worldly magnificence of the chair's owner. This chair illustrates the ostentatious display of luxury and refinement that disgusted Puritans considered signs of the vanity and false pride that distracted people from seeking and following God's Truth.

Courtesy of Huntington Antiques Ltd., Gloucestershire, England.

As Winthrop reminded the first settlers in his *Arbella* sermon, each family was a "little commonwealth" that mirrored the hierarchy among all God's creatures. Just as humankind was subordinate to God, so young people were subordinate to their elders, children to their parents, and wives to their husbands. The immigrants' family ties reinforced their religious beliefs with universally understood notions of hierarchy and mutual dependence. Whereas immigrants to the Chesapeake were disciplined mostly by the coercions of servitude and the caprices of the tobacco market, immigrants to New England entered a social order defined by the interlocking institutions of family, church, and community.

REVIEW Why did the Puritans immigrate to North America?

The Evolution of New England Society

The New England colonists, unlike their counterparts in the Chesapeake, settled in small towns, usually located on the coast or by a river (see Map 4.1). Massachusetts Bay colonists founded 133 towns during the seventeenth century, each with one or more churches. Church members' fervent piety, buttressed by the institutions of local government, enforced remarkable religious and social conformity in the small New England settlements. During the century, tensions within the Puritan faith and changes in New England communities splintered religious orthodoxy and weakened Puritan zeal. By 1700, however, Puritanism still maintained a distinctive influence in New England.

Church, Covenant, and Conformity

Puritans believed that the church consisted of men and women who had entered a solemn covenant with one another and with God. Winthrop and three other men signed the original covenant of the first Boston church in 1630, agreeing to "Promisse, and bind our selves, to walke in all our wayes according to the Rule of the Gospell, and in all sincere Conformity to His holy Ordinaunces." Each new member of the covenant had to persuade existing members that she or he had fully experienced conversion. By 1635, the Boston church had added more than 250 names to the four original subscribers to the covenant.

Puritans embraced a distinctive version of Protestantism derived from **Calvinism**, the doctrines of John Calvin, a sixteenth-century Swiss Protestant theologian. Calvin insisted that Christians strictly discipline their behavior to conform to God's commandments announced in the Bible. Like Calvin, Puritans believed in **predestination**—the idea that the all-powerful God, before the creation of the world, decided which few human souls would receive eternal life. Only God knows the identity of these fortunate, predestined individuals—the "elect" or "saints." Nothing a person did in his or her lifetime could alter God's inscrutable choice or provide assurance that the person was predestined for salvation with the elect or damned to hell with the doomed multitude. The gloomy inevitability and exclusivity of predestination contrasted sharply with Catholic doctrines that all human beings could potentially be granted eternal life by God, acting through the Catholic Church.

Despite the looming uncertainty about God's choice of the elect, Puritans believed that if a person lived a rigorously godly life—constantly winning the daily battle against sinful temptations—his or her behavior was likely to be a hint, a visible sign, that he or she was one of God's chosen few. Puritans thought that "sainthood" would become visible in individuals' behavior, especially if they were privileged to know God's Word as revealed in the Bible.

The connection between sainthood and saintly behavior, however, was far from certain. Some members of the elect, Puritans believed, had not heard God's Word as revealed in the Bible, and therefore their behavior did not necessarily signal their sainthood. One reason Puritans required all town residents to attend church services was to enlighten anyone who was ignorant of God's Truth. The slippery relationship between saintly behavior—observable by anybody—and God's predestined election—invisible and unknowable to anyone—caused Puritans to worry constantly that individuals who acted like saints were fooling themselves and others. Nevertheless, Puritans thought that "visible saints"—persons who passed their demanding tests of conversion and church membership—probably, though not certainly, were among God's elect.

Members of Puritan churches ardently hoped that God had chosen them to receive eternal life

The Puritan Challenge to the Status Quo
The World Turn'd Upside Down, a pamphlet printed in London in 1647, satirizes the Puritan notion that the contemporary world was deeply flawed. The pamphlet refers to the "distracted Times" of the Puritan Revolution in England. The drawing on the title page ridicules criticisms of English society that also were common among New England Puritans.
By permission of The British Library.

READING THE IMAGE: The drawing shows at least a dozen examples of the conventional world of seventeenth-century England turned upside down. Can you identify them?
CONNECTIONS: Puritans would claim that the artist had it wrong—that the conventional world turned God's order upside down. How might the drawing have been different if a devout Puritan had drawn it?

FOR MORE HELP ANALYZING THIS IMAGE, see the visual activity for this chapter in the Online Study Guide at bedfordstmartins.com/roark.

Remember that thou keepe holy ye Sabboth Day
The profane Iſralite, that durſt aſſay,
In gathering ſticks, to breake the Sabboth day,
Is ſtonde to death, for like Contumacy
The Lord hath ſworne, that every Soule ſhall dye.

A Woman and her two Daughters pill and dry
flax on the Lords day, are all burnt

Sabbath Breakers

These seventeenth-century prints show some of the punishments to which Sabbath breakers could be subjected by man and God. In the upper illustration, a person who gathered sticks on the Sabbath is stoned to death as Puritans believed the Bible commanded. In the lower print, three women who broke the Sabbath by preparing flax to be spun and woven into linen suffer God's retribution when they are burned to death. New Englanders differed about exactly when the Sabbath began. Some thought it started at sunset on Saturday evening, but John Winthrop believed the Sabbath began about three o'clock Saturday afternoon. Given the extreme punishments inflicted on Sabbath breakers, New Englanders needed to be careful about what they did between Saturday afternoon and Monday morning.

Divine Examples of God's Severe Judgements upon Sabbath-Breakers (London, 1671).

and tried to demonstrate saintly behavior. Their covenant bound them to help each other attain salvation and to discipline the entire community by saintly standards. Church members kept an eye on the behavior of everybody in town. Infractions of morality, order, or propriety were reported to Puritan elders, who summoned the wayward to a church inquiry. By overseeing every aspect of life, the visible saints enforced a remarkable degree of righteous conformity in Puritan communities. Total conformity, however, was never achieved. Ardent Puritans differed among themselves; non-Puritans shirked orthodox rules. But Puritan doctrine spelled out the fiery punishment for failure to conform: A servant in Roxbury declared that "if hell were ten times hotter, [I] had rather be there than [I] would serve [my] master."

Despite the central importance of religion, churches played no direct role in the civil government of New England communities. Puritans did not want to mimic the Church of England, which they considered a puppet of the king rather than an independent body that served the Lord. They were determined to insulate New England churches from the contaminating influence of the civil state and its merely human laws. Although ministers were the most highly respected figures in New England towns, they were prohibited from holding government office.

Puritans had no qualms, however, about their religious beliefs influencing New England governments. As much as possible, the Puritans tried to bring public life into conformity with their view of God's law. For example, fines were issued for Sabbath-breaking activities such as working, traveling, playing a flute, smoking a pipe, and visiting neighbors.

Puritans mandated other purifications of what they considered corrupt English practices. They refused to celebrate Christmas or Easter because the Bible did not mention either one. They outlawed religious wedding ceremonies; couples were married by a magistrate in a civil ceremony (the first wedding in Massachusetts performed by a minister occurred in 1686). They prohibited elaborate clothing and finery such as lace trim and short sleeves—"whereby the nakedness of the arm may be discovered." They banned cards, dice, shuffleboard, and other games of chance, as well as music and dancing. The distinguished minister

Increase Mather insisted that "Mixt or Promiscuous Dancing . . . of Men and Women" could not be tolerated since "the unchaste Touches and Gesticulations used by Dancers have a palpable tendency to that which is evil." On special occasions, Puritans proclaimed days of fasting and humiliation, which, as one preacher boasted, amounted to "so many Sabbaths more."

Government by Puritans for Puritanism

It is only a slight exaggeration to say that seventeenth-century New England was governed by Puritans for Puritanism. The charter of the Massachusetts Bay Company empowered the company's stockholders, known as freemen, to meet as a body known as the General Court and make the laws needed to govern the company's affairs. The colonists transformed this arrangement for running a joint stock company into a structure for governing the colony. Hoping to ensure that godly men would decide government policies, the General Court expanded the number of freemen in 1631 to include all male church members. Only freemen had the right to vote for governor, deputy governor, and other colonial officials. As new settlers were recognized as freemen, the size of the General Court grew too large to meet conveniently. So in 1634, the freemen in each town agreed to send two deputies to the General Court to act as the colony's legislative assembly. All other men were classified as "inhabitants," and they had the right to vote, hold office, and participate fully in town government.

A "town meeting," composed of a town's inhabitants and freemen, chose the selectmen and other officials who administered local affairs. New England town meetings routinely practiced a level of popular participation in political life that was unprecedented elsewhere in the world during the seventeenth century. Almost every adult man could speak out in town meetings and fortify his voice with a vote. However, all women—even church members—were prohibited from voting, and towns did not permit "contrary-minded" men to become or remain inhabitants. Although town meeting participants wrangled from time to time, widespread political participation tended to reinforce conformity to Puritan ideals.

One of the most important functions of New England government was land distribution. Settlers who desired to establish a new town entered a covenant and petitioned the General Court for a grant of land. The court granted town sites to suitably pious petitioners but did not allow settlement until the Indians who inhabited a grant agreed to relinquish their claim to the land, usually in exchange for manufactured goods. For instance, William Pynchon purchased the site of Springfield, Massachusetts, from the Agawam Indians for "eighteen fathams [arm's lengths] of Wampum, eighteen coates, 18 hatchets, 18 hoes, [and] 18 knives."

Old Ship Meeting House
Built in Hingham, Massachusetts, in 1681, this meetinghouse is one of the oldest surviving buildings used for church services in English North America. The unadorned walls and windows reflect the austere religious aesthetic of New England Puritanism. The family pews mark boundaries of kinship and piety visible to all. The elevated pulpit bathed in light signals the illumination of God's Word as preached by the minister.
Old Ship Church, Hingham, MA, photo by Bruce Benedict.

Having obtained their grant, town founders apportioned land among themselves and any newcomers they permitted to join them. Normally, each family received a house lot large enough for an adjacent garden as well as one or more strips of agricultural land on the perimeter of the town. Although there was a considerable difference between the largest and smallest family plots, most clustered in the middle range—roughly fifty to one hundred acres—resulting in a more nearly equal distribution of land in New England than in the Chesapeake.

The physical layout of New England towns encouraged settlers to look inward toward their neighbors, multiplying the opportunities for godly vigilance. Most people considered the forest that lay just beyond every settler's house an alien environment that was interrupted here and there by those oases of civilization, the towns. Footpaths connecting one town to another were so rudimentary that even John Winthrop once got lost within half a mile of his house and spent a sleepless night in the forest, circling the light of his small campfire and singing psalms.

The Splintering of Puritanism

Almost from the beginning, John Winthrop and other leaders had difficulty enforcing their views of Puritan orthodoxy. In England, persecution as a dissenting minority had unified Puritan voices in opposition to the Church of England. In New England, the promise of a godly society and the Puritans' emphasis on individual Bible study led New Englanders toward different visions of godliness. Puritan leaders, however, interpreted dissent as an error caused either by a misguided believer or by the malevolent power of Satan. Whatever the cause, errors could not be tolerated. As one Puritan minister proclaimed, "The Scripture saith . . . there is no Truth but one."

Shortly after banishing Roger Williams, Winthrop confronted another dissenter, this time a devout Puritan woman steeped in Scripture and absorbed by religious questions: Anne Hutchinson. The mother of fourteen children, Hutchinson served her neighbors as a skilled midwife. After she settled into her new home in Boston in 1634, women gathered there to hear her weekly lectures on recent sermons. As one listener observed, she was a "Woman that Preaches better Gospell then any of your black-coates . . . [from] the Ninneversity." As the months passed, Hutchinson began to lecture twice a week, and crowds of sixty to eighty women and men gathered to listen to her.

Hutchinson expounded on the sermons of John Cotton, her favorite minister. Cotton stressed what he termed the "covenant of grace"—the idea that individuals could be saved only by God's grace in choosing them to be members of the elect. Cotton contrasted this familiar Puritan doctrine with the "covenant of works," the erroneous belief that a person's behavior—one's works—could win God's favor and ultimately earn a person salvation. Belief in the covenant of works and in the possibility of salvation for all was known as Arminianism. Cotton's sermons strongly hinted that many Puritans, including ministers, embraced Arminianism, which claimed—falsely, Cotton declared—that human beings could influence God's will. Anne Hutchinson agreed with Cotton. Her lectures emphasized her opinion that many of the colony's leaders affirmed the Arminian covenant of works. Like Cotton, she preached that only God's covenant of grace led to salvation.

The meetings at Hutchinson's house alarmed her nearest neighbor, John Winthrop, who believed that she was subverting the good order of the colony. In 1637, Winthrop had formal charges brought against Hutchinson and denounced her lectures as "not tolerable nor comely in the sight of God nor fitting for your sex." He told her, "You have stept out of your place, you have rather bine a Husband than a Wife and a preacher than a Hearer; and a Magistrate than a Subject."

In court, Winthrop interrogated Hutchinson, fishing for a heresy he could pin on her. Winthrop and other Puritan elders referred to Hutchinson and her followers as **antinomians**, people who believed that Christians could be saved by faith alone and did not need to act in accordance with God's law as set forth in the Bible and as interpreted by the colony's leaders. Hutchinson nimbly defended herself against the accusation of antinomianism. Yes, she acknowledged, she believed that men and women were saved by faith alone; but no, she did not deny the need to obey God's law. "The Lord hath let me see which was the clear ministry and which the wrong," she said. Finally, Winthrop had cornered her. How could she tell which ministry was which? "By an immediate revelation," she replied, "by the voice of [God's] own spirit to my soul." Winthrop spotted in this statement the heresy of prophecy, the view that God revealed

> As one listener observed, Hutchinson was a "Woman that Preaches better Gospell then any of your black-coates . . . [from] the Ninneversity."

his will directly to a believer instead of exclusively through the Bible, as every right-minded Puritan knew.

In 1638, the Boston church formally excommunicated Hutchinson. The minister decreed, "I doe cast you out and . . . deliver you up to Satan that you may learne no more to blaspheme[,] to seduce and to lye. . . . I command you . . . as a Leper to withdraw your selfe out of the Congregation." Banished, Hutchinson and her family moved first to Roger Williams's Rhode Island and then to present-day New York, where she and most of her family were killed by Indians.

The strains within Puritanism exemplified by Anne Hutchinson and Roger Williams caused communities to splinter repeatedly during the seventeenth century. Thomas Hooker, a prominent minister, clashed with Winthrop and other leaders over the composition of the church. Hooker argued that men and women who lived godly lives should be admitted to church membership even if they had not experienced conversion. This issue, like most others in New England, had both religious and political dimensions, for only church members could vote in Massachusetts. In 1636, Hooker led an exodus of more than eight hundred colonists from Massachusetts to the Connecticut River valley, where they founded Hartford and neighboring towns. In 1639, the towns adopted the Fundamental Orders of Connecticut, a quasi-constitution that could be altered by the vote of freemen, who did not have to be church members, though nearly all of them were.

Other Puritan churches divided and subdivided throughout the seventeenth century as acrimony developed over doctrine and church government. Sometimes churches split over the appointment of a controversial minister. Sometimes families who had a long walk to the meetinghouse simply decided to form their own church nearer their houses. These schisms arose from ambiguities and tensions within Puritan belief. As the colonies matured, other tensions developed as well.

Religious Controversies and Economic Changes

A revolutionary transformation in the fortunes of Puritans in England had profound consequences in New England. Disputes between King Charles I and Parliament, dominated by Puritans, escalated in 1642 to civil war in England, a conflict known as the Puritan Revolution. Parliamentary forces led by the staunch Puritan Oliver Cromwell were victorious, executing Charles I in 1649 and proclaiming England a Puritan republic. From 1649 to 1660, England's rulers were not monarchs who suppressed Puritanism but believers who championed it. In a half century, English Puritans had risen from a harassed group of religious dissenters to a dominant power in English government.

When the Puritan Revolution began, the stream of immigrants to New England dwindled to a trickle, creating hard times for the colonists. They could no longer consider themselves a city on a hill setting a godly example for humankind. English society was being reformed by Puritans in England, not New England. Furthermore, when immigrant ships became rare, the colonists faced sky-high prices for scarce English goods and few customers for their own colonial products. As they searched to find new products and markets, they established the enduring patterns of New England's economy.

New England's rocky soil and short growing season ruled out cultivating the southern colonies' crops of tobacco and rice that found a ready market in Atlantic ports. Exports that New Englanders could not get from the soil they took instead from the forest and the sea. During the first decade of settlement, colonists traded with the Indians for animal pelts, which were in demand in Europe. By the 1640s, fur-bearing animals had become scarce unless traders ventured far beyond the **frontiers** of English settlement. Trees from the seemingly limitless forests of New England proved a longer-lasting resource. Masts for ships and staves for barrels of Spanish wine and West Indian sugar were crafted from New England timber.

But the most important New England export was fish. During the turmoil of the Puritan Revolution, English ships withdrew from the rich North Atlantic fishing grounds, and New England fishermen quickly took their place. Dried, salted codfish found markets in southern Europe and the West Indies. The fish trade also stimulated colonial shipbuilding and trained generations of fishermen, sailors, and merchants, creating a commercial network that endured for more than a century. But this export economy remained peripheral to most New England colonists. Their lives revolved around their farms, their churches, and their families.

Although immigration came to a standstill in the 1640s, the population continued to boom, doubling every twenty years. In New England, almost everyone married, and women often had eight or nine children. Long, cold winters minimized the warm-weather ailments of the southern colonies and reduced New England mortality. The descendants of the immigrants of the 1630s multiplied, boosting the New England population to roughly equal that of the southern colonies (Figure 4.1).

During the second half of the seventeenth century, under the pressures of steady population growth and integration into the Atlantic economy, the red-hot piety of the founders cooled. After 1640, the population grew faster than church membership. All residents attended sermons on pain of fines and punishment, but many could not find seats in the meetinghouses. Boston's churches in 1650 could house only about a third of the city's residents. By the 1680s, women were the majority of church members throughout New England. In some towns, only 15 percent of the adult men were members. A growing fraction of New Englanders, especially men, embraced what one historian has termed "horse-shed Christianity": They attended sermons but loitered outside near the horse shed, gossiping about the weather, fishing, their crops, or the scandalous behavior of neighbors. This slackening of piety led the Puritan minister Michael Wigglesworth to ask, in verse,

> How is it that I find
>   In stead of holiness Carnality,
> In stead of heavenly frames an Earthly mind,
>   For burning zeal luke-warm Indifferency,
>   For flaming love, key-cold Dead-heartedness,
>   For temperance (in meat, and drinke, and
>   cloaths) excess?
> Whence cometh it, that Pride, and Luxurie
>   Debate, Deceit, Contention, and Strife,
> False-dealing, Covetousness, Hypocrisie
>   (With such Crimes) amongst them are so rife,
> That one of them doth over-reach another?
>   And that an honest man can hardly
>   trust his Brother?

Most alarming to Puritan leaders, many of the children of the visible saints of Winthrop's generation failed

> New England communities treated Quakers with ruthless severity. Some Quakers were branded on the face "with a red-hot iron with [an] H. for heresie."

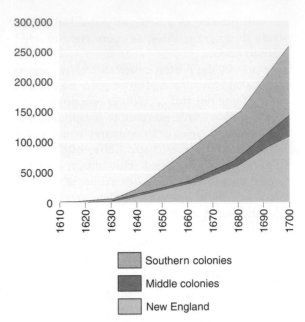

FIGURE 4.1   Population of the English North American Colonies in the Seventeenth Century
The colonial population grew at a steadily accelerating rate during the seventeenth century. New England and the southern colonies each accounted for about half the total colonial population until after 1680, when growth in Pennsylvania and New York contributed to a surge in the population of the middle colonies.

to experience conversion and attain full church membership. Puritans tended to assume that sainthood was inherited—that the children of visible saints were probably also among the elect. Acting on this premise, churches permitted saints to baptize their infant sons and daughters, symbolically cleansing them of their contamination with original sin. As these children grew up during the 1640s and 1650s, however, they seldom experienced the inward transformation that signaled conversion and qualification for church membership. The problem of declining church membership and the watering-down of Puritan orthodoxy became urgent during the 1650s when the children of saints, who had grown to adulthood in New England but had not experienced conversion, began to have children themselves. Their sons and daughters—the grandchildren of the founders of the colony—could not receive the protection that baptism afforded against the terrors of death because their parents had not experienced conversion.

Puritan churches debated what to do. To allow anyone, even the child of a saint, to become a church member without conversion was an unthinkable retreat from fundamental Puritan doctrine. In 1662, a synod of Massachusetts ministers reached a compromise known as the **Halfway Covenant**. Unconverted children of saints would be permitted to become "halfway" church members. Like regular church members, they could baptize their infants. But unlike full church members, they could not participate in communion or have the voting privileges of church membership. The Halfway Covenant generated a controversy that sputtered through Puritan churches for the remainder of the century. With the Halfway Covenant, Puritan churches came to terms with the lukewarm piety that had replaced the founders' burning zeal.

Nonetheless, New England communities continued to enforce piety with holy rigor. Beginning in 1656, small bands of Quakers—or members of the Society of Friends, as they called themselves—began to arrive in Massachusetts. Many of their beliefs were at odds with orthodox Puritanism. Quakers believed that God spoke directly to each individual through an "inner light," and that individuals needed neither a preacher nor the Bible in order to discover God's Word. Maintaining that all human beings were equal in God's eyes, Quakers refused to conform to mere temporal powers such as laws and governments unless God requested otherwise. For example, Quakers refused to observe the Sabbath because, they insisted, God had not set aside any special day for worship, expecting believers to worship faithfully every day. Women often took a leading role in Quaker meetings, in contrast to Puritan congregations, where women usually outnumbered men but remained subordinate.

New England communities treated Quakers with ruthless severity. Some Quakers were branded on the face "with a red-hot iron with [an] H. for heresie." When Quakers refused to leave Massachusetts, Boston officials hanged four of them between 1659 and 1661.

New Englanders' partial success in realizing the promise of a godly society ultimately undermined the intense appeal of Puritanism. In the pious Puritan communities of New England, leaders tried to eliminate sin. In the process, they diminished the sense of utter human depravity that was the wellspring of Puritanism. By 1700,

David, Joanna, and Abigail Mason
This 1670 painting depicts the children of Joanna and Anthony Mason, a wealthy Boston baker. The artist lavished attention on the children's elaborate clothing. Fashionable slashed sleeves, fancy lace, silver-studded shoes, six-year-old Joanna's and four-year-old Abigail's necklaces, and nine-year-old David's silver-headed cane suggest not only the Masons' wealth but also their desire to display and memorialize their possessions and adornments. The painting hints that the children themselves were adornments—young sprouts of the Mason lineage, which could afford such finery. The portrait is unified not by signs of warm affection, innocent smiles, or familial solidarity, but by trappings of wealth and sober self-importance. The painting expresses the growing respect for wealth and its worldly rewards in seventeenth-century New England.
Fine Arts Museums of San Francisco. Gift of Mr. and Mrs. John D. Rockefeller III.

New Englanders did not doubt that human beings sinned, but they were more concerned with the sins of others than with their own.

Witch trials held in Salem, Massachusetts, signaled the erosion of religious confidence and assurance. In 1692, the frenzied Salem proceedings accused more than one hundred people of witchcraft, a capital crime. (See "Historical Question," p. 122.) The Salem court executed nineteen accused witches, signaling enduring

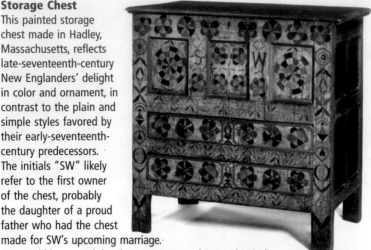

Storage Chest
This painted storage chest made in Hadley, Massachusetts, reflects late-seventeenth-century New Englanders' delight in color and ornament, in contrast to the plain and simple styles favored by their early-seventeenth-century predecessors. The initials "SW" likely refer to the first owner of the chest, probably the daughter of a proud father who had the chest made for SW's upcoming marriage. SW would have used the chest to store textiles, another indication that by the late seventeenth century, prosperous New England families owned more than they required for daily use and needed a place to store the surplus.
Pocumtuck Valley Memorial Association Memorial Hall Museum.

belief in the supernatural origins of evil and gnawing doubt about the strength of Puritan New Englanders' faith.

REVIEW Why did Massachusetts Puritans adopt the Halfway Covenant?

The Founding of the Middle Colonies

South of New England and north of the Chesapeake, a group of middle colonies were founded in the last third of the seventeenth century. Before the 1670s, few Europeans settled in the region. For the first two-thirds of the seventeenth century, the most important European outpost in the area was the relatively small Dutch colony of New Netherland. By 1700, however, the English monarchy had seized New Netherland, renamed it New York, and encouraged the creation of a Quaker colony led by William Penn. Unlike the New England colonies, the middle colonies of New York, New Jersey, and Pennsylvania originated as **land grants** by the English monarch to one or more proprietors,

> A minister complained that several groups of Jews had recently arrived, adding to the religious mixture of "Papists, Mennonites and Lutherans among the Dutch [and] many Puritans . . . and many other atheists . . . who conceal themselves under the name of Christians."

who then possessed both the land and the extensive, almost monarchical, powers of government (Map 4.2). These middle colonies attracted settlers of more diverse European origins and religious faiths than were found in New England.

From New Netherland to New York

In 1609, the Dutch East India Company dispatched Henry Hudson to search for a Northwest Passage to the Orient. Hudson sailed along the Atlantic coast and ventured up the large river that now bears his name until it dwindled to a stream that obviously did not lead to China. A decade later, the Dutch government granted the West India Company—a group of Dutch merchants and shippers—exclusive rights to trade with the Western Hemisphere. In 1626, Peter Minuit, the resident director of the company, purchased Manhattan Island from the Manhate Indians for trade goods worth the equivalent of a dozen beaver pelts. New Amsterdam, the small settlement established at the southern tip of Manhattan Island, became the principal trading center in New Netherland and the colony's headquarters.

Unlike the English colonies, New Netherland did not attract many European immigrants. Like New England and the Chesapeake colonies,

MAP 4.2 Middle Colonies in the Seventeenth Century
For the most part, the middle colonies in the seventeenth century were inhabited by settlers who clustered along the Hudson and Delaware rivers. The vast geographic extent of the colonies shown in this map reflects land grants authorized in England. Most of this area was inhabited by Native Americans rather than settled by colonists.

New Amsterdam

The settlement on Manhattan Island—complete with a windmill—appears in the background of this 1673 Dutch portrait of New Amsterdam. Wharves connect Manhattan residents to the seaborne commerce of the Atlantic world. In the foreground, the Dutch artist placed native inhabitants of the mainland, drawing them in such a way that they resemble Africans rather than Lenni Lenape (Delaware) Indians. Dutch merchants carried tens of thousands of African slaves to New World ports, including New Amsterdam. The artist probably had never seen Indians, had never been to New Amsterdam, and depended on well-known artistic conventions about the appearance of Africans to create his Native Americans. The portrait contrasts orderly, efficient, businesslike New Amsterdam with the exotic natural environment of America, to which the native woman clings as if she is refusing to succumb to the culture represented by those neat rows of rectangular houses across the river.

© Collection of the New-York Historical Society.

New Netherland never realized its sponsors' dreams of great profits. The company tried to stimulate immigration by granting patroonships—allotments of eighteen miles of land along the Hudson River—to wealthy stockholders who would bring fifty families to the colony and settle them as serflike tenants on their huge domains. Only one patroonship succeeded; the others failed to attract settlers, and the company eventually recovered much of the land.

Though few in number, New Netherlanders were remarkably diverse, especially compared with the homogeneous English settlers to the north and south. Religious dissenters and im-migrants from Holland, Sweden, France, Germany, and elsewhere made their way to the colony. A minister of the Dutch Reformed Church complained to his superiors in Holland that several groups of Jews had recently arrived, adding to the religious mixture of "Papists, Mennonites and Lutherans among the Dutch [and] many Puritans . . . and many other atheists . . . who conceal themselves under the name of Christians."

The West India Company struggled to govern the motley colonists. Peter Stuyvesant, governor from 1647 to 1664, tried to enforce conformity to the Dutch Reformed Church, but the

Why Were Some New Englanders Accused of Being Witches?

Almost everybody in seventeenth-century North America—whether Native Americans, slaves, or colonists—believed that supernatural spirits could cause harm and misfortune. Outside New England, however, few colonists were legally accused of being witches—that is, persons who had become possessed by Satan. More than 95 percent of all legal accusations of witchcraft in the North American colonies occurred in New England, a hint of the Puritans' enduring preoccupation with sin and evil. In 1691 and 1692, an epidemic of witchcraft accusations broke out in Salem, Massachusetts, but long before that, many New Englanders had whispered privately that particular individuals were witches. To accuse a person of witchcraft was a serious matter. A 1641 Massachusetts law stated, "If any man or woman be a witch . . . they shall be put to death." The other New England colonies had identical laws. During the seventeenth century, courts carried out the letter of the law: Thirty-four accused witches were legally executed, nineteen of them during the Salem outbreak.

To understand the peculiar New England obsession with witchcraft, historians have gathered a great deal of information about accused witches and the dark deeds their accusers

attributed to them. Almost anyone could be accused of being a witch, but 80 percent of the accusations were leveled against women. About two-thirds of the accused women were over forty years old, past the normal age of childbearing. About half of the men who were accused as witches were relatives of accused women. Usually, one family member did not accuse another. Nor did accusers single out a stranger as a witch. Instead, accusers pointed to a neighbor they knew well.

Almost always, the accused person denied the charge. Occasionally, the accused confessed to having made a pact with the devil. A confession could sometimes win sympathy and a reduced punishment from officials. During the Salem witch-hunt, those who confessed usually saved their own skins by naming other people as witches. The testimony of a confessed witch was then used to accuse others. At Salem, authorities sought to obtain a confession from accused witch Giles Corey by piling stones on his chest until he was crushed to death.

Accusers of all descriptions stepped forward to testify against alleged witches. Witchcraft investigations often stretched over weeks, months, or even years as courts accumulated evidence against (and sometimes in favor of) the accused.

About 90 percent of accusers were adults, about six out of ten of them men. Young women between the ages of sixteen and twenty-five made up almost all of the remaining 10 percent of accusers; typically, they claimed to be tortured by the accused.

At Salem, for example, afflicted young girls shrieked in pain, their limbs twisted into strange, involuntary contortions as they pointed out the witches who tortured them. At the trial of Bridget Bishop in Salem, the court record noted that if Bishop "but cast her eyes on them [the afflicted], they were presently struck down. . . . But upon the touch of her hand upon them, when they lay in their swoons, they would immediately revive." The bewitched girls testified that "the shape of the prisoner did oftentimes very grievously pinch them, choke them, bite them, and afflict them; urging them to write their names in a book"—the devil's book.

Such sensational evidence of torture by a witch was relatively rare in witch-hunts and trials. Usually, accusers attributed some inexplicable misfortune they had suffered to the evil influence of an accused witch. In Bridget Bishop's trial, for instance, one man testified that when he bought a pig from Bishop's husband, Bishop became angry because she "was hin-

Witches Show Their Love for Satan
Mocking pious Christians' humble obeisance to God, witches willingly debased themselves by standing in line to kneel and kiss Satan's buttocks—or so it was popularly believed. This seventeenth-century print portrays Satan with clawlike hands and feet, the tail of a rodent, the wings of a bat, and the head of a lustful ram attached to the torso of a man. Notice that women predominate among the witches eager to express their devotion to Satan and to do his bidding.
UCSF Library/Center for Knowledge Management.

dered from fingering the money," and soon afterward the pig—obviously bewitched—"was taken with strange fits; jumping, leaping, and knocking [its] head against the fence." One woman testified against a woman who, she insisted, had bewitched her cow, causing it to give discolored milk. Another woman accused a witch who she feared would "smite my chickens," and "quickly after [the suspected witch went away] one chicken died." A man was accused as a witch because his "spirit bewitched the pudding," which was inexplicably "cut lengthwise . . . as smooth as any knife could cut it." Mary Parsons testified that she suspected her husband, Hugh, of being a witch "because almost all that he sells to anybody does not prosper."

From our present-day perspective, the accusers seem to have been victims not of witchcraft but of simple accidents, of overheated imaginations, or—in the case of the possessed young women—of emotional distress. But why did seventeenth-century New Englanders find the testimony of accusers persuasive?

Seventeenth-century New Englanders believed that almost nothing happened by chance. Supernatural power, whether God's or Satan's, suffused the world and influenced the smallest event, even the color of a cow's milk. When something bad happened, an unhappy God may have caused it to show his displeasure with the victim, who had perhaps sinned in some way. But maybe the victim was not in fact responsible for the misfortune. Maybe Satan, acting through a witch, had caused it. If misfortunes could be pinned on a witch in thrall to Satan, the accuser was absolved from responsibility. The accuser became a helpless victim rather than a guilty party. Witches were an explanation for the disorder that continually crept into New England communities, an explanation that attributed the disorder not to chance or to the faults of individuals but to the witches' evil deeds, commanded by Satan.

Accusers usually targeted a vulnerable neighbor, such as an older, often poor woman. Historians have noted that accusers often complained that the accused individuals were quarrelsome, grumbled about being mistreated, muttered vague threats about getting even, and seemed to be dissatisfied with their lives. Researchers have pointed out that many New Englanders had such feelings after about 1650, but most people did not express them openly or, if they did, felt guilty about doing so. Accused witches often expressed and acted on feelings that other people shared but considered inappropriate, shameful, or sinful in their zeal to lead the saintly lives prescribed by their Puritan religion. Witches made it somewhat easier for New Englanders to consider themselves saints rather than sinners.

company declared that "the consciences of men should be free and unshackled," making a virtue of New Netherland necessity. The company never permitted the colony's settlers to form a representative government. Instead, the company appointed government officials who established policies, including taxes, that many colonists deeply resented.

In 1664, New Netherland became New York. Charles II, who became king of England in 1660 when Parliament restored the monarchy, gave his brother James, the Duke of York, an enormous grant of land that included New Netherland. Of course, the Dutch colony did not belong to the king of England, but that legal technicality did not deter the king or his brother. The duke quickly organized a small fleet of warships, which appeared off Manhattan Island in late summer 1664, and demanded that Stuyvesant surrender. With little choice, he did.

As the new proprietor of the colony, the Duke of York exercised almost the same unlimited authority over the colony as had the West India Company. The duke never set foot in New York, but his governors struggled to impose order on the unruly colonists. Like the Dutch, the duke permitted "all persons of what Religion soever, quietly to inhabit . . . provided they give no disturbance to the publique peace, nor doe molest or disquiet others in the free exercise of their religion." This policy of religious toleration was less an affirmation of liberty of conscience than a recognition of the reality of the most heterogeneous colony in seventeenth-century North America.

New Jersey and Pennsylvania

The creation of New York led indirectly to the founding of two other middle colonies, New Jersey and Pennsylvania (see Map 4.2). In 1664, the Duke of York subdivided his grant and gave the portion between the Hudson and Delaware rivers to two of his friends. The proprietors of this new colony, New Jersey, quarreled and called in a prominent English Quaker, William Penn, to arbitrate their dispute. Penn eventually worked out a settlement that continued New Jersey's proprietary government. In the process, Penn became intensely interested in what he termed a "holy experiment" of establishing a genuinely Quaker colony in America.

> Quakers allowed women to assume positions of religious leadership. "In souls there is no sex," they said.

Unlike most Quakers, William Penn came from an eminent family. His father had served both Cromwell and Charles II and had been knighted. Born in 1644, the younger Penn trained for a military career, but the ideas of dissenters from the reestablished Church of England appealed to him, and he became a devout Quaker. By 1680, he had published fifty books and pamphlets and spoken at countless public meetings, although he had not won official toleration for Quakers in England.

The Quakers' concept of an open, generous God who made his love equally available to all people manifested itself in behavior that continually brought them into conflict with the English government. Quaker leaders were ordinary men and women, not specially trained preachers. Quakers allowed women to assume positions of religious leadership. "In souls there is no sex," they said. Since all people were equal in the spiritual realm, Quakers considered social hierarchy false and evil. They called everyone "friend" and shook hands instead of curtsying or removing their hats—even when meeting the king. These customs enraged many non-Quakers and provoked innumerable beatings and worse. Penn was jailed four times for such offenses, once for nine months.

Despite his many run-ins with the government, Penn remained on good terms with Charles II. Partly to rid England of the troublesome Quakers, in 1681 Charles made Penn the proprietor of a new colony of some 45,000 square miles called Pennsylvania.

Toleration and Diversity in Pennsylvania

Quakers flocked to Pennsylvania in numbers exceeded only by the great Puritan migration to New England fifty years earlier. Between 1682 and 1685, nearly eight thousand immigrants arrived, most of them from England, Ireland, and Wales. They represented a cross section of the **artisans**, farmers, and laborers who predominated among English Quakers. Quaker missionaries also encouraged immigrants from the European continent, and many came, giving Pennsylvania greater ethnic diversity than any other English colony except New York. The Quaker colony prospered, and the capital city, Philadelphia, soon rivaled New York as a center of commerce. By 1700, the city's five thousand inhabitants participated in a thriving trade exporting flour and

William Penn

This portrait was drawn about a decade after the founding of Pennsylvania. At a time when extravagant clothing and a fancy wig proclaimed that the wearer was an important person, Penn is portrayed informally, lacking even a coat, his natural hair neat but undressed—all a reflection of his Quaker faith. Penn's full face and double chin show that his faith did not make him a stranger to the pleasures of the table. No hollow-cheeked ascetic or wild-eyed enthusiast, Penn appears sober and observant, as if sizing up the viewer and reserving judgment. The portrait captures the calm determination—anchored in faith—that inspired Penn's hopes for his new colony.
Historical Society of Pennsylvania.

other food products to the West Indies and importing English textiles and manufactured goods.

Penn was determined to live in peace with the Indians who inhabited the region. His Indian policy expressed his Quaker ideals and contrasted sharply with the hostile policies of the other English colonies. As he explained to the chief of the Lenni Lenape (Delaware) Indians, "God has written his law in our hearts, by which we are taught and commanded to love and help and do good to one another . . . [and] I desire to enjoy [Pennsylvania lands] with your love and consent." Penn instructed his agents to obtain the Indians' consent by purchasing their land, respecting their claims, and dealing with them fairly.

Penn declared that the first principle of government was that every settler would "enjoy the free possession of his or her faith and exercise of worship towards God." Accordingly, Pennsylvania tolerated Protestant sects of all kinds as well as Roman Catholics. All voters and officeholders had to be Christians, but the government did not compel settlers to attend religious services, as in Massachusetts, or to pay taxes to maintain a state-supported church, as in Virginia.

Despite its toleration and diversity, Pennsylvania was as much a Quaker colony as New England was a stronghold of Puritanism. Penn had no hesitation about using civil government to enforce religious morality. One of the colony's first laws provided severe punishment for "all such offenses against God, as swearing, cursing, lying, profane talking, drunkenness, drinking of healths, [and] obscene words . . . which excite the people to rudeness, cruelty, looseness, and irreligion."

As proprietor, Penn had extensive powers, subject only to review by the king. He appointed a governor, who maintained the proprietor's power to veto any laws passed by the colonial council, which was elected by property owners who possessed at least one hundred acres of land or who paid taxes. The council had the power to originate laws and administer all the affairs of government. A popularly elected assembly served as a check on the council; its members had the authority to reject or approve laws framed by the council.

> Penn declared that the first principle of government was that every settler would "enjoy the free possession of his or her faith and exercise of worship towards God."

Penn stressed that the exact form of government mattered less than the men who served in it. In Penn's eyes, "good men" staffed Pennsylvania's government because Quakers dominated elective and appointive offices. Quakers, of course, differed among themselves. Members of the assembly struggled to win the right to debate and amend laws, especially tax laws. They finally won the battle in 1701 when a new Charter of Privileges gave the proprietor the power to appoint the council and in turn stripped the council of all its former powers and gave them to the assembly, which became the only single-house legislature in all the English colonies.

REVIEW How did Quaker ideals shape the colony of Pennsylvania?

The Colonies and the English Empire

Proprietary grants to faraway lands were a cheap way for the king to reward friends. As the colonies grew, however, the grants became more valuable. After 1660, the king took initiatives to channel colonial trade through English hands and to consolidate royal authority over colonial governments. Occasioned by such economic and political considerations and triggered by King Philip's War between colonists and Native Americans, these initiatives defined the basic relationship between the colonies and England that endured until the American Revolution (Map 4.3).

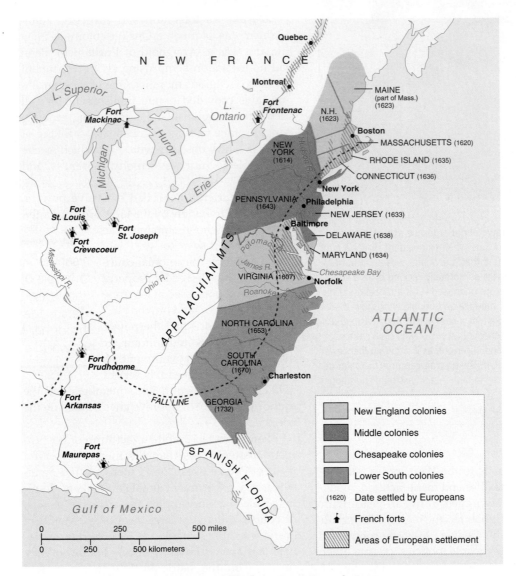

MAP 4.3   American Colonies at the End of the Seventeenth Century

By the end of the seventeenth century, settlers inhabited a narrow band of land that stretched more or less continuously from Boston to Norfolk, with pockets of settlement farther south. The colonies' claims to enormous tracts of land to the west were contested by Native Americans as well as by France and Spain.

READING THE MAP: What geographic feature acted as the western boundary for colonial territorial claims? Which colonies were the most settled and which the least?

CONNECTIONS: The map divides the colonies into four regions. Can you think of an alternative organization? On what criteria would it be based?

FOR MORE HELP ANALYZING THIS MAP, see the map activity for this chapter in the Online Study Guide at bedfordstmartins.com/roark.

Pine Tree Shilling

Currency was in short supply in the colonies. Since England prohibited the export of its coins, the precious currency circulating in the North American colonies tended to be Spanish, Dutch, French, or Portuguese. In violation of English rules that forbade colonies from issuing their own currency, John Hull, a wealthy Boston merchant and shipowner, began to mint coins in 1652. Shown here is one of his pine tree shillings, both sides boldly announcing its Massachusetts/New England origins. A shilling was worth twelve pennies; twenty shillings equaled one pound sterling. Despite Hull's attempt to ease the currency shortage, the legal tender most colonists used consisted of such commonly available items as bushels of corn or wheat, skins of beavers or deer, and, following Native American practice, wampum.

Courtesy of the Museum of the American Numismatic Association.

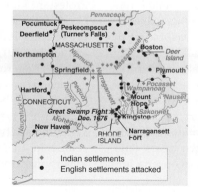

Royal Regulation of Colonial Trade

English economic policies toward the colonies were designed to yield customs revenues for the monarchy and profitable business for English merchants and shippers. Also, the policies were intended to divert the colonies' trade from England's enemies, especially the Dutch and the French.

The Navigation Acts of 1650, 1651, 1660, and 1663 (see chapter 3) set forth two fundamental rules governing colonial trade. First, goods shipped to and from the colonies had to be transported in English ships using primarily English crews. Second, the Navigation Acts listed ("enumerated," in the language of the time) colonial products that could be shipped only to England or to other English colonies. While these regulations prevented Chesapeake **planters** from shipping their tobacco directly to the European continent, they interfered less with the commerce of New England and the middle colonies, whose principal exports—fish, lumber, and flour— were not enumerated and could legally be sent directly to their most important markets in the West Indies.

By the end of the seventeenth century, colonial commerce was defined by regulations that subjected merchants and shippers to royal supervision and gave them access to markets throughout the English empire. In addition, colonial commerce received protection from the English navy. By 1700,

colonial goods (including those from the West Indies) accounted for one-fifth of all English imports and for two-thirds of all goods reexported from England to the European continent. In turn, the colonies absorbed more than one-tenth of English exports. The commercial regulations gave economic value to England's proprietorship of the American colonies.

King Philip's War and the Consolidation of Royal Authority

The monarchy also took steps to exercise greater control over colonial governments. Virginia had been a royal colony since 1624; Maryland, South Carolina, and the middle colonies were proprietary colonies with close ties to the crown. The New England colonies possessed royal charters, but they had developed their own distinctively Puritan governments. Charles II, whose father, Charles I, had been executed by Puritans in England, took a particular interest in harnessing the New England colonies more firmly to the English empire. The occasion was a royal investigation following King Philip's War.

In 1675, warfare between Indians and colonists erupted in the Chesapeake and New England. Massachusetts settlers had massacred hundreds of Pequot Indians in 1637, but they had established relatively peaceful relations with the more potent Wampanoags. In the decades that

King Philip's War, 1675

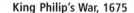

Pennacook

Pocumtuck
Deerfield • Peskeompscut (Turner's Falls)

MASSACHUSETTS
Northampton
Nipmuck
Boston
Deer Island

Springfield
Narragansett
Plymouth

Hartford
Pequot
Wampanoag
Pocasset

CONNECTICUT
Great Swamp Fight
Dec. 1675
Mount Hope
Sakonnet
Nauset

Mohegan
Kingston

New Haven
RHODE ISLAND
Narragansett Fort

♦ Indian settlements
● English settlements attacked

Wampanoag War Club
This seventeenth-century war club was used to kill King Philip, according to the Anglican missionary who obtained it from Indians early in the eighteenth century. Although the missionary's tale is probably a legend, the club is certainly a seventeenth-century Wampanoag weapon that might well have been used in King Philip's War. The heavy ball carved into the head of the club could deliver a disabling, even fatal, blow. Unlike a bow and arrow, the club needed to be wielded at very close range. For this reason, it was most useful against a wounded or utterly unaware enemy.
Courtesy of the Fruitlands Museums, Harvard, Massachusetts.

> King Philip's War left the New England colonists with an enduring hatred of Indians, a large war debt, and a devastated frontier.

followed, New Englanders steadily encroached on Indian land, and in 1675 the Wampanoags struck back with attacks on settlements in western Massachusetts. Metacomet—the chief of the Wampanoags (and son of Massasoit), whom the colonists called King Philip—probably neither planned the attacks nor masterminded a conspiracy with the Nipmucks and the Narragansetts, as the colonists feared. But when militias from Massachusetts and other New England colonies counterattacked all three tribes, a deadly sequence of battles killed more than a thousand colonists and thousands more Indians. The Indians destroyed thirteen English settlements and partially burned another half dozen. By the spring of 1676, Indian warriors ranged freely within seventeen miles of Boston. The colonists finally defeated the Indians, principally with a scorched-earth policy of burning their food supplies. King Philip's War left the New England colonists with an enduring hatred of Indians, a large war debt, and a devastated frontier. And in 1676, an agent of the king arrived to investigate whether New England was abiding by English laws.

Not surprisingly, the king's agent found all sorts of deviations from English rules, and the monarchy decided to govern New England more directly. In 1684, an English court revoked the Massachusetts charter, the foundation of the distinctive Puritan government. Two years later, royal officials incorporated Massachusetts and the other colonies north of Maryland into the Dominion of New England. To govern the dominion, the English sent Sir Edmund Andros to Boston. Some New England merchants cooperated with Andros, but most colonists were offended by his flagrant disregard of such Puritan traditions as keeping the Sabbath. Worst of all, the Dominion of New England invalidated all land titles, confronting every landowner in New England with the horrifying prospect of losing his or her land.

Events in England, however, permitted Massachusetts colonists to overthrow Andros and retain title to their property. When Charles II died in 1685, he was succeeded by his brother James II, a zealous Catholic. James's aggressive campaign to appoint Catholics to government posts engendered such unrest that in 1688, a group of Protestant noblemen in Parliament invited the Dutch ruler William III of Orange, James's son-in-law, to claim the English throne. When William III landed in England at the head of a large army, James fled to France and William III and his wife, Mary II (James's daughter), became corulers in the relatively bloodless "Glorious Revolution," reasserting Protestant influence in England and its empire. Rumors of the revolution raced across the Atlantic and emboldened colonial uprisings against royal authority in Massachusetts, New York, and Maryland.

In Boston in 1689, rebels tossed Andros and other English officials in jail, destroyed the Dominion of New England, and reestablished the former charter government. New Yorkers followed the Massachusetts example. Under the leadership of Jacob Leisler, rebels seized the royal governor in 1689 and ruled the colony for more than a year. That same year in Maryland, the Protestant Association, led by John Coode, overthrew the colony's pro-Catholic government, fearing it would not recognize the new Protestant king.

But these rebel governments did not last. When King William III's governor of New York arrived in 1691, he executed Leisler for treason. Coode's men ruled Maryland until the new royal governor arrived in 1692 and ended both Coode's rebellion and Lord Baltimore's proprietary government. In Massachusetts, John Winthrop's city on a hill became another royal colony in 1691. The new charter said that the governor of the colony would be appointed by

John Sheldon's Door and Snowshoes
John Sheldon, a resident of Deerfield, Massachusetts—first settled by colonists in 1669—
lived in a house accessed by this heavily fortified door, one of only two seventeenth-
century doors that survive. The thick, nail-studded door protected against frigid New
England winters and attacks from French and Indian raiders, who plagued Deerfield.
Sheldon wore the snowshoes to rescue more than one hundred colonists taken
hostage by the French and their Indian allies during the Deerfield Raid of 1704.
The design of snowshoes, which colonists in 1666 called "a Rackett tyed to
each foote," was adopted from the Native Americans, who had used them for centuries.
Pocumtuck Valley Memorial Association Memorial Hall Museum.

the king rather than elected by the colonists' representatives. But perhaps the most unsettling change was the new qualification for voting. Possession of property replaced church membership as a prerequisite for voting in colony-wide elections. Wealth replaced God's grace as the defining characteristic of Massachusetts citizenship.

Much as colonists chafed under increasing royal control, they still valued English protection from hostile neighbors. While the northern colonies were distracted by the Glorious Revolution, French forces from the fur-trading regions along the Great Lakes and in Canada attacked villages in New England and New York. (See "Beyond America's Borders," page 130.) Known as King William's War, the conflict with the French was a colonial outgrowth of William's war against France in Europe. The war dragged on until 1697 and ended inconclusively in both

New France and the Indians: The English Colonies' Northern Borderlands

North of New England, French explorers, traders, and missionaries carved out a distinctive North American colony that contrasted, competed, and periodically fought with the English colonies to the south.

King Louis XIV officially made New France a royal colony in 1663, but by then representatives of France had been active for more than a century in the region that stretched along the St. Lawrence River to the Great Lakes and beyond. The explorer Jacques Cartier sailed into the St. Lawrence in 1535 and claimed the region for France. Cartier's attempts to found a permanent colony failed, but French ships followed in his wake and began to trade with Native Americans for wild animal pelts. By the seventeenth century, the fur trade had become the economic foundation of New France.

Wealthy consumers in France and elsewhere in Europe coveted the thick, lustrous furs grown by beavers, bears, wolves, and other mammals during the frigid winters of what is now eastern Canada. Skilled French furriers cut and sewed the animal skins into fashionable hats, coats, and other garments prized by consumers to stay warm and to display their wealth and good taste. Aware of the strong demand for North American furs, the French monarchy granted monopoly rights to a succession of fur-trading companies.

The crown hoped to channel the fur trade through French hands into the broader European market and to compete against rival Dutch traders, whose headquarters at Albany (in what is now New York) funneled North American furs down the Hudson River to markets in the Netherlands. The French monarchy also hoped the fur trade would allow the creation of a North American colony on the cheap.

The fur trade required little investment other than the construction and staffing of trading outposts at Quebec, Montreal, and elsewhere. In exchange for textiles and various metal trade goods, the Iroquois, Huron, Ottawa, Ojibwa, and other Native Americans did the arduous, time-consuming, and labor-intensive work of tracking, trapping, and skinning the animals and transporting the pelts—usually by canoe—to French traders waiting for business in their fortifications on the St. Lawrence. The fur trade harnessed the knowledge and skills learned by Native Americans over many millennia to drain the northern wilderness of animal pelts. Unlike the English colonies, which attracted numerous settlers to engage in agriculture and produce food as well as valuable export crops of tobacco, rice, and wheat, New France needed only a few colonists to keep the trading posts open and to maintain friendly relations with their Indian suppliers. By

1660, English colonists in North America outnumbered their French counterparts by more than 20 to 1.

After England seized control of New York in 1664, English fur traders replaced the Dutch at Albany and eagerly competed to divert the northern fur trade away from New France. By then, the Iroquois—strategically located between the supply of furs to the north and west, New France to the east, and New York to the south—had become middlemen, collecting pelts from Huron, Ottawa, and other Indians and swapping them with French or English traders, depending on which offered the better deal. Able to mobilize scores of fierce warriors to threaten European traders (as well as their Indian suppliers) with traditional Native American weapons and firearms obtained mostly from the English, the Iroquois managed to play the French and English off against each other and to maintain a near choke hold on the supply of furs.

Native Americans preferred English trade goods, which tended to be of higher quality and less expensive than those available at French outposts, but New France cultivated better relationships with the Indians. When English colonists had the required military strength, they seldom hesitated to kill Indians, especially those who occupied land the colonists craved. The small number of colonists in New France never had as much military power as the English colonists to mobilize against the Indians. Instead of separating themselves from the Native Americans, as the English colonists usually did, the French colonists sought to stay on relatively peaceful and friendly terms with them. French men commonly married or cohabited with Indian women, an outgrowth of both the shortage of French women among the colonists and the relative acceptance of such couplings, compared to the strong taboo prevalent in the English colonies.

Jesuit missionaries led the spiritual colonization of New France. Zealous enemies of what they considered Protestant heresies and stout defenders of Catholicism, the Jesuits fanned out to Indian villages throughout New France, determined to convert the Native Americans and to preserve the colony as a Catholic stronghold. The missionaries focused on Huron villages, posing a challenge to Iroquois control of the fur supply and increasing Iroquois hostility toward New France. Unwittingly, the missionaries also spread European diseases among the Native Americans, repeatedly causing deadly epidemics. Above all, the missionaries worked hand in hand with the fur traders and royal officials to make New France a low-cost Catholic colony on the thinly defended borders of the predominantly Protestant English colonies.

To extend the boundaries of New France far to the west and south, almost encircling the English colonies along the Atlantic coast, royal officials in 1673 sponsored a voyage by the explorer Louis Jolliet and the priest Jacques Marquette to explore the vast interior of the North American continent by canoeing down the Mississippi River to what is now Arkansas. There they learned from local Indians that the river did not drain into the Pacific Ocean, opening the pathway to Asia they had hoped to find, but rather into the Gulf of Mexico. Jolliet and Marquette made grandiose claims to the Mississippi Valley, but these claims amounted to little more than a colored patch on European maps since these assertions were not defended on the ground.

England and France clashed repeatedly in North America over the fur trade and in a colonial extension of their rivalry at home. English

forces captured Quebec in 1629 but returned it to French control three years later. European conflict between France and England spread to North America during King William's War (1689–1697), during which the colonists and their Indian allies carried out numerous deadly raids. These

raids had no permanent consequences in the seventeenth century except to mark the boundary between New France and the English colonies as a bloody, contested zone controlled by none of its claimants or inhabitants.

Europe and the colonies. But it made clear to many colonists that along with English royal government came a welcome measure of military security.

> **REVIEW** Why did the Glorious Revolution in England lead to uprisings in the American colonies?

Conclusion: An English Model of Colonization in North America

By 1700, the diverse English colonies in North America had developed along lines quite different from the example New Spain had set in 1600. In the North American colonies, English immigrants and their descendants created societies of settlers unlike the largely Indian societies in New Spain ruled by a tiny group of Spaniards. Although many settlers came to North America from other parts of Europe and a growing number of Africans arrived in bondage, English laws, habits, ideas, and language dominated all the colonies.

Economically, the English colonies thrived on agriculture and trade instead of mining silver and exploiting Indian labor as in New Spain. Southern colonies grew huge crops of tobacco and rice with the labor of indentured servants and slaves, while farmers in the middle colonies planted wheat and New England fishermen harvested the sea. Although servants and slaves could be found throughout the North American colonies, many settlers depended principally on the labor of family members. Relations between settlers and Native Americans often exploded in bloody warfare, but Indians seldom served as an important source of labor for settlers, as they did in New Spain.

Protestantism prevailed in the North American settlements, relaxed in some colonies and straitlaced in others. The convictions of Puritanism that motivated John Winthrop and others to build a new England in the colonies became muted as the New England colonies matured and dissenters such as Roger Williams multiplied. Catholics, Quakers, Anglicans (members of the Church of England), Jews, and others settled in the middle and southern colonies, cre-

ating considerable religious toleration, especially in Pennsylvania and New York.

Politics and government differed from colony to colony, although the imprint of English institutions and practices existed everywhere. And everywhere, local settlers who were free adult white men had an extraordinary degree of political influence, far beyond that of colonists in New Spain or ordinary citizens in England. A new world of settlers that Columbus could not have imagined, that Powhatan only glimpsed, had been firmly established in English North America by 1700. During the next half century, that English colonial world would undergo surprising new developments built on the achievements of the seventeenth century.

Selected Bibliography

General Works

Virginia DeJohn Anderson, *Creatures of Empire: How Domestic Animals Transformed Early America* (2004).

Colin G. Calloway, *New Worlds for All: Indians, Europeans, and the Remaking of Early America* (1998).

Peter A. Coclanis, ed., *The Atlantic Economy during the Seventeenth and Eighteenth Centuries* (2005).

Alison Games, *Migration and the Origins of the English Atlantic World* (1999).

David D. Hall, *Worlds of Wonder, Days of Judgment: Popular Religious Belief in Early New England* (1989).

Neil Kamil, *Fortress of the Soul: Violence, Metaphysics, and Material Life in the Huguenots' New World, 1517–1751* (2005).

Cathy Matson, ed., *The Economy of Early America: Historical Perspective and New Directions* (2006).

Carla Gardina Pestana, *The English Atlantic in the Age of Revolution, 1640–1661* (2004).

Native Americans

Russell Bourne, *Gods of War, Gods of Peace: How the Meeting of Native and Colonial Religions Shaped Early America* (2002).

Roger M. Carpenter, *The Renewed, the Destroyed, and the Remade: The Three Thought Worlds of the Huron and the Iroquois, 1609–1675* (2004).

Richard W. Cogley, *John Eliot's Mission to the Indians before King Philip's War* (1999).

James David Drake, *King Philip's War: Civil War in New England, 1675–1676* (2000).

Jill Lepore, *The Name of War: King Philip's War and the Origins of American Identity* (1998).

Michael Leroy Oberg, *Dominion and Civility: English Imperialism and Native America, 1585–1685* (1999).

Ann Marie Plane, *Colonial Intimacies: Indian Marriages in Early New England* (2000).

New England

Louise A. Breen, *Transgressing the Bounds: Subversive Enterprises among the Puritan Elite in Massachusetts, 1630–1692* (2001).

James F. Cooper Jr., *Tenacious of Their Liberties: The Congregationalists in Colonial Massachusetts* (1999).

Cornelia Hughes Dayton, *Women before the Bar: Gender, Law, and Society in Connecticut, 1639–1789* (1995).

Brian Donahue, *The Great Meadow: Farmers and the Land in Colonial Concord* (2004).

Lisa M. Gordis, *Opening Scriptures: Bible Reading and Interpretive Authority in Puritan New England* (2003).

Jane Kamensky, *Governing the Tongue: The Politics of Speech in Early New England* (1997).

Eve LaPlante, *American Jezebel: The Uncommon Life of Anne Hutchinson, the Woman Who Defied the Puritans* (2005).

Edmund S. Morgan, *Roger Williams: The Church and the State* (1967).

Mary Beth Norton, *In the Devil's Snare: The Salem Witchcraft Crisis of 1692* (2002).

Mark A. Peterson, *The Price of Redemption: The Spiritual Economy of Puritan New England* (1998).

Nathaniel Philbrick, *Mayflower: A Story of Courage, Community, and War* (2006).

Lisa Wilson, *Ye Heart of a Man: The Domestic Life of Men in Colonial New England* (1999).

Michael P. Winship, *Making Heretics: Militant Protestantism and Free Grace in Massachusetts, 1636–1641* (2002).

Middle Colonies

Richard S. Dunn and Mary Maples Dunn, eds., *The World of William Penn* (1986).

Cathy Matson, *Merchants and Empire: Trading in Colonial New York* (1998).

Donna Merwick, *The Shame and the Sorrow: Dutch-Amerindian Encounters in New Netherland* (2006).

David E. Narrett, *Inheritance and Family Life in Colonial New York City* (1992).

Russell Shorto, *The Island at the Center of the World: The Epic Story of Dutch Manhattan and the Forgotten Colony That Shaped America* (2004).

Allen Tully, *Forming American Politics: Ideals, Interests, and Institutions in Colonial New York and Pennsylvania* (1994).

▶ For more books about topics in this chapter, see the Online Bibliography at bedfordstmartins.com/roark.

▶ For additional firsthand accounts of this period, see Chapter 4 in Michael Johnson, ed., *Reading the American Past*, Fourth Edition.

▶ For Web sites, images, and documents related to topics and places in this chapter, visit bedfordstmartins.com/makehistory.

REVIEWING THE CHAPTER

Follow these steps to review and strengthen your understanding of the chapter.

STEP 1: *Study the **Key Terms** and **Timeline** to identify the significance of each item listed.*

STEP 2: *Answer the **Review Questions**, drawing on key terms and dates to support your answers.*

STEP 3: *Drawing on the Key Terms, Timeline, and Review Questions, answer the broader **Making Connections** questions.*

KEY TERMS

Who

Roger Williams (p. 103)
Henry VIII (p. 105)
Elizabeth I (p. 105)
James I (p. 105)
Charles I (p. 105)
Pilgrims (p. 107)
William Bradford (p. 107)
Wampanoag Indians (p. 107)
John Winthrop (p. 108)
John Calvin (p. 113)
"visible saints" (p. 113)
Anne Hutchinson (p. 116)
John Cotton (p. 116)
antinomians (p. 116)
Thomas Hooker (p. 117)
Oliver Cromwell (p. 117)
Quakers (p. 118)
Peter Stuyvesant (p. 121)
Charles II (p. 124)

Duke of York (p. 124)
William Penn (p. 124)
Pequot Indians (p. 127)
Metacomet (p. 128)
Edmund Andros (p. 128)
James II (p. 128)
William III of Orange (p. 128)
Jacob Leisler (p. 128)
John Coode (p. 128)

What

Puritanism (p. 104)
English Reformation (p. 105)
Act of Supremacy (p. 105)
Church of England (p. 105)
separatism (p. 107)
Mayflower Compact (p. 107)
Plymouth (p. 107)
royal charter (p. 107)
Massachusetts Bay Company (p. 107)

Arbella (p. 108)
Calvinism (p. 113)
predestination (p. 113)
General Court (p. 115)
town meeting (p. 115)
covenant of grace (p. 116)
covenant of works (p. 116)
Arminianism (p. 116)
Fundamental Orders of Connecticut
    (p. 117)
Puritan Revolution (p. 117)
Halfway Covenant (p. 119)
Manhattan Island (p. 120)
Charter of Privileges (p. 125)
Navigation Acts (p. 127)
King Philip's War (p. 127)
Dominion of New England (p. 128)
Glorious Revolution (p. 128)
Protestant Association (p. 128)
King William's War (p. 129)

TIMELINE

◄ **1534** • King Henry VIII breaks with Roman Catholic Church.

1609 • Henry Hudson searches for Northwest Passage.

1620 • Plymouth colony founded.

1626 • Manhattan Island purchased and New Amsterdam founded.

1629 • Massachusetts Bay Company receives royal charter.

1630 • John Winthrop leads Puritan settlers to Massachusetts Bay.

1636 • Rhode Island colony established.
        • Connecticut colony founded.

1638 • Anne Hutchinson excommunicated.

1642 • Puritan Revolution inflames England.

1649 • English Puritans win civil war and execute Charles I.

REVIEW QUESTIONS

1. Why did Henry VIII initiate the English Reformation? (pp. 105–6)

2. Why did the Puritans immigrate to North America? (pp. 107–12)

3. Why did Massachusetts Puritans adopt the Halfway Covenant? (pp. 112–20)

4. How did Quaker ideals shape the colony of Pennsylvania? (pp. 120–25)

5. Why did the Glorious Revolution in England lead to uprisings in the American colonies? (pp. 126–32)

MAKING CONNECTIONS

1. How did the religious dissenters who flooded into the northern colonies address the question of religious dissent in their new homes? Comparing two colonies, discuss their different approaches and the implications of those approaches for colonial development.

2. In his sermon aboard the *Arbella*, John Winthrop spoke of the Massachusetts Bay Colony as "a city upon a hill." What did he mean? How did this expectation influence life in New England during the seventeenth century? In your answer, be sure to consider the relationship between religious and political life in the colony.

3. Religious conflict and political turmoil battered England in the seventeenth century. How did political developments in England affect life in the colonies? In your answer, consider the establishment of the colonies and the crown's attempts to exercise authority over them.

4. Although both were settled by the English, colonial New England was dramatically different from the colonial Chesapeake. How did they differ and why? In your answer, consider the economies, systems of governance, and patterns of settlement in each colony.

▶ FOR PRACTICE QUIZZES, A CUSTOMIZED STUDY PLAN, AND OTHER STUDY TOOLS, see the Online Study Guide at bedfordstmartins.com/roark.

1656 • Quakers arrive in Massachusetts and are persecuted there.

1660 • Monarchy restored in England; Charles II becomes king.

1662 • Many Puritan congregations adopt Halfway Covenant.

1664 • English seize Dutch colony; rename it New York.
• Colony of New Jersey created.

1675 • King Philip's War.

1681 • William Penn receives charter for colony of Pennsylvania.

1686 • Dominion of New England created.

1688 • England's Glorious Revolution; William III and Mary II become new rulers.

1692 • Salem witch trials.

PRINTED HANDKERCHIEF

This eighteenth-century handkerchief instructs servants about the life-changing virtue of industry and the vice of idleness. The story of the good servant, William Goodchild, and the bad servant, Jack Idle, starts in the upper left corner and proceeds clockwise around the handkerchief. While William stays busy at his loom, "Sluggard" Jack loafs and will be "cloathed in Rags." While William kneels and prays on Sunday, Jack fights, then foolishly goes to sea. "Faithful Servant" William is rewarded by his master with greater responsibilities, then with marriage to the boss's daughter. Soon enough, William rises to sheriff of London, a step on his path to the "Riches and Honour" of the city's highest office, mayor. Jack, in contrast, commits robbery, is turned in by his coworkers, and is finally carted off to execution because of his "own Iniquities." William's "Frugality & Industry" lead to the colonial "Trade & Commerce" (lower left) that were the lifeblood of the eighteenth-century British empire, while idle servants who avoided the gallows, unlike Jack, ended up in the colonies hoeing tobacco alongside slaves (lower right). The handkerchief displays a parable of eighteenth-century values from the perspective of masters who sought frugal, industrious, and obedient servants rather than those who were profligate, lazy, and disorderly. Ideally, the parable suggests, servants' obedience to their masters would displace their subordination to God. What does the parable suggest about the values of freedom and individualism? How might the parable be different if it adopted the viewpoint of servants rather than masters or of female servants rather than males? How might a seventeenth-century version of this parable differ, if at all?

Colonial Williamsburg Foundation.

Colonial America in the Eighteenth Century
1701–1770

- **A Growing Population and Expanding Economy in British North America** 138

- **New England: From Puritan Settlers to Yankee Traders** 140
  Natural Increase and Land Distribution 140
  Farms, Fish, and Atlantic Trade 141

- **The Middle Colonies: Immigrants, Wheat, and Work** 142
  German and Scots-Irish Immigrants 143
  Pennsylvania: "The Best Poor [White] Man's Country" 147

- **The Southern Colonies: Land of Slavery** 151
  The Atlantic Slave Trade and the Growth of Slavery 151
  Slave Labor and African American Culture 155
  Tobacco, Rice, and Prosperity 156

- **Unifying Experiences** 158
  Commerce and Consumption 158
  Religion, Enlightenment, and Revival 158
  Borderlands and Colonial Politics in the British Empire 163

- **Conclusion: The Dual Identity of British North American Colonists** 170

THE BROTHERS AMBOE ROBIN JOHN and Little Ephraim Robin John and their cousin Ancona Robin John lived during the 1750s and 1760s in Old Calabar on the Bight of Biafra in West Africa. The Robin Johns were part of a slave-trading dynasty headed by their kinsman Grandy King George, one of the most powerful leaders of the Efik people. Grandy King George owned hundreds of slaves whom he employed to capture and trade for still more slaves in the African interior. He sold these captives to captains of European slave ships seeking to fill their holds with human cargo for the transatlantic voyage to the sugar, tobacco, and rice fields in the New World. During the half century after 1725, Old Calabar exported about 80,000 slaves, almost all of them aboard British ships. It was a major contributor to the massive flow of more than 1.2 million slaves from the Bight of Biafra to the New World during the eighteenth century.

Grandy King George nearly monopolized the Old Calabar slave trade during the 1760s, allowing him to live in luxury, surrounded by fine British trade goods such as gold-headed canes, fancy mirrors, lace-trimmed clothing, and pewter chamber pots. British slave ship captains and Grandy King George's African rivals resented his choke hold on the supply of slaves and in 1767 conspired to trap the king and the Robin Johns, seize hundreds of their slaves, and destroy the king's monopoly. In the bloody melee, Grandy King George suffered eleven musket wounds but managed to escape. Other members of his family were less fortunate. Amboe Robin John was beheaded by the leader of the African attackers. Little Ephraim and Ancona Robin John were enslaved, packed aboard the ship *Duke of York* with more than 330 other slaves, and transported across the Atlantic to the West Indian island of Dominica, which the British had recently acquired from the French.

Unlike most slaves, the Robin Johns understood, spoke, and even wrote English, an essential skill they had learned as slave traders in Old Calabar. A French physician bought the Robin Johns and, according to Ancona, "treated [them] . . . upon ye whole not badly." After seven months, the Robin Johns heard that a certain ship captain would take them back to Africa. They escaped from their owner and boarded the captain's ship "determined to get home," Little Ephraim wrote. But the captain took them to Virginia instead and sold them as slaves to a merchant who traded between the Chesapeake and Bristol, England. Their new owner, John Thompson, "would tie me up & whip me many times for nothing at all," Ancona testified, adding that Thompson "was exceedingly badly man ever I saw." After Thompson died in

Colonial Slave Drum

An African in Virginia made this drum sometime around the beginning of the eighteenth century. He probably was enslaved in Africa, transported across the Atlantic in the hold of a slave ship, and sold to a tobacco planter in the Chesapeake. The drum combines deerskin and cedarwood from North America with African workmanship and designs. During rare moments of respite from their work, slaves played drums to accompany dances learned in Africa. They also drummed out messages from plantation to plantation. Whites knew that slaves used drums for communication, but they could not decipher the meanings of the rhythms and sounds. Fearful that drums signaled rebellious uprisings, whites outlawed drumming but could not eliminate it. Most likely, the messages sent included lamentations about the drummers' lives of bondage.
Trustees of the British Museum.

1772, the Robin Johns heard that a slave ship from Old Calabar had recently arrived in Virginia, and the captain promised to take them back to Africa if they would run away and come aboard his ship. Instead, he took the Robin Johns to Bristol and sought to sell them as slaves yet again.

While imprisoned "in this Deplorable condition" on a ship in Bristol harbor, the Robin Johns managed to smuggle letters to a Bristol slave trader they had known and dealt with in Old Calabar. With help from him and other English sympathizers, the Robin Johns appeared before Lord Mansfield, the chief justice of England, and appealed for their freedom on the grounds that they "were free people . . . [who] had not done anything to forfeit our liberty" and were thus unjustly enslaved. After complex negotiations, they won legal recognition of their freedom.

As free Africans in Bristol, the Robin Johns converted to Christianity under the ministry of the famous Methodists John and Charles Wesley, who wrote that the Robin Johns "received both the outward and visible signs of the inward & spiritual grace in a wonderful manner & measure." Although the Robin Johns had many friends and admirers among English Methodists, they longed to return to Africa. In 1774, they sailed from Bristol as free men on another slave ship bound for Old Calabar, where they resumed their careers as slave traders.

The Robin Johns' unrelenting quest to escape enslavement and redeem their freedom was shared but not realized by millions of Africans who were victims of slave traders such as Grandy King George and numberless merchants, ship captains, and colonists. They came involuntarily to the New World; in contrast, tens of thousands of Europeans voluntarily crossed the Atlantic to seek opportunities in North America—opportunities many purchased by agreeing to several years of contractual servitude. Both groups illustrate the undertow of violence and deceit just beneath the surface of eighteenth-century Atlantic commerce linking Britain, Africa, the West Indies, and British North America. In the flux and uncertainty of the eighteenth-century world, many, like the Robin Johns, turned to the consolations of religious faith as a source of meaning and hope in an often cruel and unforgiving society.

The flood of free and unfree migrants crossing the Atlantic contributed to unprecedented population growth in eighteenth-century British North America. In contrast, the Spanish and French colonies remained thinly populated outposts of European empires interested principally in maintaining a toehold in the vast continent. While adaptations to varied natural, economic, and social environments reinforced regional differences among New England, the middle colonies, and the southern colonies, other commercial, cultural, and political trends built common experiences, aspirations, and assumptions among the British colonists. These unifying trends would lay the groundwork for what would become in 1776 the United States of America.

A Growing Population and Expanding Economy in British North America

The most important fact about eighteenth-century British America is its phenomenal population growth: In 1700, colonists numbered about 250,000; by 1770, they tallied well over 2 million. An index of the emerging significance of colonial North America is that in 1700, there were nineteen people in England for every American colonist; by 1770, there were only three. The eightfold growth of the colonial population signaled the maturation of a distinctive colonial society. That society was by no means homogeneous. Colonists of different ethnic groups, races, and religions lived in varied environments under thirteen different colonial governments, all of them part of the British empire.

In general, the growth and diversity of the eighteenth-century colonial population derived from two sources: immigration and natural increase (growth through reproduction). Natural increase contributed about three-fourths of the population growth, immigration about one-fourth. Immigration shifted the ethnic and racial balance among the colonists, making them by 1770 less English and less white than ever before. Fewer than 10 percent of eighteenth-century immigrants came from England; about 36 percent were Scots-Irish, mostly from northern Ireland; 33 percent arrived from Africa, almost all of them slaves; nearly 15 percent had left the many German-language principalities (the nation of Germany did not exist until 1871); and almost 10 percent came from Scotland. In 1670, more than 9 out of 10 colonists were of English ancestry, and only 1 out of 25 was of African ancestry. By 1770, only about half of the colonists were of English descent,

while more than 20 percent descended from Africans. Thus, by 1770, the people of the colonies had a distinctive colonial—rather than English—profile (Map 5.1, page 140).

The booming population of the colonies hints at a second major feature of eighteenth-century colonial society: an expanding economy. In 1700, after almost a century of settlement, nearly all the colonists lived within fifty miles of the Atlantic coast. The almost limitless wilderness stretching westward made land relatively cheap. Land in the colonies commonly sold for a fraction of its price in the Old World. The abundance of land in the colonies made labor precious, and the colonists always needed more. The colonists' insatiable demand for labor was the fundamental economic environment that sustained the mushrooming population. Economic historians estimate that free colonists (those who were not **indentured servants** or slaves) had a higher standard of living than the majority of people elsewhere in the Atlantic world. The unique achievement of the eighteenth-century colonial economy was this modest economic welfare of the vast bulk of the free population.

> **REVIEW** How did the North American colonies achieve the remarkable population growth of the eighteenth century?

"Dummy Board" of Phyllis, a New England Slave
This life-size portrait of a slave woman named Phyllis, a mulatto who worked as a domestic servant for her owner, Elizabeth Hunt Wendell, was painted sometime before 1753. Known as a "dummy board," it was propped against a wall or placed in a doorway or window to suggest that the residence was occupied and to discourage thieves. Phyllis's dress and demeanor suggest that she was capable, orderly, and efficient. She illustrates the integration of the mundane tasks of housekeeping with the shifting currents of transatlantic commerce. Although tens of thousands of slaves were brought from Africa to British North America during the eighteenth century, Phyllis was probably not one of them. Instead, she was most likely born in the colonies of mixed black and white parentage.
Courtesy of Historic New England.

READING THE IMAGE: Compare this image to that of Mrs. Willing on page 150. What differences and similarities do you see in their styles of dress?
CONNECTIONS: What do these differences suggest about life in colonial America? How were women like Phyllis and Mrs. Willing affected by the burgeoning transatlantic trade in the colonies?

FOR MORE HELP ANALYZING THIS IMAGE, see the visual activity for this chapter in the Online Study Guide at bedfordstmartins.com/roark.

MAP 5.1 Europeans and Africans in the Eighteenth Century
This map illustrates regions where Africans and certain immigrant groups clustered. It is important to avoid misreading the map. Predominantly English and German regions, for example, also contained colonists from other places. Likewise, regions where African slaves resided in large numbers also included many whites, slave masters among them. The map suggests the diversity of eighteenth-century colonial society.

New England: From Puritan Settlers to Yankee Traders

The New England population grew sixfold during the eighteenth century but lagged behind the growth in the other colonies. Why did New England fail to keep pace? Most immigrants chose other destinations because of New England's relatively densely settled land and because Puritan orthodoxy made these colonies comparatively inhospitable to religious dissenters and those indifferent to religion. As the population grew, many settlers in search of farmland dispersed from towns, and Puritan communities lost much of their cohesion. Nonetheless, networks of economic exchange laced New Englanders to their neighbors, to Boston merchants, and to the broad currents of Atlantic commerce. In many ways, trade became a faith that competed strongly with the traditions of **Puritanism**.

Natural Increase and Land Distribution

The New England population grew mostly by natural increase, much as it had during the seventeenth century. Nearly every adult woman married. Most married women had children—often many children, thanks to the relatively low mortality rate in New England. The perils of childbirth gave wives a shorter life expectancy than husbands, but wives often lived to have six, seven, or eight babies. When a wife died, her husband usually remarried quickly. Anne Franklin and her husband, Josiah, a soap and candle maker in Boston, had seven children. Four months after Anne died, Josiah married his second wife, Abiah, and the couple had ten more children, including their son Benjamin, who became one of the most prominent colonial leaders of the eighteenth century.

The growing New England population pressed against a limited amount of land. Compared to colonies farther south, New England had less land for the expansion of settlement (see Map 5.1). Moreover, as the northernmost group of British colonies, New England had a contested northern and western **frontier**. Powerful Native Americans, especially the Iroquois and Mahican tribes, jealously guarded their territory. The French (and Catholic) colony of New France also menaced the British (and mostly **Protestant**) New England colonies when provoked by colonial or European disputes. (See chapter 4, "Beyond America's Borders," page 130.)

During the seventeenth century, New England towns parceled out land to individual families. In most cases, the original settlers practiced partible inheritance (that is, they subdivided land more or less equally among sons). By the eighteenth century, the original land allotments had to be further subdivided to accommodate grandsons and great-grandsons, and many plots of land became too small to support a family. Sons who could not hope to inherit sufficient land to farm had to move away from the town where they were born.

During the eighteenth century, colonial governments in New England abandoned the seventeenth-century policy of granting land to towns. Needing revenue, the governments of both Connecticut and Massachusetts sold land directly to individuals, including speculators. Now money, rather than membership in a community bound by a church **covenant**, determined whether a person could obtain land. The new land policy eroded the seventeenth-century pattern of settlement. As colonists moved into western Massachusetts and Connecticut and north into present-day New Hampshire and Maine, they tended to settle on individual farms rather than in the towns and villages that characterized the seventeenth century. New Englanders still depended on their relatives and neighbors for help in clearing land, raising a house, worshipping God, and having a good time. But far more than in the seventeenth century, they regulated their behavior in newly settled areas by their own individual choices.

Farms, Fish, and Atlantic Trade

A New England farm was a place to get by, not to get rich. New England farmers grew food for their families, but their fields did not produce a huge marketable surplus. Instead of one big crop, farmers grew many small ones. If they had extra, they sold to or traded with neighbors. Poor roads made travel difficult, time-consuming, and expensive, especially with bulky and heavy agricultural goods. The one major agricultural product the New England colonies exported—livestock—walked to market on its own legs. By 1770, New Englanders had only one-fourth as much wealth per capita as free colonists in the southern colonies.

As consumers, New England farmers participated in a diversified commercial economy that linked remote farms to markets throughout the Atlantic world. Merchants large and small stocked imported goods—British textiles, ceramics, and metal goods; Chinese tea; West Indian sugar; and Chesapeake tobacco. Farmers' needs for sturdy shoes, warm coats, sturdy carts, and solid buildings supported local shoemakers, tailors, wheelwrights, and carpenters. Larger towns, especially Boston, housed skilled tradesmen such as cabinetmakers, silversmiths, and printers. Shipbuilders tended to do better than other **artisans** because they served the most dynamic sector of the New England economy.

Boston Common in Needlework

Hannah Otis embroidered this exquisite needlework portrait of Boston Common in 1750, when she was eighteen years old. From the perspective of the twenty-first century, the scene gives few hints of city life. Otis populated the cityscape with more animals than people and more plants than paving stones. The large house (center right) belonged to the Hancock family. John Hancock, who later signed the Declaration of Independence, is shown on horseback in the foreground. Eighteenth-century Bostonians owned slaves, as Otis shows. What features of this portrait would suggest a city to an eighteenth-century viewer? How does Otis's portrait of urban Boston compare to the rural farm of Marten Van Bergen on page 148? Photograph © 2008 Museum of Fine Arts, Boston.

Many New Englanders made their fortunes at sea, as they had since the seventeenth century. Fish accounted for more than a third of New England's eighteenth-century exports; livestock and timber made up another third. The West Indies absorbed two-thirds of all New England's exports. Slaves on Caribbean sugar plantations ate dried, salted cod-fish caught by New England fisher-men, filled barrels crafted from New England timber with molasses and refined sugar, and loaded those bar-rels aboard ships bound ultimately for Europeans with a sweet tooth. Almost all of the rest of New En-gland's exports went to Britain and continental Europe (Map 5.2). This Atlantic commerce benefited the entire New England economy, providing jobs for laborers and tradesmen, as well as for ship captains, clerks, merchants, and sailors. (See "Seeking the American Promise," page 144.)

> A Connecticut traveler wrote from England in 1764, "We in New England know nothing of poverty and want, we have no idea of the thing, how much better do our poor people live than 7/8 of the people on this much famed island."

Merchants dominated Atlantic commerce. The largest and most successful merchants lived in Boston at the hub of trade between local folk and the international market. Merchants not only bought and sold goods, but they also owned and insured the ships that carried the merchandise throughout the Atlantic world. Shrewd, diligent, and lucky merchants could make a fortune. The magnificence of a wealthy Boston merchant's home stunned John Adams, a thrifty Massachusetts lawyer who became a leader during the American Revolution and ultimately the second president of the United States. To Adams, the merchant's house seemed fit "for a noble Man, a Prince," furnished with "Turkey Carpets, . . . painted Hangings, . . . Marble Tables, . . . rich Beds . . . , [and a] beautiful Chimney Clock, . . . [in all] the most magnificent of any Thing I have ever seen." Such luxurious Boston homes contrasted with the modest dwellings of Adams and other New Englanders, an indication of the polarization of wealth that developed in Boston and other seaports during the eighteenth century. By 1770, the richest 5 percent of Bostonians owned about half the city's wealth; the poorest two-thirds of the population owned less than one-tenth.

While the rich got richer and everybody else had a smaller share of the total wealth, the incidence of genuine poverty did not change much. About 5 percent of New Englanders qualified for poor relief throughout the eighteenth century. Overall, colonists were better off than most people in England. A Connecticut traveler wrote from England in 1764, "We in New England know nothing of poverty and want, we have no idea of the thing, how much better do our poor people live than 7/8 of the people on this much famed island."

The contrast with English poverty had meaning because the overwhelming majority of New Englanders traced their ancestry to England. New England was more homogeneously English than any other colonial region. People of African ancestry (almost all of them slaves) numbered more than 15,000 by 1770, but they barely diversified the region's 97 percent white majority. Most New Englanders had no hesitation about acquiring slaves, and many Puritan ministers owned one or two. In the Narragansett region of Rhode Island, large landowners imported numerous slaves to raise livestock. But most New Englanders had little use for slaves on their family farms. Instead, slaves concentrated in towns, especially Boston, where most of them worked as domestic servants and laborers.

By 1770, the population, wealth, and commercial activity of New England differed from what they had been in 1700. Ministers still enjoyed high status, but Yankee traders had replaced Puritan saints as the symbolic New Englanders. Atlantic commerce competed with religious convictions in ordering New Englanders' daily lives.

> **REVIEW**   Why did settlement patterns in New England change from the seventeenth to the eighteenth century?

The Middle Colonies: Immigrants, Wheat, and Work

In 1700, almost twice as many people lived in New England as in the middle colonies of Pennsylvania, New York, New Jersey, and Delaware. But by 1770, the population of the middle colonies had multiplied tenfold—mainly from an influx of German, Irish, Scottish, and other immigrants—and nearly equaled the population of New England. Immigrants made the middle colonies a uniquely diverse society. By 1800, barely one-third of Pennsylvanians and less than half the total population of the middle colonies traced their ancestry to England.

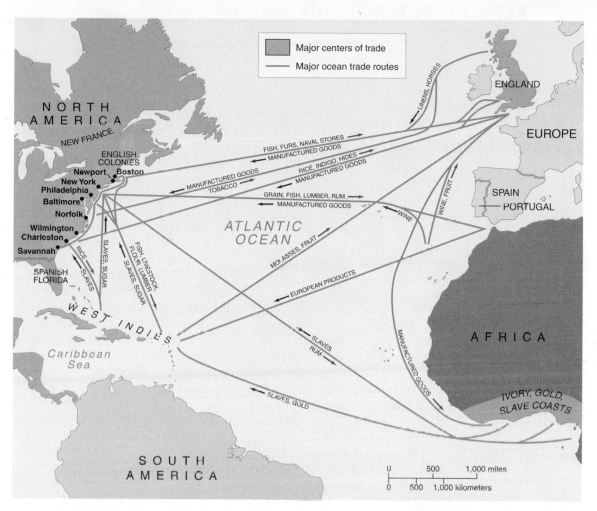

MAP 5.2 **Atlantic Trade in the Eighteenth Century**
This map illustrates the economic outlook of the colonies in the eighteenth century—east toward
the Atlantic world rather than west toward the interior of North America. The long distances involved
in the Atlantic trade and the uncertainties of ocean travel suggest the difficulties Britain experienced
governing the colonies and regulating colonial commerce.

READING THE MAP: What were the major markets for trade coming out of Europe? What goods did the
British colonies import and export?
CONNECTIONS: In what ways did the flow of raw materials from the colonies affect British industry?
How did British colonial trade policies influence the Atlantic trade?

FOR MORE HELP ANALYZING THIS MAP, see the map activity for this chapter in the Online Study Guide at
bedfordstmartins.com/roark.

German and Scots-Irish Immigrants

Germans made up the largest contingent of
migrants from the European continent to the
middle colonies. By 1770, about 85,000 Germans
had arrived in the colonies. Their fellow colonists
often referred to them as "Pennsylvania Dutch,"
an English corruption of *Deutsch*, the word the
immigrants used to describe themselves.

Most German immigrants came from what is
now southwestern Germany, where, one
observer noted, peasants were "not as well off

as cattle elsewhere." Devastating French invasions of Germany during Queen Anne's War
(1702–1713) made bad conditions worse and triggered the first large-scale migration. German immigrants included numerous artisans and a few
merchants, but the great majority were farmers
and laborers. Economically, they represented
"middling folk," neither the poorest (who could
not afford the trip) nor the better-off (who did not
want to leave).

By the 1720s, Germans who had established
themselves in the colonies wrote back to their

A Sailor's Life in the Eighteenth-Century Atlantic World

Although most eighteenth-century North American colonists made their living on farms, tens of thousands manned the vessels that ferried people, animals, commodities, consumer goods, ideas, microorganisms, and much more from port to port throughout the Atlantic world. Built almost entirely from wood crafted into hulls, masts, and fittings and from fiber twisted into ropes or woven into sails, ships were the most complex machines in the eighteenth century. Sailing them required learning a specialized vocabulary that was indecipherable to landlubbers. When the mate shouted, "The Helm's A-Lee, Fore-Sheet, Fore Top-Bowline, Jib and Stay-Sail Sheets Let Go!" the seamen had no time to ask questions and fumble around. They needed to know how to handle the intricacies of a vessel's working parts quickly, smoothly, and reliably. The ship, the cargo, and their own lives depended on such knowledge and dexterity. They also had to endure hard physical labor for weeks or months on end in a cramped space packed with cargo and crew. Sailors followed "one of the hardest and dangerousest callings," one old salt declared.

Despite the certainty of strenuous work and spartan accommodations, young men like Ashley Bowen made their way to wharves in small ports such as Marblehead, Massa-

chusetts—Bowen's hometown—or large commercial centers such as Boston, Philadelphia, New York, and Charleston. There they boarded vessels and launched a life of seafaring, seeking the promise of a future wafted on the surface of the deep rather than rooted below the surface of the soil.

Born in 1728, Bowen grew up in Marblehead, one of the most important fishing ports in North America. Like other boys who lived in or near ports, Bowen probably watched ships come and go; heard tales of adventure, disaster, and intrigue; and learned from neighbors and pals how to maneuver small, shallow-draft boats within sight of land. Young girls sometimes learned to handle a small boat, but they almost never worked as sailors aboard Atlantic vessels. When Bowen was only eleven years old, he sailed as a ship's boy aboard a vessel captained by the father of a friend who traveled down the coast to North Carolina to pick up a load of tar bound for Bristol, England. Upon arrival in Bristol, the crew—except underage Bowen and his friend—were pressed (that is, forced, involuntarily) into the British navy. The vessel picked up a new crew and a cargo of coal in Wales and carried it to Boston, where Bowen, now twelve, arrived with a yearlong seafaring education under his belt.

Most commonly, young men first went to sea when they were fifteen to eighteen years old. Like Bowen,

they were single, living with their parents, and casting about for work. They usually sailed with friends, neighbors, or kinfolk, and they sought an education in the ways of the sea. Also like Bowen, they aspired to earn some wages, to rise in the ranks eventually from seaman to mate and possibly to master (the common term for captain), to save enough to marry and support a family, and after twenty years or so to retire from the rigors of the seafaring life with a "competency"—that is, enough money to live modestly.

It typically took about four years at sea to become a fully competent seaman. Shortly after Bowen returned from his first voyage, his father apprenticed him to a sea captain for seven years. In return for a hefty payment, the captain agreed to tutor young Bowen in the art of seafaring, which ideally promised to ease his path to become a captain himself. In reality, the captain employed him as a cabin boy, taught him little except to obey, and beat him for trivial mistakes, causing Bowen to run away after four years of servitude.

Now seventeen years old, Bowen had already sailed to dozens of ports in North America, the West Indies, the British Isles, and Europe. For the next eighteen years, he shipped out as a common seaman on scores of vessels carrying nearly every kind of cargo afloat on the Atlantic. He sailed mostly aboard merchant freighters, but he also worked on whalers, fishing boats, privateers, and warships. He survived sickness, imprisonment, foul weather, accidents, and innumerable close calls. But when he retired from seafaring at age thirty-five, he still had not managed to attain command. In twenty-four years at sea, he had worked as either a common seaman or a mate, with the exception of two or three voyages that he commanded. He tried again and again to be hired as a shipmaster, but shipowners refused to employ him, despite his experience. For whatever reason, when shipowners eyed Bowen, they did not see a man they would trust to command their vessels.

Careful study of other eighteenth-century colonial seamen discloses that Bowen did better than some, about as well as many, and less well than the most successful. Unlike Bowen, about three out of ten seamen died at sea. Many drowned or died as a result of injuries, but most succumbed to tropical diseases usually picked up in the West Indies. Bowen had a hardy constitution and lived to the age of eighty-

five. After his retirement, he worked in Marblehead as a rigger, crafting nautical fittings for sailing vessels. Like Bowen, about three out of ten seamen spent their entire seafaring careers as seamen or mates, earning five dollars a month or so in wages. This was roughly comparable to wages for farm laborers, who often received payment in kind rather than in currency. About one in four seamen attained the status and improved earnings of shipmasters. Masters earned two to five times as much as common seamen and could profit handsomely from the privilege of carrying and selling their own private cargoes in available space aboard the vessels they commanded.

Although Ashley Bowen failed to attain the ultimate goal of his seafaring career, he maintained his connection to seafaring with his trade as a rigger, and he lived out his life in Marblehead within sight, sound, and smell of the sea. When Bowen was about sixty, he wrote the only autobiography ever written by an eighteenth-century common seaman, chronicling the promise, achievements, adventures, and problems of a seafaring life. When Bowen, like thousands of other seafarers in the colonies, looked at the world, his gaze did not turn west toward the farms and forests of the interior, but east toward the promise of the masts and sails in the harbor and the Atlantic deep beyond

Ashley Bowen's Journal

Ashley Bowen painted these watercolors of ships he sailed aboard in 1754, 1755, and 1756. Befitting an experienced seaman, he paid attention to the distinctive rigging and flags of each vessel, and he kept notes about the vessels' owners, masters, mates, passengers, and destinations. As the focus of Bowen's fascination, the vessels dwarf the buildings of Marblehead, Massachusetts, in the background. To Bowen, each ship had distinctive features. Can you spot the differences that caught his eye? Why might such differences be important to Bowen?

Photo courtesy of The Marblehead Historical Society, Marblehead, MA.

German Hymnal

This manuscript hymnal, once owned by Benjamin Franklin, contains words and music created by Johann Conrad Beissel, the founder of the Seventh-Day Baptists and among the earliest musical composers in the colonies. A German sect that migrated to Pennsylvania in 1732, the Seventh-Day Baptists, like many other German immigrants, continued to worship in their native German long after arriving in the British colonies. The hymns evoke the Seventh-Day Baptists' vision of "The Bitter good, or . . . the Christian church here on earth, in the valley of sadness."

Roger Foley/Library of Congress.

worshipped in Lutheran or German Reformed churches; many others belonged to dissenting sects such as the Mennonites, Moravians, and Amish, whose adherents sought relief from persecution they had suffered in Europe for their refusal to bear arms and to swear oaths, practices they shared with the Quakers. In contrast, the Scots-Irish tended to be militant Presbyterians who seldom hesitated to bear arms or swear oaths. Like German settlers, however, Scots-Irish immigrants were clannish, residing when they could among relatives or neighbors from the old country.

In the eighteenth century, wave after wave of Scots-Irish immigrants arrived, beginning in 1717, cresting every twelve or fifteen years thereafter, and culminating in a flood of immigration in the years just before the American Revolution. Deteriorating economic conditions in northern Ireland, Scotland, and England pushed many toward America. Most of the immigrants were farm laborers or tenant farmers fleeing droughts, crop failures, high food prices, or rising rents. They came, they told inquisitive British officials, because of "poverty," "tyranny of landlords," and their desire to "do better in America."

Both Scots-Irish and Germans probably heard the common saying "Pennsylvania is heaven for farmers [and] paradise for

friends and relatives, as one reported, "of the civil and religious liberties [and] privileges, and of all the goodness I have heard and seen." Such letters prompted still more Germans to pull up stakes and embark for America, to exchange the miserable certainties of their lives in Europe for the uncertain attractions of life in the middle colonies.

Similar motives propelled the Scots-Irish, who considerably outnumbered German immigrants. The term *Scots-Irish* was another misleading label coined in the colonies. Immigrants labeled "Scots-Irish" actually hailed from northern Ireland, Scotland, and northern England. Like the Germans, the Scots-Irish were Protestants, but with a difference. Most German immigrants

Weathercock

To twenty-first-century eyes, this mid–eighteenth-century rooster seems an appropriate weather vane for a farmhouse or barn. In fact, however, it crowned the first Lutheran church in Schoharie, New York, where it reminded believers of Christ's prediction at the Last Supper that his devoted disciple Peter would betray him three times before the cock crowed. Lutheran and German Reform churches often displayed such weathercocks to warn that even the most devout and faithful Christians frequently succumbed to the weaknesses of the flesh and the temptations of sin.

Schoharie County Historical Society, Old Stone Fort Museum.

artisans," but they almost certainly did not fully understand the risks of their decision to leave their native lands. Ship captains, aware of the hunger for labor in the colonies, eagerly signed up the penniless emigrants as "redemptioners," a variant of indentured servants. A captain would agree to provide transportation to Philadelphia, where redemptioners would obtain the money to pay for their passage by borrowing it from a friend or relative who was already in the colonies or, as most did, by selling themselves as servants. Many redemptioners traveled in family groups, unlike impoverished Scots-Irish emigrants, who usually traveled alone and paid for their passage by contracting as indentured servants before they sailed to the colonies.

Redemptioners and indentured servants were packed aboard ships "as closely as herring," one migrant observed. Seasickness compounded by exhaustion, poverty, poor food, bad water, inadequate sanitation, and tight quarters encouraged the spread of disease. On the sixteen immigrant ships arriving in Philadelphia in 1738, over half the passengers died en route. When one ship finally approached land, a traveler wrote, "everyone crawls from below to the deck . . . and people cry for joy, pray, and sing praises and thanks to God." Unfortunately, their troubles were far from over. Redemptioners and indentured servants had to stay on board until somebody came to purchase their labor. Unlike indentured servants, redemptioners negotiated independently with their purchasers about their period of servitude. Typically, a healthy adult redemptioner agreed to four years of labor. Indentured servants commonly served five, six, or seven years. Children usually had to serve as indentured servants until they reached twenty-one.

Pennsylvania: "The Best Poor [White] Man's Country"

New settlers, whether free or in servitude, poured into the middle colonies because they perceived unparalleled opportunities, particularly in Pennsylvania, "the best poor Man's Country in the World," as an indentured servant wrote in 1743. Although the servant reported that "the Condition of bought Servants is very hard" and masters often failed to live up to their promise to provide decent food and clothing, opportunity abounded because there was more work to be done than workers to do it.

Most servants toiled in Philadelphia, New York City, or one of the smaller towns or villages.

Artisans, small manufacturers, and shopkeepers prized the labor of male servants. Female servants made valuable additions to households, where nearly all of them cleaned, washed, cooked, or minded children. From the masters' viewpoint, servants were a bargain. A master could purchase five or six years of a servant's labor for approximately the wages a common laborer would earn in four months. Wage workers could walk away from their jobs when they pleased, and they did so often enough to be troublesome for employers. Servants, however, could not walk away; they were legally bound to work for their masters until their terms expired.

> Both Scots-Irish and Germans probably heard the common saying "Pennsylvania is heaven for farmers [and] paradise for artisans," but they almost certainly did not fully understand the risks of their decision to leave their native lands.

Since a slave cost at least three times as much as a servant, only affluent colonists could afford the long-term investment in slave labor. Like many other prosperous urban residents, Benjamin Franklin purchased a few slaves after he became wealthy. But most farmers in the middle colonies used family labor, not slaves. Wheat, the most widely grown crop, did not require more labor than farmers could typically muster from relatives, neighbors, and a hired hand or two. Consequently, although people of African ancestry (almost all slaves) increased to more than 30,000 in the middle colonies by 1770, they accounted for only about 7 percent of the total population and much less outside the cities.

Most slaves, like the Robin Johns, came to the middle colonies and New England after a stopover in the West Indies. Very few came directly from Africa. Enough slaves arrived to prompt colonial assemblies to pass laws that punished slaves much more severely than servants for the same transgressions. "For the least trespass," an indentured servant reported, slaves "undergo the severest Punishment." In practice, both servants and slaves were governed more by their masters than by the laws. But in cases of abuse, servants could and did charge masters with violating the terms of their indenture contracts. The terms of a slave's bondage were set forth in a master's commands, not in a written contract.

Small numbers of slaves managed to obtain their freedom, though few of them as dramatically as the Robin Johns. But free African Americans did not escape whites' firm convictions about black inferiority and white supremacy. Whites' racism and blacks' lowly social

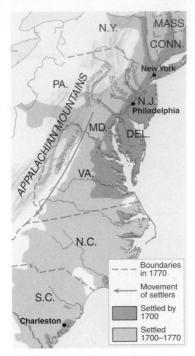

Patterns of Settlement, 1700–1770

Boundaries in 1770
Movement of settlers
Settled by 1700
Settled 1700–1770

status made African Americans scapegoats for European Americans' suspicions and anxieties. In 1741, when arson and several unexplained thefts plagued New York City, officials suspected a murderous slave conspiracy. On the basis of little evidence other than the slaves' "insolence" (refusal to conform fully to whites' expectations of servile behavior), city authorities had thirteen slaves burned at the stake and eighteen others hanged. Although slaves were certifiably impoverished, they were not among the poor for whom the middle colonies were reputed to be the best country in the world.

Immigrants swarmed to the middle colonies because of the availability of land. The Penn family encouraged immigration to bring in potential buyers for their enormous tracts of land in Pennsylvania. From the beginning, Pennsylvania followed a policy of negotiating with Indian tribes to purchase additional land. This policy reduced the violent frontier clashes more common elsewhere in the colonies. Yet the Penn family did not shrink from pushing its agreements with Indians

to the limit and beyond. In a dispute with tribes on the northern Delaware River in 1737, the Penns pulled out a document showing that local Indians had granted the colonists land that stretched as far as a man could walk in a day and a half. Under the terms of this infamous "Walking Purchase," the Penns sent out three runners, two of whom collapsed before the thirty-six hours expired. The third runner raced more than sixty miles, doubling the size of the Penns' claim.

Few colonists drifted beyond the northern boundaries of Pennsylvania. Owners of the huge estates in New York's Hudson valley preferred to rent rather than sell their land, and therefore they attracted fewer immigrants. The Iroquois dominated the lucrative fur trade of the St. Lawrence valley and eastern Great Lakes, and they vigorously defended their territory from colonial encroachment. Few settlers chose to risk having their scalps lifted by Iroquois warriors in northern New York when they could settle instead in the comparatively safe environs of Pennsylvania.

The price of farmland depended on soil quality, access to water, distance from a market town, and extent of improvements. One hundred acres of improved land that had been cleared, plowed, fenced, and ditched, and perhaps had a house and barn built on it, cost three or four times more than the same acreage of uncleared,

Marten Van Bergen Farm

This rare 1730s painting by a local artist depicts the farm of Marten and Catarina Van Bergen, prosperous Dutch colonists in New York's Hudson valley. Commissioned by the Van Bergens to hang over their fireplace mantel, the painting portrays the farm as a peaceable, small-scale kingdom governed by the couple and populated by their seven children, their slaves and indentured servants, and neighboring Native Americans, as well as assorted pets, livestock, and poultry. Carved out of the forest at the foot of the Catskill Mountains, the farm is connected to the wider world, represented by the foreboding darkness beyond the fence, by a road along which people, goods, and information traveled. Rather than a place of fields and crops, which are absent from the painting, the farm is the locus of a happy, orderly family revolving around Marten and Catarina and the warm hearth just behind them. What ideas and attitudes are suggested by the clothing of the people in the painting? What do the design and construction of the house and outbuildings suggest about the influence of different cultures at the farm?

Bethlehem, Pennsylvania

This view of the small community of Bethlehem, Pennsylvania, in 1757 dramatizes the profound transformation of the natural landscape wrought in the eighteenth century by highly motivated human labor. Founded by Moravian immigrants in 1740, Bethlehem must have appeared at first like the dense woods on the upper left horizon. In less than twenty years, precisely laid-out orchards and fields replaced forests and glades. By carefully penning their livestock (lower center right) and fencing their fields (lower left), farmers safeguarded their livelihoods from the risks and disorders of untamed nature. Individual farmsteads (lower center) and impressive multistory brick town buildings (upper center) integrated the bounty of the land with the delights of community life. Few eighteenth-century communities were as orderly as Bethlehem, but many effected a comparable transformation of the environment.

Print Collection, Miriam and Ira D. Wallack Division of Art, Prints and Photographs, The New York Public Library. Astor, Lenox, and Tilden Foundations.

READING THE IMAGE: What does this painting indicate about the colonists' priorities?

CONNECTIONS: Why might Pennsylvanians have been so concerned about maintaining order?

FOR MORE HELP ANALYZING THIS IMAGE, see the visual activity for this chapter in the Online Study Guide at bedfordstmartins.com/roark.

---

unimproved land. Since the cheapest land always lay at the margin of settlement, would-be farmers tended to migrate to promising areas just beyond already improved farms. From Philadelphia, settlers moved north along the Delaware River and west along the Schuylkill and Susquehanna rivers. By midcentury, settlement had reached the eastern slopes of the Appalachian Mountains, and newcomers spilled south down the fertile valley of the Shenandoah River into western Virginia and the Carolinas. Thousands of settlers migrated from the middle colonies through this back door to the South.

Farmers made the middle colonies the breadbasket of North America. They planted a wide variety of crops to feed their families, but they grew wheat in abundance. Flour milling was the number one industry and flour the number one export, constituting nearly three-fourths of all exports from the middle colonies. Pennsylvania flour fed residents in other colonies, in southern Europe, and, above all, in the West Indies (see Map 5.2). For farmers, the grain market in the Atlantic world proved risky but profitable. Grain prices rose steadily after 1720. By 1770, a bushel of wheat was worth twice as much (adjusted for inflation) as it had been fifty years earlier.

The standard of living in rural Pennsylvania was probably higher than in any other agricultural region of the eighteenth-century world. The comparatively widespread prosperity of all the middle colonies permitted residents to indulge in a half-century shopping spree for British imports. The middle colonies' per capita consumption of imported goods from Britain more than doubled between 1720 and 1770, far outstripping the per capita consumption of British goods in New England and the southern colonies.

At the crossroads of trade in wheat exports and British imports stood Philadelphia. By 1776, Philadelphia had a larger population than any other city in the entire British empire except London. Merchants occupied the top stratum of Philadelphia society. In a city where only 2 percent of the residents owned enough property to qualify to vote, merchants built grand homes and dominated local government. Many of Philadelphia's wealthiest merchants were Quakers. Quaker traits of industry, thrift, honesty, and sobriety encouraged the accumulation of wealth. A colonist complained that a Quaker "prays for his neighbor on First Days [the Sabbath] and then preys on him the other six."

The ranks of merchants reached downward to aspiring tradesmen such as Benjamin Franklin.

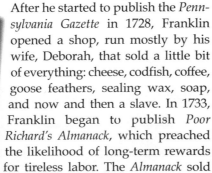

After he started to publish the *Pennsylvania Gazette* in 1728, Franklin opened a shop, run mostly by his wife, Deborah, that sold a little bit of everything: cheese, codfish, coffee, goose feathers, sealing wax, soap, and now and then a slave. In 1733, Franklin began to publish *Poor Richard's Almanack*, which preached the likelihood of long-term rewards for tireless labor. The *Almanack* sold thousands of copies, quickly becoming Franklin's most profitable product.

The popularity of *Poor Richard's Almanack* suggests that many Pennsylvanians thought less about the pearly gates than about their pocketbooks. Poor Richard's advice that "God gives all Things to Industry" might be considered the

Mrs. Charles Willing
This portrait of Mrs. Charles Willing of Philadelphia illustrates the prosperity achieved by numerous women and men in the eighteenth-century colonies. Painted by the Philadelphia artist Robert Feke in 1746, the portrait depicts the close connections between Europe and the North American colonies made possible by the thriving transatlantic commerce. Scholars have discovered that Anna Maria Garthwaite, an established textile designer in Spitalfields — a silk-weaving center near London — designed the material used to make Mrs. Willing's dress. A Spitalfields weaver, Simeon Julins, then wove the fabric and sold it to a merchant, who exported it to Philadelphia in 1744. Mrs. Willing must have spotted the silk in a shop and purchased enough to have this fashionable gown made for her portrait. The portrait demonstrates that, like other prosperous colonists, Mrs. Willing kept abreast of the latest London fashions available in the shops of colonial merchants.
Courtesy, Winterthur Museum, gift of Mrs. George P. Bissell Jr.

motto for the middle colonies. The promise of a worldly payoff made work a secular faith. Poor Richard advised, "Work as if you were to live 100 years, Pray as if you were to die Tomorrow."

William Penn's Quaker utopia became a center of worldly affluence whose most famous citizen, Franklin, was neither a Quaker nor a utopian. Quakers remained influential, but Franklin spoke for most colonists with his aphorisms of work, discipline, and thrift that echoed Quaker rules for outward behavior. Franklin's maxims did not look to the Quakers' divine inner light for guidance. They depended instead on the spark of ambition and the glow of gain.

> **REVIEW** Why did immigrants flood into Pennsylvania during the eighteenth century?

The Southern Colonies: Land of Slavery

Between 1700 and 1770, the population of the southern colonies of Virginia, Maryland, North Carolina, South Carolina, and Georgia grew almost ninefold. By 1770, about twice as many people lived in the South as in either the middle colonies or New England. As elsewhere, natural increase and immigration accounted for the rapid population growth. Many Scots-Irish and German immigrants funneled from the middle colonies into the southern backcountry. Other immigrants were indentured servants (mostly English and Scots-Irish) who followed their seventeenth-century predecessors. But slaves made the most striking contribution to the booming southern colonies, transforming the racial composition of the population. Slavery became the defining characteristic of the southern colonies during the eighteenth century, shaping the region's economy, society, and politics.

The Atlantic Slave Trade and the Growth of Slavery

The number of southerners of African ancestry (nearly all of them slaves) rocketed from just over 20,000 in 1700 to well over 400,000 in 1770. The black population increased nearly three times faster than the South's briskly growing white population. Consequently, the proportion of southerners of African ancestry grew from 20 percent in 1700 to 40 percent in 1770.

Southern colonists clustered into two distinct geographic and agricultural zones. The colonies in the upper South, surrounding the Chesapeake Bay, specialized in growing tobacco, as they had since the early seventeenth century. Throughout the eighteenth century, nine out of ten southern whites and eight out of ten southern blacks lived in the Chesapeake region. The upper South retained a white majority during the eighteenth century.

Charleston Harbor
This 1730s painting of Charleston, South Carolina, depicts the intersecting currents of international trade and local commerce in the variety of vessels conveying goods and people between ship and shore. More African slaves arrived in Charleston than in any other North American port, yet no slaves appear in this painting. Without slaves, however, Charleston harbor would have been virtually empty, and the prosperous city shown in the background would have been little more than a swampy outpost.
Colonial Williamsburg Foundation.

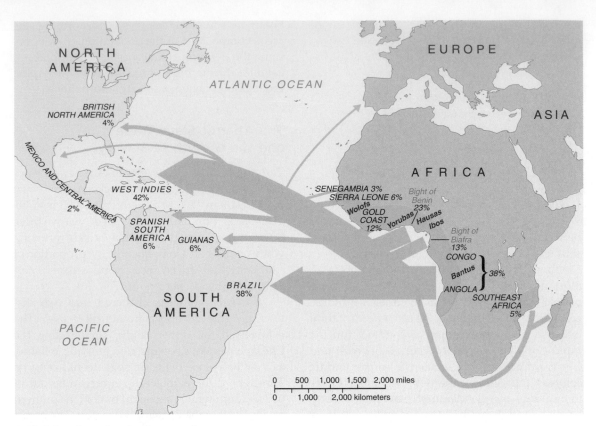

MAP 5.3   The Atlantic Slave Trade

Although the Atlantic slave trade lasted from about 1450 to 1870, its peak occurred during the eighteenth century, when more than six million African slaves were imported to the New World. Only a small fraction of these slaves were taken to British North America. Most went to sugar plantations in Brazil and the Caribbean.

READING THE MAP: Where in Africa did most slaves originate? Approximately how far was the trip from the busiest ports of origin to the two most common New World destinations?

CONNECTIONS: Why were so many more African slaves sent to the West Indies and Brazil than to British North America?

FOR MORE HELP ANALYZING THIS MAP, see the map activity for this chapter in the Online Study Guide at bedfordstmartins.com/roark.

In the lower South, a much smaller cluster of colonists inhabited the coastal region and specialized in the production of rice and indigo (a plant used to make blue dye). Lower South colonists made up only 5 percent of the total population of the southern colonies in 1700 but inched upward to 15 percent by 1770. South Carolina was the sole British colony along the southern Atlantic coast until 1732, when Georgia was founded. (North Carolina, founded in 1711, was largely an extension of the Chesapeake region.) Blacks in South Carolina, in contrast to every other British mainland colony, outnumbered whites almost two to one; in some low-country districts, the ratio of blacks to whites exceeded ten to one.

The enormous growth in the South's slave population occurred through natural increase and the flourishing Atlantic slave trade (Map 5.3 and Table 5.1). Slave ships brought almost 300,000 Africans to British North America be-

TABLE 5.1	SLAVE IMPORTS, 1451–1870
Estimated Slave Imports to the Western Hemisphere	
1451–1600	275,000
1601–1700	1,341,000
1701–1810	6,100,000
1811–1870	1,900,000

tween 1619 and 1780. Of these Africans, 95 percent arrived in the South and 96 percent arrived during the eighteenth century. Unlike indentured servants or redemptioners, these Africans did not choose to come to the colonies. Like the Robin Johns, most of them had been born into free families in villages located within a few hundred miles of the West African coast. Although they shared African origins, they came from many different African **cultures**, including Akan, Angolan, Asante, Bambara, Gambian, Igbo, Mandinga, and others. They spoke different languages, worshipped different deities, observed different rules of kinship, grew different crops, and recognized different rulers.

The most important experience they had in common was enslavement. Captured in war, kidnapped, or sold into slavery by other Africans, they were brought to the coast, sold to African traders like the Robin Johns who assembled slaves for resale, and sold again to European or colonial slave traders or ship captains, who packed two hundred to three hundred or more aboard ships that carried them on the **Middle Passage** across the Atlantic and then sold them yet again to a colonial slave merchant or a southern **planter**.

Olaudah Equiano published an account of his enslavement that hints at the stories that might have been told by the millions of other Africans swept up in the slave trade. Equiano wrote that he was born in 1745 in the interior of what is now Nigeria. "I had never heard of white men or Europeans, nor of the sea," he recalled.

One day when he was eleven years old, he was kidnapped by Africans, who sold him to other Africans, who in turn eventually sold him to a slave ship on the coast. Equiano feared that he was "going to be killed" and "eaten by those white men with horrible looks, red faces, and loose hair." Once the ship set sail, many of the slaves, crowded together in suffocating heat fouled by filth of all descriptions, died from sickness. "The shrieks of the women and the groans of the dying rendered the whole a scene of horror almost inconceivable," Equiano recalled. Most of the slaves on the ship were sold in Barbados, but Equiano and other leftovers were shipped off to Virginia, where he "saw few or none of our native Africans and not one soul who could talk to me." Equiano felt isolated and "exceedingly miserable" because he "had no person to speak to that I could understand." Finally, the captain of a tobacco ship bound for England purchased Equiano, and he traveled as a slave between North America, England, and the West Indies for ten years until he succeeded in buying his freedom in 1766.

Only about 15 percent of the slaves brought into the southern colonies came aboard ships from the West Indies, as Equiano and the Robin Johns did. All the other slaves brought into the southern colonies came directly from Africa, and almost all the ships that brought them (roughly 90 percent) belonged to British merchants. Most of the slaves on board were young adults, with men usually outnumbering women two to one. Children under the age of fourteen, like Equiano, typically accounted for no more than 10 to 15 percent of a cargo.

Olaudah Equiano
This portrait shows Equiano more than a decade after he had bought his freedom. The portrait evokes Equiano's successful acculturation to the customs of eighteenth-century England. His clothing and hairstyle reflect the fashions of a respectable young Englishman. In his *Interesting Narrative*, Equiano explained that he had learned to speak and understand English while he was a slave. He wrote that he "looked upon [the English] . . . as men superior to us [Africans], and therefore I had the stronger desire to resemble them, to imbibe their spirit and imitate their manners; I therefore embraced every occasion of improvement, and every new thing that I observed I treasured up in my memory." Equiano's embrace of English culture did not cause him to forsake his African roots. He honored his dual identity by campaigning against slavery. His *Narrative* was one of the most important and powerful antislavery documents of the time.
Library of Congress.

Negro's houses

a fire

Boys playing under that Rooff

a Woman with her Child on her back

a door

The African Slave Trade

The African slave trade existed to satisfy the New World's demand for labor and Europe's voracious appetite for such New World products as sugar, tobacco, and rice. African men, women, and children, like those pictured in this early-eighteenth-century engraving of a family residence in Sierra Leone, were kidnapped or captured in wars—typically by other Africans—and enslaved. Uprooted from their homes and kin, they were usually taken to coastal enclaves where African traders and European ship captains negotiated prices, made deals, and often branded the newly enslaved people. The collaboration between Europeans and their African trading partners is evident in the seventeenth-century Benin bronze box in the shape of a royal palace in Nigeria. The palace is guarded by two massive predatory birds and two Portuguese soldiers. Jammed into the holds of slave ships, enslaved Africans made the dreaded Middle Passage to the New World. The model of a slave ship shown here was used in parliamentary debates by antislavery leaders in Britain to demonstrate the inhumanity of shipping people as if they were cargo. The model does not show another typical feature of slave ships: weapons. Slaves vastly outnumbered the crews aboard the ships, and crew members justifiably feared slave uprisings.

Benin bronze box: Staatliche Museen Zu Berlin, Preussischer Kulturbesitz; Engraving: Courtesy, Earl Gregg Swen Library, College of William and Mary, Williamsburg, Virginia; Slave ship model: Wilberforce House, Hull City Museums and Art Galleries, UK/Bridgeman Art Library.

Mortality during the Middle Passage varied considerably from ship to ship. On average, about 15 percent of the slaves died, but sometimes half or more perished. The average mortality among the white crew of slave ships was often nearly as bad. In general, the longer the voyage lasted, the more people died. Recent studies suggest that many slaves succumbed not only to virulent epidemic diseases such as smallpox and dysentery, but also to acute dehydration caused by fluid loss from perspiration, vomiting, and diarrhea combined with a severe shortage of drinking water.

Normally, an individual planter purchased at any one time a relatively small number of newly arrived Africans, or "new Negroes," as they were called. New Negroes were often profoundly depressed, demoralized, and disoriented. Planters expected their other slaves—either those born into slavery in the colonies (often called "country-born" or "creole" slaves) or Africans who had arrived earlier—to help new Negroes become accustomed to their strange new surroundings.

Planters' preferences for slaves from specific regions of Africa aided slaves' acculturation (or "seasoning," as it was called) to the routines of bondage in the southern colonies. Chesapeake planters preferred slaves from Senegambia, the Gold Coast, or—like Equiano and the Robin Johns—the Bight of Biafra, which combined accounted for 40 percent of all Africans imported to the Chesapeake. South Carolina planters favored slaves from the central African Congo and Angola regions, the origin of about 40 percent of the African slaves they imported (see Map 5.3). Although slaves within each of these regions spoke many different languages, enough linguistic and cultural similarities existed that they could usually communicate with other Africans from the same region.

Seasoning acclimated new Africans to the physical as well as the cultural environment of the southern colonies. Slaves who had just endured the Middle Passage were poorly nourished, weak, and sick. In this vulnerable state, they encountered the alien diseases of North America without having developed a biological arsenal of acquired immunities. As many as 10 to 15 percent of newly arrived Africans, sometimes more, died during their first year in the southern colonies. Nonetheless, the large number of newly enslaved Africans made the influence of African culture in the South stronger in the eighteenth century than ever before—or since.

While newly enslaved Africans poured into the southern colonies, slave mothers bore children, which caused the slave population in the South to grow rapidly. Slave owners encouraged these births. Thomas Jefferson explained, "I consider the labor of a breeding [slave] woman as no object, that a [slave] child raised every 2 years is of more profit than the crop of the best laboring [slave] man." Although slave mothers loved and nurtured their children, the mortality rate among slave children was high, and the ever-present risk of being separated by sale brought grief to many slave families. Nonetheless, the growing number of slave babies set the southern colonies apart from other New World slave societies, where mortality rates were so high that deaths exceeded births. The high rate of natural increase in the southern colonies meant that by the 1740s, the majority of southern slaves were country-born.

Slave Labor and African American Culture

Southern planters expected slaves to work from sunup to sundown and beyond. George Washington wrote that his slaves should "be at their work as soon as it is light, work til it is dark, and be diligent while they are at it." The conflict between the masters' desire for maximum labor and the slaves' reluctance to do more than necessary made the threat of physical punishment a constant for eighteenth-century slaves. Masters preferred black slaves to white indentured servants, not just because slaves served for life but also because colonial laws did not limit the force masters could use against slaves. As a traveler observed in 1740, "A new negro . . . [will] let a hundred men show him how to hoe, or drive a wheelbarrow; he'll still take the one by the bottom and the other by the wheel and . . . often die before [he] can be conquered." Slaves, the traveler noted, resisted their masters' demands because of their "greatness of soul"—their stubborn unwillingness to conform to their masters' definition of them as merely slaves.

> George Washington wrote that his slaves should "be at their work as soon as it is light, work til it is dark, and be diligent while they are at it."

Some slaves escalated their acts of resistance to direct physical confrontation with the master, the mistress, or an overseer. But a hoe raised in anger, a punch in the face, or a desperate swipe with a knife led to swift and predictable retaliation by whites. Throughout the southern colonies, the balance of physical power rested securely in the hands of whites.

Rebellion occurred, however, at Stono, South Carolina, in 1739. Before dawn on a September Sunday, a group of about twenty slaves attacked a country store, killed the two storekeepers, and confiscated the store's guns, ammunition, and powder. Enticing other slaves to join, the group plundered and burned more than half a dozen plantations and killed more than twenty white men, women, and children. A mounted force of whites quickly suppressed the rebellion. They placed the rebels' heads atop mileposts along the road, grim reminders of the consequences of rebellion. The Stono rebellion illustrated that eighteenth-century slaves had no chance of overturning slavery and very little chance of defending themselves in any bold strike for freedom. After the rebellion, South Carolina legislators enacted repressive laws designed to guarantee that whites would always have the upper hand. No other similar uprisings occurred during the colonial period.

Slaves maneuvered constantly to protect themselves and to gain a measure of autonomy within the boundaries of slavery. In Chesapeake tobacco fields, most slaves were subject to close supervision by whites. In the lower South, the task system gave slaves some control over the pace of their work and some discretion in the use of the rest of their time. A "task" was typically defined as a certain area of ground to be cultivated or a specific job to be completed. A slave who completed the assigned task might use the remainder of the day, if any, to work in a garden, fish, hunt, spin, weave, sew, or cook. When masters sought to boost productivity by increasing tasks, slaves did what they could to defend their customary work assignments.

Eighteenth-century slaves also planted the roots of African American lineages that branch out to the present. Slaves valued family ties, and, as in West African societies, kinship structured slaves' relations with one another. Slave parents often gave a child the name of a grandparent, aunt, or uncle. In West Africa, kinship identified a person's place among living relatives and linked the person to ancestors in the past and to descendants in the future. Newly imported African slaves usually arrived alone, like Equiano, without kin. Often slaves who had traversed the Middle Passage on the same ship adopted one another as "brothers" and "sisters." Likewise, as new Negroes were seasoned and incorporated into existing slave communities, established families often adopted them as "fictive" kin.

When possible, slaves expressed many other features of their West African origins in their lives on New World plantations. They gave their children traditional dolls and African names such as Cudjo or Quash, Minda or Fuladi. They grew food crops they had known in Africa, such as yams and okra. They constructed huts with mud walls and thatched roofs similar to African residences. They fashioned banjos, drums, and other

> The extravagant lifestyle of one gentry family astonished a tutor from New Jersey, who noted that during the winter, the family kept twenty-eight large fires roaring, requiring six oxen to haul four cartloads stacked with slave-cut firewood to the house every day.

musical instruments, held dances, and observed funeral rites that echoed African practices. In these and many other ways, slaves drew upon their African heritages as much as the oppressive circumstances of slavery permitted.

Tobacco, Rice, and Prosperity

Slaves' labor bestowed prosperity on their masters, British merchants, and the monarchy. The southern colonies supplied 90 percent of all North American exports to Britain. Rice exports from the lower South exploded from less than half a million pounds in 1700 to eighty million pounds in 1770, nearly all of it grown by slaves. Exports of indigo also boomed. Together, rice and indigo made up three-fourths of lower South exports, nearly two-thirds of them going to Britain and most of the rest to the West Indies, where sugar-growing slaves ate slave-grown rice. Tobacco was by far the most important export from British North America; by 1770, it represented almost one-third of all colonial exports and three-fourths of all Chesapeake exports. And under the provisions of the Navigation Acts (see chapter 4), nearly all of it went to Britain, where the monarchy collected a lucrative tax on each pound. British merchants then reexported more than 80 percent of the tobacco to the European continent, pocketing a nice markup for their troubles.

These products of slave labor made the southern colonies by far the richest in North America. The per capita wealth of free whites in the South was four times greater than that in New England and three times that in the middle colonies. At the top of the wealth pyramid stood the rice grandees of the lower South and the tobacco gentry of the Chesapeake. These elite families commonly resided on large estates in handsome mansions adorned by luxurious gardens, all maintained and supported by slaves. The extravagant lifestyle of one gentry family astonished a young tutor from New Jersey, who noted that during the winter months, the family kept twenty-eight large fires roaring, requiring six oxen to haul four cartloads stacked with slave-cut firewood to the house every day. In contrast, **yeoman** families—who supported themselves on small plots of land without slaves—cut their own firewood and normally warmed themselves around just one fire.

The vast differences in wealth among white southerners engendered

Eliza Lucas Pinckney's Gown

When Eliza Lucas was sixteen years old in 1738, she took over day-to-day management of her father's rice plantations when he was called to duty in the British army. Highly educated, independent, and energetic, Lucas relished her duties and introduced numerous innovations on the plantations, including the cultivation of indigo—which became a major export crop in South Carolina—and silkworms. She married Charles Pinckney, a wealthy rice planter, in 1744 and continued her interest in agricultural innovation while raising four children. The gown shown here was made for her out of silk produced on her plantation and sent to England to be dyed and woven.

Smithsonian Institution, Washington, D.C.

envy and occasional tension between rich and poor, but remarkably little open hostility. In private, the planter elite spoke disparagingly of humble whites, but in public the planters acknowledged their lesser neighbors as equals, at least in belonging to the superior—in their minds—white race. Looking upward, white yeomen and tenants (who owned neither land nor slaves) sensed the gentry's condescension and veiled contempt. But they also appreciated the gentry for granting favors, upholding white supremacy, and keeping slaves in their place. Although racial slavery made a few whites much richer than others, it also gave those who did not get rich a powerful reason to feel similar (in race) to those who were so different (in wealth).

The slaveholding gentry dominated the politics and economy of the southern colonies. In Virginia, only adult white men who owned at least one hundred acres of unimproved land or twenty-five acres of land with a house could vote. This property-holding requirement prevented about 40 percent of white men in Virginia from voting for representatives to the House of Burgesses. In South Carolina, the property requirement was only fifty acres of land, and therefore most adult white men qualified to vote. In both colonies, voters elected members of the gentry to serve in the colonial legislature. The gentry passed elected political offices from generation to generation, almost as if they were hereditary. Politically, the gentry built a self-perpetuating oligarchy—rule by the elite few—with the votes of their many humble neighbors.

The gentry also set the cultural standard in the southern colonies. They entertained lavishly, gambled regularly, and attended Anglican (Church of England) services more for social than for religious reasons. Above all, they cultivated the leisurely pursuit of happiness. They did not condone idleness, however. Their many pleasures and responsibilities as plantation owners kept them busy. Thomas Jefferson, a phenomenally productive member of the gentry, recalled that his earliest childhood memory was of being carried on a pillow by a family slave—a powerful image of the slave hands supporting the gentry's leisure and achievement.

REVIEW   How did slavery influence the society and economy of the southern colonies?

Unifying Experiences

The societies of New England, the middle colonies, and the southern colonies became more sharply differentiated during the eighteenth century, but colonists throughout British North America also shared unifying experiences that eluded settlers in the Spanish and French colonies. The first was economic. All three British colonial regions had their economic roots in agriculture. Colonists sold their distinctive products in markets that, in turn, offered to consumers throughout British North America a more or less uniform array of goods. A second unifying experience was a decline in the importance of religion. Some settlers called for a revival of religious intensity, but most people focused less on religion and more on the affairs of the world than they had in the seventeenth century. Third, white inhabitants throughout British North America became aware that they shared a distinctive identity as *British* colonists. Thirteen different governments presided over these North American colonies, but all of them answered to the British monarchy. British policies governed not only trade but also military and diplomatic relations with the Indians, French, and Spanish arrayed along colonial borderlands. Royal officials who expected loyalty from the colonists often had difficulty obtaining obedience. The British colonists asserted their prerogatives as British subjects to defend their special colonial interests.

Commerce and Consumption

Eighteenth-century commerce whetted colonists' appetites to consume. Colonial products spurred the development of mass markets throughout the Atlantic world (Figure 5.1). Huge increases in the supply of colonial tobacco and sugar brought the price of these small luxuries within the reach of most free whites. Colonial goods brought into focus an important lesson of eighteenth-century commerce: Ordinary people, not just the wealthy elite, would buy the things that they desired in addition to what they absolutely needed. Even news, formerly restricted mostly to a few people through face-to-face conversations or private letters, became an object of public consumption through the innovation of newspapers. (See "The Promise of Technology," page 160.) With the appropriate stimulus, market demand seemed unlimited.

The Atlantic commerce that took colonial goods to markets in Britain brought objects of consumer desire back to the colonies. British merchants and manufacturers recognized that colonists made excellent customers, and the Navigation Acts gave British exporters privileged access to the colonial market. By midcentury, export-oriented industries in Britain were growing ten times faster than firms attuned to the home market. Most British exports went to the vast European market, where potential customers outnumbered those in the colonies by more than one hundred to one. But as European competition stiffened, colonial markets became increasingly important. British exports to North America multiplied eightfold between 1700 and 1770, outpacing the rate of population growth after midcentury (see Figure 5.1). When the colonists' eagerness to consume exceeded their ability to pay, British exporters willingly extended credit, and colonial debts soared.

Imported mirrors, silver plate, spices, bed and table linens, clocks, tea services, wigs, books, and more infiltrated parlors, kitchens, and bedrooms throughout the colonies. Despite the many differences among the colonists, the consumption of British exports built a certain material uniformity across region, religion, class, and status. Consumption of British exports made the colonists look and feel more British even though they lived at the edge of a wilderness an ocean away from Britain.

The rising tide of colonial consumption had other less visible but no less important consequences. Consumption presented women and men with a novel array of choices. In many respects, the choices might appear trivial: whether to buy knives and forks, teacups, or a clock. But such small choices confronted eighteenth-century consumers with a big question: What do you want? As colonial consumers defined and expressed their desires with greater frequency during the eighteenth century, they became accustomed to thinking of themselves as individuals who had the power to make decisions that influenced the quality of their lives—attitudes of significance in the hierarchical world of eighteenth-century British North America.

Religion, Enlightenment, and Revival

Eighteenth-century colonists could choose from almost as many religions as consumer goods. Virtually all of the bewildering variety of religious

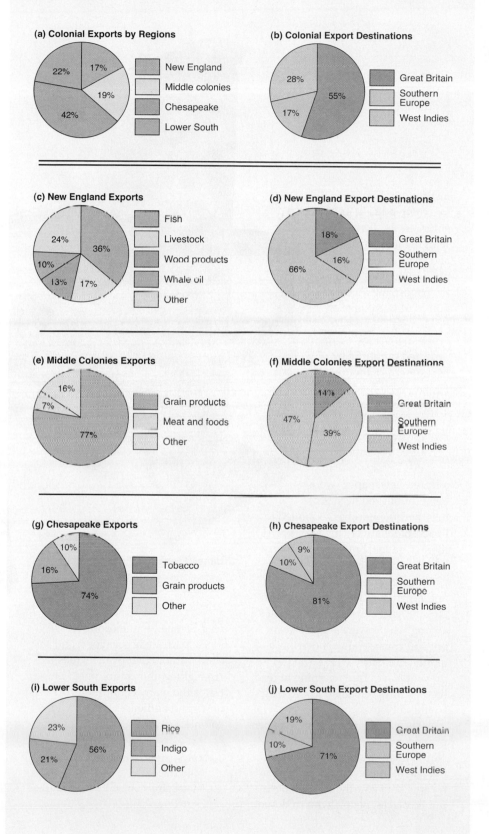

(a) Colonial Exports by Regions

- 17% New England
- 19% Middle colonies
- 42% Chesapeake
- 22% Lower South

(b) Colonial Export Destinations

- 55% Great Britain
- 17% Southern Europe
- 28% West Indies

(c) New England Exports

- 36% Fish
- 17% Livestock
- 13% Wood products
- 10% Whale oil
- 24% Other

(d) New England Export Destinations

- 18% Great Britain
- 16% Southern Europe
- 66% West Indies

(e) Middle Colonies Exports

- 77% Grain products
- 7% Meat and foods
- 16% Other

(f) Middle Colonies Export Destinations

- 14% Great Britain
- 39% Southern Europe
- 47% West Indies

(g) Chesapeake Exports

- 74% Tobacco
- 16% Grain products
- 10% Other

(h) Chesapeake Export Destinations

- 81% Great Britain
- 9% Southern Europe
- 10% West Indies

(i) Lower South Exports

- 56% Rice
- 21% Indigo
- 23% Other

(j) Lower South Export Destinations

- 71% Great Britain
- 10% Southern Europe
- 19% West Indies

FIGURE 5.1
Colonial Exports, 1768–1772

These pie charts provide an overview of the colonial export economy in the 1760s. The first two show that almost two-thirds of colonial exports came from the South and that the majority of the colonies' exports went to Great Britain. The remaining charts illustrate the distinctive patterns of exports in each colonial region. Fish, livestock, and wood products were New England's most important exports; they were sent primarily to the West Indies. Grain products made up three-fourths of all exports from the middle colonies; most of these went to the West Indies and southern Europe. The Chesapeake also exported some grain, but tobacco accounted for three-fourths of that region's export trade. Nearly all of it went to Great Britain, as mandated by the Navigation Acts. Rice and indigo accounted for three-fourths of the exports from the lower South; the bulk of this was sent to Great Britain. Taken together, these charts reveal Britain's economic interest in the exports of the North American colonies.

Newspapers: "The Spring of Knowledge"

In the eighteenth century, colonial printers began to publish newspapers. Since the 1630s, colonial printers had used presses to churn out books, pamphlets, broadsides, government announcements, legal forms, invitations, and even promissory notes. The innovation of compiling newsworthy information and publishing it on a regular schedule began in 1704 with the appearance of the *Boston News-Letter*, which was usually printed on both sides of a single sheet of paper smaller than conventional typing paper. Each week the *News-Letter* contained reprints of articles that had appeared in British newspapers, along with a few tidbits of local news such as deaths, fires, storms, and ship arrivals.

For years, the audience for such information remained small; the editor complained in 1719 that he could not sell three hundred copies of each issue. Nonetheless, a competing newspaper, the *Boston Gazette*, began publication in that year. It was printed by James Franklin on his press, which he had brought from England. Both the *Gazette* and the *News-Letter* submitted their copy to the governor for official approval before the newspapers were printed. Frustrated by this official scrutiny, Franklin started a new paper, the *New England Courant*, which set out to thumb its nose at officialdom, both government and religious institutions. The *Courant* pledged "to entertain the Town with the most comical and diverting Incidents of Humane Life" and to "expose the Vice and Follies of Persons of all Ranks and Degrees." Franklin's press—operated faithfully by his apprentice brother, Benjamin—broadcast to the reading public dissenting opinions previously confined to private conversations.

By 1740, more than a dozen newspapers were being published in the colonies, and the number continued to increase. Relatively high rates of literacy gave them a large audience. In the northern colonies, readers included well over half of adult men and nearly half of adult women. In the southern colonies, literacy rates among whites were slightly lower but still considerably above those in England. Since whites tried to prevent slaves from learning to read, literacy rates remained low among southern blacks.

The information that newspapers printed spread far beyond readers. Newspapers were often read aloud, not just at home but in workshops, taverns, and courthouses. In these public places, people who could not

James Franklin's Printing Press
Newport Historical Society.

read listened to the controversial ideas, partisan accusations, and salacious rumors that printers relished. An eighteenth-century poem illustrates the many connections between news and audiences cultivated by colonial newspapers:

> News-papers are the spring of knowledge,
> The gen'ral source throughout the nation.

Of ev'ry modern conversation.
What would this mighty people do,
If there, alas! were nothing new?

A News-paper is like a feast,
Some dish there is for ev'ry guest;
Some large, some small, some
strong, some tender,
For ev'ry stomach, stout or slender;
Those who roast beef and ale de-
light in,
Are pleas'd with trumpets, drums,
and fighting;
For those who are more puny
made,
Are arts and sciences, and trade;
For fanciful and am'rous blood,
We have a soft poetic food;
For witty and satyric folks,
High-season'd, acid, BITTER
JOKES;
And when we strive to please the
mob,
A jest, a quarrel, or a job.

If any gentleman wants a wife,
(A partner, as 'tis termed, for life)
An advertisement does the thing,
And quickly brings the pretty thing

If you want health, consult our pages,
You shall be well, and live for ages. . . .

Our services you can't express,
The good we do you hardly guess;
There's not a want of human kind,
But we a remedy can find.

When newspapers employed the technology of printing to publish everything from political news to advertisements for a spouse, all kinds of information and ideas began to spread more readily beyond official channels and to help form public opinion. Combining the old technology of printing with the new currents of commerce, dissent, and enlightenment, eighteenth-century newspapers created a novel awareness of the problems and possibilities of public life.

Numb. XIII.

THE
New-York Weekly JOURNAL,

Containing the freſheſt Advices, Foreign, and Domeſtick.

MUNDAY January 28, 1733.

Lege fr.enata omnis poteſtas Eſto.
BRACTON.

SIR,

MEN in a Torrent of Proſperity ſeldom think of a Day of Diſtreſs, or Great Men that their greatneſs will ever Ceaſe. This ſeems to be a Sort of a Curſe upon Power, a Vanity and Infatuation blended with the Nature of it: As if it were Poſſible nay eaſy to bind the Fickleneſs of Fortune, and enſure Happyneſs for a Term of Years. Tis from this Aſſureance, often cleaving to very able Men that thoſe in Authority often act with ſuch Boldneſs and Inſolence as if their Reign were never to End, and they were for ever ſecure againſt all After-reckonings, all caſualties and diſgrace. From whence elſe comes it, but from ſuch blindSecurity in the Permanence of their Condition, and in the Impunity of their Actions, that Miniſters have ſometimes concerted SCHEMES OF GENERAL OPPRESSION AND PILLAGE, SCHEMES TO DEPRECIATE OR EVADE THE LAWs, RESTRAINTS UPON LIBERTY AND PROIECTS FOR ARBITRARY WILL? Had they thought that ever they themſelves ſhould ſuffer in the common Oppreſſion would they have adviſed *Methods of Oppreſſing*? Should they have been for *Weakning* or *abrogating the Laws*, had they Dreamed that they ſhould come to want THE PROTECTION OF THE LAW? Would they have aimed at *Aboliſhing Liberty*, had they apprehended that they were at any time to fall from Power; or at eſtabliſhing *deſpotick Rule*, but for the Sake of *having the Direction of it* againſt others, without feeling ITS Weight and Terrors in their own Particulars?

How few Men in Power have ſecured to themſelves a Reſource of Friendſhip and Affection from the Publick, in Caſe of a Storm at Court and the Frowns of a Croun! Nay what ſome of them have done to ſerve the Crown againſt the People, has been a Motive with the Crown (and a politic Motive, tho not always a juſt one, at leaſt not generous) to Sacrifice them to the Pleaſure and Revenge of the People, thus *Cæſar Borgio*, uſed *Romiro D'orco* Governour of *Rumagna*, one firſt employed to commit Cruelties then executed for having committed them. Thus were EMPSON and DUDLEY uſed, and thus the great Turk often uſes his Baſhaws.

The GENERAL SECURITY, is the only certain Security of particulars; and tho'Deſperate Men often find ſafety in publick Deſtruction, yet they cannot inſure the ſame ſafety to their Children, who muſt ſuffer with the reſt in the miſery of all. If Great wicked Men would conſider this, the World would not be plagued with their Ambition, their Poſterity ſcarce ever miſs to reap the bitter Fruits of their Actions, and the Curſe of their iniquities rarely fails to follow them to the third and fourth Generation.

The INSTRUMENTS OF PUBLICK RUIN have generally at once intailed miſery upon their Country and their own Race. Thoſe who were the Inſtruments and Miniſters of *Cæſar* and *Auguſtus*, and put the Common Wealth under their Feet AND THEM ABOVE THE LAWS, did not conſider that they were not only forging Chains for their Country, but whetting Swords againſt their own Families, who were all cut off under ſucceeding Tyrants: Nay, moſt of their Children fell

early

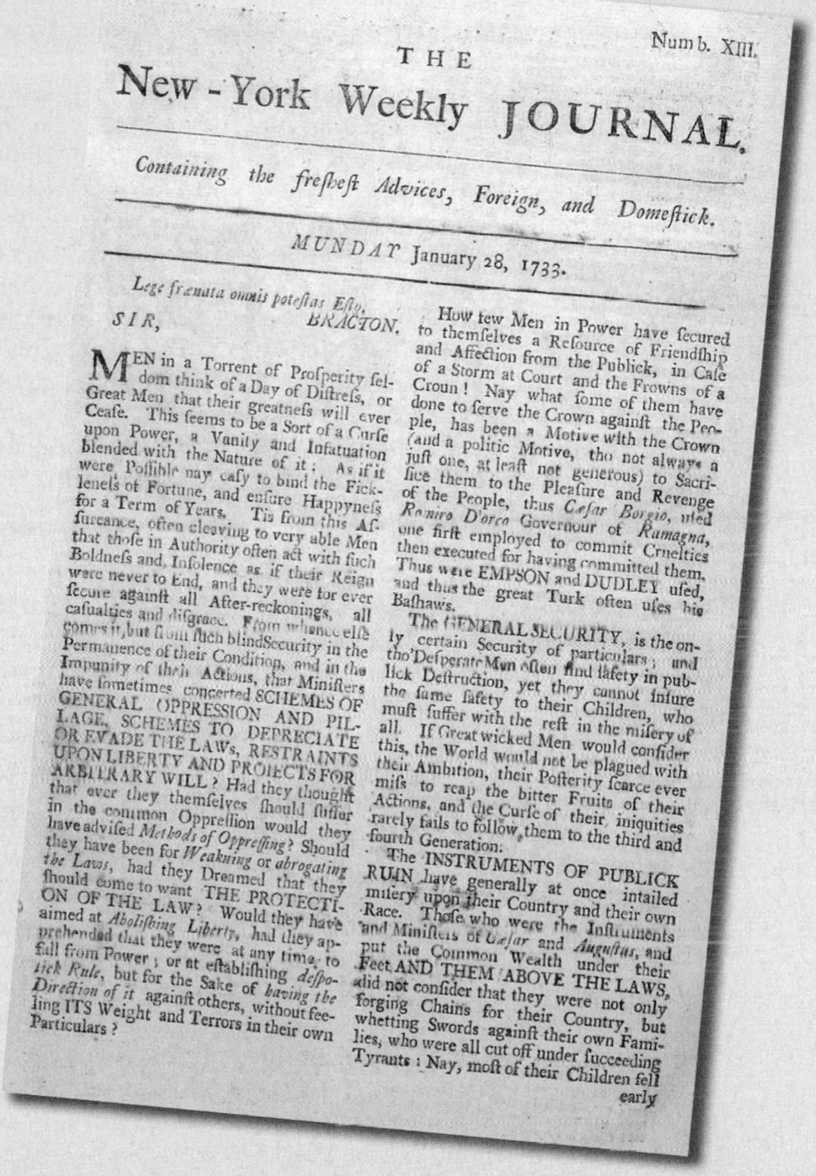

John Peter Zenger's Newspaper

This issue of John Peter Zenger's *New-York Weekly Journal* contained on the third of its four pages an article criticizing New York's governor. For this and other critical articles, the governor had Zenger tried for seditious libel in 1735. The jury sided with Zenger and acquitted him, although the law favored the governor. Like Zenger, printers throughout the colonies continued to be harassed by public officials who tried to censor irreverent and independent publishers. But colonial governments were too weak to suppress dissenting opinions for very long. Vigorous political commentary like that featured on the page shown here found an avid audience among colonial readers.

Courtesy, American Antiquarian Society.

denominations represented some form of Christianity, almost all of them Protestant. Slaves made up the largest group of non-Christians. A few slaves converted to Christianity in Africa or after they arrived in North America, but most continued to embrace elements of indigenous African religions. Roman Catholics concentrated in Maryland as they had since the seventeenth century, but even there they were outnumbered by Protestants.

The varieties of Protestant faith and practice ranged across a broad spectrum. The middle colonies and the southern backcountry included militant Baptists and Presbyterians. Huguenots who had fled persecution in Catholic France peopled congregations in several cities. In New England, old-style Puritanism splintered into strands of Congregationalism that differed over fine points of theological doctrine. The Congregational Church was the official established church in New England, and all residents paid taxes for its support. Throughout the plantation South and in urban centers such as Charleston, New York, and Philadelphia, prominent colonists belonged to the Anglican Church, which received tax support in the South. But dissenting faiths grew everywhere, and in most colonies their adherents won the right to worship publicly, although the established churches retained official support.

Many educated colonists became deists, looking for God's plan in nature more than in the Bible. Deists shared the ideas of eighteenth-century European **Enlightenment** thinkers, who tended to agree that science and reason could disclose God's laws in the natural order. In the colonies as well as in Europe, Enlightenment ideas encouraged people to study the world around them, to think for themselves, and to ask whether the disorderly appearance of things masked the principles of a deeper, more profound natural order. From New England towns to southern drawing rooms, individuals met to discuss such matters. Philadelphia was the center of these conversations, especially after the formation of the American Philosophical Society in 1769, an outgrowth of an earlier group organized by Benjamin Franklin, who was a deist. Leading colonial thinkers such as Franklin and Thomas Jefferson, among many other members, communicated with each other seeking both to understand nature and to find ways to improve society. Franklin's interest in electricity, stoves,

> A minister in Charleston observed that on the Sabbath, "the Taverns have more Visitants than the Churches."

and eyeglasses exemplified the shift of focus among many eighteenth-century colonists from heaven to the here and now.

Most eighteenth-century colonists went to church seldom or not at all, although they probably considered themselves Christians. A minister in Charleston observed that on the Sabbath, "the Taverns have more Visitants than the Churches." In the leading colonial cities, church members were a small minority of eligible adults, no more than 10 to 15 percent. Anglican parishes in the South rarely claimed more than one-fifth of eligible adults as members. In some regions of rural New England and the middle colonies, church membership embraced two-thirds of eligible adults, while in other areas, only one-quarter of the residents belonged to a church. The dominant faith overall was religious indifference. As a late-eighteenth-century traveler observed, "Religious indifference is imperceptibly disseminated from one end of the continent to the other."

The spread of religious indifference, of deism, of denominational rivalry, and of comfortable backsliding profoundly concerned many Christians. A few despaired that, as one wrote, "religion . . . lay a-dying and ready to expire its last breath of life." To combat what one preacher called the "dead formality" of church services, some ministers set out to convert nonbelievers and to revive the piety of the faithful with a new style of preaching that appealed more to the heart than to the head. Historians have termed this wave of revivals the **Great Awakening**. In Massachusetts during the mid-1730s, the fiery Puritan minister Jonathan Edwards reaped a harvest of souls by reemphasizing traditional Puritan doctrines of humanity's utter depravity and God's vengeful omnipotence. The title of Edwards's most famous sermon, "Sinners in the Hands of an Angry God," conveys the flavor of his message. In Pennsylvania and New Jersey, William Tennent led revivals that dramatized spiritual rebirth with accounts of God's miraculous powers, such as raising Tennent's son from the dead.

The most famous revivalist in the eighteenth-century Atlantic world was George Whitefield. An Anglican, Whitefield preached well-worn messages of sin and salvation to large audiences in England using his spellbinding, unforgettable voice. Whitefield visited the North American colonies seven times, staying for more than three years during the mid-1740s and attracting tens of thousands to his sermons, including Benjamin Franklin and Olaudah Equiano. Whitefield's preaching transported many in his audience to emotion-choked states of religious ecstasy. About one revival he wrote, "The bitter cries and groans were enough to pierce the hardest heart. Some of the people were as pale as death; others were wringing their hands; others lying on the ground; others sinking into the arms of their friends; and most lifting their eyes to heaven, and crying to God for mercy. They seemed like persons . . . coming out of their graves to judgment."

Whitefield's successful revivals spawned many lesser imitations. Itinerant preachers, many of them poorly educated, toured the colonial backcountry after midcentury, echoing Whitefield's medium and message as best they could. Bathsheba Kingsley, a member of Jonathan Edwards's flock, preached the revival message informally—as did an unprecedented number of other women throughout the colonies—causing her congregation to brand her a "brawling woman" who had "gone quite out of her place."

The revivals awakened and refreshed the spiritual energies of thousands of colonists struggling with the uncertainties and anxieties of eighteenth-century America. The conversions at revivals did not substantially boost the total number of church members, however. After the revivalists moved on, the routines and pressures of everyday existence reasserted their primacy in the lives of many converts. But the revivals communicated the important message that every soul mattered, that men and women could choose to be saved, that individuals had the power to make a decision for everlasting life or death. Colonial revivals expressed in religious terms many of the same democratic and egalitarian values expressed in economic terms by colonists' patterns of consumption. One colonist noted the analogy by referring to itinerant revivalists as "Pedlars in divinity." Like consumption, revivals contributed to a set of common experiences that bridged colonial divides of faith, region, class, and status.

George Whitefield

An anonymous artist portrayed George Whitefield preaching, emphasizing the power of his sermons to transport his audience to a revived awareness of divine spirituality. Light from above gleams off his forehead. His crossed eyes and faraway gaze suggest that he spoke in a semihypnotic trance. Notice the absence of a Bible on the pulpit. Rather than elaborating on God's Word as revealed in Scripture, Whitefield speaks from his own inner awareness. The young woman bathed in light below his hands appears transfixed, her focus on some inner realm illuminated by his words. Her eyes and Whitefield's do not meet, yet the artist's use of light suggests that she and Whitefield see the same core of holy Truth. The other people in Whitefield's audience appear not to have achieved this state, failing so far to be ignited by the divine spark.

National Portrait Gallery, London.

Borderlands and Colonial Politics in the British Empire

The plurality of peoples, faiths, and communities that characterized the North American colonies arose from the somewhat haphazard policies of

GLOBAL COMPARISON

Large Warships in European Navies, 1660–1760

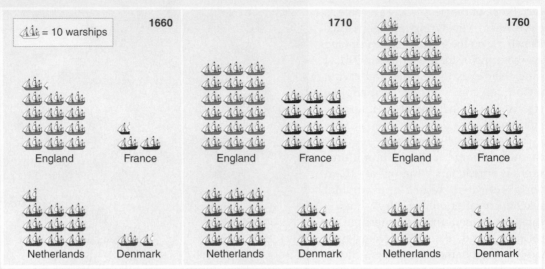

Note: Comparable data does not exist for Spain.

The large warships in England's navy usually outnumbered those of rival nations from 1660 to 1760. During the eighteenth century, the British fleet grew dramatically, while the fleets of rival nations declined. The British monarchy paid the enormous cost of building, manning, and maintaining the largest European navy because defending commerce and communication with its far-flung colonies was fundamental to the integrity of its empire. Britain's North American colonies benefited from defense by the most powerful navy in the Atlantic. However, since supremacy in the number of warships never translated automatically into supremacy in a particular naval battle, Britain's colonists constantly worried about surprise attacks by other nations, whose warships might sail into a harbor or capture a merchant vessel while British warships were someplace else. Why do you think British warships outnumbered those of their competitors? What might account for the changing numbers of warships between 1660 and 1760?

A colonial official observed in 1761, "A modern Indian cannot subsist without Europeans. . . . [The European goods that were] only conveniency at first [have] now become necessity."

the eighteenth-century British empire. Since the Puritan Revolution of the mid-seventeenth century, British monarchs had valued the colonies' contributions to trade and encouraged their growth and development. Unlike Spain and France—whose policies of excluding Protestants and foreigners kept the population of their North American colonial territories tiny—Britain kept the door to its colonies open to anyone, and tens of thousands of non-British immigrants settled in the North American colonies and raised families. The open door did not extend to trade, however, as the seventeenth-century Navigation Acts restricted colonial trade to British ships and traders. These policies evolved because they served the interests of the monarchy and of influential groups in Britain and the colonies. The policies also gave the colonists a common framework of political expectations and experiences.

At a minimum, British power defended the colonists from Indian, French, and Spanish enemies on their borders—as well as from foreign powers abroad. Each colony organized a militia, and privateers sailed from every port to prey on foreign ships. But the British navy and army bore ultimate responsibility for colonial defense. (See "Global Comparison.")

Royal officials warily eyed the small North American settlements of New France and New Spain for signs of threats to the colonies. Alone, neither New France nor New Spain jeopardized British North America, but with Indian allies, they could become a potent force that kept colonists on their guard (Map 5.4). Native Americans' impulse to defend their territory from colonial incursions warred with their desire for trade, which tugged them toward the settlers. As a colonial official observed in 1761, "A modern Indian cannot subsist without Europeans. . . . [The European goods that were] only conveniency at first [have] now become necessity." To obtain such necessities as guns, ammunition, clothing, sewing utensils, and much more that was manufactured largely by the British, Indians trapped beavers, deer, and other fur-bearing animals throughout the interior.

Colonial traders and their respective empires competed to control the fur trade. British, French, Spanish, and Dutch officials monitored the trade to prevent their competitors from deflecting the flow of furs toward their own markets. Indians took advantage of this competition to improve their own prospects, playing one trader and empire off against another. The Iroquois, for example, promised the French exclusive access to the furs and territory of the Great Lakes region and at the same time made the same pledge of exclusive rights to the British. Indian tribes and confederacies also competed among themselves for favored trading rights with one colony or another, a competition colonists encouraged.

The shifting alliances and complex dynamics of the fur trade struck a fragile balance along the frontier. The threat of violence from all sides was ever present, and the threat became reality often enough for all parties to be prepared for the worst. In the Yamasee War of 1715, Yamasee and Creek Indians—with French encouragement—mounted a coordinated attack against colonial settlements in South Carolina and inflicted heavy casualties. The Cherokee Indians, traditional enemies of the Creeks, refused to join the attack. Instead, they protected their access to British trade goods by allying with the colonists and turning the tide of battle, thus triggering a murderous rampage of revenge by the colonists against the Creek and Yamasee tribes.

Relations between Indians and colonists differed from colony to colony and from year to year. But the British colonists' nagging perceptions of menace on the frontier kept them continually hoping for help from the British to keep the Indians at bay and to maintain the essential flow of trade. In 1754, the British colonists' endemic competition with the French flared into the Seven Years' War (also known as the French and Indian War), which would inflame the frontier for years (see chapter 6). Before the 1760s, neither

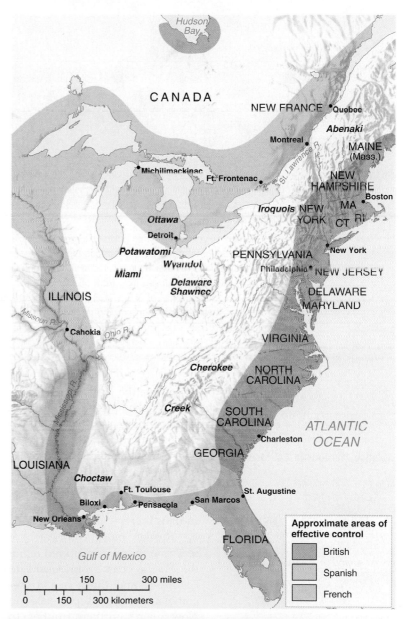

MAP 5.4 Zones of Empire in Eastern North America
The British zone, extending west from the Atlantic coast, was much more densely settled than the zones under French, Spanish, and Indian control. The comparatively large number of British colonists made them more secure than the relatively few colonists in the vast regions claimed by France and Spain or the settlers living among the many Indian peoples in the huge area between the Mississippi River and the Appalachian Mountains. Yet the British colonists were not powerful enough to dominate the French, Spanish, or Indians. Instead, they had to guard against attacks by powerful Indian groups allied with the French or Spanish.

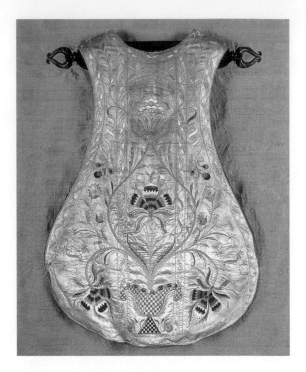

Mission Carmel

This eighteenth-century drawing portrays a reception for a Spanish visitor at Mission Carmel in what is now Carmel, California. Lines of mission Indians, dressed in robes, flank the entrance to the chapel, where a priest and his assistants await the visitor. During worship, priests wore lavishly decorated chasubles, like the one shown here from Mission Santa Clara. The intricate and colorful embroidery signified the magnificence of divine authority, embodied in the priests—God's representatives on earth—and their Spanish sponsors. The reception ritual dramatized the strict hierarchy that governed relations between Spanish missionaries, ruling officials, and the subordinate Indians.

Reception: University of California at Berkeley, Bancroft Library; Chasuble: de Saisset Museum, Santa Clara University.

the British colonists nor the British themselves developed a coherent policy toward the Indians. But both agreed that Indians made deadly enemies, profitable trading partners, and powerful allies. As a result, the British and their colonists kept an eye on the Spanish empire to the west and relations with the Indians there.

Russian hunters in search of seals and sea otters ventured along the Pacific coast from Alaska to California and threatened to become a permanent presence on New Spain's northern frontier. To block Russian access to present-day California, officials in New Spain mounted a campaign to build forts (called *presidios*) and missions there.

In 1769, an expedition headed by a military man, Gaspar de Portolá, and a Catholic priest, Junípero Serra, traveled north from Mexico to present-day San Diego, where they founded the first California mission, San Diego de Alcalá. They soon journeyed all the way to Monterey, which became the capital of Spanish California. There Portolá established a presidio in 1770 "to defend us from attacks by the Russians," he wrote. The same year, Serra founded Mission San Carlos Borroméo de Carmelo in Monterey to convert the Indians and recruit them to work to support the soldiers and other Spaniards in the presidio. By 1772, Serra had founded other missions along the path from San Diego to Monterey.

One Spanish soldier praised the work of the missionaries, writing that "with flattery and presents [the missionaries] attract the savage Indians and persuade them to adhere to life in society and to receive instruction for a knowledge of the Catholic faith, the cultivation of the land, and the arts necessary for making the instruments most needed for farming." Yet for the Indians, the Spaniards' California missions had horrendous consequences, as they had else-

Spanish Missions in California

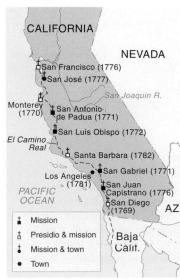

where in the Spanish borderlands. European diseases decimated Indian populations, Spanish soldiers raped Indian women, and missionaries beat Indians and subjected them to near slavery. Indian uprisings against the Spaniards occurred repeatedly (see "Documenting the American Promise," page 168), but the presidios and missions endured as feeble projections of the Spanish empire along the Pacific coast.

British attempts to exercise political power in their colonial governments met with success so long as British officials were on or very near the sea. Colonists acknowledged—although they did not always readily comply with—British authority to collect customs duties, inspect cargoes, and enforce trade regulations. But when royal officials tried to wield their authority on land in the internal affairs of the colonies, they invariably encountered colonial resistance. A governor appointed by the king in each of the nine royal colonies (Rhode Island and Connecticut selected their own governors) or by the proprietors in Maryland and Pennsylvania headed the government of each colony. The British envisioned colonial governors as mini-monarchs able to exert influence in the colonies much as the king did in Britain. But colonial governors were not kings, and the colonies were not Britain.

Eighty percent of colonial governors had been born in England, not in the colonies. Some governors stayed in England, close to the source of royal patronage, and delegated the grubby details of colonial affairs to subordinates. Even the best-intentioned colonial governors had difficulty developing relations of trust and respect with influential colonists because their terms of office averaged just five years and could be terminated at any time. Colonial governors controlled few patronage positions to secure political friendships in the colonies. Officials who administered the colonial customs service, for example, received their appointments through patronage networks centered in England rather than from colonial governors. In obedience to Britain, colonial governors fought incessantly with the colonists' assemblies. They battled over governors' vetoes of colonial legislation, removal of colonial judges, creation of new courts, dismissal of the representative assemblies, and other local issues. Some governors developed a working

Ambush of Spanish Expedition

This detail from a remarkable hide painting depicts an ambush of a Spanish expedition by French soldiers and their Pawnee and Oto allies in August 1720. Two and a half months earlier, the governor of New Mexico had sent forty-three Spanish soldiers along with sixty Pueblo Indians to expel French intruders from the northern borderlands of New Spain. When the expedition reached the confluence of the Platte and Loup rivers in present-day Nebraska, they were attacked by the French and their Indian allies, who killed thirty-three Spaniards and twelve Pueblos and drove the expedition back to New Mexico. Shortly afterward, an artist—whether Indian or Spanish is unknown—recorded the disastrous ambush of the Spaniards. The priest in the center of the detail shown here is Father Juan Minguez, the first priest assigned to Albuquerque; he was killed in the ambush. The Indian directly in front of him is Joseph Naranjo, who also was killed; he came from the Santa Clara Pueblo. He was the leader of the Spaniards' Pueblo allies and the son of Domingo Naranjo, a leader of the Pueblo Revolt against the Spaniards in 1680.
Courtesy of the Museum of New Mexico, Neg. No. 149804.

Missionaries Report on California Missions

Catholic missionaries sent regular reports to their superiors in Mexico City, New Spain's capital city. The reports described what the missionaries considered their successes in converting pagan Indians—whom they called gentiles—as well as the difficulties caused by the behavior of both Spaniards and Indians.

DOCUMENT 1
Father Luís Jayme Describes Conditions at Mission San Diego de Alcalá, 1772

Father Luís Jayme, a Franciscan missionary, reported on the deplorable behavior of some of the Spanish soldiers at Mission San Diego de Alcalá, who frequently raped Indian women, causing many Indians to resist the efforts of the missionaries.

With reference to the Indians, I wish to say that great progress [in converting Indians] would be made if there was anything to eat and the soldiers would set a good example. We cannot give them anything to eat because what Don Pedro [the governor] has given is not enough to last half a year for the Indians from the Californias who are here. Thus little progress will be made under present conditions.

As for the example set by the soldiers, no doubt some of them are good exemplars and deserve to be treated accordingly, but very many of them deserve to be hanged on account of the continuous outrages which they are committing in seizing and raping the women. There is not a single mission where all the gentiles have not been scandalized, and even on the roads, so I have been told. Surely, as the gentiles themselves state, they [the soldiers] are committing a thousand evils, particularly of a sexual nature. . . .

At one of these Indian villages near this mission of San Diego, which said village is very large, and which is on the road to Monterey, the gentiles therein many times have been on the point of coming here to kill us all, and the reason for this is that some soldiers went there and raped their women, and other soldiers who were carrying the mail to Monterey turned their animals into their fields and they ate up their crops. Three other Indian villages . . . [near] here have reported the same thing to me several times. For this reason on several occasions when . . . I have gone to see these Indian villages, as soon as they saw us they fled from their villages and fled to the woods or other remote places. . . . They do this so that the soldiers will not rape their women as they have already done so many times in the past.

No wonder the Indians here were bad when the mission was first founded. To begin with, they did not know why [the Spaniards] had come, unless they wanted to take their lands away from them. Now they all want to be Christians because they know that there is a God who created the heavens and earth and all things, that there is a Hell and Glory, that they have souls, etc., but when the mission was first founded . . . they thought they were like animals, and . . . they were very loath to pray, and they did not want to be Christians at all. . . . [Now] they all know the natural law, which, so I am informed, they have observed as well or better than many Christians elsewhere. They do not have idols; they do not go on drinking sprees; they do not marry relatives; and they have but one wife. The married men sleep with their wives only. . . . Some of the first adults whom we baptized, when we pointed out to them that it was wrong to have sexual intercourse with a woman to whom they were not married, told me that they already knew that, and that among them it was considered to be very bad, and so they do not do so at all. "The soldiers," they told me, "are Christians and, although they know that God will punish them in Hell, do so, having sexual intercourse with our wives." "We," they said, "although we did not know that God would punish us for that in Hell, considered it to be very

relationship with the colonists' assemblies. But during the eighteenth century, the assemblies gained the upper hand.

Since British policies did not clearly define the colonists' legal powers, colonial assemblies seized the opportunity to make their own rules. Gradually, the assemblies established a strong tradition of representative government analogous, in their eyes, to the British Parliament. Voters often returned the same representatives to the assem-

bad, and we did not do it, and even less now that we know that God will punish us if we do so." When I heard this, I burst into tears to see how these gentiles were setting an example for us Christians.

SOURCE: Maynard Geiger, trans. and ed., *The Letter of Luís Jayme, O.F.M.: San Diego, October 17, 1772* (Los Angeles, 1970): 38–42.

DOCUMENT 2
Father Junípero Serra Describes the Indian Revolt at Mission San Diego de Alcalá, 1775

Father Junípero Serra, the founder of many of the California missions, reported to his superiors in Mexico City that an Indian uprising had destroyed Mission San Diego de Alcalá. He recommended rebuilding and urged officials to provide additional soldiers to defend the missions, but not to punish the rebellious Indians.

As we are in the vale of tears, not all the news I have to relate can be pleasant. And so I make no excuses for announcing . . . the tragic news that I have just received of the total destruction of the San Diego Mission, and of the death of the senior of its two religious ministers, called Father Luís Jayme, at the hand of the rebellious gentiles and of the Christian neophytes [Indians who lived in the mission]. All this happened, November 5th, about one or two o'clock at night. The gentiles came together from forty rancherías, according to

information given me, and set fire to the church, after sacking it. They then went to the storehouse, the house where the Fathers lived, the soldiers' barracks, and all the rest of the buildings. They killed a carpenter . . . and a blacksmith. . . . They wounded with their arrows the four soldiers, who alone were on guard at the . . . mission. . . .

And now, after the Father has been killed, the Mission burned, its many and valuable furnishings destroyed, together with the sacred vessels, its paintings, its baptismal, marriage, and funeral records, and all the furnishings for the sacristy, the house, and the farm implements—now the forces [of soldiers] of both presidios [nearby] come together to set things right. . . . What happened was that before they set about reestablishing the Mission, they wanted to . . . lay hands on the guilty ones who were responsible for the burning of the Mission, and the death of the Fathers, and chastise them. The harassed Indians rebelled anew and became more enraged. . . . And so the soldiers there are gathered together in their presidios, and the Indians in their state of heathenism. . . .

While the missionary is alive, let the soldiers guard him, and watch over him, like the pupils of God's very eyes. That is as it should be. . . . But after the missionary has been killed, what can be gained by campaigns [against the rebellious Indians]? Some will say to frighten them and prevent them from killing others. What I say is that, in order to

prevent them from killing others, keep better guard over them than they did over the one who has been killed; and, as to the murderer, let him live, in order that he should be saved—which is the very purpose of our coming here, and the reason which justifies it.

SOURCE: Antonine Tibesar, O.F.M., ed., *The Writings of Junípero Serra.* (Washington, D. C., 1956), 2: 401–7. Reprinted by permission of the American Academy of Franciscan History.

QUESTIONS FOR ANALYSIS AND DEBATE

1. In what ways did Jayme and Serra agree about the motivations of Indians in and around Mission San Diego de Alcalá? In what ways did they disagree? How would Serra's recommendations for rebuilding the mission have addressed the problems identified by Jayme that caused the revolt?

2. How did the goals and activities of the Spanish soldiers compare with those of the Catholic missionaries? What accounted for the differences and similarities?

3. How did the religious convictions of Jayme and Serra influence their reports? What might Spanish soldiers or Indians have said about these events? What might they have said about missionaries like Jayme and Serra?

blies year after year, building continuity in power and leadership that far exceeded that of the governor. By 1720, colonial assemblies had won the power to initiate legislation, including tax laws and authorizations to spend public funds. Al-though all laws passed by the assemblies (except in Maryland, Rhode Island, and Connecticut) had to be approved by the governor and then by the Board of Trade in Britain, the difficulties in communication about complex subjects over long distances effectively ratified the assemblies' decisions. Years often passed before colonial laws were repealed by British authorities, and in the meantime, the assemblies' laws prevailed.

The heated political struggles between royal governors and colonial assemblies that occurred throughout the eighteenth century taught colonists a common set of political lessons. They learned to employ traditionally British ideas of representative government to defend their own colonial interests. They learned that power in the British colonies rarely belonged to the British government.

> **REVIEW** What experiences tended to unify the colonists in British North America during the eighteenth century?

Conclusion: The Dual Identity of British North American Colonists

During the eighteenth century, a society that was both distinctively colonial and distinctively British emerged in British North America. Tens of thousands of immigrants and slaves like the Robin Johns gave the colonies an unmistakably colonial complexion and contributed to the colonies' growing population and expanding economy. People of different ethnicities and faiths sought their fortunes in the colonies, where land was cheap, labor was dear, and—as Benjamin Franklin preached—work promised to be rewarding. Indentured servants and redemptioners risked a temporary period of bondage for the potential reward of better opportunities in the colonies than on the Atlantic's eastern shore. Slaves endured lifetime servitude, which they neither chose nor desired but from which their masters greatly benefited.

Identifiably colonial products from New England, the middle colonies, and the southern colonies flowed to the West Indies and across the Atlantic. Back came unquestionably British consumer goods along with fashions in ideas, faith, and politics. The bonds of the British empire required colonists to think of themselves as British subjects and, at the same time, encouraged them to consider their status as colonists.

People of European origin in the North American colonies of Spain and France did not share in the emerging political identity of the British colonists. They also did not participate in the cultural, economic, social, and religious changes experienced by their counterparts in British North America. Unlike the much more numerous colonists in British North America, North American Spanish and French colonists did not develop societies that began to rival the European empires that sponsored and supported them.

By 1750, British colonists in North America could not imagine that their distinctively dual identity—as British and as colonists—would soon become a source of intense conflict. But by 1776, colonists in British North America had to choose whether they were British or American.

Selected Bibliography

General Works

Ira Berlin, *Generations of Captivity: A History of African-American Slaves* (2003).

Mary Sarah Bilder, *The Transatlantic Constitution: Colonial Legal Culture and the Empire* (2004).

Holly Brewer, *By Birth or Consent: Children, Law, and the Anglo-American Revolution in Authority* (2005).

Peter A. Coclanis, ed., *The Atlantic Economy during the Seventeenth and Eighteenth Centuries: Organization, Operation, Practice, and Personnel* (2005).

Kathleen DuVal, *The Native Ground: Indians and Colonists in the Heart of the Continent* (2006).

Patrick Griffin, *The People with No Name: Ireland's Ulster Scots, America's Scots Irish, and the Creation of a British Atlantic World, 1689–1764* (2001).

Cathy Matson, ed., *The Economy of Early America: Historical Perspective and New Directions* (2006).

Martha Saxton, *Being Good: Women's Moral Values in Early America* (2003).

Nancy Shoemaker, *A Strange Likeness: Becoming Red and White in Eighteenth-Century North America* (2005).

New England

Richard Aquila, *The Iroquois Restoration: Iroquois Diplomacy on the Colonial Frontier, 1701–1754* (1997).

Elaine Forman Crane, *Ebb Tide in New England: Women, Seaports, and Social Change, 1630–1800* (1998).

Christopher Grasso, *A Speaking Aristocracy: Transforming Public Discourse in Eighteenth-Century Connecticut* (1999).

Phyllis Whitman Hunter, *Purchasing Identity in the Atlantic World: Massachusetts Merchants, 1670–1780* (2001).

George M. Marsden, *Jonathan Edwards: A Life* (2003).

Lisa Norling, *Captain Ahab Had a Wife: New England Women and the Whale Fishery, 1720–1870* (2000).

Daniel Vickers, *Young Men and the Sea: Yankee Seafarers in the Age of Sail* (2005).

Middle Colonies

Leslie M. Harris, *In the Shadow of Slavery: African Americans in New York City, 1626–1863* (2003).

Eric Hinderaker, *Elusive Empires: Constructing Colonialism in the Ohio Valley, 1673–1800* (1997).

Jill Lepore, *New York Burning: Liberty, Slavery, and Conspiracy in Eighteenth-Century Manhattan* (2005).

Brendan J. McConville, *These Darling Disturbers of the Public Peace: The Struggle for Property and Power in Early New Jersey* (1999).

James H. Merrell, *Into the American Woods: Negotiators on the Pennsylvania Frontier* (1999).

Jane T. Merritt, *At the Crossroads: Indians and Empires on a Mid-Atlantic Frontier, 1700–1763* (2003).

Donna Merwick, *The Shame and the Sorrow: Dutch-Amerindian Encounters in New Netherland* (2006).

Simon P. Newman, *Embodied History: The Lives of the Poor in Early Philadelphia* (2003).

Southern Colonies

Vincent Carretta, *Equiano the African: Biography of a Self-Made Man* (2005).

Emma Christopher, *Slave Ship Sailors and Their Captive Cargoes, 1730–1807* (2006).

Steven W. Hackel, *Children of Coyote, Missionaries of Saint Francis: Indian-Spanish Relations in Colonial California, 1769–1850* (2005).

Robert H. Jackson, *Missions and the Frontiers of Spanish America* (2005).

Catherine Kerrison, *Claiming the Pen: Women and Intellectual Life in the Early American South* (2006).

Philip D. Morgan, *Slave Counterpoint: Black Culture in the Eighteenth-Century Chesapeake and Low Country* (1998).

Robert Olwell, *Masters, Slaves, and Subjects: The Culture of Power in the South Carolina Low Country, 1740–1790* (1998).

Jon F. Sensbach, *Rebecca's Revival: Creating Black Christianity in the Atlantic World* (2005).

Randy Sparks, *The Two Princes of Calabar: An Eighteenth-Century Atlantic Odyssey* (2004).

David J. Weber, *Bárbaros: Spaniards and Their Savages in the Age of Enlightenment* (2005).

Bradford J. Wood, *This Remote Part of the World: Regional Formation in Lower Cape Fear, North Carolina, 1725–1775* (2004).

▶ For more books about topics in this chapter, see the Online Bibliography at bedfordstmartins.com/roark.

▶ For additional firsthand accounts of this period, see Chapter 5 in Michael Johnson, ed., *Reading the American Past*, Fourth Edition.

▶ For Web sites, images, and documents related to topics and places in this chapter, visit bedfordstmartins.com/makehistory.

REVIEWING THE CHAPTER

Follow these steps to review and strengthen your understanding of the chapter.
STEP 1: *Study the* **Key Terms** *and* **Timeline** *to identify the significance of each item listed.*
STEP 2: *Answer the* **Review Questions***, drawing on key terms and dates to support your answers.*
STEP 3: *Drawing on the Key Terms, Timeline, and Review Questions, answer the broader* **Making Connections** *questions.*

KEY TERMS

Who

the Robin Johns (p. 137)
Benjamin Franklin (p. 140)
Iroquois Indians (p. 140)
Mahican Indians (p. 140)
Pennsylvania Dutch (p. 143)
middling folk (p. 143)
Scots-Irish (p. 146)
redemptioners (p. 147)
Olaudah Equiano (p. 153)
"new Negroes" (p. 154)
"country-born" or "creole" slaves
   (p. 155)
Jonathan Edwards (p. 162)
George Whitefield (p. 162)
Yamasee Indians (p. 165)

Creek Indians (p. 165)
Cherokee Indians (p. 165)
Gaspar de Portolá (p. 166)
Junípero Serra (p. 166)

What

natural increase (p. 139)
partible inheritance (p. 140)
Queen Anne's War (p. 143)
Poor Richard's Almanack (p. 150)
Middle Passage (p. 153)
"seasoning" (p. 155)
Senegambia (p. 155)
Gold Coast (p. 155)
Bight of Biafra (p. 155)
Congo (p. 155)

Angola (p. 155)
Stono rebellion (p. 155)
task system (p. 156)
gentry (p. 157)
property-holding requirement (p. 157)
mass markets (p. 158)
Congregational Church (p. 162)
Enlightenment (p. 162)
American Philosophical Society (p. 162)
deism (p. 162)
Great Awakening (p. 162)
fur trade (p. 165)
Yamasee War of 1715 (p. 165)
Seven Years' War (p. 165)
presidios (p. 166)
San Diego de Alcalá (p. 166)

TIMELINE

1702 • Queen Anne's War triggers German migration to North America.

      1711 • North Carolina founded.

         1715 • Yamasee War.

           1717 • Scots-Irish immigration increases.

               1730s • Jonathan Edwards promotes Great Awakening.

               1732 • Georgia founded.

               1733 • Benjamin Franklin begins to
                       publish *Poor Richard's Almanack*.

                    1739 • Stono rebellion.

REVIEW QUESTIONS

1. How did the North American colonies achieve the remarkable population growth of the eighteenth century? (pp. 138–39)

2. Why did settlement patterns in New England change from the seventeenth to the eighteenth century? (pp. 140–42)

3. Why did immigrants flood into Pennsylvania during the eighteenth century? (pp. 142–51)

4. How did slavery influence the society and economy of the southern colonies? (pp. 151–57)

5. What experiences tended to unify the colonists in British North America during the eighteenth century? (pp. 158–70)

MAKING CONNECTIONS

1. Colonial products such as tobacco and sugar transformed consumption patterns on both sides of the Atlantic in the eighteenth century. How did consumption influence the relationship between the American colonies and Britain? In your answer, consider how it might have strengthened and weakened connections.

2. Why did the importance of religion decline throughout the colonies from the seventeenth to the eighteenth century? How did American colonists respond to these changes?

3. How did different colonies attempt to manage relations with the Indians? How did the Indians attempt to manage relationships with the Europeans? In your answer, consider disputes over territory and trade.

4. Varied immigration patterns contributed to important differences between the British colonies. Compare and contrast patterns of immigration to the middle and southern colonies. Who came, and how did they get there? How did they shape the economic, cultural, and political character of each colony?

▶ FOR PRACTICE QUIZZES, A CUSTOMIZED STUDY PLAN, AND OTHER STUDY TOOLS, see the Online Study Guide at bedfordstmartins.com/roark.

1740s • George Whitefield preaches religious revival in North America.

• Majority of southern slaves are country-born.

1745 • Olaudah Equiano born.

1750s • Colonists begin to move down Shenandoah Valley.

1754 • Seven Years' War begins.

1769 • American Philosophical Society founded.

• First California mission, San Diego de Alcalá, established.

1770 • Mission and presidio established at Monterey, California.

• British North American colonists number more than two million.

1775 • Indians destroy San Diego mission.

PATRICK HENRY'S MAP DESK

Like many of the leading gentry of 1760s Virginia, Patrick Henry pursued land speculation as a way to gain wealth. From 1767 to 1773, he engaged in half a dozen land ventures, buying up thousands of acres of frontier land in regions that are now part of Kentucky—purchases that would soon figure in the emerging crisis of empire. This odd little table was Henry's map desk. Its fold-out extensions provided support for the large maps required to represent Virginia's vast western land claims, and its light weight allowed Henry to position it near the best light source in his law office. As is often the case with speculative purchases, Henry's land deals entailed risk: Many of his properties were occupied by the Cherokee, who did not recognize his claim of ownership. The British government, fearing war between the Indians and settlers, tried to choke off risky land speculation in 1763 by establishing an imaginary line along the crest of the Appalachian Mountains beyond which settlement was prohibited. But men like Henry continued to buy land cheap in the hopes of selling dear at a later time. As a leading planter and powerful orator, Henry quickly became a spokesman in the growing imperial struggle with Britain. When he gained election to the Virginia House of Burgesses in 1765, he skillfully maneuvered that assembly into the startling repudiation of British power known as the Virginia Resolves. By 1775, he favored independence from Britain, a position that eventually would unleash settlers looking to buy land in the West. In 1776, he was elected the first governor of the Commonwealth of Virginia. Patrick Henry ultimately had seventeen children, fourteen of whom survived to adulthood. Through astute land purchases, he managed to establish each with a landed estate.

Courtesy of Scotchtown, photo by Katherine Wetzel.

The British Empire and the Colonial Crisis

1754–1775

- **The Seven Years' War, 1754–1763** 176
  French-British Rivalry in the Ohio Country 177
  The Albany Congress and Intercolonial Defense 179
  The War and Its Consequences 180
  British Leadership, Pontiac's Uprising, and the Proclamation of 1763 182

- **The Sugar and Stamp Acts, 1763–1765** 186
  Grenville's Sugar Act 186
  The Stamp Act 187
  Resistance Strategies and Crowd Politics 187
  Liberty and Property 192

- **The Townshend Acts and Economic Retaliation, 1767–1770** 193
  The Townshend Duties 193
  Nonconsumption and the Daughters of Liberty 194
  Military Occupation and "Massacre" in Boston 196

- **The Tea Party and the Coercive Acts, 1770–1774** 197
  The Calm before the Storm 197
  Tea in Boston Harbor 198
  The Coercive Acts 199
  Beyond Boston: Rural Massachusetts 200
  The First Continental Congress 201

- **Domestic Insurrections, 1774–1775** 204
  Lexington and Concord 204
  Rebelling against Slavery 206

- **Conclusion: How Far Does Liberty Go?** 207

I N 1771, THOMAS HUTCHINSON became the royal governor of the colony of Massachusetts. Unlike most royal governors, who were British aristocrats sent over by the king for short tours of duty, Hutchinson was a fifth-generation American. A Harvard-educated member of the Massachusetts elite, from a family of successful merchants, Hutchinson had served two decades in the Massachusetts general assembly. In 1758, he was appointed lieutenant governor, and in 1760 he also became chief justice of the colony's highest court. He lived in the finest mansion in Boston. Wealth, power, and influence were his in abundance. He was proud of his connection to the British empire and loyal to his king.

Hutchinson had the misfortune to be a loyal colonial leader during the two very tumultuous decades leading up to the American Revolution. He worked hard to keep the British and colonists aligned in interests, even promoting a plan to unify the colonies into a single defensive unit (the Albany Plan of Union) to ward off Indian wars. The plan of union failed, and a major war ensued—the Seven Years' War, pitting the British and colonists against the French and their Indian allies in the backcountry of the American colonies. When the war ended and the British government began to think about taxing colonists to pay for it, Hutchinson had no doubt that the new British policies were legitimate. Unwise, perhaps, in their specific formulation, but certainly legitimate.

Not everyone in Boston shared his opinion. Fervent, enthusiastic crowds protested against a succession of British taxation policies enacted after 1763—the Sugar Act, the Stamp Act, the Townshend duties, the Tea Act, all landmark events on the road to the American Revolution. But Hutchinson maintained his steadfast loyalty to Britain. His love of order and tradition inclined him to unconditional support of the British empire, and he was, by nature, a measured and cautious man. "My temper does not incline to enthusiasm," he once wrote.

Privately, he lamented the stupidity of the British acts that provoked trouble, but his sense of duty required him to defend the king's policies, however misguided. Quickly, he became an inspiring villain to the emerging revolutionary movement. Governor Hutchinson came to personify all that was wrong with British and colonial relations. The man not inclined to enthusiasm unleashed popular enthusiasm all around him. He never appreciated that irony.

In another irony, Thomas Hutchinson was actually one of the first Americans to recognize the difficulties of maintaining full rights and privileges for colonists so far from their supreme government, the king and Parliament in Britain. In 1769, when British troops occupied Boston in an effort to provide civil order, he wrote privately to a friend in England, "There must be an abridgement of what are called English liberties. . . . I doubt whether it is possible to project a system of government in which a colony three thousand miles distant from the parent state shall enjoy all the liberty of the parent state." What he could not imagine was the possibility of giving up the parent state and creating an independent government closer to home.

Thomas Hutchinson was a loyalist; in the 1750s, most English-speaking colonists were af-fectionately loyal to Britain. But the Seven Years' War, which Britain and its colonies fought together as allies, shook that affection, and imperial policies in the decade following the war (1763 to 1773) shattered it completely. Over the course of that decade, colonists insistently raised serious questions about American liberties and rights, especially over the issues of taxation and representation. Many came to believe what Thomas Hutchinson could never credit—that a tyrannical Britain had embarked on a course to enslave the colonists by depriving them of their traditional English liberties.

The opposite of **liberty** was slavery, a condition of nonfreedom and coercion. Political rhetoric about liberty, tyranny, and slavery heated up emotions of white colonists during the many crises of the 1760s and 1770s. But this rhetoric turned out to be a two-edged sword. The call for an end to tyrannical slavery meant one thing when sounded by Boston merchants whose commercial shipping rights had been revoked; the same call meant something quite different in 1775 when sounded by black Americans locked in the bondage of slavery.

All of this was set in motion by the Seven Years' War. The British victory at first fortified loyalty to the mother country, but its aftermath, taxation, stirred up discussions of rights, fueled white colonists' fear of enslavement by king and Parliament, and produced a potent political vocabulary with unexpected consequences.

Thomas Hutchinson

The only formal portrait of Thomas Hutchinson still in existence shows an assured young man in ruffles and hair ribbons. Decades of turmoil in Boston failed to puncture his self-confidence. Doubtless he sat for other portraits, as did all the Boston leaders in the 1760s to 1780s, but no other likeness has survived. One other portrait of him hung in his summer house outside Boston; a revolutionary crowd mutilated it and stabbed out the eyes. In 1775, Hutchinson fled to Britain, the country he regarded as his cultural home, only to realize how very American he was.
Courtesy of the Massachusetts Historical Society.

The Seven Years' War, 1754–1763

For the first fifty years of the eighteenth century, Britain was at war intermittently with France or Spain. Often the colonists in America experienced reverberations from these conflicts, most acutely along the French **frontier** in northern New England, which bumped up against New France, an area of French settlement along the St. Lawrence River with population centers at Montreal and Quebec. In the 1750s, international tensions mounted again, but this time over events originating in America. The conflict began in 1754 over contested land in the Ohio Valley, variously claimed by Virginians, Pennsylvanians, the French, and the Indians already living there. The result was the costly Seven Years' War (its British name), which spread in 1756 to encompass much of Europe, the Caribbean, and even India. The American colonists experienced nearly ten years of warfare, not seven, in what they called the French and Indian War. (In Canada, it is called the War of the Conquest, marking the takeover of French Canada by the British.) British and American soldiers shared the hardships of battle and the glory of victory over the French and Indians. But the immense costs of the war—in money, death, and desire for revenge by losers and even winners—laid the groundwork for the imperial crisis of the 1760s between the British and Americans.

French-British Rivalry in the Ohio Country

For several decades, French traders had cultivated alliances with the Indian tribes in the Ohio Country, a frontier region they regarded as part of New France (see Map 6.1, page 178). Cementing their relationships with gifts, the French established a profitable trade of manufactured goods for beaver furs. But in the 1740s, aggressive Pennsylvania traders traveled west and began to infringe on their territory, underselling French traders and threatening to reorient Indian loyalties. Adding to the tensions, a group of wealthy Virginians, including the brothers Lawrence and Augustine Washington, also asserted claim to the same large territory. The Virginians formed the Ohio Company in 1747 and obtained a **land grant** from the British king to some five hundred square miles of land, including the strategically important forks of the Ohio River (present-day Pittsburgh). In contrast to the French, who had no plans to settle colonists in the Ohio Country, the Virginians were primarily interested in land speculation, fueled by an exploding Anglo-American population seeking new land.

In response to these incursions, the French sent soldiers to build a series of military forts to secure their trade routes and to create a western barrier to American population expansion. In 1753, the royal governor of Virginia, Robert Dinwiddie, himself a shareholder in the Ohio Company, sent a messenger to warn the French that they were trespassing on Virginia land.

The messenger on this dangerous mission was George Washington, younger half-brother of the Ohio Company leaders. Though only twenty-one, Washington was an ambitious youth whose imposing height (six feet two) and air of silent competence convinced the governor he could do the job. The middle child in a family of eight,

Washington did not stand to inherit great wealth, so he sought to gain public reputation and impress the Virginia elite by volunteering for this perilous duty. Accompanied by six other Virginians, only one of whom spoke French, Washington delivered Dinwiddie's message to a French outpost near Lake Erie in late 1753 and returned home with crucial intelligence about French military plans.

Impressed, Dinwiddie appointed the youth to lead a small military expedition west to assert and, if need be, defend Virginia's claim. Imperial officials in London, concerned about the French fortifications, had authorized the governor "to repell force by force," but only if the French attacked first. By early 1754, the French had built Fort Duquesne at the forks of the Ohio River; Washington's difficult assignment was to chase the French away without actually being the aggressor.

In the spring of 1754, Washington set out with 160 Virginians, soon accompanied by a contingent of Mingo Indians, who opposed the increasing French military presence in the Ohio Country. Washington's game plan was not well formed, and he followed the lead of Tanaghrisson, the Mingo chief, who guided a detachment of Virginians in the early-morning hours to a very small encampment of French soldiers in the woods. The French, just rising, suddenly feared attack, and in a few panicked minutes, both sides commenced shooting. This May morning marked the violent start of the Seven Years' War. Who fired first was later a matter of dispute, but fourteen Frenchmen (and no Virginians) were wounded. Washington, lacking a translator, struggled to communicate with the injured French commander, who himself was on a diplomatic mission to deliver a message to the Virginians. But Tanaghrisson and his men intervened to kill and then scalp the wounded men, starting with the commander, probably with the strategic aim of inflaming hostilities between the French and the colonists.

This sudden massacre violated Washington's instructions to avoid being the aggressor and raised the stakes considerably. Fearing retaliation, Washington ordered his men to fortify their position; the flimsy "Fort Necessity" was the result. Reinforcements amounting to several hundred more Virginians arrived; but the Mingos,

Ohio River Valley, 1753

British fort

French fort

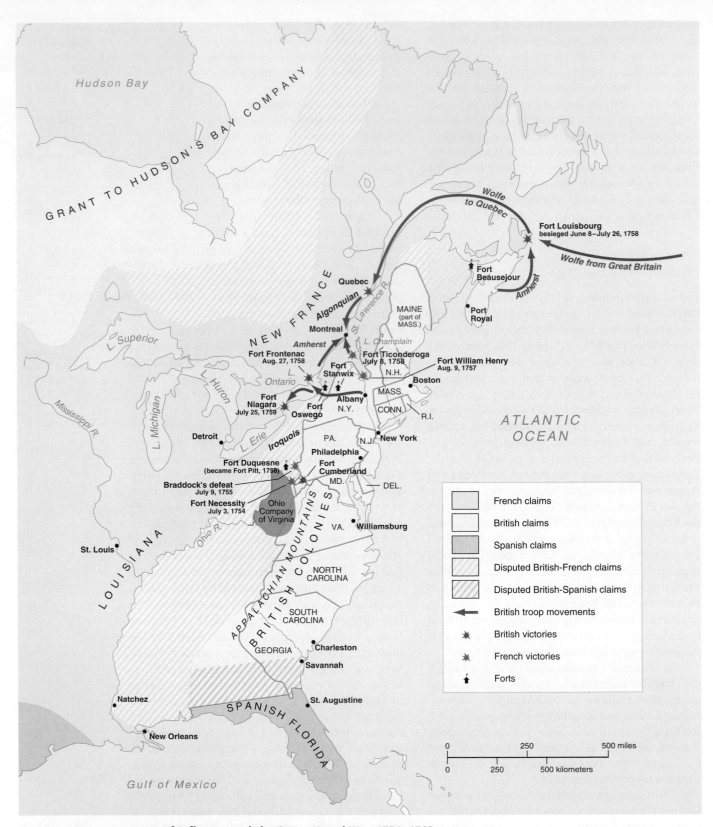

MAP 6.1   European Areas of Influence and the Seven Years' War, 1754–1763

In the mid-eighteenth century, France, Britain, and Spain claimed vast areas of North America, many of them already inhabited by various Indian peoples. The early flash points of the Seven Years' War were in regions of disputed claims where the French had allied with powerful native groups—the Iroquois and the Algonquian tribes—to put pressure on the westward-moving British and Americans.

sensing disaster and displeased by Washington's style of command, fled. (Tanaghrisson later said, "The Colonel was a good-natured man, but had no experience; he took upon him to command the Indians as his slaves, [and] would by no means take advice from the Indians.") In early July, more than six hundred French soldiers aided by one hundred Shawnee and Delaware warriors attacked Fort Necessity, killing or wounding a third of Washington's men. The message was clear: The French would not depart from the disputed territory.

The Albany Congress and Intercolonial Defense

Even as Virginians, Frenchmen, and Indians fought and died in the Ohio Country, British imperial leaders hoped to prevent a larger war. One obvious strategy was to strengthen British alliances with seemingly neutral Indian tribes. To this end, British authorities directed the governor of New York to convene a colonial conference.

In June and July of 1754, twenty-four delegates from seven colonies met in Albany, New York. Also attending were Iroquois Indians of the Six Nations, a confederacy of tribes (Mohawk, Oneida, Onondaga, Cayuga, Seneca, and Tuscarora) inhabiting the central and western parts of present-day New York. Albany was the traditional meeting place of the Covenant Chain, a trade alliance first created in 1692 between New York leaders and Mohawk Indians, the most easterly of the Six Nations. In 1753, the aged and venerable Mohawk leader Hendrick accused the New York colonials of breaking the Covenant Chain. A prime goal of the Albany Congress was to repair trade relations with the Mohawk and secure their help—or at least their neutrality—against the French threat.

Two delegates at the congress had more ambitious plans. Benjamin Franklin of Pennsylvania and Thomas Hutchinson of Massachusetts, both rising political stars in their home colonies, coauthored the Albany Plan of Union, a proposal for a unified colonial government limited to war and defense policies. In the course of the meeting, the Albany delegates learned of Washington's defeat at Fort Necessity and understood instantly the escalating risk of war with France; they approved the plan. Key features included a president general appointed by the crown and a grand council of forty-eight representatives, all to meet annually to consider questions of war, peace, and trade with the Indians.

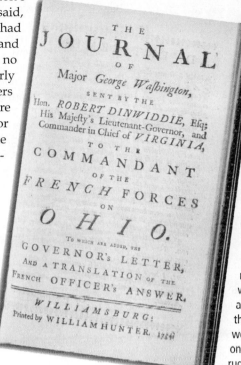

Washington's Journal, 1754
When George Washington returned from his first mission to the French, Governor Dinwiddie asked him to write a full report of what he had seen of the countryside, the Indians, and French troop strength. Washington obliged, writing about seven thousand words in less than two days (roughly equivalent to a twenty-five-page double-spaced paper). He coolly narrated scenes of personal danger: traveling in deep snow and freezing temperatures, falling off a raft into an icy river, and being shot at by a lone Indian. Dinwiddie printed Washington's report, along with his own letter and the French commander's defiant answer, in a thirty-two-page pamphlet that was soon reprinted in London. The governor's aim was to inform Virginians and British leaders about the French threat in the West. But the pamphlet suited Washington's aims as well. At age twenty-two, he became known on both sides of the Atlantic for resolute and rugged courage.

The writers of the Albany Plan humbly reaffirmed Parliament's authority; this was no bid for enlarged autonomy of the colonies.

To Franklin's surprise, not a single colony approved the Albany Plan. The Massachusetts assembly feared it was "a Design of gaining power over the Colonies," especially the power of taxation. Others objected that it would be impossible to agree on unified policies toward scores of quite different Indian tribes. The British government never backed the Albany Plan either, which perplexed both Franklin and Hutchinson. Instead, British authorities centralized dealings with Indians by appointing, in 1755, two superintendents of Indian affairs, one for the northern and another for the southern colonies, each with exclusive powers to negotiate treaties, trade, and land sales with all tribes.

The Indians at the Albany Congress were not impressed with the Albany Plan either. The Covenant Chain alliance with the Mohawk tribe was reaffirmed, but the other nations left without pledging to help the British battle the French. At this very early point in the Seven Years' War, the Iroquois figured that the French military presence around the Great Lakes would discourage the westward push of American colonists and therefore better serve their interests.

The brave old Hendrick the great Sachem or Chief of the Mohawk Indians one of the Six Nations now in Alliance with & Subject to the King of Great Britain. Sold by Eliz Bakewell opposit Birchin Lane in Cornhill.

Chief Hendrick and John Caldwell

Dress is a symbol system that conveys status and self-presentation to others. Might it also change the way the dresser thinks about himself or herself? Chief Hendrick (top) worked closely with the British in New York to maintain the trade alliance known as the Covenant Chain. In 1740, when he was sixty, he traveled to England, was presented at the royal court, and sat for this portrait. His blue coat, ruffled shirt, three-cornered hat, and cravat are all signs of a well-dressed English gentleman. But Hendrick holds a tomahawk in one hand and wampum in the other, and his long white hair is conspicuously un-curled, unlike an eighteenth-century gent's wig. John Caldwell (bottom) also holds a tomahawk, which goes with his Indian garb: feather headdress, blankets, leggings, and moccasins. During the Revolutionary War, Caldwell was stationed at Fort Detroit, a British garrison that provided aid to tribes in the Ohio Valley battling Americans. Caldwell acquired this outfit for a formal diplomatic mission to the Shawnee Indians in 1780. He took the clothes back to England and wore them for this portrait.

Hendrick: Courtesy of the John Carter Brown Library at Brown University; Caldwell: The Board of Trustees of the National Museums & Galleries on Merseyside (King's Regiment Collection).

READING THE IMAGE: What might it mean that Chief Hendrick dressed in English clothes and John Caldwell wore native attire when posing for these portraits? **CONNECTIONS:** Do you think these examples of imitation indicate a willingness to cross cultural boundaries? Is the co-opting of dress just play or a sign of something deeper?

FOR MORE HELP ANALYZING THIS IMAGE, see the visual activity for this chapter in the Online Study Guide at bedfordstmartins.com/roark.

The War and Its Consequences

By 1755, Washington's frontier skirmish had turned into a major mobilization of British and American troops against the French. At first, the British hoped for quick victory on three fronts. General Edward Braddock, recently arrived from England, planned to rout the French at Fort Duquesne in western Pennsylvania. In Massachusetts, Governor William Shirley aimed his soldiers at Fort Niagara, critically located between Lakes Erie and Ontario. And William Johnson, a New Yorker recently appointed superintendent of Indian affairs, led forces north toward Lake Champlain, in an effort to push the French back to Canada (see Map 6.1). Unfortunately for the British, the French were prepared to fight and had cemented respectful alliances with many Indian tribes from Canada down through the Great Lakes region and into the Ohio Country.

Braddock's march west was the first of a series of disasters for the British. Accompanied by George Washington and his Virginia soldiers, Braddock led 2,000 troops into the backcountry in July 1755, expecting an easy victory with his big artillery and over-whelming numbers. Indian guidance and support amounted to a mere 8 Oneida warriors. One day short of Fort Duquesne, in heavy woods where their cannons were useless, the British were am-bushed by 250 French soldiers aided by 640 Indian warriors, in-cluding Ottawas, Ojibwas, Potawatomis, Shawnees, and Delawares. In the bloody Battle of the Monongahela, named for a nearby river, nearly a thousand on the British side were killed or wounded.

Washington was unhurt, though two horses in succession were shot out from under him; General Braddock was killed. Washington's bravery in battle caused the governor of Virginia to promote him to commander of the Virginia army. At age twenty-two, Washington was beginning to realize his ambitions.

News of Braddock's defeat caused the other two British armies, then hacking their way through the dense forests of northern New York, to retreat from action. For the next two years, the British stumbled badly on the American front. They lacked adequate troops and supplies, and they received scant help from the American colonial assemblies. Most Indian tribes actively supported the French, figuring that sparsely populated fur trading French settlements were better for them than the fast-growing, westward-pushing American colonies.

What finally turned the war around was the rise to power of William Pitt, who became Britain's prime minister in 1757. Willing to commit massive resources to fight France and its ally Spain throughout the world, he paid colonial assemblies to raise and equip provincial soldiers, and he mounted military assaults in Europe, Canada, and the Caribbean. In America, British and American troops captured Forts Duquesne, Niagara, and Ticonderoga by 1759. Next, the British navy sailed up the St. Lawrence River to the isolated French cities of Quebec and Montreal. The decisive victory on the North American continent was the capture of the seemingly invincible fortress city of Quebec in September 1759 by the young British general James Wolfe. Montreal surrendered in 1760.

The American colonists rejoiced, but the worldwide war was not over yet. Battles continued in the Caribbean, where the French sugar islands Martinique and Guadeloupe fell to the British. Battles raged in Austria and Prussia and extended to India. In 1762, the British laid siege to Spanish Cuba because Spain was France's ally in the global conflict. The costly water invasion of Havana required some four thousand provincial soldiers from New York and New England. By the end of 1762, the fighting was over. France and Spain capitulated, and the Treaty of Paris was signed in 1763.

The triumph was sweet but short-lived. The complex peace negotiations reorganized the map of North America but stopped short of providing Britain with the full spoils of victory. Britain gained control of Canada, eliminating the French threat from the north and west. British and American title to the eastern half of North America, precisely what Britain had claimed before the war, was confirmed. But all French territory west of the Mississippi River, including New Orleans, was transferred to Spain as compensation for Spain's assistance to France during the war. Stranger still, Cuba was returned to Spain, and Martinique and Guadeloupe were returned to France (Map 6.2).

In truth, the French islands in the Caribbean were hardly a threat to Americans, for they

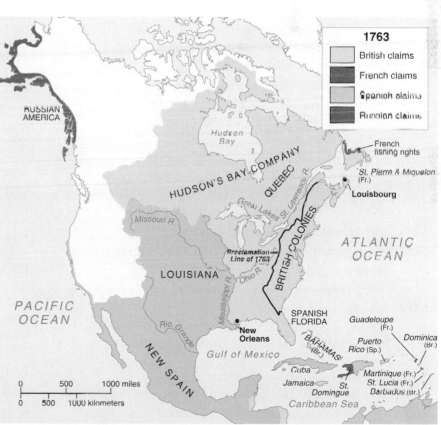

MAP 6.2   North America after the Seven Years' War
In the peace treaty of 1763, France ceded its interior territory but retained fishing rights and islands in the far north and several sugar islands in the Caribbean. Much of France's claim to Louisiana went not to Britain but to Spain.

READING THE MAP: How did European land claims change from 1754 (see Map 6.1) to 1763, as shown here?
CONNECTIONS: What was the goal of the Proclamation of 1763?

FOR MORE HELP ANALYZING THIS MAP, see the map activity for this chapter in the Online Study Guide at bedfordstmartins.com/roark.

provided a profitable trade in smuggled molasses. The main threat to the colonists came instead from the Indians. The Treaty of Paris ignored them and assigned their lands to British rule. With the French gone, the Indians lost the advantage of having two opponents to play off against each other, and they now had to cope with the westward-moving Americans. Indian policy would soon become a serious point of contention between the British government and the colonists.

> Braddock's defeat "gave us Americans," Franklin wrote, "the first suspicion that our exalted ideas of the prowess of British regulars had not been well founded."

Britain's version of the victory of 1763 awarded all credit to the mighty British army, successful despite inadequate support by ungrateful colonists. Worse still, some colonists had engaged in smuggling—notably a lively trade in beaver pelts with French fur traders and an illegal molasses trade in the Caribbean. American traders, grumbled the British leaders, were really traitors. William Pitt was convinced that the illegal trade "principally, if not alone, enabled France to sustain and protract this long and expensive war."

Colonists read the lessons of the war differently. American colonial soldiers had turned out in force, they claimed, but had been relegated to grunt work by arrogant British leaders and subjected to unexpectedly harsh military discipline, ranging from floggings to executions. One soldier recalled watching three New England soldiers endure whippings of eight hundred lashes for some "trifling offense" at the hands of the British. Americans bristled at stories of British disdain, such as the remark of the impetuous General Wolfe, the British hero of Quebec, who said the American soldiers were "contemptible dogs." General Braddock had foolishly bragged to Benjamin Franklin that "these savages may, indeed, be a formidable enemy to your raw American militia, but upon the king's regular and disciplined troops, sir, it is impossible they should make any impression." Braddock's defeat "gave us Americans," Franklin wrote, "the first suspicion that our exalted ideas of the prowess of British regulars had not been well founded."

The human costs of the war were etched especially sharply in the minds of New England colonists. About one-third of all Massachusetts men between fifteen and thirty had seen service. Many families lost loved ones, a cost not soon forgotten. The assault on Havana in Cuba, for example, took the lives of some two thousand Americans, half the provincial force that had been sent there.

The enormous expense of the war caused by Pitt's no-holds-barred military strategy cast another huge shadow over the victory. By 1763, Britain's national debt, double what it had been when Pitt took office, posed a formidable challenge to the next decade of leadership in Britain.

The Seven Years' War

1692–1750s English and Iroquois create and affirm the Covenant Chain alliance in western New York.

1700–1740s French settlers enjoy exclusive trade with Indians in Ohio Valley.

1747 Ohio Company receives land grant from British king.

1753 Mohawk chief Hendrick accuses English of breaking Covenant Chain.
French soldiers advance from Canada into Ohio Country.
George Washington delivers message telling French they are trespassing.

1754 French build Fort Duquesne.
Washington returns to Ohio Country with troops and Mingo allies.
May Washington, guided by Mingo chief Tanaghrisson, attacks French.
June–July Albany Congress convenes.
July French and Indian soldiers defeat Washington at Fort Necessity.

1755 British authorities appoint two superintendents of Indian affairs.
July Braddock defeated in the Battle of the Monongahela.

1756 William Pitt becomes British prime minister.

1758 British capture Fort Duquesne.

1759 British capture Forts Niagara and Ticonderoga.

1760 British capture Montreal.

1762 British capture Cuba.

1763 Treaty of Paris signed.

British Leadership, Pontiac's Uprising, and the Proclamation of 1763

In 1760, in the middle of the Seven Years' War, twenty-two-year-old George III came to the British throne. Timid and insecure, the new king trusted only his Scottish tutor, the Earl of Bute, an outsider to power circles in London, and made him head of his cabinet of ministers. Bute committed blunders and did not last long, but he made one significant decision—to keep a standing army in the colonies after the last battle was over in 1760. In both financial and political terms, this was a costly move.

The ostensible reason for stationing British troops in America was to maintain the peace between the colonists and the Indians. This was not a misplaced concern. The defeat and withdrawal of the French from North America had left their Indian allies—who did not accept defeat—in a state of alarm. Just three months after the Treaty of Paris was signed in 1763, Pontiac, chief of the Ottawa tribe in the northern Ohio region, attacked the British garrison near Detroit. Six more attacks on forts quickly followed, and frontier settlements were also raided by nearly a dozen tribes from western New York, the Ohio Valley, and the Great Lakes region. By the fall, every fort west of Detroit had been captured; more than four hundred British soldiers were dead and another two thousand colonists killed or taken captive. Pontiac's uprising was quelled in December 1763 by the combined efforts of British and colonial soldiers, but tensions remained high. (See "Historical Question," page 184.)

To minimize the violence, the British government issued the Proclamation of 1763, forbidding colonists to settle west of the Appalachian Mountains. The Proclamation chiefly aimed to separate Indians and settlers, but it also limited trade with Indians to traders licensed by colonial governors, and it forbade private sales of Indian land. The Proclamation's language took care not to identify western lands as belonging to the Indians. Instead, it spoke of

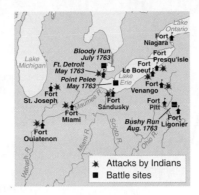

Pontiac's Uprising, 1763

Indians "who live under our protection" on "such parts of our Dominions and Territories as, not having been ceded to or purchased by Us, are reserved to them, as their Hunting Grounds." Other parts of the Proclamation of 1763 referred to American and even French colonists in Canada as "our loving subjects," entitled to English rights and privileges. In contrast, the Indians were clearly rejected as British subjects, and instead described more vaguely as "Tribes of Indians with whom We are connected." Of course, the British were not really well connected with any Indians, nor did they wish connections to form among the tribes. As William Johnson, the superintendent of northern Indian affairs, advised in 1764, "It will be expedient to treat with each nation separately . . . for could they arrive at a perfect union, they must prove very dangerous Neighbours."

The 1763 boundary proved impossible to enforce. Surging population growth had already sent many hundreds of settlers west of the Appalachians, and land speculators, such as those of Virginia's Ohio Company, had no desire to lose opportunities for profitable resale of their land grants. Bute's decision to post a standing army in the colonies was thus a cause for concern among western settlers, eastern speculators, and Indian tribes alike.

REVIEW How did the Seven Years' War erode relations between colonists and British authorities?

Silver Medal to Present to Indians
After Pontiac's uprising ended, the British attempted to mend relations with the insurgent Indians by honoring them with gifts. This silver medal, minted in 1766, displays a profile of King George III on the front and a cozy depiction of an Indian and a Briton smoking a peace pipe on the back. The Latin words on the front announce George's name, title, and kingly dominions. Both this inscription and the English words on the back would have been equally unintelligible to the recipients of the gift. Imagine a conversation between an Indian chief and an English translator who tried to explain what the slogan HAPPY WHILE UNITED might mean. The scene depicted—two men with relaxed, friendly body language—illustrates HAPPY and UNITED. The WHILE, conveying a sense of temporariness and contingency, might have been trickier to explain. Why?
The American Numismatic Society.

How Long Did the Seven Years' War Last in Indian Country?

France had been defeated on the North American continent in 1761, and the Peace of Paris officially ended the global war between France and Britain in 1763. But there was no lasting peace for the Indian nations of the Ohio Valley and Great Lakes region. In 1761, a Chippewa chief named Minavavana clearly explained the reasons why, in an ominous speech delivered to a British trader at Fort Michilimackinac, a British outpost that guarded the Straits of Mackinac where Lakes Huron and Michigan meet. "Englishman," he said, "although you have conquered the French, you have not yet conquered us! We are not your slaves. These lakes, these woods and mountains were left to us by our ancestors. They are our inheritance; and we will part with them to none." Furthermore, Minavavana pointedly noted, "your king has never sent us any presents, nor entered into any treaty with us, wherefore he and we are still at war; and until he does these things we must consider that we have no other father, nor friend, among the white men than the King of France."

Minavavana and other Indians of the region had cause to be alarmed. With the exit of the French, British regiments took over the French-built forts all over the old Northwest. Fort Duquesne, renamed Fort Pitt in honor of the British leader who had authorized the war-winning strategy, underwent two years of fortification. No one could mistake the new walls—sixty feet thick at their base, ten at the top—for the external facade of a friendly fur trading post. Nonmilitary Americans were moving into Fort Pitt's neighborhood, too, complicating matters.

Minavavana's complaint about the lack of British presents was a far more serious problem than the British military leaders thought. Gifts exchanged in Indian **culture** cemented social relationships; they symbolized honor and established obligation. Over many decades, the French had mastered the subtleties of gift exchange, distributing clothing, textiles, and hats and receiving in return calumets (ornamented ceremonial pipe stems) as symbols of friendship. The British military leaders, new to the practice, often discarded the calumets as trivial trinkets, thereby insulting the givers. Major General Jeffery Amherst was sometimes willing to offer gifts to particular Indian leaders, positioning the "gift" as a bribe in the British frame of reference. But Amherst saw extensive gift exchange as demeaning to the British, forcing them to pay tribute to people whom he considered inferior. "It is not my intention ever to attempt to gain the friendship of Indians by presents," Amherst declared. The Indian view was the opposite: Generous givers expressed dominance and protection, not subordination, in the act of giving. Sir William Johnson, superintendent of Indian affairs, warned Amherst that he was insulting the Indians, but the imperious Amherst would not listen.

A religious revival in 1760–1761, fueled by prophetic visions, greatly enhanced the prospects of frontier war in the old Northwest. The new spiritual message was delivered by a Delaware leader named Neolin in the upper Ohio Valley. Neolin predicted a swift decline for all the tribes unless they altered their ways; gave up quarreling with each other; shunned trade in guns, alcohol, and other trade goods; and curbed their overkilling of animals for the pelt trade. Neolin's preachings spread quickly, gaining credence as the British bungled diplomacy and American settlers continued to penetrate western lands.

A renewal of commitment to Indian ways and the formation of tribal alliances led to open warfare in 1763, called (by the British) Pontiac's Rebellion. (The Indians would not have credited Pontiac with sole leadership. In its impressive and coordinated extent, the war was the work of many men.) Amherst, never a shrewd observer of Indian relations, flatly declared in April 1763 that reports of impending attack were "Meer Bugbears." By mid-May, the British commander at Detroit knew the threat was real. Pontiac, chief of the Ottawas, along with Potawatomi and Huron warriors, attacked Fort Detroit and laid siege for two months. In late May, within two weeks of Pontiac's first move, Forts Sandusky, St. Joseph, Miami, and Ouiatenon were captured by Indians, all through ruses in which Indians pretending to have peaceful business gained entry to the garrisons. Far north at Fort Michilimackinac, Ojibwas engaged in their regular sporting event, a form of lacrosse, outside the fort. After several hours of strenuous play, the ball landed near the fort's open gate, and the enthralled British spectators realized too late that the convergence of players on the ball was really a rush of warriors into the fort. The players seized tomahawks that had been hidden under blankets worn by Indian women on the sidelines. Michili-mackinac fell to Ojibwa control.

By the end of June, thirteen British garrisons had either fallen or been evacuated under threat of attack. Yet the three most important forts—Detroit, Niagara, and Pitt—besieged by Indians, were kept by the British. At Fort Pitt, two ostensibly friendly Delaware Indians showed up at the end of May to suggest that the British should leave to avoid attack. Fort Pitt's commander thanked them but declined their suggestion, then sent them on their way with his idea of a gift: two blankets and a handkerchief, lately used by British smallpox patients in the fort. "We hope it will have the desired effect," wrote a militiaman whose diary is the source for this story. Two months later, in July, Amherst suggested to a subordinate that spreading smallpox should be considered as a method of war. "We must use Every Stratagem in our Power to Reduce them." Annihilating the Indians was his ultimate goal; he did not flinch from what a later age would call germ or poison warfare.

Yet there is no evidence that the infected blankets actually propagated smallpox or that Amherst's suggestion was put into effect.

From late summer through the early months of 1764, Indian country was the scene of bloodshed. Indians targeted British supply routes and civilian settlements, resulting in several thousand deaths. Not all of the attacks came from Indians. In one unique event in December 1763, some fifty Pennsylvania vigilantes known as the Paxton Boys descended on a peaceful village of Conestoga Indians—friendly Indians, not very far west into Pennsylvania—and murdered and scalped twenty of them. The vigilantes, now numbering five hundred and out to make war on all Indians, marched on Philadelphia to try to capture and murder some Christian Indians held in protective custody there. British troops prevented that, but the Paxton Boys escaped all punishment for their murderous attack on the Conestoga village.

In 1764, the rebellion faded. The Indians were short on ammunition;

the British were tired and broke. Amherst's superiors in Britain blamed him for mishandling the conflict, and when he was recalled home, his own soldiers toasted his leaving. A new military leader, Thomas Gage, took command and made good on the advice of William Johnson by distributing gifts profusely among the Indians.

Was the Seven Years' War finally over for the Indians, ten years after it started? If 1764 represents an end, it was only a brief one. Periodic raids and killings punctuated the rest of the 1760s and early 1770s, climaxing in the late 1770s as Indians joined the British to fight the Americans in the Revolutionary War. Warfare and massacres extended from New England and New York down to South Carolina and Georgia, especially in the Ohio Country. The American Revolution eventually ended, at least the war between the British and the Americans, but the frontier war continued on and off until 1815, when the War of 1812 ended. Perhaps from the Indians' point of view, the Seven Years' War could be called the Sixty-One Years' War.

Subduing Pontiac's Uprising

As the Indian revolt of 1763–1764 weakened, British colonel Henry Bouquet took his 1,500-man army deep into the Ohio Country to threaten and subdue the Shawnee, Delaware, and Mingo tribes. Among his soldiers was one Thomas Hutchins, a cartographer from New Jersey, who produced a detailed topographical map of the region, with this illustration in one corner. The British flag waves over Bouquet's encampment, and one tent is opened up for the treaty negotiation. Bouquet and his aides command the table and chairs in the tent, while the Indians sit on a log or on the ground. Note the soldier in a kilt with a gun and sword; five hundred Scottish Highlanders were part of Bouquet's force. Attention is focused on the man standing by the fire, whose hand gestures suggest that he is speaking. Another Indian smokes a calumet pipe, a symbol of peacemaking. A third, on the log, appears to weep. Bouquet demanded the return of all captives taken by these tribes since the start of the Seven Years' War in exchange for his promise to spare Indian villages from further attack. He took two hostages from each tribe, to be held at Fort Pitt until all the captives were returned. In all, close to three hundred white captives were released.

William L. Clements Library.

The Sugar and Stamp Acts, 1763–1765

Lord Bute lost power in 1763, and the young King George turned to a succession of leaders throughout the 1760s, searching for a prime minister he could trust. A half dozen ministers in seven years took turns dealing with one basic, underlying British reality: A huge war debt, amounting to £123 million and growing due to interest, needed to be serviced, and the colonists, as British subjects, should help to pay it off. To many Americans, however, that proposition seemed in deep violation of what they perceived to be their rights and liberties as British subjects, and it created resentment that eventually erupted in rebellion. The first provocative revenue acts were the work of Sir George Grenville, prime minister from 1763 to 1765.

Grenville's Sugar Act

To find revenue, George Grenville scrutinized the customs service, which monitored the shipping trade and collected all import and export duties in both Britain and America. Grenville found that the salaries of customs officers cost the government four times what was collected in revenue. The shortfall was due in part to bribery and smuggling, so Grenville began to insist on rigorous attention to paperwork and a strict accounting of collected duties.

The hardest duty to enforce was the one imposed by the Molasses Act of 1733—a stiff tax of six pence per gallon on any molasses purchased from non-British sources. The purpose of the tax was to discourage trade with French Caribbean islands and redirect the molasses trade to British sugar islands, but it did not work. French molasses remained cheap and abundant because French **planters** on Martinique and Guadeloupe had no use for it. A by-product of sugar production, molasses was a key ingredient in rum, a drink the French scorned. Rum-loving Americans were eager to buy French molasses, and they had ignored the tax law for decades.

Grenville's ingenious solution was the Revenue Act of 1764, popularly dubbed the "Sugar Act." It lowered the duty on French molasses to three pence, making it more attractive for shippers to obey the law, and at the same time raised penalties for smuggling. The act appeared to be in the tradition of navigation acts meant to regulate trade, but Grenville's actual

George Grenville, Prime Minister 1763–1765
George Grenville was a thrifty man. He worked for years in the British treasury and navy departments, banking his salary and living off the interest. His argumentative style often annoyed other politicians. He gained the prime minister's job in 1763 at a point when King George was short of competent alternatives, but the king found him irksome: "When he has wearied me for two hours, he looks at his watch, to see if he may not tire me for an hour more," King George said. The king sacked him in July 1765 for being insolent, not for his controversial colonial policies. *The Earl of Halifax, Garrowby, Yorkshire.*

intent was to raise revenue. He was using an established form of law for new ends and accomplishing his goal by the novel means of lowering a duty.

The Sugar Act toughened enforcement policies. From now on, all British naval crews could act as impromptu customs officers, boarding suspicious ships and seizing cargoes found to be in violation. Smugglers caught without proper paperwork would be prosecuted, not in a friendly civil court with a local jury but in a vice-admiralty court located in Halifax, Nova Scotia, where a single judge presided. The implication was that justice would be sure and severe.

Grenville hoped that the new Sugar Act would reform American smugglers into law-abiding shippers and in turn generate income for the empire. Unfortunately, the decrease in duty was not sufficient to offset the attractions of smuggling. The vigilant customs officers made bribery harder to accomplish, and several ugly confrontations occurred in port cities. Reaction to the Sugar Act foreshadowed questions about Britain's right to tax Americans, but in 1764 objections to the act came principally from Americans in the shipping trades inconvenienced by the law.

From the British point of view, the Proclamation of 1763 and the Sugar Act seemed to be reasonable efforts to administer the colonies. To the Americans, however, the British supervision appeared to be a disturbing intrusion into the long colonial practice of centering taxation powers in colonial assemblies composed of elected representatives. Philadelphian Benjamin Franklin, living in London as the agent for Pennsylvania, warned that "two distinct Jurisdictions or Powers of Taxing cannot well subsist together in the same country. If a Tax is propos'd with us, how dare we venture to lay it, as the next Ship perhaps may bring us an Account of some heavy Tax propos'd by you?"

The Stamp Act

By his second year in office, Grenville had made almost no dent in the national debt. Continued evasion prevented the Sugar Act from becoming the moneymaker he had hoped it would be. So in February 1765, he escalated his revenue program with the Stamp Act, precipitating a major conflict between Britain and the colonies over Parliament's right to tax. The Stamp Act imposed a tax on all paper used for official documents—newspapers, pamphlets, court documents, licenses, wills, ships' cargo lists— and required an affixed stamp as proof that the tax had been paid. Unlike the Sugar Act, which regulated trade, the Stamp Act was designed plainly and simply to raise money. It affected nearly everyone who used any taxed paper, but most of all those in the business and legal communities, who relied heavily on official documents.

Grenville was no fool. Anticipating that the stamp tax would be unpopular—Thomas Hutchinson had forewarned him—he delegated the administration of the act to Americans, to avoid taxpayer hostility toward British enforcers. In each colony, local stamp distributors would be hired at a handsome salary of 8 percent of the revenue collected.

English tradition held that taxes were a gift of the people to their monarch, granted by the people's representatives. This view of taxes as a freely given gift preserved an essential concept of English political theory: the idea that citizens have the liberty to enjoy and use their property without fear of confiscation. The king could not demand money; only the House of Commons could grant it. Grenville quite agreed with the notion of taxation by consent, but he argued that the colonists were already "virtually" represented in Parliament. The House of Commons, he insisted, represented all British subjects, wherever they were.

Colonial leaders emphatically rejected this view, arguing that **virtual representation** could not withstand the stretch across the Atlantic. The stamp tax itself, levied by a distant Parliament on unwilling colonies, illustrated the problem. Daniel Dulany, a Maryland lawyer, wrote a best-selling pamphlet explaining that virtual representation was "a mere cob-web, spread to catch the unwary, and entangle the weak."

> Benjamin Franklin warned that "two distinct Jurisdictions or Powers of Taxing cannot well subsist together in the same country."

Resistance Strategies and Crowd Politics

News of the Stamp Act arrived in the colonies in April 1765, seven months before it was to take effect on November 1. There was time, therefore, to object. Governors were unlikely to challenge the law, for most of them owed their office to the king. Instead, the colonial assemblies took the lead; eight of them held discussions on the Stamp Act.

Virginia's assembly, the House of Burgesses, was the first. At the end of its May session, after two-thirds of the members had left, Patrick Henry, a young political newcomer, presented a series of resolutions on the Stamp Act that were debated and passed, one by one. They became known as the Virginia Resolves.

Henry's resolutions inched the assembly toward radical opposition to the Stamp Act. The first three stated the obvious: that Virginians were British citizens, that they enjoyed the same rights and privileges as Britons, and that self-taxation was one of those rights. The fourth resolution noted that Virginians had always taxed themselves, through their representatives in the House of Burgesses. The fifth took a radical leap by pushing the other four unexceptional statements to one logical conclusion—that the Virginia assembly alone had the right to tax Virginians.

Newspapers Protest the Stamp Act
The Stamp Act affected newspaper publishers more than any other businessmen. From New Hampshire to South Carolina, papers issued on October 31, 1765, used dark black mourning lines and funereal language to herald the date the Stamp Act went into effect. The editor of the *Pennsylvania Journal*, a Son of Liberty in Philadelphia, designed his paper to look like a tombstone, with coffins and skulls throughout its four pages. A New Hampshire editor dramatically declared, "I *must Die*, or Submit to that which *is worse* than Death, Be Stamped, and lose my Freedom." All colonial newspapers resumed publication within a week or two, defiantly operating without stamps. One stampless New Haven, Connecticut, editor wrote, "The press is the test of truth, the bulwark of public safety, the guardian of freedom." Library of Congress.

Two more fiery resolutions were debated as Henry pressed the logic of his case to the extreme. The sixth resolution denied legitimacy to any tax law originating outside Virginia, and a seventh boldly called anyone who disagreed with these propositions an enemy of Virginia. This was too much for the other representatives. They voted down resolutions six and seven and later rescinded their vote on number five as well.

Their caution hardly mattered, however, because newspapers in other colonies printed all seven Virginia Resolves, creating the impression that a daring first challenge to the Stamp Act had occurred. Consequently, other assemblies were willing to consider even more radical questions, such as this: By what authority could Parliament legislate for the colonies without also taxing them? No one disagreed, in 1765, that Parliament had legislative power over the colonists, who were, after all, British subjects. Several assemblies advanced the argument that there was a distinction between *external* taxes, imposed to regulate trade, and *internal* taxes, such as a stamp tax or a property tax, which could only be self-imposed.

Reaction to the Stamp Act ran far deeper than political debate in assemblies. Every person whose livelihood required official paper had to decide whether to comply with the act. There were only three options: boycotting, which was within the law but impractical because of the reliance on paper; defying the law and using unstamped paper; or preventing distribution of the stamps at the source, before the law took effect, thus ensuring universal noncompliance.

The first organized resistance to the Stamp Act began in Boston in August 1765 under the direction of town leaders, chief among them Samuel Adams, John Hancock, and Ebenezer Mackintosh. The first two had Harvard educations and were elected officials in Boston. Adams, in his forties, had shrewd political instincts and a gift for organizing. Hancock, though not yet thirty, had recently inherited his uncle's mercantile shipping business and was one of the wealthiest men in Massachusetts. Mackintosh, the same age as Hancock, was a shoemaker and highly experienced street activist. Many other artisans, tradesmen, printers, tavern keepers, dockworkers, and sailors—the middling and lower orders—mobilized in resistance to the Stamp Act, taking the name "Sons of Liberty" from an impassioned speech given in Parliament by a member opposed to the act.

The plan hatched in Boston called for a large street demonstration highlighting a ritualized mock execution designed to convince Andrew Oliver, the designated stamp distributor, to resign. With no distributor, no stamps could be sold. On August 14, 1765, a crowd of two thousand to three thousand demonstrators, led by Mackintosh, hung an effigy of Oliver in a tree and then paraded it around town before finally beheading and burning it. In hopes of calming tensions, the royal governor Francis Bernard took no action. The flesh-and-blood Oliver stayed in hiding; the next day he resigned his office in a well-publicized announcement. The Sons of Liberty were elated. (See "Seeking the American Promise," page 190.)

The demonstration provided lessons for everyone. Oliver learned that stamp distributors would be very unpopular people. Governor Bernard, with no police force to call on, learned the limitations of his power to govern. The demonstration's leaders learned that street action was effective. And hundreds of ordinary men not only learned what the Stamp Act was all about but also gained pride in their ability to have a decisive impact on politics.

Twelve days later, a second crowd action showed how well these lessons had been learned. On August 26, a crowd visited the houses of three detested customs and admiralty court officials, breaking windows and raiding wine cellars. A fourth target was the finest dwelling in Massachusetts, owned by Andrew Oliver's stiff-necked brother-in-law, Thomas Hutchinson. Rumors abounded that Hutchinson had urged Grenville to adopt the Stamp Act. Although he had actually done the opposite, Hutchinson refused to set the record straight, saying curtly, "I am not obliged to give an answer to all the questions that may be put me by every lawless person." The crowd attacked his house and, after removing his furniture and personal effects, demolished it. By daybreak only the exterior walls were standing. Governor Bernard gave orders to call out the militia, but he was told that many militiamen were among the crowd.

The destruction of Hutchinson's house brought a temporary halt to protest activities in Boston. The town meeting issued a statement of sympathy for Hutchinson, but a large reward for the arrest and conviction of rioters failed to produce a single lead. Hutchinson assumed that Mackintosh had led the attack, under orders issued by Samuel Adams, but Adams denied involvement and professed shock at the "truly mobbish Nature" of the violence.

Nonetheless, the opponents of the Stamp Act in Boston had triumphed; no one volunteered to replace Oliver as distributor. When the Stamp Act took effect on November 1, customs officers were unable to prevent ships lacking properly stamped clearance papers from passing through the harbor. Hutchinson, as chief justice of the Massachusetts court, could not tolerate this defiance of the law, but he could not bring the lawbreakers to justice in his court. So he did the only thing he could do as a principled man: He resigned his judgeship. He remained lieutenant governor, however, and within five years he would agree to become the royal governor.

> Contrary to rumors, Hutchinson had not urged Grenville to adopt the Stamp Act, but he refused to set the record straight, saying curtly, "I am not obliged to give an answer to all the questions that may be put me by every lawless person."

Symbolic Death to Stamp Agents

Crowds of protesters in many American towns staged threatening demonstrations designed to make any stamp distributor think twice about selling the hated stamps. In this contemporary cartoon, a dummy wearing a hat and waistcoat is being led to destruction. One protester carries a hangman's gallows, another a large bundle of sticks to burn the dummy after it is hanged. Do you think the cartoonist was in sympathy with the demonstrators? Why or why not?

Granger Collection.

Pursuing Liberty, Protesting Tyranny

In August 1765, a little-known Boston shoemaker gained sudden prominence as the leader of crowd actions opposing the Stamp Act. Ebenezer Mackintosh boldly encouraged thousands of ordinary men in Massachusetts to assert a claim to liberty against what they identified as British tyranny. The story of Mackintosh offers a glimpse into the political thinking of the man in the street during a difficult decade of pre-Revolutionary turmoil. By 1776, this quest for liberty would be a defining feature of the fledgling United States.

Born in poverty in 1737, Ebenezer Mackintosh lacked family resources to ease his way in the world. His ancestors had settled in Dedham, a town near Boston, in the Puritan migration of the 1630s. A century later, they remained at the bottom of the town's hierarchy. Ebenezer's father, Moses, who had been orphaned at a young age, struggled against bad fortune. He owned no land and lacked a trade; he moved frequently and married and buried wives at least three times. The best Moses could do for fourteen-year-old Ebenezer after his mother died was to apprentice him to a shoemaker in Boston. During the Seven Years' War, Ebenezer joined the army to secure a signing bonus, a common recourse for poor young men. He saw action in the Ticonderoga campaign and returned to Boston seven months later, in 1758, to resume shoemaking. He was twenty-one.

A major fire in Boston in 1760 marked a dramatic change in direction for Mackintosh. In the aftermath of the fire, which gutted four hundred buildings, town authorities looked to younger, able-bodied men to reinvigorate the volunteer fire companies. Ebenezer was invited to join a select firemen's association in the city's South End. Ebenezer was likely proud of his new status, for as John Adams once remarked, "It is of some Importance in Boston to belong to a fire Clubb and to choose and get admitted to a good one." Fighting fires as a volunteer demonstrated one's sense of civic duty and manly responsibility. Fire clubs also generated fraternal sociability, with firemen regularly meeting in taverns over pitchers of beer, cementing the team spirit so critical to successful firefighting.

Mackintosh proved to be a leader of men in times of emergency. Gaining confidence from his involvement in the firemen's association, Mackintosh in 1764 assumed leadership of the South End gang, which staged a mock battle every year on Pope's Day (Guy Fawkes Day in England) against the rival North End gang. (The English holiday commemorated a failed plot by English Catholics, led by Guy Fawkes, to assassinate the Protes-

tant king in 1605.) In this traditional street festival, Mackintosh gained direct experience managing the often rowdy crowd. Expertise in fire and crowd control paved the way for Mackintosh's transition from community leader to community activist in 1765. Stamp Act protests erupted twice in August of that year. In the first event, Mackintosh presided over the mock hanging of a dummy representing Andrew Oliver, the stamp distributor, at a century-old elm tree known as the Liberty Tree. The shoemaker next led the several thousand protesters in a march around the governor's office and to a building rumored to be the new stamp office, which was pulled down and burned. Twelve days later, a smaller but far more destructive demonstration almost certainly led by Mackintosh demolished the mansion of Governor Thomas Hutchinson. Hutchinson ordered Mackintosh arrested, but no witnesses cared to identify him, and hours later the sheriff—a member of Mackintosh's fire company—released him, predicting worse trouble if he was kept in jail.

The shoemaker continued to lead large demonstrations in November and December, on one occasion forcing Andrew Oliver to repudiate his stamp distributor duties. Ordinary people like Mackintosh exerted a new authority and confidence that day, commanding their social betters to do their bidding.

In 1766, the Stamp Act was repealed, and Mackintosh went back to shoemaking. He married Elizabeth Maverick and had two children by 1769. Perhaps he took a break from activism; no record links him to protest activities when British troops came to town in 1769–1770, nor was his presence recorded at the Boston Massacre in March 1770. (However, one of the five men killed that night was his wife's nineteen-year-old cousin, Samuel Maverick.) In 1773, he was apparently back at it, bragging later in life that he led the group of men who threw tea into Boston harbor.

A well-publicized rumor spread in 1774 that a ship en route from London carried official orders to arrest four rebellious subjects: John Hancock, John Rowe, Samuel Adams, and Mackintosh. Hancock, Rowe, and Adams readied themselves for the trouble to come, but Mackintosh, still lacking resources and at a low moment in life—his young wife

had recently died—decided that flight was his best option. He set off on foot, carrying his two young children and his meager belongings with him. He traveled more than 150 miles north to the village of Haverhill, New Hampshire, where he set up shop as a shoemaker and carpenter. He served locally and briefly as a soldier in the war, then remarried and fathered four more children.

An especially telling clue to Mackintosh's idealization of liberty appears in the unusual name he gave his son born in 1769: Paschal Paoli

Mackintosh, in honor of Pasquale Paoli of Corsica, an antimonarchical freedom fighter who was much publicized in American newspapers in 1767–1769. Mackintosh enjoyed his brief moment of fame, and he lived to see liberty defined and enshrined in the foundational documents of the United States. Although he ended his life in 1816 in obscurity, as he had begun it, his activism in 1765 helped ensure that the thousands of people he mobilized learned a new political language of rights and liberties—a language that still resonates loudly today.

Mackintosh the Fireman

Mackintosh's signature, from a 1774 legal document, demonstrates his facility with a pen. Note the use of a common abbreviation, the superscript *r* instead of *er*, and the *s* written old style, like an *f*. The woodcut depicts a Boston fire engine of the 1760s. Underground water mains brought fresh pond water to Boston's center via wooden logs bored out four inches in diameter. Firemen punched a hole in the log to tap the water, moving it via hose or bucket brigade; both methods are in use here. (A *fireplug* resealed the hole.) Teams of vigorous men pumped the water by hand up into the hose with sufficient force to spray it on the fire. Demolition to halt the spread of fires was also essential work. Mackintosh's fire-control skills transferred easily to anti–Stamp Act actions, whether burning effigies and small buildings or pulling down Hutchinson's house.

Signature: Publications of the Colonial Society of Massachusetts; Fire engine. Granger Collection.

Liberty and Property

Boston's crowd actions of August sparked similar eruptions by groups calling themselves Sons of Liberty in nearly fifty towns throughout the colonies, and stamp distributors everywhere hastened to resign. One Connecticut distributor was forced by a crowd to throw his hat and powdered wig in the air while shouting a cheer for "Liberty and property!" This man fared better than another Connecticut stamp agent, who was nearly buried alive by Sons of Liberty. Only when the thuds of dirt sounded on his coffin did he have a sudden change of heart, shouting out his resignation to the crowd above. Luckily, he was heard. In Charleston, South Carolina, the stamp distributor resigned after crowds burned effigies and chanted "Liberty! Liberty!"

Some colonial leaders, disturbed by the riots, sought a more moderate challenge to parliamentary authority. Twenty-seven delegates representing nine colonial assemblies met in New York City in October 1765 as the Stamp Act Congress. For two weeks, the men hammered out a petition about taxation addressed to the king and Parliament. Their statement closely resembled the first five Virginia Resolves, claiming that taxes were "free gifts of the people," which only the people's representatives could give. They dismissed virtual representation: "The people of these colonies are not, and from their local circumstances, cannot be represented in the House of Commons." At the same time, the delegates carefully affirmed their subordination to Parliament and monarch in deferential language. (Even so, the elected president of the congress, wealthy Timothy Ruggles of Hardwick, Massachusetts, refused to sign the document, fearing it was too radical. When he returned home, his townsmen challenged his lukewarm attitude, ending his long career in politics.) Although the Stamp Act Congress's deference to the king defined a moderate path, the mere fact of its meeting advanced a radical potential—the notion of intercolonial political action.

The rallying cry of "Liberty and property" made perfect sense to many white Americans of all social ranks, who feared that the Stamp Act threatened their traditional right to liberty as British subjects. In this case, the liberty in question was the right to be taxed only by representative government. "Liberty and property" came from a trinity of concepts—"life, liberty, property"—that had come to be regarded as the birthright of freeborn British subjects since at least the seventeenth century. A powerful tradition of British political thought invested representative government with the duty to protect individual lives, liberties, and property (possessions or money) against potential abuse by royal authority. Up to 1765, Americans had consented to accept Parliament as a body that in some way represented them. But now, in this matter of taxation via stamps, Parliament seemed a distant body that had failed to protect Americans' liberty and property against royal authority.

Alarmed, some Americans began to speak and write about a plot by British leaders to enslave them. The opposite of liberty was slavery, the condition of being under the control of someone else. A Maryland writer warned that if the colonies lost "the right of exemption from all taxes without their consent," that loss would "deprive them of every privilege distinguishing freemen from slaves." In Virginia, a group of planters headed by Richard Henry Lee issued a document called the Westmoreland Resolves, claiming that the Stamp Act was an attempt "to reduce the people of this country to a state of abject and detestable slavery." The opposite meanings of *liberty* and *slavery* were utterly clear to white Americans, but they stopped short of applying similar logic to the half million black Americans they held in bondage. Many blacks, however, could see the contradiction. When a crowd of Charleston blacks paraded with shouts of "Liberty!"

Teapots for Patriots
Colonists could purchase commemorative teapots to celebrate the repeal of the Stamp Act. The one heralding AMERICA: LIBERTY RESTORED proclaims NO STAMP ACT on the back. Both of these pots were British imports. Can you think of any reason why a British pottery manufacturer might also have celebrated the repeal of the Stamp Act? Do you think one or both of these teapots might have found a market in Britain, too? Remember that in 1765, teapots were just teapots; the symbolic significance of tea lay several years in the future. During the political struggles over tea in 1770–1774, no British manufacturer is known to have made a souvenir teapot for the American market.
Liberty Restored: Northeast Auctions, Portsmouth, New Hampshire; Stamp Act Repeal'd: Peabody Essex Museum, Salem, Massachusetts.

just a few months after white Sons of Liberty had done the same, the town militia turned out to break up the demonstration.

Politicians and merchants in Britain reacted with distress to the American demonstrations and petitions. Merchants particularly feared trade disruptions and pressured Parliament to repeal the Stamp Act. By late 1765, yet another new minister, the Marquess of Rockingham, headed the king's cabinet and sought a way to repeal the act without losing face. The solution came in March 1766—the Stamp Act was repealed—but with it came the Declaratory Act, which asserted Parliament's right to legislate for the colonies "in all cases whatsoever." Perhaps the stamp tax had been inexpedient, but the power to tax—one prime case of a legislative power—was stoutly upheld.

> **REVIEW** Why did the Sugar Act and the Stamp Act draw fierce opposition from colonists?

The Townshend Acts and Economic Retaliation, 1767–1770

Rockingham did not last long as prime minister. By the summer of 1766, George III had persuaded William Pitt to resume that position. Pitt appointed Charles Townshend to be chancellor of the exchequer, the chief financial minister. Facing both the old war debt and the continuing cost of stationing British troops in America, Townshend turned again to taxation. But his knowledge of the changing political climate in the colonies was limited, and his simple yet naive idea to raise revenue touched off coordinated boycotts of British goods in 1768 and 1769. Even women were politicized as self-styled "Daughters of Liberty." Boston led the uproar, causing the British to send peacekeeping soldiers to assist the royal governor. The stage was thus set for the first fatalities in the brewing revolution.

The Townshend Duties

Townshend proposed new taxes in the old form of a navigation act. Officially called the Revenue Act of 1767, it established new duties on tea, glass, lead, paper, and painters' colors imported into the colonies, to be paid by the importer but passed on to consumers in the retail price. A year before, the duty on French molasses had been reduced from three pence to one pence per gallon, and finally the Sugar Act was pulling in a tidy revenue of about £45,000 annually. So it was not unreasonable to suppose that duties on additional trade goods might also improve the cash flow. Townshend assumed that external taxes on transatlantic trade would be more acceptable to Americans than internal taxes, such as the stamp tax.

The Townshend duties were not especially burdensome, but the principle they embodied—taxation through trade duties—looked different to the colonists in the wake of the Stamp Act crisis. Although Americans once distinguished between external and internal taxes, accepting external duties as presumably wise governmental policy designed to direct the flow of trade, that distinction was wiped out by an external tax meant only to raise money. John Dickinson, a Philadelphia lawyer, articulated this view in a series of articles titled *Letters from a Farmer in Pennsylvania*, widely reprinted in the winter of 1767–68. "We are taxed without our consent. . . . We are therefore—SLAVES," Dickinson wrote, calling for "a total denial of the power of Parliament to lay upon these colonies any 'tax' whatever."

> "We are taxed without our consent. . . . We are therefore—SLAVES," wrote Philadelphia lawyer John Dickinson, calling for "a total denial of the power of Parliament to lay upon these colonies any 'tax' whatever."

A controversial provision of the Townshend duties directed that some of the revenue generated would pay the salaries of royal governors. Before 1767, local assemblies set the salaries of their own officials, giving them significant influence over crown-appointed officeholders. Townshend wanted to strengthen the governors' position as well as to curb the growing independence of the assemblies.

The New York assembly, for example, seemed too defiant to Townshend. It had refused to enforce a British rule of 1765 called the Quartering Act, which directed the colonies to furnish shelter and provisions for the British army left in place after the Seven Years' War. The assembly argued that the Quartering Act was really a tax measure because it required New Yorkers to pay money by order of Parliament. Townshend came down hard on the assembly. He orchestrated a parliamentary order, the New York Suspending Act, which declared all the assembly's acts null and void until it met its obligations to the army. Both measures—the new way to pay royal governors' salaries and the

Edenton Tea Ladies

American women in many communities renounced British apparel and tea during the early 1770s. Women in Edenton, North Carolina, publicized their pledge and drew hostile fire in the form of a British cartoon. The cartoon's message is that brazen women who meddled in politics would undermine their femininity. Neglected babies, urinating dogs, wanton sexuality, and mean-looking women would be some of the dire consequences, according to the artist. The cartoon works as humor for the British because of the gender reversals it predicts and because of the insult it directs at American men.

Library of Congress.

suspension of the governance functions of the New York assembly—struck a chill throughout the colonies. Many wondered whether legislative government was at all secure.

Massachusetts again took the lead in protesting the Townshend duties. Samuel Adams, an elected member of the provincial assembly, argued that any form of parliamentary taxation was unjust because Americans were not repre-

sented in Parliament. Further, he argued that the new way to pay governors' salaries subverted the proper relationship between the people and their rulers. The assembly circulated a letter with Adams's arguments to other colonial assemblies for their endorsement. As with the Stamp Act Congress of 1765, colonial assemblies were starting to coordinate their protests.

In response to Adams's letter, the new man in charge of colonial affairs in Britain, Lord Hillsborough, instructed Massachusetts governor Bernard to dissolve the assembly if it refused to repudiate the letter. The assembly refused, by a vote of 92 to 17, and Bernard carried out his instruction. In the summer of 1768, Boston was in an uproar.

Nonconsumption and the Daughters of Liberty

The Boston town meeting had already passed resolutions, termed "nonconsumption agreements," calling for a boycott of all British-made goods. Dozens of other towns passed similar resolutions in 1767 and 1768. For example, prohibited purchases in the town of New Haven, Connecticut, included carriages, furniture, hats, clothing, lace, clocks, and textiles. The idea was to encourage home manufacture and to hurt trade, causing London merchants to pressure Parliament for repeal of the duties.

Nonconsumption agreements were very hard to enforce. With the Stamp Act, there was one hated item, a stamp, and a limited number of official distributors. In contrast, an agreement to boycott all British goods required coordination on many fronts, from shippers to merchants to consumers. It also required serious personal sacrifice. Some merchants were wary of nonconsumption because it hurt their pocketbooks, and a few continued to import in readiness for the end of nonconsumption (or to sell on the side to people choosing to ignore nonconsumption). In Boston, such merchants found themselves blacklisted in newspapers and broadsides.

A more direct blow to trade came from nonimportation agreements, but it proved more difficult to get merchants to agree to these. There was always the risk that merchants in other colonies might continue to trade with the British and thus receive handsome profits if neighboring colonies prohibited trade. Not until late 1768 could Boston merchants agree to suspend trade through a nonimportation agreement lasting one year starting January 1, 1769. Sixty signed the agreement. New York merchants soon followed suit, as did Philadelphia and Charleston merchants in 1769.

Doing without British products, whether luxury goods, tea, or textiles, no doubt was a hardship. But it also presented an opportunity, for many of the British products specified in nonconsumption agreements were household goods traditionally under the control of the "ladies." By 1769, male leaders in the patriot cause clearly understood that women's cooperation in nonconsumption and home manufacture was beneficial to their cause. The Townshend duties thus provided an unparalleled opportunity for encouraging female patriotism. During the Stamp Act crisis, Sons of Liberty took to the streets in protest. During the difficulties of 1768 and 1769, the concept of "Daughters of Liberty" emerged to give shape to a new idea—that women might play a role in public affairs.

Any woman could express affiliation with the colonial protest through conspicuous boycotts of British made goods. In Boston, more than three hundred women signed a petition to abstain from tea, "sickness excepted," in order to "save this abused Country from Ruin and Slavery." A Philadelphia woman inscribed some "patriotic poesy" in praise of women boycotters in her notebook in 1768, ending with the lines, "Stand firmly resolved and bid Grenville to see, / That rather than Freedom, we'll part with our Tea." A nine-year-old girl visiting the royal governor's house in New Jersey took the tea she was offered, curtsied, and tossed the beverage out a nearby window.

Homespun cloth became a prominent symbol of patriotism. A young Boston girl learning to spin called herself "a daughter of liberty," noting that "I chuse to wear as much of our own manufactory as pocible." A stylish matron in Massachusetts who pieced together a patchwork petticoat sewn from dozens of old remnants was deemed exemplary and therefore newsworthy by a Boston newspaper. In the boycott period of 1768 to 1770, newspapers reported on spinning matches, or bees, in some sixty New England towns, in which women came together in public to make yarn. Nearly always, the bee was held at the local minister's house, and the yarn produced was charitably handed over to him for distribution to the poor. Newspaper accounts variously called the spinners "Daughters of Liberty" or "Daughters of Industry."

> Homespun cloth became a prominent symbol of patriotism. A young Boston girl learning to spin called herself "a daughter of liberty," noting that "I chuse to wear as much of our own manufactory as pocible."

Spinning Wheel

A lot of skill was needed to spin high-quality thread and yarn. This wheel was used for spinning flax (a plant with a long fibrous stem) into linen thread. It is likely the type used in the politicized 1768–1769 spinning bees in which Daughters of Liberty proclaimed their boycott of British textiles. A foot treadle controls the turning of the wheel, and a spindle holds the thread produced. The art of spinning was all in the spinster's hand, which controlled the tension on the thread and the speed of the twisting. The spinning Daughters of Liberty were praised for their virtuous industry. Responding to such praise, one young woman complained, in a Rhode Island newspaper, that young male patriots were deficient in virtue: "Alas! We hear nothing of their working matches, nothing of their concern for the honor of their King or for the safety or liberties of their country." Instead, the news was of "nocturnal Carousals and Exploits; of their drinking, gaming & whoring matches; and how they disturb the quiet of honest people."

Smithsonian Institution, Washington, D.C.

This surge of public spinning was related to the politics of the boycott, which infused traditional women's work with new political purpose. But the women spinners were not equivalents of the Sons of Liberty. The Sons marched in streets, burned effigies, threatened hated officials, and celebrated anniversaries of their successes with raucous drinking and feasting in taverns. The Daughters manifested their patriotism quietly, in ways marked by piety, industry, and charity. The difference was due in part to cultural ideals of gender, which prized masculine self-assertion but feminine selflessness. It also was due to class. The Sons were a cross-class alliance, with leaders from the middling orders reliant on men and boys of the lower ranks to fuel their crowds. The Daughters, dusting off spinning wheels and shelving their teapots, were genteel ladies used to buying British goods. The difference between the Sons and Daughters also speaks to two views of how best to challenge authority. Which was the more effective strategy: violent threats and street actions, or the self-disciplined, self-sacrificing boycott of goods?

> After a short pause, someone yelled "Fire!" and the other soldiers shot into the crowd, hitting eleven men, killing five of them.

On the whole, the anti-British boycotts were a success. Imports fell by more than 40 percent; British merchants felt the pinch and let Parliament know it. In Boston, the Hutchinson family also endured losses, but even more alarming to the rigid lieutenant governor, Boston seemed overrun with anti-British sentiment. The Sons of Liberty staged annual rollicking celebrations of the Stamp Act riot, and both Hutchinson and Governor Bernard concluded that British troops were necessary to restore order.

Military Occupation and "Massacre" in Boston

In the fall of 1768, three thousand uniformed troops arrived to occupy Boston. The soldiers drilled conspicuously on the Common, played loud music on the Sabbath, and in general grated on the nerves of Bostonians. Although the situation was frequently tense, no major troubles occurred during that winter and through most of 1769. But as January 1, 1770, approached, marking the end of the nonimportation agreement, it was clear that some merchants—such as Thomas Hutchinson's two sons, both importers—were ready to break the boycott.

Trouble began in January, when a crowd defaced the door of the Hutchinson brothers' shop by "Hillsborough paint," a potent mixture of human excrement and urine. In February, a crowd surrounded the house of customs official Ebenezer Richardson, who panicked and fired a musket, accidentally killing a young boy passing on the street. The Sons of Liberty mounted a massive funeral procession to mark this first instance of violent death in the struggle with Britain.

For the next week, tension gripped Boston. The climax came on Monday evening, March 5, 1770, when a crowd taunted eight British soldiers guarding the customs house. Onlookers threw snowballs and rocks and dared the soldiers to fire; finally one did. After a short pause, someone yelled "Fire!" and the other soldiers shot into the crowd, hitting eleven men, killing five of them.

The Boston Massacre, as the event quickly became called, was over in minutes. In the immediate aftermath, Hutchinson (now acting governor after Bernard's recall to Britain) showed courage in addressing the crowd from the balcony of the statehouse. He quickly removed the regiments to an island in the harbor to prevent further bloodshed, and he jailed Captain Thomas Preston and his eight soldiers for their own protection, promising they would be held for trial.

The Sons of Liberty staged elaborate martyrs' funerals for the five victims. Significantly, the one nonwhite victim shared equally in the public's veneration. Crispus Attucks, a sailor and rope maker in his forties, was the son of an African man and a Natick Indian woman. A slave in his youth, he was at the time of his death a free laborer at the Boston docks. Attucks was one of the first American partisans to die in the American Revolution, and certainly the first African American.

The trial of the eight soldiers came in the fall of 1770. They were defended by two young Boston attorneys, Samuel Adams's cousin John Adams and Josiah Quincy. Because Adams and Quincy had direct ties to the leadership of the Sons of Liberty, their decision to defend the British soldiers at first seems odd. But Adams was deeply committed to the idea that even unpopular defendants deserved a fair trial. Samuel Adams respected his cousin's decision to take the case, for there was a tactical benefit as well. It showed that the Boston leadership was not lawless but could be seen as defenders of British liberty and law.

The Bloody Massacre Perpetrated in King Street, Boston, on March 5, 1770
This mass-produced engraving by Paul Revere sold for six pence per copy. In this patriot version of events, the soldiers fire on an unarmed crowd under orders of their captain. The tranquil dog is an artistic device used to signal the crowd's peaceful intent; not even a deaf dog could have held that pose during the melee. Among the five killed was Crispus Attucks, a black sailor, but Revere shows only whites among the casualties. Anne S. K. Brown Military Collection, Providence, R.I.

READING THE IMAGE: How does this picture attempt to sway its viewers' sympathies?
CONNECTIONS: Does this picture accurately represent the events of the Boston Massacre? What might account for its biases?

FOR MORE HELP ANALYZING THIS IMAGE, see the visual activity for this chapter in the Online Study Guide at bedfordstmartins.com/roark.

The five-day trial, with dozens of witnesses, resulted in acquittal for Preston and for all but two of the soldiers, who were convicted of manslaughter, branded on the thumbs, and released. Nothing materialized in the trial to indicate a conspiracy or concerted plan to provoke trouble by either the British or the Sons of Liberty. To this day, the question of responsibility for the Boston Massacre remains obscure.

REVIEW   Why did British authorities send troops to occupy Boston in the fall of 1768?

The Tea Party and the Coercive Acts, 1770–1774

In the same week as the Boston Massacre, yet another new British prime minister, Frederick North, acknowledged the harmful impact of the boycott on trade and recommended repeal of the Townshend duties. A skillful politician, Lord North took office in 1770 and kept it for twelve years; at last King George had stability at the helm.

Seeking peace with the colonies and prosperity for British merchants, North persuaded Parliament to remove all the duties except the tax on tea, kept as a symbol of Parliament's power.

The renewal of trade and the return of cooperation between Britain and the colonies gave men like Thomas Hutchinson hope that the worst of the crisis was behind them. For nearly two years, peace seemed possible, but tense incidents in 1772, followed by a renewed struggle over the tea tax in 1773, precipitated a full-scale crisis that by 1775 resulted in war.

The Calm before the Storm

Repeal of the Townshend duties brought an end to nonimportation, despite the tax on tea. Trade boomed in 1770 and 1771, driven by pent-up demand. Moreover, the leaders of the popular movement seemed to be losing their power. Samuel Adams, for example, ran for a minor local office in Boston and lost to a conservative merchant.

Then in 1772, several incidents again brought the conflict with Britain into sharp focus. One was the burning of the *Gaspée*, a Royal Navy ship pursuing suspected smugglers off the coast of

Rhode Island. A British investigating commission failed to arrest anyone but announced that it would send suspects, if any were found, to Britain for trial on charges of high treason. This ruling seemed to fly in the face of the traditional English right to trial by a jury of one's peers.

When news of the *Gaspée* investigation spread, it was greeted with disbelief in other colonies. Patrick Henry, Thomas Jefferson, and Richard Henry Lee in the Virginia House of Burgesses proposed that a network of standing committees be established to link the colonies and pass along alarming news. By mid-1773, every colonial assembly except Pennsylvania's had a "committee of correspondence."

Another British action in 1772 further spread the communications network. Lord North proposed to pay the salaries of superior court justices out of the tea revenue, similar to Townshend's plan for paying royal governors. The Boston town meeting, fearful that judges would now be in the pockets of their new paymasters, established a committee of correspondence and urged all Massachusetts towns to do likewise. The first vital message, circulated in December 1772, attacked the judges' salary policy as the latest proof of a British plot to undermine traditional "liberties": unjust taxation, military occupation, massacre, now capped by the subversion of justice. By the spring of 1773, more than half the towns in Massachusetts had set up committees of correspondence, providing local forums for debate. These committees politicized ordinary townspeople, sparking a revolutionary language of rights and constitutional duties. They also bypassed the official flow of power and information through the colony's royal government.

> Patrick Henry, Thomas Jefferson, and Richard Henry Lee proposed that a network of standing committees be established to link the colonies and pass along alarming news. By mid-1773, every colonial assembly except Pennsylvania's had a "committee of correspondence."

The final incident shattering the relative calm of the early 1770s was the Tea Act of 1773. Americans had resumed buying the taxed British tea, but they were also smuggling large quantities of Dutch tea, cutting into the sales of Britain's East India Company. So Lord North proposed legislation giving favored status to the East India Company, allowing it to sell tea directly to government agents rather than through public auction to independent merchants. The hope was to lower the price of the East India tea, including the duty, below that of smuggled Dutch tea, motivating Americans to obey the law.

Tea in Boston Harbor

In the fall of 1773, news of the Tea Act reached the colonies. Parliamentary legislation to make tea inexpensive struck many colonists as an insidious plot to trick Americans into buying large quantities of the dutied tea. The real goal, some argued, was the increased revenue, which would be used to pay the royal governors and judges. The Tea Act was thus a painful reminder of Parliament's claim to the power to tax and legislate for the colonies.

But how to resist the Tea Act? Nonimportation was not viable, because the tea trade was too lucrative to expect all merchants to give it up willingly. Consumer boycotts had proved ineffective, because it was impossible to distinguish between dutied tea (the object of the boycott) and smuggled tea (illegal but politically clean) once it was in the teapot. The act's appointment of tea agents, parallel to the Stamp Act distributors, suggested one solution. In every port city, revived Sons of Liberty pressured tea agents to resign; without agents, governors yielded, and tea cargoes either landed without paperwork or were sent home.

Governor Hutchinson, however, would not bend any rules. Three ships bearing tea arrived in Boston in November 1773. They cleared customs and unloaded their other cargoes but not the tea. Sensing the town's extreme tension, the captains wished to return to England, but Hutchinson would not grant them clearance to leave without paying the tea duty. Also, there was a time limit on the stay allowed in the harbor. After twenty days, the duty had to be paid, or local authorities would confiscate the tea.

For the full twenty days, pressure built in Boston. Daily mass meetings energized citizens from Boston and surrounding towns, alerted by the committees of correspondence. On the final day, December 16, when for a final time Hutchinson refused clearance for the ships, a large crowd gathered at Old South Church to debate a course of action. No solution emerged at that meeting, but immediately following it, somewhere between 100 and 150 men, thinly disguised as Indians, boarded the ships and dumped thousands of pounds of tea into the water while a crowd of 2,000 watched. John Adams rejoiced over the bold destruction of the tea in a diary entry the following day: "There is a Dignity, a Majesty, a Sublimity, in this last Effort of the Patriots, that I greatly admire. . . . This Destruction of the Tea is so bold, so daring, so firm, intrepid and inflexible, and it must have so important Consequences."

Tossing the Tea

This colored engraving appeared in an English book published in 1789 recounting the history of North America from its earliest settlement to "becoming united, free, and independent states." Men on the ship break into the chests and dump the contents; a few are depicted in Indian disguise, with topknots of feathers or hair. A large crowd on the shore looks on. The red rowboat is clearly stacked with tea chests, suggesting that some of the raiders were stealing rather than destroying the tea. However, the artist, perhaps careless, shows the rowboat heading toward the ship instead of away. This event was not dubbed the "Tea Party" until the 1830s, when a later generation celebrated the illegal destruction of the tea and made heroes out of the few surviving participants, by then in their eighties and nineties. Library of Congress.

The Coercive Acts

Lord North's response was swift and stern: He persuaded Parliament to issue the Coercive Acts, four laws meant to punish Massachusetts for destroying the tea. In America, those laws, along with a fifth one, the Quebec Act, were soon known as the Intolerable Acts.

The first act, the Boston Port Act, closed Boston harbor to all shipping as of June 1, 1774, until the destroyed tea was paid for. Britain's objective was to halt the commercial life of the city.

The second act, the Massachusetts Government Act, altered the colony's charter, underscoring Parliament's claim to supremacy over Massachusetts. The royal governor's powers were greatly augmented, and the council became an appointive, rather than elective, body. Further, the governor could now appoint all judges, sheriffs, and officers of the court. No town meeting beyond the annual spring election of town selectmen could be held without the governor's approval, and every agenda item likewise required prior approval. Every Massachusetts town was affected.

The third Coercive Act, the Impartial Administration of Justice Act, stipulated that any royal official accused of a capital crime—for example, Captain Preston and his soldiers at the Boston Massacre—would be tried in a court in Britain. It did not matter that Preston had received a fair trial in Boston. What this act ominously suggested was that down the road, more Captain Prestons and soldiers might be firing into unruly crowds.

The fourth act amended the 1765 Quartering Act and permitted military commanders to lodge soldiers wherever necessary, even in private households. In a related move, Lord North appointed General Thomas Gage, commander of the Royal

Hutchinson the Traitor Faces Death

This hideous engraving enlivened the cover of the *Massachusetts Calendar, or an Almanac for . . . 1774*, published in Boston in December 1773, just as the high drama over the tea tax unfolded. It shows Thomas Hutchinson with the devil behind him holding up a list of his many crimes and a skeleton representing death about to spear him. The caption below the picture read: "The wicked Statesman, or the Traitor to his Country, at the Hour of DEATH." Almanacs were the most common publications kept in colonial homes. The monthly calendar pages noted highly practical knowledge, such as sunrise and sunset, phases of the moon, and tides. People often used them to record family or business events and the daily weather. On page 2, readers of this anti-Hutchinson diatribe were invited to think about "the Horrors that Man must endure, who owes his Greatness to his Country's Ruin." The color here is probably a later addition.

Granger Collection.

also gave Quebec control of disputed land (and control of the lucrative fur trade) throughout the Ohio Valley, land also claimed by Virginia, Pennsylvania, and a number of Indian tribes.

The five Intolerable Acts spread alarm in all the colonies. If Britain could squelch Massachusetts—change its charter, suspend local government, inaugurate military rule, and on top of that give Ohio to Catholic Quebec—what liberties were secure? Fearful royal governors in half a dozen colonies dismissed the sitting assemblies, adding to the sense of urgency. A few of the assemblies defiantly continued to meet in new locations. Through the committees of correspondence, colonial leaders arranged to convene in Philadelphia in September 1774 to respond to the crisis.

Beyond Boston: Rural Massachusetts

By the time delegates assembled in Philadelphia, all of Massachusetts had arrived at the brink of open insurrection. With a British general occupying the governorship and some three thousand troops controlling Boston, the revolutionary momentum shifted from urban radicals to rural farmers who protested the Massachusetts Government Act in dozens of spontaneous, dramatic showdowns. In some towns, the last authorized town meeting simply continued to meet, as a dodge against the prohibition on new meetings, while more defiant towns just ignored the law. Gage's call for elections for a new provincial assembly under his control sparked elections for a competing and unauthorized assembly. In all counties except one, crowds of hundreds and even thousands of armed men converged to prevent the opening of county courts run by crown-appointed jurists. No judges were physically harmed, but they were forced to resign and made to doff their judicial wigs or run a humiliating gantlet. In Suffolk County, the courts met in troop-filled Boston, making mass intimidation of judges impossible. One by one, however, the citizen jurors called to serve in court refused. By late August 1774, farmers and artisans all over Massachusetts had effectively taken local control away from the crown.

In this early phase of the struggle, confrontations did not lead to bloodshed. But one incident, the Powder Alarm, nearly provoked violence and showed just how ready New England farmers were to take up arms. Gage sent troops

Army in New York, governor of Massachusetts. Thomas Hutchinson was out, relieved at long last of his duties. Military rule, including soldiers, returned once more to Boston.

Ill timed, the fifth act—the Quebec Act—had nothing to do with the four Coercive Acts, but it fed American fears. It confirmed the continuation of French civil law and government form, as well as Catholicism, for Quebec—all an affront to **Protestant** New Englanders recently denied their own representative government. The act

to capture a supply of gunpowder just outside Boston on September 1, and in the surprise and scramble of the attack, false news spread that the troops had fired on men defending the powder, killing six. Within twenty-four hours, thousands of armed men from Massachusetts and Connecticut set out on foot for Boston to avenge the first blood spilled. (See "Documenting the American Promise," page 202.) Once the error was corrected and the crisis defused, the men returned home peaceably. But Gage could no longer doubt the speed, size, and determination of the rebellious subjects he was told to subdue.

All this had occurred without orchestration by Boston radicals, Gage reported. But British leaders found it hard to believe, as one put it, that "a tumultuous Rabble, without any Appearance of general Concert, or without any Head to advise, or Leader to conduct" could pull off such effective resistance. Repeatedly in the years to come, the British would seriously underestimate their opponents.

Ordinary Massachusetts citizens, unfettered by the crown, began serious planning for the crisis everyone assumed would come. Town militias acquired two pounds of gunpowder per man "in case of invasion." Judges who had been willing crown appointees recanted and confessed their errors—or started packing to leave. The new provincial assembly convinced towns to withhold tax money from the royal governor and divert it to military supplies. Gage beefed up fortifications around Boston, sent armed soldiers to stop meetings that quickly dispersed, and in general rattled his sword loudly. Any bolder action would have to wait until he could acquire a larger army.

The First Continental Congress

Every colony except Georgia sent delegates to Philadelphia in September 1774 to discuss the looming crisis in what was later called the First Continental Congress. The gathering included notables such as Samuel Adams and John Adams from Massachusetts and George Washington and Patrick Henry from Virginia. A few colonies purposely sent men who opposed provoking Britain, such as Pennsylvania's Joseph Galloway, to keep the congress from becoming too radical.

Delegates sought to articulate their liberties as British subjects and the powers Parliament held over them, and they debated possible responses to the Coercive Acts. Some wanted a total ban on trade with Britain to force repeal, while others, especially southerners dependent on tobacco and rice exports, opposed halting trade. Samuel Adams and Patrick Henry were eager for a ringing denunciation of all parliamentary control. The conservative Joseph Galloway proposed a plan (quickly defeated) to

Tarring and Feathering Cartoon
In 1774, a Boston customs collector named John Malcolm felt the sting of a Boston crowd that tarred and feathered him as punishment for extorting money from shippers. This ritualized humiliation involved stripping a man, painting him with tar, and dipping him in chicken feathers. Local committees of public safety often used threats of this treatment as a weapon to enforce boycotts. In actuality, however, it happened far less often than it was threatened. This cartoon, of English origin, is hostile to Americans, who are shown with cruelly gleeful faces, forcing tea down Malcolm's throat. The Liberty Tree has become a gallows; posted to it is the Stamp Act, upside down. The dumping of tea in the harbor is depicted in the background. Library of Congress.

How News of the Powder Alarm Traveled

In the fall of 1774, tension in Massachusetts built under the pressure of the Massachusetts Government Act, which prohibited official town meetings and packed the police and judicial system (sheriffs, justices, and judges) with crown-appointed loyalists. In defiance, farmers and artisans flouted the law by holding unofficial meetings to govern. Armed men marched on county courts and forced loyalist judges to resign. Tensions climaxed on September 1, when Governor Thomas Gage sent British troops to capture a cache of gunpowder in Charlestown, across the river from Boston, in what became known as the Powder Alarm. A false rumor quickly spread that six Americans had been killed in the raid, sparking thousands of armed Massachusetts and Connecticut men to head to Boston in retaliation. When the error became known, the men returned home, but Gage now fully realized the depth of American fear and anger. The following accounts illustrate the different ways news of the Powder Alarm spread.

DOCUMENT 1
A Call to Rally the Forces via Committees of Correspondence, September 3–4, 1774

The horrifying report of six fatalities and a call for help moved the 220 miles from Boston to New York City in three days via a network of eight committees of correspondence. Individual endorsements of leading citizens gave greater authenticity to the rumor and indicated the route the news should travel.

POMFRET, CONNECTICUT, *September 3, 1774.* CAPTAIN CLEVELAND: Mr. *Keys* this moment brought us the news that the men-of-war and troops began to fire upon the people last night at sunset at *Boston*, when a post was immediately sent off to inform the country. He informs, that the artillery played all night; that the people were universally rallying from *Boston* as far as here, and desire all the assistance possible. The first was occasioned by the country's being robbed of their powder from *Boston* as far as *Framingham*, and when found out, the persons who went to take them were immediately fired upon; six of our number were killed the first shot, and a number wounded, and beg you will rally all the forces you can, and be upon the march immediately for the relief of *Boston*, and the people that way. ISRAEL PUTNAM.

Send an express along to *Norwich* and elsewhere. AARON CLEVELAND.

Forwarded from *Norwich* per *JOHN DURKEE.*

NEW-LONDON, *September* 3. Pray send forward an express to *Saybrook*, and elsewhere on the sea shore, and to *East Haddam*, immediately. I desire those towns to forward expresses to their neighbouring towns.
RICHARD LAW, NATHANIEL SHAW, SAMUEL H. PARSONS.

To Messrs. *John Lay*, Esquire, and the rest of the Committee of Correspondence at *Lyme*. NEW-LONDON, *September* 3. You will see, by a Letter to your Committee of Correspondence, the necessity of rallying all your forces immediately. Pray let every man who values his own, or his country's liberty, appear immediately. We shall march before noon to-morrow. I came home to-day; shall set out with our forces on the morrow. Let your Captains call their men as early as possible, and make no delay in joining. S. PARSONS.

To the Committee of Correspondence in SAYBROOK, *or to the Selectmen in* SAYBROOK: It is desired that this may be forwarded to *Killingsworth*, to be forwarded westward. *Ele. Matther, John Lay*, 2d, *John McCurdy, William Noyes, Samuel Matther*, Jun., Committee of Correspondence.

TO DR. NATHANIEL RUGGLES, AND SAMUEL BROWN, ESQUIRE. GENTLEMEN: You will doubtless think it prudent, on the receipt of this intelligence, to forward it at least as far as *New-Haven*, where, doubtless, intelligence will be received by the upper road. AARON ELLIOTT, BENJAMIN GALE.

GUILFORD, *September* 4. Forwarded by the subscriber to *Branford.* SAMUEL BROWN.

BRANFORD, *September* 4. Forwarded to *John Whiting*, Esquire, and the rest of the Committee of Correspondence at *New-Haven*, per SAMUEL BAKER, SAMUEL JONES.

NEW-HAVEN, *September* 4. GENTLEMEN: We have to communicate the fatal news of an attack by the King's fleet and troops upon the town of *Boston*. Enclosed you have the foundation and conveyance of the melancholy intelligence. We thought it necessary and expedient to communicate by express, expecting your speedy aid to forward the same to the Congress at *Philadelphia*. We are, gentlemen, your friends and brethren in the common cause. Signed for the Committee of Correspondence. TIMOTHY JONES, *Clerk of the said Committee.* To the Committee of Correspondence of *New-York*.

SOURCE: Peter Force, *American Archives,* volume 1: 325. © 2004 Northern Illinois University Libraries. Reprinted with permission.

DOCUMENT 2
Ezra Stiles's Account of Mr. McNeil's Experience on September 2, 1774

A Connecticut merchant named McNeil was at an inn in Shrewsbury, in central Massachusetts, and witnessed how news of the Powder Alarm traveled by word of mouth. He described the commotion over rumored fatalities to his friend Ezra Stiles, a minister in New Haven, Connecticut, a few weeks later. Stiles's diary entry reveals the nearly instantaneous determination shown by men, women, and children in rural Massachusetts to rush into battle against the British.

[McNeil] went to bed [on September 1, 1774] without hearing any Thing. But about midnight or perhaps one o'clock he was suddenly waked up, somebody violently rapping up the Landlord, telling the doleful Story that the Powder was taken, six men killed, & all the people between there & Boston arming & marching down to the Relief of their Brethren at Boston; and within a qr. or half an hour he judges fifty men were collected at the Tavern tho' now deep in Night, equipping themselves & sending off Posts every Way to the neighboring Towns. . . .

In the Morning, being fryday Sept. 2, Mr. McNeil rode forward & passed thro' the whole at the very Time of the Convulsion. He said he never saw such a Scene before—all along were armed Men rushing forward some on foot some on horseback, at every house Women & children making Cartridges, running Bullets, making Wallets, baking Biscuit, crying & bemoaning & at the same time animating their Husbands & Sons to fight for their Liberties, tho' not knowing whether they should ever see them again. I asked whether the Men were Cowards or disheartened or appeared to want Courage? No. Whether the tender Distresses of weeping Wives & Children softened effeminated & overcome the Men and set them Weeping to? No—nothing of this—but a firm and intrepid Ardor, hardy eager & courageous Spirit of Enterprize, a Spirit for revenging the Blood of their Brethren & rescue our Liberties, all this & an Activity corresponding with such Emotions appeared all along the whole Tract of above fourty Miles from Shrewsbury to Boston . . . for they all believed the Action commenced between the Kings Troops & the Provincials.

SOURCE: Reprinted in *The First American Revolution: Before Lexington and Concord* by Ray Raphael. Copyright © 2002, New Press, pp. 128–29. Reprinted with permission.

DOCUMENT 3
Newspaper Accounts beyond Massachusetts, September 1774

This newspaper item purported to come from Boston and within a week was reprinted in papers in Salem, Massachusetts; Portsmouth, New Hampshire; and Philadelphia, Pennsylvania, all weekly publications. The item reports on the size of the sudden mobilization in Connecticut converging to defend Boston. In December, the Massachusetts Provincial Congress, meeting illegally in Salem, directed towns to arm and train a subset of town militiamen to be "minutemen," ready to respond at a minute's notice, in order to formalize what had happened during the Powder Alarm.

BOSTON, Thursday, Sept. 8. By letters from Connecticut, and by several credible gentlemen arrived from thence, we are informed that there were not less than 40,000 men in motion, and under arms, on their way to Boston, on Saturday, Sunday and Monday last, having heard a false report, that the troops had fired upon Boston, and had killed several of the inhabitants: Twelve hundred arrived at Hartford from Farmington, and other places forty miles beyond Hartford, on Sunday last, on their way to this place, so rapidly did the news fly. But being informed by expresses that it was a false report, they returned home, declaring themselves ready at a minute's warning to arm again, and fight for their country, and distressed brethren of Boston.

SOURCE: Early American Newspapers online, Readex Corporation, *Essex Gazette*, Massachusetts, September 13, 1774; *New Hampshire Gazette and Historical Chronicle*, September 16, 1774; *Dunlap's Pennsylvania Packet*, or the *General Advertiser*, September 19, 1774

QUESTIONS FOR ANALYSIS AND DEBATE

---

1. Compare and contrast the different ways news of the Powder Alarm traveled: a hand-delivered letter passed by committees of correspondence, word of mouth as described by Ezra Stiles, and newspaper articles. How do these accounts differ in terms of speed of transmission, reliability, and authenticity?

2. What was the point of having members of Connecticut's committees of correspondence add their names to the letter in the first document as it made its way to New York City?

3. What message about women and war does the second document convey? What does this suggest about the colonists' readiness to fight the British in 1774?

4. Do you think it likely that the third document was actually first printed in a Boston newspaper? What constraints might have operated in Boston in September 1774 that could have affected what got printed there? What or who else might have been the source of the article in the three other papers?

create a secondary parliament in America to assist the British Parliament in ruling the colonies.

The congress met for seven weeks and produced a declaration of rights couched in traditional language: "We ask only for peace, liberty and security. We wish no diminution of royal prerogatives, we demand no new rights." But from Britain's point of view, the rights assumed already to exist were radical. Chief among them was the claim that Americans were not represented in Parliament and so each colonial government had the sole right to govern and tax its own people. The one slight concession to Britain was a carefully worded agreement that the colonists would "cheerfully consent" to trade regulations for the larger good of the empire— so long as trade regulation was not a covert means of raising revenue.

To put pressure on Britain, the delegates agreed to a staggered and limited boycott of trade—imports prohibited this year, exports the following, and rice totally exempted (to keep South Carolinians happy). To enforce the boycott, they called for a Continental Association, with chapters in each town variously called committees of public safety or of inspection, to monitor all commerce and punish suspected violators of the boycott (sometimes with a bucket of tar and a bag of feathers). Its work done in a month, the congress disbanded in October, with agreement to convene a second time in May 1775.

> Thomas Gage realized how desperate the British position was. The people, he wrote, were "numerous, worked up to a fury, and not a Boston rabble but the freeholders and farmers of the country."

The committees of public safety, the committees of correspondence, the regrouped and defiant colonial assemblies, and the Continental Congress were all political bodies functioning without any constitutional authority. British officials did not recognize them as legitimate, but many Americans who supported the patriot cause instantly accepted them. A key reason for the stability of such unauthorized governing bodies was that they were composed of many of the same men who had held elective office before.

Britain's severe reaction to Boston's destruction of the tea finally succeeded in making many colonists from New Hampshire to Georgia realize that the problems of British rule went far beyond questions of taxation. The Coercive Acts infringed on liberty and denied self-government; they could not be ignored. With one colony already subordinated to military rule and a British army at the ready in Boston, the threat of a general war was on the doorstep.

> **REVIEW**   Why did Parliament pass the Coercive Acts in 1774?

Domestic Insurrections, 1774–1775

Before the Second Continental Congress could meet, violence and bloodshed came to Massachusetts, raising the stakes considerably. General Thomas Gage, military commander and royal governor, knew that it would take more than a mere show of force to subdue the domestic insurrection unfolding in Massachusetts. He requested more soldiers and, under pressure from above, initiated a march on the towns of Lexington and Concord in April 1775. As in the Powder Alarm of 1774, New England farmers were ready, justifying their preparations for war as a defense of their homes and liberties against an intrusive power bent on enslaving them. To the south, a different and inverted version of the same story began to unfold, as thousands of enslaved black men and women seized an unprecedented opportunity to mount a different kind of insurrection—against planter-patriots who looked over their shoulders uneasily whenever they called out for liberty from the British.

Lexington and Concord

During the winter of 1774–75, Americans pressed on with boycotts. Optimists hoped to effect a repeal of the Coercive Acts; pessimists started stockpiling arms and ammunition. In Massachusetts, gunpowder and shot were secretly stored, and militia units known as minutemen prepared to respond at a minute's notice to any threat from the British troops in Boston.

Thomas Gage soon realized how desperate the British position was. The people, Gage wrote Lord North, were "numerous, worked up to a fury, and not a Boston rabble but the freeholders and farmers of the country." Gage requested twenty thousand reinforcements. He also strongly advised repeal of the Coercive Acts, but leaders in Britain could not admit failure. Instead, they ordered Gage in mid-April 1775 to

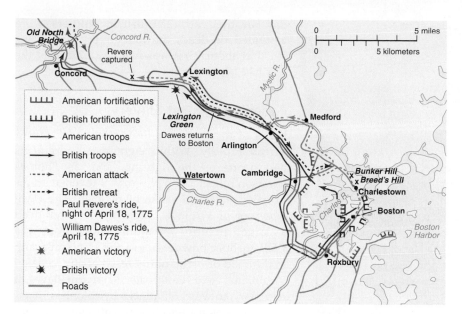

MAP 6.3   Lexington and Concord, April 1775

Under pressure from Britain, some nine hundred British forces at Boston staged a raid on a suspected patriot arms supply in Concord, Massachusetts, starting the first battle of the Revolutionary War. The routes of the two men sent to warn the patriots are marked. Paul Revere went by boat from Boston to Charlestown and then continued by horse through Medford to Lexington. William Dawes casually passed British sentries guarding the only land route out of Boston, a land bridge called the Neck, then rode his horse at full speed to Lexington. Revere and Dawes reached Samuel Adams and John Hancock, guests in a Lexington home, and urged them to flee to avoid capture. The two couriers then went on to Concord to warn residents of the impending attack.

READING THE MAP: William Dawes was, like Paul Revere, a messenger who raced ahead of British troops to warn the minutemen of British plans for raiding their supply of weapons. How did Dawes's route differ from Revere's? What kinds of terrain and potential dangers did each man face during his ride, according to the map?

CONNECTIONS: Why might it have mattered who shot first on the Lexington green? What was at stake for each side in claiming the other shot first?

FOR MORE HELP ANALYZING THIS MAP, see the map activity for this chapter in the Online Study Guide at bedfordstmartins.com/roark.

---

arrest the troublemakers immediately, before the Americans got better organized.

Gage quickly planned a surprise attack on a suspected ammunition storage site at Concord, a village eighteen miles west of Boston (Map 6.3). Near midnight on April 18, 1775, British soldiers moved west across the Charles River. Boston silversmith Paul Revere and William Dawes, a tanner, raced ahead to alert the minutemen. When the soldiers got to Lexington, a village five miles east of Concord, they were met by some seventy armed men assembled on the village green. The British commander barked out, "Lay down your arms, you damned rebels, and disperse." The militiamen hesitated and began

to comply, turning to leave the green, but then someone—nobody knows who—fired. In the next two minutes, more firing left eight Americans dead and ten wounded.

The British units continued their march to Concord, any pretense of surprise gone. Three companies of minutemen nervously occupied the town center but offered no challenge to the British as they searched in vain for the ammunition. Finally, at Old North Bridge in Concord, troops and minutemen exchanged shots, killing two Americans and three British soldiers.

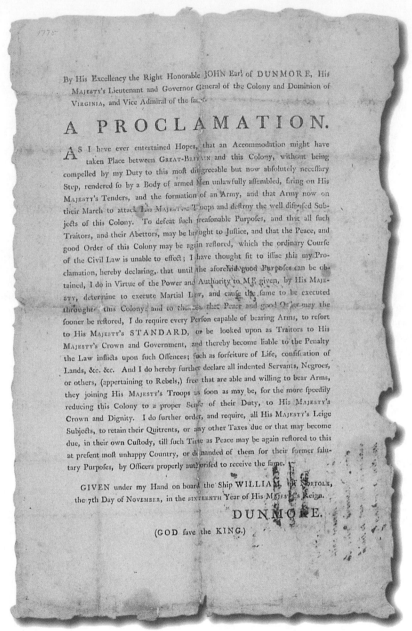

Lord Dunmore's Proclamation

In November 1775, Lord Dunmore of Virginia offered freedom to "all indented Servants, Negroes, or others, (appertaining to Rebels)" who would help put down the rebellion. Dunmore issued multiple printed copies in broadside form from the safety of a ship anchored at Norfolk, Virginia.

Special Collections, University of Virginia, Alderman Library.

By now, both sides were very apprehensive. The British had failed to find the expected arms, and the Americans had failed to stop their raid. As the British returned to Boston along a narrow road, militia units in hiding attacked from the sides of the road in the bloodiest fighting of the day. In the end, 273 British soldiers were wounded or dead; the toll for the Americans stood at about 95. It was April 19, 1775, and the war had begun.

Rebelling against Slavery

News of the battles of Lexington and Concord spread rapidly. Within eight days, Virginians had heard of the fighting, and, as Thomas Jefferson reflected, "a phrenzy of revenge seems to have seized all ranks of people." The royal governor of Virginia, Lord Dunmore, removed a large quantity of gunpowder from the Williamsburg powder house and put it on a ship in the dead of night, out of reach of any frenzied Virginians. Next, he threatened to arm slaves, if necessary, to ward off attacks by colonists.

This was an effective threat; Dunmore understood full well how to produce panic among the planters. He did not act on his warning until November 1775, when he issued an official proclamation promising freedom to defecting able-bodied slaves who would fight for the British. Although Dunmore wanted to scare the planters, he had no intention of liberating all the slaves or starting a real slave rebellion. Female, young, and elderly slaves were not welcome behind British lines, and many were sent back to face irate masters. Astute blacks noticed that Dunmore neglected to free his own slaves. A Virginia barber named Caesar declared that "he did not know any one foolish enough to believe him [Dunmore], for if he intended to do so, he ought first to set his own free."

By December 1775, around fifteen hundred slaves in Virginia had fled to Lord Dunmore, who armed them and called them his "Ethiopian Regiment." Camp diseases quickly set in: dysentery, typhoid fever, and, worst of all, smallpox. When Dunmore sailed for England in mid-1776, he took just three hundred black survivors with him. But the association of freedom with the British authorities had been established, and throughout the war, thousands more southern slaves made bold to run away as soon as they heard the British army was approaching.

In the northern colonies as well, slaves clearly recognized the evolving political struggle with Britain as an ideal moment to bid for freedom. A twenty-one-year-old Boston domestic slave employed biting sarcasm in a 1774 newspaper essay to call attention to the hypocrisy of local slave owners: "How well the Cry for Liberty, and the reverse Disposition for exercise of oppressive Power over others agree,—I humbly think it does not require the Penetration of a Philosopher to Determine." This extraordinary young woman, Phillis Wheatley, had already gained international recognition through a book of poems, endorsed by Governor Thomas Hutchinson and Boston merchant John Hancock and published in London in 1773. Possibly neither man fully appreciated the irony of his endorsement, however, for Wheatley's poems spoke of "Fair Freedom" as the "Goddess long desir'd" by Africans enslaved in America. At the urging of his wife, Wheatley's master freed the young poet in 1775.

Wheatley's poetic ideas about freedom found concrete expression among other discontented groups. Some slaves in Boston petitioned Thomas Gage, promising to fight for the British if he would liberate them. Gage turned them down. In Ulster County, New York, along the Hudson River, two blacks were overheard discussing gunpowder, and thus a plot unraveled that involved at least twenty slaves in four villages discovered to have ammunition stashed away.

In Maryland, soon after the news of the Lexington battle arrived, blacks exhibited impatience with their status as slaves, causing one Maryland planter to report that "the insolence of the Negroes in this county is come to such a height, that we are under a necessity of disarming them. . . . We took about eighty guns, some bayonets, swords, etc." In North Carolina, a planned uprising was uncovered, and scores of slaves were arrested. Ironically, it was the revolutionary committee of public safety that ordered the whippings to punish this quest for liberty.

By 1783, when the Revolutionary War ended, as many as twenty thousand blacks had voted against slavery with their feet by seeking refuge with the British army. Most failed to achieve the liberation they were seeking. The British generally used them for menial labor, and disease, especially smallpox, devastated encampments of runaways. But some eight thousand to ten thousand persisted through the war and later, under the protection of the British army, left America to start new lives of freedom in Canada's Nova Scotia or Africa's Sierra Leone.

REVIEW How did enslaved people in the colonies react to the stirrings of revolution?

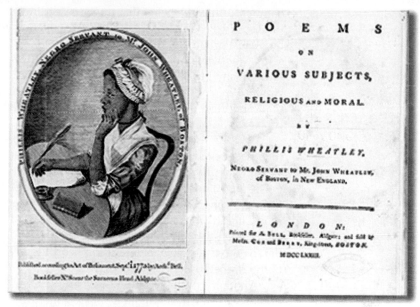

Phillis Wheatley's Title Page
Phillis, born in Africa, was sold to John Wheatley of Boston at age seven. Remarkably gifted in learning English, she published her first poem at age twelve, in 1766. By age sixteen, she could read the Bible with ease and composed many poems. Her master took her to London in 1773, where this book was published, gaining her great literary notice. Wheatley's eloquent achievement captured the attention of American leaders, and in 1776 she met with George Washington. The Wheatleys freed Phillis, but John Wheatley's early death left her without resources. An unhappy marriage to a free black man followed. Two of their three children died in infancy, and her husband deserted her. Poetry alone could not support her, and she found work in a boarding-house. By the end of 1784, Phillis and her remaining child had died.
Library of Congress.

Conclusion: How Far Does Liberty Go?

The Seven Years' War set the stage for the imperial crisis of the 1760s and 1770s by creating distrust between Britain and its colonies and by running up a huge deficit in the British treasury. The years 1763 to 1775 brought repeated attempts by the British government to subordinate the colonies into taxpaying partners in the larger scheme of empire.

American resistance grew slowly but steadily over those years. In 1765, loyalist Thomas Hutchinson shared with patriot

> One Maryland planter reported that "the insolence of the Negroes in this county is come to such a height, that we are under a necessity of disarming them."

Samuel Adams the belief that it was exceedingly unwise for Britain to assert a right to taxation, because Parliament did not adequately represent Americans. By temperament and office, Hutchinson had to uphold British policy. Adams, in contrast, protested the policy and made political activists out of thousands in the process.

By 1775, events propelled many Americans to the conclusion that a concerted effort was afoot to deprive them of all their liberties, the most important of which were the right to self-taxation, the right to live free of an occupying army, and the right to self-rule. Hundreds of minutemen converged on Concord, prepared to die for those liberties. April 19 marked the start of their rebellion.

Another rebellion under way in 1775 was doomed to be short-circuited. Black Americans who had experienced actual slavery listened to shouts of "Liberty!" from white crowds and appropriated the language of revolution swirling around them that spoke to their deepest needs and hopes. Defiance of authority was indeed contagious.

The emerging leaders of the patriot cause were mindful of a delicate balance they felt they had to strike. To energize the American public about the crisis with Britain, they had to politicize masses of men—and eventually women, too—and infuse them with a keen sense of their rights and liberties. But in so doing, they became fearful of the unintended consequences of teaching a vocabulary of rights and liberties. They worried that the rhetoric of enslavement might go too far.

The question of how far the crisis could be stretched before something snapped was largely unexamined in 1765. Patriot leaders in that year wanted a correction, a restoration of an ancient liberty of self-taxation that Parliament seemed to be ignoring. But events from 1765 to 1775 convinced many that a return to the old ways was impossible. Challenging Parliament's right to tax had led, step by step, to challenging Parliament's right to legislate over the colonies in any matter. If Parliament's sovereignty was set aside, who actually had authority over the American colonies? By 1775, with the outbreak of fighting and the specter of slave rebellions, American leaders turned to the king for the answer to that question.

Selected Bibliography

General Works

Edward Countryman, *The American Revolution* (2003).

Merrill Jensen, *The Founding of a Nation: A History of the American Revolution, 1763–1776* (2004).

Robert Middlekauff, *The Glorious Cause: The American Revolution, 1763–1789* (2005).

Gordon Wood, *The Radicalism of the American Revolution* (1992).

Alfred F. Young, *The American Revolution: Explorations in the History of American Radicalism* (1984).

Native Americans and the Seven Years' War

Fred Anderson, *Crucible of War: The Seven Years' War and the Fate of Empire in British North America, 1754–1766* (2000).

Greg Evans Dowd, *War under Heaven: Pontiac, the Indian Nations and the British Empire* (2002).

James H. Merrell, *Into the American Woods: Negotiators on the Pennsylvania Frontier* (1999).

Timothy J. Shannon, *Indians and Colonists at the Crossroads of Empire: The Albany Congress of 1754* (1999).

Richard White, *The Middle Ground: Indians, Empires, and Republics in the Great Lakes Region, 1650–1815* (1991).

The Revolutionary Crisis of the 1760s and 1770s

Bernard Bailyn, *The Ordeal of Thomas Hutchinson* (1974).

Carol Berkin, *Revolutionary Mothers: Women in the Struggle for America's Independence* (2005).

T. H. Breen, *The Marketplace of Revolution: How Consumer Politics Shaped American Independence* (2004).

Benjamin L. Carp, *Rebels Rising: Cities and the American Revolution* (2007).

Edward Countryman, *A People in Revolution: The American Revolution and Political Society in New York, 1760–1790* (1981).

John E. Ferling, *The First of Men: A Life of George Washington* (1988).

David Hackett Fischer, *Paul Revere's Ride* (1994).

Robert A. Gross, *The Minutemen and Their World* (1976).

Joan Gundersen, *To Be Useful to the World: Women in Revolutionary America, 1740–1790* (1996).

Dirk Hoerder, *Crowd Action in Revolutionary Massachusetts, 1765–1780* (1977).

Woody Holton, *Forced Founders: Indians, Debtors, Slaves, and the Making of the American Revolution in Virginia* (1999).

Rhys Isaac, *The Transformation of Virginia, 1740–1790* (1982).

Pauline Maier, *From Resistance to Revolution: Colonial Radicals and the Development of American Opposition to Britain, 1765–1776* (1972).

Henry Mayer, *A Son of Thunder: Patrick Henry and the American Republic* (1992).

Edmund S. and Helen M. Morgan, *The Stamp Act Crisis: Prologue to Revolution* (1995).

Gary B. Nash, *The Urban Crucible: Social Change, Political Consciousness, and the Origins of the American Revolution* (1979).

Mary Beth Norton, *Liberty's Daughters: The Revolutionary Experience of American Women, 1750–1800* (1980).

Ray Raphael, *The First American Revolution: Before Lexington and Concord* (2002).

Steven Rossman, *Arms, Country, and Class: The Philadelphia Militia and the "Lower Sort" during the American Revolution* (1987).

Ann Fairfax Withington, *Toward a More Perfect Union: Virtue and the Formation of American Republics* (1991).

Alfred F. Young, *The Shoemaker and the Tea Party: Memory and the American Revolution* (1999).

Slavery

Sylvia Frey, *Water from the Rock: Black Resistance in a Revolutionary Age* (1991).

Winthrop D. Jordan, *White over Black: American Attitudes toward the Negro, 1550–1812* (1968).

Sidney Kaplan and Emma Nogrady Kaplan, *The Black Presence in the Era of the American Revolution* (1989).

Philip Morgan, *Slave Counterpoint* (1998).

▶ **For more books about topics in this chapter,** see the Online Bibliography at bedfordstmartins.com/roark.

▶ **For additional firsthand accounts of this period,** see Chapter 6 in Michael Johnson, ed., *Reading the American Past*, Fourth Edition.

▶ **For Web sites, images, and documents related to topics and places in this chapter,** visit bedfordstmartins.com/makehistory.

REVIEWING THE CHAPTER

Follow these steps to review and strengthen your understanding of the chapter.

STEP 1: *Study the **Key Terms** and **Timeline** to identify the significance of each item listed.*

STEP 2: *Answer the **Review Questions**, drawing on key terms and dates to support your answers.*

STEP 3: *Drawing on the Key Terms, Timeline, and Review Questions, answer the broader **Making Connections** questions.*

KEY TERMS

Who

Thomas Hutchinson (p. 175)
Robert Dinwiddie (p. 177)
George Washington (p. 177)
Tanaghrisson (p. 177)
Benjamin Franklin (p. 179)
Edward Braddock (p. 180)
William Pitt (p. 181)
George III (p. 182)
Pontiac (p. 183)
George Grenville (p. 186)
Patrick Henry (p. 187)
Samuel Adams (p. 188)
Ebenezer Mackintosh (p. 188)
Andrew Oliver (p. 188)
Charles Townshend (p. 193)
Thomas Preston (p. 196)
Frederick North (p. 197)

Thomas Gage (p. 199)
minutemen (p. 203)
Paul Revere (p. 205)
Lord Dunmore (p. 206)
Phillis Wheatley (p. 207)

What

Seven Years' War (p. 176)
Ohio Company (p. 177)
Fort Duquesne (p. 177)
Fort Necessity (p. 177)
Covenant Chain (p. 179)
Albany Plan of Union (p. 179)
Treaty of Paris (p. 181)
Proclamation of 1763 (p. 182)
Molasses Act of 1733 (p. 186)
Sugar Act (Revenue Act of 1764) (p. 186)
Stamp Act (p. 187)

virtual representation (p. 187)
Virginia Resolves (p. 187)
Sons of Liberty (p. 188)
Stamp Act Congress (p. 192)
Declaratory Act (p. 193)
Townshend duties (p. 193)
nonconsumption agreements (p. 194)
nonimportation agreements (p. 194)
Daughters of Liberty (p. 195)
Boston Massacre (p. 196)
Gaspée (p. 197)
committees of correspondence (p. 198)
Tea Act of 1773 (p. 198)
Coercive Acts (p. 199)
Powder Alarm (p. 200)
First Continental Congress (p. 201)
Continental Association (p. 204)
committees of public safety (p. 204)

TIMELINE

◀ **1747** • Ohio Company of Virginia formed.

1754 • Seven Years' War begins in North America.
• Albany Congress proposes Plan of Union (never implemented).

1755 • Braddock defeated in western Pennsylvania.

1757 • William Pitt fully commits Britain to war effort.

1759 • Quebec falls to British.

1760 • Montreal falls to British.
• George III becomes British king.

1763 • Treaty of Paris ends Seven Years' War.
• Pontiac's uprising.
• Proclamation of 1763.
• Paxton Boys massacre friendly Indians in Pennsylvania.

1764 • Parliament enacts Revenue (Sugar) Act.

1765 • Parliament enacts Stamp Act.
• Virginia Resolves challenge Stamp Act.
• Dozens of crowd actions by Sons of Liberty.
• Stamp Act Congress meets.

REVIEW QUESTIONS

1. How did the Seven Years' War erode relations between colonists and British authorities? (pp. 176–83)

2. Why did the Sugar Act and the Stamp Act draw fierce opposition from colonists? (pp. 186–93)

3. Why did British authorities send troops to occupy Boston in the fall of 1768? (pp. 193–97)

4. Why did Parliament pass the Coercive Acts in 1774? (pp. 197–204)

5. How did enslaved people in the colonies react to the stirrings of revolution? (pp. 204–7)

MAKING CONNECTIONS

1. In the mid-eighteenth century, how did Native Americans influence relations between European nations? Between Britain and the colonies?

2. Why did disputes over taxation figure so prominently in the deteriorating relations between Britain and the colonies? In your answer, refer to specific disputed British attempts to raise revenue and the colonial response.

3. How did the colonists organize to oppose British power so effectively? In your answer, discuss the role of communication in facilitating the colonial resistance, being sure to cite specific examples.

▶ FOR PRACTICE QUIZZES, A CUSTOMIZED STUDY PLAN, AND OTHER STUDY TOOLS, see the Online Study Guide at bedfordstmartins.com/roark.

1766 • Parliament repeals Stamp Act and passes Declaratory Act.

1767 • Parliament enacts Townshend duties.

1768 • British station troops in Boston.

1769 • Merchants sign nonimportation agreements.

1770 • Boston Massacre.
• Parliament repeals Townshend duties.

1772 • British navy ship *Gaspée* burned.
• Committees of correspondence begin forming.

1773 • Parliament passes Tea Act.
• Dumping of tea in Boston harbor.

1774 • Parliament passes Coercive Acts (Intolerable Acts).
• Powder Alarm shows colonists' readiness to bear arms.
• First Continental Congress meets; Continental Association formed.

1775 • Battles of Lexington and Concord.
• Lord Dunmore promises freedom to defecting slaves.

CONTINENTAL ARMY UNIFORM WORN AT THE SIEGE OF FORT STANWIX, 1777

In 1775, the Continental Congress faced the daunting prospect of fielding an army to fight the largest military force in the world. Money was scarce, soldiers were hastily trained and short of equipment, and uniforms were hard to come by. (Many were purchased from France.) At the start of the war, ordinary enlisted men often wore brown work clothes, and although this outfit gave them a unified look, it did not allow for easy categorization of soldiers by their units. When General Washington finally issued dress specifications, he chose the color already preferred by many officers— dark blue—and then specified the variety of colors to be used for the facings and linings of the coat to establish the rank and the unit of each soldier. Officers especially needed distinctive clothing to distinguish them from ordinary soldiers and from other officers, so that the military hierarchy could be maintained at all times. The coat pictured here belonged to a brigadier general, Peter Gansevoort, who was twenty-eight in 1777 and in command of Fort Stanwix in the Mohawk Valley of New York. The coat has a buff-colored lining (seen inside the coattails) and bright red facings on the collar, lapels, and cuffs, marking him as a New York soldier. The color of the shoulder ribbons (red) reveals Gansevoort's rank. The ribbons could be easily replaced with a new color, enabling a man to ascend in rank without having to get a new coat. Young Gansevoort became a celebrated hero when he successfully defended Fort Stanwix against an attack by British and Indians. His grandson, the author Herman Melville, named his second son Stanwix in honor of the event.

National Museum of American History, Smithsonian Institution, Washington, D.C.

CHAPTER

7

The War for America
1775–1783

■ **The Second Continental Congress** 215
Assuming Political and Military Authority 215
Pursuing Both War and Peace 218
Thomas Paine, Abigail Adams, and the Case for Independence 220
The Declaration of Independence 221

■ **The First Year of War, 1775–1776** 222
The American Military Forces 223
The British Strategy 225
Quebec, New York, and New Jersey 225

■ **The Home Front** 228
Patriotism at the Local Level 228
The Loyalists 229
Who Is a Traitor? 233
Financial Instability and Corruption 236

■ **The Campaigns of 1777–1779: The North and West** 236
Burgoyne's Army and the Battle of Saratoga 236
The War in the West: Indian Country 239
The French Alliance 240

■ **The Southern Strategy and the End of the War** 241
Georgia and South Carolina 241
The Other Southern War: Guerrillas 242
Surrender at Yorktown 243
The Losers and the Winners 244

■ **Conclusion: Why the British Lost** 246

LIKE MANY OF THE MEN who fought in the Revolutionary War on the American side, Robert Shurtliff of Massachusetts enlisted in the Continental army in 1782 for several different reasons. Early in the war, a desire to fight British oppression motivated many recruits, especially those from Massachusetts, the colony under direct attack. But late in the war, deciding to enlist required more than idealism, and even the promise of a pay envelope and future frontier acreage no longer sufficed. To meet their draft quotas, towns offered cash bounties as high as $50 in silver. Young, single, poor, and unsettled in life, Shurtliff responded to that powerful incentive. Tall (five feet seven) and muscular, with an adventurous disposition, the young recruit readily won assignment in the army's elite light infantry unit.

Shurtliff's reported age was eighteen, not unusual for the new recruits of 1782 in the seventh year of a difficult war. Some quarter of a million soldiers, ages sixteen to sixty, served in either the Continental army or state militia units, and as the war wound down, manpower was in short supply. Beardless boys populated Washington's army—boys who had been just ten years old when the British marched on Lexington. The need for an army of thousands persisted well past the decisive American victory at Yorktown in the fall of 1781 because the British army refused to end its occupation of New York City until a peace treaty was signed. Consequently, the Americans had to field an army to hold the British in check. For nearly two years after Yorktown, Washington's force of 10,000 men camped along the Hudson River north of the city, skirmishing with the enemy.

That is, 10,000 men and 1 woman. In fact, "Robert Shurtliff" was actually Deborah Sampson, age twenty-three, from Middleborough, Massachusetts. For seventeen months, Sampson masqueraded as a man, marching through the woods, handling and firing a musket, and spending seemingly interminable time in camp. Misrepresenting her age enabled her to blend in with the beardless boys, as did her unusual competence as a soldier. With privacy at a minimum, she faced constant risks of discovery. Soldiers slept six to a tent, "spooning" their bodies together for warmth. Yet somehow, Sampson managed to escape detection. Certainly, she was helped by the poor standards of hygiene of the day. With no centralized shower or bathing facilities, she was not compelled to disrobe in front of her comrades.

Although many thousands of women served the army as cooks, laundresses, and caregivers, they were never allowed in combat positions. Not only was Sampson defrauding the military (and the town that had paid her bounty), but she was also violating a biblical prohibition on cross-dressing that was punishable under Massachusetts law. Why did she run this risk?

Deborah Sampson
In the mid-1790s, Deborah Sampson sat for this small portrait painted by Massachusetts folk artist Joseph Stone. An engraved copy of it illustrated *The Female Review*, a short book about Sampson's unusual military career and life published in 1797. Sampson, by then a wife and mother, displays femininity in this picture. Note her long curly hair, the necklace, and the stylish gown with a low, lace-trimmed neckline filled in (for modesty's sake) with a puffy white neckerchief. Sampson the soldier had used a cloth band to compress her breasts; Sampson the matron wore a satin band to define her bustline.
Rhode Island Historical Society.

A hard-luck childhood had left Sampson both impoverished and unusually plucky. By the time she was five, her father had deserted the family, causing her mother to place her children in foster care. Deborah lived with a succession of families, learning household skills appropriate to a servant's life. More unusually, she also learned to plow a field and to read and write. Freed from servitude at age eighteen, she earned a living as a weaver and then a teacher, both low-wage jobs but also ones without supervising bosses. Marriage would have been her normal next step, but either lack of inclination or a wartime shortage of men kept her single and "masterless," something few women could claim to be in the eighteenth century. But like most single females, she was also poor, and the $50 bounty enticed her to enlist.

Sampson was unmasked after seventeen months of service, when she suffered a battle-related injury, and the treatment revealed her sex. She was discharged immediately, but her fine record kept her superiors from prosecuting her for cross-dressing. Sampson spent many years seeking a pension from the government to compensate her for her war injury, but to no avail.

What eventually made Sampson famous was not her war service alone, but her effort to capitalize on it by selling her story to the public. In 1797, now a middle-aged mother of three, she cooperated with a young author to tell her life story (a blend of fact and fiction) in a short book. During 1802–1803, she reenacted her wartime masquerade on a speaking tour of New England and New York. Once again, she was crossing gender boundaries, since women normally did not speak from public stages (except as actresses) or travel without a male escort.

Except for her disguised sex, Sampson's Revolutionary War experience was similar to that of most Americans. Disruptions caused by the war affected everyone's life, whether in military service or on the home front. Wartime shortages of all kinds caused women and children to step in and replace male labor. Soldiers fought for ideas, but they also fought to earn money. Hardship was widely endured. And Sampson's quest for personal independence—a freedom from the constraints of being female—was echoed in the general quest for political independence that many Americans identified as a major goal of the war.

Political independence was not everyone's primary goal, however, at least not at first. For more than a year after the war began, the Continental Congress in Philadelphia resisted declaring America's independence. Some delegates were cautiously hoping for reconciliation with Britain. Yet with fighting already under way, the congress had to raise an army, finance it, and seek alliances with foreign countries—all while exploring diplomatic channels for peace.

When King George III rejected all peace overtures, Americans loudly declared their independence, and the war moved into high gear. In part a classic war with professional armies and textbook battles, the Revolutionary War was also a civil war and at times even a brutal **guerrilla war** between committed rebels and loyalists. It also had complex ethnic dimensions, pitting some Indian tribes allied with the British against others allied with the Americans. And it provided an unprecedented opportunity for enslaved African Americans to win their freedom, some by joining the British, who openly encouraged slaves to desert their masters, and others by joining the Continental army or state militias, fighting alongside white Americans.

The Second Continental Congress

On May 10, 1775, nearly one month after the fighting at Lexington and Concord, the Second Continental Congress assembled in Philadelphia. The congress immediately set to work on two crucial and seemingly contradictory tasks: to raise and supply an army and to explore reconciliation with Britain. To do the former, they needed soldiers and a commander to come to the aid of the Massachusetts militiamen, they needed money, and they needed to work out a declaration of war. To do the latter, however, they needed diplomacy to approach the king. But the king was not receptive, and by 1776, as the war progressed and hopes of reconciliation faded, delegates at the congress began to ponder the treasonous act of declaring independence—said by some to be plain common sense.

Assuming Political and Military Authority

Like members of the First Continental Congress (see chapter 6), the delegates to the second were well-established figures in their home colonies, but they still had to learn to know and trust each other; they did not always agree. The Adams cousins John and Samuel defined the radical end of the spectrum, favoring independence. John Dickinson of Pennsylvania, no longer the eager revolutionary who had dashed off *Letters from a Farmer* back in 1767, was now a moderate, seeking reconciliation with Britain. Benjamin Franklin, fresh off a ship from an eleven-year residence in London, was feared by some to be a British spy. Mutual suspicions flourished easily when the undertaking was so dangerous, opinions were so varied, and a misstep could spell disaster.

Most of the delegates were not yet prepared to break with Britain. Several legislatures instructed their delegates to oppose independence. Some felt that government without a king was unworkable, while others feared it might be suicidal to lose Britain's protection against its traditional enemies, France and Spain. Colonies that traded actively with Britain feared undermining their economies. Probably the vast majority of ordinary Americans were unable to envision independence. From the Stamp Act of 1765 to the Coercive Acts of 1774 (see chapter 6), the constitutional struggle with Britain had turned on the issue of parliamentary power. During that decade, almost no one had questioned the legitimacy of the monarchy.

The few men at the Continental Congress who did think that independence was desirable were, not surprisingly, from Massachusetts. Their colony had been stripped of civil government under the Coercive Acts, their capital was occupied by the British army, and blood had been shed at Lexington and Concord. Even so, those men knew that it was premature to push for a break with Britain. John Adams wrote to his wife, Abigail, in June 1775: "America is a great, unwieldy body. Its progress must be slow. It is like a large fleet sailing under convoy. The fleetest sailors must wait for the dullest and slowest."

> John Adams wrote in June 1775: "America is a great, unwieldy body. Its progress must be slow. It is like a large fleet sailing under convoy. The fleetest sailors must wait for the dullest and slowest."

As slow as the American colonies were in sailing toward political independence, they needed to take swift action to coordinate a military defense, for the Massachusetts countryside was under threat of further attack. Even the hesitant moderates in the congress agreed that a military buildup was necessary. Around the country, militia units from New York to Georgia collected arms and drilled on village greens in anticipation. (See "The Promise of Technology," page 216.) On June 14, the congress voted to create the Continental army. Choosing the commander in chief offered an opportunity to demonstrate that this was no local war of a single rebellious colony. The congress bypassed Artemas Ward from Massachusetts, a veteran of the Seven Years' War, then already commanding the soldiers massed around Boston, and instead chose a Virginian, George Washington. Washington's appointment sent the clear message to Britain that there was widespread commitment to war beyond New England.

Next the congress drew up a document titled "A Declaration on the Causes and Necessity of Taking Up Arms," which rehearsed familiar arguments about the tyranny of Parliament and the need to defend English liberties. This declaration was first drafted by a young Virginia **planter**, Thomas Jefferson, a newcomer to the congress and a radical on the question of independence. The moderate John Dickinson, fearing that the declaration would offend Britain and rule out reconciliation, was allowed to rewrite it. However, he left intact much of Jefferson's highly charged language about choosing "to die freemen rather than to live slaves." Even a man as reluctant for independence as Dickinson

Arming the Soldiers: Muskets and Rifles

How combat-ready was the American side in the Revolutionary War? Were there adequate numbers of firearms along with men trained in their use? These lively and important questions have recently generated sharp debate among historians. A book published in 2000 argued that gun ownership was surprisingly rare in the 1770s, occurring in only one out of seven households. This finding did not square with historians' largely untested assumption that a militia-based defense system implied that nearly all households contained a gun. The ensuing controversy quickly became a firestorm, involving activists on both sides of the modern gun control debate as well as historians. In consequence, the examination of evidence and methods to evaluate gun ownership has been considerably sharpened.

What were eighteenth-century guns like? Guns called fowling pieces fired shot (small pellets) and were useful for hunting ducks, turkeys, and small game such as raccoons and squirrels. For larger game and for warfare, muskets, a sixteenth-century invention, were the preferred weapon. By the mid-eighteenth century, the musket had an improved flintlock ignition system: The trigger released a spring-held cock that caused a hammer to strike a flint, creating sparks; the sparks set off a small charge in a priming pan, producing a larger explosion in the gun barrel. To load a musket, the shooter first put the hammer on half cock to prevent an accidental firing. He next put a small quantity of gunpowder (carried in a powder horn) in the priming pan and closed it, poured more gunpowder down the smooth gun barrel, dropped in the projectile (usually a one-ounce lead ball), and with a ramrod wadded paper down the gun barrel to hold the loose ball in place. He then raised the gun to firing position, put the hammer on full cock, and fired. The whole procedure took highly experienced shooters 45 to 90 seconds.

The range of muskets extended only about 50 to 100 yards. They were notoriously inaccurate because of the poor fit between ball and barrel and the considerable kick produced by firing, which interfered with aiming. Far more accurate were the longer-barreled rifles, used in frontier regions where big-game hunting was more common. Spiral grooves inside the rifle barrel imparted spin to the lead ball as it traversed the barrel, stabilizing and lengthening its flight and enabling expert marksmen to hit small targets at 150 to 200 yards. Yet militiamen preferred muskets. Rifles took twice as long to load and fire, and their longer barrels made them unwieldy for soldiers on the march. Inaccurate muskets were quite deadly enough when fired by a group of soldiers in unison at targets 50 yards away.

How many American men actually owned fowling pieces, muskets, or rifles? A partial answer can be gleaned from probate inventories, many thousands of which exist in state archives. Inventories listed a decedent's possessions to facilitate settling the estate and to make sure creditors were paid off. Yet these sources are fraught with problems. For one thing, many inventories are not complete: If few of them itemized clothing, can we conclude the decedents went nude? If no firearm is listed, can we conclude that the decedent *never* owned a gun? Clearly not. In addition, probate inventories were made for only a subset of dead property owners, primarily for the use of creditors and heirs, so they are biased by age (older), sex (male), and wealth (more).

Despite complexities, scholars have worked with probate inventories to establish a baseline figure for gun ownership. It takes sophistication with statistical sampling technique as well as the ability to read old handwriting to use the evidence, since the thousands of inventories cannot all be tallied. Recent careful studies based on this source yield estimates on overall gun ownership that range from 40 to 50 percent of all probated estates in the 1770s.

A second way to assess gun ownership is to look at the arms procurement experiences of state legislatures and the Continental Congress as they geared up for war. In the early months of 1775, New England patriot leaders had a keen interest to know how many armed soldiers could be mobilized in the event of war. One scholar has located militia returns from thirty towns in Massachusetts, New Hampshire, and Rhode Island. Scattered returns from other states exist in archives. At their most complete, these records form a census of soldiers and equipment taken on a militia training day. A particularly detailed list from Salem, Massachusetts, notes next to each man's name his ownership of a firelock, a bayonet, a sword, a pouch, a cartouche box, a cartridge, a flint, lead balls, gunpowder, a knapsack, and priming wires. Salem's list appears to support the conclusion that 100 percent of adult men owned guns, yet the scholar seeking to calculate gun ownership must ask: Who is not on this list? Who failed to report to the muster exercise? This careful study concludes that in 1775, probably three-quarters of all men ages sixteen to sixty in New England owned guns.

These high rates of ownership, however, are not matched by a final kind of evidence: reports from militia officers to state legislatures complaining of being underarmed. A New Hampshire captain complained of his unit's plight in June 1775: "We are in want of both arms and ammunition. There is but very little, nor none worth mentioning—perhaps one pound of powder to twenty men, and not one-half our men have arms." A militia officer in Pennsylvania noted that men who owned high-quality muskets and rifles were often reluctant to report for active duty with them unless assured they would be reimbursed in the event of loss of the valuable possession. A Prussian general who volunteered his expertise to the Continental army arrived at Valley Forge in 1778 and was shocked to find "muskets, carbines, fowling pieces, and rifles" all in the same company of troops.

Lack of uniformity in guns posed considerable problems for supplying appropriate ammunition. Yet scattered complaints about underarmed troops must be weighed against the much larger number of militia leaders who failed to lodge similar complaints, perhaps because they found their troops adequately armed. Historians must take care not to be misled by stray documents or quotations that may be atypical.

Certainly, the Continental Congress knew that more guns were needed. Before 1774, American artisans imported British-made gunlocks (the central firing mechanisms) and added the wooden stock and iron barrel to produce muskets. But in October 1774, the British Parliament, anticipating trouble, prohibited all gunlock and firearm exports to the colonies. Congress then turned to French and Dutch suppliers to purchase gunlocks, gunpowder, and finished muskets.

Muskets and even fowling pieces worked well enough for the Revolutionary War, where similarly armed combatants engaged in massed, synchronized firing at close range. In individual use, however, muskets were clumsy, inaccurate, and not highly lethal. High rates of musket ownership did not translate to high rates of successful homicide or accidental deaths by shooting. Sixty years after the Revolution, all

that changed with the advent of machine-tooled firearms such as the Colt revolver and the Remington rifle. Those new repeat-fire weapons were cheaper, more accurate, and far more deadly. Comparing ownership rates of muskets and revolvers—or assault weapons—across time may not be the most meaningful path to understanding this country's historic relationship with guns.

Powder Horn

James Pike, a twenty-three-year-old New England militiaman, made and then personalized this powder horn, a hollow cow's horn capped on both ends with leather. The stopper was designed to be pulled off by the teeth so that the hands of the user would be free to hold the musket barrel and pour the powder. Pike's carvings suggest his motivation for fighting. Above his name is a scene dated April 19, 1775, in which British soldiers, labeled "the Aggressors," fire through the Liberty Tree at "Provincials, Defending." Pike was not at Lexington or Concord; his first combat experience came two months later at the battle of Bunker Hill, where he saw his brother killed and was himself wounded in the shoulder.
Chicago Historical Society.

Committee of Safety Musket

This gun was one of the small number of American-made muskets produced in 1775 in a German region of Pennsylvania where blacksmith shops were numerous. The smithy forged and fashioned the gun barrel and attached it to an imported gunlock, the mechanism over the trigger. A wooden stock completed the design.
York County Historical Society.

acknowledged the necessity of military defense against an invading army.

To pay for the military buildup, the congress authorized a currency issue of $2 million. The Continental dollars were merely paper; they did not represent gold or silver, for the congress owned no precious metals. The delegates somewhat naively expected that the currency would be accepted as valuable on trust as it spread in the population through the hands of soldiers, farmers, munitions suppliers, and beyond.

In just two months, the Second Continental Congress had created an army, declared war, and issued its own currency. It had taken on the major functions of a legitimate government, both military and financial, without any legal basis for its authority, for it had not—and would not for a full year—declare independence from the authority of the king.

Pursuing Both War and Peace

Three days after the congress approved a Continental army, one of the bloodiest battles of the Revolution occurred. The British commander in Boston, Thomas Gage, had recently received troop reinforcements, three talented generals (William Howe, John Burgoyne, and Henry Clinton), and new instructions to root out the rebels around Boston. But before Gage could take the offensive, the Americans fortified the hilly terrain of Charlestown, a peninsula just north of Boston, on the night of June 16, 1775.

The British generals could have nipped off the peninsula where it met the mainland, to box in the Americans. But General Howe insisted on a bold frontal assault, sending his 2,500 soldiers across the water and up the hill in an intimidating but potentially costly attack. The American troops, 1,400 strong, listened to the British drummers pacing the uphill march and held their fire until the British were about twenty yards away. At that distance, the musket volley was sure and deadly, and the British turned back. Twice more, General Howe sent his men up the hill and received the same blast of firepower; each time they had to step around the bodies of men felled in the previous attempts.

On the third assault, the British took the hill, mainly because the American ammunition supply gave out, and the defenders quickly retreated. The battle of Bunker Hill was thus a British victory, but an expensive one. The dead numbered 226 on the British side, with more than 800 wounded; the Americans suffered 140 dead, 271 wounded, and 30 captured. As General Clinton later remarked, "It was a dear bought victory; another such would have ruined us."

Instead of pursuing the fleeing Americans, Howe pulled his army back to Boston, unwilling to risk more raids into the countryside. If the British had had any grasp of the basic instability of the American units gathered around Boston, they might have pushed westward and perhaps decisively defeated the Continental army in its infancy. Instead, they lingered in Boston, abandoning it without a fight nine months later. Howe used the time in Boston to inoculate his army against smallpox, because a new epidemic of the deadly disease was spreading in port cities along the Atlantic. Inoculation worked by producing a light but real (and therefore risky) case of smallpox, followed by lifelong immunity. Howe's instinct was right: From 1775 to 1782, the years coinciding with the American Revolution, some 130,000 people on the American continent, most of them Indians, died of smallpox. Nearly 500 uninoculated Bostonians contracted smallpox, and Howe booted them out of Boston, causing American leaders to fear that the British intended to spread the disease as a "weapon of defense."

A week after Bunker Hill, when General Washington arrived to take charge of the new Continental army, he found enthusiastic but undisciplined troops. Sanitation was an unknown concept, with inadequate latrines fouling the campground. Drunkenness on duty was common, and soldiers came and went at will. The amazed general attributed the disarray to the New England custom of letting militia units elect their own officers, a custom he felt undermined deference. A captain from a Connecticut regiment was spotted shaving one of his own men, an inappropriate gesture of personal service by a superior officer. But in civilian life the captain was a barber; he had been elected an

Battle of Bunker Hill, 1775

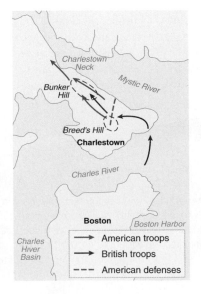

An Exact View of the Late Battle at Charlestown, June 17th 1775

This dramatic panorama is the earliest visual representation of the battle of Bunker Hill. On sale to the public six weeks after the battle, the engraving shows Charlestown in flames (center back) and British and American soldiers in fixed formation firing muskets at each other. The Americans, to the left, are dug in along the crest of the hill; British casualties have begun to litter the field of battle. The artist, Bernard Romans, was a noted cartographer, military engineer, linguist, and mathematician. Born in the Netherlands, he came to America as a British-paid surveyor, but he took the American side in the Revolution. His maps of war zones were bought by Americans eager to track the geography of the war. His large depiction of Bunker Hill, produced in multiple copies—some of which were hand-colored like this one—likely decorated many a patriot's wall. It was advertised for sale in newspapers in Philadelphia and Virginia, and a half-size copy was engraved and inserted in an issue of the *Pennsylvania Magazine,* a monthly periodical edited by Thomas Paine. One ad for the picture promised that "Every well-wisher to this country cannot but delight in seeing a plan of the ground on which our brave American Army conquered the British Ministerial Forces." Technically, the British won the battle by taking the hill, but that was not the story told by this picture.
Colonial Williamsburg Foundation.

George Washington's Camp Chest

This portable camp chest (or mess kit) belonged to George Washington during the Revolutionary War. The wooden box, covered in leather and lined with wool fabric, held an elaborate setup neatly collapsed into a small space: four tin pots with detached handles, five tin plates, three tin platters, two tin boxes, two knives, three forks, eight glass bottles with cork stoppers, salt and pepper shakers, and a woolen sack with six compartments. The chest also contained a tinderbox, which held kindling and a flint for starting a fire, and a gridiron (or grate) with collapsed legs for cooking over the fire. Washington—or, more likely, a subordinate preparing his food—would have used this chest when the army was on the move. It was an officer's chest, presented to the general by a Philadelphia merchant in 1776. Enlisted men would have had something much more basic, if anything. Washington saved the chest for two decades after the war. After his death, it was auctioned off and donated to the federal government by the new owner. It is now owned by the Smithsonian Institution in Washington, D.C.
National Museum of American History, Smithsonian Institution, Behring Center.

officer by the men of his town, who saw nothing strange in his practicing his trade in the camp. Washington quickly imposed more hierarchy and authority. "Discipline is the soul of the army," he stated.

While military plans moved forward, the Second Continental Congress pursued its second, contradictory objective: reconciliation with Britain. Delegates from the middle colonies (Pennsylvania, Delaware, and New York), whose merchants depended on trade with Britain, urged that channels for negotiation remain open. In July 1775, congressional moderates led by John Dickinson engineered an appeal to the king called the Olive Branch Petition. The petition affirmed loyalty to the monarchy and blamed all the troubles on the king's ministers and on Parliament. It proposed that the American colonial assemblies be recognized as individual parliaments, under the umbrella of the monarchy. By late fall 1775, however, reconciliation was out of the question. King George III rejected the Olive Branch Petition and heatedly condemned the Americans, calling them rebels and traitors. Thereafter, it was hard to blame only the king's ministers, and not the king himself, for the conflict.

Thomas Paine, Abigail Adams, and the Case for Independence

Pressure for independence started to mount in January 1776, when a pamphlet titled *Common Sense* appeared in Philadelphia. Thomas Paine, its author, was an English **artisan** and coffeehouse intellectual who had befriended Benjamin Franklin in London. He came to America in the fall of 1774 with letters of introduction from Franklin to several Philadelphia printers. He landed a job with the *Pennsylvania Magazine* and soon met delegates from the Second Continental Congress. With their encouragement, he wrote *Common Sense* to lay out a lively and compelling case for complete independence.

In simple yet forceful language, Paine elaborated on the absurdities of the British monarchy. Why should one man, by accident of birth, claim extensive power over others? he asked. A king might be foolish or wicked. "One of the strongest natural proofs of the folly of hereditary right in kings," Paine wrote, "is that nature disapproves it; otherwise she would not so frequently turn it into ridicule by giving mankind *an ass for a lion*."

> "Do not put such unlimited power into the hands of the Husbands," Abigail Adams advised. "Remember all Men would be tyrants if they could."

Calling the British king an ass broke through the automatic deference most Americans still had for the monarchy. To replace monarchy, Paine advocated **republican** government, based on the consent of the people. Rulers, according to Paine, were only representatives of the people, and the best form of government relied on frequent elections to achieve the most direct **democracy** possible.

Paine's pamphlet sold more than 150,000 copies in a matter of weeks. Newspapers reprinted it; men read it aloud in taverns and coffeehouses; John Adams, a delegate in Philadelphia, sent a copy to his wife, Abigail, who passed it around to neighbors in Braintree, Massachusetts. New Englanders desired independence, but other colonies, under no immediate threat of violence, remained cautious.

Abigail Adams was impatient not only for independence but also for other legal changes that would revolutionize the new country. In a series of astute letters to her husband, she outlined obstacles and gave advice. She worried that southern slave owners might shrink from a war in the name of **liberty**: "I have sometimes been ready to think that the passion for Liberty cannot be Equally strong in the Breasts of those who have been accustomed to deprive their fellow Creatures of theirs." And in March 1776, she expressed her hope that women's legal status would improve under the new government: "In the new Code of Laws which I suppose it will be necessary for you to make I desire you would Remember the Ladies, and be more generous and favourable to them than your ancestors." Her chief concern was husbands' legal dominion over wives: "Do not put such unlimited power into the hands of the Husbands," she advised. "Remember all Men would be tyrants if they could." Abigail Adams anticipated a more radical end to tyranny than did Thomas Paine.

The Continental Congress was, in fact, not rewriting family law; that task was left to individual states in the 1780s. John Adams lightly dismissed his wife: "As to your extraordinary Code of Laws, I cannot but Laugh." Men were too smart to repeal their "Masculine Systems," John assured her, needing structured male dominance to avoid the "despotism of the petticoat." To a male politician and friend, Adams privately rehearsed the reasons why women (and men who were free blacks, or young, or propertyless) should remain excluded from political participation. Even though he concluded that nothing should change, at least Abigail's letter had forced him to ponder the exclusion, something few men—or women—did in 1776. Urgent talk of political independence was seen as radical enough. Few could imagine even more radical change in social and political relations.

The Declaration of Independence

In addition to Paine's *Common Sense*, another key factor hastening official independence was the prospect of an alliance with France, Britain's archrival. France was willing to provide military supplies and naval power, but not without firm assurance that the Americans would separate from Britain. News that the British were negotiating to hire German mercenary soldiers further solidified support for independence. By May, all but four colonies were agitating for a declaration. The holdouts were Pennsylvania, Maryland, New York, and South Carolina, the latter two containing large loyalist populations. An exasperated Virginian wrote to his friend in the congress, "For God's sake, why do you dawdle in the Congress so strangely? Why do you not at once declare yourself a separate independent state?" But a more pessimistic southerner feared that independence was "in truth a delusive bait which

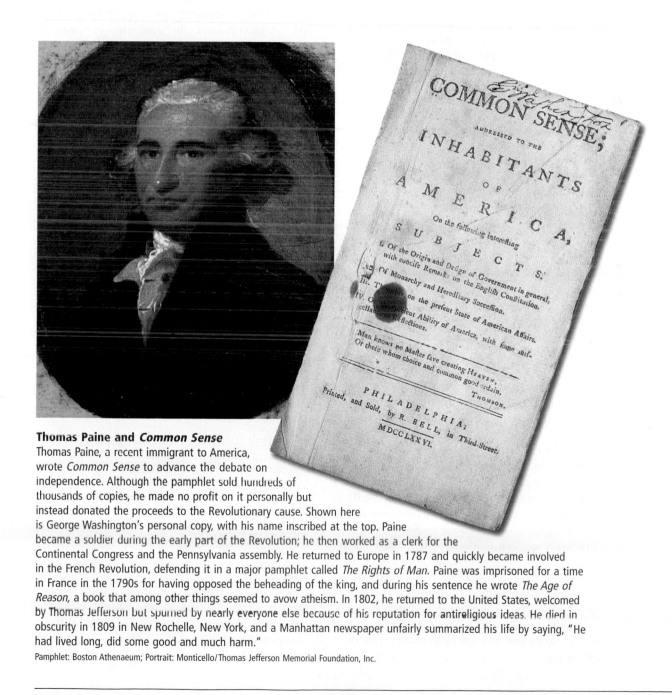

Thomas Paine and *Common Sense*
Thomas Paine, a recent immigrant to America, wrote *Common Sense* to advance the debate on independence. Although the pamphlet sold hundreds of thousands of copies, he made no profit on it personally but instead donated the proceeds to the Revolutionary cause. Shown here is George Washington's personal copy, with his name inscribed at the top. Paine became a soldier during the early part of the Revolution; he then worked as a clerk for the Continental Congress and the Pennsylvania assembly. He returned to Europe in 1787 and quickly became involved in the French Revolution, defending it in a major pamphlet called *The Rights of Man*. Paine was imprisoned for a time in France in the 1790s for having opposed the beheading of the king, and during his sentence he wrote *The Age of Reason*, a book that among other things seemed to avow atheism. In 1802, he returned to the United States, welcomed by Thomas Jefferson but spurned by nearly everyone else because of his reputation for antireligious ideas. He died in obscurity in 1809 in New Rochelle, New York, and a Manhattan newspaper unfairly summarized his life by saying, "He had lived long, did some good and much harm."
Pamphlet: Boston Athenaeum; Portrait: Monticello/Thomas Jefferson Memorial Foundation, Inc.

Jefferson's Laptop Writing Desk

On a long stagecoach ride from Virginia to Philadelphia in May 1776, thirty-three-year-old Thomas Jefferson sketched out a design for a portable laptop writing desk. On arrival, he hired a Philadelphia cabinetmaker to produce it in mahogany. The adjustable book rest shown here (notice the notches) could also unfold on its hinges to create a large writing surface. Pens, quills, ink, and paper were stored below. The desk weighed five pounds. Jefferson used this desk to pen rough drafts of the Declaration of Independence. Near the end of his life, he gave the desk to his granddaughter's husband, expressing the hope that it might become esteemed for its connection to the Declaration. The man replied that he would revere the desk as something "no longer inanimate, and mute, but as something to be interrogated and caressed." In 1876, it was a featured exhibit at a centennial exhibition in Philadelphia celebrating the founding of the nation.

National Museum of American History, Smithsonian Institution, Washington, D.C.

men inconsiderably snatch at, without knowing the hook to which it is affixed."

In early June, Richard Henry Lee of the Virginia delegation introduced a resolution calling for independence. The moderates still commanded enough support to postpone a vote on the measure until July, so they could go home and consult about this extreme step. In the meantime, the congress appointed a committee, with Thomas Jefferson and others, to draft a longer document setting out the case for independence.

On July 2, after intense politicking, all but one state voted for independence; New York abstained. The congress then turned to the document drafted by Jefferson and his committee. Jefferson began with a preamble that articulated philosophical principles about natural rights, equality, the right of revolution, and the consent of the governed as the only true basis for government. He then listed more than two dozen grievances against King George. The congress merely glanced at the political philosophy, finding nothing exceptional in it. The ideas about natural rights and the consent of the governed were seen as "self-evident truths," just as the document claimed. In itself, this absence of comment showed a remarkable transformation in political thinking since the end of the Seven Years' War. The single phrase declaring the natural equality of "all men" was also passed over without comment; no one elaborated on its radical implications.

For two days, the congress wrangled over the list of grievances, especially the issue of slavery. Jefferson had included an impassioned statement blaming the king for slavery, which delegates from Georgia and South Carolina struck out. They had no intention of denouncing their labor system as an evil practice. But the congress let stand another of Jefferson's fervent grievances, blaming the king for mobilizing "the merciless Indian Savages" into bloody **frontier** warfare, a reference to Pontiac's uprising (see chapter 6).

On July 4, the amendments to Jefferson's text were complete, and the congress formally adopted the document. (See appendix I, page A-1.) A month later, the delegates gathered to sign the official parchment copy, handwritten by an exacting scribe. Four men, including John Dickinson, declined to sign; several others "signed with regret . . . and with many doubts," according to John Adams. The document was then printed, widely distributed, and read aloud in celebrations everywhere. A crowd in New York listened to a public reading of it and then toppled a lead statue of George III on horseback to melt it down for bullets. On July 15, the New York delegation switched from abstention to endorsement, making the vote on independence unanimous.

Printed copies of the Declaration of Independence did not include the signers' names, for they had committed treason, a crime punishable by death. On the day of signing, they indulged in gallows humor. When Benjamin Franklin paused before signing to look over the document, John Hancock of Massachusetts teased him, "Come, come, sir. We must be unanimous. No pulling different ways. We must all hang together." Franklin replied, "Indeed we must all hang together. Otherwise we shall most assuredly hang separately."

REVIEW   Why were many Americans reluctant to pursue independence from Britain?

The First Year of War, 1775–1776

Both sides approached the war for America with uneasiness. The Americans, with inexperienced militias, opposed the mightiest military power in the world. Also, their country was not unified, many remained loyal to Britain. The British faced serious obstacles as well. Their disdain for the fighting abilities of the Americans required reassessment in light of the Bunker Hill battle. The logistics of supplying an army with food across three thousand miles of water were daunting. And since the British goal was to regain allegiance, not to destroy and conquer, the army was often constrained in its actions. These patterns—undertrained American troops and British troops strangely unwilling to press their advantage—played out repeatedly in the first year of war when the Americans invaded Canada, the British invaded New York, and the two sides chased each other up and down the length of New Jersey.

The American Military Forces

Americans claimed that the initial months of war were purely defensive, triggered by the British army's invasion. But the war also quickly became a rebellion, an overthrowing of long-established authority. As both defenders and rebels, Americans were generally highly motivated to fight, and the potential manpower that could be mobilized was in theory very great.

Local defense in the colonies had long rested with a militia requiring participation from able-bodied men over age sixteen. When the main threat to public safety was the occasional Indian attack, the local militia made sense. But such attacks were now mostly limited to the frontier. Southern militias trained with potential slave rebellions in mind, but these, too, were rare. The annual muster day in most communities had evolved into a holiday of drinking, marching, and shooting practice with small fowling guns or muskets.

Militias were best suited for limited engagements and not for extended wars requiring military campaigns far from home. In forming the Continental army, the congress set enlistment at one year, but army leaders soon learned that was inadequate to train soldiers and carry out campaigns. A three-year enlistment earned a new soldier a $20 bonus, while men who committed for the duration of the war were promised a postwar **land grant** of one hundred acres. For this inducement to be effective, of course, recruits had to believe that the Americans would win. Over the course of the war, some 230,000 men spent time in military service, amounting to roughly one-quarter of the white male population over age sixteen. (See "Global Comparison," page 224.)

Women also served in the Continental army, cooking, washing, and nursing the wounded.

Backcountry Riflemen
A German officer with the British army drew this sketch of two American riflemen, dressed in rustic hunting shirts and leggings. One wears moccasins; the other is barefoot. Their celebrated ability to hit small targets at great distances and their willingness to snipe from behind trees and aim particularly at officers made them a terror to the British. Ten companies of riflemen were recruited in 1775 from western Pennsylvania and Virginia. General Washington worried that they were too undisciplined to make good soldiers, but others suggested that the trademark hunting shirt should become the Continental army uniform for all soldiers, just for the fear it provoked in the enemy. The stiff shirts, made of coarse linen (or, more rarely, deerskin), functioned like coats, with wool layers worn underneath for warmth. Decorated with fringe, the shirts were dyed "the shade of a fallen dry leaf," offering excellent camouflage. A tie belt closed the shirt; typically, two essentials, a tomahawk and a hunting knife (absent here), were suspended from the belt. The leather hats here closely resemble the cone-shaped headgear worn by Hessian soldiers. Some American militiamen did sport such caps, but with the turned-up bill in the back, not the front as shown here. (Note the word "Congress" tooled in the leather bill.) The German officer depicted a fixed bayonet on what was represented to be a rifle, but only muskets had bayonets. Artistic errors aside, the debt of western riflemen to Indian apparel is evident.
Anne S. K. Brown Military Collection, Brown University Library.

The British army established a ratio of one woman to every ten men; in the Continental army, the ratio was set at one woman to fifteen men. Close to 20,000 "camp followers," as they were called, served during the war, probably most of them wives of men in service. Children

GLOBAL COMPARISON

How Tall Were Eighteenth-Century Men on Average?

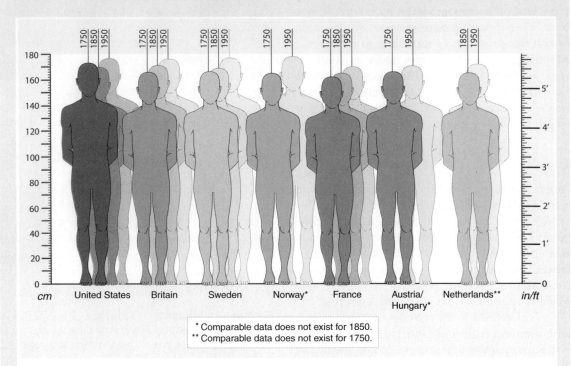

Average Heights of Males

Although individuals within a population vary in height for genetic as well as nutritional reasons, variations between populations are generally due to pervasive differences in the basic standard of living. A key factor is inadequate nutrition, which typically stunts childhood growth and leads to shorter adults. Military enlistment records provide large data sets on height (but for males only), allowing historians to gain insight into comparative standards of living. This figure shows that American men during the Revolution were on average 8 centimeters (cm) or about 3 inches taller than their British opponents. Americans also were taller than all other Europeans. Clearly, Americans enjoyed more abundant food and suffered from fewer endemic diseases than did Europeans. Revolutionary soldiers from the South and New England showed a modest but distinct height difference of 1.3 cm. A much wider spread occurred in Britain, where officers from the gentry were a full 15 cm taller on average than soldiers recruited from the working class. What might account for these differences?

Studies of stature show that average height generally declined in the mid-nineteenth century in Europe and the United States, as urbanization, industrialization, and the disease environment changed. Major gains were posted in the twentieth century, but in recent decades, average height in the United States has stagnated, while European males continue to grow. The tallest men in the world are, on average, the Dutch, at 179 cm. Young Dutch men now average 183 cm, which shows how recent these gains are. The U.S. average, calculated for native-born men, remains at 175 cm.

tagged along as well, and babies were born in the camps and on the road.

Black Americans were at first excluded from the Continental army, by slave owner George Washington's orders. But as manpower needs increased, the northern states welcomed free blacks into service; slaves in some states could serve with their masters' permission. About 5,000 black men served in the Revolutionary War on the rebel side, nearly all from the northern states. Black Continental soldiers sometimes were segregated into separate units; two battalions from Rhode Island were entirely black. Just under 300 blacks joined regiments from Connecticut. Whereas some of these men were **draftees**, others were clearly inspired by the ideals of freedom being voiced in a war against tyranny. For example, twenty-three blacks gave "Liberty," "Freedom," or "Freeman" as their surname at the time of enlistment. (Southern slaves did not join the Continental army, but in large numbers they deserted their owners for the protection of the British instead.)

Military service helped politicize Americans during the early stages of the war. In early 1776, independence was a risky idea, potentially treasonous. But as the war heated up and recruiters demanded commitment, some Americans discovered that apathy had its dangers as well. Anyone who refused to serve ran the risk of being called a traitor to the cause. Military service became a prime way of defining and demonstrating political allegiance.

The American army was at times raw and inexperienced, and often woefully undermanned. It never had the precision and discipline of European professional armies. But it was never as bad as the British continually assumed. The British would learn that it was a serious mistake to underrate the enemy.

The British Strategy

The American strategy was straightforward—to repulse and defeat an invading army. The British strategy was not nearly so clear. Britain wanted to put down a rebellion and restore monarchical power in the colonies, but the question was how to accomplish this. A decisive defeat of the Continental army was essential but not sufficient to end the rebellion, for the British would still have to contend with an armed and motivated insurgent population.

Furthermore, there was no single political nerve center whose capture would spell certain victory. The Continental Congress moved from place to place, staying just out of reach of the British. During the course of the war, the British captured and occupied every major port city, but that brought no serious loss to the Americans, 95 percent of whom lived in the countryside.

Britain's delicate task was to restore the old governments, not to destroy an enemy country. Hence, the British generals were reluctant to ravage the countryside, confiscate food, or burn villages and towns. There were thirteen distinct political entities to capture, pacify, and then restore to the crown, and they stretched in a long line from New Hampshire to Georgia. Clearly, a large land army was required for the job. Without the willingness to seize food from the locals, the British needed hundreds of supply ships bringing food for storage—hence their desire to capture the ports. The British strategy also assumed that many Americans remained loyal to the king and would come to their aid. Without substantial numbers of loyal subjects, the plan to restore old royal governments made no sense.

The overall British plan was a divide-and-conquer approach, focusing first on New York, the state judged to harbor the greatest number of loyal subjects. New York offered a geographic advantage as well: Control of the Hudson River would allow the British to isolate those troublesome New Englanders. British armies could descend from Canada and move up from New York City along the Hudson River into western Massachusetts. Squeezed between a naval blockade on the eastern coast and army raids in the west, Massachusetts could be driven to surrender. New Jersey and Pennsylvania would fall in line, the British thought, due to loyalist strength. Virginia was a problem, like Massachusetts, but the British were confident that the Carolinas would help them isolate and subdue Virginia.

Quebec, New York, and New Jersey

In late 1775, an American expedition was swiftly launched to capture the cities of Montreal and Quebec before British reinforcements could arrive (Map 7.1, page 226). This offensive was a clear sign that the war was not purely a reaction to the invasion of Massachusetts. The two cities were symbolic as well as strategic goals, having been sites of bloody contest in the Seven Years' War (see chapter 6). A force of New York Continentals commanded by General Richard Montgomery took Montreal easily in September 1775 and then advanced on Quebec. Meanwhile, a second contingent of Continentals led by Colonel Benedict Arnold moved north through Maine to Quebec, a punishing trek through freezing rain with woefully inadequate supplies;

> Some black Continental soldiers were clearly inspired by the ideals of freedom being voiced in a war against tyranny. For example, twenty-three blacks gave "Liberty," "Freedom," or "Freeman" as their surname at the time of enlistment.

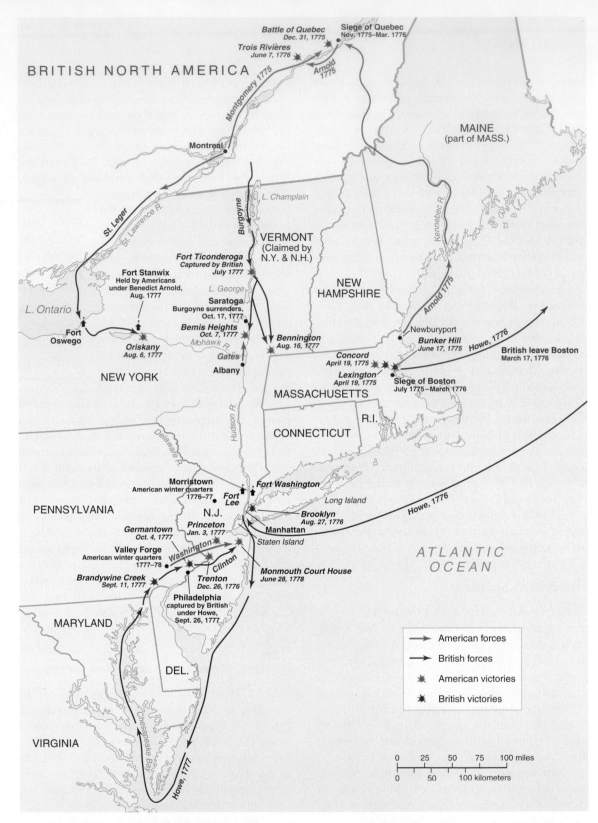

Battle of Quebec
Dec. 31, 1775

Siege of Quebec
Nov. 1775–Mar. 1776

Trois Rivières
June 7, 1776

Montgomery 1775

Arnold 1775

BRITISH NORTH AMERICA

MAINE
(part of MASS.)

Montreal

L. Champlain

St. Leger

St. Lawrence R.

Burgoyne

VERMONT
(Claimed by
N.Y. & N.H.)

NEW
HAMPSHIRE

Kennebec R.

Arnold 1775

Fort Ticonderoga
Captured by British
July 1777

Fort Stanwix
Held by Americans
under Benedict Arnold,
Aug. 1777

L. George

L. Ontario

Saratoga
Burgoyne surrenders,
Oct. 17, 1777

Bemis Heights
Oct. 7, 1777

Newburyport

Bunker Hill
June 17, 1775

Howe, 1776

British leave Boston
March 17, 1776

Fort
Oswego

Oriskany
Aug. 6, 1777

Mohawk R.

Bennington
Aug. 16, 1777

Concord
April 19, 1775

Siege of Boston
July 1775–March 1776

Gates

NEW YORK

Albany

Lexington
April 19, 1775

MASSACHUSETTS

Hudson R.

CONNECTICUT

R.I.

Delaware R.

Morristown
American winter quarters
1776–77

Fort Washington

Fort
Lee

Long Island

Howe, 1776

PENNSYLVANIA

N.J.

Brooklyn
Aug. 27, 1776

Howe, 1776

Germantown
Oct. 4, 1777

Princeton
Jan. 3, 1777

Manhattan

Washington

Staten Island

Valley Forge
American winter quarters
1777–78

Clinton

Monmouth Court House
June 28, 1778

ATLANTIC
OCEAN

Brandywine Creek
Sept. 11, 1777

Trenton
Dec. 26, 1776

Philadelphia
captured by British
under Howe,
Sept. 26, 1777

MARYLAND

DEL.

Chesapeake Bay

American forces

British forces

American victories

British victories

VIRGINIA

Howe, 1777

| 0 | 25 | 50 | 75 | 100 miles |

| 0 | | 50 | | 100 kilometers |

MAP 7.1 The War in the North, 1775–1778
After the early battles in Massachusetts in 1775, rebel forces invaded Canada but failed to capture Quebec. A large British army landed in New York in August 1776, turning New Jersey into a continual battle site in 1777 and 1778. Burgoyne arrived from England to secure Canada and made his attempt to pinch off New England along the Hudson River, but he was stopped at Saratoga in 1777 in the key battle of the early war.

READING THE MAP: Which general's troops traveled the farthest in each of these years: 1775, 1776, and 1777? How did the availability of water routes affect British and American strategy? **CONNECTIONS:** Why did the French wait until early 1778 to join American forces against the British? What did they hope to gain from participating in the war?

FOR MORE HELP ANALYZING THIS MAP, see the map activity for this chapter in the Online Study Guide at bedfordstmartins.com/roark.

A View of the Attack against Fort Washington and Rebel Redouts near New York on the 16 of November 1776 by the British and Hessian Brigades Drawn on the spot by Cap Davies Cap R.A. of Artillery.

"A View of the Attack against Fort Washington"

An eyewitness sketched this scene of Hessian troops attacking Fort Washington in mid-November 1775. The fort, manned by 3,000 American soldiers, sat on well-secured high ground between the Harlem and Hudson rivers. A British lieutenant colonel at the scene wrote home that "we could not be masters of York Island or indeed secure of New York" while the Americans held the fort. Yet attempting to take it was dangerous. The boatloads of attacking soldiers could not land under protective cover of their own fire because of "the shortness of artillery," and the open boats and steep hillside denuded of leaves made the attackers easy pickings for American gunners. "So smart was the fire that the Sailors abandoned their oars & hid themselves in the bottom of the Boats," the British officer wrote. The British and Hessians attacked from three sides, and the fort finally surrendered, losing cannons, two months' supply of food, and all 3,000 men, who became prisoners of war. General Washington watched the attack in despair from Fort Lee, on the New Jersey side of the Hudson. His decision to defend the fort instead of evacuating it was one of his most costly mistakes in the war. The victors promptly renamed their prize Fort Knyphausen, for the German general who led the attack.

The Phelps Stokes Collection, Miriam and Ira D. Wallach Division of Art, Prints, and Photographs, The New York Public Library. Astor, Lenox, and Tilden Foundations.

many men died. Arnold's determination to get to Quebec was heroic, but in human costs, the campaign was a tragedy. Arnold and Montgomery jointly attacked Quebec in December but failed to take the city. Worse yet, they encountered smallpox, which killed more men than had been felled by the British.

The main action of the first year of the war came not in Canada, however, but in New York, so crucial to Britain. In August 1776, some 45,000 British troops (including 8,000 German mercenaries, called Hessians) landed south of New York City, under the command of General Howe. General Washington had anticipated that New York would be Howe's target and had moved his army, numbering about 20,000, south from Massachusetts. The battle of Long Island, in late August 1776, pitted the well-trained British "redcoats" (common slang referring to the red British uniforms) against a very green Continental army. Howe attacked, inflicting many casualties (1,500 dead and wounded) and spreading panic among the American soldiers, who fled to the western edge of Long Island. A British general called it "a field day," as though the battle had been a military parade. "If a good bleeding can bring those Bible-faced Yankees to their senses, the fever of independency should soon abate," he said. Howe failed to press forward, however, perhaps remembering the costly victory of Bunker Hill, and Washington evacuated his troops to Manhattan Island in the dead of a foggy night.

Washington knew it would be hard to hold Manhattan, so he withdrew farther north to two forts on either side of the Hudson River. For two months, the armies engaged in limited skirmishing, but in November, Howe finally captured Fort Washington and Fort Lee, taking nearly 3,000 prisoners. (See "Beyond America's Borders," page 230.) Washington retreated quickly across New Jersey into Pennsylvania. Yet again Howe unaccountably failed to press his advantage. Had he attacked Washington's army at Philadelphia, he probably would have taken the city. Instead, he parked his German troops in winter quarters along the Delaware River. Perhaps he knew that many of the Continental soldiers' enlistment periods ended on December 31, so he felt confident that the Americans would not attack him. But he was wrong.

On December 25, near midnight, as sleet and hail rained down, Washington stealthily moved his large army across the icy Delaware River and in the early morning made a quick capture of the unsuspecting German soldiers encamped at Trenton. This impressive victory lifted the sagging morale of the patriot side. For the next two weeks, Washington remained on the offensive, capturing supplies in a clever attack on British units at Princeton on January 3. Soon he was safe in Morristown, in northern New Jersey, where he settled his troops in for the winter. Washington finally had time to administer mass smallpox inoculations and see his men through the abbreviated course of the disease. Future recruits also would face inoculation.

All in all, in the first year of declared war, the rebellious Americans had a few isolated moments to feel proud of but also much to worry about. The very inexperienced Continental army had barely hung on in the New York campaign. Washington had shown exceptional daring and admirable restraint, but what really saved the Americans may have been the repeated reluctance of the British to follow through militarily when they had the advantage.

REVIEW   Why did the British exercise restraint in their efforts to defeat the rebellious colonies?

The Home Front

Battlefields alone did not determine the outcome of the war. Struggles on the home front were equally important. In 1776, each community contained small numbers of highly committed people on both sides and far larger numbers who were uncertain about whether independence was worth a war. Both persuasion and force were used to gain the allegiance of the many neutrals. Revolutionaries who took control of local government often used it to punish loyalists and intimidate neutrals, while loyalists worked to reestablish British authority. The struggle to secure political allegiance was complicated greatly by a shaky wartime economy. The creative financing of the fledgling government brought hardships as well as opportunities, forcing Americans to confront new manifestations of virtue and corruption.

Patriotism at the Local Level

Committees of correspondence, of public safety, and of inspection dominated the political landscape in patriot communities. These committees took on more than customary local governance; they enforced boycotts, picked army draftees, and policed suspected traitors. They sometimes invaded homes to search for contraband goods such as British tea or textiles.

Loyalists were dismayed by the increasing show of power by patriots. A man in Westchester, New York, described his response to intrusions by committees: "Choose your committee or suffer it to be chosen by a half dozen fools in your neighborhood—open your doors to them—let them examine your tea-cannisters and molasses-jugs, and your wives' and daughters' petty coats—bow and cringe and tremble and quake—fall down and worship our sovereign lord the mob. . . . Should any pragmatical committee-gentleman come to my house and give himself airs, I shall show him the door." Oppressive or not, the local committees were rarely challenged. Their persuasive powers convinced many middle-of-the-road citizens that neutrality was not a comfortable option.

Another group new to political life—white women—increasingly demonstrated a capacity for patriotism as wartime hardships dramatically altered their work routines. Many wives whose husbands were away on military or political service took on masculine duties. Their competence to tend farms and make business decisions encouraged some to assert competence in politics as well. Abigail Adams managed the family farm in Massachusetts while John Adams was away for several years doing politics, in which Abigail took a keen interest. Eliza Wilkinson managed a South Carolina plantation and talked revolutionary politics with women friends. "None were greater politicians than the several knots of ladies who met together," she remarked, alert to the unusual turn female conversations had taken. "We commenced perfect statesmen."

Women from prominent Philadelphia families took more direct action, forming the Ladies Association in 1780 to collect money for Continental soldiers. A published broadside, "The Sentiments of an American Woman," defended their female patriotism: "The time is arrived to display the same sentiments which animated us at the beginning of the Revolution, when we renounced the use of teas [and] when our republican and laborious hands spun the flax." The broadside's author was Esther Reed, wife of Pennsylvania's governor.

Even young girls found ways to participate in the rebellion. Three feisty fifteen-year-olds on Martha's Vineyard, an island south of Massachusetts, decided to destroy a cherished liberty pole in their town rather than let a British navy captain take it to replace a broken spar on his ship. (Liberty poles, like liberty trees, had come to symbolize Americans' quest for liberty.) The town's leaders capitulated to the captain's demand that they sell him the tall, mastlike pole or face violent attack. Under cover of night, the girls drilled holes in the pole; deposited gunpowder in the holes, using rags as fuses; and touched off an explosion with hot coals. The pole was ruined for any naval use but saved as a symbol. Town leaders were so totally mystified by the act of destruction that the angry navy captain left without launching an attack. More than fifty years later, the aged and poor Mary Daggett Hillman petitioned the U.S. Congress for a reward for her bold deed.

Abigail Adams

Abigail Smith Adams was twenty-two when she sat for this pastel portrait in 1766. A wife for two years and a mother for one, Adams exhibits a steady, intelligent gaze. Pearls and a lace collar anchor her femininity, while her facial expression projects a confidence and maturity not often credited to young women of the 1760s. A decade later, she was running the family's Massachusetts farm while her husband, John, attended the Continental Congress in Philadelphia. Her frequent letters gave him the benefit of her sage advice on politics and the war.
Courtesy of the Massachusetts Historical Society.

The Loyalists

Around one-fifth of the American population remained loyal to the crown in 1776, and another two-fifths were probably neutral. With proper cultivation, this large base might have sustained the British empire in America, if only the British army leaders had known how to use it. In general, loyalists had strong cultural and economic ties to England; they thought that social stability depended on a government anchored by monarchy and aristocracy. Perhaps most of all, they feared democratic tyranny. They understood that dissolving the automatic respect that subjects had for their king could lead to a society where deference to one's social betters might come under challenge. Patriots seemed to them to be unscrupulous, violent, self-interested men who simply wanted power for themselves.

The most visible loyalists (called Tories by their enemies) were royal officials, not only governors such as Thomas Hutchinson of Massachusetts

Prisoners of War in the Eighteenth Century

The taking of captives was essential to eighteenth-century warfare, both to reduce an adversary's troop strength and to create opportunities for prisoner exchange. Although no formal international law governed the status of prisoners of war, many European nation-states had developed shared expectations of decent treatment, recognizing that captured soldiers were not common criminals subject to punishing incarceration. Among the expectations were provision of rations and such comforts as clean bedding straw. Customarily, prisoners' expenses (for food, clothes, blankets, and laundry) were paid by their own government, to guarantee adequate supplies. All captives could hope for release through prisoner exchange of men of parallel rank. Officers could be ransomed or released on "parole," giving their solemn word of honor not to resume active military duty once freed.

George Washington fully expected the British to honor these customary civilities. But British leaders refused to recognize the colonies as a sovereign nation; the war was precisely about denying their independence. According to King George III, captured Americans were traitorous rebels—worse than common criminals and certainly not entitled to honorable and humane treatment.

The consequences of this point of view became apparent when the British invaded Long Island in August 1776 and captured more than 1,000 Continental soldiers. Prisoners were crammed into New York City's one jail and stashed in several sugar re-fineries, the only large buildings in the city. In November, when another 3,000 Americans surrendered at nearby Fort Washington, the British imprisoned the overflow captives on ships moored in the East River. Treatment was far from humane, and almost no means of release was honored, at least not at first. For the war's duration, some two dozen vessels anchored in Wallabout Bay, off Brooklyn, became death ships for thousands of prisoners captured from New England to Georgia.

The most infamous of these vessels was the very large HMS *Jersey*, built in the 1720s but now just a hulk stripped of its masts and guns. Built to house a crew of 400, the *Jersey* was packed with nearly three times that number of captives. Surviving prisoners described the dark, crowded, stinking space below-decks where men died daily, wasted and parched from extreme thirst. Prisoners were allowed on deck once a day, in shifts. Food, water, and sanitation facilities were inadequate. A twenty-year-old captive seaman described his first view of the hold: "Here was a motley crew, covered with rags and filth; visages pallid with disease, emaciated with hunger and anxiety, and retaining hardly a trace of their original appearance. Here were men . . . now shriveled by a scanty and unwholesome diet, ghastly with inhaling an impure atmosphere, exposed to contagion and disease, and surrounded with the horrors of sickness and death."

Following the European model, the prisoners were supposed to receive two-thirds the rations of regular soldiers and sailors, and the Continental Congress supplied some funds and food toward that end. But only a fraction of the provisions reached the prisons. Throughout the war, the British had trouble supplying their own soldiers, and corrupt commissaries diverted food for British use. Washington fumed at General Howe and threatened severe treatment of British prisoners; Howe remained uncooperative.

Treating the captives as common criminals instead of prisoners of war potentially triggered the Anglo-American right of habeas corpus, a central feature of English law since the thirteenth century, which guaranteed every prisoner the right to challenge his detention before a judge and learn the charges against him. To remove that possibility, Parliament voted in early 1777 to suspend habeas corpus specifically for "persons taken in the act of high treason" in any of the colonies.

That suspension grievously troubled a group of Britons. The horrors of the Brooklyn prison ships were not close at hand, but there were two well-known prisons in Britain where several thousand captured American sailors languished, inadequately fed and housed. Denied prisoner of war privileges, and denied the right to challenge their detention, these men were in legal limbo. Their British sympathizers raised funds to buy them food.

As the war dragged on, some prisoner exchanges were negotiated out of necessity, when the British were desperate to regain valued officers. But for ordinary soldiers and seamen, death—or the rare escape—was their fate. Six to ten corpses left the prison ships daily and were buried along the shore by prisoner work crews. For decades after, skeletons washed out of the bay's embankments. Historians estimate that more than 15,000 men en-

The British Prisoner Ship HMS *Jersey*

American Robert Sheffield escaped from a prison ship (most likely the HMS *Jersey*) in 1778 after just six days and told a Connecticut newspaper of the torturous treatment of prisoners. "Their sickly Countenances and ghastly Looks were truly horrible," he reported. "Some [were] swearing and blaspheming; some crying, praying, and wringing their Hands, and stalking about like Ghosts and Apparitions; others delirious, void of Reason, raving, and storming; some groaning and dying—all panting for Breath; some dead and corrupting. The air so foul at Times, that a Lamp could not be kept burning, by Reason of which three Boys were not missed till they had been dead ten Days."

Granger Collection.

dured captivity in the New York jails and prison ships during the war. More than two-thirds of them died, a larger number than those who died in battle.

Despite that horror, General Washington insisted that captured British soldiers be properly treated. More than 3,000 British and Germans taken at Saratoga in 1778 spent the next five years in various locations from Massachusetts to Virginia, moving each time the theater of war drew near. Quartered in self-built barracks and guarded by local townsmen, the captives typically could cultivate small gardens, move about freely during the day, and even hire themselves out to farmers suffering wartime labor shortages. Officers with money purchased lodging with private families and mixed socially with Americans. Officers on parole enjoyed freedom to travel locally; many were allowed to keep their guns.

At the end of the war, prisoners on both sides were released and allowed to return home. But the war's end came too late for the many thousands of Americans who died in captivity.

In 1785, shortly after the Revolution, three American diplomats in Europe—Thomas Jefferson, Benjamin Franklin, and John Adams—negotiated a friendly treaty of commerce with Prussia that included a ground-breaking paragraph requiring humane treatment of prisoners of war. Prisoners "shall not be confined in dungeons, prison ships, nor prisons" and shall have "air & exercise," roomy barracks, and full rations—all concerns directly arising out of the American experience in the Revolution. It was the historic first in a series of steps leading to the twentieth-century Geneva conventions designed to protect prisoners of war.

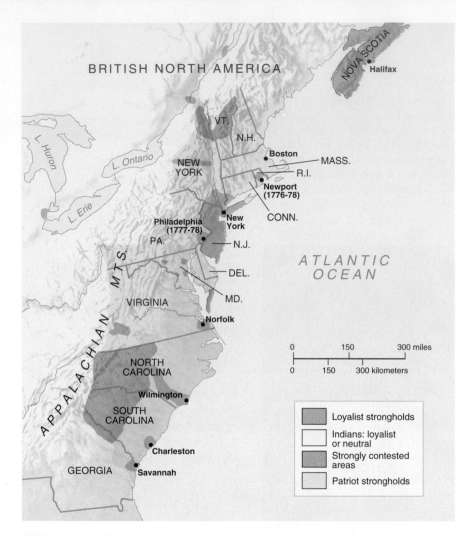

BRITISH NORTH AMERICA

NOVA SCOTIA
Halifax

L. Huron

L. Ontario

L. Erie

VT.

N.H.

NEW YORK

Boston

MASS.

R.I.

Newport (1776-78)

Philadelphia (1777-78)

New York

CONN.

PA.

N.J.

DEL.

VIRGINIA

MD.

Norfolk

ATLANTIC OCEAN

APPALACHIAN MTS.

NORTH CAROLINA

Wilmington

SOUTH CAROLINA

Charleston

GEORGIA   Savannah

0   150   300 miles
0   150   300 kilometers

Loyalist strongholds

Indians: loyalist or neutral

Strongly contested areas

Patriot strongholds

MAP 7.2   Loyalist Strength and Rebel Support
The exact number of loyalists can never be known. No one could have made an accurate count at the time, and political allegiance often shifted with the wind. This map shows the regions of loyalist strength on which the British relied—most significantly, the lower Hudson valley and the Carolina Piedmont.

READING THE MAP: Which forces were stronger, those loyal to Britain or those rebelling? (Consider the size of their respective areas, centers of population, and vital port locations.) What areas were contested? If the contested areas ultimately sided with the British, how would the balance of power change?
CONNECTIONS: Who was more likely to be a loyalist and why? How many loyalists left the United States? Where did they go?

FOR MORE HELP ANALYZING THIS MAP, see the map activity for this chapter in the Online Study Guide at bedfordstmartins.com/roark.

but also local judges and customs officers. Wealthy merchants gravitated toward loyalism to maintain the trade protections of navigation acts and the British navy. Conservative urban lawyers admired the stability of British law and order. Some colonists chose loyalism simply to oppose traditional adversaries. For example, backcountry farmers in the Carolinas tended to

be loyalists out of resentment over the political and economic power of the lowlands gentry, generally of patriot persuasion. And, of course, southern slaves had their own resentments against the white slave-owning class and looked to Britain for hope of freedom.

Many Indian tribes hoped to remain neutral at the war's start, seeing the conflict as a civil war between English and American brothers. Eventually, however, most were drawn in, many taking the British side. The powerful Iroquois confederacy divided: The Mohawk, Cayuga, Seneca, and Onondaga peoples lined up with the British; the Oneida and Tuscarora tribes aided Americans. One young Mohawk leader, Thayendanegea (known also by his English name, Joseph Brant), traveled to England in 1775 to complain to King George about American settlers cheating his people of land. "It is very hard when we have let the King's subjects have so much of our lands for so little value," he wrote, "they should want to cheat us in this manner of the small spots we have left for our women and children to live on. We are tired out in making complaints & getting no redress." Brant pledged Indian support for the king in exchange for protection from encroaching settlers. In the Ohio Country, parts of the Shawnee and Delaware tribes started out pro-American but shifted to the British side by 1779 in the face of repeated betrayals by American settlers and soldiers.

Pockets of loyalism thus existed everywhere—in the middle colonies, in the backcountry of the southern colonies, and out beyond the Appalachian Mountains in Indian country (Map 7.2). Even New England towns at the heart of the turmoil, such as Concord, Massachusetts, had a small and increasingly silenced core of loyalists who refused to countenance armed revolution. On occasion, husbands and wives, fathers and sons disagreed completely on the war. (See "Documenting the American Promise," page 234.)

Loyalists were most vocal between 1774 and 1776, when the possibility of a full-scale rebellion against Britain was still uncertain. Loyalists challenged the emerging patriot side in pamphlets and newspapers. In New York City, 547 loyalists signed and circulated a broadside titled "A Declaration of Dependence," in rebuttal to the congress's July 4, 1776, declaration. The broadside denounced the "most unnatural, unprovoked Rebellion that ever disgraced the annals of Time."

Speeches delivered by ministers in the pulpit and others at open-air meetings bolstered the loyalist cause. At a backcountry rally in South Carolina in 1775, a loyalist warned listeners of the superior might of the British army and of the damage to trade that war would bring. Most effectively, he played on white farmers' resentment of coastal planters' wealth and political power. It is ironic, he said, that "the charge of our intending to enslave you should come oftenest from the mouths of those lawyers who in your southern provinces, at least, have long made you slaves to themselves."

Joseph Brant

The Mohawk leader Thayendanegea, called Joseph Brant by the Americans, had been educated in English ways at Eleazar Wheelock's New England school (which became Dartmouth College in 1769). In 1775, the thirty-four-year-old Brant traveled to England with another Mohawk to negotiate the tribe's support for the British. During his extended stay in London, he had his portrait painted by the English artist George Romney. Notice that Brant wears a metal gorget around his neck over his English shirt, along with an Indian sash, headdress, and armbands. A gorget was a piece of armor worn by feudal knights to protect the throat. Many military men, both white and Indian, wore smaller versions when they dressed formally for portraits—or for war. National Gallery of Canada.

Who Is a Traitor?

The rough treatment that loyalists experienced at the hands of the revolutionaries seemed to substantiate their worst fears. In June 1775, the First Continental Congress declared all loyalists to be traitors. Over the next year, state laws defined as treason acts such as joining or provisioning the British army, saying or printing anything that undermined patriot morale, or discouraging men from enlisting in the Continental army. Punishments ranged from house arrest and suspension of voting privileges to confiscation of property and deportation. And sometimes self-appointed committees of Tory-hunters bypassed the judicial niceties and terrorized loyalists, raiding their houses or tarring and feathering them.

Were wives of loyalists also traitors? When loyalist families fled the country, their property was typically confiscated. In the rare case that a wife stayed behind, courts usually allowed her to keep one-third of the property, the amount due her if widowed, and confiscated the rest, so long as she was known to be "a steady and true and faithful friend to the American states," in the case of one Connecticut woman. But even when a wife fled with her husband, was she necessarily a loyalist, too? If the husband insisted, was she not obligated to leave with him? Such questions were adjudicated in lawsuits after the Revolution, when descendants of refugee loyalists tried to regain property that had entered the family through the mother's inheritance or marriage dowry. In one well-publicized Massachusetts case in 1805, the outcome confirmed the traditional view of women as political blank slates. The American son of loyalist refugee Anna Martin recovered her dowry property on the grounds that she had no independent will to be a loyalist.

Tarring and feathering, property confiscation, deportation, terrorism—to the loyalists, such denials of liberty of conscience and of freedom to own private property proved that democratic tyranny was more to be feared than the monarchical variety. A Boston loyalist named Mather Byles aptly expressed this point: "They call me a brainless Tory, but tell me . . . which is better—to be ruled by one tyrant three thousand miles away, or by three thousand tyrants not a mile away?" Byles was soon sentenced to deportation.

Throughout the war, probably 7,000 to 8,000 loyalists fled to England, and 28,000 found closer

> Mather Byles expressed his fear of democratic tyranny: "They call me a brainless Tory, but tell me . . . which is better—to be ruled by one tyrant three thousand miles away, or by three thousand tyrants not a mile away?"

Families Divide over the Revolution

Generalizing about rebels versus loyalists is a complex historical task. Sometimes categorizing by class, race, and geographical descriptors helps explain the split. But beyond economic interests or cultural politics, sometimes the loyalist-patriot divide cut across families—and cut deeply. These documents reveal men and women pitted against loved ones over wartime allegiance.

DOCUMENT 1
A Loyalist Wife Writes to Her Patriot Husband, 1778

Mary Gould Almy, wife and mother, lived in Newport, Rhode Island, an island town occupied by the British army in 1778. She was a Quaker and a loyalist, in contrast to her Anglican husband, Benjamin Almy, who joined the Continental army. Mary wrote to Benjamin in September 1778, sending him her account of the monthlong siege of the town by the French fleet and American troops.

September 02, 1778. Once more, my dear Mr. Almy, I am permitted to write you. . . . I am to give you an account of what passes during the siege; but first let me tell you, it will be done with spirit, for my dislike to the nation that you call your friends, is the same as when you knew me, knowing there is no confidence to be placed in them. . . .

[The 1st day]: At nine in the morning a signal was made for a fleet in sight; at ten o'clock was discovered the number to be eleven large ships . . . the French fleet. . . . With a distressed heart, I endeavor to comfort my poor children by saying, that they would not come in till morning, and then began to secure my papers and plate in the ground.

[The 9th day]: Heavens! what a scene of wretchedness before this once happy and flourishing island. . . . Neither sleep to my eyes, nor slumber to my eyelids, this night; but judge you, what preparation could I make, had I been endowed with as much presence of mind as ever woman was; six children hanging around me, the little girls crying out, "Mamma, will they kill us?" The boys endeavor to put on an air of manliness, and strive to assist, but slip up to the girls, in a whisper, "Who do you think will hurt you? Ain't your papa coming with them?" Indeed this cut me to the soul.

[The 18th day]: Still carting, still fortifying; your people encroaching nearer, throwing up new works every night. . . . And really, Mr. Almy, my curiosity was so great, as to wish to behold the entrenchment that I supposed you were behind; . . . different agitations as by turns took hold upon me. Wishing most ardently to call home my wanderer, at the same time, filled with resentment against those he calls his friends.

[The 24th day]: They kept up a smart firing till two o'clock, and then they began to bury the dead and bring in the wounded. . . . The horrors of that day will never be quite out of my remembrance. I quitted company and hid myself to mourn in silence, for the wickedness of my country. Never was a heart more differently agitated than mine. Some of my good friends in the front of the battle here; and Heaven only knows how many of the other side. . . . At last I shut myself from the family, to implore Heaven to protect you, and keep you from imprisonment and death.

SOURCE: *Mrs. Almy's Journal: Siege of Newport, R.I., August 1778* (Newport, R.I.: Newport Historical Publishing Company, 1881, pp. 19–31). Reprinted with permission. Available online in select college libraries in the electronic database: *North American Women's Letters and Diaries,* Alexander Street Press.

DOCUMENT 2
Patriot Benjamin Franklin and Loyalist Son William Correspond, 1784

Benjamin Franklin, a keen advocate of the Revolution, had a son who stayed loyal to the crown. William was Benjamin's illegitimate son, resulting from a youthful indiscretion. He was raised in the Franklin family and accompanied Benjamin to England in 1757 for four years' service as Pennsylvania's colonial agent. Thanks to his father, William acquired connections at court, and in 1762, at the age of thirty-one, he was appointed royal governor of New Jersey, a post he held until 1776. When the war began, he was declared a traitor to the patriot cause and placed under house arrest. Father and son did not communicate for the next nine years, even when William was confined in a Connecticut prison for eight months. During this time, Benjamin took charge of William's oldest son, an illegitimate child born before William's legal marriage. After the war, William moved to England, and in 1784 he wrote to his father, then in Paris, asking for a meeting of reconciliation. He did not apologize for his loyalism.

Dear and honored Father,
Ever since the termination of the unhappy contest between Great Britain and America, I have been anxious to write to you. . . . There are narrow illiberal Minds in all Parties. In that

which I took, and on whose Account I have so much suffered, there have not been wanting some who have insinuated that my Conduct has been founded on Collusion with you, that one of us might succeed whichever Party should prevail. . . . The Falsity of such Insinuation in our Case you well know, and I am happy that I can with Confidence appeal not only to you but to my God, that I have uniformly acted from a strong Sense of what I conceived my Duty to my King, and Regard to my Country, required. If I have been mistaken, I cannot help it. It is an Error of Judgment what the maturest Reflection I am capable of cannot rectify; and I verily believe were the same Circumstances to occur again Tomorrow, my Conduct would be exactly similar to what it was heretofore.

The father replied:

Dear Son,

I am glad to find that you desire to revive the affectionate Intercourse, that formerly existed between us. It will be very agreeable to me; indeed nothing has ever hurt me so much and affected me with such keen Sensations, as to find myself deserted in my old age by my only Son; and not only deserted, but to find him taking up Arms against me, in a Cause, wherein my good Fame, Fortune and Life were all at Stake. You conceived, you say, that your Duty to your King and regard for your Country requir'd this. I ought not to blame you for differing in Sentiment with me in Public Affairs. We are Men, all subject to errors. Our opinions are not in our own Power; they are form'd and govern'd much by Circumstances, that are often as inexplicable as they are irresistible. Your Situation was such that few would have censured your remaining Neuter, tho' there are *Natural Duties* which preceded political ones,

and cannot be extinguish'd by them.

This is a disagreeable Subject. I drop it. And we will endeavor, as you propose mutually to forget what has happened relating to it, as well as we can. I send your Son over to pay his Duty to you. . . . He is greatly esteem'd and belov'd in this Country, and will make his Way anywhere. . . . Wishing you Health, and more happiness than it seems you have lately experienced, I remain your affectionate father,

B. Franklin

SOURCE: Courtesy of the American Philosophical Society, <www.amphilsoc.org>.

DOCUMENT 3
Two Oneida Brothers Confront Their Different Allegiances, 1779

Mary Jemison was captured as a girl during the Seven Years' War and adopted into the Seneca tribe of western New York, where she remained for life. When she was eighty, her narrative was taken down and published. In this story from her narrative, she relates how some Oneida warriors siding with the British captured two Indians guiding General Sullivan's 1779 campaign of terror in central New York. One of the captors recognized his own brother.

Envy and revenge glared in the features of the conquering savage, as he advanced to his brother (the prisoner) in all the haughtiness of Indian pride, heightened by a sense of power, and addressed him in the following manner:

"Brother, you have merited death! The hatchet or the war-club shall finish your career! When I begged of you to follow me in the fortunes of war, you was deaf to my cries—you spurned my entreaties!

"Brother! You have merited death and shall have your deserts!

When the rebels raised their hatchets to fight their good master, you sharpened your knife, you brightened your rifle and led on our foes to the fields of our fathers! You have merited death and shall die by our hands! When those rebels had drove us from the fields of our fathers to seek out new homes, it was you who could dare to step forth as their pilot, and conduct them even to the doors of our wigwams, to butcher our children and put us to death! No crime can be greater! But though you have merited death and shall die on this spot, my hands shall not be stained in the blood of a brother! *Who will strike?*"

Little Beard, who was standing by, as soon as the speech was ended, struck the prisoner on the head with his tomahawk, and dispatched him at once.

SOURCE: James E. Seaver, *A narrative of the life of Mrs. Mary Jemison, who was taken by the Indians, in the year 1755, when only about twelve years of age, and has continued to reside amongst them to the present time* (1824), chapter VII, Project Gutenberg, <http://www.ibiblio.org/gutenberg/etext04/jemsn10.txt> (accessed June 19, 2006).

QUESTIONS FOR ANALYSIS AND DEBATE

1. Why was Mary Almy "cut . . . to the soul" by the remarks of her sons? She was frightened for her husband's safety. Was she also angry with him? Why or why not?

2. What did Benjamin Franklin mean by the emphasized words *"Natural Duties"*? Do you think Franklin really believed that his son was entitled to his own political opinions on the Revolutionary War? What factors help explain why William remained loyal to the crown?

3. Why did the Oneida warrior believe that his brother merited death?

haven in Canada. But many chose to remain in the new United States and tried to swing with the changing political winds. In some instances, that proved difficult. In New Jersey, for example, 3,000 Jerseyites felt protected (or scared) enough by the occupying British army in 1776 to swear an oath of allegiance to the king. But then General Howe drew back to New York City, leaving them to the mercy of local patriot committees. British strategy depended on using loyalists to hold occupied territory, but the New Jersey experience showed how poorly that strategy was carried out.

Financial Instability and Corruption

Wars cost money—for arms and ammunition, for food and uniforms, for soldiers' pay. The Continental Congress printed money, but its value quickly deteriorated because the congress held no reserves of gold or silver to back the currency. In practice, it was worth only what buyers and sellers agreed it was worth. When the dollar eventually bottomed out at one-fortieth of its face value, a loaf of bread that once sold for two and a half cents then sold for a dollar. States, too, were printing paper money to pay for wartime expenses, further complicating the economy.

As the currency depreciated, the congress turned to other means to procure supplies and labor. One method was to borrow **hard money** (gold or silver coins) from wealthy men in exchange for certificates of debt (public securities) promising repayment with interest. The certificates of debt were similar to present-day **government bonds**. To pay soldiers, the congress issued land grant certificates, written promises of acreage usually located in frontier areas such as central Maine or eastern Ohio. Both the public securities and the land grant certificates quickly became forms of negotiable currency. A soldier with no cash, for example, could sell his land grant certificate to get food for his family. These certificates soon depreciated, too.

Depreciating currency inevitably led to rising prices, as sellers compensated for the falling value of the money. The wartime economy of the late 1770s, with its unreliable currency and price inflation, was extremely demoralizing to Americans everywhere. In 1778, in an effort to impose stability, local committees of public safety began to fix prices on essential goods such as

flour. Inevitably, some turned this unstable situation to their advantage. Money that fell fast in value needed to be spent quickly; being in debt was suddenly advantageous because the debt could be repaid in devalued currency. A brisk black market sprang up in prohibited luxury imports, such as tea, sugar, textiles, and wines, even though these items came from Britain. A New Hampshire delegate to the congress denounced the violation of the homespun association agreements of just a few years before: "We are a crooked and perverse generation, longing for the fineries and follies of those Egyptian task masters from whom we have so lately freed ourselves."

> **REVIEW**   How did the patriots promote support for their cause in the colonies?

The Campaigns of 1777–1779: The North and West

In early 1777, the Continental army faced bleak choices. General Washington had skillfully avoided outright defeat, but the minor victories in New Jersey lent only faint optimism to the American side. Meanwhile, British troops moved south from Quebec, aiming to isolate New England from the rest of the colonies by taking control of the Hudson River. Their presence drew the Continental army up into central New York, polarizing Indian tribes of the Iroquois nation and turning the Mohawk Valley into a bloody war zone. By 1779, tribes in western New York and in Indian country in the Ohio Valley were fully involved in the Revolutionary War; most sided with the British and against the Americans. The Americans had some success in this period, such as the victory at Saratoga, but the involvement of Indians and the continuing strength of the British forced the American government to look toward France for help.

Burgoyne's Army and the Battle of Saratoga

In 1777, British general John Burgoyne assumed command of an army of 7,800 soldiers in Canada and began the northern squeeze on the Hudson River valley. His goal was to capture Albany, near the intersection of the Hudson and Mohawk rivers (see Map 7.1). Accompanied by 1,000 "camp followers" (cooks, laundresses, and musicians) and some 400 Indian warriors, Burgoyne's army did not travel light. In addition to food and supplies for 9,200 people, the army carried food for the 400 horses hauling heavy artillery. Burgoyne also carted thirty trunks of personal belongings, including fine wines and elegant clothing.

In July, Burgoyne captured Fort Ticonderoga with ease. Some 3,000 American troops stationed there spotted the approaching British and abandoned the fort without a fight. The British continued to move south, but the large army moved slowly on primitive roads through heavily forested land. Burgoyne lost a month hacking his way south; meanwhile, his supply lines back to Canada were severely stretched. Soldiers sent out to forage for food were beaten back by local militia units.

The logical second step in isolating New England should have been to advance troops up the Hudson from New York City to meet Burgoyne, who was expecting them. George Washington expected this move, too, in light of American surveillance indicating that General Howe in Manhattan was readying his men for a major expedition in August 1777. But Howe surprised everyone by sailing south, to attack Philadelphia.

Now Burgoyne could only hope for crucial support to arrive from the west, along the Mohawk River in central New York. Close to 1,000 soldiers, including British regulars, German mercenaries, Canadians, and refugee loyalists, sailed from Montreal to Lake Ontario under the leadership of British general Barry St. Leger. Once in New York, a thousand Mohawk and Seneca Indians joined them, along with hundreds more local loyalists fighting against their rebel neighbors. St. Leger believed, wrongly, that the large community of Palatine Germans in the Mohawk Valley also would be heavily loyalist, so he expected little trouble getting to Albany. These Germans were descendants of some 10,000 immigrants who had come to New York around 1710 from the Palatinate, a region of Germany near the Rhine River.

A hundred miles west of their goal, in August 1777, the British encountered a small force of American Continental soldiers at Fort Stanwix who refused to surrender. On August 3, the British laid siege to the fort, causing local militia units forty miles away to rush to the aid of the Continentals. The 800 militiamen were mostly Palatine Germans, joined by 40 Oneida

A Soldier's Canteen
This wooden canteen belonged to Noah Allen, whose name and regiment number are carved into the side. Allen was from the Sixth Continental Regiment from Massachusetts. Almost no piece of equipment surpassed in importance the soldier's canteen.
Fort Ticonderoga Museum.

Indians. St. Leger dispatched the Mohawks and Senecas, under the leadership of the Mohawk chief Joseph Brant, and a loyalist regiment to stop the militia. Brant, with his detailed knowledge of the terrain, selected as the site of the ambush a deep ravine that the militia would have to traverse. On August 6, as the thirsty militiamen drank at Oriskany Creek in the ravine, the Indians and loyalists opened fire and inflicted heavy losses, killing nearly 500 out of 840 Americans and Indians. On Brant's side, some 90 men were killed. The battle of Oriskany was notable not only for its high death rate but also for the fact that all the combatants were American-born.

While the Oriskany battle raged, the Continentals at Fort Stanwix repelled the British and Indians besieging them and forced the attackers to retreat (see Map 7.1). Taken together, the Oriskany and Fort Stanwix battles were complexly multiethnic, pitting Indians against Indians, German Americans (the Palatines) against German mercenaries, New York patriots against New York loyalists, and English Americans against British soldiers.

The British retreat at Fort Stanwix was complete when the American general Benedict Arnold in Albany mobilized troops to chase St. Leger back to Canada, depriving General Burgoyne of the reinforcements he expected to carry out his Hudson River strategy. Camped at a small village called Saratoga, Burgoyne was isolated, with food supplies dwindling and men deserting. His adversary at Albany, General Horatio Gates, began moving 7,000 Continental soldiers toward him. Burgoyne decided to attack first because every day his army weakened. The British prevailed, but at the great cost of 600 dead or wounded redcoats. Three weeks later, an American attack on Burgoyne's forces at Saratoga cost the British another 600 men and

> Accompanied by 1,000 "camp followers" (cooks, laundresses, and musicians) and some 400 Indian warriors, Burgoyne's army did not travel light.

Death of Jane McCrea

This 1804 painting by John Vanderlyn memorializes the martyr legend of Jane McCrea. McCrea, daughter of an American patriot family in northern New York, was in love with a young American loyalist who joined Burgoyne's Army. In July 1777 she eloped to join her fiancé, guided by Indians sent by the British to escort her. But she was killed on the short journey—either shot in the crossfire of battle, as the British claimed, or murdered by savage Indians allied with the British, in the patriots' version. The American general Horatio Gates sent Burgoyne an accusatory letter. "The miserable fate of Miss McCrea was particularly aggravated by her being dressed to meet her promised husband," Gates wrote, "but she met her murderers employed by you." Gates skillfully used the story of the vulnerable, innocent maiden dressed in alluring clothes as propaganda to inspire his soldiers' drive for victory at Saratoga.

Wadsworth Atheneum, Hartford.

READING THE IMAGE: How does the artist portray McCrea? How does he portray the Indians?
CONNECTIONS: Had McCrea been a man, her flight would have been traitorous. Why was she treated differently?

FOR MORE HELP ANALYZING THIS IMAGE, see the visual activity for this chapter in the Online Study Guide at **bedfordstmartins.com/roark.**

Battle of Saratoga, 1777

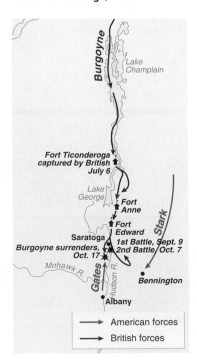

most of their cannons. General Burgoyne finally surrendered to the American forces on October 17, 1777.

Americans on the side of the rebellion were jubilant. After the battle of Saratoga, the first decisive victory for the Continental army, a popular dance called "General Burgoyne's Surrender" swept through the country, and bookies in the major cities set odds at five to one that the war would be won in six months.

General Howe, meanwhile, had succeeded in occupying Philadelphia in September 1777. Figuring that the Saratoga loss was balanced by the capture of Philadelphia, the British government proposed a negotiated settlement—not including independence—to end the war. The American side refused.

Patriot optimism was not well-founded. Spirits ran high, but supplies of arms and food ran precariously low. Washington moved his troops into winter quarters at Valley Forge, just west of Philadelphia. Quartered in drafty huts, the men lacked blankets, boots, stockings, and food. Some 2,000 men at Valley Forge died of disease; another 2,000 deserted over the bitter six-month encampment.

Washington blamed the citizenry for lack of support, and indeed, evidence of corruption and profiteering was abundant. Army suppliers too often provided defective food, clothing, and gunpowder. When a shipment of blankets arrived, they turned out to be one-quarter their customary size. Preserved meat arrived rotten because the brine had been drained from the barrels in order to lighten the load and thereby reduce transportation costs. Selfishness and greed seemed to infect the American side. As one Continental officer said, "The people at home are destroying the Army by their conduct much faster than Howe and all his army can possibly do by fighting us."

The War in the West: Indian Country

Burgoyne's defeat in the fall of 1777 and Washington's long stay at Valley Forge up to June 1778 might suggest that the war paused for a time; and it did, on the Atlantic coast. But in the interior western areas—the Mohawk Valley, the Ohio Valley, and Kentucky—the war of Indians against the American pro-independence side was heating up. For native tribes, the struggle was not about taxation, representation, or monarchical rule; it was about independence, freedom, and land.

The ambush and slaughter at Oriskany in August 1777 marked the beginning of three years of terror for the inhabitants of the Mohawk Valley. Loyalists and Indians together engaged in many raids on farms throughout 1778, capturing or killing the residents. In retaliation, American militiamen destroyed Joseph Brant's home village, Onaquaga, but failed to capture any warriors; several children in hiding were killed. A month later, Brant's warriors attacked the town of Cherry Valley, killing 32 townspeople and 16 soldiers and taking 71 people captive.

The following summer, General Washington authorized a campaign to wreak "total destruction and devastation" on all the Iroquoian villages of central New York. Some 4,500 troops commanded by General John Sullivan carried out a deliberate campaign of terror in the fall of 1779. Forty Indian towns met with total obliteration; the soldiers looted and torched the dwellings, then burned cornfields and orchards. In a few towns, women and children were slaughtered; but in most, the inhabitants managed to escape, fleeing to the British at Fort Niagara. Thousands of Indian refugees, sick and starving, camped around the fort in one of the most miserable winters on record.

Much farther to the west, beyond Fort Pitt, another complex story of alliances and betrayals between American militiamen and Indians unfolded. Some 150,000 native people lived between the Appalachian Mountains and the Mississippi River, and by 1779, neutrality was no longer an option. Most sided with the British, who maintained a major garrison at Fort Detroit, but a portion of the Shawnee and Delaware tribes at first sought peace with the Americans. In mid-1778, the Delaware chief White Eyes negotiated a treaty at Fort Pitt, pledging Indian support for the Americans in exchange for supplies and trade goods. But escalating violence undermined the agreement. That fall, when American soldiers killed two friendly Shawnee chiefs, Cornstalk and Red Hawk, the Continental Congress hastened to apologize, as did the governors of Pennsylvania and Virginia, but the soldiers who stood trial for the murders were acquitted. Two months later, White Eyes, still nominally an ally and an informant for the Americans, died under mysterious circumstances, almost certainly murdered by militiamen, who repeatedly had trouble honoring distinctions between allied and enemy Indians.

In far western North Carolina (today's Tennessee), a frontier war zone heated up in the South in 1779, when militias attacked Cherokee settlements, destroying thirty-six villages and burning fields and livestock. Indian raiders from north of the Ohio River, in alliance with the British, repeatedly attacked white settlements such as Boonesborough (in present-day Kentucky) that had sprouted up in defiance of the Proclamation of 1763 (Map 7.3, page 240). In retaliation, a young Virginian, George Rogers Clark, led Kentucky militiamen into what is now Illinois, his men attacking and taking the British fort at Kaskaskia. Clark's men wore native clothing—hunting shirts and breech cloths—but their dress was not a sign of solidarity with the Indians. When they attacked British-held Fort Vincennes in 1779, Clark's troops tomahawked Indian captives and threw their still-live bodies into the river in a gory spectacle witnessed by the redcoats. "To excel them in barbarity is the only way to make war upon Indians," Clark announced. And, he might have added, it was a good way to terrorize British soldiers as well.

> "To excel them in barbarity is the only way to make war upon Indians," George Rogers Clark announced.

By 1780, very few Indians remained neutral. Violent raids by Americans drove Indians into the arms of the British at Detroit and Niagara, or into the arms of the Spanish, who still held much of the land west of the Mississippi River. Said one officer on the Sullivan campaign, "Their nests are destroyed but the birds are still on the wing." For those who stayed near their native lands, chaos and confusion prevailed. Rare as it was, Indian support for the American side occasionally emerged out of a strategic sense that the Americans were unstoppable in their westward pressure and that it was better to work out an alliance than to lose in a war. But American treatment of even friendly Indians showed that there was no winning strategy for them.

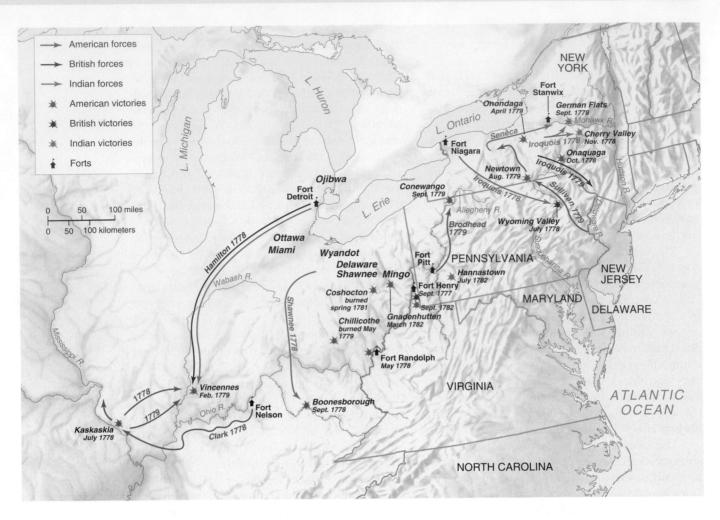

MAP 7.3   The Indian War in the West, 1777–1782
The American Revolution involved many Indian tribes, most of them supporting the British. Iroquois Indians, with British aid, attacked American towns in New York's Mohawk Valley throughout 1778. In 1779, the Continental army marched on forty Iroquois villages in central New York and destroyed them. Shawnee and Delaware Indians to the west of Fort Pitt tangled with American militia units in 1779, while tribes supported by the British at Fort Detroit conducted raids on Kentucky settlers, who hit back with raids of their own. George Rogers Clark led Kentucky militiamen against Indians in the Illinois region. Sporadic fighting continued in the West through 1782, ending with Indian attacks on Hannastown, Pennsylvania, and Fort Henry, on the Ohio River. By the late 1780s, occasional fighting resumed, sparked by American settlers pressing west onto Indian land.

The French Alliance

On their own, the Americans could not have defeated Britain, especially as pressure from hostile Indians increased. Essential help arrived as a result of the victory at Saratoga, which convinced the French to enter the war; a formal alliance was signed in February 1778. France recognized the United States as an independent nation and promised full military and commercial support throughout the war. Most crucial was the French navy, which could challenge Britain's transatlantic shipment of supplies and troops and aid the Americans in taking and holding prisoners of war.

Although France had been waiting for a promising American victory to justify a formal declaration of war, the French had been providing aid to the Americans in the form of cannons, muskets, gunpowder, and highly trained military advisers since 1776. Still, monarchical France was understandably cautious about endorsing a democratic revolution attacking the principles of kingship. For France, the main attraction of an alliance was the opportunity it provided to defeat archrival Britain. A victory would also open pathways to trade and perhaps result in France acquiring the coveted British West Indies. Even American defeat would not be a full disaster for France if the war lasted many years and drained Britain of men and money.

French support materialized slowly. The navy arrived off the Virginia coast in July 1778 but then sailed south to the West Indies to defend the French sugar-producing islands. French help would prove indispensable to the American victory, but the alliance's first months brought no dramatic victories, and some Americans grumbled that the partnership would prove worthless.

REVIEW   Why did the Americans need assistance from the French to ensure victory?

The Southern Strategy and the End of the War

When France joined the war, some British officials wondered whether the fight was worth continuing. A troop commander, arguing for an immediate negotiated settlement, shrewdly observed that "we are far from an anticipated peace, because the bitterness of the rebels is too widespread, and in regions where we are masters the rebellious spirit is still in them. The land is too large, and there are too many people. The more land we win, the weaker our army gets in the field." The commander of the British navy argued for abandoning the war, and even Lord North, the prime minister, agreed. But the king was determined to crush the rebellion, and he encouraged a new strategy for victory focusing on the southern colonies, thought to be more persuadably loyalist. It was a brilliant but desperate plan, and ultimately unsuccessful. Southern colonists were not all that loyal and in fact were willing to engage in guerrilla warfare against the British. The southern strategy thus led to a British defeat at Yorktown and the end of the war.

Georgia and South Carolina

The new strategy called for British forces to abandon New England and focus on the South, with its valuable crops—tobacco, rice, and indigo—and its large slave population, potentially a powerful destabilizing factor that might keep rebellious white southerners in line. Georgia and the Carolinas appeared to hold large numbers of loyalists, providing a base for the British to recapture the southern colonies one by one, moving north to the more problematic middle colonies and saving prickly New England for last.

Georgia, the first target, fell at the end of December 1778 (Map 7.4, page 242). A small army of British soldiers occupied Savannah and Augusta, and a new royal governor and loyalist assembly were quickly installed. Taking Georgia was easy because the bulk of the Continental army was in New York and New Jersey, keeping an eye on General Henry Clinton, Howe's replacement as commander in chief, and the French were in the West Indies. The British in Georgia quickly organized twenty loyal militia units, and 1,400 Georgians swore an oath of allegiance to the king. So far, the southern strategy looked as if it might work.

Next came South Carolina. The Continental army put ten regiments into the port city of Charleston to defend it from attack by British troops shipped south from New York under the command of General Clinton. For five weeks in early 1780, the British laid siege to the city, then took it in May 1780, sending 3,300 American soldiers (a tremendous loss) into British captivity. Again, the king's new strategy seemed to be on target.

Clinton returned to New York, leaving the task of pacifying the rest of South Carolina to General Charles Cornwallis and 4,000 troops. A bold commander, Lord Cornwallis quickly chased out the remaining Continentals and established military rule of South Carolina by midsummer. He purged rebels from government office and disarmed rebel militias. The export of South Carolina's main crop, rice, resumed, and as in Georgia, pardons were offered to Carolinians who swore loyalty oaths to the crown and then proved their loyalty by taking up arms for the British.

By August, American troops arrived from the North to strike back at Cornwallis. General Gates, the hero of the battle of Saratoga, led 3,000 troops, half of them experienced Continental soldiers and others newly recruited militiamen, into battle against Cornwallis at Camden, South Carolina, on August 16 (see Map 7.4). The militiamen panicked at the sight of the approaching enemy cavalry; men threw down unfired muskets and ran. When regiment leaders tried to regroup the next day, only 700 soldiers showed up; a thousand Americans were dead or wounded, another thousand captured, and three hundred were still in flight. The battle of Camden was a devastating defeat, the worst of the entire war; prospects seemed very grim for the Americans.

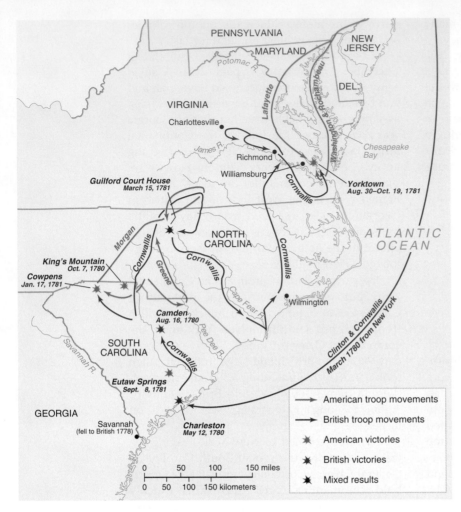

MAP 7.4   The War in the South, 1780–1781

After taking Charleston in May 1780, the British advanced into South Carolina and the foothills of North Carolina, leaving a bloody civil war in their wake. When the American general Horatio Gates and his men fled from the humiliating battle of Camden, Gates was replaced by General Nathanael Greene and General Daniel Morgan, who pulled off major victories at King's Mountain and Cowpens. The British general Cornwallis then moved north and invaded Virginia but was bottled up and finally overpowered at Yorktown in the fall of 1781.

Britain's southern strategy succeeded in 1780 in part because of information about American troop movements secretly passed on to the British by an American traitor: Benedict Arnold. The hero of several American battles, Arnold was a brilliant military talent but also a deeply insecure man who never felt he got his due in either honor or financial reward. Sometime in 1779, he opened secret negotiations with General Clinton in New York, trading information for money and hinting that he could deliver far more of value. When General Washington made him commander of West Point, a new fort sixty miles north of New York City on the Hudson River, Arnold's plan crystal-

lized. West Point controlled the Hudson; its easy capture by the British might well have meant victory in the war.

Arnold's plot to sell a West Point victory to the British was foiled in the fall of 1780 when Americans captured the man carrying plans of the fort's defense from Arnold to Clinton. News of Arnold's treason created shock waves. Arnold represented all of the patriots' worst fears about themselves: greedy self-interest, like that of the war profiteers; the unprincipled abandonment of war aims, like that of turncoat southern Tories; panic, like that of the terrified soldiers at Camden. Plus, the war was going badly for the Americans; what if Arnold's choice to switch sides was really the smart choice? All these deeply troubling questions could be submerged by making Arnold into a moral monster. His treachery was publicly and ritually denounced in a kind of displacement of the anxieties of the moment. Vilifying Arnold allowed Americans to stake out a wide distance between themselves and dastardly conduct. It inspired a renewal of patriotism at a particularly low moment.

The Other Southern War: Guerrillas

Shock over Gates's defeat at Camden and Arnold's treason revitalized rebel support in western South Carolina, an area that Cornwallis believed to be pacified and loyal. The backcountry of the South soon became the site of guerrilla warfare. In hit-and-run attacks, both sides burned and ravaged not only opponents' property but the property of anyone claiming to be neutral. Loyalist militia units organized by the British were met by fierce rebel militia units who figured they had little to lose. In South Carolina, some 6,000 men became active partisan fighters, and they entered into at least twenty-six engagements with loyalist units. Some were classic battles, but on other occasions the fighters were more like bandits than soldiers. Guerrilla warfare soon spread to Georgia and North Carolina. Both sides committed murders and atrocities and plundered property, clear deviations from standard military practice.

The British southern strategy depended on sufficient loyalist strength to hold reconquered territory as Cornwallis's army moved north. The backcountry civil war proved this assumption false. The Americans won few major battles in the South, but they ultimately succeeded by harassing the British forces and preventing them from foraging for food. Cornwallis moved the war into North Carolina in the fall of 1780, not because he thought South Carolina was secure—it was not—but because the North Carolinians were supplying the South Carolina rebels with arms and men (see Map 7.4). Then news of a brutal massacre of loyalist units by 1,400 frontier riflemen at the battle of King's Mountain, in western South Carolina, sent him hurrying back. The British were stretched too thin to hold on to even two of their onetime colonies.

Surrender at Yorktown

By early 1781, the war was going very badly for the British. Their defeat at King's Mountain was quickly followed by a second major defeat at the battle of Cowpens in South Carolina in January 1781. Cornwallis moved back to North Carolina again and thence to Virginia, where he captured Williamsburg in June. A raiding party proceeded to Charlottesville, the seat of government, capturing members of the Virginia assembly but not Governor Thomas Jefferson, who escaped the soldiers by a mere ten minutes. (More than a dozen of Jefferson's slaves chose this moment to seek refuge with the British.) These minor victories allowed Cornwallis to imagine that he was gaining

"The Swamp Fox" of South Carolina

Francis Marion first gained military experience fighting Cherokee Indians in the 1750s. Two decades later, when the British invaded his home state, Marion mobilized a band of guerrilla fighters to stalk the redcoats, raid their supply depots, and viciously attack their loyalist supporters. To avoid capture, the guerrillas retreated to swamps—hence Marion's nickname, "the Swamp Fox." Marion was mythologized in several nineteenth-century biographies, the first by Parson Weems, the same author who gave birth to the story of George Washington and the cherry tree. In this 1850 painting, titled *Marion Crossing the Pedee*, artist William T. Ranney wraps a strong, silent Marion in a brown cloak. His loyal followers are an appealing and diverse mix. Mythologizing of Marion has continued to the present, most recently in the Hollywood film *The Patriot* (2000), which was very loosely based on Marion's life.

Marion Crossing the Pedee, by William T. Ranney, 1850, oil on canvas, 1983.126. Amon Carter Museum, Fort Worth, Texas.

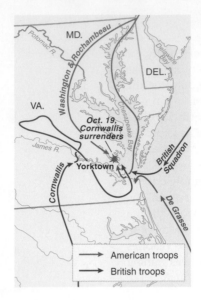

Siege of Yorktown, 1781

the upper hand in Virginia. He next marched to Yorktown, near the Chesapeake Bay, to await the arrival of backup troops by ship from New York City, still held by the British.

At this juncture, the French-American alliance came into play. Already, French regiments commanded by the Comte de Rochambeau had joined General Washington in Newport, Rhode Island, in mid-1780, and now in 1781 warships under the Comte de Grasse sailed from France. Washington, Rochambeau, and de Grasse fixed their attention on the Chesapeake Bay in Virginia. The French fleet got there ahead of the British troop ships from New York; a five-day naval battle left the French navy in clear control of the Virginia coast. This proved to be the decisive factor, because it eliminated the possibility of reinforcements for Cornwallis's army, dug in at Yorktown, and made rescue by the British navy impossible.

On land, General Cornwallis and his 7,500 troops faced a combined French and American army numbering more than 16,000. For twelve days, the Americans and French bombarded the British fortifications at Yorktown; Cornwallis ran low on food and ammunition. An American observer keeping a diary noted that "the enemy, from want of forage, are killing off their horses in great numbers. Six or seven hundred of these valuable animals have been killed, and their carcasses are almost continually floating down the river." Realizing that escape was impossible, Cornwallis signaled his intention to surrender. On October 19, 1781, he formally capitulated.

What began as a promising southern strategy in 1778 turned into a discouraging defeat by 1781. British attacks in the South had energized American resistance, as did the timely exposure of Benedict Arnold's treason. The arrival of the French fleet sealed the fate of Cornwallis at the battle of Yorktown, and major military operations came to a halt.

The Losers and the Winners

The surrender at Yorktown proved to be the decisive end to the war with Britain, but it took two years for the principals to realize that. Frontier areas in Kentucky, Ohio, and Illinois still blazed with battles and sieges pitting Americans against

Lafayette at Yorktown

An enthusiast for American liberty, the young French nobleman Lafayette came to the United States in 1777 at age twenty to volunteer his services to General Washington. After proving his leadership in several northern campaigns, he went to Virginia in 1781 to fight Cornwallis. In Richmond, he met James, a slave belonging to William Armistead, who loaned him to Lafayette. At the siege of Yorktown, James, pretending to be an escaped slave, infiltrated the British command, giving them misinformation and bringing crucial intelligence back to Lafayette. At the surrender, Cornwallis saw James at Lafayette's headquarters and realized he'd been had. The French artist Jean Baptiste Le Paon painted the two men in 1783 without ever having laid eyes on James. His heroic portrait focuses on Lafayette; James, with plumed hat, fancy improbable costume, and generic face, is a mere ornament to his white general. James obtained his freedom in 1786, after Lafayette wrote a letter on his behalf to the Virginia assembly. In honor of his friend, he took the name James Armistead Lafayette. Art Gallery, Williams Center, Lafayette College.

"The Ballance of Power," 1780

This cartoon was published in England soon after Spain and the Netherlands declared an alliance with France to support the war in America. On the left, Britannia, a female figure representing Great Britain, cannot be moved by all the lightweights on the right-hand side of the scale. France wears a ruffled shirt, Spain has a feather in his hat, and a Dutch boy has just hopped on, saying, "I'll do anything for Money." The forlorn Indian maiden, the standard icon representing America in the eighteenth century, sits on the scale, head in hand, wailing, "My Ingratitude is Justly punished." The poem printed below the cartoon predicts, "The Americans too will with Britons Unite." This fanciful prediction was punctured nine months after it appeared, when the British surrendered to the Americans and the French at Yorktown in 1781.

Print Collection, Miriam and Ira D. Wallach Division of Art, Prints, and Photographs, The New York Public Library, Astor, Lenox, and Tilden Foundations.

READING THE IMAGE: What does this cartoon reveal about British perceptions of the American Revolution?

CONNECTIONS: How did British attitudes toward the colonies contribute to the British defeat in the war?

FOR MORE HELP ANALYZING THIS IMAGE, see the visual activity for this chapter in the Online Study Guide at bedfordstmartins.com/roark.

---

various Indian tribes. The British army still occupied three coastal cities, including New York City with 13,000 soldiers, causing the Continental army at an augmented strength of 10,000 to remain in the field, stationed north of the city near West Point and Newburgh, New York. Occasional skirmishes broke out, like the one in which light infantryman Deborah Sampson saw action and sustained a wound, thereby revealing her cross-gender masquerade.

The peace treaty took six months to negotiate. Commissioners from America, Britain, and France met in Paris and worked out eighty-two articles of peace. The first article went to the heart of the matter: "His Britannic Majesty acknowledges the said United States to be free Sovereign and independent States." Other articles set the western boundary of the new country at the Mississippi River and guaranteed that creditors on both sides could collect debts owed them in sterling money, a provision especially important to British merchants. Britain agreed to withdraw its troops quickly; more than a decade later, this promise still had not been fully kept. The Treaty of Paris was signed on September 2, 1783.

Like the treaty ending the Seven Years' War, this treaty failed to recognize the Indians as players in the conflict. As one American told the Shawnee people, "Your Fathers the English have made Peace with us for themselves, but forgot you their Children, who Fought with them, and neglected you like Bastards." Indian lands were assigned to the victors as though they were uninhabited. Some Indian refugees fled west into present-day Missouri and Arkansas, and others, such as Joseph Brant's Mohawks, relocated to Canada. But significant numbers remained within the new United States, occupying their traditional homelands in areas west and north of the Ohio River. For them, the Treaty of Paris brought no peace at all; their longer war against the Americans would extend at least until 1795 and for some until 1813. The Indians' ally, Britain, conceded defeat, but the Indians did not.

With the treaty finally signed, the British began their evacuation of New York, Charleston, and Savannah, a process complicated by the sheer numbers involved—soldiers, fearful loyalists, and runaway slaves by the thousands. In New York City, more than 27,000 soldiers and 30,000 loyalists sailed on hundreds of ships for England in the late fall of 1783. In a final act of mischief, on the November day when the last ships left, the losing side raised the British flag at the southern tip of Manhattan, cut away the ropes used to hoist it, and greased the flagpole.

REVIEW   Why did the British southern strategy ultimately fail?

Conclusion: Why the British Lost

The British began the war for America convinced that they could not lose. They had the best-trained army and navy in the world; they were familiar with the landscape from the Seven Years' War; they had the willing warrior-power of most of the native tribes of the backcountry; and they easily captured every port city of consequence in America. Probably one-fifth of the population was loyalist, and another two-fifths were undecided. Why, then, did the British lose?

One continuing problem the British faced was the uncertainty of supplies. Unwilling to ravage the countryside, the army depended on a steady stream of supply ships from home. Insecurity about food helps explain their reluctance to pursue the Continental army aggressively. A further obstacle was their continual misuse of loyalist energies. Any plan to repacify the colonies required the cooperation of the loyalists, as well as new support from the many neutrals. But repeatedly, the British failed to back the loyalists, leaving them to the mercy of vengeful rebels. In the South, they allowed loyalist militias to engage in vicious guerrilla warfare that drove away potential converts among the rest of the population.

French aid looms large in any explanation of the British defeat. Even before the formal alliance, French artillery and ammunition proved vital for the Continental army. After 1780, the French army brought a new infusion of troops to a war-weary America, and the French navy made the Yorktown victory possible. Finally, the British abdicated civil power in the colonies in 1775 and 1776, when royal officials fled to safety, and they never really regained it. For seven years, the Americans created their own government structures, from the Continental Congress to local committees and militias. Staffed by many who before 1775 had been the political elites, these new government agencies had remarkably little trouble establishing their authority to rule. The basic British goal—to turn back the clock to imperial rule—receded into impossibility as the war dragged on.

The war for America had lasted just over six years, from Lexington to Yorktown; negotiations and the evacuation took two more. It profoundly disrupted the lives of Americans everywhere. It was a war for independence from Britain, but it was more. It was a war that required men and women to think about politics and the legitimacy of authority. The precise disagreement with Britain about representation and political participation had profound implications for the kinds of governance the Americans would adopt, both in the moment of emergency and in the longer run of the late 1770s and early 1780s when states began to write their constitutions. The rhetoric employed to justify the revolution against Britain put words such as *liberty*, *tyranny*, *slavery*, *independence*, and *equality* into common usage.

These words carried far deeper meanings than a mere complaint over taxation without representation. The Revolution unleashed a dynamic of equality and liberty that was largely unintended and unwanted by many of the American leaders of 1776. But that dynamic emerged as a potent force in American life in the decades to come.

Selected Bibliography

General Works

Edward Countryman, *The American Revolution* (1985).

Piers Mackesy, *The War for America, 1775-1783* (1964).

Gary B. Nash, *The Unknown American Revolution: The Unruly Birth of Democracy and the Struggle to Create America* (2005).

Ray Raphael, *A People's History of the American Revolution: How Common People Shaped the Fight for Independence* (2001).

Charles Royster, *A Revolutionary People at War: The Continental Army and American Character, 1775-1783* (1979).

Stanley Weintraub, *Iron Tears: America's Battle for Freedom, Britain's Quagmire: 1775-1783* (2005).

Gordon S. Wood, *The Radicalism of the American Revolution* (1992).

The Wartime Confederation and Its Leaders

Joseph J. Ellis, *His Excellency: George Washington* (2004).

John E. Ferling, *Setting the World Ablaze: Washington, Adams, Jefferson, and the American Revolution* (2000).

Eric Foner, *Tom Paine and Revolutionary America* (1976).

Edith Gelles, *Portia: The World of Abigail Adams* (1992).

Pauline Maier, *American Scripture: Making the Declaration of Independence* (1997).

Jackson Turner Main, *The Sovereign States, 1775-1783* (1973).

Jack N. Rakove, *The Beginnings of National Politics: An Interpretive History of the Continental Congress* (1979).

Campaigns, Battles, and Soldiers

Lawrence E. Babits, *A Devil of a Whipping: The Battle of Cowpens* (1998).

Wayne K. Bodle, *The Valley Forge Winter: Civilians and Soldiers in War* (2004).

W. Jeffrey Bolster, *Black Jacks: African American Seamen in the Age of Sail* (1998).

Edwin G. Burrows, *The Prisoners of New York* (2008).

Colin G. Calloway, *The American Revolution in Indian Country: Crisis and Diversity in Native American Communities* (1995).

E. Wayne Carp, *To Starve the Army at Pleasure: Continental Army Administration and American Political Culture, 1775-1783* (1984).

David Hackett Fischer, *Washington's Crossing* (2004).

Joseph R. Fischer, *A Well-Executed Failure: The Sullivan Campaign against the Iroquois, July–September 1779* (1997).

Sylvia Frey, *The British Soldier in America: A Social History of Military Life in the Revolutionary Period* (1965).

Robert Gross, *The Minutemen and Their World* (1976).

M. Thomas Hatley, *The Dividing Paths: Cherokees and South Carolinians through the Era of Revolution* (1993).

Sidney Kaplan and Emma Nogrady Kaplan, *The Black Presence in the Era of the American Revolution* (1989).

Lee Kennett, *The French Forces in America, 1780-1783* (1977).

Richard M. Ketchum, *Saratoga: Turning Point of America's Revolutionary War* (1997).

John Komlos, ed., *Stature, Living Standards, and Economic Development: Essays in Anthropometric History* (1994).

David G. Martin, *The Philadelphia Campaign: June 1777-1778* (2003).

James Kirby Martin, *Benedict Arnold, Revolutionary Hero: An American Warrior Reconsidered* (1997).

Holly A. Mayer, *Belonging to the Army: Camp Followers and Community during the American Revolution* (1996).

David McCullough, *1776* (2005).

John E. Walsh, *The Execution of Major André* (2001).

Alfred F. Young, *Masquerade: The Life and Times of Deborah Sampson, Continental Soldier* (2004).

▶ **For more books about topics in this chapter,** see the Online Bibliography at bedfordstmartins.com/roark.

▶ **For additional firsthand accounts of this period,** see Chapter 7 in Michael Johnson, ed., *Reading the American Past*, Fourth Edition.

▶ **For Web sites, images, and documents related to topics and places in this chapter,** visit bedfordstmartins.com/makehistory.

REVIEWING THE CHAPTER

Follow these steps to review and strengthen your understanding of the chapter.

STEP 1: *Study the **Key Terms** and **Timeline** to identify the significance of each item listed.*

STEP 2: *Answer the **Review Questions**, drawing on key terms and dates to support your answers.*

STEP 3: *Drawing on the Key Terms, Timeline, and Review Questions, answer the broader **Making Connections** questions.*

KEY TERMS

Who

Deborah Sampson (p. 213)
John Dickinson (p. 215)
George Washington (p. 215)
Thomas Jefferson (p. 215)
Thomas Gage (p. 218)
William Howe (p. 218)
George III (p. 220)
Thomas Paine (p. 220)
Abigail Adams (p. 220)
camp followers (p. 223)
Richard Montgomery (p. 225)
Benedict Arnold (pp. 225, 242)
Hessians (p. 227)
redcoats (p. 227)
Tories (p. 229)

Joseph Brant (Thayendanegea) (p. 232)
John Burgoyne (p. 236)
Horatio Gates (p. 237)
John Sullivan (p. 239)
White Eyes (p. 239)
Henry Clinton (p. 241)
Charles Cornwallis (p. 241)
Comte de Rochambeau (p. 244)

What

Second Continental Congress (p. 215)
Continental army (p. 215)
battle of Bunker Hill (p. 217)
smallpox (p. 218)
Olive Branch Petition (p. 220)
Common Sense (p. 220)

Declaration of Independence (p. 221)
battle of Long Island (p. 227)
Ladies Association (p. 229)
Fort Ticonderoga (p. 237)
Fort Stanwix (p. 237)
battle of Oriskany (p. 237)
battle of Saratoga (p. 238)
Valley Forge (p. 238)
Mohawk Valley (p. 239)
Fort Pitt (p. 239)
southern strategy (p. 241)
battle of Camden (p. 241)
West Point (p. 242)
battle of King's Mountain (p. 243)
battle of Yorktown (p. 244)
Treaty of Paris (p. 246)

TIMELINE

1775
• Second Continental Congress convenes.
• British win battle of Bunker Hill.
• King George rejects Olive Branch Petition.
• Americans lose battle of Quebec.

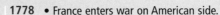

    1776
    • *Common Sense* published.
    • British evacuate Boston.
    • **July 4.** Congress adopts Declaration of Independence.
    • British take Manhattan.

        1777
        • British take Fort Ticonderoga.
        • Ambush at Oriskany.
        • Americans hold Fort Stanwix.
        • British occupy Philadelphia.
        • British surrender at Saratoga.
        • Continental army endures winter at Valley Forge.

            1778
            • France enters war on American side.
            • American militiamen destroy Mohawk chief Joseph Brant's village.
            • White Eyes negotiates treaty with Americans; later mysteriously dies.

REVIEW QUESTIONS

1. Why were many Americans reluctant to pursue independence from Britain? (pp. 215–22)

2. Why did the British exercise restraint in their efforts to defeat the rebellious colonies? (pp. 222–28)

3. How did the patriots promote support for their cause in the colonies? (pp. 228–36)

4. Why did the Americans need assistance from the French to ensure victory? (pp. 236–41)

5. Why did the British southern strategy ultimately fail? (pp. 241–46)

MAKING CONNECTIONS

1. Even before the colonies had committed to independence, they faced the likelihood of serious military conflict. How did they mobilize for war? In your answer, discuss specific challenges they faced, noting any unintended consequences of their solutions.

2. Congress's adoption of the Declaration of Independence confirmed a decisive shift in the conflict between the colonies and Britain. Why did the colonies make this decisive break in 1776? In your answer, discuss some of the arguments for and against independence.

3. The question of whether the colonists' loyalty would be to the new government or to the old king was pivotal during the Revolutionary War. Discuss the importance of loyalty in the outcome of the conflict. In your answer, consider both military and political strategy.

4. American colonists and British soldiers were not the only participants in the Revolutionary War. Discuss the role of Native Americans in the war. How did they shape the conflict? What benefits did they hope to gain? Did they succeed?

▶ FOR PRACTICE QUIZZES, A CUSTOMIZED STUDY PLAN, AND OTHER STUDY TOOLS, see the Online Study Guide at bedfordstmartins.com/roark.

1779 • Militias attack Cherokee settlements in far western North Carolina.
• Americans destroy forty Iroquois villages in New York.
• Americans take Forts Kaskaskia and Vincennes.

1780 • Philadelphia Ladies Association raises money for soldiers.
• British take Charleston, South Carolina.
• French army arrives in Newport, Rhode Island.
• British win battle of Camden.
• Benedict Arnold exposed as traitor.
• Americans win battle of King's Mountain.

1781 • British forces invade Virginia.
• French fleet blockades Chesapeake Bay.
• Cornwallis surrenders at Yorktown; concedes British defeat.

1783 • Treaty of Paris ends war; United States gains all land to Mississippi River.

A CHAIR FOR THE NEW NATION

George Washington sat in this splendid and
unique chair for three hot months in the summer
of 1787, presiding over a convention of fifty-five
delegates engaged in writing a document that
would define the government of the United
States. Made of mahogany and topped with a
carved sun painted in gold, the chair signaled
dignity and respect for Washington's role.
Mercifully, a padded leather seat provided
him with some comfort as he sat for long
hours. At just over six feet, Washington was a
tall man by the standards of his day. Even so,
this chair was sufficiently tall (five feet) that his
head did not obscure the gold embellishment.
After weeks of serious debate and heated disagreement, most of the delegates lined up on
the last day of the convention to sign the new
Constitution of the United States. Among them
was the ever-observant Benjamin Franklin.
James Madison took note of Franklin's words
during the signing: "Whilst the last members
were signing it Doctr. FRANKLIN looking towards
the Presidents Chair, at the back of which a rising sun happened to be painted, observed to a
few members near him, that Painters had found
it difficult to distinguish in their art a rising from
a setting sun. I have said he, often and often in
the course of the Session, and the vicissitudes
of my hopes and fears as to its issue, looked at
that behind the President without being able to
tell whether it was rising or setting: But now at
length I have the happiness to know that it is a
rising and not a setting Sun."

Independence National Historic Park.

Building a Republic

1775–1789

■ **The Articles of
Confederation** 252
Congress, Confederation, and
the Problem of Western Lands 253
Running the New Government 255

■ **The Sovereign States** 255
The State Constitutions 255
Who Are "the People"? 256
Equality and Slavery 258
Legal Changes to Slavery,
1777–1804 259

■ **The Confederation's
Problems** 262
Financial Chaos and Paper Money 263
The Treaty of Fort Stanwix 264
Land Ordinances and
the Northwest Territory 265
Shays's Rebellion, 1786–1787 269

■ **The United States
Constitution** 271
From Annapolis to Philadelphia 271
The Virginia and New Jersey Plans 274
Democracy versus Republicanism 275

■ **Ratification of
the Constitution** 275
The Federalists 276
The Antifederalists 277
The Big Holdouts:
Virginia and New York 278

■ **Conclusion: The "Republican
Remedy"** 282

J AMES MADISON GRADUATED from Princeton College in New Jersey in 1771, not knowing what to do next with his life. Certainly, the twenty-year-old had an easy fallback position. As the firstborn son of a wealthy plantation owner, he could return home to the foothills of Virginia and wait to inherit substantial land and a large force of slaves. But Madison was an intensely studious young man, uninterested in farming and reluctant to leave the collegiate environment. Five years at boarding school had given him fluency in Greek, Latin, French, and mathematics, and three years at Princeton had acquainted him with the great thinkers, both ancient and modern. Driven by a thirst for learning, young Madison slept only five hours a night, perhaps undermining his health. Protesting that he was too ill to travel, he hung around Princeton for six months after graduation.

In 1772, he returned home, still adrift. He tried studying law, but his unimpressive oratorical talents discouraged him. Instead, he swapped reading lists and ideas about political theory by letter with a Princeton classmate, prolonging his student life. While Madison struggled for direction, the powerful winds before the storm of the American Revolution swirled through the colonies. In May 1774, he traveled north to deliver his brother to boarding school and was in Philadelphia when the startling news broke that Britain had closed the port of Boston in retaliation for the destruction of the tea. Turbulent protests over the Coercive Acts turned him into a committed revolutionary.

Back in Virginia, Madison joined his father on the newly formed committee of public safety. For a few days in early 1775, the twenty-four-year-old took up musket practice, but his continued poor health ruled out the soldier's life. His special talent lay in the science of politics, and in the spring of 1776, he gained election to the Virginia Convention, a Revolutionary assembly replacing the defunct royal government. The convention's main task was to hammer out a state constitution with innovations such as frequent elections and limited executive power. Shy, self-effacing, and still learning the ropes, Madison mostly stayed on the sidelines, but Virginia's elder statesmen noted the young man's logical, thoughtful contributions. When his county failed to return him to the assembly in the next election, he was appointed to the governor's council, where he spent two years gaining experience in a wartime government.

In early 1780, Madison represented Virginia in the Continental Congress. Not quite twenty-nine, unmarried, and supported by his father's money, he was free of the burdens that made distant political service difficult for so many others. He stayed in the North for three years, working with men such as Alexander Hamilton of New York and Robert Morris of Pennsylvania as the congress wrestled with the chaotic economy and the ever-precarious war effort. In one crisis, Madison's negotiating skills proved crucial: He broke the deadlock over the ratification of the Articles of Confederation by arranging for the cession of Virginia's vast western lands. Those lands would soon appear on maps as the Northwest Territory, calling forth a series of western land ordinances, planned out by Madison's friend Thomas Jefferson, that exemplified the promise and high hopes for the future of the new confederation government. But more often, service in the congress proved frustrating to Madison because the confederation government seemed to lack essential powers, chief among them the power to tax.

Madison resumed a seat in the Virginia assembly in 1784. But he did not retreat to a local point of view as so many other state politicians of the decade did. The difficult economic hardships created by heavy state taxation programs—which in Massachusetts led to a full-fledged rebellion against state government—spurred Madison to pursue means to strengthen the government of the thirteen new states. In this, he was in the minority: It was by no means clear to many Americans that the Articles of Confederation needed any major revamping.

Madison thought it did. He worked hard to bring about an all-state convention in Philadelphia in the late spring of 1787, where he took the lead in steering the delegates to a complete rewrite of the structure of the national government, investing it with considerably greater powers. True to form, Madison spent the months before the convention in feverish study of the great thinkers he had read in college, searching out the best way to constitute a government on **republican** principles. His lifelong passion for scholarly study, seasoned by a dozen years of energetic political experience, paid off handsomely. The United States Constitution was the result.

By the end of the 1780s, James Madison had had his finger in every kind of political pie, on the local, state, confederation, and finally national level. He had transformed himself from a directionless and solitary youth into one of the leading political thinkers of the Revolutionary period. His personal history over the 1780s was deeply entwined with the path of the emerging United States.

The Articles of Confederation

For five years after declaring independence, the Second Continental Congress continued to meet in Philadelphia and other cities without any formal constitutional basis. Delegates first had to work out a plan of government that embodied Revolutionary principles. With monarchy gone,

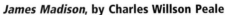

James Madison, **by Charles Willson Peale**
A short and slight man, Madison appeared younger than he was. This miniature portrait, made in 1783 when he was thirty-two, shows him with natural hair (no wig) and a boyishly smooth face. Madison commissioned the portrait on the occasion of his first serious romance. The Philadelphia artist Charles Willson Peale painted matching miniatures of Madison and his fiancée, Kitty Floyd, the sixteen-year-old daughter of a New York delegate to the Continental Congress. Madison and his Virginia friend Thomas Jefferson both boarded with the Floyd family while the congress met in Philadelphia. Jefferson, a very recent widower, encouraged the shy Madison and assured him that Kitty "will render you happier than you can possibly be in a single state." Madison's portrait was mounted in a brooch (note the pin sticking out on the right) so that his lady love might wear it on her person; the back of the brooch held a neatly plaited lock of Madison's hair. The companion miniature of Kitty no longer holds a lock of her hair, if it ever did, for Kitty soon jilted Madison for a suave younger man and returned the Madison miniature to the grieving bachelor. Eleven years later, Madison tried romance again when New York congressman Aaron Burr introduced him to a Virginia widow named Dolley Payne Todd, seventeen years his junior. Madison was forty-three, and Todd was twenty-six; they married four months after meeting.
Library of Congress.

where would sovereignty lie? What would be the nature of representation? Who would hold the power of taxation? Who should vote; who should rule? The resulting plan, called the Articles of Confederation, proved to be surprisingly difficult to implement, mainly because the thirteen states had serious disagreements about how to manage areas to the west whose political ownership was contested. Once the Articles were finally ratified and the confederation was formally constituted, that arena of government seemed to many to be far less relevant or interesting than the state governments.

Congress, Confederation, and the Problem of Western Lands

Only after declaring independence did the Continental Congress turn its attention to creating a written document that would specify what powers the congress had and by what authority it existed. There was widespread agreement on key government powers: pursuing war and peace, conducting foreign relations, regulating trade, and running a postal service. But there was serious disagreement about the powers of the congress over the western boundaries of the states. Virginia and Connecticut, for example, had old colonial charters that located their western boundaries at the Mississippi River. States without extensive land claims insisted on redrawing those colonial boundaries.

This was no mere quarrel over lines on a map. In the 1780s, more than 100,000 Americans had moved west of the Appalachian Mountains, and another 100,000 were moving from eastern towns to newly opened land in northern Vermont and western New York and Pennsylvania, as well as to Kentucky, Georgia, and beyond. Who owned the land, who protected it, who governed it? These were major and pressing questions.

For more than a year, the congress tinkered with drafts of the Articles of Confederation, reaching agreement only in November 1777. The Articles defined the union as a loose confederation of states, characterized as "a firm league of friendship" existing mainly to foster a common defense. The structure of the government paralleled that of the existing Continental Congress. There was no national executive (that is, no president) and no national judiciary. The congress was composed of two to seven delegates from each state, selected annually by the state legislatures and prohibited from serving more than three years out of any six. The actual number of delegates was not critical, since each state delegation cast a single vote.

Routine decisions in the congress required a simple majority of seven states; for momentous decisions, such as declaring war, nine states needed to agree. To approve or amend the Articles required the unanimous consent both of the thirteen state delegations and of the thirteen state legislatures. The congressional delegates undoubtedly thought they were guaranteeing that no individual state could be railroaded by the other twelve in fundamental constitutional matters. But what this requirement really did was to hamstring the government. Any single state could—and did—hold the rest of the country hostage to its demands.

On the delicate question of taxes, needed to finance the war, the Articles provided an ingenious but ultimately troublesome solution. Each state was to contribute in proportion to the property value of the state's land. Large and populous states would give more than small or sparsely populated states. The actual taxes would be levied by the state legislatures, not by the congress, to preserve the Revolution's principle of taxation only by direct representation. However, no mechanism was created to compel states to contribute their fair share.

The lack of centralized authority in the confederation government was exactly what many state leaders wanted in the late 1770s. A league of states with rotating personnel, no executive branch, no power of taxation, and a requirement of unanimity for any major change seemed to be a good way to avoid the kind of tyranny experienced under the rule of the British monarchy.

Yet there were problems. The requirement for unanimous approval, for example, stalled the acceptance of the Articles for four additional years. The key dispute involved the problem of land claims west of the existing states (Map 8.1, page 254). Five states, all lacking land claims—Maryland, Delaware, New Jersey, Rhode Island, and Pennsylvania—insisted that the congress control western lands as a national domain that would eventually constitute new states. The other eight states refused to yield their colonial-era claims and opposed giving the congress power to alter boundaries. In all the heated debate, few seemed to remember that those same western lands were inhabited by many thousands of Indians not party to the disputes.

The eight land-claiming states were ready to sign the Articles of Confederation in 1777.

MAP 8.1   Cession of Western Lands, 1782–1802
The thirteen new states found it hard to ratify the Articles of Confederation without settling their conflicting land claims in the west, an area larger than the original states and occupied by Indian tribes. The five states objecting to the Articles' silence over western lands policy were Maryland, Delaware, New Jersey, Rhode Island, and Pennsylvania.

READING THE MAP: Which states had the largest claims on western territory? What disputed territory became the fourteenth state?
CONNECTIONS: In what context did the first dispute regarding western lands arise? How was it resolved? Does the map suggest a reason why Pennsylvania, a large state, joined the four much smaller states on this issue?

FOR MORE HELP ANALYZING THIS MAP, see the map activity for this chapter in the Online Study Guide at bedfordstmartins.com/roark.

Three states without claims, Rhode Island, Pennsylvania, and New Jersey, eventually capitulated and signed, "not from a Conviction of the Equality and Justness of it," said a New Jersey delegate, "but merely from an absolute Necessity there was of complying to save the Continent." But Delaware and Maryland continued to hold out, insisting on a national domain policy. In 1779, the disputants finally compromised: Any land a state volunteered to relinquish would become the national domain. When James Madison and Thomas Jefferson ceded

Virginia's huge land claim in 1781, the Articles were at last unanimously approved.

The western lands issue demonstrated that powerful interests divided the thirteen new states. The apparent unity of purpose inspired by fighting the war against Britain papered over sizable cracks in the new confederation.

Running the New Government

No fanfare greeted the long-awaited inauguration of the new government. The congress continued to sputter along, its problems far from solved by the signing of the Articles. Lack of a quorum often hampered day-to-day activities. The Articles required representation from seven states to conduct business and a minimum of two men from each state's delegation. But some days, fewer than fourteen men in total showed up. State legislatures were slow to select delegates, and many of those appointed were reluctant to attend, especially if they had wives and children at home. Consequently, some of the most committed delegates were young bachelors, such as James Madison, and men in their fifties and sixties whose families were grown, such as Samuel Adams.

Many politicians preferred to devote their energies to state governments, especially when the congress seemed deadlocked or, worse, irrelevant. It also did not help that the congress had no permanent home. During the war, when the British army threatened Philadelphia, the congress relocated to small Pennsylvania towns such as Lancaster and York and then to Baltimore. After hostilities ceased, the congress moved from Trenton to Princeton to Annapolis to New York City.

To address the difficulties of an inefficient congress, executive departments of war, finance, and foreign affairs were created in 1781 to handle purely administrative functions. When the department heads were ambitious—as was Robert Morris, a wealthy Philadelphia merchant who served as superintendent of finance—they could exercise considerable executive power. The Articles of Confederation had deliberately refrained from setting up an executive branch, but a modest one was being invented by necessity.

REVIEW Why was the confederation government's authority so limited?

The Sovereign States

In the first decade of independence, the states were sovereign and all-powerful. Relatively few functions, such as declaring war and peace, had been transferred to the confederation government. As Americans discarded their British identity, they thought of themselves instead as Virginians or New Yorkers or Rhode Islanders. Familiar and close to home, state governments claimed the allegiance of citizens and became the arena in which the Revolution's innovations would first be tried. States defined who was a voter, and they also defined who would be free. The question of slavery quickly became a front-burner issue, as all the states were forced to figure out whether or how Revolutionary ideals could coexist with lifelong bondage for African Americans. Northern states had more success ending inconsistency than did southern states, where slavery was deeply entrenched in the economy.

The State Constitutions

In May 1776, the congress recommended that all states draw up constitutions based on "the authority of the people." By 1778, ten states had done so, and three more (Connecticut, Massachusetts, and Rhode Island) had adopted and updated their original colonial charters. Having been denied unwritten British **liberties**, Americans wanted written contracts that guaranteed basic principles.

A shared feature of all the state constitutions was the conviction that government ultimately rests on the consent of the governed. Political writers in the late 1770s embraced the concept of republicanism as the underpinning of the new governments. Republicanism meant more than popular elections and representative institutions. For some, republicanism invoked a way of thinking about who leaders should be: autonomous, virtuous citizens who placed civic values above private interests. For others, it suggested direct **democracy**, with nothing standing in the way of the will of the people. For all, it meant government that promoted the people's welfare.

Widespread agreement about the virtues of republicanism went hand in hand with the idea that republics could succeed only in relatively small units. Distant government could easily become tyrannical; that was the lesson of the 1760s. Nearly every state continued the colonial practice of a two-chamber assembly but greatly augmented the powers of the lower house, since it was closer to the people. Two states, Pennsylvania and Georgia, abolished the more elite upper house altogether, and most states severely limited the term and powers of the governor. The lower houses of the state legislatures, with annual elections and guaranteed rotation in office, could be most responsive to popular majorities. If a representative displeased his constituents, he could be out of office in a matter of months. James Madison's unsuccessful attempt to win reelection to the Virginia assembly in 1777 offers an example of quick rotation in office. He was sure he had lost because he had failed to campaign in the traditional style, with the abundant liquor and glad-handing that his constituents had come to expect. Shy and retiring, Madison was not capable of running for election in this manner. His series of increasingly significant political posts from 1778 to 1787 all came as a result of appointment, not popular election.

Six of the state constitutions included bills of rights—lists of basic individual liberties that government could not abridge. Virginia debated and passed the first bill of rights in June 1776, and many of the other states borrowed from it. Its language bears a close resemblance to the wording of the Declaration of Independence, which Thomas Jefferson was drafting that same June in Philadelphia: "That all men are by nature equally free and independent, and have certain inherent rights, of which, when they enter into a state of society, they cannot by any compact deprive or divest their posterity; namely, the enjoyment of life and liberty, with the means of acquiring and possessing property, and pursuing and obtaining happiness and safety." Along with these inherent rights went more specific rights to freedom of speech, freedom of the press, and trial by jury.

> Virginia passed the first bill of rights in June 1776. Its language bears a close resemblance to the wording of the Declaration of Independence: "That all men are by nature equally free and independent, and have certain inherent rights."

Who Are "the People"?

When the Continental Congress called for state constitutions based on "the authority of the people," and when the Virginia bill of rights granted "all men" certain rights, who was meant by "the people"? Who exactly were the citizens of this new country, and how far would the principle of democratic government extend? Different people answered these questions differently, but in the 1770s certain limits to full political participation by all Americans were widely agreed upon.

One limit was defined by property. In nearly every state, candidates for the highest offices had to meet substantial property qualifications. In Maryland, a candidate for governor had to be worth £5,000, a large sum of money. Voters in Maryland had to own fifty acres of land or £30, a barrier to one-third of adult white males. In the most democratic state, Pennsylvania, voters and candidates needed to be taxpayers, owning enough property to owe taxes. Only property owners were presumed to possess the necessary independence of mind to make wise political choices. Are not propertyless men, asked John Adams, "too little acquainted with public affairs to form a right judgment, and too dependent upon other men to have a will of their own?" In addition, the requirement drew logic from the claim that propertyless men should not have a voice in decisions about tax levies since they paid no taxes.

Property qualifications probably **disfranchised** from one-quarter to one-half of adult white males in all the states. Not all of them took their nonvoter status quietly. One Maryland man wondered what was so special about being worth £30: "Every poor man has a life, a personal liberty, and a right to his earnings; and is in danger of being injured by government in a variety of ways." Why then restrict such a man from voting? Others pointed out that propertyless men were fighting and dying in the Revolutionary War; surely they were expressing an active concern about politics. Finally, a few radical voices challenged the notion that owning property transformed men into good citizens. Perhaps it did the opposite: The richest men might well be greedy and selfish and therefore bad citizens. But ideas like this were outside the mainstream. The writers of the new constitutions, themselves men of property, viewed the right to own and preserve property as a central principle of the Revolution.

Another exclusion from voting—women—was so ingrained that few stopped to question it. Yet the logic of allowing propertied females to vote did occur to at least two well-placed women. Abigail Adams wrote to her husband, John, in 1782, "Even in the freest countrys our property is subject to the controul and disposal of our partners, to whom the Laws have given a

A Possible Voter in Essex County, New Jersey
Mrs. Elizabeth Alexander Stevens was married to John Stevens, a New Jersey delegate to the Continental Congress in 1783. Widowed in 1792, she would have then been eligible to vote in state elections according to New Jersey's unique enfranchisement of property-holding women. Mrs. Stevens's family was a prominent one. Her father had been surveyor general of New Jersey and New York; her husband was active in politics and was secretary to the governor of New York. Her son John was the inventor of steamboat and locomotive innovations; her daughter Mary married Robert R. Livingston of New York, also a delegate to the Continental Congress and a man who later built a fortune in steamboating. Essex County, where Elizabeth Stevens lived, was said to be the place where female suffrage was exercised most actively. This portrait, done around 1793–1794, represents the most likely face of that rare bird, the eighteenth-century female voter. The widow Stevens died in 1799, before suffrage was redefined to be the exclusive right of males.
New Jersey Historical Society.

his reply does: "You complain that widows are not represented, and that being temporary possessors of the estates, ought not to be liable to the tax." Yet, he continued, women would be "out of character . . . to press into those tumultuous assemblies of men where the business of choosing representatives is conducted."

Only three states specified that voters had to be male, so powerful was the unspoken assumption that only men could vote. Still, in one state, small numbers of women began to turn out at the polls in the 1780s. New Jersey's constitution of 1776 enfranchised all free inhabitants worth more than £50, language that in theory opened the door to free blacks as well as unmarried women who met the property requirement. (Married women owned no property, for by law their husbands held title to everything, and few free blacks would meet the property qualification.) Little fanfare accompanied this radical shift, and some historians have inferred that the inclusion of unmarried women and blacks was an oversight. Yet other parts of the **suffrage** clause pertaining to residency and property were extensively debated when it was put in the state constitution, and no objections were raised at that time to its gender- and race-free language. Thus other historians have concluded that the law was intentionally inclusive. In 1790, a revised election law used the words *he or she* in reference to voters, making woman suffrage explicit. As one New Jersey legislator declared, "Our Constitution gives this right to maids or widows *black* or *white*." However, that legislator was complaining, not bragging, so his expansive words should not be taken as a sign that egalitarian suffrage was an accepted fact.

In 1790, only about 1,000 free black adults of both sexes lived in New Jersey, a state with a population of 184,000. The number of unmarried adult white women was probably also small, mainly widows. In view of the property requirement, the voter bloc enfranchised under this law could not have been decisive in elections. Still, this highly unusual situation lasted until 1807, when a new state law specifically disfranchised both blacks and women. Henceforth, independence of mind, that essential precondition of voting, was redefined to be sex- and race-specific.

In the 1780s, voting everywhere was class-specific, due to the property restrictions. John Adams urged the framers of the Massachusetts constitution not even to discuss the scope of suffrage but simply to adopt the traditional colonial property qualifications. If suffrage is brought up

sovereign Authority. Deprived of a voice in Legislation, obliged to submit to those Laws which are imposed upon us, is it not sufficient to make us indifferent to the publick Welfare?" A wealthy Virginia widow named Hannah Corbin wrote to her brother, Richard Henry Lee, to complain of her taxation without the corresponding representation. Her letter no longer exists, but

for debate, he warned, "there will be no end of it. New claims will arise; women will demand a vote; lads from twelve to twenty-one will think their rights not enough attended to; and every man who has not a farthing, will demand an equal voice with any other." Adams was astute enough to anticipate complaints about excluding women, youths, and poor men from political life, but it did not even occur to him to worry about another group: slaves.

Equality and Slavery

Restrictions on political participation did not mean that propertyless people enjoyed no civil rights and liberties. The various state bills of rights applied to all individuals who had, as the Virginia bill so carefully phrased it, "enter[ed] into a state of society." No matter how poor, a free person was entitled to life, liberty, property, and freedom of conscience. Unfree people, however, were another matter.

The author of the Virginia bill of rights was George Mason, a plantation owner with 118 slaves. When he penned the sentence "All men are by nature equally free and independent," he

> When George Mason penned the sentence "All men are by nature equally free and independent," he did not have slaves in mind; he instead was asserting that Americans (meaning white Americans) could not be denied the liberties of British citizens.

did not have slaves in mind; he instead was asserting that Americans (meaning white Americans) were the equals of the British and could not be denied the liberties of British citizens. But other Virginia legislators worried that the words could be construed to apply to slaves. So they added the phrase specifying that rights belonged only to people who had entered civil society. As one wrote, with relief, "Slaves, not being constituent members of our society, could never pretend to any benefit from such a maxim."

One month later, the Declaration of Independence used essentially the same phrase about equality, this time without the modifying clause about entering society. Two state constitutions, for Pennsylvania and Massachusetts, also included the inspiring language about equality without limiting it, as had Virginia. When the Massachusetts constitution was sent around to be ratified, town by town, the town of Hardwick suggested rewording the phrase "All men are born free and equal" to read "All men, whites and blacks, are born free and equal." The clear endorsement of racial equality was not implemented.

The only other state to draft language about equality was Vermont, whose 1777 constitution explicitly outlawed slavery and based its logic on the equality phrase of the Declaration. (Vermont had very few slaves within its borders and did not win recognition as a state until 1791, due to competing claims to its territory by New York and New Hampshire.) Reluctance to include equality language in other state bills of rights and constitutions indicates an uneasy recognition that such language might indeed threaten the institution of slavery.

Paul Cuffe's Silhouette
Captain Paul Cuffe of Martha's Vineyard, off the Massachusetts coast, was the son of a Wampanoag Indian woman and an African man named Kofi, who had purchased his own freedom from a Quaker owner. Young Paul took his father's African name for his last name, though with a different spelling. He studied navigation and went to sea at age sixteen during the American Revolution, enduring several months of imprisonment by the British. After the war, he and his brother John protested that Massachusetts taxed free blacks who lacked the privilege of voting, in other words taxation without representation. In his thirty-year career as a shipbuilder and master mariner, Cuffe traveled extensively. By 1812, when this engraving with silhouette was made, Cuffe had explored the African country of Sierra Leone as a possible site for resettlement of American blacks and had met with African kings, English dukes, and an American president.
Library of Congress.

Northern enslaved blacks challenged their bondage in petitions citing Revolutionary ideals of equality. In 1773, four enslaved men in Massachusetts petitioned the state legislature for their "natural right" to freedom, offering a plan to resettle in Africa. Three years later, several more Massachusetts slaves presented their claim to a "natural & unalienable right to that freedom which the great Parent of the Universe hath bestowed equally on all mankind." Their modest request, for freedom for their children at age twenty-one, met with rejection. In 1779, similar petitions in Connecticut and New Hampshire also were unsuccessful. In 1780, seven Massachusetts freemen, including the mariner brothers Paul and John Cuffe, refused to pay taxes for three years on the grounds that they could not vote and so were not represented. The Cuffe brothers went to jail for tax evasion, but their petition to the state legislature spurred the extension of suffrage to taxpaying free blacks in 1783.

Legal Changes to Slavery, 1777–1804

Another way to bring the issue before lawmakers was to sue in court. In 1781, a woman called Mum Bett was the first to win freedom in a Massachusetts court, basing her case on the just-passed state constitution that declared "all men are born free and equal." (See "Seeking the American Promise," page 260.) Later that year, another Massachusetts slave, Quok Walker, charged his master with assault and battery, arguing that he was de facto a free man under that same constitutional phrase. Walker won the case and was set free, a decision confirmed in an appeal to the state's superior court in 1783. Several similar cases followed, and by 1789 slavery had been effectively abolished by a series of judicial decisions in Massachusetts.

Legal wheels sometimes turned far more slowly. Pennsylvania politicians ended slavery by a gradual **emancipation** law in 1780. Only infants born to a slave mother on or after March 1, 1780, would be freed, but not until age twenty-eight. Thus no current slave in Pennsylvania would in theory gain freedom until 1808; well into the nineteenth century, those blacks born before 1780 would still be slaves. Not until 1847 did Pennsylvania fully abolish slavery. But slaves did not wait for such slow implementation. Untold numbers in Pennsylvania simply ran away from their owners and claimed their freedom, sometimes with the help of sympathetic whites. One estimate holds that more than half of young slave men in Philadelphia took flight in the 1780s and joined the ranks of free blacks. Owners generally did not pursue them. By 1790, free blacks outnumbered slaves in Pennsylvania by nearly two to one.

Rhode Island and Connecticut adopted gradual emancipation laws in 1784. In 1785, New York expanded the terms under which individual owners could free slaves, but only in 1799 did the state adopt a gradual emancipation law; New Jersey followed suit in 1804. These were the two northern states with the largest number of slaves: New York in 1800 with 20,000, New Jersey with more than 12,000. In contrast, slaves in Pennsylvania numbered just 1,700. Gradual emancipation illustrates the tension between radical and conservative implications of republican ideology. Republican government protected people's liberties and property, yet slaves were both people and property. Gradual emancipation balanced the civil rights of blacks and the property rights of their owners by delaying the promise of freedom.

South of Pennsylvania, in Delaware, Maryland, and Virginia, where slavery was so important to the economy, emancipation bills were rejected. All three states, however, eased legal restrictions and allowed individual acts of emancipation for adult slaves below the age of forty-five under new manumission laws passed in 1782 (Virginia), 1787 (Delaware), and 1790 (Maryland). By 1790, close to 10,000 newly freed Virginia slaves had formed local free black communities complete with schools and churches.

In the deep South—the Carolinas and Georgia—freedom for slaves was unthinkable among whites. Yet several thousand slaves had defected to the British during the war,

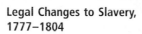

Legal Changes to Slavery, 1777–1804

BRITISH
NORTH AMERICA

MAINE
(MASS.)

L. Ontario

VT. 1777
N.H. 1783

N.Y. 1799

MASS. 1783
CONN. 1784

Hudson R.

R.I. 1784

PA. 1780

N.J. 1804

MD. 1790

DEL. 1787

VA. 1782

N.C.

ATLANTIC OCEAN

Abolished slavery

Gradual emancipation

Individual cases of emancipation

A Slave Sues
for Her Freedom

The stirring language about liberty, equality, and freedom that inspired American revolutionaries in the 1770s was written into many state constitutions in the 1780s. Yet unfree people, held as property, had little recourse to challenge their status.

Massachusetts law presented an unusual opportunity because it recognized slaves as persons with legal standing to bring lawsuits against whites. Less than 2 percent of the state's population consisted of slaves, numbering well under four thousand and living preponderantly in the coastal cities. Before 1780, some thirty Massachusetts slaves had sued for their freedom, but their cases had turned on particular circumstances, such as an owner's unfulfilled promise to emancipate or a dispute over a slave's parentage. In 1780, a new Massachusetts state constitution boldly declared that "all men are born free and equal," opening the door to lawsuits based on a broad right to freedom. The first to bring suit under the new constitution was Bett, a thirty-year-old slave living in the western Massachusetts town of Sheffield.

Born of African parents in the early 1740s, Bett and her sister Lizzie grew up as slaves in Claverack, New York, in the wealthy Dutch American family of Pieter Hogeboom. When Hogeboom died in 1758, Bett and Lizzie were transported twenty-four miles east into Massachusetts, where Hogeboom's daughter Hannah lived with her husband, Colonel John Ashley. A town tax list of 1771 shows that Colonel Ashley owned five slaves. Clusters of slaves appeared in western Massachusetts towns such as Sheffield and Stockbridge because of a pattern of eastward migration of both whites and blacks from the relatively slave-dense Hudson River region of New York. Sheffield, a town with two hundred to three hundred families, probably had three dozen to four dozen unfree blacks. Bett was not an isolated slave.

Colonel Ashley was the richest man in Sheffield, and among the oldest, having been born in 1709. His title derived from militia service; he was also a judge and a respected leader in the patriot cause. He was known as a kind and gentle man, but as one account suggests, his wife was "a shrew untamable" and "the most despotic of mistresses." One day, Hannah Ashley became enraged with Lizzie and heaved a hot kitchen shovel at her. Bett interceded to protect her sister, sustaining a burn on her arm that left a lifetime scar.

On another occasion, in 1773, Bett was, in her own words, "keepin'

still and mindin' things" while she served refreshments to a dozen white men gathered at her master's house to draw up a protest petition against the British. Colonel Ashley took the lead in drafting a set of resolutions, the first of which read: "Resolved, That mankind in a state of nature are equal, free, and independent of each other, and have a right to the undisturbed enjoyment of their lives, their liberty and property." The import of their discussion was well noted by Bett.

In the fall of 1780, Bett overheard conversations at the Ashleys' about the new Massachusetts state constitution. Bett pondered the words proclaiming equality and reasonably concluded that they applied to her. She sought out a young lawyer named Theodore Sedgwick, who had been present at the petition meeting in 1773. Sedgwick, Sheffield's representative in the new Massachusetts legislature, filed a writ in April 1781 requesting the recovery of unlawfully held property—in this case, the human property of Bett and a second plaintiff owned by Ashley, a man identified only as Brom, "a Negro man" and a "labourer." (Brom, a common Dutch nickname for Abraham, probably also came from Claverack.) Ashley contested the writ, and the case, officially called *Brom and Bett v. J. Ashley, Esq.*, went to court.

When the case came to trial, a jury agreed that Bett and Brom were entitled to freedom and ordered Ashley to pay each plaintiff 30 shillings in damages, as well as all the

and between 3,000 and 4,000 shipped out of Savannah and Charleston, destined for freedom. Adding northern blacks evacuated from New York City in 1783, the probable total of emancipated blacks who left the United States was between 8,000 and 10,000. Some went to Canada, some to England, and some to Sierra Leone, on the west coast of Africa. Many hundreds took refuge with the Seminole and Creek Indians, becoming permanent members of their communities in Spanish Florida and western Georgia.

court costs. The brief court records do not reveal the legal arguments or evidence presented, but the later boast among Sedgwick descendants was that Theodore Sedgwick had invoked the Massachusetts constitution to argue that slavery could not exist in the state.

Bett chose a new name to go with her new status: Elizabeth Freeman. She left Colonel Ashley's employ and became a paid housekeeper in the Sedgwick family, virtually raising the children when their mother became incapacitated by mental illness. "Her spirit spurned slavery," a Sedgwick daughter wrote, offering this quotation from Bett as evidence: "Anytime, anytime while I was a slave, if one minute's freedom had been offered to me, and I had been told I must die at the end of that minute, I would have taken it—just to stand one minute, I would have taken it just to stand one minute on God's earth a free woman—I would."

The Sedgwicks were especially grateful to Freeman for her commanding presence of mind during Shays's Rebellion in 1786 (see page 269). Because Sedgwick represented the legal elite of the county, he was the target of hostile crowd action. Freeman was home alone when insurgents demanded entry, searching for Sedgwick and for valuables to plunder. Unable to prevent their entry, Freeman let the dissidents in but followed the men around with a large shovel and threatened to flatten anyone who damaged any property.

Freeman died in 1829 and was buried in the Sedgwick family plot. Her will, signed with an X, indicates that she had children and grandchildren. A Sedgwick son paid her this tribute: "If there could be a practical refutation of the imagined superiority of our race to hers, the life and character of this woman would afford that refutation. . . . Even in her humble station, she had, when occasion required it, an air of command which conferred a degree of dignity."

Freeman's lawsuit of 1781 inspired others to sue, and in 1783, the judge of the Massachusetts Supreme Court in another case declared that "slavery is in my judgment as effectively abolished as it can be by the granting of rights and privileges" in the state constitution. It took several more legal challenges and additional time for that news to trickle out—no newspaper reported the change—but the slow erosion of slavery in Massachusetts gradually picked up speed as blacks demanded manumission or wages for work, or simply walked away from their masters. In 1790, the federal census listed 5,369 "other free persons" (that is, nonwhites) in the state and not a single slave.

Elizabeth Freeman

Solo portraits of African American women in the early Republic are incredibly rare. This 1811 watercolor of Mum Bett was the work of Susan Ridley Sedgwick, wife of one of the Sedgwick sons. It indicates the importance of Freeman to the Sedgwick household. Upon her death, one of the Sedgwick sons wrote: "She was born a slave and remained a slave for nearly thirty years. She could neither read nor write, yet in her own sphere she had no superior nor equal. . . . She was the most efficient helper, and the tenderest friend." The blue dress, gathered at the bustline and topped by a white neckerchief, was standard dress for an older woman of the late eighteenth century but out-of-date in 1811. (Compare the earlier portrait of Mrs. Stevens on page 257.) Freeman very likely lacks a corset, an essential undergarment surely worn by the white women in the Sedgwick household. In this she was lucky.
Massachusetts Historical Society.

All these instances of emancipation were gradual, small, and certainly incomplete, but their symbolic importance was enormous. Every state from Pennsylvania north acknowledged explicitly that slavery was fundamentally inconsistent with Revolutionary ideology. On some level, white southerners also understood this, but their inability to imagine a free biracial society prevented them from taking much action. George Washington owned 390 slaves and freed not one of them in the 1780s, even when his friend the French general Lafayette urged him to do so as a

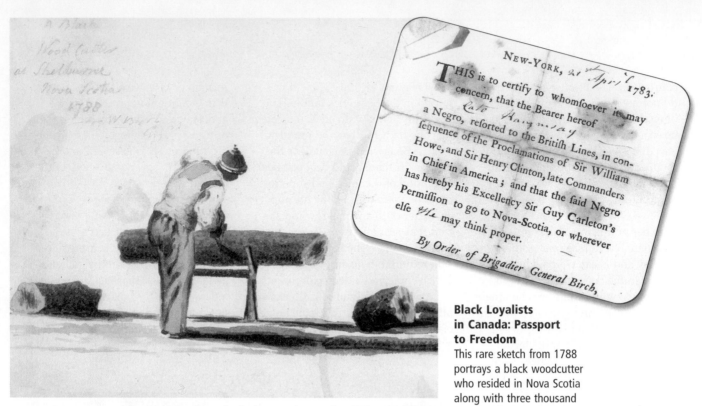

Black Loyalists in Canada: Passport to Freedom
This rare sketch from 1788 portrays a black woodcutter who resided in Nova Scotia along with three thousand other black loyalists who had escaped to northeastern Canada between 1783 and 1785. The inset is a passport issued by the British high command to Cato Rammsay, permitting him to leave New York in 1783. Very few of the Nova Scotia refugees were able to acquire land, and after 1786 the British authorities stopped provisioning them. Most, like the man pictured here, were forced to become servants or day laborers for whites. Low wages created dissatisfaction, and racial tensions mounted. In 1791–1792, nearly a third of the black refugees in Nova Scotia left for Sierra Leone, in West Africa, where British officials promised them land and opportunities for self-rule.
Sketch: William Booth, National Archives of Canada C-401621; Passport: Nova Scotia Archives & Records Management.

model for others. In his will, written in 1799, the guilt-stricken Washington provided for the eventual freedom of his slaves—but only after his wife, Martha, died. One year after his death, Martha Washington freed them, preferring loss of income to the uneasy situation of her life being the only barrier to her slaves' freedom.

Emancipation in the 1780s, limited as it was, shows that the phrase of the Declaration of Independence—"all men are created equal"— was beginning to acquire real force as a basic principle. Yet a geographical pattern was taking shape: From the 1780s on, the North was associated with freedom and the South with slavery, with profound consequences for the next two centuries of American history.

REVIEW   How did states determine who would be allowed to vote?

The Confederation's Problems

After the Revolution concluded in 1783, the confederation government turned to its three main and interrelated areas of concern: paying down the large war debt, making formal peace with the Indians, and dealing with western settlement. The debt was a vexing problem, since the Articles of Confederation lacked the power to tax. Western lands provided a promising source of income, once it was clear who owned them and who could sell them. Virginia's cession of its vast western territory in 1781 had opened the way for the ratification of the Articles, but there were still conflicts over territory, most crucially in the area that is now western New York, where Massachusetts and tribes of the Iroquois confederacy had legitimate claims. In the years from 1784 to 1786, the congress struggled mightily with these issues. Some leaders were gripped by a sense of crisis, fearing that the Articles of

Confederation were too weak. Others defended the Articles as the best guarantee of individual liberty, because real governance occurred at the state level, closer to the people. A major outbreak of civil disorder in western Massachusetts quickly crystallized the debate and propelled the critics of the Articles into decisive and far-reaching action.

Financial Chaos and Paper Money

Seven years of war produced a chaotic economy in the 1780s. The confederation and the individual states had run up huge war debts, financed by printing paper money and borrowing from private sources. Some $400 million to $500 million in paper currency had been injected into the economy, and prices and wages fluctuated wildly. Private debt and rapid expenditure flourished, as people quickly bought what goods they could with the depreciating currency. In many localities, legal suits between debtors and creditors quadrupled over prewar levels. A laborer in central Massachusetts, William Manning, described the economic trouble brewing: "With the prices of labor and produce falling very fast, creditors began calling for old debts and saying that they would not take payment in paper money. . . . Property was selling almost every day by execution [court-ordered foreclosures] for less than half its value. The jails were crowded with debtors." A serious postwar depression settled in by the mid-1780s and did not lift until the 1790s.

The confederation government itself was in a terrible financial fix. Continental dollars had lost almost all value: In 1781, it took 146 of them to buy what one dollar had bought in 1775. Desperate times required desperate measures. The congress chose Robert Morris, Philadelphia merchant and newly reelected delegate, to be superintendent of finance. Morris had a gift for financial dealings but had resigned from the congress in 1778 amid accusations that he had unfairly profited from public service. Now his talents were again needed, and from 1781 to 1784, he took charge of the confederation's economic problems.

To augment the government's revenue, Morris first proposed a 5 percent impost (an import tax). Since the Articles of Confederation did not authorize taxation, an amendment was needed, but unanimous agreement proved impossible.

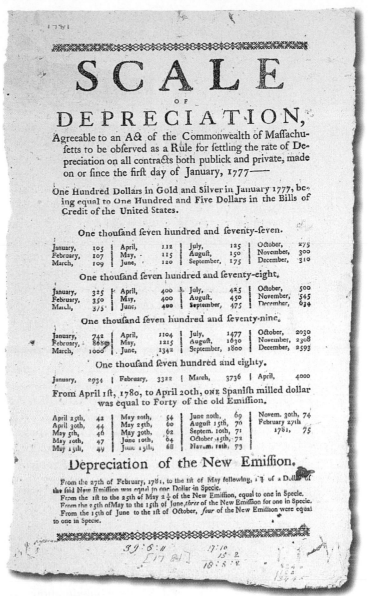

Scale of Depreciation

This chart shows the declining monthly value of two emissions of paper dollars from January 1777 to October 1781 as stipulated by the government of Massachusetts. From early in 1777 to April 1780, the paper dollar dropped to a fortieth of its value, requiring $4,000 paper dollars to equal the buying power of $100 in gold or silver. Starting in April 1780, the chart pegged the paper dollar against the Spanish dollar coin, at a 1:40 ratio, and by the end of February 1781, the ratio fell to 1:75. Then a new emission of paper money in February tried to restore the U.S. dollar to the value of the Spanish dollar, and it too fell in four months to a 1:4 ratio. Such a chart was needed when debtors and creditors settled accounts contracted at one time and paid off later in greatly depreciated dollars.

Courtesy, American Antiquarian Society.

READING THE IMAGE: What level of arithmetic and chart-reading skills were required to read this chart? Notice the handwritten figuring at the bottom of the chart. Do these arithmetic notations and operations look familiar to you?

CONNECTIONS: How easy would it have been to keep one's head above water in an economy with such fast currency depreciation?

FOR MORE HELP ANALYZING THIS IMAGE, see the visual activity for this chapter in the Online Study Guide at bedfordstmartins.com/roark.

Rhode Island and New York, whose bustling ports provided ample state revenue, preferred to keep their money and simply refused to agree to a national impost.

Morris's next idea was the creation of the Bank of North America. This private bank would enjoy a special relationship with the confederation, holding the government's **hard money** (gold and silver coins) as well as private deposits, and providing it with short-term loans. The bank's contribution to economic stability came in the form of banknotes, pieces of paper inscribed with a dollar value. Unlike paper money, banknotes were backed by hard money in the bank's vaults and thus would not depreciate. Morris hoped this form of money would retain value; the congress agreed and voted to approve the bank in 1781. But the bank had limited success curing the confederation's economic woes because it issued very little currency; its charter was allowed to expire in 1786.

If Morris could not resuscitate the economy in the 1780s, probably no one could have done it. Because the Articles of Confederation reserved most economic functions to the states, the congress was helpless to tax trade, control inflation, curb the flow of state-issued paper money, or pay the mounting public debt. However, the confederation had one source of enormous potential wealth: the huge western territories, attractive to the fast-growing white population but inhabited by Indians.

The Treaty of Fort Stanwix

Since the Indians had not been party to the Treaty of Paris of 1783, the confederation government needed to formalize a treaty with them to conclude hostilities and secure land cessions. The most pressing problem was the land inhabited by the Iroquois League of Six Nations, now urgently claimed by the states of New York and Massachusetts based on colonial charters granted by the king (see Map 8.1). Both states hoped to ease heavy war debts by selling land to speculators and settlers. The Massachusetts claim was legally stronger because its charter predated New York's by four decades, but New York felt entitled because it bordered the territory. The dispute in the congress between the two states was so tense that it struck a southern delegate as "the seeds of dissension which I think will not end without a civil war."

The congress tried to solve the dispute by calling the Six Nations to a meeting in October

Cornplanter
Cornplanter, whose Indian name was Kaintwakon ("what one plants"), headed the Seneca delegation at Fort Stanwix in 1784. Raised fully Indian, he was the son of a fur trader from a prominent Dutch family in Albany, New York, and a highborn Seneca woman of the Wolf Clan. Evidently, the Dutch trader did not stick around for long, as Cornplanter never learned either Dutch or English. During the Revolution, when his father was married to a German woman in the Mohawk Valley and faced capture by Indians, Cornplanter recognized him by his name and released him. The Seneca chief sat for this formal portrait in full finery in the 1790s, wearing a plumed headdress, an earring and nose ring, a gorget around his neck, and metal armbands. Despite the feathered tobacco pipe, smoke wafting from it, Cornplanter lived to be about 90, dying in 1836.
© Collection of the New-York Historical Society.

1784 at Fort Stanwix, on the upper reaches of the Mohawk River. The Articles of Confederation gave the congress (as opposed to individual states) the right to manage diplomacy, war, and "all affairs with the Indians, not members of any of the States." But New York leaders seized on this ambiguous language to claim that the Iroquois were in fact "members" of their state and that New York alone should negotiate with them.

To scoop both the congress and Massachusetts, New York's governor called his own meeting with the Iroquois at Fort Stanwix in

September. Suspecting that New York's claim to authority might be superseded by the congress, the most important chiefs declined to come. Instead, they sent deputies who lacked the authority to negotiate. The Mohawk leader Joseph Brant shrewdly identified the problem of divided authority that afflicted the confederation government: "Here lies some Difficulty in our Minds, that there should be two separate bodies to manage these Affairs." No deal was struck with New York.

Three weeks later, U.S. commissioners opened proceedings at Fort Stanwix with the Seneca chief Cornplanter and Captain Aaron Hill, a Mohawk leader. Six hundred Indians from the six tribes attended the meeting. The U.S. commissioners came with a security detail of one hundred New Jersey militiamen.

The Americans demanded a return of prisoners of war; recognition of the confederation's authority to negotiate, rather than that of individual states; and an all-important cession of a strip of land from Fort Niagara due south, which established U.S.-held territory adjacent to the border with Canada. This crucial change enclosed the Iroquois land within the United States and made it impossible for the Indians to claim to be *between* the United States and Canada. When the tribal leaders balked, one of the commissioners sternly replied, "You are mistaken in supposing that, having been excluded from the treaty between the United States and the King of England, you are become a free and independent nation and may make what terms you please. It is not so. You are a subdued people."

In the end, the treaty was signed, gifts were given, and six high-level Indian hostages were kept at the fort awaiting the release of the American prisoners taken during the war, most of whom were women and children. In addition, a significant side deal sealed for $5,000 the release of much of the Seneca tribe's claim to the Ohio Valley to the United States. This move was a major surprise and disappointment to the Delaware, Mingo, and Shawnee Indians who lived there. In the months to come, the Iroquois and other tribes not at the meeting tried to disavow the Treaty of Fort Stanwix as a document signed under coercion by virtual hostages. But the confederation government

ignored those complaints and made plans to survey and develop the Ohio Territory.

New York's governor understood that the confederation government's power to implement the treaty terms it had gained was limited. The U.S. government's financial coffers were nearly empty, and its leadership was stretched. So New York quietly began surveying and then selling the very land it had failed to secure by individual treaty with the Indians. As that fact became generally known, it pointed up the weakness of the confederation government. One Connecticut leader wondered, "What is to defend us from the ambition and rapacity of New-York, when she has spread over that vast territory, which she claims and holds? Do we not already see in her the seeds of an over-bearing ambition?"

> When tribal leaders balked, one of the commissioners replied, "You are mistaken in supposing that . . . you are become a free and independent nation and may make what terms you please. It is not so. You are a subdued people."

Land Ordinances and the Northwest Territory

The congress ignored western New York and turned instead to the Ohio Valley to make good on the promise of western expansion. Delegate Thomas Jefferson, charged with drafting a policy, proposed dividing the territory north of the Ohio River and east of the Mississippi—called the Northwest Territory—into nine new states with evenly spaced east-west boundaries and townships ten miles square. He at first advocated giving the land to settlers, rather than selling it, arguing that future property taxes on the improved land would be payment enough. Jefferson's aim was to encourage rapid and democratic settlement, to build a nation of freeholders (as opposed to renters), and to avoid land speculation. Jefferson also insisted on representative governments in the new states; they would not become colonies of the older states. Finally, Jefferson's draft prohibited slavery in the ten new states.

The congress adopted parts of Jefferson's plan in the Ordinance of 1784: the rectangular grid, the ten states, and the guarantee of self-government and eventual statehood. What the congress found too radical was the proposal to give away the

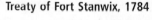

Treaty of Fort Stanwix, 1784

Lake Ontario

Fort Niagara

CANADA

Lake Erie

NEW YORK

IROQUOIS LANDS

Ceded to U.S., 1784

PENNSYLVANIA

Thomas Jefferson, by John Trumbull

This miniature of Thomas Jefferson at age forty-five was painted in 1788 by an American artist who visited Jefferson during his diplomatic assignment in Paris. Jefferson requested three replicas of the miniature to bestow as gifts. One went to his daughter Martha, another to a very attractive (but married) American woman in London, and the third to the also married Maria Cosway, a British artist with whom Jefferson shared an intense infatuation during his stay in France. A widower, Jefferson never remarried, but a scandal over his private life erupted in 1802, when a journalist charged that he had fathered several children by his slave Sally Hemings. In 1998, a careful DNA study concluded that uniquely marked Jefferson Y chromosomes were common to male descendants in both the Hemings and Jefferson lines. The DNA evidence, when combined with historical evidence about Jefferson's whereabouts at the start of each of Hemings's six pregnancies, makes a powerful case that Jefferson fathered some and probably all of her children. What cannot be known is the nature of the relationship between the two. Was it coerced or voluntary, or somewhere in between? Was a voluntary relationship even possible, given the power differential between master and slave? In all his voluminous writings, Jefferson left no comment about Sally Hemings, and the record on her side is entirely mute. Two of her four surviving children were allowed to slip away to freedom in the 1820s; the other two were freed in Jefferson's will.

Monticello/Thomas Jefferson Memorial Foundation, Inc.

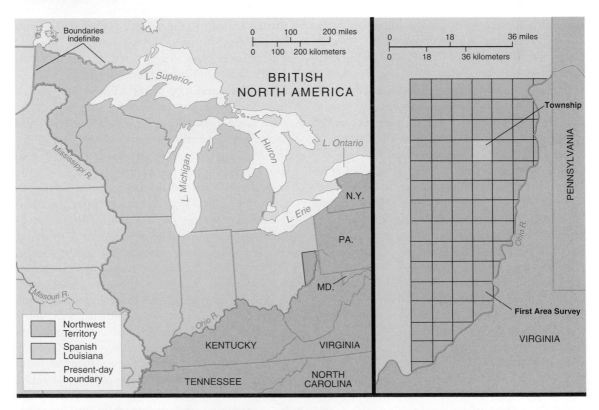

MAP 8.2 The Northwest Territory and Ordinance of 1785

Surveyors mapping the eastern edge of the Northwest Territory followed the Ordinance of 1785, using the stars as well as poles and chains (standard surveying equipment) to run long boundary lines. The result was a blanket of six-mile-square townships, subdivided into one-mile squares each containing sixteen 40-acre farms. Jefferson got his straight lines and right angles after all. Compare this map to his on page 267.

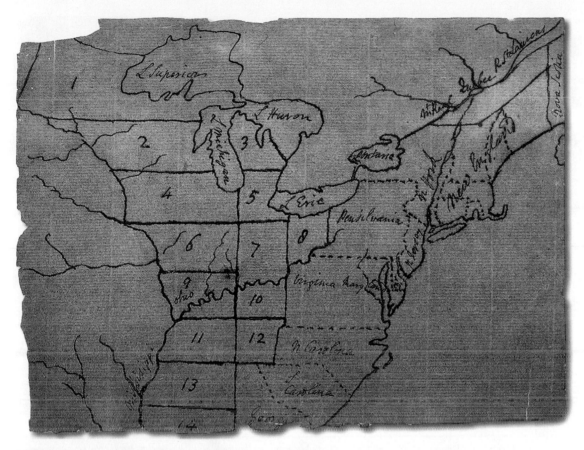

Jefferson's Map of the Northwest Territory

Thomas Jefferson sketched out borders for nine new states in his initial plan for the Northwest Territory in 1784 and additional anticipated states below the Ohio River. Straight lines and right angles held a strong appeal for him. But such regularity ignored inconvenient geographic features such as rivers and even more inconvenient political features such as Indian territorial claims, most unlikely to be ceded by treaty in orderly blocks. Jefferson also submitted ten distinctive names for the states. Number 9, for example, was Polypotamia, "land of many rivers" in Greek. Other proposed names were Sylvania, Michigania, Assenisipia, and Metropotamia. William L. Clements Library.

READING THE IMAGE: What does this map indicate about Jefferson's vision of the Northwest Territory?
CONNECTIONS: What were the problems with Jefferson's design for the division of the territory? Why did the congress alter it in the land ordinances of 1784, 1785, and 1787?

FOR MORE HELP ANALYZING THIS IMAGE, see the visual activity for this chapter in the Online Study Guide at bedfordstmartins.com/roark.

---

land; the national domain was the confederation's only source of independent wealth. The slavery prohibition also failed, by a vote of seven to six states.

A year later, the congress revised the legislation with procedures for mapping and selling the land. The Ordinance of 1785 called for three to five states (instead of ten) divided into townships six miles square, further divided into thirty-six sections of 640 acres, or one mile square, each section enough for four family farms (Map 8.2). Property was thus reduced to

precise and easily mappable squares. One lot in each township was earmarked for educational purposes. Land would be sold by public auction, at a minimum price of one dollar an acre, with highly desirable land bid up for more. Two further restrictions applied: The minimum purchase was 640 acres, and payment must be in hard money or in certificates of debt from Revolutionary days. This effectively meant that the land's first owners would be prosperous speculators. The grid of invariant squares further enhanced speculation, allowing buyers and

View of a Farm Near Detroit, 1789
In French, *Detroit* means "the narrows," in this case the narrow river connecting two of Michigan's
Great Lakes, Lake Huron and Lake Erie. Detroit was founded in 1701 by the French military leader
Cadillac, who recognized a good place for a fort when he saw one. The settlement stayed small for
another century, passing from French to British and then to American hands. In 1783, it became
part of the Northwest Territory—in theory. In reality, the British failed to vacate until the Jay Treaty
of 1795 forced them out. This watercolor scene painted on a piece of silk by Anne Powell shows
a farm near Detroit's fort. Settlers in eighteenth-century clothing stroll around a pond. Judge William
Dummer Powell, Anne's brother, came to Detroit from Canada in 1789 to preside over a British court.
The Powells were Boston-born loyalists who fled north during the Revolution. When the Americans
took over the fort and the village, the Powells moved back to Canada.
Royal Ontario Museum.

sellers to operate without ever setting foot on the
acreage. The commodification of land had been
taken to a new level.

Speculators usually held the land for resale
rather than inhabiting it. Thus they avoided
direct contact with the most serious obstacle to settlement: the dozens of Indian tribes that claimed
the land as their own. The treaty signed at Fort
Stanwix in 1784 was followed by the Treaty of

Fort McIntosh in 1785, which similarly coerced
partial cessions of land from the Delaware,
Huron, and Miami tribes. Finally, in 1786, a
united Indian meeting near Detroit issued an ul-
timatum: No cession would be valid without
unanimous consent of the tribes. The Indians advised the United States to "prevent your surveyors and other people from coming upon our side
of the Ohio river." For two more decades, violent

Indian wars in Ohio and Indiana would continue to impede white settlement (see chapter 9).

In 1787, a third land act, called the Northwest Ordinance, set forth a three-stage process by which settled territories would advance to statehood. First, the congress would appoint officials for a sparsely populated territory who would adopt a legal code and appoint local magistrates to administer justice. When the free male population of voting age and landowning status (fifty acres) reached 5,000, the territory could elect its own legislature and send a nonvoting delegate to the congress. When the population of voting citizens reached 60,000, they could write a state constitution and apply for full admission to the Union. At all three territorial stages, the inhabitants were subject to taxation to support the Union, in the same manner as were the original states.

The Northwest Ordinance of 1787 was perhaps the most important legislation passed by the confederation government. It ensured that the new United States, so recently released from colonial dependency, would not itself become a colonial power at least not with respect to white citizens. The mechanism it established allowed for the successful and orderly expansion of the United States across the continent in the next century.

Nonwhites were not forgotten or neglected in the 1787 ordinance. The brief document acknowledged the Indian presence in the Northwest Territory and promised that "the utmost good faith shall always be observed towards the Indians; their lands and property shall never be taken from them without their consent; and, in their property, rights, and liberty, they shall never be invaded or disturbed, unless in just and lawful wars authorized by Congress." The 1787 ordinance further pledged that "laws founded in justice and humanity, shall from time to time be made for preventing wrongs being done to them, and for preserving peace and friendship with them." These promises were full of noble intentions, but they were not generally honored in the decades to come.

Jefferson's original and remarkable suggestion to prohibit slavery in the Northwest Territory resurfaced in the 1787 ordinance, passing this time without any debate. Probably the addition of a fugitive slave provision in the act set southern congressmen at ease: Escaped slaves caught north of the Ohio River would be returned south. The ordinance thus acknowledged and supported slavery even as it prohibited it in one region. Further, abundant territory south of the Ohio remained available for the spread of slavery. Still, the prohibition of slavery in the Northwest Territory perpetuated the dynamic of gradual emancipation in the North. North-South sectionalism based on slavery was slowly taking shape.

Shays's Rebellion, 1786–1787

Without an impost amendment, and with public land sales projected but not yet realized, the confederation turned to the states in the 1780s to contribute revenue voluntarily. Struggling with their own war debts, most state legislatures were reluctant to tax their constituents too heavily. Massachusetts, however, had a fiscally conservative legislature, dominated by the coastal commercial centers. For four years, the legislature passed tough tax laws that called for payment in hard money, not cheap paper. Farmers in the western two-thirds of the state found it increasingly difficult to comply and repeatedly petitioned against what they called oppressive taxation. In July 1786, when the legislature adjourned having yet again ignored their complaints, dissidents held a series of conventions and called for revisions to the state constitution to promote democracy, eliminate the elite upper house, and move the capital farther west in the state.

> The Northwest Ordinance of 1787 promised that "the utmost good faith shall always be observed towards the Indians; their lands and property shall never be taken from them without their consent."

Still unheard in Boston, the dissidents targeted the county courts, the local symbol of state authority. In the fall of 1786, several thousand armed men marched on courthouses in six Massachusetts counties and forced bewildered judges to close their courts until the state constitution was revised. Sympathetic local militias did not intervene. The insurgents were not predominantly poor or debt-ridden farmers; they included veteran soldiers and officers in the Continental

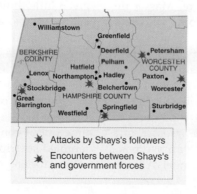

Shays's Rebellion, 1786–1787

* Attacks by Shays's followers
* Encounters between Shays's and government forces

Two Rebel Leaders and a Silver Bowl for an Anti-Shays General
A Boston almanac of 1787 yields the only rough depiction of Daniel Shays
in existence. Shays is standing with another rebel leader, Job Shattuck, from
the town of Groton. This particular almanac series was quite pro-Constitution in
1788, so very likely this picture was intended to mock the rebels by showing them
in fancy uniforms and armed with swords, trappings beyond their presumed lowly
means. The silver bowl was a present to an official general, William Shepard of Springfield,
who honored his victory over the insurgents. Presentational silver conveyed a double message: It announced
gratitude and praise in engraved words, and it transmitted considerable monetary value in the silver itself.
General Shepard could display his trophy on a shelf, use it as a punch bowl, will it to descendants to keep
his moment of fame alive, or melt it down in hard times.
Bowl: Yale University Art Gallery, Mabel Brady Garvan Collection; Illustration: National Portrait Gallery, Smithsonian Institution/Art Resource, NY.

army as well as town leaders. One was a farmer and onetime army captain, Daniel Shays, from the town of Pelham.

The governor of Massachusetts, James Bowdoin, who had once organized protests against British taxes, now characterized the western dissidents as illegal rebels. He vilified Shays as the chief leader, and a Boston newspaper claimed Shays planned to burn Boston to the ground and overthrow the government, clearly an overreaction. Another former radical, Samuel Adams,

> Benjamin Franklin shrewdly observed that in 1776, Americans had feared "an excess of power in the rulers" but now the problem was perhaps "a defect of obedience" in the subjects.

took the extreme position that "the man who dares rebel against the laws of a republic ought to suffer death." Those aging revolutionaries had given little thought to the possibility that popular majorities, embodied in a state legislature, could seem to be just as oppressive as monarchs. The dissidents challenged the assumption that popularly elected governments would always be fair and just.

Members of the Continental Congress worried that the Massachusetts insurgency was spinning out of control. In October, the congress attempted to triple the size of the federal army, calling for 660 new recruits from Massachusetts and another 560 from the rest of New England; fewer than 100 enlisted in the troubled state. So Governor Bowdoin raised a private army, gaining the services of some 3,000 by paying them bounties provided by wealthy and fearful Boston merchants (and later repaid by the state).

In January 1787, the insurgents learned of the private army marching their way, and 1,500 of them moved swiftly to capture a federal armory in Springfield to gain weapons. But a militia band loyal to the state government beat them to the weapons facility and met their attack with gunfire; 4 rebels were killed and another 20 wounded. The final and bloodless encounter came at Petersham, where Bowdoin's army surprised the rebels on a freezing February morning and took 150 prisoners; the others fled into the woods. Shays took off for Canada and other leaders left the state, but more than 1,000 dissidents were rounded up and jailed.

In the end, 2 men were executed for rebellion; 16 more sentenced to hang were reprieved at the last moment on the gallows. Some 4,000 men gained leniency by confessing their misconduct and swearing an oath of allegiance to the state. A special Disqualification Act prohibited the penitent rebels from voting, holding public office, serving on juries, working as schoolmasters, or operating taverns for up to three years.

Shays's Rebellion caused leaders throughout the country to worry about the confederation's ability to handle civil disorder. Inflammatory Massachusetts newspapers wrote about bloody mob rule; perhaps, some feared, similar "combustibles" in other states were awaiting the spark that would set off a dreadful political conflagration. New York lawyer John Jay wrote to George Washington, "Our affairs seem to lead to some crisis, some revolution—something I cannot foresee or conjecture. I am uneasy and apprehensive; more so than during the war." Benjamin Franklin, in his eighties, shrewdly observed that in 1776, Americans had feared "an excess of power in the rulers" but now the problem was perhaps "a defect of obedience" in the subjects. Among such leaders, the sense of crisis in the confederation had greatly deepened.

REVIEW Why did farmers in western Massachusetts revolt against the state legislature?

The United States Constitution

Shays's Rebellion provoked an odd mixture of fear and hope that the government under the Articles of Confederation was losing its grip on power. A small circle of Virginians decided to try one last time to augment the powers granted to the government by the Articles. Their call for a meeting to discuss trade regulation led, more quickly than they could have imagined in 1786, to a total reworking of the national government.

From Annapolis to Philadelphia

The Virginians took their lead from James Madison, now thirty-five and a member of the Virginia assembly. Madison convinced the confederation congress to allow a meeting of delegates at Annapolis, Maryland, in September 1786, to try again to revise the trade regulation powers of the Articles, but only five states participated. Like Madison, the dozen men who attended felt a foreboding of crisis, and they rescheduled the meeting for Philadelphia in May 1787. The congress reluctantly endorsed the Philadelphia meeting and limited its scope to "the sole and express purpose of revising the Articles of Confederation." But at least one representative at the Annapolis meeting had more ambitious plans. Alexander Hamilton of New York hoped the Philadelphia meeting would do whatever was necessary to strengthen the federal government. Hamilton got his wish, as the meeting soon turned into a constitutional convention.

Hamilton was, by nature, suited for such bold steps. The illegitimate son of a poor mother in the West Indies, he trained as a bookkeeper and prospered under the intellectual mentorship of a local minister. In 1773, the bright lad greatly impressed an American trader, who sent him to New York City for a college education. Hamilton soon got swept up in the military enthusiasm of 1776 and by 1777 had joined George Washington's staff, serving at the general's side through much of the Revolution. After the war, he studied law, married into a New York merchant family, and sat in the Continental Congress for two years. Despite his stigmatized and impoverished childhood, the aspiring Hamilton identified with the elite classes and their fear of democratic disorder.

City Tavern

Philadelphia's City Tavern, built in 1773, became a favorite gathering place for political delegates who traveled to that city for the Continental Congress. Taverns provided important public meeting spaces for business and social functions; they were critical nodes on the information network of the day, the place to learn news from travelers, newspapers, or local gossip. John Adams called the City Tavern "the most genteel one in America." Here, in the Long Room on the second floor, delegates toasted each other on the first anniversary of the Declaration of Independence, July 4, 1777. The men who wrote the Constitution in the summer of 1787 took meals and drinks at the tavern, using dinner plates like the ones shown here. This engraving and others like it aided in the complete reconstruction of the tavern on its original site in the 1970s. Today, it is open to the public as a period restaurant, complete with staff in costume.

Illustration: Rare Book Department, The Free Library of Philadelphia; Plates: Independence National Historic Park.

The Pennsylvania Statehouse
The constitutional convention assembled at the Pennsylvania statehouse to sweat out the summer of 1787. Despite the heat, the delegates nailed the windows shut to eliminate the chance of being heard by eavesdroppers, so intent were they on secrecy. The statehouse, built in the 1740s to house the colony's assembly, accommodated the Continental Congress at various times in the 1770s and 1780s. The building is now called Independence Hall, in honor of the signing of the Declaration of Independence there in 1776.
Historical Society of Pennsylvania.

The fifty-five men who assembled at Philadelphia in May 1787 were generally those who had already concluded that there were weaknesses in the Articles of Confederation. Few attended who were opposed to revising the Articles. Patrick Henry, author of the Virginia Resolves in 1765 and more recently state governor, refused to go to the convention, saying he "smelled a rat." Rhode Island refused to send delegates. Two New York representatives left in dismay in the middle of the convention, leaving Alexander Hamilton as the sole delegate from New York.

This gathering of white men included no **artisans** or day laborers or even farmers of middling wealth. Two-thirds of the delegates were lawyers. The majority had served in the confederation congress and knew its strengths and weaknesses; half had been officers in the Continental army. Seven men had been governors of their states and knew firsthand the frustrations of thwarted executive power. A few elder statesmen attended, such as Benjamin Franklin and George Washington, but on the whole, the delegates were young, like Madison and Hamilton.

The Virginia and New Jersey Plans

The convention worked in secrecy, so the men could freely explore alternatives without fear that their honest opinions would come back to haunt them. The Virginia delegation first laid out a fifteen-point plan for a complete restructuring of the government. This Virginia Plan was a total repudiation of the principle of a confederation of states. Largely the work of Madison, the plan set out a three-branch government composed of a two-chamber legislature, a powerful executive, and a judiciary. It practically eliminated the voices of the smaller states by pegging representation in both houses of the congress to population. The theory was that government operated directly on people, not on states. Among the breathtaking powers assigned to the congress were the rights to veto state legislation and to coerce states militarily to obey national laws. To prevent the congress from having absolute power, the executive and judiciary could jointly veto its actions.

In mid-June, a delegate from New Jersey, after caucusing with delegates from other small states, unveiled an alternative proposal. The New Jersey Plan, as it was called, maintained the existing single-house congress of the Articles of Confederation in which each state had one vote. Acknowledging the need for an executive, it created a plural presidency to be shared by three men elected by the congress from among its membership. Where it sharply departed from the existing government was in the sweeping powers it gave to the new congress: the right to tax, to regulate trade, and to use force on unruly state governments. In favoring national power over **states' rights**, it aligned itself with the Virginia Plan. But the New Jersey Plan retained the confederation principle that the national government was to be an assembly of states, not of people.

For two weeks, delegates debated the two plans, focusing on the key issue of representation. The small-state delegates conceded that one house in a two-house legislature could be apportioned by population, but they would never agree that both houses could be. Madison was equally vehement about bypassing representation by state, which he viewed as the fundamental flaw in the Articles.

> Using "all other Persons" as a substitute for "slaves" indicates the discomfort delegates felt in acknowledging in the Constitution the existence of slavery.

The debate seemed deadlocked, and for a while the convention was "on the verge of dissolution, scarce held together by the strength of a hair," according to one of the delegates. Only in mid-July did the so-called Great Compromise break the stalemate and produce the basic structural features of the emerging United States Constitution. Proponents of the competing plans agreed on a bicameral legislature. Representation in the lower house, the House of Representatives, would be apportioned by population, and representation in the upper house, the Senate, would come from all the states equally. Instead of one vote per state in the upper house, as in the New Jersey Plan, the compromise provided two senators who voted independently.

Representation by population turned out to be an ambiguous concept once it was subjected to rigorous discussion. Who counted? Were slaves, for example, people or property? As people, they would add weight to the southern delegations in the House of Representatives, but as property they would add to the tax burdens of those states. What emerged was the compromise known as the three-fifths clause: All free persons plus "three-fifths of all other Persons" constituted the numerical base for the apportionment of representatives.

Using "all other Persons" as a substitute for "slaves" indicates the discomfort delegates felt in acknowledging in the Constitution the existence of slavery. The words *slave* and *slavery* appear nowhere in the document, but slavery figured in two other places besides the three-fifths clause. Trade regulation, for example, a power of the new House of Representatives, naturally included regulation of the slave trade. In euphemistic language, a compromise between southern and northern states specified that "the Migration or Importation of such Persons as any of the States now shall think proper to admit, shall not be prohibited by the Congress prior to the Year one thousand eight hundred and eight." A third provision guaranteed the return of fugitive slaves: "No person, held to Service or Labour in one State, under the Laws thereof, escaping into another, shall, in Consequence of any Law or Regulation therein, be discharged from such Service or Labour but shall be delivered up on Claim of the party to whom such Service or Labour may be due." Slavery was nowhere named, but it was recognized, guaranteed, and thereby perpetuated by the U.S. Constitution.

Democracy versus Republicanism

The delegates in Philadelphia made a distinction between *democracy* and *republicanism* new to American political vocabulary. Pure democracy was now taken to be a dangerous thing. As a Massachusetts delegate put it, "The evils we experience flow from the excess of democracy." The delegates still favored republican institutions, but they created a government that gave direct voice to the people only in the House and that granted a check on that voice to the Senate, a body of men elected not by direct popular vote but by the state legislatures. Senators served for six years, with no limit on reelection; they were protected from the whims of democratic majorities, and their long terms fostered experience and maturity in office.

Similarly, the presidency evolved into a powerful office out of the reach of direct democracy. The delegates devised an electoral college whose only function was to elect the president and vice president. Each state's legislature would choose the electors, whose number was the sum of representatives and senators for the state, an interesting blending of the two principles of representation. The president thus would owe his office not to the Congress, the states, or the people, but to a temporary assemblage of distinguished citizens who could vote their own judgment on the candidates.

The framers had developed a far more complex form of federal government than that provided by the Articles of Confederation. To curb the excesses of democracy, they devised a government with limits and checks on all three branches of government. They set forth a powerful president who could veto Congress, but they gave Congress power to override presidential vetoes. They set up a national judiciary to settle disputes between states and citizens of different states. They separated branches of government not only by functions and by reciprocal checks but by deliberately basing the election of each branch on different universes of voters— voting citizens (the House), state legislators (the Senate), and the electoral college (the presidency).

The convention carefully listed the powers of the president and of Congress. The president could initiate policy, propose legislation, and veto acts of Congress; he could command the military and direct foreign policy; and he could appoint the entire judiciary, subject to Senate approval. Congress held the purse strings: the power to levy taxes, to regulate trade, and to coin money and control the currency. States were expressly forbidden to issue paper money. Two more powers of Congress—to "provide for the common defence and general Welfare" of the country and "to make all laws which shall be necessary and proper" for carrying out its powers—provided elastic language that came closest to Madison's wish to grant sweeping powers to the new government.

The Constitution was a product of lengthy debate and compromise; no one was entirely satisfied with every line. Madison himself, who soon became its staunchest defender, remained unsure that the most serious flaws of the Articles had been expunged. But when the final vote was taken at the Philadelphia convention in September 1787, only three dissenters refused to endorse the document. The thirty-nine who signed it (thirteen others had gone home early) no doubt wondered how to sell this plan, with its powerful executive and Congress and its deliberate limits on pure democracy, to the American public. The Constitution specified a mechanism for ratification that avoided the dilemma faced earlier by the confederation government: Nine states, not all thirteen, had to ratify it, and special ratifying conventions elected only for that purpose, not state legislatures, would make the crucial decision.

> Pure democracy was now taken to be a dangerous thing. As a Massachusetts delegate put it, "The evils we experience flow from the excess of democracy."

REVIEW Why did the government proposed by the constitutional convention employ multiple checks on each branch?

Ratification of the Constitution

Had a popular vote been taken on the Constitution in the fall of 1787, it would probably have been rejected. In the three most populous states—Virginia, Massachusetts, and New York—substantial majorities opposed a powerful new national government. North Carolina and Rhode Island refused to call ratifying conventions. Seven of the eight

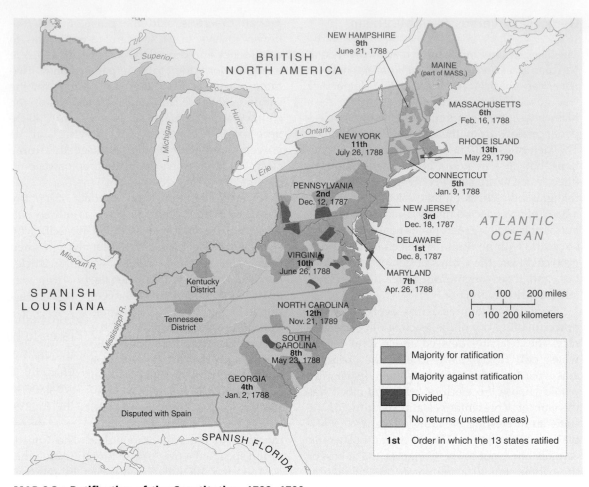

MAP 8.3   Ratification of the Constitution, 1788–1790
Populated areas cast votes for delegates to state ratification conventions. This map shows Antifederalist strength generally concentrated in backcountry, noncoastal, and non-urban areas, but with significant exceptions (for example, Rhode Island).

Reading the map: Where was Federalist strength concentrated? How did the distribution of Federalist and Antifederalist sentiment affect the order of state ratifications of the Constitution?
Connections: What objections did Antifederalists have to the new United States Constitution? How did their locations affect their view of the Federalist argument?

For more help analyzing this map, see the map activity for this chapter in the Online Study Guide at bedfordstmartins.com/roark.

remaining states were easy victories for the Constitution, but securing the approval of the ninth proved difficult. Pro-Constitution forces, called Federalists, had to strategize very shrewdly to defeat anti-Constitution forces, called Antifederalists.

The Federalists

Proponents of the Constitution moved into action swiftly. To silence the criticism that they had gone beyond their charge (which indeed they had), they sent the document to the congress.

The congress withheld explicit approval but resolved to send the Constitution to the states for their consideration. The pro-Constitution forces shrewdly secured another advantage by calling themselves "Federalists." By all logic, this label was more suitable for the backers of the confederation concept, because the Latin root of the word *federal* means "league." Their opponents became known as "Antifederalists," a label that made them sound defensive and negative, lacking a program of their own.

To gain momentum, the Federalists targeted the states most likely to ratify quickly. Delaware provided unanimous ratification by early December, before the Antifederalists had even begun to campaign. Pennsylvania, New Jersey, and Georgia followed within a month (Map 8.3). Delaware and New Jersey were small states surrounded by more powerful neighbors; a government that would regulate trade and set taxes according to population was an attractive proposition. Georgia sought the protection that a stronger national government would afford against hostile Indians and Spanish Florida to the south. "If a weak State with the Indians on its back and the Spaniards on its flank does not see the necessity of a General Government there must I think be wickedness or insanity in the way," said Federalist George Washington.

Another three easy victories came in Connecticut, Maryland, and South Carolina. As in Pennsylvania, merchants, lawyers, and urban artisans in general favored the new Constitution, as did large landowners and slaveholders. This tendency for the established political elite to be Federalist enhanced the prospects of victory, for Federalists already had power and influence disproportionate to their number. Antifederalists in these states tended to be rural, western, and noncommercial, men whose access to news was limited and whose participation in state government was tenuous.

Massachusetts was the only early state that gave the Federalists difficulty. The vote to select the ratification delegates decidedly favored the Antifederalists, whose strength lay in the western areas of the state, home to Shays's Rebellion. One rural delegate from Worcester County voiced widely shared suspicions: "These lawyers and men of learning and money men that talk so finely, and gloss over matters so smoothly, to make us poor illiterate people swallow down the pill, expect to get into Congress themselves; they expect to be the managers of the Constitution and get all the power and all the money into their own hands, and then they will swallow up all us little folks." Nevertheless, the Antifederalist lead was slowly eroded by a vigorous newspaper campaign. In the end, the Federalists won by a very slim margin and only with promises that amendments to the Constitution would be taken up in the first Congress.

By May 1788, eight states had ratified; only one more was needed. North Carolina and Rhode Island were hopeless for the Federalist cause, and New Hampshire seemed nearly as bleak. More worrisome was the failure to win over the largest and most important states, Virginia and New York.

The Antifederalists

The Antifederalists were a composite group, united mainly in their desire to block the Constitution. Although much Antifederalist strength came from backcountry areas long suspicious of eastern elites, many Antifederalist leaders came from the same social background as Federalist leaders; economic class alone did not differentiate them. Antifederalism also drew strength in states already on sure economic footing, such as New York, that could afford to remain independent. Probably the biggest appeal of antifederalism lay in the long-nurtured fear that distant power might infringe on people's liberties. The language of the earlier Revolutionary movement was not easily forgotten.

But by the time eight states had ratified, the Antifederalists faced a far harder task than they had once imagined. First, they were no longer defending the status quo now that the momentum lay with the Federalists. Second, it was difficult to defend the confederation government with its admitted flaws. Even so, they remained genuinely fearful that the new government would be too distant from the people and could thus become corrupt or tyrannical. "The difficulty, if not impracticability, of exercising the equal and equitable powers of government by a single legislature over an extent of territory that reaches from the Mississippi to the western lakes, and from them to the Atlantic ocean, is an insuperable objection to the adoption of the new system," wrote one articulate Antifederalist in a compelling and much-read political pamphlet by "A Columbia Patriot." The Columbia Patriot was the alias for Mercy Otis Warren, a Massachusetts woman whose father, brother, and husband had all been active leaders in the Revolutionary movement in Boston.

The new government was indeed distant. In the proposed House of Representatives, the only directly democratic element of the Constitution, one member represented some 30,000 people. How could that member really know or communicate with his whole constituency, the Antifederalists wondered. In contrast, one wrote, "the members of our state legislatures are annually elected—they are subject to instructions—they are chosen within small circles— they are sent but a small distance from their

> One rural delegate voiced widely shared suspicions: "These lawyers and men of learning . . . expect to be the managers of the Constitution and get all the power and all the money into their own hands, and then they will swallow up all us little folks."

respective homes. Their conduct is constantly known to their constituents. They frequently see, and are seen, by the men whose servants they are."

The Antifederalists also worried that elected representatives would always be members of the elite. Such men "will be ignorant of the sentiments of the middling and much more of the lower class of citizens, strangers to their ability, unacquainted with their wants, difficulties, and distress," a Maryland man worried. None of this would be a problem under a confederation system, according to the Antifederalists, because real power would continue to reside in the state governments.

> Madison called a national government "a republican remedy for the diseases most incident to republican government."

The Federalists generally agreed that the elite would be favored for election to the House of Representatives, not to mention the Senate and the presidency. That was precisely what they hoped. Federalists wanted power to flow to intelligent, virtuous, public-spirited leaders like themselves. They did not envision a government constituted of every class of people. "Fools and knaves have voice enough in government already," argued a New York Federalist, without being guaranteed representation in proportion to the total population of fools. Alexander Hamilton claimed that mechanics and laborers preferred to have their social betters represent them. The Antifederalists challenged the notion that any class could be sufficiently selfless to rule disinterestedly for others. One complained that "in reality, there will be no part of the people represented, but the rich. . . . It will literally be a government in the hands of the few to oppress and plunder the many." (See "Historical Question," page 280.)

Antifederalists fretted over many specific features of the Constitution. It prohibited state-issued paper money. It regulated the time and place of congressional elections, leading to fears that only one inconvenient polling place might be authorized, to disfranchise rural voters. The most widespread objection to the Constitution was its glaring omission of any guarantees of individual liberties in a bill of rights, like those contained in many state constitutions.

Despite Federalist campaigns in the large states, it was a small state—New Hampshire—that provided the decisive ninth vote for ratification, on June 21, 1788. Federalists there succeeded in getting the convention postponed

from February to June and in the interim conducted an intense and successful lobbying effort on specific delegates.

The Big Holdouts: Virginia and New York

Four states still remained outside the new union, and a glance at a map demonstrated the necessity of pressing the Federalist case in the two largest, Virginia and New York (see Map 8.3). Although Virginia was home to Madison and Washington, an influential Antifederalist group led by Patrick Henry and George Mason made the outcome uncertain. The Federalists finally but barely won ratification by proposing twenty specific amendments that the new government would promise to consider.

New York voters tilted toward antifederalism out of a sense that a state so large and powerful need not relinquish so much authority to the new federal government. But New York was also home to some of the most persuasive Federalists. Starting in October 1787, Alexander Hamilton collaborated with James Madison and New York lawyer John Jay on a series of eighty-five essays on the political philosophy of the new Constitution, published in New York newspapers and later republished as *The Federalist Papers*. The essays brilliantly set out the failures of the Articles of Confederation and offered an analysis of the complex nature of federalism. In one of the most compelling essays, number 10, Madison challenged the Antifederalists' heartfelt conviction that republican government had to be small-scale. Madison argued that a large and diverse population was itself a guarantee of liberty. In a national government, no single faction could ever be large enough to subvert the freedom of other groups. "Extend the sphere, and you take in a greater variety of parties and interests; you make it less probable that a majority of the whole will have a common motive to invade the rights of other citizens," Madison asserted. He called it "a republican remedy for the diseases most incident to republican government."

At New York's ratifying convention, Antifederalists predominated, but impassioned debate and lobbying—plus the dramatic news of Virginia's ratification—finally tipped the balance to the Federalists. Still, the Antifederalists' approval of the document was delivered with a list of twenty-four individual rights they hoped would be protected and thirty-three structural

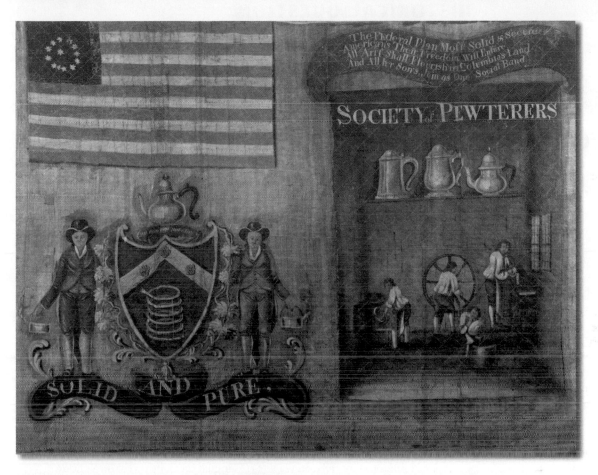

Silk Banner of the New York Society of Pewterers
As soon as nine states ratified the Constitution, the Federalists held spectacular victory celebrations meant to demonstrate national unity behind the new government. New York City's parade, coming three days before the state's own ratification vote in July 1788, involved five thousand participants marching under seventy-six occupational banners. Foresters and farmers headed the procession; coopers, tanners, cutlers, brewers, wig makers, tobacconists, chocolate makers, lawyers, and other tradesmen, artisans, professionals, and workers followed. This banner was carried by the Society of Pewterers, men who made household utensils from an alloy of tin, copper, and lead. Despite the broad spectrum of male workers represented in the parade, many of whom could not vote, no working women—milliners, dressmakers, or household servants—participated. Why? Note that the pewterers jumped the gun a bit with their thirteen-star flag.
© Collection of the New-York Historical Society.

changes they hoped to see in the Constitution. New York's ratification ensured the solidity and legitimacy of the new government. It took another year and a half for Antifederalists in North Carolina to come around. Fiercely independent Rhode Island held out until May 1790, and even then it ratified by only a two-vote margin.

In less than twelve months, the U.S. Constitution was both written and ratified. (See appendix I, page A-7.) An amazingly short time by twenty-first-century standards, it is even more remarkable for the late eighteenth century, with its horse-powered transportation and hand-printed communications. The Federalists had faced a formidable task, but by building momentum and assuring consideration of a **Bill of Rights**, they did indeed carry the day.

> **REVIEW**   Why did Antifederalists oppose the Constitution?

Was the New United States a Christian Country?

Rebecca Samuel, a Jewish resident of Virginia, conveyed her excitement about the new U.S. Constitution when she wrote her German parents in 1791 that finally "Jew and Gentile are as one" in the realm of politics and citizenship. Other voices were distinctly less approving. An Antifederalist pamphlet warned that the pope could become president; another feared that "a Turk, a Jew, a Roman Catholic, and what is worse than all, a Universalist, may be President."

The document that produced such wildly different readings was indeed remarkable in its handling of religion. The Constitution did not invoke Christianity as a state religion. It made no reference to an almighty being, and it specifically promised, in Article 6, section 3, that "no religious test shall ever be required as a qualification to any office or public trust under the United States." The six largest congregations of Jews—numbering about two thousand and located in Newport, New York, Philadelphia, Baltimore, Charleston, and Savannah—were delighted with this nearly unprecedented statement of political equality and wrote George Washington to express their hearty thanks.

But more than a few Christian leaders were stunned at the Constitution's near silence on religion. It seemed to represent a complete turnabout from the state consti-

tutions of the 1770s and 1780s. A New Yorker warned that "should the Citizens of America be as irreligious as her Constitution, we will have reason to tremble, lest the Governor of the universe . . . crush us to atoms." A delegate to North Carolina's ratifying convention played on anti-immigrant fears by predicting that the Constitution was "an invitation for Jews and pagans of every kind to come among us." A concerned Presbyterian minister asked Alexander Hamilton why religion was not in the Constitution. Hamilton reportedly quipped, "Indeed, Doctor, we forgot it."

Measured against the practices of state governments, Hamilton's observation is hardly credible. The men who wrote and debated the state and federal constitutions from 1775 to 1787 actively thought about principles of inclusion and exclusion when they defined citizenship, voting rights, and officeholding. They carefully considered property ownership, race, gender, and age in formulating rules about who could participate. And they also thought about religious qualifications.

Most leaders of the 1780s took for granted that Christianity was the one true faith and the essential foundation of morality. All but two state constitutions assumed the primacy of **Protestantism**, and one-third of them collected public taxes to support Christian churches. Every state

but New York required a Christian oath as a condition for officeholding. Every member of Pennsylvania's legislature swore to "acknowledge the Scripture of the Old and New Testament to be given by divine inspiration." North Carolina's rule was even more restrictive, since it omitted Catholics: "No person who shall deny the being of God or the truth of the Protestant religion, or the divine authority of the Old or New Testaments" could hold office. In South Carolina, all voters had to be Protestants.

Other common political practices affirmed that the United States was a Christian country. Governors proclaimed days of public thanksgiving in the name of the Holy Trinity. Chaplains led legislatures in Christian prayer. Jurors and witnesses in court swore Christian oaths. New England states passed Sabbath laws prohibiting all work or travel on Sunday. Blasphemy laws punished people who cursed the Christian God or Jesus.

Close to half the state constitutions included the right to freedom of religion as an explicit guarantee. But freedom of religion meant only that difference would be tolerated; it did not guarantee political equality. How then did the U.S. Constitution come to be such a break from the immediate past? Had the framers really just forgotten about religion?

Not James Madison of Virginia. Madison arrived at the 1787 convention fresh from a hard-won victory in Virginia to establish religious liberty. At the end of 1786, he had finally secured passage of a bill written by Thomas Jefferson seven years earlier called the Virginia Statute of Religious Freedom. "All men shall be free to profess, and by argument to maintain, their opinions in matters of religion, and that the same shall

Touro Synagogue

A Jewish community inhabited the coastal shipping city of Newport, Rhode Island, as early as the 1650s. In 1759, the thriving group built a synagogue, the oldest Jewish house of worship still standing in the United States. The building blends a Georgian brick exterior with elements of Sephardic Jewish origin. It is sited diagonally on its property so that worshippers face east, the direction of Jerusalem. President Washington visited Newport in 1790 and wrote to "the Hebrew Congregation" a few days later: "It is now no more that toleration is spoken of, as if it was by the indulgence of one class of people, that another enjoyed the exercise of their inherent natural rights."

Touro Synagogue/photo John T. Hopf.

in no wise diminish, enlarge, or affect their civil capacities," the bill read. Madison had convinced both the Episcopalians and the Baptist dissenters, at war with each other over state support, that to grant either or both churches tax money would be to concede to the state the authority to endorse one religion—and by implication to crush another. The statute separated church from state to protect religion. Further, it went beyond mere toleration to guarantee that religious choice was independent of civil rights.

In Madison's judgment, it was best for the U.S. Constitution to say as little as possible about religion, especially since state laws reflected a variety of positions. When Anti-federalists demanded a bill of rights, Madison drew up a list for the first Congress to consider. Two items dealt with religion, but only one was approved. One became part of the First Amendment: "Congress shall make no law respecting an establishment of religion, or prohibiting the free exercise thereof." In a stroke, Madison set religious worship and the privileging of any one church beyond Congress's power. Significantly, his second proposal failed to pass: "No State shall violate the equal rights of conscience." Evidently, the states wanted to be able to keep their Christian-only rules without federal interference. Different faiths would be tolerated—but not guaranteed equal standing. And the very same session of Congress proceeded to hire Christian chaplains and proclaim days of thanksgiving.

Gradually, states deleted restrictive laws, but as late as 1840 Jews still could not hold public office in four states. Into the twentieth century, some states maintained Sunday laws that forced business closings on the Christian Sabbath, working enormous hardship on those whose religion required Saturday closings. The guarantee of freedom of religion was embedded in state and federal founding documents in the 1770s and 1780s, but it has taken many years to fulfill Jefferson's vision of what true religious liberty means: the freedom for religious belief to be independent of civil status.

Conclusion:
The "Republican Remedy"

Thus ended one of the most intellectually tumultuous and creative periods in American history. American leaders experimented with ideas and drew up plans to embody their evolving and conflicting notions of how a society and a government ought to be formulated. There was widespread agreement that government should derive its power and authority from the people, but a narrow vision of "the people" prevailed. With limited exceptions—New Jersey, for example—free blacks and women were excluded from government. Indians, even when dubiously called "members" of a state, were outside the sovereign people authorizing government, as were all slaves. Even taking free white males as "the people," men disagreed fiercely over the degree of democracy—the amount of direct control of government by the people—that would be workable in American society.

The period began in 1775 with a confederation government that could barely be ratified because of its requirement of unanimity, but there was no reaching unanimity on the western lands, an impost, or the proper way to respond to unfair taxation in a republican state. The new Constitution offered a different approach to these problems by loosening the grip of impossible unanimity and by embracing the ideas of a heterogeneous public life and a carefully balanced government that together would prevent any one part of the public from tyrannizing another. The genius of James Madison was to anticipate that diversity of opinion was not only an unavoidable reality but a hidden strength of the new society beginning to take shape. This is what he meant in his tenth *Federalist* essay when he spoke of the "republican remedy" for the troubles most likely to befall a government where the people are the source of authority.

Despite Madison's optimism, political differences remained keen and worrisome to many. The Federalists still hoped for a society in which leaders of exceptional wisdom would discern the best path for public policy. They looked backward to a society of hierarchy, rank, and benevolent rule by an aristocracy of talent, but they created a government with forward-looking **checks and balances** as a guard against corruption, which they figured would most likely emanate from the people. The Antifederalists also looked backward, but to an old order of small-scale direct democracy and local control, where virtuous people kept a close eye on potentially corruptible rulers. Antifederalists feared a national government led by distant, self-interested leaders who needed to be held in check. In the 1790s, these two conceptions of republicanism and of leadership would be tested in real life.

Selected Bibliography

General Works

Lance Banning, *The Sacred Fire of Liberty: James Madison and the Founding of the Federal Republic* (1995).
Gary B. Nash, *The Unknown American Revolution: The Unruly Birth of Democracy and the Struggle to Create America* (2006).
Peter S. Onuf and Cathy D. Matson, *A Union of Interests: Political and Economic Thought in Revolutionary America* (1990).
Robert E. Shalhope, *The Roots of Democracy: American Thought and Culture, 1760–1800* (2004).
Alan Taylor, *The Divided Ground: Indians, Settlers, and the Northern Borderland of the American Revolution* (2006).
Gordon Wood, *The Creation of the American Republic, 1776–1787* (1969).
Alfred F. Young, ed., *Beyond the American Revolution: Explorations in the History of American Radicalism* (1993).

The Confederation Government and the States

Daniel M. Friedenberg, *Life, Liberty, and the Pursuit of Land: The Plunder of Early America* (1992).
Marc W. Kruman, *Between Authority and Liberty: State Constitution Making in Revolutionary America* (1997).
Jackson Turner Main, *The Sovereign States, 1775–1783* (1973).
Peter S. Onuf, *Statehood and Union: A History of the Northwest Ordinance* (1987).
Jack N. Rakove, *The Beginnings of National Politics: An Interpretive History of the Continental Congress* (1979).

Citizenship

Ira Berlin, *Many Thousands Gone: The First Two Centuries of Slavery in North America* (1998).
Linda K. Kerber, *Women of the Republic: Intellect and Ideology in Revolutionary America* (1980).
Joanne Pope Melish, *Disowning Slavery: Gradual Emancipation and "Race" in New England, 1780–1860* (1998).
Gary B. Nash and Jean R. Sonderlund, *Freedom by Degrees: Emancipation in Pennsylvania and Its Aftermath* (1991).
Leonard L. Richards, *Shays's Rebellion: The American Revolution's Final Battle* (2002).

Marylynn Salmon, *Women and the Law of Property in Early America* (1986).

Rosemarie Zagarri, *A Woman's Dilemma: Mercy Otis Warren and the American Revolution* (1995).

The Constitution and Ratification

John K. Alexander, *The Selling of the Constitutional Convention: A History of News Coverage* (1990).

Carol Berkin, *A Brilliant Solution: Inventing the American Constitution* (2003).

Stephen R. Boyd, *The Politics of Opposition: Anti-federalists and the Acceptance of the Constitution* (1979).

Richard Brookhiser, *Gentleman Revolutionary: Gouverneur Morris, the Rake Who Wrote the Constitution* (2003).

Saul Cornell, *The Other Founders: Anti-Federalism and the Dissenting Tradition in America, 1788–1828* (1999).

Michael Allen Gillespie and Michael Lienesch, eds., *Ratifying the Constitution* (1989).

Merrill Jensen and Ed Countryman, *The Anti-Federalists: Critics of the Constitution, 1781–1788* (2003).

John P. Kaminski and Richard Leffler, *Federalists and Antifederalists: The Debate over the Constitution* (1998).

Cecelia M. Kenyon, *Men of Little Faith: Selected Writings by Cecelia Kenyon* (2003).

Leonard W. Levy, *The Establishment Clause: Religion and the First Amendment* (1994).

Elizabeth P. McCaughey, *Government by Choice: Inventing the United States Constitution* (1987).

William Lee Miller, *The First Liberty: Religion and the American Republic* (1986).

Richard B. Morris, *Witnesses at the Creation: Hamilton, Madison, Jay, and the Constitution* (1985).

Jack N. Rakove, *Original Meanings: Politics and Ideas in the Making of the Constitution* (1996).

► **For more books about topics in this chapter,** see the Online Bibliography at bedfordstmartins.com/roark.

► **For additional firsthand accounts of this period,** see Chapter 8 in Michael Johnson, ed., *Reading the American Past,* Fourth Edition.

► **For Web sites, images, and documents related to topics and places in this chapter,** visit bedfordstmartins.com/makehistory.

REVIEWING THE CHAPTER

Follow these steps to review and strengthen your understanding of the chapter.
STEP 1: *Study the **Key Terms** and **Timeline** to identify the significance of each item listed.*
STEP 2: *Answer the **Review Questions**, drawing on key terms and dates to support your answers.*
STEP 3: *Drawing on the Key Terms, Timeline, and Review Questions, answer the broader **Making Connections** questions.*

KEY TERMS

Who

James Madison (p. 251)
Alexander Hamilton (p. 251)
Thomas Jefferson (p. 252)
John Adams (p. 256)
Abigail Adams (p. 256)
George Mason (p. 258)
Paul and John Cuffe (p. 259)
Elizabeth Freeman (Mum Bett) (p. 259)
Quok Walker (p. 259)
Robert Morris (p. 263)
Iroquois Indians (p. 264)
Delaware Indians (p. 265)
Mingo Indians (p. 265)
Shawnee Indians (p. 265)
Huron Indians (p. 268)

Miami Indians (p. 268)
Daniel Shays (p. 270)
James Bowdoin (p. 270)
Patrick Henry (p. 273)
Federalists (p. 276)
Antifederalists (p. 276)

What

Virginia Convention (p. 251)
Continental Congress (p. 253)
Articles of Confederation (p. 253)
republicanism (p. 255)
bills of rights (p. 256)
suffrage (p. 257)
gradual emancipation (p. 259)
manumission law (p. 259)

impost (p. 263)
Bank of North America (p. 264)
Treaty of Fort Stanwix (p. 265)
Northwest Territory (p. 265)
Ordinance of 1784 (p. 265)
Ordinance of 1785 (p. 265)
Treaty of Fort McIntosh (p. 267)
Northwest Ordinance (p. 268)
Disqualification Act (p. 269)
constitutional convention (p. 271)
Virginia Plan (p. 274)
New Jersey Plan (p. 274)
Great Compromise (p. 274)
U.S. Constitution (p. 274)
three-fifths clause (p. 274)
The Federalist Papers (p. 278)

TIMELINE

1775 • Second Continental Congress begins to meet.

  1776 • Virginia adopts state bill of rights.

    1777 • Articles of Confederation sent to states.

      1778 • State constitutions completed.

        1780 • Pennsylvania institutes gradual emancipation.

          1781 • Articles of Confederation ratified.

              • Creation of executive departments.

              • Bank of North America chartered.

              • Slaves Mum Bett and Quok Walker successfully sue for freedom in Massachusetts.

            1782 • Virginia relaxes state manumission law.

              1783 • Treaty of Paris signed, ending the Revolutionary War.

                • Massachusetts extends suffrage to taxpaying free blacks.

                1784 • Gradual emancipation laws passed in Rhode Island and Connecticut.

                • Treaty of Fort Stanwix.

REVIEW QUESTIONS

1. Why was the confederation government's authority so limited? (pp. 252–55)

2. How did states determine who would be allowed to vote? (pp. 255–62)

3. Why did farmers in western Massachusetts revolt against the state legislature? (pp. 262–71)

4. Why did the government proposed by the constitutional convention employ multiple checks on each branch? (pp. 271–75)

5. Why did Antifederalists oppose the Constitution? (pp. 275–79)

MAKING CONNECTIONS

1. Leaders in the new nation held that voting should be restricted to citizens who possessed independence of mind. Why? What did they mean by independence of mind? How did this principle limit voters in the early Republic?

2. Why did many Revolutionary leaders shaping the government of the new nation begin to find the principle of democracy troubling? How did they attempt to balance democracy with other concerns in the new government?

3. Twenty-first-century Americans see a profound tension between the Revolutionary ideals of liberty and equality and the persistence of American slavery. Did Americans in the late eighteenth century see a tension? In your answer, be sure to discuss factors that might have shaped varied responses, such as region, race, and class.

4. The Northwest Territory was the confederation's greatest asset. Discuss the proposals to manage settlement of the new territory. How did they shape the nation's expansion? Which proposals succeeded and which failed?

▶ FOR PRACTICE QUIZZES, A CUSTOMIZED STUDY PLAN, AND OTHER STUDY TOOLS, see the Online Study Guide at bedfordstmartins.com/roark.

1786 • Virginia adopts Statute of Religious Freedom.

• Shays's Rebellion begins.

　1787 • Shays's Rebellion crushed.

• Northwest Ordinance.

• Delaware provides manumission law.

• Constitutional convention meets in Philadelphia.

　　1788 • U.S. Constitution ratified.

　　　1789 • Slavery ended in Massachusetts by judicial decision.

　　　　1790 • Maryland provides manumission law.

　　　　　1799 • Gradual emancipation law passed in New York.

　　　　　　1804 • Gradual emancipation law passed in New Jersey.

WASHINGTON STANDS OUTSIDE OF TIME

A French clockmaker and artist produced this piece of Washington memorabilia after the death of the president. Washington's trim figure, rendered in gilt bronze, sports a spiffy uniform complete with fringed epaulets. One gloved hand rests on a sword; the other holds a rolled parchment, offered up in front of an eagle, the symbol of America's strength. Below the eagle a familiar motto is inscribed: "E Pluribus Unum" — "Out of many, one" — a reference to the political unity of the sovereign states. Below the clock is a motto about Washington that was first uttered in his funeral eulogy: "First in War, First in Peace, and First in the Hearts of his Countrymen." Death elevated Washington to celebrity status, and Americans immortalized him by purchasing souvenirs, many of them European-made.

The Warner Collection of Gulf States Paper Corporation.

CHAPTER 9

The New Nation Takes Form

1789–1800

- **The Search for Stability** 289
  Washington Inaugurates
  the Government 289
  The Bill of Rights 290
  The Republican Wife and Mother 291

- **Hamilton's Economic Policies** 294
  Agriculture, Transportation,
  and Banking 294
  The Public Debt and Taxes 295
  The First Bank of the United States
  and the *Report on Manufactures* 298
  The Whiskey Rebellion 299

- **Conflicts West, East, and South** 302
  To the West: The Indians 302
  Across the Atlantic: France
  and Britain 306
  To the South:
  The Haitian Revolution 309

- **Federalists and Republicans** 310
  The Election of 1796 310
  The XYZ Affair 311
  The Alien and Sedition Acts 312

- **Conclusion: Parties Nonetheless** 316

ALEXANDER HAMILTON was just thirty-four years old when President George Washington appointed him secretary of the treasury, giving him control over all economic and domestic policy in the new nation. Young and brilliant, Hamilton had been called a "colossus" for his gigantic mental abilities by Thomas Jefferson, the new secretary of state. But he also proved to be the most polarizing figure of the 1790s, leading to the collapse of the tight political alliance that had unified Federalists in the 1780s.

Through force of personality, Hamilton overcame a disadvantaged childhood on the small West Indies island of Nevis. His parents never married. His father, the impoverished fourth son of a Scottish lord, disappeared when Alexander was nine, and his mother, a woman with a checkered past, died two years later. Jeered as a "whore child," Hamilton developed a fierce ambition to make good. After serving an apprenticeship to a merchant, he made his way to the mainland colony of New York. In a mere six months, he sufficiently mastered Greek and Latin to gain admission to King's College (now Columbia University), from which he graduated in three years. Articles he wrote for a New York newspaper brought him to the attention of General Washington, who made the twenty-year-old an officer in the Continental army and hired him as a close aide. After the war, Hamilton practiced law in New York and then played a central role at the constitutional convention in Philadelphia. His astute *Federalist* essays—more than fifty drafted in just six months—helped secure the ratification of the Constitution.

Hamilton's private life was similarly upwardly mobile. Handsome and now well connected, he married Betsey Schuyler, whose father was one of the richest men in New York. He had a magnetic personality that attracted both men and women eager to experience his charm, which was on full display at dinner parties and social gatherings. Late-night events, however, never interfered with his prodigious capacity for work.

As secretary of the treasury, Hamilton quickly moved into high gear. "If a Government appears to be confident of its own powers, it is the surest way to inspire the same confidence in others," he once remarked. He immediately secured big loans from two banks and started to track tax revenues from trade, the government's main source of income. Most trade was with Britain, so Hamilton sought ways to protect Anglo-American relations. Next he tackled the country's unpaid Revolutionary War debt, writing in three months a forty-thousand-word report for Congress laying out a plan that both funded the debt and pumped millions of dollars into the U.S. economy. In short order,

***Alexander Hamilton,* by John Trumbull**

Hamilton was confident, handsome, audacious, brilliant, and very hardworking. Ever slender, in marked contrast to the more corpulent leaders of his day, he posed for this portrait in 1792, at the age of thirty-seven and at the height of his power. Yale University Art Gallery.

he drafted a bold plan for a national banking system to enhance and control the money supply. Finally, he turned his attention to industrial development, writing a richly detailed analysis of ways to promote manufacturing via government subsidies and tariff policies.

Hamilton was both visionary and practical. No one could doubt that he was a gifted man with remarkable political intuitions. It is strange, then, that this magnetic man made enemies in the 1790s, as the "Founding Fathers" of the Revolution and Constitution became competitors and even bitter rivals. To some extent, jealousy over Hamilton's talents and his access to President Washington explains the chill, but serious disagreement about political philosophy drove the divisions deeper.

Personalities clashed. Hamilton's charm no longer worked with James Madison, now a representative in Congress and at odds with Hamilton on all his plans. His charm had never worked with John Adams, the new vice president, who privately called him "the bastard brat of a Scotch pedlar," who was motivated by "disappointed Ambition and unbridled malice and revenge." Abigail Adams thought Hamilton a second Napoleon Bonaparte, an uncomplimentary reference to the belligerent leader of war-torn France. Years later, when asked why he deserted Hamilton, Madison replied, "Colonel Hamilton deserted me."

Hamilton assumed that government was safest when in the hands of "the rich, the wise, and the good"—in other words, America's commercial elite. For Hamilton, economic and political power naturally belonged together, creating an energetic force for economic growth. In contrast, Jefferson and Madison trusted most those whose livelihood was tied to the land. Agrarian values ran deep with them, and they were suspicious of get-rich-quick speculators, financiers, and manufacturing development. Differing views of European powers also loomed large in the rivalries. Whereas Hamilton was an unabashed admirer of everything British, Jefferson was enchanted by France, where he had lived in the 1780s. These loyalties governed foreign relations in the late 1790s, when the United States was in a war or near war with both of these overseas rivals.

The personal and political antagonisms of this first generation of American leaders left their mark on the young country. No one was prepared for the intense and passionate polarization that emerged over economic and foreign policy. The disagreements were articulated around particular events and policies: taxation and the public debt, a new farmers' rebellion in a western region, policies favoring commercial development, a treaty with Britain, a rebellion in Haiti, and the Quasi-War with France that led to severe strictures on ideas of sedition and free speech. But at their heart, these disagreements arose out of opposing ideological stances on the value of **democracy**, the nature of leadership, and the limits of federal power. About the only major policy development that did not replicate or intensify these antagonisms among political leaders was Indian policy in the new republic. Out in war-torn western Ohio, three forts named for Washington, Hamilton, and Jefferson symbolized the government's unified stance on Indians.

By 1800, the opposing politics ripening between Hamiltonian and Jeffersonian politicians would begin to crystallize into political parties, the Federalists and the Republicans. To the men of that day, this was an unhappy development.

The Search for Stability

After the struggles and discord of the 1780s, the most urgent task in establishing the new government under the Constitution was to secure stability. Leaders sought ways to heal old divisions and maximize unity, and the first presidential election offered the means to do that in the person of George Washington, who enjoyed widespread veneration. People trusted him to exercise the untested and perhaps elastic powers of the presidency, and his precedent-setting decisions would have a decisive impact on the success of the enterprise.

Congress had important work as well in initiating the new government. Many Antifederalists had insisted on changing the new Constitution to include a **Bill of Rights**, and Federalists now agreed. And beyond politics, cultural changes were mobilized to promote stability in the fledgling government. One important shift involved rethinking gender. Cultural commentators began to argue for the importance of a private virtue in women that would bolster the public virtue of male citizens. Despite the fact that women could not vote, **republicanism** was forcing a rethinking of women's relation to the state.

Washington Inaugurates the Government

The election of George Washington in February 1789 was quick work, the tallying of the sixty-nine unanimous votes by the electoral college a mere formality. Everyone's first choice, Washington perfectly embodied the republican ideal of disinterested, public-spirited leadership. Indeed, he cultivated that image through astute ceremonies such as the dramatic surrender of his sword to the Continental Congress at the end of the war, symbolizing the subservience of military power to the law.

With attractive modesty, Washington at first feigned reluctance to accept the presidency. He wrote his wartime confidant, Alexander Hamilton, for advice: Could he hesitate to accept but then ultimately take the office without seeming to be too ambitious? Hamilton replied that he must accept the office; public sentiment was universally for it. "No other man," Hamilton urged him, "can sufficiently unite the public opinion or can give the requisite weight to the office in the commencement of the government." The unanimous ballot for Washington supported Hamilton's claim. John Adams of Massachusetts, the vice presidential candidate, won only thirty-four votes, with the other thirty-five votes split among a variety of candidates, a result that deeply wounded Adams's pride.

Once in office, Washington calculated his moves, knowing that every step set a precedent and any misstep could be dangerous for the fragile government. How kingly should a president be? Congress debated a range of titles, such as "His Highness, the President of the United States of America and Protector of Their Liberties" and "His Majesty, the President"; Washington was known to favor "His High Mightiness." (Opponents of such lofty titles joked that the vice president should be called "His Rotundity" or "Duke of Braintree," Adams's home village in Massachusetts.) But in the end, republican simplicity prevailed. The final title was simply "President of the United States of America," and the established form of address became "Mr. President," a subdued yet dignified title in a society where only property-owning adult white males could presume to be called "Mister."

Liverpool Souvenir Pitcher, 1789
A British pottery manufacturer produced this commemorative pitcher for the American market to capture sales at the time of George Washington's inauguration in 1789. The design shows Liberty as a woman dressed in a golden gown, her liberty cap on a pole. She is holding a laurel wreath (signifying classical honors) over Washington's head. Fifteen labeled links encircle the scene, representing the states, although in 1789, Rhode Island and North Carolina had not yet ratified the Constitution, and Vermont and Kentucky were merely anticipated states. The Liverpool manufacturer was looking ahead; commemorative pitchers, jugs, and mugs were commonplace articles of consumer culture produced in Britain for the American market.
Smithsonian Institution, Washington, D.C.

Washington's genius in establishing the presidency lay in his capacity for implanting his own reputation for integrity into the office itself. He was not a brilliant thinker or a shrewd political strategist. He was not even a particularly congenial man. In the political language of the day, he was *virtuous*, meaning that he took pains to elevate the public good over private interest and projected honesty and honor over ambition. He remained aloof, resolute, and dignified, to the point of appearing wooden at times. He encouraged pomp and ceremony to create respect for the office, traveling with six sleekly oiled white horses to pull his coach, hosting formal balls, and surrounding himself with uniformed servants. He even held weekly "levees," as European monarchs did. At these hour-long audiences granted to distinguished visitors (including women), Washington appeared attired in black velvet, with a feathered hat and a polished sword. The president and his guests bowed, avoiding the egalitarian familiarity of a handshake. But he always managed, perhaps just barely, to avoid the extreme of royal splendor.

Washington chose talented and experienced men to preside over the newly created Departments of War, Treasury, and State. For the Department of War, Washington chose General Henry Knox, former secretary of war in the confederation government. For the Treasury—an especially tough job in view of revenue conflicts during the Confederation (see chapter 8)—the president picked Alexander Hamilton, known for his general brilliance and financial astuteness. To lead the Department of State, the foreign policy arm of the executive branch, Washington chose Thomas Jefferson, a master of the intricacy of diplomatic relations and the current minister to France. For attorney general, Washington picked Edmund Randolph, a Virginian who had attended the constitutional convention but had turned Anti-federalist during ratification. For chief justice of the Supreme Court, Washington designated John Jay, a New York lawyer who, along with Madison and Hamilton, had vigorously defended the Constitution in *The Federalist Papers*.

Washington liked and trusted all these men, and by 1793, in his second term, he was meeting regularly with them, thereby establishing the precedent of a presidential cabinet. (Vice President John Adams was not included; his only official duty, to preside over the Senate, he found "a punishment" because he could not participate in legislative debates. To his wife he complained, "My country has in its wisdom contrived for me

the most insignificant office.") Yet deep philosophical differences separated key appointees. No one anticipated that two decades of party turbulence would emerge from the brilliant but explosive mix of Washington's first cabinet.

The Bill of Rights

An early order of business in the First Congress was the passage of a Bill of Rights. Seven states had ratified the Constitution on the condition that guarantees of individual liberties and limitations to federal power be swiftly incorporated. The Federalists of 1787 had thought an enumeration of rights unnecessary, but in 1789 Congressman James Madison understood that healing the divisions of the 1780s was of prime importance. "It will be a desirable thing to extinguish from the bosom of every member of the community, any apprehensions that there are those among his countrymen who wish to deprive them of the liberty for which they valiantly fought and honorably bled," Madison said.

Madison pulled much of his wording of rights directly from various state constitutions with bills of rights. He enumerated guarantees of freedom of speech, press, and religion; the right to petition and assemble; and the right to be free from unwarranted searches and seizures. One amendment asserted the right to keep and bear arms in support of a "well-regulated militia," to which Madison added, "but no person religiously scrupulous of bearing arms, shall be compelled to render military service in person." That provision for what a later century would call "conscientious objector" status failed to gain acceptance in Congress.

In September 1789, Congress approved a set of twelve amendments and sent them to the states for approval; ten were eventually ratified. The First through Eighth Amendments dealt with individual liberties, and the Ninth and Tenth concerned the boundary between federal and state authority. (See the amendments to the U.S. Constitution in appendix I, page A-12.) One proposal that failed to pass suggested a formula for fine-tuning the ratio of representation as population grew; the other required that any congressional pay raise voted in would not take effect until after the next election (not until 1992 did this amendment—the Twenty-seventh—pass). The process of state ratification took another two years, but there was no serious doubt about the outcome.

Still, not everyone was entirely satisfied. State ratifying conventions had submitted some eighty proposed amendments. Congress never considered proposals to change structural features of the new government, and Madison had no intention of reopening debates about the length of the president's term or the power to levy excise taxes.

Significantly, no one complained about one striking omission in the Bill of Rights: the right to vote. Only much later was voting seen as a fundamental **liberty** requiring protection by constitutional amendment—indeed, by four amendments. The Constitution deliberately left the definition of voters to the states because of the existing wide variation in local voting practices. Most of these practices were based on property qualifications, but some touched on religion and, in one unusual case (New Jersey), on sex and race (see chapter 8, page 258).

The Republican Wife and Mother

The exclusion of women from political activity did not mean they had no civic role or responsibility. A flood of periodical articles in the 1790s by both male and female writers reevaluated courtship, marriage, and motherhood in light of republican ideals. Tyrannical power in the ruler, whether king or husband, was now declared a thing of the past. Affection, not duty, bound wives to their husbands and citizens to their government. In republican marriages, the writers claimed, women had the capacity to reform the morals and manners of men. One male author promised women that "the solidity and stability of the liberties of your country rest with you; since Liberty is never sure, 'till Virtue reigns triumphant. . . . While you thus keep our country virtuous, you maintain its independence." (For the relatively few American voices that raised questions about what rights women might have, see "Beyond America's Borders," page 292.)

Until the 1790s, public virtue was strictly a masculine quality. But another sort of virtue enlarged in importance: sexual chastity, a private asset prized as a feminine quality. Essayists of the 1790s explicitly advised young women to use sexual virtue to increase public virtue in men. "Love and courtship . . . invest a lady with more authority than in any other situation that falls to the lot of human beings," one male essayist proclaimed. If women spurned selfish suitors, they could promote good morals more than any social institution could, essayists promised.

Republican ideals also cast motherhood in a new light. Throughout the 1790s, advocates for female education, still a controversial proposition, argued that education would produce better mothers, who in turn would produce better citizens. Benjamin Rush, a Pennsylvania physician and educator, called for female education because "our ladies should be qualified . . . in instructing their sons in the principles of liberty and government." A series of published essays by Judith Sargent Murray of Massachusetts favored education that would remake women into self-confident, rational beings, poised to become

Republican Womanhood: Judith Sargent Murray
The twenty-one-year-old in this portrait, completed in 1772, became known eighteen years later as America's foremost spokeswoman for woman's equality. Judith Sargent Murray frequently wrote essays for the *Massachusetts Magazine* under the pen name "Constantia." In "On the Equality of the Sexes," published in 1790, she confidently asserted that women had "natural powers" of mind fully the equal of men's. Murray, the wife of a Universalist minister, also wrote plays that were performed on the Boston stage. In 1798, she published her collected "Constantia" essays in a book titled *The Gleaner*; George Washington and John Adams each bought a copy. Murray was the only woman of the era to keep an indexed letter book, which contains copies of nearly two thousand letters that she wrote during her lifetime.

John Singleton Copley, *Portrait of Mrs. John Stevens* (Judith Sargent, later Mrs. John Murray), 1770–1772, oil on canvas, 50 × 40 inches, Terra Foundation for America, Chicago/Art Resource, NY.

France, Britain, and Woman's Rights in the 1790s

During the 1770s and 1780s, only rarely did anyone in America wonder about rights for women. Abigail Adams's letter to her husband, John, in 1776, asking him to "Remember the Ladies" when writing new laws, stayed a private document for a century. Boycotts by the Daughters of Liberty before the Revolution did not challenge gender hierarchy, nor did New Jersey's handful of women voters (see chapter 8). Simply replacing a monarchy with a republic did not lead to an immediate or substantial challenge to women's subordinate status. Instead, it was influence from abroad that initially sparked new ideas about women's place in American society.

In France between 1789 and 1793, the revolution against monarchy enlarged ideas about citizenship and led some women to argue for the concept of the *citoyenne*, the female citizen. Women's political clubs, such as the Society of Republican Revolutionary Women in Paris, sent petitions and gave speeches to the National Assembly, demanding education, voting rights, and a curbing of the paternal and marital powers of men over women. In 1791, Frenchwoman Olympe de Gouges rewrote the male revolutionaries' document *The Rights of Man* into *The Rights of Woman,* asserting that "all women are born free and remain equal to men in rights." Another prominent woman, Théroigne de Méricourt,

held a feminist salon, marched around Paris in masculine riding attire, and took part in an attack on a palace. Her vision went beyond political rights to the social customs that dictated women's subordination: "It is time for women to break out of the shameful incompetence in which men's ignorance, pride, and injustice have so long held us captive."

Although the male National Assembly never approved voting rights for French women in that era, it did reform French civil and family law in the early 1790s. Marriage was removed from the control of the church, divorce was legalized, and the age of majority for women was lowered. A far-reaching advance in inheritance law required division of a patriarch's estate among all his children, regardless of age, sex, and even legitimacy. Henceforth, daughters could inherit along with sons; no longer did a woman from a family of means need to marry money—or indeed, to marry at all. In contrast, most American states adopted traditional English family law virtually unchanged.

French **feminism** traveled across the Channel to England and directly inspired a talented woman named Mary Wollstonecraft. In 1792, she published *A Vindication of the Rights of Woman,* arguing for the intellectual equality of the sexes, economic independence for women, and women's participation in

representative government. Most radically, she called marriage legalized prostitution.

Wollstonecraft's book created a sensation in America. Excerpts appeared immediately in Philadelphia and Boston periodicals, bookstores stocked the London edition, and by 1795 there were three American reprints. Some women readers were cautious. A sixty-year-old Philadelphian, Elizabeth Drinker, reflected in her diary, "In very many of her sentiments, she, as some of our friends say, speaks my mind; in some others, I do not altogether coincide with her. I am not for quite so much independence." Other women embraced Wollstonecraft's ideas. In 1794, a woman much younger than Drinker, Priscilla Mason, gave a biting commencement address at the new Young Ladies' Academy in Philadelphia, using Wollstonecraft as the inspiration for her rousing speech condemning "the high and mighty lords" (men) who denied women education and professional opportunities in church, law, and politics. "Happily, a more liberal way of thinking begins to prevail. . . . Let us by suitable education, qualify ourselves for those high departments," Mason said. She concluded with unwarranted optimism, "They will open before us." Many women's letters report lively debates stimulated by *A Vindication of the Rights of Woman.*

Male readers' responses were varied as well. Aaron Burr, a senator from New York, called the book "a work of genius." A Fourth of July speaker in New Jersey in 1793 proclaimed that "the Rights of Woman are no longer strange sounds to an American ear," and he hoped they would soon be embedded in state law codes. A more negative orator on that same holiday in New York argued that woman's rights really meant a woman's duty "to submit to the control of that government she has voluntarily chosen"—namely, the government of a husband. And a New Hampshire orator advanced this tart joke: "Every man, by the Constitution, is born with an equal right to be elected to the highest office. And every woman is born with an equal right to be the wife of the most eminent man." For some, it was clearly hard to think seriously about gender equality.

The notion of equal rights for women had a long incubation period in the United States. In the 1790s, ideas of equality were too closely associated with the radicalism of the French Revolution, a divisive topic in America, and the unhappy fate of de Gouges, guillotined in France in 1794 for her feminist polemic, was widely reported in the American press. Soon revelations of Wollstonecraft's unconventional personal life as an unwed mother dampened enthusiasm for her pioneering book. Not until the 1830s and 1840s would a new generation of women, led by Sarah Grimké, raise new and insistent questions about woman's equality (see chapter 11, page 384, and also chapter 12, page 425). Most Americans of the 1790s preferred a moderate stance, praising women's contributions to civil society through their influence on the family—the "republican motherhood" concept, as historians have called it. Although this fell far short of an egalitarian claim to rights, it did justify—and this was no small gain—women's formal education. A young woman speaker at a Fourth of July picnic in Connecticut in 1799 summed it up perfectly for her all-female audience: "As mothers, wives, sisters, and daughters, we may all be important, [and] teach our little boys, the inestimable value of Freedom, how to blend and harmonize the natural and social rights of man, and as early impressions are indelible, thus assist our dear country, to be as glorious in maintaining, as it was great in gaining her immortal independence."

FRONTISPIECE.

Publish'd at Philad.ᵃ Dec.ʳ 1.ˢᵗ 1792.

Woman's Rights in the *Lady's Magazine*, 1792

This frontispiece appeared in the first volume of the Philadelphia periodical the *Lady's Magazine and Repository of Entertaining Knowledge*, published in December 1792. Excerpts from Mary Wollstonecraft's *Vindication of the Rights of Woman* also appeared in that issue. (The editor was a literary man, Charles Brockden Brown.) The caption identified the kneeling figure as "the Genius of the *Lady's Magazine*." She is accompanied by "the Genius of Emulation," carrying a trumpet and a laurel wreath. (*Genius* here meant a spirit; *emulation* meant ambition to excel. Thus, the genius of emulation was the spirit of ambition—women's ambition in this case.) The spirit representing the *Lady's Magazine* kneels before Liberty, identified by her liberty cap on a pole, and presents a paper titled "Rights of Woman." Study the objects arranged below Liberty: a book, a musical instrument, an artist's palette, a globe, and a page of geometrical shapes. The kneeling figure seems to gesture toward them. What do they suggest about the nature of the "rights of woman" that this picture endorses?

Library Company of Philadelphia.

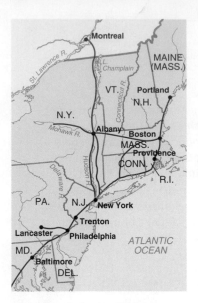

Major Roads in the 1790s

the equals of men. Her first essay, published in 1790, was boldly titled "On the Equality of the Sexes." A subsequent essay on education asserted that educated women "will accustom themselves to reflection; they will investigate accurately, and reason will point their conclusion; Yet they will not be assuming; the characteristic trait [sweetness] will still remain." Even Murray had to dress her advanced ideas in the cloak of republican motherhood, justifying female education in the context of family duty.

Although women's obligations as wives and mothers were now infused with political meaning, traditional gender relations remained unaltered. The analogy between marriage and civil society worked precisely because of the self-subordination inherent in the term *virtue*. Men should put the public good first, before selfish desires, just as women must put their husbands and families first, before themselves. Women might gain literacy and knowledge, but only in the service of improved domestic duty. In Federalist America, wives and citizens alike should feel affection for and trust in their rulers; neither should ever rebel.

> **REVIEW**   How did political leaders in the 1790s attempt to overcome the divisions of the 1780s?

Hamilton's Economic Policies

The new government had the lucky break to be launched in relatively flush economic times. Compared to the severe financial instability of the 1780s, the 1790s brimmed with opportunity and prosperity, as seen in increased agricultural trade and improvements in transportation and banking. In 1790, the federal government moved from New York City to Philadelphia, a more central location with a substantial mercantile class. There, Alexander Hamilton, secretary of the treasury, embarked on his innovative plan to solidify the government's economic base. But contro-

versy arose at every turn. Hamilton's plan to combine the large national debt, unpaid and unfunded, with unpaid state debts produced an early crisis in the first Congress. And his plan to raise revenues via taxation brought on the young country's first domestic conflict, the Whiskey Rebellion.

Agriculture, Transportation, and Banking

Dramatic increases in international grain prices motivated American farmers to boost agricultural production for the export trade. Europe's rising population needed grain, and the French Revolutionary and Napoleonic Wars that engulfed Europe for a dozen years after 1793 severely compromised production there. From the Connecticut River valley to the Chesapeake, farmers planted more wheat, generating new jobs for millers, coopers, dockworkers, and ship and wagon builders.

Cotton production also underwent a boom, spurred by market demand and a mechanical invention. Limited amounts of smooth-seed cotton had long been grown in the coastal areas of the South, but this variety of cotton did not prosper in the drier, inland regions. Green-seed cotton grew well inland, but its rough seeds stuck to the cotton fibers and were difficult to remove. In 1793, Yale graduate Eli Whitney visited Georgia and devised a machine called a gin that separated out the seeds. Cotton production soared—from 138,000 pounds in 1782 to 35 million in 1800—with the cleaned cotton shipped to English factories to be made into textiles.

A surge of road building also stimulated the economy. Before 1790, a series of bumpy post roads ran from Maine to Georgia, but with the establishment of the U.S. Post Office in 1792, six times as many miles of roads were quickly constructed to facilitate the transport of mail. Privately chartered companies also built roads. The first toll road in the nation was the Lancaster Turnpike of 1794, connecting Philadelphia with Lancaster, Pennsylvania. Another turnpike linked Boston with Albany, New York. Farther inland, a major road extended southwest down the Shenandoah Valley, while another joined Richmond, Virginia, with the Tennessee towns of Knoxville and Nashville.

By 1800, a dense network of dirt, gravel, or plank roadways connected cities and towns in southern New England and the Middle Atlantic states, spurring commercial stage companies to regularize and speed up passenger traffic. A trip from New York to Boston took four days; from New York to Philadelphia, less than two (Map 9.1). In 1790, Boston had only three stagecoach companies; by 1800, there were twenty-four. Transport of goods by road was still expensive per mile compared to water transport on navigable rivers or along the coast, but at least it was possible.

A third development signaling economic resurgence was the growth of commercial banking. During the 1790s, the number of banks nationwide multiplied tenfold, from three to twenty-nine in 1800. Banks drew in money chiefly through the sale of stock. They then made loans in the form of banknotes, paper currency backed by the gold and silver that stockholders paid in. Because banks issued two or three times as much money in banknotes as they held in **hard money**, they were creating new money for the economy.

The U.S. population expanded along with economic development, propelled by large average family size and better than adequate food and land resources. As measured by the first two federal censuses, in 1790 and 1800, population grew from 3.9 million to 5.3 million, an increase of 35 percent. (See "Global Comparison," page 297.)

The Public Debt and Taxes

The upturn in the economy, plus the new taxation powers of the government, suggested that the government might soon repay its wartime debt, amounting to more than $52 million owed to foreign and domestic creditors. Much of the debt originated when the Continental Congress needed supplies and manpower but had no independent source of revenue. Soldiers paid in government IOUs often sold them for as little as 15 percent of their face value, reflecting the widespread belief that the confederation government could never make good on them.

Treasury Secretary Hamilton attacked the debt problem in his *Report on Public Credit* in January 1790. He recommended that the debt be

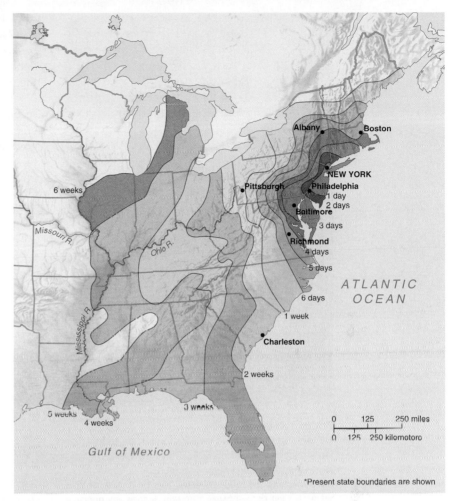

MAP 9.1 Travel Times from New York City in 1800
Notice that travel out of New York extends over a much greater distance in the first week than in subsequent weeks. River corridors in the West and East speeded up travel—but only if one were going downriver. Also notice that travel by sea (north and south along the coast) was much faster than land travel.

READING THE MAP: Compare this map to the map "Major Roads in the 1790s" (page 294) and to Map 9.2 (page 304). What physical and cultural elements account for the slower travel times west of Pittsburgh?
CONNECTIONS: Why did Americans in the 1790s become so interested in traveling long distances? How did travel times affect the American economy?

FOR MORE HELP ANALYZING THIS MAP, see the map activity for this chapter in the Online Study Guide at bedfordstmartins.com/roark.

funded—but not repaid immediately—at full value. This meant that old certificates of debt would be rolled over into new bonds, which would earn interest until they were retired several years later. There would still be a public debt, but it would be secure, supported by citizens' presumed confidence in the new government. The bonds would circulate as owners bought and sold them, in effect injecting millions of dollars of new money into the economy. "A national

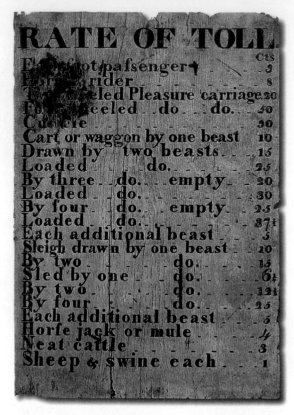

RATE OF TOLL

	Cts
Each foot passenger	9
Each rider	8
Three wheeled Pleasure carriage	20
Four wheeled do. do.	50
Curricle	30
Cart or waggon by one beast	10
Drawn by two beasts	15
Loaded do.	25
By three do. empty	20
Loaded do.	30
By four do. empty	25
Loaded do.	37½
Each additional beast	5
Sleigh drawn by one beast	10
By two do.	15
Sled by one do.	6¼
By two do.	12½
By four do.	25
Each additional beast	5
Horse jack or mule	4
Neat cattle	3
Sheep & swine each	1

Bridge Toll Sign, 1796
This sign lists an amazing variety of tolls charged for crossing a bridge over the Connecticut River between Cornish, New Hampshire, and Windsor, Vermont, in 1796. Owners of bridges and toll roads collected fees from users of their privately built rights-of-way. Can you deduce any principle of pricing in this list? Is the list exhaustive? What if a boy with a dog attempted to cross the bridge? Do you imagine there were traffic jams at the tollgate?
New Hampshire Historical Society.

debt if not excessive will be to us a national blessing; it will be a powerfull cement of our union," Hamilton wrote to a financier. The holders of the national debt would be investors in the country, men with a direct financial stake in the success of the new government. The debt was the "price of liberty," he further argued, and had to be honored, not repudiated. But not paid off either: Hamilton's goal was to make the new country creditworthy, not debt-free.

Funding the debt in full was controversial mainly because a large part of the old debt had been bought up cheaply by speculators in the late 1780s, and Hamilton's report touched off another round of turbulent speculation. (Hamilton himself held no certificates; he was careful to divest himself of anything that posed a conflict of interest. However, his father-in-law had certifi-

cates with a face value of $60,000.) Philadelphia and New York speculators sent agents deep into backcountry regions looking for certificates of debt whose unwary owners were ignorant about the proposed face-value funding.

Hamilton compounded controversy with a second breathtaking proposal: to add to the federal debt another $25 million that some state governments still owed to individuals. During the war, all the states had obtained supplies by issuing IOUs to farmers, merchants, and money-lenders. Some states, such as Virginia and New York, had paid off these debts entirely. Others, such as Massachusetts, had partially paid them off through heavy taxation of the people. About half the states had made little headway. Hamilton called for the federal government to assume these state debts and combine them with the federal debt, in effect consolidating federal power over the states. This large-scale debt consolidation—called *assumption* at the time—struck critics as expensive, unnecessary, unfair, and, worse, a power grab by the new government to subordinate the states.

Congressman James Madison strenuously objected to putting windfall profits in the pockets of speculators. Up to this point, he and Hamilton had been friends, but they broke over this issue of "discrimination"—of whether or not to discriminate between original and later debt holders. Madison proposed a complex scheme to pay both the original holders of the federal debt and the speculators, each at fair fractions of the face value. Hamilton countered that tracking the history of traded certificates would be impossible. When the vote on discrimination was tallied, Madison lost by a vote of 36 to 13. Madison also strongly objected to assumption of all the states' debts. His Virginia constituents had responsibly paid down their state debt, but now they would be taxed to pay the debts of other states. Furthermore, a large debt was dangerous, Madison warned, especially because it would lead to high taxation. Secretary of State Jefferson also was fearful of Hamilton's proposals. "No man is more ardently intent to see the public debt soon and sacredly paid off than I am. This exactly marks the difference between Colonel Hamilton's views and mine, that I would wish the debt paid tomorrow; he wishes it never to be paid, but always to be a thing where with to corrupt and manage the legislature."

A solution to this impasse over assumption arrived when Jefferson invited Hamilton and Madison to dinner. Good food evidently softened

GLOBAL COMPARISON

National Census Taking Worldwide

Taking a regular census is now a routine activity of most centralized governments, but in 1787, when the U.S. Constitution was written, it was an innovative and ambitious idea. Just a few nations had recently begun the practice, building on new Enlightenment theories of statecraft, which held that population size was a direct measure of the power and resources of a country. Regular censuses helped rulers discern eceonomic trends, anticipate food supply needs, and judge military preparedness. In ancient times, a small number of governments conducted isolated censuses, but only the Roman Republic managed a regular census at five-year intervals, conducted by "Censors." Throughout history, some subject populations have worried that government enumeration was a form of surveillance that might trigger increased taxation or military conscription. In the nineteenth century, many censuses expanded to collect social data useful to monitor the health and wealth of the nation. The U.S. census had one additional purpose that was truly pathbreaking and distinctive in its time: Its primary justification was to apportion political representation in the House of Representatives. Numbers became the foundation of representative democracy.

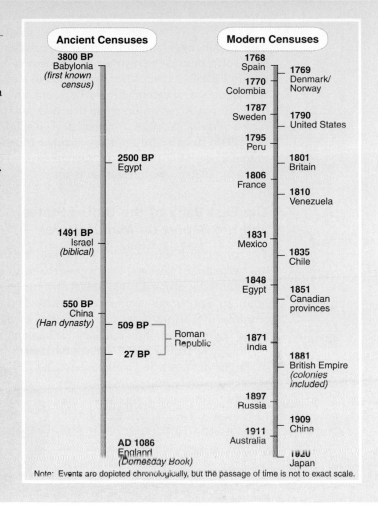

Ancient Censuses

3800 BP	Babylonia *(first known census)*
2500 BP	Egypt
1491 BP	Israel *(biblical)*
550 BP	China *(Han dynasty)*
509 BP	Roman Republic
27 BP	Roman Republic
AD 1086	England *(Domesday Book)*

Modern Censuses

1768	Spain
1769	Denmark/Norway
1770	Colombia
1787	Sweden
1790	United States
1795	Peru
1801	Britain
1806	France
1810	Venezuela
1831	Mexico
1835	Chile
1848	Egypt
1851	Canadian provinces
1871	India
1881	British Empire *(colonies included)*
1897	Russia
1909	China
1911	Australia
1920	Japan

Note: Events are depicted chronologically, but the passage of time is not to exact scale.

The Return for SOUTH CAROLINA having been made since the foregoing Schedule was originally printed, the whole Enumeration is here given complete, except for the N. Western Territory, of which no Return has yet been published.

DISTICTS	Free white Males of 16 years and upwards, including heads of families.	Free white Males under fixteen years.	Free white Females, including heads of families.	All other free persons.	Slaves.	Total.
Vermont	22435	22328	40505	255	16	85539
N. Hampshire	36086	34851	70160	630	158	141885
Maine	24384	24748	46870	538	NONE	96540
Maſſachuſetts	95453	87289	190582	5463	NONE	378787
Rhode Iſland	16019	15799	32652	3407	948	68825
Connecticut	60523	54403	117448	2808	2764	237946
New York	83700	78122	152320	4654	21324	340120
New Jerſey	45251	41416	83287	2762	11423	184139
Pennſylvania	110788	106948	206363	6537	3737	434373
Delaware	11783	12143	22384	3899	8887	59094
Maryland	55915	51339	101395	8043	103036	319728
Virginia	110936	116135	215046	12866	292627	747610
Kentucky	15154	17057	28922	114	12430	73677
N. Carolina	69988	77506	140710	4975	100572	393751
S. Carolina	35576	37722	66880	1801	107094	249073
Georgia	13103	14044	25739	398	29264	82548
	807094	791850	1541263	59150	694280	3893635
Total number of Inhabitants of the United States exclusive of S. Weſtern and N. Territory.	Free white Males of 21 years and upwards.	Free Males under 21 years of age.	Free white Females.	All other perſons.	Slaves.	Total
S. W. territory	6271	10277	15365	361	3417	35691
N. Ditto	—	—	—	—	—	—

1790 Census Page

This page provides a published tally of the final results of the first federal census in 1790, mandated by the U.S. Constitution as the means by which representation in Congress and proportional taxation on the states would be determined. Notice the choice of five classifications for the count: free white males age sixteen or older, free white males under age sixteen, free white females, all other free persons, and slaves. To implement the Constitution's three-fifths clause (counting slaves as three-fifths of a person), slaves had to be counted separately from all free persons. Separating white males into two broad age groups at sixteen provides a measure of military strength, something important for the government to gauge at a time of continuing and threatened Indian wars. U.S. Census Bureau.

READING THE IMAGE: Which northern states still had slaves? Which state had the largest population? Which had the largest white population?

CONNECTIONS: Why did the census separate males from females? Who might "all other free persons" include? Since women, children, and "all other free persons" counted for purposes of apportionment, could it be said that those groups were represented in the new government?

FOR MORE HELP ANALYZING THIS IMAGE, see the visual activity for this chapter in the Online Study Guide at bedfordstmartins.com/roark.

their animosity; Hamilton secured the reluctant Madison's promise to restrain his opposition. In return, Hamilton pledged to back efforts to locate the nation's new capital city in the South, along the Potomac River, an outcome that was sure to please Virginians. (See "Historical Question," page 300.) In early July, Congress voted for the Potomac site, and in late July, Congress passed the debt package, assumption and all.

The First Bank of the United States and the *Report on Manufactures*

The second and third major elements of Hamilton's economic plan were his proposal to create a national Bank of the United States and his program to encourage domestic manufacturing. Arguing that banks were the "nurseries of national wealth," Hamilton modeled his bank plan on European central banks, such as the Bank of England, a private corporation that used its government's money to invigorate the British economy. According to Hamilton's bold plan, the central bank was to be capitalized at $10 million, a sum larger than all the hard money in the entire nation. The federal government would hold 20 percent of the bank's stock, making the bank in effect the government's fiscal agent, holding its revenues derived from import duties, land sales, and various other taxes. The other 80 percent of the bank's capital would come from private investors, who could buy stock in the bank with either hard money (silver or gold) or federal securities. Because of its size and the privilege of being the only national bank, the central bank would help stabilize the economy by exerting prudent control over credit, interest rates, and the value of the currency. The bank had twenty-five directors, five appointed by the government and the other twenty chosen from the bank's stockholders, sure to be merchants from the world of high finance.

Concerned that a few rich bankers might have undue influence over the economy, Madison tried but failed to stop the plan in Congress; it passed by a vote of 39 to 20 in the House, with the principal division one of North versus South. The Senate passed it easily, so bank opponents next looked to the president to veto it. Secretary of State Jefferson advised President Washington

A discouraged Madison reported that in New York, "the Coffee House is an eternal buzz with the gamblers," some of them self-interested congressmen intent on "public plunder."

that the Constitution did not permit Congress to charter banks. Hamilton, however, pointed out that the Constitution gave Congress specific powers to regulate commerce and a broad right "to make all laws which shall be necessary and proper for carrying into execution the foregoing powers." Washington sided with Hamilton and signed the Bank of the United States into law in February 1791, with a charter allowing it to operate for twenty years.

When the bank's privately held stock went on sale in Philadelphia, Boston, and New York City in July, it sold out in a few hours, touching off an immediate mania of speculation in resale that lasted for more than a month and drew in many hundreds of urban merchants and artisans. A discouraged Madison reported that in New York, "the Coffee House is an eternal buzz with the gamblers," some of them self-interested congressmen intent on "public plunder." Stock prices shot upward, then crashed in mid-August. Hamilton shrewdly managed to cushion the crash to an extent, but Jefferson worried about the risk to morality inherent in gambling in stocks: "The spirit of gaming, once it has seized a subject, is incurable. The tailor who has made thousands in one day, tho' he has lost them the next, can never again be content with the slow and moderate earnings of his needle."

The third key component of Hamilton's plan was issued in December 1791 in the *Report on Manufactures*, a proposal to encourage the production of American-made goods and thus make the country less reliant on European imports, a dependence that had proved crippling during the Revolution. Domestic manufacturing was in its infancy, and Hamilton aimed to mobilize the new powers of the federal government to grant subsidies to manufacturers and to impose moderate tariffs on those same products from overseas. This would protect the nascent industries at home and give them extra incentive to get established. Hamilton's plan targeted manufacturing of iron goods, arms and ammunition, coal, textiles, wood products, and glass. Among the blessings of manufacturing, he counted the new employment opportunities that would open to children and unmarried young women, who he felt were underutilized in agricultural societies. The *Report on Manufactures*, however, was never approved by Congress, and indeed never even voted on. Many confirmed agriculturalists in Congress remained cautious about endorsing

One Man's Tribute to the New Nation
In the early seventeenth century, David Thatcher's ancestors helped settle the Massachusetts seacoast town of Yarmouth, where generations of Thatchers made a living from the sea. In 1790, Thatcher installed this dramatic overmantel on the wall above his fireplace. The artist, Jonathan Edes, painted scenes of fish and freedom in a massive wooden frame. Codfish harvested from the sea dry on hillside tables (top), a lighthouse guides large sailing ships (left), and an island fort guards Boston harbor (right). A profile of President George Washington holds center place for Thatcher, a patriot in the 1770s and a pro-Constitution Federalist. Thatcher served in the Massachusetts assembly for a record twenty-seven consecutive years, and Yarmouth men chose him to represent the town in the state convention that ratified the federal constitution in 1788.
Peabody Essex Museum, Salem, MA.

manufacturing, fearing that it would prove to be a curse rather than a blessing. Madison and Jefferson in particular were deeply alarmed by the prospect of stretching the "general welfare" clause of the Constitution to include public subsidies to private businesses.

The Whiskey Rebellion

Hamilton's plan to restore public credit required new taxation to pay the interest on the large national debt, swollen to some $77 million. Hamilton did not propose a general increase in import duties, in deference to the merchant class, nor did he propose land taxes, which would have fallen hardest on the nation's wealthiest landowners. Instead, he convinced Congress in 1791 to pass a 25 percent excise tax on whiskey, to be paid by farmers when they brought their grain to the distillery, then passed on to individual whiskey consumers in the form of higher prices. Members of Congress from eastern areas favored the tax—especially those from New England, where the favorite drink was rum. A New Hampshire representative cheerfully observed that the country would be "drinking down the national debt," an idea he evidently found acceptable. Virginia representative James Madison took a different but approving view of the tax, which he hoped might promote "sobriety and thereby prevent disease and untimely deaths."

Not surprisingly, the new excise tax proved unpopular with cash-short grain farmers in the western regions and whiskey drinkers everywhere. In 1791, farmers in the western parts of Pennsylvania, Virginia, Maryland, and the Carolinas, as well as throughout Kentucky, forcefully conveyed to Congress their resentment of Hamilton's tax. One farmer complained that he already paid half his grain to the local distillery

How Did Washington, D.C., Become the Federal Capital?

Why didn't Boston, Philadelphia, or New York City become the capital of the United States? The great cities of London and Paris were great precisely because political power was situated at the heart of commerce and culture in those European countries. Although much smaller in scale, several American cities boasted elegant houses, cultural institutions, lively economies, newspapers, food markets, taverns, coffeehouses, and stagecoach and shipping lines—nearly everything necessary to accommodate the political elites who would be running the new government. Instead, the infant United States chose marshy, vacant acreage along the Maryland shore of the Potomac River for its permanent capital.

Although the choice of that particular site was by no means inevitable, the country's leaders agreed that there should be only one site. During the war years, the Continental Congress had jumped around many times, from Philadelphia, Lancaster, and York in Pennsylvania to Princeton and Trenton in New Jersey, and down to Baltimore, often on the run from the British army. Even after the war, the Congress continued to circulate, meeting in Trenton, in Annapolis and Georgetown in Maryland, and finally in New York City. When the confederation government commissioned an equestrian statue of George Washington to inspire and dignify its meetings, a humorist suggested that the marble horse be fitted with wheels so it could be towed from place to place.

For some, a floating capital symbolized the precarious status of the confederation. But the alternative, a fixed location, put the federal government at the mercy of the particular state in which it sat. If irate citizens stormed the congress, as had happened once in Philadelphia in 1783, could the local state militia always be counted on to protect it? The writers of the Constitution thus came up with a novel solution. They decided to locate the capital on land not controlled by any state. The 1788 Constitution specified a square district, not exceeding ten miles on a side, where Congress would have sole jurisdiction, but it deferred the complicated choice of the exact site to the First Congress.

In 1790, more than forty cities and towns clamored for consideration, from Kingston and Newburgh in New York's Hudson River valley down to Richmond and Williamsburg in Virginia. Eleven contenders clustered along the Delaware River between New Jersey and Pennsylvania, roughly the demographic center of the country. Six more sites fell in the interior of Pennsylvania, along the Susquehanna River, each claiming to be the future geographic center as the country grew westward. Another eleven locations dotted the Potomac River from Chesapeake Bay to the Appalachians. Clearly, river transportation figured heavily in all these plans, and investors in canal and river navigation companies took special notice.

The First Congress struggled to reconcile private interests, regional jealousies, and genuine dilemmas of citizen access. A Pennsylvania proposal naming a Susquehanna River site finally passed the House but not the Senate. Virginians held out for the Potomac, drawing objections from New Englanders fearful of disease-laden southern swamps. Philadelphians insisted that their city, the premier cultural and economic center of America, was the only logical choice. In short, the situation was at a stalemate.

Another, unrelated stalemate obstructed Congress in early 1790. Alexander Hamilton presented Congress with his controversial bill to fund the public debt by assuming state debts (called the "assumption bill"). James Madison objected and wrested the necessary votes from Hamilton—at first.

Hamilton approached Robert Morris of Pennsylvania to propose a deal: If Morris would deliver votes for the assumption bill, the influential Hamilton would back a capital site in Pennsylvania. But Morris could not command enough congressional votes, so Hamilton next approached Thomas Jefferson, secretary of state, who invited him to dinner with James Madison. There, the three reached an agreement: enough southern votes for assumption in exchange for a Potomac River site. Madison could not bring himself to vote for assumption, but he rounded up the necessary votes from men representing districts along the river. In the final bill, Philadelphia was named the interim capital until 1800, by which time a site on the Potomac River, to be selected by President Washington, would be developed and the government open for business there. Robert Morris gloated that the Virginians had been tricked; he felt sure that Philadelphia's charms would ensnare the government permanently. Assumption quickly passed, by six votes.

Washington, drawing on his surveying expertise, took another year to select the hill-banked plain east of Georgetown, after scouting far up the river. No matter what location he chose, the Potomac Company—a canal-building enterprise of which Washington himself was president and principal investor—stood to benefit, but this was not considered a conflict of interest in the 1790s. Indeed, Washington had extensive landholdings up the Potomac and into the Ohio Valley, so the decision to site the capital on the Potomac River was much to his personal benefit. What made the Potomac advantageous both for a capital site and for investment in navigation was that it penetrated the farthest inland of any East Coast river, traversing the lowest point in the Appalachian Mountains. Washington's scouting trips convinced him that with short portages, water routes could connect Chesapeake Bay to western Pennsylvania and beyond that to the Ohio and Mississippi rivers.

Next, the rural site had to be purchased from the Maryland farmers who owned it. Washington and Jefferson purposely deployed surveyors in widely scattered locations up and down the river to keep local owners from guessing where the capital would finally rest within the district—and thus to keep a lid on land prices. The president also deputized friends to purchase the land "as if for yourselves, and to conduct your propositions so as to excite no suspicion that they are on behalf of the public."

Washington then hired a French-born master designer to plan the capital. Pierre L'Enfant, an architect living in New York City, mapped out a grid of streets slashed dramatically by wide diagonal boulevards. L'Enfant

envisioned a mall surrounded by grand government buildings. The rest of his map showed small lots intended for private buyers, who, it was hoped, would provide housing and services for those working in the government. The proceeds of the land sales would fund construction, so that a city could be built without having to draw on the U.S. Treasury at all.

In the end, the capital landed in the South because a major east-west river was there and because the South had crucial votes to trade on the assumption bill. Washington, D.C., represented the geographic but not

the demographic center of the thirteen states. Its placement exerted a southern tug on the federal government, augmented by the fact that five of the first seven presidents were southerners. In all the political horse-trading over choosing the site, nobody thought it worthy to note that the capital of the Republic sat in the heart of a slave society. But it would turn out to be of major significance some sixty years later, when the capital of President Abraham Lincoln was surrounded by slavery, with many of its inhabitants of doubtful loyalty to the Union.

Plan for Washington, D.C., on a Handkerchief

In 1791 and 1792, the pressure was high to get a detailed map of the proposed capital city into circulation so that prospective land buyers could be lined up. A Philadelphia engraving firm produced this plan of the future city with each block numbered. It was reproduced on large handkerchiefs in an early marketing strategy to entice buyers. At the time, the actual site consisted of fields and marshes.
Library of Congress.

for distilling his rye, and now the distiller was taking the new whiskey tax out of the farmer's remaining half. This "reduces the balance to less than one-third of the original quantity. If this is not an oppressive tax, I am at a loss to describe what is so," the farmer wrote. Congress responded with modest modifications to the tax in 1792, but even so, discontent was rampant.

Simple evasion of the law was the most common response; the tax proved hard to collect. In some places, crowds threatened to tar and feather federal tax collectors, and some distilleries underreported their production. Four counties in Pennsylvania established committees of correspondence and held assemblies to carry their message to Congress. President Washington issued a warning that the protests had to stop, and for a time, things cooled down. Still, noncompliance continued, and an embarrassed Hamilton admitted to Congress that the revenue was far less than anticipated. But rather than abandon the law, he tightened up the prosecution of tax evaders.

In western Pennsylvania, Hamilton had one ally, a stubborn tax collector named John Neville, who refused to quit even after a group of spirited farmers burned him in effigy. In May 1794, Neville filed charges against seventy-five farmers and distillers for tax evasion. In July, he and a federal marshal were ambushed in Allegheny County by a group of forty men. Neville's house was then burned to the ground by a crowd estimated at five hundred, and one man in the crowd was killed. At the end of July, seven thousand Pennsylvania farmers planned a march—or perhaps an attack, some thought—on Pittsburgh to protest the hated tax.

The governor of Pennsylvania refused to call out the militia, preferring to allow arrests and judicial authority to handle illegal acts. In response, President Washington nationalized the Pennsylvania militia and set out, with Hamilton at his side urging him on, at the head of thirteen thousand soldiers. (This event remains the only time in the country's history that a president in military uniform led an army in anticipated action.) A worried Philadelphia newspaper criticized the show of force: "Shall Pennsylvania be converted into a human slaughter house because the dignity of the United States will not admit of conciliatory measures? Shall torrents of blood be spilled to support an odious excise system?" But

One farmer complained about the new whiskey tax: "If this is not an oppressive tax, I am at a loss to describe what is so."

in the end, no blood was spilled. By the time the army arrived in late September, the demonstrators had dispersed. No battles were fought, and no shots were exchanged. Twenty men were rounded up as rebels and charged with high treason, but only two were convicted, and both were soon pardoned by Washington.

Had the federal government overreacted? Thomas Jefferson thought so; he saw the event as a replay of Shays's Rebellion of 1786, when a protest against government taxation had been met with unreasonable government force (see chapter 8). The rebel farmers agreed; they felt entitled to protest oppressive taxation. Hamilton and Washington, however, thought that laws passed by a republican government must be obeyed. The Whiskey Rebellion presented an opportunity for the new federal government to flex its muscles and stand up to civil disorder.

REVIEW   Why were Hamilton's economic policies controversial?

Conflicts West, East, and South

While the whiskey rebels challenged federal leadership from within the country, disorder threatened the United States from external sources as well. From 1790 onward, serious trouble brewed in three directions. To the west, a powerful confederation of Indian tribes in the Ohio Country resisted white encroachment, resulting in a brutal war. At the same time, conflicts between the major European powers forced Americans to take sides and nearly thrust the country into another war, this time across the Atlantic. And to the south, a Caribbean slave rebellion raised fears that racial war would be imported to the United States. Despite these conflicts, and the grave threats they posed to the young country, Washington won reelection to the presidency unanimously in the fall of 1792.

To the West: The Indians

In the 1783 Treaty of Paris, Britain had yielded all land east of the Mississippi River to the United States without regard to the resident Indian population. The 1784 Treaty of Fort Stanwix (see chapter 8) had attempted to solve that omis-

George Washington Reviewing Troops, 1795
This painting shows President Washington reviewing army troops at Fort Cumberland, in western Maryland, at the start of the Whiskey Rebellion. Washington did lead an army into western Pennsylvania and very likely did inspect his men at attention from the heights of a horse, but the scene is an artist's reconstruction. The soldiers stretch in lines far to the right horizon; note all the tents on a distant hill. The artist, Frederick Kemmelmeyer, was a German immigrant living in Baltimore. He painted portrait miniatures and signage for a living.
The Metropolitan Museum of Art, Gift of Edgar William and Bernice Chrysler Garbisch, 1963 (63.201.1). Photograph © 1983 the Metropolitan Museum of Art.

sion by establishing terms between the new confederation government and native peoples, but the key tribes of the Ohio Valley—the Shawnee, Delaware, and Miami—had not been involved in those negotiations. To confuse matters further, British troops still occupied a half dozen forts in the northwest, protecting an ongoing fur trade between British traders and Indians and thereby sustaining Indians' claims to that land.

The doubling of the American population from two million in 1770 to nearly four million in 1790 greatly intensified the pressure for western land. Several thousand settlers a year moved down the Ohio River in the mid-1780s. Most headed for Kentucky, on the south bank of the river, but some eyed the forests to the north, in Indian country. By the late 1780s, government land sales in eastern Ohio had commenced, although actual settlement lagged.

Meanwhile, the U.S. army entered the western half of Ohio, where white settlers did not dare to go. Fort Washington, built on the Ohio River in 1789 at the site of present-day Cincinnati, became the command post for three major invasions of Indian country (Map 9.2, page 304). General Josiah Harmar, under orders to subdue the Indians of western Ohio, marched with 1,400 men into Ohio's northwest region in

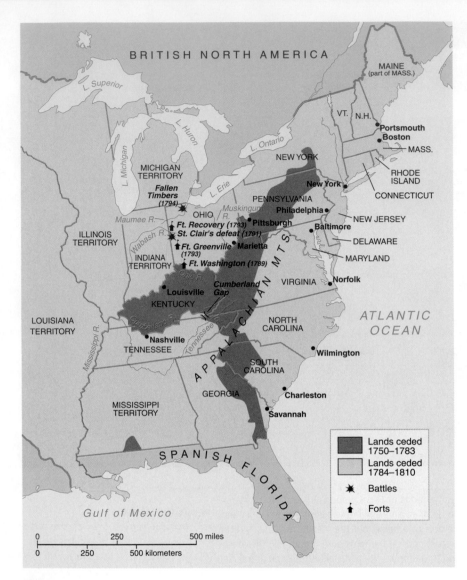

MAP 9.2   Western Expansion and Indian Land Cessions to 1810
By the first decade of the nineteenth century, intense Indian wars had resulted in significant cessions of land to the U.S. government by treaty.

READING THE MAP: Locate the Appalachians. The Proclamation Line of 1763 that ran along these mountains forbade colonists to settle west of the line. How well was that purpose met?
CONNECTIONS: How much did the population of the United States grow between 1750 and 1790? How did this growth affect western settlement?

FOR MORE HELP ANALYZING THIS MAP, see the map activity for this chapter in the Online Study Guide at bedfordstmartins.com/roark.

General Arthur St. Clair, the military governor of the Northwest Territory, had pursued peaceful tactics in the 1780s, signing treaties with Indians for land in eastern Ohio—dubious treaties, as it happened, since the Indian negotiators were not authorized to yield land. In the wake of Harmar's bungled operation, St. Clair geared up for military action, and in the fall of 1791, he led two thousand men (accompanied by two hundred women camp followers) north from Fort Washington to claim Ohio territory from the Miami and Shawnee tribes. Along the route, St. Clair's men quickly built two forts, named for Hamilton and Jefferson. However, when the Indians attacked at daybreak on November 4, at the headwaters of the Wabash River, St. Clair's army was not protected by fortifications.

Before noon, 55 percent of the Americans were dead or wounded; only three of the women escaped alive. "The savages seemed not to fear anything we could do," wrote an officer afterward. "They could skip out of reach of bayonet and return, as they pleased. The ground was literally covered with the dead. . . . It appeared as if the officers had been singled out, as a very great proportion fell. The men being thus left with few officers, became fearful, despaired of success, gave up the fight." The Indians captured valuable weaponry, scalped and dismembered the dying, and pursued fleeing survivors for miles. With more than nine hundred lives lost, this was the most stunning American loss in the history of the U.S.-Indian wars. President Washington fumed that St. Clair "was worse than a murderer" and demanded his resignation. An angry Congress issued subpoenas and launched its first-ever investigation of the executive branch, looking beyond St. Clair to learn what had gone wrong. Grisly tales of St. Clair's defeat became instantly infamous, increasing the level of terror that Americans brought to their confrontations with the Indians.

Washington doubled the U.S. military presence in Ohio and appointed a new commander, General Anthony Wayne of Pennsylvania, nick-

the fall of 1790, burning Indian villages. His inexperienced troops were ambushed by Miami and Shawnee Indians led by their chiefs, Little Turtle and Blue Jacket. Harmar lost one-eighth of his soldiers.

Harmar's defeat—so humiliating that he was court-martialed—spurred efforts to clear Ohio for permanent American settlement.

named "Mad Anthony" for his headstrong, hard-drinking style of leadership. About the Ohio natives, Wayne wrote, "I have always been of the opinion that we never should have a permanent peace with those Indians until they were made to experience our superiority." With some 3,500 men, Wayne established two new military camps, Fort Greenville and Fort Recovery, deep in Indian territory in western Ohio, the latter on the site of St. Clair's defeat. Wayne's men had to pick through skeletal remains to build the fort.

Throughout 1794, Wayne's army engaged in skirmishes with Shawnee, Delaware, and Miami Indians. Chief Little Turtle of the Miami tribe advised negotiation; in his view, Wayne's large army looked overpowering. But Blue Jacket of the Shawnees counseled continued warfare, and his view prevailed. The decisive action came in August 1794 at the battle of Fallen Timbers, near the Maumee River where a recent tornado had felled many trees. The confederated Indians—mainly Ottawas, Potawatomis, Shawnees, and Delawares and numbering around eight hundred—ambushed the Americans but were underarmed, and Wayne's troops made effective use of their guns and bayonets. The Indians withdrew and sought refuge at nearby Fort Miami, still held by the British. Their former allies, however, locked the gate and refused protection. The surviving Indians fled to the woods, their ranks decimated.

Fallen Timbers was a major defeat for the Indians. The Americans had destroyed cornfields and villages on the march north, and with winter approaching, the Indians' confidence was sapped. They reentered negotiations in a much less powerful bargaining position. In 1795, about a thousand Indians representing nearly a dozen tribes met with Wayne and other American emissaries to work out the Treaty of Greenville. The Americans offered treaty goods (calico shirts, axes, knives, blankets, kettles, mirrors, ribbons, thimbles, and abundant wine and liquor casks) worth $25,000 and promised additional shipments every year. The government's idea was to create a dependency on American goods to keep the Indians friendly. In exchange, the Indians ceded most of Ohio to the Americans; only the northwest part of the territory was reserved solely for the Indians.

The treaty brought temporary peace to the region; however, it did not restore a peaceful

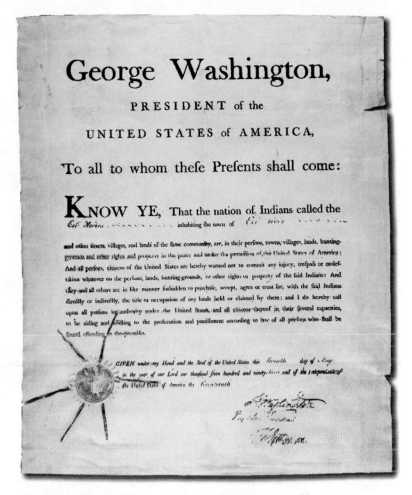

Washington's Proclamation Protecting Indian Territory
The president's name, in bold print, prefaces a warning that American citizens were forbidden to injure Indians or trespass on their lands in the Northwest Territory. When the federal government signed treaties with Indian tribes ceding land to the United States, it often guaranteed protections for land not ceded. This poster of 1793, designed to be tacked up on trees, announced federal protection for Indians around the Eel River in Ohio. Such warnings were not very effective. Washington wrote in 1796, "I believe scarcely any thing short of a Chinese Wall, or line of Troops will restrain LandJobbers, and the Incroachment of Settlers, upon Indian Territory." (A jobber was a middleman operating between buyers and sellers.)
The Huntington Library and Art Collections, San Marino, California.

life to the Indians. The annual allowance from the United States too often came in the form of liquor. "More of us have died since the Treaty of Greenville than we lost by the years of war before, and it is all owing to the introduction of liquor among us," said Chief Little Turtle in 1800. "This liquor that they introduce into our country is more to be feared than the gun and tomahawk."

"This liquor that they introduce into our country is more to be feared than the gun and tomahawk," said Chief Little Turtle in 1800.

Treaty of Greenville, 1795

This painting by an unknown artist of the 1790s purports to depict the signing of the Treaty of Greenville in 1795. The treaty was signed by General Anthony Wayne, Chief Little Turtle of the Miami tribe, and Chief Tarhe the Crane of the Wyandot tribe. An American officer kneels in front of a group of other officers, apparently writing something down—not a likely posture in which to draft a formal treaty. One Indian of the three pictured seems to be gesturing with emphasis, as if to dictate terms to the Americans, but in fact the treaty was most favorable to the United States. Although many Indians from a dozen Ohio tribes congregated at the signing of the treaty, this picture shows unrealistically open spaces and very few Indians. The treaty medal commemorates the event. It is one of probably dozens distributed to Indian participants by U.S. officials. Why might "E Pluribus Unum"—"Out of many, one"—appear on the medal?
Painting: Chicago Historical Society; Medal: Indiana Historical Society.

Across the Atlantic:
France and Britain

While Indian battles engaged the American military in the west, another war overseas to the east was also closely watched. Since 1789, revolution had been raging in France. In its first five years, the general American reaction was positive, for it was flattering to think that the American Revolution had inspired imitation in France. As monarchy and privilege were overthrown in the name of republicanism in France, towns throughout America celebrated the victory of the French people with civic feasts and public festivities. Dozens of pro-French political clubs, called democratic or republican societies, sprang up around the country. The societies mobilized farmers and mechanics, issued circular letters, injected pro-French (and anti-British) feelings into local elections, and in general heightened popular participation and public interest in foreign policy.

Many American women also joined in the pro-French enthusiasm. Clothing accessories provided a striking way to make a political statement, leading some women to sport a sash and an ornamental French cockade made with ribbons of red, white, and blue—a badge of solidarity with revolutionary France.

Pro-French headgear for committed women included an elaborate turban, leading one horrified Federalist newspaper editor to chastise the "fiery frenchified dames" thronging Philadelphia's streets. Staged female celebrations of France's new liberty occurred in New England, Pennsylvania, and the South, where one most extraordinary event made the columns of South Carolina's *Charleston City Gazette and Daily Advertiser* in 1793. It centered on a public marriage ceremony uniting two women as partners, one French and one American, who repudiated their husbands "on account of ill treatment" and pledged mutual "union and friendship." A militia fired a salute to seal the pledge, while male dignitaries beamed on the women and their blended multichild family. Most likely, this ceremony was not the country's first civil union but instead a richly metaphorical piece of street theater in which the spurned husbands repre-

sented Britain. The paper did not report names for the two women but did print recognizably local names of male sponsors and officiants.

Anti–French Revolution sentiments also ran deep. Vice President John Adams, who lived in France in the 1780s, said he trembled for the outcome. Radicals in France worried him, just as radicals in America did. "Too many Frenchmen, after the example of too many Americans, pant for the equality of persons and property," Adams said. "The impracticability of this, God Almighty has decreed, and the advocates for liberty, who attempt it, will surely suffer for it."

Support for the French Revolution remained a matter of personal conviction until 1793, when Britain and France went to war and French versus British loyalty became a critical foreign policy debate. France had helped America substantially during the American Revolution, and the confederation government had signed an

Revolutionary Solidarity

In the early 1790s, some Americans showed enthusiasm for the French Revolution by wearing a tricolor cockade — a distinctive bow made from red, white, and blue ribbons. A woman seeking the full pro-French look could copy Parisian revolutionary outfits, as in this style described in a Philadelphia newspaper in 1790: a black beaver hat with cockade and feathers; a dark blue jacket with a white collar, red cuffs, and yellow buttons; a white blouse; a blue skirt with white trim; and black shoes. Another pro-French statement appeared in several marriage announcements in Boston, Hartford, and Philadelphia newspapers in the early months of 1793. In these announcements, men often adopted *Citizen* as their title of address, with the corresponding term *Citess* for women. (*Citess* was invented on the spot and spelled eighteenth-century style with a character shaped like the letter "f.") In France, *Citoyen* and *Citoyenne* enjoyed widespread use as egalitarian titles of address.

Outfit: Bibliothèque Nationale de France; Announcement: Courtesy, American Antiquarian Society.

MARRIED, By Citizen *Thacher*, Citizen FREDERICK W. GEYER, jun. toCitefs REBECCA, daughter toCitizen NATHAN FRAZER.——On Thurfday Eveninglaft, by Citizen *Lathrop*, Citizen JONATHAN WILD, to Citefs MARY, daughter to Citizen SAMUEL RIDGWAY.

alliance in 1778 promising aid if France were ever under attack. Some Americans, optimistic about the eventual outcome of the French Revolution, wanted to deliver on that promise. Others, including those shaken by the report of the guillotining of thousands of French people, as well as those with strong commercial ties to Britain, sought ways to stay neutral. In particular, the startling news of the beheading of King Louis XVI and Queen Marie Antoinette quickly dampened the uncritical enthusiasm for everything French. Those who fondly remembered the excitement and risk of the American Revolution were still likely to regard France with optimism. But the reluctant revolutionaries of the 1770s and 1780s, who had worried about excessive democracy and social upheaval in America, deplored the far greater violence occurring in the name of republicanism as France in 1793 moved into the Reign of Terror, with its surge of executions.

In May 1793, President Washington issued the Neutrality Proclamation, which contained friendly assurances to both sides. But tensions at home flared in response to official neutrality. "The cause of France is the cause of man, and neutrality is desertion," wrote H. H. Brackenridge, a congressman from western Pennsylvania, voicing the sentiments of thousands. The Neutrality Proclamation fit Washington's goal of staying out of European wars. Yet American ships continued to trade between the French West Indies and France. In late 1793 and early 1794, the British expressed their displeasure by capturing more than three hundred of these vessels near the West Indies. Clearly, something had to be done to assert American power.

President Washington sent John Jay, the chief justice of the Supreme Court and a man of strong pro-British sentiments, to England to negotiate commercial relations in the British West Indies and secure compensation for the seizure of American ships. In addition, Jay was supposed to resolve several long-standing problems. Southern **planters** wanted reimbursement for the slaves lured away by the British army during the war, and western settlers wanted Britain to vacate the frontier forts still occupied because of their proximity to the Indian fur trade.

Jay returned from his diplomatic mission in 1795 with a treaty that no one could love. First,

> "The nation has been . . . divorced from France, and most clandestinely married to Great Britain: we are taken from the embraces of a loving wife, and find ourselves in the arms of a detestable and abandoned whore," one newspaper said of the Jay Treaty.

the treaty failed to address the captured cargoes or the lost property in slaves. Second, it granted the British a lenient eighteen months to withdraw from the frontier forts, as well as continued rights in the fur trade. (Even with the delay, however, the provision disheartened the Indians just then negotiating the Treaty of Greenville in Ohio. It was a significant factor in their decision to make peace.) Finally, the Jay Treaty called for repayment with interest of the debts that some American planters still owed to British firms dating from the Revolutionary War. In exchange for such generous terms, Jay secured limited trading rights in the West Indies and agreement that some issues—boundary disputes with Canada and the damage and loss claims of shipowners—would be decided later by arbitration commissions.

The Senate debated the treaty in secrecy, knowing how explosive its terms would be, and passed it by a vote of 20 to 10. President Washington signed it, but with misgivings. When newspapers published the terms of the treaty, powerful opposition emerged from Maine to Georgia. In Massachusetts, this graffiti appeared on a wall: "Damn John Jay! Damn everyone who won't damn John Jay! Damn everyone who won't stay up all night damning John Jay!" Bonfires in many places burned effigies of Jay and copies of the treaty. A newspaper in New Jersey used graphic imagery to explain to its readers the implications of the Jay Treaty:

> The nation has been secretly, I will not say treacherously, divorced from France, and most clandestinely married to Great Britain: we are taken from the embraces of a loving wife, and find ourselves in the arms of a detestable and abandoned whore, covered with crimes, rottenness, and corruption.

When Alexander Hamilton appeared at a public meeting in New York City to defend the treaty, he was hissed and booed, and several stones were thrown at him. Within days, he was challenging opponents to fights, but no one took up his challenge. A Connecticut newspaper, in reporting with cautious approval on unmarried females voting in a New Jersey election, openly wondered whether "a certain treaty" might have "obtained better terms" had it been negotiated by a widow instead of "a MALE minister," a clear insult to Jay's competence.

Some representatives in the House, led by Madison, tried to undermine the Senate's approval by insisting on a separate vote on the funding provisions of the treaty, on the grounds that the House controlled all money matters. Finally, in 1796, the House approved funds to implement the various commissions mandated by the treaty, but by only a three-vote margin. The vote in both houses of Congress divided along the same lines as the Hamilton-Jefferson split on economic policy. It was the most bitter political split yet in the country's short history.

To the South: The Haitian Revolution

In addition to the Indian wars in Ohio and the European wars across the Atlantic, a third bloody conflict to the south polarized and even terrorized many Americans in the 1790s. The western third of the large Caribbean island of Hispaniola, just to the east of Cuba, became engulfed in revolution starting in 1791. The eastern portion of the island was a Spanish colony called Santo Domingo; the western part, in bloody conflagration, was the French Saint Domingue. War raged in Saint Domingue for more than a decade, resulting in 1804 in the birth of the Republic of Haiti, the first and only independent black state to arise out of a successful slave revolution.

The Haitian Revolution was a complex event involving many participants, including the diverse local population and, eventually, three European countries. Some 30,000 whites ruled the island in 1790, running sugar and coffee plantations with close to half a million enslaved blacks, two-thirds of them of African birth. The white French colonists were not the only plantation owners, however. About 28,000 free, mixed-race people (*gens de couleur*) also lived in Saint Domingue; they owned one-third of the island's plantations and nearly a quarter of the slave labor force. Despite their economic status, these mixed-race planters were barred from political power, but they aspired to it.

The French Revolution of 1789 was the immediate catalyst for rebellion in this already tense society. First, white colonists challenged the white royalist government in an effort to link Saint Domingue with the new revolutionary government in France. Next, the mixed-race planters rebelled in 1791, demanding equal civil rights with the whites. No sooner was this revolt viciously suppressed than another part of the island exploded as thousands of enslaved blacks armed with machetes and torches wreaked devastation and slaughter. In 1793, the civil war escalated to include French, Spanish, and British troops fighting the inhabitants and also each other. Slaves led by Toussaint L'Ouverture in alliance with Spain occupied the northern regions of the island, leaving a thousand plantations in ruins and tens of thousands of people dead. Thousands of white and mixed-race planters, along with some of their slaves, fled to Spanish Louisiana and southern cities in the United States.

White Americans followed the revolution in fascinated horror through newspapers and refugees' accounts. A few sympathized with the impulse for liberty, but many more shuddered at the violent atrocities. White refugees were welcomed in Charleston, Norfolk, and Richmond; but French-speaking blacks, whether free or slave, were eventually barred from entry in all southern states except Virginia. White southerners clearly feared that violent black insurrection might be imported from Haiti into their own society.

Many black American slaves also followed the revolution, hearing about it from dockworkers; black sailors; anxious whites, who spoke of it over dinner or in taverns, where blacks waited on tables; and French-speaking blacks themselves, who arrived in Virginia ports in significant numbers after 1793. Amazing news—the success of the first massive revolution by slaves—traveled quickly in this oral **culture**. Southern whites complained of behaviors among slaves that might prefigure plots and conspiracies, such as increased insolence and higher runaway rates.

The Haitian Revolution provoked naked fear of a race war in white southerners. Jefferson, agonizing over the contagion of liberty in 1797, wrote another Virginia slaveholder that "if something is not done, and soon done, we shall be the murderers of our own children . . . ; the revolutionary storm, now sweeping the globe, will be upon us, and happy if we make timely provision to give it an easy passage over our

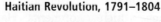

Haitian Revolution, 1791–1804

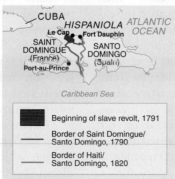

CUBA
HISPANIOLA ATLANTIC OCEAN
Le Cap Fort Dauphin
SAINT DOMINGUE (France) SANTO DOMINGO (Spain)
Port-au-Prince

Caribbean Sea

Beginning of slave revolt, 1791

Border of Saint Domingue/ Santo Domingo, 1790

Border of Haiti/ Santo Domingo, 1820

land. From the present state of things in Europe and America, the day which brings our combustion must be near at hand; and only a single spark is wanting to make that day to-morrow."

Jefferson's cataclysmic fears were not shared by New Englanders. Timothy Pickering of Massachusetts, in Washington's cabinet since 1795, chastised the inconsistent Jefferson for supporting French revolutionaries while condemning black Haitians fighting for freedom just because they had "a skin not colored like our own." Not that Pickering supported either type of violent revolutionary— he did not. But he and his political allies, soon to be called the Federalists, were far more willing to contemplate trade and diplomatic relations with the emerging black republic of Haiti.

> Pickering chastised the inconsistent Jefferson for supporting French revolutionaries while condemning black Haitians fighting for freedom just because they had "a skin not colored like our own."

REVIEW   Why did the United States feel vulnerable to international threats in the 1790s?

Federalists and Republicans

By the mid-1790s, polarization over the French Revolution, Haiti, the Jay Treaty, and Hamilton's economic plans had led to two distinct and consistent rival political groups: Federalists and Republicans. Politicians and newspapers adopted these labels, words that summarized conflicting political positions. Federalist leaders supported Britain in foreign policy and commercial interests at home, while Republicans rooted for liberty in France and worried about monarchical Federalists at home. The labels did not yet describe full-fledged political parties, which were still thought to be a sign of failure of the experiment in government. Washington's decision not to seek a third term led to serious partisan electioneering in the presidential and congressional elections of 1796. Federalist John Adams won the presidency, but party strife accelerated over failed diplomacy in France, bringing the United States to the brink of war. Pro-war and antiwar antagonism created a major crisis over political free speech, militarism, and fears of sedition and treason.

The Election of 1796

Washington struggled to appear to be above party politics, and in his farewell address, he stressed the need to maintain a "unity of government" reflecting a unified body politic. He also urged the country to "steer clear of permanent alliances with any portion of the foreign world." The leading contenders for his position, John Adams of Massachusetts and Thomas Jefferson of Virginia, in theory agreed with him, but around them raged a party contest split along pro-British versus pro-French lines.

Adams and Jefferson were not adept politicians in the modern sense, skilled in the arts of persuasion and intrigue. Bruised by his conflicts with Hamilton, Jefferson had resigned as secretary of state in 1793 and retreated to Monticello, his home in Virginia. Adams's job as vice president kept him closer to the political action, but his personality often put people off. He was temperamental, thin-skinned, and quick to take offense.

The leading Federalists informally caucused and chose Adams as their candidate, with Thomas Pinckney of South Carolina to run with him. The Republicans settled on Aaron Burr of New York to pair with Jefferson. The Constitution did not anticipate parties and tickets. Instead, each electoral college voter could cast two votes for any two candidates, but on only one ballot. The top vote-getter became president, and the next-highest assumed the vice presidency. (This procedural flaw was corrected by the Twelfth Amendment, adopted in 1804.) With only one ballot, careful maneuvering was required to make sure the chief rivals for the presidency did not land in the top two spots.

Into that maneuverable moment stepped Alexander Hamilton. No longer in the cabinet, Hamilton had returned to his law practice in 1795, but he kept a firm hand on political developments. Hamilton did not trust Adams; he preferred Pinckney, and he tried to influence electors to throw their support to the South Carolinian. But his plan backfired: Adams was elected president with 71 electoral votes; Jefferson came in second with 68 and thus became vice president. Pinckney got 59 votes, while Burr trailed with 30.

Adams's inaugural speech pledged neutrality in foreign affairs and respect for the French people, which made Republicans hopeful. To please Federalists, Adams retained three cabinet

**Washington's Farewell Address
Printed on a Textile, 1806**
This small square of fabric, suitable for framing or tacking to
the wall, was one of many items that served to immortalize
Washington as the benevolent savior of the young Republic.
Known well by close associates as a man with ordinary
human failings—one Federalist member of his last cabinet
complained that he was "vain and weak and ignorant"—
Washington in death became a demigod, a genius of inspired leadership and faultless integrity. This 1806 textile
features the final paragraph of Washington's 1796 farewell
address, one highlighting his modesty and self-deprecation.
At the bottom, the American eagle and the British lion flank
two sailing ships (one close, one far-off) under the words
"Commercial Union." This textile picture was in fact an
implicit criticism of President Thomas Jefferson (1801–1809),
whose leadership was producing deteriorating relations
with Britain that would finally result in the War of 1812.
Collection of Janice L. and David J. Frent.

members from Washington's administration—
the secretaries of state, treasury, and war. But the
three were Hamilton loyalists, passing off
Hamilton's judgments and advice as their own
to the unwitting Adams. Vice President Jefferson
extended a conciliatory hand to Adams when the
two old friends met in Philadelphia, still the capital. They even took temporary lodging in the
same boardinghouse, as if expecting to work
closely together. But the Hamiltonian cabinet
ruined the honeymoon. Jefferson's advice was
spurned, and he withdrew from active counsel
of the president.

The XYZ Affair

From the start, Adams's presidency was in crisis.
France retaliated for the British-friendly Jay
Treaty by abandoning its 1778 alliance with the
United States. French privateers—armed private
vessels—started detaining American ships
carrying British goods; by March 1797, more
than three hundred American vessels had been
seized. To avenge these insults, Federalists
started murmuring openly about war with
France. Adams preferred negotiations and dispatched a three-man commission to France in

the fall of 1797. When the three commissioners
arrived in Paris, French officials would not
receive them. Finally, the French minister of
foreign affairs, Talleyrand, sent three French
agents—unnamed and later known to the
American public as X, Y, and Z—to the
American commissioners with the information
that $250,000 might grease the wheels of diplo-
macy and a $12 million loan to the French gov-
ernment would be the price of a peace treaty.
Incensed, the commissioners brought news of
the bribery attempt to the president.

Americans reacted to the XYZ affair with
shock and anger. Even staunch pro-French
Republicans began to reevaluate their allegiance.
The Federalist-dominated Congress appropriated money for an army of ten thousand soldiers
and repealed all prior treaties with France. In
1798, twenty naval warships launched the
United States into its first undeclared war, called
the Quasi-War by historians to underscore its uncertain legal status. The main scene of action was
the Caribbean, where more than one hundred
French ships were captured.

There was no home-front unity in this time
of undeclared war; antagonism only intensified
between Federalists and Republicans. Because

John Adams, by John Trumbull
In 1793, a year after painting a portrait of the youthful secretary of the treasury Alexander Hamilton (see page 288), Trumbull painted Vice President John Adams, then age fifty-eight. A friend once listed Adams's shortcomings as a politician: "He can't dance, drink, game, flatter, promise, dress, swear with gentlemen, and small talk and flirt with the ladies."
National Portrait Gallery, Smithsonian Institution/Art Resources, NY.

there seemed to be very little chance of a land invasion by France, leading Republicans feared, with some justification, that the Federalists' real aim might be to raise the army to threaten domestic dissenters. Some claimed that Hamilton had masterminded the army buildup and was lobbying to be second in command, behind the aging Washington. President Adams was increasingly mistrustful, but his cabinet backed the military buildup, and Adams was too weak politically to prevail. He was, moreover, beginning to suspect that his cabinet was more loyal to Hamilton than to the president.

Republican newspapers heaped abuse on Adams. Pro-French mobs roamed the capital, and Adams, fearing for his personal safety, stocked weapons in his presidential quarters. Federalists, too, went on the offensive. In Newburyport, Massachusetts, they lit a huge bonfire and burned issues of the state's Republican newspapers. One Federalist editor ominously declared that "he who is not for us is against us."

The Alien and Sedition Acts

With tempers so dangerously high, and fears that political dissent was perhaps akin to treason, Federalist leaders moved to muffle the opposition. In mid-1798, Congress hammered out the Sedition Act, which not only made conspiracy and revolt illegal but also penalized speaking or writing anything that defamed the president or Congress. Criticizing government leaders became a criminal offense. One Federalist in Congress justified his vote for the law this way: "Let gentlemen look at certain papers printed in this city and elsewhere, and ask themselves whether an unwarrantable and dangerous combination does not exist to overturn and ruin the government by publishing the most shameless falsehoods against the representatives of the people." In all, twenty-five men, almost all Republican newspaper editors, were charged with sedition; twelve were convicted. (See "Documenting the American Promise," page 314.)

Congress also passed two Alien Acts. The first extended the waiting period for an alien to achieve citizenship from five to fourteen years and required all aliens to register with the federal government. The second empowered the president in time of war to deport or imprison without trial any foreigner suspected of being a danger to the United States. The clear intent of these laws was to harass French immigrants already in the United States and to discourage others from coming.

Republicans strongly opposed the Alien and Sedition Acts on the grounds that they were in conflict with the Bill of Rights, but they did not have the votes to revoke the acts in Congress, nor could the federal judiciary, dominated by Federalist judges, be counted on to challenge them. Jefferson and Madison turned to the state legislatures, the only other competing political arena, to press their opposition. Each man drafted a set of resolutions condemning the acts and had the legislatures of Virginia and Kentucky present them to the federal government in late fall 1798. The Virginia and Kentucky Resolutions tested the novel argument that state legislatures have the right to judge the constitutionality of federal laws and to **nullify** laws that infringe on the liberties of the people as defined in the Bill of Rights. The resolutions made little dent in the Alien and Sedition Acts, but the idea of a state's right to nullify federal law did not disappear. It would resurface several times in decades to come, most notably in a

Cartoon of the Matthew Lyon Fight in Congress
The political tensions of 1798 were not merely intellectual. A February session in Congress degenerated from name-calling to a brawl. Roger Griswold, a Connecticut Federalist, called Matthew Lyon, a Vermont Republican, a coward. Lyon responded with some well aimed spit, the first departure from the gentle man's code of honor. Griswold responded by raising his cane to Lyon, whereupon Lyon grabbed nearby fire tongs to beat back his assailant. Madison wrote to Jefferson that the two should have dueled: "No man ought to reproach another with cowardice, who is not ready to give proof of his own courage" by negotiating a duel, the honorable way to avenge insults in Virginia's planter class. But Lyon, a Scots-Irish immigrant, did not come from a class or culture that cultivated the art of the duel. Rough-and-tumble fighting was his first response to insult.
Library of Congress.

READING THE IMAGE: What was the cartoonist trying to convey about the tone of Congress and its members? What is the picture on the back wall?
CONNECTIONS: How did the Constitution's political ideals contrast with the actual behavior of politicians in the 1790s?

FOR MORE HELP ANALYZING THIS IMAGE, see the visual activity for this chapter in the Online Study Guide at bedfordstmartins.com/roark.

---

major tariff dispute in 1832 and in the sectional arguments that led to the Civil War.

Amid all the war hysteria and sedition fears in 1798, President Adams regained his balance. He was uncharacteristically restrained in pursuing opponents under the Sedition Act, and he finally refused to declare war on France, as extreme Federalists wished. No doubt he was beginning to realize how much he had been the dupe of Hamilton. He also shrewdly realized that France was not eager for war and that a peaceful settlement might be close at hand. In January 1799, a peace initiative from France arrived in the form of a letter assuring Adams that diplomatic channels were open again and that new commissioners would be welcomed in France. Adams accepted this overture and appointed new negotiators. By late 1799, the Quasi-War with

The Crisis of 1798: Sedition

As President John Adams inched toward an undeclared war with France, criticism of his foreign policy reached an all-time high. Newspaper editors and politicians favorable to France blasted him with such intemperate language that his supporters feared the United States could be pushed to the brink of civil war. Federalists in Congress tried to muffle the opposition by criminalizing seditious words, believing it the only way to preserve the country. Republicans just redoubled their opposition.

DOCUMENT 1
Abigail Adams Complains of Sedition, 1798

Throughout the spring of 1798, a beleaguered Abigail Adams complained repeatedly in confidential letters to her sister Mary Cranch about the need for a sedition law to put a stop to the political criticisms of her husband, the president, by Benjamin Bache, the pro-French editor of the Philadelphia Aurora.

(April 26): . . . Yet dairingly do the vile incendaries keep up in Baches paper the most wicked and base, voilent & calumniating abuse—It was formerly considerd as leveld against the Government, but now it . . . insults the Majesty of the Sovereign People. But nothing will have an Effect until Congress passes a Sedition Bill. . . . (April 28): . . . We are now wonderfully popular except with Bache & Co who in his paper calls the President old, querilous, Bald, blind, cripled, Toothless Adams. (May 10): . . . This Bache is cursing & abusing daily. If that fellow . . . is not surpressd, we shall come to a civil war. (May 26): . . . I wish the Laws of our Country were competant to punish the stirer up of sedition, the writer and Printer of base and unfounded calumny. This would contribute as much to the Peace and harmony of our Country as any measure. . . . (June 19): . . . In any other Country Bache & all his papers would have been seazd and ought to be here, but congress are dilly dallying about passing a Bill enabling the President to seize suspisious persons, and their papers. (June 23): . . . I wish our Legislature would set the example & make a sedition act, to hold in order the base Newspaper calumniators. In this State, you could not get a verdict, if a prosecution was to be commenced.

SOURCE: *New Letters of Abigail Adams, 1788–1801* by Stewart Mitchell, ed., pp. 165, 167, 172, 179, 193, 196. Copyright © 1974 by The American Antiquarian Society. Reprinted by permission of Houghton Mifflin Company. All rights reserved.

DOCUMENT 2
The Sedition Act of 1798

On July 14, 1798, Congress approved a bill making sedition with malicious intent a crime.

SECTION 1. . . . if any persons shall unlawfully combine or conspire together, with intent to oppose any measure or measures of the government of the United States . . . , or to impede the operation of any law of the United States, or to intimidate or prevent any person holding . . . office in or under the government of the United States, from undertaking, performing or executing his trust or duty, and if any person or persons, with intent as aforesaid, shall counsel, advise or attempt to procure any insurrection, riot, unlawful assembly, or combination . . . , he or they shall be deemed guilty of a high misdemeanor, and on conviction . . . shall be punished by a fine not exceeding five thousand dollars, and by imprisonment during a term not less than six months nor exceeding five years. . . .

SEC. 2. . . . If any person shall write, print, utter or publish, or shall cause or procure to be written, printed, uttered or published . . . , any false, scandalous and malicious writing or writings against the government of the United States, or either house of the Congress of the United States, or the President of the United States, with intent to defame the said government . . . or to bring them . . . into contempt or disrepute; or to excite against them . . . the hatred of the good people of the United States . . . , or to aid, encourage or abet any hostile designs of any foreign nation against the United States . . . , then such person, being thereof convicted . . . shall be punished by a fine not exceeding two thousand dollars, and by imprisonment not exceeding two years.

SOURCE: Excerpted text from Congressional bill, July 14, 1798.

DOCUMENT 3
Matthew Lyon Criticizes John Adams, 1798

Matthew Lyon, a member of Congress from Vermont, published this criticism of President Adams in a letter to the editor of Spooner's Vermont Journal *(July 31, 1798). It became the first of three counts against him in a sedition trial. Lyon drew a four-month sentence and a fine of $1,000. From jail, he ran for reelection to Congress—and won.*

As to the Executive, when I shall see the efforts of that power bent on the promotion of the comfort, the happiness, and the accommodation of the people, that Executive shall have my zealous and uniform support. But when I see every consideration of the public welfare swallowed up in a continual grasp for power, in an unbounded thirst for ridiculous pomp, foolish adulation, or selfish avarice; when I shall behold men of real merit daily turned out of office for no other cause but independence of sentiment; when I shall see men of firmness, merit, years, abilities, and experience, discarded on their application for office, for fear they possess that independence; and men of meanness preferred for the ease with which they take up and advocate opinions, the consequence of which they know but little of; when I shall see the sacred name of religion employed as a State engine to make mankind hate and persecute one another, I shall not be their humble advocate.

SOURCE: Matthew Lyon, Letter in *Spooner's Vermont Journal*, July 31, 1798. Quoted *Matthew Lyon: New Man of the Democratic Revolution, 1749–1822* by Aleine Austin, pp. 108–9. Copyright © 1981 Aleine Austin. Reprinted with permission of Pennsylvania State University Press.

DOCUMENT 4
The Virginia Resolution, December 24, 1798

James Madison drafted the Virginia Resolution and had a trusted ally present it to the Virginia legislature, which was dominated by Republicans. (Jefferson did the same for Kentucky.) The Virginia document denounces the Alien and Sedition Acts and declares that states have the right to "interpose" to stop unconstitutional actions by the federal government.

RESOLVED . . . That this assembly most solemnly declares a warm attachment to the Union of the States, to maintain which it pledges all its powers; and that for this end, it is their duty to watch over and oppose every infraction of those principles which constitute the only basis of that Union, because a faithful observance of them, can alone secure its existence and the public happiness.

That this Assembly doth explicitly and peremptorily declare, that it views the powers of the federal government, as resulting from the compact, to which the states are parties; as limited by the plain sense and intention of the instrument constituting the compact; as no further valid that they are authorized by the grants enumerated in that compact; and that in case of a deliberate, palpable, and dangerous exercise of other powers, not granted by the said compact, the states who are parties thereto, have the right, and are in duty bound, to interpose for arresting the progress of the evil, and for maintaining within their respective limits, the authorities, rights and liberties appertaining to them. . . .

That the General Assembly doth particularly protest against the palpable and alarming infractions of the Constitution, in the two late cases of the "Alien and Sedition Acts" . . . ; the first of which exercises a power no where delegated to the federal government . . . ; and the other of which acts, exercises in like manner, a power not delegated by the constitution, but on the contrary, expressly and positively forbidden by one of the amendments thereto; a power, which more than any other, ought to produce universal alarm, because it is levelled against that right of freely examining public characters and measures, and of free communication among the people thereon, which has ever been justly deemed, the only effectual guardian of every other right.

SOURCE: Avalon Project, Yale Law School, 1996. www.yale.edu. © 1996–2007 The Avalon Project at Yale Law School. Reprinted with permission.

QUESTIONS FOR ANALYSIS AND DEBATE

1. Why did the Federalists believe that the Sedition Act was necessary? What exactly was the threat, according to Abigail Adams? What threat is implied by the wording of the act?

2. Does Matthew Lyon's criticism of President Adams rise to the level of threat that the Federalists feared? How do you explain his guilty verdict? His reelection to Congress?

3. What might Madison have meant by "interpose" as the desired action by states? What could states actually do?

4. Which side had the stronger argument in 1798–1799? Do you think there should be limits on what can be said publicly about high government officials? Why or why not?

France had subsided, and in 1800 the negotiations resulted in a treaty declaring "a true and sincere friendship" between the United States and France. But Federalists were not pleased; Adams lost the support of a significant part of his own party and sealed his fate as the first one-term president of the United States.

The election of 1800 was openly organized along party lines. The self-designated national leaders of each group met to handpick their candidates for president and vice president. Adams's chief opponent was Thomas Jefferson. When the election was finally over, President Jefferson mounted the inaugural platform to announce, "We are all republicans, we are all federalists," an appealing rhetoric of harmony appropriate to an inaugural address. But his formulation perpetuated a denial of the validity of party politics, a denial that ran deep in the founding generation of political leaders.

> **REVIEW** Why did Congress pass the Alien and Sedition Acts in 1798?

Conclusion: Parties Nonetheless

American political leaders began operating the new government in 1789 with great hopes of unifying the country and overcoming selfish factionalism. The enormous trust in President Washington was the central foundation for those hopes, and Washington did not disappoint, becoming a model "Mr. President" with a blend of integrity and authority. Stability was further aided by easy passage of the Bill of Rights (to appease Antifederalists) and by attention to cultivating a virtuous citizenry of upright men supported and rewarded by republican womanhood. Yet the hopes of the honeymoon period soon turned to worries and then fears as major political disagreements flared up.

At the core of the conflict was a group of talented men—Hamilton, Madison, Jefferson, and Adams—so recently allies but now opponents. They diverged over Hamilton's economic program, over relations with the British and the Jay Treaty, over the French and Haitian revolutions, and over preparedness for war abroad and free speech at home. Hamilton was perhaps the driving force in these conflicts, but the antagonism was not about mere personality. Parties were taking shape not around individuals, but around principles, such as ideas about what constituted enlightened leadership, how powerful the federal government should be, who was the best ally in Europe, and when oppositional political speech turned into treason. The Federalists were pro-British, pro-commerce, and ever alarmed about the potential excesses of democracy. The Republicans celebrated, up to a point, the radical republicanism of France and opposed the Sedition Act as an alarming example of an overbearing government cutting off freedom of speech.

When Jefferson in his inaugural address of 1800 offered his conciliatory assurance that Americans were at the same time "all republicans" and "all federalists," he probably mystified some listeners. Possibly, he meant to suggest that both groups shared two basic ideas—the value of republican government, in which power derived from the people, and the value of the unique federal system of shared governance structured by the Constitution. But by 1800, *Federalist* and *Republican* defined competing philosophies of government. To at least some of his listeners, Jefferson's assertion of harmony across budding party lines could only have seemed bizarre. For the next two decades, these two groups would battle each other, each fearing that the success of the other might bring the demise of the country. And for the next two decades, leaders continued to worry that partisan spirit itself was a bad thing.

Selected Bibliography

Politics

Akhil Reed Amar, *The Bill of Rights: Creation and Reconstruction* (2000).

Bernard Bailyn, *To Begin the World Anew: The Genius and Ambiguities of the American Founders* (2003).

Kenneth R. Bowling, *The Creation of Washington, D.C.: The Idea and Location of the American Capital* (1991).

Ron Chernow, *Alexander Hamilton* (2004).

Jerry A. Clouse, *The Whiskey Rebellion: Southwestern Pennsylvania's Frontier People Test the American Constitution* (1995).

Stanley Elkins and Eric McKitrick, *The Age of Federalism: The Early American Republic, 1788–1800* (1993).

Joseph J. Ellis, *Founding Brothers: The Revolutionary Generation* (2000).

John E. Ferling, *A Leap in the Dark: The Struggle to Create the American Republic* (2003).

Carolyn E. Fick, *The Making of Haiti: The Saint Domingue Revolution from Below* (1991).

David Barry Gaspar and David Patrick Geggus, eds., *A Turbulent Time: The French Revolution and the Greater Caribbean* (1997).

Peter P. Hill, *French Perceptions of the Early American Republic, 1783–1793* (1988).

Ralph Ketcham, *Presidents above Party: The First American Presidency, 1789–1829* (1984).

Leonard Levy, *The Emergence of a Free Press* (1985).

David McCullough, *John Adams* (2001).

Jeffrey L. Pasley, *The Tyranny of Printers: Newspaper Politics in the Early American Republic* (2001).

James Rogers Sharp, *American Politics in the Early Republic: The New Nation in Crisis* (1993).

Thomas P. Slaughter, *The Whiskey Rebellion: Frontier Epilogue to the American Revolution* (1986).

Larry E. Tise, *The American Counterrevolution: A Retreat from Liberty, 1783–1800* (1999).

Richard J. Twomey, *Jacobins and Jeffersonians: Anglo-American Radicalism in the United States, 1790–1820* (1989).

Henry Wiencek, *An Imperfect God: George Washington, His Slaves, and the Creation of America* (2003).

Society and Culture

Susan Branson, *These Fiery Frenchified Dames: Women and Political Culture in Early National Philadelphia* (2001).

Richard D. Brown, *Knowledge Is Power: The Diffusion of Information in Early America, 1700–1865* (1989).

Nancy Cott, *The Bonds of Womanhood: Women's Sphere in New England, 1780–1835* (1977).

Joanne B. Freeman, *Affairs of Honor: National Politics in the New Republic* (2001).

Richard R. John, *Spreading the News: The American Postal System from Franklin to Morse* (1996).

Linda Kerber, *Women of the Republic: Intellect and Ideology in Revolutionary America* (1980).

Clare A. Lyons, *Sex among the Rabble: An Intimate History of Gender and Power in the Age of Revolution, Philadelphia, 1730–1830* (2006).

Bruce H. Mann, *Republic of Debtors: Bankruptcy in the Age of American Independence* (2002).

Simon P. Newman, *Parades and the Politics of the Street: Festive Culture in the Early American Republic* (2000).

Sheila L. Skemp, *Judith Sargent Murray: A Brief Biography with Documents* (1998).

David Waldstreicher, *In the Midst of Perpetual Fetes: The Making of American Nationalism, 1776–1820* (1997).

Indians and the Frontier

Andrew R. L. Cayton, *Frontier Republic: Ideology and Politics in the Ohio Country, 1780–1825* (1989).

Gregory E. Dowd, *A Spirited Resistance: The North American Indian Struggle for Unity, 1745–1815* (1992).

R. Douglas Hurt, *The Ohio Frontier: Crucible of the Old Northwest, 1720–1830* (1998).

Wiley Sword, *President Washington's Indian War: The Struggle for the Old Northwest, 1790–1795* (1985).

► **For more books about topics in this chapter,** see the Online Bibliography at bedfordstmartins.com/roark.

► **For additional firsthand accounts of this period,** see Chapter 9 in Michael Johnson, ed., *Reading the American Past,* Fourth Edition.

► **For Web sites, images, and documents related to topics and places in this chapter,** visit bedfordstmartins.com/makehistory.

REVIEWING THE CHAPTER

Follow these steps to review and strengthen your understanding of the chapter.

STEP 1: *Study the* **Key Terms** *and* **Timeline** *to identify the significance of each item listed.*

STEP 2: *Answer the* **Review Questions***, drawing on key terms and dates to support your answers.*

STEP 3: *Drawing on the Key Terms, Timeline, and Review Questions, answer the broader* **Making Connections** *questions.*

KEY TERMS

Who

Alexander Hamilton (pp. 287, 290, 295, 298)

Thomas Jefferson (pp. 287, 290)

James Madison (pp. 288, 290, 298)

George Washington (p. 289)

John Jay (pp. 290, 308)

Judith Sargent Murray (p. 291)

Mary Wollstonecraft (p. 292)

Eli Whitney (p. 294)

Robert Morris (p. 300)

Pierre L'Enfant (p. 301)

Josiah Harmar (p. 303)

Arthur St. Clair (p. 304)

Anthony Wayne (p. 304)

Little Turtle (p. 304)

Blue Jacket (p. 304)

Toussaint L'Ouverture (p. 309)

Talleyrand (p. 311)

What

Revolutionary War debt (p. 287)

Bill of Rights (p. 289)

republican motherhood (p. 293)

Report on Public Credit (p. 295)

assumption (p. 296)

Washington, D.C. (pp. 298, 300)

Bank of the United States (p. 298)

Report on Manufactures (p. 298)

Whiskey Rebellion (p. 299)

Fort Washington (p. 304)

Fort Greenville (p. 305)

Fort Recovery (p. 305)

battle of Fallen Timbers (p. 305)

Treaty of Greenville (p. 305)

French Revolution (p. 307)

Neutrality Proclamation (p. 308)

Jay Treaty (p. 308)

Haitian Revolution (p. 309)

Federalists (p. 310)

Republicans (p. 310)

XYZ affair (p. 311)

Quasi-War (p. 311)

Sedition Act (p. 312)

Alien Acts (p. 312)

Virginia and Kentucky Resolutions (p. 312)

TIMELINE

1789 • George Washington inaugurated first president.

• French Revolution begins.

• First Congress meets.

• Fort Washington erected in western Ohio.

1790 • Congress approves Hamilton's debt plan.

• Judith Sargent Murray publishes "On the Equality of the Sexes."

• Shawnee and Miami Indians in Ohio defeat General Josiah Harmar.

1791 • States ratify Bill of Rights.

• Congress and president charter Bank of the United States.

• Ohio Indians defeat General Arthur St. Clair.

• Congress passes whiskey tax.

• Haitian Revolution begins.

• Hamilton issues *Report on Manufactures*.

1793 • Napoleonic Wars break out between France and Britain.

• Washington issues Neutrality Proclamation.

• Eli Whitney invents cotton gin.

REVIEW QUESTIONS

1. How did political leaders in the 1790s attempt to overcome the divisions of the 1780s? (pp. 289–94)

2. Why were Hamilton's economic policies controversial? (pp. 294–302)

3. Why did the United States feel vulnerable to international threats in the 1790s? (pp. 302–10)

4. Why did Congress pass the Alien and Sedition Acts in 1798? (pp. 310–16)

MAKING CONNECTIONS

1. Why did the Federalist alliance fracture in the 1790s? Why was this development troubling to the nation? In your answer, cite specific ideological and political developments that compromised cooperation.

2. What provoked the Whiskey Rebellion? How did the government respond? In your answer, discuss the foundations and precedents of the conflict, as well as the significance of the government's response.

3. Americans held that virtue was pivotal to the success of their new nation. What did they mean by virtue? How did they hope to ensure that their citizens and their leaders possessed virtue?

4. The domestic politics of the new nation were profoundly influenced by conflicts beyond the nation's borders. Discuss how conflicts abroad contributed to domestic political developments in the 1790s.

▶ FOR PRACTICE QUIZZES, A CUSTOMIZED STUDY PLAN, AND OTHER STUDY TOOLS, see the Online Study Guide at bedfordstmartins.com/roark.

1794 • Whiskey Rebellion.
• Battle of Fallen Timbers.

1795 • Treaty of Greenville.
• Jay Treaty.

1796 • Federalist John Adams elected second president.

1797 • XYZ affair.

1798 • Quasi-War with France erupts.
• Alien and Sedition Acts.
• Virginia and Kentucky Resolutions.

1800 • Republican Thomas Jefferson elected third president.

PATRIOTIC PITCHER, 1800

This pitcher, a humble piece of everyday tableware, celebrates American military readiness. A militia officer strikes a springy pose, ready for action. Two naval frigates lie offshore; a cannon juts out aggressively. Banners proclaim "Success to America Whose Militia Is Better Than Standing Armies" and "May Its Citizens Emulate Soldiers, and Its Soldiers Heroes." The picture's swagger implies a military preparedness that was woefully off the mark. In 1800, the U.S. navy had only six frigates, some of which were still under construction. Serious trouble was brewing in the Mediterranean, where North African privateers attacked American ships with impunity. In 1801, President Jefferson received the first official declaration of war against the United States, from the leader of Tripoli. Marines, not militiamen, were needed.

Earthenware pitchers emblazoned with patriotic messages all came from English manufacturers in Liverpool, with its good clay and ready supply of coal for high-temperature firing. Thousands of American-themed pitchers—with eagles and flags, Miss Liberty and George Washington—were made and sold. Pitchers saw daily use in the early Republic wherever people gathered to eat or drink. Water or milk, ale or apple juice, hot rum toddies or mulled cider—early Americans' beverage choices were more limited than ours today, and everyone gathered around the table typically drank the same beverage from the shared pitcher.

Kahn Fine Antiques/photo courtesy of Antiques and Fine Arts.

Republicans in Power

1800–1824

■ **Jefferson's Presidency** 322
Turbulent Times:
Election and Rebellion 323
The Jeffersonian Vision
of Republican Simplicity 326
The Judiciary and the
Midnight Judges 327
The Promise of the West:
The Louisiana Purchase and the
Lewis and Clark Expedition 328
Challenges Overseas:
The Barbary Wars 330
More Transatlantic Troubles:
Impressment and Embargo 331

■ **The Madisons in
the White House** 331
Women in Washington City 332
Indian Troubles in the West 333
The War of 1812 333
Washington City Burns:
The British Offensive 335

■ **Women's Status in
the Early Republic** 337
Women and the Law 337
Women and Church Governance 340
Female Education 340

■ **Monroe and Adams** 344
From Property to Democracy 345
The Missouri Compromise 346
The Monroe Doctrine 348
The Election of 1824 349
The Adams Administration 351

■ **Conclusion:
Republican Simplicity
Becomes Complex** 352

T HE NAME TECUMSEH translates as "Shooting Star," a fitting name for the Shawnee chief who reached meteoric heights of fame among Indians during Thomas Jefferson's presidency. From Canada south to Georgia and from the Atlantic west to the Mississippi, Tecumseh was accounted a charismatic leader, for which white Americans praised (and feared) him. Graceful, eloquent, compelling, and astute: Tecumseh was all these and more. A gifted natural commander, he was equal parts politician and warrior.

The Ohio Country, where Tecumseh was born in 1768, was home to about a dozen Indian tribes, including the Shawnee, recently displaced from the South. During the Revolutionary War, the region became a battleground with the "Big Knives," as the Shawnee people called the Americans. Tecumseh's childhood was marked by repeated violence and the loss of his father and two brothers in battle. Five times between 1774 and 1782, the boy fled raids by American soldiers that left his home in flames and his village destroyed. The Treaty of Paris in 1783 brought no peace to Indian country. American settlers pushed west, and the youthful Tecumseh honed his warrior skills by ambushing pioneers running flatboats down the Ohio River. He fought at the battle of Fallen Timbers, a major Indian defeat in 1794, but avoided the 1795 negotiations of the Treaty of Greenville, in which half a dozen dispirited tribes ceded much of Ohio to the Big Knives. In frustration, he watched as seven treaties between 1802 and 1805 whittled away more Indian land.

Some Indians, resigned and tired, looked for ways to accommodate, taking up farming, trade, and even intermarriage with the Big Knives. Others spent their treaty payments on alcohol. Tecumseh's younger brother Tenskwatawa led an embittered life of idleness and drink. But Tecumseh rejected assimilation and inebriation and instead campaigned for a return to ancient ways. Donning traditional animal-skin garb, he traveled around the Great Lakes region after 1805, persuading tribes to join his pan-Indian confederacy. The American territorial governor of Indiana, William Henry Harrison, reported, "For four years he has been in constant motion. You see him today on the Wabash, and in a short time hear of him on the shores of Lake Erie or Michigan, or on the banks of the Mississippi, and wherever he goes he makes an impression favorable to his purpose." In 1811, the leader named Shooting Star traveled among tribes in the South while an especially brilliant comet illuminated the night sky.

Even his dissolute brother was born anew. After a near-death experience in 1805, Tenskwatawa revived and recounted a startling vision of meeting the Master of Life. Renaming himself the Prophet, he urged Indians everywhere to regard whites as children of the Evil Spirit, destined to be destroyed. Tecumseh and the Prophet established a new village called Prophetstown,

Tecumseh
Several portraits of Tecumseh exist, but they all present a different visage, and none of them enjoys verified authenticity. This one perhaps comes closest to how Tecumseh actually looked. It is an 1848 engraving adapted from an earlier drawing that no longer exists, sketched by a French trader in Indiana named Pierre Le Dru in a live sitting with the Indian leader in 1808. The engraver has given Tecumseh a British army officer's uniform, showing that he fought on the British side in the War of 1812. Notice the head covering and the medallion around Tecumseh's neck, marking his Indian identity.
Library of Congress.

located in present-day Indiana, offering a potent blend of spiritual regeneration and political unity that attracted thousands of followers. Governor Harrison admired and feared Tecumseh, calling him "one of those uncommon geniuses which spring up occasionally to produce revolutions."

President Thomas Jefferson worried about an organized Indian confederacy and its potential for a renewed alliance with the British in Canada. Those worries became a reality during Jefferson's second term in office (1805–1809). Although his first term (1801–1805) brought notable successes, such as the Louisiana Purchase and the Lewis and Clark expedition, his second term was consumed by the threat of war with either Britain or France, in a replay of the late-1790s tensions. When war came in 1812, the

enemy was Britain, bolstered by a reenergized Indian-British alliance. Among the causes of the war were insults over international shipping rights, the capture of U.S. vessels, and the impressment of American sailors. But the war also derived compelling strength from Tecumseh's confederacy, now pledged to help the British in Canada. Significant battles pitted U.S. soldiers against Indians in the Great Lakes, Tennessee, and Florida.

In the end, the War of 1812 settled little between the United States and Britain, but it was tragically conclusive for the Indians. Eight hundred warriors led by Tecumseh helped defend Canada against U.S. attacks, but the British did not reciprocate when the Indians were under threat. Tecumseh died on Canadian soil at the battle of the Thames in the fall of 1813. No Indian leader with his star power would emerge again east of the Mississippi.

The briefly unified Indian confederacy under Tecumseh had no counterpart in the young Republic's confederation of states, where widespread unity and enthusiasm behind a single leader proved impossible to achieve. Republicans did battle with Federalists during the Jefferson and Madison administrations, but then Federalists doomed their party by opposing the War of 1812 and after 1815 ceased to be a major force in political life. The next two presidents, James Monroe and John Quincy Adams, congratulated themselves on the Federalists' demise and Republican unity, but in fact divisions within their own party were extensive. Wives of politicians increasingly inserted themselves into this dissonant mix, managing their husbands' politicking and jockeying for power in the Capitol and enabling them to appear above the fray and maintain the fiction of a nonpartisan state. That it was a fiction became sharply apparent in the most serious political crisis of this period, the Missouri Compromise of 1820.

Jefferson's Presidency

The nerve-wracking election of 1800, decided in the House of Representatives, enhanced fears that party divisions would ruin the country. A panicky Federalist newspaper in Connecticut predicted that Jefferson's victory would produce a bloody civil war and usher in an immoral reign of "murder, robbery, rape, adultery and incest." Similar fears were expressed in the South, where a frightful slave uprising seemed a possible outcome of Jefferson's victory. But nothing nearly so dramatic occurred. Jefferson later called his election the "revolution of 1800," referring to his repudiation of monarchical practices, his undoing of Federalist judicial appointments, and his cutbacks in military spending and taxes.

Jefferson did radically transform the presidency, away from the Federalists' vision of a powerful executive branch and toward **republican** simplicity and limited government. Yet even Jefferson found that circumstances sometimes required him to draw on the expansive powers of the presidency. The rise of Napoleon in France brought France and Britain into open warfare again in 1803, creating unexpected opportunities and challenges for Jefferson. One major opportunity arrived in the spectacular purchase from France of the Louisiana Territory; a significant challenge arose when pirates threatened American ships off the north coast of Africa and when British and French naval forces nipped at American ships—and American honor—in the Atlantic Ocean.

Turbulent Times: Election and Rebellion

The result of the election of 1800 remained uncertain from polling time in November to repeated roll call votes in the House of Representatives in February 1801. Federalist John Adams, never secure in his leadership of the Federalist Party, was no longer in the presidential race once it got to the House. Instead, the contest was between Jefferson and his running mate, Senator Aaron Burr of New York. Republican voters in the electoral college slipped up, giving Jefferson and Burr an equal number of votes, an outcome possible because of the single balloting to choose both president and vice president (Map 10.1). (To fix this problem, the Twelfth Amendment to the Constitution, adopted four years later, provided for distinct ballots for the two offices.) The vain and ambitious Burr declined to concede, so the Federalist-dominated House of Representatives took up its constitutional mandate to choose which Republican would become president.

Each state delegation had one vote, and a candidate needed nine votes to win. Some Federalists preferred Burr, believing that his character flaws made him especially susceptible to Federalist pressure. But the influential Alexander Hamilton, though no friend of Jefferson, recognized that the high-strung Burr

would be more dangerous than Jefferson in the presidency. Jefferson was a "contemptible hypocrite" in Hamilton's opinion, but at least he was not corrupt. (In 1804, Burr shot and killed Hamilton in a formal but illegal duel. See "Historical Question," page 324.) Jefferson received the votes of eight states on the first ballot. Thirty-six ballots and six days later, he got the critical ninth vote, as well as a tenth. This election demonstrated a remarkable feature of the new constitutional government: No matter how hard fought the campaign, the leadership of the nation could shift from one group to a distinctly different group in a peaceful transfer of power effected by ballots, not bullets.

As the country struggled over its white leadership crisis, a twenty-four-year-old blacksmith named Gabriel, the slave of Thomas Prossor, plotted rebellion in Virginia. Inspired by the Haitian Revolution (see chapter 9), and perhaps directly informed of it by French slaves new to the Richmond area, Gabriel was said to be organizing a thousand slaves to march on the state capital of Richmond and take the governor, James Monroe, hostage. On the appointed day, however, a few nervous slaves went to the authorities, and within days, scores of implicated conspirators were jailed and brought to trial.

MAP 10.1 The Election of 1800

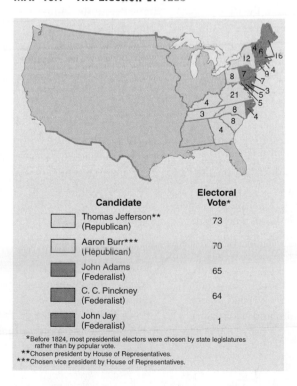

Candidate	Electoral Vote*
Thomas Jefferson** (Republican)	73
Aaron Burr*** (Republican)	70
John Adams (Federalist)	65
C. C. Pinckney (Federalist)	64
John Jay (Federalist)	1

*Before 1824, most presidential electors were chosen by state legislatures rather than by popular vote.
**Chosen president by House of Representatives.
***Chosen vice president by House of Representatives.

How Could a Vice President Get Away with Murder?

On July 11, 1804, the vice president of the United States, Aaron Burr, shot Alexander Hamilton, the architect of the Federalist Party, in a duel on a narrow ledge below the cliffs of Weehawken, New Jersey, across the Hudson River from New York City. The pistol blast tore through a rib, demolished Hamilton's liver, and splintered his spine. The forty-nine-year-old Hamilton died the next day, in agonizing pain.

How could it happen that a sitting vice president and a prominent political leader could put themselves at such risk? Why did men who made their living by the legal system go outside the law and turn to the centuries-old ritual of the duel? Here were two eminent attorneys, skilled in the legalistic negotiations meant to substitute for violent resolution of disputes, firing .54-caliber hair-trigger weapons at ten paces. Did anyone try to stop them? How did the public react? Was Hamilton's death a criminal act? How could Burr continue to fulfill his federal office as vice president and preside over the U.S. Senate?

Burr challenged Hamilton in late June after learning about a newspaper report that Hamilton "looked upon Mr. Burr to be a dangerous man, and one who ought not be trusted with the reins of government." Burr knew that Hamilton had long held a very low opinion of him and had never hesitated to say so in private, but now his private disparagement had made its way into print. Compounding the insult were political consequences: Burr was sure that Hamilton's remark cost him election to the governorship of New York.

Quite possibly, he was right. Knowing that Jefferson planned to dump him from the federal ticket in the 1804 election, Burr had chosen to run for New York's highest office. His opponent was an obscure Republican judge; Burr's success depended on the support of the old Federalist leadership in the state. Up to the eve of the election, he appeared to have it—until Hamilton's remark was circulated.

So on June 18, Burr challenged Hamilton to a duel if he did not disavow his comment. Over the next three weeks, the men exchanged several letters clarifying the nature of the insult that had aggrieved Burr. Hamilton the lawyer evasively quibbled over words, causing Burr finally to rail against his focus on syntax and grammar. At heart, Hamilton could not deny the insult, nor could he spurn the challenge without injury to his reputation for integrity and bravery. Both Burr and Hamilton were locked in a highly ritualized procedure meant to uphold a gentleman's code of honor.

Each man had a trusted "second," in accord with the code of dueling, who helped frame and deliver the letters and finally assisted at the duel site. Only a handful of close friends knew of the challenge, and no one tried to stop it. Hamilton did not tell his wife. He wrote her a tender farewell letter the night before, to be opened in the event of his death. He knew full well the pain dueling brought to loved ones, for his nineteen-year-old son Philip had been killed in a duel three years earlier, on the same Weehawken ledge, as a result of heated words exchanged at a New York theater. Even when Hamilton's wife

***Aaron Burr*, by John Vanderlyn**
Aaron Burr was fifty-three years old at the time of this portrait, painted in 1809 by the New York artist John Vanderlyn.
Collection of The New-York Historical Society.

was called to her husband's deathbed, she was first told he had terrible spasms from an illness. Women were completely shut out of the masculine world of dueling.

News of Hamilton's death spread quickly in New York and then throughout the nation. On the day of the funeral, church bells tolled continuously, and New York merchants shut down their businesses. Thousands joined the procession, and the city council declared a six-week mourning period. Burr fled to Philadelphia, fearing retribution by the crowd.

While northern newspapers expressed indignation over the illegal duel and the tragic death of so prominent a man, response in the South was more subdued. Dueling was fully accepted there as an extralegal remedy for insult, and Burr's grievance fit perfectly the sense of violated honor that legitimated duels. In addition, southerners had never been particularly fond of the Federalist Hamilton. Many northern states, in contrast, had criminalized dueling recently, treating a challenge as a misdemeanor and a dueling death as a homicide. Even after death, the loser of an illegal duel could endure one final penalty— being buried without a coffin, having a stake driven through the body, being strung up in public until the body rotted, or, more horrible still for the time, being donated to medical students for dissection. By dishonoring the corpse, northern lawmakers hoped to discourage dueling. Hamilton's body was spared such a fate. But two ministers in succession refused to administer Holy Communion to him in his dying hours because he was a duelist; one finally relented.

The public demanded to know the reasons for the duel, so the seconds prepared the correspondence between the principals for publication.

A coroner's jury in New York soon indicted Burr on misdemeanor charges for issuing a challenge; a grand jury in New Jersey indicted him for murder. By that time, Burr was a fugitive from justice hiding out with sympathetic friends in South Carolina.

But not for long. Amazingly, he returned to Washington, D.C., in November 1804 to resume presiding over sessions of the Senate, a role he continued to perform until his term ended in March 1805. Federalists snubbed him, but eleven Republican senators petitioned New Jersey to drop its indictment on the grounds that "civilized nations" do not treat dueling deaths as "common murders." New Jersey did not pursue the murder charge. Burr freely visited New Jersey and New York for three more decades, paying no penalty for killing Hamilton.

Few would doubt that Burr was a scoundrel, albeit a brilliant one. A few years later, he was indicted for treason against the U.S. government in a presumed plot to break off part of the United States and start his own country in the Southwest. (He dodged that bullet, too, in a spectacular trial presided over by John Marshall, chief justice of the Supreme Court.) Hamilton certainly thought Burr a scoundrel, and when that opinion reached print, Burr had cause to defend his honor under the etiquette of dueling. The accuracy of Hamilton's charge was of absolutely no account. Dueling redressed questions of honor, not questions of fact.

Dueling continued to be a feature of southern society for many more decades, but in the North the custom became extremely rare by the 1820s, discouraged by the tragedy of Hamilton's death and by the rise of a legalistic society that now preferred evidence, interrogation, and monetary judgments to avenge injury.

Pistols from the Burr-Hamilton Duel
Alexander Hamilton's brother-in-law John B. Church purchased this pair of dueling pistols in London in 1797. Church used them once in a duel with Aaron Burr, occasioned by Church's calling Burr a scoundrel in public; neither man was hurt. Hamilton's son Philip had borrowed them for his own fatal duel three years before. When Burr challenged Hamilton, the latter also turned to Church for the weapons. The guns stayed in the Church family until 1930, when they were given to the Chase Manhattan Bank in New York City, chartered in 1799 as the Manhattan Company. (Burr, Church, and Hamilton all served on the bank's board of directors.) When the pistols were cleaned in 1874, a hidden hair trigger came to light. It could be cocked by moving the trigger forward one-eighth inch. It then required only a half-pound pull, instead of a ten-pound pull, to fire the gun. If Hamilton knew about the hair trigger, he gained no advantage from it.
Courtesy of Chase Manhattan Archives.

One of the jailed rebels compared himself to the most venerated icon of the early Republic: "I have nothing more to offer than what General Washington would have had to offer, had he been taken by the British and put to trial by them." Such talk invoking the specter of a black George Washington worried white Virginians, and in September and October 1800, twenty-seven black men were hanged for allegedly contemplating rebellion. Finally, President Jefferson advised Governor Monroe that the hangings had gone far enough. "The world at large will forever condemn us if we indulge a principle of revenge," Jefferson wrote.

The Jeffersonian Vision of Republican Simplicity

Jefferson sidestepped the problem of slavery and turned his attention to establishing his administration in clear contrast to the Federalists. For his inauguration, held in the village optimistically called Washington City, he dressed in everyday clothing, to strike a tone of republican simplicity, and he walked to the Capitol for the modest swearing-in ceremony. Once in office, he continued to emphasize unfussy frugality. He scaled back Federalist building plans for Washington and cut the government budget. He wore plain clothes, appearing "neglected but not slovenly," according to one onlooker. He cultivated a casual style, wearing slippers to greet important guests, avoiding the formality of state parties and liveried servants. Jefferson's apparent carelessness was very deliberate.

> For his inauguration, held in the village optimistically called Washington City, Jefferson dressed in everyday clothing, to strike a tone of republican simplicity.

Martha Washington and Abigail Adams had received the wives of government officials at weekly teas, thereby creating and cementing social relations in the governing class. But Jefferson, a longtime widower, disdained female gatherings and avoided the women of Washington City. He abandoned George Washington's practice of holding weekly formal receptions, limiting these drop-in gatherings to just two a year. His preferred social event was the small dinner party with carefully chosen politicos, either all Republicans or all Federalists (and all male). At these intimate dinners, the president demonstrated his version of statecraft, exercising influence and strengthening informal relationships that would help him govern.

Jefferson's paramount goal was to roll back federal power. He was no Antifederalist. He had supported the Constitution in 1788, although he

Thomas Jefferson at Age Seventy-eight
When Jefferson was a diplomat in Paris in the 1780s, he honored his post and his country by wearing fancy clothes—an elaborately embroidered silk waistcoat under a greatcoat trimmed with gold lace. In contrast, during his presidency he preferred simple clothes to make a point about republican manners. Sometimes that dismayed guests. One senator who visited the president in 1802 found him "dressed, or rather undressed, with an old brown coat, red waistcoat, old corduroy small clothes, much soiled, woolen hose, and slippers without heels." Artist Thomas Sully painted Jefferson at his home, Monticello, in 1821. His clothes were still simple and understated, perhaps a function of Jefferson's financial difficulties but also a result of a recent change in men's fashions away from tight, colorful vests and knee breeches and toward the plain black suit. At Jefferson's neck, we see a white collar and a touch of a red vest; his black suit jacket is topped by a fur-trimmed greatcoat. The sitting took place in March, usually a cool month in Virginia, and Jefferson was known for keeping the temperature inside his home low to conserve firewood. Monticello, Thomas Jefferson Memorial Foundation, Inc.

had qualms about the unrestricted reelection allowed to the president. But events of the 1790s had caused him to worry about the stretching of powers in the executive branch. Jefferson had watched with distrust as Hamiltonian policies refinanced the public debt, established a national bank, and secured commercial ties with Britain (see chapter 9). These policies seemed to Jefferson to promote the interests of greedy speculators at the expense of the rest of the country.

Jefferson's Duplicating Machine

Jefferson wrote tens of thousands of letters during his lifetime. For some years, he kept copies of his work by using a patented slow-drying ink and special tissue paper obtained in England. The very thin tissue could be pressed against a manuscript page whose ink was still wet and then carefully peeled off to create a copy. In 1804, Jefferson acquired his first polygraph, or duplicating machine, which could produce four identical copies of a handwritten page. No doubt the stepped-up business of the presidency (and his small clerical staff) made this machine very useful. Patented by an Englishman and a Philadelphian in 1803, the polygraph linked up to five pens. The motion of the first pen, held in Jefferson's hand, was perfectly mimicked by the other pens, poised over tautly held paper.

National Museum of American History, Smithsonian Institution, Behring Center.

Jefferson was not at all anticommerce, but financial schemes that seemed merely to allow rich men to become richer were corrupt and worthless, he believed, and their promotion by the federal government was not authorized by the Constitution. In Jefferson's vision, the source of true **liberty** in America was the independent farmer, someone who owned and worked his land both for himself and for the market.

Jefferson set out to dismantle Federalist innovations. He reduced the size of the army by a third, leaving only three thousand soldiers, and he kept the navy small, with just half a dozen ships. Peacetime defense, he felt, should rest with "a well-disciplined militia," not a standing army. With the consent of Congress, he abolished all federal internal taxes based on population or whiskey. A national tax on population had been tried just once, in 1798, and had proved as burdensome and expensive as taking a census. Government revenue would now derive solely from customs duties and from the sale of western land. This strategy was of particular benefit to the South, because the three-fifths clause of the Constitution counted slaves for both representation and taxation. The South could exercise its extra influence in the House of Representatives without the threat of extra taxes. By the end of his first term, Jefferson had deeply reduced Hamilton's cherished national debt.

A properly limited federal government, according to Jefferson, was responsible merely for running a postal system, maintaining the federal courts, staffing lighthouses, collecting customs duties, and conducting a census once every ten years. Government jobs were kept to a minimum. The president had just one private secretary, a young man named Meriwether Lewis, to help with his correspondence, and Jefferson paid him out of his own pocket. The Department of State employed only 8 people: Secretary James Madison, 6 clerks, and a messenger. The Treasury Department was by far the largest unit, with 73 revenue commissioners, auditors, and clerks, plus 2 watchmen. The entire payroll of the executive branch amounted to a mere 130 people in 1801.

The Judiciary and the Midnight Judges

One large set of government workers lay beyond Jefferson's command. His predecessor, John Adams, had seized the few weeks between his election defeat and Jefferson's inauguration to appoint 217 Federalists to various judicial, diplomatic, and military posts.

Most of this windfall of appointments came to Adams as a result of the Judiciary Act of 1801, passed in the final month of his presidency. Its predecessor, the Judiciary Act of 1789, had established a six-man Supreme Court and six circuit courts. The new law authorized sixteen circuit courts, each headed by a new judge. If he acted quickly, Adams could appoint sixteen circuit court judges with lifetime tenure, plus dozens more attorneys, marshals, and clerks for each court. The 1801 act also reduced the Supreme Court from six to five justices. Prior to its passage, however, Adams appointed solidly Federalist Virginian John Marshall to a vacant sixth seat. After the 1801 act became law, a future president would not be able to fill the next empty seat.

In the last weeks of February 1801, Adams and Marshall worked feverishly to secure agreements from the new appointees. In view of the slowness of the mail, achieving 217 acceptances was astonishing. The two men were at work until 9 p.m. on the last night Adams was president, signing and delivering commissions (appointment papers) to the new officeholders.

The appointment of the "midnight judges" infuriated the Republicans. Jefferson, upon taking office, immediately canceled the appointments of the nontenured men and refused to honor the few appointments that had not yet been delivered. One of them was addressed to William Marbury, who soon decided to sue the new secretary of state, James Madison, for failure to make good on the appointment. This action gave rise to a landmark Supreme Court case, *Marbury v. Madison*, decided in 1803. The Court, presided over by John Marshall, ruled that although Marbury's commission was valid and the new president should have delivered it, the Court could not compel him to do so. What made the case significant was little noted at the time: The Court found that the grounds of Marbury's suit, resting in the Judiciary Act of 1789, were in conflict with the Constitution. For the first time, the Court acted to disallow a law on the grounds that it was unconstitutional. John Marshall quietly established the concept of judicial review; the Supreme Court in effect assumed the legal authority to **nullify** acts judged in conflict with the Constitution.

> John Marshall quietly established the concept of judicial review; the Supreme Court in effect assumed the legal authority to nullify acts judged in conflict with the Constitution.

The Promise of the West: The Louisiana Purchase and the Lewis and Clark Expedition

The reach of the *Marbury* decision went largely unnoticed in 1803 because the president and Congress were preoccupied with other major issues, among them the acquisition of the Louisiana Territory. Up through the Seven Years' War (see chapter 6), France claimed but only lightly settled a large expanse of land west of the Mississippi River, only to lose it to Spain in the 1763 Treaty of Paris. Spain never sent adequate forces to control or settle the land, and Spanish power in North America remained precarious everywhere outside New Orleans. Meanwhile, American farming families were settling Kentucky and Tennessee, along rivers emptying into the upper Mississippi, and for a time, the Spanish allowed them to ship their agricultural produce downriver and even encouraged American settlements across the river, in an effort to augment the population. By 1801, Americans made up a sizable minority of the population around the lower Mississippi. Publicly, Jefferson protested the luring of Americans to Spanish territory, but privately he welcomed it as a potential move toward appropriating territory immediately west of the Mississippi. He wrote, "I wish a hundred thousand of our inhabitants would accept the invitation; it will be the means of delivering to us peaceably, what may otherwise cost us a war."

Jefferson's fears of war were not unrealistic. In 1802, the Spanish governor revoked American shipping privileges through or past New Orleans. Congressmen began muttering about taking the city by force. Talk of war, especially in Federalist newspapers, became commonplace.

In the same year, rumors reached Jefferson that Spain had struck a secret bargain with France to hand over a large part of Spain's trans-Mississippi territory to Napoleon in exchange for some land in Italy. Spain had proved a weak western neighbor, but France was another story. Jefferson was so alarmed that he instructed Robert R. Livingston, America's minister in France, to try to buy New Orleans. At first, the French denied they owned the city. But when Livingston hinted that the United States might simply seize it if buying was not an option, the French negotiator suddenly asked him to name his price for the entire Louisiana Territory, from the Gulf of Mexico north to Canada. Livingston stalled, and the Frenchman made suggestions: $125 million? $60 million? Livingston shrewdly stalled some more, and within days the French sold the entire territory for the bargain price of $15 million (Map 10.2). The French, motivated sellers, needed cash because of their impending war with Britain and the recent failure, despite committing twenty thousand troops, to prevent Haitian independence.

Jefferson and most of Congress were delighted with the outcome of the diplomatic mission. Still, Jefferson had some qualms about the Louisiana Purchase. The price was right, and the enormous territory fulfilled Jefferson's dream of abundant farmland for future generations. But by what authority expressed in the Constitution could he justify the purchase? His frequent criticism of Hamilton's stretching of the Constitution came back to haunt him. His legal reasoning told him he needed a constitutional amendment to authorize the addition of territory; more expedient minds told him the treaty-making powers of the president were sufficient. Expediency won out. In late 1803, the American army took formal control of the Louisiana Territory, and the United States grew by 828,000 square miles.

Even before the Louisiana Purchase, Jefferson had eyed the trans-Mississippi West

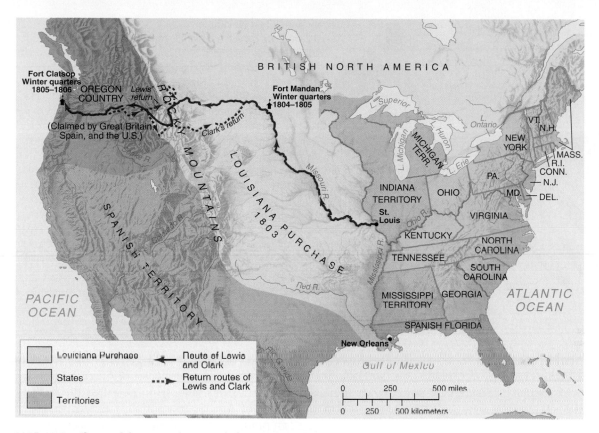

MAP 10.2   The Louisiana Purchase and the Lewis and Clark Expedition

Robert Livingston's bargain buy of 1803 far exceeded his initial assignment to acquire the city of New Orleans. New England Federalists, worried that their geographically based power in the federal government would someday be eclipsed by the West, voted against the purchase. The Indians who inhabited the vast region, unaware that their land had been claimed by either the French or the Americans, got their first look at Anglo-American and African American men when the Lewis and Clark expedition explored the territory in 1804–1806.

READING THE MAP: What natural boundaries defined the Louisiana Purchase? How did the size of the newly acquired territory compare to the land area of the existing American states and territories?
CONNECTIONS: What political events in Europe created the opportunity for the Jefferson administration to purchase Louisiana? What constitutional obstacles to expansion did Jefferson have to contend with? How did the acquisition of Louisiana affect Spain's hold on North America?

FOR MORE HELP ANALYZING THIS MAP, see the map activity for this chapter in the Online Study Guide at bedfordstmartins.com/roark.

---

with intense curiosity. In early 1803, he had arranged congressional funding for a secret scientific and military mission into Spanish and Indian territory. Jefferson appointed twenty-eight-year-old Meriwether Lewis, his personal secretary, to head the expedition, instructing him to investigate Indian **cultures**, to collect plant and animal specimens, and to chart the geography of the West. Congress had more traditional goals in mind: The expedition was to scout locations for military posts, open commercial agreements

for the fur trade, and locate any possible waterway between the East and West coasts.

For his co-leader, Lewis chose Kentuckian William Clark, a veteran of the 1790s Indian wars. Together, they handpicked a crew of forty-five, including expert rivermen, gunsmiths, hunters, interpreters, a cook, and a slave named York, who belonged to Clark. The explorers left St. Louis in the spring of 1804, working their way northwest up the Missouri River. They camped for the winter at a Mandan village in what is now central North Dakota. The

Grizzly Bear Claw Necklace

Lewis and Clark collected hundreds of Indian artifacts on their expedition, but until December 2003, only six were known still to exist. Then this grizzly bear claw necklace unexpectedly turned up at Harvard University's Peabody Museum of Archaeology and Ethnology, stored by mistake in a South Pacific collection. Curators instantly recognized it as a necklace missing since 1899 that had been part of a Lewis and Clark museum exhibit in the mid-nineteenth century. In their expedition journal, the famed explorers noted seeing bear claw necklaces on Shoshoni warriors in the Rocky Mountains; possibly one of these warriors gave his necklace to the travelers. The thirty-eight impressive claws, each three to four inches long, are strung together by rawhide thongs. At least two grizzly bears would have been required to make the necklace. Male grizzlies are large—six to seven feet tall and five hundred to nine hundred pounds—and aggressive. What would it be like to wear this necklace? It seems certain that a sense of the bears' power would be bestowed on the wearer.

Peabody Museum, Harvard University, Photo 99-12-10/99700.

Mandan Indians were familiar with British and French traders from Canada, but the black man York created a sensation. Reportedly, the Indians rubbed moistened fingers over the man's skin to see if the color was painted on.

The following spring, the explorers headed west, accompanied by a sixteen-year-old Shoshoni woman named Sacajawea. Kidnapped by Mandans at about age ten, she had been sold to a French trapper as a slave/wife. Hers was not a unique story among Indian women; such women knew several languages, making them valuable translators and mediators. Further, Sacajawea and her new baby allowed the American expedition to appear peaceful to suspicious tribes. As Lewis wrote in his journal, "No woman ever accompanies a war party of Indians in this quarter."

The Lewis and Clark expedition reached the Pacific Ocean at the mouth of the Columbia River in November 1805. When Lewis and Clark returned home the following year, they were greeted as national heroes. They had established favorable relations with dozens of Indian tribes; they had collected invaluable information on the peoples, soils, plants, animals, and geography of the West; and they had inspired a nation of restless explorers and solitary imitators.

Challenges Overseas: The Barbary Wars

The inspiring opportunity of westward exploration was matched at the same time by a frustrating challenge from the Middle East, leading to the first declaration of war against the United States. For well over a century, four Muslim states on the northern coast of Africa—Morocco, Algiers, Tunis, and Tripoli—called the Barbary States by Americans, controlled all Mediterranean shipping traffic by demanding large annual payments (called "tribute") for safe passage. Countries electing not to pay the tribute found their ships at risk for seizure, with cargoes plundered and crews captured and sold into slavery. Up to 1776, American ships flew the British flag and thus were protected. Once independent, the United States began to pay the tribute, which rose by the mid-1790s to $50,000 a year. The trade was apparently worth maintaining. About a hundred American merchant ships annually traversed the Mediterranean, trading lumber, tobacco, sugar, and rum for regional delicacies such as raisins, figs, capers, and opium, the last an essential ingredient in many medicines. Some 20 percent of all American exports went to the Middle East.

In May 1801, when the pasha (military head) of Tripoli failed to secure a large increase in his tribute, he declared war on the United States. Jefferson had long considered such payments extortion, and he sent four warships to the Mediterranean to protect U.S. shipping. From 1801 to 1803, U.S. frigates engaged in skirmishes with Barbary privateers.

Then, in late 1803, the USS *Philadelphia* ran aground near Tripoli harbor. Its three-hundred-man crew was captured along with the ship. In retaliation, seventy men led by navy lieutenant Stephen Decatur sailed into the harbor after dark, guided by an Arabic-speaking pilot to fool harbor sentries. They drew up to the *Philadelphia*, boarded it, and set it on fire, then escaped. Decatur was an instant hero in America. A second foray into the harbor to try to blow up the entire Tripoli fleet with a bomb-laden boat failed when the explosives detonated prematurely; eleven Americans were killed.

In 1804, William Eaton, an American officer stationed in Tunis, felt the humiliation of his country's ineffectiveness. He wrote to Secretary of State James Madison to ask for a thousand marines to invade Tripoli. Madison rejected the plan and another scheme to ally with the pasha's exiled brother to effect a regime change. On his own, Eaton contacted the brother, assembled a force of four hundred men (more than three hundred Egyptian mercenaries and a handful of marines), and marched them over five hundred miles of desert for a surprise attack on Tripoli's second-largest city. Amazingly, he succeeded. The pasha of Tripoli yielded, released the prisoners taken from the *Philadelphia*, and negotiated a treaty with the United States. Peace with the other Barbary States came in a second treaty in 1812.

The Barbary Wars of 1801–1805 cost Jefferson's government more money than the tribute demanded. But the honor of the young country was thought to be at stake. At political gatherings, the slogan "Millions for defense, but not a cent for tribute" became a popular toast.

More Transatlantic Troubles: Impressment and Embargo

Jefferson easily retained the presidency in the election of 1804, with his 162 electoral votes trouncing the 14 won by the Federalist candidate, Charles Cotesworth Pinckney of South Carolina. But governing in his second term was not easy, due to seriously escalating tensions between the United States and both France and Britain. Beginning in 1803, both European rivals, embroiled in a war with each other, repeatedly warned the United States not to ship arms to the other. Britain acted on these threats in 1806, stopping U.S. ships to inspect cargoes for military aid to France and seizing suspected deserters from the British navy, along with many Americans. Ultimately, 2,500 sailors were "impressed" (taken by force) by the British. In retaliation, Jefferson convinced Congress to pass nonimportation laws banning certain British-made goods.

One incident made the usually cautious Jefferson nearly belligerent. In June 1807, the American ship *Chesapeake*, harboring some British deserters, was ordered to stop by the British frigate *Leopard*. The *Chesapeake* refused, and the *Leopard* opened fire, killing three Americans—right at the mouth of the Chesapeake Bay, well within U.S. territory. In response, Congress passed the Embargo Act of 1807, banning all importation of British goods into the country. Though surely a drastic measure, the embargo was meant to forestall war: The goal was to make Britain suffer. All foreign ports were declared off-limits to American merchants, to discourage illegal trading through secondary ports. Jefferson was convinced that Britain needed America's agricultural products far more than America needed British goods. He also was wary of Federalist shipowners who might circumvent the ban.

The Embargo Act of 1807 was a disaster. From 1790 to 1807, U.S. exports had increased fivefold, but the embargo brought commerce to a standstill. In New England, the heart of the shipping industry, unemployment rose. Grain plummeted in value, river traffic halted, tobacco rotted in the South, and cotton went unpicked. Protest petitions flooded Washington. The federal government suffered, too, for import duties were a significant source of revenue. Jefferson paid political costs as well. The Federalist Party, in danger of fading away after its weak showing in the election of 1804, began to revive.

The *Chesapeake* Incident, June 22, 1807

REVIEW How did Jefferson attempt to undo the Federalist innovations of earlier administrations?

The Madisons in the White House

In mid-1808, Jefferson indicated that he would not run for a third term. Secretary of State James Madison got the nod from the Republican caucuses—informal political groups that orchestrated the selection of candidates for state and local elections. The Federalist caucuses again chose Charles Cotesworth Pinckney, their candidate in 1804. Madison won, but Pinckney received

47 electoral votes, nearly half of Madison's total. Support for the Federalists remained centered in New England, and Republicans still held the balance of power nationwide.

As president, James Madison continued Jefferson's policy of economic pressure on Britain and France with a modified embargo, but he broke new ground in the domestic management of the executive office, with the aid of his astute and talented wife, Dolley Madison. Under her leadership, the president's house was designated the White House—something close to a palace, but a palace many Americans were welcome to visit. Under his leadership, the country went to war in 1812 with Britain and with Tecumseh's Indian confederacy. In 1814, British forces burned the White House and Capitol nearly to the ground.

Women in Washington City

During her first eight years in Washington, as wife of the highest-ranking cabinet officer, Dolley Madison developed elaborate social networks that, in the absence of a First Lady, constituted the top level of female politicking in the highly political city. Although women could not vote and supposedly left politics to men, the women of Washington took on several overtly political functions that greased the wheels of the affairs of state. They networked through dinners, balls, receptions, and the intricate custom of "calling," in which men and women paid brief visits and left calling cards at each other's homes. Webs of friendship and influence in turn facilitated female political lobbying. It was not uncommon for women in this social set to write letters of recommendation for men seeking government work. Hostessing was no trivial or leisured business; it significantly influenced the federal government's patronage system.

When James Madison became president, Dolley Madison, called by some the "presidentress," struck a balance between queenliness and republican openness. She dressed the part in resplendent clothes, choosing a plumed velvet turban for her headdress at her husband's inauguration. She opened three large, elegant rooms in the executive mansion for a weekly party called "Mrs. Madison's crush" or "squeeze." In contrast to George and Martha Washington's stiff, brief receptions, the Madisons' parties went on for hours, with scores or even hundreds of

> Dolley Madison, called by some the "presidentress," struck a balance between queenliness and republican openness.

guests milling about, talking, and eating. Members of Congress, cabinet officers, distinguished guests, envoys from foreign countries, and their womenfolk attended with regularity. Even people who hated parties—or these gatherings in particular—attended. Mrs. Madison's "squeeze" was an essential event for gaining political access, trading information, and establishing informal channels that would smooth the governing process.

In 1810–1811, the Madisons' house acquired its present name, the White House, probably in reference to its white-painted sandstone exterior. In 1810, a Baltimore newspaper heralded the name as "the people's name" for the people's house, because the words were simple and commonplace. The many guests at the weekly parties experienced simultaneously the splendor of

Dolley Madison, **by Gilbert Stuart**

The "presidentress" of the Madison administration sat for this official portrait in 1804. She wears an empire-style dress, at the height of French fashion in 1804 and a style worn by many women at the coronation of the emperor Napoleon in Paris. The hallmarks of such a dress were a light fabric (muslin or chiffon), short sleeves, a high waistline from which the fabric fell straight to the ground, and usually a low, open neckline, as shown here. The artist made a companion likeness of James Madison, and the two portraits hung in the drawing room of the Madisons' Virginia estate, Montpelier.

© White House Historical Association.

the executive mansion and the atmosphere of republicanism that made it accessible to so many. Dolley Madison, ever an enormous political asset to her rather shy husband, understood well the symbolic function of the White House to enhance the power and legitimacy of the presidency.

Indian Troubles in the West

While the Madisons cemented alliances at home, difficulties with Britain and France overseas and with Indians in the old Northwest Territory continued to increase. The Shawnee chief Tecumseh actively solidified his confederacy, while the more northern tribes renewed their ties with supportive British agents and fur traders in Canada, a potential source of food and weapons. If the United States went to war with Britain, there would clearly be serious repercussions on the **frontier**.

Shifting demographics raised the stakes for both sides. The 1810 census counted some 230,000 Americans in Ohio only seven years after it achieved statehood. Another 40,000 Americans inhabited the territories of Indiana, Illinois, and Michigan. The Indian population of the entire region (the old Northwest Territory) was much smaller, probably about 70,000, a number unknown (because uncounted) to the Americans but certainly gauged by Tecumseh during his extensive travels.

Up to 1805, Indiana's territorial governor, William Henry Harrison, had negotiated a series of treaties in a divide-and-conquer strategy aimed at extracting Indian lands for paltry payments. But with the rise to power of Tecumseh and his brother Tenskwatawa, the Prophet, Harrison's strategy faltered. A fundamental part of Tecumseh's message was the assertion that all Indian lands were held in common by all the tribes. "No tribe has the right to sell [these lands], even to each other, much less to strangers . . . ," Tecumseh said. "Sell a country! Why not sell the air, the great sea, as well as the earth? Didn't the Great Spirit make them all for the use of his children?" In 1809, while Tecumseh was away on a recruiting trip, Harrison assembled the leaders of the Potawatomi, Miami, and Delaware tribes to negotiate the Treaty of Fort Wayne. After promising (falsely) that this was the last cession of land the United States would seek, Harrison secured three million acres at about two cents per acre (Map 10.3, page 334).

When he returned, Tecumseh was furious with both Harrison and the tribal leaders. Leaving his brother in charge at Prophetstown

***Tenskwatawa,* by George Catlin**
Tenskwatawa, the Prophet, and his brother Tecumseh led the spiritual and political efforts of a number of Indian tribes to resist land-hungry Americans moving west in the decade before the War of 1812. George Catlin portrays the Prophet wearing beaded necklaces, metal arm and wristbands, and earrings. Compare the metal gorget here with the one worn by Joseph Brant (page 233).
National Museum of American Art, Washington, D.C./Art Resource, NY.

on Tippecanoe River, the Shawnee chief left to seek alliances with tribes in the South. In November 1811, Harrison decided to attack Prophetstown with a thousand men. The two-hour battle resulted in the deaths of sixty-two Americans and forty Indians before the Prophet's forces fled the town, which Harrison's men set on fire. The battle of Tippecanoe was heralded as a glorious victory for the Americans, but Tecumseh was now more ready than ever to make war on the United States.

The War of 1812

The Indian conflicts in the old Northwest Territory soon merged into the wider conflict with Britain, now known as the War of 1812. Between 1809 and 1812, President Madison teetered between declaring either Britain or France America's primary enemy, as attacks by both countries on American ships continued. In 1809, Congress replaced Jefferson's stringent embargo with the

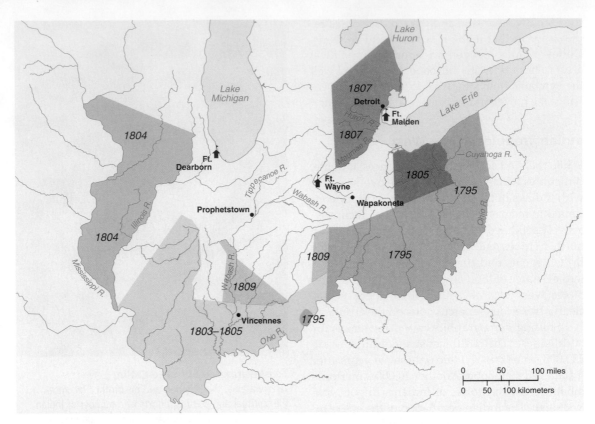

MAP 10.3   Indian Lands Ceded by Treaties in the Northwest Territory, 1795–1809

The Treaty of Greenville (1795) transferred two-thirds of Ohio to the Americans. For more than a decade thereafter, officials such as William Henry Harrison managed to acquire for the United States vast tracts along the Ohio and Mississippi rivers by negotiating with Indians whose authority to speak for their tribes was often unclear or dubious.

"Land Cessions in the Old Northwest, 1795–1809." From *Tecumseh: A Life* by John Sugden. Copyright 1997 by John Sugden. Reprinted with the permission of Henry Holt and Company LLC.

Battle of Tippecanoe, 1811

Non-Intercourse Act, which prohibited trade only with Britain and France and their colonies, thus opening up other trade routes to alleviate somewhat the anguish of shippers, farmers, and **planters**. By 1811, the country was seriously divided and in a deep quandary. To some, the United States seemed, appropriately, on the verge of war. To others, war with either Britain or France meant disaster for commerce.

A new Congress arrived in Washington in March 1811. Several dozen of the younger Republican members were eager to avenge the insults from abroad. Thirty-four-year-old Henry Clay from Kentucky and twenty-nine-year-old John C. Calhoun from South Carolina became the center of a group informally known as the **War Hawks**. They saluted Harrison's victory at Tippecanoe and urged the country to war. Mostly lawyers by profession, they came from the West and South and welcomed a war with Britain both to justify attacks on the Indians and to bring an end to impressment. Many were also expansionists, looking to occupy Florida and threaten Canada. Clay was elected Speaker of the House, an extraordinary honor for a newcomer. Calhoun won a seat on the Foreign Relations Committee. The War Hawks approved major defense expenditures, and the army soon quadrupled in size.

In June 1812, Congress declared war on Great Britain in a vote divided along sectional lines: New England and some Middle Atlantic states opposed the war, while the South and West were strongly for it. Ironically, Britain had just announced that it would stop the search and seizure of American ships, but the war momentum would not be slowed. The Foreign Relations

Committee issued an elaborate justification titled *Report on the Causes and Reasons for War*, written mainly by Calhoun and containing extravagant language about Britain's "lust for power," "unbounded tyranny," and "mad ambition." These were fighting words in a war that was in large measure about insult and honor.

The War Hawks proposed an invasion of Canada, confidently predicting victory in four weeks. Instead, the war lasted two and a half years, and Canada never fell. The northern invasion turned out to be a series of blunders that revealed America's grave unpreparedness for war against the unexpectedly powerful British and Indian forces. Detroit quickly fell, as did Fort Dearborn, site of the future Chicago (Map 10.4). By the fall of 1812, the outlook was grim.

Worse, the New England states dragged their feet in raising troops, and some New England merchants carried on illegal trade with Britain. While President Madison fumed about Federalist disloyalty, Bostonians drank India tea in Liverpool cups. The fall presidential election pitted Madison against DeWitt Clinton of New York, nominally a Republican but able to attract the Federalist vote. Clinton picked up all of New England's electoral votes, with the exception of Vermont's, and also took New York, New Jersey, and part of Maryland. Madison won in the electoral college, 128 to 89, but his margin of victory was considerably smaller than in 1808.

In late 1812 and early 1813, the tide began to turn in the Americans' favor. First came some reassuring victories at sea. Then the Americans attacked York (now Toronto), the capital of Upper Canada, and burned it in April 1813. A few months later, Commodore Oliver Hazard Perry defeated the British fleet at the western end of Lake Erie. Emboldened, General Harrison drove an army into Canada from Detroit and in October 1813 defeated the British and Indians at the battle of the Thames, where Tecumseh was killed.

The Indians in the South who had allied with Tecumseh's confederacy were also plunged into all-out war. Some fifty villages, home to 10,000 Creek Indians in the southern region of the Mississippi Territory, put up a spirited fight against American militia for ten months in 1813–1814. Even without Tecumseh's recruitment trip of 1811 or the War of 1812, the Creeks had grievances aplenty, sparked by American settlers moving into their territory. Using guns obtained in the panhandle of Spanish Florida, the Creeks mounted a strong defense. But the Creek War ended suddenly in March 1814, when a general

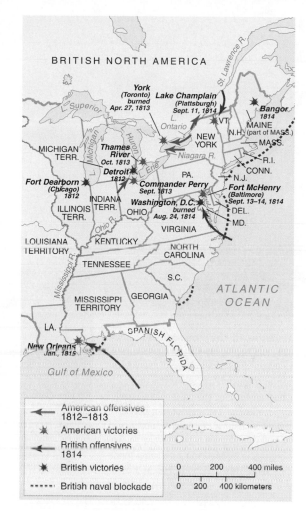

MAP 10.4 The War of 1812
During the War of 1812, battles were fought along the Canadian border and in the Chesapeake region. The most important American victory came in New Orleans two weeks after a peace agreement had been signed in England.

named Andrew Jackson led 2,500 Tennessee militiamen in a bloody attack called the Battle of Horseshoe Bend. More than 550 Indians were killed, and several hundred more died trying to escape across a river. Later that year, General Jackson extracted from the defeated Creek tribe a treaty relinquishing thousands of square miles of their land to the United States.

Washington City Burns: The British Offensive

In August 1814, British ships sailed into the Chesapeake Bay, landing 5,000 troops and throwing the capital into a panic. Families evacuated, banks hid their money, and government clerks carted away boxes of important papers.

forces dramatically carried the day. The British suffered between 2,000 and 3,000 casualties, the Americans fewer than 80. Jackson became an instant hero. The battle of New Orleans was the most glorious victory the Americans had experienced, allowing some Americans to boast that the United States had won a second war of independence from Britain. No one in the United States knew that negotiators in Europe had signed a peace agreement two weeks earlier.

The Treaty of Ghent, signed in December 1814, settled few of the surface issues that had led to war. Neither country could claim victory, and no land changed hands. Instead, the treaty reflected a mutual agreement to give up certain goals. The Americans dropped their plea for an end to impressments, which in any case subsided as soon as Britain and France ended their war in 1815. They also gave up any claim to Canada; the British agreed to abandon aid to the Indians. Nothing was said about shipping rights. The most concrete result was a plan for a commission to determine the exact boundary between the United States and Canada.

Antiwar Federalists in New England could not gloat over the war's ambiguous conclusion, because of an ill-timed and seemingly unpatriotic move on their part. The region's leaders had convened a secret meeting in Hartford, Connecticut, in December 1814, to discuss dramatic measures to curb the South's power. They proposed amending the Constitution to abolish the three-fifths clause as a basis of representation; to specify that congressional powers to impose embargoes, admit states, or declare war should require a two-thirds vote instead of a simple majority; and to limit the president to one term and prohibit the election of successive presidents from the same state. The cumulative effect of these proposals would have been to reduce the South's political power and break the monopoly held by Virginians on the presidency. New England wanted to make sure that no sectional party could again lead the country into war against the clear interests of another. The Federalists at Hartford even discussed secession from the Union but rejected that path. Coming just as peace was achieved, however, the Hartford Convention suddenly looked very unpatriotic. The Federalist Party never recovered

Remains of the President's House
This watercolor sketch documents the burning of the White House in Washington in August 1814, when the British attacked the city. The light-colored walls still stood, but the interior had been gutted by the fire. Some British soldiers engaged in plundering that night. Shown here is James Madison's personal medicine chest, taken back to England by a British soldier. A descendant of his returned the souvenir to President Franklin D. Roosevelt in 1939.
Watercolor: Library of Congress; Medicine chest: FDR Library.

Dolley Madison, with dinner for guests cooking over the fire (see "The Promise of Technology," page 338), fled with her husband's papers and a portrait of George Washington. British commanders ate Mrs. Madison's meal before burning her house. They also burned the Capitol, a newspaper office, and a well-stocked arsenal. Instead of trying to hold the city, the British headed north and attacked Baltimore, but a fierce defense by the Maryland militia thwarted that effort.

In another powerful offensive that same month, British troops marched from Canada into New York State, but a series of mistakes cost them a naval skirmish at Plattsburgh on Lake Champlain, and they retreated to Canada. Five months later, another large British army landed in lower Louisiana and, in early January 1815, encountered General Andrew Jackson and his militia just outside New Orleans. Jackson's

its grip, and within a few years, it was reduced to a shadow of its former self, even in New England.

No one really won the War of 1812. Americans celebrated as though they had, however, with parades and fireworks. The war gave rise to a new spirit of **nationalism**. The paranoia over British tyranny evident in the 1812 declaration of war was laid to rest, replaced by pride in a more equal relationship with the old mother country. Indeed, in 1817 the two countries signed the Rush-Bagot disarmament treaty (named after its two negotiators), which limited each country to a total of four naval vessels, each with just a single cannon, to patrol the vast watery border between them. The Rush-Bagot treaty was perhaps the most successful disarmament treaty for a century to come.

The biggest winners in the War of 1812 were the young men, once called War Hawks, who took up the banner of the Republican Party and carried it in new, expansive directions. These young politicians favored trade, western expansion, internal improvements, and the energetic development of new economic markets. The biggest losers of the war were the Indians. Tecumseh was dead, his brother the Prophet was discredited, the prospects of an Indian confederacy were dashed, the Creeks' large homeland was seized, and the British protectors were gone.

> **REVIEW** Why did Congress declare war on Great Britain in 1812?

Women's Status in the Early Republic

General esteem for Dolley Madison's pioneering role as "presidentress" showed that at the pinnacles of power, elite women of the early nineteenth century could be a visible and even active presence in civic affairs. But as with the 1790s cultural compromise that endorsed female education chiefly so that women could be better wives and mothers (see chapter 9), Mrs. Madison and her female circle practiced politics in service to their husbands' careers. Any argument for an independently grounded "rights of woman" movement fizzled after the English feminist Mary Wollstonecraft was exposed as an unwed mother.

From 1800 to 1825, key institutions central to the shaping and constraining of women's lives—

the legal system, marriage, and religion—proved fairly, but not completely, resistant to change. State legislatures and the courts grappled with the legal dependency of married white women in a country whose defining (and symbolic) characteristic for men was independence. Marriage laws for whites continued to support unequal power between men and women, but this was far less true for blacks. Religious organizations struggled to redefine the role of women in church governance, at a time when church membership rates for women were skyrocketing beyond those for men. The most dramatic opportunity for women came with the flowering of female academies, whose rigorous curricula fostered high-level literacy and rational thought. Even when advertised as institutions to prepare girls to be intelligent mothers, many academies built up their students' self-confidence and implanted expectations that their knowledge and mental training would find a use beyond the kitchen and nursery.

Dolley Madison, with dinner for guests cooking over the fire, fled with her husband's papers and a portrait of George Washington. British commanders ate Mrs. Madison's meal before burning her house.

Women and the Law

The Anglo-American view of women, implanted in English common law, was that wives had no independent legal or political personhood. The legal doctrine of *feme covert* (covered woman) held that a wife's civic life was completely subsumed by her husband's. A wife was obligated to obey her husband; her property was his, her domestic and sexual services were his, and even their children were legally his. Women had no right to keep their wages, to make contracts, or to sue or be sued. Any crime committed by a wife in the presence of her husband was chargeable to him, with two exceptions: treason against the state and keeping a brothel. The fundamental assumption of coverture was that husbands did—and ought to—control their wives.

State legislatures generally passed up the opportunity to rewrite the laws of domestic relations even though they redrafted other British laws in light of republican principles. The standard and much consulted legal treatise on family law, published in 1816, was titled *The Law of Baron and Feme*—meaning "the law of lord and woman." The title perfectly captured how lawyers framed husband-wife power relations: unequal and unchallenged.

Stoves Transform Cooking

The cookstove, one of the most underrated achievements of the technology of daily life, fundamentally changed the way men and women labored to put food on the table. Its slow development can be traced in the nearly one thousand patents registered between 1815 and 1850 by inventors tinkering to control heat, devise convenient cooking surfaces, and improve fuel efficiency.

Before 1815, nearly all household cooking was done in wood-burning fireplaces. Daily fires used for cooking and heating consumed immense amounts of wood; in cold climates, a household might require 40 cords of wood per year. Supplying each cord (a pile measuring 4 by 4 by 8 feet) was laborious men's work; the difficult and dangerous tasks of cooking and maintaining the fire fell to women. Great skill was needed to time the peak heat to coordinate with the varying temperature needs of baking, stewing, and roasting. Muscles and stamina were required to hoist 20-pound iron pots and cauldrons onto the hooks that suspended them over the fire. Cooks worked dangerously close to open flames when tending a roasting joint of meat on a spit or raking smaller fires out of the large one to heat frying skillets set on trivets on the hearth. Women wearing long skirts risked clothing fires, and children running about sometimes collided with hot pots and burning logs at floor level. The heavy lifting and exposure to the blasting heat, especially uncomfortable on hot summer days, exacted a toll on every cook.

In 1744, Benjamin Franklin developed a heating stove that enclosed a wood fire on three sides in a small cast-iron box, which radiated heat to the room. (The open fourth side allowed a pleasing view of the dancing flames.) The Franklin stove cut fuel costs, but it did not catch on for another half century as an alternative to heating by fireplace. Its inadequate venting of smoke was one problem not fixed until the 1790s. Further, cast iron was expensive and wood was cheap, and the Franklin stove offered no provision for cooking. As long as wood remained affordable, Americans preferred the look of a log fire and the taste of food cooked over one.

Then, between 1800 and 1815, a serious fuel shortage driven by the depletion of forests caused wood prices to double along the East Coast. At the same time, domestic iron manufacturing started to flourish, encouraged by Jefferson's shipping embargo and the War of 1812. With wood rising and iron falling in price, the conditions were right for the start of serious cookstove manufacture. Many inventors got to work.

The cast-iron contraptions advertised around 1815 were larger than the Franklin stove and had a flat surface on top where pots and pans could be heated by the fire burning below. One challenge was to find a simple way to modulate the fire by varying the amount of air feeding it. This was accomplished through better design of the damper system. Dampers were valves or movable plates that controlled the draft of air to the fire and hence the rate of combustion. A related challenge was to manage the temperatures of the cooking spaces and surfaces. This could be done by moving pots around, by raising and lowering the grate that held the logs inside the firebox, or even by using cranks to rotate the fire.

Most of the new stoves raised the cooking surface nearly to waist level, offering relief from the backbreaking labor required by fireplace cookery. They fully enclosed the fire, minimizing the risk of clothing fires; they prevented sparks from jumping on floors and carpets; and they piped sooty air with combustion pollutants out of the house. For all these reasons, stove cooking was a great advance in safety.

New stoves changed not only the way people cooked but also the way they ate. On a hearth, separate dishes required separate fires, so cooks generally limited meals to one-pot stews. Using the new stoves, cooks could prepare several different

---

The one aspect of family law that changed in the early Republic was divorce. Before the Revolution, only New England jurisdictions recognized a limited right to divorce; by 1820, every state except South Carolina did so. However, divorce was uncommon and difficult and in many states could be obtained only by petition to the state's legislature, a daunting obstacle for many ordinary people. A mutual wish to terminate a marriage was never sufficient grounds for a legal divorce. A New York judge affirmed that "it would be aiming a deadly blow at public morals to decree a dissolution of the marriage contract merely because the parties requested it. Divorces

dishes with just one fire, and meals became more varied. Not everyone was pleased, however. Many complained that the convenience of stoves came at the price of food quality. Oven-baked meat was nearly universally regarded as less savory than meat roasted over a fire, and in flavor and crustiness, oven-baked bread did not measure up to bread baked in the brick chamber of a fireplace wall. Nonetheless, convenience triumphed.

The cookstove changed home labor for both men and women. It shrank men's role in meal preparation by curtailing the work of procuring wood. No such reduction occurred for women. Replacing the hours of careful fire tending that women had once done were hours spent maintaining and cleaning the stoves—removing the ashes, cleaning soot from the flues and dampers, and blacking the stoves weekly with a thick paste to keep them from rusting.

From 1815 to the mid-nineteenth century, the cookstove was a work in progress; the many imperfections in the initial designs sent inventors back to the workbench again and again to try to perfect this new cooking system. Nonetheless, women wanted stoves for their safety and convenience, and men liked them for their fuel efficiency. In the late 1840s, the widespread popularity of cookstoves became evident along wagon trails heading west. Many families had packed up their stoves for the trip—evidence they embraced the new style of cooking—

but had to abandon them along the way when forced to lighten their loads. One young traveler wrote, "We heard great talk of things being thrown away on the road but we saw little that was any good excepting stoves and there were plenty of them." Cookstoves had become America's first popular "consumer durable."

An Early Cookstove
A stove of the 1820s, patented by W. T. James, sits in this reconstructed historical site adjacent to the fireplace it replaced. A stovepipe vents combustion fumes through the old chimney. A large, flat surface over the fire provides a cooktop, shown here with a copper pot and a teakettle whose extremely large base speeds water to a boil. The round container on the lower ledge of the stove is a reflector oven, called a "tin kitchen," first used with fireplaces and then adapted for cookstoves. A spit inside held meat, and a crank (visible on the end) was used to turn the food. Put against the fire, the tin oven cooked meat by direct and reflected heat, while the round bottom preserved the juices. In this scene, the old fireplace has been bricked up and is used for storing wood for the stove. Householders of the 1820s would have seen this setup as a highly modern convenience offering improvements in safety, fuel efficiency, and heat control.
Old Sturbridge Village

should never be allowed, except for the protection of the innocent party, and for the punishment of the guilty." States upheld the institution of marriage both to protect persons they thought of as naturally dependent (women and children) and to regulate the use and inheritance of property. (Unofficial self-divorce, desertion, and bigamy were remedies that ordinary people sometimes chose to get around the strictness of marriage law. But powerful social sanctions against such behavior usually prevailed.) Legal enforcement of marriage as an unequal relationship played a major role in maintaining gender inequality in the nineteenth century.

Single adult women could own and convey property, make contracts, initiate lawsuits, and pay taxes. They could not vote (except in New Jersey before 1807), serve on juries, or practice law, so their civil status was limited. Single women's economic status was often limited as well, by custom as much as by law. Unless they had inherited adequate property or could live with married siblings, single adult women in the early Republic were very often poor.

None of the legal institutions that structured white gender relations applied to black slaves. As property themselves, slaves could not freely consent to any contractual obligations, including marriage. The protective features of state-sponsored unions were thus denied to black men and women in slavery, who were controlled by a more powerful authority: the slave owner. But this also meant that slave unions did not establish unequal power relations between partners, backed by the force of law, as did marriages among the free.

Women and Church Governance

In most **Protestant** denominations around 1800, white women made up the majority of congregants, as they had for some time. Yet the church hierarchy—ordained ministers and elders—was exclusively male, and the governance of most denominations rested in men's hands.

There were some exceptions, however. In Baptist congregations in New England, women served along with men on church governance committees, deciding on the admission of new members, voting on hiring ministers, and even debating doctrinal points. Quakers, too, had a history of recognizing women's spiritual talents. Quaker women who felt a special call were accorded the status of minister, which meant they were capable of leading and speaking in Quaker meetings.

Between 1790 and 1820, a small and highly unusual set of women emerged who actively engaged in open preaching. Most were from Freewill Baptist groups centered in New England and upstate New York. Others came from small Methodist sects, and yet others rejected any formal religious affiliation. Probably fewer than a hundred such women existed, but several dozen traveled beyond their local communities, creating converts and controversy. They spoke from

> In Baptist congregations in New England, women served along with men on church governance committees, deciding on the admission of new members, voting on hiring ministers, and even debating doctrinal points.

the heart, without prepared speeches, often exhibiting trances and claiming to exhort (counsel or warn) rather than to preach. None of these women were ordained ministers with official credentials to preach or perform baptisms.

The best-known exhorting woman was Jemima Wilkinson, who called herself "the Publick Universal Friend." After a near-death experience from a high fever in 1776, Wilkinson proclaimed her body no longer female or male but the incarnation of the "Spirit of Light." She dressed in men's clothes, wore her hair in a masculine style, shunned gender-specific pronouns, and preached openly in Rhode Island and Philadelphia. In the early nineteenth century, Wilkinson withdrew to a settlement called New Jerusalem in western New York with some 250 followers. Her fame was sustained by periodic newspaper articles that fed public curiosity about her lifelong transvestism and her unfeminine forcefulness.

The decades from 1790 to the 1820s marked a period of unusual confusion, ferment, and creativity in American religion. New denominations blossomed, new styles of religiosity gripped adherents, and an extensive periodical press devoted to religion popularized all manner of theological and institutional innovations. Congregations increasingly attracted vibrant female participation, often eclipsing the percentage of male congregants. In such a climate, the age-old tradition of gender subordination came into question here and there among the most radically **democratic** of the churches. But the presumption of male authority over women was deeply entrenched in American culture. Even denominations that had allowed women to participate in church governance began to pull back, and most churches reinstated patterns of hierarchy along gender lines.

Female Education

Starting in the North and eventually spreading to the South, states and localities began investing in public schools to foster an educated citizenry deemed essential to the good functioning of a republic. Young girls attended such schools, called district schools, sometimes along with boys or, in rural areas, more often in separate summer sessions. Basic literacy and numeracy formed the curriculum taught to white children aged roughly six to eleven. By 1830, girls had made rapid gains, in many places approaching male literacy rates. (Far fewer schools addressed the needs of free black children, whether male or female.)

Women and the Church: Jemima Wilkinson
In this early woodcut, Jemima Wilkinson, "the Publick Universal Friend," wears a clerical collar and body-obscuring robe, in keeping with the claim that the former Jemima was now a person without gender. Her hair is pulled back tight on her head and curled at the neck in a masculine style of the 1790s. Did she become masculinized, or did she truly transcend gender?
Rhode Island Historical Society.

More advanced education for girls was provided by a growing number of private academies, which attracted teenage girls with parents willing and able to invest in their education. Judith Sargent Murray, the Massachusetts author who had called for an equality of the sexes around 1790 (see chapter 9), predicted in 1800 that "a new era in female history" would emerge because "female academies are everywhere establishing." Some dozen female academies were established in the 1790s, and by 1830 that number had grown to nearly two hundred. Many of the earliest female academies were in New England and Pennsylvania, but others soon followed in the South, for example in Salem and Warrenton, North Carolina; in Lexington, Kentucky; and in Columbia, South Carolina.

Candidates for admission were primarily daughters of elite families, as well as those of middling families with elite or intellectual aspirations, such as ministers' daughters.

The curriculum in the three-year course of study included both ornamental arts and solid academics. The ornamental program developed the skills of female gentility: drawing, needlework, music, dancing, and conversing in French. The academic subjects typically advanced well beyond prior levels of female education to include English grammar, literature, history, the natural sciences, geography, and elocution (the art of effective public speaking). Academy catalogs show that by the 1820s, the courses and reading lists at the top female academies equaled those at male colleges such as Harvard, Yale, Dartmouth, and Princeton. The girls at these academies studied Latin, rhetoric, logic, theology, moral philosophy, algebra, geometry, and even chemistry and physics.

The most rigorous schools called themselves seminaries, to set themselves a notch above the academies. The two best-known female seminaries were the Troy Female Seminary in New York, founded by Emma Willard in 1821, and the Hartford Seminary in Connecticut, founded by Catharine Beecher in 1822. (See "Seeking the American Promise," page 342.) Both schools prepared their students to teach. This was especially true of the Hartford Seminary, where half the students did not have a father (thus making them legally orphans) and hence were in special need of practical training for employment. Willard and Beecher argued that women made better teachers than men. Author Harriet Beecher Stowe, educated at her sister's school and then a teacher there, agreed: "If men have more knowledge they have less talent at communicating it. Nor have they the patience, the long-suffering, and gentleness necessary to superintend the formation of character."

The most immediate value of advanced female education lay in the self-cultivation and confidence it provided. Following the model of male colleges, female graduation exercises required speeches, recitations, and demonstrations of learning from each student, generally performed in front of a mixed-sex audience of family, friends, and local notables. Here, their elocution studies paid off; they had learned the art of persuasion along with correct pronunciation and the skill of fluent speaking.

One Woman's Quest to Provide Higher Education for Women

Talented young men seeking the mental enrichment and career boost of higher education saw their opportunities expand rapidly in the early Republic. In addition to the dozen colonial colleges and universities, another five dozen institutions opened their doors between 1790 and 1830. From Vermont's Middlebury College in the North to Georgia's Franklin College in the South and Kentucky's Transylvania University to the west, private and state-chartered schools trained young men in science, history, religion, literature, and philosophy. Not a single college of these dozens admitted females.

What, then, of bright young women harboring intellectual ambitions? With the spread of district schools and female academies, the number of girls trained for advanced study was on the rise. The winning rationale for female education—that mothers molded the character of rising generations—worked well to justify basic and ornamental schooling. But a highly intellectual woman, negatively termed a "bluestocking," was thought to put at risk her femininity, her mothering capacities, and her attractiveness to men. Some critics sounded a more practical note: "When girls become scholars, who is to make the puddings and pies?"

Emma Hart of Connecticut had high academic aspirations. Born in 1787 near Hartford, she was the second to youngest in a farm family of seventeen children. Encouraged by her father, who read Shakespeare at night to his large brood, Emma attended the local district school and then an academy for girls. After graduating, she taught for a term at the district school before moving to Vermont to head the Middlebury Female Academy, founded in 1800. There, she taught sixty adolescents in an underheated building.

Emma ran the academy for two years until her marriage in 1809 to a Middlebury physician and banker named John Willard, a widower twenty-eight years her senior. Marriage for white women usually brought an end to employment outside the home, and this was true for Emma. Yet despite caring for a baby and attending to her domestic duties, she found time to read books from her husband's well-stocked library. She read widely, from political philosophy to medical treatises, physiology texts, and even Euclid's geometry. In this environment, Emma nurtured a talent and taste for advanced learning.

Four years into their marriage, John Willard suffered severe financial losses in his banking business. This turn of events led Emma Willard to open an advanced girls' school in her home. She patterned her courses on those at nearby Middlebury College for men, and her rigorous curriculum soon drew students from all over the Northeast. One satisfied father with political connections persuaded the Willards to relocate to his home state of New York with the promise to help them secure state funding for a school.

Emma drew up a formal proposal in 1819, arguing that advanced female education would not merely enhance motherhood but also supply excellent teachers needed for a projected state-supported system of universal schooling. Her proposal gained impressive endorsements from Governor DeWitt Clinton, John Adams, and Thomas Jefferson, but the New York assembly failed to fund it. In the end, Willard decided to locate her school in Troy, on the Hudson River, where local citizens supplied her with a building. The Troy Female Seminary opened in 1821 with students coming from many states. In naming the school, Willard deliberately chose the modest term "seminary" instead of "college" to avoid exciting concerns that "we mean to intrude upon the province of the men." Yet her rigorous curriculum did intrude into what were commonly thought of as masculine domains. In addition to the modern languages and literature taught at other female academies, Willard included Latin, Greek, mathematics, and science. She taught geometry and trigonometry herself and hired other teachers for classes in astronomy, botany, geology, chemistry, and zoology. She soon forged a cooperative alliance with the neighboring Rensselaer Polytechnic Institute, the nation's first engineering school, founded in 1824. "Lady mathematics took its rise" at the Troy Female Seminary, Willard claimed. In direct emulation of Harvard and

Princeton, her seminary embraced another hallmark of male education: a required course in moral philosophy, taught by Willard to all senior students using the same texts employed at the male colleges.

To demonstrate the reasoning powers of her students, Willard invited the public to weeklong examinations. Students solved algebra problems and geometry proofs on chalkboards and gave twenty-minute discourses on history and philosophy. Educated men were particularly encouraged to question the students, to put to rest any "lurking suspicion, that the learning which a female possesses must be superficial." One minister was astonished, and pleased, to see "Euclid discussed by female lips." In the early nineteenth century, geometry enjoyed exalted status because it required pure abstract reasoning and insistent logic, as opposed to subjects learned by memorization. By emphasizing it, Willard vindicated her claim that women could equal men in logic and reasoning. But she took pains to make sure her students did not damage their femininity. "Above all, preserve feminine delicacy," she admonished them, and "avoid the least indelicacy of language or behavior, such as too much exposure of the person."

More than the rigorous curriculum inspired these young women. Willard was an exemplary role model, beloved by many of her students for her dedication and confidence. A teacher at Troy in the 1820s said, "She taught with the enthusiasm of an originator, thus enkindling the enthusiasm of her pupils." One student recalled that her "great distinction seemed to me to be a supreme confidence in herself, and, as a consequence, a stubborn faith in

the capacity of her own sex." A student named Elizabeth Cady, who attended the seminary in the 1830s and later became an important figure in the woman's rights movement, recalled that Willard had a "profound self respect (a rare quality in a woman) which gave her a dignity truly regal." Willard graciously gave much of the credit to her unusually supportive husband: "He entered into the full spirit of my views, with a disinterested zeal for the sex whom, as he had come to believe, his own had unjustly neglected."

The Troy Female Seminary flourished throughout the nineteenth century and beyond; it still exists today as the Emma Willard School.

From 1821 to 1871, more than 12,000 girls attended; it was larger than most men's colleges. Not all of the students paid full tuition. Ministers' daughters received a discount, and many girls were allowed to defer payment of tuition until they were wage-earning teachers. Nearly 5,000 graduates in the first fifty years became teachers, and some 150 directed their own schools scattered across the nation.

Emma Willard strategically chose the name "seminary," but when the marquis de Lafayette, aging hero of the American Revolution, visited her school in 1824, he pronounced it a "Female University." Surely, Willard took pleasure in his recognition of her success.

Portrait of Emma Willard
Emma Hart Willard's calm composure shines through in this portrait.
Emma Willard School.

Home and Away: The New Boarding School
These two engravings show "before" and "after" pictures of a young woman around 1820 whose family enrolled her in one of the new female academies. The artist, Philadelphia painter John Lewis Krimmel, worked as a drawing master at such an academy.
Library Company of Philadelphia.

READING THE IMAGE: What seem to be the family's expectations as they send the young woman off to school? How is she changed when she returns? According to the artist's depiction, did she acquire a practical or an ornamental education?
CONNECTIONS: Since the artist worked at a female academy, should we presume that his depiction is accurate? What do these pictures reveal about the options for young women in this period? Do you detect any anxiety about the wisdom of educating women?

FOR MORE HELP ANALYZING THIS IMAGE, see the visual activity for this chapter in the Online Study Guide at bedfordstmartins.com/roark.

Many schools took care to assure parents that their pupils would retain a pleasing female modesty. Female pedantry or intellectual immodesty triggered the stereotype of the "bluestocking," a British term of hostility for a too-learned woman, doomed to fail in the marriage market.

By the mid-1820s, the total annual enrollment at the female academies and seminaries equaled the male enrollment at the five dozen male colleges in the United States. Both groups accounted for only about 1 percent of their age cohorts in the country at large, indicating that advanced education was clearly limited to a privileged few. Among the men, this group disproportionately filled the future rosters of ministers, lawyers, judges, political leaders, and writers of influence and note. Most female graduates in time married and raised families, but first many of them became teachers at academies and district schools. And a large number of the women became authors, contributing essays, stories, and poetry to newspapers and periodicals; editing publications; and publishing novels. The new attention to the training of female minds laid the foundation for major changes in the gender system as girl students of the 1810s matured into adult women of the 1830s.

> **REVIEW** How did the civil status of American women and men differ in the early Republic?

Monroe and Adams

With the elections of 1816 and 1820, Virginians continued their hold on the presidency. In 1816, James Monroe beat Federalist Rufus King of New York, garnering 183 electoral votes to King's 34. In 1820, Monroe was reelected with all but one electoral vote. That near unanimity did not necessarily reflect voter satisfaction, however, for barely one-quarter of eligible voters went to the polls. At the state level, elections for governors, congressmen, and state assemblymen engaged voters as never before, and a drive for universal white male suffrage sparked political debate in all the states that maintained property qualifications for voting.

After Monroe's first victory, the apparent collapse of the Federalist Party at the national level led one overly optimistic newspaper to proclaim the arrival of the "Era of Good Feelings," as though a period of one-party government was destined to be harmonious. The harmony did not last long. Monroe and his aloof wife, Elizabeth, sharply curtailed social gatherings at the White House, driving the hard work of social networking into different and competing channels. Ill feelings were stirred by a sectional crisis over the admission of Missouri to the Union, and foreign policy questions involving European claims to Latin America animated sharp disagreements as well. The election of 1824 brought forth an abundance of candidates, all claiming to be Republicans. The winner was John Quincy Adams, in an election decided by the House of Representatives and, many believed, a backroom bargain. Put to the test of practical circumstances, the one-party political system failed and then fractured.

From Property to Democracy

Presidential elections occurred at a remove from ordinary voters, since the electoral college (or occasionally the House of Representatives) ultimately chose the president. But state elections were another matter, generating widespread popular involvement and driving an insistent pressure for greater democratization that ultimately spilled over into presidential elections from 1824 on.

In the 1780s, twelve of the original thirteen states enacted property qualifications for voting, usually specified at a minimum (and sometimes substantial) threshold. This policy was based on the time-honored theory that only male freeholders—landowners, as distinct from tenants or servants—had sufficient independence of mind and attachment to community to be entrusted with the vote. Of course, not everyone accepted that restricted idea of the people's role in government (see chapter 8). In the 1790s, Vermont entered the Union as the first state to enfranchise all adult males, and four other states soon substituted "taxpayer" for "freeholder." This change in terminology broadened suffrage considerably, since owning a few acres or even just a cow required the paying of taxes in many states. These were early signs of the trend toward greater democratization that gripped all the states between 1800 and 1830. Petitions and lively newspaper exchanges finally led to a series of state constitutional conventions, where questions of suffrage, balloting procedures, apportionment, and representation were hotly debated. Both political philosophy and practical politics were entwined in these debates: Who are

Eli Terry's Pillar and Scroll Clock
Before the 1790s, sundials and church bells answered most timekeeping needs; clocks were objects of art, not utility. The Connecticut clockmaker Eli Terry realized that affordable clocks might change all that. First he switched from brass to wood for the clock's internal movement. Then he designed machinery to mass-produce the parts, achieving the first successful system of "interchangeable parts" and turning out thousands of clocks a year. In 1814, Terry developed this inexpensive compact clock and sold tens of thousands over the next dozen years. Affordable clocks revolutionized timekeeping, enabling workers to arrive before the factory bell and travelers to make stagecoach and canal boat departure times. Employers could demand punctuality, a moral virtue made possible by the pervasiveness of clocks. For good or ill, clocks did not merely measure time; they helped speed up the pace of life.
American Clock & Watch Museum, Bristol, CT. Photo by C. R. Lang Photography.

"the people" in a government founded on **popular sovereignty**, and whose party or interest group gains the most from expanded suffrage?

For underpopulated western states entering the Union before 1830, a further consideration was whether a restrictive property qualification made any sense if it kept the voter pool extremely small. Congress had set a fifty-acre freehold as the threshold for voting in several territories, but in Illinois, fewer than three hundred men met that test at the time of statehood. When Indiana, Illinois, and Mississippi became states, their constitutions granted suffrage to all taxpayers. Five additional new western states abandoned property and taxpayer qualifications altogether.

The most heated battles over extending suffrage occurred in East Coast states, where expanding numbers of commercial men, renters, and mortgage holders of all classes contended with entrenched landed political elites who, not surprisingly, tended to favor the status quo. From 1800 to 1812, seven of the original eastern states debated suffrage reform, which then passed in three but failed in four. After the War of 1812, states again took up the issue of democracy. Contentious state constitutional conventions in Massachusetts, Connecticut, and New York finally abolished the freehold qualification and opened the franchise to all whites who paid any tax or rendered militia service.

The defenders of substantial freehold qualifications put up a fight and in several states managed to delay expanded suffrage for two more decades. But it was increasingly hard to persuade the **disfranchised** that landowners alone had a stake in government. Proponents of the status quo began to argue instead that the "industry and good habits" necessary to achieve a propertied status in life were what gave landowners the right character to vote. Opponents fired back blistering attacks. One delegate to New York's constitutional convention said, "More integrity and more patriotism are generally found in the labouring class of the community than in the higher orders." Owning land was no more predictive of wisdom and good character than it was of a person's height or strength, said another.

> Regarding property qualifications for voting, one delegate to New York's constitutional convention said, "More integrity and more patriotism are generally found in the labouring class of the community than in the higher orders."

Both sides of the debate generally agreed that character mattered, and many ideas for ensuring an electorate of proper wisdom came up for discussion. The exclusion of paupers and felons convicted of "infamous crimes" found favor in legislation in many states. Literacy tests and raising the voting age to a figure in the thirties were debated but ultimately discarded. The exclusion of women required no discussion in the constitutional conventions, so firm was the legal power of *feme covert*. But in one exceptional moment, at the Virginia convention in 1829, a delegate who wondered aloud why unmarried women over the age of twenty-one could not vote was quickly silenced with the argument that all women lacked the "free agency and intelligence" necessary for wise voting.

Free black men's enfranchisement was another story, generating much discussion at all the conventions. Under existing freehold qualifications, a small number of propertied black men could vote; universal or taxpayer suffrage would inevitably enfranchise many more. Many delegates at the various state conventions spoke against that extension, claiming that blacks as a race lacked prudence, independence, and knowledge. With the exception of New York, which retained the existing property qualification for black voters as it removed it for whites, the general pattern was one of expanded suffrage for whites and a total eclipse of suffrage for blacks.

The Missouri Compromise

The politics of race lay at the heart of one of the most divisive issues to confront the Monroe administration. In February 1819, Missouri applied for statehood. Since 1815, four other states had joined the Union (Indiana, Mississippi, Illinois, and Alabama), following the blueprint laid out by the Northwest Ordinance of 1787. But Missouri posed a problem. Although much of its area was on the same latitude as the free state of Illinois, its territorial population included ten thousand slaves brought there by southern white planters.

Missouri's unusual combination of geography and demography led a New York congressman, James Tallmadge Jr., to propose two amendments to the statehood bill. The first stipulated that slaves born in Missouri after statehood would be free at age twenty-five, and the second declared that no new slaves could be imported into the state. Tallmadge modeled the first amendment on New York's gradual **emancipation** law of 1799. It did not strip slave owners of their current property, and it allowed them full use of the labor of newborn slaves well into their prime productive years. Still, southerners in Congress objected, because in the long run the amendments would make Missouri a free state, presumably no longer allied with southern economic and political interests. Just as southern economic power rested on slave labor, southern political power drew extra strength from the slave population because of the three-fifths rule. In 1820, the South owed seventeen of its seats in the House of Representatives to its slave population.

A View of St. Louis from an Illinois Town, 1835
Just fifteen years after the Missouri Compromise, St. Louis was already a booming city, having gotten its start
in the eighteenth century as a French fur-trading village. It was incorporated as a town in 1809 and chartered
as a city in 1822. In this 1835 view, commercial buildings and steamships line the riverfront; a ferry on the
Illinois shore prepares to transport travelers across the Mississippi River. Black laborers (in the foreground)
handle loading tasks. Illinois was a free state; Missouri, where the ferry will land, was a slave state.
A View of St. Louis from an Illinois Town, 1835: Private collection.

READING THE IMAGE: What kind of city was St. Louis?

CONNECTIONS: Does this image of St. Louis conform to the usual depiction of the slave states as agricultural?

FOR MORE HELP ANALYZING THIS IMAGE, see the visual activity for this chapter in the Online Study Guide at
bedfordstmartins.com/roark.

Tallmadge's amendments passed in the House by a close and sharply sectional vote of North against South. The ferocious debate led a Georgia representative to observe that the question had started "a fire which all the waters of the ocean could not extinguish. It can be extinguished only in blood." The Senate, with an even number of slave and free states, voted down the amendments, and Missouri statehood was postponed until the next congressional term.

In 1820, a compromise emerged. Maine, once part of Massachusetts, applied for statehood as a free state, balancing against Missouri as a slave state. The Senate further agreed that the southern boundary of Missouri—latitude 36°30'—extended west, would become the per-manent line dividing slave from free states, guaranteeing the North a large area where slavery was banned (Map 10.5, page 348). The House also approved the compromise, thanks to expert deal brokering by Kentucky's Henry Clay, who earned the nickname "the Great Pacificator" for his superb negotiating skills. The whole package passed because seventeen northern congressmen decided that minimizing sectional conflict was the best course and voted with the South.

President Monroe and former president Jefferson at first worried that the Missouri crisis would reinvigorate the Federalist Party as the party of the North. But even ex-Federalists agreed that the split between free and slave states was too dangerous a fault line to be permitted to become a shaper of national politics. When new parties did develop in the 1830s, they took pains to bridge geography, each party developing a presence in both North and South. Monroe and Jefferson also worried about the future of slavery. Both understood slavery to be deeply problematic, but, as Jefferson said, "we have the wolf by the ears, and we can neither hold him, nor safely let him go. Justice is in one scale, and self-preservation in the other."

The Monroe Doctrine

New foreign policy challenges arose even as Congress struggled with the slavery issue. In 1816, U.S. troops led by General Andrew Jackson invaded Spanish Florida in search of Seminole

Indians harboring escaped slaves. Once there, Jackson declared himself the commander of northern Florida, demonstrating his power in 1818 by executing two British men who he claimed were dangerous enemies. In asserting rule over the territory, and surely in executing the two British subjects on Spanish land, Jackson had gone too far. Privately, President Monroe was distressed and pondered court-martialing Jackson, prevented only by Jackson's immense popularity as the hero of the battle of New Orleans. Instead, John Quincy Adams, the secretary of state, negotiated with Spain the Adams-Onís Treaty, which delivered Florida to the United States in 1819. In exchange, the Americans agreed to abandon any claim to Texas or Cuba. Southerners viewed this as a large concession,

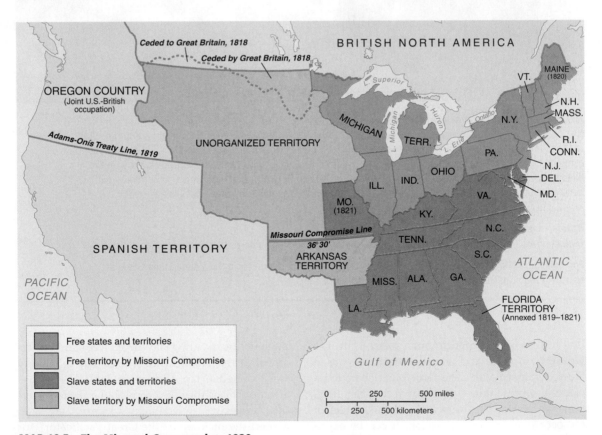

MAP 10.5 The Missouri Compromise, 1820

After a difficult battle in Congress, Missouri entered the Union in 1821 as part of a package of compromises. Maine was admitted as a free state to balance slavery in Missouri, and a line drawn at latitude 36°30′ put most of the rest of the Louisiana Territory off-limits to slavery in the future.

READING THE MAP: How many free and how many slave states were there prior to the Missouri Compromise? What did the admission of Missouri as a slave state threaten to do?

CONNECTIONS: Who precipitated the crisis over Missouri, what did he propose, and where did the idea come from? Who proposed the Missouri Compromise, and who benefited from it?

FOR MORE HELP ANALYZING THIS MAP, see the map activity for this chapter in the Online Study Guide at bedfordstmartins.com/roark.

having eyed both places as potential acquisitions for future slave states.

Spain at that moment was preoccupied with its colonies in South America. One after another, Chile, Colombia, Peru, and finally Mexico declared themselves independent in the early 1820s. To discourage Spain or France from reconquering these colonies, Monroe formulated a declaration of principles on South America. Incorporated into his annual message to Congress in December 1823, the declaration became known in later years as the **Monroe Doctrine**. The president warned that "the American Continents, by the free and independent condition which they have assumed and maintain, are henceforth not to be considered as subjects for future colonization by any European power." Any attempt to interfere in the Western Hemisphere would be regarded as "the manifestation of an unfriendly disposition towards the United States." In exchange for noninterference by Europeans, Monroe pledged that the United States would stay out of European struggles. At that time, Monroe did not intend his statement to lay a foundation for U.S. intervention in South America. Indeed, the small American navy could not realistically defend Chile or Peru against Spain or France. The doctrine was Monroe's idea of sound foreign policy, but it did not have the force of law.

The Election of 1824

Monroe's nonpartisan administration was the last of its kind, a throwback to eighteenth-century ideals, led by the last president to wear a powdered wig and knee breeches. Monroe's cabinet contained men of sharply different philosophies, all calling themselves Republicans. Secretary of State John Quincy Adams represented the urban Northeast; South Carolinian John C. Calhoun spoke for the planter aristocracy as secretary of war; and William H. Crawford of Georgia, secretary of the treasury, was a proponent of Jeffersonian **states' rights** and limited federal power. Even before the end of Monroe's first term, these men and others began to maneuver for the election of 1824.

Crucially helping them to maneuver were their wives, who accomplished some of the work of modern campaign managers by courting men—and women—of influence. The parties not thrown by Elizabeth Monroe were now given all over town by women whose husbands were jockeying for political favor. Louisa Catherine

Adams remodeled her house and had a party every Tuesday night for guests numbering in the hundreds. The somber Adams lacked charm—"I am a man of reserved, cold, austere, and forbidding manners," he once wrote—but his abundantly charming (and hardworking) wife made up for that. She attended to the etiquette of social calls, sometimes making two dozen in a morning, and counted sixty-eight members of Congress as her regular Tuesday guests.

Since 1800, the congressional caucus of each party had met to identify and lend its considerable but still informal support to the party's leading candidate. In 1824, with only one party alive—and alive with five serious candidates—the caucus system splintered. Since such a large number of candidates reduced the chances of anyone securing a majority in the electoral college, many expected that the final election would be decided by the House of Representatives. Having sixty-eight members of Congress on one's regular guest list was thus smart politics.

John Quincy Adams (and Louisa Catherine) very much wanted the presidency, an ambition fed by John's sense of rising to his father's accomplishment. Candidate Henry Clay, Speaker of the House and a man of vast congressional experience, had engaged in high-level diplomacy in negotiating the Treaty of Ghent with Britain in 1814. Clay promoted his "American System," a package of protective tariffs to encourage manufacturing and federal expenditures for extensive internal improvements such as roads and canals. Treasurer William Crawford was a favorite of Republicans from Virginia and New York, even after he suffered an incapacitating stroke in mid-1824. Calhoun was another serious contender, having served in Congress and in several cabinets. Like Clay, he favored internal improvements and protective tariffs, which gained him support in northern states.

The final candidate was an outsider and a latecomer: General Andrew Jackson of Tennessee. Jackson had much less national political experience than the others, having served one year in the House and two in the Senate. His fame derived from his reputation as a military leader. In January 1824, on the anniversary of the battle of New Orleans, the Adamses threw a spectacular ball with five hundred guests in honor of General Jackson. No doubt Adams hoped that

> President Monroe warned that "the American Continents, by the free and independent condition which they have assumed and maintain, are henceforth not to be considered as subjects for future colonization by any European power."

Election Sewing or Trinket Boxes from 1824
Women could express their support for a presidential candidate by purchasing a sewing box emblazoned with his face. On the left is a box with John Quincy Adams's picture inside the cover, created with a lithographic process—just coming into widespread use in the 1820s—that made possible the production of thousands of pictures from a single master stone plate. (Wood and copper plates, the earlier technology, produced prints numbering only in the hundreds before deteriorating under pressure.) The top of the Adams box (not visible here) has a velvet pincushion printed with the slogan "Be Firm for Adams." The competing box on the right features Andrew Jackson's likeness under glass on top of the cover. The lithographic portrait was hand-colored with watercolors. Notice that Jackson is shown in his military uniform, with the title of general and a rather younger-looking face than he actually had in 1824.
Collection of Janice L. and David J. Frent.

some of Jackson's charisma would rub off on him; he was not yet thinking of Jackson as a rival for office. But later in 1824, Jackson's supporters put his name in play, and voters in the West and South reacted with enthusiasm. Calhoun soon dropped out of the race and shifted his attention to winning the vice presidency.

The 1824 election was the first presidential contest in which candidates' popularity with ordinary voters could be measured. Along with expanding the suffrage to nearly all white males, the recent conventions to rewrite the state constitutions had put the power to choose members of the electoral college directly in the hands of voters. (Only six states out of the full twenty-four kept that power in the hands of the state legislature.) Jackson was by far the most popular candidate with voters, winning 153,544 votes. Adams was second with 108,740, Clay won 47,136 votes, and the debilitated Crawford

> Andrew Jackson felt that the election of 1824 had been stolen from him, and he wrote bitterly that "the Judas of the West [Clay] has closed the contract and will receive the thirty pieces of silver."

garnered 46,618. This was still not a large voter turnout, probably amounting to just over a quarter of adult white males. But in its tortured outcome, the election of 1824 forever changed popular voting for the presidency. Partisanship energized the electorate; apathy and a low voter turnout would not recur until the twentieth century.

In the electoral college, Jackson received 99 votes, Adams 84, Crawford 41, and Clay 37 (Map 10.6). Jackson did not have a majority, so the election went to the House of Representatives, for the second (and last) time in American history. Each state delegation had one vote; according to the Twelfth Amendment to the Constitution, passed in 1804, only the top three candidates could enter the runoff. Thus Henry Clay was out of the race and in a position to bestow his support on another candidate.

Jackson's supporters later characterized the election of 1824 as the "corrupt bargain." Clay backed Adams, and Adams won by one vote in the House, in a vote in February 1825. Clay's support made sense on several levels. Despite strong mutual dislike, he and Adams agreed on issues such as federal support to build roads and canals, and Clay was uneasy with Jackson's volatile temperament and unstated political views and with Crawford's diminished capacity. What made Clay's decision look "corrupt" was that immediately after the election, Adams offered to appoint Clay secretary of state—and Clay accepted.

In fact, there probably was no concrete bargain; Adams's subsequent cabinet appointments demonstrated his lack of political astuteness. But Andrew Jackson felt that the election had been stolen from him, and he wrote bitterly that "the Judas of the West [Clay] has closed the contract and will receive the thirty pieces of silver."

The Adams Administration

John Quincy Adams, like his father, was a one-term president. His career had been built on diplomacy, not electoral politics, and despite his wife's deftness in the art of political influence, his own political horse sense was not well developed. With his cabinet choices, he welcomed his opposition into his inner circle. He asked Crawford to stay on in the Treasury. He retained an openly pro-Jackson postmaster general even though that position controlled thousands of nationwide patronage appointments. He even asked Jackson to become secretary of war. With Calhoun as vice president (elected without opposition by the electoral college) and Clay at the State Department, the whole argumentative crew would have been thrust into the executive branch. Crawford and Jackson had the good sense to decline the appointments.

Adams had lofty ideas for federal action during his presidency, and the plan he put before Congress was so sweeping that it took Henry Clay aback. Adams called for federally built roads, canals, and harbors. He proposed a national university in Washington as well as government-sponsored scientific research. He wanted to build observatories to advance astronomical knowledge and to promote precision in timekeeping, and he backed a decimal-based system of weights and measures. In all these endeavors, Adams believed he was continuing the Jefferson and Madison legacy, using the powers of government

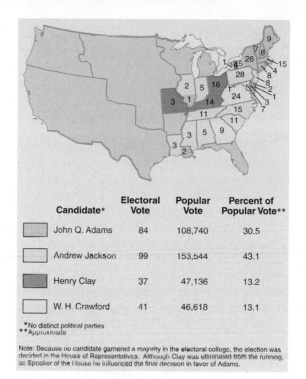

Candidate*	Electoral Vote	Popular Vote	Percent of Popular Vote**
John Q. Adams	84	108,740	30.5
Andrew Jackson	99	153,544	43.1
Henry Clay	37	47,136	13.2
W. H. Crawford	41	46,618	13.1

*No distinct political parties
**Approximate

Note: Because no candidate garnered a majority in the electoral college, the election was decided in the House of Representatives. Although Clay was eliminated from the running, as Speaker of the House he influenced the final decision in favor of Adams.

MAP 10.6 The Election of 1824

to advance knowledge. But his opponents feared he was too Hamiltonian, using federal power inappropriately to advance commercial interests.

Whether he was more truly Federalist or Republican was a moot point. Lacking the give-and-take political skills required to gain congressional support, Adams was unable to implement much of his program. He scorned the idea of courting voters to gain support and using the patronage system to enhance his power. He often made appointments (to posts such as customs collectors) to placate enemies rather than reward friends. A story of a toast offered to the president may well have been mythical, but as humorous folklore it made the rounds during his term and came to summarize Adams's precarious hold on leadership. A dignitary raised a glass and said, "May he strike confusion to his foes," to which another voice scornfully chimed in, "as he has already done to his friends."

REVIEW How did the collapse of the Federalist Party influence the administrations of James Monroe and John Quincy Adams?

Conclusion: Republican Simplicity Becomes Complex

The Jeffersonian Republicans tried at first to undo much of what the Federalists had created in the 1790s, but their promise of a simpler government gave way to the complexities of domestic and foreign issues. The sudden acquisition of the Louisiana Purchase promised land and opportunity to settlers but also complicated the country's political future with the issues central to the Missouri Compromise. Antagonism from both foreign and Indian nations led to complex and costly policies such as embargoes, treaties, and military action, culminating in the War of 1812, a war motivated less by concrete economic or political issues than by questions of honor. Its conclusion at the battle of New Orleans allowed Americans to foster the illusion that they had fought a second war of independence.

The War of 1812 was the Indians' second *lost* war for independence. Tecumseh's vision of an unprecedentedly large confederacy of Indian tribes that would halt westward expansion by white Americans was cut short by the war and by his death. Without British support, the Indians probably could not have successfully challenged for long the westward dynamic of American settlement. But when Canada was under attack, the British valued its defense more than they valued their promises to help the Indians.

The war elevated to national prominence General Andrew Jackson, whose popularity with voters in the 1824 election surprised traditional politicians—and their politically astute wives—and threw the one-party rule of Republicans into a tailspin. John Quincy Adams had barely assumed office in 1825 before the election campaign of 1828 was off and running. Appeals to the people—the mass of white male voters—would be the hallmark of all elections after 1824. It was a game Adams could not easily play.

Politics in this entire period was a game that women could not play either. Except for the political wives of Washington, women, whether white or free black, had no place in government. Male legislatures maintained women's *feme covert* status, keeping wives dependent on husbands.

A few women found a pathway to greater personal autonomy through religion. Meanwhile, the routine inclusion of girls in public schools and the steady spread of female academies planted seeds that would blossom into a major transformation of gender in the 1830s and 1840s.

The War of 1812 started another chain of events that would prove momentous in later decades. Jefferson's long embargo and Madison's wartime trade stoppages gave strong encouragement to American manufacturing, momentarily protected from competition with British factories. When peace returned in 1815, the years of independent development burst forth into a period of sustained economic growth that continued nearly unabated into the mid-nineteenth century.

Selected Bibliography

Politics

Robert J. Allison, *The Crescent Obscured: The United States and the Muslim World, 1776–1815* (1995).

Lance Banning, *The Jeffersonian Persuasion: Evolution of a Party Ideology* (1978).

Saul Cornell, *The Other Founders: Anti-Federalism and the Dissenting Tradition in America, 1788–1828* (1999).

Joseph J. Ellis, *American Sphinx: The Character of Thomas Jefferson* (1997).

Joanne B. Freeman, *Affairs of Honor: National Politics in the New Republic* (2001).

Annette Gordon-Reed, *Thomas Jefferson and Sally Hemings: An American Controversy* (1997).

Ralph Ketcham, *Presidents above Party: The First American Presidency, 1789–1829* (1984).

Alexander Keyssar, *The Right to Vote: The Contested History of Democracy in the United States* (2000).

Jon Kukla, *A Wilderness So Immense: The Louisiana Purchase and the Destiny of America* (2003).

Jan Ellen Lewis and Peter S. Onuf, eds., *Sally Hemings and Thomas Jefferson: History, Memory, and Civic Culture* (1999).

Drew R. McCoy, *The Last of the Fathers: James Madison and the Republican Legacy* (1989).

Michael B. Oren, *Power, Faith, and Fantasy: America in the Middle East: 1776 to the Present* (2007).

Jeffrey L. Pasley, Andrew W. Robertson, and David Waldstreicher, *Beyond the Founders: New Approaches to the Political History of the Early American Republic* (2003).

Stephen Watts, *The Republic Reborn: War and the Making of Liberal America, 1790–1820* (1987).

Sean Wilentz, *The Rise of American Democracy: Jefferson to Lincoln* (2005).

Indians, the War of 1812, and the West

Stephen E. Ambrose, *Undaunted Courage: Meriwether Lewis, Thomas Jefferson, and the Opening of the American West* (1996).

James M. Banner, *To the Hartford Convention: The Federalists and the Origins of Party Politics in Massachusetts, 1789–1815* (1969).

Carl Benn, *The Iroquois in the War of 1812* (1998).

Pierre Berton, *The Invasion of Canada* (1980).

James F. Brooks, *Captives and Cousins: Slavery, Kinship, and Community in the Southwest Borderlands* (2002).

Gregory E. Dowd, *A Spirited Resistance: The North American Indian Struggle for Unity, 1745–1815* (1992).

R. David Edmunds, *Tecumseh and the Quest for Indian Leadership* (1984).

Albert Furtwangler, *Acts of Discovery: Visions of America in the Lewis and Clark Journals* (1993).

John Sugden, *Tecumseh: A Life* (1997).

Richard White, *The Middle Ground: Indians, Empires, and Republics in the Great Lakes Region, 1650–1815* (1991).

Slavery

Douglas Egerton, *Gabriel's Rebellion* (1993).

James Oliver Horton and Lois E. Horton, *In Hope of Liberty: Culture, Community, and Protest among Northern Free Blacks, 1700–1860* (1997)

Gary B. Nash, *Forging Freedom: The Formation of Philadelphia's Black Community, 1720–1840* (1988).

Shane White, *Somewhat More Independent: The End of Slavery in New York City, 1710–1810* (1991).

Women, Marriage, and Religion

Catherine Allgor, *Parlor Politics: In Which the Ladies of Washington Help Build a City and a Government* (2000).

Norma Basch, *In the Eyes of the Law: Women, Marriage, and Property in Nineteenth-Century New York* (1982).

Norma Basch, *Framing American Divorce: From the Revolutionary Generation to the Victorians* (1999).

Catherine A. Brekus, *Strangers and Pilgrims: Female Preaching in America, 1740–1845* (1998).

Nancy Cott, *Public Vows: A History of Marriage and the Nation* (2001).

Susan Juster, *Disorderly Women: Sexual Politics and Evangelicalism in Revolutionary New England* (1994).

Mary Kelley, *Learning to Stand and Speak: Women, Education, and Public Life in America's Republic* (2006).

Marylynn Salmon, *Women and the Law of Property in Early America* (1986).

Mary Beth Sievens, *Stray Wives: Marital Conflict in Early National New England* (2005).

▶ **FOR MORE BOOKS ABOUT TOPICS IN THIS CHAPTER,** see the Online Bibliography at bedfordstmartins.com/roark.

▶ **FOR ADDITIONAL FIRSTHAND ACCOUNTS OF THIS PERIOD,** see Chapter 10 in Michael Johnson, ed., *Reading the American Past,* Fourth Edition.

▶ **FOR WEB SITES, IMAGES, AND DOCUMENTS RELATED TO TOPICS AND PLACES IN THIS CHAPTER,** visit bedfordstmartins.com/makehistory.

REVIEWING THE CHAPTER

Follow these steps to review and strengthen your understanding of the chapter.

STEP 1: *Study the* **Key Terms** *and* **Timeline** *to identify the significance of each item listed.*

STEP 2: *Answer the* **Review Questions**, *drawing on key terms and dates to support your answers.*

STEP 3: *Drawing on the Key Terms, Timeline, and Review Questions, answer the broader* **Making Connections** *questions.*

KEY TERMS

Who

Tecumseh (p. 321)
Tenskwatawa (the Prophet) (p. 321)
Thomas Jefferson (p. 322)
Aaron Burr (p. 323)
Alexander Hamilton (p. 323)
John Marshall (p. 325)
James Madison (pp. 327, 331)
Meriwether Lewis (p. 329)
William Clark (p. 329)
Sacajawea (p. 330)
Dolley Madison (p. 332)
William Henry Harrison (p. 333)
Henry Clay (pp. 334, 347)
John C. Calhoun (p. 334)
Andrew Jackson (p. 335)
Jemima Wilkinson (p. 340)

Emma Willard (p. 341)
Catharine Beecher (p. 341)
James Monroe (p. 344)
James Tallmadge Jr. (p. 346)
John Quincy Adams (p. 348)

What

Treaty of Greenville (p. 321)
Gabriel's rebellion (p. 323)
Judiciary Act of 1801 (p. 327)
Marbury v. Madison (p. 328)
Louisiana Purchase (p. 328)
impressment (p. 331)
Chesapeake (p. 331)
Embargo Act of 1807 (p. 331)
Treaty of Fort Wayne (p. 333)
battle of Tippecanoe (p. 333)

War of 1812 (p. 333)
War Hawks (p. 334)
Creek War (p. 335)
battle of New Orleans (p. 336)
Treaty of Ghent (p. 336)
Hartford Convention (p. 336)
Rush-Bagot disarmament treaty (p. 337)
feme covert (p. 337)
district schools (p. 340)
female academies (p. 341)
female seminaries (p. 341)
Troy Female Seminary (p. 341)
"Era of Good Feelings" (p. 344)
suffrage qualifications (p. 345)
Missouri Compromise (p. 346)
Adams-Onís Treaty (p. 348)
Monroe Doctrine (p. 349)

TIMELINE

◄ **1789** • Judiciary Act establishes six Supreme Court justices.

1800 • Republicans Thomas Jefferson and Aaron Burr tie in electoral college.
   • Fears of slave rebellion led by Gabriel in Virginia result in twenty-seven executions.

1801 • Judiciary Act reduces Supreme Court justices to five, increases number of circuit courts.
   • House of Representatives elects Thomas Jefferson president after thirty-six ballots.

1803 • *Marbury v. Madison.*
   • Britain and France warn United States not to ship war-related goods to each other.
   • United States purchases Louisiana Territory.

1804– • Lewis and Clark expedition goes to Pacific Ocean.
1806

1807 • British attack and search *Chesapeake*.
   • Embargo Act.

1808 • Republican James Madison elected president; Dolley Madison soon dubbed "presidentress."

1809 • Treaty of Fort Wayne.
   • Non-Intercourse Act.

1811 • Battle of Tippecanoe.

REVIEW QUESTIONS

1. How did Jefferson attempt to undo the Federalist innovations of earlier administrations? (pp. 322–31)

2. Why did Congress declare war on Great Britain in 1812? (pp. 331–37)

3. How did the civil status of American women and men differ in the early Republic? (pp. 337–44)

4. How did the collapse of the Federalist Party influence the administrations of James Monroe and John Quincy Adams? (pp. 344–51)

MAKING CONNECTIONS

1. When Jefferson assumed the presidency following the election of 1800, he expected to transform the national government. Describe his republican vision and his successes and failures in implementing it. Did subsequent Republican presidents advance the same objectives?

2. How did the United States expand and strengthen its control of territory in North America in the early nineteenth century? In your answer, discuss the roles of diplomacy, military action, and political leadership in contributing to this development.

3. Regional tensions emerged as a serious danger to the American political system in the early nineteenth century. Discuss specific conflicts that had regional dimensions. How did Americans resolve, or fail to resolve, these tensions?

4. Although the United States denied its female citizens equality in public life, some women were able to exert considerable influence. How did they do so? In your answer, discuss the legal, political, and educational status of women in the early Republic.

► For practice quizzes, a customized study plan, and other study tools, see the Online Study Guide at bedfordstmartins.com/mark.

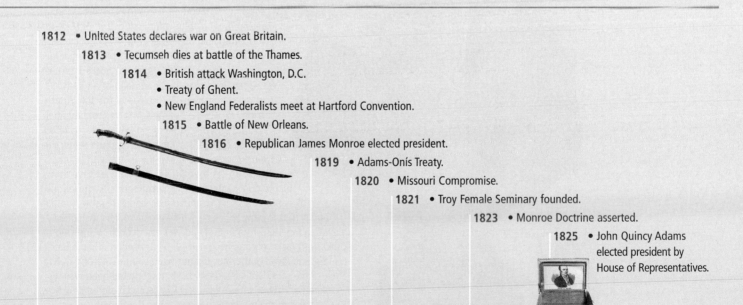

1812 • United States declares war on Great Britain.

1813 • Tecumseh dies at battle of the Thames.

1814 • British attack Washington, D.C.
• Treaty of Ghent.
• New England Federalists meet at Hartford Convention.

1815 • Battle of New Orleans.

1816 • Republican James Monroe elected president.

1819 • Adams-Onís Treaty.

1820 • Missouri Compromise.

1821 • Troy Female Seminary founded.

1823 • Monroe Doctrine asserted.

1825 • John Quincy Adams elected president by House of Representatives.

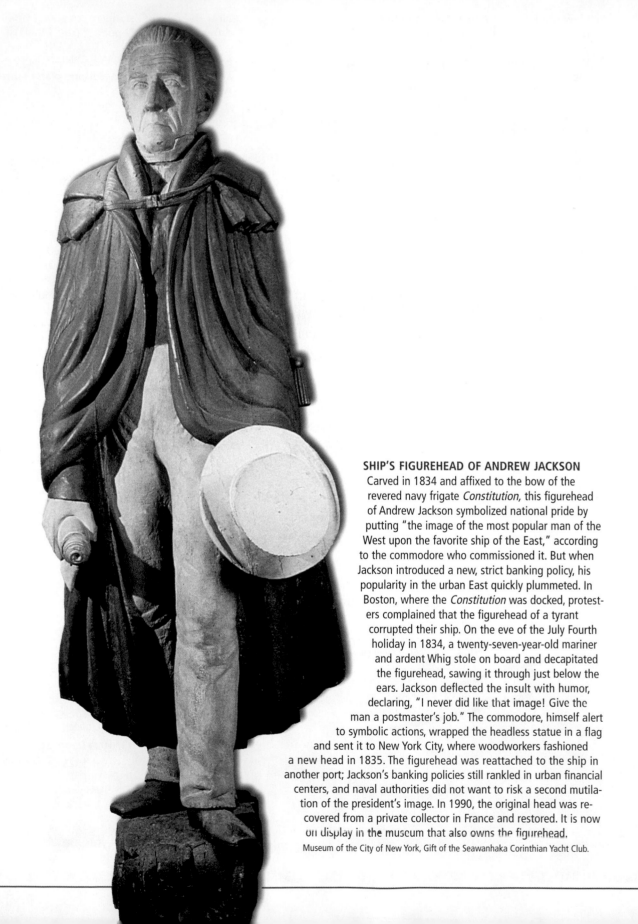

SHIP'S FIGUREHEAD OF ANDREW JACKSON

Carved in 1834 and affixed to the bow of the revered navy frigate *Constitution,* this figurehead of Andrew Jackson symbolized national pride by putting "the image of the most popular man of the West upon the favorite ship of the East," according to the commodore who commissioned it. But when Jackson introduced a new, strict banking policy, his popularity in the urban East quickly plummeted. In Boston, where the *Constitution* was docked, protesters complained that the figurehead of a tyrant corrupted their ship. On the eve of the July Fourth holiday in 1834, a twenty-seven-year-old mariner and ardent Whig stole on board and decapitated the figurehead, sawing it through just below the ears. Jackson deflected the insult with humor, declaring, "I never did like that image! Give the man a postmaster's job." The commodore, himself alert to symbolic actions, wrapped the headless statue in a flag and sent it to New York City, where woodworkers fashioned a new head in 1835. The figurehead was reattached to the ship in another port; Jackson's banking policies still rankled in urban financial centers, and naval authorities did not want to risk a second mutilation of the president's image. In 1990, the original head was recovered from a private collector in France and restored. It is now on display in the museum that also owns the figurehead.

Museum of the City of New York, Gift of the Seawanhaka Corinthian Yacht Club.

The Expanding Republic

1815–1840

■ **The Market Revolution** 358
Improvements in Transportation 359
Factories, Workingwomen, and
Wage Labor 361
Bankers and Lawyers 365
Booms and Busts 365

■ **The Spread of Democracy** 366
Popular Politics and
Partisan Identity 367
The Election of 1828 and
the Character Issue 367
Jackson's Democratic Agenda 368

■ **Jackson Defines
the Democratic Party** 369
Indian Policy and the Trail of Tears 369
The Tariff of Abominations
and Nullification 373
The Bank War and
Economic Boom 373

■ **Cultural Shifts, Religion,
and Reform** 375
The Family and Separate Spheres 376
The Education and
Training of Youths 378
The Second Great Awakening 379
The Temperance Movement and
the Campaign for Moral Reform 380
Organizing against Slavery 381

■ **Van Buren's One-Term
Presidency** 385
The Politics of Slavery 385
The Election of 1836 386
Two Panics and the
Election of 1840 386

■ **Conclusion: The Age of Jackson
or the Era of Reform?** 390

PRESIDENT ANDREW JACKSON was the dominant figure of his age, yet his precarious childhood little foretold the fame, fortune, and influence he would enjoy in the years after 1815. Jackson was born in the Carolina backcountry in 1767. His Scots-Irish father had recently died, leaving a poor, struggling mother to support three small boys. During the Revolution, Andrew followed his brothers into the militia, where both died of disease, as did his mother. Orphaned at fourteen, Jackson drifted around, drinking, gambling, and brawling.

Then at seventeen, his prospects began to improve. He studied under a lawyer for three years and moved to Nashville, a **frontier** community full of opportunities for a young man with legal training and an aggressive temperament. He became a public prosecutor, married into a leading family, and acquired land and slaves. When Tennessee became a state in 1796, Jackson, then twenty-nine, was elected to Congress and served a single term. In 1802, he became major general of the Tennessee militia, cultivating a fierce style of military leadership.

Jackson captured national attention in 1815 by leading the United States to victory at the battle of New Orleans. With little else to celebrate about the War of 1812, many Americans seized on the Tennessee general as the champion of the day. Songs, broadsides, and an admiring biography set him up as the original self-made man—the parentless child magically responsible for his own destiny. Jackson seemed to have created himself—a gritty, forceful personality extracting opportunities from the dynamic, turbulent frontier.

Jackson was more than a man of action, however. He was also strong-willed, reckless, and quick to anger, impulsively challenging men to duels, sometimes on slight pretexts. In one legendary fight in 1806, Jackson deliberately let his opponent, an expert marksman, shoot first. The bullet hit him in a rib, but Jackson masked all sign of injury under a loose cloak and an immobile face. He then took careful aim at the astonished man and killed him. Such steely courage chilled his political opponents.

Jackson's image as a tough frontier hero set him apart from the learned and privileged gentlemen from Virginia and Massachusetts who had occupied the presidency up to 1828. When he lost the 1824 election to John Quincy Adams, an infuriated Jackson vowed to fight a rematch. He won in 1828 and again in 1832, capturing large majorities. His appeal stretched across the urban working classes of the East, frontier voters of the West, and slaveholders in the South, who all saw something of themselves in Jackson. Once

President Andrew Jackson
Boston painter Ralph E. W. Earl traveled to Nashville, Tennessee, in 1817 to paint the hero of the battle of New Orleans. There, Earl met and married Mrs. Jackson's niece. When the niece died a year later in childbirth, Earl moved into the Hermitage, the Jacksons' plantation home. He stayed ten years and then moved with Andrew Jackson to the White House. The two men were fast friends. Earl was Jackson's "court painter," producing three dozen portraits of him, hundreds of which were sold as lithographic copies to Jackson's supporters. Earl was a shrewd publicist, manufacturing a kindly, subdued, gentle Jackson to counteract the many satirical cartoons that generally portrayed him as a villain (see page 370). Earl stayed with Jackson throughout his presidency. He died in 1838.
North Carolina Museum of Art, purchased with funds from the State of North Carolina.

elected, he brought a combative style to politics and enlarged the powers of the presidency.

The confidence and even recklessness of Jackson's personality mirrored the new confidence of American society in the years after 1815. An entrepreneurial spirit gripped the country, producing a market revolution of unprecedented scale. Old social hierarchies eroded; ordinary men dreamed of moving high up the ladder of success, just as Jackson had done. Stunning advances in transportation and economic productivity fueled such dreams and propelled thousands to move west or to cities. Urban growth and technological change fostered the diffusion of a distinctive and vibrant public

culture, spread mainly through the increased circulation of newspapers, which allowed popular opinions to coalesce and intensify. Jackson's sudden nationwide celebrity was a case in point.

Expanded communication transformed politics dramatically. Sharp disagreements over the best way to promote individual **liberty**, economic opportunity, and national prosperity in the new market economy defined key differences between Jackson and Adams and the parties they gave rise to in the 1830s. The process of party formation brought new habits of political participation and party loyalty to many thousands more adult white males. Religion became democratized as well. A nationwide **evangelical** revival brought its adherents the certainty that salvation and perfection were now available to all.

As president from 1829 to 1837, Jackson presided over all these changes, fighting some and supporting others in his vigorous and volatile way. As with his own stubborn personality, there was a dark underside to the confidence and expansiveness of American society. Steamboats blew up, banks and businesses periodically collapsed, alcoholism rates soared, Indians were killed or relocated farther west, and slavery continued to expand. The brash confidence that turned some people into rugged, self-promoting, Jackson-like individuals inspired others to think about the human costs of rapid economic expansion and thus about reforming society in dramatic ways. The common denominator was a faith that people and societies could shape their own destinies.

The Market Revolution

The return of peace in 1815 unleashed powerful forces that revolutionized the organization of the economy. Spectacular changes in transportation facilitated the movement of commodities, information, and people, while textile mills and other factories created many new jobs, especially for young unmarried women. Innovations in banking, legal practices, and tariff policies promoted swift economic growth.

This was not yet an industrial revolution, as was beginning in Britain, but a market revolution, fueled by traditional sources—water, wood, beasts of burden, and human muscle. What was new was the accelerated pace of economic activity and the scale of the distribution of goods. Men and women were drawn out of old patterns of rural self-sufficiency into the wider realm of national market relations. At the same time, the nation's money supply enlarged considerably, leading to speculative investments in commerce, manufacturing, transportation, and land. The new nature and scale of production and consumption changed Americans' economic behavior, attitudes, and expectations. But in 1819 and again in 1837 and 1839, serious crashes of the economy punctured those optimistic expectations.

Improvements in Transportation

Before 1815, transportation in the United States was slow and expensive; it cost as much to ship a crate over thirty miles of domestic roads as it did to send it across the Atlantic Ocean. The fastest stagecoach trip from Boston to New York took four days. But between 1815 and 1840, networks of roads, canals, steamboats, and finally railroads dramatically raised the speed and lowered the cost of travel (Map 11.1). The young Andrew Jackson spent weeks traveling west from North Carolina to Nashville, Tennessee, in the 1780s along old Indian trails, but when he journeyed east in 1829, it took only days for the new president to get to Washington, D.C., by steamboat and turnpike.

Improved transportation moved goods into wider markets. It moved passengers, too, broadening their horizons and allowing young people as well as adults to take up new employment in cities and factory towns. Transportation also facilitated the flow of political information via the U.S. mail with its bargain postal rates for newspapers, periodicals, and books.

Enhanced public transport was expensive and produced uneven economic benefits, so presidents from Jefferson to Monroe were reluctant to fund it with federal dollars. Only the

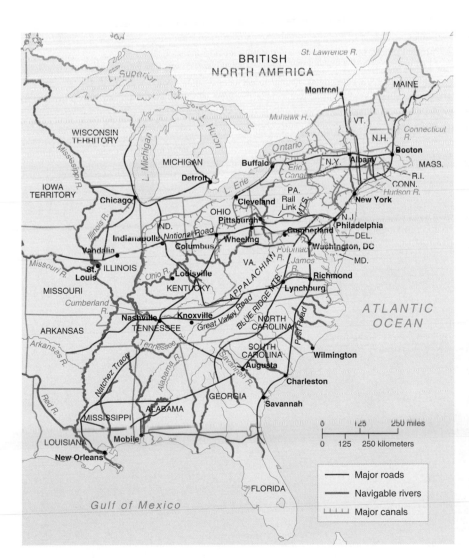

MAP 11.1   Routes of Transportation in 1840

By the 1830s, transportation advances had cut travel times significantly. By way of the Erie Canal, goods and people could move from New York City to Buffalo in four days, a trip that had taken two weeks by road in 1800. Similarly, the trip from New York to New Orleans, which had taken four weeks in 1800, could now be accomplished in less than half that time on steamboats plying the western rivers.

READING THE MAP: In what parts of the country were canals built most extensively? Were most of them within a single state's borders, or did they encourage interstate travel and shipping? **CONNECTIONS:** What impact did the Erie Canal have on the development of New York City? How did improvements in transportation affect urbanization in other parts of the country?

FOR MORE HELP ANALYZING THIS MAP, see the map activity for this chapter in the Online Study Guide at bedfordstmartins.com/roark.

National Road, begun in 1806, was government sponsored. By 1818, it linked Baltimore with Wheeling, in western Virginia. In all other cases, private investors pooled resources and chartered transport companies, receiving significant subsidies and **monopoly** rights from state governments. Turnpike and roadway mileage increased dramatically after 1815, reducing shipping costs. Stagecoach companies proliferated, and travel time on main routes was cut in half.

Water travel was similarly transformed. In 1807, Robert Fulton's steam-propelled boat, the *Clermont*, churned up the Hudson River from New York City to Albany in thirty-two hours, compared with two days for the land route, touching off a steamboat craze. In 1820, a dozen boats left New York City daily, and scores more operated on midwestern rivers and the Great Lakes. A voyager on one of the first steamboats to go down the Mississippi reported that the Chickasaw Indians called the vessel a "fire canoe" and considered it "an omen of evil." By the early 1830s, more than seven hundred steamboats were in operation on the Ohio and Mississippi rivers. A journey upriver from New Orleans to Louisville, Kentucky, took only one week.

Steamboats were not benign advances, however. The urgency to cut travel time led to over-stoked furnaces, sudden boiler explosions, and terrible mass fatalities. (See "The Promise of Technology," page 362.) By 1838, nearly three thousand Americans had been killed in steamboat acci-

View of the Erie Canal at Lockport

The Erie Canal struck many as the eighth wonder of the world when it was completed in 1825, not only for its length of 350 miles but also for its impressive elevation. Eighty-three locks were required to move canal boats over the combined ascent and descent of 680 feet. The biggest challenge of the entire route came at Lockport, 20 miles northeast of Buffalo, where the canal had to traverse a steep slate escarpment. Work crews—mostly immigrant Irishmen—used gunpowder and grueling physical labor to blast a deep artificial gorge out of the cliff; note the raw cut rock on the left. Next, five double locks were constructed to move boats in stages up and down the 60-foot elevation. Passengers would take the stairs that separated the locks, while barge animals would take the towpath on the far side. Even with double locks, bottlenecks occurred. Not surprisingly, a village grew up here to service waiting passengers and crews. Its name, Lockport, was probably an obvious choice. Library of Congress.

dents, leading to initial federal attempts—at first unsuccessful—to regulate safety on ships used for interstate commerce. Environmental costs were also very high. Steamboats had to load fuel—"wood up"—every twenty miles or so, causing serious deforestation. By the 1830s, the banks of many main rivers were denuded of trees, and forests miles back from the rivers fell to the ax. As steamboats burned wood, they transferred the carbon stored in trees into the atmosphere, creating America's first significant air pollution.

Canals were another major innovation of the transportation revolution. These shallow highways of water (typically just four feet deep) allowed passage for barges and boats pulled by horses or mules trudging on a towpath along the embankment. Travel speed was slow—under five miles per hour. The economy in comparison to land travel came from increased loads. The low-friction water allowed one horse to pull a fifty-ton barge. Pennsylvania in 1815 and New York in 1817 commenced major state-sponsored canal enterprises. Pennsylvania's Schuylkill Canal stretched 108 miles west from Philadelphia when it was completed in 1826. Much more impressive was the Erie Canal, finished in 1825. It spanned 350 miles from Albany to Buffalo, New York, thus linking the port of New York City (via the Hudson River) with the entire Great Lakes region. Wheat and flour moved east, household goods and tools moved west, and passengers went in both directions. By the 1830s, the cost of shipping by canal fell to less than a tenth of the cost of overland transport, and New York City quickly blossomed into the premier commercial city in the United States.

In the 1830s, private railroad companies began to give canals stiff competition, and by the 1840s railroads eclipsed canal boats as passenger conveyances, leaving them to haul freight only. The nation's first railroad, the Baltimore and Ohio, laid thirteen miles of track in 1829. During the 1830s, three thousand more miles of track materialized nationwide, the result of a speculative fever in railroad construction masterminded by bankers, locomotive manufacturers, and state legislators, who provided subsidies, charters, and land rights-of-way. Rail lines in the 1830s were generally short, on the order of twenty to one hundred miles. They did not yet provide an efficient distribution system for goods, but passengers flocked to experience the marvelous speeds of fifteen to twenty miles per hour. Railroads and other advances in transportation made possible enormous change by unifying the country culturally and economically.

Factories, Workingwomen, and Wage Labor

Transportation advances promoted the expansion of manufacturing after 1815, creating an ever-expanding market for goods. The two leading industries, textiles and shoes, altered methods of production and labor relations. Textile production was greatly spurred by the development of water-driven machinery, built near fast-coursing rivers. Shoe manufacturing, still using the power and skill of human hands, involved only a reorganization of production. Both mechanized and manual manufacturing pulled young women into wage-earning labor for the first time.

The earliest factory was built by English immigrant Samuel Slater in Pawtucket, Rhode Island, in the 1790s. It featured a mechanical spinning machine that produced thread and yarn. By 1815, nearly 170 spinning mills had been built along streams and rivers in lower New England. In British manufacturing cities, entire families worked in factories where wages were low and conditions unhealthy. In contrast, American factories targeted young women as employees. Mill girls provided cheap labor because of their limited employment options and because they would soon "retire" to marriage, to be replaced by fresh recruits earning a beginner's wage.

In 1821, a group of Boston entrepreneurs founded the town of Lowell, Massachusetts, on the Merrimack River. There, they centralized all aspects of cloth production: combing, shrinking, spinning, weaving, and dyeing. By 1830, the eight mills in Lowell employed more than five thousand young women, most between the ages of sixteen and twenty-three. A key innovation was the close moral supervision of these workers, who lived in company-owned boardinghouses. Corporation rules required church attendance and prohibited drinking and unsupervised courtship; dorms were locked at 10 p.m. The typical mill worker earned $2 to $3 for a seventy-hour week. That was more than a seamstress or domestic servant could earn but less than a young man's wages. The job consisted of tending noisy power looms in rooms kept hot and humid—ideal conditions for thread but not for people.

Despite the discomforts, young women embraced factory work as

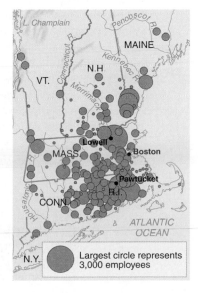

Cotton Textile Industry, 1839

Largest circle represents 3,000 employees

Early Steamboats

Steamboats revolutionized travel in the early nineteenth century. The basic technology consisted of an engine powered by the steam from a boiler heated by a wood-burning furnace. The steam first collected in a cylinder and then cooled and condensed to create a vacuum that drove a piston, which in turn propelled a paddle wheel mounted on the side or stern of the boat. From the 1780s to 1807, several inventors sought the ideal combination of engine size, boat size, and paddle wheel type. Robert Fulton's *Clermont* of 1807 was not the first American steamboat, but it was the first long-distance, commercially successful endeavor.

Two advantages marked Fulton's effort: He imported a superior British-made engine—a low-pressure model built with many precision parts—and he formed a partnership with New York businessman Robert R. Livingston. In 1798, Livingston had acquired from the New York legislature the right to a twenty-year monopoly on all steam transportation on the Hudson River, on the condition that he produce a boat capable of traveling four miles per hour upriver. The *Clermont* met that test.

In 1811, Fulton and Livingston launched the first steamboat on the Mississippi River. Their low-pressure engine, operating at about two pounds per square inch of pressure in the cylinder, failed to maneuver against the river's shifting currents and many obstructions. A high-pressure steam engine developed by Delaware entrepreneur Oliver Evans proved far more suitable. Generating pressures from eighty to one hundred pounds per square inch, it required 30 percent more fuel, but at that time wood was plentiful along western waterways. By the 1830s, there were many hundreds of boats on the Mississippi, Ohio, and lower Missouri rivers, run by companies competing to reduce travel time. An upriver trip from New Orleans to Louisville that took nearly a month in the 1810s took less than a week in the 1830s. The American traveling public fell in love with steamboats for their speed and power.

Steamboats offered luxury as well as speed. They often were floating palaces, carrying several hundred passengers and providing swank accommodations to ladies and gentlemen paying first-class fares. A few boats had private cabins, but most often there were two large rooms, one for each sex, filled with chairs that converted to beds. (The separation of the sexes answered an important need in addition to bodily modesty: Women travelers often expressed their disgust over the spit-drenched carpets in the men's cabin.) Dining rooms with elegant appointments served elaborate meals. Many steamboats had gambling rooms as well.

Low-fare passengers, typically men, occupied the lower decks, finding sleeping space out in the open or in crowded berths in public rooms. Often these men were pressed into service loading wood at the frequent fueling stops.

The fire and smoke of a steamboat proved awesome and even terrifying to many. An older gent making his first trip in 1836 wrote, "I went on board, and passing the fireroom, where they were just firing up, I stopped, with unfeigned horror, and asked myself if, indeed, I was prepared to die!" But many others were enthralled by the unprecedented power represented by the belching smoke. Impromptu boat racing became a popular sport. A German traveler identified a competitive streak in American passengers: "When two steamboats happen to get alongside each other, the passengers will encourage the captains to run a race. . . . The boilers intended for a pressure of only 100 pounds per square inch, are by the accelerated generation of steam, exposed to a pressure of 150, and even 200 pounds, and this goes sometimes so far, that the trials end with an explosion."

Steamboats were far from safe. Between 1811 and 1851, accidents destroyed nearly a thousand boats— a third of all steam vessels built in that period. More than half the sinkings resulted from underwater debris that penetrated the boats' hulls. Fires, too, were fearsome hazards in wooden boats that commonly carried highly combustible cargoes, such as raw cotton in burlap bags. The development of sheet metal, which

a means to earn spending money and build savings before marriage. Also welcome was the unprecedented, though still limited, personal freedom of living in an all female social space, away from parents and domestic tasks. In the evening, the women could engage in self-improvement activities, such as attending lectures or writing for the company's periodical, the *Lowell Offering*.

In the mid-1830s, worldwide changes in the cotton market impelled mill owners to speed up work and lower wages. The workers protested, emboldened by their communal living arrange-

strengthened hulls and protected wooden surfaces near the smokestacks from sparks, was a major safety advance.

Boiler explosions were the most horrifying cause of accidents. By far the greatest loss of life came from scalding steam, flying wreckage, and fire, which could engulf a boat in a matter of minutes. In the 1830s alone, 89 boiler explosions caused 861 deaths and many more injuries. The cause of an explosion was often mysterious: Was it excessive steam pressure or weak metal? Exactly how much pressure could plate iron fastened with rivets withstand? Did a dangerous or explosive gas develop in the boiler when the water level fell too low? Or was the principal cause human error—reckless or drunk pilots (none of them licensed) or captains bent on breaking speed records?

And who was responsible for public safety? When the three-week-old *Moselle* blew up near Cincinnati in 1838, with the loss of 150 lives, a citizens committee fixed blame on the twenty-eight-year-old captain, who had ordered the fires stoked with pitch and the safety valves shut to build up a bigger head of steam. "Such disasters have their foundation in the present mammoth evil of our country, an inordinate love of gain," said the committee. "We are not satisfied with getting rich, but we must get rich in a day. We are not satisfied with traveling at a speed of ten miles an hour, but we must fly. Such is the effect of competition that everything must be done cheap; boiler iron must be cheap, traveling must be done

"The Awful Conflagration of the Steamboat *Lexington* in Long Island Sound," 1840

The *Lexington* was six years old in 1840 and equipped with many extra safety features, such as a fire engine and pump, but with only three lifeboats. The lifeboats could accommodate only half of the passengers; they were quickly swamped in the emergency and rendered useless. Only 4 people survived; many of the 139 victims froze to death in the icy January waters. Thousands of copies of this lithograph were made for sale. Who would buy this kind of artistic reproduction?

The Mariners Museum, Newport News, VA.

Awful Conflagration of the Steam Boat LEXINGTON In Long Island Sound on Monday Eve' Jan'y 13th 1840, by which melancholy occurrence; over 100 PERSONS PERISHED.

cheap, freight must be cheap, yet everything must be speedy. A steamboat must establish a reputation of a few minutes 'swifter' in a hundred miles than others, before she can make fortunes fast enough to satisfy the owners."

In 1830, the federal government awarded a grant to the Franklin Institute of Philadelphia to study the causes of boiler explosions. But not until 1852 did public safety become a federal responsibility with the passage of regulations by Congress mandating steamboat inspections. After the Civil War, affordable sheet steel and the development of new welding techniques produced boilers that were much stronger and safer.

ment and by their relative independence as temporary employees. In 1834 and again in 1836, hundreds of women at Lowell went out on strike. All over New England, female mill workers led strikes and formed unions. In 1834, women at a mill in Dover, New Hampshire, de-

nounced their owners for trying to turn them into "slaves": "However freely the epithet of 'factory slaves' may be bestowed upon us, we will never deserve it by a base and cringing submission to proud wealth or haughty insolence." Their assertiveness surprised many, but in the

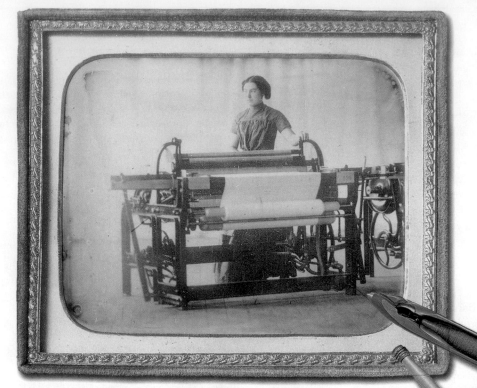

Mill Worker Tending a Power Loom, 1850
This daguerreotype (the earliest form of photograph) shows a young woman tending a power loom in a textile mill. Her main task was to replace the spindle when it ran out of thread and load a new spindle into the shuttle. Spindles carried the woof—the crosswise threading—that was woven into the warp already mounted on the loom. The close-up shows spindles of pink and blue thread next to a shuttle. Factory workers had to be constantly alert for sudden breaks in the warp, which required a fast shutdown of the loom and a quick repair of the thread. In the 1830s, women weavers generally tended two machines at a time. In the 1840s, some companies increased the workload to four.
Mill worker: American Textile History Museum; Shuttle with spindles: Picture Research Consultants & Archives.

end their bargaining power was undercut by the ease with which factory owners could replace them. In the 1840s, owners began to shift to immigrant families as their primary labor source.

Other manufacturing enterprises of the 1820s and 1830s, such as shoemaking, innovated by employing women in ever-larger numbers. New modes of organizing the work allowed manufacturers to step up production, control waste and quality, and decrease wages by hiring women, including wives. Male shoemakers still cut the leather and made the soles, but now the stitching of the upper parts of the shoes, called shoebinding, became women's work, performed at home so that it could be done in conjunction with domestic chores. Although women's wages were lower than men's, shoebinders were in the vanguard of a new trend as wage-earning wives, contributing additional cash to family income.

In the economically turbulent 1830s, shoebinder wages fell. The fact that shoebinders worked at home, in isolation, was a serious hindrance to organized protest. In Lynn, Massachusetts, a major shoemaking center, women used female church networks to organize resistance, communicating via religious newspapers. The Lynn shoebinders who demanded higher wages in 1834 built on a collective sense of themselves as women even though they did not work together daily. "Equal rights should be extended to all—to the weaker sex as well as the stronger," they wrote in a document establishing the Female Society of Lynn.

In the end, the Lynn shoebinders' protests failed to achieve wage increases. Isolated workers all over New England continued to accept low wages, and even in Lynn, many women shied away from organized protest, preferring to situate their work in the context of family duty (helping their husbands to finish the shoes) instead of market relations.

Bankers and Lawyers

Entrepreneurs such as the Lowell factory owners relied on innovations in the banking system to finance their ventures. Between 1814 and 1816, the number of state-chartered banks in the United States more than doubled, from fewer than 90 to 208. By 1830, there were 330, and by 1840 hundreds more. Banks stimulated the economy by making loans to merchants and manufacturers and by enlarging the money supply. Borrowers were issued loans in the form of banknotes—certificates unique to each bank—which were used as money for all transactions. Neither federal nor state governments issued paper money, so banknotes became the country's currency.

In theory, a note could always be traded in at a bank for its **hard-money** equivalent in gold or silver. This transaction was known as a "specie payment." A note from a solid local bank might be worth exactly what it was written for, but the face value of a note from a distant or questionable bank would be discounted. Buying and selling banknotes in this era required knowledge and caution. Not surprisingly, counterfeiting flourished.

Bankers exercised great power over the economy, deciding who would get loans and what the discount rates would be. The most powerful bankers sat on the board of directors for the second Bank of the United States, headquartered in Philadelphia. The twenty-year charter of the first Bank of the United States had expired in 1811. The second Bank of the United States, with eighteen branches throughout the country, opened for business in 1816 under another twenty-year charter. The rechartering of this bank would be a major issue in Andrew Jackson's reelection campaign in 1832.

Accompanying the market revolution was a revolution in commercial law, fashioned by politicians to enhance the prospects of private investment. In 1811, states started to rewrite their laws of incorporation (allowing the chartering of businesses by states), and the number of corporations expanded rapidly, from about twenty in 1800 to eighteen hundred by 1817. Incorporation protected individual investors from being held liable for corporate debts. State lawmakers also wrote laws of eminent domain, empowering states to buy land for roads and canals even from unwilling sellers. They drafted legislation on contributory negligence, relieving employers of the responsibility for workplace injuries. In such ways, entrepreneurial lawyers of the 1820s and 1830s created the legal foundation for an economy that would give priority to ambitious individuals interested in maximizing their own wealth.

Not everyone applauded these developments. Andrew Jackson, himself a skillful lawyer turned politician, spoke for a large and mistrustful segment of the population when he warned about the potential abuses of power "which the moneyed interest derives from a paper currency which they are able to control, from the multitude of corporations with exclusive privileges which they have succeeded in obtaining in the different states, and which are employed altogether for their benefit." Jacksonians believed that ending government-granted privileges was the way to maximize individual liberty and economic opportunity.

> Andrew Jackson spoke for a large and mistrustful segment of the population when he warned about the potential abuses of power "which the moneyed interest derives from a paper currency which they are able to control."

Booms and Busts

One aspect of the economy that the lawyer-politicians could not control was the threat of financial collapse. The boom years from 1815 to 1818 exhibited a volatility that resulted in the

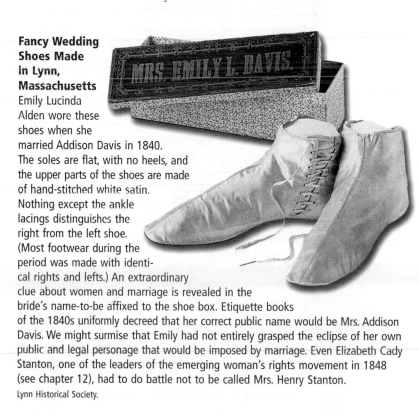

Fancy Wedding Shoes Made in Lynn, Massachusetts Emily Lucinda Alden wore these shoes when she married Addison Davis in 1840. The soles are flat, with no heels, and the upper parts of the shoes are made of hand-stitched white satin. Nothing except the ankle lacings distinguishes the right from the left shoe. (Most footwear during the period was made with identical rights and lefts.) An extraordinary clue about women and marriage is revealed in the bride's name-to-be affixed to the shoe box. Etiquette books of the 1840s uniformly decreed that her correct public name would be Mrs. Addison Davis. We might surmise that Emily had not entirely grasped the eclipse of her own public and legal personage that would be imposed by marriage. Even Elizabeth Cady Stanton, one of the leaders of the emerging woman's rights movement in 1848 (see chapter 12), had to do battle not to be called Mrs. Henry Stanton. Lynn Historical Society.

first sharp, large-scale economic downturn in U.S. history. Americans called this downturn a "panic," and the pattern was repeated in the 1830s. Rapidly rising consumer demand stimulated price increases, and speculative investment opportunities offering the possibility of high payoffs abounded—in bank stocks, western land sales, urban real estate, and commodities markets. High inflation made some people wealthy but created hardships for workers on fixed incomes.

When the bubble burst in 1819, the overnight rich suddenly became the overnight poor. Some blamed the panic of 1819 on the second Bank of the United States, which had failed to exercise control over the state banks. Many of those state banks had suspended specie payments—the exchange of gold or silver for banknotes—in their eagerness to expand the economic bubble. By mid-1818, when the Bank of the United States started to call in its loans and insisted that the state banks do likewise, the contracting of the money supply sent tremors throughout the economy. The crunch was made worse by a financial crisis in Europe in the spring of 1819. Overseas, prices for American cotton, tobacco, and wheat plummeted by more than 50 percent. Thus, when the Bank of the United States and the state banks called in their outstanding loans, American debtors involved in the commodities trade could not come up with the money. The number of business and personal bankruptcies skyrocketed. The intricate web of credit and debt relationships meant that almost everyone with even a toehold in the new commercial economy was affected by the panic. Thousands of Americans lost their savings and property, and unemployment estimates suggest that half a million people lost their jobs.

A farmer compared credit to "a man pissing in his breeches on a cold day to keep his arse warm—very comfortable at first but I dare say . . . you know how it feels afterwards."

Recovery took several years. Unemployment rates fell, but bitterness lingered, ready to be stirred up by politicians in the decades to come. The dangers of a system that was dependent on extensive credit were clear to many. In one folksy formulation that circulated around 1820, a farmer compared credit to "a man pissing in his breeches on a cold day to keep his arse warm— very comfortable at first but I dare say . . . you know how it feels afterwards."

By the mid-1820s, the economy was back on track, driven by increases in productivity, consumer demand for goods, and international trade, as well as a restless and calculating people moving goods, human labor, and investment capital in expanding circles of commerce. Despite the panic of 1819, credit financing continued to fuel the system. With the growth of manufacturing and transportation networks, buyers and sellers operated in a much larger arena, using credit transactions on paper instead of moving actual (and scarce) hard money around. A merchant in Ohio who bought goods in New York City on credit hoped to repay the loan with interest when he sold the merchandise—often on credit—for a profit. Slave owners might obtain loans to purchase additional land or slaves, using currently owned slaves as collateral. A network of credit and debt relations grew dense by the 1830s in a system that encouraged speculation and risk taking. A pervasive optimism about continued growth supported the elaborate system, but a single business failure could produce many innocent victims. Well after the panic of 1819, an undercurrent of anxiety about rapid economic change continued to shape the political views of many Americans.

REVIEW Why did the United States experience a market revolution after 1815?

The Spread of Democracy

Just as the market revolution held out the promise, if not the reality, of economic opportunity for all who worked, the political transformation of the 1830s held out the promise of political opportunity for hundreds of thousands of new voters. During Andrew Jackson's presidency (1829–1837), the second American party system took shape. Not until 1836, however, would the parties have distinct names and consistent programs transcending the particular personalities running for office. Over those years, more men could and did vote, responding to new methods of arousing voter interest. In 1828, Jackson's charismatic personality defined his party, and his victory over incumbent president John Quincy Adams turned on questions of character. Once in office, Jackson championed ordinary citizens against the power elite— **democracy** versus aristocracy in Jackson's terminology. A lasting contribution of the Jackson years was the notion that politicians needed to have the common touch in their dealings with voters.

Popular Politics and Partisan Identity

The election of 1828 was the first presidential contest in which the popular vote determined the outcome. In twenty-two out of twenty-four states, voters—not state legislatures—designated the number of electors committed to a particular candidate. More than a million voters participated in the election—three times the number in 1824 and nearly half the free male population, reflecting the high stakes that voters perceived in the Adams-Jackson rematch. Throughout the 1830s, voter turnout continued to rise and reached 70 percent in some localities, partly due to the disappearance of property qualifications in all but three states and partly due to heightened political interest.

The 1828 election inaugurated new campaign styles. State-level candidates routinely gave speeches at rallies, picnics, and banquets. Adams and Jackson still declined such appearances as undignified, but Henry Clay of Kentucky, campaigning for Adams, earned the nickname "the Barbecue Orator." Campaign rhetoric became more informal and even blunt. The Jackson camp established many Hickory Clubs, trading on Jackson's popular nickname, "Old Hickory," from a common Tennessee tree suggesting resilience and toughness. (Jackson was the first presidential candidate to have an affectionate and widely used nickname.)

Partisan newspapers in ever-larger numbers defined issues and publicized political personalities as never before. Improved printing technology and rising literacy rates fueled a great expansion of newspapers of all kinds (Table 11.1). Party leaders dispensed subsidies and other favors to secure the support of papers, even in remote towns and villages. In New York State, where party development was most advanced, a pro-Jackson group called the Bucktails controlled fifty weekly publications. Stories from the leading Jacksonian paper in Washington, D.C., were reprinted two days later in a Boston or Cincinnati paper, for example, as fast as the mail stage could carry them. Presidential campaigns were now coordinated in a national arena.

Politicians at first identified themselves as Jackson or Adams men, honoring the fiction of Republican Party unity. By 1832, however, the terminology had evolved to National Republicans, favoring federal action to promote commercial development, and Democratic Republicans, who promised to be responsive to the will of the majority. Between 1834 and 1836, National Republicans came to be called Whigs, while Jackson's party became simply the Democrats.

The Election of 1828 and the Character Issue

The campaign of 1828 was the first national election in which scandal and character questions reigned supreme. They became central issues because voters used them to comprehend the kind of public officer each man would make. Character issues conveyed in shorthand larger questions about morality, honor, and discipline. Jackson and Adams presented two radically different styles of manhood.

John Quincy Adams was vilified by his opponents as an elitist, a bookish academic, and perhaps even a monarchist. Critics pointed to his White House billiard table and ivory chess set as symbols of his aristocratic degeneracy. They also attacked his "corrupt bargain" of 1824—the alleged election deal between Adams and Henry Clay (see chapter 10). Adams's supporters returned fire with fire. They played on Jackson's fatherless childhood to portray him as the bastard son of a prostitute. Worse, the cloudy circumstances around his marriage to Rachel Donelson Robards in 1791 gave rise to the story that Jackson was a seducer and an adulterer, having married a woman whose divorce from her first husband was not entirely legal. Pro-Adams newspapers howled that Jackson was sinful and impulsive, while portraying Adams as pious, learned, and virtuous.

Editors in favor of Adams played up Jackson's violent temper, as evidenced by the many duels, brawls, and canings in which he had been involved. Jackson's supporters used the same stories to project Old Hickory as a tough frontier hero who knew how to command obedience. As for learning, Jackson's rough frontier education gave him a "natural sense," wrote a Boston editor,

> The campaign of 1828 was the first national election in which scandal and character questions reigned supreme.

TABLE 11.1	THE GROWTH OF NEWSPAPERS, 1820–1840			
	1820	*1830*	*1835*	*1840*
U.S. population (in millions)	9.6	12.8	15.0	17.1
Number of newspapers published	500	800	1,200	1,400
Daily newspapers	42	65	—	138

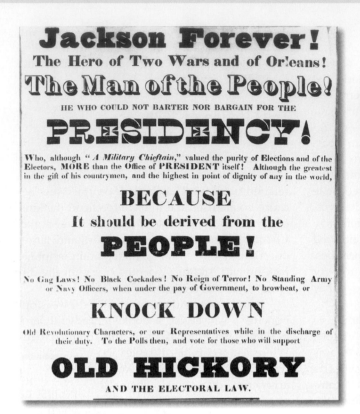

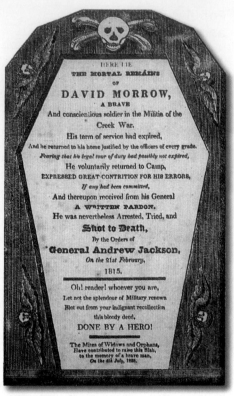

Campaign Posters from 1828

The poster on the left praises Andrew Jackson as a war hero and "man of the people" and reminds readers that Jackson, who won the largest popular vote in 1824, did not stoop to "bargain for the presidency," as John Quincy Adams presumably had in his dealings with Henry Clay (see chapter 10). What "two wars" does this poster refer to? The poster with the ominous tombstone and coffin graphics accuses Jackson of the unjustified killing of a Kentucky militiaman (one of six executed) during the Creek War in 1815. The text implores readers to think of the "hero" as a man capable of "this bloody deed."

Pro-Jackson broadside: © Collection of the New-York Historical Society; Anti-Jackson broadside: Smithsonian Institution, Washington, D.C.

that "can never be acquired by reading books— it can only be acquired, in perfection, by reading men."

Jackson won a sweeping victory, 56 percent of the popular vote and 178 electoral votes to Adams's 83 (Map 11.2). Old Hickory took most of the South and West and carried Pennsylvania and New York as well; Adams carried the remainder of the East. Jackson's vice president was John C. Calhoun, who had just served as vice president under Adams but had broken with Adams's policies.

After 1828, national politicians no longer deplored the existence of political parties. They were coming to see that parties mobilized and delivered voters, sharpened candidates' differences, and created party loyalty that surpassed loyalty to individual candidates and elections. Adams and Jackson clearly symbolized the competing ideas of the emerging parties: a moralis-

tic, top-down party (the Whigs) ready to make major decisions to promote economic growth competing against a contentious, energetic party (the Democrats) ready to embrace liberty-loving individualism.

Jackson's Democratic Agenda

Before the inauguration in March 1829, Rachel Jackson died. Certain that the ugly campaign had hastened his wife's death, the president went into deep mourning, his depression worsened by constant pain from the bullet still lodged in his chest from the 1806 duel and by mercury poisoning from the medicines he took. At sixty-two years old, Jackson carried only 140 pounds on his six-foot-one frame. His adversaries doubted that he would make it to a second term. His supporters, however, went wild at the inauguration. Thousands cheered his ten-minute inaugural address, the shortest in history. An open reception at the White House turned into a near riot as well-wishers jammed the premises, used windows as doors, stood on furniture for a better view of the great man, and broke thousands of dollars' worth of china and glasses.

During his presidency, Jackson continued to offer unprecedented hospitality to the public. Twenty spittoons newly installed in the East Room of the White House accommodated the tobacco chewers among the throngs that arrived daily to see the president. The courteous Jackson, committed to his image as president of the "common man," held audiences with unannounced visitors throughout his two terms.

Jackson's appointments marked a departure from past presidential policy. Earlier presidents had tried to lessen party conflict by including men of different factions in their cabinets, but Jackson would have only loyalists, a political tactic followed by most later presidents. For secretary of state, the key job, he tapped New Yorker Martin Van Buren, one of the shrewdest politicians of the day. Throughout the federal government, from postal clerks to ambassadors, Jackson removed competent civil servants and installed party loyalists. "To the victor belong the spoils," said a Democratic senator from New York, expressing his approval of patronage-driven appointments. Jackson's approach to civil service employment got tagged the **spoils system**; it was a concept the president strenuously defended.

Jackson's agenda quickly emerged. He favored a Jeffersonian limited federal government, fearing that intervention in the economy inevitably favored some groups at the expense of others. He therefore opposed federal support of transportation and grants of monopolies and charters that privileged wealthy investors. Like Jefferson, he anticipated the rapid settlement of the country's interior, where land sales would spread economic democracy to settlers. Thus, establishing a federal policy to remove the Indians from this area was a priority for Jackson. Unlike Jefferson, Jackson exercised his presidential veto power over Congress. In 1830, he vetoed a highway project in Maysville, Kentucky—Henry Clay's home state—that Congress had voted to support with federal dollars. The Maysville Road veto articulated Jackson's principled stand that citizens' federal tax dollars could be spent only on projects of a "general, not local" character. In all, Jackson used the veto twelve times; all previous presidents had exercised that right a total of nine times.

> **REVIEW** Why did Andrew Jackson defeat John Quincy Adams so dramatically in the 1828 election?

Jackson Defines the Democratic Party

In his two terms as president, Andrew Jackson worked to implement his vision of a politics of opportunity for all white men. To open land for white settlement, he favored the relocation of all eastern Indian tribes. He dramatically confronted John C. Calhoun and South Carolina when that state tried to nullify the tariff of 1828. Disapproving of all government-granted privilege, Jackson challenged what he called the "monster" Bank of the United States and took it down to defeat. In all this, he greatly enhanced the power of the presidency.

Indian Policy and the Trail of Tears

Probably nothing defined Jackson's presidency more than his efforts to solve what he saw as the Indian problem. Thousands of Indians lived in the South and the old Northwest, and not a few remained in New England and New York. Jackson, who rose to fame fighting the Creek and Seminole tribes in the 1810s, declared in

MAP 11.2   The Election of 1828

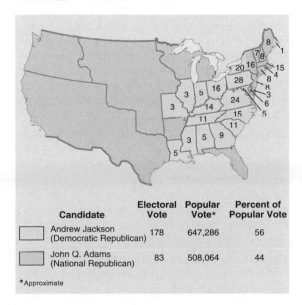

Candidate	Electoral Vote	Popular Vote*	Percent of Popular Vote
Andrew Jackson (Democratic Republican)	178	647,286	56
John Q. Adams (National Republican)	83	508,064	44

*Approximate

Peace Medal on an Indian Necklace

U.S. presidents continued the British and French practice of presenting peace medals to Indian leaders on ceremonial occasions, such as a treaty signing or a tribal delegation's visit to Washington, D.C. The silver medals carried the likeness of the current president and came in three sizes, dispensed according to the status of the recipient. Medals became valued badges of friendship and power. Indian leaders often wore them in portraits and were buried with them. When Andrew Jackson became president, he delayed authorizing a new medal. Removal, not friendship or appeasement, was his policy. Yet federal agents along the frontier desperately needed them, and finally in 1832, nearly three years into Jackson's first term, 242 medals were struck. Shown here is a Jackson medal incorporated into an Indian necklace crafted with beadwork, shells, and eagle claws.

National Museum of American History, Smithsonian Institution (158354), photo by Walter Lattimore.

1829, in his first message to Congress, that removing the Indians to territory west of the Mississippi was the only way to save them. White civilization destroyed Indian resources and thus doomed the Indians, he claimed: "That this fate surely awaits them if they remain within the limits of the states does not admit of a doubt. Humanity and national honor demand that every effort should be made to avert so great a calamity." Jackson never publicly wavered from this seemingly noble theme, returning to it in his next seven annual messages.

Prior administrations had experimented with different Indian policies. Starting in 1819, Congress granted $10,000 a year to various missionary associations eager to "civilize" native peoples by converting them to Christianity and encouraging English literacy and agricultural practices. Missionaries also promoted white gender customs, but Indian women were reluctant to embrace practices that accorded them less power than their tribal systems did. The federal government also had pursued aggressive treaty making with many tribes, dealing with the Indians as if they were foreign nations (see chapter 10, page 333).

Privately, Jackson thought it was "absurd" to treat the Indians as foreigners; he saw them as subjects of the United States. Jackson also did not

Andrew Jackson as "the Great Father"

In 1828, a new process of cheap commercial lithography found immediate application in a colorful presidential campaign aimed at capturing popular votes, and with it, a rich tradition of political cartoons was born. Jackson inspired at least five dozen satirical cartoons centering on caricatures of him. Strikingly, only one of them featured his Indian policy, controversial as it was, and only a single copy still exists. At some point, this cartoon was cropped at the bottom and top, and thus we do not have the cartoonist's caption or signature, both important for more fully understanding the artist's intent. Still, the sarcastic visual humor of Jackson cradling Indians packs an immediate punch.

William L. Clements Library.

Reading the image: Examine the body language conveyed in the various characters' poses. Are the Indians depicted as children or as powerless, miniature adults? What is going on in the picture on the wall?

Connections: Does the cartoon suggest that Jackson offers protection to Indians? What does the picture on the wall contribute to our understanding of the artist's opinion of Jackson's Indian removal policy?

For more help analyzing this image, see the visual activity for this chapter in the Online Study Guide at **bedfordstmartins.com/roark.**

approve of assimilation; that way lay extinction, he said. In his 1833 message to Congress, he wrote, "They have neither the intelligence, the industry, the moral habits, nor the desire of improvement which are essential. . . . Established in the midst of a superior race . . . they must necessarily yield to the force of circumstances and ere long disappear." Congress backed Jackson's goal and passed the Indian Removal Act of 1830, appropriating $500,000 to relocate eastern tribes west of the Mississippi. About 100 million acres of eastern land would be vacated for eventual white settlement under this act authorizing ethnic expulsion (Map 11.3, page 372).

Jackson's explanation that removal would save the Indians from extinction was in part formulated in response to the widespread controversy generated by the act. Newspapers, public lecturers, and local clubs debated Jackson's proposed policy, and in an unprecedented move, thousands of northern white women launched a petition drive to protest the expulsion law. The right to petition for redress of grievances, part of the Constitution's First Amendment, had long been used by individual women acting on personal cause, as when a widow requested a benefit based on a dead husband's military service. But mass petitioning by women was something new; it challenged the prevailing assumptions that women were not political actors and should let their husbands speak for them. Between 1830 and 1832, women's petitions rolled into Washington, arguing specifically that the Cherokee Indians of Georgia were a sovereign people, on the road to Christianity and with a right to stay on their land. The petitions had little effect on Jackson's policy.

For the northern tribes, their numbers diminished by years of war, gradual removal was already well under way. But not all the Indians went quietly. In 1832 in western Illinois, Black Hawk, a leader of the Sauk and Fox Indians who had fought in alliance with Tecumseh in the War of 1812 (see chapter 10, page 335), resisted removal. Volunteer militias attacked and chased the Indians into southern Wisconsin, where, after several skirmishes and a deadly battle (later called the Black Hawk War), Black Hawk was captured and about four hundred of his people were massacred.

The southern tribes proved even more resistant to removal. The powerful Creek, Chickasaw, Choctaw, and Cherokee tribes refused to relocate. A second Seminole War broke out in Florida as the Indians there—a mixture of Seminoles and escaped black slaves who had intermarried with the tribe—took up arms against relocation in 1836–1837.

The Cherokee tribe of Georgia responded with a unique legal challenge to being treated as subjects. More than any other southern tribe, the seventeen thousand Cherokees had incorporated white political and economic practices into their tribal life. Spurred by dedicated missionaries, they had adopted written laws, including, in 1827, a constitution modeled on the U.S. Constitution. Two hundred of the wealthiest Cherokees had intermarried with whites and had adopted white styles of housing, dress, and cotton agriculture, including the ownership of a thousand slaves. They had developed a written alphabet and published a newspaper and Christian prayer books in their language. These features helped make their cause attractive to the northern white women who petitioned the government on their behalf.

In 1831, after Georgia announced that it would subject the Indians to state law and seize their property, the Cherokee tribe appealed to the U.S. Supreme Court to restrain Georgia. Chief Justice John Marshall found for Georgia on the grounds that the tribe did not have standing to sue. When Georgia jailed two missionaries under an 1830 state law forbidding missionary aid to Indians without permission, the tribe brought suit again, naming one of the missionaries as plaintiff. In the 1832 case *Worcester v. Georgia*, the Supreme Court upheld the territorial sovereignty of the Cherokee people, recognizing their existence as "a distinct community, occupying its own territory, in which the laws of Georgia can have no force." Ignoring the Court's decision, an angry President Jackson pressed the Cherokee tribe to move west: "If they now refuse to accept the liberal terms offered, they can only be liable for whatever evils and difficulties may arise. I feel conscious of having done my duty to my red children."

The Cherokee tribe remained in Georgia for two more years without significant violence. Then, in 1835, a small, unauthorized faction of the tribe signed a treaty selling all the tribal lands to the state, which rapidly resold the land to whites. Chief John Ross, backed by several thousand Cherokees, petitioned the U.S. Congress to ignore the bogus treaty. "By the stipulations of this instrument," he wrote, "we are stripped of every attribute of freedom and eligibility for legal self-defense. Our property may be plundered before our eyes; violence may be committed on our persons; even our lives may be taken away. . . . We are denationalized; we are **disfranchised**."

Most of the Cherokees refused to move, so in May 1838, the deadline for voluntary evacuation, federal troops sent by Jackson's successor, Martin Van Buren, arrived to remove them. Under armed guard, the Cherokees embarked on a 1,200-mile journey west that came to be called the Trail of Tears. A newspaperman in Kentucky described the forced march: "Even aged females, apparently, nearly ready to drop into the grave, were traveling with heavy burdens attached to the back. . . . They buried fourteen to fifteen at every stopping place." Nearly a quarter of the Cherokees died en route. The survivors joined the fifteen thousand Creek, twelve thousand Choctaw, five thousand Chickasaw, and several thousand Seminole Indians also forcibly relocated to Indian Territory (which became the state of Oklahoma in 1907).

In his farewell address to the nation in 1837, Jackson professed his belief in the benefit of Indian removal: "This unhappy race . . . are now placed in a situation where we may well hope that they will share in the blessings of civilization and be saved from the degradation and destruction to which they were rapidly hastening while they remained in the states." Perhaps Jackson genuinely believed that exile to the West was necessary to save these Indian cultures from destruction. But for the forcibly removed tribes, the costs of relocation were high.

MAP 11.3   Indian Removal and the Trail of Tears

The federal government under President Andrew Jackson pursued a vigorous policy of Indian removal in the 1830s. Tribes were forcibly moved west to land known as Indian Territory (present-day Oklahoma). As many as a quarter of the Cherokee Indians died on the route known as the Trail of Tears in 1838.

READING THE MAP: From which states were most of the Native Americans removed? Through which states did the Trail of Tears go?

CONNECTIONS: Before Jackson's presidency, how did the federal government view Native Americans, and what policy initiatives were undertaken by the government and private groups? How did Jackson change the government's policy toward Native Americans?

FOR MORE HELP ANALYZING THIS MAP, see the map activity for this chapter in the Online Study Guide at bedfordstmartins.com/roark.

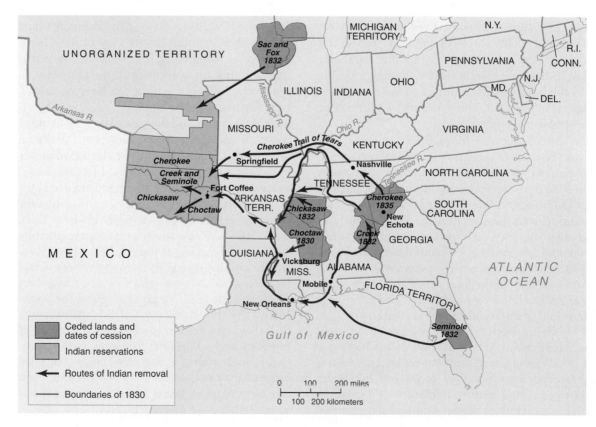

The Tariff of Abominations and Nullification

Jackson's Indian policy happened to harmonize with the principle of **states' rights**: The president supported Georgia's right to ignore the Supreme Court's decision in *Worcester v. Georgia*. But in another pressing question of states' rights, Jackson contested South Carolina's attempt to ignore federal tariff policy.

Federal tariffs as high as 33 percent on imports such as textiles and iron goods had been passed in 1816 and again in 1824, in an effort to favor new American manufacturers and shelter them from foreign competition, as well as to raise federal revenue. Some southern congressmen opposed the steep tariffs, fearing they would decrease overseas shipping and hurt cotton exports. During John Quincy Adams's administration (1825–1829), tariff policy generated heated debate. In 1828, Congress passed a revised tariff that came to be known as the Tariff of Abominations. A bundle of conflicting duties—some as high as 50 percent—the legislation contained provisions that pleased and angered every economic and sectional interest. Drafted mostly by southern congressmen, who loaded it with duties on raw materials needed by New England manufacturers, it also contained protectionist elements favored by those same manufacturers.

South Carolina in particular suffered from the Tariff of Abominations. Worldwide prices for cotton had declined in the late 1820s, and the fall-off in shipping caused by the high tariffs further hurt the South. In 1828, a group of South Carolina politicians headed by John C. Calhoun advanced a doctrine called **nullification**. The Union, they argued, was a confederation of states that had yielded some but not all power to the federal government. When Congress overstepped its powers, states had the right to nullify Congress's acts. As precedents, they pointed to the Virginia and Kentucky Resolutions of 1798, which had attempted to invalidate the Alien and Sedition Acts (see chapter 9). Congress had erred in using tariff policy as an instrument to benefit specific industries, the South Carolinians claimed; tariffs should be used only to raise revenue.

On assuming the presidency in 1829, Jackson ignored the South Carolina statement of nullification and shut out Calhoun, his new vice president, from influence or power. Tariff revisions in early 1832 brought little relief to the South. Sensing futility, Calhoun resigned the vice presidency in 1832 and accepted election by the South Carolina legislature to a seat in the U.S. Senate, where he could better argue his state's antitariff stance. Strained to their limit, the South Carolina leaders took the radical step of declaring the federal tariffs null and void in their state as of February 1, 1833. Finally, the constitutional crisis was out in the open.

Opting for a dramatic confrontation, Jackson sent armed ships to Charleston harbor and threatened to invade the state. He pushed through Congress a bill, called the Force Bill, defining the Carolina stance as treason and authorizing military action to collect federal tariffs. At the same time, Congress moved quickly to pass a revised tariff that was more acceptable to the South. The conciliating Senator Henry Clay rallied support for a moderate bill that gradually reduced tariffs down to the 1816 level. On March 1, 1833, Congress passed both the new tariff and the Force Bill. South Carolina responded by withdrawing its nullification of the old tariff—and then nullifying the Force Bill. It was a symbolic gesture, since Jackson's show of muscle was no longer necessary. Both sides were satisfied with the immediate outcome. Federal power had prevailed over a dangerous assertion of states' rights, and South Carolina got the lower tariff it wanted.

> The implied threat behind nullification was secession, a position articulated in 1832 by some South Carolinians whose concerns went beyond tariff policy.

Yet the question of federal power versus states' rights was far from settled. The implied threat behind nullification was secession, a position articulated in 1832 by some South Carolinians whose concerns went beyond tariff policy. In the 1830s, the political moratorium on discussions of slavery agreed on at the time of the Missouri Compromise (see chapter 10) was coming unglued, and new northern voices opposed to slavery gained increasing attention. If and when a northern-dominated federal government decided to end slavery, the South Carolinians thought, the South might want to nullify such laws, or even remove itself from the Union.

The Bank War and Economic Boom

Along with the tariff and nullification, President Jackson fought another political battle, over the Bank of the United States. After riding out the panic of 1819, the bank finally prospered. It handled the federal government's deposits, extended credit and loans, and issued banknotes—

by 1830, the most stable currency in the country. Now having twenty-nine branches, it benefited the whole nation. Jackson, however, did not find the bank's functions sufficiently valuable to offset his criticism of the concept of a national bank. In his first two annual messages to Congress, in 1829 and 1830, he claimed that the bank concentrated undue economic power in the hands of a few.

National Republican (Whig) senators Daniel Webster and Henry Clay decided to force the issue. They convinced the bank to apply for charter renewal in 1832, well before the fall election, even though the existing charter ran until 1836. They fully expected that Congress's renewal would force Jackson to follow through on his rhetoric with a veto, that the unpopular veto would cause Jackson to lose the election, and

that the bank would survive on an override vote by a new Congress swept into power on the anti-Jackson tide.

At first, the plan seemed to work. The bank applied for rechartering, Congress voted to renew, and Jackson, angry over being manipulated, issued his veto. But it was a brilliantly written veto, full of fierce language about the privileges of the moneyed elite who oppress the democratic masses in order to enrich themselves. "Many of our rich men have not been content with equal protection and equal benefits, but have besought us to make them richer by act of Congress," Jackson wrote.

Clay and his supporters found Jackson's economic ideas so absurd and his language of class antagonism so shocking that they distrib-

Fistfight between Old Hickory and Bully Nick
This 1834 cartoon represents President Andrew Jackson squaring off against Nicholas Biddle, the director of the Bank of the United States. Pugilism as a semiprofessional sport gained great popularity in the 1830s. The joke here is that the aged Jackson and the aristocratic Biddle would strip to revealing tight pants and engage in open combat. To Biddle's left are his seconds, Daniel Webster and Henry Clay. Behind the president is his vice president, Martin Van Buren. Whiskey and port wine lubricate the action.
The Library Company of Philadelphia.

uted thousands of copies of the bank veto as campaign material for their own party. A confident Henry Clay headed his party's ticket for the presidency. But the plan backfired. Jackson's translation of the bank controversy into a language of class antagonism and egalitarian ideals resonated with many Americans. Old Hickory won the election easily, gaining 55 percent of the popular vote and 219 electoral votes to Clay's 49. Jackson's party still controlled Congress, so no override was possible. The second Bank of the United States would cease to exist after 1836.

Jackson, however, wanted to destroy the bank sooner. Calling it a "monster," he ordered the sizable federal deposits to be removed from its vaults and redeposited into Democratic-inclined state banks. In retaliation, the Bank of the United States raised interest rates and called in loans. This action caused a brief decline in the economy in 1833 and actually enhanced Jackson's claim that the bank was too powerful for the good of the country.

Unleashed and unregulated, the economy went into high gear in 1834. Just at this moment, an excess of silver from Mexican mines made its way into American banks, giving bankers license to print ever more banknotes. From 1834 to 1837, inflation soared; prices of basic goods rose more than 50 percent. States quickly chartered hundreds of new private banks. Each bank issued its own banknotes and set interest rates as high as the market would bear. Entrepreneurs borrowed and invested money, much of it funneled into privately financed railroads and canals. With money cheap, the webs of credit and debt relationships that were the hallmark of the American economy grew denser yet.

The market in western land sales heated up. In 1834, about 4.5 million acres of the public domain had been sold, the highest annual volume since 1818. By 1836, the total reached an astonishing 20 million acres (Figure 11.1). Some of this was southern land in Mississippi and Louisiana, which slave owners rushed to bring under cultivation, but much more was in the North, where land offices were deluged with buyers. The Jackson administration worried that the purchasers were overwhelmingly eastern capitalists, land speculators instead of self-reliant **yeoman** farmers who intended to settle on the land.

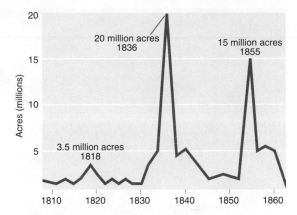

FIGURE 11.1 **Western Land Sales, 1810–1860**
Land sales peaked in the 1810s, 1830s, and 1850s as Americans rushed to speculate in western land sold by the federal government. The surges in 1818 and 1836 demonstrate the volatile, speculative economy that suddenly collapsed in the panics of 1819 and 1837.

In one respect, the economy attained an admirable goal: The national debt disappeared, and, for the first and only time in American history, from 1835 to 1837 the government had a monetary surplus. But much of that surplus consisted of questionable bank currencies—"bloated, diseased" currencies, in Jackson's vivid terminology. While the boom was on, however, few stopped to worry about the consequences if and when the bubble burst.

REVIEW Why did Jackson promote Indian removal?

Cultural Shifts, Religion, and Reform

The growing economy, moving steadily upward in the 1820s and then booming in the mid-1830s, transformed far more than just productive activity. For increasing numbers of families, especially in the commercialized Northeast, standards of living rose, consumption patterns changed, and the nature and location of work altered. All of these changes had a direct impact on the duties of men and women and on the training of youths for the economy of the future.

Along with economic change came an unprecedented revival of evangelical religion known as the **Second Great Awakening**. Just as

The Talcott Family at Home, 1832
Folk art depicting family life became popular and affordable in the early Republic. Samuel Talcott, twenty-eight, a farmer in Madison County, New York, poses with his wife, Betsey, twenty; his recently widowed mother, Mary, seventy; and daughters Clarissa, three, and Emily, three months. (Three more children were born over the next ten years.) The couple wear quite fashionable clothes: Betsey's enormous sleeves are a hallmark of the 1830s, as is Samuel's "cutaway" waistcoat with its stiff, high collar. A broad black cravat molds his white shirt collar into two sharp points. The artist, Deborah Goldsmith, grew up in a neighboring village. She painted other local families, including the Throops, whose son she soon married. She died suddenly in 1836, a few months after the birth of her second child, cutting short her artistic career.
Abby Aldrich Rockefeller Folk Art Center, Williamsburg, VA.

universal male **suffrage** allowed all white men to vote, democratized religion offered salvation to all who chose to embrace it. Among the most serious adherents of evangelical **Protestantism** were men and women of the new merchant classes, whose self-discipline in pursuing market ambitions meshed well with the message of self-discipline in pursuit of spiritual perfection. Not content with individual perfection, many of these people sought to perfect society as well, by defining excessive alcohol consumption, non-marital sex, and slavery as three major evils of modern life in need of correction.

The Family and Separate Spheres

The centerpiece of new ideas about gender relations was the notion that husbands found their status and authority in the new world of work, leaving wives to tend the hearth and home. Sermons, advice books, periodicals, and novels reinforced the idea that men and women inhabited **separate spheres** and had separate duties. "To woman it belongs . . . to elevate the intellectual character of her household [and] to kindle the fires of mental activity in childhood," wrote Mrs. A. J. Graves in a popular book titled *Advice to American Women*. For men, in contrast, "the absorbing passion for gain, and the pressing demands of business, engross their whole attention." In particular, the home, now the exclusive domain of women, was sentimentalized as the source of intimacy, love, and safety, a refuge from the cruel and competitive world of market relations.

Some new aspects of society gave substance to this formulation of separate spheres. Men's work was undergoing profound change after

GLOBAL COMPARISON

Changing Trends in Age at First Marriage for Women

	Nineteenth Century		Twentieth Century		
	1800	*1850*	*1900*	*1960*	*2000*
United States	21	23	23	20	25
England	20	24	24	22	28
Netherlands	—	28	26	25	28
Russia	—	19	—	25	22

Note: Dates are approximate. Dashes indicate a lack of reliable information.

Average age at first marriage is a remarkably complex indicator of social, economic, and cultural factors in all societies. It is also a number that is dauntingly hard to determine for historical populations, because marriage registration before the twentieth century rarely included age data. Historical demographers have developed techniques to link brides' birth and marriage records in small community studies. For larger populations, sophisticated quantitative methods can generate data on mean age at marriage based on reported age and marital status in a census. In general, conditions favoring a low age at marriage for women are those that provide young couples with early financial support: abundant affordable farmland, coresidence with parents, or steady employment for men at a wage that can support a family. Factors that postpone marriage include a lack of farmland, deterioration in male employment prospects, a changed economy requiring more years of prejob education and training, or enhanced employment for women that makes the job market more attractive than the marriage market. The low mean ages in this table reflect abundant farmland (1800, United States), factory wage labor (1800, England), and serfdom (1850, Russia). In Europe and the United States, age at marriage for women rose steeply in the nineteenth century. The northeastern United States led the way in the 1820s and 1830s. Can you suggest reasons why? One immediate consequence of later marriage was a decline in completed family size, since brides shaved two years off their exposure to the risk of pregnancy. Finally, demographers note that in some cases, rising age at first marriage is accompanied by rising rates of nonmarriage, sometimes as high as 20 percent. How might these two trends be connected?

1815 and increasingly brought cash to the household, especially in the manufacturing and urban Northeast. Farmers and tradesmen sold products in a market, and bankers, bookkeepers, shoemakers, and canal diggers got pay envelopes. Furthermore, many men performed jobs outside the home, at an office or store. For men who were not farmers, work indeed seemed newly disconnected from life at home.

A woman's domestic role was more complicated than the cultural prescriptions indicated. (See "Global Comparison.") Although the vast majority of married white women did not hold paying jobs, the home continued to be a site of time-consuming labor. But the advice books treated household tasks as loving familial duties; housework as *work* was thereby rendered invisible in an economy that evaluated work by how much cash it generated. In reality, wives contributed directly to family income in many ways. Some took in boarders; others engaged in outwork, earning pay for shoebinding, hatmaking, or needlework done at home. Wives in the poorer classes of society, including most free black wives, did not have the luxury of husbands earning adequate wages; for them, work as servants or laundresses helped augment family income.

Idealized notions about the feminine home and the masculine workplace gained acceptance in the 1830s (and well beyond) because of the

Women Graduates of Oberlin College, Class of 1855
Oberlin College, founded in Ohio by evangelical and abolitionist activists in the 1830s, admitted men and women, both white and black. In the early years, the black students were all male, and the women students were all white. Instruction was not coeducational; the women attended classes in the separate Ladies' Department. By 1855, as this daguerreotype shows, black women had integrated the Ladies' Department. The two older women wearing bonnets are the principal and a member of the board. Each student is dressed in the latest fashion: a dark taffeta dress with sloping shoulders, a tight bodice, and a detachable white lace collar. Hairstyles were similarly uniform for women of all ages throughout the 1850s: hair parted down the middle, dressed with oil, and lustrously coiled over the ears. Compare these women with the mill worker pictured on page 364. What differences do you see?
Oberlin College Archives, Oberlin, Ohio.

cultural dominance of the middle and upper classes of the Northeast, expressed through books and periodicals that reflected these gender ideals. Men seeking manhood through work and pay would embrace competition and acquisitiveness, while women established femininity through dutiful service to home and family. This particular formulation of gender difference helped smooth the path for the first generation of Americans experiencing the market revolution, and both men and women of the middle classes benefited. Men were set free to pursue wealth, and women gained moral authority within the home. Beyond white families of the middle and upper classes, however, these new gender ideals had limited applicability. Despite their apparent dominance in printed material of the period, they were never all-pervasive.

The Education and Training of Youths

The market economy, with its new expectations for men and women, required expanded opportunities for training youths of both sexes. By the 1830s, in both the North and South, state-supported public school systems were the norm, designed to produce pupils able, by age twelve or fourteen, to read, write, and participate in marketplace calculations. Girls usually received the same basic education as boys. Literacy rates for white females climbed dramatically, rivaling the rates for white males for the first time. The fact that taxpayers paid for children's education created an incentive to seek an inexpensive teaching force. By the 1830s, school districts began replacing male teachers with young females, for, as a Massachusetts state report on education put it, "females can be educated cheaper, quicker, and better, and will teach cheaper after they are qualified." Like mill workers, female teachers were in their late teens and regarded the work as temporary. Many were trained in private female academies, now numbering in the hundreds (see chapter 10).

Advanced education continued to expand in the 1830s, with an additional two dozen colleges for men and several more female seminaries offering education on a par with the male colleges. Mount Holyoke Seminary in western Massachusetts, founded by educator Mary Lyon in 1837, developed a rigorous scientific curriculum drawing on resources from the science program at nearby Amherst College. And Oberlin College in Ohio, founded by Presbyterians in 1835, became the first coeducational college when it opened its doors to women in 1837. Oberlin's goal was to train young men for the ministry and to prepare young women to be minister's wives.

Still, only a very small percentage of young people attended institutions of higher learning. The vast majority of male youths left public school at age fourteen to apprentice in specific trades or to embark on business careers by seeking entry-level clerkships, abundant in the growing urban centers. Young girls also headed for mill towns or for cities in unprecedented numbers, seeking work in the expanding service sector as seamstresses and domestic servants. Changes in patterns of youth employment meant that large numbers of youngsters escaped the watchful eyes of their parents. Moralists fretted about the dangers of unsupervised youths, and following the lead of the Lowell mill owners, some established apprentices' libraries and uplifting lecture series to keep young people honorably occupied. Advice books published by the hundreds instructed youths in the virtues of hard work and delayed gratification.

The Second Great Awakening

A newly invigorated version of Protestantism gained momentum in the 1820s and 1830s as the economy reshaped gender and age relations. The earliest manifestations of this fervent piety appeared in 1801 in Kentucky, when a crowd of ten thousand people camped out on a hillside at Cane Ridge for a revival meeting that lasted several weeks. By the 1810s and 1820s, "camp meetings" had spread to the Atlantic seaboard states, finding especially enthusiastic audiences in western New York and Pennsylvania. The outdoor settings permitted huge attendance, which itself intensified the emotional impact of the experience. "For more than a half mile, I could see people on their knees before God in humble prayer," recalled one Cane Ridge worshipper.

The gatherings attracted women and men hungry for a more immediate access to spiritual peace, one not requiring years of soul-searching. One eyewitness at a revival reported that "some of the people were singing, others praying, some crying for mercy. . . . At one time I saw at least five hundred swept down in a moment as if a battery of a thousand guns had been opened upon them, and then immediately followed shrieks and shouts that rent the very heavens."

From 1800 to 1820, church membership doubled in the United States, much of it among the evangelical groups. Methodists, Baptists, and Presbyterians formed the core of the new movement; Episcopalians, Congregationalists, Unitarians, Dutch Reformed, Lutherans, and Catholics maintained strong skepticism about the emotional enthusiasm. Women more than men were attracted to the evangelical movement, and wives and mothers typically recruited husbands and sons to join them.

The leading exemplar of the Second Great Awakening was a lawyer turned minister named Charles Grandison Finney. Finney lived in western New York, where the completion of the Erie Canal in 1825 fundamentally altered the social and economic landscape overnight. Towns swelled with new inhabitants who brought in remarkable prosperity along with other, less admirable side effects, such as prostitution, drinking, and gaming. Finney saw New York canal towns as especially ripe for evangelical awakening. In Rochester, New York, he sustained a six-month revival through the winter of 1830–31, generating thousands of converts.

> One eyewitness at a revival reported that "at one time I saw at least five hundred swept down in a moment as if a battery of a thousand guns had been opened upon them, and then immediately followed shrieks and shouts that rent the very heavens."

Finney's message was directed primarily at women and men of the business classes. He argued that a reign of Christian perfection loomed, one that required public-spirited outreach to the less-than-perfect to foster their salvation. Evangelicals promoted Sunday schools to bring piety to children; they battled to end mail delivery, stop public transport, and close shops on Sundays to honor the Sabbath. Many women formed missionary societies, which distributed

Charles G. Finney and His Broadway Tabernacle

The Reverend Charles Grandison Finney (shown here in a portrait done in 1834) took his evangelical move-ment to New York City in the early 1830s, operating first out of a renovated theater. In 1836, the Broadway Tabernacle was built for his pastorate. In its use of space, the tabernacle resembled a theater more than a traditional church, but it departed radically from one very theaterlike tradition of churches—the custom of charging pew rents. In effect, most churches required worshippers to purchase their seats. Finney insisted that all the seats in his house were free, unreserved, and open to anyone.

Oberlin College Archives, Oberlin, Ohio.

READING THE IMAGE: How does the engraving of Finney's sermon at the Broadway Tabernacle reflect his preaching style?

CONNECTIONS: How did Finney's preaching style differ from that of ministers in more established sects?

FOR MORE HELP ANALYZING THIS IMAGE, see the visual activity for this chapter in the Online Study Guide at bedfordstmartins.com/roark.

---

millions of Bibles and religious tracts. Through such avenues, evangelical religion offered women expanded spheres of influence. Finney adopted the tactics of Jacksonian-era politi-cians—publicity, argumentation, rallies, and speeches—to sell his cause. His object, he said, was to get Americans to "vote in the Lord Jesus Christ as the governor of the Universe."

The Temperance Movement and the Campaign for Moral Reform

The evangelical disposition—a combination of faith, energy, self-discipline, and righteousness—animated vigorous campaigns to eliminate al-cohol abuse and eradicate sexual sin. Millions of Americans took the temperance pledge to abstain from strong drink, and thousands be-came involved in efforts to end prostitution.

Alcohol consumption had risen steadily in the decades up to 1830, when the average person over age thirteen annually consumed an aston-ishing nine gallons of hard liquor plus thirty gallons of hard cider, beer, and wine. All classes imbibed. A lively saloon culture fostered mascu-line camaraderie along with extensive alcohol con-sumption among laborers, while in elite homes, the after-dinner whiskey or sherry was common-place. Colleges before 1820 routinely served stu-dents a pint of ale with meals, and the army and navy included rum in the standard daily ration.

Organized opposition to drinking first sur-faced in the 1810s among health and religious re-formers. In 1826, Lyman Beecher, a Connecticut minister of an "awakened" church, founded the American Temperance Society, which warned that drinking led to poverty, idleness, crime, and family violence. Adopting the methods of evangelical ministers, temperance lecturers traveled the country expounding the damage of drink. By 1833, some six thousand local affiliates of the American Temperance Society boasted more than a million members. Middle-class drinking began a steep decline. One powerful tool of persuasion was the temperance pledge, which many manufacturers and business owners began to require of employees.

In 1836, leaders of the **temperance movement** regrouped into a new society, the American Temperance Union, which demanded total abstinence of its adherents. The intensified war against alcohol moved beyond individual moral suasion into the realm of politics, as reformers sought to deny taverns liquor licenses. By 1845, temperance advocates had put an impressive dent in alcohol consumption, which diminished to one-quarter of the per capita consumption of 1830. In 1851, Maine became the first state to ban entirely the manufacture and sale of all alcoholic beverages.

More controversial than temperance was a social movement called "moral reform," which first aimed at public morals in general but quickly narrowed to a campaign to eradicate sexual sin, especially prostitution. In 1833, a group of Finneyite women started the New York Female Moral Reform Society. Its members insisted that uncontrolled male sexual expression posed a serious threat to society in general and to women in particular. The society's nationally distributed newspaper, the *Advocate of Moral Reform*, was the first major paper in the country that was written, edited, and typeset by women. In it, they condemned men who visited brothels or seduced innocent women. Within five years, more than four thousand auxiliary groups of women had sprung up, mostly in New England, New York, Pennsylvania, and Ohio.

In its analysis of the causes of licentiousness and its conviction that women had a duty to speak out about unspeakable things, the Moral Reform Society pushed the limits of what even the men in the evangelical movement could tolerate. Yet these women did not regard themselves as radicals. They were simply pursuing the logic of a gender system that defined home protection and morality as women's special sphere and a religious conviction that called for the eradication of sin.

Organizing against Slavery

More radical still was the movement in the 1830s to abolish the sin of slavery. The abolitionist movement had its roots in Great Britain in the late 1700s. (See "Beyond America's Borders," page 382.) Previously, the American Colonization Society, founded in 1817 by some Maryland and Virginia **planters**, aimed to promote gradual individual **emancipation** of slaves followed by **colonization** in Africa. By the early 1820s, several thousand ex-slaves had been transported to Liberia on the West African coast. (See chapter 12, "Beyond America's Borders," page 428.) But not surprisingly, newly freed men and women were often not eager to emigrate; their African roots were three or more generations in the past. Colonization was too gradual (and expensive) to have much impact on American slavery.

Around 1830, northern challenges to slavery surfaced with increasing frequency and resolve, beginning in free black communities. In 1829, a Boston printer named David Walker published *An Appeal . . . to the Coloured Citizens of the World*, which condemned racism, invoked the egalitarian language of the Declaration of Independence, and hinted at racial violence if whites did not change their prejudiced ways. In 1830, at the inaugural National Negro Convention meeting in Philadelphia, forty blacks from nine states discussed the racism of American society

A Cold Water Army Fan
This fan was a keepsake for children enlisted in the Reverend Thomas Hunt's Cold Water Army of 1836, which advocated abstinence from alcohol. Hunt, a Presbyterian, figured that preventing children from starting to drink would be an effective strategy against future alcoholism. "Prevention is better than cure" was his motto.
Museum of American Political Life.

Transatlantic Abolition

Abolitionism blossomed in the United States in the 1830s, but its roots stretched back to the 1780s in both Britain and America. Developments on both sides of the Atlantic reinforced each other, leading to a transatlantic antislavery movement with shared ideas, strategies, activists, songs, and, eventually, victories.

An important source of antislavery sentiment derived from the Quaker religion, with its deep convictions regarding human equality. But moral sentiment alone does not make a political movement; something needs to galvanize it. English Quakers, customarily an apolitical group, awoke to sudden antislavery zeal in 1783, triggered in part by the loss of the imperial war for America and the debate it spurred about citizenship and slavery. The end of the war also brought a delegation of Philadelphia Quakers to meet with the London group, and an immediate result was the first petition, signed by 273 Quaker men in 1783, requesting that Parliament abolish the slave trade.

The English Quakers, now joined by a scattering of evangelical Anglicans and Methodists, formed the Society for Effecting the Abolition of the Slave Trade in 1787 and in just five years became a force to be reckoned with. They amassed thousands of signatures on petitions to Parliament. They organized a boycott of slave-produced sugar from the British West Indies—a boycott said to have involved 300,000 Britons. (Women, the traditional cooks of English families, were essential to the effort.) In 1789, the society scored a publicity coup by publishing two chilling illustrations of slave ships stacked with human cargo. These images, reprinted by the thousands, created a sensation. The society's Reverend Thomas Clarkson distributed them in Paris and in northern U.S. cities along with a book he wrote detailing the shipboard tortures inflicted on slaves by the use of shackles, handcuffs, whips, and branding irons. The society mobilized the resulting groundswell of antislavery sentiment to pressure Parliament once again. A sympathetic member of that body, the Methodist William Wilberforce, brought the anti–slave trade issue to a debate and vote in 1791; it lost.

Meanwhile, Pennsylvania Quakers in 1784 launched their own Society for Promoting the Abolition of Slavery, which non-Quakers Benjamin Franklin and Thomas Paine joined. It worked to end slavery in that state and petitioned the confederation congress—unsuccessfully—to put an end to American participation in the international slave trade. A French group, the Société des Amis des Noirs (Society of the Friends of Blacks), sprang up in Paris in 1788. All three groups, in close communication, agreed that ending the slave trade was the critical first step in abolishing slavery.

In lockstep with the British campaign, American Quakers petitioned the U.S. Congress in 1790 to end the slave trade immediately. Congress

International Abolitionists

George Thompson (middle), a leading figure in the British antislavery campaign, brought his lecture tour to the United States in 1834 and 1835. Although he had some success in converting audiences to abolition, some newspapers called him the "imported incendiary" and claimed that he had proposed that all slave owners' throats be cut, a charge he denied. William Lloyd Garrison (left) promoted Thompson's speaking tour in his antislavery newspaper, the *Liberator*. Wendell Phillips (right), a young Boston lawyer, heard Thompson speak and was inspired to make abolition his lifework. All three attended the World Antislavery Convention in 1840. They met again in 1850 when Thompson returned to the United States, providing the occasion for this historic picture.

Historical Library of Swarthmore College.

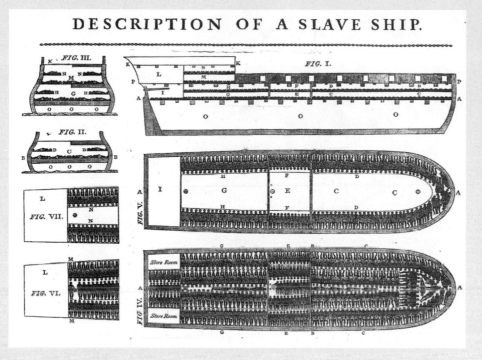

DESCRIPTION OF A SLAVE SHIP.

Description of a Slave Ship

This powerful and often-reprinted image combines a precise technical rendering of a British ship (normally evoking pride in Britons) with the horrors of a crowded mass of dark human flesh.
Peabody Essex Museum, Salem, MA.

tabled the petition, pointing to the U.S. Constitution's clause that prohibited federal regulation of the trade before 1808. In response, a bolder appeal came the next day, calling for an end not only to the slave trade but to slavery itself. The petitioners suggested that the constitutional power to make laws "necessary and proper" to ensure the "general welfare" of the country could include "Liberty for all Negroes" as crucial to the country's general welfare. Congress debated slavery for the first time, and by a close vote (29 to 25) rejected the petition. It also set an important precedent by resolving that slavery was under the sole control of the states where it existed.

Over the next three decades, the antislavery cause in Britain and America moved forward in piecemeal fashion. In 1807, Parliament finally made it illegal for British ships to transport Africans into slavery. A year later, in 1808, the United States also banned the slave trade. The rapid natural increase of the African American population made passage of this law relatively easy. Older slave states along the coast supported the ban because it actually increased the value of their native-born slaves sold and transported west in the domestic slave trade.

British antislavery forces took a new tack in the 1820s, when women became active and pushed beyond the ban on trade. Quaker widow Elizabeth Heyrick authored *Immediate Not Gradual Abolition* in 1824, prompting the formation of scores of all-women societies. American women abolitionists soon followed suit.

Abolitionists again bombarded Parliament with a massive petition campaign, and of the 1.3 million signatures submitted in 1833, 30 percent were women's. That year, Parliament finally passed the Abolition of Slavery Act, which freed all slave children under age six and gradually phased out slavery for everyone older during a four-year apprenticeship. The act also provided financial compensation for owners (£20 million), a key proviso made possible by the relatively small number of slave owners in the British slaveholding colonies.

The success of the British movement generated even greater transatlantic communication. In 1840, British and American abolitionists came together in full force at the World Antislavery Convention in London. Among the 409 delegates to the convention were Rev. Clarkson, who presided; William Lloyd Garrison of Boston; and Philadelphia Quaker Lucretia Mott, a lifelong antislavery activist. Most of the delegates were from Britain and the West Indies, although 53 Americans and a half dozen French delegates also attended. Only about a quarter of the attendees were Quakers. Ten days of meetings produced speeches and reports on the worldwide practice of slavery, along with debates over various economic and religious strategies to end it. A key plan was to publicize throughout America the British movement's success in achieving emancipation. The delegates closed their meeting fully energized by their international congress, called to propose international solutions to an international problem.

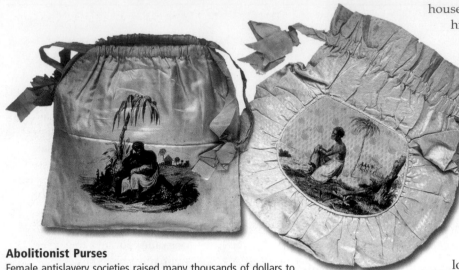

Abolitionist Purses
Female antislavery societies raised many thousands of dollars to support the abolitionist cause by selling handcrafted items at giant antislavery fairs. Toys, infant clothes, quilts, caps and collars, purses, wax flowers, inlaid boxes—the list was endless. Items were often emblazoned with abolitionist mottoes, such as "Let My People Go," "Liberty," and "Loose the Bonds of Wickedness." These pink silk drawstring bags are decorated with pictures of the "hapless slave woman," an object of compassion. Money raised at antislavery fairs supported the travels of abolitionist speakers, as well as the publication and distribution of many antislavery books and articles.
The Daughters of the American Revolution Museum, Washington, D.C. Gift of Mrs. Erwin L. Broecker.

and proposed emigration to Canada. In 1832, a twenty-eight-year-old black woman named Maria Stewart delivered public lectures for black audiences in Boston on slavery and racial prejudice. Although her arguments against slavery were welcomed, her voice—that of a woman—created problems even among her sympathetic audiences. Few American-born women had yet engaged in public speaking beyond theatrical performances or religious prophesying. Stewart was breaking a social taboo, an offense made more challenging by her statements suggesting that black women should rise above housework: "How long shall the fair daughters of Africa be compelled to bury their minds and talents beneath a load of iron pots and kettles?" She retired from the platform in 1833 but took up writing and published her lectures in a national publication called the *Liberator*, giving them much wider circulation.

The *Liberator*, founded in 1831 in Boston, took antislavery agitation to new heights. Its founder and editor, an uncompromising twenty-six-year-old white printer named William Lloyd Garrison, advocated immediate abolition: "On this subject, I do not wish to think, or speak, or write, with moderation. No! No! Tell a man whose house is on fire to give a moderate alarm; tell him to moderately rescue his wife from the hands of the ravisher; tell the mother to gradually extricate her babe from the fire into which it has fallen;—but urge me not to use moderation in a cause like the present."

In 1832, Garrison's supporters started the New England Anti-Slavery Society. Similar groups were organized in Philadelphia and New York in 1833. Soon a dozen antislavery newspapers and scores of antislavery lecturers were spreading the word and inspiring the formation of new local societies, which numbered thirteen hundred by 1837. Entirely confined to the North, their membership totaled a quarter of a million men and women.

Many white northerners were not prepared to embrace the abolitionist call for emancipation, immediate or gradual. They might oppose slavery as a blot on the country's ideals or as a rival to the **free-labor** system of the North, but at the same time most white northerners remained antiblack and therefore antiabolition. From 1834 to 1838, there were more than a hundred eruptions of serious mob violence against abolitionists or free blacks. On one occasion, antislavery headquarters in Philadelphia and a black church and orphanage were burned to the ground. In another incident, Illinois abolitionist editor Elijah Lovejoy was killed by a rioting crowd attempting to destroy his printing press.

Women played a prominent role in abolition, just as they did in moral reform and evangelical religion. They formed women's auxiliaries and held fairs to sell handmade crafts to support male lecturers in the field. They circulated antislavery petitions, presented to the U.S. Congress with tens of thousands of signatures. Up to 1835, women's petitions were framed as respectful memorials to Congress about the evils of slavery, but by mid-decade these petitions called for Congress to outlaw slavery in the District of Columbia (the only area under Congress's sole power). By 1836, women were signing petitions using urgent and strident abolitionist language. They were asserting their claim to be heard on political issues without their husbands' permission and their privilege to instruct members of Congress.

Garrison particularly welcomed women's activity. When a southern plantation daughter named Angelina Grimké wrote to him about her personal repugnance for slavery, Garrison published the letter in the *Liberator* and brought her overnight fame. In 1837, Grimké and her older sister, Sarah, became antislavery lecturers targeting women, but their powerful eyewitness speeches attracted men as well, causing leaders of the Congregational Church in Massachusetts to warn all ministers not to let the Grimké sisters use their pulpits. Like Maria Stewart, the Grimkés had violated a gender norm by presuming to instruct men.

In the late 1830s, the cause of abolition divided the nation as no other issue did. Even among abolitionists, significant divisions emerged. The Grimké sisters, radicalized by the public reaction to their speaking tour, began to write and speak about woman's rights. They were opposed by moderate abolitionists who were unwilling to mix the new and controversial issue of woman's rights with their first cause, the rights of blacks. A few radical men, such as Garrison, embraced woman's rights fully, working to get women leadership positions in the national antislavery group.

The many men and women active in reform movements in the 1830s found their initial inspiration in evangelical Protestantism's dual message: Salvation was open to all, and society needed to be perfected. Their activist mentality squared well with the interventionist tendencies of the party forming in opposition to Andrew Jackson's Democrats. Generally, reformers gravitated toward the Whig Party, the males as voters and the females as rallying supporters in the 1830s campaigns.

REVIEW How did evangelical Protestantism contribute to the social reform movements of the 1830s?

Van Buren's One-Term Presidency

By the mid-1830s, a vibrant and tumultuous political culture occupied center stage of American life. A colorful military hero had left his stamp on the nation, for good or for ill, but both by custom and by the old man's infirmity, another reelection of Andrew Jackson was out of the question. The northerner Martin Van Buren, Old Hickory's vice president and handpicked successor, inherited a strong Democratic organization, but he faced doubts from slave-owning Jacksonians as well as opposition from increasingly combative Whigs. Abolitionist tactics had pushed slavery into the political debate, but Van Buren managed to defuse that conflict somewhat and even use it to his advantage. What could not be forestalled, however, was the collapse of the economic boom so celebrated by both Democrats and Whigs. The shattering panic of 1837, followed by another panic in 1839, brought the country its worst economic depression yet. The difficult times did not let up for six years.

The Politics of Slavery

Sophisticated party organization was Martin Van Buren's specialty. Nicknamed "the Little Magician" and "the Red Fox" for his consummate political skills, the redheaded New Yorker had built his career by pioneering many of the loyalty-enhancing techniques the Democrats used in the 1830s. After serving as senator and then governor, he became Jackson's secretary of state in 1828. Four years later, he replaced South Carolinian John C. Calhoun as Jackson's running mate. His eight years in the volatile Jackson administration required the full measure of his political deftness as he sought repeatedly to save Jackson from both his enemies and his own obstinacy.

> John C. Calhoun tried to discredit Martin Van Buren among southern proslavery Democrats. Van Buren spent the next year assuring them that he was a "northern man with southern principles."

Jackson made it known that he favored Van Buren for the nomination in 1836, but starting in 1832, the major political parties had moved to formal nominating conventions to choose their candidates. To help ensure a Van Buren victory, Democratic leaders agreed to hold their nominating convention a year early, in 1835. The convention voted unanimously for the vice president, to the dismay of his archrival, Calhoun, who tried to discredit Van Buren among southern proslavery Democrats. Van Buren spent the next year assuring them that he was a "northern man with southern principles."

This should not have been hard for the vice president. His Dutch family hailed from the Hudson River counties where New York slavery had once flourished, and his own family had owned at least one slave as late as the 1810s, although he chose not to broadcast that fact. (Slavery was only gradually phased out in New

York starting in 1799; see chapter 8, page 259.) Calhoun's partisans whipped up controversy over Van Buren's support of suffrage for New York's propertied free blacks at the 1821 state convention on suffrage. Van Buren's partisans developed a proslavery spin by emphasizing that the Little Magician had argued that the mass of "poor, degraded blacks" were incapable of voting; he had merely favored retaining the existing stiff property qualifications for the handful of elite blacks who had always voted in New York, while simultaneously removing all such qualifications for white men.

Calhoun was able to stir up trouble for Van Buren because in 1835, southerners were increasingly alarmed by the rise of northern antislavery sentiment. When, in late 1835, abolitionists prepared to circulate in the South a million pamphlets condemning slavery, a mailbag of their literature was hijacked at the post office in Charleston, South Carolina, and ceremoniously burned along with effigies of leading abolitionists. President Jackson condemned the theft but issued approval for individual postmasters to exercise their own judgment about whether to allow incendiary materials to reach their destination. Abolitionists saw this as undue censorship of the mail.

The petitioning tactics of abolitionists escalated sectional tensions. As petitions demanding Congress to "purify" the site of the national government by outlawing slavery in the District of Columbia grew into the hundreds, proslavery congressmen sought to short-circuit the appeals by passing a "**gag rule**" in 1836. The gag rule prohibited entering the documents into the public record on the grounds that what the abolitionists prayed for was unconstitutional and, further, an assault on the rights of white southerners, as one South Carolina representative put it.

Van Buren shrewdly seized on both mail censorship and the gag rule to express his prosouthern sympathies. Abolitionists were "fanatics," he repeatedly claimed, possibly under the influence of "foreign agents" (British abolitionists). He dismissed the issue of abolition in the District of Columbia as "inexpedient" and said that if he was elected president, he would not allow any interference in southern "domestic institutions."

The Election of 1836

The Democrats had evolved from a coalition into a party, and Martin Van Buren had a clear shot at the presidency. Although the elections of 1824, 1828, and 1832 clearly bore the stamp of Jackson's personality, by 1836 the party apparatus was sufficiently developed to support itself. Local and state committees existed throughout the country. Democratic candidates ran in every state election, succeeding even in old Federalist states such as Maine and New Hampshire. More than four hundred newspapers declared themselves Democratic.

Van Buren was a backroom politician, not a popular public figure, and the Whigs hoped that he might be defeatable. In many states, Whigs had captured high office in 1834, shedding the awkward National Republican label and developing statewide organizations to rival those of the Democrats. However, no figure yet commanded nationwide support, and so three regional candidates opposed Van Buren in 1836. Senator Daniel Webster of Massachusetts could deliver New England, home to reformers, merchants, and manufacturers; Senator Hugh Lawson White of Tennessee attracted proslavery voters still suspicious of the northern Magician; and the aging General William Henry Harrison, now residing in Ohio and memorable for his Indian war heroics in 1811, pulled in the western, anti-Indian vote. Not one of the three candidates had the ability to win the presidency, but together they came close to denying Van Buren a majority vote. Van Burenites called the three-Whig strategy a deliberate plot to derail the election and move it to the House of Representatives, setting the stage perhaps for another allegedly stolen election, as in 1824 (see chapter 10).

In the end, Van Buren won the election of 1836 by 170 electoral votes, while the other three received a total of 113. The popular vote told a somewhat different story. Van Buren's narrow majorities, where he won, were far below those Jackson had commanded. Although Van Buren had pulled together a national Democratic Party, with wins in both the North and the South, he had done it at the cost of committing northern Democrats to the proslavery agenda. And running three candidates had maximized the Whigs' success by drawing Whigs into office at the state level.

Two Panics and the Election of 1840

The day Martin Van Buren took office in March 1837, the financial markets were already quaking; by April, the country was plunged into crisis. The causes of the panic of 1837 were multiple and far-ranging. Bad harvests in Europe and a large trade imbalance between Britain and the United States caused the Bank of England to

The Panic of 1837
A sad family with an unemployed father faces sudden privation in this cartoon showing the consequences
of the panic of 1837. The wife and children complain of hunger, the house is nearly stripped bare, and rent
collectors loom in the doorway. Faint pictures on the wall show Andrew Jackson and Martin Van Buren
presiding over the economic devastation of the family. The only support system for the unemployed in 1837
was the local almshouse, where families were split up and living conditions were harsh.
Library of Congress.

raise its interest rates in 1836 and to start calling
in loans to American merchants, demanding
money and not banknotes in payment. Failures
in various crop markets and a 30 percent downturn in cotton prices on the international market
fed the growing disaster. Cotton merchants in
the South could no longer meet their obligations
to creditors in New York City, and brokerage
firms in the nation's financial capital began to
fail—ninety-eight of them in March and April
1837 alone. Frightened citizens thronged the
banks to try to get their money out, and businesses rushed to liquefy their remaining assets
to pay off debts. Prices of stocks, bonds, and real
estate fell 30 to 40 percent. The familiar events of
the panic of 1819 unfolded again, with terrifying
rapidity, and the credit market tumbled like
a house of cards. (See "Seeking the American
Promise," page 388.)

Some Whig leaders were certain that Jackson's antibank and hard-money policies were
responsible for the ruin. New Yorker Philip
Hone, a wealthy Whig, called the Jackson administration "the most disastrous in the annals
of the country" for its "wicked interference" in
banking and monetary matters. Others framed
the devastation as retribution for an immoral
frenzy of speculation that had gripped the nation. A religious periodical in Boston hoped that
Americans would now moderate their greed:
"We were getting to be almost insane upon the
subject of wealth. . . . We were getting to think
that there was no end to the wealth, and could be
no check to the progress of our country; that
economy was not needed, that prudence was
weakness." In this view, the panic was a wake-
up call, a blessing in disguise. Others identified
the competitive, profit-maximizing capitalist
economic system as the cause of the wrecked
economy and looked across the Atlantic, to
Britain and France, for new socialist ideas calling
for the common ownership of land and of the

Going Ahead or *Gone to Smash*: An Entrepreneur Struggles in the 1830s

The spectacular economic boom of the 1830s gave life to the dream of get-rich-quick entrepreneurship, leading many to expect overnight wealth. America's abundance and progress promised a level of comfort and even opulence previously unimagined. A new slang term, *go-aheadism*, captured the enthusiasm of the day. It was used to characterize men who were ambitious, competitive, and confident. But there was a downside to this enthusiasm, identified by a New York diarist who lamented that *go-aheadism* had made Americans "the most careless, reckless, headlong people on the face of the earth." Soon enough, a rich vocabulary also defined business failure: *gone to smash, fizzled, wiped out, busted, up a tree,* and *GTT*—for "gone to Texas," a location outside the United States (until 1845) and therefore out of reach of U.S. law.

Benjamin Rathbun of Buffalo, New York, epitomized both *go-aheadism* and *gone to smash* failure in the turbulent 1830s. Born in Connecticut in 1790, Rathbun arrived in Buffalo at age thirty and by 1825 owned the opulent Eagle Hotel. A shy man who was never seen to smile, he shrewdly identified Buffalo as the perfect location for his new business venture. Buffalo was a boomtown, occupying the crucial node between the western end of the new Erie Canal and the eastern Great Lakes gateway to the interior of the country. Scores of steamboats departed Buffalo daily for Cleveland, Detroit, and Chicago. The town's population nearly doubled from 1830 to 1835, and then doubled again by 1840 to eighteen thousand inhabitants, close to the size of Washington, D.C. Fueling this boom were brokerage houses that lined Buffalo's streets, lending money at high interest rates to borrowers speculating in real estate and business.

The success of the Eagle Hotel enabled Rathbun to become Buffalo's biggest self-made man. In eight years, he built an empire of real estate, building construction, banks, and transportation. He bought and sold city lots; he constructed ninety-nine buildings, including stores, mansions, hotels, churches, and a large jail. To supply the construction, he owned lumber mills, brick works, and stone quarries. He operated the mail stage lines out of town and the city omnibuses within it; his livery stables housed hundreds of horses. He opened stores selling groceries, dry goods, and carpets; he invested in three out-of-state banks. More than two thousand employees—more than a third of all adult males in Buffalo—were on his payroll.

This empire, with its daily cash flow of $10,000, required business acumen, astute management, and a steady influx of borrowed banknotes issued by New York City creditors. Rathbun's trusted younger brother, Lyman, headed financial operations, while Rathbun kept his eye on the big picture: designing the grand architecture of Buffalo and buying up all the land on the American side of Niagara Falls for profitable resale. Some people even said that Rathbun owned the falls themselves.

Collapse came suddenly in 1836. On a buying trip to New York City, Rathbun learned that his creditors there were selling his IOUs to brokers at a steep discount, a process known as "note shaving." Those creditors had lost faith in Rathbun, and the new note holders were charging him much higher interest rates (by a multiple of five or ten). To cover the increased interest, the Rathbuns negotiated more loans, supposedly backed by a dozen cosigners from the Buffalo business community guaranteeing payment if the brothers failed. When Rathbun applied for a $500,000 loan in an attempt to consolidate his debt, the dozen endorsements were revealed to be forgeries. Benjamin Rathbun went to jail; brother Lyman disappeared with trunks full of money—"GTT," many people said. Rathbun was convicted of fraud and sentenced to five years' hard labor in state prison.

Rathbun's spectacular failure plunged Buffalo into a severe depression eight months in advance of the panic of 1837. He was the talk of the national business community, the canary in the mine—had anyone chosen to heed the warning. Although deliberate fraud brought him down, his *wipeout* highlighted the inherent difficulties in an economy of note shaving and discounting, where loans of millions of dollars were granted on the basis of a few signatures. Who could trust that even an authentic endorsement of a debt indicated creditworthiness? Rathbun's failure differed only in scale from the many failures of the 1830s, when, historians calculate, something like a fifth of all businessmen *fizzled* or *went up a tree.*

Massive failures in the five years after 1837 led to two striking innovations in business law and loan practices. First, the federal government passed the U.S. Bankruptcy Act of 1841, a controversial and short-term law that enabled failed debtors to wipe debts away legally, paying creditors a fraction of what was owed and generating a sizable revenue stream for the agencies that administered the law. Bankruptcies thus benefited lawyers, court officers, auctioneers, and even the newspaper publishers who collected fees for managing, selling, and advertising foreclosed property. Debtors gained release from crushing debt but had to endure the humiliation of having notices of their bankruptcies printed in the newspapers.

Second, the credit reporting industry was born in 1841 when a failed businessman opened the Mercantile Agency in New York City. For a $50 subscription fee, lenders could tap into large books containing confidential information gathered by hundreds of agents around the country who assessed the creditworthiness of local businessmen. Agents might be postmasters, bank cashiers, attorneys, bill collectors, even ministers—men in positions to know not just the financial but also the moral worth of a man. Operating as spies, the agents furnished evaluations such as: "Is smart enough to carry on his business" and "Loafer—Bad." Church (and saloon) attendance, family stability, and punctuality were frequent factors in grading businessmen's reputations for prudence and reliability.

Had it been in existence in 1836, the Mercantile Agency (renamed Dun & Bradstreet in the 1850s) might have unmasked Rathbun's fraud through semiannual checks on his reputation.

The Bankruptcy Act no doubt helped the many debt-saddled Buffalo men who had been caught out by Rathbun's failure. Luckily for many ordinary citizens of Buffalo, his liquidated estate paid out first to the thousands of workers on his payroll, second to the lawyers, and third to preferred creditors, leaving several hundred thousands of dollars of debt unpaid.

When Rathbun left prison in 1843, he rejoined his wife, now running a boardinghouse in Buffalo to make ends meet. Soon the Rathbuns moved to New York City, where the onetime proprietor of Buffalo's Eagle Hotel returned to his first occupation. With financial help from cousins, he leased a building on lower Broadway, the first in a series of increasingly seedy hotels that he ran until his death four decades later.

The Eagle Hotel, Buffalo, 1825
Benjamin Rathbun (shown here scowling) bought this three-story building in 1825, doubled it in size with a building behind it, and turned it into the finest hotel west of New York City. Located on Main Street in Buffalo, the Eagle became the meeting place for all civic and professional groups in early Buffalo. The marquis de Lafayette, French hero of the American Revolution, stayed at the Eagle in 1825 on his U.S. tour.
Buffalo and Erie County Historical Society.

means of production. American socialists were not large in number during this period, but they were vocal and imaginative, and in the early 1840s, several thousand developed utopian alternatives (see chapter 12, page 424).

The panic of 1837 subsided somewhat by 1838, as banks suspended payouts in hard money, stopping the outflow of deposits and even resuming loan activity. But in 1839, another run on the banks and ripples of business failures deflated the economy, creating a second panic. President Van Buren called a special session of Congress to consider creating an independent treasury system to perform some of the functions of the defunct Bank of the United States. Such a system, funded by government deposits, would deal only in hard money, forcing commercial banks to restrict their issuance of paper currency, and it would not make loans, thus avoiding the danger of speculative meddling in the economy. In short, an independent treasury system could exert a powerful moderating influence on inflation and the credit market without being directly involved in the market. But Van Buren encountered strong resistance in Congress, even among Democrats. The treasury system finally won approval in 1840, but by then Van Buren's chances of winning a second term in office were virtually nil because of the tumultuous economy.

In 1840, the Whigs settled on William Henry Harrison to oppose Van Buren. The campaign drew on voter involvement as no presidential campaign ever had. The Whigs borrowed tricks from the Democrats: Harrison was touted as a common man born in a log cabin (in reality, he was born on a Virginia plantation), and raucous campaign parades featured toy log cabins held aloft. His Indian-fighting days, now thirty years behind him, were played up to give him a Jacksonian aura. Whigs staged festive rallies all over the country, drumming up mass appeal with candlelight parades and song shows, and women participated in rallies as never before. Some 78 percent of eligible voters cast ballots—the highest percentage ever in American history. Harrison took 53 percent of the popular vote and won a resounding 234 electoral college votes to Van Buren's 60. A Democratic editor lamented, "We have taught them how to conquer us!"

REVIEW   How did slavery figure as a campaign issue in the election of 1836?

Conclusion: The Age of Jackson or the Era of Reform?

Harrison's election closed a decade that had brought the common man and democracy to the forefront of American politics. Economic transformations loom large in explaining the fast-paced changes of the 1830s. Transportation advances put goods and people in circulation, augmenting urban growth and helping to create a national culture, and water-powered manufacturing began to change the face of wage labor. Trade and banking mushroomed, and western land once occupied by Indians was auctioned off in a landslide of sales. Two periods of economic downturn—including the panic of 1819 and the panics of 1837 and 1839—offered sobering lessons about speculative fever.

Andrew Jackson symbolized this age of opportunity for many. His fame as an aggressive general, Indian fighter, champion of the common man, and defender of slavery attracted growing numbers of voters to the emergent Democratic Party, which championed personal liberty, free competition, and egalitarian opportunity for all white men.

Jackson's constituency was challenged by a small but vocal segment of the population troubled by serious moral problems that Jacksonians preferred to ignore. Reformers drew sustenance from the message of the Second Great Awakening: that all men and women were free to choose salvation and that personal and societal sins could be overcome. Reformers targeted personal vices (illicit sex and intemperance) and social problems (prostitution, poverty, and slavery), and joined forces with evangelicals and wealthy lawyers and merchants (North and South) who appreciated a national bank and protective tariffs. The Whig Party was the party of activist moralism and state-sponsored entrepreneurship. Whig voters were, of course, male, but thousands of reform-minded women broke new ground by signing political petitions on the issues of Indian removal and slavery.

National politics in the 1830s were more divisive than at any time since the 1790s. The new party system of Democrats and Whigs reached far deeper into the electorate than had the Federalists and Republicans. Stagecoaches and steamboats carried newspapers from the cities to the backwoods, politicizing voters and creating party loyalty. Politics acquired immediacy and excitement, causing nearly four out of five white men to cast ballots in 1840.

High rates of voter participation would continue into the 1840s and 1850s. Unprecedented urban growth, westward expansion, and early industrialism marked those decades, sustaining the Democrat-Whig split in the electorate. But critiques of slavery, concerns for free labor, and an emerging protest against women's second-class citizenship complicated the political scene of the 1840s, leading to third-party political movements. One of these third parties, called the Republican Party, would achieve dominance in 1860 with the election of an Illinois lawyer, Abraham Lincoln, to the presidency.

Selected Bibliography

The Market Revolution

Edward J. Balleisen, *Navigating Failure: Bankruptcy and Commercial Society in Antebellum America* (2001).

Mary H. Blewett, *Men, Women, and Work: Class, Gender, and Protest in the New England Shoe Industry, 1780–1910* (1988).

Jeanne Boydston, *Home and Work: Housework, Wages, and the Ideology of Labor in the Early Republic* (1990).

Thomas Dublin, *Transforming Women's Work: New England Lives in the Industrial Revolution* (1994).

Charles G. Sellers, *The Market Revolution: Jacksonian America, 1815–1846* (1991).

Carol Sheriff, *The Artificial River: The Erie Canal and the Paradox of Progress, 1817–1862* (1996).

Richard B. Stott, *Workers in the Metropolis: Class, Ethnicity, and Youth in Antebellum New York City* (1990).

Politics

Hendrik Booraem, *Young Hickory: The Making of Andrew Jackson* (2001).

Andrew Burstein, *The Passions of Andrew Jackson* (2003).

Jonathan H. Earle, *Jacksonian Antislavery and the Politics of Free Soil* (2004).

John Ehle, *Trail of Tears: The Rise and Fall of the Cherokee Nation* (1997).

Daniel Feller, *The Jacksonian Promise: America, 1815–1840* (1995).

Sean Michael O'Brien, *In Bitterness and in Tears: Andrew Jackson's Destruction of the Creeks and Seminoles* (2003).

Theda Perdue, *Cherokee Women: Gender and Culture Change, 1700–1835* (1998).

Merrill D. Peterson, *The Great Triumvirate: Webster, Clay, and Calhoun* (1987).

Robert V. Remini, *The Life of Andrew Jackson* (2001).

Harry L. Watson, *Liberty and Power: The Politics of Jacksonian America* (1990).

Sean Wilentz, *The Rise of American Democracy, Jefferson to Lincoln* (2005).

Culture, Religion, and Reform

Robert Abzug, *Cosmos Crumbling: American Reform and the Religious Imagination* (1994).

Christopher Leslie Brown, *Moral Capital: Foundations of British Abolitionism* (2006).

Bruce Dorsey, *Reforming Men & Women: Gender in the Antebellum City* (2002).

Lori D. Ginzberg, *Women and the Work of Benevolence: Morality, Politics, and Class in the Nineteenth-Century United States* (1990).

Stanley Harrold, *Subversives: Antislavery Community in Washington, D.C., 1828–1865* (2003).

Nathan O. Hatch, *The Democratization of American Christianity* (1991).

Helen Lefkowitz Horowitz, *Rereading Sex: Battles over Sexual Knowledge and Suppression in Nineteenth-Century America* (2002).

Julie Roy Jeffrey, *The Great Silent Army of Abolitionism: Ordinary Women in the Antislavery Movement* (1998).

Richard R. John, *Spreading the News: The American Postal System from Franklin to Morse* (1995).

Catherine E. Kelly, *In the New England Fashion: Reshaping Women's Lives in the Nineteenth Century* (1999).

Bruce Laurie, *Beyond Garrison: Antislavery and Social Reform* (2005).

Richard S. Newman, *The Transformation of American Abolitionism: Fighting Slavery in the Early Republic* (2002).

Alisse Portnoy, *Their Right to Speak: Women's Activism in the Indian and Slave Debates* (2005).

Patrick Rael, *Black Identity and Black Protest in the Antebellum North* (2002).

Scott A. Sandage, *Born Losers: A History of Failure in America* (2005).

Carroll Smith-Rosenberg, *Disorderly Conduct: Visions of Gender in Victorian America* (1985).

Ronald J. Zboray, *Literary Dollars and Social Sense: A People's History of the Mass Market Book* (2005).

▶ **FOR MORE BOOKS ABOUT TOPICS IN THIS CHAPTER,** see the Online Bibliography at bedfordstmartins.com/roark.

▶ **FOR ADDITIONAL FIRSTHAND ACCOUNTS OF THIS PERIOD,** see Chapter 11 in Michael Johnson, ed., *Reading the American Past,* Fourth Edition.

▶ **FOR WEB SITES, IMAGES, AND DOCUMENTS RELATED TO TOPICS AND PLACES IN THIS CHAPTER,** visit bedfordstmartins.com/makehistory.

REVIEWING THE CHAPTER

Follow these steps to review and strengthen your understanding of the chapter.

STEP 1: *Study the **Key Terms** and **Timeline** to identify the significance of each item listed.*

STEP 2: *Answer the **Review Questions**, drawing on key terms and dates to support your answers.*

STEP 3: *Drawing on the Key Terms, Timeline, and Review Questions, answer the broader **Making Connections** questions.*

KEY TERMS

Who

Andrew Jackson (p. 357)
Robert Fulton (p. 360)
John Quincy Adams (p. 366)
Henry Clay (p. 367)
John C. Calhoun (p. 368)
Martin Van Buren (p. 369)
Black Hawk (p. 371)
Charles Grandison Finney (p. 379)
Lyman Beecher (p. 380)
David Walker (p. 381)
Maria Stewart (p. 384)
William Lloyd Garrison (p. 384)
Angelina and Sarah Grimké (p. 385)
William Henry Harrison (p. 386)

What

Erie Canal (p. 360)
Baltimore and Ohio Railroad (p. 361)

Lowell mills (p. 361)
specie payment (p. 365)
second Bank of the United States (p. 366)
panic of 1819 (p. 366)
Hickory Clubs (p. 367)
Bucktails (p. 367)
Whigs (p. 367)
Democrats (p. 367)
Maysville Road veto (p. 369)
Indian Removal Act of 1830 (p. 371)
Black Hawk War (p. 371)
second Seminole War (p. 371)
Worcester v. Georgia (p. 371)
Trail of Tears (p. 372)
Tariff of Abominations (p. 373)
nullification (p. 373)
Force Bill (p. 373)
Second Great Awakening (p. 375)

separate spheres (p. 376)
Oberlin College (p. 379)
American Temperance Society (p. 380)
American Temperance Union (p. 381)
New York Female Moral Reform Society (p. 381)
American Colonization Society (p. 381)
National Negro Convention (p. 381)
Liberator (p. 384)
New England Anti-Slavery Society (p. 384)
gag rule of 1836 (p. 386)
panic of 1837 (p. 386)
panic of 1839 (p. 390)
treasury system (p. 390)

TIMELINE

◀ **1807** • Robert Fulton's *Clermont* sets off steamboat craze.

    1816 • Second Bank of the United States chartered.

      1817 • American Colonization Society founded.

        1818 • National Road links Baltimore to western Virginia.

          1819 • Economic panic.

            1821 • Mill town of Lowell, Massachusetts, founded.

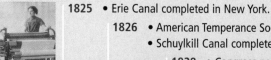

              1825 • Erie Canal completed in New York.

                1826 • American Temperance Society founded.
                       • Schuylkill Canal completed in Pennsylvania.

                  1828 • Congress passes Tariff of Abominations.
                       • Democrat Andrew Jackson elected president.

                    1829 • David Walker's *Appeal . . . to the Coloured Citizens of the World* published.
                       • Baltimore and Ohio Railroad begun.

REVIEW QUESTIONS

1. Why did the United States experience a market revolution after 1815? (pp. 358–66)

2. Why did Andrew Jackson defeat John Quincy Adams so dramatically in the 1828 election? (pp. 366–69)

3. Why did Jackson promote Indian removal? (pp. 369–75)

4. How did evangelical Protestantism contribute to the social reform movements of the 1830s? (pp. 375–85)

5. How did slavery figure as a campaign issue in the election of 1836? (pp. 385–90)

MAKING CONNECTIONS

1. Describe the market revolution that began in the 1810s. How did it affect Americans' work and domestic lives? In your answer, be sure to consider how gender contributed to these developments.

2. Andrew Jackson's presidency coincided with important changes in American politics. Discuss how Jackson benefited from, and contributed to, the vibrant political culture of the 1830s. Cite specific national developments in your answer.

3. Describe Andrew Jackson's response to the "Indian problem" during his presidency. How did his policies revise or continue earlier federal policies toward Native Americans? How did Native Americans respond to Jackson's actions?

4. While a volatile economy buffeted the United States in the 1830s, some Americans looked to reform the nation. Discuss the objectives and strategies of two reform movements. What was the relationship of these reform movements to larger political and economic trends of the 1830s?

▶ For practice quizzes, a customized study plan, and other study tools, see the Online Study Guide at bedfordstmartins.com/roark.

1830 • Indian Removal Act; Women's petitions for Indian rights begin.

    1831 • William Lloyd Garrison starts *Liberator*.
        • Charles Grandison Finney preaches in Rochester, New York.

        1832 • Massacre of Sauk and Fox Indians under Chief Black Hawk.
           • *Worcester v. Georgia.*
           • Jackson vetoes charter renewal of Bank of the United States.
           • New England Anti-Slavery Society founded.

           1833 • Nullification of federal tariffs declared in South Carolina.
               • New York and Philadelphia antislavery societies founded.
               • New York Female Moral Reform Society founded.

               1834 • Female mill workers strike in Lowell, Massachusetts, and again in 1836.

                  1836 • Democrat Martin Van Buren elected president.
                    • American Temperance Union founded.

                    1837 • Economic panic.

                      1838 • Trail of Tears: Cherokees forced to relocate west.

                        1839 • Economic panic.

                          1840 • Whig William Henry Harrison elected president.

GOLD NUGGETS

Gold! Nuggets like these scooped from a California river drove easterners crazy with excitement. A quarter of a million people joined the great rush for western riches in the five years after gold's discovery in 1848. Men from the East and around the world sought to escape routine jobs and mundane lives by "making their pile" in California. The carnival that was the gold rush fulfilled the hopes of only a few, but the rest participated in one of the great adventures of the nineteenth century and rarely regretted their experiences.

The Oakland Museum.

The New West and Free North

1840–1860

■ **Economic and Industrial Evolution** 397
Agriculture and Land Policy 397
Manufacturing and Mechanization 398
Railroads: Breaking the Bonds of Nature 399

■ **Free Labor: Promise and Reality** 402
The Free-Labor Ideal: Freedom plus Labor 402
Economic Inequality 405
Immigrants and the Free-Labor Ladder 405

■ **The Westward Movement** 407
Manifest Destiny 407
Oregon and the Overland Trail 408
The Mormon Exodus 411
The Mexican Borderlands 412

■ **Expansion and the Mexican-American War** 414
The Politics of Expansion 414
The Mexican-American War, 1846–1848 416
Victory in Mexico 419
Golden California 420

■ **Reforming Self and Society** 424
The Pursuit of Perfection: Transcendentalists and Utopians 424
Woman's Rights Activists 425
Abolitionists and the American Ideal 426

■ **Conclusion: Free Labor, Free Men** 430

EARLY IN NOVEMBER 1842, Abraham Lincoln and his new wife, Mary, moved into their first home in Springfield, Illinois, a rented room measuring eight by fourteen feet on the second floor of the Globe Tavern. A busy blacksmith shop next door filled the Lincolns' room with the clamor of iron being pounded into horseshoes and other useful objects. The small, noisy room above the tavern was the nicest place that Abraham Lincoln had ever lived; it was the worst place that Mary Todd Lincoln had ever inhabited. She had grown up in Lexington, Kentucky, attended by slaves in the elegant home of her father, a prosperous merchant, banker, and politician. When she came to Illinois as a young single woman, she lived with relatives, who were among the local elite. Less than twenty years after their marriage, in March 1861, the Lincolns moved into what would prove to be their last home, the presidential mansion in Washington, D.C.

Abraham Lincoln climbed from the Globe Tavern to the White House by relentless work, unslaked ambition, and immense talent—traits he had honed since boyhood. Lincoln and many others celebrated his rise from humble origins as an example of the opportunities that beckoned in the free-labor economy of the North and West. They attributed his spectacular ascent to his individual qualities and tended to ignore the help he received from Mary and many others.

Born in a Kentucky log cabin in 1809, Lincoln grew up on small, struggling farms as his family migrated west. His father, Thomas, had left Virginia, where he had been born, and settled in Kentucky. Thomas Lincoln never learned to read and, as his son recalled, "never did more in the way of writing than to bunglingly sign his own name." Lincoln's mother, Nancy, could neither read nor write. In December 1816, Thomas Lincoln moved his young family from Kentucky to the Indiana wilderness. They lived for two frozen months in a crude lean-to while Thomas, a skilled carpenter, built a cabin. On the Indiana farmstead, Abraham learned the arts of agriculture practiced by families throughout the nation. Although only eight years old, he "had an axe put into his hands at once" and used it "almost constantly" for the next fifteen years, as he recalled later. He worked for neighbors for twenty-five cents a day and gave the money to his father. When he could be spared from work, the boy attended school, less than a year in all. "There was absolutely nothing to excite ambition for education," Lincoln recollected. In contrast, Mary Todd received ten years of schooling in Lexington's best private academies for young women.

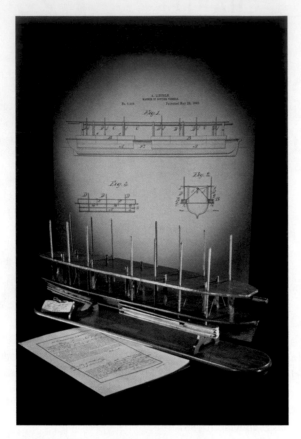

Abraham Lincoln's Patent

In 1849, lawyer Abraham Lincoln applied for a patent based on this model illustrating his idea of using inflatable rubberized bags (the long white objects under the lower deck) to lift riverboats over stretches of shallow water. Lincoln knew firsthand the difficulties of transporting goods on the nation's rivers, having rafted two loads of farm products all the way from the Midwest to New Orleans as a young man. His desire to solve practical problems grew out of his firm belief "that heads and hands should cooperate as friends," a key ingredient of the widespread free-labor ideology. Lincoln received his patent, becoming the only patent holder ever to serve as president. Although his patented idea never caught on, tens of thousands of other Americans sought to bring together knowledge and ingenuity in their quest for progress and to patent their schemes to profit from their inventiveness.
Smithsonian Institution, National Museum of American History.

In 1830, Thomas Lincoln decided to move farther west. The Lincolns hitched up the family oxen and headed to central Illinois, where they built another log cabin. The next spring, Thomas moved yet again, but this time Abraham stayed behind and set out on his own, a "friendless, uneducated, penniless boy," as he described himself. By dogged striving, Abraham Lincoln gained an education and the respect of his Illinois neighbors, although a steady income eluded him for years. Mary Todd had many suitors, including Stephen A. Douglas, Lincoln's eventual political rival. She told a friend that she "would rather marry a good man—a man of mind—with hope and bright prospects ahead for position—fame and power." After she married Lincoln, she said, "Intellectually my husband towers above Douglas . . . [and he] has no equal in the United States." The newlyweds received help from Mary's father, including eighty acres of land and a yearly allowance of about $1,100 for six years that helped them move out of their room above the Globe Tavern. Abraham eventually built a thriving law practice in Springfield, Illinois, and served in the state legislature and then in Congress. Mary helped him in many ways, rearing their sons, tending their household, and integrating him into her wealthy and influential extended family in Illinois and Kentucky. Mary also shared Abraham's keen interest in politics and ambition for power and prestige. With Mary's encouragement and support, Abraham's political success ultimately propelled them into the White House, where he became the first president born west of the Appalachian Mountains.

Like Lincoln, millions of Americans believed they could make something of themselves, whatever their origins, so long as they were willing to work. Individuals who refused to work—who were lazy, undisciplined, or foolish—had only themselves to blame if they failed. Work was a prerequisite for success, not a guarantee. This emphasis on work highlighted the individual efforts of men and tended to slight the many crucial contributions of women, family members, neighbors, and friends to the successes of men like Lincoln. In addition, the rewards of work were skewed toward white men and away from women and free African Americans. Nonetheless, the promise of rewards from hard work spurred efforts that shaped the contours of America, pushing the boundaries of the nation south to the Rio Grande, north to the Great Lakes, and ever westward to the Pacific Ocean. During Lincoln's presidency, Abraham and Mary talked about moving west to California at the end of his term. The economic, political, and geographic expansion that the Lincolns exemplified raised anew the question of whether slavery should also move west, the question that Lincoln and other Americans confronted again and again following the Mexican-American War, yet another outgrowth of the nation's ceaseless westward movement.

Economic and Industrial Evolution

During the 1840s and 1850s, Americans experienced a profound economic transformation that had been under way since the start of the nineteenth century. Since 1800, the total output of the U.S. economy had multiplied twelvefold. Four fundamental changes in American society fueled this remarkable economic growth.

First, millions of Americans—Abraham Lincoln among them—moved from farms to towns and cities. Even so, 80 percent of the nation's 31 million people remained in rural areas in 1860. Second, the number of Americans who worked in factories, mainly in urban centers, grew to about 20 percent of the labor force by 1860. This trend contributed to the nation's economic growth because, in general, factory workers produced twice as much (per unit of labor) as agricultural workers.

Third, a shift from water-power to steam as a source of energy raised productivity, especially in factories and transportation. In the 1840s, mines in Pennsylvania, Ohio, and elsewhere began to excavate millions of tons of coal for industrial fuel, accelerating the shift to steam power. Between 1840 and 1860, coal production multiplied eight fold, cutting prices in half and permitting coal-fired steam engines to power ever more factories, railroads, and ships. Nonetheless, by 1860 coal supplied less than a fifth of the nation's energy consumption, and the muscles of people and work animals still provided thirty times more energy for manufacturing than steam.

A fourth fundamental change propelling America's economic development was the rise in agricultural productivity, which nearly doubled during Lincoln's lifetime. More than any other single factor, agricultural productivity spurred the nation's economic growth. While cities, factories, and steam engines multiplied throughout the nation—particularly in the North and West—the roots of the United States' economic growth lay in agriculture.

Historians often refer to this cascade of changes in farms, cities, factories, power, and transportation as an industrial revolution. However, these changes did not cause an abrupt discontinuity in America's economy or society. The United States remained overwhelmingly agricultural. Old methods of production continued alongside the new. The changes in the American economy during the 1840s and 1850s might better be termed "industrial evolution."

Agriculture and Land Policy

A French traveler in the United States noted that Americans had "a general feeling of hatred against trees." Although the traveler exaggerated, his observation contained an important truth. Trees limited agricultural productivity because farmers had to spend a great deal of time and energy clearing land for planting. But as farmers pushed westward in a quest for cheap land, they encountered the Midwest's comparatively treeless prairie, where they could spend less time with an ax and more time with a plow and hoe. Rich prairie soils yielded bumper crops, enticing farmers such as the Lincolns to migrate to the Midwest by the tens of thousands between 1830 and 1860. The populations of Indiana, Illinois, Michigan, Wisconsin, and Iowa exploded tenfold between 1830 and 1860, four times faster than the growth of the nation as a whole. Lincoln's home state of Illinois added more people during the 1850s than any other state in the Union.

Laborsaving improvements in farm implements also hiked agricultural productivity. The cast-iron plow in use since the 1820s proved too weak for the thick turf and dense soil of the mid-western prairie. In 1837, John Deere patented a strong, smooth steel plow that sliced through prairie soil so cleanly that farmers called it the "singing plow." Deere's company became the leading plow manufacturer in the Midwest, turning out more than ten thousand plows a year by the late 1850s. Energy for plowing still came from human and animal muscles, but better plows permitted farmers to break more ground and plant more crops.

Improvements in wheat harvesting also multiplied farmers' productivity. In 1850, most farmers harvested wheat by hand, cutting two or three acres a day with backbreaking labor. In the 1840s, Cyrus McCormick and others experimented with designs for mechanical reapers, and by the 1850s, a McCormick reaper that cost between $100 and $150 allowed a farmer to harvest twelve acres a day. Farmers had purchased about eighty thousand reapers by 1860, but most continued to cut their grain by hand. Still, improved reapers and plows, usually powered by horses or oxen, allowed farmers to cultivate more land, doubling the corn and wheat harvests between 1840 and 1860.

Harvesting Grain with Cradles
This late-nineteenth-century painting shows a grain harvest during the mid-nineteenth century at Bishop Hill, Illinois, a Swedish community where the artist, Olof Krans, and his parents settled in 1850. The men swing cradles, slowly cutting a swath through the grain; the women gather the cut grain into sheaves to be hauled away later for threshing. Bishop Hill, a well-organized community, could call upon the labor of a large number of men and women at harvesttime. Most farmers had only a few family members and a hired hand or two to help with the harvest. Notice that although the grain field appears level enough to be ideal for a mechanical reaper, all the work is done by hand; there is no machine in sight.
Private Collection/Art Resource, NY.

Federal land policy made possible the agricultural productivity that fueled the nation's economy. Up to 1860, the United States continued to be land-rich and labor-poor. Territorial acquisitions made the nation a great deal richer in land, adding more than a billion acres with the Louisiana Purchase (see chapter 10) and the annexation of Florida, Oregon, and vast territories following the Mexican-American War (see page 416). The federal government made most of this land available for purchase to attract settlers and to generate revenue. Wily speculators found ways to claim large tracts of the most desirable plots and sell them to settlers at a generous markup. But millions of ordinary farmers bought federal land for just $1.25 an acre, or $50 for a forty-acre farm that could support a family. Millions of other farmers could not afford that much. They squatted on unclaimed federal land, carved out a farm, and, if they still lacked funds to buy the land after a few years, usually moved farther west to squat on federal land elsewhere. By making land available to millions of Americans on relatively easy terms, the federal government achieved the goal of attracting settlers to the new territories in the West, which in due course joined the Union as new states. Above all, federal land policy created the basic precondition for the increase in agricultural productivity that underlay the nation's impressive economic growth.

Manufacturing and Mechanization

Changes in manufacturing arose from the nation's land-rich, labor-poor economy. Britain and other European countries had land-poor, labor-rich economies; there, meager opportunities in agriculture kept factory laborers plentiful and wages low. In the United States, western expansion and government land policies buoyed agriculture, keeping millions of people on the farm and thereby limiting the supply of workers for manufacturing and elevating wages. Because of this relative shortage of workers, manufacturers searched constantly for ways to save labor.

Mechanization allowed manufacturers to produce more with less labor. The practice of manufacturing and then assembling interchangeable parts spread from gun making to other industries and became known as the "American system." Mechanization became so integral to American manufacturing that some machinists specialized in what was called the machine tool industry, which made parts for machinery. Standardized parts produced by machine allowed manufacturers to employ unskilled workers who were much cheaper and more readily available than highly trained craftsmen. A visitor to a Springfield, Massachusetts, gun factory in 1841 noted, for example, that unskilled workers "in every machine shop and manufactory throughout the country" could now make guns because standardized parts made the trained gunsmith's "skill of the eye and the hand, [previously] acquired by practice alone . . . no longer indispensable." Even in heavily mechanized industries, factories remained fairly small; few had more than twenty or thirty employees.

Manufacturing and agriculture meshed into a dynamic national economy. New England led the nation in manufacturing, shipping goods such as guns, clocks, plows, and axes west and south, while southern and western states sent commodities such as wheat, pork, whiskey, tobacco, and cotton north and east. Manufacturers specialized in producing for the gigantic domestic market rather than for export. British goods dominated the international market and, on the whole, were cheaper and better than American-made products. U.S. manufacturers supported tariffs to minimize British competition, but their best protection from British competitors was to strive harder to please their American customers, most of them farmers. The burgeoning national economy was further fueled by the growth of the railroads, which served to link farmers and factories in new ways.

Railroads: Breaking the Bonds of Nature

Railroads incorporated the most advanced developments of the age. A Swedish visitor in 1849 noticed that American schoolboys drew sketches of locomotives, always in motion, belching smoke. Railroads captured Americans' imaginations because they seemed to break the bonds of nature. When canals and rivers froze in winter or became impassable during summer droughts, trains steamed ahead. When becalmed sailing ships went nowhere, locomotives kept on chugging, averaging over twenty miles an hour during the 1850s. Above all, railroads gave cities not blessed with canals or navigable rivers a way to compete for rural trade.

By 1850, trains steamed along 9,000 miles of track, almost two-thirds of it in New England and the Middle Atlantic states. By 1860, several railroads spanned the Mississippi River, connecting frontier farmers to the nation's 30,000 miles of track, approximately as much as in all of the rest of the world combined (Map 12.1, page 400). In 1857, for example, France had 3,700 miles of track; England and Wales had a total of 6,400 miles. The massive expansion of American railroads helped catapult the nation into position as the world's second-greatest industrial power (after Great Britain).

> A visitor to a Springfield, Massachusetts, gun factory in 1841 noted that standardized parts made the trained gunsmith's "skill of the eye and the hand, [previously] acquired by practice alone . . . no longer indispensable."

In addition to speeding transportation, railroads propelled the growth of other industries, such as iron and communications. Iron production grew five times faster than the population during the decades up to 1860, in part to meet the demand for rails, wheels, axles, locomotives, and heavy, gravity-defying iron bridges. Railroads also stimulated the fledgling telegraph industry. (See "The Promise of Technology," page 402.) In 1844, Samuel F. B. Morse persuasively demonstrated the potential of his telegraph by transmitting a series of dots and dashes that instantly conveyed an electronic message along forty miles of wire strung between Washington, D.C., and Baltimore. By 1861, more than fifty thousand miles of wire stretched across the continent to the Pacific Ocean, often alongside railroad tracks, making trains safer and more efficient and accelerating communications of all sorts.

Private corporations built and owned almost all railroads, in contrast to government ownership of railroads common in other industrial nations. But privately owned American railroads received massive government aid, especially federal **land grants**. Up to 1850, the federal government had granted a total of seven million acres of federal land to various turnpike,

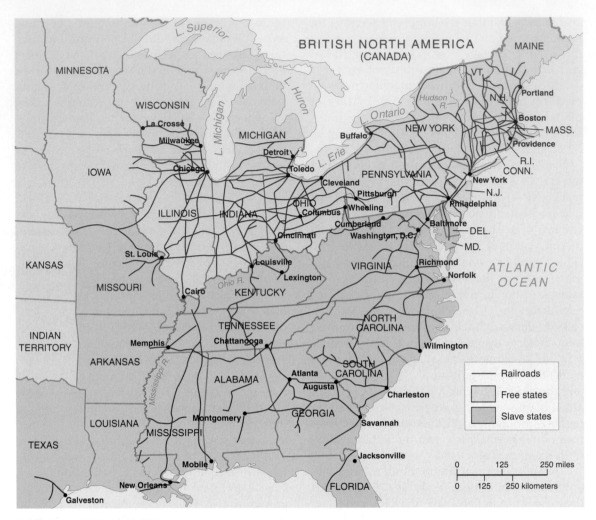

MAP 12.1   Railroads in 1860

Railroads were a crucial component of the revolutions in transportation and communications that transformed nineteenth-century America. The railroad system reflected the differences in the economies of the North and South.

READING THE MAP: In which sections of the country was most of the railroad track laid by the middle of the nineteenth century? What cities served as the busiest railroad hubs?

CONNECTIONS: How did the expansion of railroad networks affect the American economy? Why was the U.S. government willing to grant more than twenty million acres of public land to the private corporations that ran the railroads?

FOR MORE HELP ANALYZING THIS MAP, see the map activity for this chapter in the Online Study Guide at bedfordstmartins.com/roark.

highway, and canal projects. In 1850, Congress approved a precedent-setting grant to railroads of six square miles of federal land for each mile of track laid. By 1860, Congress had granted railroads more than twenty million acres of federal land, thereby underwriting construction costs and promoting the expansion of the rail network, the settlement of federal land, and the integration of the domestic market.

The railroad boom of the 1850s signaled the growing industrial might of the American economy. But railroads, like other industries, succeeded because they served both farms and cities. Older forms of transportation remained significant. By 1857, for example, trains carried only about one-third of the mail; most of the rest still went by stagecoach or horseback. In 1860, most Americans were far more familiar with horses than with locomotives.

Westward the Star of Empire Takes Its Way—near Council Bluffs, Iowa
This painting by Andrew Melrose depicts the mid–nineteenth-century landscape of agricultural and technological progress. On the right, the dark forest is boldly transformed by railroad tracks that interrupt the irregularity of nature with a level roadbed and straight iron rails. A hard-charging locomotive illuminates the path of progress and bears down on a group of innocent deer frightened by the unstoppable industrial power so alien to their familiar natural world. On the left, a frontier family stands in the shadow of their log cabin, surveying their progress in clearing trees to transform forest into fields. Their cozy domestication of nature, suggested by the grazing milk cows, the laundry hanging to the left of the cabin, and the smoke rising from the chimney, is linked to the urban and industrial world beyond their gaze by the cinder-spouting locomotive that passes along the edge of their clearing, making their farm economically and culturally far more valuable than the untamed nature on the other side of the tracks. Notice that the family is not watching the natural beauty of the rising or setting sun to the left, but instead the artificial blaze of the locomotive's headlight.
Museum of the American West, Autry National Center, 92.147.1.

READING THE IMAGE: How does the artist use light to suggest the environment of progress? How are trees depicted in this painting?
CONNECTIONS: What messages about nature and progress does the artist suggest? How does the title of the painting contribute to your understanding of this message?

FOR MORE HELP ANALYZING THIS IMAGE, see the visual activity for this chapter in the Online Study Guide at bedfordstmartins.com/roark.

The economy of the 1840s and 1850s linked an expanding, westward-moving population in farms and cities with muscles, animals, machines, steam, and railroads. Abraham Lincoln cut trees, planted corn, and split rails as a young man before he moved to Springfield, Illinois, and became a successful attorney who defended, among others, railroad corporations. His mobility—westward, from farm to city, from manual to mental labor, and upward—illustrated the direction of economic change and the opportunities that beckoned enterprising individuals.

> **REVIEW** Why did the United States become a leading industrial power in the nineteenth century?

The Telegraph: The "Wonder Working Wire"

The telegraph played as important a role as the railroad in opening the West and uniting the nation. Telegraph wires often paralleled railroad lines, and the two developments were allies in the nineteenth-century communications revolution. Both delivered what nineteenth-century Americans craved—speed and efficiency and the ability to overcome vast distances.

Samuel F. B. Morse is credited with inventing the telegraph because of his patent of June 20, 1840, but, as is the case with many inventions, the assumption of "one man, one invention" exaggerates the contribution of a single individual. The telegraph grew out of scientific knowledge gradually acquired in the eighteenth and nineteenth centuries by a number of scientists, especially André Ampère of France, Alessandro Volta of Italy, and Joseph Henry of the United States, who pioneered in the field of electromagnetism and experimented with sending electrical signals through wires.

Morse was no scientist—he was an acclaimed painter—but beginning in the early 1830s, he devoted himself to creating a machine that transmitted messages electrically. As one contemporary observed, Morse's talent consisted of "combining and applying the discoveries of others in the invention of a particular instrument and process for telegraphic purposes." This was no small achievement. In addition, Morse's system depended on a code he devised that represented each letter and number with dots and dashes. With a series of taps on a telegraph key, operators sent short and long pulses of electricity—a dash was three times as long as a dot. At the receiver's end, the code was originally written out by an electrically activated stylus on a moving strip of paper and then read off. But soon skilled operators found that by listening to the taps, they could interpret the message and write it down. Morse code became the universal language of the telegraph.

The breakthrough moment for Morse's invention came in 1842 when Congress voted $30,000 to build an experimental line between Washington, D.C., and Baltimore. Four years earlier, a congressional report had declared that if Morse's invention succeeded, "space will be, to all practical purposes of information, completely annihilated between the States of the Union." Congress was eager to find out whether the invention would work. Morse strung the line, and from the Supreme Court in Washington on May 22, 1844, he tapped out a biblical phrase. In Baltimore, forty-one miles away, a receiver transcribed: "What hath God wrought!" The trial was a stunning technical success, as well as a public relations coup, for the entire nation stood awed by the speed and precision of the "wonder working wire."

Free Labor: Promise and Reality

The nation's impressive economic performance did not reward all Americans equally. Native-born white men tended to do better than immigrants. With few exceptions, women were excluded from opportunities open to men. Tens of thousands of women worked as seamstresses, laundresses, domestic servants, factory hands, and teachers but had little opportunity to aspire to higher-paying jobs. In the North and West, slavery was slowly eliminated in the half century after the American Revolution, but most free African Americans were relegated to dead-end jobs as laborers and servants. Discrimination against immigrants, women, and free blacks did not trouble most white men. With certain notable exceptions, they considered it proper and just.

The Free-Labor Ideal: Freedom plus Labor

During the 1840s and 1850s, leaders throughout the North and West emphasized a set of ideas that seemed to explain why the changes under way in their society benefited some people more than others. They referred again and again to the advantages of what they termed **free labor**. (The word *free* referred to laborers who were not slaves. It did not mean laborers who worked for

The telegraph spread almost as swiftly as news of its existence. By 1846, most eastern cities were connected by telegraph. By 1850, of the states east of the Mississippi River, only Florida remained without it. More than fifty thousand miles of wires webbed the nation by 1861, when the telegraph reached California. Despite the cost—initially, an astronomical $1 a word—the line between San Francisco and the East chattered with dots and dashes.

The telegraph obliterated distance, and cheap, efficient, and fast communication changed American businesses, newspapers, government, and everyday life. The telegraph made it possible to synchronize clocks, which in turn allowed railroads to run safely according to precise schedules. Businesses of every kind could send and receive information and orders almost instantaneously. Investors from across the country could learn the latest stock prices from the New York Stock Exchange. Newspapers could gather information from around the country and have it in the headlines within hours. As early as 1848, Americans followed the war in Mexico from reports brought not by messengers on horseback or on ships, but by the magical wire. After 1866, when an underwater transatlantic cable linked Europe and the United States, the federal government used the telegraph to monitor international affairs and to respond swiftly to crises. On a personal level, families scattered across the continent could communicate more quickly than letter writing allowed. The telegraph met the needs of the vigorous, sprawling nation.

It is one thing to conceive of and build an innovative device. It is another to develop the idea into a profitable business. Unlike Eli Whitney, who made little from his invention of the cotton gin, Morse was a skilled entrepreneur who grew rich from his invention. Patent rights, which he defended vigorously and successfully, allowed the Morse telegraph to dominate the United States and most of the non-British world. Morse's technology made him wealthy and worked powerfully to draw the far-flung young nation together, even as it began to pull apart politically.

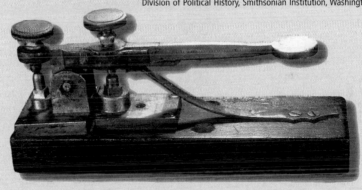

Telegraph Transmitter
This is Samuel Morse's telegraph key—the one that sent the first message in 1844.
Division of Political History, Smithsonian Institution, Washington, D.C.

nothing.) By the 1850s, free-labor ideas described a social and economic ideal that accounted for both the successes and the shortcomings of the economy and society taking shape in the North and West.

Free-labor spokesmen celebrated hard work, self-reliance, and independence. They proclaimed that the door to success was open not just to those who inherited wealth or status but also to self-made men such as Abraham Lincoln. Free labor, Lincoln argued, was "the just and generous, and prosperous system, which opens the way for all—gives hope to all, and energy, and progress, and improvement of condition to all." Free labor permitted farmers and artisans to enjoy the products of their own labor, and it also benefited wageworkers. "The prudent, penniless beginner in the world," Lincoln asserted, "labors for wages awhile, saves a surplus with which to buy tools or land, for himself; then labors on his own account another while, and at length hires another new beginner to help him." Wage labor was the first rung on the ladder toward eventual self-employment and hiring others.

The free-labor ideal affirmed an egalitarian vision of human potential. Lincoln and other spokesmen stressed the importance of universal education to permit "heads and hands [to] cooperate as friends." (See "Global Comparison," page 404.)

> Free labor, Abraham Lincoln argued, was "the just and generous, and prosperous system, which opens the way for all."

GLOBAL COMPARISON

Nineteenth-Century School Enrollment and Literacy Rates

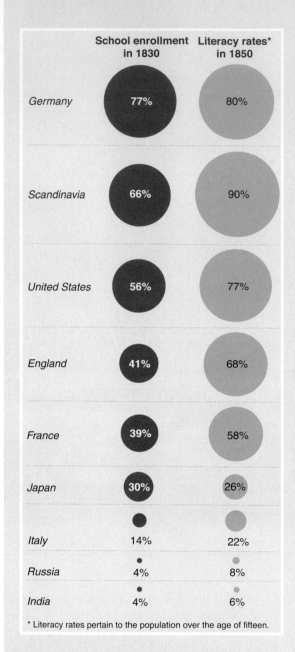

	School enrollment in 1830	Literacy rates* in 1850
Germany	77%	80%
Scandinavia	66%	90%
United States	56%	77%
England	41%	68%
France	39%	58%
Japan	30%	26%
Italy	14%	22%
Russia	4%	8%
India	4%	6%

* Literacy rates pertain to the population over the age of fifteen.

In the first half of the nineteenth century, school enrollment and literacy rates in northern and western Europe and the United States were high compared to those in the rest of the world. U.S. figures would be even higher but for the South, where less than 10 percent of black slaves were literate and whites were less likely to attend school than in the North. The ability to read and write facilitates communication, business transactions, acquisition of skills, and perhaps even greater openness to change, all building blocks of rapid economic growth. But mass literacy has not always been a prerequisite for economic development. When England underwent industrialization between 1780 and 1830, less than half of the nation's children attended school. By 1850, England was the world's greatest industrial power, but where did it rank in literacy? Literacy levels may actually have fallen in Lancashire, a region of England that experienced great industrial growth, as children went to work in factories rather than attend school.

Throughout the North and West, communities supported public schools to make the rudiments of learning available to young children. By 1860, many cities and towns boasted that up to 80 percent of children ages seven to thirteen attended school at least for a few weeks each year. In rural areas, where the labor of children was more difficult to spare, schools typically enrolled no more than half the school-age chil-

dren. Lessons included more than arithmetic, penmanship, and a smattering of other subjects. Textbooks and teachers—most of whom were young women—drummed into students the lessons of the free-labor system: self-reliance, discipline, and, above all else, hard work. "Remember that all the ignorance, degradation, and misery in the world is the result of indolence and vice," one textbook intoned. In school and out, free-labor ideology emphasized labor as much as freedom.

Economic Inequality

The free-labor ideal made sense to many Americans, especially in the North and West, because it seemed to describe their own experiences. Lincoln frequently referred to his humble beginnings as a hired laborer and implicitly invited his listeners to consider how far he had come. In 1860, his wealth of $17,000 easily placed him in the top 5 percent of the population. The opportunities presented by the expanding economy made a few men much, much richer. In 1860, the nation had about forty millionaires. Most Americans, however, measured success in far more modest terms. The average wealth of adult white men in the North in 1860 barely topped $2,000. Nearly half of American men had no wealth at all; about 60 percent owned no land. Because property possessed by married women was normally considered to belong to their husbands, women had less wealth than men. Free African Americans had still less; 90 percent of them were propertyless.

Free-labor spokesmen considered these economic inequalities a natural outgrowth of freedom—the inevitable result of some individuals being more able and willing to work and luckier. These inequalities also demonstrate the gap between the promise and the performance of the free-labor ideal. Economic growth permitted many men to move from being landless squatters to landowning farmers and from being hired laborers to independent, self-employed producers. But many more Americans remained behind, landless and working for wages. Even those who realized their aspirations often had a precarious hold on their independence. Bad debts, market volatility, crop failure, sickness, or death could quickly eliminate a family's gains.

Seeking out new opportunities in pursuit of free-labor ideals created restless social and geographic mobility. Whereas fortunate people such as Abraham Lincoln rose far beyond their social origins, others shared the misfortune of a merchant who, an observer noted, "has been on the sinking list all his life." In search of better prospects, roughly two-thirds of the rural population moved every decade, and population turnover in cities was even greater. This constant coming and going weakened community ties to neighbors and friends and threw individuals even more on their own resources in times of trouble.

Miner with Pick, Pan, and Shovel
This young man exhibits the spirit of individual effort that was the foundation of free-labor ideals. Posing with a pick and shovel to loosen gold-bearing deposits and a pan to wash away debris, the man appears determined to succeed as a miner by his own muscles and sweat. Hard work with these tools, the picture suggests, promised rewards and maybe riches.
Collection of Matthew Isenburg.

Immigrants and the Free-Labor Ladder

The risks and uncertainties of free labor did not deter millions of immigrants from entering the United States during the 1840s and 1850s. Almost 4.5 million immigrants arrived between 1840 and 1860, six times more than had come during the previous two decades (Figure 12.1, page 406). The half million immigrants who came in 1854 accounted for nearly 2 percent of the entire U.S. population, a higher proportion than in any other single year of the nation's history. By 1860, foreign-born residents made up about one-eighth of the U.S. population, a fraction that held steady well into the twentieth century.

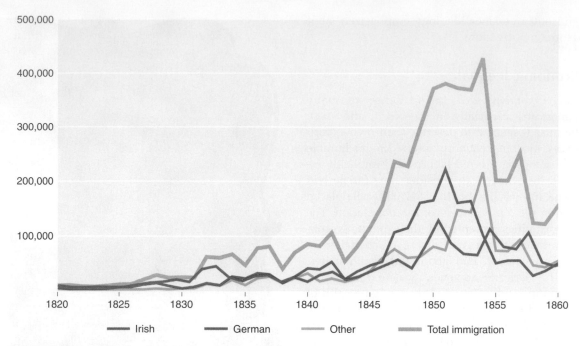

FIGURE 12.1 Antebellum Immigration, 1820–1860
After increasing gradually for several decades, immigration shot up in the mid-1840s.
Between 1848 and 1860, nearly 3.5 million immigrants entered the United States.

Irish Laborer

Landless, jobless, often uneducated, and confronting famine in Ireland, tens of thousands of Irish laborers, like the young man photographed here, immigrated to the United States in the 1850s. They frequently encountered anti-Irish prejudice, as indicated by the title of the sheet music shown here, because of their appearance, language, religion, and what respectable folk considered their rowdy habits. Undeterred, most Irish immigrants found jobs as day laborers and domestic servants, and formed thriving communities in many American cities.

Photo: Unknown photographer, from "Ireland in Old Photos" compiled by Sean Sexton, Bullfinch Press Book © 1994; Music: Special Collections, Milton S. Eisenhower Library, The Johns Hopkins University.

Nearly three out of four immigrants who arrived in the United States between 1840 and 1860 came from Germany or Ireland. The vast majority of the 1.4 million Germans who entered during these years were skilled tradesmen and their families. They left Germany to escape deteriorating economic conditions, and they had little difficulty finding work in the expanding U.S. economy. German immigrants settled most heavily in the Midwest. German butchers, bakers, beer makers, carpenters, shopkeepers, machinists, and others tended to congregate in cities. Roughly a quarter of German immigrants were farmers, most of whom scattered throughout the Midwest, although some settled in Texas. On the whole, German Americans settled into that middle stratum of sturdy independent producers celebrated by free-labor spokesmen; relatively few Germans occupied the bottom rung of the free-labor ladder as wage laborers or domestic servants.

Irish immigrants, in contrast, entered at the bottom of the free-labor ladder and struggled to climb up. Nearly 1.7 million Irish immigrants arrived between 1840 and 1860, nearly all of them desperately poor and often weakened by hunger and disease. Potato blight struck Ireland in 1845 and returned repeatedly in subsequent years, spreading a catastrophic famine throughout the island. Many of the lucky ones, half-starved, crowded into the holds of ships and set out for America, where they congregated in northeastern cities. As one immigrant group declared, "All we want is to get out of Ireland; we must be better anywhere than here." Death trailed after them. So many died crossing the Atlantic that ships from Ireland were often termed "coffin ships."

Roughly three out of four Irish immigrants worked as laborers or domestic servants. Irish men dug canals, loaded ships, laid railroad track, and took what other work they could find. Irish women hired out to cook, wash and iron, mind children, and clean house. Almost all Irish immigrants were Catholic, a fact that set them apart from the overwhelmingly **Protestant** native-born residents. Many natives regarded the Irish as hard-drinking, obstreperous, half-civilized folk. Such views lay behind the discrimination reflected in job announcements that commonly stated, "No Irish need apply." Despite such prejudices, native residents hired Irish immigrants because they accepted low pay and worked hard.

In America's labor-poor economy, Irish laborers could earn more in one day than in several weeks in Ireland, if they could find work there. In America, one immigrant explained in 1853, there was "plenty of work and plenty of wages plenty to eat and no land lords thats enough what more does a man want." But some immigrants wanted more, especially respect and decent working conditions. One immigrant complained that he was "a slave for the Americans as the generality of the Irish . . . are."

Such testimony illustrates that the free-labor system, whether for immigrants or native-born laborers, often did not live up to the optimistic vision outlined by Abraham Lincoln and others. Many wage laborers could not realistically aspire to become independent, self-sufficient property holders, despite the claims of free-labor proponents.

> **REVIEW** How did the free-labor ideal account for economic inequality?

The Westward Movement

In the 1840s, the nation's swelling population, booming economy, and boundless confidence propelled a new era of rapid westward migration. Until then, the overwhelming majority of Americans lived east of the Mississippi River. Native Americans inhabited the plains, deserts, and rugged coasts to the west. The British claimed the Oregon Country, and the Mexican flag flew over the vast expanse of the Southwest. But by 1850, the boundaries of the United States stretched to the Pacific, and the nation had more than doubled in size. By 1860, the great migration had carried four million Americans west of the Mississippi River.

Frontier settlers took the land and then, with the exception of the Mormons, lobbied their government to acquire the territory they had settled. The human cost of aggressive expansionism was high. The young Mexican nation lost a war and half of its territory. Two centuries of Indian wars east of the Mississippi ended during the 1830s, but the fierce struggle between native inhabitants and invaders continued for another half century in the West. Americans believed it was their destiny to conquer the continent.

> In America, one immigrant explained in 1853, there was "plenty of work and plenty of wages plenty to eat and no land lords thats enough what more does a man want."

Manifest Destiny

Most Americans believed that the superiority of their institutions and white **culture** bestowed on them a God-given right to spread their civilization across the continent. They imagined the West as a howling wilderness, empty and undeveloped. If they recognized Indians and Mexicans at all, they dismissed them as primitive drags on progress who would have to be redeemed, shoved aside, or exterminated. The West provided young men

***Cathedral Forest,* by Albert Bierstadt**
Born and trained in Germany, Albert Bierstadt visited the American West for the first time in 1859 with a U.S. government expedition searching for shortcuts through the Rocky Mountains. The West captured his imagination. In a series of monumental paintings, he portrayed a new Eden, an epic landscape of spectacular beauty and unlimited economic potential that silently beckoned a restless, questing young nation. Here, cloud-piercing giant sequoias dwarf the tiny figures in their midst. Some easterners gave thanks for Providence's gift of magnificent natural cathedrals; others calculated the board feet of lumber in a single tree. Images such as this inspired both tourists and entrepreneurs to head west.
Private Collection/Art Resource, NY.

especially an arena in which to "show their manhood." The sense of uniqueness and mission was as old as the Puritans, but by the 1840s, the conviction of superiority had been bolstered by the United States' amazing success. Most Americans believed that the West needed the civilizing power of the hammer and the plow, the ballot box and the pulpit, which had transformed the East.

In 1845, a New York political journal edited by John L. O'Sullivan coined the term **manifest destiny** as the latest justification for white settlers to take the land they coveted. O'Sullivan called on Americans to resist any foreign power—British, French, or Mexican—that attempted to thwart "the fulfillment of our manifest destiny to overspread the continent allotted by Providence for the free development of our yearly multiplying millions . . . [and] for the development of the great experiment of liberty and federative self-government entrusted to us." Almost overnight, the magic phrase *manifest destiny* swept the nation and provided an ideological shield for conquering the West.

As important as national pride and racial arrogance were to manifest destiny, economic gain made up its core. Land hunger drew hundreds of thousands of average Americans westward. Some politicians, moreover, had become convinced that national prosperity depended on capturing the rich trade of the Far East. To trade with Asia, the United States needed the Pacific coast ports that stretched from San Diego to Puget Sound. No one was more eager to extend American trade in the Pacific than Missouri senator Thomas Hart Benton. "The sun of civilization must shine across the sea: socially and commercially," he declared. The United States and Asia must "talk together, and trade together. Commerce is a great civilizer." In the 1840s, American economic expansion came wrapped in the rhetoric of uplift and civilization.

Oregon and the Overland Trail

The Oregon Country—a vast region bounded on the west by the Pacific Ocean, on the east by the Rocky Mountains, on the south by the forty-second parallel, and on the north by Russian Alaska—caused the pulse of American expansionists to race. But the British also coveted the area. They argued that their claim lay with Sir Francis Drake's discovery of the Oregon coast in 1579. Americans countered with historic claims of their own. Unable to agree, the United States and Great Britain decided in 1818 on "joint occupation" that would leave Oregon "free and open" to settlement by both countries. A handful of American fur traders and "mountain men" roamed the region in the 1820s, but expansionists soon made the Oregon Country an early target of manifest destiny.

By the late 1830s, settlers began to trickle along the Oregon Trail, following a path blazed by the mountain men (Map 12.2). The first wagon trains headed west in 1841, and by 1843 about 1,000 emigrants a year set out from

Independence, Missouri. By 1869, when the first transcontinental railroad was completed, approximately 350,000 migrants had traveled west to the Pacific in wagon trains.

Emigrants encountered the Plains Indians, a quarter of a million Native Americans who populated the area between the Rocky Mountains and the Mississippi River. Some were farmers who lived peaceful, sedentary lives, but a majority—the Sioux, Cheyenne, Shoshoni, and Arapaho of the central plains and the Kiowa, Wichita, and Comanche of the southern plains— were horse-mounted, nomadic, nonagricultural peoples whose warriors symbolized the "savage Indian" in the minds of whites.

Horses, which had been brought to North America by Spaniards in the sixteenth century, permitted the Plains tribes to become highly mobile hunters of buffalo. They came to depend on buffalo for nearly everything—food, clothing,

shelter, and fuel. Competition for buffalo led to war between the tribes. Young men were introduced to warfare early, learning to ride ponies at breakneck speed while firing off arrows and, later, rifles with astounding accuracy. "A Comanche on his feet is out of his element," observed western artist George Catlin, "but the moment he lays his hands upon his horse, his *face* even becomes handsome, and he gracefully flies away like a different being."

The Plains Indians struck fear in the hearts of whites on the wagon trains. But Native Americans had far more to

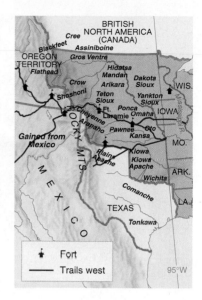

Plains Indians and Trails West in the 1840s and 1850s

MAP 12.2 Major Trails West

In the 1830s, wagon trains began snaking their way to the Southwest and the Pacific coast. Deep ruts, some of which can still be seen today, soon marked the most popular routes.

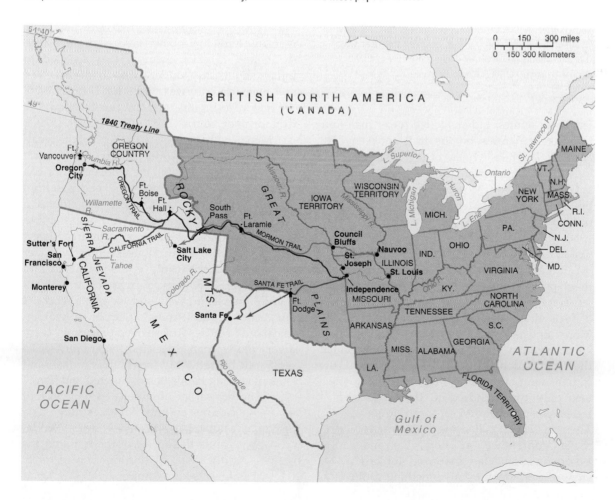

Kee-O-Kuk, the Watchful Fox, Chief of the Tribe, George Catlin, 1835
In the 1830s, Pennsylvania-born artist George Catlin traveled the West painting Native American portraits, rituals, and landscapes. Though not the first artist to paint Indians, he was the first to portray them in their own environments and one of the few to present them as human beings, not savages. Convinced that western Indian cultures would soon disappear, Catlin sought to document Indian life through hundreds of paintings and prints. Keokuk, chief of the Sauk and Fox, struggled with the warrior Black Hawk (see chapter 11) about the proper strategy for dealing with whites. Black Hawk fought American expansion; Keokuk believed that war was fruitless and signed over land in Illinois, Missouri, and Wisconsin.
Smithsonian American Art Institution, Washington, D.C. Gift of Mrs. Joseph Harrison Jr.

be done to protect them from the ravages of the wagon trains. Instead, U.S. government negotiators persuaded the chiefs to sign agreements that cleared a wide corridor for wagon trains by restricting Native Americans to specific areas that whites promised they would never violate. This policy of concentration became the seedbed for the subsequent policy of reservations. But whites would not keep out of Indian territory, and Indians would not easily give up their traditional ways of life. Struggle for control of the West meant warfare for decades to come.

Still, Indians threatened emigrants less than life on the trail did. The men, women, and children who headed west each spring could count on at least six months of grueling travel. With nearly two thousand miles to go and traveling no more than fifteen miles a day, the pioneers endured parching heat, drought, treacherous rivers, disease, physical and emotional exhaustion, and, if the snows closed the mountain passes before they got through, freezing and starvation. Women sometimes faced the dangers of trailside childbirth. It was said that a person could walk from Missouri to the Pacific stepping only on the graves of those who had died heading west. Such tribulations led one miserable woman, trying to keep her children dry in a rainstorm and to calm them as they listened to Indian shouts, to wonder "what had possessed my husband, anyway, that he should have thought of bringing us away out through this God forsaken country."

Men usually found Oregon "one of the greatest countries in the world." From "the Cascade mountains to the Pacific, the whole country can be cultivated," exclaimed one eager settler. When women reached Oregon, they found a wilderness. Neighbors were few and far between, and things were in a "primitive state." One young wife set up housekeeping with her new husband with only one stew kettle and three knives. Necessity blurred the traditional division between men's and women's work. "I am maid of all traids," one busy woman remarked in 1853. Work seemed unending. "I am a very old woman," declared twenty-nine-year-old Sarah Everett. "My face is thin sunken and wrinkled, my hands bony withered and hard." Another settler observed, "A woman that can not endure almost as much as a horse has no business here." Yet despite the ordeal of the trail and the difficulties of starting from scratch, emigrants kept coming.

fear from whites. Indians killed fewer than four hundred emigrants on the trail between 1840 and 1860, while whites brought alcohol and deadly epidemics of smallpox, measles, cholera, and scarlet fever. Moreover, whites killed the buffalo, often slaughtering them for sport. The buffalo still numbered some twelve million in 1860, but the herds were shrinking rapidly, intensifying conflict among the Plains tribes.

Emigrants insisted that the federal government provide them with more protection. The government responded by constructing a chain of forts along the Oregon Trail (see Map 12.2). More important, it adopted a new Indian policy: "concentration." First, the government rescinded the "permanent" buffer it had granted the Indians west of the ninety-fifth meridian, which was only two hundred to three hundred miles west of the Mississippi River. Then, in 1851, it called the Plains tribes to a conference at Fort Laramie, Wyoming. Some ten thousand Indians showed up, hopeful that something could

Pioneer Family on the Trail West

In 1860, W. G. Chamberlain photographed these unidentified travelers momentarily at rest by the upper Arkansas River in Colorado. We do not know their fates, but we can only hope that they fared better than the Sager family. Henry and Naomi Sager and their six children set out from St. Joseph, Missouri, in 1844. "Father," one of Henry and Naomi's daughters remembered, "was one of those restless men who are not content to remain in one place long at a time. [He] had been talking of going to Texas. But mother, hearing much said about the healthfulness of Oregon, preferred to go there." Still far from Oregon, Henry Sager died of fever. Twenty-six days later, Naomi died, leaving seven children, the last delivered on the trail. The Sager children, under the care of other families in the wagon train, pressed on. After traveling two thousand miles in seven months, the migrants arrived in Oregon, where Marcus and Narcissa Whitman, whose own daughter had drowned, adopted all seven of the Sager children. Denver Public Library, Western History Division # F3226.

READING THE IMAGE: Based on this photograph, what were some of the difficulties faced by pioneers traveling west?

CONNECTIONS: How did wagon trains change the western United States?

FOR MORE HELP ANALYZING THIS IMAGE, see the visual activity for this chapter in the Online Study Guide at bedfordstmartins.com/roark.

The Mormon Exodus

Not every wagon train heading west was bound for the Pacific Slope. One remarkable group of religious emigrants halted near the Great Salt Lake in what was then Mexican territory. The Mormons deliberately chose the remote site as a refuge. After years of persecution in the East, they fled west to find religious freedom and communal security.

In 1830, Joseph Smith Jr., who was only twenty-four, published *The Book of Mormon* and founded the Church of Jesus Christ of Latter-Day Saints (the Mormons). A decade earlier, the upstate New York farm boy had begun to experience revelations that were followed, he said, by a visit from an angel who led him to golden tablets buried near his home. With the aid of magic stones, Smith translated the mysterious language on the tablets to produce *The Book of Mormon*. It told the story of an ancient Hebrew civilization in the New World and predicted the appearance of an American prophet who would reestablish Jesus Christ's undefiled kingdom in America. Converts, attracted to the promise of a pure faith in the midst of **antebellum** America's social turmoil and rampant materialism, flocked to the new church.

Neighbors branded Mormons heretics and drove Smith and his followers from New York to Ohio, then to Missouri, and finally in 1839 to Nauvoo, Illinois, where they built a prosperous community. But a rift in the church developed after Smith sanctioned "plural marriage" (polygamy). Non-Mormons caught wind of the controversy and eventually arrested Smith and his brother. On June 27, 1844, a mob stormed the jail and shot both men dead.

The embattled church turned to an extraordinary new leader, Brigham Young, who immediately began to plan a great exodus. In 1846, traveling in 3,700 wagons, 12,000 Mormons made their way to eastern Iowa. The following year, they arrived at their new home beside the Great Salt Lake. Young described the region as a barren waste, "the paradise of the lizard, the cricket and the rattlesnake." Within ten years, however, the Mormons developed an irrigation system that made the desert bloom. They accomplished the feat through cooperative labor, not the individualistic and competitive enterprise common among most emigrants. Under Young's stern leadership, the Mormons built a thriving community.

In 1850, the Mormon kingdom was annexed to the United States as Utah Territory. The nation's attention focused on Utah in 1852 when Brigham Young announced that many Mormons practiced polygamy. Although only one Mormon man in five had more than one wife (Young had twenty-three), Young's statement caused a popular outcry that forced the U.S. government to establish its authority in Utah. In 1857, 2,500 U.S. troops invaded Salt Lake City in what was known as the Mormon War. The bloodless occupation illustrates that most Americans viewed the Mormons as a threat to American morality, law, and institutions. The invasion did not dislodge the Mormon Church from its central place in Utah, however, and for years to come, most Americans perceived the Mormon settlement as strange and suitably isolated.

The Mexican Borderlands

In the Mexican Southwest, westward-moving Anglo-American pioneers confronted northern-moving Spanish-speaking frontiersmen. On this frontier as elsewhere, national cultures, interests, and aspirations collided. Since 1821, when Mexico won its independence from Spain, the Mexican flag had flown over the vast expanse that stretched from the Gulf of Mexico to the Pacific and from the Oregon Country to Guatemala (Map 12.3). Mexico's borders remained ill defined, and its northern provinces were sparsely populated. Moreover, severe problems plagued the young nation: civil wars, economic crises, quarrels with the Roman Catholic Church, and devastating raids by the Comanche, Apache, and Kiowa. Mexico found it increasingly difficult to defend its borderlands, especially when faced with a northern neighbor convinced of its superiority and bent on territorial acquisition.

The American assault began quietly. In the 1820s, Anglo-American trappers, traders, and settlers drifted into Mexico's far northern provinces. Santa Fe, a remote outpost in the province of New Mexico, became a magnet for American enterprise. Each spring, American traders gathered at Independence, Missouri, for the long trek southwest along the Santa

MAP 12.3 Texas and Mexico in the 1830s
As Americans spilled into lightly populated and loosely governed northern Mexico, Texas and then other Mexican provinces became contested territory.

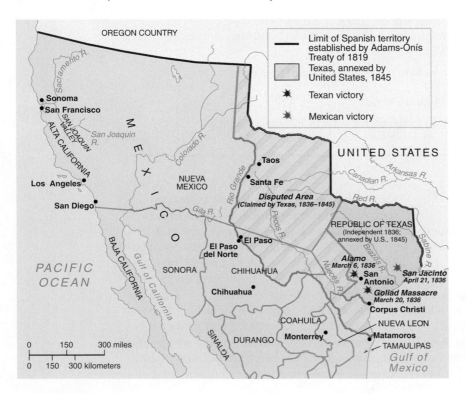

***Fandango,* by Theodore Gentilz, 1844**
Although Spanish and Mexican authorities failed to entice many Hispanic settlers to distant provinces such as Texas, a small and resourceful Tejano community managed to develop a ranching economy in the harsh frontier conditions. The largest Hispanic population was concentrated in the vicinity of San Antonio, where settlers reproduced as best they could the cultural traditions they carried with them. Here, a group of animated, well-dressed men and women perform a Spanish dance called the fandango while musicians play in triple time.
Daughters of the Republic of Texas Library, Alamo Collection.

Fe Trail (see Map 12.2). They crammed their wagons with inexpensive American manufactured goods and returned home with Mexican silver, furs, and mules.

The Mexican province of Texas attracted a flood of Americans who had settlement, not long-distance trade, on their minds (see Map 12.3). Wanting to populate and develop its northern territory, the Mexican government granted the American Stephen F. Austin a huge tract of land along the Brazos River. In the 1820s, Austin became the first Anglo-American *empresario* (colonization agent) in Texas, offering land at only ten cents an acre. Thousands of Americans poured across the border. Most were Southerners who brought cotton and slaves with them.

By the 1830s, the settlers had established a thriving plantation economy in Texas. Americans numbered 35,000, while the *Tejano* (Spanish-speaking) population was less than 8,000. Few Anglo-American settlers were Roman Catholic, spoke Spanish, or cared about assimilating into Mexican culture. Afraid of losing Texas to the new arrivals, the Mexican government in 1830 banned further immigration to Texas from the United States and outlawed the introduction of additional slaves. The Anglo-Americans complained loudly and made it increasingly clear that they wanted to be rid of the "despotism of the sword and the priesthood" and to govern themselves. In Mexico City, however, General Antonio López de Santa Anna seized political power and set about restoring order to the northern frontier.

Faced with what they considered tyranny, the Texan settlers rebelled. Santa Anna ordered the Mexican army northward and in February 1836 arrived at the outskirts of San Antonio.

Texas War for Independence, 1836

Commanded by Colonel William B. Travis from Alabama, the rebels included the Tennessee frontiersman David Crockett and the Louisiana adventurer James Bowie, as well as a handful of Tejanos. They took refuge in a former Franciscan mission known as the Alamo. Santa Anna sent wave after wave of his 2,000-man army crashing against the walls until the attackers finally broke through and killed all 187 rebels. A few weeks later, outside the small town of Goliad, Mexican forces surrounded and captured a garrison of Texans. Following orders from Santa Anna, Mexican firing squads executed almost 400 of the men as "pirates and outlaws." In April 1836, at San Jacinto, General Sam Houston's army adopted the massacre of Goliad as a battle cry and crushed Santa Anna's troops in a predawn attack. The Texans had succeeded in establishing the Lone Star Republic, and the following year, the United States recognized the independence of Texas from Mexico.

Earlier, in 1824, in an effort to increase Mexican migration to the thinly settled province of California, the Mexican government granted *ranchos*—huge estates devoted to cattle raising—to new settlers. *Rancheros* ruled over near-feudal empires worked by Indians whose condition sometimes approached that of slaves. Not satisfied, the *rancheros* coveted the vast lands controlled by the Franciscan missions. In 1834, they persuaded the Mexican government to confiscate the missions and make their lands available to new settlement, a development that accelerated the decline of the California Indians. Devastated by disease, the Indians, who had numbered approximately 300,000 when the Spanish arrived in 1769, had declined to half that number by 1846.

Despite the efforts of the Mexican government, California in 1840 counted a population of only 7,000 Mexican settlers. Non-Mexican settlers numbered only 380, but among them were Americans who championed manifest destiny. They sought to woo American emigrants to California. In the 1840s, wagon after wagon left the Oregon Trail to head southwest on the California Trail (see Map 12.2). As the trickle of Americans became a river, Mexican officials grew alarmed. As a New York newspaper put it in 1845, "Let the tide of emigration flow toward California and the American population will soon be sufficiently numerous to play the Texas game." Only a few Americans in California wanted a war for independence, but many dreamed of living again under the U.S. flag.

The U.S. government made no secret of its desire to acquire California. In 1835, President Andrew Jackson tried unsuccessfully to purchase it. In 1846, American settlers in the Sacramento Valley took matters into their own hands. Prodded by John C. Frémont, a former army captain and explorer who had arrived with a party of sixty buckskin-clad frontiersmen spoiling for a fight, the Californians raised an independence movement known as the Bear Flag Revolt. By then, James K. Polk, a champion of aggressive expansion, sat in the White House.

REVIEW   Why did westward migration expand dramatically in the mid-nineteenth century?

Expansion and the Mexican-American War

Although emigrants acted as the advance guard of American empire, there was nothing automatic about the U.S. annexation of territory in the West. Acquiring territory required political action. In the 1840s, the politics of expansion became entangled with sectionalism and the slavery question. Texas, Oregon, and the Mexican borderlands thrust the United States into dangerous diplomatic crises with Great Britain and Mexico.

Aggravation between Mexico and the United States escalated to open antagonism in 1845 when the United States annexed Texas. Absorbing territory still claimed by Mexico ruptured diplomatic relations between the two countries and set the stage for war. But it was President James K. Polk's insistence on having Mexico's other northern provinces that made war certain. The war was not as easy as Polk anticipated, but it ended in American victory and the acquisition of a new American West.

The Politics of Expansion

Texans had sought admission to the Union almost since winning their independence from Mexico in 1836. Almost constant border warfare between Mexico and the Republic of Texas in the decade following the revolution underscored the precarious nature of independence. Any suggestion of adding another slave state to the Union outraged most Northerners, however. Although Northerners applauded westward expansion, they imagined the expansion of American liberty, not the spread of slavery. Annexing Texas also risked precipitating war, because Mexico had never relinquished its claim to its lost province.

President John Tyler, who became president in April 1841 when William Henry Harrison died one month after taking office, understood that Texas was a dangerous issue. Adding to the danger, Great Britain began sniffing around Texas, apparently contemplating adding the young republic to its growing empire. Tyler, an ardent expansionist, decided to risk annexing the Lone Star Republic.

In April 1844, John C. Calhoun, Tyler's secretary of state, laid an annexation treaty before the Senate. But when Calhoun linked annexation to the defense of slavery, he doomed the treaty. Howls of protest erupted across the North. In Massachusetts, future senator Charles Sumner deplored the "insidious" plan to annex Texas and carve from it "great slaveholding states." The Senate soundly rejected the treaty, and it appeared that Tyler had succeeded only in inflaming sectional conflict. In Texas, one newspaper observed that a "general gloom seems to rest over every section of the Republic."

The issue of Texas had not died down by the 1844 election. In an effort to appeal to northern voters, the Whig nominee for president, Henry Clay, came out against the immediate annexation of Texas. "Annexation and war with Mexico are identical," he declared. The Democrats chose Tennessean James K. Polk, who was as strongly in favor of the annexation of Texas as Clay was against it. To make annexation palatable to Northerners, the Democrats shrewdly yoked Texas to Oregon, thus tapping the desire for expansion in the free states of the North as well as in the slave states of the South. The Democratic platform called for the "reannexation of Texas" and the "reoccupation of Oregon." The suggestion that the United States was merely reasserting existing rights was poor history but good politics.

When Clay finally recognized the popularity of expansion, he waffled, hinting that under certain circumstances, he might accept the annexation of Texas. His retreat won little support in the South and succeeded only in alienating antislavery opinion in the North. James G. Birney, the candidate of the fledgling Liberty Party, picked up the votes of thousands of disillusioned Clay supporters. In the November election, Polk received 170 electoral votes and Clay 105. New York's 35 electoral votes proved critical to Clay's defeat. A shift of just one-third of Birney's 15,000 votes to Clay would have given Clay the state and the presidency.

On March 4, 1845, in his inaugural address, Polk confirmed his faith in America's manifest destiny and aggressive **nationalism**. "This heaven-favored land," he declared, enjoyed the "most admirable and wisest system of well-regulated self-government . . . ever devised by human minds." He asked, "Who shall assign limits to the achievements of free minds and free hands under the protection of this glorious Union?"

The nation did not have to wait for Polk's inauguration in March 1845 to see results from his victory. One month after the election, President Tyler announced that the triumph of the Democratic Party provided a mandate for the annexation of Texas "promptly and immediately." In February 1845, after a fierce debate between antislavery and proslavery forces, Congress approved a joint resolution offering the Republic of Texas admission to the United States. Texas entered as the fifteenth slave state.

Polk and Dallas Banner, 1844

In 1844, Democratic presidential nominee James K. Polk and vice presidential nominee George M. Dallas campaigned under this cotton banner. The extra star spilling over into the red and white stripes symbolizes Polk's vigorous support for annexing the huge slave republic of Texas, which had declared its independence from Mexico eight years earlier. Henry Clay, Polk's Whig opponent, ran under a banner that was similar but conspicuously lacked the additional star.

Collection of Janice L. and David J. Frent.

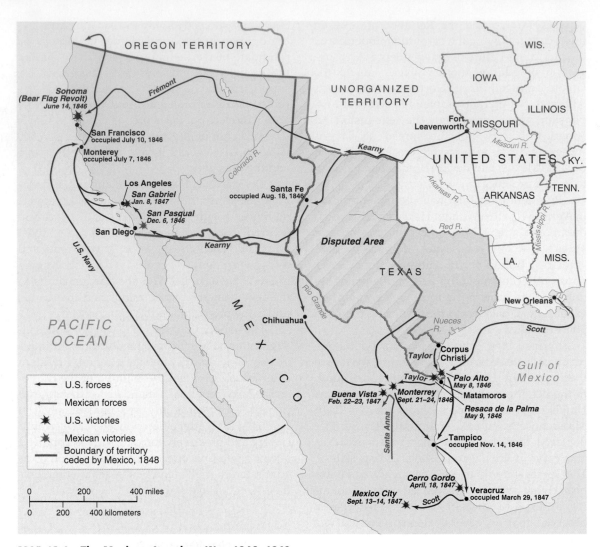

MAP 12.4   The Mexican-American War, 1846–1848
American and Mexican soldiers skirmished across much of northern Mexico, but the major battles took place between the Rio Grande and Mexico City.

Tyler delivered Texas, but Polk had promised Oregon, too. Westerners particularly demanded that the new president make good on the Democrats' pledge "Fifty-four Forty or Fight"— that is, all of Oregon, right up to Alaska (54°40' was the southern latitude of Russian Alaska). But Polk was close to war with Mexico and could not afford a war with Britain over U.S. claims in Canada. After the initial bluster, he muted the all-of-Oregon refrain and renewed an old offer to divide Oregon along the forty-ninth parallel. When Britain accepted the compromise, some Americans cried betrayal, but most celebrated the agreement that gave the nation an enormous territory peacefully. When the Senate finally approved the treaty in June 1846, the United States and Mexico were already at war.

The Mexican-American War, 1846–1848

From the day he entered the White House, Polk craved Mexico's remaining northern provinces: California and New Mexico, land that today makes up California, Nevada, and Utah, most of New Mexico and Arizona, and parts of Wyoming and Colorado. Polk hoped to buy the territory, but when the Mexicans refused to sell, he concluded that military force would be needed to realize the United States' manifest destiny.

Polk had already ordered General Zachary Taylor to march his 4,000-man army 150 miles south from its position on the Nueces River, the southern boundary of Texas according to the Mexicans, to the banks of the Rio Grande, the boundary claimed by Texans (Map 12.4). Viewing the American advance as aggression, the Mexican general in Matamoros ordered Taylor back to the Nueces. Taylor refused, and on April 25, Mexican cavalry attacked a party of American soldiers, killing or wounding sixteen and capturing the rest. Even before news of the battle arrived in Washington, Polk had obtained his cabinet's approval of a war message.

On May 11, 1846, the president told Congress, "Mexico has passed the boundary of the United States, has invaded our territory, and shed American blood upon American soil." Thus "war exists, and, notwithstanding all our efforts to avoid it, exists by the act of Mexico herself." Congress passed a declaration of war and began raising an army. Despite years of saber rattling toward Mexico and Britain, the U.S. army was pitifully small, only 8,600 soldiers. Faced with the nation's first foreign war, against a Mexican army that numbered more than 30,000, Polk called for volunteers. Of the men who rushed to the colors, 40 percent were immigrants. Eventually, more than 112,000 white Americans (blacks were banned) joined the army to fight in Mexico.

Despite the flood of volunteers, the war divided the nation. Northern Whigs in particular condemned the war as the bullying of a weak neighbor. The Massachusetts legislature claimed that the war was being fought for the "triple object of extending slavery, of strengthening the slave power, and of obtaining control of the free states." On January 12, 1848, a gangly freshman Whig representative from Illinois rose from his back-row seat in the House of Representatives to deliver his first important speech in Congress. Before Abraham Lincoln sat down, he had questioned Polk's intelligence, honesty, and sanity. The president simply ignored the upstart representative, but antislavery, antiwar Whigs kept up the attack throughout the conflict. In their effort to undercut national support, they labeled it "Mr. Polk's War."

> On May 11, 1846, President Polk told Congress, "War exists, and, notwithstanding all our efforts to avoid it, exists by the act of Mexico herself."

Since most Americans backed the war, it was not really Polk's war, but the president acted as if it were. Although he had no military experience, he directed the war personally. He planned a short war in which U.S. armies would occupy Mexico's northern provinces and defeat the Mexican army in a decisive battle or two, after which Mexico would sue for peace and the United States would keep the territory its armies occupied.

At first, Polk's strategy seemed to work. In May 1846, Zachary Taylor's troops drove south from the Rio Grande and routed the Mexican army, first at Palo Alto, then at Resaca de la Palma (see Map 12.4). "Old Rough and Ready," as Taylor was affectionately known among his adoring troops, became an instant war hero. Polk rewarded Taylor for his victories by making him commander of the Mexican campaign.

A second prong of the campaign to occupy Mexico's northern provinces centered on Colonel

Shako Hat

American soldiers fighting in the Mexican-American War were a colorful lot. U.S. army regulars wore as a dress uniform a dark blue wool tailcoat and sky-blue wool trousers, topped with the shako, a full-dress cap made of leather, crowned with black feathers, and adorned with a decorative plate showing the eagle spreading its wings—the symbol of manifest destiny.

One veteran criticized the army for "dressing up men within an inch of their lives, until they looked more like a flock of eastern flamingos . . . than the descendants of the race of men who fought and bled to establish civil liberty and republican simplicity in our country." General Winfield Scott, nicknamed "Old Fuss and Feathers" by his men, expected his troops to follow "regulations of dress, hair, whiskers, and so forth." Other commanders, most notably General Zachary Taylor, were notoriously lax, especially for volunteer troops, who were required to furnish their own uniforms. One junior officer serving under Taylor observed: "We wear all kinds of uniforms here, each one to his taste, some shirtsleeves, some white, some purple, some fancy jackets and all colors of cottonelle pants, some straw and some Quaker hats, and that is just the way, too, that our fellows went into battle."

Chicago Historical Society.

***Batalla del Sacramento,* by Julio Michaud y Thomas**
Most images of the Mexican-American War were created by artists from the United States, but Mexicans also recorded the war. In this hand-colored lithograph, the Mexican artist Julio Michaud y Thomas offers his interpretation of the battle that took place in February 1847 when 1,100 American troops engaged 3,000 Mexicans on the banks of the Sacramento River in northern Mexico. Michaud accurately portrays the first moments of the bold Mexican cavalry charge at the American center, but he neglects to finish the story. American artillery forced the Mexican lancers to retreat, with "great confusion in their ranks." When the fighting ended, 700 Mexicans had been killed, wounded, or captured. American casualties amounted to one man killed and six wounded. The battle made a national hero of the American commander, Colonel Alexander Doniphan, who watched the battle with one leg hooked around his saddle horn, whittling a stick in full view of the enemy.
Yale Collection of Western Americana, Beinecke Rare Book and Manuscript Library.

Stephen Watts Kearny, who led a 1,700-man army from Missouri into New Mexico. Without firing a shot, U.S. forces took Santa Fe in August 1846. Polk then ordered Kearny to California. Pushing on with only 300 troops, Kearny marched into San Diego three months later, encountering a major Mexican rebellion against American rule. In January 1847, after several clashes and severe losses, the U.S. forces occupied Los Angeles. California and New Mexico were in American hands.

By then, Taylor had driven deep into the interior of Mexico. In September 1846, after a five-day siege and house-to-house fighting, he took the fortified city of Monterrey. With reinforcements and fresh supplies, Taylor pushed his 5,000 troops southwest, where the Mexican hero of the Alamo, General Antonio López de Santa Anna, was concentrating an army of 21,000. On February 23, 1847, Santa Anna's troops attacked Taylor at Buena Vista. Superior American artillery and accurate musket fire won the day, but the Americans suffered heavy casualties, including Henry Clay Jr., the son of the man who had opposed Texas annexation for fear it would precipitate war. The Mexicans suffered even greater losses (some 3,400 dead, wounded, and missing, compared with 650 Americans). During the night, Santa Anna withdrew his battered army, much to the "profound disgust of the troops," one Mexican officer remembered. "They are filled with grief that they were going to lose the benefit of all the sacrifices that they had made; that the conquered field would be abandoned, and that the victory would be given to the enemy." Retreat, he complained, fed the belief "that it was impossible to conquer the Americans."

The series of uninterrupted victories in northern Mexico certainly fed the American troops' sense of superiority. "No American force has ever thought of being defeated by any amount of Mexican troops," one soldier declared. The Americans worried about other hazards, however. "I can assure you that fighting is the least dangerous & arduous part of a soldier's life," one young man declared. Letters home told of torturous marches across arid wastes alive with tarantulas, scorpions, and rattlesnakes. Others recounted dysentery, malaria, smallpox, cholera, and yellow fever. Of the 13,000 American soldiers who died (some 50,000 Mexicans perished), fewer than 2,000 fell to Mexican bullets and shells. Disease killed most of the others. Medicine was so primitive and conditions so harsh that, as one Tennessee man observed, "nearly all who take sick die."

Victory in Mexico

Although the Americans won battle after battle, President Polk's strategy misfired. Despite heavy losses on the battlefield, Mexico refused to trade land for peace. One American soldier captured the Mexican mood: "They cannot submit to be deprived of California after the loss of Texas, and nothing but the conquest of their Capital will force them to such a humiliation." Polk had arrived at the same conclusion. The president tapped another general to carry the war to Mexico City. While Taylor occupied the north, General Winfield Scott would land his army on the Gulf coast of Mexico and march 250 miles inland to the capital. Polk's plan entailed enormous risk because Scott would have to cut himself off from supplies and lead his men deep into enemy country against a much larger army.

After months of careful planning, an amphibious landing on March 9, 1847, near Veracruz put some 10,000 American troops ashore without the loss of a single life. After a siege of two weeks and furious shelling, Veracruz surrendered on March 29, 1847. In early April 1847, the U.S. army moved westward, following the path blazed more than three centuries earlier by Hernán Cortés to "the halls of the Montezumas" (see chapter 2).

After the defeat at Buena Vista, Santa Anna had returned to Mexico City. He rallied his ragged troops and marched them east to set a trap for Scott in the mountain pass at Cerro Gordo. Knifing through Mexican lines, the Americans almost captured Santa Anna, who fled the field on foot. So complete was the victory that Scott gloated to Taylor, "Mexico no longer has an army." But Santa Anna, ever resilient, again rallied the Mexican army. Some 30,000 troops took up defensive positions on the outskirts of Mexico City and began melting down church bells to cast new cannons.

In August, Scott began his assault on the Mexican capital. The fighting proved the most brutal of the war. Santa Anna backed his army into the city, fighting each step of the way. At the battle of Churubusco, the Mexicans took 4,000 casualties in a single day and the Americans more than 1,000. At the castle of Chapultepec, American troops scaled the walls and fought the Mexican defenders hand to hand. After Chapultepec, Mexico City officials persuaded Santa Anna to evacuate the city to save it from destruction, and on September 14, 1847, General Winfield Scott rode in triumphantly. The ancient capital of the Aztecs had fallen once again to an invading army.

Mexican Family

This family had its portrait taken in 1847, in the middle of the war. Where were the adult males? Mexican civilians were vulnerable to atrocities committed by the invading army. Volunteers, a large portion of the American troops, received little training and resisted discipline. The "lawless Volunteers stop at no outrage," Brigadier General William Worth declared. "Innocent blood has been basely, cowardly, and barbarously shed in cold blood." Generals Zachary Taylor and Winfield Scott gradually tamed the volunteers with stern military justice.

Mexican Family, unknown, ca. 1847, Daguerreotype, Amon Carter Museum, Fort Worth, Texas.

On February 2, 1848, American and Mexican officials signed the Treaty of Guadalupe Hidalgo in Mexico City. Mexico agreed to give up all claims to Texas north of the Rio Grande and to cede the provinces of New Mexico and California—more than 500,000 square miles—to the United States (see Map 12.4). The United States agreed to pay Mexico $15 million and to assume $3.25 million in claims that American citizens had against Mexico. Some Americans clamored for all of Mexico, some for none of it, but in March 1848, the Senate ratified the treaty. Polk had his Rio Grande border, his Pacific ports, and all the land that lay between.

The American triumph had enormous consequences. Less than three-quarters of a century after its founding, the United States had achieved its self-proclaimed manifest destiny to stretch from the Atlantic to the Pacific (Map 12.5). It would enter the industrial age with vast new natural resources and a two-ocean economy, while Mexico faced a sharply diminished economic future. Mexicans neither forgot nor forgave Americans for tearing away the northern half of their country. In 1915, in south Texas, Tejanos killed dozens of white farmers in a violent effort to return the American Southwest to Mexico. The wave of lynchings and vigilantism that followed cost thousands of Tejanos their lives.

Golden California

Another consequence of the Mexican defeat in the war with the United States was that California gold poured into American, not Mexican, pockets. On a cold January morning in 1848, just

---

MAP 12.5 Territorial Expansion by 1860

Less than a century after its founding, the United States spread from the Atlantic seaboard to the Pacific coast. War, purchase, and diplomacy had gained a continent.

Reading the map: List the countries from which the United States acquired land. Which nation lost the most land because of U.S. expansion?

Connections: Who coined the phrase *manifest destiny*? When? What does it mean? What areas targeted for expansion were the subjects of debate during the presidential campaign of 1844?

For more help analyzing this map, see the map activity for this chapter in the Online Study Guide at bedfordstmartins.com/roark.

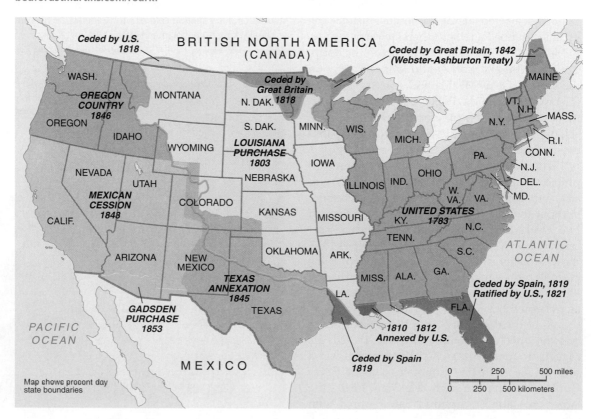

View of San Francisco
San Francisco stood at the entrance to a huge bay offering the best deep-water port on the Pacific coast. When gold was discovered in 1848 only ninety miles away, the Sacramento and San Joaquin rivers provided access to gold country. As this illustration from the early 1850s shows, a shortage of housing forced some new arrivals to camp on the city's outskirts. Behind them lies what is already an imposing urban scene, complete with a harbor jammed with ships from around the world. Early San Francisco fattened itself on exports of gold and silver and imports of everything the miners needed.
University of California at Berkeley, Bancroft Library.

weeks before the formal transfer of territory, James Marshall discovered gold in the American River in the foothills of the Sierra Nevada. Marshall's discovery set off the California gold rush, one of the wildest mining stampedes in the world's history. Between 1849 and 1852, more than 250,000 "forty-niners," as the would-be miners were known, descended on the Golden State. In less than two years, Marshall's discovery transformed California from foreign territory to statehood.

News of gold quickly spread around the world. Soon, a stream of men, of various races and nationalities, all bent on getting rich, arrived in California, where they remade the quiet world of Mexican ranches into a raucous, roaring mining and town economy. (See "Historical Question," page 422.) Forty-niners rarely had much money or mining experience, but as one witness observed, "No capital is required to obtain this gold, as the laboring man wants nothing but his pick, shovel, and tin pan, with which to dig and wash the gravel; and many frequently pick gold

out of the crevices of rock with their butcher knives in pieces from one to six ounces." Only a few struck it rich, and life in the goldfields was nasty, brutish, and often short. Men faced miserable living conditions, sometimes sheltering in holes and brush lean-tos. They also faced cholera and scurvy, exorbitant prices for food (eggs cost a dollar apiece), deadly encounters with claim jumpers, and endless backbreaking labor. An individual with gold in his pocket could find only temporary relief in the saloons, card games, dogfights, gambling dens, and brothels that flourished in the mining camps.

By 1853, San Francisco had grown into a raw, booming city of 50,000 that depended as much on gold as did the mining camps inland. Like all the towns that dotted the San Joaquin and Sacramento valleys, it suffered from overcrowding, fire, crime, and violence. But enterprising individuals had learned that there was money to be made tending to the needs of the miners. Hotels, saloons, restaurants, laundries,

Who Rushed for California Gold?

When news of James Marshall's discovery reached the East in the fall of 1848, gold proved irresistible. Newspapers went crazy with stories about prospectors who extracted half a pan of gold from every pan of gravel they scooped from western streams. Soon, cities reverberated with men singing:

Oh Susannah, don't you cry for me;
I'm gone to California with
my wash-bowl on my knee.

Scores of ships sailed from East Coast ports, headed either around South America to San Francisco or across the Gulf of Mexico to Panama, where the passengers made their way by foot and canoe to the Pacific and waited for a ship to carry them north. Even larger numbers of gold seekers took riverboats to the Missouri River and then set out in wagons, on horseback, or by foot for the West.

Young men everywhere contracted gold fever. As stories of California gold circled the globe, Chinese and Germans, Mexicans and Irish, Australians and French, Chileans and Italians, and people of dozens of other nationalities set out to strike it rich. Louisa Knapp Clappe, wife of a minister and one of the few women in gold country, remarked that when she walked through Indian Bar, the little mining town where she lived, she heard English, French, Spanish, German, Italian, Kanaka (Hawaiian), Asian Indian, and American Indian languages. Hangtown, Hell's Delight, Gouge Eye, and a hundred other crude mining camps became temporary homes to a diverse throng of nationalities and peoples.

One of the largest groups of new arrivals was the Chinese. Between 1848 and 1854, Chinese men numbering 45,000 (but almost no Chinese women) arrived in California. Most considered themselves "sojourners," temporary residents who planned to return home as soon as their savings allowed. The majority came under a Chinese-controlled contract labor system in which each immigrant worked out the cost of his transportation. In the early years, most became wage laborers in mining. By the 1860s, they dominated railroad construction in the West. Ninety percent of the Central Pacific Railroad's 10,000 workers were Chinese. The Chinese also made up nearly half of San Francisco's labor force, working in the shoe, tobacco, woolen, laundry, and sewing trades. By 1870, the Chinese population in California had grown to 63,200, including 4,500 women. They constituted nearly 10 percent of the state's people and 25 percent of its wage-earning force.

The presence of peoples from around the world shattered the Anglo-American dream of a racially and ethnically homogeneous West, but ethnic diversity did nothing to increase the tolerance of Anglo-American prospectors. In their eyes, no "foreigner" had a right to dig for gold. In 1850, the California legislature passed the Foreign Miners' Tax Law, which levied high taxes on non-Americans to drive them from the goldfields, except as hired laborers working on claims owned by Americans. Stubborn foreign miners were sometimes hauled before "Judge Lynch." Among the earliest victims of lynching in the goldfields were a Frenchman and a Chilean.

Anglo-Americans considered the Chinese devious and unassimilable. They also feared that hardworking, self-denying Chinese labor would undercut white labor and drive it from the country. As a consequence, the Chinese were segregated residentially and occupationally and made ineligible for citizenship. Along with blacks and Indians, Chinese were denied public education and the right and shops and stores of all kinds exchanged services and goods for miners' gold.

In 1851, the Committee of Vigilance determined to bring order to the city. Members pledged that "no thief, burglar, incendiary or assassin shall escape punishment, either by the quibbles of the law, the insecurity of prisons, the carelessness or corruption of the police, or a laxity of those who pretended to administer justice." Lynchings proved that the committee meant business. In time, merchants, **artisans**, and professionals made the city their home and brought their families from back east. Gradually, gunfights declined and theaters sprouted, but many years would pass before anyone pacified San Francisco.

to testify in court. In addition to exclusion, they suffered from violence. Mobs drove them from Eureka, Truckee, and other mining towns.

American prospectors swamped the *Californios*, Spanish and Mexican settlers who had lived in California for generations. Soon after the American takeover, raging prejudice and discriminatory laws pushed Hispanic *rancheros*, professionals, merchants, and artisans into the ranks of unskilled labor. Americans took their land even though the U.S. government had pledged to protect Mexican and Spanish land titles after the cession of 1848. Anglo forty-niners branded Spanish-speaking miners, even native-born Californios, "foreigners" and drove them from the diggings. Mariano Vallejo, a leading Californio, said of the forty-niners, "The good ones were few and the wicked many."

For Native Americans, the gold rush was a catastrophe. Numbering about 150,000 in 1848, the Indian population of California fell to 25,000 in 1856. The Californios had exploited the native peoples, but the forty-niners wanted to eradicate them. Starvation, disease, and a declining birthrate took a heavy toll. Indians also fell victim to wholesale murder. "That a war of extermination will continue to be waged between the two races until the Indian race becomes extinct must be expected," declared California governor Peter W. Burnett in 1851. The nineteenth-century historian Hubert Howe Bancroft described

white behavior toward Indians during the gold rush as "one of the last human hunts of civilization, and the basest and most brutal of them all." To survive, Indians moved to the most remote areas of the state and tried to stay out of the way.

The forty-niners created dazzling wealth—in 1852, 81 million ounces of gold, nearly half of the world's production. Only a few prospectors struck it rich, however. The era of the prospector panning in streams quickly gave way to corporate-owned deep-shaft mining. The larger the mining operations became, the smaller individual miners' opportunities were. Most forty-niners eventually took up farming, opened small businesses, or worked for wages for the corporations that pushed them out. But because of gold, a flood of people had roared into California. Anglo-Americans were the most numerous, but the gold rush also brought a rainbow of other nationalities. Anglo dominance developed early, however, and not everyone shared equally in the bonanza. Both Anglo-American ascendancy and ethnic and racial diversity in the West were among the most significant legacies of the gold rush.

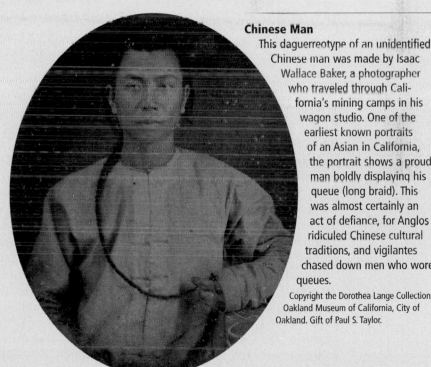

Chinese Man

This daguerreotype of an unidentified Chinese man was made by Isaac Wallace Baker, a photographer who traveled through California's mining camps in his wagon studio. One of the earliest known portraits of an Asian in California, the portrait shows a proud man boldly displaying his queue (long braid). This was almost certainly an act of defiance, for Anglos ridiculed Chinese cultural traditions, and vigilantes chased down men who wore queues.

Copyright the Dorothea Lange Collection, Oakland Museum of California, City of Oakland. Gift of Paul S. Taylor.

Establishing civic order on a turbulent frontier was made more difficult by Anglo bigotry and by the welter of nationalities, ethnicities, and races drawn to California. The Chinese attracted special scrutiny. By 1851, 25,000 Chinese lived in California, and their religion, language, dress, queues (long pigtails), eating habits, and opium convinced many Anglos that they were not fit citizens of the Golden State. As early as 1852, opponents demanded a halt to Chinese immigration. Chinese leaders in San Francisco fought back. Admitting deep cultural differences, they insisted that "in the important matters we are good men. We honor our parents; we take care of our children; we are industrious and peaceable; we trade much; we are trusted for small and large sums; we pay our debts; and are honest, and of course must tell the truth." Their protestations offered little protection, however, and racial violence braided with forty-niner optimism and energy.

Westward expansion did not stop at the California shore. California's ports were connected to a vast trade network throughout the Pacific. American seafarers and merchants traded furs, hides and tallow, and lumber and engaged in whaling and the China trade. Still, as California's first congressional representative observed, the state was separated "by thousands of miles of plains, deserts, and almost impossible mountains" from the rest of the Union. Some dreamers imagined a railroad that would someday connect the Golden State with the booming agriculture and thriving industry of the East. Others imagined an America transformed not by transportation, but by progressive individual and institutional reform.

REVIEW   Why was the annexation of Texas such a controversial policy?

Reforming Self and Society

While manifest destiny, the Mexican-American War, and the California gold rush transformed the nation's geography, many Americans sought personal and social reform. The emphasis on self-discipline and individual effort at the core of the free-labor ideal led Americans to believe that insufficient self-control caused the major social problems of the era. **Evangelical** Protestants struggled to control individuals' propensity to sin, and **temperance** advocates exhorted drinkers to control their urge for alcohol. In the midst of the worldly disruptions of geographic expansion and economic change, evangelicals brought more Americans than ever before into churches. Historians estimate that church members accounted for about one-third of the American population by 1850. Most Americans remained outside churches, as did Abraham Lincoln. But the influence of evangelical religion reached far beyond those who belonged to churches. The evangelical temperament—a conviction of righteousness coupled with energy, self-discipline, and faith that the world could be improved—animated most reformers.

A few activists pointed out that certain fundamental injustices lay beyond the reach of individual self-control. Transcendentalists and utopians believed that perfection could be attained only by rejecting the competitive, individualistic values of mainstream society. Woman's rights activists and abolitionists sought to reverse the subordination of women and to eliminate the enslavement of blacks by changing laws and social institutions as well as attitudes and customs. They confronted the daunting challenge of repudiating widespread assumptions about male supremacy and white supremacy and somehow subverting the entrenched institutions that reinforced those assumptions: the family and slavery.

The Pursuit of Perfection: Transcendentalists and Utopians

A group of New England writers that came to be known as transcendentalists believed that individuals should conform neither to the dictates of the materialistic world nor to the dogma of formal religion. Instead, people should look within themselves for truth and guidance. The leading transcendentalist, Ralph Waldo Emerson—an essayist, poet, and lecturer—proclaimed that the power of the solitary individual was nearly limitless. Henry David Thoreau, Margaret Fuller, and other transcendentalists agreed with Emerson that "if the single man plant himself indomitably on his instincts, and there abide, the huge world will come round to him." In many ways, the inward gaze and confident egoism of transcendentalism represented less an alternative to mainstream values than an exaggerated form of the rampant individualism of the age.

Unlike transcendentalists who sought to turn inward, a few reformers tried to change the world by organizing utopian communities as alternatives to prevailing social arrangements. Although these communities never attracted more than a few thousand people, the activities of their members demonstrated both dissatisfaction with the larger society and their efforts to realize their visions of perfection. Some communities functioned as retreats for those who did not want to sever ties with the larger society. Brook Farm, organized in 1841 in West Roxbury, Massachusetts, briefly provided a haven for a few literary and artistic New Englanders trying to balance bookish pursuits with manual labor.

Other communities set out to become models of perfection that they hoped would point the way toward a better life for everyone. During the 1840s, more than two dozen communities organized around the ideas of Charles Fourier, a

Mary Cragin, Oneida Woman

A founding member of the Oneida community, Mary Cragin had a passionate sexual relationship with John Humphrey Noyes even before the community was organized. Within the bounds of complex marriage as practiced by the Oneidans, Cragin's magnetic sexuality made her a favorite partner of many men. In her journal, she confessed that "every evil passion was very strong in me from my childhood, sexual desire, love of dress and admiration, deceit, anger, pride." Oneida, however, transformed evil passion to holy piety. Cragin wrote, "In view of [God's] goodness to me and of his desire that I should let him fill me with himself, I yield and offer myself, to be penetrated by his spirit, and desire that love and gratitude may inspire my heart so that I shall sympathize with his pleasure in the thing, before my personal pleasure begins, knowing that it will increase my capability for happiness." Oneida's sexual practices were considered outrageous and sinful by almost all other Americans. Even Oneidans did not agree with all of Noyes's ideas about sex. "There is no reason why [sex] should not be done in public as much as music and dancing," he declared. It would display the art of sex, he explained, and watching "would give pleasure to a great many of the older people who now have nothing to do with the matter." Nonetheless, public sex never caught on among Oneidans. Oneida Community Mansion House.

French critic of contemporary society. Members of Fourierist phalanxes, as these communities were called, believed that individualism and competition were evils that denied the basic truth that "men . . . are brothers and not competitors." Phalanxes aspired to replace competition with harmonious cooperation based on communal ownership of property. But Fourierist communities failed to realize their lofty goals, and few survived more than two or three years.

The Oneida community went beyond the Fourierist notion of communalism. John Humphrey Noyes, the charismatic leader of Oneida, believed that American society's commitment to private property made people greedy and selfish. Noyes claimed that the root of private property lay in marriage, in men's conviction that their wives were their exclusive property. Drawing from a substantial inheritance, Noyes organized the Oneida community in New York in 1848 to abolish marital property rights through the practice of what he called "complex marriage." Sexual intercourse was not restricted to married couples but was permitted between any consenting man and woman in the community. Noyes also required all members to relinquish their economic property to the community, which developed a lucrative business manufacturing animal traps. Oneida's sexual and economic communalism attracted several hundred members, but most of their neighbors considered Oneidans adulterers, blasphemers, and worse. Yet the practices that set Oneida apart from its mainstream neighbors strengthened the community, and it survived long after the Civil War.

Woman's Rights Activists

Women participated in the many reform activities that grew out of evangelical churches. Women church members outnumbered men two to one and worked to put their religious ideas into practice by joining peace, temperance, anti-slavery, and other societies. Involvement in reform organizations gave a few women activists practical experience in such political arts as speaking in public, running a meeting, drafting resolutions, and circulating petitions. Along with such experience came confidence. The abolitionist Lydia Maria Child pointed out in 1841 that "those who urged women to become missionaries and form tract societies . . . have changed the household utensil to a living energetic being and they have no spell to turn it into a broom again."

In 1848, about three hundred reformers led by Elizabeth Cady Stanton and Lucretia Mott gathered at Seneca Falls, New York, for the first national woman's rights convention in the United States. As Stanton recalled, "The general discontent I felt with women's portion as wife, mother, housekeeper, physician, and spiritual guide, [and] the wearied anxious look of the majority of women impressed me with a strong feeling that some active measure should be taken to right the wrongs of society in general, and of women in particular." The Seneca Falls Declaration of Sentiments set an ambitious agenda to right the wrongs of women and society. The declaration proclaimed that "the history of mankind is a history of repeated injuries and usurpations on the part of man toward woman, having in direct object the establishment of an absolute tyranny over her." In the style of the Declaration of Independence (see appendix I, page A-1), the Seneca Falls declaration denounced men who "endeavored in every way . . . to destroy her confidence in her own powers, to lessen her self-respect, and to make her willing to lead a dependent and abject life." The declaration demanded that women "have immediate

> The Declaration of Sentiments demanded that women "have immediate admission to all the rights and privileges which belong to them as citizens of the United States," particularly the "inalienable right to the elective franchise."

admission to all the rights and privileges which belong to them as citizens of the United States," particularly the "inalienable right to the elective franchise."

Nearly two dozen other woman's rights conventions assembled before 1860, repeatedly calling for **suffrage** and an end to discrimination against women. But women had difficulty receiving a respectful hearing, much less achieving legislative action. No state came close to permitting women to vote. Politicians and editorialists held that a woman's place was in the home, rearing her children and civilizing her man. Even so, the Seneca Falls declaration served as a pathbreaking manifesto of dissent against male supremacy and of support for woman suffrage, and it inspired many women to challenge the barriers that limited their opportunities.

Stanton and other activists sought fair pay and expanded employment opportunities for women by appealing to free-labor ideology. Woman's rights advocate Paula Wright Davis pointed out that "every able bodied Man, inured to Labor . . . is worth a dollar a day and can readily command it. . . . But the sister of this same faithful worker, equally careful, intelligent, and willing to do anything honest and reputable for a living . . . [is] fortunate if . . . she can earn five or six dollars per month." Davis urged Americans to stop discriminating against able and enterprising women: "Let [women] . . . open a Store, . . . plant and tend an Orchard, . . . learn any of the lighter mechanical Trades, . . . study for a Profession, . . . be called to the lecture-room, [and] . . . the Temperance rostrum . . . [and] let her be appointed [to serve in the Post Office]." Some women pioneered in these and many other occupations during the 1840s and 1850s. Woman's rights activists also succeeded in protecting married women's rights to their own wages and property in New York in 1860. (See chapter 14, "Seeking the American Promise," page 494.) But discrimination against women persisted, as most men believed that free-labor ideology required no compromise of male supremacy.

Bloomers and Woman's Emancipation

This 1851 British cartoon lampoons bloomers, the trouserlike garment worn beneath shortened skirts by two cigar-smoking American women. Bloomers were invented in the United States as an alternative to the uncomfortable, confining, and awkward dresses worn by fashionable women, suggested here by the clothing of the "respectable" British women on the right. In the 1850s, Elizabeth Cady Stanton and other woman's rights activists wore bloomers and urged all American women to do likewise. Critics, as suggested by the cartoon, ridiculed "bloomerism" as unfeminine, eventually causing American reformers to abandon bloomers and instead focus on other, more important woman's rights issues. The bloomer controversy illustrates the immense power of conventional notions of femininity confronted by woman's rights advocates.

Miriam and Ira D. Wallach Division of Art, Prints and Photographs, The New York Public Library. Astor, Lenox and Tilden Foundations.

BLOOMERISM—AN AMERICAN CUSTOM.

Abolitionists and the American Ideal

During the 1840s and 1850s, abolitionists continued to struggle to draw the nation's attention to the plight of slaves and the need for emancipation. Former slaves such as Frederick Douglass, Henry Bibb, and Sojourner Truth lectured to reform audiences throughout the North about the cruelties of slavery. Abolitionists published newspapers, held conventions, and petitioned Congress, but they never attracted a mass following among white Americans. Many white Northerners became convinced that slavery was wrong, but they still believed that blacks were inferior. Many other white Northerners shared the common view of white Southerners that slavery was necessary and even desirable. The geographic expansion of the nation during the 1840s offered abolitionists an opportunity to link their unpopular ideal to a goal that many white Northerners found much more attractive— limiting the geographic expansion of slavery, an issue that moved to the center of national politics during the 1850s (see chapter 14).

Black leaders rose to prominence in the abolitionist movement during the 1840s and 1850s. African Americans had actively opposed slavery for decades, but a new generation of leaders came to the forefront in these years. Frederick Douglass, Henry Highland Garnet, William Wells Brown, Martin R. Delany, and others became impatient with white abolitionists' appeals to the conscience of the white majority. In 1843, Garnet proclaimed that slaves had "little hope of Redemption without the shedding of blood" and urged them to choose "Liberty or Death" and rise in insurrection against their masters, an idea that alienated almost all white people and carried little influence among slaves. To express their own uncompromising ideas, black abolitionists founded their own newspapers and held their own antislavery conventions, although they still cooperated with sympathetic whites.

The commitment of black abolitionists to battling slavery grew out of their own experiences with white supremacy. The 250,000 free African Americans in the North and West constituted less than 2 percent of the total population. They confronted the humiliations of racial discrimination in nearly every arena of daily life. Only Maine, Massachusetts, New Hampshire, and Vermont permitted black men to vote; New York imposed a special property-holding requirement on black—but not white—voters, effectively excluding most black men from the **franchise**. The pervasive racial discrimination both handicapped and energized black abolitionists. Some cooperated with the American Colonization Society's efforts to send freed slaves and other black Americans to Liberia in West Africa. (See "Beyond America's Borders," page 428.) Others sought to move to Canada, Haiti, or someplace else, convinced that, as an

Abolitionist Meeting
This rare daguerreotype was made by Ezra Greenleaf Weld in August 1850 at an abolitionist meeting in Cazenovia, New York. Frederick Douglass, who had escaped from slavery in Maryland twelve years earlier, is seated on the platform next to the woman at the table. One of the nation's most brilliant and eloquent abolitionists, Douglass also supported equal rights for women. The man immediately behind Douglass gesturing with his outstretched arm is Gerrit Smith, a wealthy New Yorker and militant abolitionist whose funds supported many reform activities. Notice the two black women in similar clothing on either side of Smith and the white woman next to Douglass. Most white Americans considered such voluntary racial proximity scandalous and promiscuous. What messages did abolitionists attempt to convey by attending such protest meetings?
Collection of the J. Paul Getty Museum, Malibu, CA.

African American from Michigan wrote, "it is impracticable, not to say impossible, for the whites and blacks to live together, and upon terms of social and civil equality, under the same government." Most black American leaders refused to embrace emigration and worked against racial prejudice in their own communities, organizing campaigns against segregation, particularly in transportation and education. Their most

Back to Africa: The United States in Liberia

In the first half of the nineteenth century, thousands of free African Americans returned to Africa. In Liberia, they established a beachhead for American culture, one that clearly remains alive today. American-sounding names (the county of Maryland); American institutions (Masonic lodges); a red, white, and blue flag patterned on the Stars and Stripes; and a restaurant that advertises Maryland-style fried chicken make it impossible to forget the American origins of this modern-day West African nation.

In 1817, white men with a range of motives founded the American Colonization Society to transport black Americans to Africa. Some colonizationists sympathized with America's oppressed blacks and urged them to return to Africa, their "natural home," to escape racism, improve their lot in life, and help "civilize" an entire continent. Other colonizationists wanted to rid the United States of what they considered a "useless, pernicious, and dangerous" people. Whatever their motivation, colonizationists agreed that the two races could not live together and that blacks should leave. Aware that British anti-slavery forces had founded Sierra Leone in West Africa as a haven for freed slaves a generation earlier, the society purchased land to the south from African chiefs. They named the colony Liberia, after **liberty**, and called its capital Monrovia, after President James Monroe.

Between 1820, when it sent the first settlers to Liberia, and the start of the American Civil War in 1861, the society transported approximately 12,000 African Americans to Africa. About 7,000 were slaves whose masters freed them (often because they were favorites or kin) on the condition that they leave America, and about 5,000 were free blacks who chose to go because they had lost hope of achieving equality in the United States. John Russwurm, a free black man, accepted the society's invitation because he concluded that blacks in America could never overcome "the odium of [an] inferior and degraded caste." The overwhelming majority of free blacks claimed America as their country and decided to make their stand at home. Frederick Douglass spoke for them in 1849 when he denounced colonizationists: "Shame upon the guilty wretches that dare propose . . . such a proposition. We live here—have lived here—have a right to live here, and mean to live here."

American settlers in Liberia found life even harder there than in the United States. Land along the coast was swampy and covered with forests, and often it lacked fresh water. The society never had enough funds to support the settlers adequately, and even though former masters provided some assistance, the newcomers faced shortages of basic necessities. Moreover, settlers and Africans clashed as the newcomers pushed inland, taking land, killing game, and attacking slave traders who kidnapped or bought people to ship as laborers to Cuba and Brazil. The outpost somehow managed to survive, but many of the Americans did not. In the first two decades of settlement, "African fever," most likely malaria, killed about one-quarter of them.

In time, the settlers established a foothold, and life grew a little less precarious. They learned to farm without horses and mules, which could not survive African diseases, and they began trading coffee, sugar, and palm oil. They stabilized the boundaries of the colony, controlling some 250 miles of coastline to a depth of 40 to 50 miles. But by the 1840s, the American Colonization Society was nearly bankrupt. When the U.S. government refused to assume sovereignty of the private colony, the society demanded that the settlers proclaim their independence. In 1847, a few thousand North American immigrants announced the Republic of Liberia and took control of a substantial piece of Africa and several hundred thousand Africans.

The settlers had fled America, but rather than cast off American culture, they clung to it, straining every muscle to re-create American life, without slavery and white supremacy, in Africa. As far as possible, they retained American habits in food, dress, manners, and housing. Liberia produced abundant crops of millet, yams, cassava, and pawpaw, but the settlers maintained a taste for flour, pork, and dried fruit, which they imported when they could. They also established American institutions, including public schools, fraternal organizations, and temperance societies. Most important, they promoted their evangelical Christian faith by building Methodist and Baptist churches everywhere they settled. Most newcomers felt a profound missionary urge to carry "the blessed Gospel" to the land of their forefathers.

Despite their African heritage, the American settlers felt little kinship with Africans. The newcomers displayed a strong sense of superiority and engaged in what they considered a providential effort to "civilize and uplift." Peyton Skipwith, an ex-slave from Virginia, declared, "It is something to think that these people are calld [sic] our ancestors. In my present thinking if we have any ancestors they could not have been like these hostile tribes . . . for you may . . . do all you can for them and they still will be your enemy." The settlers labored to maintain the distinctions between themselves and the Gola, Kru, and Vai peoples who surrounded them. Africa was populated, Matilda Skipwith insisted, with "the most savage, & blud thirsty people I ever saw." But opposition to Africans did not mean that the American settler community was united. The settlers carried with them old tensions and divisions, especially those between the freeborn and slaveborn. Light-skinned freeborn African Americans often arrived with more money, education, and skills than darker-skinned ex-slaves, and they quickly enjoyed greater wealth and political power.

The settlers did agree, however, that they had found in Africa what they had primarily come for—dignity and freedom. Despite the continuing heartache of leaving family behind and the stubborn reality of physical hardship, they refused to return to America. In 1848, one African American said, "I will never consent to leave the country . . . for this is the only place where a colored person can enjoy his liberty, for there exists no prejudice of color in this country, and every man is free and equal."

In the second half of the nineteenth century, when European powers sliced Africa into colonies, Liberia managed to retain its political independence. But in the 1920s, an American corporation, the Firestone Rubber Company, made Liberia a kind of economic colony, and the dominant Americo-Liberians did not allow the indigenous people to vote until 1946. Finally, in 1980, the African majority rose up in bloody rebellion against the Americo-Liberian elite. In 2007, although Liberians of American descent accounted for only about 5 per-

cent of the country's population, they continued to wield disproportionate power.

Years of civil war have largely wrecked the country, trapping its people in fear and starvation. Liberians have implored the United States, which some call "big brother," to recognize its historic connection with the African nation and fulfill what Liberians see as its continuing responsibilities by intervening with peacekeeping forces. During the twentieth century, black Americans developed a sense of kinship with all Africans, particularly in the 1950s and 1960s, when they recognized the interconnectedness of the freedom struggles on both sides of the Atlantic. But the U.S. government has been slower to acknowledge historic ties with Liberia. In August 2003, under intense pressure from the international community, the Bush administration successfully pressured Liberian president Charles

Contemporary Liberia

Taylor to resign and sent in a handful of peacekeeping troops. Three years later, in 2006, a United Nations–backed tribunal indicted Taylor on eleven counts of war crimes, and Ellen Johnson-Sirleaf, an American-trained economist, was inaugurated as Liberia's president. (She is Africa's first female head of state.) In 2007, fifteen thousand United Nations troops helped preserve the country's fragile peace.

Liberian Crowds Await the U.S. President
In April 1978, Americans and Liberians await the arrival of President Jimmy Carter at the airport outside Monrovia. Flying side by side, the two national flags offer dramatic evidence of Liberia's American origins and the United States' continuing influence on the country.
Smithsonian Institution, National Museum of American History.

notable success came in 1855 when Massachusetts integrated its public schools. Elsewhere, white supremacy continued unabated.

Outside the public spotlight, free African Americans in the North and West contributed to the antislavery cause by quietly aiding fugitive slaves. Harriet Tubman escaped from slavery in Maryland in 1849 and repeatedly risked her freedom and her life to return to the South to escort slaves to freedom. When the opportunity arose, free blacks in the North provided fugitive slaves with food, a safe place to rest, and a helping hand. An outgrowth of the antislavery sentiment and opposition to white supremacy that unified nearly all African Americans in the North, this "underground railroad" ran mainly through black neighborhoods, black churches, and black homes.

> **REVIEW**   Why were women especially prominent in many nineteenth-century reform efforts?

Conclusion: Free Labor, Free Men

During the 1840s and 1850s, a cluster of interrelated developments—steam power, railroads, and the growing mechanization of agriculture and manufacturing—meant greater economic productivity, a burst of output from farms and factories, and prosperity for many. Diplomacy and war handed the United States 1.2 million square miles and more than 1,000 miles of Pacific coastline. One prize of manifest destiny, California, almost immediately rewarded its new owners with tons of gold. To most Americans, new territory and vast riches were appropriate accompaniments to the nation's stunning economic progress.

To Northerners, industrial evolution confirmed the choice they had made to eliminate slavery and promote free labor as the key to independence, equality, and prosperity. Like Abraham Lincoln, millions of Americans could point to their personal experiences as evidence of the practical truth of the free-labor ideal. But millions of others had different stories to tell. They knew that in the free-labor system, poverty and wealth continued to rub shoulders. By 1860,

more than half of the nation's free-labor workforce still toiled for someone else. Free-labor enthusiasts denied that the problems were inherent in the country's social and economic systems. Instead, they argued, most social ills—including poverty and dependency—sprang from individual deficiencies. Consequently, many reformers focused on self-control and discipline, on avoiding sin and alcohol. Other reformers focused on woman's rights and slavery. They challenged widespread conceptions of male supremacy and black inferiority, but neither group managed to overcome the prevailing free-labor ideology, based on individualism, racial prejudice, and notions of male superiority.

By midcentury, the nation was half slave and half free, and each region was animated by different economic interests, cultural values, and political aims. Not even the victory over Mexico could bridge the deepening divide between North and South.

Selected Bibliography

The Economy and Free Labor

Jeanne Boydston, *Home and Work: Housework, Wages, and the Ideology of Labor in the Early Republic* (1990).

Stuart Bruchey, *Enterprise: The Dynamic Economy of a Free People* (1990).

J. Matthew Gallman, *Receiving Erin's Children: Philadelphia, Liverpool, and the Irish Famine Migration, 1854–1855* (2000).

Jonathan A. Glickstein, *Concepts of Free Labor in the Antebellum United States* (1991).

Donald R. Hoke, *Ingenious Yankees: The Rise of the American System of Manufactures in the Private Sector* (1990).

Robert A. Margo, *Wages and Labor Markets in the United States, 1820–1860* (2000).

David R. Meyer, *The Roots of American Industrialization* (2003).

Scott A. Sandage, *Born Losers: A History of Failure in America* (2005).

Kenneth J. Winkle, *The Young Eagle: The Rise of Abraham Lincoln* (2001).

Westward Expansion and the Mexican-American War

Leonard J. Arrington and Davis Bitton, *The Mormon Experience: A History of the Latter-Day Saints* (1979).

H. W. Brand, *Lone Star Nation* (2004).

David Dary, *The Oregon Trail: An American Saga* (2004).

John Mack Faragher, *Women and Men on the Overland Trail* (1979).

Paul W. Foos, *A Short, Offhand, Killing Affair: Soldiers and Social Conflict during the Mexican-American War* (2002).

Amy S. Greenberg, *Manifest Manhood and the Antebellum American Empire* (2005).

Julie Roy Jeffrey, *Frontier Women: The Trans-Mississippi West, 1840–1880* (1979).

Benjamin Heber Johnson, *Revolution in Texas: How a Forgotten Rebellion and Its Bloody Suppression Turned Mexicans into Americans* (2003).

Susan Lee Johnson, *Roaring Camp: The Social World of the California Gold Rush* (2000).

Patricia Nelson Limerick, *The Legacy of Conquest: The Unbroken Past of the American West* (1987).

David Montejano, *Anglos and Mexicans in the Making of Texas, 1836–1986* (1987).

Gregory H. Nobles, *American Frontiers: Cultural Encounters and Continental Conquest* (1997).

Malcolm Rohrbough, *Days of Gold: The California Gold Rush and the American Nation* (1997).

James A. Sandos, *Converting California: Indians and Franciscans in the Missions* (2004).

Joel H. Sibley, *Storm over Texas: The Annexation Controversy and the Road to Civil War* (2005).

Robert M. Utley, *The Indian Frontier of the American West, 1846–1890* (1984).

Richard White, *"It's Your Misfortune and None of My Own": A New History of the American West* (1993).

Richard Bruce Winders, *Mr. Polk's Army: The American Military Experience in the Mexican War* (1997).

Antebellum Culture and Reform

Bruce Dorsey, *Reforming Men and Women: Gender in the City* (2002).

Lori D. Ginzberg, *Untidy Origins: A Story of Women's Rights in Antebellum New York* (2005).

Bruce Laurie, *Beyond Garrison: Antislavery and Social Reform* (2005).

Timothy Patrick McCarthy and John Stauffer, eds., *Prophets of Protest: Reconsidering the History of American Abolitionism* (2006).

Patrick Rael, *Black Identity and Black Protest in the Antebellum North* (2002).

Susan M. Ryan, *The Grammar of Good Intentions: Race and the Antebellum Culture of Benevolence* (2003).

Beth A. Salerno, *Sister Societies: Women's Antislavery Organizations in Antebellum America* (2005).

John Stauffer, *The Black Hearts of Men: Radical Abolitionists and the Transformation of Race* (2002).

Susan Zaeske, *Signatures of Citizenship: Petitioning, Antislavery, and Women's Political Identity* (2003).

▶ **For more books about topics in this chapter,** see the Online Bibliography at bedfordstmartins.com/roark.

▶ **For additional firsthand accounts of this period,** see Chapter 12 in Michael Johnson, ed., *Reading the American Past,* Fourth Edition.

▶ **For Web sites, images, and documents related to topics and places in this chapter,** visit bedfordstmartins.com/makehistory.

REVIEWING THE CHAPTER

Follow these steps to review and strengthen your understanding of the chapter.

STEP 1: *Study the* **Key Terms** *and* **Timeline** *to identify the significance of each item listed.*

STEP 2: *Answer the* **Review Questions**, *drawing on key terms and dates to support your answers.*

STEP 3: *Drawing on the Key Terms, Timeline, and Review Questions, answer the broader* **Making Connections** *questions.*

KEY TERMS

Who

Abraham Lincoln (p. 395)
Mary Todd Lincoln (p. 395)
John Deere (p. 397)
Cyrus McCormick (p. 397)
Samuel F. B. Morse (p. 399)
John L. O'Sullivan (p. 408)
Joseph Smith Jr. (p. 411)
Brigham Young (p. 412)
Stephen F. Austin (p. 413)
Antonio López de Santa Anna (p. 413)
Sam Houston (p. 414)
John C. Frémont (p. 414)
James K. Polk (p. 414)
John Tyler (p. 415)
John C. Calhoun (p. 415)
Henry Clay (p. 415)
Zachary Taylor (p. 416)
Stephen Watts Kearny (p. 418)
Winfield Scott (p. 419)
Ralph Waldo Emerson (p. 424)

Elizabeth Cady Stanton (p. 425)
Lucretia Mott (p. 425)
Frederick Douglass (p. 426)
Henry Highland Garnet (p. 427)
Harriet Tubman (p. 430)

What

industrial evolution (p. 397)
singing plow (p. 397)
mechanical reaper (p. 397)
American system (p. 399)
free-labor ideal (p. 405)
manifest destiny (p. 408)
Oregon Trail (p. 408)
policy of concentration (p. 410)
Fort Laramie conference (p. 410)
The Book of Mormon (p. 411)
Church of Jesus Christ of Latter-Day Saints (p. 411)
Utah Territory (p. 412)
Mormon War (p. 412)

Santa Fe Trail (p. 413)
Alamo (p. 414)
Goliad (p. 414)
San Jacinto (p. 414)
Lone Star Republic (p. 414)
ranchos (p. 414)
California Trail (p. 414)
Bear Flag Revolt (p. 414)
Republic of Texas (p. 415)
Mexican-American War (p. 416)
Treaty of Guadalupe Hidalgo (p. 420)
California gold rush (p. 421)
transcendentalism (p. 424)
utopian communities (p. 424)
Brook Farm (p. 424)
Fourierist phalanxes (p. 425)
Oneida community (p. 425)
Seneca Falls Declaration of Sentiments (p. 426)
American Colonization Society (p. 427)
underground railroad (p. 430)

TIMELINE

◄ **1836** • Texas declares independence from Mexico.

1837 • John Deere patents steel plow.

1840s • Practical mechanical reapers created.

1841 • First wagon trains head west on Oregon Trail.
• Vice President John Tyler becomes president when William Henry Harrison dies.
• Brook Farm organized.

1844 • Democrat James K. Polk elected president.
• Samuel F. B. Morse demonstrates telegraph.

1845 • Term *manifest destiny* coined.
• United States annexes Texas, which enters Union as slave state.
• Potato blight in Ireland spurs immigration to United States.

1846 • Bear Flag Revolt in California.
• Congress declares war on Mexico.
• United States and Great Britain agree to divide Oregon Country.

REVIEW QUESTIONS

1. Why did the United States become a leading industrial power in the nineteenth century? (pp. 397–401)

2. How did the free-labor ideal account for economic inequality? (pp. 402–7)

3. Why did westward migration expand dramatically in the mid-nineteenth century? (pp. 407–14)

4. Why was the annexation of Texas such a controversial policy? (pp. 414–24)

5. Why were women especially prominent in many nineteenth-century reform efforts? (pp. 424–30)

MAKING CONNECTIONS

1. Varied political, economic, and technological factors promoted westward migration in the mid-nineteenth century. Considering these factors, discuss migration to two different regions (for instance, Texas, Oregon, Utah, or California). What drew migrants to the region? How did the U.S. government contribute to their efforts?

2. How did the ideology of manifest destiny contribute to the mid–nineteenth-century drive for expansion? Discuss its implications for individual migrants and the nation. In your answer, consider how manifest destiny built on, or revised, earlier understandings of the nation's history and racial politics.

3. The Mexican-American War reshaped U.S. borders and more. Discuss the consequences of the war for national political and economic developments in subsequent decades. What resources did the new territory give the United States? How did debate over annexation revive older political disputes?

4. Some nineteenth-century reform movements drew on the free-labor ideal, while others challenged it. Discuss the free-labor ideal in relation to two reform movements (such as abolitionism and utopian communalism). How did they draw on the ideal to pursue specific reforms? How did these minority movements try to influence national developments?

▶ **FOR PRACTICE QUIZZES, A CUSTOMIZED STUDY PLAN, AND OTHER STUDY TOOLS**, see the Online Study Guide at bedfordstmartins.com/roark.

1847 • Mormons settle in Utah.

    1848 • Treaty of Guadalupe Hidalgo.

        • Oneida community organized in New York.

        • First U.S. woman's rights convention takes place at Seneca Falls, New York.

        1849 • California gold rush begins.

            1850 • Mormon community annexed to United States as Utah Territory.

                1851 • Conference in Laramie, Wyoming, marks the beginning of government policy of concentration.

                    1855 • Massachusetts integrates public schools.

                        1857 • U.S. troops invade Salt Lake City in Mormon War.

CLAY JUG

Enslaved African American potters created tens of thousands of ceramic pots to hold water and store food. Pottery sometimes went beyond the utilitarian and became art. The most renowned slave potter, Dave, worked in Edgefield District, South Carolina, an area with rich deposits of high-quality clay and a concentration of white-owned pottery shops. Many of Dave's vessels are huge. This pot, completed on August 24, 1857, is nearly three feet tall and holds more than twenty-five gallons. Beyond their extraordinary size, Dave's pots are unusual for their inscriptions. At a time when teaching slaves to read and write was illegal, Dave signed his work with a grand flourish: "Dave" or "Dave the potter." He also inscribed some of his pots with verse. His rhymes provide glimpses into his life. For example, "I wonder where is all my relations / Friendship to all and every nation" probably refers to the slave sales that sent some of his family to Louisiana.

Collection of McKissick Museum, University of South Carolina.

13

The Slave South

1820–1860

■ **The Growing Distinctiveness of the South** 436
Cotton Kingdom, Slave Empire   437
The South in Black and White   437
The Plantation Economy   442

■ **Masters, Mistresses, and the Big House** 448
Plantation Masters   448
Plantation Mistresses   450

■ **Slaves and the Quarter** 456
Work 456
Family, Religion, and Community   457
Resistance and Rebellion   459

■ **Black and Free: On the Middle Ground** 461
Precarious Freedom   461
Achievement despite Restrictions   462

■ **The Plain Folk** 462
Plantation Belt Yeomen   463
Upcountry Yeomen   463
Poor Whites   464
The Culture of the Plain Folk   466

■ **The Politics of Slavery** 466
The Democratization of the Political Arena   467
Planter Power   468

■ **Conclusion: A Slave Society** 469

NAT TURNER WAS BORN A SLAVE in Southampton County, Virginia, in October 1800. People in his neighborhood claimed that he had always been different. His parents noticed special marks on his body, which they said were signs that he was "intended for some great purpose." His master said that he learned to read without being taught. As an adolescent, he adopted an austere lifestyle of Christian devotion and fasting. In his twenties, he received visits from the "Spirit," the same spirit, he believed, that had spoken to the ancient prophets. In time, Turner began to interpret these things to mean that God had appointed him an instrument of divine vengeance for the sin of slaveholding.

In the early morning of August 22, 1831, he set out with six trusted friends—Hark, Henry, Sam, Nelson, Will, and Jack—to punish slave owners. Turner struck the first blow, an ax to the head of his master, Joseph Travis. The rebels killed all of the white men, women, and children they encountered in each household they attacked. By noon, they had visited eleven farms and slaughtered fifty-seven whites. Along the way, they had added fifty or sixty men to their army. Word spread quickly, and soon the militia and hundreds of local whites gathered in response. By the next day, whites had captured or killed all of the rebels except Turner, who hid out for about ten weeks before being captured in nearby woods. Within a week, he was tried, convicted, and executed. By then, forty-five slaves had stood trial, twenty had been convicted and hanged, and another ten had been banished from Virginia. Frenzied whites had killed another hundred or more blacks—insurgents and innocent bystanders—in their counterattack against the rebellion.

Virginia's governor, John Floyd, asked how Turner's band of "assassins and murderers" could have assaulted the "unsuspecting and defenseless" citizens of "one of the fairest counties in the Commonwealth." White Virginians prided themselves on having the "mildest" slavery in the South, but sixty black rebels on a rampage challenged the comforting theory of the contented slave. Nonetheless, whites found explanations that allowed them to feel safer. They placed the blame on outside agitators. In 1829, David Walker, a freeborn black man living in Boston, had published his *Appeal . . . to the Coloured Citizens of the World,* an invitation to slaves to rise up in bloody rebellion, and copies had fallen into the hands of Virginia slaves. Moreover, on January 1, 1831, in Boston, the Massachusetts abolitionist William Lloyd Garrison had published the first issue of the *Liberator,* his fiery newspaper. White Virginians also dismissed the rebellion's leader, Nat Turner, as insane. "He is a complete fanatic, or plays his part admirably," wrote Thomas R. Gray, the lawyer who was assigned to defend Turner.

Horrid Massacre in Virginia
There are no known contemporary images of Nat Turner. This woodcut simply imagines the rebellion as
a nightmare in which black brutes took the lives of innocent whites. Although there was never another
rebellion as large as Turner's, images of black violence continued to haunt white imaginations.
Library of Congress.

In the months following the insurrection, white Virginians debated the future of slavery in their state. Although some expressed substantial doubts, the Virginia legislature reaffirmed the state's determination to preserve black bondage. Delegates passed a raft of laws strengthening the institution of slavery and further restricting free blacks. A thirty-year-old professor at the College of William and Mary, Thomas R. Dew, published a vigorous defense of slavery that became the bible of Southerners' proslavery arguments. More than ever, the nation was divided along the "Mason-Dixon line," the surveyors' mark that in colonial times had established the boundary between Maryland and Pennsylvania but half a century later divided the free North and the slave South.

Black slavery increasingly molded the South into a distinctive region. In the decades after 1820, Southerners, like Northerners, raced westward, but unlike Northerners who spread small farms and free labor, Southerners spread slavery, cotton, and plantations. Geographic expansion meant that slavery became more vigorous and profitable than ever, embraced more people, and increased the South's political power. **Antebellum** Southerners included diverse people who at times found themselves at odds with one another—not only slaves and free people but also women and men; Indians, Africans, and Europeans; and aristocrats and common folk. Nevertheless, beneath this diversity, a distinctively southern society and **culture** were forming. The South became a slave society, and most white Southerners were proud of it.

The Growing Distinctiveness of the South

From the earliest settlements, inhabitants of the southern colonies had shared a great deal with northern colonists. Most whites in both sections were British and **Protestant**, spoke a common language, and shared an exuberant pride in their victorious revolution against British rule. The creation of the new nation under the Constitution in 1789 forged strong political ties that bound all Americans. The beginnings of a national economy fostered economic interdependence and communication across regional boundaries. White Americans everywhere celebrated the achievements of the prosperous young nation, and they looked forward to its seemingly boundless future.

Despite these national similarities, Southerners and Northerners grew increasingly different. The French political observer Alexis de Tocqueville believed he knew why. "I could easily prove," he asserted in 1831, "that almost all the differences which may be noticed between the character of the Americans in the Southern and Northern states have originated in slavery." Slavery made the South different, and it was the differences between the North and South, not the similarities, that increasingly shaped antebellum American history.

Cotton Kingdom, Slave Empire

In the first half of the nineteenth century, millions of Americans migrated west. In the South, the stampede began after the Creek War of 1813–1814, which divested the Creek Indians of 24 million acres and initiated the government campaign to remove Indian people living east of the Mississippi River to the West (see chapters 10 and 11). Eager slaveholders seeking virgin acreage for new plantations, struggling farmers looking for patches of land for small farms, herders and drovers pushing their hogs and cattle toward fresh pastures—anyone who was restless and ambitious felt the pull of Indian land. Southerners pushed westward relentlessly, until by midcentury the South encompassed nearly a million square miles. Contemporaries spoke of this vast region as the Lower South, those states where cotton was dominant, and the Upper South, where cotton was less important.

The South's climate and geography were ideally suited for the cultivation of cotton. Advancing Southerners encountered a variety of terrain, soil, and weather, but cotton's requirements are minimal: two hundred frost-free days from planting to picking and plentiful rain, conditions found in much of the South. By the 1830s, cotton fields stretched from southern Virginia to central Texas. Heavy southern and westward migration led to statehood for Arkansas in 1836 and for Texas and Florida in 1845. Production soared from 300,000 bales in 1830 to nearly 5 million in 1860, when the South produced three-fourths of the world's supply. The South—especially that tier of states from South Carolina west to Texas—had become the cotton kingdom (Map 13.1, page 438).

The cotton kingdom was also a slave empire. The South's cotton boom rested on the backs of slaves, who grew 75 percent of the crop on plantations, toiling in gangs in broad fields under the direct supervision of whites. As cotton agriculture expanded westward, whites shipped more than 300,000 slaves out of the old seaboard states. Victims of this brutal but thriving domestic slave trade marched hundreds of miles to new plantations in the Lower South. Cotton, slaves, and plantations moved west together.

The slave population grew enormously. Southern slaves numbered fewer than 700,000 in 1790, about 2 million in 1830, and almost 4 million by 1860, an increase of almost 600 percent in seven decades. By 1860, the South contained more slaves than all the other slave societies in the New World combined. The extraordinary growth was not the result of the importation of slaves, which the federal government outlawed in 1808. Instead, the slave population grew through natural reproduction. By the nineteenth century, most slaves were native born Southerners. In comparison, Cuba and Brazil, slave societies that kept their slave trades open until the mid-nineteenth century, had more African-born slaves and thus stronger ties to Africa.

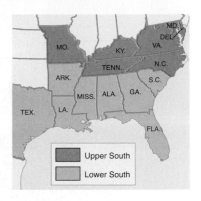

The Upper and Lower South

The South in Black and White

By 1860, one in every three Southerners was black (approximately 4 million blacks and 8 million whites). In the Lower South states of Mississippi and South Carolina, blacks were the majority (Figure 13.1, page 439). The contrast with the North was striking: In 1860, only one Northerner in seventy-six was black (about 250,000 blacks to 19 million whites).

The presence of large numbers of African Americans had profound consequences for the South. Southern culture—language, food, music, religion, and even accents—was in part shaped by blacks. But the most direct consequence of the South's biracialism was southern whites' commitment to white supremacy. Northern whites believed in racial superiority, too, but they lived in a society in which blacks made up barely 1 percent of the population. Their dedication to white supremacy lacked the intensity and urgency increasingly felt by white Southerners who lived among millions of blacks. White Southerners despised blacks because they considered them

The French political observer Alexis de Tocqueville asserted in 1831, "Almost all the differences which may be noticed between the character of the Americans in the Southern and Northern states have originated in slavery."

Slave population, 1820

One dot equals 200 slaves

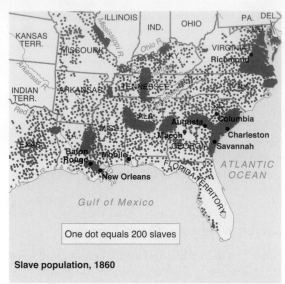

Slave population, 1860

One dot equals 200 slaves

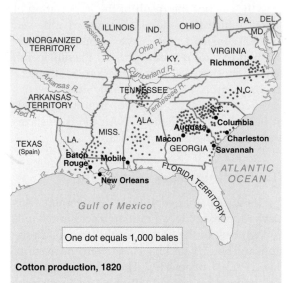

Cotton production, 1820

One dot equals 1,000 bales

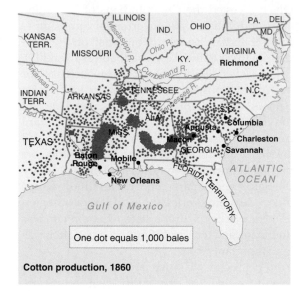

Cotton production, 1860

One dot equals 1,000 bales

MAP 13.1   Cotton Kingdom, Slave Empire: 1820 and 1860
As the production of cotton soared, the slave population increased dramatically. Slaves continued to toil in tobacco and rice fields along the Atlantic seaboard, but increasingly they worked on cotton plantations in Alabama, Mississippi, and Louisiana.

READING THE MAP: Where was slavery most prevalent in 1820? In 1860? How did the spread of slavery compare with the spread of cotton?

CONNECTIONS: How much of the world's cotton was produced in the American South in 1860? How did the number of slaves in the American South compare to that in the rest of the world? What does this suggest about the South's cotton kingdom?

FOR MORE HELP ANALYZING THIS MAP, see the map activity for this chapter in the Online Study Guide at bedfordstmartins.com/roark.

members of an inferior race, further degraded by their status as slaves. They also feared blacks because they realized that slaves had every reason to hate them and to strike back, as Nat Turner had.

Attacks on slavery after 1820—from blacks and a handful of white antislavery advocates within the South and from abolitionists outside—jolted southern slaveholders into a distressing awareness that they lived in a dangerous and fragile world. As the only slave society embedded in an egalitarian, democratic republic, the South made extraordinary efforts to strengthen slavery. State legislatures constructed slave codes (laws) that required the total submission of slaves to their masters and to white society in general. As the Louisiana code stated, a slave "owes his master . . . a respect without bounds, and an absolute obedience." The laws underlined the authority of all whites, not just masters. Any white could "correct" slaves who did not stay "in their place."

Intellectuals joined legislators in the campaign to strengthen slavery. Beginning in earnest in the 1820s, the South's academics, writers, and clergy constructed a proslavery argument that sought to unify the region's whites around slavery and provide ammunition for the emerging war of words with northern abolitionists. With the intellectuals' guidance, white Southerners gradually moved away from defending slavery as a "necessary evil"—the halfhearted argument

popular in Jefferson's day—and toward a full-throated, aggressive defense of slavery as a "positive good." John C. Calhoun, an influential southern politician, declared that in the states where slavery had been abolished, "the condition of the African, instead of being improved, has become worse," while in the slave states, the Africans "have improved greatly in every respect." (See "Documenting the American Promise," page 440.)

Slavery's champions employed every imaginable defense. In the South, slaves were legal property, and wasn't the protection of property the bedrock of American **liberty**? They also used historical evidence to endorse slavery. Weren't the great civilizations—such as those of the Hebrews, Greeks, and Romans—slave societies? They argued that the Bible, properly interpreted, also sanctioned slavery. Old Testament patriarchs owned slaves, they observed, and in the New Testament, Paul returned the runaway slave Onesimus to his master. Some proslavery spokesmen played on the fears of Northerners

FIGURE 13.1 Black and White Populations in the South, 1860

Blacks represented a much larger fraction of the population in the South than in the North, but considerable variation existed from state to state. Only one Missourian in ten, for example, was black, while Mississippi and South Carolina had black majorities. States in the Upper South were "whiter" than states in the Lower South, despite the Upper South's greater number of free blacks.

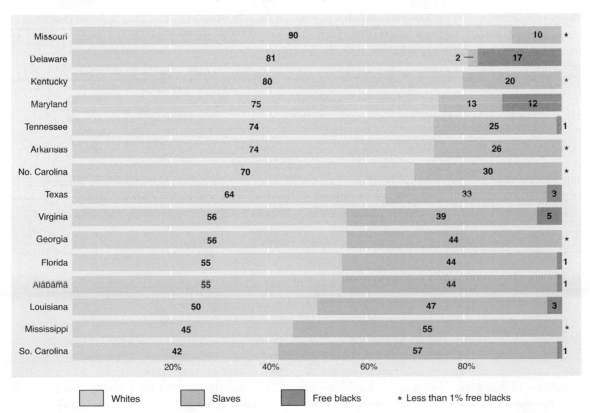

State	Whites	Slaves	Free blacks
Missouri	90	10	*
Delaware	81	2	17
Kentucky	80	20	*
Maryland	75	13	12
Tennessee	74	25	1
Arkansas	74	26	*
No. Carolina	70	30	*
Texas	64	33	3
Virginia	56	39	5
Georgia	56	44	*
Florida	55	44	1
Alabama	55	44	1
Louisiana	50	47	3
Mississippi	45	55	*
So. Carolina	42	57	1

20%   40%   60%   80%

Whites   Slaves   Free blacks   * Less than 1% free blacks

Defending Slavery

White Southerners who defended slavery were rationalizing their economic interests and racial privileges, of course, but they also believed what they said about slavery being just, necessary, and godly. Politicians, planters, clergymen, and academics wrote essays on economics, religion, morality, science, political theory, and law to defend the southern way of life and justify slavery. Whatever their specific arguments, they agreed with the Charleston Mercury that without slavery, the South would become a "most magnificent jungle."

DOCUMENT 1
John C. Calhoun, Speech before the U.S. Senate, 1837

When abolitionists began to flood Congress with petitions that denounced slavery as sinful and odious, John C. Calhoun, the South's leading proslavery politician, rose to defend the institution as "a positive good." Calhoun devoted part of his speech to the argument that enslavement benefited the slaves themselves.

Be it good or bad, it [slavery] has grown up with our society and institutions, and is so interwoven with them, that to destroy it would be to destroy us as a people. But let me not be understood as admitting, even by implication, that the existing relations between the two races in the slaveholding States is an evil: far otherwise; I hold it to be a good, as it has thus far proved to be to both, and will continue to prove so if not disturbed by the fell spirit of abolition. I appeal to facts. Never before has the black race of Central Africa, from the dawn of history to the present day, attained a condition so civilized and so improved, not only physically, but morally and intellectually. It came to us in a low, degraded, and savage condition, and in the course of a few generations, it has grown up under the fostering care of our institutions, reviled they have been, to its present comparatively civilized condition. This, with the rapid increase of numbers, is conclusive proof of the general happiness of the race, in spite of all the exaggerated tales to the contrary. . . .

I hold that in the present state of civilization, where two races of different origin, and distinguished by color, and other physical differences, as well as intellectual, are brought together, the relation now existing in the slaveholding States between the two, is, instead of an evil, a good—a positive good. . . .

I may say with truth, that in few countries so much is left to the share of the laborer, and so little exacted from him, or where there is more kind attention paid to him in sickness or infirmities of age. Compare his condition with the tenants of the poor houses in the more civilized portions of Europe—look at the sick, and the old and infirm slave, on one hand, in the midst of his family and friends, under the kind superintending care of his master and mistress, and compare it with the forlorn and wretched condition of the pauper in the poor house.

SOURCE: John C. Calhoun, "Speech on the Reception of Abolition Petitions, Delivered in the Senate, February 6th, 1837," in *Speeches of John C. Calhoun, Delivered in the House of Representatives and in the Senate of the United States*. Edited by Richard K. Cralle (Appleton, 1853), 625–33.

DOCUMENT 2
William Harper, *Memoir on Slavery*, 1837

Unlike Calhoun, who defended slavery by pointing to what he considered slavery's concrete benefits for blacks, William Harper—judge, politician, and academic—defended slavery by denouncing abolitionists, particularly the "atrocious philosophy" of "natural equality and inalienable rights" that they used to support their attacks on slavery.

All men are born free and equal. Is it not palpably nearer the truth to say that no man was ever born free, and

and Southerners alike by charging that giving blacks equal rights would lead to the sexual mixing of the races, or **miscegenation**. Others attacked the economy and society of the North. George Fitzhugh of Virginia argued that behind the North's grand slogan of **free labor** lay a heartless philosophy: "Every man for himself, and the devil take the hindmost." Gouging capitalists exploited wageworkers unmercifully, Fitzhugh declared, and he contrasted the North's vicious free-labor system with the humane relations that he claimed prevailed between masters and slaves because slaves were valuable capital that masters sought to protect.

But at the heart of the defense of slavery lay the claim of black inferiority. Black enslavement

that no two men were ever born equal? . . . Wealth and poverty, fame or obscurity, strength or weakness, knowledge or ignorance, ease or labor, power or subjection, mark the endless diversity in the condition of men. . . .

It is the order of nature and of God, that the being of superior faculties and knowledge, and therefore of superior power, should control and dispose of those who are inferior. It is as much in the order of nature, that men should enslave each other, as that other animals should prey upon each other. I admit that he does this under the highest moral responsibility, and is most guilty if he wantonly inflicts misery or privation on beings more capable of enjoyment or suffering than brutes, without necessity or any view to the great good which is to result. . . .

Moralists have denounced the injustice and cruelty which have been practiced towards our aboriginal Indians, by which they have been driven from their native seats and exterminated. . . . No doubt, much fraud and injustice has been practiced in the circumstances and manner of their removal. Yet who has contended that civilized man had no moral right to possess himself of the country? That he was bound to leave this wide and fertile continent, which is capable of sustaining uncounted myriads of a civilized race, to a few roving and ignorant barbarians? Yet if any thing is certain, it is certain that there were no means by which he could possess the country, without exterminating or enslaving them. Slave and civilized man cannot live together, and the savage can only be tamed by being enslaved or by having slaves.

SOURCE: William Harper, *Memoir of Slavery* (J.S. Burges, 1838).

DOCUMENT 3
Thornton Stringfellow, "The Bible Argument: or, Slavery in the Light of Divine Revelation," 1856

Reverend Thornton Stringfellow, a Baptist minister from Virginia, offered a defense of human bondage based on his reading of the Bible. In these passages, he makes a case that Jesus himself approved of the relationship between master and slave.

Jesus Christ recognized this institution [slavery] as one that was lawful among men, and regulated its relative duties.

. . . I affirm then, first, (and no man denies,) that Jesus Christ has not abolished slavery by a prohibitory command: and second, I affirm, he has introduced no new moral principle which can work its destruction, under the gospel dispensation; and that the principle relied on for this purpose, is a fundamental principle of the Mosaic law, under which slavery was instituted by Jehovah himself. . . .

To the church at Colosse, a city of Phrygia, in the lesser Asia, Paul in his letter to them, recognizes the three relations of wives and husbands, parents and children, servants and masters, as relations existing among the members . . . and to the servants and masters he thus writes: "Servants obey in all things your masters, according to the flesh: not with eye service, as men pleasers, but in singleness of heart, fearing God: and whatsoever you do, do it heartily, as to the Lord and not unto men; knowing that of the Lord ye shall receive the reward of the inheritance, for ye serve the Lord Christ. . . . Masters give unto your servants that which is just and equal, knowing that you also have a master in heaven."

SOURCES: *Slavery Defended: The Views of the Old South* by Eric L. McKitrick, editor. Published by Prentice-Hall, 1963. Reprinted with permission. *Cotton Is King and Pro-Slavery Arguments* by Thornton Stringfellow (Pritchard, Abbott & Loomis, 1860), 459–546.

QUESTIONS FOR ANALYSIS AND DEBATE

1. According to John C. Calhoun, what were slavery's chief benefits for blacks? How did his proslavery convictions shape his argument?

2. Why do you suppose William Harper interjected Americans' treatment of Indians into his defense of slavery?

3. According to Thornton Stringfellow, the Bible instructs both masters and slaves about their duties. What are their respective obligations?

was both necessary and proper, antebellum defenders argued, because Africans were lesser beings. Rather than exploitative, slavery was a mass civilizing effort that lifted lowly blacks from barbarism and savagery, taught them disciplined work, and converted them to soul-saving Christianity. According to Virginian Thomas R. Dew, most slaves were grateful. He declared that "the slaves of a good master are his warmest, most constant, and most devoted friends."

Black slavery encouraged whites to unify around race rather than to divide by class. The grubbiest, most tobacco-stained white man could proudly proclaim his superiority to all blacks and his equality with the most refined southern patrician. Because of racial slavery,

Georgia attorney Thomas R. R. Cobb observed, every white Southerner "feels that he belongs to an elevated class. It matters not that he is no slaveholder; he is not of the inferior race; he is a freeborn citizen." Consequently, the "poorest meets the richest as an equal; sits at his table with him; salutes him as a neighbor; meets him in every public assembly, and stands on the same social platform." In the South, Cobb boasted, "there is no war of classes."

In reality, slavery did not create perfect harmony among whites or ease every strain along class lines. But by providing every antebellum white Southerner membership in the ruling race, slavery helped whites bridge differences in wealth, education, and culture. Slavery meant white dominance, white superiority, and white equality.

The Plantation Economy

As important as slavery was in unifying white Southerners, only about a quarter of the white population lived in slaveholding families. Most slaveholders owned fewer than five slaves. Only

---

The Fruits of Amalgamation

White Southerners and Northerners alike generally agreed that giving blacks equal rights would lead to miscegenation (also known as "amalgamation"). In this lithograph from 1839, Edward W. Clay of Philadelphia attacked abolitionists by imagining the outcome of their misguided campaign. He drew a beautiful white woman with her two black children, one suckling at her breast, while her dark-skinned, ridiculously overdressed husband, resting his feet in his wife's lap, reads an abolitionist newspaper. The couple is attended by a white servant. Another interracial couple—perhaps the man is abolitionist William Lloyd Garrison himself—has come calling. Hanging on the wall is a picture entitled *Othello & Desdemona*, based on Shakespeare's *Othello*, a tragic play about a couple who crossed the color line. A black dog and a white dog play indiscriminately on the floor. Abolitionists denied the charge of amalgamation and pointed to the lasciviousness of southern slaveholders as the true source of miscegenation in antebellum America.
Courtesy, American Antiquarian Society.

THE FRUITS OF AMALGAMATION.

about 12 percent of slave owners owned twenty or more, the number of slaves that historians consider necessary to distinguish a **planter** from a farmer. Although they were hugely outnumbered, planters nevertheless dominated the southern economy. In 1860, 52 percent of the South's slaves lived and worked on plantations. Plantation slaves produced more than 75 percent of the South's export crops, the backbone of the region's economy. Slavery was dying elsewhere in the New World (only Brazil and Cuba still defended slavery at midcentury), but slave plantations increasingly dominated southern agriculture.

The South's major cash crops—tobacco, sugar, rice, and cotton—grew on plantations (Map 13.2). Tobacco, the original plantation crop in North America, had shifted westward in the nineteenth century from the Chesapeake to Tennessee and Kentucky. Large-scale sugar production began in 1795, when Étienne de Boré built a modern sugar mill in what is today New Orleans, and sugar plantations were confined almost entirely to Louisiana. Commercial rice production began in the seventeenth century, and like sugar, rice was confined to a small geographic area, a narrow strip of coast stretching from the Carolinas into Georgia.

Tobacco, sugar, and rice were labor-intensive crops that relied on large numbers of slaves to do the backbreaking work. Most phases of tobacco cultivation—planting, transporting, thinning, picking off caterpillars, cutting, drying, packing—required laborers to stoop or bend down. Work on sugarcane plantations was reputed to be the most physically demanding. During the harvest, slaves worked eighteen hours a day, and so hard was the slaves' task that one visitor concluded that "nothing but 'involuntary servitude' could go through the toil and suffering required to produce sugar." Working in water and mud in the heat of a Carolina summer regularly threatened slaves involved in rice production with malaria, yellow fever, and other diseases. As a consequence, blacks accounted for 90 percent of the population in the coastal area.

If tobacco, sugar, and rice were the princes of plantation agriculture, cotton was the king. Cotton became commercially significant in the 1790s after the invention of a new cotton gin

MAP 13.2   The Agricultural Economy of the South, 1860
Cotton dominated the South's agricultural economy, but the region grew a variety of crops and was largely self-sufficient in foodstuffs.

READING THE MAP: In what type of geographical areas were rice and sugar grown? After cotton, what crop commanded the greatest agricultural area in the South? In which region of the South was this crop predominantly found?
CONNECTIONS: What role did the South play in the U.S. economy in 1860? How did the economy of the South differ from that of the North?

FOR MORE HELP ANALYZING THIS MAP, see the map activity for this chapter in the Online Study Guide at bedfordstmartins.com/roark.

by Eli Whitney dramatically increased the production of raw cotton. (See "Beyond America's Borders," page 444.) Cotton was relatively easy to grow and took little capital to get started—just enough to purchase land, seed, and simple tools. Thus, small farmers as well as planters grew the white fluffy stuff. But planters, whose fields were worked by slaves, produced three-quarters of the South's cotton, and cotton made planters rich.

Plantation slavery also enriched the nation. By 1840, cotton accounted for more than 60 percent of American exports. Much of the profit from the sale of cotton overseas returned to planters, but some went to northern middlemen who bought, sold, insured, warehoused, and shipped cotton to the mills in Great Britain and

White Gold: The International Empire of Cotton

Although farmers had grown cotton for more than five thousand years, it wasn't until 1793 that the invention of a simple device enabled the once localized cotton market to spread into an international empire. The kind of cotton that grew best in the American South—green-seed cotton—was filled with sticky seeds that clung to the fibers. Many a pioneer family spent long winter evenings seated around the fire tediously plucking the fluff from each seed. Farmwives made the little clean cotton produced by handpicking into homespun on family spinning wheels and hand looms. The problem of sticky seeds attracted the attention of mechanics from India to Santo Domingo, but no one was able to solve this problem. Machines for separating cotton fibers from seeds—cotton gins (the word *gin* is short for *engine*)—had been around for centuries, but none cleaned cotton quickly and efficiently.

In 1792, a young New Englander accepted a position as tutor to the children of a Georgia planter. The teaching post did not work out, but Eli Whitney stayed on at the Savannah River plantation of Catherine Greene, widow of Nathanael Greene, who had been a hero of the American Revolution. On September 11, 1793, Whitney wrote his sister, "I have . . . heard much said of the extreme difficulty of ginning cotton. That is, separating it from its seed." He had met "a number of respectable Gentlemen . . .

who all agreed that if a machine could be invented which would clean cotton with expedition, it would be a great thing both to the country and the inventor."

Whitney succeeded in building a simple little device for separating the fibers from the seeds. It consisted of wire teeth set in a wooden cylinder that, when rotated, reached through narrow slats to pull cotton fibers away from the seeds while a brush swept the fibers from the revolving teeth. It was crude, but news of the invention spread like wildfire. Just days later, South Carolina planter Pierce Butler wrote a friend, "There is a young Man at Mrs Greene's in Georgia, who has made a Cotton Ginn that with two Boys cleans of the green seed cotton 64 p[oun]ds of clean cotton in about nine hours." In his application for a patent, Whitney emphasized that his gin was "entirely new & constructed in a different manner and upon different principles from any other Cotton Ginn." His invention enabled cotton growers for the first time to supply huge quantities of clean cotton for the world market.

Almost overnight, cotton production soared, and cotton quickly pushed out rice, then tobacco, as the South's major cash crop. In just a few years, Whitney's gin helped transform the entire economy of the South. The commercial production of cotton bound millions of African Americans to perpetual slavery. For them, the promise of this particular piece of

technology proved tragically hollow. Cotton also wielded power in the Midwest, which sold millions of dollars' worth of food to cotton producers in the South, and the East, which sold boatloads of manufactured goods to Southerners and whose ships carried cotton to the world. In 1860, the South produced an astonishing 2.2 billion pounds of clean cotton, enough to satisfy the cotton-hungry textile factories of the North and of Europe.

Whitney's invention spawned a worldwide cotton industry and initiated an international economic and social transformation. Not only did mill towns spring up in New England, but American cotton also became central to the industrializing economies of Europe, particularly in Britain, France, and Belgium. Cotton utterly transformed the face of Britain. The steam engine, other mechanical advances in the spinning of yarn and the weaving of cloth, and almost unlimited amounts of cotton from America's South changed the production of British textiles from a family-based endeavor to a roaring industrial enterprise. Cotton made the north of England a vast beehive of manufacturing activity, the epicenter of the first truly industrial society. Armies of workers trudged to massive cotton factories in Manchester and other booming industrial cities in the county of Lancashire. By the mid-nineteenth century, almost one-fourth of the English population depended in some way on the textile industry, and cotton cloth made up half of England's exports.

Before the American Civil War (1861–1865), most of the cotton that fed textile mills in Europe was grown by slaves in the South. When the war temporarily interrupted the flow of cotton (see chapter 15), European imperial powers looked increasingly to their territories—especially those in Asia and Africa—for more of their cotton. The temporary cessation of American cotton production helped propel what has been called the Second British Empire—the nineteenth-century expansion of mercantile imperialism that brought India and other far-flung areas of the world into the emerging global cotton economy.

The Civil War abolished slavery, but it did not end the South's fixation on cotton. Indeed, by the end of the nineteenth century, the South produced more than twice as much cotton with free labor as it had forty years earlier with slaves. With the end of the war, most of Britain's cotton again came from the American South, and the South remained integral to the new global trading and manufacturing cotton complex. Not only did America dominate the world market for raw cotton for 150 years, but by 1897 it also surpassed Britain as the largest manufacturer of cotton cloth in the world.

The cotton fields of the South and the textile mills of Europe and New England brought cotton cloth within the reach of everyone. Before Eli Whitney's cotton gin, the world was clothed in flax and wool, and cotton fabrics were luxury items. In 1793, only about 4 percent of all the clothing in Europe and the United States was made from cotton. A century later, that figure had grown to 73 percent. Around the world, cotton became the cloth of everyman, accessible to people of all classes, races, and nationalities.

Cotton Transport in India

For centuries, India stood at the center of the world's production of handmade cotton textiles, but beginning in the eighteenth century Britain needed raw cotton, not finished cloth, for its burgeoning mechanized textile industry. This 1862 watercolor portrays a caravan of ox-drawn, wooden-wheeled carts heavily laden with raw cotton snaking its way through a traditional village. This was the first step on the long trip to Britain, the heart of the new global cotton economy.

Cotton Transport, India, 1862 (w/c over pencil heightened with white) by William Simpson (1823–1899) © Private Collection/Photo © Bonhams, London, UK/The Bridgeman Art Library. Nationality/copyright status: Scottish/out of copyright.

The Cotton Gin

By the 1790s, the British had succeeded in mechanizing the manufacture of cotton cloth, but they were unable to get enough raw cotton. The South could grow cotton in unimaginable quantities, but cotton stuck to seeds was useless in British textile mills. In 1793, Eli Whitney, a Northerner who was living on a Savannah River plantation, built a simple device for separating the cotton from the seed. Widespread use of the cotton gin broke the bottleneck in the commercial production of cotton and eventually bound millions of African Americans to slavery.

Smithsonian Institution, Washington, D.C.

Arise! Arise! and weep no more
dry up your tears, we shall part
no more, come rose we go to
Tennessee,
that happy shore. To old virginia
never — never — return.

Slave Traders: Sold to Tennessee

Slave trading—or "Negro speculation," as it was called by contemporaries—was a booming business in the antebellum South. This color drawing by Lewis Miller portrays slaves walking from Virginia to Tennessee under the watchful eyes of professional slave traders. A few children accompany the adults, some of whom may be their parents. Forced migrations almost always resulted in the separation of black family members.
Abby Aldrich Rockefeller Folk Art Center, Williamsburg, VA.

elsewhere. As one New York merchant observed, "Cotton has enriched all through whose hands it has passed." As middlemen invested their profits in the booming northern economy, industrial development received a burst of much-needed capital. Furthermore, southern plantations benefited northern industry by providing an important market for textiles, agricultural tools, and other manufactured goods.

The economies of the North and South steadily diverged. While the North developed a mixed economy—agriculture, commerce, and manufacturing—the South remained overwhelmingly agricultural. Since planters were earning healthy profits, they saw little reason to diversify. Year after year, they funneled the profits they earned from land and slaves back into more land and slaves. With its capital flowing into agriculture, the South did not develop many factories. By 1860, only 10 percent of the nation's industrial workers lived in the South.

> One New York merchant observed, "Cotton has enriched all through whose hands it has passed."

Some cotton mills sprang up, but the region that produced 100 percent of the nation's cotton manufactured less than 7 percent of its cotton textiles.

Without significant economic diversification, the South developed fewer cities than the North and West (Map 13.3). In 1860, it was the least urban region in the country. Whereas nearly 37 percent of New England's population lived in cities, less than 12 percent of Southerners were urban dwellers. Southern cities also differed from those elsewhere in the nation. They were mostly port cities on the periphery of the region and busy principally with exporting the agricultural products of plantations in the interior. Urban merchants provided agriculture with indispensable services, such as hauling, insuring, and selling cotton, rice, and sugar, but they were the tail on the plantation dog. Southern cities could claim something no northern city desired: 140,000 slaves in 1860. In some southern cities, slaves made up half the population, and they worked in nearly every conceivable occupation, helping the southern economy thrive.

Because the South had so few cities and industrial jobs, it attracted relatively small numbers of European immigrants. Seeking economic opportunity, not competition with slaves (whose labor would keep wages low), immigrants steered well north of the South's slave-dominated, agricultural economy. In 1860, 13 percent of all Americans were born abroad. But in nine of the fifteen slave states, only 2 percent or less of the population was foreign-born. As in the North, immigrants were concentrated in the cities.

Not every Southerner celebrated the region's plantation economy. Critics lambasted the excessive commitment to cotton and slaves and bemoaned what one called the "deplorable scarcity" of factories. Diversification, reformers promised, would make the South economically independent and more prosperous. State governments encouraged economic development by helping to create banking systems that supplied credit for a wide range of projects and by constructing railroads, but they also failed to create some of the essential services modern economies

required. By the mid-nineteenth century, for example, no southern legislature had created a state-wide public school system. The dominant slaveholders failed to see any benefit in educating small farmers, especially with their tax money. Despite the flurry of railroad building, the South's mileage in 1860 was less than half that of the North. Moreover, whereas railroads crisscrossed the North carrying manufactured goods as well as agricultural products, most railroads in the South ran from port cities back into farming areas and were built to export cotton (see Map 12.1, page 400).

Northerners claimed that slavery was a backward and doomed labor system, but few Southerners perceived economic weakness in their region. In

▨	Less than 10%
▨	10–19%
▨	20–29%
▨	More than 30%

Immigrants as a Percentage of State Populations, 1860

MAP 13.3 Major Cities in 1860

By 1860, northern cities were more numerous and larger than southern cities. In the slave states, cities were usually seaports or river ports that served the needs of agriculture, especially cotton.

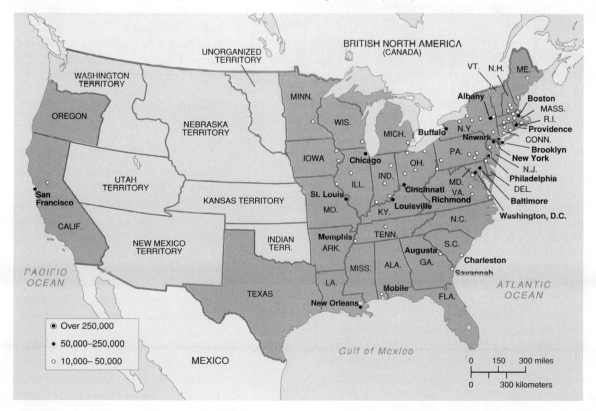

fact, planters' pockets were never fuller than in the 1850s. Compared with Northerners, Southerners invested less of their capital in industry, transportation, and public education. Planters' decisions to reinvest in agriculture ensured the momentum of the plantation economy and the political and social relationships rooted in it.

REVIEW Why did the nineteenth-century southern economy remain primarily agricultural?

The *Henry Frank*, New Orleans
The steamboat *Henry Frank* sits dangerously overloaded with cotton bales at the New Orleans levee in 1854. The banner flying from the flagstaff indicates that captains boasted about the number of bales their boats carried. The crowd on hand to greet the *Henry Frank* suggests that it might have carried a record-breaking load. The magnitude of the cotton trade in the South's largest city and major port is difficult to capture. Six years earlier, a visitor, Solon Robinson, had expressed awe: "It must be seen to be believed; and even then, it will require an active mind to comprehend acres of cotton bales standing upon the levee, while miles of drays [carts] are constantly taking it off to the cotton presses. . . . Boats are constantly arriving, so piled up with cotton, that the lower tier of bales on deck are in the water." Amid the mountains of cotton, few Southerners doubted that cotton was king.
Historic New Orleans Collection.

READING THE IMAGE: How does the image of the *Henry Frank* demonstrate the centrality of cotton to southern agriculture and southern people?

CONNECTIONS: Where did most of the cotton on the *Henry Frank* likely come from?

FOR MORE HELP ANALYZING THIS IMAGE, see the visual activity for this chapter in the Online Study Guide at bedfordstmartins.com/roark.

Masters, Mistresses, and the Big House

Nowhere was the contrast between northern and southern life more vivid than on the plantations of the South. Located on a patchwork of cleared fields and dense forests, a plantation typically included a "big house" and a slave quarter. Scattered about were numerous outbuildings, each with a special function. Near the big house were the kitchen, storehouse, smokehouse (for curing and preserving meat), and hen coop. More distant were the barns, toolsheds, **artisans'** workshops, and overseer's house. Large plantations sometimes had an infirmary and a chapel for slaves. Depending on the crop, there was a tobacco shed, a rice mill, a sugar refinery, or a cotton gin house. Lavish or plain, plantations everywhere had an underlying similarity (Figure 13.2).

The plantation was the home of masters, mistresses, and slaves. Slavery shaped the lives of all the plantation's inhabitants, from work to leisure activities, but it affected each differently. A hierarchy of rigid roles and duties governed relationships. Presiding was the master, who ruled his wife, children, and slaves, none of whom had many legal rights and all of whom were designated by the state as dependents under his dominion and protection.

Plantation Masters

Whereas smaller planters supervised the labor of their slaves themselves, larger planters hired overseers who went to the fields with the slaves, leaving the planters free to concentrate on marketing, finance, and general affairs of the plantation. Planters also found time to escape to town to discuss cotton prices, to the courthouse and legislature to debate politics, and to the woods to hunt and fish.

Increasingly in the nineteenth century, planters characterized their mastery in terms of what they called

"Christian guardianship" and what historians have called **paternalism**. The concept of paternalism denied that the form of slavery practiced in the South was brutal and exploitative. Instead, it defined southern slavery as a set of reciprocal obligations between masters and slaves. In exchange for the slaves' labor and obedience, masters provided basic care and necessary guidance. As owners of blacks, masters argued, they had the responsibility of caring for a childlike, dependent people. In 1814, Thomas Jefferson captured the essence of the advancing ideal: "We should endeavor, with those whom fortune has thrown on our hands, to feed & clothe them well, protect them from ill usage, require such reasonable labor only as is performed voluntarily by freemen, and be led by no repugnancies to abdicate them, and our duties to them." A South Carolina rice planter insisted, "I manage them as my children."

Paternalism was part propaganda and part self-delusion. But it was also economically shrewd. Masters increasingly recognized slaves as valuable assets, particularly after the nation closed its external slave trade in 1808. They realized that the expansion of the slave labor force could come only from natural reproduction. As one planter declared in 1849, "It behooves those who own them to make them last as long as possible." Another planter instructed his overseer to pay attention to "whatever tends to promote their health and render them prolific."

One consequence of this paternalism and economic self-interest was a small improvement in slaves' welfare. Diet improved, although nineteenth-century slaves still ate mainly fatty pork and cornmeal. Housing improved, although the cabins still had cracks large enough, slaves said, for cats to slip through. Clothing improved, although slaves seldom received much more than two crude outfits a year and perhaps a pair of cheap shoes. In the fields, workdays remained sunup to sundown, but planters often provided a rest period in the heat of the day. And most owners ceased the colonial practice of punishing slaves by branding and mutilation.

Paternalism should not be mistaken for "Ol' Massa's" kindness and goodwill. It encouraged better treatment because it made economic sense to provide at least minimal care for valuable slaves. Nor did paternalism require that planters put aside their whips. They could flail away and still claim that they were only fulfilling their respon-

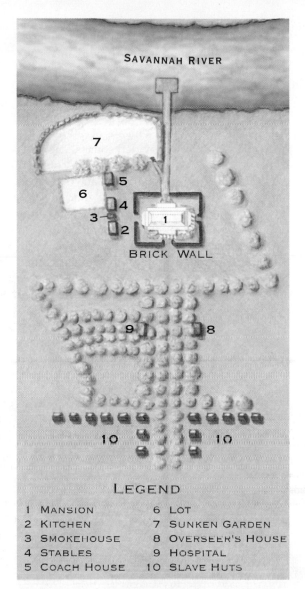

FIGURE 13.2 A Southern Plantation

Slavery determined how masters laid out their plantations, where they situated their "big houses" and slave quarters, and what kinds of buildings they constructed. This model of the Hermitage, the mansion built in 1830 for Henry McAlpin, a Georgia rice planter, shows the overseer's house poised in a grove of oak trees halfway between the owner's mansion and the slave huts. The placement of the mansion at the end of an extended road leading up from the river underscored McAlpin's affluence and authority.

Adapted from *Back of the Big House: The Architecture of Plantation Slavery* by John Michael Vlach. Copyright © 1993 by the University of North Carolina Press. Reprinted with permission of the University of North Carolina Press. Original illustration property of the Historic American Buildings Survey, a division of the National Park Service.

sibilities as guardians of their naturally lazy and at times insubordinate dependents. State laws gave masters nearly "uncontrolled authority over the body" of the slave, according to one North

Carolina judge. Paternalism offered slaves some informal protection against the most brutal punishments, but whipping remained the planters' essential form of coercion. (See "Historical Question," page 452.)

With its notion that slavery imposed on masters a burden and a duty, paternalism provided slaveholders with a means of rationalizing their rule. But it also provided some slaves with leverage in controlling the conditions of their lives. Slaves learned to manipulate the slaveholder's need to see himself as a good and decent master. To avoid a reputation as a cruel tyrant, planters sometimes negotiated with slaves, rather than just resorting to the whip. Masters sometimes granted slaves small garden plots in which they could work for themselves after working all day in the fields, or they gave slaves a few days off and a dance when they had gathered the last of the cotton.

The Virginia statesman Edmund Randolph argued that slavery created in white southern men a "quick and acute sense of personal liberty" and a "disdain for every abridgement of personal independence." Indeed, prickly individualism and aggressive independence became crucial features of the southern concept of honor. Social standing, political advancement, and even self-esteem rested on an honorable reputation. Defending honor became a male passion. Andrew Jackson's mother reportedly told her son, "Never tell a lie, nor take what is not your own, nor sue anybody for slander or assault and battery. *Always settle them cases yourself.*" Among planters, such advice sometimes led to duels. Dueling arrived from Europe in the eighteenth century. It died out in the North, but in the South, even after legislatures banned it, gentlemen continued to defend their honor with pistols at ten paces.

Southerners also expected an honorable gentleman to be a proper patriarch. Nowhere in America was masculine power more accentuated. Slavery buttressed the power of white men, and planters brooked no opposition from any of their dependents, black or white. The master's absolute dominion sometimes led to miscegenation. Laws prohibited interracial sex, and some masters practiced self-restraint. Others merely urged discretion. How many trips masters and their sons made to slave cabins is impossible to tell, but as long as slavery gave white men extraordinary power, slave women were forced to submit to the sexual appetites of the men who owned them.

Individualistic impulses were strong among planters, but duty to family was paramount. In time, as the children of one elite family married the children of another, ties of blood and kinship, as well as economic interest and ideology, linked planters to one another. Conscious of what they shared as slaveholders, planters worked together to defend their common interests. The values of the big house—slavery, honor, male domination—washed over the boundaries of plantations and flooded all of southern life.

Southern Man with Children and Their Mammy
Obviously prosperous and looking like a man accustomed to giving orders and being obeyed, this patriarch poses around 1848 with his young daughters and their nurse. The black woman is clearly a servant, a status indicated by her race and her attire. Why does she appear in the daguerreotype? The absent mother may be dead. Her death might account for the inclusion of the African American woman in the family circle. In any case, her presence signals her importance in the household. Fathers left the raising of daughters to mothers and nurses.
Collection of the J. Paul Getty Museum, Malibu, CA.

Plantation Mistresses

Like their northern counterparts, southern ladies were expected to possess the feminine virtues of piety, purity, chastity, and obedience within the context of marriage, motherhood, and domesticity. Southerners also expected ladies to mirror all that was best in plantation society. Countless toasts praised the southern lady as the perfect complement to her husband, the commanding

Bird Store, 626 Royal Street, New Orleans
Most elite white women in the antebellum South lived isolated existences on rural plantations. But some lived in cities, while others visited them from time to time, and going shopping was a prominent feature of such visits. Teenager Gertrude Clanton, who lived in Augusta, Georgia, wore store-bought clothes that she described endlessly in letters to her friends. Here a wealthy mother and daughter shop for a pet in a New Orleans bird store. The attentive proprietor and attractive shop provide everything they need—birds, cages, food, even an inviting couch and blanket in case they want to rest before moving on. Elite white women themselves were, in a way, like birds kept in golden cages. Could it be that they were attracted to the thought of owning birds of their own, something they could care for, train, and control?
Historic New Orleans Collection.

patriarch. She was physically weak, "formed only for the less laborious occupations," and thus dependent on male protection. To gain this protection, she was naturally modest and delicate, possessed beauty and grace, and cultivated refinement and charm.

For women, this image of the southern lady was no blessing. Chivalry—the South's romantic ideal of male-female relationships—glorified the lady while it subordinated her. Chivalry's underlying assumptions about the weakness of women and the protective authority of men resembled the paternalistic defense of slavery. Indeed, the most articulate spokesmen for slavery

also vigorously defended the subordination of women. George Fitzhugh insisted that "a woman, like children, has but one right and that is the right to protection. The right to protection involves the obligation to obey. A husband, a lord and master, nature designed for every woman. . . . If she be obedient she stands little danger of maltreatment." Just as the slaveholder's mastery was written into law, so too were the paramount rights of husbands. Married women lost almost all their property rights to their husbands. Women throughout the nation found divorce difficult, but southern women found it almost impossible.

How Often Were Slaves Whipped?

As important as this question is to historians, and obviously was to slaves, we have very little reliable evidence on the frequency of whipping. We know from white sources that whipping was the prescribed method of physical punishment on most antebellum plantations. Masters' instructions to overseers authorized whippings and often set limits on the number of strokes an overseer could administer. Some planters allowed fifteen lashes, some fifty, and some one hundred. But slave owners' instructions, as revealing as they are, tell us more about the severity of beatings than about their frequency.

Remembrances of former slaves confirm that whipping was widespread and frequent. In the 1930s, a government program gathered testimony from more than 2,300 elderly African Americans about their experiences as slaves. Their accounts offered grisly evidence of the cruelty of slavery. "You say how did our Master treat his slaves?" asked one woman. "Scandalous, they treated them just like dogs." She was herself whipped "till the blood dripped to the ground." A few slaves remembered kind masters and never personally felt the sting of the lash. Bert Strong was one such slave, but he also recalled hearing slaves on other farms "hollering when they get beat." He said, "They beat them till it a pity." Beatings occurred often, but how often?

A remarkably systematic record of whippings over a sustained period of time comes from the diary of Bennet H. Barrow, the master of Highland plantation in West Feliciana Parish, Louisiana. For a twenty-three-month period in 1840–1841, Barrow meticulously recorded every whipping he administered or ordered. On most large plantations, overseers handled the business of day-to-day management, but in 1838 Barrow concluded that overseers were "good for nothing" and "a perfect nuisance." He dismissed his white overseer and, assisted only by a black driver, began managing his own plantation.

What does the Barrow evidence show? In 1840, according to the federal census, Barrow owned 129 slaves. In the twenty-three-month period, Barrow recorded 160 whippings. That means that, on the average, a slave was whipped every four and a half days. Sixty of the 77 slaves who worked in the fields were whipped at least once. Most of the 17 field slaves who escaped being beaten were children and pregnant women. Eighty percent of male cotton pickers and 70 percent of female cotton pickers were whipped at least once in this period. Dave Barley received eight floggings, more than any other Barrow slave, and Patience received six whippings, more than any other female slave.

In most instances, Barrow recorded not only the fact of a whipping but also its cause. All sorts of "misconduct," "rascallity," and "disorderly acts" made Barrow reach for his whip. The provocations included family quarrels in the slave quarter, impudence, running away, and failure to keep curfew. But nearly 80 percent of the acts he recorded were related to poor work. Barrow gave beatings for "not picking as well as he can," for picking "very trashy cotton," and for failing to pick the prescribed weight of cotton. One slave claimed to have lost his eyesight and for months refused to work, until Barrow "gave him 25 cuts yesterday morning & ordered him to work Blind or not."

Whippings should not be mistaken for spankings. Some planters used whips that raised welts, caused blisters, and bruised. Others resorted to rawhide and cowhide whips that broke the skin, caused scarring, and sometimes permanently maimed. Occasionally, slaves were beaten to death. Whipping was not Barrow's only means of inflicting pain. His diary mentions confining slaves to a plantation jail, putting them in chains, shooting them, breaking a "sword cane" over one slave's head, having slaves mauled by dogs, placing them in stocks, "staking down" slaves for hours, "hand sawing" them, holding their heads under water, and a variety of punishments intended to ridicule and to shame, including making men wear women's clothing and do "women's work," such as the laundry. Still, Barrow's preferred instrument of punishment was the whip.

On the Barrow plantation, as on many others, whipping was public. Victims were often tied to a stake in the quarter, and the other slaves were made to watch. In a real sense, the entire slave population on the plantation experienced a whipping every four and a half days. Even though some never felt the lash personally, all were familiar with its terror and agony.

Was whipping effective? Did it produce a hardworking, efficient, and conscientious labor force? Not according to Barrow's own record. No evidence indicates that whipping changed the slaves' behavior. What Barrow considered bad work continued. Unabated whipping is itself evidence of the failure of punishment to achieve the master's will. Slaves knew the rules, yet they continued to act "badly." And they continued to suffer. It was a gruesome drama—the master seeking from his slaves hard labor, and the slaves denying their master what he most wanted, day after day.

Did Barrow whip with the same frequency as other planters? We simply do not know. As much as we would like to answer the question precisely, because of the lack of quantifiable evidence, we will never know exactly how often whippings occurred. Still, the Barrow evidence allows us to speculate profitably on the frequency of whipping by large planters. We do know that Barrow did not consider himself a cruel man. He bitterly denounced his neighbor as "the most cruel Master i ever knew of" for castrating three of his slaves. Moreover, Barrow had dispensed with his overseer in part because of the overseer's "brutal feelings" toward slaves. Like most whites, he believed that the lash was essential to get the work done. He used it no more than he believed absolutely necessary.

Most masters, including Barrow, tried to encourage work with promises of small gifts and brief holidays, but punishment was their most important motivator. We will never know if the typical slave was beaten once a year as on the Barrow plantation, but the admittedly scanty evidence suggests that on large plantations, the whip fell on someone's back every few days.

More than a half century after emancipation, the sharpest recollections of former slaves usually involved punishment. They remembered the pain, the injustice, and their bitter resentment. They evaluated their former masters according to how frequently they reached for the whip. According to one former slave, "Some was good and some was bad, and about the most of them was bad."

Gordon

This photograph of Gordon, a runaway slave from Baton Rouge, Louisiana, was taken on April 2, 1863, and sent home from the Civil War by Frederick W. Mercer, an assistant surgeon with the Forty-seventh Massachusetts Regiment. Mercer examined four hundred other runaways and found many "to be as badly lacerated." Masters claimed that they whipped only when they had to and only as hard as they had to, but slave testimony and photographic evidence refute their defense of slavery as a benign institution.

Courtesy of the Massachusetts Historical Society.

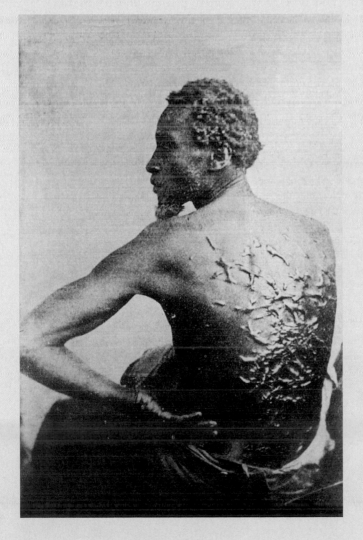

Daughters of planters confronted chivalry's demands at an early age. Their education aimed at fitting them to become southern ladies. At their private boarding schools, they read literature, learned languages, and studied the appropriate drawing-room arts. Elite women began courting at a young age and married early. Kate Carney exaggerated only slightly when she despaired in her diary: "Today, I am seventeen, getting quite old, and am not married." Yet marriage meant turning their fates over to their husbands and making enormous efforts to live up to their region's lofty ideal. One mother warned her daughter: "A single life has fewer troubles; but then it is not the one for which our maker designed us."

> One mother warned her daughter: "A single life has fewer troubles; but then it is not the one for which our maker designed us."

Proslavery ideologues claimed that slavery freed white women from drudgery. Surrounded "by her domestics," declared Thomas R. Dew, "she ceases to be a mere beast of burden" and "becomes the cheering and animating center of the family circle." In reality, however, having servants required the plantation mistress to work long hours. Like her husband, she had managerial responsibilities. She managed the big house, directly supervising as many as a dozen slaves. But unlike her husband, the mistress had no overseer. All house servants answered directly to her. She assigned them tasks each morning, directed their work throughout the day, and punished them when she found fault. In addition to supervising a complex household, she had responsibility for the henhouse and dairy. On some plantations, she directed the slave hospital and nursery and rationed supplies for the slave quarter. Women also bore the dangers of childbearing and the responsibilities of child rearing. Southern ladies did not often lead lives of leisure.

Whereas masters used their status as slaveholders as a springboard into public affairs, mistresses' lives were circumscribed by the plantation. Masters left the plantation when they pleased, but mistresses needed chaperones to travel. When they could, they went to church, but women spent most days at home, where they often became lonely. In 1853, Mary Kendall wrote how much she enjoyed her sister's letter: "For about three weeks I did not have the pleasure of seeing one white female face, there being no white family except our own upon the plantation." In their few leisure hours, plantation mistresses read and wrote letters, but they pre-

Tools of a Plantation Mistress: Keys and Key Basket

Almost every plantation mistress supervised the big house's storerooms and oversaw the distribution of the supplies kept there. To protect the goods from sticky-fingered house servants, each mistress kept the supplies under lock and key and carried the keys with her in a basket. The large five-inch key would have opened a door, and the four smaller keys on a ring would have opened boxes that held valuable foodstuffs such as sugar and tea. Throughout the day, slaves came to the mistress for access to household goods: "I keep all the keys and if anything is wanted they are obliged to come to me," one white woman declared.

Keys: Valentine Museum, Cook Collection; Basket: Courtesy June Lambert.

The Price of Blood

This 1868 painting by T. S. Noble depicts a transaction between a slave trader and a rich planter. The trader nervously pretends to study the contract, while the planter waits impatiently for the completion of the sale. The planter's mulatto son, who is being sold, looks away. The children of white men and slave women were property and could be sold by the father/master.

Morris Museum of Art, Augusta, GA.

READING THE IMAGE: Who is absent from the painting, and what does this suggest about the tragedy of miscegenation?

CONNECTIONS: The white, male planter represented the pinnacle of southern society. How did white women, black men, and black women fit into this strict hierarchy?

FOR MORE HELP ANALYZING THIS IMAGE, see the visual activity for this chapter in the Online Study Guide at bedfordstmartins.com/roark.

ferred the company of friends. Grand parties and balls occasionally broke the daily routine, but the burden of planning and supervising the preparation of the food and drink fell on mistresses.

As members of slaveholding families, mistresses lived privileged lives. But they also had significant grounds for discontent. No feature of plantation life generated more anguish among mistresses than miscegenation. A perceptive observer of plantation society, Mary Boykin Chesnut of Camden, South Carolina, confided in her diary, "Ours is a monstrous system, a wrong and iniquity. Like the patriarchs of old, our men live all in one house with their wives and their concubines; and the mulattos one sees in every family partly resemble the white children. Any lady is ready to tell you who is the father of all the mulatto children in everybody's household but her own. Those, she seems to think drop from the clouds."

Most planters' wives, including Chesnut, accepted slavery. After all, the mistress's world rested on slave labor, just as the master's did. By acknowledging the realities of male power, mistresses enjoyed the rewards of their class and race. But these rewards came at a price. Still, the heaviest burdens of slavery fell not on those who lived in the big house, but on those who toiled to support them.

> **REVIEW** Why did the ideology of paternalism gain currency among planters in the nineteenth century?

Slaves and the Quarter

On most plantations, only a few hundred yards separated the big house and the slave quarter. The distance was short enough to ensure whites easy access to the labor of blacks, yet great enough to provide slaves with some privacy. Out of eyesight and earshot of the big house, slaves drew together and built lives of their own. They created families, worshipped God, and developed an African American community. Individually and collectively, slaves found subtle and not so subtle ways to resist their bondage.

Despite the rise of plantations, a substantial minority of slaves lived and worked elsewhere. Most labored on small farms, where they wielded a hoe alongside another slave or two and perhaps their master. But by 1860, almost half a million slaves (one in eight) did not work in agriculture at all. Some were employed in towns and cities as domestics, day laborers, bakers, barbers, tailors, and more. Others, far from urban centers, toiled as fishermen, lumbermen, and railroad workers. Slaves could also be found in most of the South's factories. Nevertheless, a majority of slaves (52 percent) counted plantations as their workplaces and homes.

> An ex-slave named Albert Todd recalled, "Work was a religion that we were taught."

Work

An ex-slave named Albert Todd recalled, "Work was a religion that we were taught." Whites enslaved blacks for their labor, and all slaves who were capable of productive labor worked. Young children were introduced to the world of work as early as age five or six. Ex-slave Carrie Hudson recalled that children who were "knee high to a duck" were sent to the fields to carry water to thirsty workers or to protect ripening crops from hungry birds. Others helped in the slave nursery, caring for children even younger than themselves, or in the big house, where they swept floors or shooed flies in the dining room. When slave boys and girls reached the age of eleven or twelve, masters sent most of them to the fields, where they learned farmwork by laboring alongside their parents. After a lifetime of labor, old women left the fields to care for the small children and spin yarn, and old men moved on to mind livestock and clean stables.

The overwhelming majority of plantation slaves worked as field hands. Planters sometimes assigned men and women to separate gangs, the women working at lighter tasks and the men doing the heavy work of clearing and breaking the land. But women also did heavy work. "I had to work hard," Nancy Boudry remembered, and "plow and go and split wood just like a man." The backbreaking labor and the monotonous routines caused one ex-slave to observe that the "history of one day is the history of every day."

A few slaves (about one in ten) became house servants. Nearly all of those (nine out of ten) were women. They cooked, cleaned, babysat, washed clothes, and did the dozens of other tasks the master and mistress required. House servants enjoyed somewhat less physically demanding work than field hands, but they were constantly on call, with no time that was entirely their own. Since no servant could please constantly, most bore the brunt of white frustration and rage. Ex-slave Jacob Branch of Texas remembered, "My poor mama! Every washday old Missy give her a beating."

Even rarer than house servants were skilled artisans. In the cotton South, no more than one slave in twenty (almost all men) worked in a skilled trade. Most were blacksmiths and carpenters, but slaves also worked as masons, mechanics, millers, and shoemakers. Slave craftsmen took pride in their skills and often exhibited the independence of spirit that caused slaveholder James H. Hammond of South Carolina to declare in disgust that when a slave became a skilled artisan, "he is more than half freed." Skilled slave fathers took pride in teaching their crafts to their sons. "My pappy was one of the black smiths and worked in the shop," John Mathews remembered. "I had to help my pappy in the shop when I was a child and I

Isaac Jefferson
In this 1845 daguerreotype, seventy-year-old Isaac Jefferson proudly poses in the apron he wore while practicing his crafts as a tinsmith and nail maker. Slaves of Thomas Jefferson, he, his wife, and their two children were deeded to Jefferson's daughter Mary when she married in 1797. Isaac worked at Jefferson's home, Monticello, until 1820, when he moved to Petersburg, Virginia. When work was slow on the home plantation, slave owners often would hire out their skilled artisans to neighbors who needed a carpenter, blacksmith, mason, or tinsmith. Special Collections Department, University of Virginia Library.

learnt how to beat out the iron and make wagon tires, and make plows."

Rarest of all slave occupations was that of slave driver. Probably no more than one male slave in a hundred worked in this capacity. These men were well named, for their primary task was driving other slaves to work harder in the fields. In some drivers' hands, the whip never rested. Ex-slave Jane Johnson of South Carolina called her driver the "meanest man, white or black, I ever see." But other drivers showed all the restraint they could. "Ole Gabe didn't like that whippin' business," West Turner of Virginia remembered. "When Marsa was there, he would lay it on 'cause he had to. But when old Marsa wasn't lookin', he never would beat them slaves."

Normally, slaves worked from what they called "can to can't," from "can see" in the morning to "can't see" at night. Even with a break at noon for a meal and rest, it made for a long day. For slaves, Lewis Young recalled, "work, work, work, 'twas all they do."

Family, Religion, and Community

From dawn to dusk, slaves worked for the master, but at night, when the labor was done, and all day Sunday and usually Saturday afternoon, slaves were left largely to themselves. Bone tired perhaps, they nonetheless used the time and space to develop and enjoy what mattered most: family, religion, and community.

In the quarter, slaves became husbands and wives, mothers and fathers, sons and daughters, preachers and singers, storytellers and conjurers. Over the generations, they created a community and a culture that buoyed them up during long hours in the fields and brought them joy and hope in the few hours they had to themselves.

One of the most important consequences of slaves' limited autonomy was the preservation and persistence of the family. Though severely battered, the black family survived slavery. No laws recognized slave marriage, and therefore no master or slave was legally obligated to honor the bond. Nevertheless, plantation records show that slave marriages were often long-lasting. Because the slave population in the South grew primarily through natural reproduction, sex ratios were approximately equal by the nineteenth century. Young men and women in the quarter fell in love, married, and set up housekeeping in cabins of their own. The primary cause of the ending of slave marriages was death, just as it was in white families. But the second most frequent cause was the sale of the husband or wife, something no white family ever had to fear. Precise figures are unavailable, but in the years 1820 to 1860, research suggests that sales destroyed at least 300,000 slave marriages.

Slave Quarter, South Carolina
On large plantations, several score of African Americans lived in cabins that were often arranged along what slaves called "the street." The dwellings in this picture of a South Carolina plantation by Civil War photographer George N. Barnard were better built than the typical rickety, one-room, dirt-floored slave cabin. Almost certainly posed, this photograph shows the inhabitants of the slave quarter: little children playing in the dirt; girls and women sitting on the steps talking and working at something; older boys and men driving carts and wagons. During the daylight hours of the workweek, when most men and women labored in the fields, the quarter was mostly empty. At night and on Sundays, it was a busy place.
Collection of the New-York Historical Society.

In 1858, a South Carolina slave named Abream Scriven wrote a letter to his wife, who lived on a neighboring plantation. "My dear wife," he began, "I take the pleasure of writing you . . . with much regret to inform you I am Sold to man by the name of Peterson, a Treader and Stays in New Orleans." Scriven promised to send some things when he got to his new home in Louisiana, but he admitted that he was not sure how he would "get them to you and my children." He asked his wife to "give my love to my father and mother and tell them good Bye for me. And if we do not meet in this world I hope to meet in heaven. . . . My dear wife for you and my children my pen cannot express the griffe I feel to be parted from you all." He closed with words no master would have permitted in a slave's marriage vows: "I remain your truly husband until Death." The letter makes clear Scriven's love for his family; it also demonstrates slavery's massive assault on family life in the quarter.

Despite their inability to fulfill the traditional roles of provider and protector, fathers gained status by doing what they could to help their families. Slave fathers and mothers divided responsibilities in the quarter along traditional gender lines: Women cooked, sewed, and cleaned; men hunted, raised hogs, cultivated gardens, and made furniture for their cabins. Slaves held their parents in high esteem, grateful for the small bits of refuge from the rigors of slavery their parents provided when they were children.

Religion also provided slaves with a refuge and a reason for living. Before the American Revolution, Baptists and Methodists began trying to convert slaves from their African beliefs. **Evangelicals** offered an emotional "religion of the heart" to which blacks (and many whites as well) responded enthusiastically. By the mid-nineteenth century, perhaps as many as one-quarter of all slaves claimed church membership, and many of the rest would not have objected to being called Christians.

Planters promoted Christianity in the quarter because they believed that the slaves' salvation was part of their obligation and that religion made slaves more obedient. South Carolina slaveholder Charles Colcock Jones, the leading missionary to the slaves, published his *Catechism for Colored Persons* in 1834. In it, he instructed slaves "to count their Masters 'worthy of all honour,' as those whom God has placed over them in this world." But slaves laughed up their sleeves at such messages. "That old white preacher just was telling us slaves to be good to our masters," one ex-slave said with a chuckle. "We ain't cared a bit about that stuff he was telling us 'cause we wanted to sing, pray, and serve God in our own way."

Meeting in their cabins or secretly in the woods, slaves created an African American Christianity that served their needs, not the masters'. Laws prohibited teaching slaves to read, but a few could read enough to struggle with the Bible. They interpreted the Christian message themselves. Rather than obedience, their faith emphasized justice. Slaves believed that God kept score and that the accounts of this world would be settled in the next. "The idea of a revolution in the conditions of the whites and blacks in the corner stone" of the slaves' religion, recalled one ex-slave. But the slaves' faith also spoke to their experiences in this world. In the Old Testament, they discovered Moses, who delivered his people from slavery, and in the New Testament, they found Jesus, who offered salvation to all. Jesus' message of equality provided a potent antidote to the planters' claim that blacks were an inferior people whom God condemned to slavery.

Christianity did not entirely drive out traditional African beliefs. Even slaves who were Christians sometimes continued to believe that conjurers, witches, and spirits possessed the power to injure and protect. Moreover, slaves' Christian music, preaching, and rituals reflected the influence of Africa, as did many of their secular activities, such as wood carving, quilt making, and storytelling. But by the mid-nineteenth century, black Christianity had assumed a central place in slaves' quest for freedom. In the words of one spiritual, "O my Lord delivered Daniel / O why not deliver me too?"

> "That old white preacher just was telling us slaves to be good to our masters," one ex-slave said with a chuckle. "We ain't cared a bit about that stuff he was telling us 'cause we wanted to sing, pray, and serve God in our own way."

Resistance and Rebellion

Slaves did not suffer slavery passively. They were, as whites said, "troublesome property." Slaves understood that accommodation to what they could not change was the price of survival, but in a hundred ways, they protested their bondage. Theoretically, the master was all-powerful and the slave powerless. But sustained by their families, religion, and community, slaves engaged in day-to-day resistance against their enslavers.

The spectrum of slave resistance ranged from mild to extreme. Telling a pointed story by the fireside in a slave cabin was probably the mildest form of protest. But when the weak got the better of the strong, as they did in tales of Br'er Rabbit and Br'er Fox (*Br'er* is a contraction of *Brother*), listeners could enjoy

Gourd Fiddle
Found in St. Marys County, Maryland, this slave-made gourd fiddle is an example of the many musical instruments that African Americans crafted and played throughout the South. Henry Wright, an ex-slave from Georgia, remembered: "I made a fiddle out of a large sized gourd—a long wooden handle was used as a neck, and the hair from a horse's tail was used for the bow. The strings were made of catgut." A hybrid of African and European elements, this fiddle offers material evidence of the cultural transformation of African slaves. Although Africans lost much in their forced journey to the Americas, Africa remained in their cultural memory. Black men and women drew on the traditions of their homeland and the South to create something new—an African American culture. Music, a crucial component of that sustaining culture, provided slaves with a creative outlet and relief from the rigors of slavery.
Smithsonian Institution/Aldo Tutino/Folio, Inc.

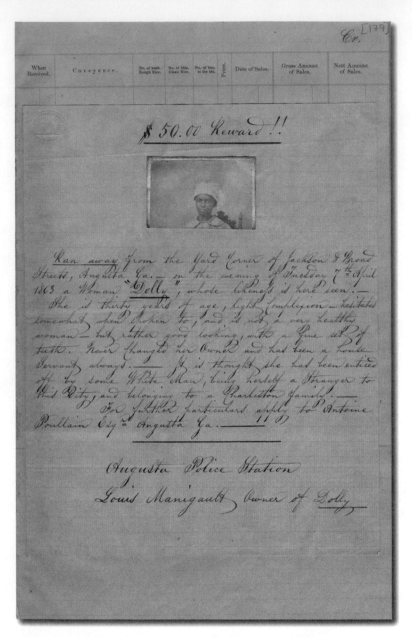

"$50.00 Reward!!"

Runaway slaves were as common as thunderstorms in the South. Slave owners often used notices—reward posters like this one and newspaper advertisements—to recover their property. Typically, notices provided precise information about the runaway's physical appearance—size, age, color, build, scars, and hairstyle—and clothing, since slaves often fled with only the clothes on their backs. Notices frequently mentioned the slave's personality and speech habits as well. Here, prominent rice planter Louis Manigault describes his slave Dolly as slow to respond when spoken to. Manigault apparently could not accept that a trusted house servant would flee on her own, and thus he suggests that "some white man" had enticed her away. But Manigault also notes that Dolly was new to Augusta, which may suggest that she was seeking to reunite with her family on the coast after Manigault had moved his white family and house servants inland seeking safety during the Civil War. What distinguishes this runaway notice from almost all others is Dolly's photograph. Manigault had apparently rewarded this favorite servant with a photograph, which he then used to track her down.

Manigault Papers, Southern Historical Collection, North Carolina Collection, The Library of the University of North Carolina, Chapel Hill, collection #P484.

the thrill of a vicarious victory over their masters. Protest in the fields was riskier and included putting rocks in their cotton bags before having them weighed, feigning illness, and pretending to be so thickheaded that they could not understand the simplest instruction. Slaves broke so many hoes that owners outfitted the tools with oversized handles. Slaves so mistreated the work animals that masters switched from horses to mules, which could absorb more abuse. Although slaves worked hard in the master's fields, they also sabotaged his interests.

Running away was a common form of protest. Some runaways sought the ultimate prize: freedom in the North or in Canada. Over the decades, thousands of slaves, almost all from the Upper South, made it. But escape from the Lower South was almost impossible, except in Texas, where several hundred slaves found freedom in Mexico. Overwhelmingly young, unattached men, runaways could hope only to escape for a few days. Seeking temporary respite from hard labor or avoiding punishment, they usually stayed close to their plantations, keeping to the deep woods or swamps and slipping back into the quarter at night to get food. "Lying out," as it was known, usually ended when the runaway, worn-out and ragged, gave up or was finally chased down by slave-hunting dogs.

Although resistance was common, outright rebellion—a violent assault on slavery by large numbers of slaves—was very rare. Major rebellions were more common elsewhere in the New World. The scarcity of revolts in the South is not evidence of the slaves' contentedness, however. Rather, conditions gave rebels almost no chance of success. By 1860, whites in the South outnumbered blacks two to one and were heavily armed. Moreover, communication between plantations was difficult, and the South provided little protective wilderness into which rebels could retreat and defend themselves. Rebellion, as Nat Turner's experience showed, was virtual suicide.

Despite the rarity of slave revolts, whites believed that they were surrounded by conspiracies to rebel. In 1822, whites in Charleston accused Denmark Vesey, a free black carpenter, of conspiring with plantation slaves to slaughter Charleston's white inhabitants. The authorities rounded up scores of suspects, who, prodded by torture and the threat of death, implicated others in the plot "to riot in blood, outrage, and rapine." Although the city fathers never found any weapons and Vesey and most of the accused steadfastly denied the charges of conspiracy, officials hanged thirty-five black men, including Vesey, and banished another thirty-seven blacks from the state.

Masters boasted that their slaves were "instinctively contented," but steady resistance and occasional rebellion proved otherwise. Slaves did not have the power to end their bondage, but by asserting themselves, they affirmed their humanity and worth. By resisting their masters' will, slaves became actors in the plantation drama, helping establish limits beyond which planters and overseers hesitated to go.

Still, slavery blunted and thwarted African Americans' hopes and aspirations. Slavery broke some and crippled others. But slavery's destructive power had to contend with the resiliency of the human spirit. Slaves fought back physically, culturally, and spiritually. They not only survived bondage, but they also created in the quarter a vibrant African American culture and community that sustained them through more than two centuries of slavery and what came after.

> **REVIEW** What types of resistance did slaves participate in, and why did slave resistance rarely take the form of rebellion?

Black and Free: On the Middle Ground

Not every black Southerner was a slave. In 1860, some 260,000 (approximately 6 percent) of the region's 4.1 million African Americans were free (see Figure 13.1, page 439). What is surprising is not that their numbers were small but that they existed at all. "Free black" seemed increasingly a contradiction to most white Southerners. According to the emerging racial thinking, blacks were supposed to be slaves. Blacks who were free stood out, and whites made them more and more targets of oppression. Free blacks stood precariously between slavery and full freedom, on what a young free black artisan in Charleston characterized in 1848 as "a middle ground." But they made the most of their freedom, and a few found success despite the restrictions placed on them by white Southerners.

Precarious Freedom

The population of free blacks swelled after the Revolution, when the natural rights philosophy of the Declaration of Independence and the egalitarian message of evangelical Protestantism joined to challenge slavery. A brief flurry of **emancipation** visited the Upper South, where the ideological assault on slavery coincided with a deep depression in the tobacco economy. Some masters freed their slaves outright; others permitted favorite slaves to buy their freedom by working after hours to accumulate money for self-purchase. By 1810, free blacks in the South numbered more than 100,000, a fact that worried white Southerners, who, because of the cotton boom, wanted more slaves, not more free blacks.

In the 1820s and 1830s, state legislatures acted to stem the growth of the free black population and to shrink the liberty of those blacks who had gained their freedom. Some laws denied masters the right to free their slaves. Other laws humiliated and restricted free blacks by subjecting them to special taxes, requiring them to register annually with the state or to choose a white guardian, prohibiting them from interstate travel, denying them the right to have schools and to participate in politics, and requiring them to carry "freedom papers" to prove they were not slaves. Increasingly, whites subjected free blacks to the same laws as slaves. They could not testify under oath in a court of law or serve on juries. Like slaves, they were liable to whipping and the treadmill, where they were made to walk on the moving steps of a wheel until they fell, exhausted. Free blacks were forbidden to strike whites, even to defend themselves. "Free negroes belong to a degraded caste of society," a South Carolina judge said in 1848. "They are in no respect on a perfect equality with the white man. . . . They ought, by law, to be compelled to demean themselves as inferiors."

> "Free negroes belong to a degraded caste of society," a South Carolina judge said in 1848. "They are in no respect on a perfect equality with the white man. . . . They ought, by law, to be compelled to demean themselves as inferiors."

The elaborate system of regulations confined most free African Americans to a constricted life of poverty and dependence. Typically, free blacks were rural, uneducated, unskilled agricultural laborers and domestic servants. Opportunities of all kinds—for work, education, or community—were slim. Planters looked on free blacks as degraded parasites, likely to set a bad example for slaves. They believed that free blacks subverted the racial subordination that was the essence of slavery.

Achievement despite Restrictions

Despite increasingly harsh laws and stepped-up persecution, free African Americans made the most of the advantages their status offered. Unlike slaves, free blacks could legally marry. They could protect their families from arbitrary disruption and pass on their heritage of freedom to their children. Freedom also meant that they could choose occupations and own property. For most, these economic rights proved only theoretical, for a majority of the South's free blacks remained propertyless.

Still, some free blacks escaped the poverty and degradation whites thrust on them. Particularly in urban areas—especially the cities of Charleston, Mobile, and New Orleans—a small elite of free blacks emerged. Urban whites enforced many of the restrictive laws only sporadically, allowing free blacks room to maneuver.

Freedom Paper

This legal document attests to the free status of the Reverend John F. Cook of Washington, D.C., his daughter Mary, and his son George. Cook was a free black man who kept his "freedom paper" in this watertight tin, which he probably carried with him at all times. Free blacks had to be prepared to prove their free status anytime a white man challenged them, for southern law presumed that a black person was a slave unless he or she could prove otherwise. Without such proof, free blacks risked enslavement.

Moorland-Spingarn Research Center, Howard University, Washington, D.C.

The elite consisted overwhelmingly of light-skinned African Americans who worked at skilled trades, and their customers were prominent whites who appreciated their able, respectful service. The free black elite operated schools for their children and traveled in and out of their states, despite laws forbidding both activities. They worshipped with whites (in separate seating) in the finest churches and lived scattered about in white neighborhoods, not in ghettos. And like elite whites, some owned slaves. Blacks could own blacks because they had the right to own property, which in the South included human property. Of the 3,200 black slaveholders (barely 1 percent of the free black population), most owned only a few slaves, who were sometimes family members whom they could not legally free. Others owned slaves in large numbers and exploited them for labor.

One free black slave owner was William Ellison of South Carolina. Ellison was born a slave in 1790, but he bought his freedom in 1816 and moved to a thriving plantation district about one hundred miles north of Charleston. He set up business as a cotton gin maker, a trade he had learned as a slave, and by 1835 he was prosperous enough to purchase the home of a former governor of the state. By the time of his death in 1861, he had become a cotton planter, with sixty-three slaves and an 800-acre plantation.

Most free blacks neither became slaveholders like Ellison nor sought to raise a slave rebellion, as whites accused Denmark Vesey of doing. Rather, most free blacks simply tried to preserve their freedom, which was under increasing attack. Unlike blacks in the North whose freedom was secure, free blacks in the South clung to a precarious freedom by seeking to impress whites with their reliability, economic contributions, and good behavior.

REVIEW   Why did many state legislatures pass laws restricting free blacks' rights in the 1820s and 1830s?

The Plain Folk

Like most free blacks, most whites in the South did not own slaves, not even one. In 1860, more than six million of the South's eight million whites lived in slaveless households. Some slaveless whites lived in cities and worked as artisans, mechanics, and traders. Others lived in the country and worked as storekeepers, parsons, and schoolteachers. But most "plain folk" were small farmers. Perhaps three out of four were **yeomen**, small farmers who owned their own land. As in the North, farm ownership provided a family with an economic foundation, social respectability, and political standing. Unlike their northern counterparts, however, southern yeomen lived in a region whose economy and society were increasingly dominated by unfree labor.

The Cotton Belt

In an important sense, the South had more than one white yeomanry. The huge southern landscape provided space enough for two yeoman societies, separated roughly along geographical lines. Yeomen throughout the South had much in common, but the life of a small farm family in the plantation belt—the flatlands that spread from South Carolina to east Texas—differed from the life of a family in the upcountry—the area of hills and mountains. And some rural, slaveless whites were not yeomen; they owned no land at all and were sometimes desperately poor.

Plantation Belt Yeomen

Plantation belt yeomen lived within the orbit of the planter class. Small farms actually outnumbered plantations in that great arc of fertile cotton land known as the cotton belt, which stretched from South Carolina to Texas, but they were dwarfed in importance. Small farmers grew mainly food crops, particularly corn, but they also devoted a portion of their land to cotton. With only family labor to draw upon, they produced only a few 400-pound bales each year, whereas large planters measured their crop in hundreds of bales. The small farmers' cotton tied them to planters. Unable to afford cotton gins or baling presses of their own, they relied on helpful neighborhood slave owners to gin and bale their cotton. With no link to merchants in the port cities, plantation belt yeomen also turned to better-connected planters to ship and sell their cotton.

A dense network of relationships laced small farmers and planters together in patterns of reciprocity and mutual obligation. Planters hired out surplus slaves to ambitious yeomen who wanted to expand cotton production. They

sometimes chose overseers from among the sons of local farm families. Plantation mistresses sometimes nursed ailing neighbors. In rural counties, adult white males, often yeomen, rode in slave patrols, which nightly scoured country roads to make certain that no slaves were moving about without permission. Family ties could span class lines, making rich and poor kin as well as neighbors. On Sundays, plantation dwellers and plain folk came together in church to worship and afterward lingered to gossip and to transact small business.

Plantation belt yeomen may have envied, and at times even resented, wealthy slaveholders, but in general small farmers learned to accommodate. Planters made accommodation easier by going out of their way to behave as good neighbors and avoid direct exploitation of slaveless whites in their community. As a consequence, rather than raging at the oppression of the planter regime, the typical plantation belt yeoman sought entry into it. He dreamed of adding acreage to his farm, buying a few slaves of his own, and retiring from exhausting field work.

Upcountry Yeomen

By contrast, the hills and mountains of the South resisted the spread of slavery and plantations. In the western parts of Virginia, North Carolina, and South Carolina; in northern Georgia and Alabama; and in eastern Tennessee and Kentucky, the higher elevation, colder climate, rugged terrain, and poor transportation made it difficult for commercial agriculture to make headway. As a result, yeomen dominated these isolated areas, and planters and slaves were scarce.

At the core of this distinctive upcountry society was the independent farm family working its own patch of land; raising hogs, cattle, and sheep; and seeking self-sufficiency and independence. Toward that end, all members of the family worked, their tasks depending on their sex and age. Husbands labored in the fields, and with their sons, they cleared, plowed, planted, and cultivated primarily food crops. Though pressed into field labor at harvesttime, wives and daughters of upcountry yeomen, like those of plantation belt yeomen, worked in and about the cabin most of the year. One up-country farmer remembered that his mother "worked in the house cooking, spinning, weaving [and doing] patchwork." Women also tended the vegetable garden, kept a cow and some chickens, preserved food, cleaned their homes, fed their families, and cared for their children. Male and female tasks were equally crucial to the farm's success, but as in other white southern households, the domestic sphere was subordinated to the will of the male patriarch.

The typical upcountry yeoman also grew a little cotton or tobacco, but production for home consumption was more important than production for the market. Not much currency changed hands in the upcountry. Barter was common. A yeoman might trade his small cotton or tobacco crop to a country store owner for a little salt, lead shot, needles, and nails. Or he might swap extra sweet potatoes for a plow from a blacksmith or for leather from a tanner. Networks of exchange and mutual assistance tied individual homesteads to the larger community. Farm families also joined together in logrolling, house and barn raising, and cornhusking.

Even the hills had some plantations and slaves, but they existed in much smaller numbers than in the plantation belt. The few upcountry folks who owned slaves usually had only two or three. As a result, slaveholders had much less direct social and economic power, and yeomen had more. But the upcountry did not oppose slavery. As long as upcountry plain folk were free to lead their own lives, they defended slavery and white supremacy just as staunchly as other white Southerners.

Poor Whites

Hardworking, landholding small farmers made up the majority of white Southerners. But Northerners had a different image of southern society. They believed that slavery had condemned most whites to poverty, brutality, and back-wardness. One antislavery advocate charged that the South harbored three classes: "the slaves on whom devolves all the regular industry, the slaveholders who reap all the fruits, and an idle and lawless rabble who live dispersed over vast plains little removed from absolute barbarism." Critics called this third class a variety of derogatory names: hillbillies, crackers, rednecks, and poor white trash. According to critics, poor whites were not just whites who were poor. They were also supposedly ignorant, diseased, and degenerate. Even slaves were known to chant, "I'd rather be a nigger an' plow ol' Beck / Than a white hillbilly with a long red neck."

Contrary to northern opinion, only about one in four nonslaveholding rural white men was landless and very poor. Some worked as tenants, renting land and struggling to make a go of it. Others survived by herding pigs and cattle. And still others worked for meager wages, ditching, mining, logging, and laying track for railroads. A Georgian remembered that his "father worked by the day when ever he could get work."

Some poor white men earned reputations for mayhem and violence. One visitor claimed that a "bowie-knife was a universal, and a pistol a not at all unusual companion." Edward Isham, an illiterate roustabout, spent about as much time fighting as he did working. When he wasn't engaged in ear-biting, eye-gouging free-for-alls, he was fighting with sticks, shovels, rocks, axes, tomahawks, knives, and guns. Working at what he could find, he took up with and abandoned many women, gambled, drank, stole, had run-ins with the law, and eventually murdered a respected slaveholder, for which he was hanged in 1860.

Unlike Isham, most poor white men did not engage in ferocious behavior but instead lived responsible lives. They sat at the bottom of the white pecking order, but they were ambitious people eager to climb into the yeomanry. The Lipscomb family illustrates the possibility of upward mobility. In 1845, Smith and Sally Lipscomb and their children abandoned their worn-out land in South Carolina for Benton County, Alabama. "Benton is a mountainous country but ther is a heep of good levil land to tend

> Most poor whites were ambitious people eager to climb into the yeomanry. Smith and Sally Lipscomb abandoned their worn-out land in South Carolina for Alabama, which, Smith said, "will be better for the rising generation if not for ourselves."

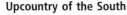

Upcountry of the South

***Gathering Corn in Virginia,* circa 1870**
In this romanticized agricultural scene, painter Felix O. C. Darley depicts members of a white farm family gathering its harvest by hand. A young black drover, who before the Civil War would have been the property of the white man or would have been rented by him from a neighboring planter, steadies the team of oxen while another man fills the wagon. Sitting before the bundled stalks, the couple shucks the ripe ears of corn. The happy moment is made complete by playful and dozing children and a sleeping dog (at lower left). In reality, growing corn was hard work. Even yeomen who grew considerable amounts of cotton also grew lots of corn, usually producing about twice the corn they needed for their families and livestock and marketing the rest. The artist, however, is less concerned with realism than with extolling rural family labor as virtuous and noble. Darley surrounds the southern yeomen with an aura of republican independence, dignity, and freedom.
Warner Collection of Gulf States Paper Corporation.

in it," Smith wrote back to his brother. Alabama, Smith said, "will be better for the rising generation if not for ourselves but I think it will be the best for us all that live any length of time." Indeed, primitive living conditions made life precarious. All of the Lipscombs fell ill, but all recovered, and the entire family went to work. Because they had no money to buy land, they squatted on seven unoccupied acres. With the help of neighbors, they built a 22-by-24-foot cabin, a detached kitchen, and two stables. From daylight to dark, Smith and his sons worked the land. Nature cooperated, and they produced enough food for the table and several bales of cotton. The women worked as hard in the cabin, and Sally contributed to the family's income by selling homemade shirts and socks. In time, the Lipscombs bought land and joined the Baptist church, completing their transformation to respectable yeomen.

Many poor whites succeeded in climbing the economic ladder, but in the 1850s upward mobility slowed. The cotton boom of that decade caused planters to expand their operations, driving the price of land beyond the reach of poor families. Whether they gained their own land or not, however, poor whites shared common cultural traits with yeomen farmers.

The Culture of the Plain Folk

Situated on scattered farms and in tiny villages, rural plain folk lived isolated, local lives. Bad roads and a lack of newspapers meant that everyday life revolved around family, a handful of neighbors, the local church, and perhaps a country store. Work occupied most hours, but plain folk still found time for pleasure. "Dancing they are all fond of," a visitor to North Carolina discovered, "especially when they can get a fiddle, or bagpipe." They also loved their tobacco. One visitor complained that the "use of tobacco is almost universal." Men smoked and chewed (and spat), while women dipped snuff. But the truly universal pastimes among men and boys were fishing and hunting. A traveler in Mississippi recalled that his host sent "two of his sons, little fellows that looked almost too small to shoulder a gun," for food. "One went off towards the river and the other struck into the forest, and in a few hours we were feasting on delicious venison, trout and turtle."

Plain folk did not usually associate "book learning" with the basic needs of life. A northern woman visiting the South in the 1850s observed, "Education is not extended to the masses here as at the North." Private academies charged fees that yeomen could not afford, and public schools were scarce. Although most people managed to pick up a basic knowledge of the "three R's," approximately one southern white man in five was illiterate in 1860, and the rate for white women was even higher. "People here prefer talking to reading," a Virginian remarked. Telling stories, reciting ballads, and singing hymns were important activities in yeoman culture.

> "Dancing they are all fond of," a visitor to North Carolina discovered, "especially when they can get a fiddle, or bagpipe."

Plain folk everywhere spent more hours in revival tents than in classrooms. Not all rural whites were religious, but many were, and the most characteristic feature of their evangelical Christian faith was the revival. The greatest of the early-nineteenth-century revivals occurred in 1801 at Cane Ridge, Kentucky, where some twenty thousand people gathered to listen to evangelical preachers who spoke day and night for a week. Ministers sought to save souls by bringing individuals to a personal conviction of sin. Revivalism crossed denominational lines, but Baptists and Methodists adopted it most readily and by midcentury had become the South's largest religious groups. By emphasizing free choice and individual worth, the plain folk's religion was hopeful and affirming. Hymns and spirituals provided guides to right and wrong—praising humility and steadfastness, condemning drunkenness and profanity. Above all, hymns spoke of the eventual release from worldly sorrows and the assurance of eternal salvation.

REVIEW   Why did yeomen dominate the upcountry?

The Politics of Slavery

By the mid-nineteenth century, all southern white men—planters and plain folk alike—had gained the vote. But even after the South's politics became **democratic** for the white male population, political power remained unevenly distributed. The nonslaveholding white majority wielded less political power than their numbers indicated. The slaveholding white minority wielded more. Self-conscious, cohesive, and with a well-developed sense of class interest, slaveholders busied themselves with party politics, campaigns, and officeholding and made demands of state governments. As a result, they received significant benefits. Nonslaveholding whites were concerned mainly with preserving their liberties and keeping their taxes low. Collectively, they asked government for little of an economic nature, and they received little.

Slaveholders sometimes worried about nonslaveholders' loyalty

***A Baptizing on the South Branch of the Potomac near Franklin, Virginia*, 1844**
In 1844, noted painter William Thompson Russell Smith undertook a geological expedition to Virginia, and there he encountered a rural baptism. Primarily a landscape painter, Smith portrayed the human figures as minor characters. If one of the participants had sketched the baptism, he or she might have emphasized the human drama, the emotional pitch of what was for evangelical Christians throughout the South a profound religious moment.
The Charleston Renaissance Gallery, Robert M. Hicklin Jr., Inc., Charleston, South Carolina.

to slavery, but since the eighteenth century, the majority of whites had accepted the planters' argument that the existing social order served *all* Southerners' interests. Slavery rewarded every white man—no matter how poor—with membership in the South's white ruling class. It also provided the means by which nonslaveholders might someday advance into the ranks of the planters. White men in the South fought furiously about many things, but they agreed that they should take land from Indians, pro-

mote agriculture, uphold white supremacy and masculine privilege, and defend slavery from its enemies.

The Democratization of the Political Arena

The political reforms that swept the nation in the first half of the nineteenth century reached deeply into the South. Southern politics became democratic politics—for white men. Southerners eliminated the wealth and property requirements that had once restricted political participation. Beginning in the 1810s, Southerners began expanding **suffrage** until, by the 1850s, every state had extended the right to vote to all adult white males. Most southern states also removed the property requirements for holding state offices. To be sure, undemocratic features lingered. Plantation districts still wielded disproportionate power in several state legislatures. Nevertheless, southern politics took place within an increasingly democratic political structure.

White male suffrage ushered in an era of vigorous electoral competition. Eager voters rushed to the polls to exercise their new rights. High turnouts—often approaching 80 percent—became a hallmark of southern electoral politics. As politics became aggressively democratic, it also grew fiercely partisan. From the 1830s to the 1850s, Whigs and Democrats battled for the electorate's favor. In the South, both parties presented themselves as the plain white folk's best friend. All candidates declared their fervent commitment to **republican** equality and pledged to defend the people's liberty. Each party sought to portray the other as a collection of rich, snobbish, selfish men who had antidemocratic designs up their silk sleeves. Each, in turn, claimed for itself the mantle of humble "servant of the people."

The Whig and Democratic parties sought to serve the people differently, however. Whigs favored government intervention in the economy, and Democrats tended to oppose it. Whigs generally backed state support of banks, railroads, and corporations, arguing that government aid would stimulate the economy, enlarge opportunity, and thus increase the general welfare. Democrats emphasized the threat to individual liberty that government intervention posed, claiming that granting favors to special economic interests would result in concentrated power, which would in turn jeopardize the common man's opportunity and equality. Beginning with the panic of 1837, the parties clashed repeatedly on concrete economic and financial issues.

Planter Power

Whether Whig or Democrat, southern officeholders were likely to be slave owners. The power slaveholders exerted over slaves did not translate directly into political authority over whites, however. In the nineteenth century, political power could be won only at the ballot box, and almost everywhere nonslaveholders were in the majority. Yet year after year, proud and noisily egalitarian common men elected wealthy slaveholders.

By 1860, the percentage of slave owners in state legislatures ranged from 41 percent in Missouri to nearly 86 percent in North Carolina (Table 13.1). Legislators not only tended to own slaves; they also often owned large numbers. The percentage of planters (individuals with twenty or more slaves) in southern legislatures in 1860 ranged from 5.3 percent in Missouri to 55.4 percent in South Carolina. In North Carolina, where only 3 percent of the state's white families belonged to the planter class, more than 36 percent of state legislators were planters. The democratization of politics in the nineteenth century meant that more ordinary citizens participated in elections, but yeomen and artisans remained rare sights in the halls of southern legislatures.

Upper-class dominance of southern politics reflected the elite's success in persuading the white majority that what was good for slaveholders was also good for them. In reality, the South had, on the whole, done well by the plain folk. Most had farms of their own. They participated as equals in a democratic political system.

TABLE 13.1	PERCENT OF SLAVEHOLDERS AND PLANTERS IN SOUTHERN LEGISLATURES, 1860	
Legislature	Slaveholders	Planters*
Virginia	67.3%	24.2%
Maryland	53.4	19.3
North Carolina	85.8	36.6
Kentucky	60.6	8.4
Tennessee	66.0	14.0
Missouri	41.2	5.3
Arkansas	42.0	13.0
South Carolina	81.7	55.4
Georgia	71.6	29.0
Florida	55.4	20.0
Alabama	76.3	40.8
Mississippi	73.4	49.5
Louisiana	63.8	23.5
Texas	54.1	18.1

*Planters: Owned 20 or more slaves.

SOURCE: Adapted from Ralph A. Wooster, *The People in Power: Courthouse and Statehouse in the Lower South, 1850–1860*, page 40. Copyright © 1975 by Ralph A. Wooster. Courtesy of the University of Tennessee Press.

They enjoyed an elevated social status, above all blacks and in theory equal to all other whites. They commanded patriarchal authority over their households. And as long as slavery existed, they could dream of joining the planter class. Slaveless white men found much to celebrate in the slave South.

Most slaveholders took pains to win the plain folk's trust and to nurture their respect. One South Carolinian told his wealthy neighbor that he had a bright political future because he never thought himself "too good to sit down & talk to a poor man." South Carolinian Mary Boykin Chesnut complained about the fawning attention her slaveholding husband showed to poor men, including one who had "mud sticking up through his toes." Smart candidates found ways to convince wary plain folk of their democratic convictions and egalitarian sentiments, whether they were genuine or not. When young John A. Quitman ran for a seat in the Mississippi legislature, he amazed a boisterous crowd of small farmers at one campaign stop by not only entering but winning contests in jumping, boxing, wrestling, and sprinting. For his finale, he outshot the area's champion marksman. Then, demonstrating his deft political touch, he gave his prize, a fat ox, to the defeated rifleman. The electorate showed its approval by sending Quitman to the state capital.

Georgia politics illustrate how well planters protected their interests in state legislatures. In 1850, about half of the state's revenues came from taxes on slaves, the characteristic form of planter wealth. However, the tax rate on slaves was trifling, only about one-fifth the rate on land. Moreover, planters benefited far more than other groups from public spending. Financing railroads—which carried cotton to market—was the largest state expenditure. The legislature also established low tax rates on land, the characteristic form of yeoman wealth, which meant that the typical yeoman's annual tax bill was small. Still, relative to their wealth, large slaveholders paid less than did other whites. Relative to their numbers, they got more in return. A sympathetic slaveholding legislature protected planters' interests and gave the impression of protecting the small farmers' interests as well.

The South's elite defended slavery in other ways. In the 1830s, whites decided that slavery was too important to debate. "So interwoven is [slavery] with our interest, our manners, our climate and our very being," one man declared in 1833, "that no change can ever possibly be effected without a civil commotion from which the heart of a patriot must turn with horror." To end free speech on the slavery question, powerful whites dismissed slavery's critics from college faculties, drove them from pulpits, and hounded them from political life. Sometimes antislavery Southerners fell victim to vigilantes and mob violence. One could defend slavery; one could even delicately suggest mild reforms. But no Southerner could any longer safely call slavery evil or advocate its destruction.

> One South Carolinian told his wealthy neighbor that he had a bright political future because he never thought himself "too good to sit down & talk to a poor man."

In the South, therefore, the rise of the common man occurred alongside the continuing, even growing, power of the planter class. Rather than pitting slaveholders against nonslaveholders, elections remained an effective means of binding the region's whites together. Elections affirmed the sovereignty of white men, whether planter or plain folk, and the subordination of African Americans. Those twin themes played well among white women as well. Though unable to vote, white women supported equality for whites and slavery for blacks. In the antebellum South, the politics of slavery helped knit together all of white society.

REVIEW   How did planters benefit from their control of state legislatures?

Conclusion: A Slave Society

By the early nineteenth century, northern states had either abolished slavery or put it on the road to extinction, while southern states were aggressively building the largest slave society in the New World. Regional differences increased over time, not merely because the South became more and more dominated by slavery, but also because developments in the North rapidly propelled it in a very different direction.

One-third of the South's population was enslaved by 1860. Bondage saddled blacks with enormous physical and spiritual burdens: hard labor, harsh treatment, broken families, and, most important, the denial of freedom itself.

Although degraded and exploited, they were not defeated. Out of African memories and New World realities, blacks created a life-affirming African American culture that sustained and strengthened them. Their families, religion, and community provided antidotes to white racist ideas and even to white power. Defined as property, they refused to be reduced to things. Perceived as inferior beings, they rejected the notion that they were natural slaves. Slaves engaged in a war of wills with masters who sought their labor, while the slaves themselves sought to live dignified, autonomous lives.

By the mid-nineteenth century, slavery was crucial to the South's distinctiveness and to the loyalty and regional identification of its whites. The South was not merely a society with slaves; it had become a slave society. Slavery shaped the region's economy, culture, social structure, and politics. Whites south of the Mason-Dixon line believed that racial slavery was necessary and just. By making all blacks a pariah class, all whites gained a measure of equality and harmony.

Racism did not erase stress along class lines, nor did the other features of southern life that helped confine class tensions: the wide availability of land, rapid economic mobility, the democratic nature of political life, and patriarchal power among all white men. Anxious slaveholders continued to worry that yeomen would defect from the proslavery consensus. But during the 1850s, a far more ominous division emerged—that between "slave states" and "free states."

Selected Bibliography

Slaveholders and the Economy

Edward E. Baptist, *Creating an Old South: Middle Florida's Plantation Frontier before the Civil War* (2002).

David L. Carlton and Peter A. Coclanis, *The South, the Nation, and the World: Perspectives on Southern Economic Development* (2003).

Steven Deyle, *Carry Me Back: The Domestic Slave Trade in American Life* (2005).

Drew G. Faust, *James Henry Hammond and the Old South: A Design for Mastery* (1982).

Richard Follett, *The Sugar Masters: Planters and Slaves in Louisiana's Cane World, 1820–1860* (2005).

Jonathan Martin, *Divided Mastery: Slave Hiring in the American South* (2004).

James David Miller, *South by Southwest: Planter Emigration and Identity in the Slave South* (2002).

Gavin Wright, *The Political Economy of the Cotton South: Households, Markets, and Wealth in the Nineteenth Century* (1978).

Jeffrey Robert Young, *Domesticating Slavery: The Master Class in Georgia and South Carolina, 1670–1837* (1999).

Slaves, Slavery, and Race Relations

Ira Berlin, *Generations of Captivity: A History of African-American Slaves* (2003).

Thomas C. Buchanan, *Black Life on the Mississippi: Slaves, Free Blacks, and the Western Steamboat World* (2004).

Eugene D. Genovese, *Roll, Jordan, Roll: The World the Slave Made* (1974).

Kenneth S. Greenberg, ed., *Nat Turner: A Slave Rebellion in History and Memory* (2002).

Gwendolyn Midlo Hall, *Slavery and African Ethnicities in the Americas: Restoring the Links* (2005).

Peter Kolchin, *American Slavery, 1619–1877* (1993).

Dylan C. Penningroth, *The Claims of Kinfolk: African American Property and Community in the Nineteenth-Century South* (2003).

Willie Lee Rose, ed., *A Documentary History of Slavery in North America* (1976).

Brenda E. Stevenson, *Life in Black and White: Family and Community in the Slave South* (1996).

Society and Culture

Ira Berlin, *Slaves without Masters: The Free Negro in the Antebellum South* (1974).

Charles C. Bolton and Scott P. Culclasure, eds., *The Confessions of Edward Isham: A Poor White Life of the Old South* (1998).

Orville Vernon Burton, *In My Father's House Are Many Mansions: Family and Community in Edgefield, South Carolina* (1985).

Victoria E. Bynum, *Unruly Women: The Politics of Social and Sexual Control in the Old South* (1992).

Craig T. Friend and Lorri Glover, eds., *Southern Manhood: Perspectives on Masculinity in the Old South* (2004).

Steven Hahn, *The Roots of Southern Populism: Yeoman Farmers and the Transformation of the Georgia Upcountry, 1850–1890* (1983).

Christine Leigh Heyrman, *Southern Cross: The Beginnings of the Bible Belt* (1997).

Michael P. Johnson and James L. Roark, *Black Masters: A Free Family of Color in the Old South* (1984).

Stephanie McCurry, *Masters of Small Worlds: Yeoman Households, Gender Relations, and the Political Culture of the Antebellum South* (1995).

James Oakes, *Slavery and Freedom: An Interpretation of the Old South* (1990).

Adam Rothman, *Slave Country: American Expansion and the Deep South* (2005).

Bertram Wyatt-Brown, *Southern Honor: Ethics and Behavior in the Old South* (1982).

Politics and Political Culture

William J. Cooper Jr., *Liberty and Slavery: Southern Politics to 1860* (1983).

Lacy K. Ford Jr., *Origins of Southern Radicalism: The South Carolina Upcountry, 1800–1860* (1988).

Robert E. May, *John A. Quitman: Old South Crusader* (1985).

Elizabeth R. Varon, *We Mean to Be Counted: White Women and Politics in Antebellum Virginia* (1998).

Peter Wallenstein, *From Slave South to New South: Public Policy in Nineteenth-Century Georgia* (1987).

▶ FOR MORE BOOKS ABOUT TOPICS IN THIS CHAPTER, see the Online Bibliography at bedfordstmartins.com/roark.

▶ FOR ADDITIONAL FIRSTHAND ACCOUNTS OF THIS PERIOD, see Chapter 13 in Michael Johnson, ed., *Reading the American Past,* Fourth Edition.

▶ FOR WEB SITES, IMAGES, AND DOCUMENTS RELATED TO TOPICS AND PLACES IN THIS CHAPTER, visit bedfordstmartins.com/makehistory.

REVIEWING THE CHAPTER

Follow these steps to review and strengthen your understanding of the chapter.

STEP 1: *Study the* **Key Terms** *and* **Timeline** *to identify the significance of each item listed.*

STEP 2: *Answer the* **Review Questions***, drawing on key terms and dates to support your answers.*

STEP 3: *Drawing on the Key Terms, Timeline, and Review Questions, answer the broader* **Making Connections** *questions.*

KEY TERMS

Who

Nat Turner (p. 435)
David Walker (p. 435)
William Lloyd Garrison (p. 435)
Thomas R. Dew (p. 436)
John C. Calhoun (p. 439)
Eli Whitney (p. 443)
Mary Boykin Chesnut (p. 455)
Denmark Vesey (p. 460)
William Ellison (p. 462)

What

Nat Turner's insurrection (p. 435)
Mason-Dixon line (p. 436)
cotton kingdom (p. 437)
slave codes (p. 439)
planter (p. 443)
plantation (p. 443)
overseer (p. 448)
paternalism (p. 449)
miscegenation (p. 450)

chivalry (p. 451)
slave driver (p. 457)
slave resistance (p. 459)
Vesey conspiracy (p. 460)
"free black" (p. 461)
emancipation (p. 461)
yeomen (p. 463)
plantation belt (p. 463)
upcountry (p. 463)

TIMELINE

◄ **1808** • External slave trade outlawed.

1810s–1850s • Suffrage extended throughout the South to all adult white males.

1813–1814 • Creek War opens Indian land to white settlement.

1820s–1830s • Southern legislatures enact slave codes to strengthen slavery.
• Southern legislatures enact laws to restrict the growth of the free black population.
• Southern intellectuals begin to fashion a systematic defense of slavery.

1829 • *Appeal...to the Coloured Citizens of the World* published.

1830 • Southern slaves number approximately two million.

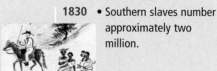

REVIEW QUESTIONS

1. Why did the nineteenth-century southern economy remain primarily agricultural? (pp. 436–48)

2. Why did the ideology of paternalism gain currency among planters in the nineteenth century? (pp. 448–56)

3. What types of resistance did slaves participate in, and why did slave resistance rarely take the form of rebellion? (pp. 456–61)

4. Why did many state legislatures pass laws restricting free blacks' rights in the 1820s and 1830s? (pp. 461–62)

5. Why did yeomen dominate the upcountry? (pp. 462–66)

6. How did planters benefit from their control of state legislatures? (pp. 466–69)

MAKING CONNECTIONS

1. By the mid-nineteenth century, the South had become a "cotton kingdom." How did cotton's profitability shape the region's antebellum development? In your answer, discuss the region's distinctive demographic and economic features.

2. How did southern white legislators and intellectuals attempt to strengthen the institution of slavery in the 1820s? What prompted them to undertake this work? In your answer, be sure to explore regional and national influences.

3. Although bondage restricted slaves' autonomy and left slaves vulnerable to extreme abuse, they resisted slavery. Discuss the variety of ways in which slaves attempted to lessen the harshness of slavery. What were the short- and long-term effects of their efforts?

4. Despite vigorous political competition in the South, by 1860 legislative power was largely concentrated in the hands of a regional minority—slaveholders. Why were slaveholders politically dominant? In your answer, be sure to consider how the region's biracialism contributed to its politics.

▶ For practice quizzes, a customized study plan, and other study tools, see the Online Study Guide at bedfordstmartins.com/roark.

1831 • Nat Turner's slave rebellion.
• First issue of *Liberator* published.

     1834 • *Catechism for Colored Persons* published.

          1836 • Arkansas admitted to the Union as a slave state.

               1840 • Cotton accounts for more than 60 percent of the nation's exports.

                    1845 • Texas and Florida admitted to the Union as slave states.

                         1860 • Southern slaves number nearly four million, one-third of the South's population.

JOHN BROWN'S PIKES

Scorning what he called "milk-and-water" abolitionists who only talked about slavery, John Brown favored "action!" In 1859, when he brought his abolitionist war to Harpers Ferry, Virginia, he carried with him 950 pikes, handsome but deadly spears made by a Connecticut blacksmith, which he expected to put into the hands of rebelling slaves. Bloody pikes, he thought, would end slavery in America. After Brown's failure at Harpers Ferry, townspeople sold many of the weapons as souvenirs.

Chicago Historical Society.

The House Divided

1846–1861

- **The Bitter Fruits of War** 476
  The Wilmot Proviso and
  the Expansion of Slavery 476
  The Election of 1848 479
  Debate and Compromise 479

- **The Sectional Balance
  Undone** 481
  The Fugitive Slave Act 481
  Uncle Tom's Cabin 484
  The Kansas-Nebraska Act 485

- **Realignment of
  the Party System** 487
  The Old Parties: Whigs
  and Democrats 487
  The New Parties: Know-Nothings
  and Republicans 490
  The Election of 1856 493

- **Freedom under Siege** 496
  "Bleeding Kansas" 496
  The *Dred Scott* Decision 497
  Prairie Republican:
  Abraham Lincoln 499
  The Lincoln-Douglas Debates 500

- **The Union Collapses** 501
  The Aftermath of
  John Brown's Raid 501
  Republican Victory in 1860 502
  Secession Winter 504

- **Conclusion: Slavery,
  Free Labor, and the Failure
  of Political Compromise** 506

OTHER THAN TWENTY CHILDREN, John Brown did not have much to show for his life in 1859. Grizzled, gnarled, and fifty-nine years old, he had for decades lived like a nomad, hauling his large family back and forth across six states as he tried desperately to better himself. He turned his hand to farming, raising sheep, running a tannery, and selling wool, but failure dogged him. The world had given John Brown some hard licks, but it had not budged his conviction that slavery was wrong and ought to be destroyed. He had learned to hate slavery at his father's knee, and in the wake of the fighting that erupted over the issue in Kansas in the 1850s, his beliefs turned violent. On May 24, 1856, he led an eight-man antislavery posse in the midnight slaughter of five allegedly proslavery men at Pottawatomie, Kansas. He told Mahala Doyle, whose husband and two oldest sons he killed, that if a man stood between him and what he thought right, he would take that man's life as calmly as he would eat breakfast.

After the killings, Brown slipped out of Kansas and reemerged in the East. More than ever, he was a man on fire for abolition. He spent thirty months begging money from New Englanders to support his vague plan for military operations against slavery. He captivated the genteel easterners, particularly the Boston elite. They were awed by his iron-willed determination and courage, but most could not accept violence. "These men are all talk," Brown declared. "What is needed is action—action!" But the hypnotic-eyed Brown convinced a handful of people that God had touched him for a great purpose, and they donated enough money for him to gather a small band of antislavery warriors.

On the night of October 16, 1859, Brown took his war against slavery into the South. With only twenty-one men, including five African Americans, he invaded Harpers Ferry, Virginia. His band quickly seized the town's armory and rifle works, but the invaders were immediately surrounded, first by local militia and then by Colonel Robert E. Lee, who commanded the U.S. troops in the area. When Brown refused to surrender, federal soldiers charged with bayonets. Seventeen men, two of whom were slaves, lost their lives. Although a few of Brown's raiders escaped, federal forces killed ten (including two of his sons) and captured seven, among them Brown.

"When I strike, the bees will begin to swarm," Brown told Frederick Douglass a few months before the raid. As slaves rushed to Harpers Ferry, he said, he would arm them with the pikes he carried with him and with weapons stolen from the armory. They would then fight a war of liberation. Brown, however, neglected to inform the slaves that he had arrived in Harpers Ferry, and the few who knew of his arrival wanted nothing to do with his enterprise. "It was not a slave insurrection," Abraham Lincoln observed.

John Brown

In this 1859 photograph, John Brown appears respectable, even statesmanlike, but contemporaries debated his mental state and moral character, and the debate still rages. Critics argue that he was a bloody terrorist, a religious fanatic who believed that he was touched by God for a great purpose, one for which he was willing to die. Admirers see a resolute and selfless hero, a rare white man who believed that black people were the equals of whites, and a shrewd political observer who recognized that only a full-scale revolt of the oppressed would end slavery in America.

National Portrait Gallery, Smithsonian Institution/ Art Resource, NY.

"It was an attempt by white men to get up a revolt among slaves, in which the slaves refused to participate. In fact, it was so absurd that the slaves, with all their ignorance, saw plainly enough it could not succeed."

Although Brown's raid ended in utter defeat, white Southerners viewed it as proof of their growing suspicion that Northerners actively sought to incite slaves in bloody rebellion. For more than a decade, Northerners and Southerners had accused one another of hostile intentions, and by 1859, emotions were raw. Sectional tension was as old as the Constitution, but hostility had escalated with the outbreak of war with Mexico in May 1846 (see chapter 12). Only three months after the war began, national expansion and the slavery issue intersected when Representative David Wilmot introduced a bill to prohibit slavery in any territory that might be acquired as a result of the war. After that, the problem of slavery in the territories became the principal wedge that divided the nation.

"Mexico is to us the forbidden fruit," South Carolina senator John C. Calhoun declared at the war's outset. "The penalty of eating it [is] to subject our institutions to political death." For a decade and a half, the slavery issue intertwined with the fate of former Mexican land, poisoning the national political debate. Slavery proved powerful enough to transform party politics into sectional politics.

Rather than Whigs and Democrats confronting one another across party lines, Northerners and Southerners eyed one another hostilely across the Mason-Dixon line. Sectional politics encouraged the South's separatist impulses. Southern separatism, a fitful tendency before the Mexican-American War, gained strength with each confrontation. As the nation lurched from crisis to crisis, southern disaffection and alienation mounted, and support for compromise and conciliation eroded. The era began with a crisis of Union and ended with the Union in even graver peril. As Abraham Lincoln predicted in 1858, "A house divided against itself cannot stand."

The Bitter Fruits of War

Between 1846 and 1848, the nation grew by 1.2 million square miles, an incredible two-thirds. The gold rush of 1849 transformed the sleepy **frontier** of California into a booming, thriving economy (see chapter 12). The 1850s witnessed new "rushes," for gold in Colorado and silver in Nevada's Comstock Lode. People from around the world flocked to the West, where they produced a vibrant agriculture as well as tons of gold and silver. But it quickly became clear that Northerners and Southerners had very different visions of the West, particularly the place of slavery in its future.

History provided contradictory precedents for handling slavery in the territories. In 1787, the Northwest Ordinance banned slavery north of the Ohio River. In 1803, slavery was allowed to remain in the newly acquired Louisiana Territory. The Missouri Compromise of 1820 prohibited slavery in part of that territory but allowed it in the rest. In 1846, when the war with Mexico suggested new territory for the United States, politicians offered various plans. But when the war ended in 1848, Congress had made no headway in solving the issue of slavery in the land acquired from Mexico, called the Mexican cession. In 1850, Congress patched together a settlement, one that Americans hoped would be permanent.

The Wilmot Proviso and the Expansion of Slavery

In the years leading up to the Civil War, Americans focused not on slavery where it existed, but on the possibility that slavery might expand into areas where it did not exist. Most

Oak Home Farm, San Joaquin County, California
The discovery of gold in California initiated a stampede west, but not everyone wanted to be a prospector. In 1860, an unknown artist painted this idyllic view of the farm of W. I. Overhiser in California's fertile San Joaquin Valley. Thousands of miles away, farmers compared farmsteads like Overhiser's with their own. Many judged life more bountiful in the West and trekked across the country to try to strike it rich in western agriculture.
University of California at Berkeley, Bancroft Library.

Americans agreed that the Constitution left the issue of slavery to the individual states to decide. Northern states had done away with slavery, while southern states had retained it. But what about slavery in the nation's territories? The Constitution states that "Congress shall have power to . . . make all needful rules and regulations respecting the territory . . . belonging to the United States." The debate about slavery, then, turned toward Congress.

The spark for the national debate was provided in August 1846 by a young Democratic representative from Pennsylvania, David Wilmot, who proposed that Congress bar slavery from all lands acquired in the war with Mexico. The Mexicans had already abolished slavery in their country, and Wilmot declared, "God forbid that we should be the means of planting this institution upon it."

Regardless of party affiliation, Northerners lined up behind the Wilmot Proviso. Many supported **free soil**, by which they meant territory in which slavery would be prohibited, on the basis of egalitarian principles. They wanted to preserve the West for **free labor**, for hardworking,

self-reliant free men, not for slaveholders and slaves. But support also came from those who were simply anti-South. New slave territories would eventually mean new slave states, and they opposed magnifying the political power of Southerners. Wilmot himself said he saw his proposal as a means of blunting "the *power* of slaveholders" in the national government.

Additional support for free soil came from Northerners who were hostile to blacks and wanted to reserve new land for whites. Wilmot understood what one Indiana man put bluntly: "The American people are emphatically a *Negro-hating* people." Wilmot himself blatantly encouraged racist support when he declared, "I would preserve for free white labor a fair country, a rich inheritance, where the sons of toil, of my own race and own color, can live without the disgrace which association with negro slavery

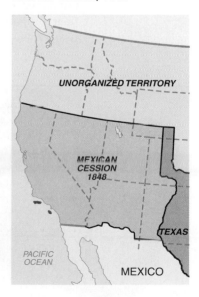

Mexican Cession, 1848

brings upon free labor." It is no wonder that some called the Wilmot Proviso the "White Man's Proviso."

The thought that slavery might be excluded outraged almost all white Southerners. They regarded the West as a ladder for economic and social opportunity. They also believed that the exclusion of slavery was a slap in the face to veterans of the Mexican-American War, at least half of whom were Southerners. "When the war-worn soldier returns home," one Alabaman asked, "is he to be told that he cannot carry his property to the country won by his blood?"

In addition, southern leaders understood the need for political parity with the North to protect the South's interests, especially slavery. The need seemed especially urgent in the 1840s, when the North's population and wealth were booming. James Henry Hammond of South Carolina predicted that ten new states would be carved from the acquired Mexican land. If free soil won, the North would "ride over us roughshod" in Congress, he claimed. "Our only safety is in *equality* of POWER."

The two sides squared off in the nation's capital. Because Northerners had a majority in the House, they easily passed the Wilmot Proviso. In the Senate, however, where slave states outnumbered free states fifteen to fourteen, Southerners defeated it in 1847. Senator John C. Calhoun of South Carolina denied that Congress had the constitutional authority to exclude slavery from the nation's territories. He argued that the territories were the "joint and common property" of all the states and that Congress could not justly deprive any state of equal rights in the territories and therefore could not bar citizens of one state from migrating with their property (including slaves) to the territories. Whereas Wilmot demanded that Congress slam shut the door to slavery, Calhoun called on Congress to hold the door wide open.

In 1847, Senator Lewis Cass of Michigan offered a compromise through the doctrine of **popular sovereignty**, by which the people who settled the territories would decide for themselves slavery's fate. This solution, Cass argued, sat squarely in the American tradition of **democracy** and local self-government. It had the added attraction of removing the incendiary issue of the expansion of slavery from the nation's capital and lodging it in distant, sleepy territorial legislatures, where it would excite fewer passions.

Popular sovereignty's most attractive feature was its ambiguity about the precise moment when settlers could determine slavery's fate. Northern advocates believed that the decision on slavery could be made as soon as the first territorial legislature assembled. With free-soil majorities likely because of the North's greater population, they would shut the door to slavery almost before the first slave arrived. Southern supporters declared that popular sovereignty guaranteed that slavery would be unrestricted throughout the entire territorial period. Only at the very end, when settlers in a territory drew up a constitution and applied for statehood, could they decide the issue of slavery. By then, slavery would have sunk deep roots. As long as the matter of timing remained vague, popular sovereignty gave hope to both sides.

When Congress ended its session in 1848, no plan had won a majority in both houses. Northerners who demanded no new slave territory anywhere, ever, and Southerners who demanded entry for their slave property into all territories, or else, staked out their extreme positions. Unresolved in Congress, the territorial question naturally became an issue in the presidential election of 1848.

General Taylor Cigar Case

This papier-mâché cigar case portrays General Zachary Taylor, Whig presidential candidate in 1848, in a colorful scene from the Mexican-American War. Shown here as a dashing, elegant officer, Taylor was in fact a short, thickset, and roughly dressed Indian fighter who had spent his career commanding small frontier garrisons. The inscription reminds voters that Taylor was a victor in the first four battles fought in the war and directs attention away from the fact that in politics, he was a rank amateur.

Collection of Janice L. and David J. Frent.

The Election of 1848

When President Polk, worn-out and ailing, chose not to seek reelection, the Democratic convention nominated Lewis Cass of Michigan, the man most closely associated with popular sovereignty. But in an effort to keep peace between their proslavery and antislavery factions, the Democrats adopted a platform that avoided a firm position on slavery in the territories. The Whigs followed a different strategy and nominated a Mexican-American War hero, General Zachary Taylor. The Whigs bet that the combination of a military hero and total silence on the slavery issue would unite their divided party, and thus they declined to adopt a party platform. Taylor, who owned more than one hundred slaves on plantations in Mississippi and Louisiana, was hailed by Georgia politician Robert Toombs as a "Southern man, a slaveholder, a cotton **planter**."

Antislavery Whigs balked and looked for an alternative. The time seemed ripe for a major political realignment. Senator Charles Sumner called for "one grand Northern party of Freedom," and in the summer of 1848, antislavery Whigs and antislavery Democrats founded the Free-Soil Party. Nearly fifteen thousand noisy Free-Soilers gathered in Buffalo, New York, where they nominated a Democrat, Martin Van Buren, for president and a Whig, Charles Francis Adams, for vice president. The platform boldly proclaimed, "Free soil, free speech, free labor, and free men."

The November election dashed the hopes of the Free-Soilers. Although they succeeded in making slavery the campaign's central issue, they did not carry a single state. The major parties went through contortions to present their candidates favorably in both North and South, and their evasions succeeded. Taylor won the all-important electoral vote, 163 to 127, carrying eight of the fifteen slave states and seven of the fifteen free states (Map 14.1). (Wisconsin had entered the Union earlier in 1848 as the fifteenth free state.) Northern voters proved that they were not yet ready for Sumner's "one grand Northern party of Freedom," but the struggle over slavery in the territories had shaken the major parties badly.

> The Free-Soil Party platform boldly proclaimed, "Free soil, free speech, free labor, and free men."

Debate and Compromise

Southern slaveholder Zachary Taylor entered the White House in March 1849 and almost immediately shocked the nation by championing a free-soil solution to the Mexican cession. Believing that he could avoid further sectional strife if California and New Mexico skipped the territorial stage, he sent agents west to persuade the settlers to apply for admission to the Union as states. Predominantly antislavery, the settlers began writing free-state constitutions. "For the first time," Mississippian Jefferson Davis lamented, "we are about permanently to destroy the balance of power between the sections."

Congress convened in December 1849, beginning one of the most contentious and most significant sessions in its history. President Taylor urged Congress to admit California as a free state immediately and to admit New Mexico, which lagged behind a few months, as soon as it applied. Southerners exploded. In their eyes, Taylor had betrayed his region. A North Carolinian declared that Southerners who would "consent to be thus degraded and enslaved, ought to be whipped through their fields by their own negroes."

Into this rancorous scene stepped Senator Henry Clay of Kentucky, known as "the Great Pacificator," the architect of Union-saving compromises in the Missouri and **nullification** crises (see chapters 10 and 11). Clay offered a series of resolutions meant to answer and balance "all questions in controversy between the free and slave

MAP 14.1 The Election of 1848

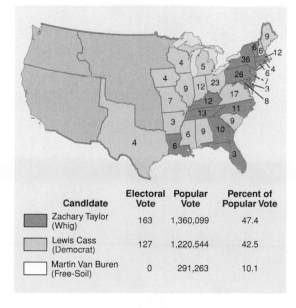

Candidate	Electoral Vote	Popular Vote	Percent of Popular Vote
Zachary Taylor (Whig)	163	1,360,099	47.4
Lewis Cass (Democrat)	127	1,220,544	42.5
Martin Van Buren (Free-Soil)	0	291,263	10.1

states, growing out of the subject of slavery." Admit California as a free state, he proposed, but organize the rest of the Southwest without restrictions on slavery. Require Texas to abandon its claim to parts of New Mexico, but compensate it by assuming its preannexation debt. Abolish the domestic slave trade in Washington, D.C., but confirm slavery itself in the nation's capital. Reassert Congress's lack of authority to interfere with the interstate slave trade and enact a more effective fugitive slave law.

Both antislavery advocates and "fire-eaters" (as radical Southerners who urged secession from the Union were called) savaged Clay's plan. Senator Salmon P. Chase of Ohio ridiculed it as "sentiment for the North, substance for the South." Senator Henry S. Foote of Mississippi denounced it as more offensive to the South than the speeches of abolitionists William Lloyd Garrison, Wendell Phillips, and Frederick Douglass combined. The most ominous response came from John C. Calhoun, who charged that unending northern agitation on the slavery question had "snapped" many of the "cords which bind these states together in one common Union." He argued that the fragile political unity of North and South depended on continued equal representation in the Senate, which Clay's plan for a free California destroyed. "As things now stand," he said in February 1850, the South "cannot with safety remain in the Union."

After Clay and Calhoun had spoken, it was time for the third member of the "great triumvirate," Senator Daniel Webster of Massachusetts, to address the Senate. (The three were later immortalized in daguerreotypes by the renowned photographer Mathew Brady. See "The Promise of Technology," page 482.) Like Clay, Webster sought to build a constituency for compromise. He told Northerners that the South had legitimate complaints that required attention. But he told Southerners that secession from the Union would mean civil war. He appealed for an end to taunts and reckless proposals and, to the dismay of many Northerners, mentioned by name the Wilmot Proviso. A legal ban on slavery in the territories was unnecessary, he said, because the harsh climate effectively prohibited the expansion of cotton and slaves into the new American Southwest. "I would not take pains uselessly to reaffirm an ordinance of nature, nor to re-enact the will of God," Webster declared.

Free-soil forces recoiled from what they saw as Webster's desertion. In Boston, clergyman and abolitionist Theodore Parker could only conclude that "the Southern men" must have offered Webster the presidency. In Washington, Senator William H. Seward of New York responded that Webster's and Clay's compromise with slavery was "radically wrong and essentially vicious." He flatly rejected Calhoun's argument that Congress lacked the constitutional authority to exclude slavery from the territories. In any case, Seward said, in the most sensational moment in his address, there was a "higher law than the Constitution"—the law of God—to ensure freedom in all the public domain. Claiming that God was a Free-Soiler did nothing to cool the superheated political atmosphere.

In May, a Senate committee produced a bill that joined Clay's resolutions into a single comprehensive package, known as the Omnibus Bill because it was a vehicle on which "every sort of passenger" could ride. Clay bet that a majority of Congress wanted compromise and that the members would vote for the package, even though it contained provisions they disliked, to

John C. Calhoun

Hollow-cheeked and dark-eyed in this 1850 daguerreotype by Mathew Brady, Calhoun had only months to live. Still, his passion and indomitable will come through. British writer Harriet Martineau once described the champion of southern rights as "the cast-iron man who looks as if he had never been born and could never be extinguished."

National Portrait Gallery, Smithsonian Institution/Art Resource, NY.

gain an overall settlement of sectional issues. But the omnibus strategy backfired. Free-Soilers and proslavery Southerners voted down the comprehensive plan.

Fortunately for those who favored a settlement, Senator Stephen A. Douglas, a rising Democratic star from Illinois, stepped in. He broke the bill into its various parts and skillfully ushered each through Congress. The agreement Douglas won in September 1850 was very much the one Clay had proposed in January. California entered the Union as a free state. New Mexico and Utah became territories where slavery would be decided by popular sovereignty. Texas accepted its boundary with New Mexico and received $10 million from the federal government. Congress ended the slave trade in the District of Columbia but enacted a more stringent fugitive slave law. In September, Millard Fillmore, who had become president when Zachary Taylor died in July, signed into law each bill, collectively known as the Compromise of 1850 (Map 14.2).

Actually, the Compromise of 1850 was not a true compromise at all. Douglas's parliamentary skill, not a spirit of conciliation, was responsible for the legislative success. Still, the nation breathed a sigh of relief, for the Compromise preserved the Union and peace for the moment. Daniel Webster declared, "We have gone through the most important crisis that has occurred since the foundation of the government." But others recognized that the Compromise scarcely touched the deeper conflict over slavery. Free-Soiler Salmon Chase observed, "The question of slavery in the territories has been avoided. It has not been settled."

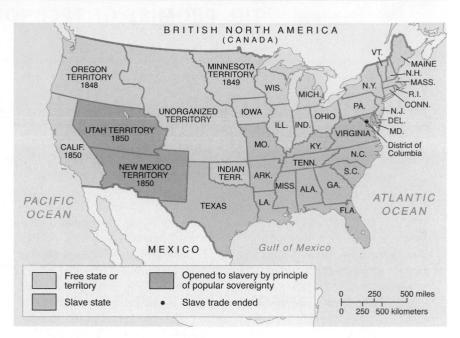

MAP 14.2   The Compromise of 1850
The patched-together sectional agreement was both clumsy and unstable. Few Americans—in either North or South—supported all five parts of the Compromise.

ously received relatively little attention. Instead of restoring calm, the Compromise brought the horrors of slavery into the North.

Millions of Northerners who had never seen a runaway slave confronted slavery in the early 1850s. Harriet Beecher Stowe's *Uncle Tom's Cabin*, a novel that vividly depicts the brutality and heartlessness of the South's "peculiar institution," aroused passions so deep that many found goodwill toward white Southerners nearly impossible to achieve. But no groundswell of antislavery sentiment compelled Congress to reopen the slavery controversy. Instead, politicians did it themselves. Four years after Congress delicately stitched the sectional compromise together, it ripped the threads out. With the Kansas-Nebraska Act, it again posed the question of slavery in the territories, the deadliest of all sectional issues.

> **REVIEW**   Why did response to the Wilmot Proviso split along sectional rather than party lines?

The Sectional Balance Undone

The Compromise of 1850 began to come apart almost immediately. The thread that unraveled it was not slavery in the Southwest, the crux of the disagreement, but runaway slaves in New England, a part of the settlement that had previ-

The Fugitive Slave Act

The Fugitive Slave Act proved the most explosive of the Compromise measures. The issue of runaways was as old as the Constitution, which contained a provision for the return of any "person held to service or labor in one state" who escaped to another. In 1793, a federal law gave muscle to the provision by authorizing slave

Daguerreotypes: The "Sunbeam Art"

Early in the nineteenth century, several Europeans working separately discovered that the shadow of an object falling on a chemically treated surface remained after the light source was removed. In the late 1830s, Frenchman Louis Daguerre learned how to keep the "shadow" from fading. "Daguerreotypomania" soon gripped Paris. News of Daguerre's success in fixing an image arrived in New York City in the spring of 1839. As Americans found, photography was not for amateurs. The daguerreotype photographic process was cumbersome and complex. Initially, a photographer's equipment included a large wooden box, a glass lens, copper plates coated with silver, vials of chemicals, and a fire for heat. Because picture taking required several minutes of exposure, candid shots were impossible. To ease the strain of sitting immobile for so long while facing the camera, an American photographer invented a vise to clamp the sitter's head from behind. The process tested the subject's patience and often led to photographs that captured grimaces and pained scowls.

Despite their considerable shortcomings, daguerreotypes were an instant success. Samuel Morris, the first American to see a daguerreotype, exclaimed, "The exquisite minuteness of the delineation cannot be conceived. No painting or engraving ever approached it." Another awed observer declared that the daguerreotype was a "perfect transcript of the thing itself." The almost three-dimensional images spooked country people, some of whom suspected magic. But by the early 1840s, photography was a booming business. Itinerant photographers rode the rural and small-town circuit, while in cities photographic galleries sprang up. In 1850, one observer declared,

"In our great cities a Daguerreotypist is to be found in almost every square; and there is scarce a county in the states that has not one or more of those industrious individuals busy at work catching 'the shadow' ere the 'substance fade.'"

Ordinary citizens could not afford to have their portraits painted, and thus few working people owned personal likenesses. Compared to paintings, daguerreotypes were cheap, and at midcentury one reporter claimed that "it is hard to find a man who has not gone through the operator's hands from once to half-a-dozen times, or who has not the shadowy faces of his wife & children done up in purple morocco and velvet. . . . Truly the sunbeam art is a most wonderful one, and the public feel it a great benefit." In the 1850s, the rage for photographs meant that Americans were buying millions of images each year. The new technology met the needs of a culture undergoing vast and rapid change. People kept their precious daguerreotypes in safe places, thankful that this "camera magic" preserved families so often parted by distance or death.

No early American photographer was more important than Mathew Brady. In 1844, he opened the Daguer-

---

owners to enter other states to recapture their slave property. Proclaiming the 1793 law a license to kidnap free blacks, northern states in the 1830s began passing "personal liberty laws" that provided fugitives with some protection.

Some northern communities also formed vigilance committees to help runaways and to obstruct white Southerners who came north to reclaim them. Each year, a few hundred slaves escaped into free states and found friendly northern "conductors" who put them aboard the "underground railroad," which was not a railroad at all but a series of secret "stations" (hideouts) on the way to Canada. Harriet Tubman, an escaped slave from Maryland, returned to the South more than a dozen times and guided more than three hundred slaves to freedom in this way.

Furious about northern interference, Southerners in 1850 insisted on the stricter fugitive slave law that was passed as part of the Compromise. To seize an alleged slave, a slaveholder simply had to appear before a commissioner and swear that the runaway was his. The commissioner earned $10 for every black returned to slavery but only $5 for those set free. Most galling to Northerners, the law stipulated that all citizens were expected to assist officials in apprehending runaways.

Horace Greeley

One of the distinguished men whose portraits Mathew Brady shot was his friend and fellow New Yorker Horace Greeley. Journalist, politician, and reformer, Greeley advocated temperance, socialism, labor unions, spiritualism, and revolutionary dietary habits. Brady's 1851 daguerreotype captures the eccentric editor of the powerful *New York Tribune* sitting on a chair with a newspaper folded in his lap.

Library of Congress.

rean Miniature Gallery at Broadway and Fulton Street in New York City. He sought to bend photography from merely personal to political ends. Brady declared that "from the first, I regarded myself as under obligation to my country to preserve the faces of its historic men and mothers." Seeing himself as a kind of historian of the nation, he shot portraits of distinguished citizens—presidents, congressmen, senators, and statesmen—as well as everyday people who walked into his gallery. Likenesses of illustrious Americans reflected Brady's devotion to the country, and he hoped that they would inspire patriotism in others. His elegant establishment was renowned as a meeting place where people of all classes mingled freely. "People used to stroll in there in those days," a writer remembered, "to see what new celebrity had been added to the little collection, and the last new portrait at Brady's was a standing topic of conversation."

In 1850, Brady sought to extend the public-spirited message of his photographs beyond his shop. He published *The Gallery of Illustrious Americans*—twelve portraits of famous statesmen, including John C. Calhoun, Daniel Webster, and Henry Clay. Anxiety framed the project. At that

moment, Washington was embroiled in bitter sectional controversy, and the United States stood on the brink of disintegration. Accurate, realistic images of eminent public men, Brady figured, would capture the "genius" of the nation and rally citizens to their beleaguered Republic. The *Gallery* was a nonpartisan, nonsectional gesture that sought to embrace Whigs and Democrats, Northerners and Southerners, and to urge them to overcome the disuniting elements in American life. The magic of daguerreotypes, Brady thought, would help bind citizens more directly, more personally to living statesmen and to the country they symbolized.

Technology, even technology married to art, could not save the nation. But such was the promise of early photography that some believed it might. Like Webster and Clay, the *Gallery* pleaded for compromise and national unity. Brady hoped that the new technology of photography would serve as a moral agent furthering political reconciliation and peace. By 1860, however, daguerreotypes had all but disappeared from American life, replaced by more efficient photographic processes, and the Union remained imperiled.

Theodore Parker, the clergyman and abolitionist, denounced the law as "a hateful statute of kidnappers." In Boston in February 1851, an angry crowd overpowered federal marshals and snatched a runaway named Shadrach from a courtroom, put him on the underground railroad, and whisked him off to Canada. Three years later, when another Boston crowd rushed the courthouse in a failed attempt to rescue Anthony Burns, who had recently fled slavery in Richmond, a guard was shot dead. Martha Russell was among the angry crowd that watched Burns being escorted to the ship that would return him to Virginia. "Did you ever feel

every drop of blood in you boiling and seething, throbbing and burning, until it seemed you should suffocate?" she asked. "I have felt all this today. I have seen that poor slave, Anthony Burns, carried back to slavery!"

To white Southerners, it seemed that fanatics of the "higher law" creed had whipped Northerners into a frenzy of massive resistance. Actually, the overwhelming majority of fugitives claimed before federal commissioners were reenslaved peacefully. Spectacular rescues such as the one that saved Shadrach were rare. But brutal enforcement of the unpopular law had a radicalizing effect in the North, particularly in

The Modern Medea

In 1855, a slave family—Robert Garner; his twenty-two-year-old wife, Margaret; their four children; and his parents—fled Kentucky. Archibald Gaines, Margaret's owner, tracked them to a cabin in Ohio. Thinking that all was lost and that her children would be returned to slavery, Margaret seized a butcher knife and cut the throat of her two-year-old daughter. She was turning on her other children when slave catchers burst in and captured her. Garner's child murder electrified the nation. Abolitionists claimed that the act revealed the horror of slavery and the tragic heroism of slave mothers. Defenders of slavery argued that the deed proved that slaves were savages. In 1867, Thomas Satterwhite Noble painted a defiant Margaret Garner standing over the bodies of two boys. Noble's departure from history was demanded by his allusion to the Greek myth about Medea killing her two children to spite her husband. In 1988, Toni Morrison's novel *Beloved*, drawing on the Garner tragedy, was awarded a Pulitzer Prize.

Harper's Weekly, May 18, 1867/Picture Research Consultants & Archives.

New England. And to Southerners it seemed that Northerners had betrayed the Compromise. "The continued existence of the United States as one nation," warned the *Southern Literary Messenger*, "depends upon the full and faithful execution of the Fugitive Slave Bill."

Uncle Tom's Cabin

The spectacle of shackled African Americans being herded south seared the conscience of every Northerner who witnessed such a scene. But even more Northerners were turned against slavery by a fictional account, a novel. Harriet Beecher Stowe, a Northerner who had never stepped foot on a plantation, made the South's slaves into flesh-and-blood human beings almost more real than life.

A member of a famous clan of preachers, teachers, and reformers, Stowe despised the slave catchers and wrote to expose the sin of slavery. Published as a book in 1852, *Uncle Tom's Cabin, or Life among the Lowly* became a blockbuster hit and sold 300,000 copies in its first year and more than 2 million copies within ten years. Stowe's characters leaped from the page. Here was the gentle slave Uncle Tom, a Christian saint who forgave those who beat him to death; the courageous slave Eliza, who fled with her child across the frozen Ohio River; and the fiendish overseer Simon Legree, whose Louisiana plantation was a nightmare of torture and death. Mother of seven children, Stowe aimed her most powerful blows at slavery's destructive impact on the family. Her character Eliza

135,000 SETS, 270,000 VOLUMES SOLD.

UNCLE TOM'S CABIN

FOR SALE HERE.

AN EDITION FOR THE MILLION, COMPLETE IN 1 Vol., PRICE 37 1-2 CENTS.
"   "   IN GERMAN, IN 1 Vol., PRICE 50 CENTS.
"   "   IN 2 Vols,. CLOTH, 6 PLATES, PRICE $1.50.
SUPERB ILLUSTRATED EDITION, IN 1 Vol., WITH 153 ENGRAVINGS,
PRICES FROM $2.50 TO $5.00.

The Greatest Book of the Age.

***Uncle Tom's Cabin* Poster**

After Congress passed the Fugitive Slave Act in 1850, Harriet Beecher Stowe's outraged sister-in-law told her, "Now Hattie, if I could use a pen as you can, I would write something that will make this whole nation feel what an accursed thing slavery is." This poster advertising the novel Stowe wrote calls it "The Greatest Book of the Age." The novel's vivid characters gripped readers' imaginations and fueled the growing antislavery crusade.

Granger Collection.

READING THE IMAGE: According to the poster, in what languages was the book available? What does this suggest about the book's readership?

CONNECTIONS: What region would not agree that *Uncle Tom's Cabin* was the greatest book of the age?

FOR MORE HELP ANALYZING THIS IMAGE, see the visual activity for this chapter in the Online Study Guide at bedfordstmartins.com/roark.

succeeds in keeping her son from being sold away, but other mothers are not so fortunate. When told that her infant has been sold, Lucy drowns herself. Driven half mad by the sale of a son and daughter, Cassy decides "never again [to] let a child live to grow up!" She gives her third child an opiate and watches as "he slept to death."

In the North, common people and literary giants alike shed tears and sang praises to *Uncle Tom's Cabin*. The poet Henry Wadsworth Longfellow judged it "one of the greatest triumphs recorded in literary history." What Northerners accepted as truth, Southerners denounced as

slander. Virginian George F. Holmes proclaimed Stowe a member of the "Woman's Rights" and "Higher Law" schools and dismissed the novel as a work of "intense fanaticism." Although it is impossible to measure precisely the impact of a novel on public opinion, *Uncle Tom's Cabin* clearly helped to crystallize northern sentiment against slavery and to confirm white Southerners' suspicion that they no longer had any sympathy in the free states.

Other writers—ex-slaves who knew life in slave cabins firsthand—also produced stinging indictments of slavery. Solomon Northup's compelling *Twelve Years a Slave* (1853) sold 27,000 copies in two years, and the powerful *Narrative of the Life of Frederick Douglass, as Told by Himself* (1845) eventually sold more than 30,000 copies. But no work touched the North's conscience like the novel by a free white woman. A decade after its publication, when Stowe visited Abraham Lincoln at the White House, he reportedly said, "So you are the little woman who wrote the book that made this great war."

> A decade after the publication of *Uncle Tom's Cabin*, when Harriet Beecher Stowe visited Abraham Lincoln at the White House, he reportedly said, "So you are the little woman who wrote the book that made this great war."

The Kansas-Nebraska Act

As the 1852 election approached, the Democrats and Whigs sought to close the sectional rifts that had opened within their parties. For their presidential nominee, the Democrats turned to Franklin Pierce of New Hampshire. Pierce's most valuable asset was his well-known sympathy with southern views on public issues. His leanings caused northern critics to include him among the "doughfaces," northern men malleable enough to champion southern causes. The Whigs were less successful in bridging differences. Adopting the formula that had proved successful in 1848, they chose another Mexican-American War hero, General Winfield Scott of Virginia. But the Whigs' northern and southern factions were hopelessly divided, and the party suffered a humiliating defeat. The Democrat Pierce carried twenty-seven states to Scott's four and won the electoral college vote 254 to 42 (see Map 14.4, page 491). In the afterglow of the Compromise of 1850, the Free-Soil Party lost almost half of the voters who had turned to it in the tumultuous political atmosphere of 1848.

Eager to leave the sectional controversy behind, the new president turned swiftly to foreign

Gadsden Purchase, 1853

expansion. **Manifest destiny** remained robust. (See "Beyond America's Borders," page 488.) Pierce's major objective was Cuba, which was owned by Spain and in which slavery flourished, but his clumsy diplomatic efforts galvanized antislavery Northerners, who blocked Cuba's acquisition to keep more slave territory from entering the Union. Pierce's fortunes improved in Mexico. In 1853, he sent diplomat James Gadsden to negotiate a $15 million purchase of some 30,000 square miles of land south of the Gila River in present-day Arizona and New Mexico. The Gadsden Purchase stemmed from the dream of a transcontinental railroad to California and Pierce's desire for a southern route through Mexican territory. The booming population of the Pacific coast made it obvious that the vast, loose-jointed Republic needed a railroad to bind it together. Talk of a railroad ignited rivalries in cities from New Orleans to Chicago as they maneuvered to become the eastern terminus. The desire for a transcontinental railroad evolved into a sectional contest, which by the 1850s inevitably involved slavery.

No one played the railroad game more enthusiastically than Illinois's Democratic senator Stephen A. Douglas. He badly wanted the transcontinental railroad for Chicago and his home state, and his chairmanship of the Senate Committee on Territories provided him with an opportunity. Any railroad that ran west from Chicago would pass through a region that Congress in 1830 had designated a "permanent" Indian reserve. Douglas proposed giving this vast area between the Missouri River and the Rocky Mountains an Indian name, Nebraska, and then throwing the Indians out. Once the region achieved territorial status, whites could survey and sell the land, establish a civil government, and build a railroad.

Nebraska lay within the Louisiana Purchase and, according to the Missouri Compromise of 1820, was closed to slavery (see chapter 10). Since Douglas could not count on New England to back western economic development, he needed southern votes to pass his Nebraska legislation. But Southerners had no incentive to create another free territory or to help a northern city win the transcontinental railroad. Southerners, however, agreed to help organize Nebraska for a price:

nothing less than repeal of the Missouri Compromise. Southerners insisted that Congress organize Nebraska according to popular sovereignty. That meant giving slavery a chance in Nebraska Territory and reopening the dangerous issue of slavery expansion, which Douglas himself had so ably helped to resolve only four years earlier.

In January 1854, Douglas introduced his bill to organize Nebraska Territory, leaving to the settlers themselves the decision about slavery. At southern insistence, and even though he knew it would "raise a hell of a storm," Douglas added an explicit repeal of the Missouri Compromise. Indeed, the Nebraska bill did raise a storm of controversy. Free-Soilers branded Douglas's plan "a gross violation of a sacred pledge" and an "atrocious plot" to transform free land into a "dreary region of despotism, inhabited by masters and slaves."

Undaunted, Douglas skillfully shepherded the explosive bill through Congress in May 1854.

Papago Indians

Major William Emory's Mexican boundary survey of the early 1850s provided Americans with glimpses of a little-known southwestern frontier. In this drawing, Papago Indian women in Arizona Territory use sticks to knock down cactus fruit. The Center for American History, The University of Texas at Austin.

Nine-tenths of the southern members (Whigs and Democrats) and half of the northern Democrats cast votes in favor of the bill. Like Douglas, most northern supporters believed that popular sovereignty would make Nebraska free territory. Ominously, however, half of the northern Democrats broke with their party and opposed the bill. In its final form, the Kansas-Nebraska Act divided the huge territory in two: Nebraska west of the free state of Iowa and Kansas west of the slave state of Missouri (Map 14.3). With this act, the government pushed the Plains Indians farther west, making way for farmers and railroads.

> **REVIEW**   Why did the Fugitive Slave Act provoke such strong opposition in the North?

longer muffled moral issues such as slavery. The new party system also thwarted political compromise and instead promoted political polarization that further jeopardized the Union.

The Old Parties: Whigs and Democrats

Distress signals could be heard from the Whig camp as early as the Mexican-American War, when members clashed over the future of slavery in annexed Mexican lands. By 1852, the Whig Party could please its proslavery southern wing or its antislavery northern wing but not both. The Whigs' miserable showing in the election of 1852 made clear that they were no longer a strong national party. By 1856, after more than two decades of contesting the Democrats, they were hardly a party at all (Map 14.4, page 491).

Realignment of the Party System

The Kansas-Nebraska Act marked a fateful escalation of the sectional conflict. Douglas's controversial measure had several consequences, none more crucial than the realignment of the nation's political parties. Since the rise of the Whig Party in the early 1830s, Whigs and Democrats had organized and channeled political conflict in the nation. This party system dampened sectionalism and strengthened the Union. To achieve national political power, the Whigs and Democrats had to retain their strength in both North and South. Strong northern and southern wings required that each party compromise and find positions acceptable to both wings.

The Kansas-Nebraska controversy shattered this stabilizing political system. In place of two national parties with bisectional strength, the mid-1850s witnessed the development of one party heavily dominated by one section and another party entirely limited to the other section. Rather than "national" parties, the country had what one critic disdainfully called "geographic" parties. Parties now sharpened ideological and policy differences between the sections and no

MAP 14.3   The Kansas-Nebraska Act, 1854
Americans hardly thought twice about dispossessing the Indians of land guaranteed them by treaty, but many worried about the outcome of repealing the Missouri Compromise and opening up the region to slavery.

READING THE MAP: How many slave states and how many free states does the map show? Estimate the percentage of new territory likely to be settled by slaveholders.
CONNECTIONS: Who would be more likely to support changes in government legislation to discontinue the Missouri Compromise, slaveholders or free-soil advocates? Why?

FOR MORE HELP ANALYZING THIS MAP, see the map activity for this chapter in the Online Study Guide at bedfordstmartins.com/roark.

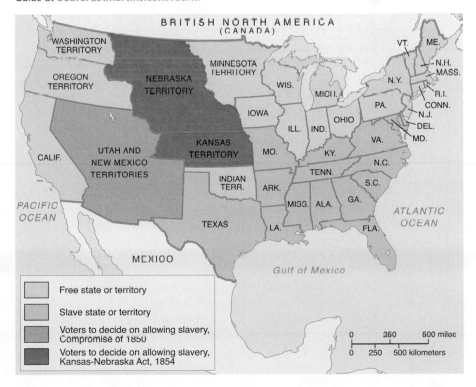

Free state or territory

Slave state or territory

Voters to decide on allowing slavery, Compromise of 1850

Voters to decide on allowing slavery, Kansas-Nebraska Act, 1854

Filibusters: The Underside of Manifest Destiny

Each year, the citizens of Caborca, Mexico, a small town in the northern state of Sonora, celebrate the defeat there in 1857 of an American army. The invaders did not wear the uniform of the U.S. army, but instead marched as a private army, the "Arizona Colonization Company." Their commander, Henry A. Crabb, a Mississippian who followed the gold rush to California, saw fresh opportunity in the civil disorder that reigned south of the border. Fierce fighting between Mexicans and Apache and Yaqui Indians made life precarious in Sonora and divided the Mexicans. When the governor of Sonora faced an insurrection, he invited Crabb, who was married to a Sonoran woman, to help him repress his enemies in exchange for mineral rights and land.

Crabb marched his band of sixty-eight heavily armed ex-miners south from Los Angeles into Mexico. But by the time the Americans arrived, the governor had put down the insurgency, and he turned on the invaders. Every American except one died either in battle or at the hands of Mexican firing squads. Crabb's head was preserved in alcohol and placed on display as a symbol of victory.

Henry Crabb was one of thousands of American adventurers, known as "filibusters" (from the Spanish *filibustero*, meaning "freebooter" or "pirate"), who in the mid-nineteenth century joined private armies that invaded foreign countries in North America, Central America, South America, and the Caribbean. Although these expeditions were illegal and violated the U.S. Neutrality Act of 1818, private American armies attacked Canada, Mexico, Ecuador, Honduras, Cuba, and Nicaragua and planned invasions of places as far away as the Hawaiian kingdom. The federal government occasionally winked at the actions of filibusters, but more often it cracked down, fearful that private invasions would jeopardize legitimate diplomatic efforts to promote trade and acquire territory.

Filibusters joined invading armies for a variety of reasons ranging from personal gain to validating manhood. Many saw themselves as carrying on the work of manifest destiny, extending America's reach beyond Texas, California, and Oregon, the prizes of the 1830s and 1840s. In addition, during the 1840s and 1850s, when Northerners insisted on containing slavery's spread to the North and West, Southerners joined filibustering expeditions to expand slavery south beyond the U.S. border. Although filibusters came from all regions of the country, their greatest numbers and support came from the proslavery forces of the South. A leading proslavery ideologue, George Fitzhugh, sought to blunt criticism of filibustering by defending it through historical comparison: "They who condemn the modern filibuster, to be consistent, must also condemn the discoverers and settlers of America, of the East Indies of Holland, and of the Indian and Pacific Oceans." Such arguments, deeply rooted in manifest destiny, failed to convince many, including the ambassador from Costa Rica, who called filibustering America's "social cancer." Northerners claimed (with some justification) that filibustering was a southern campaign to extend "the empire of the lash."

One of the most vigorous filibusters to appeal to southern interests was not an American. Narciso Lopez was a Venezuelan-born Cuban who dedicated himself to the liberation of Cuba from Spanish rule. In his first attempt in 1849, he recruited an army of several hundred would-be liberators but got no farther than New York harbor, where U.S. marshals intercepted his fleet. Thereafter, he resolved to "rest his hopes on the men of the bold West and chivalric South." Lopez claimed that Spain was planning to free Cuba's slaves, and he told Southerners that "self-preservation" demanded that they seize the island. When Governor John Quitman of Mississippi joined his scheme, Lopez shifted his headquarters to New Orleans. Early in 1850, Lopez and an army of more than 500 landed on the northwest coast of Cuba, but Spanish troops quickly drove them off. Two months later, with 450 troops, he tried again. This time, the Spanish crushed the invasion, killing 200 filibusters, shipping 160 prisoners to Spain, executing 50 invaders by firing squad, and publicly garroting Lopez. John Quitman gathered another army of several thousand, but federal authorities seized one of his ships and ended the threat to Cuba.

The most successful of all filibusters was William Walker of Tennessee, a restless dreamer who longed for an empire of his own south of the border. Walker cut his filibustering teeth with expeditions to Baja California and Sonora, but when they failed, he turned to Central America. He believed that Southerners paid too much attention to Kansas and that instead they should expand slavery in tropical America. In May 1855, Walker and an army of fifty-six men sailed from San Francisco to the west coast of Nicaragua. Two thousand reinforcements and a civil war in Nicaragua gave Walker his victory. He had himself proclaimed president, legalized slavery, and called on Southerners to come raise cotton, sugar, and coffee in "a magnificent country." Hundreds of Southerners took up **land grants**, but Walker's regime survived only until 1857, when a coalition of Central American countries allied with the Nicaraguans and sent Walker packing. Walker doggedly launched four other attacks on Nicaragua. In 1860, Honduran forces captured and shot him.

Filibustering had lost steam by 1861, but the battle-hardened adventurers found new employment in the armies of the Civil War, particularly in the service of the Confederate military. The Confederacy paid a diplomatic price for its association with filibustering, however. The Guatemalan minister Antonio Jose de Irisarri declared that there was "no foreign Nation which can have less cause for sympathy with the enemies of the American Union, than the Republics of Central America, because from the Southern States were set on foot those filibustering expeditions." No Central American nation recognized Confederate independence.

The peoples of Central America and the Caribbean, like the inhabitants of Sonora, still harbor bitter memories of filibusters' private wars of **imperialism** and honor those who fought off American advances. When U.S. marines occupied Nicaragua in the 1920s, insurgents found inspiration in their country's defeat of William Walker's army of freebooters eighty years earlier. In 1951, on the centennial of Lopez's invasion, Cubans erected a monument at the very spot where his ill-fated army came ashore. Costa Ricans celebrate Juan Santamaria as their national martyr for his courage in battling William Walker. Memories of the invasions by nineteenth-century filibusters set the stage for anti-American sentiment in Latin America that lingers to this day.

Filibustering in Nicaragua
In this image of a pitched battle in Nicaragua in 1856, Costa Ricans on foot fight American filibusters on horseback. Costa Rican soldiers and their Central American allies defeated William Walker's *filibusteros* in 1857. Before then, the Pierce administration had extended diplomatic recognition to Walker's regime, and white Southerners had cheered Walker's attempt to "introduce civilization" in Nicaragua and to develop its rich resources "with slave labor."
London Illustrated Times, May 24, 1856.

The Realignment of Political Parties

Whig Party

1848   Whig Party divides into two factions over slavery; Whigs adopt no platform and nominate war hero Zachary Taylor, who is elected president.

1852   Whigs nominate war hero General Winfield Scott for president; deep divisions in party result in humiliating loss.

1856   Shattered by sectionalism, Whig Party fields no presidential candidate.

Democratic Party

1848   President Polk declines to run again; Democratic Party nominates Lewis Cass, the man most closely associated with popular sovereignty, but avoids firm platform position on expansion of slavery.

1852   To bridge rift in party, Democrats nominate northern war veteran with southern views, Franklin Pierce, for president; he wins with 50.9 percent of popular vote.

1856   Democrat James Buchanan elected president on ambiguous platform; his prosouthern actions in office alienate northern branch of party.

1860   Democrats split into northern Democrats and southern Democrats; each group fields its own presidential candidate.

Free-Soil Party

1848   Breakaway antislavery Democrats and antislavery Whigs found Free-Soil Party; presidential candidate Martin Van Buren takes 10.1 percent of popular vote, mainly from Whigs.

1852   Support for Free-Soil Party ebbs in wake of Compromise of 1850; Free-Soil presidential candidate John P. Hale wins only 5 percent of popular vote.

American (Know-Nothing) Party

1851   Anti-immigrant American (Know-Nothing) Party formed.

1854–   American Party succeeds in state elections and attracts votes
1855   from northern and southern Whigs in congressional elections.

1856   Know-Nothing presidential candidate Millard Fillmore wins only Maryland; party subsequently disbands.

Republican Party

1854   Republican Party formed to oppose expansion of slavery in territories; attracts northern Whigs, northern Democrats, and Free-Soilers.

1856   Republican presidential candidate John C. Frémont wins all but five northern states, establishing Republicans as main challenger to Democrats.

1860   Republican Abraham Lincoln wins all northern states except New Jersey and is elected president in four-way race against divided Democrats and southern Constitutional Union Party.

The collapse of the Whig Party left the Democrats as the country's only national party. Although the Democrats were not immune to the disruptive pressures of the territorial question, they discovered in popular sovereignty a doctrine that many Democrats could support. Even so, popular sovereignty very nearly undid the party. When Stephen Douglas applied the doctrine to the part of the Louisiana Purchase where slavery had been barred, he divided northern Democrats and destroyed the dominance of the Democratic Party in the free states. After 1854, the Democrats became a southern-dominated party. Nevertheless, the Democrats, unlike the Whigs, remained a national political organization. Gains in the South more than balanced Democratic losses in the North. During the 1850s, Democrats elected two presidents and won majorities in Congress in almost every election.

The breakup of the Whigs and the disaffection of significant numbers of northern Democrats set many Americans politically adrift. As they searched for new political harbors, Americans found that the death of the old party system created a multitude of fresh political alternatives. The question was which party would attract the drifters.

The New Parties: Know-Nothings and Republicans

Dozens of new political organizations vied for voters' attention. Out of the confusion, two emerged as true contenders. One grew out of the slavery controversy, a spontaneous coalition of indignant antislavery Northerners. The other arose from an entirely different split in American society, between Roman Catholic immigrants and native **Protestants**.

The tidal wave of immigrants that broke over America from 1845 to 1855 produced a nasty backlash among Protestant Americans, who believed that the American Republic was about to drown in a sea of Roman Catholics from Ireland and Germany (see Figure 12.1, page 406). Most immigrants became Democrats because they perceived that party as more tolerant of newcomers than were the Whigs. But in the 1850s, they met sharp political opposition when **nativists** (individuals who were anti-immigrant) began to organize, first into secret fraternal societies and then in 1854 into a political party. Recruits swore never to vote for either foreign-born or Roman Catholic candidates and not to reveal any information about the organization. When questioned, they said, "I know nothing."

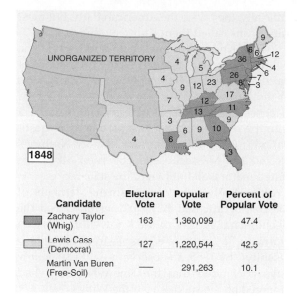

Candidate	Electoral Vote	Popular Vote	Percent of Popular Vote
Zachary Taylor (Whig)	163	1,360,099	47.4
Lewis Cass (Democrat)	127	1,220,544	42.5
Martin Van Buren (Free-Soil)	—	291,263	10.1

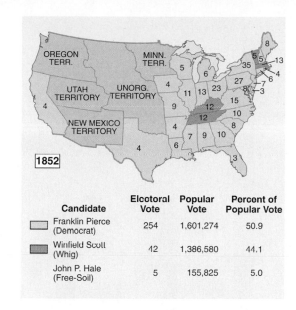

Candidate	Elcotoral Vote	Popular Vote	Percent of Popular Vote
Franklin Pierce (Democrat)	254	1,601,274	50.9
Winfield Scott (Whig)	42	1,386,580	44.1
John P. Hale (Free-Soil)	5	155,825	5.0

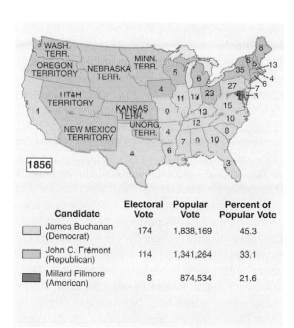

Candidate	Electoral Vote	Popular Vote	Percent of Popular Vote
James Buchanan (Democrat)	174	1,838,169	45.3
John C. Frémont (Republican)	114	1,341,264	33.1
Millard Fillmore (American)	8	874,534	21.6

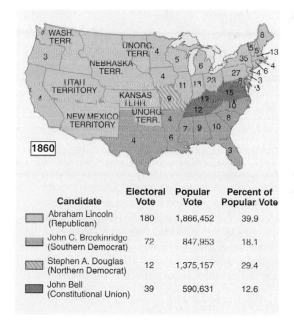

Candidate	Electoral Vote	Popular Vote	Percent of Popular Vote
Abraham Lincoln (Republican)	180	1,866,452	39.9
John C. Breckinridge (Southern Democrat)	72	847,953	18.1
Stephen A. Douglas (Northern Democrat)	12	1,375,157	29.4
John Bell (Constitutional Union)	39	590,631	12.6

MAP 14.4 Political Realignment, 1848–1860

In 1848, slavery and sectionalism began taking their toll on the country's party system. The Whig Party was an early casualty. By 1860, national parties—those that contended for votes in both North and South—had been replaced by regional parties.

READING THE MAP: Which states did the Democrats pick up in 1852 compared to 1848? Which of these states did the Democrats lose in 1856? Compare the general geographical location of the states won by the Republicans in 1856 versus those won in 1860.
CONNECTIONS: In the 1860 election, which party benefited the most from the western and midwestern states added to the Union since 1848? Why do you think these states chose to back the Republicans over the Democrats?

FOR MORE HELP ANALYZING THIS MAP, see the map activity for this chapter in the Online Study Guide at bedfordstmartins.com/roark.

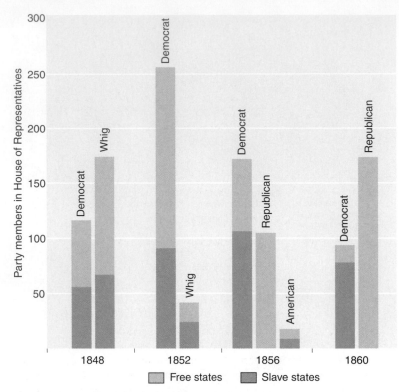

FIGURE 14.1 Changing Political Landscape, 1848–1860
The polarization of American politics between free states and slave states occurred in little more than a decade.

Know-Nothing Banner

Convinced that the incendiary issue of slavery had blinded Americans to the greater dangers of uncontrolled immigration and foreign influence, the Know-Nothing Party nominated Millard Fillmore for president in 1856. There is more than a little irony in this banner's appeal to "Native Americans" to stem the invasion from abroad. The Know-Nothings were referring to native-born Americans, but bona fide Native Americans—American Indians—also faced an invasion, and to them it made little difference whether the aggressors were fresh off the boat or born in the USA.

Milwaukee County Historical Society.

Officially, they were the American Party, but most Americans called them Know-Nothings.

The Know-Nothings exploded onto the political stage in 1854 and 1855 with a series of dazzling successes. They captured state legislatures in the Northeast, West, and South and claimed dozens of seats in Congress. Their greatest triumph came in Massachusetts, a favorite destination for Irish immigrants. Know-Nothings elected the Massachusetts governor, all of the state senators, all but two of the state representatives, and all of the congressmen. Members of the Democratic and Whig parties described the phenomenal success of the Know-Nothings as a "tornado," a "hurricane," and "a freak of political insanity." By 1855, an observer might reasonably have concluded that the Know-Nothings had emerged as the successor to the Whigs.

The Know-Nothings were not the only new party making noise, however. One of the new antislavery organizations provoked by the Kansas-Nebraska Act called itself the Republican Party. The Republicans attempted to unite all the dissidents and political orphans—Whigs, Free-Soilers, anti-Nebraska Democrats, even Know-Nothings—who opposed the extension of slavery into any territory of the United States.

The Republican creed tapped into the basic beliefs and values of the northern public. Slavery, the Republicans argued, degraded the dignity of white labor by associating work with blacks and servility. Three-quarters of the South's white population, claimed one Republican, "retire to the outskirts of civilization, where they live a semi-savage life, sinking deeper and more hopelessly into barbarism with every succeeding generation." They warned that the insatiable slaveholders of the South, whom antislavery Northerners called the "Slave Power," were conspiring through their control of the Democratic Party to expand slavery, subvert **liberty**, and undermine the Constitution. Only if slavery was restricted to the South, Republicans believed, could the system of free labor flourish elsewhere. The ideal of free labor respected the dignity of work and provided anyone willing to toil a chance for a decent living and advancement (see chapter 12). In the North, one Republican declared in 1854, "every man holds his fortune in his own right arm; and his position in society, in life, is to be tested by his own individual character." These powerful images of liberty and opportunity attracted a wide range of Northerners to the Republican cause (Figure 14.1).

Women as well as men rushed to the new Republican Party. Indeed, three women helped found the party in Ripon, Wisconsin, in 1854. Although women could not vote before the Civil War and suffered from a raft of other legal handicaps, they nevertheless participated in partisan politics by writing campaign literature, marching in parades, giving speeches, and working to influence voters. Women's antislavery fervor attracted them to the Republican Party, and participation in party politics in turn nurtured the woman's rights movement. Susan B. Anthony, who attended Republican meetings throughout the 1850s, found that her political activity made her **disfranchisement** all the more galling. She and other women worked throughout the country to secure both woman suffrage and the right of married women to control their own property. (See "Seeking the American Promise," page 494.)

The Election of 1856

The election of 1856 revealed that the Republicans had become the Democrats' main challenger, and slavery in the territories, not nativism, was the election's principal issue. When the Know-Nothings insisted on a platform that endorsed the Kansas-Nebraska Act, most of the Northerners walked out, and the party came apart. The few Know-Nothings who remained nominated ex-president Millard Fillmore.

The Republicans adopted a platform that focused almost exclusively on "making every territory free." When they labeled slavery a "relic of barbarism," they signaled that they had written off the South. For president, they nominated the dashing soldier and California adventurer John C. Frémont, "Pathfinder of the West." Frémont lacked political credentials, but his wife, Jessie, the daughter of Senator Thomas Hart Benton of Missouri, knew the political map as well as her husband knew the western trails. Though careful to maintain a proper public image, the vivacious young mother and antislavery zealot helped attract voters and draw women into politics.

The Democrats, successful in 1852 in bridging sectional differences by nominating a northern man with southern principles, chose another "doughface," James Buchanan of Pennsylvania. They took refuge in the ambiguity of popular sovereignty and portrayed the Republicans as extremists ("Black Republican Abolitionists") whose support for the Wilmot Proviso risked pushing the South out of the Union.

The Democratic strategy carried the day for Buchanan, but Frémont did astonishingly well. Buchanan won 174 electoral votes against Frémont's

John and Jessie Frémont Poster
The election of 1856 marked the first time a candidate's wife appeared on campaign items. Smart and ambitious, and the daughter of Senator Thomas Hart Benton, Jessie Benton Frémont made the breakthrough. In this poster—made from paper letters and figures cut from an English hunting print—Jessie and her husband, John C. Frémont, the Republican Party's presidential nominee, ride spirited horses. The scene emphasizes their youth (John was forty-three and Jessie thirty-one), their vigor, and their outdoor exuberance. Jessie helped plan her husband's campaign, coauthored his election biography, and drew northern women into political activity as never before. "What a shame that women can't vote!" declared abolitionist Lydia Maria Child. "We'd carry 'our Jessie' into the White House on our shoulders, wouldn't we." Critics of Jessie's violation of women's traditional sphere ridiculed both Frémonts. A man who met the couple in San Francisco pronounced her "the better man of the two." Jessie Frémont was, as Abraham Lincoln observed ambivalently, "quite a female politician."
Museum of American Political Life.

114 and Fillmore's 8 (see Map 14.4, page 491). Campaigning under the banner "Free soil, Free men, Frémont," the Republican carried all but five of the states north of the Mason-Dixon line. The election made clear that the Whigs had disintegrated, the Know-Nothings would not ride nativism to national power, and the Democrats were badly strained. But the big news was what the press called the "glorious defeat" of the Republicans. Despite being a brand-new party and purely sectional, the Republicans had seriously challenged for national power. Sectionalism had fashioned a new party system, one that spelled danger for the Republic. Indeed, war had already broken out between proslavery and antislavery forces in distant Kansas Territory.

REVIEW Why did the Whig Party disintegrate in the 1850s?

"A Purse of Her Own": Petitioning for the Right to Own Property

In the early Republic, as today, having money and deciding how to spend it was a fundamental aspect of independent adulthood. Yet antebellum married women were denied this privilege, due to the laws of *coverture*, which placed wives under the full legal control of their husbands (see chapter 10). By law, husbands made all the financial decisions in a household. Even money that a wife earned or brought into a marriage from gifts or inheritance was not hers to control as long as she remained married. Ernestine Potowsky Rose of New York City thought that was wrong. She was not alone in thinking this, but being unusually plucky and enterprising, she became the first woman in the United States to take action to change the law.

Ernestine Potowsky, born in Poland in 1810, was a precocious child. Her mother died when she was young, and her father, a rabbi, homeschooled his daughter in religious texts as if she were a son. Yet as a daughter, her destiny was fixed: an arranged marriage, many children, and a life strictly governed by religious law. Ernestine rejected this fate and left home. At age nineteen, she arrived in London and joined a circle of radical intellectuals who proposed socialistic solutions to the problems of poverty and industrialization. She married William Rose, a like-minded intellectual, and at the age of twenty-six emigrated with him to the United States.

The couple settled in New York City, where William, a jeweler, started a business. Ernestine soon learned of a starkly egalitarian bill presented in 1837 in the New York assembly proposing that married women, "equally with males and unmarried females, possess the rights of *life*, *liberty*, and PROPERTY, and are equally entitled to be protected in all three." The bill's author was Thomas Herttell, a New York labor advocate, assembly member, and "freethinker" (one who rejects all formal religion). Rose, having abandoned Judaism and embraced English socialism, easily gravitated to Herttell's group. She went door-to-door soliciting women's support for the bill but met with indifference. Opponents feared that it would undermine a central pillar of marriage: the assumption that husband and wife shared identical interests. How could a wife not trust her husband to control the money? Herttell's utopian bill predictably failed to pass.

The devastating panics of 1837 and 1839, and the resulting bankruptcies, soon changed some traditionalists' minds about wives and property. Men in several state legislatures crafted laws that shielded a wife's inherited property from creditors collecting debts from her husband. Mississippi led the way in 1839, and by 1848 eighteen states had modified property laws in the name of family protection.

In New York, support for a liberalized law grew in the late 1840s. Protecting family assets from creditors remained important for elite men married to women from wealthy families. Ernestine Rose broadened the debate to mobilize a new constituency of women activists around the far more egalitarian argument that married women should be able to own and control property, just as married men did. She circulated petitions and spoke from public platforms, often joined by Elizabeth Cady Stanton, a young wife from western New York. In April 1848, three months before the Seneca Falls woman's rights convention (see chapter 12), the New York assembly finally awarded married women sole authority over property they brought to a marriage.

Rose welcomed the new law but recognized its key shortcoming: It made no provision for wages earned by a married woman. It also did nothing to alter inheritance laws that limited a widow's share of her husband's estate. Speaking at every national woman's rights convention from 1850 to 1860, Rose argued for women's economic independence. She challenged lawmakers with her well-honed debating skills and regaled audiences with her sharp sense of humor. In an 1853 speech, she itemized the limited belongings allowed to a widow if her husband died without a will: "As to the personal property, after all debts and liabilities are discharged, the widow receives one-half of it; and, in addition, the law allows her, her own wearing apparel, her own ornaments, proper to her station, one bed, with appurtenances for the same, a stove, the Bible, family

Ernestine Rose

Ernestine Rose, in her mid-forties when this photograph was taken, managed to hold a smile for the several minutes required to capture her image on a photographic plate.
Schlesinger Library, Radcliffe Institute for Advanced Study, Harvard University.

failed to support their dependents. Anthony, herself a lifelong single woman, recalled that "as I passed from town to town I was made to feel the great evil of women's utter dependence on man. I never before took in so fully the grand idea of pecuniary independence. Woman must have a purse of her own."

Rose's efforts paid off. In 1860, New York amended its law to include a wife's wages as her own, but only if she earned the money outside the household. Money earned selling eggs or butter or caring for boarders, even when fully the product of the wife's labor, still went directly into the husband's pocket. Perhaps the most significant beneficiaries of this law were women whose husbands were incompetent to support them or who had deserted them. These husbands now had no right to their wives' hard-earned nest eggs.

The revision of the New York law made other important changes to coverture. A wife could now sue (or be sued) and make legal contracts of her own. In addition, the wife was established as joint guardian of the children, "with equal powers, rights and duties in regard to them, with the husband." These changes, adopted in many states after 1860, began the long process of elevating married women to near equality with men, a process that still continues today.

Ever keen with sarcasm, Ernestine Rose produced great laughter shortly after the passage of the revised law at the 1860 woman's rights convention in New York City when she commented: "We 'woman's rights women' have redeemed our last legislature, by inducing them to give us one good act, among so many corrupt ones, and it strikes me that they owe us as many thanks as we owe them!"

pictures, and all the school-books; also all spinning wheels and weaving looms, one table, six chairs, ten cups and saucers, one tea-pot, one sugar dish, and six spoons." While her audience laughed appreciatively, Rose questioned whether the spoons would be teaspoons, "since a widow might live on tea only," and why no kettles or pots were included. Spinning wheels, long gone in 1853,

needed no elaboration from her to make the law sound pathetically out-of-date.

Of particular concern to Rose was the plight of the many wives not from wealthy families. She and Susan B. Anthony traveled the state of New York and encountered women trapped in marriages with spendthrift or heartless husbands who drained family resources and

Freedom under Siege

Events in Kansas Territory in the mid-1850s provided the young Republican organization with an enormous boost and help explain its strong showing in the election of 1856. Republicans organized around the premise that the slaveholding South provided a profound threat to "free soil, free labor, and free men," and now Kansas reeled with violence that Republicans argued was southern in origin. Kansas, Republicans claimed, opened a window to southern values and intentions. Republicans also pointed to the brutal beating by a Southerner of a respected northern senator on the floor of Congress. Even the Supreme Court, in the Republicans' view, reflected the South's drive toward tyranny and minority rule in its decision in the *Dred Scott* case. Then, in 1858, the issues dividing North and South received an extraordinary airing in a senatorial contest in Illinois, when the nation's foremost Democrat debated a resourceful Republican.

"Bleeding Kansas"

Three days after the House of Representatives approved the Kansas-Nebraska Act in 1854, Senator William H. Seward of New York boldly challenged the South. "Come on then, Gentlemen of the Slave States," he cried, "since there is no escaping your challenge, I accept it in behalf of the cause of freedom. We will engage in competition for the virgin soil of Kansas, and God give the victory to the side which is stronger in numbers as it is in right." Because of Stephen Douglas, popular sovereignty would determine whether Kansas became slave or free. Free-state and slave-state settlers both sought a majority at the ballot box, claimed God's blessing, and kept their rifles ready.

In both North and South, emigrant aid societies sprang up to promote settlement from free states or slave states. The most famous, the New England Emigrant Aid Company, sponsored some 1,240 settlers in 1854 and 1855. In the South, tiny rural communities from Virginia to Texas raised money to support proslavery settlers. Missourians,

"Bleeding Kansas," 1850s

KANSAS TERRITORY

MISSOURI

Missouri R.

Kansas R.

Leavenworth

Topeka

Lecompton

Shawnee Mission

Kansas City

Lawrence
May 21, 1856

Osawatomie
Aug. 31, 1856

Marais des Cygnes R.

Pottawatomie Creek
May 24, 1856

Marais des Cygnes
May 19, 1858

★ Major violent outbreaks

already bordered on the east by the free state of Illinois and on the north by the free state of Iowa, especially thought it important to secure Kansas for slavery. Thousands of rough frontiersmen, egged on by Missouri senator David Rice Atchison, invaded Kansas. "There are eleven hundred coming over from Platte County to vote," Atchison reported, "and if that ain't enough we can send five thousand—enough to kill every God-damned abolitionist in the Territory." Not surprisingly, proslavery candidates swept the territorial elections in November 1854. When Kansas's first territorial legislature met, it enacted a raft of proslavery laws. Antislavery men, for example, were barred from holding office or serving on juries. Ever-pliant President Pierce endorsed the work of the fraudulently elected legislature. Free-soil Kansans did not. They elected their own legislature, which promptly banned both slaves and free blacks from the territory. Organized into two rival governments and armed to the teeth, Kansans verged on civil war.

Fighting broke out on the morning of May 21, 1856, when several hundred proslavery men raided the town of Lawrence, the center of free-state settlement. Only one man died, but the "Sack of Lawrence," as free-soil forces called it, inflamed northern opinion. Elsewhere in Kansas, news of events in Lawrence provoked John Brown, a free-soil settler, to "fight fire with fire." Announcing that "it was better that a score of bad men should die than that one man who came here to make Kansas a Free State should be driven out," he led the posse that massacred five allegedly proslavery settlers along Pottawatomie Creek. After that, **guerrilla war** engulfed the territory.

Just as "Bleeding Kansas" gave the fledgling Republican Party fresh ammunition for its battle against the "Slave Power," so too did an event that occurred in the national capital. In May 1856, Senator Charles Sumner of Massachusetts delivered a speech titled "The Crime against Kansas," which included a scalding personal attack on South Carolina senator Andrew P. Butler. Sumner described Butler as a "Don Quixote" who had taken as his mistress "the harlot, slavery." Preston Brooks, a young South Carolina member of the House and a kinsman of Butler's, felt compelled to defend the honor of both his aged relative and his state. On May 22, Brooks entered the Senate, where he found Sumner working at his desk. He beat Sumner over the head with his cane until Sumner lay bleeding and uncon-

Armed Settlers Near Lawrence, Kansas, and "Southern Rights" Flag
Armed with rifles, knives, swords, and pistols, these tough antislavery men
gathered for a photograph near Lawrence in 1856. Equally well-armed proslavery
men marched under the red "Southern Rights" flag. This flag was adopted by the Palmetto
Guards, a group formed by South Carolinians living in Kansas and named after the tree that symbol
ized their state. When proslavery forces attacked and occupied Lawrence in 1856, this flag flew briefly
over the free-soil town.
Kansas State Historical Society.

scious on the floor. Brooks resigned his seat in
the House, only to be promptly reelected. In the
North, the southern hero became an archvillain.
Like "Bleeding Kansas," "Bleeding Sumner" provided the Republican Party with a potent symbol
of the South's "twisted and violent civilization."

The *Dred Scott* Decision

Political debate over slavery in the territories became so heated in part because the Constitution
lacked precision on the issue. Only the Supreme
Court speaks definitively about the meaning of
the Constitution, and in 1857, in the case of *Dred
Scott v. Sandford*, the Court announced its judgment of the issue of slavery in the territories. The
Court's decision demonstrated that it enjoyed no
special immunity from the sectional and partisan
passions that convulsed the land.

In 1833, John Emerson, an army doctor,
bought the slave Dred Scott in St. Louis, Missouri, and took him as his personal servant to
Fort Armstrong, Illinois. Two years later, Scott

accompanied Emerson when he transferred to
Fort Snelling in Wisconsin Territory. Emerson
eventually returned Scott to St. Louis, where in
1846, Scott, with the help of white friends, sued
to prove that he and his family were legally
entitled to their freedom. Scott based his claim
on his travels and residences. He argued that
living in Illinois, a free state, and Wisconsin, a
free territory, had made his family free, and that
they remained free even after returning to
Missouri, a slave state.

In 1857, the U.S. Supreme Court ruled in the
case. Chief Justice Roger B. Taney hated Republicans and detested racial equality, and the Court's
majority decision, which he wrote, reflected
those prejudices. First, the Court ruled that Dred
Scott could not legally claim violation of his constitutional rights because he was not a citizen of
the United States. In 1787, when the Constitution
was written, Taney said, blacks "were regarded
as beings of an inferior order . . . so far inferior,
that they had no rights which the white man was
bound to respect." Second, the laws of Dred

The *Dred Scott* Case, 1857
The *Dred Scott* case aroused enormous curiosity about the man suing for freedom. This portrait of Dred Scott was painted in 1857, the year of the Supreme Court's decision. A journalist who traveled to St. Louis to interview Scott "found him on examination to be a pure-blooded African, perhaps fifty years of age, with a shrewd, intelligent, good-natured face, of rather light frame, being not more than five feet six inches high." African Americans in the North were particularly alarmed by the Court's ruling. The poster announces that two black leaders, Charles L. Remond and Robert Purvis, will speak at a public meeting about the "atrocious decision."

Poster: © Private Collection/Peter Newark American Pictures/The Bridgeman Art Library; Nationality/copyright status: American/out of copyright; Portrait: Collection of the New-York Historical Society.

Scott's home state, Missouri, determined his status, and thus his travels in free areas did not make him free. Third, Congress's power to make "all needful rules and regulations" for the territories did not include the right to prohibit slavery. The Court explicitly declared the Missouri Compromise unconstitutional, even though it had already been voided by the Kansas-Nebraska Act.

The Taney Court's extreme proslavery decision outraged Republicans. By denying the federal government the right to exclude slavery in the territories, it cut the legs out from under the Republican Party. Moreover, as the *New York Tribune* lamented, the decision cleared the way for "all our Territories . . . to be ripened into Slave States." Particularly frightening to African Americans in the North was the Court's declaration that free blacks were not citizens and had no rights.

> As the *New York Tribune* lamented, the *Dred Scott* decision cleared the way for "all our Territories . . . to be ripened into Slave States."

The Republican rebuttal to the *Dred Scott* ruling relied heavily on the dissenting opinion of Justice Benjamin R. Curtis. Scott *was* a citizen of the United States, Curtis argued. At the time of the writing of the Constitution, free black men could vote in five states and participated in the ratification process. Scott *was* free. Because slavery was prohibited in Wisconsin, the "involuntary servitude of a slave, coming into the Territory with his master, should cease to exist." The Missouri Compromise *was* constitutional. The Founders had meant exactly what they said: Congress had the power to make "*all* needful rules and regulations" for the territories, including barring slavery.

In a seven-to-two decision, the Court rejected Curtis's arguments, thereby validating an extreme statement of the South's territorial rights. John C. Calhoun's claim that Congress had no authority to exclude slavery became the law of the land. White Southerners cheered, but the *Dred Scott* decision actually strengthened the young Republican Party. Indeed, that "outrageous" decision, one Republican argued, was "the best thing that could have happened." It provided dramatic evidence of the Republicans' claim that a hostile "Slave Power" conspired against northern liberties. Only the capture of the Supreme Court by the "slavocracy," Republicans argued, could explain the tortured and historically inaccurate decision.

As for Dred Scott, although the Court rejected his suit, he did in the end gain his freedom. In May 1857, a white man purchased and freed Scott and his family. On September 17, 1858, Dred Scott died in obscurity. Nevertheless, his case changed the political landscape and brought new Republican politicians to the fore.

Prairie Republican: Abraham Lincoln

By reigniting the sectional flames, the *Dred Scott* case provided Republican politicians with fresh challenges and fresh opportunities. Abraham Lincoln had long since put behind him his hardscrabble log-cabin beginnings in Kentucky and Indiana. He lived in a fine two-story house in Springfield, Illinois, and earned good money as a lawyer. The law provided Lincoln's living, but politics was his life. "His ambition was a little engine that knew no rest," observed his law partner William Herndon. Lincoln had served as a Whig in the Illinois state legislature and in the House of Representatives, but he had not held public office since 1849.

The disintegration of the Whig Party meant that Lincoln had no political home. His credo— opposition to "the *extension* of slavery"—made the Republicans his only choice, and in 1856 Lincoln joined the party. Convinced that slavery was a "monstrous injustice," a "great moral wrong," and an "unqualified evil to the negro, the white man, and the State," Lincoln condemned Douglas's Kansas-Nebraska Act of 1854 for giving slavery a new life. He accepted that the Constitution permitted slavery in those states where it existed, but he believed that Congress could contain its spread. Penned in, Lincoln believed, plantation slavery would wither, and in time Southerners would end slavery themselves. By providing fresh land for slavery in the territories, Douglas had put it "on the high road to extension and perpetuity."

Lincoln held what were, for his times, moderate racial views. Like a majority of Republicans, Lincoln defended black humanity without challenging white supremacy. Although

The Herald in the Country, by William Sidney Mount, 1853
William Sidney Mount was the first American painter to achieve fame for his vivid depictions of everyday life. His motto was "Never paint for the few but for the many." Here, two men from the country, one with a rifle and a dead bird at his feet and the other taking a break from his work in a hay field, keep up with the news by reading a copy of the *New York Herald*. Men like these increasingly accepted Abraham Lincoln's portrait of the Republican Party as the guardian of the common people's liberty and economic opportunity. When Lincoln claimed that southern slaveholders threatened free labor and democracy, northern men listened.
The Long Island Museum of American Art, History and Carriages. Gift of Mr. and Mrs. Ward Melville, 1955.

he denounced slavery as immoral, he also viewed black equality as impractical and unachievable. "Negroes have natural rights . . . as other men have," he said, "although they cannot enjoy them here." Insurmountable white prejudice made it impossible to extend full citizenship and equality to blacks in America, he believed. Freeing blacks and allowing them to remain in this country would lead to a race war. In Lincoln's mind, social stability and black progress required that slavery end and that blacks leave the country.

Lincoln envisioned the western territories as "places for poor people to go to, and better their conditions." The "*free* labor system," he said, "opens the way for all—gives hope to all, and energy, and progress, and improvement of condition to all." But slavery's expansion threatened free men's basic right to succeed. The Kansas-Nebraska Act and the *Dred Scott* decision persuaded him that slaveholders were engaged in a dangerous conspiracy to nationalize slavery. The next step, Lincoln warned, would be "another Supreme Court decision, declaring that the Constitution of the United States does not permit a State to exclude slavery from its limits." Unless the citizens of Illinois woke up, he warned, the Supreme Court would make "Illinois a slave State."

> The "*free* labor system," Lincoln said, "opens the way for all—gives hope to all, and energy, and progress, and improvement of condition to all."

In Lincoln's view, the nation could not "endure, permanently half slave and half free." Either opponents of slavery would arrest its spread and place it on the "course of ultimate extinction," or its advocates would see that it became legal in "*all* the States, *old* as well as *new*— *North* as well as *South*." Lincoln's convictions that slavery was wrong, that Congress must stop its spread, and that it must be put on the road to extinction formed the core of the Republican ideology. Lincoln so impressed his fellow Republicans in Illinois that in 1858, they chose him to challenge the nation's premier Democrat, who was seeking reelection to the U.S. Senate.

The Lincoln-Douglas Debates

When Stephen Douglas learned that the Republican Abraham Lincoln would be his opponent for the Senate, he confided in a fellow Democrat: "He is the strong man of the party— full of wit, facts, dates—and the best stump speaker, with his droll ways and dry jokes, in the West. He is as honest as he is shrewd, and if I beat him my victory will be hardly won."

Not only did Douglas have to contend with a formidable foe, but he also carried the weight of a burden not of his own making. The previous year, the nation's economy had experienced a sharp downturn. Prices had plummeted, thousands of businesses had failed, and unemployment had risen. As a Democrat, Douglas had to go before the voters as a member of the party whose policies stood accused of causing the panic of 1857.

Douglas's response to another crisis in 1857, however, helped shore up his standing in Illinois. Proslavery forces in Kansas met in the town of Lecompton, drafted a proslavery constitution, and applied for statehood. Everyone knew that free-soilers outnumbered proslavery settlers, but President Buchanan instructed Congress to admit Kansas as the sixteenth slave state. Republicans denounced the "Lecompton swindle." Senator Douglas broke with the Democratic administration and came out against the Lecompton constitution; Congress killed the Lecompton bill. (When Kansans reconsidered the Lecompton constitution in an honest election, they rejected it six to one. Kansas entered the Union in 1861 as a free state.) By denouncing the fraudulent proslavery constitution, Douglas declared his independence from the South and, he hoped, made himself acceptable at home.

A relative unknown and a decided underdog in the Illinois election, Lincoln challenged Douglas to debate him face-to-face. The two met in seven communities for what would become a legendary series of debates. To the thousands who stood straining to see and hear, they must have seemed an odd pair. Douglas was five feet four inches tall, broad, and stocky; Lincoln was six feet four inches tall, angular, and lean. Douglas was in perpetual motion, darting across the platform, shouting, and jabbing the air; Lincoln stood still and spoke deliberately. Douglas wore the latest fashions and dazzled audiences with his flashy vests; Lincoln wore good suits but managed to look rumpled anyway. The differences in physical appearance and style, however, were of little importance. The men debated the central issues of the age—slavery and freedom—and showed the citizens of Illinois (and much of the nation because of widespread press coverage) the difference between an anti-Lecompton Democrat and a true Republican.

Lincoln badgered Douglas with the question of whether he favored the spread of slavery. He tried to force Douglas into the damaging admission that the Supreme Court had repudiated Douglas's own territorial solution, popular sovereignty. In the debate at Freeport, Illinois, Douglas admitted that settlers could not now pass legislation barring slavery, but he argued that they could ban slavery just as effectively by not passing protective laws, such as those found in slave states. Southerners condemned Douglas's "Freeport Doctrine" and charged him with trying to steal the victory they had gained with the *Dred Scott* decision. Lincoln chastised his opponent for his "don't care" attitude about slavery, for "blowing out the moral lights around us."

Douglas worked the racial issue. He called Lincoln an abolitionist and an egalitarian enamored of "our colored brethren." Put on the defensive, Lincoln came close to staking out positions on race that were as **conservative** as Douglas's. Lincoln reaffirmed his faith in white rule: "I will say, then, that I am not, nor ever have been, in favor of bringing about in any way the social and political equality of the white and black race." But unlike Douglas, who told racist jokes, Lincoln was no negrophobe. He tried to steer the debate back to what he considered the true issue: the morality and future of slavery. "Slavery is wrong," Lincoln repeated, because "a man has the right to the fruits of his own labor."

As Douglas predicted, the election was hard-fought and closely contested. Until the adoption of the Seventeenth Amendment in 1911, citizens voted for state legislators, who in turn selected U.S. senators. Since Democrats won a slight majority in the Illinois legislature, the members returned Douglas to the Senate. But the debates thrust Lincoln, the prairie Republican, into the national spotlight.

> **REVIEW** Why did the *Dred Scott* decision strengthen northern suspicions of a "Slave Power" conspiracy?

The Union Collapses

Lincoln's thesis that the "slavocracy" conspired to make slavery a national institution now seems exaggerated. But from the northern perspective, the Kansas-Nebraska Act, the Brooks-Sumner affair, the *Dred Scott* decision, and the Lecompton constitution amounted to irrefutable evidence of the South's aggressiveness. White Southerners, of course, saw things differently. They were the ones who were under siege, they declared. Signs were everywhere that the North planned to use its numerical advantage to attack slavery, and not just in the territories. Republicans had made it clear that they were unwilling to accept the *Dred Scott* ruling as the last word on the issue of slavery expansion. And John Brown's attempt to incite a slave insurrection in Virginia in 1859 proved that Northerners were unwilling to be bound by Christian decency and reverence for life.

Threats of secession increasingly laced the sectional debate. Talk of leaving the Union had been heard for years, but until the final crisis, Southerners had used secession as a ploy to gain concessions within the Union, not to destroy it. Then the 1850s delivered powerful blows to Southerners' confidence that they could remain Americans and protect slavery. When the Republican Party won the White House in 1860, many Southerners concluded that they would have to leave.

The Aftermath of John Brown's Raid

For his attack on Harpers Ferry, John Brown stood trial for treason, murder, and incitement of slave insurrection. "To hang a fanatic is to make a martyr of him and fledge another brood of the same sort," cautioned one southern newspaper. But on December 2, 1859, Virginia executed Brown. In life, Brown was a ne'er-do-well, but he died with courage and dignity. He told his wife that he was "determined to make the utmost possible out of a defeat." He told the court: "If it is deemed necessary that I should forfeit my life for the furtherance of the ends of justice, and mingle my blood further with the blood of . . . millions in this slave country whose rights are disregarded by wicked, cruel, and unjust enactments, I say, let it be done."

> In life, John Brown was a ne'er-do-well, but he died with courage and dignity. He told his wife that he was "determined to make the utmost possible out of a defeat."

After Brown's heroic death, northern denunciation of Brown as a dangerous fanatic gave way to grudging respect. Some even celebrated his "splendid martyrdom." Abolitionist Lydia Maria Child likened Brown to Christ and declared that he made "the scaffold . . . as glorious as the Cross of Calvary." Some abolitionists explicitly endorsed Brown's resort to violence. Abolitionist William Lloyd Garrison, who usually professed pacifism, announced, "I am prepared to say 'success to every slave insurrection at the South and in every country.'"

Most Northerners did not advocate bloody rebellion, however. Like Lincoln, they concluded that Brown's noble antislavery ideals could not "excuse violence, bloodshed, and treason." Still, when many in the North marked John Brown's execution with tolling bells, hymns, and prayer vigils, white Southerners contemplated what they had in common with people who "regard John Brown as a martyr and a Christian hero, rather

***John Brown Going to His Hanging,* by Horace Pippin, 1942**
The grandparents of Horace Pippin, a Pennsylvania artist, were slaves. His grandmother witnessed the hanging of John Brown, and this painting recalls the scene she so often described to him. Pippin used a muted palette to establish the bleak setting and to tell the grim story, but he managed to convey a striking intensity nevertheless. Historically accurate, the painting depicts Brown tied and sitting erect on his coffin, passing resolutely before the silent, staring white men. The black woman in the lower right corner presumably is Pippin's grandmother.

Romare Bearden, a leading twentieth-century African American artist, recalled the central place of John Brown in black memory: "Lincoln and John Brown were as much a part of the actuality of the Afro-American experience, as were the domino games and the hoe cakes for Sunday morning breakfast. I vividly recall the yearly commemorations for John Brown and see my grandfather reading Brown's last speech to the court, which was a regular part of the ceremony at Pittsburgh's Shiloh Baptist Church."
Pennsylvania Academy of Fine Arts, Philadelphia. John Lambert Fund.

READING THE IMAGE: What was the artist trying to convey about the tone of John Brown's execution? According to the painting, what were the feelings of those gathered to witness the event?
CONNECTIONS: How did Brown's trial and execution contribute to the growing split between North and South?

FOR MORE HELP ANALYZING THIS IMAGE, see the visual activity for this chapter in the Online Study Guide at
bedfordstmartins.com/roark.

than a murderer and robber." Georgia senator Robert Toombs announced solemnly that Southerners must "never permit this Federal government to pass into the traitorous hands of the black Republican party." At that moment, the presidential election was only months away.

Republican Victory in 1860

Events between Brown's hanging and the presidential election only heightened sectional hostility and estrangement. A southern business convention meeting in Nashville shocked the

Abraham Lincoln
Lincoln actively sought the Republican presidential nomination in 1860. While in New York City to give a political
address, he had his photograph taken by Mathew Brady.
"While I was there I was taken to one of the places
where they get up such things," Lincoln explained, sound-
ing more innocent than he was, "and I suppose they got
my shadow, and can multiply copies indefinitely." Multiply
they did. Later, Lincoln credited his victory to his New York
speech and to this dignified photograph by Brady.
The Lincoln Museum, Fort Wayne, Indiana, #0-17.

nation (including many Southerners) by calling
for the reopening of the African slave trade,
closed since 1808 and considered an abomination
everywhere in the Western world. Chief Justice
Taney provoked new indignation when the
Supreme Court ruled northern personal liberty
laws unconstitutional and reaffirmed the
Fugitive Slave Act. Then, the normally routine
business of electing a Speaker of the House
threatened to turn bloody as Democrats and
Republicans battled over control of the office.
After two months of acrimonious debate left the
House deadlocked, one congressman observed
that the "only persons who do not have a re-

volver and a knife are those who have two
revolvers." A last-minute compromise may
have averted a shootout. Finally, Mississippian
Jefferson Davis demanded that the Senate adopt
a federal slave code for the territories, a goal of extreme proslavery
Southerners for several years. Not
only was Congress powerless to
block slavery's spread, he argued, but it was obligated to offer slavery all "needful protection."

When the Democrats converged on
Charleston for their convention in April 1860,
fire-eating Southerners denounced Stephen
Douglas and demanded a platform that included
federal protection of slavery in the territories.
But northern Democrats knew that northern voters would not stomach a federal slave code.
When the delegates approved a platform with
popular sovereignty, representatives from the
entire Lower South and Arkansas stomped out
of the convention. The remaining Democrats adjourned to meet a few weeks later in Baltimore,
where they nominated Douglas for president.

When southern Democrats met, they nominated Vice President John C. Breckinridge of
Kentucky and approved a platform with a federal slave code. Southern moderates, however,
refused to support Breckinridge. They formed
the Constitutional Union Party to provide voters
with a Unionist choice. Instead of adopting a
platform and confronting the slavery question,
the Constitutional Union Party merely approved
a vague resolution pledging "to recognize no political principle other than *the Constitution . . . the
Union . . . and the Enforcement of the Laws.*" For
president, they picked former senator John Bell
of Tennessee.

The Republicans smelled victory, but they
estimated that they needed to carry nearly all the
free states to win. To make their party more appealing, they expanded their platform beyond
antislavery. They hoped that free homesteads, a
protective tariff, a transcontinental railroad,
and a guarantee of immigrant political rights
would provide an economic and social agenda
broad enough to unify the North. While reasserting their commitment to stop the spread of slavery, they also denounced John Brown's raid as
"among the gravest of crimes" and confirmed
the security of slavery in the South.

Republicans cast about for a moderate candidate to go with their evenhanded platform.
The foremost Republican, William H. Seward,
had made enemies with his radical "higher law"
doctrine and "irrepressible conflict" speech.

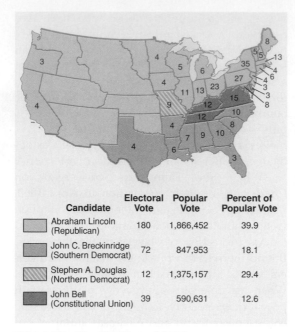

Candidate	Electoral Vote	Popular Vote	Percent of Popular Vote
Abraham Lincoln (Republican)	180	1,866,452	39.9
John C. Breckinridge (Southern Democrat)	72	847,953	18.1
Stephen A. Douglas (Northern Democrat)	12	1,375,157	29.4
John Bell (Constitutional Union)	39	590,631	12.6

MAP 14.5   The Election of 1860

Lincoln, however, since bursting onto the national scene in 1858 had demonstrated his clear purpose, good judgment, and solid Republican credentials. That, and his residence in Illinois, a crucial state, made him attractive to the party. On the third ballot, the delegates chose Lincoln. Defeated by Douglas in a state contest less than two years earlier, Lincoln now stood ready to take him on for the presidency.

The election of 1860 was like none other in American politics. It took place in the midst of the nation's severest crisis. Four major candidates crowded the presidential field. Rather than a four-cornered contest, however, the election broke into two contests, each with two candidates. In the North, Lincoln faced Douglas; in the South, Breckinridge confronted Bell. So outrageous did Southerners consider the Republican Party that they did not even permit Lincoln's name to appear on the ballot in ten of the fifteen slave states.

An unprecedented number of voters cast their ballots on November 6, 1860. Approximately 82 percent of eligible northern men and nearly 70 percent of eligible southern men went to the polls. Lincoln swept all of the eighteen free states except New Jersey, which split its electoral votes between him and Douglas. Although Lincoln received only 39 percent of the popular vote, he won easily in the electoral college with 180 votes, 28 more than he needed for victory (Map 14.5). Lincoln did not win because his opposition was splintered. Even if the votes of his three opponents had been combined, Lincoln would still have won. He won because his votes were concentrated in the free states, which contained a majority of electoral votes. Ominously, however, Breckinridge, running on a southern-rights platform, won the entire Lower South, plus Delaware, Maryland, and North Carolina.

Secession Winter

The telegraphs had barely stopped tapping out the news of Lincoln's victory when anxious Southerners began debating what to do. Although Breckinridge had carried the South, a vote for "southern rights" was not necessarily a vote for secession. Besides, slightly more than half of the Southerners who had voted had cast ballots for Douglas and Bell, two stout defenders of the Union.

Southern Unionists tried to calm the fears that Lincoln's election triggered. Let the dust settle, they pleaded. Former congressman Alexander Stephens of Georgia asked what Lincoln had done to justify something as extreme as secession. Had he not promised to respect slavery where it existed? In Stephens's judgment, the fire-eater cure would be worse than the Republican disease. Secession might lead to war, which would loosen the hinges of southern society, possibly even open the door to slave insurrection. "Revolutions are much easier started than controlled," he warned. "I consider slavery much more secure in the Union than out of it."

Secessionists emphasized the dangers of delay. "Mr. Lincoln and his party assert that this doctrine of equality applies to the negro," former Georgia governor Howell Cobb declared, "and necessarily there can exist no such thing as property in our equals." Lincoln's election without a single electoral vote from the South meant that Southerners were no longer able to defend themselves within the Union, Cobb argued. Why wait, he said, for Lincoln to appoint abolitionist judges, marshals, customs collectors, and postmasters to federal posts throughout the South? As for

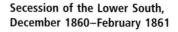

Secession of the Lower South, December 1860–February 1861

war, there would be none. The Union was a voluntary compact, and Lincoln would not coerce patriotism. If Northerners did resist with force, secessionists argued, one southern woodsman could whip five of Lincoln's greasy mechanics.

For all their differences, southern whites agreed that they had to defend slavery. John Smith Preston of South Carolina spoke for the overwhelming majority when he declared, "The South cannot exist without slavery." They disagreed about whether the mere presence of a Republican in the White House made it necessary to exercise what they considered a legitimate right to secede.

The debate about what to do was briefest in South Carolina; it seceded from the Union on December 20, 1860. By February 1861, the six other Lower South states marched in South Carolina's footsteps. In some states, the vote was close. In general, slaveholders spearheaded secession, while nonslaveholders in the Piedmont and mountain counties, where slaves were relatively few, displayed the greatest attachment to the Union. On February 4, representatives from South Carolina, Georgia, Florida, Alabama, Mississippi, Louisiana, and Texas met in Montgomery, Alabama, where three days later they celebrated the birth of the Confederate States of America. Jefferson Davis became president, and Alexander Stephens, who had spoken so eloquently about the dangers of revolution, became vice president. In March 1861, Stephens declared that the Confederacy's "cornerstone" was "the great truth that the negro is not equal to the white man; that slavery, subordination to the superior race, is his natural and moral condition."

Lincoln's election had split the Union. Now secession split the South. Seven slave states seceded during the winter, but the eight slave states of the Upper South rejected secession, at least for the moment. The Upper South had a smaller stake in slavery. Barely half as many white families in the Upper South held slaves (21 percent) as in the Lower South (37 percent). Slaves represented twice as large a percentage of the population in the Lower South (48 percent) as in the Upper South (23 percent). Consequently, whites in the Upper South had fewer fears that Republican ascendancy meant economic catastrophe, social chaos, and racial war. Lincoln would need to do more than just be elected to provoke them into secession.

The nation had to wait until March 4, 1861, when Lincoln took office, to see what he would do. (Presidents-elect waited four months to take

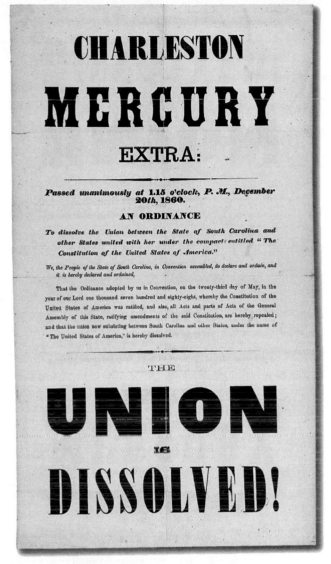

"The Union Is Dissolved!"
On December 20, 1860, the *Charleston Mercury* put out this special edition of the paper to celebrate South Carolina's secession from the Union. Six weeks earlier, upon hearing the news that Lincoln had won the presidency, it had predicted as much. "The tea has been thrown overboard," the *Mercury* announced. "The revolution of 1860 has been initiated."
Chicago Historical Society.

office until 1933, when the Twentieth Amendment to the Constitution shifted the inauguration to January 20.) After his election, Lincoln chose to stay in Springfield and to say nothing. "Lame-duck" president James Buchanan sat in Washington and did nothing. Buchanan demonstrated, William H. Seward said mockingly, that "it is the President's duty to enforce the laws, unless somebody opposes him." In Congress, efforts at cobbling together a peace-saving compromise came to nothing.

Lincoln began his inaugural address with reassurances to the South. He had "no lawful right" to interfere with slavery where it existed, he declared again, adding for emphasis that he had "no inclination to do so." In filling federal posts, he would not "force obnoxious strangers" on the South. Conciliatory about slavery, Lincoln proved inflexible about the Union. The Union, he declared, was "perpetual." Secession was "anarchy" and "legally void." The Constitution required him to execute the law "in all the States." He would hold federal property, collect federal duties, and deliver the mail.

> The Union, Lincoln declared, was "perpetual." Secession was "anarchy" and "legally void."

The decision for civil war or peace rested in the South's hands, Lincoln said. "You can have no conflict, without being yourselves the aggressors. *You* have no oath registered in Heaven to destroy the government, while *I* shall have the most solemn one to 'preserve, protect, and defend' it." What Confederates in Charleston held in their hands at that very moment were the cords for firing the cannons aimed at the federal garrison at Fort Sumter.

> **REVIEW** Why did some southern states secede immediately after Lincoln's election?

Conclusion: Slavery, Free Labor, and the Failure of Political Compromise

As their economies, societies, and **cultures** diverged in the nineteenth century, Northerners and Southerners expressed different concepts of the American promise and the place of slavery within it. Their differences crystallized into political form in 1846 when David Wilmot proposed banning slavery in any territory won in the Mexican-American War. "As if by magic," a Boston newspaper observed, "it brought to a head the great question that is about to divide the American people." Discovery of gold and other precious metals in the West added urgency to the controversy over slavery in the territories. Although Congress addressed the issue with the Compromise of 1850, the Fugitive Slave Act quickly brought conflict between free and slave states. Matters worsened with the 1852 publication of *Uncle Tom's Cabin*, which further hardened northern sentiments against slavery and confirmed southern suspicions of northern ill will. The bloody violence that erupted in Kansas in 1856 and the incendiary *Dred Scott* decision in 1857 further eroded hope for a solution to this momentous question.

During the extended crisis of the Union that stretched from 1846 to 1861, the slavery question braided with national politics. The traditional Whig and Democratic parties struggled to hold together, as new parties, most notably the Republican Party, emerged. Politicians fixed their attention on the expansion of slavery, but from the beginning, the nation recognized that the controversy had less to do with slavery in the territories than with the future of slavery in America.

For more than seventy years, statesmen had found compromises that accepted slavery and preserved the Union. But as each section grew increasingly committed to its labor system and the promise it provided, Americans discovered that accommodation had limits. In 1859, John Brown's militant antislavery pushed white Southerners to the edge. In 1860, Lincoln's election convinced whites in the Lower South that slavery and the society they had built on it were at risk in the Union, and they seceded. In his inaugural address, Lincoln pleaded, "We are not enemies but friends. We must not be enemies." By then, however, seven southern states had ceased to sing what he called "the chorus of the Union." It remained to be seen whether disunion would mean war.

Selected Bibliography

General Works

Don E. Fehrenbacher, *The Slaveholding Republic: An Account of the United States Government's Relations to Slavery* (2001).

Paul Finkelman, *An Imperfect Union: Slavery, Federalism, and Comity* (1981).

Michael Holt, *Fate of Their Country: Politicians, Slavery Extension, and the Coming of the Civil War* (2004).

Bruce C. Levine, *Half Slave and Half Free: The Roots of the Civil War* (1992).

James M. McPherson, *Ordeal by Fire: The Civil War and Reconstruction* (1982).

Mark E. Neely, *Boundaries of American Political Culture in the Civil War Era* (2005).

Eric H. Walther, *The Shattering of the Union: America in the 1850s* (2004).

Northern Sectionalism

Tom Chaffin, *Pathfinder: John Charles Frémont and the Course of American Empire* (2002).

Eric Foner, *Free Labor, Free Soil, Free Men: The Ideology of the Republican Party before the Civil War* (1970).

William E. Gienapp, *The Origins of the Republican Party, 1852–1856* (1987).

Susan-Mary Grant, *North over South: Northern Nationalism and American Identity in the Antebellum Era* (2000).

David Grimsted, *American Mobbing, 1828–1865: Toward Civil War* (1998).

Joan D. Hedrick, *Harriet Beecher Stowe: A Life* (1994).

Pamela Herr, *Jessie Benton Frémont: A Biography* (1987).

Nancy Isenberg, *Sex and Citizenship in Antebellum America* (1998).

Michael D. Pierson, *Free Hearts and Free Homes: Gender and American Antislavery Politics* (2003).

David S. Reynolds, *John Brown, Abolitionist: The Man Who Killed Slavery, Sparked the Civil War, and Seeded Civil Rights* (2005).

James Brewer Stewart, *Wendell Phillips, Liberty's Hero* (1986).

Wendy Hamand Venet, *Neither Ballots nor Bullets: Women Abolitionists and the Civil War* (1991).

Douglas L. Wilson, *Honor's Voice: The Transformation of Abraham Lincoln* (1998).

David Zarefsky, *Lincoln, Douglas, and Slavery: In the Crucible of Public Debate* (1990).

Southern Sectionalism

William J. Cooper Jr., *The South and the Politics of Slavery, 1828–1856* (1978).

John Patrick Daly, *When Slavery Was Called Freedom: Evangelicalism, Proslavery, and the Causes of the Civil War* (2002).

Lacy K. Ford Jr., *Origins of Southern Radicalism: The South Carolina Upcountry, 1800–1860* (1988).

William W. Freehling, *The Road to Disunion*, vol. 1, *Secessionists at Bay, 1776–1854* (1990).

William A. Link, *Roots of Secession: Slavery and Politics in Antebellum Virginia* (2002).

Robert E. May, *Manifest Destiny's Underworld: Filibustering in Antebellum America* (2002).

Christopher J. Olsen, *Political Culture and Secession in Mississippi: Masculinity, Honor, and the Antiparty Tradition, 1830–1860* (2002).

Manisha Sinha, *The Counterrevolution of Slavery: Politics and Ideology in Antebellum South Carolina* (2000).

Mitchell Snay, *Gospel of Disunion: Religion and Separatism in the Antebellum South* (1993).

Secession

Daniel Crofts, *Reluctant Confederates: Upper South Unionists in the Secession Crisis* (1989).

Charles B. Dew, *Apostles of Disunion: Southern Secession Commissioners and the Causes of the Civil War* (2001).

Michael P. Johnson, *Toward a Patriarchal Republic: The Secession of Georgia* (1977).

David M. Potter, *Lincoln and His Party in the Secession Crisis* (1942).

Lorman A. Ratner and Dwight L. Teeter Jr., *Fanatics and Fire Eaters: Newspapers and the Coming of the Civil War* (2003).

▶ FOR MORE BOOKS ABOUT TOPICS IN THIS CHAPTER, see the Online Bibliography at bedfordstmartins.com/roark

▶ FOR ADDITIONAL FIRSTHAND ACCOUNTS OF THIS PERIOD, see Chapter 14 in Michael Johnson, ed., *Reading the American Past*, Fourth Edition.

▶ FOR WEB SITES, IMAGES, AND DOCUMENTS RELATED TO TOPICS AND PLACES IN THIS CHAPTER, visit bedfordstmartins.com/makehistory.

REVIEWING THE CHAPTER

Follow these steps to review and strengthen your understanding of the chapter.
STEP 1: *Study the **Key Terms** and **Timeline** to identify the significance of each item listed.*
STEP 2: *Answer the **Review Questions**, drawing on key terms and dates to support your answers.*
STEP 3: *Drawing on the Key Terms, Timeline, and Review Questions, answer the broader **Making Connections** questions.*

KEY TERMS

Who

John Brown (p. 475)
David Wilmot (p. 476)
John C. Calhoun (p. 476)
Lewis Cass (p. 478)
Martin Van Buren (p. 479)
Zachary Taylor (p. 479)
Henry Clay (p. 479)
Daniel Webster (p. 480)
William H. Seward (p. 480)
Stephen A. Douglas (pp. 481, 486)
Millard Fillmore (p. 481)
Harriet Beecher Stowe (p. 481)
Franklin Pierce (p. 485)
Winfield Scott (p. 485)
James Gadsden (p. 486)
John C. Frémont (p. 493)
Jessie Frémont (p. 493)

James Buchanan (p. 493)
Ernestine Rose (p. 494)
Charles Sumner (p. 496)
Roger B. Taney (p. 497)
Abraham Lincoln (p. 499)
John C. Breckinridge (p. 503)
Jefferson Davis (p. 503)

What

John Brown's raid on Harpers Ferry (p. 475)
Wilmot Proviso (p. 477)
popular sovereignty (p. 478)
Democratic Party (pp. 479, 487)
Whig Party (pp. 479, 487)
Free-Soil Party (p. 479)
Omnibus Bill (p. 480)
Compromise of 1850 (p. 481)

Fugitive Slave Act (p. 481)
underground railroad (p. 482)
Uncle Tom's Cabin (pp. 481, 484)
Gadsden Purchase (p. 486)
Kansas-Nebraska Act (p. 487)
Know-Nothing Party (p. 490)
Republican Party (p. 492)
free labor (p. 492)
"Bleeding Kansas" (p. 496)
"Sack of Lawrence" (p. 496)
"Bleeding Sumner" (p. 497)
Dred Scott decision (p. 498)
panic of 1857 (p. 500)
Lecompton constitution (p. 500)
Lincoln-Douglas debates (p. 500)
Constitutional Union Party (p. 503)
Confederate States of America (p. 505)

TIMELINE

◄ **1820** • Missouri Compromise.

1846 • Wilmot Proviso introduced in Congress.

1847 • Wilmot Proviso defeated in Senate.
• Compromise of "popular sovereignty" offered.

1848 • Free-Soil Party founded.
• Whig Zachary Taylor elected president.

1849 • California gold rush.

1850 • Taylor dies; Vice President Millard Fillmore becomes president.
• Compromise of 1850 becomes law.

1852 • *Uncle Tom's Cabin* published.
• Democrat Franklin Pierce elected president.

1853 • Gadsden Purchase.

1854 • American (Know-Nothing) Party emerges.
• Kansas-Nebraska Act.
• Republican Party founded.

REVIEW QUESTIONS

1. Why did response to the Wilmot Proviso split along sectional rather than party lines? (pp. 476–81)

2. Why did the Fugitive Slave Act provoke such strong opposition in the North? (pp. 481–87)

3. Why did the Whig Party disintegrate in the 1850s? (pp. 487–93)

4. Why did the *Dred Scott* decision strengthen northern suspicions of a "Slave Power" conspiracy? (pp. 496–501)

5. Why did some southern states secede immediately after Lincoln's election? (pp. 501–6)

MAKING CONNECTIONS

1. The process of compromise that had successfully contained tensions between slave and free states since the nation's founding collapsed with secession. Why did compromise fail at this moment? In your answer, address specific political conflicts and attempts to solve them between 1846 and 1861.

2. In the 1850s, many Americans supported popular sovereignty as the best solution to the explosive question of slavery in the western territories. Why was this solution so popular, and why did it ultimately prove inadequate? In your answer, be sure to address popular sovereignty's varied critics as well as its champions.

3. In the 1840s and 1850s, the United States witnessed the realignment of its long-standing two-party system. Why did the old system fall apart, what emerged to take its place, and how did this process contribute to the coming of the Civil War?

4. Abraham Lincoln believed that he had staked out a moderate position on the question of slavery, avoiding the extremes of immediate abolitionism and calls for unlimited protection of slavery. Why, then, did some southern states determine that his election necessitated the radical act of secession?

▶ FOR PRACTICE QUIZZES, A CUSTOMIZED STUDY PLAN, AND OTHER STUDY TOOLS, see the Online Study Guide at bedfordstmartins.com/roark

---

1856 • "Bleeding Kansas."
• Preston Brooks canes Charles Sumner.
• Pottawatomie massacre.
• Democrat James Buchanan elected president.

    1857 • *Dred Scott* decision.
• Congress rejects Lecompton constitution.
• Panic of 1857.

        1858 • Abraham Lincoln and Stephen A. Douglas debate slavery; Douglas wins Senate seat.

          1859 • John Brown raids Harpers Ferry, Virginia.

            1860 • Republican Abraham Lincoln elected president.
• South Carolina secedes from Union.

              1861 • Six other deep South states secede.
• Confederate States of America formed.
• Lincoln takes office.

FORT SUMTER STARS AND STRIPES

This U.S. flag flew over Fort Sumter throughout the Confederate bombardment that started the Civil War on April 12, 1861. Shrapnel from thirty-three hours of cannon fire shredded the flag, but when Union major Robert Anderson surrendered on April 13, he and his men marched out of the fort under this tattered banner. The governor of South Carolina cheered what he called the humbling of the flag of the United States. Northerners bridled at this insult, and within days flags sprouted across the Union. The Civil War stitched the flag and American nationalism together and made the Stars and Stripes the powerful symbol it is today. When Anderson returned to Fort Sumter in April 1865, he triumphantly raised this very flag.

Confederate Museum, United Daughters of the Confederacy.

15

The Crucible of War

1861–1865

■ **"And the War Came"** 513
Attack on Fort Sumter 513
The Upper South Chooses Sides 514

■ **The Combatants** 515
How They Expected to Win 515
Lincoln and Davis Mobilize 517

■ **Battling It Out, 1861–1862** 518
Stalemate in the
Eastern Theater 518
Union Victories in the
Western Theater 522
The Atlantic Theater 523
International Diplomacy 524

■ **Union *and* Freedom** 524
From Slaves to Contraband 525
From Contraband to Free People 528
War of Black Liberation 529

■ **The South at War** 530
Revolution from Above 531
Hardship Below 534
The Disintegration of Slavery 535

■ **The North at War** 536
The Government and
the Economy 537
Women and Work on
the Home Front 537
Politics and Dissent 538

■ **Grinding Out Victory,
1863–1865** 539
Vicksburg and Gettysburg 539
Grant Takes Command 540
The Election of 1864 545
The Confederacy Collapses 546

■ **Conclusion: The Second
American Revolution** 547

O N THE RAINY NIGHT OF SEPTEMBER 21, 1862, in Wilmington, North Carolina, twenty-four-year-old William Gould and seven other black men crowded into a small boat on the Cape Fear River and quietly pushed away from the dock. Knowing that the authorities would sound the alarm for eight runaway slaves at daybreak, they rowed hard throughout the night. By dawn, the runaways had traveled twenty-eight miles to where the river flowed into the Atlantic Ocean. They plunged into the swells and made for the Union navy patrolling offshore to disrupt the flow of goods in and out of Wilmington, a major Confederate port. At 10:30 that morning, the USS *Cambridge* took the men aboard.

Astonishingly, on the same day that Gould reached the federal ship, President Abraham Lincoln announced to his cabinet in Washington, D.C., that he intended to issue a proclamation of **emancipation** freeing the slaves in the Confederate states. Because the proclamation would not take effect until January 1863, Gould was not legally free in the eyes of the U.S. government. But the U.S. navy, suffering from a shortage of sailors, cared little about the formal status of runaway slaves. Within days, all eight runaways became sailors "for three years," Gould said, "first taking the Oath of Allegiance to the Government of Uncle Samuel."

Unlike most slaves, William Gould could read and write, and he began making almost daily entries in a remarkable diary, apparently the only diary kept during the war by a sailor who had been a slave. In some ways, Gould's naval experience looked like that of a white sailor. He found duty on a ship in the blockading squadron both boring and exhilarating. He often recorded comments such as "All hands painting, cleaning" and "Cruised as usual." But long days of tedious work were sometimes interrupted by a "period of daring exploit" as enemy ships engaged in combat. When Gould's ship closed on one Confederate vessel, he declared that "we told them good morning in the shape of a shot." In a five-day period in 1862, his ship and two other blockaders captured four blockade runners and ran another aground. In October 1863, Gould transferred to the USS *Niagara* and sailed for European waters to search for Confederate cruisers abroad.

But Gould's Civil War experience was shaped by his race. Most white Northerners fought to preserve their government and society, while most black men in the Union military saw service as an opportunity to fight slavery. From the beginning, Gould linked union and freedom, which he called "the holiest of all causes."

Nevertheless, Gould witnessed a number of racial incidents on federal ships. "There was A malee [melee] on Deck between the white and colard [colored] men," he declared. Later, when a black regiment came aboard, "they were treated verry rough by the crew," he observed. The white sailors "refused to let them eat off the mess pans and called them all kinds of names[;] . . . in all they was treated shamefully." Recording another incident, Gould stated, "This Morning four or fiv[e] white fellows beat Jerry Jones (co[lored]). He was stabd in his left shoulder. Verry bad."

Still, Gould was proud of his service in the navy and monitored the progress of racial equality during the war. On shore leave in 1863, he cheered the "20th Regmt of U.S. (collard)

The Crew of the USS *Hunchback*

African Americans served as sailors in the federal military long before they were permitted to become soldiers. Blacks initially served only as coal heavers, cooks, and stewards, but within a year, some black sailors joined their ships' gun crews. The *Hunchback* was one of the Union's innovative ironclad ships. Although ironclads made wooden navies obsolete, they were far from invincible. During the assault on Charleston in 1863, five of the nine federal ironclads were partially or wholly disabled.
National Archives.

Volunteers, the first collard Regement raised in New York pronounce[d] by all to be A splendid Regement." In March 1865, he celebrated the "passage of an amendment of the Con[sti]tution prohibiting slavery througho[ut] the United States." And a month later, he thrilled to the "Glad Tidings that the Stars and Stripe[s] had been planted over the Capital of the D—nd Confederacy by the invincible Grant." He added, we must not forget the "Mayrters to the cau[se] of Right and Equality."

Slaves like the eight runaways from Wilmington took the first steps toward making the war for union also a war for freedom. Early in the fighting, black abolitionist Frederick Douglass challenged the friends of freedom to "*be up and doing;—now is your time.*" But for the first eighteen months of the war, Union soldiers fought solely to uphold the Constitution and preserve the nation. With the Emancipation Proclamation, however, the northern war effort took on a dual purpose: to save the Union and to free the slaves.

Even if the Civil War had not touched slavery, the conflict still would have transformed America. As the world's first modern war, it mobilized the entire populations of North and South, harnessed the productive capacities of both economies, and produced battles that fielded 200,000 soldiers and created casualties in the tens of thousands. The carnage lasted four years and cost the nation an estimated 633,000 lives, nearly as many as in all of its other wars combined. The war helped mold the modern American nation-state, and the federal government emerged with new power and responsibility over national life. The war encouraged industrialization. It tore families apart and pushed women into new work and roles. But because the war for union also became a war against slavery, the northern victory had truly revolutionary meaning. Defeat and emancipation destroyed the slave society of the Old South and gave birth to a different southern society.

Recalling the Civil War years, Frederick Douglass said, "It is something to couple one's name with great occasions." It *was* something— for William Gould and millions of other Americans. Whether they fought for the Confederacy or the Union, whether they labored behind the lines to supply Yankee or rebel soldiers, whether they prayed for the safe return of Northerners or Southerners, all Americans experienced the crucible of war. But the war affected no group more than the 4 million African Americans who saw its beginning as slaves and emerged as free people.

"And the War Came"

Abraham Lincoln faced the worst crisis in the history of the nation: disunion. He revealed his strategy on March 4, 1861, in his inaugural address, which was firm yet conciliatory. First, he sought to stop the contagion of secession by avoiding any act that would push the skittish Upper South (North Carolina, Virginia, Maryland, Delaware, Kentucky, Tennessee, Missouri, and Arkansas) out of the Union. Second, he sought to buy time so that emotions could cool by reassuring the seceding Lower South (South Carolina, Georgia, Florida, Alabama, Mississippi, Louisiana, and Texas) that the Republicans would not abolish slavery. Lincoln believed that Unionists there would assert themselves and overturn the secession decision. Always, Lincoln denied the right of secession and upheld the Union.

His counterpart, Jefferson Davis, fully intended to establish the Confederate States of America as an independent republic. To achieve permanence, Davis had to sustain the secession fever that had carried the Lower South out of the Union. Even if the Lower South held firm, however, the Confederacy would remain weak without additional states. Davis watched for opportunities to add new stars to the Confederate flag.

Neither man sought war; both wanted to achieve their objectives peacefully. As Lincoln later observed, "Both parties deprecated war, but one of them would *make* war rather than let the nation survive, and the other would *accept* war rather than let it perish. And the war came."

Fort Sumter after the Bombardment
Located on an artificial island inside the entrance to Charleston harbor, Fort Sumter had walls eight to twelve feet thick. The fort was so undermanned that when Confederate shells began raining down on April 12, 1861, U.S. troops could answer back with only a few of the fort's forty-eight guns. Confederate artillery lobbed more than 4,000 rounds. Cannonballs pulverized the walls, while hot shot ignited the wooden buildings inside.
Minnesota Historical Society.

Attack on Fort Sumter

Major Robert Anderson and some eighty U.S. soldiers occupied Fort Sumter, which was perched on a tiny island at the entrance to Charleston harbor. The fort with its American flag became a hated symbol of the nation that Southerners had abandoned, and they wanted federal troops out. Sumter was also a symbol to Northerners, a beacon affirming federal sovereignty in the seceded states.

Lincoln decided to hold Fort Sumter, but to do so, he had to provision it, for Anderson was running dangerously short of food. In the first week of April 1861, Lincoln authorized a peaceful expedition to bring supplies, but not military reinforcements, to the fort. The president understood that he risked war, but his plan honored his inaugural promises to defend federal property and to avoid using military force unless first attacked. Masterfully, Lincoln had shifted the fateful decision of war or peace to Jefferson Davis.

On April 9, Jefferson Davis and his cabinet met to consider the situation in Charleston harbor. The territorial integrity of the Confederacy demanded the end of the federal presence, Davis argued. But his secretary of state, Robert Toombs of Georgia, pleaded against military action. "Mr. President," he declared, "at this time it is suicide, murder, and will lose us every friend at the North. You will wantonly strike a hornet's nest which extends from mountain to ocean, and legions now quiet will swarm out and sting us to death." Davis rejected Toombs's prophecy and sent word to Confederate troops in Charleston to take the fort before the relief expedition arrived. Thirty-three hours of bombardment on April 12 and 13 reduced the fort to rubble. Miraculously, not a single Union soldier died. On April 14, with the fort ablaze, Major Anderson offered his surrender and lowered the U.S. flag. The Confederates had Fort Sumter, but they also had war.

On April 15, when Lincoln called for 75,000 militiamen to serve for ninety days to put down the rebellion, several times that number rushed to defend the flag. Democrats responded as fervently as Republicans. Stephen A. Douglas, the recently defeated Democratic candidate for president, pledged his support. "There are only two sides to the question," he said. "Every man must be for the United States or against it. There can be no neutrals in this war, *only patriots—or traitors.*" But the people of the Upper South found themselves torn.

> "There are only two sides to the question," Stephen A. Douglas said. "Every man must be for the United States or against it. There can be no neutrals in this war, *only patriots—or traitors.*"

The Upper South Chooses Sides

The Upper South faced a horrendous choice: either to fight against the Lower South or to fight against the Union. Many who only months earlier had rejected secession now embraced the Confederacy. To vote against southern independence was one thing, to fight fellow Southerners another. Thousands felt betrayed, believing that Lincoln had promised to achieve a peaceful reunion by waiting patiently for Unionists to retake power in the seceding states. One man furiously denounced the conflict as a "politician's war,"

conceding that "this is no time now to discuss the causes, but it is the duty of all who regard Southern institutions of value to side with the South, make common cause with the Confederate States and sink or swim with them."

One by one, the states of the Upper South jumped off the fence. In April and May 1861, Virginia, Arkansas, Tennessee, and North Carolina joined the Confederacy (Map 15.1). But in the border states of Delaware, Maryland, Kentucky, and Missouri, Unionism triumphed. Only in Delaware, where slaves accounted for less than 2 percent of the population, was the victory easy. In Maryland, Unionism needed a helping hand. Rather than allow the state to secede and make Washington, D.C., a federal island in a Confederate sea, Lincoln suspended the writ of habeas corpus, essentially setting aside constitutional guarantees that protect citizens from illegal and arbitrary arrest and detention, and he ordered U.S. troops into Baltimore. Maryland's legislature rejected secession.

The struggle turned violent in the West. In Missouri, Unionists won a narrow victory, but southern-sympathizing **guerrilla** bands roamed the state for the duration of the war, terrorizing civilians and soldiers alike. In Kentucky, Unionists also narrowly defeated secession, but the prosouthern minority claimed otherwise. The Confederacy, not especially careful about

MAP 15.1   Secession, 1860–1861
After Lincoln's election, the fifteen slave states debated what to do. Seven states quickly left the Union, four left after the firing on Fort Sumter, and four remained loyal to the Union.

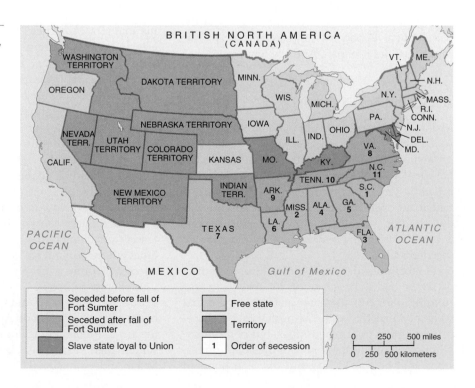

counting votes, eagerly made Missouri and Kentucky the twelfth and thirteenth stars on the Confederate flag.

Throughout the border states, but especially in Kentucky, the Civil War divided families. Seven of Henry Clay's grandsons fought: four for the Confederacy and three for the Union. Lincoln understood that the border states—particularly Kentucky—contained indispensable resources, population, and wealth and also controlled major rivers and railroads. "I think to lose Kentucky is nearly the same as to lose the whole game," Lincoln said. "Kentucky gone, we can not hold Missouri, nor, as I think, Maryland. These all against us, . . . we would as well consent to separation at once."

In the end, only eleven of the fifteen slave states joined the Confederate States of America. Moreover, the four seceding Upper South states contained significant numbers of people who felt little affection for the Confederacy. Dissatisfaction was so rife in the western counties of Virginia that in 1863, citizens there voted to create the separate state of West Virginia, loyal to the Union. Still, the acquisition of four new states greatly strengthened the Confederacy's drive for national independence.

> **REVIEW** Why did both the Union and the Confederacy consider control of the border states crucial?

The Combatants

Only slaveholders had a direct economic stake in preserving slavery (estimated at some $3 billion in 1860), but most whites in the Confederacy defended the institution, the way of life built on it, and the Confederacy itself. The degraded and subjugated status of blacks elevated the status of the poorest whites. "It matters not whether slaves be actually owned by many or by few," one Southerner declared. "It is enough that one simply belongs to the superior and ruling race, to secure consideration and respect." Moreover, Yankee "aggression" was no longer a mere threat; it was real and at the South's door. Southern whites equated the secession of 1861 with the declaration of independence from tyrannical British rule in 1776. As one Georgia

woman observed, Southerners wanted "nothing from the North but—to *be let alone*."

For Northerners, rebel "treason" threatened to destroy the best government on earth. The South's failure to accept the **democratic** election of a president and its firing on the nation's flag challenged the rule of law, the authority of the Constitution, and the ability of the people to govern themselves. As an Indiana soldier told his wife, a "good government is the best thing on earth. Property is nothing without it, because it is not protected; a family is nothing without it, because they cannot be educated." Only a Union victory, Lincoln declared, would secure America's promise "to elevate the condition of man."

Northerners and Southerners rallied behind their separate flags, fully convinced that they were in the right and that God was on their side. But no one could argue that the South's resources and forces equaled the North's. A glance at the census figures contradicted such a notion. Yankees took heart from their superior power, but the rebels believed they had advantages that nullified every northern strength. Both sides mobilized swiftly in 1861, and each devised what it believed would be a winning military and diplomatic strategy.

How They Expected to Win

The balance sheet of northern and southern resources reveals enormous advantages for the Union (Figure 15.1, page 516). The twenty-three states remaining in the Union had a population of 22.3 million; the eleven Confederate states had a population of only 9.1 million, of whom 3.67 million (40 percent) were slaves. The North's economic advantages were even more overwhelming. So mismatched were the Union and the Confederacy that the question becomes, Was not the South's cause lost before Confederates fired the first rounds at Fort Sumter? The answer quite simply is "no." Southerners expected to win—for some good reasons—and they came very close to doing so.

Southerners knew they bucked the military odds, but hadn't the **liberty**-loving colonists in 1776 also done so? "Britain could not conquer three million," a Louisianan proclaimed, and "the world cannot conquer the South." How could anyone doubt the outcome of a contest between lean, hard, country-born rebel warriors defending family, property, and liberty, and soft, flabby, citified Yankee mechanics waging an unconstitutional war?

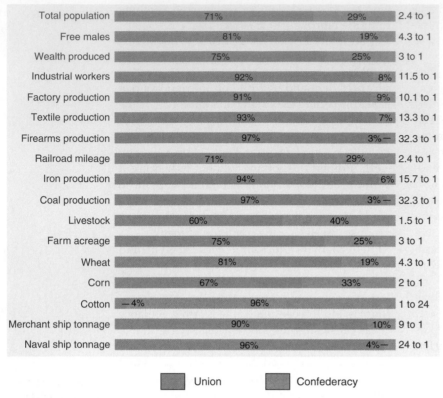

	Union	Confederacy	
Total population	71%	29%	2.4 to 1
Free males	81%	19%	4.3 to 1
Wealth produced	75%	25%	3 to 1
Industrial workers	92%	8%	11.5 to 1
Factory production	91%	9%	10.1 to 1
Textile production	93%	7%	13.3 to 1
Firearms production	97%	3%	32.3 to 1
Railroad mileage	71%	29%	2.4 to 1
Iron production	94%	6%	15.7 to 1
Coal production	97%	3%	32.3 to 1
Livestock	60%	40%	1.5 to 1
Farm acreage	75%	25%	3 to 1
Wheat	81%	19%	4.3 to 1
Corn	67%	33%	2 to 1
Cotton	4%	96%	1 to 24
Merchant ship tonnage	90%	10%	9 to 1
Naval ship tonnage	96%	4%	24 to 1

FIGURE 15.1   Resources of the Union and Confederacy
The Union's enormous statistical advantages failed to convince Confederates that their cause was doomed.

The South's confidence also rested on its belief that northern prosperity depended on the South's cotton. It followed that without cotton, New England textile mills would stand idle. And without southern **planters** purchasing northern manufactured goods, northern factories would drown in their own unsold goods. And without the foreign exchange earned by the overseas sales of cotton, the financial structure of the entire Yankee nation would collapse. A Virginian spoke for most Confederates when he declared that in the South's ability to "withhold the benefits of our trade, we hold a power over the North more powerful than a powerful army in the field."

Cotton would also make Europe a powerful ally of the Confederacy, Southerners reasoned. After all, they said, Britain's economy (and, to a lesser degree, France's) also depended on cotton. Of the 900 million pounds of cotton Britain imported annually, more than 700 million pounds came from the South. If the supply was interrupted, sheer economic need would make Britain (and perhaps France) a Confederate ally. And because the British navy ruled the seas, the North would find Britain a formidable foe.

Southerners' confidence may seem naive today, but even tough-minded European military observers picked the South to win. Offsetting the Union's power was the Confederacy's expanse. The North, Europeans predicted, could not conquer the vast territory (750,000 square miles) extending from the Potomac to the Rio Grande. To defeat the South, the Union would need to raise and equip a massive invading army and protect supply lines that would stretch farther than any in modern history.

Indeed, the South enjoyed major advantages, and the Confederacy devised a military strategy to exploit them. It recognized that a Union victory required the North to defeat and subjugate the South, but a Confederate victory required only that the South stay at home, blunt invasions, avoid battles that risked annihilating its army, and outlast the North's will to fight. When an opportunity presented itself, the South would strike the invaders. Like the American colonists, the South could win independence by not losing the war.

If the North did nothing, the South would by default establish itself as a sovereign nation. The Lincoln administration, therefore, adopted an offensive strategy that applied pressure at many points. Lincoln declared a naval blockade of the Confederacy to deny the South the advantages offered by its most valuable commodity—cotton. Without the sale of cotton abroad, the South would have far fewer dollars to pay for war goods. Even before the North could mount an effective blockade, however, Jefferson Davis decided voluntarily to cease exporting cotton. He wanted to create a cotton "famine" that would enfeeble the northern economy and precipitate European intervention. But the cotton famine Davis created devastated the South, not the North, and left Europe on the diplomatic sidelines. Lincoln also ordered the Union army into Virginia, at the same time planning a march through the Mississippi valley that would cut the Confederacy in two. This ambitious strategy took advantage of the Union's superior resources.

Neither side could foresee the magnitude and duration of the war. Americans thought of war in terms of their most recent experience, the Mexican-American War of the 1840s. In Mexico, fighting had taken place between relatively small armies, had cost relatively few lives, and had inflicted only light damage on the countryside. On the eve of the Civil War, they could not know that four ghastly years of bloodletting lay ahead.

Lincoln and Davis Mobilize

Mobilization required effective political leadership, and at first glance, the South appeared to have the advantage. Jefferson Davis brought to the Confederate presidency a distinguished political career, including experience in the U.S. Senate. He was also a West Point graduate, a combat veteran and authentic hero of the Mexican-American War, and a former secretary of war. Dignified and ramrod straight, with "a jaw sawed in steel," Davis appeared to be everything a nation could want in a wartime leader.

In contrast, Abraham Lincoln brought to the White House one lackluster term in the House of Representatives and almost no administrative experience. His sole brush with anything military was as a captain in the militia in the Black Hawk War, a brief struggle in Illinois in 1832 in which whites expelled the last Indians from the state. Lincoln later joked about his service in the Black Hawk War as the time when he survived bloody encounters with mosquitoes and led raids on wild onion patches. The lanky, disheveled Illinois lawyer-politician looked anything but military or presidential in his bearing.

Davis, however, proved to be less than he appeared. Although he worked hard, he had no gift for military strategy yet intervened often in military affairs. He was an even less able political leader. Quarrelsome and proud, he had an acid tongue that made enemies the Confederacy could ill afford. He insisted on dealing with every scrap of paper that came across his desk, and he grew increasingly unbending and dogmatic. The Confederacy's intimidating problems might have defeated an even more talented leader, however. For example, **state sovereignty**, which was enshrined in the Confederate constitution, made Davis's task of organizing a new nation and fighting a war difficult in the extreme.

With Lincoln, in contrast, the North got far more than met the eye. He proved himself a master politician and a superb leader. When forming his cabinet, Lincoln appointed the ablest men, no matter that they were often his chief rivals and critics. He appointed Salmon P. Chase secretary of the treasury, knowing that Chase had presidential ambitions. As secretary of state, he chose his chief opponent for the Republican nomination in 1860, William H. Seward. Despite his civilian background, Lincoln displayed an innate understanding of military strategy. No one was more crucial in mapping the Union war plan. Further, Lincoln wrote beautifully and through letters and speeches reached out to the North's people, helping to galvanize them in defense of the nation he called "the last best hope of earth."

Excavating for a New Junction at Devereux Station, Virginia
Confederates burned southern railroads and bridges to slow Union advances, cut federal supply lines, and protect Confederate retreats. Brigadier General Hermann Haupt, chief of construction and transportation for U.S. military railroads, was responsible for rebuilding what the Confederates destroyed. Here he is shown standing on the bank supervising work on a new junction for the Orange and Alexandria Railroad. Although railroads were first used as an instrument of war in the Crimea in the 1850s, they took on revolutionary importance in the Civil War. Railroads allowed for vastly increased overland mobility, more rapid deployment of men and materiel, and greater concentration of forces.
National Archives.

The Minié Ball

The Union army was one of the best-equipped armies in history, but none of its weaponry proved more vital than a French innovation by Captain Claude Minié. In 1848, Minié created an inch-long bullet that was rammed down a rifle barrel and would spin at great speed as it left the muzzle. The spin gave the bullet greater distance and accuracy than bullets fired from smoothbore weapons. When the war began, most soldiers carried smoothbore muskets, but by 1863 infantry on both sides fought with rifles. Bullets caused more than 90 percent of battle wounds, and minié balls proved extremely destructive to human bodies on impact.

Picture Research Consultants & Archives.

Lincoln and Davis began gathering their armies. Confederates had to build almost everything from scratch, and Northerners had to channel their superior numbers and industrial resources to the purposes of war. On the eve of the war, the federal army numbered only 16,000 men, most of them scattered over the West subjugating Indians. One-third of the officers followed the example of the Virginian Robert E. Lee, resigning their commissions and heading south. The U.S. navy was in better shape. Forty-two ships were in service, and a large merchant marine would in time provide more ships and sailors for the Union cause. Possessing a much weaker navy, the South pinned its hopes on its armies.

The Confederacy made prodigious efforts to build new factories to produce tents, blankets, shoes, and its gray uniforms, but many rebel soldiers slept in the open air without proper clothes and sometimes without shoes. Even when factories managed to produce what the soldiers needed, southern railroads often could not deliver the goods. And each year, more railroads were captured, destroyed, or left in disrepair. Food production proved less of a problem, but food sometimes rotted before it reached the soldiers. The one bright spot was the Confederacy's Ordnance Bureau, headed by Josiah Gorgas, a near miracle worker when it came to manufacturing gunpowder, cannons, and rifles. In April 1864, Gorgas proudly observed: "Where three years ago we were not making a gun, a pistol nor a sabre, no shot nor shell . . . —a pound of powder—we now make all these in quantities to meet the demands of our large armies."

Recruiting and supplying huge armies required enormous new revenues. At first, the Union and the Confederacy sold war bonds, which essentially were loans from patriotic citizens. In addition, both sides turned to taxes. The North raised one-fifth of its wartime revenue from taxes; the South raised only one-twentieth. Eventually, both began printing paper money. Inflation soared, but the Confederacy suffered more because it financed a greater part of its wartime costs through the printing press. Prices in the Union rose by about 80 percent during the war, while inflation in the Confederacy topped 9,000 percent.

Within months of the bombardment of Fort Sumter, both sides found men to fight and ways to supply and support them. But the underlying strength of the northern economy gave the Union the decided advantage. With their military and industrial muscles beginning to ripple, Northerners became itchy for action. They wanted an invasion that once and for all would smash the rebellion. Horace Greeley's *New York Tribune* began to chant: "Forward to Richmond! Forward to Richmond!"

> **REVIEW** Why did the South believe it could win the war despite numerical disadvantages?

Battling It Out, 1861–1862

During the first year and a half of the war, armies fought major campaigns in both East and West. Because the rival capitals—Richmond and Washington, D.C.—were only ninety miles apart and each was threatened more than once with capture, the eastern campaign was especially dramatic. But the battles in the West proved more decisive. As Yankee and rebel armies pounded each other on land, the navies fought on the seas and on the rivers of the South. In Europe, Confederate and U.S. diplomats competed for advantage in the corridors of power. All the while, casualty lists on both sides reached appalling lengths.

Stalemate in the Eastern Theater

Irvin McDowell, commanding general of the Union army assembling outside Washington, had no thought of taking his raw recruits into battle during the summer of 1861. Lincoln, however,

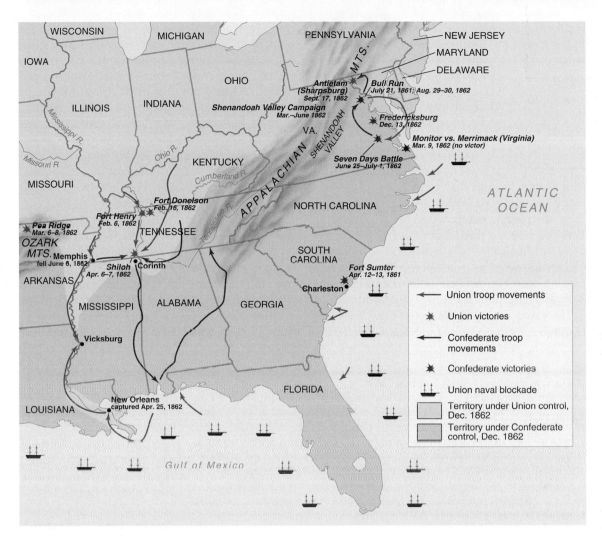

MAP 15.2   The Civil War, 1861–1862

While most eyes were focused on the eastern theater, especially the ninety-mile stretch of land between Washington, D.C., and the Confederate capital of Richmond, Virginia, Union troops were winning strategic victories in the West.

READING THE MAP: In which states did the Confederacy and the Union each win the most battles during this period? Which side used or followed water routes most for troop movements and attacks?

CONNECTIONS: Which major cities in the South and West fell to Union troops in 1862? Which strategic area did those Confederate losses place in Union hands? How did this outcome affect the later movement of troops and supplies?

FOR MORE HELP ANALYZING THIS MAP, see the visual activity for this chapter in the Online Study Guide at bedfordstmartins.com/roark.

ordered him to prepare his 35,000 troops for an attack on the 20,000 Confederates defending Manassas, a railroad junction in Virginia about thirty miles southwest of Washington. On July 21, the Union army forded Bull Run, a branch of the Potomac River, and engaged the southern forces (Map 15.2). But fast-moving southern reinforcements blunted the Union attack and then counterattacked. What began as an orderly Union retreat turned into a panicky stampede. Demoralized federal troops ran over shocked civilians as the soldiers raced back to Washington.

By Civil War standards, the casualties (wounded and dead) at Bull Run (or Manassas, as Southerners called the battle) were light, about 2,000 Confederates and 1,600 Federals. The significance of the battle lay in the lessons Northerners and Southerners drew from it. For

Southerners, it confirmed the superiority of rebel fighting men and the inevitability of Confederate nationhood. Manassas was *"one of the decisive battles of the world,"* a Georgian proclaimed. It *"has* secured our independence." While victory elevated southern pride, defeat sobered Northerners. It was a major setback, admitted the *New York Tribune,* but "let us go to work, then, with a will." Bull Run taught Lincoln that victory would be neither quick nor easy. Within four days of the disaster, the president authorized the enlistment of 1 million men for three years.

> "If General McClellan does not want to use the army I would like to *borrow* it," Lincoln declared in frustration.

Lincoln also found a new general, replacing McDowell with young George B. McClellan. Having been born in Philadelphia of well-to-do parents and graduated from West Point second in his class, the thirty-four-year-old McClellan believed that he was a great soldier and that Lincoln was a dunce, the "original Gorilla." A superb administrator and organizer, McClellan came to Washington as commander of the newly named Army of the Potomac. McClellan energetically whipped his dispirited army into shape but was reluctant to send his soldiers into battle. For all his energy, McClellan lacked decisiveness. Lincoln wanted a general who would advance, take risks, and fight, but McClellan went into winter quarters. "If General McClellan does not want to use the army I would like to *borrow* it," Lincoln declared in frustration.

Finally, in May 1862, McClellan launched his long-awaited offensive. He transported his highly polished army, now 130,000 strong, to the mouth of the James River and began slowly moving up the Yorktown peninsula toward Richmond. When he was within six miles of the Confederate capital, General Joseph Johnston hit him like a hammer. In the assault, Johnston was wounded and was replaced by Robert E. Lee, who would become the South's most celebrated general. Lee named his command the Army of Northern Virginia.

The contrast between Lee and McClellan could hardly have been greater. McClellan brimmed with conceit and braggadocio; Lee was courteous and reserved. On the battlefield, McClellan grew timid and irresolute, and Lee became audaciously, even recklessly, aggressive. And Lee had at his side in the peninsula campaign military men of real talent: Thomas J. Jackson, nicknamed "Stonewall" for holding the line at Manassas, and James E. B. ("Jeb") Stuart, a dashing twenty-nine-year-old cavalry commander who rode circles around Yankee troops.

Lee's assault initiated the Seven Days Battle (June 25–July 1) and began McClellan's march back down the peninsula. By the time McClellan reached the safety of the Union navy, 30,000 men from both sides

The Battle of Savage's Station, by Robert Knox Sneden, 1862

In 1862, thirty-year-old Robert Sneden joined the Fortieth New York Volunteers and soon found himself in Virginia, part of George McClellan's peninsula campaign. A gifted artist in watercolors as well as an eloquent writer, Sneden captured an early Confederate assault in what became known as the Seven Days Battle. "The immense open space in front of Savage's [house] was densely thronged with wagon trains, artillery, caissons, ammunition trains, and moving troops," Sneden observed. The "storm of lead was continuous and deadly on the approaching lines of the Rebels. They bravely rushed up, however, to within twenty feet of our artillery, when bushels of grape and canister from the cannon laid them low in rows." Over the next three years, Sneden produced hundreds of vivid drawings and eventually thousands of pages of remembrances, providing one of the most complete accounts of a Union soldier's Civil War experience.

© 1996, Lora Robbins Collection of Virginia Art, Virginia Historical Society.

had died or been wounded. Although Southerners suffered twice the casualties of Northerners, Lee had saved Richmond and achieved a strategic success. Lincoln wired McClellan to abandon the peninsula campaign and replaced him with General John Pope.

In August, north of Richmond, at the second battle of Bull Run, Lee's smaller army battered Pope's forces and sent them scurrying back to Washington. Lincoln ordered Pope to Minnesota to pacify the Indians and restored McClellan to command. Lincoln had not changed his mind about McClellan's capacity as a warrior, but he reluctantly acknowledged that "if he can't fight himself, he excels in making others ready to fight."

Lee could fight, and sensing that he had the enemy on the ropes, Lee sought to land the knockout punch. He pushed his army across the Potomac and invaded Maryland. A victory on northern soil would dislodge Maryland from the Union, Lee reasoned, and might even cause Lincoln to sue for peace. On September 17, 1862, McClellan's forces engaged Lee's army at Antietam Creek (see Map 15.2). Earlier, a Union soldier had found a copy of Lee's orders to his army wrapped around some cigars dropped by a careless Confederate officer, so McClellan had a clear picture of Lee's position. McClellan's characteristic caution, however, cost him the opportunity to destroy the opposing army. Still, he did severe damage. With "solid shot . . . cracking skulls like eggshells," according to one observer, the armies went after each other. At Miller's Cornfield, the firing was so intense that "every stalk of corn in the . . . field was cut as closely as could have been done with a knife." By nightfall, 6,000 men lay dead or dying on the battlefield, and 17,000 more had been wounded. The battle of Antietam would be the bloodiest day of the war. More American soldiers died in a single day than died in the entire Revolutionary War. Instead of being the war-winning fight Lee had anticipated when he came north, Antietam sent the battered Army of Northern Virginia limping back home. McClellan claimed to have saved the North, but Lincoln again removed him

The Dead of Antietam
In October 1862, photographer Mathew Brady opened an exhibition at his New York gallery that shocked the nation. Titled The Dead of Antietam, the exhibition consisted of ninety-five photographs that presented the battle of Antietam as the soldiers saw it. The photograph included here shows fallen Confederate soldiers along a rail fence on the Hagerstown Pike. Among the thousands of visitors to the exhibit was a reporter for the *New York Times* who observed, "Mr. Brady has done something to bring to us the terrible reality and earnestness of the war. If he has not brought bodies and laid them in our door-yards and along [our] streets, he has done something very like it."
Library of Congress.

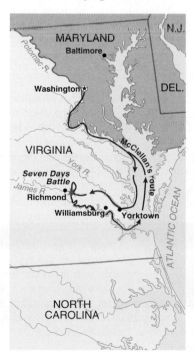

Peninsula Campaign, 1862

from command of the Army of the Potomac and appointed General Ambrose Burnside.

Though bloodied, Lee found an opportunity in December to punish the enemy at Fredericksburg, Virginia, where Burnside's 122,000 Union troops faced 78,500 Confederates dug in behind a stone wall on the heights above the Rappahannock River. Half a mile of open ground separated the armies. "A chicken could not live on that field when we open on it," a Confederate artillery officer predicted. Yet Burnside ordered a frontal assault. When the shooting ceased, the Federals counted nearly 13,000 casualties, the Confederates fewer than 5,000. The battle of Fredericksburg was one of the Union's worst defeats. As 1862 ended, the North seemed no nearer to ending the rebellion than it had been when the war began. Rather than checkmate, military struggle in the East had reached stalemate.

Union Victories in the Western Theater

While most eyes focused on events in the East, the decisive early encounters of the war were taking place between the Appalachian Mountains and the Ozarks (see Map 15.2). The West's rivers—the Mississippi, the Tennessee, and the Cumberland—became the keys to the military situation. Looking northward along the three rivers, Southerners spied Missouri and Kentucky, states they claimed but did not control. Looking southward, Northerners saw that if they controlled the Mississippi River, they would split Arkansas, Louisiana, and Texas from the Confederacy. Moreover, the Cumberland and Tennessee rivers penetrated Tennessee, one of the Confederacy's main producers of food, mules, and iron—all vital resources.

Before Union forces could march on Tennessee, they needed to secure Missouri to the west. Union troops commanded by General Samuel R. Curtis swept across Missouri to the border of Arkansas, where in March 1862, they encountered General Earl Van Dorn's 16,000-man Confederate army, which included three regiments of Indians from the Five Civilized Tribes in Indian Territory. Although Indians fought on both sides during the war, Native Americans who sided with the South hoped that the Confederacy would grant them more independence than had the United States. Curtis's victory at the battle of Pea Ridge left Missouri free of Confederate troops, but Missouri was not free of Confederate guerrillas. Guerrilla bands led by the notorious William Clarke Quantrill and "Bloody Bill" Anderson burned, tortured, scalped, and murdered Union civilians and soldiers until the final year of the war.

Even farther west, Confederate armies sought to fulfill Jefferson Davis's vision of a slaveholding empire stretching all the way to the Pacific. Both sides recognized the immense value of the gold and silver mines of California, Nevada, and Colorado. A quick strike by Texas troops took Santa Fe, New Mexico, in the winter of 1861–62. Then in March 1862, a band of Colorado miners ambushed and crushed southern forces at Glorieta Pass, outside Santa Fe. Confederate military failures in the far West meant that there would be no Confederate empire beyond Texas.

The principal western battles took place in Tennessee, where General Ulysses S. Grant emerged as the key northern commander. Grant had graduated from West Point and served bravely in Mexico. When the Civil War began, he was a thirty-nine-year-old dry-goods clerk in Galena, Illinois. Gentle at home, he became pugnacious on the battlefield. "The art of war is simple," he said. "Find out where your enemy is, get at him as soon as you can and strike him

Native American Recruits
Both the Union and the Confederacy sought soldiers from tribes in Indian Territory. Here, a Union recruiter swears in Indian recruits, but it was the Confederacy that signed treaties with the so-called Five Civilized Tribes—the Choctaw, Chickasaw, Creek, Seminole, and Cherokee—in 1861. The Confederates promised to assume the financial obligations of the old treaties with the United States, guarantee slavery, respect the independence of the tribes, and permit the tribes to send delegates to Richmond. John Ross, chief of the Cherokee, prayed that he had chosen the right side. "We are in the situation of a man standing upon a low naked spot of ground," he said, "with the water rising all around him. . . . The tide carries by him, in its mad course, a drifting log. . . . By refusing it he is a doomed man. By seizing hold of it he has a chance for his life." Approximately 20,000 Indians fought in blue and in gray uniforms. In some battles in Arkansas, Indians fought Indians.
Wisconsin Historical Society.

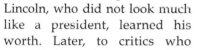

as hard as you can, and keep moving on." Grant's philosophy of war as attrition would take a huge toll in human life, but it played to the North's strength: superiority in manpower. In his private's uniform and slouch hat, Grant did not look much like a general. But Lincoln, who did not look much like a president, learned his worth. Later, to critics who wanted the president to sack Grant because of his drinking, Lincoln would say, *"I can't spare this man. He fights."*

Battle of Glorieta Pass, 1862

In February 1862, operating in tandem with U.S. navy gunboats, Grant captured Fort Henry on the Tennessee River and Fort Donelson on the Cumberland (see Map 15.2). Defeat forced the Confederates to withdraw from all of Kentucky and most of Tennessee, but Grant followed. On April 6, General Albert Sidney Johnston's army surprised him at Shiloh Church in Tennessee. Grant's troops were badly mauled the first day, but Grant remained cool and brought up reinforcements throughout the night. The next morning, the Union army counterattacked, driving the Confederates before it. The battle of Shiloh was terribly costly to both sides; there were 20,000 casualties, among them General Johnston. Grant later said that after Shiloh, he "gave up all idea of saving the Union except by complete conquest."

Although no one knew it at the time, Shiloh ruined the Confederacy's bid to control the theater of operations in the West. In short order, the Yankees captured the strategic town of Corinth, Mississippi; the river city of Memphis; and the South's largest city, New Orleans. By the end of 1862, the far West and most—but not all—of the Mississippi valley lay in Union hands. At the same time, the outcome of the struggle in another theater of war was also becoming clearer.

The Atlantic Theater

Both sides recognized the importance of the naval theater in the Atlantic. When the war began, the U.S. navy's blockade fleet consisted of about three dozen ships to patrol more than 3,500 miles of southern coastline, and rebel merchant ships were able to slip in and out of south-

ern ports nearly at will. Taking on cargoes in the Caribbean, sleek Confederate blockade runners brought in vital supplies—guns and medicine. But with the U.S. navy commissioning a new blockader almost weekly, the naval fleet eventually numbered 150 ships on duty, and the Union navy dramatically improved its score.

Unable to build a conventional navy equal to the expanding U.S. fleet, the Confederates experimented with a radical new maritime design: the ironclad warship. At Norfolk, Virginia, they layered the wooden hull of the frigate *Merrimack* with two-inch-thick armor plate. Rechristened *Virginia*, the ship steamed out in March 1862 and sank two wooden federal ships, killing at least 240 Union sailors (see Map 15.2). When the *Virginia* returned to finish off the federal blockaders the next morning, it was challenged by the *Monitor*, a federal ironclad of even more radical design, topped with a revolving turret holding two eleven-inch guns. On March 9, the two ships hurled shells at each other for two hours, but neither could penetrate the other's armor, and the battle ended in a draw.

The Confederacy never found a way to break the Union blockade despite exploring

Major Battles of the Civil War, 1861–1862

April 12–13, 1861	Attack on Fort Sumter
July 21, 1861	First battle of Bull Run (Manassas)
February 6, 1862	Battle of Fort Henry
February 16, 1862	Battle of Fort Donelson
March 6–8, 1862	Battle of Pea Ridge
March 9, 1862	Battle of the *Merrimack* (the *Virginia*) and the *Monitor*
March 26, 1862	Battle of Glorieta Pass
April 6–7, 1862	Battle of Shiloh
May–July 1862	McClellan's peninsula campaign
June 6, 1862	Fall of Memphis
June 25–July 1, 1862	Seven Days Battle
August 29–30, 1862	Second battle of Bull Run (Manassas)
September 17, 1862	Battle of Antietam
December 13, 1862	Battle of Fredericksburg

many naval innovations, including a new underwater vessel—the submarine. (See "The Promise of Technology," page 526.) It placed its greatest hope in destroying enough Union ships to force the blockading squadrons to withdraw to protect the northern merchant marine. The British-built Confederate cruiser *Alabama* sank or captured sixty-four Union merchant ships before the USS *Kearsarge* sank it off the coast of France in 1864. But each month, the Union fleet tightened its noose. By 1863, the South had abandoned its embargo policy and desperately wanted to ship cotton to pay for imports of arms, bullets, shoes, and uniforms needed to fight the war. The growing effectiveness of the federal blockade, a southern naval officer observed, "shut the Confederacy out from the world, deprived it of supplies, weakened its military and naval strength." By 1865, the blockaders were intercepting about half of the southern ships attempting to break through. The Confederacy was sealed off, with devastating results.

International Diplomacy

What the Confederates could not achieve on the seas, they sought to achieve through international diplomacy. Confederates and Unionists both recognized that the world was watching the struggle in North America. Nationalists everywhere understood that the American Civil War involved issues central to their own nation-building efforts. The Confederates rested their claims to separate nationhood on the principles of self-determination and rightful rebellion against tyrannical power, and they desperately wanted Europe to intervene. The Lincoln administration explained why the Union had to be preserved and Europe had to remain neutral. "The question," Lincoln explained, is "whether a constitutional republic, or a democracy—a government of the people, by the same people—can or cannot, maintain its territorial integrity, against its own domestic foes."

More practically, the Confederates based their hope for European support on King Cotton. In theory, cotton-starved European nations would have no choice but to break the Union blockade and recognize the Confederacy. Southern hopes were not unreasonable, for at the height of the "cotton famine" in 1862, when 2 million British workers were unemployed, Britain tilted toward

> As the great English liberal John Stuart Mill declared, a Confederate victory "would give courage to the enemies of progress and damp the spirits of its friends all over the civilized world."

recognition. Along with several other European nations, Britain granted the Confederacy "belligerent" status, which enabled it to buy goods and build ships in European ports. But no country challenged the blockade or recognized the Confederate States of America as a nation, a bold act that probably would have drawn that country into war with the United States and perhaps tipped the balance in the South's favor.

King Cotton diplomacy failed for several reasons. A bumper cotton crop in 1860 meant that the warehouses of British textile manufacturers bulged with surplus cotton throughout 1861. In 1862, when a cotton shortage did occur, European manufacturers found new sources in India, Egypt, and elsewhere. (See "Global Comparison.") In addition, the development of a brisk trade between the Union and Britain—British war materiel for American grain and flour—helped offset the decline in textiles and encouraged Britain to remain neutral.

Europe's temptation to intervene disappeared for good in 1862. Union military successes in the West made Britain and France think twice about linking their fates to the struggling Confederacy. Moreover, in September 1862, five days after the Union victory at Antietam, Lincoln announced a new policy that made an alliance with the Confederacy an alliance with slavery—a commitment the French and British, who had outlawed slavery in their empires and looked forward to its eradication worldwide, were not willing to make. After 1862, the South's cause was linked irrevocably with slavery and reaction, and the Union's cause was linked with freedom and democracy. As the great English liberal John Stuart Mill declared, a Confederate victory "would give courage to the enemies of progress and damp the spirits of its friends all over the civilized world." The Union, not the Confederacy, had won the diplomatic stakes.

REVIEW   Why did the Confederacy's bid for international support fail?

Union *and* Freedom

For a year and a half, Lincoln insisted that the North fought strictly to save the Union and not to abolish slavery. Despite Lincoln's repeated pronouncements, however, the war for union became a war for African American freedom. Each month the conflict dragged on, it became clearer

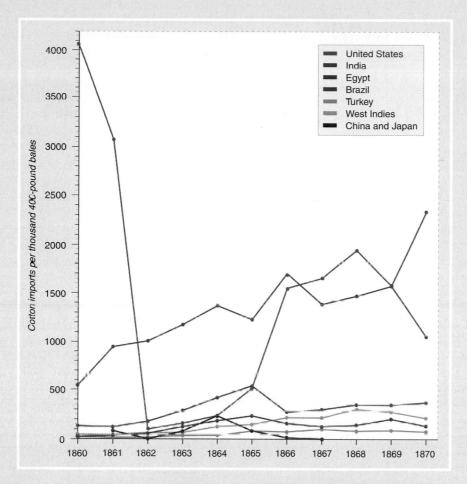

In 1860, the South enjoyed a near monopoly in supplying cotton to Europe's textile mills, but the Civil War almost entirely halted its exports. Figures for Europe's importation of cotton for 1861 to 1865 reveal one of the reasons the Confederacy's King Cotton diplomacy failed: Europeans found other sources of cotton. Which countries were most important in filling the void? When the war ended in 1865, cotton production resumed in the South, and exports to Europe again soared. Did the South regain its near monopoly? How would you characterize the United States' competitive position five years after the war?

that the Confederate war machine depended heavily on slavery. Rebel armies used slaves to build fortifications, haul materiel, tend horses, and perform camp chores. On the home front, slaves labored in ironworks and shipyards, and they grew the food that fed both soldiers and civilians. Slavery undergirded the Confederacy as certainly as it had the Old South. Union military commanders and politicians alike gradually realized that to defeat the Confederacy, the North would have to destroy slavery. "I am a slow walker," Lincoln said, "but I never walk back."

From Slaves to Contraband

Lincoln detested human bondage, but as president he felt compelled to act prudently in the interests of the Union. He doubted his right under the Constitution to tamper with the "domestic institutions" of any state, even states in rebellion. An astute politician, Lincoln worked within the tight limits of public opinion. The issue of black freedom was particularly explosive in the loyal border states, where slaveholders threatened to jump into the arms of the Confederacy at even

CSS *H. L. Hunley:* The World's First Successful Submarine

The Confederacy had no navy when it was born in 1861, and without major shipyards, it could never build a fleet to match that of the Union. As the federal blockade of southern ports gradually began to strangle Confederate shipping, Southerners were forced to innovate in naval technology: the ironclad, floating mines (called torpedoes), and, most spectacular of all, the submarine.

On the bone-chilling night of February 17, 1864, a lookout aboard the USS *Housatonic,* the largest ship among the Union blockaders off Charleston, noticed something in the water. It might have been just a log or a porpoise, but he was jumpy because of rumors of a Confederate secret weapon roaming the ocean— something Union sailors called the "infernal machine"—and he sounded the alarm. The *Housatonic's* cannons could not target something so low in the water, and the ship's crew soon discovered that rifle and revolver rounds did not stop it.

Just below the surface of the Atlantic, eight sweating men at hand cranks propelled their peculiar vessel—a submarine named the *H. L. Hunley*—toward the Union blockader. The *Hunley* rammed a 135-pound explosive, which was lashed to a spar protruding from its bow, into the *Housatonic* just below its waterline, then quickly backed out as the 150-foot detonation rope played out. Within seconds, an explosion ripped the big Union ship, and it quickly sank to the bottom. Five sailors lost their lives, as the *Housatonic* became the first ship ever sunk by a submarine. The *Hunley* then surfaced, and the crew flashed a light to their comrades onshore to signal a successful mission. Minutes later, the *Hunley* and its crew vanished, never to resurface again.

Three years of trial-and-error experimentation and wartime innovation had produced the *Hunley.* Shortly after the war began, a group of New Orleans engineers and investors, including H. L. Hunley, imagined a new kind of ship—an underwater vessel that could defend the city from federal naval assaults. First, they built the *Pioneer,* a cigar-shaped submarine with a crew of two, but Admiral David Farragut's Union fleet captured New Orleans before the *Pioneer* could go into action. Hunley and his partners moved their operations to Mobile, Alabama, where they built a second underwater ship, the *American Diver*, with a four-man crew. The builders experimented with propelling the submarine with an electromagnetic engine, but when the device failed to generate enough power, they returned to the hand-crank design. Stormy seas sank the *American Diver* in February 1863, but within weeks, the civilian builders, now joined by the Confederate military, began work on a third submarine, the *H. L. Hunley.*

A sleek, forty-foot, nine-man version based on previous efforts, the *Hunley* was an engineering marvel that exhibited both sophisticated technology and primitive features. Ballast tanks at both ends of the hull could be flooded to submerge the craft and emptied to make it rise to the surface. Two lateral fins, or adjustable dive planes, adjusted the ship's underwater depth. The captain steered the sub with a vertical rod attached to the rudder, perhaps the world's first joystick for navigating a vessel. A 4,000-pound keel ensured that the ship would remain upright as it slipped through the water. Eight men, squeezed into a space no more than four feet high, turned a crankshaft connected to a propeller. The ship had two towers

---

the hint of emancipation. Black freedom also raised alarms in the free states. The Democratic Party gave notice that emancipation would make the war strictly a Republican affair. Democrats marched under the banner "The Constitution As It Is, the Union As It Was."

Moreover, many white Northerners were not about to risk their lives to satisfy what they considered abolitionist "fanaticism." "We Won't Fight to Free the Nigger," one popular banner read. They feared that emancipation would propel "two or three million semi-savages" northward, where they would crowd into white neighborhoods, compete for white jobs, and mix with white "sons and daughters." Thus, emancipation threatened to dislodge the loyal slave states from

with manholes secured by hatch covers fitted with watertight rubber gaskets that the crew secured from inside. Each tower also had small round windows. The vessel had a kind of snorkel for air, but it never worked, which meant that the sub had to surface every half hour or so for fresh air. The *Hunley* also was outfitted with a mercury depth gauge, a compass, and a single wax candle for light, which also provided a warning when oxygen was dangerously low.

Desperate to break the Union blockade in Charleston, General P. G. T. Beauregard ordered the *Hunley* loaded on a train and shipped from Mobile to Charleston harbor. Test runs began immediately, and the sub sank twice, with the loss of thirteen men, including H. L. Hunley. The sinkings were apparently caused by accidents, not design flaws. After the second accident, however, Beauregard declared, "I can have nothing more to do with that submarine boat. It is more dangerous to those who use it than the enemy." But Charleston's plight caused him to raise the sub and man it with an all-volunteer crew. After the *Hunley* destroyed the *Housatonic* and itself sank for the third and final time, no other submarine would sink an enemy ship until World War I, more than half a century later.

Much of what we know about the world's first successful submarine rests on the discovery of the *Hunley* in May 1995. It was found four miles off Sullivan's Island, South Carolina, in thirty feet of water and under three feet of sand. One marine **archaeologist** has described it as "the find of the century." Raised in August 2000 and deposited in a large steel tank filled with 55,000 gallons of cold fresh water to protect it from further deterioration, the *Hunley* is now the object of intensive investigation. Archaeologists, metallurgists, neuroscientists, forensic scientists, and historians are successfully teasing evidence of its past from its remains. Essentially a time capsule, the *Hunley* has not yet given an answer to the question of why it did not return safely to Charleston harbor, but investigators are closing in on the mystery.

The C.S.S. H. L. Hunley *at Charleston, 6 December 1863*, by Conrad Wise Chapman This striking image of the *Hunley* makes clear why General P. G. T. Beauregard felt compelled to explain to men who were considering volunteering for its crew the "desperately hazardous nature of the service required." The artist contrasts the grim reality of the submarine with the beautiful (and safe) sailboat in the distance. U.S. Naval Historical Center.

the Union, alienate the Democratic Party, deplete the armies, and perhaps even spark race warfare.

Yet proponents of emancipation pressed Lincoln as relentlessly as the anti-emancipation forces. Abolitionists argued that by seceding, Southerners had forfeited their right to the protection of the Constitution, and that Lincoln could—as the price of their treason—legally confiscate their property in slaves. When Lincoln refused, abolitionists scalded him. Frederick Douglass labeled him "the miserable tool of traitors and rebels." Abolitionists won increasing numbers of converts during the war, especially among the radical faction of the Republican Party.

The Republican-dominated Congress declined to leave slavery policy entirely in President

Lincoln's hands. In August 1861, Congress approved the Confiscation Act, which allowed the seizure of any slave employed directly by the Confederate military. It also fulfilled the **free-soil** dream of prohibiting slavery in the territories and abolished slavery in Washington, D.C. Democrats and border-state representatives voted against even these mild measures, but Congress's attitude was clearly stiffening against slavery.

> In 1862, Lincoln defended colonization to a delegation of black visitors to the White House. One of the visitors told the president, "This is our country as much as it is yours, and we will not leave."

Slaves, not politicians, became the most insistent force for emancipation. By escaping their masters by the tens of thousands and running away to Union lines, they forced slavery on the North's wartime agenda. Runaways precipitated a series of momentous decisions. Were the runaways now free, or were they still slaves who, according to the fugitive slave law, had to be returned to their masters? At first, Yankee military officers sent the fugitives back. But Union armies needed laborers, and some officers accepted the runaways and put them to work. At Fort Monroe, Virginia, General Benjamin F. Butler refused to turn them over to their owners, calling them "contraband of war," meaning "confiscated property." Congress made Butler's practice national policy in March 1862 when it forbade returning fugitive slaves to their masters. Slaves were still not legally free, but there was a tilt toward emancipation.

Lincoln's policy of noninterference with slavery gradually crumbled. To calm Northerners' racial fears, Lincoln offered **colonization**, the deportation of African Americans from the United States to Haiti, Panama, or elsewhere. (For earlier colonization efforts to Liberia, see chapter 12, "Beyond America's Borders," page 428.) In the summer of 1862, he defended colonization to a delegation of black visitors to the White House. He told them that deep-seated racial prejudice made it impossible for blacks to achieve equality in this country. One of the visiting African Americans told the president, "This is our country as much as it is yours, and we will not leave." Congress voted a small amount of money to underwrite colonization, but after one miserable experiment on a small island in the Caribbean, practical limitations and black opposition sank further efforts.

While Lincoln was developing his own initiatives, he snuffed out actions that he believed would jeopardize northern unity. He was particularly alert to Union commanders who tried to dictate slavery policy from the field. In August 1861, when John C. Frémont, former Republican presidential nominee and now commander of federal troops in Missouri, freed the slaves belonging to Missouri rebels, Lincoln forced the general to revoke his edict and then removed him from command. The following May, when General David Hunter freed the slaves in Georgia, South Carolina, and Florida, Lincoln countermanded his order. Events moved so rapidly, however, that Lincoln found it impossible to control federal policy on slavery.

From Contraband to Free People

On August 22, 1862, Lincoln replied to an angry abolitionist who demanded that he attack slavery. "My paramount objective in this struggle *is* to save the Union," Lincoln said deliberately, "and is *not* either to save or destroy slavery. If I could save the Union without freeing *any* slave I would do it, and if I could save it by freeing *all*

Human Contraband

This grainy photograph shows a black family approaching Union lines in 1862, seeking sanctuary with the federal army. Most slaves fled with little more than the clothes on their backs, but not all escaped slavery empty-handed. The mules, wagon, and goods seen here could have been procured by a number of means—purchased during slavery, "borrowed" from the former master, or found during flight. Refugees who possessed draft animals and a wagon had many more economic opportunities than those who had only their labor to sell.

National Archives.

the slaves I would do it; and if I could save it by freeing some and leaving others alone I would also do that." Instead of simply restating his old position that union was the North's sole objective, Lincoln announced that slavery was no longer untouchable and that he would emancipate every slave if doing so would preserve the Union.

By the summer of 1862, events were tumbling rapidly toward emancipation. On July 17, Congress adopted the second Confiscation Act. The first had confiscated slaves employed by the Confederate military; the second declared all slaves of rebel masters "forever free of their servitude." In theory, this breathtaking measure freed most Confederate slaves, for slaveholders formed the backbone of the rebellion. Congress had traveled far since the war began.

Lincoln had, too. On July 21, the president informed his cabinet that he was ready "to take some definitive steps in respect to military action and slavery." The next day, he read a draft of a preliminary emancipation proclamation that promised to free *all* the slaves in the seceding states on January 1, 1863. Lincoln described emancipation as an "act of justice," but it was the lengthening casualty lists that finally brought him around. Emancipation, he declared, was "a military necessity, absolutely essential to the preservation of the Union." Only freeing the slaves would "strike at the heart of the rebellion." On September 22, Lincoln issued his preliminary Emancipation Proclamation promising freedom to slaves in areas still in rebellion on January 1, 1863.

The limitations of the proclamation—it exempted the loyal border states and the Union-occupied areas of the Confederacy—caused some to ridicule the act. The *Times* (London) observed cynically, "Where he has no power Mr. Lincoln will set the negroes free, where he retains power he will consider them as slaves." But Lincoln had no power to free slaves in loyal states, and invading Union armies would liberate slaves in the Confederacy as they advanced.

By presenting emancipation as a "military necessity," Lincoln hoped he had disarmed his **conservative** critics. Emancipation would deprive the Confederacy of valuable slave laborers, shorten the war, and thus save lives. Democrats, however, fumed that the "shrieking and howling abolitionist faction" had captured the White House and made it "a nigger war." Democrats made political hay out of Lincoln's action in the November 1862 elections, gaining thirty-four congressional seats. House Democrats quickly proposed a resolution branding emancipation "a high crime against the Constitution." The Republicans, who maintained narrow majorities in both houses of Congress, beat it back.

As promised, on New Year's Day 1863, Lincoln issued the final Emancipation Proclamation. In addition to freeing the slaves in the rebel states, the edict also committed the federal government to the fullest use of African Americans to defeat the Confederate enemy.

War of Black Liberation

Even before Lincoln proclaimed freedom a Union war aim, African Americans in the North had volunteered to fight. But the War Department, doubtful of their abilities and fearful of white reaction to serving side by side with them, refused to make black men soldiers. Instead, the army employed black men as manual laborers; black women sometimes found employment as laundresses and cooks. The navy, however, accepted blacks from the outset, including runaway slaves such as William Gould.

As the Union experienced manpower shortages, Northerners gradually and reluctantly turned to African Americans to fill the Union army's blue uniforms. With the Militia Act of July 1862, Congress authorized enrolling blacks in "any military or naval service for which they may be found competent." After the Emancipation Proclamation, whites—like it or not—were fighting and dying for black freedom, and few insisted that blacks remain out of harm's way behind the lines. Indeed, whites insisted that

> Emancipation, Lincoln declared, was "a military necessity, absolutely essential to the preservation of the Union." Only freeing the slaves would "strike at the heart of the rebellion."

blacks share the danger, especially after March 1863, when Congress resorted to the **draft** to fill the Union army.

The military was far from color-blind. The Union army established segregated black regiments, paid black soldiers $10 per month rather than the $13 it paid whites, refused blacks the opportunity to become commissioned officers, punished blacks as if they were slaves, and assigned blacks to labor battalions rather than to combat units. Still, when the war ended, 179,000 African American men had served in the Union military, approximately 10 percent of the total army. An astounding 71 percent of black men ages eighteen to forty-five in the free states wore Union blue, a participation rate that was substantially higher than that of white men. More than 130,000 black soldiers came from the slave states, perhaps 100,000 of them ex-slaves.

In time, whites allowed blacks to put down their shovels and to shoulder rifles. At the battles of Port Hudson and Milliken's Bend on the Mississippi River and at Fort Wagner in Charleston harbor, black courage under fire finally dispelled notions that African Americans could not fight. More than 38,000 black soldiers died in the Civil War, a mortality rate that was higher than that of white troops. Blacks played a crucial role in the triumph of the Union and the destruction of slavery in the South. (See "Seeking the American Promise," page 532.)

REVIEW Why did the Union change policy in 1863 to allow black men to serve in the army?

The South at War

By seceding, Southerners brought on themselves a firestorm of unimaginable fury. Monstrous losses on the battlefield nearly bled the Confederacy to death. White Southerners on the home front also suffered, even at the hands of their own government. Efforts by the Davis administration in Richmond to centralize power in order to fight the war effectively convinced some men and women that the Confederacy had betrayed them. Wartime economic changes hurt everyone, some more than others. By 1863, planters and **yeomen** who had stood together began to drift apart. Most disturbing of all, slaves became open participants in the destruction of slavery and the Confederacy.

Black Soldiers at Work on the Dutch Gap Canal in Virginia, November 1864
Although African Americans joined the Union army to strike at slavery, they often found themselves wielding picks and shovels rather than rifles. Five months before this photograph was taken, Union officials had banned excessive fatigue duty for black troops. Many commanders ignored the rules, however, and continued to make discriminatory labor assignments.
Chicago Historical Society.

Confederate Soldiers and Their Slaves
Soldiers of the Seventh Tennessee Cavalry pose with their slaves. Many slaveholders took "body servants" with them to war. These slaves cooked, washed, and cleaned for the white soldiers. In 1861, James H. Langhorne reported to his sister: "Peter . . . is charmed with being with me & 'being a soldier.' I gave him my old uniform overcoat & he says he is going to have his picture taken . . . to send to the servants." Do you think Peter was "puttin' on ol' massa" or just glad to be free of plantation labor?

Daguerreotype courtesy of Tom Farish. Photographed by Michael Latil.

READING THE IMAGE: What can we glean from this image about a Confederate soldier's life in the military? **CONNECTIONS:** This daguerreotype likely was not taken for any purpose other than to capture the camaraderie of four southern cavalrymen, yet the inclusion of the two slaves speaks volumes. What are the possible ramifications of slaveholders bringing "body servants" to war?

FOR MORE HELP ANALYZING THIS IMAGE, see the visual activity for this chapter in the Online Study Guide at
bedfordstmartins.com/roark.

Revolution from Above

As a Confederate general observed, Southerners were engaged in a total war "in which the whole population and the whole production . . . are to be put on a war footing, where every institution is to be made auxiliary to war." Jefferson Davis faced the task of building an army and navy from scratch, supplying them from factories that were scarce and anemic, and paying for it all from a treasury that did not exist. Finding eager soldiers proved easiest. Hundreds of officers defected from the U.S. army, and hundreds of thousands of eager young rebels volunteered to follow them. Very quickly, the Confederacy developed formidable striking power.

The Confederacy's economy and finances proved tougher problems. Because of the Union blockade, the government had no choice but to build an industrial sector itself. Government-owned clothing and shoe factories, mines, arsenals, and powder works sprang up. The government also harnessed private companies, such as the huge Tredegar Iron Works in Richmond, to the war effort. Paying for the war became the most difficult task. A flood of paper money caused debilitating inflation. By 1863, people in Charleston paid ten times more for food than they had paid at the start of the war. By Christmas 1864, a Confederate soldier's monthly pay no longer bought a pair of socks. Despite bold measures, the Davis administration failed to transform the agricultural economy into a modern industrial one. The Confederacy manufactured much more than most people imagined possible, but it never produced all that the South needed. Each month, the gap between the North's and the South's production widened.

Richmond's war-making effort brought unprecedented government intrusion into the private lives of Confederate citizens. In April 1862, the Confederate Congress passed the first **conscription** (draft) law in American history. All able-bodied white males between the ages of eighteen and thirty-five (later seventeen and fifty) were liable to serve in the rebel army. The government adopted a policy of impressment, which allowed officials to confiscate food, horses, wagons, and whatever else they wanted from private citizens and to pay for them at below-market rates. After March 1863, the Confederacy legally impressed slaves, employing them as military laborers.

War necessitated much of the government's unprecedented behavior, but citizens found it arbitrary and inequitable. Richmond's centralizing efforts ran head-on into the South's traditional values of **states' rights** and unfettered individualism. The states lashed out at what Georgia governor Joseph E. Brown denounced as the "dangerous usurpation by Congress of the reserved

> One Confederate general observed that Southerners were engaged in a total war "in which the whole population and the whole production . . . are to be put on a war footing, where every institution is to be made auxiliary to war."

The Right to Fight: Black Soldiers in the Civil War

When unprecedented bloodletting at Shiloh, Antietam, and elsewhere caused the flood of military volunteers to slow to a trickle, first the Confederacy and then the Union had to resort to the draft to force white men into their armies. But one group of Americans beat at the doors of the War Department, begging to enroll in the Union army. "A war undertaken and brazenly carried on for the perpetual enslavement of colored men, calls logically and loudly for colored men to help suppress it," black leader Frederick Douglass declared. Speaking for free blacks in the North and fugitive slaves in the South, he said, "Would to God you would let us do something. We lack nothing but your consent. We are ready and would go. . . . But you won't let us go."

The lengthening casualty lists gradually turned the Lincoln administration around. In 1863, the Union eagerly began recruiting black soldiers. In February of that year, four days after the 54th Massachusetts Colored Regiment opened its recruiting office, James Henry Gooding, a twenty-six-year-old seaman from New Bedford, enlisted. For the next year, Gooding documented his experiences in vivid letters published by his hometown newspaper, the *New Bedford Mercury*. He appealed for new recruits, but black soldiers earned even less than white soldiers, and he understood that many black men did

not want to join the army and leave their families "destitute." Still, he said, "we are all determined to act like men, and fight, money or not." His heart filled with pride when he saw African Americans rush to the flag, refuting the notion that "the black race are incapable of patriotism, valor or ambition."

Like most black soldiers, Gooding viewed military service as a great opportunity to strike blows against slavery and white prejudice. Slavery in the South was vulnerable, Gooding observed, but "it depends on the free black men of the North, whether it will die or not—those who are in bonds must have some one to open the door; when the slave sees the white soldier approach, he dares not trust him and why? Because he has heard that *some* have treated him worse than their owners in rebellion. But if the slave sees a black soldier, he knows he has got a friend." Fighting for the Union also offered a chance to attack white prejudice. In military service lay "the germs of the elevation of a downtrodden and despised race," Gooding argued, the chance for African Americans "to make themselves a people." In the words of the 54th Massachusetts Colored Regiment, "We came to fight For Liberty justice & Equality."

Fighting, Gooding believed, offered blacks a chance to destroy the "foul aspersion that they were not men." According to the white

commander of the 59th U.S. Colored Infantry, when an ex-slave put on a uniform of army blue, "he was completely metamorphosed, not only in appearance and dress, but in character and relations also." The change, he said, was dramatic: "Yesterday a filthy, repulsive 'nigger,' to-day a neatly-attired man; yesterday a slave, to-day a freeman; yesterday a civilian, to-day a soldier." Others noticed the same transformation: "Put a United States uniform on his back and the *chattel* is a *man*." Black veterans agreed. One black soldier remembered, "This was the biggest thing that ever happened in my life. I felt like a man with a uniform and a gun in my hand." Another said, "I felt freedom in my bones."

Black courage under fire ended skepticism about the capabilities of African American troops. As one white officer observed after a battle, "They seemed like men who were fighting to vindicate their manhood and they did it well." The truth is, another remarked, "they have fought their way into the respect of all the army." After the 54th fought courageously in South Carolina, Gooding reported: "It is not for us to blow our horn; but when a regiment of white men gave us three cheers as we were passing them, it shows that we did our duty as men should."

Yet discrimination within the Union army continued. At first, blacks were assigned to manual labor rather than fighting. Even so, Gooding advised, "If it is to wield the shovel and pick, do it faithfully; if it is to haul siege guns, or load and unload transports, our motto is, work faithfully and willingly." Few issues disturbed Gooding and the 54th more than the government's refusal to pay blacks the same as whites. The 54th refused to accept unequal pay. Gooding wrote to President Lincoln himself to explain his regiment's decision: "Now the main question is, Are we Soldiers, or are we Labourers? . . . Now your Excellency, we have done a Soldier's Duty. Why Can't we have a Soldier's pay?" Gooding's eloquence and the 54th's principled stance helped reverse the government's position. In June 1864, Congress equalized the pay of black and white soldiers.

As Union troops advanced deeper into the collapsing Confederacy, countless former slaves greeted black soldiers as heroes. Gooding observed, "The contrabands did not believe we were coming; one [of] them said, 'I nebber bleeve black Yankee come here help culer men.' They think now the kingdom is coming sure enough." The white officer of a black regiment that occupied Wilmington, North Carolina, in March 1865 reported that black soldiers "stepped like lords & conquerors. The frantic demonstrations of the negro population will never die out of my memory. Their cheers & heartfelt 'God bress ye's' & cries of 'De chains is broke; De chains is broke,' mingled sublimely with the lusty shout of our brave soldiery."

Hardened and disciplined by their military service, black soldiers drew tremendous strength from their participation in the Union effort. Although blacks remained second-class soldiers, army life proved to be a great counterweight to the degradation and dependency of slavery. Black veterans emerged from the war with new confidence, proud of their contributions and convinced that their military service had earned them and their race full citizenship. Eager to shoulder the rights, privileges, and responsibilities of freedom, black veterans often took the lead in the hard struggle for equality after the war. Black soldiers made up a significant portion of the Union army that occupied the South after 1865,

Company E, 4th U.S. Colored Infantry, Fort Lincoln, Virginia
The Lincoln administration was slow to accept black soldiers into the Union army, in part because of lingering doubts about their ability to fight. But eventually, the battlefield valor of black troops eroded white skepticism. Colonel Thomas W. Higginson, the white commander of the Union's First South Carolina Infantry, which was made up of former slaves, celebrated the courage his men displayed in their first skirmish: "No officer in this regiment now doubts that the key to the successful prosecution of this war lies in the unlimited employment of black troops. . . . Instead of leaving their homes and families to fight they are fighting for their homes and families." Before the war was over, ex-slaves and free blacks filled 145 Union regiments.
Library of Congress.

and they assumed a special obligation to protect the lives and property of former slaves. "The fact is," one black chaplain said, "when colored soldiers are about they [whites] are afraid to kick colored women and abuse colored people on the Streets, as they usually do."

Black veterans fervently believed that their military service entitled African Americans not only to freedom but also to civil and political rights. Black sergeant Henry Maxwell announced: "We want two more boxes besides the cartridge box—the ballot and the jury box."

Having learned to read and write in the army, many veterans became schoolteachers. Others, having developed leadership skills, became politicians. Black soldiers had demonstrated what they could do if permitted to become warriors; they now demanded the chance to perform as citizens.

James Henry Gooding did not have a chance to participate in the postwar struggle for equal rights. Captured at the battle of Olustee in Florida, he was sent to the infamous Confederate prison Andersonville, where he died on July 19, 1864.

The Texas Brigade in Camp, 1861
Rebel soldiers who did not have slave servants to attend them spent much of their time doing chores. Standing in front of their winter quarters near Dumfries, Virginia, the Texans here are busy washing dishes, washing clothes, chopping firewood, and cooking. The soldier with the skillet displays the corn bread he has just cooked. Confederate troops ate salted meat and corn bread more than anything else. A federal officer marching through an abandoned rebel camp near Sharpsburg, Maryland, in 1862 recalled that "huge corn cakes, 2 inches thick and 12 to 15 inches wide, lay in piles and were kicked along the road by our men." Southerners learned to appreciate anything on their plates, but soldiers grew very tired of the old standbys. "If any person offers me cornbread after this war comes to a close," a Louisianan declared just before Lee's surrender, "I shall probably tell him to—go to hell!"

Photograph: Atlanta History Center, Austin Public Library; Skillet: Concord Museum, Concord, MA; Sifter: Museum of the Confederacy.

right of the States." Richmond and the states struggled for control of money, supplies, and soldiers, with damaging consequences for the war effort. Individuals also remembered that Davis had promised to defend southern "liberty" against Republican "despotism."

Hardship Below

Hardships on the home front fell most heavily on the poor. Salt—necessary for preserving meat—shot up from $2 to $60 a bag during the first year of the war. Flour, which cost three or four cents a pound in 1861, cost thirty-five cents in 1863. The draft stripped yeoman farms of men, leaving the women and children to grow what they ate. Government agents took 10 percent of farmwives' harvests as a "tax-in-kind" on agriculture. Like inflation, shortages afflicted the entire population, but the rich lost luxuries while the poor

lost necessities. In the spring of 1863, bread riots broke out in a dozen cities and villages across the South. In Richmond, a mob of nearly a thousand hungry women broke into shops and took what they needed.

"Men cannot be expected to fight for the Government that permits their wives & children to starve," a southern leader observed in November 1862. Although a few wealthy individuals shared their bounty and the Confederate and state governments made efforts at social welfare, every attempt fell short. In late 1864, one desperate farmwife told her husband, "I have always been proud of you, and since your connection with the Confederate army, I have been prouder of you than ever before. I would not have you do anything wrong for the world, but before God, Edward, unless you come home, we must die." When the war ended, one-third of the soldiers had already gone home. A Mississippi deserter explained, "We are poor men and are willing to defend our country but our families [come] first."

Yeomen perceived a profound inequality of sacrifice. They called it "a rich man's war and a poor man's fight." The draft law permitted a man who had money to hire a substitute to take his place. Moreover, the "twenty-Negro law" exempted one white man on every plantation with

Maria Isabella ("Belle") Boyd, Spy

Most southern white women, in addition to keeping their families fed and safe, served the Confederate cause by sewing uniforms, knitting socks, rolling bandages, and nursing the sick and wounded. But Belle Boyd became a spy. Only seventeen when the war broke out, she became, in the words of a northern journalist, "insanely devoted to the rebel cause." Her first act for the Confederacy came on July 3, 1861, when she shot a drunken federal soldier who barged into her Virginia home and insulted her mother. Her relations with occupying northern troops improved, and soon this compelling young woman was eavesdropping on officers' conversations and slipping messages to Confederate armies. Boyd's information handed Stonewall Jackson an easy victory at Front Royal, Virginia, in May 1862. "I thank you," the general wrote Boyd, ". . . for the immense service that you have rendered your country today." Imprisoned several times for spying, Boyd took up a theatrical career when the war ended. Courtesy Warren Rifles Confederate Museum, Front Royal, VA.

twenty or more slaves. The government intended this law to provide protection for white women and to see that slaves tended the crops, but yeomen perceived it as rich men evading military service. A Mississippian complained that stay-at-home planters sent their slaves into the fields to grow cotton while in plain view "poor soldiers' wives are plowing with *their own* hands to make a subsistence for themselves and children—while their husbands are suffering, bleeding and dying for their country." In fact, most slaveholders went off to war, but the extreme suffering of common folk and the relative immunity of planters fueled class animosity.

> "Men cannot be expected to fight for the Government that permits their wives & children to starve," a southern leader observed in November 1862.

The Richmond government hoped that the crucible of war would mold a region into a nation. Officials and others worked to promote a southern **nationalism** that would "excite in our citizens an ardent and enduring attachment to our Government and its institutions." Clergymen assured their congregations that God had blessed slavery and the new nation. Patriotic songwriters, poets, authors, and artists extolled southern **culture**. Jefferson Davis asked citizens to observe national days of fasting and prayer. But these efforts failed to win over thousands of die-hard Unionists, and friction between yeomen and planters increased rather than decreased. The war also threatened to rip the southern social fabric along its racial seam.

The Disintegration of Slavery

The legal destruction of slavery was the product of presidential proclamation, congressional legislation, and eventually constitutional amendment, but the practical destruction of slavery was the product of war—what Lincoln called war's "friction and abrasion." War exposed the illusion of slave contentment. Slaves took advantage of the upheaval to reach for freedom. Some half a million of the South's 4 million slaves ran away to Union military lines. More than 100,000 runaways took up arms as federal soldiers and sailors and attacked slavery directly. Other men and women stayed in the slave quarter, where they staked their claim to more freedom.

War disrupted slavery in a dozen ways. Almost immediately, it called the master away, leaving the mistress to assume responsibility for the plantation. But mistresses could not maintain traditional standards of slave discipline in wartime, and the balance of power shifted. Slaves got to the fields late, worked indifferently, and quit early. Some slaveholders responded violently; most saw no alternative but to strike bargains—offering gifts or part of the crop—to keep slaves at home and at work. An Alabama woman complained that she "begged . . . what little is done." Slaveholders had believed that they "knew" their slaves, but they learned that they did not. When the war began, a North Carolina woman praised her slaves as "diligent and respectful." When it ended, she said, "As to the idea of a *faithful servant, it is all a fiction.*"

As military action sliced through the South's farms and plantations, some slaveholders fled, leaving their slaves behind. Many more took their slaves with them, but flight meant additional chaos and offered slaves new opportunities to resist bondage. Whites' greatest fear—retaliatory violence—rarely occurred, however. Slaves who stayed home steadily undermined white mastery and expanded control over their own lives.

REVIEW How did wartime hardship in the South contribute to class animosity?

The North at War

Although the North was largely untouched by the fighting, Northerners could not avoid being touched by the war. Almost every family had a son, husband, father, or brother in uniform. Moreover, total war blurred the distinction between home front and battlefield. As in the South, men marched off to fight, but preserving the country was also women's work. For civilians as well as soldiers, for women as well as men, war was transforming.

The need to build and fuel the Union war machine boosted the economy. The Union sent nearly 2 million men into the military and still increased production in almost every area. But because the rewards and burdens of patriotism were distributed unevenly, the North experienced sharp, even violent, divisions. Workers confronted employers, whites confronted blacks, and Democrats confronted Republicans. Still, Northerners on the home front remained fervently attached to the Union.

Union Ordnance, Yorktown, Virginia
As the North successfully harnessed its enormous industrial capacity to meet the needs of the war, cannons, mortars, and shells poured out of its factories. A fraction of that abundance is seen here at Yorktown in 1862, ready for transportation to Union troops in the field. Two years later, Abraham Lincoln observed that the Union was "gaining strength, and may if need be maintain the contest indefinitely. . . . Material resources are now more complete and abundant than ever. . . . The national resources are unexhausted, and, as we believe, inexhaustible." Library of Congress.

READING THE IMAGE: What does this image indicate about northern military might in the Civil War?
CONNECTIONS: What role did the North's industrial power play in its victory in the war?

FOR MORE HELP ANALYZING THIS IMAGE, see the visual activity for this chapter in the Online Study Guide at bedfordstmartins.com/roark.

The Government and the Economy

When the war began, the United States had no national banking system, no national currency, and no federal income or excise taxes. But the secession of eleven slave states cut the Democrats' strength in Congress in half and destroyed their capacity to resist Republican economic programs. The Legal Tender Act of February 1862 created a national currency—paper money that Northerners called "greenbacks." With the passage of the National Banking Act in February 1863, Congress established a system of national banks that by the 1870s had largely replaced the **antebellum** system of decentralized state banks. Congress also enacted a series of sweeping tax laws. The Internal Revenue Act created the Bureau of Internal Revenue to collect taxes. In addition, Congress enacted a higher tariff to increase revenue and protect manufacturers against foreign competition. By revolutionizing the country's banking, monetary, and tax structures, the Republicans generated enormous economic power.

The Republicans' wartime legislation also aimed at integrating the West more thoroughly into the Union. In May 1862, Congress approved the Homestead Act, which offered 160 acres of public land to settlers who would live and labor on it. The Homestead Act bolstered western loyalty and in time resulted in more than a million new farms. The Pacific Railroad Act in July 1862 provided massive federal assistance for building a transcontinental railroad that ran from Omaha to San Francisco when completed in 1869. Congress further bound East and West by subsidizing the Pony Express mail service and a transcontinental telegraph.

Two additional initiatives had long-term consequences for agriculture and industry. Congress created the Department of Agriculture and passed the Land-Grant College Act (also known as the Morrill Act after its sponsor, Representative Justin Morrill of Vermont), which set aside public land to support universities that emphasized "agriculture and mechanical arts." The Lincoln administration immeasurably strengthened the North's effort to win the war, but its ideas also permanently changed the nation.

Women and Work on the Home Front

More than a million farm men were called to the military, so farm women added men's chores to their own. "I met more women driving teams on the road and saw more at work in the fields than men," a visitor to Iowa reported in the fall of 1862. Rising production testified to their success in plowing, planting, and harvesting. Rapid mechanization assisted farm women in their new roles. Cyrus McCormick sold 165,000 of his reapers during the war years. The combination of high prices for farm products and increased production ensured that war and prosperity joined hands in the rural North.

A few industries, such as textiles (which depended on southern cotton), declined during the war, but many more grew. Huge profits prompted one Pennsylvania ironmaster to remark, "I am in no hurry for peace." With orders pouring in and a million nonfarmworkers at war, unemployment declined and wages often rose. The boom proved friendlier to owners than to workers, however. Inflation and taxes cut so deeply into workers' paychecks that their standard of living actually fell.

> "I met more women driving teams on the road and saw more at work in the fields than men," a visitor to Iowa reported in the fall of 1862.

In cities, women stepped into jobs vacated by men, particularly in manufacturing, and also into essentially new occupations such as government secretaries and clerks. Women made up about one-quarter of the manufacturing workforce when the war began and one-third when it ended. As more and more women entered the workforce, employers cut wages. In 1864, New York seamstresses working fourteen-hour days earned only $1.54 a week. Urban workers resorted increasingly to strikes to wrench decent salaries from their employers, but their protests rarely succeeded. Nevertheless, tough times failed to undermine the patriotism of most workers.

Most middle-class white women stayed home and contributed to the war effort in traditional ways. They sewed, wrapped bandages, and sold homemade goods at local fairs to raise money to aid the soldiers. Other women expressed their patriotism in an untraditional way—as wartime nurses. Thousands of women on both sides defied prejudices about female delicacy and volunteered to nurse the wounded. Many northern female volunteers worked through the U.S. Sanitary Commission, a civilian organization that bought and distributed clothing, food, and medicine and recruited doctors and nurses.

Some volunteers went on to become paid military nurses. For example, Dorothea Dix, well known for her efforts to reform insane asylums,

Women Doing Laundry for Federal Soldiers, circa 1861
Northern women eagerly joined the Union war effort. Thousands aided in the work of the U.S. Christian
Commission, the U.S. Sanitary Commission, and other philanthropic organizations to provide soldiers
with Bibles, fresh food, and new socks. But some women were forced by their desperate financial circumstances to wash soldiers' dirty clothes to make a living. Army camps were difficult places for "respectable"
women to work. One Union soldier discouraged his wife even from visiting, noting, "It is not a fit place
for any woman, for there is all kinds of talk, songs and everything not good for them 2 hear."
© Bettmann/Corbis.

was named superintendent of female nurses in
April 1861. Eventually, some 3,000 women
served under her. Most nurses worked in hospitals behind the battle lines, but some, like Clara
Barton, who later founded the American Red
Cross, worked in battlefield units. At Antietam,
as Barton was giving a wounded man a drink, a
bullet ripped through her sleeve, striking and
killing the soldier. Women who served in the war
went on to lead the postwar movement to establish training schools for female nurses.

Politics and Dissent

At first, the bustle of economic and military mobilization seemed to silence politics, but bipartisan
unity did not last. Within a year, Democrats were
labeling the Republican administration a "reign of
terror," and Republicans were calling Democrats
the party of "Dixie, Davis, and the Devil." Demo-

crats denounced Republican policies—emanci-
pating the slaves, subsidizing private business, and
expanding federal power—as unconstitutional,
arguing that the "Constitution is as binding in war
as in peace."

In September 1862, in an effort to stifle opposition to the war, Lincoln placed under military
arrest any person who discouraged enlistments,
resisted the draft, or engaged in "disloyal" practices. Before the war ended, his administration
imprisoned nearly 14,000 individuals, most in
the border states. The campaign fell short of a
reign of terror, for the majority of the prisoners
were not northern Democratic opponents but
Confederates, blockade runners, and citizens of
foreign countries, and most of those arrested
gained quick release. Still, the administration's
heavy-handed tactics did suppress free speech.

When the Republican-dominated Congress
enacted the draft law in March 1863, Democrats

had another grievance. The law required that all men between the ages of twenty and forty-five enroll and make themselves available for a lottery that would decide who went to war. What poor men found particularly galling were provisions that allowed a draftee to hire a substitute or simply to pay a $300 fee and get out of his military obligation. As in the South, common folk could be heard chanting, "A rich man's war and a poor man's fight."

Linking the draft and emancipation, Democrats argued that Republicans employed an unconstitutional means (the draft) to achieve an unconstitutional end (emancipation). In the summer of 1863, antidraft, antiblack mobs went on rampages in northern cities. In New York City, Democratic Irish workingmen—crowded into filthy tenements, gouged by inflation, enraged by the draft, and dead set against fighting to free blacks—erupted in four days of rioting. The draft riots killed at least 105 people, most of them black, and left the Colored Orphan Asylum a smoking ruin.

Racist mobs failed to achieve their purpose: the subordination of African Americans. Free black leaders had lobbied aggressively for emancipation, and after Lincoln's proclamation, they fanned out over the North agitating for equality. They won a few small victories. Illinois and Iowa overturned laws that excluded blacks from entering those states. Illinois and Ohio began permitting blacks to testify in court. But significant progress toward black equality would have to wait until the war ended.

> **REVIEW** Why was the U.S. Congress able to pass such a bold legislative agenda during the war?

Grinding Out Victory, 1863–1865

In the early months of 1863, the Union's prospects looked bleak, and the Confederate cause stood at high tide. Then, in July 1863, the tide began to turn. The military man most responsible for this shift was Ulysses S. Grant. Lifted from obscurity by his successes in the West, Grant became the "great man of the day, perhaps of the age," one man observed in July 1864. Elevated to supreme command, Grant knit together a powerful war machine that integrated

a sophisticated command structure, modern technology, and complex logistics and supply systems. But the arithmetic of this plain man remained unchanged: Killing more of the enemy than he kills of you equaled "the complete overthrow of the rebellion."

The North ground out the victory battle by bloody battle. The balance tipped in the Union's favor in 1863, but Southerners were not deterred. The fighting escalated in the last two years of the war. As national elections approached in the fall of 1864, Lincoln expected a war-weary North to reject him. Instead, northern voters declared their willingness to continue the war in the defense of the ideals of union and freedom.

Vicksburg and Gettysburg

Vicksburg, Mississippi, situated on the eastern bank of the Mississippi River, stood between Union forces and complete control of the river. Impenetrable terrain made the city impossible to take from the north. To get his army south of Vicksburg, Grant marched it down the swampy western bank of the Mississippi. Union forces crossed the Mississippi, marched north more than one hundred miles, and attacked the city. Confederates beat back the assault, and in May, Grant decided to lay siege to the city and starve

Major Battles of the Civil War, 1863–1865

May 1–4, 1863	Battle of Chancellorsville
July 1–3, 1863	Battle of Gettysburg
July 4, 1863	Fall of Vicksburg
September 16–20, 1863	Battle of Chickamauga
November 23–25, 1863	Battle of Chattanooga
May 5–7, 1864	Battle of the Wilderness
May 7–19, 1864	Battle of Spotsylvania Court House
June 3, 1864	Battle of Cold Harbor
June 27, 1864	Battle of Kennesaw Mountain
September 2, 1864	Fall of Atlanta
November–December 1864	Sheridan sacks Shenandoah Valley Sherman's "March to the Sea"
December 15–16, 1864	Battle of Nashville
December 22, 1864	Fall of Savannah
April 2–3, 1865	Fall of Petersburg and Richmond
April 9, 1865	Lee surrenders at Appomattox Court House

out the enemy. Civilian residents of Vicksburg moved into caves to escape the incessant Union bombardment, and as the siege dragged on, they ate mules and rats to survive.

After six weeks, on July 4, 1863, nearly 30,000 rebels marched out of Vicksburg, stacked their arms, and surrendered unconditionally. A Yankee captain wrote home to his wife: "The backbone of the Rebellion is this day broken. The Confederacy is divided. . . . Vicksburg is ours. The Mississippi River is opened, and Gen. Grant is to be our next President."

On the same Fourth of July, word arrived that Union forces had crushed General Lee at Gettysburg, Pennsylvania (Map 15.3). Emboldened by his victory at Chancellorsville in May and hoping to relieve Virginia of the burden of the fighting, Lee and his 75,000-man army had invaded Pennsylvania. On June 28, Union forces under General George G. Meade intercepted the Confederates at the small town of Gettysburg, where Union soldiers occupied the high ground. Three days of furious fighting involving 165,000 troops could not dislodge the Federals from the hills. Lee ached for a decisive victory, and on July 3 he ordered a major assault against the Union center on Cemetery Ridge. Open, rolling fields provided the dug-in Yankees with three-quarters of a mile of clear vision, and they raked the mile-wide line of Confederate soldiers under General George E. Pickett with cannon and rifle fire. Gettysburg cost Lee more than one-third of his army— 28,000 casualties. "It's all my fault," he lamented. In a drenching rain on the night of July 4, 1863, he marched his battered army back to Virginia.

The twin disasters at Vicksburg and Gettysburg proved to be the turning point of the war. The Confederacy could not re-

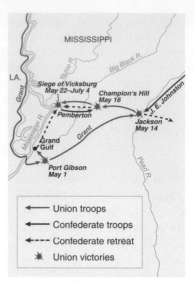

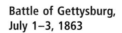

Vicksburg Campaign, 1863

Battle of Gettysburg,
July 1–3, 1863

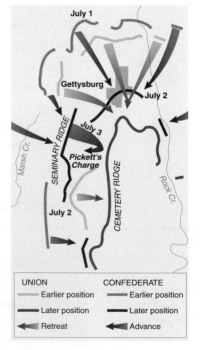

place the nearly 60,000 soldiers who were captured, wounded, or killed. Lee never launched another major offensive north of the Mason-Dixon line. It is hindsight, however, that permits us to see the pair of battles as decisive. At the time, the Confederacy still controlled the heartland of the South, and Lee still had a vicious sting. War-weariness threatened to erode the North's will to win before Union armies could destroy the Confederacy's ability to go on.

Grant Takes Command

Toward the end of September 1863, Union general William Rosecrans placed his army in a dangerous situation in Chattanooga, Tennessee, where he had retreated after defeat at the battle of Chickamauga earlier in the month (see Map 15.3). Rebels surrounded the disorganized bluecoats and threatened to starve them into submission. Grant, now commander of Union forces between the Mississippi River and the Appalachians, arrived in Chattanooga in October. Within weeks, he opened an effective supply line, broke the siege, and routed the Confederate army. The victory at Chattanooga on November 25 opened the door to Georgia. It also confirmed Lincoln's estimation of Grant. In March 1864, the president asked Grant to come east to become the general in chief of all Union armies.

In Washington, General Grant implemented his grand strategy for a war of attrition. He ordered a series of simultaneous assaults from Virginia all the way to Louisiana. Two actions proved particularly significant. In one, General William Tecumseh Sherman, whom Grant appointed his successor to command the western armies, plunged southeast toward Atlanta. In the other, Grant, who took control of the Army of the Potomac, went

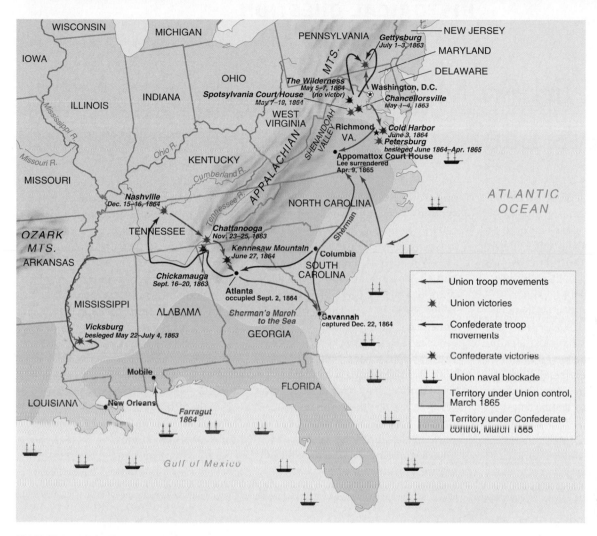

MAP 15.3   The Civil War, 1863–1865
Ulysses S. Grant's victory at Vicksburg divided the Confederacy at the Mississippi River. William Tecumseh Sherman's march from Chattanooga to Savannah divided it again. In northern Virginia, Robert E. Lee fought fiercely, but Grant's larger, better-supplied armies prevailed.

READING THE MAP: Describe the difference between Union and Confederate naval capacity. Were the battles shown on the map fought primarily in Union-controlled or Confederate-controlled territory? (Look at the land areas on the map.)

CONNECTIONS: Did former slaves serve in the Civil War? If so, on which side(s), and what did they do?

FOR MORE HELP ANALYZING THIS MAP, see the map activity for this chapter in the Online Study Guide at bedfordstmartins.com/roark.

---

head-to-head with Lee for almost four straight weeks in Virginia.

Grant and Lee met in the first week of May 1864 in northern Virginia in a dense tangle of scrub oaks and small pines. Often unable to see more than ten paces, the armies pounded away at each other until approximately 18,000 Yankees and 11,000 rebels had fallen. The savagery of the battle of the Wilderness did not compare with

that at Spotsylvania Court House a few days later. Frenzied men fought hand to hand for eighteen hours in the rain. One veteran remembered men "piled upon each other in some places four layers deep, exhibiting every ghastly phase of mutilation." (See "Historical Question," page 542.) Spotsylvania cost Grant another 18,000 casualties and Lee 10,000, but the Yankee bulldog would not let go. Grant kept moving

Why Did So Many Soldiers Die?

From 1861 to 1865, Americans killed Americans on a scale never before seen. Not until the First World War, a half century later, would the Western world match (and surpass) the killing fields at Shiloh, Antietam, and Gettysburg (Figure 15.2). Why were the Civil War totals so horrendous? Why did 260,000 rebel soldiers and 373,000 Union soldiers die?

By the mid-nineteenth century, the balance between the ability to kill and the ability to save lives had tipped disastrously toward death. The sheer size of the armies—some battles involved more than 200,000 soldiers—ensured that battlefields would turn red with blood. Moreover, armies fought with antiquated Napoleonic strategy. In the generals' eyes, the ideal soldier was trained to advance with his comrades in a compact, close-order formation. Theory also emphasized frontal assaults.

By the 1860s, modern technology had made such strategy appallingly deadly. Weapons with rifled barrels were replacing smoothbore muskets and cannons. Rifles propelled spinning bullets four times as far as muskets—about 320 yards. The rifle's greater range and accuracy, along with the ability of rifled cannons to fire canisters filled with flesh-ripping, bone-breaking steel shot, made sitting ducks of charging infantry units and gave an enormous advantage to entrenched defensive forces. As a result, battles took thousands of lives in a single day. On July 2, 1862, the morning after the battle at Malvern Hill in eastern Virginia, a Union officer surveyed the scene: "Over 5,000 dead and wounded men were on the ground . . . enough were alive and moving to give to the field a singular crawling effect."

Wounded soldiers often lay on battlefields for hours, sometimes days, without water or care of any kind. When the Civil War began, no one anticipated casualty lists with thousands of names. Union and Confederate medical departments could not cope with skirmishes, much less large-scale battles. They had no ambulance corps to remove the wounded from the scene. They had no field hospitals. Early in the war, someone in the U.S. Quartermaster Department, which was responsible for constructing Union hospitals, responded to demands that it do something to improve the care of the wounded by saying, "Men need guns, not beds." Only the shock of massive casualties compelled reform. A lack of resources meant that the South lagged behind the North, but gradually both North and South organized effective ambulance corps, built hospitals, and hired trained surgeons and nurses.

Soldiers did not always count speedy transportation to a field hospital as a blessing. As one Union soldier said, "I had rather risk a battle than the Hospitals." Medicine remained primitive. Physicians gained a reputation as butchers, and soldiers dreaded the operating table more than they did entrenched riflemen. Serious wounds to a leg or an arm usually meant amputation and, after major battles, surgeons worked among piles of severed limbs.

A wounded man's real enemy was medical ignorance. Physicians had almost no knowledge of the cause

---

FIGURE 15.2   Civil War Deaths
The loss of life in the Civil War—633,000—was almost equal to the losses in all other American wars through the Vietnam War combined.

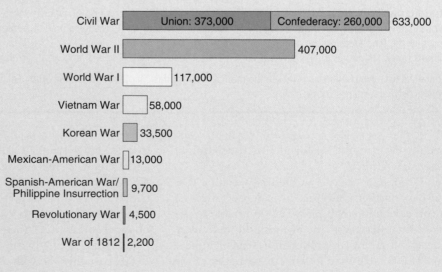

Civil War	Union: 373,000 Confederacy: 260,000 633,000
World War II	407,000
World War I	117,000
Vietnam War	58,000
Korean War	33,500
Mexican-American War	13,000
Spanish-American War/ Philippine Insurrection	9,700
Revolutionary War	4,500
War of 1812	2,200

Wounded Men at Savage's Station

Misery did not end when the cannons ceased firing. Northern and southern surgeons performed approximately 60,000 amputations with simple instruments such as those included in this surgical kit. The wounded men shown here were but a fraction of those injured or killed during General George McClellan's peninsula campaign in 1862.

Photo: Library of Congress; Surgical kit: Chicago Historical Society.

and transmission of disease or the benefits of **antiseptics**. Not aware of basic germ theory, they spread infection almost every time they operated. Doctors wore the same bloody smocks for days and washed their hands and their scalpels and saws in buckets of dirty water. When they had difficulty threading their needles, they wet the thread with their own saliva. Soldiers often did not survive amputations, not because of the operations but because of the infections that inevitably followed. Of the Union soldiers whose legs were amputated above the knee, more than half died. A Union doctor discovered in 1864 that bromine arrested gangrene, but the best that most amputees could hope for was maggots, which ate dead flesh on the stump and thus inhibited the spread of in-fection. During the Civil War, nearly one of every five wounded rebel soldiers died, and one of every six Yankees. A century later, in Vietnam, only one wounded American soldier in four hundred died.

Soldiers who avoided battlefield wounds and hospital infections still faced sickness. Deadly diseases swept through crowded army camps, where latrines were often dangerously close to drinking-water supplies and mos-quitoes, flies, and body lice were more than nuisances. The principal killers were dysentery and typhoid, but pneumonia and malaria also cut down thousands. Quinine from South America was an effective treatment for malaria, but by the end of the war, the going price was $500 an ounce. Treatments often added to the misery.

Doctors prescribed doses of turpentine for patients with typhoid, they fought respiratory problems with mustard plasters, and they at-tacked intestinal disorders by blister-ing the skin with sulfuric acid.

Thousands of nurses, including Dorothea Dix and Clara Barton, im-proved the wounded men's odds and alleviated their suffering. Civilian re-lief agencies promoted hygiene in army camps and made some head-way. Nevertheless, disease killed nearly twice as many soldiers as did combat. Many who died of disease were prisoners of war. Approxi-mately 30,000 Northerners died in Confederate prisons, and approxi-mately 26,000 Southerners died in Union prisons.

and tangled with Lee again at Cold Harbor, where he suffered 13,000 additional casualties to Lee's 5,000.

Twice as many Union soldiers as rebel soldiers died in four weeks of fighting in Virginia in May and June, but because Lee had only half as many troops as Grant, his losses were equivalent to Grant's. Grant knew that the South could not replace the losses. Moreover, the campaign carried Grant to the outskirts of Petersburg, just south of Richmond, where he abandoned the costly tactic of the frontal assault and began a

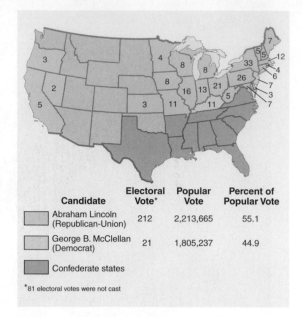

Candidate	Electoral Vote*	Popular Vote	Percent of Popular Vote
Abraham Lincoln (Republican-Union)	212	2,213,665	55.1
George B. McClellan (Democrat)	21	1,805,237	44.9
Confederate states			

*81 electoral votes were not cast

MAP 15.4   The Election of 1864

Grant Planning the Attack at Cold Harbor

On June 2, 1864, General Ulysses S. Grant moved his headquarters to Bethesda Church, Maryland, carried the pews outdoors, and planned the attack he would make at Cold Harbor. Here, Grant leans over a pew to study a map. The next day, he ordered frontal assaults against entrenched Confederate forces, resulting in enormous Union losses. "I am disgusted with the generalship displayed," young Brigadier General Emory Upton observed. "Our men have, in many cases, been foolishly and wantonly slaughtered." Years later, Grant said that he regretted the assault at Cold Harbor, but in 1864 he kept pushing toward Richmond.
Library of Congress.

siege that immobilized both armies and dragged on for nine months.

Simultaneously, Sherman invaded Georgia. Grant instructed Sherman to "get into the interior of the enemy's country as far as you can, inflicting all the damage you can against their War resources." In early May, Sherman moved 100,000 men south against 65,000 rebels. Skillful maneuvering, constant skirmishing, and one pitched battle, at Kennesaw Mountain, brought Sherman to Atlanta, which fell on September 2.

Intending to "make Georgia howl," Sherman marched out of Atlanta on November 15 with 62,000 battle-hardened veterans, heading for Savannah, 285 miles away on the Atlantic coast. One veteran remembered, "[We] destroyed all we could not eat, stole their niggers, burned their cotton & gins, spilled their sorghum, burned & twisted their R. Roads and raised Hell generally." Sherman's "March to the Sea" aimed at destroying the will of the southern people. A few weeks earlier, General Philip H. Sheridan had carried out his own scorched-earth campaign in the Shenandoah Valley, complying with Grant's order to turn the valley into "a barren waste . . . so that crows flying over it for the balance of this season will have to carry their provender [food] with them." When Sherman's troops entered an undefended Savannah in mid-December, the general telegraphed Lincoln that he had "a Christmas gift" for him. A month earlier, Union voters had bestowed on the president an even greater gift.

The Election of 1864

In the summer of 1864, with Sherman temporarily checked outside Atlanta and Grant bogged down in the siege of Petersburg, the Democratic Party smelled victory in the fall elections. Rankled by a seemingly never-ending war, inflation, the draft, the attack on civil liberties, and the commitment to blacks, Northerners appeared ready for a change. Lincoln himself concluded, "It seems exceedingly probable that this administration will not be re-elected."

The Democrats were badly divided, however. "Peace" Democrats insisted on an armistice, while "war" Democrats supported the conflict but opposed Republican means of fighting it. The party tried to paper over the chasm by nominating a war candidate, General George McClellan, but adopting a peace platform that demanded that "immediate efforts be made for a cessation of hostilities." Republicans denounced the peace plank as a cut-and-run plan that "virtually proposed to surrender the country to the rebels in arms against us."

The capture of Atlanta on September 2 turned the political tide in favor of the Republicans. Lincoln received 55 percent of the popular vote, but his electoral margin was a whopping 212 to McClellan's 21 (Map 15.4). The Republicans also gained large margins over the Democrats in the

> Democrats were badly divided over the war. "Peace" Democrats insisted on an armistice, while "war" Democrats supported the conflict but opposed Republican means of fighting it.

The Dead Line, by Robert Sneden, Andersonville Prison, 1864
The train carrying prisoner of war Robert Sneden arrived at Andersonville on the last day of February 1864 as the Confederates were completing the stockade that surrounded their newest prison. Soon the sixteen and a half acres in southwestern Georgia were crammed with humanity. By June, the prison had to be expanded. Andersonville's 33,000 Union prisoners made it the fifth-largest city in the Confederacy. Sneden sketched this scene of a man being shot by a guard while trying to take part of a fence (the "dead line" that prisoners could not cross) for firewood. More than 13,000 prisoners perished at Andersonville. Smallpox, dysentery, scurvy, malnutrition, and infections proved far greater threats to them than bullets.
© 1996, Lora Robbins Collection of Virginia Art, Virginia Historical Society.

The dead line Andersonville Prison. Georgia.
Shot by the guard while taking a part of the dead line for firewood.

congressional elections. Lincoln's party won a resounding victory, one that gave him a mandate to continue the war until slavery and the Confederacy were dead.

The Confederacy Collapses

As 1865 dawned, military disaster littered the Confederate landscape. With the destruction of John B. Hood's army at Nashville in December 1864, the interior of the Confederacy lay in Yankee hands (see Map 15.3). Sherman's troops, resting momentarily in Savannah, eyed South Carolina hungrily. Farther north, Grant had Lee's army pinned down in Petersburg, a few miles from Richmond.

Some Confederates turned their backs on the rebellion. News from the battlefield made it difficult not to conclude that the Yankees had beaten them. Soldiers' wives begged their husbands to return home to keep their families from starving, and the stream of deserters grew dramatically. In most cases, when white Southerners lost the will to continue, it was not because they lost faith in independence but because they had been battered into submission. Despite the deep divisions within the Confederacy, white Southerners had demonstrated a remarkable endurance for their cause. Half of the 900,000 Confederate soldiers had been killed or wounded, and ragged, hungry women and children had sacrificed throughout one of the bloodiest wars then known to history.

The end came with a rush. On February 1, 1865, Sherman's troops stormed out of Savannah into South Carolina, the "cradle of the Confederacy." In Virginia, Lee abandoned Petersburg on April 2, and Richmond fell on April 3. Grant pursued Lee until he surrendered on April 9, 1865, at Appomattox Court House, Virginia. Grant offered generous peace terms. He allowed Lee's men to return home and to keep their horses to help "put in a crop to carry themselves and their families through the next winter." With Lee gone, the remaining Confederate armies lost hope and gave up within two weeks. After four years, the war was over.

No one was more relieved than Lincoln, but his celebration was restrained. He told his cabinet that his postwar burdens would weigh almost as heavily as those of wartime. Seeking a distraction, Lincoln attended Ford's Theatre on the evening of Good Friday, April 14,

Robert E. Lee and Friends, by Mathew Brady, 1865
One week after his surrender at Appomattox Court House, Robert E. Lee, again wearing his uniform, sat for this portrait by Mathew Brady, the country's most famous photographer. Lee is joined by his eldest son, Major General George Washington Custis Lee (left), and a longtime aide, Lieutenant Colonel Walter H. Taylor (right). Lee's sober, weary expression reflects four hard years of war and his final defeat. Already a matchless hero among white Southerners, Lee was well on his way toward saintly immortality. In 1868, one woman described Lee as "bathed in the white light which falls directly upon him from the smile of an approving and sustaining God."
Library of Congress.

Richmond, Virginia, 1865
As the Confederate government evacuated Richmond during the evening of April 2, 1865, demolition squads set fire to everything that had military or industrial value. Huge explosions devastated the arsenal, the ruins of which are shown here. As one witness observed, "The old war-scarred city seemed to prefer annihilation to conquest."
Library of Congress.

1865. John Wilkes Booth, an actor with southern sympathies, slipped into the president's box and shot Lincoln in the head. He died at 7:22 the following morning. Vice President Andrew Johnson became president. The man who had led the nation through the war would not lead it during the postwar search for a just peace.

REVIEW   Why were the siege of Vicksburg and the battle of Gettysburg crucial to the outcome of the war?

Conclusion: The Second American Revolution

A transformed nation emerged from the crucible of war. Antebellum America was decentralized politically and loosely integrated economically. To bend the resources of the country to a Union victory, Congress enacted legislation that reshaped the nation's political and economic character. It created a national currency and banking system and turned to free land, a transcontinental railroad, and miles of telegraph lines to bind the West to the rest of the nation. Congress also established the sovereignty of the federal government and permanently increased its power. To most citizens before the war, Washington meant the local post office and little more. During the war, the federal government drafted, taxed, and judged Americans in unprecedented ways. The massive changes brought about by the war—the creation of a national government, a national economy, and a national spirit—led one historian to call the American Civil War the "Second American Revolution."

The Civil War also had a profound effect on individual lives. When the war began in 1861, millions of men dropped their hoes, hammers, and pencils; put on blue or gray uniforms; and fought and suffered for what they passionately believed was right. The war disrupted families, leaving women at home with additional responsibilities while offering new opportunities to others for wartime work in factories, offices, and hospitals. It offered blacks new and more effective ways to resist slavery and agitate for equality.

The war devastated the South. Three-fourths of southern white men of military age served in the Confederate army, and at least half of them were captured, wounded, or killed or died of disease. The war destroyed two-fifths of the South's livestock, wrecked half of the farm machinery, and blackened dozens of cities and towns. The immediate impact of the war on the North was more paradoxical. The struggle cost the North a heavy price: 373,000 lives. But rather than devastating the land, the war set the countryside and cities humming with business activity. The radical shift in power from South to North signaled a new direction in American development: the long decline of agriculture and the rise of industrial capitalism.

Most revolutionary of all, the war ended slavery. Ironically, the South's war to preserve slavery destroyed it. Nearly 200,000 black men, including ex-slave William Gould, dedicated their wartime service to its eradication. Because slavery was both a labor and a racial system, the institution was entangled in almost every aspect of southern life. Slavery's uprooting inevitably meant fundamental change. But the full meaning of abolition remained unclear in 1865. Determining the new economic, political, and social status of nearly 4 million ex-slaves would be the principal task of reconstruction.

Selected Bibliography

General Works

James M. McPherson, *The Battle Cry of Freedom: The Civil War Era* (1988).

James M. McPherson and William J. Cooper Jr., *Writing the Civil War: The Quest to Understand* (1998).

Military History

Mark Grimsley, *The Hard Hand of War: Union Military Policy toward Southern Civilians, 1861–1865* (1995).

James M. McPherson, *What They Fought For, 1861–1865* (1994).

Reid Mitchell, *Civil War Soldiers: Their Expectations and Their Experiences* (1988).

Brooks D. Simpson, *Ulysses S. Grant: Triumph over Adversity, 1822–1865* (2000).

Emory M. Thomas, *Robert E. Lee: A Biography* (1995).

Russell F. Weigley, *A Great Civil War: A Military and Political History, 1861–1865* (2000).

The North and South at War

Stephen V. Ash, *When the Yankees Came: Conflict and Chaos in the Occupied South, 1861–1865* (1995).

Iver Bernstein, *The New York City Draft Riots: Their Significance for American Society and Politics in the Age of the Civil War* (1990).

Stephen W. Berry II, *All That Makes a Man: Love and Ambition in the Civil War South* (2003).

William A. Blair, *Virginia's Private War: Feeding Body and Soul in the Confederacy, 1861–1865* (1998).

Richard J. Carwardine, *Lincoln* (2003).

William J. Cooper, *Jefferson Davis, American* (2000).

Drew Gilpin Faust, *The Creation of Confederate Nationalism: Ideology and Identity in the American Civil War* (1996).

William W. Freehling, *The South vs. the South: How Anti-Confederate Southerners Shaped the Course of the Civil War* (2001).

Gary W. Gallagher, *The Confederate War* (1997).

Judith Ann Giesberg, *Civil War Sisterhood: The U.S. Sanitary Commission and Women's Politics in Transition* (2000).

Randall M. Miller, Harry S. Stout, and Charles Reagan Wilson, eds., *Religion and the American Civil War* (1998).

Mark E. Neely Jr., *The Fate of Liberty: Abraham Lincoln and Civil Liberties* (1991).

George C. Rable, *Civil Wars: Women and the Crisis of Southern Nationalism* (1989).

Heather Cox Richardson, *The Greatest Nation of the Earth: Republican Economic Policies during the Civil War* (1997).

James L. Roark, *Masters without Slaves: Southern Planters in the Civil War and Reconstruction* (1977).

Anne Sarah Rubin, *A Shattered Nation: The Rise and Fall of the Confederacy, 1861–1868* (2005).

Nina Silber, *Daughters of the Union: Northern Women Fight the Civil War* (2006).

Margaret M. Storey, *Loyalty and Loss: Alabama's Unionists in the Civil War and Reconstruction* (2004).

LeeAnn Whites, *The Civil War as a Crisis in Gender* (2000).

The Struggle for Freedom

Ira Berlin et al., eds., *Freedom: A Documentary History of Emancipation, 1861–1867,* 4 vols. (1982–1993).

Dudley Taylor Cornish, *The Sable Arm: Negro Troops in the Union Army, 1861–1865* (1966).

Louis Gerteis, *From Contraband to Freedom: Federal Policy toward Southern Blacks, 1861–1865* (1973).

Joseph T. Glatthaar, *Forged in Battle: The Civil War Alliance of Black Soldiers and White Officers* (1990).

William B. Gould IV, ed., *Diary of a Contraband: The Civil War Passage of a Black Sailor* (2002).

Bruce Levine, *Confederate Emancipation: Southern Plans to Free and Arm Slaves during the Civil War* (2006).

William S. McFeely, *Frederick Douglass* (1991).

▶ FOR MORE BOOKS ABOUT TOPICS IN THIS CHAPTER, see the Online Bibliography at bedfordstmartins.com/roark.

▶ FOR ADDITIONAL FIRSTHAND ACCOUNTS OF THIS PERIOD, see Chapter 15 in Michael Johnson, ed., *Reading the American Past,* Fourth Edition.

▶ FOR WEB SITES, IMAGES, AND DOCUMENTS RELATED TO TOPICS AND PLACES IN THIS CHAPTER, visit bedfordstmartins.com/makehistory.

REVIEWING THE CHAPTER

Follow these steps to review and strengthen your understanding of the chapter.

STEP 1: *Study the* **Key Terms** *and* **Timeline** *to identify the significance of each item listed.*

STEP 2: *Answer the* **Review Questions***, drawing on key terms and dates to support your answers.*

STEP 3: *Drawing on the Key Terms, Timeline, and Review Questions, answer the broader* **Making Connections** *questions.*

KEY TERMS

Who

Frederick Douglass (p. 512)
Abraham Lincoln (pp. 513, 517)
Jefferson Davis (pp. 513, 516)
Salmon P. Chase (p. 517)
William H. Seward (p. 517)
George B. McClellan (p. 520)
Joseph Johnston (p. 520)
Robert E. Lee (p. 520)
Ambrose Burnside (p. 521)
Samuel R. Curtis (p. 522)
William Clarke Quantrill (p. 522)
"Bloody Bill" Anderson (p. 522)
Ulysses S. Grant (p. 522)
Benjamin F. Butler (p. 528)
Dorothea Dix (p. 537)
Clara Barton (p. 538)
George G. Meade (p. 540)
George E. Pickett (p. 540)

William Tecumseh Sherman (p. 540)
Philip H. Sheridan (p. 544)

What

Fort Sumter (p. 513)
battle of Bull Run/Manassas (p. 519)
peninsula campaign (p. 520)
Seven Days Battle (p. 520)
battle of Antietam (p. 521)
battle of Fredericksburg (p. 521)
battle of Pea Ridge (p. 522)
Fort Henry (p. 523)
Fort Donelson (p. 523)
battle of Shiloh (p. 523)
Union blockade (p. 523)
Merrimack/Virginia (p. 523)
Monitor (p. 523)
King Cotton diplomacy (p. 524)
Confiscation Act (p. 528)

contraband of war (p. 528)
second Confiscation Act (p. 529)
Emancipation Proclamation (p. 529)
bread riots (p. 534)
National Banking Act (p. 537)
Homestead Act (p. 537)
Pacific Railroad Act (p. 537)
Land-Grant College Act (Morrill Act) (p. 537)
U.S. Sanitary Commission (p. 537)
American Red Cross (p. 538)
Union draft law (p. 538)
New York City draft riots (p. 539)
siege of Vicksburg (p. 540)
battle of Gettysburg (p. 540)
battle of Chattanooga (p. 540)
battle of the Wilderness (p. 541)
Sherman's "March to the Sea" (p. 544)
"peace" Democrats (p. 545)

TIMELINE

1861 • **April.** Attack on Fort Sumter.
• **April–May.** Four Upper South states join Confederacy.
• **July.** Union forces routed in first battle of Bull Run.
• **August.** First Confiscation Act.

1862 • **February.** Grant captures Fort Henry and Fort Donelson.
• **March.** Confederates defeated at battle of Glorieta Pass.
• Union victory at battle of Pea Ridge.
• **April.** Battle of Shiloh in Tennessee ends Confederate bid to control Mississippi valley.
• Confederate Congress authorizes draft.
• **May.** Homestead Act.
• **May–July.** Union forces defeated during Virginia peninsula campaign.
• **July.** Second Confiscation Act.
• Militia Act.
• **September.** Battle of Antietam stops Lee's advance into Maryland.

REVIEW QUESTIONS

1. Why did both the Union and the Confederacy consider control of the border states crucial? (pp. 513–15)

2. Why did the South believe it could win the war despite numerical disadvantages? (pp. 515–18)

3. Why did the Confederacy's bid for international support fail? (pp. 518–24)

4. Why did the Union change policy in 1863 to allow black men to serve in the army? (pp. 524–30)

5. How did wartime hardship in the South contribute to class animosity? (pp. 530–36)

6. Why was the U.S. Congress able to pass such a bold legislative agenda during the war? (pp. 536–39)

7. Why were the siege of Vicksburg and the battle of Gettysburg crucial to the outcome of the war? (pp. 539–47)

MAKING CONNECTIONS

1. Despite loathing slavery, Lincoln embraced emancipation as a war objective late and with great caution. Why? In your answer, trace the progression of Lincoln's position, considering how legal, political, military, and moral concerns influenced his policies.

2. The Emancipation Proclamation did not accomplish the destruction of slavery on its own. How did a war over union bring about the end of slavery? In your answer, consider the direct actions of slaves and Union policymakers as well as indirect factors within the Confederacy.

3. In addition to restoring the Union and destroying slavery, what other significant changes did the war produce on the home front and in the nation's capital? In your answer, discuss economic, governmental, and social developments, being attentive to regional variations.

4. Brilliant military strategy alone did not determine the outcome of the war; victory also depended on generating revenue, materiel mobilization, diplomacy, and politics. In light of these considerations, explain why the Confederacy believed it would succeed and why it ultimately failed.

▶ For practice quizzes, a customized study plan, and other study tools, see the Online Study Guide at bedfordstmartins.com/roark.

1863 • **January.** Emancipation Proclamation becomes law.
• **February.** National Banking Act.
• **March.** Congress authorizes draft.
• **July.** Fall of Vicksburg to Union forces.
• Lee defeated at battle of Gettysburg.
• New York City antidraft riots.

1864 • **March.** Grant appointed Union general in chief.
• **May–June.** Wilderness campaign.
• **September.** Fall of Atlanta to Sherman.
• **November.** Lincoln reelected.
• **December.** Fall of Savannah to Sherman.

1865 • **April 2–3.** Fall of Petersburg and Richmond.
• **April 9.** Lee surrenders to Grant.
• **April 15.** Lincoln dies from bullet wound; Vice President Andrew Johnson becomes president.

CARPETBAG

A carpetbag was a nineteenth-
century suitcase made from carpet, often brightly
colored. Applied first to wildcat bankers on the western frontier,
"carpetbagger" was a derogatory name for rootless and penniless adventurers who
could carry everything they owned in a single bag. Critics of Republican administrations
in the South hurled the name "carpetbaggers" at white Northerners who moved South
during Reconstruction and became active in politics. According to white Southerners,
carpetbaggers exploited gullible ex-slaves to gain power and wealth. In fact, many
Northerners who came to the South joined with blacks and some southern whites to
form Republican state and local governments that were among the most progressive
anywhere in the nineteenth century.

Private Collection/Picture Research Consultants & Archives.

16

Reconstruction

1863–1877

■ **Wartime Reconstruction** 555
"To Bind Up the
Nation's Wounds" 555
Land and Labor 556
The African American Quest
for Autonomy 557

■ **Presidential Reconstruction** 561
Johnson's Program
of Reconciliation 561
White Southern Resistance
and Black Codes 562
Expansion of Federal Authority
and Black Rights 564

■ **Congressional
Reconstruction** 565
The Fourteenth Amendment
and Escalating Violence 565
Radical Reconstruction
and Military Rule 568
Impeaching a President 570
The Fifteenth Amendment
and Women's Demands 571

■ **The Struggle in the South** 572
Freedmen, Yankees, and Yeomen 572
Republican Rule 573
White Landlords,
Black Sharecroppers 578

■ **Reconstruction Collapses** 579
Grant's Troubled Presidency 580
Northern Resolve Withers 582
White Supremacy Triumphs 583
An Election and a Compromise 585

■ **Conclusion: "A Revolution
But Half Accomplished"** 586

I N 1856, JOHN RAPIER, a free black barber in Florence, Alabama, urged his four freeborn sons to flee the increasingly repressive and dangerous South. Searching for a color-blind society, three of the brothers scattered to New York, California, and Panama. The fourth, James T. Rapier, chose Canada, where he went to live with his uncle in a largely black community and studied Greek and Latin in a log schoolhouse. After his conversion at a Methodist revival, James wrote to his father: "I have not thrown a card in 3 years[,] touched a woman in 2 years[,] smoked nor drunk any Liquor in going on 2 years." And he vowed, "I will endeavor to do my part in solving the problems [of African Americans] in my native land."

The approaching Union victory in the Civil War gave James Rapier the opportunity to redeem his pledge. Defeat promised to turn the South upside down. With the Confederacy dead and slavery gone, blacks could push for equality. A few months before the war ended, after eight years of exile, the twenty-seven-year-old Rapier returned to the South. He participated in a freedmen's convention in Tennessee and then went home to Alabama, where he presided over the first political gathering of former slaves in the state. The Alabama freedmen produced a petition that called on the federal government to thoroughly reconstruct the South, to grant blacks the vote, and to guarantee free speech, free press, free schools, and equal rights for all men, regardless of color.

Rapier soon discovered that Alabama's whites found it agonizingly difficult to accept defeat and black freedom. They responded to the revolutionary changes under the banner "White Man—Right or Wrong—Still the White Man!" In 1868, when Rapier and other Alabama blacks vigorously supported the Republican presidential candidate, former Union general Ulysses S. Grant, the recently organized Ku Klux Klan went on a bloody rampage of whipping, burning, and shooting. In September, a mob of 150 outraged whites scoured Rapier's neighborhood seeking four black politicians they claimed were trying to "Africanize Alabama." They caught and hanged three, but the "nigger carpetbagger from Canada" escaped. Badly shaken, Rapier considered fleeing the state, but he decided to stay and fight.

Tall, handsome, knowledgeable, and quick-witted, Rapier emerged in the early 1870s as Alabama's most prominent black leader. He demanded that the federal government end the violence against ex-slaves and guarantee their civil rights. He called for debt relief for black sharecroppers and tenant farmers, the end of racial segregation in public places, and land for freedmen. In 1872, he won election to the House of Representatives and joined six other black congressmen in Washington, D.C. Even those who sought to destroy him and overthrow so-called "Negro rule" admitted that Rapier was "the

J. T. Rapier

Only two years after emancipation, ex-slaves in the United States gained full political rights and wielded far more political power than former bondsmen anywhere else in the New World. Black suffrage sent fourteen African American congressmen to Washington, D.C., during Reconstruction, among them James T. Rapier of Alabama. Temporarily at least, he and his black colleagues helped shape post-emancipation society. In 1874, Rapier spoke passionately in favor of a civil rights bill. He described the humiliation of being denied service at inns all along his route from Montgomery to Washington. Elsewhere in the world, he said, class and religion were invoked to defend discrimination. In Europe, "they have princes, dukes, lords"; in India, "brahmans or priests, who rank above the sudras or laborers." But in America, "our distinction is color."

Alabama Department of Archives and History.

Brown. After more than a dozen trips scouting the possibilities in Kansas, Rapier purchased land and urged Alabama's blacks to escape with him. Buoyant and confident when he returned to Alabama in 1865, he had over the years grown profoundly pessimistic that blacks could ever achieve equality and prosperity in the South. In 1883, however, before he could leave Alabama, Rapier died of tuberculosis at the age of forty-five.

In 1865, Carl Schurz had foreseen many of the troubles Rapier would encounter in the postwar South. A Union general who undertook a fact-finding mission to the former Confederate states immediately after the war, Schurz concluded that the Civil War was "a revolution but half accomplished." Northern victory had freed the slaves, but it had not changed former slaveholders' minds about blacks' unfitness for freedom. Left to themselves, Schurz believed, whites would "introduce some new system of forced labor, not perhaps exactly slavery in its old form but something similar to it." To defend their freedom, Schurz concluded, blacks would need federal protection, land of their own, and voting rights. Until whites "cut loose from the past, it will be a dangerous experiment to put Southern society upon its own legs."

As Schurz discovered, the end of the war did not mean peace. The United States was one of only two societies in the New World in which slavery ended in bloody war. (The other was Haiti, where a slave revolt that began in 1791 eventually swept slavery away.) Not surprisingly, racial turmoil continued in the South after the armies quit fighting in 1865. The nation entered one of its most chaotic and conflicted eras—Reconstruction, a violent period that would define the defeated South's status within the Union and the meaning of freedom for ex-slaves.

The place of the South within the nation and the extent of black freedom were determined not only in Washington, D.C., where the federal government played an active role, but also in the state legislatures and county seats of the South, where blacks participated in the process. Moreover, on farms and plantations from Virginia to Texas, ex-slaves struggled to become free people while ex-slaveholders clung to the Old South.

In the midst of Reconstruction's racial flux and economic chaos, a small band of crusading women sought to achieve gender equality. Their attempts to secure voting rights for women as well as blacks were blunted, and they soon turned their attention solely to the feminist cause.

best intellect under a colored skin in Alabama." Defeated for reelection in 1874 in a fraudulent campaign of violence and ballot box stuffing, Rapier turned to cotton farming, generously giving thousands of dollars of his profits to black schools and churches.

Rapier's black constituents celebrated him as a hero, but in the eyes of dominant whites, he was "nothing but a nigger." Embittered by persistent black poverty and illiteracy, demoralized by continuing racial violence and a federal government that refused to stop it, Rapier again chose exile. Kansas attracted him because of its millions of acres of cheap land and because it was, before the war, home to that fiery enemy of slavery John

Reconstruction witnessed a gigantic struggle to determine the consequences of Confederate defeat and **emancipation**. In the end, white Southerners prevailed. Their **New South** was a different South from the one to which most whites wished to return but also vastly unlike the one of which James Rapier dreamed.

Wartime Reconstruction

Reconstruction did not wait for the end of war. As the odds of a northern victory increased, thinking about reunification quickened. Immediately, a question arose: Who had authority to devise a plan for reconstructing the Union? President Abraham Lincoln believed firmly that reconstruction was a matter of executive responsibility. Congress just as firmly asserted its jurisdiction. Fueling the argument about who had the authority to set the terms of reconstruction were significant differences about the terms themselves. Lincoln's primary aim was the restoration of national unity, which he sought through a program of speedy, forgiving political reconciliation. Congress feared that the president's program amounted to restoring the old southern ruling class to power. It wanted greater assurances of white loyalty and greater guarantees of black rights.

In their eagerness to formulate a plan for political reunification, neither Lincoln nor Congress gave much attention to the South's land and labor problems. But as the war rapidly eroded slavery and traditional plantation agriculture, Yankee military commanders in the Union-occupied areas of the Confederacy had no choice but to oversee the emergence of a new labor system.

"To Bind Up the Nation's Wounds"

On March 4, 1865, President Lincoln delivered his second inaugural address. He surveyed the history of the long, deadly war and then looked ahead to peace. "With malice toward none; with charity for all; with firmness in the right, as God gives us to see the right," Lincoln said, "let us strive on to finish the work we are in; to bind up the nation's wounds . . . to do all which may achieve and cherish a just, and a lasting peace." Lincoln had contemplated reunion for nearly two years. While deep compassion for the enemy guided his thinking about peace, his plan

for reconstruction aimed primarily at shortening the war and ending slavery.

In his Proclamation of Amnesty and Reconstruction, issued in December 1863, Lincoln offered a full pardon to rebels willing to renounce secession and to accept emancipation. (Pardons were valuable because they restored all property, except slaves, and full political rights.) His offer excluded only high-ranking Confederate military and political officers and a few other groups. When merely 10 percent of a state's voting population had taken an oath of allegiance, the state could organize a new government. Lincoln's plan did not require ex-rebels to extend social or political rights to ex-slaves, nor did it anticipate a program of long-term federal assistance to freedmen. Clearly, the president looked forward to the speedy restoration of the broken Union.

Lincoln's easy terms enraged abolitionists such as Wendell Phillips of Boston, who charged that the president "makes the negro's freedom a mere sham." He "is willing that the negro should be free but seeks nothing else for him," Phillips declared. He compared Lincoln to the most passive of the Civil War generals: "What McClellan was on the battlefield— 'Do as little hurt as possible!'— Lincoln is in civil affairs—'Make as little change as possible!'" Phillips and other northern radicals called instead for a thorough overhaul of southern society. Their ideas proved to be too drastic for most Republicans during the war years, but Congress agreed that Lincoln's plan was inadequate. In July 1864, Congress put forward a plan of its own.

> Lincoln "is willing that the negro should be free but seeks nothing else for him," Wendell Phillips declared.

Congressman Henry Winter Davis of Maryland and Senator Benjamin Wade of Ohio jointly sponsored a bill that demanded that at least half of the voters in a conquered rebel state take the oath of allegiance before reconstruction could begin. Moreover, the Wade-Davis bill banned all ex-Confederates from participating in the drafting of new state constitutions. Finally, the bill guaranteed the equality of freedmen before the law. Congress's reconstruction would be neither as quick nor as forgiving as Lincoln's. When Lincoln exercised his right not to sign the bill and let it die instead, Wade and Davis charged the president with usurpation of power. They warned Lincoln to confine himself to "his executive duties—to obey and execute, not make the laws—to suppress by arms armed rebellion, and leave political organization to Congress."

Military Auction of Condemned Property, Beaufort, South Carolina, 1865
During the war, thousands of acres of land in the South came into federal hands as abandoned property or as a result of seizures due to nonpayment of taxes. The government authorized the sale of some of this land at public auction. This rare photograph shows expectant blacks (and a few whites) gathered in Beaufort, South Carolina, for a sale. Very few former slaves could raise enough money to purchase land, and even when they pooled their resources, they usually lost out to northern army officers, government officials, or speculators with deeper pockets. Several of the individuals here are wearing Union army caps, strong affirmation of their political loyalties.
The Huntington Library, San Marino, California.

Undeterred, Lincoln continued to nurture the formation of loyal state governments under his own plan. Four states—Louisiana, Arkansas, Tennessee, and Virginia—fulfilled the president's requirements, but Congress refused to seat representatives from the "Lincoln states." In his last public address in April 1865, Lincoln defended his plan but for the first time expressed publicly his endorsement of **suffrage** for southern blacks, at least "the very intelligent, and . . . those who serve our cause as soldiers." The announcement demonstrated that Lincoln's thinking about reconstruction was still evolving. Four days later, he was dead.

Land and Labor

Of all the problems raised by the North's victory in the war, none proved more critical than the South's transition from slavery to **free labor**. As federal armies invaded and occupied the Confederacy, hundreds of thousands of slaves became free workers. Union armies controlled vast territories in the South where legal title to land had become unclear. The wartime Confiscation Acts punished "traitors" by taking away their property. The question of what to do with federally occupied land and how to organize labor on it engaged former slaves, former slaveholders, Union military commanders, and federal government officials long before the war ended.

Up and down the Mississippi valley, occupying federal troops announced a new labor code. The code required slaveholders to sign contracts with ex-slaves and to pay wages. It obligated employers to provide food, housing, and medical care. It outlawed whipping, but it reserved to the army the right to discipline blacks who refused to work. The code required black laborers to enter into contracts, work diligently, and remain subordinate and obedient. Military leaders clearly had no intention of promoting a social or economic revolution. Instead, they sought to restore plantation agriculture with wage labor. The effort resulted in a hybrid system that one contemporary called "compulsory free labor," something that satisfied no one. Depending on one's point of view, it provided either too little or too much of a break with the past.

Planters complained because the new system fell short of slavery. Blacks could not be "transformed by proclamation," a Louisiana sugar planter warned. Yet under the new system, blacks "are expected to perform their new obligations without coercion, & without the fear of punishment which is essential to stimulate the idle and correct the vicious." Without the right to whip, he argued, the new labor system did not have a chance.

African Americans found the new regime too reminiscent of slavery to be called free labor. Its chief deficiency, they believed, was the failure to provide them with land of their own. "What's the use of being free if you don't own land enough to be buried in?" one man asked. Freedmen believed they had a moral right to land because they and their ancestors had worked it without compensation for more than two centuries. Moreover, several wartime developments led them to believe that the federal government planned to undergird black freedom with land-ownership.

In January 1865, General William Tecumseh Sherman set aside part of the coast south of Charleston for black settlement. He devised the plan to relieve himself of the burden of thousands of impoverished blacks who trailed desperately after his army. By June 1865, some 40,000 freedmen sat on 400,000 acres of "Sherman land." In addition, in March 1865, Congress passed a bill establishing the Bureau of Refugees, Freedmen, and Abandoned Lands. The Freedmen's Bureau, as it was called, distributed food and clothing to destitute Southerners and eased the transition of blacks from slaves to free persons. Congress also authorized the agency to divide abandoned and confiscated land into 40-acre plots, to rent them to freedmen, and eventually to sell them "with such title as the United States can convey." By June 1865, the bureau had situated nearly 10,000 black families on a half million acres abandoned by fleeing planters. Hundreds of thousands of other ex-slaves eagerly anticipated farms of their own.

Despite the flurry of activity, wartime reconstruction failed to produce agreement about whether the president or Congress had the authority to devise and direct policy or what proper policy should be. As Lincoln anticipated, the nation faced postwar dilemmas almost as trying as those of the war.

The African American Quest for Autonomy

Ex-slaves never had any doubt about what they wanted from freedom. They had only to contemplate what they had been denied as slaves. (See "Documenting the American Promise," page 558.) Slaves had to remain on their plantations; freedom allowed blacks to go wherever they pleased. Thus, in the first heady weeks after emancipation, freedmen often abandoned their plantations just to see what was on the other side of the hill. Slaves had to be at work in the fields by dawn; freedom permitted blacks to taste the formerly forbidden pleasure of sleeping through a sunrise. Freedmen also tested the etiquette of racial subordination. "Lizzie's maid passed me today when I was coming from church *without speaking to me*," huffed one plantation mistress.

> "The way we can best take care of ourselves is to have land," one former slave declared in 1865, "and turn it and till it by our own labor."

To whites, emancipation looked like pure anarchy. Blacks, they said, had reverted to their natural condition: lazy, irresponsible, and wild. Without the discipline of slavery, whites predicted, blacks would go the way of "the Indian and the buffalo." Actually, former slaves were experimenting with freedom, but they could not long afford to roam the countryside, neglect work, and casually provoke whites. Soon, most were back at work in whites' kitchens and fields.

But other items on ex-slaves' agenda of freedom endured. They continued to dream of land and economic independence. "The way we can best take care of ourselves is to have land," one former slave declared in 1865, "and turn it and till it by our own labor." Another explained that he wanted land, "not a Master or owner[,] Neither a driver with his Whip."

Antebellum southern whites had deliberately kept blacks illiterate, and freedmen wanted to learn to read and write. Many black soldiers had become literate in the Union army, and they understood the value of the pen and book. "I wishes the Childern all in School," one black veteran asserted. "It is beter for them then to be their Surveing a mistes [mistress]."

Moreover, bondage had denied slaves secure family lives, and the restoration of their families became a persistent black aspiration. Thousands of black men and women took to the roads in 1865 to look for kin who had been sold away or to free those who were being held illegally as slaves. A black soldier from Missouri

The Meaning of Freedom

On New Year's Day 1863, President Abraham Lincoln issued the Emancipation Proclamation. It states that "all persons held as slaves" within the states still in rebellion "are, and henceforward shall be, free." Although the Proclamation in and of itself did not free any slaves, it transformed the character of the war. Despite often intolerable conditions, black people focused on the possibilities of freedom.

DOCUMENT 1
Letter from John Q. A. Dennis to Edwin M. Stanton, July 26, 1864

John Q. A. Dennis, formerly a slave in Maryland, wrote to ask Secretary of War Edwin M. Stanton for help in reuniting his family.

Boston

Dear Sir I am Glad that I have the Honour to Write you afew line I have been in troble for about four yars my Dear wife was taken from me Nov 19th 1859 and left me with three Children and I being a Slave At the time Could Not do Anny thing for the poor little Children for my master it was took me Carry me some forty mile from them So I Could Not do for them and the man that they live with half feed them and half Cloth them & beat them like dogs & when I was admitted to go to see them it use to brake my heart & Now I say again I am Glad to have the honour to write to you to see if you Can Do Anny thing for me or for my poor little Children I was keap in Slavy untell last Novr 1863. then the Good lord sent the Cornel borne

[federal Colonel William Birney?] Down their in Marland in worsester Co So as I have been recently freed I have but letle to live on but I am Striveing Dear Sir but what I went too know of you Sir is it possible for me to go & take my Children from those men that keep them in Savery if it is possible will you pleas give me a permit from your hand then I think they would let them go. . . .

Hon sir will you please excuse my Miserable writeing & answer me as soon as you can I want get the little Children out of Slavery, I being Criple would like to know of you also if I Cant be permited to rase a Shool Down there & on what turm I Could be admited to Do so No more At present Dear Hon Sir

Source: *Freedom: A Documentary History of Emancipation, 1861–1867*, ser. 1, vol. 1, *The Destruction of Slavery*, 386, by Ira Berlin, Joseph P. Reidy, and Leslie S. Rowland, eds. Copyright © 1985. Reprinted with the permission of Cambridge University Press.

DOCUMENT 2
Report from Reverend A. B. Randall, February 28, 1865

Freedom prompted ex-slaves to seek legal marriages, which under slavery had been impossible. Writing from Little Rock, Arkansas, to the adjutant general of the Union army, A. B. Randall, the white chaplain of a black regiment, affirmed the importance of marriage to freed slaves and emphasized their conviction that emancipation was only the first step toward full freedom.

Weddings, just now, are very popular, and abundant among the Colored People. They have just learned, of the Special Order No. 15. of Gen Thomas [Adjutant General Lorenzo Thomas] by which, they may not only be lawfully married, but have their Marriage Certificates, Recorded; in a book furnished by the Government. This is most desirable. . . . Those who were captured . . . at Ivy's Ford, on the 17th of January, by Col Brooks, had their Marriage Certificates, taken from them; and destroyed; and then were roundly cursed, for having such papers in their posession. I have married, during the month, at this Post; Twenty five couples; mostly, those, who have families; & have been living together for years. I try to dissuade single men, who are soldiers, from marrying, till their time of enlistment is out: as that course seems to me, to be most judicious.

The Colord People here, generally consider, this war not only; their exodus, from bondage; but the road, to Responsibility; Competency; and an honorable Citizenship—God grant that their hopes and expectations may be fully realized.

Source: *Freedom: A Documentary History of Emancipation, 1861–1867*, ser. 2, vol. 1, *The Black Military Experience*, 712, by Ira Berlin, Joseph P. Reidy, and Leslie S. Rowland, eds. Copyright © 1982. Reprinted with the permission of Cambridge University Press.

DOCUMENT 3
Petition "to the Union Convention of Tennessee Assembled in the Capitol at Nashville," January 9, 1865

Early efforts at political reconstruction prompted petitions from former slaves demanding civil and political rights.

In January 1865, black Tennesseans petitioned a convention of white Unionists debating the reorganization of state government.

We the undersigned petitioners, American citizens of African descent, natives and residents of Tennessee, and devoted friends of the great National cause, do most respectfully ask a patient hearing of your honorable body in regard to matters deeply affecting the future condition of our unfortunate and long suffering race.

First of all, however, we would say that words are too weak to tell how profoundly grateful we are to the Federal Government for the good work of freedom which it is gradually carrying forward; and for the Emancipation Proclamation which has set free all the slaves in some of the rebellious States, as well as many of the slaves in Tennessee. . . .

We claim freedom, as our natural right, and ask that in harmony and co-operation with the nation at large, you should cut up by the roots the system of slavery, which is not only a wrong to us, but the source of all the evil which at present afflicts the State. For slavery, corrupt itself, corrupted nearly all, also, around it, so that it has influenced nearly all the slave States to rebel against the Federal Government, in order to set up a government of pirates under which slavery might be perpetrated.

In the contest between the nation and slavery, our unfortunate people have sided, by instinct, with the former. We have little fortune to devote to the national cause, for a hard fate has hitherto forced us to live in poverty, but we do devote to its success, our hopes, our toils, our whole heart, our sacred honor, and our lives. We will work, pray, live, and, if need be, die for the Union, as cheerfully as ever a white patriot died for his country. The color of our skin does not lessen in the least degree, our love either for God or for the land of our birth. . . .

We know the burdens of citizenship, and are ready to bear them. We know the duties of the good citizen, and are ready to perform them cheerfully, and would ask to be put in a position in which we can discharge them more effectually. . . .

This is a democracy—a government of the people. It should aim to make every man, without regard to the color of his skin, the amount of his wealth, or the character of his religious faith, feel personally interested in its welfare. Every man who lives under the Government should feel that it is his property, his treasure, the bulwark and defence of himself and his family, his pearl of great price, which he must preserve, protect, and defend faithfully at all times, on all occasions, in every possible manner.

This is not a Democratic Government if a numerous, law-abiding, industrious, and useful class of citizens, born and bred on the soil, are to be treated as aliens and enemies, as an inferior degraded class, who must have no voice in the Government which they support, protect and defend, with all their heart, soul, mind, and body, both in peace and war. . . .

The possibility that the negro suffrage proposition may shock popular prejudice at first sight, is not a conclusive argument against its wisdom and policy. No proposition ever met with more furious or general opposition than the one to enlist colored soldiers in the United States army. The opponents of the measure exclaimed on all hands that the negro was a coward; that he would not fight; that one white man, with a whip in his hand could put to flight a regiment of them; that the experiment would end in the utter rout and ruin of the Federal army. Yet the colored man has fought so well, on almost every occasion, that the rebel government is prevented, only by its fears and distrust of being able to force him to fight for slavery as well as he fights against it, from putting half a million of negroes into its ranks.

The Government has asked the colored man to fight for its preservation and gladly has he done it. It can afford to trust him with a vote as safely as it trusted him with a bayonet.

Source: *Freedom: A Documentary History of Emancipation, 1861–1867*, ser. 2, vol. 1, *The Black Military Experience*, 811–16, by Ira Berlin, Joseph P. Reidy, and Leslie S. Rowland, eds. Copyright © 1982. Reprinted with the permission of Cambridge University Press.

QUESTIONS FOR ANALYSIS AND DEBATE

1. How does John Q. A. Dennis interpret his responsibility as a father?

2. Why do you think ex-slaves wanted their marriages legalized?

3. Why, according to petitioners to the Union Convention of Tennessee, did blacks deserve voting rights?

Samuel Dove Ad, 1865, and Harry Stephens and Family, 1866
Dressed in their Sunday best, this Virginia family sits proudly for a photograph. Many black families were not as fortunate as the Stephens family. Separated by slavery or war, former slaves desperately sought news of missing family members through newspaper advertisements like the one posted by Samuel Dove in August 1865. We do not know whether he succeeded in locating his mother, brother, and sisters.

Ad: Chicago Historical Society; Family: The Metropolitan Museum of Art, Gilman Collection, Purchase, The Horace W. Goldsmith Foundation Gift, 2005 (2005.100.277)

SAML. DOVE wishes to know of the whereabouts of his mother, Areno, his sisters Maria, Neziah, and Peggy, and his brother Edmond, who were owned by Geo. Dove, of Rockingham county, Shenandoah Valley, Va. Sold in Richmond, after which Saml. and Edmond were taken to Nashville, Tenn., by Joe Mick; Areno was left at the Eagle Tavern, Richmond

Respectfully yours,
SAML. DOVE.

Utica, New York, Aug. 5, 1865–3m

U. S. Christian Commission,
Nashville, Tenn., July 19, 1865.

wrote his daughters that he was coming for them. "I will have you if it cost me my life," he declared. "Your Miss Kitty said that I tried to steal you," he told them. "But I'll let her know that god never intended for a man to steal his own flesh and blood." And he swore that "if she meets me with ten thousand soldiers, she [will] meet her enemy."

Another hunger was for independent worship. African Americans greeted freedom with a mass exodus from white churches, where they had been required to worship when slaves. Some joined the newly established southern branches of all-black northern churches, such as the African Methodist Episcopal Church. Others formed black versions of the major southern denominations, Baptists and Methodists. Slaves had comprehended their tribulations through the lens of their deeply felt Christian faith, and freedmen continued to interpret the events of the Civil War and reconstruction as people of faith. One black woman thanked Lincoln for the Emancipation Proclamation, declaring, "When you are dead and in Heaven, in a thousand years that action of yours will make the Angels sing your praises I know it."

REVIEW   Why did Congress object to Lincoln's wartime plan for reconstruction?

Presidential Reconstruction

Abraham Lincoln died on April 15, 1865, just hours after John Wilkes Booth shot him at a Washington, D.C., theater. Chief Justice Salmon P. Chase immediately administered the oath of office to Vice President Andrew Johnson of Tennessee. Congress had adjourned in March, which meant that legislators were away from Washington when Lincoln was killed. They would not reconvene until December. Throughout the summer and fall, therefore, the "accidental president" made critical decisions about the future of the South without congressional advice. Like Lincoln, Johnson believed that responsibility for restoring the Union lay with the president. With dizzying speed, he drew up and executed a plan of reconstruction.

Congress returned to the capital in December to find that, as far as the president and former Confederates were concerned, reconstruction was already decided. Most Republicans, however, thought Johnson's modest demands of ex-rebels made a mockery of the sacrifice of Union soldiers. Instead of honoring the dead by insisting on "a new birth of freedom," as Lincoln had promised in his 1863 speech at Gettysburg, Johnson had acted as midwife to the rebirth of the Old South and the stillbirth of black **liberty**. To let his program stand, Republican legislators said, would mean that the North's dead had indeed died in vain. They proceeded to dismantle it and substitute a program of their own, one that southern whites found ways to resist.

Johnson's Program of Reconciliation

Born in 1808 in Raleigh, North Carolina, Andrew Johnson was the son of illiterate parents. Self-educated and ambitious, Johnson moved to Tennessee, where he worked as a tailor, accumulated a fortune in land, acquired five slaves, and built a career in politics championing the South's common white people and assailing its "illegitimate, swaggering, bastard, scrub aristocracy." The only senator from a Confederate state to remain loyal to the Union, Johnson held the planter class

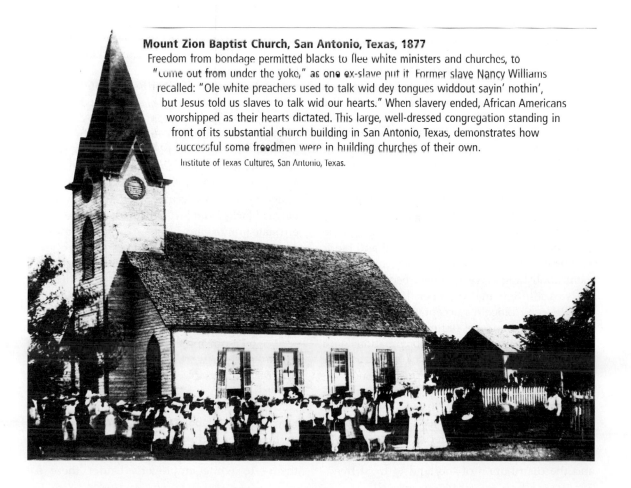

Mount Zion Baptist Church, San Antonio, Texas, 1877
Freedom from bondage permitted blacks to flee white ministers and churches, to "come out from under the yoke," as one ex-slave put it. Former slave Nancy Williams recalled: "Ole white preachers used to talk wid dey tongues widdout sayin' nothin', but Jesus told us slaves to talk wid our hearts." When slavery ended, African Americans worshipped as their hearts dictated. This large, well-dressed congregation standing in front of its substantial church building in San Antonio, Texas, demonstrates how successful some freedmen were in building churches of their own.
Institute of Texas Cultures, San Antonio, Texas.

responsible for secession. Less than two weeks before he became president, he made it clear what he would do to planters if he ever had the chance: "I would arrest them—I would try them—I would convict them and I would hang them."

Despite such statements, Johnson was no friend of the Republicans. A southern Democrat all his life, Johnson occupied the White House only because the Republican Party in 1864 had needed a vice presidential candidate who would appeal to loyal, Union-supporting Democrats. Johnson favored traditional Democratic causes, vigorously defending **states' rights** (but not secession) and opposing Republican efforts to expand the power of the federal government. A steadfast defender of slavery, Johnson had owned slaves until 1862, when Tennessee rebels, angry at his Unionism, confiscated them. He only grudgingly accepted emancipation. When he did, it was more because he hated planters than sympathized with slaves. "Damn the negroes," he said. "I am fighting those traitorous aristocrats, their masters." At a time when the nation confronted the future of black Americans, the new president harbored unshakable racist convictions. Africans, Johnson said, were "inferior to the white man in point of intellect—better calculated in physical structure to undergo drudgery and hardship."

Like Lincoln, Johnson stressed reconciliation between the Union and the defeated Confederacy and rapid restoration of civil government in the South. Like Lincoln, he promised to pardon most, but not all, ex-rebels. Johnson recognized the state governments created by Lincoln but set out his own requirements for restoring the other rebel states to the Union. All that the citizens of a state had to do was to renounce the right of secession, deny that the debts of the Confederacy were legal and binding, and ratify the Thirteenth Amendment abolishing slavery, which became part of the Constitution in December 1865. Johnson's plan ignored Lincoln's acceptance near the end of his life of some form of limited black voting.

Johnson's eagerness to restore relations with southern states and his lack of sympathy for blacks also led him to return to pardoned ex-Confederates all confiscated and abandoned land, even if it was in the hands of freedmen. Reformers were shocked. They had expected the president's hatred of planters to mean the permanent confiscation of the South's plantations and the distribution of the land to loyal freed-

> Not a single southern state granted any black—no matter how educated, wealthy, or refined—the right to vote.

men. Instead, his instructions canceled the promising beginnings made by General Sherman and the Freedmen's Bureau to settle blacks on land of their own. As one freedman observed, "Things was hurt by Mr. Lincoln getting killed."

White Southern Resistance and Black Codes

In the summer of 1865, delegates across the South gathered to draw up the new state constitutions required by Johnson's plan of reconstruction. Rather than take their medicine, delegates choked on even the president's mild requirements. Refusing to renounce secession, the South Carolina and Georgia conventions merely "repudiated" their secession ordinances, preserving in principle their right to secede. South Carolina and Mississippi refused to disown their Confederate war debts. Mississippi rejected the Thirteenth Amendment outright, and Alabama rejected it in part. Despite these defiant acts, Johnson did nothing. By failing to draw a hard line, he rekindled southern resistance. White Southerners began to think that by standing up for themselves they—not victorious Northerners—would shape reconstruction. In the fall of 1865, newly elected southern legislators set out to reverse what they considered the "retreat into barbarism" that followed emancipation.

State governments across the South adopted a series of laws known as *black codes*, which made a travesty of black freedom. The codes sought to keep ex-slaves subordinate to whites by subjecting them to every sort of discrimination. Several states made it illegal for blacks to own a gun. Mississippi made insulting gestures and language by blacks a criminal offense. The codes barred blacks from jury duty. Not a single southern state granted any black—no matter how educated, wealthy, or refined—the right to vote.

At the core of the black codes, however, lay the matter of labor. Faced with the death of slavery, legislators sought to hustle freedmen back to the plantations. South Carolina attempted to limit blacks to either farmwork or domestic service by requiring them to pay annual taxes of $10 to $100 to work in any other occupation. Mississippi declared that blacks who did not possess written evidence of employment could be declared vagrants and be subject to involuntary plantation labor. Most states allowed judges to bind black children—orphans and others whose parents they deemed unable to support them—to white employers. Under these so-

The Black Codes
Titled "Selling a Freeman to Pay His Fine at Monticello, Florida," this 1867 drawing from a northern magazine equates black codes with the reinstitution of slavery. The laws stopped short of reenslavement but sharply restricted blacks' freedom. In Florida, as in other southern states, certain acts, such as breaking a labor contract, were made criminal offenses, the penalty for which could be involuntary plantation labor for a year.
Granger Collection.

called apprenticeship laws, courts bound thousands of black children to work for planter "guardians."

Johnson refused to intervene. A staunch defender of states' rights, he believed that the citizens of every state, even those who attempted to destroy the Union, should be free to write their own constitutions and laws. Moreover, since Johnson was as eager as other white Southerners to restore white supremacy and black subordination, the black codes did not offend him.

But Johnson also followed the path that he believed would offer him the greatest political return. A **conservative** Tennessee Democrat at the head of a northern Republican Party, he began to look southward for political allies.

Despite tough talk about punishing traitors, he personally pardoned fourteen thousand wealthy or high-ranking ex-Confederates. By pardoning powerful whites, by acquiescing in the black codes, and by accepting governments even when they failed to satisfy his minimal demands, he won useful southern friends.

In the fall elections of 1865, white Southerners dramatically expressed their mood. To represent them in Congress, they chose former Confederates, not loyal Unionists. Of the eighty senators and representatives they sent to Washington, fifteen had served in the Confederate army, ten of them as generals. Another sixteen had served in civil and judicial posts in the Confederacy. Nine others had served in the Confederate Congress.

One—Alexander Stephens—had been vice president of the Confederacy. In December, this remarkable group arrived on the steps of the nation's Capitol building to be seated in Congress. As one Georgian remarked, "It looked as though Richmond had moved to Washington."

Expansion of Federal Authority and Black Rights

Southerners had blundered monumentally. They had assumed that what Andrew Johnson was willing to accept, Republicans would accept as well. But southern intransigence compelled even moderates to conclude that ex-rebels were a "generation of vipers," still untrustworthy and dangerous. So angry were Republicans with the rebels that the federal government refused to supply artificial limbs to disabled Southerners, as they did for Union veterans. (See "The Promise of Technology," page 566.)

The black codes became a symbol of southern intentions to "restore all of slavery but its name." Northerners were hardly saints when it came to racial justice, but black freedom had become a hallowed war aim. "We tell the white men of Mississippi," the *Chicago Tribune* roared, "that the men of the North will convert the State of Mississippi into a frog pond before they will allow such laws to disgrace one foot of the soil in which the bones of our soldiers sleep and over which the flag of freedom waves."

The moderate majority of the Republican Party wanted only assurance that slavery and treason were dead. They did not champion black equality or the confiscation of plantations or black voting, as did the radicals, a minority within the party. But southern obstinacy had succeeded in forging unity (at least temporarily) among Republican factions. In December 1865, exercising Congress's right to determine

> The *Chicago Tribune* roared, "The men of the North will convert the State of Mississippi into a frog pond before they will allow [black codes] to disgrace one foot of the soil in which the bones of our soldiers sleep."

the qualifications of its members, Republicans refused to seat the southern representatives. Rather than accept Johnson's claim that the "work of restoration" was done, Congress challenged his executive power. Congressional Republicans enjoyed a three-to-one majority over the Democrats, and if they could agree on a program of reconstruction, they could easily pass legislation and even override presidential vetoes.

Senator Lyman Trumbull of Illinois declared that the president's policy meant that the ex-slave would "be tyrannized over, abused, and virtually reenslaved without some legislation by the nation for his protection." Early in 1866, the moderates produced two bills that strengthened the federal shield. The first, the Freedmen's Bureau bill, prolonged the life of the agency established by the previous Congress. Since the end of the war, it had distributed food, supervised labor contracts, and sponsored schools for freedmen. Arguing that the Constitution never contemplated a "system for the support of indigent persons," President Andrew Johnson vetoed the bill. Congress failed by a narrow margin to override the president's veto.

The moderates designed their second measure, the Civil Rights Act, to nullify the black codes by

Confederate Flag Dress
While politicians in Washington, D.C., debated the future of the South, white Southerners were coming to grips with the reality of Confederate defeat. They began to refer to their failure to secede from the Union as the "Lost Cause." They enshrined the memory of certain former Confederates, especially Robert E. Lee, whose nobility and courage represented the white South's image of itself, and they made a fetish of the Confederate flag. White Southerners incorporated symbols of the Lost Cause into their daily lives. This dress, made from material embossed with the rebel flag, did double duty. It both memorialized the Confederacy and, through the sale of the cloth, raised funds for the Confederate Soldiers' Home in Richmond, Virginia.
Valentine Museum, Cook Collection.

affirming African Americans' rights to "full and equal benefit of all laws and proceedings for the security of person and property as is enjoyed by white citizens." The act boldly required the end of legal discrimination in state laws and represented an extraordinary expansion of black rights and federal authority. The president argued that the civil rights bill amounted to "unconstitutional invasion of states' rights" and vetoed it. In essence, he denied that the federal government possessed the authority to protect the civil rights of blacks.

In April 1866, an incensed Republican Party again pushed the civil rights bill through Congress and overrode the presidential veto. In July, it passed another Freedmen's Bureau bill and overrode Johnson's veto. For the first time in American history, Congress had overridden presidential vetoes of major legislation. As a worried South Carolinian observed, Johnson had succeeded in uniting the Republicans and probably touched off "a fight this fall such as has never been seen."

> **REVIEW** How did the North respond to the passage of black codes in the southern states?

Congressional Reconstruction

By the summer of 1866, President Andrew Johnson and Congress had dropped their gloves and stood toe-to-toe in a bare-knuckle contest unprecedented in American history. Johnson made it clear that he would not budge on either constitutional issues or policy. Moderate Republicans responded by amending the Constitution. But the obstinacy of Johnson and white Southerners pushed Republican moderates ever closer to the radicals and to acceptance of additional federal intervention in the South. In time, Congress debated whether to give the ballot to black men. Congress also voted to impeach the president. Outside of Congress, blacks championed color-blind voting rights, while women sought to make voting sex-blind as well.

The Fourteenth Amendment and Escalating Violence

In June 1866, Congress passed the Fourteenth Amendment to the Constitution, and two years later it gained the necessary ratification of three-fourths of the states. The most important provisions of this complex amendment made all native-born or naturalized persons American citizens and prohibited states from abridging the "privileges and immunities" of citizens, depriving them of "life, liberty, or property without due process of law," and denying them "equal protection of the laws." By making blacks national citizens, the amendment provided a national guarantee of equality before the law. In essence, it protected blacks against violation by southern state governments.

The Fourteenth Amendment also dealt with voting rights. It gave Congress the right to reduce the congressional representation of states that withheld suffrage from some of its adult male population. In other words, white Southerners could either allow black men to vote or see their representation in Washington slashed.

Whatever happened, Republicans stood to benefit from the Fourteenth Amendment. If southern whites granted voting rights to freedmen, Republicans, entirely a northern party, would gain valuable black votes, establish a wing in the South, and secure their national power. If whites refused, representation of southern Democrats would plunge, and Republicans would still gain political power.

The Fourteenth Amendment's suffrage provisions completely ignored the small band of politicized and energized women who had emerged from the war demanding "the ballot for the two disenfranchised classes, negroes and women." Founding the American Equal Rights Association in 1866, Susan B. Anthony and Elizabeth Cady Stanton lobbied for "a government by the people, and the whole people; for the people and the whole people." They felt betrayed when their old anti-slavery allies, who now occupied positions of national power, proved to be fickle and refused to work for their goals. "It was the Negro's hour," Frederick Douglass later explained. Senator Charles Sumner suggested that woman suffrage could be "the great question of the future."

> Susan B. Anthony and Elizabeth Cady Stanton lobbied for "a government by the people, and the whole people; for the people and the whole people."

The Fourteenth Amendment dashed women's expectations. It provided for punishment of any state that excluded voters on the basis of race but not on the basis of sex. The amendment also introduced the word *male* into the Constitution when it referred to a citizen's right to vote. Stanton predicted that "if that word 'male' be inserted, it will take us a century at least to get it out."

Filling the "Empty Sleeve": Artificial Limbs

Industrial and technological developments that had made the war so destructive also came to the aid of maimed veterans during national reconstruction. A new kind of ammunition used in the war, the minié ball, proved extremely destructive to human flesh. In attempts to save lives, northern and southern surgeons performed approximately 60,000 amputations. Confederate nurse Kate Cummings observed that amputations were so common in her hospital that they were "scarcely noticed." Approximately 45,000 of the amputees survived, and as the nation began reconstructing the Union, it also sought the literal reconstruction of disabled veterans.

Once their wounds had healed, most amputees were eager to fill an empty sleeve or pant leg with an artificial limb. The federal government provided limbs to those who had fought for the Union, and individual southern states provided limbs for Confederate veterans. Innovations in design and production began during the war and accelerated sharply as the enormous demand produced a surge of interest in prosthetic technology. In the fifteen years before the war, 34 patents were issued for artificial limbs and assisting devices; in the twelve years from the beginning of the war to 1873, 133 patents for limbs were issued, nearly a 300

percent increase. As Oliver Wendell Holmes Jr., an army veteran and future Supreme Court justice, observed, if "war unmakes legs," then "human skill must supply their places."

The search for a functional, lightweight, artificial limb drew on a number of advancing fields, including photography, physiology, physics, mathematics, and psychology. For example, in 1859 photographers in Edinburgh and New York succeeded in taking a rapid succession of fast-speed pictures of pedestrians and breaking their strides down into minute parts. Photographs of individuals frozen in mid-step provided new information about human movement that helped make better artificial limbs. The application of photography is but one example of the growing application of science and technology to the alleviation of human suffering in the late nineteenth century.

As excited designers sought to overcome problems of noise, weight, appearance, and discomfort, artificial limbs advanced quickly from crude peg legs to hollow willow legs with movable ankles that simulated the natural motions of the foot. Newly invented vulcanized rubber (called India rubber) increased strength and flexibility and allowed disabled veterans to dispense with

metal bolts and springs in their new limbs. Limb makers sought to erase the line between nature and technology, to merge "bodies with machines," as one manufacturer promised. One doctor boasted: "In our time, limb-making has been carried to such a state of perfection that both in form and function they so completely resemble the natural extremity that those who wear them pass unobserved and unrecognized in walks of business and pleasure." He exaggerated, for the artificial limbs of the 1860s were crude by today's standards, but they did represent significant technological advances.

Less than two years after the war, the manufacture of artificial limbs had become, according to Oliver Wendell Holmes Jr., "a great and active branch of history." Before the war, locksmiths, gunsmiths, toolmakers, harness makers, and cabinetmakers made peg legs and artificial arms individually as sidelines to their principal tasks. After the war, the great demand for artificial limbs prompted businesses to apply industrial manufacturing processes to limbs. Soon American factories—high-volume, mechanized, uniform—were producing untold numbers of sewing machines, bicycles, typewriters, and artificial limbs.

The postwar business of prosthetics was highly competitive. With the federal and state governments placing large, lucrative orders, dozens of manufacturers entered the market. Very quickly, buyers could choose from English, French, German, and American models. With so many choices, men had to be persuaded that one leg was better than another. Aggressive advertising campaigns announced the new products. Northern manufacturers used government military and pension registration rolls to mail brochures directly to the homes of Union veterans. Manufacturers in New York, Philadelphia, and Boston established dazzling showrooms on major shopping streets. They also sponsored "cripple races" to test and promote their products.

Politics sometimes entered into decisions. Southern manufacturers proclaimed that they were "home manufacturers" and deserved contracts from former Confederate states more than their northern competitors did. Confederate general John B. Hood made a controversial admission when he declared that his "Yankee leg was the best of all." Another disabled Southerner, however, disliked his northern-manufactured leg, which, he concluded, "like the majority of Yankee inventions proved to be a 'humbug.'"

Disabled veterans sometimes found their postwar struggle to find work, to overcome the stigma of being disabled, and to regain confidence as difficult as their battlefield experiences. To help them, some prosthetic manufacturers dabbled in medicine that wedded technological and psychological efforts to renew wholeness. New York, for example, was host to an annual left-handed penmanship contest to encourage men who had lost their right hands to learn to write with their left. Well into the twentieth century, a veteran's "empty sleeve" remained both a badge of courage and a sign of permanent loss—a wound that national reconstruction could never heal.

"Before and After"

These photographic images, one showing a veteran with two amputations and the other showing him wearing his artificial legs, come from the back of an A. A. Marks business card in about 1878. This manufacturer of artificial limbs sent a clear message: Marks legs make maimed men whole again. Marks promised that, thus restored, the wounded man would be the "equal of his fellowmen in every employment of life."

Warshaw Collection, National Museum of American History, Smithsonian Institution.

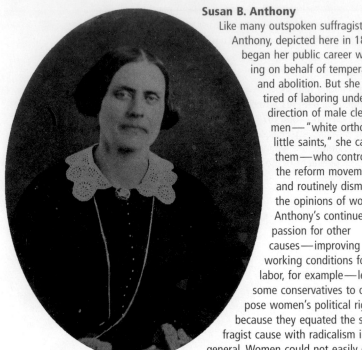

Susan B. Anthony
Like many outspoken suffragists, Anthony, depicted here in 1852, began her public career working on behalf of temperance and abolition. But she grew tired of laboring under the direction of male clergymen—"white orthodox little saints," she called them—who controlled the reform movements and routinely dismissed the opinions of women. Anthony's continued passion for other causes—improving working conditions for labor, for example—led some conservatives to oppose women's political rights because they equated the suffragist cause with radicalism in general. Women could not easily overcome such views, and the long struggle for the vote eventually drew millions of women into public life.
Susan B. Anthony House, Inc.

convention, thirty-four blacks died. In Memphis, white mobs crashed through the black sections of town, killing at least forty-six people. The slaughter shocked Northerners and renewed skepticism about Johnson's claim that southern whites could be trusted. "Who doubts that the Freedmen's Bureau ought to be abolished forthwith," a New Yorker observed sarcastically, "and the blacks remitted to the paternal care of their old masters, who 'understand the nigger, you know, a great deal better than the Yankees can.'"

The 1866 elections resulted in an overwhelming Republican victory in which the party retained its three-to-one congressional majority. Johnson had bet that Northerners would not support federal protection of black rights and that a racist backlash would blast the Republican Party. But the war was still fresh in northern minds, and as one Republican explained, southern whites "with all their intelligence were traitors, the blacks with all their ignorance were loyal."

Radical Reconstruction and Military Rule

The 1866 election should have taught southern whites the folly of relying on Andrew Johnson to guide them through reconstruction. But when Johnson continued to urge Southerners to reject the Fourteenth Amendment, every southern state except Tennessee voted it down. "The last one of the sinful ten," thundered Representative James A. Garfield of Ohio, "has flung back into our teeth the magnanimous offer of a generous nation." After the South rejected the moderates' program, the radicals seized the initiative.

Each act of defiance by southern whites had boosted the standing of the radicals within the Republican Party. Except for freedmen themselves, no one did more to make freedom the "mighty moral question of the age." Radicals such as Massachusetts senator Charles Sumner and Pennsylvania representative Thaddeus Stevens did not speak with a single voice, but they united in demanding civil and political equality. They insisted on extending to ex-slaves the same opportunities that northern working people enjoyed under the free-labor system. Southern states were "like clay in the

Tennessee approved the Fourteenth Amendment in July, and Congress promptly welcomed the state's representatives and senators back. Had President Johnson counseled other southern states to ratify this relatively mild amendment and warned them that they faced the fury of an outraged Republican Party if they refused, they might have listened. Instead, Johnson advised Southerners to reject the Fourteenth Amendment and to rely on him to trounce the Republicans in the fall congressional elections.

Johnson had decided to make the Fourteenth Amendment the overriding issue of the 1866 congressional elections and to gather its white opponents into a new conservative party, the National Union Party. The president's strategy suffered a setback when whites in several southern cities went on rampages against blacks—an escalation of the violence that had never really ceased. When a mob in New Orleans assaulted delegates to a black suffrage

Reconstruction Military Districts, 1867

hands of the potter," Stevens declared in January 1867, and he called on Congress to begin reconstruction all over again.

In March 1867, Congress overturned the Johnson state governments and initiated military rule of the South. The Military Reconstruction Act (and three subsequent acts) divided the ten unreconstructed Confederate states into five military districts. Congress placed a Union general in charge of each district and instructed him to "suppress insurrection, disorder, and violence" and to begin political reform. After the military had completed voter registration, which would include black men, voters in each state would elect delegates to conventions that would draw up new state constitutions. Each constitution would guarantee black suffrage. When the voters of each state had approved the constitution and the

state legislature had ratified the Fourteenth Amendment, the state could submit its work to Congress. If Congress approved, the state's senators and representatives could be seated, and political reunification would be accomplished.

Radicals proclaimed the provision for black suffrage "a prodigious triumph," for it extended far beyond the limited suffrage provisions of the Fourteenth Amendment. Republicans united in the conviction that only the voting power of ex-slaves could bring about a permanent revolution in the South. Indeed, suffrage provided blacks with a powerful instrument of change and self-protection. When combined with the **disfranchisement** of thousands of ex-rebels, it promised to cripple any neo-Confederate resurgence and guarantee Republican state governments in the South.

Memphis Riots, May 1866

On May 1, 1866, two carriages, one driven by a white man and the other by a black man, collided on a busy street in Memphis, Tennessee. This minor incident led to three days of bloody racial violence in which dozens of blacks and two whites died. Racial friction was common in postwar Memphis, and white newspapers routinely heaped abuse on black citizens. "Would to God they were back in Africa, or some other seaport town," the *Memphis Argus* shouted two days before the riot erupted, "anywhere but here." South Memphis, pictured in this lithograph from *Harper's Weekly*, was a shantytown where the families of black soldiers stationed at nearby Fort Pickering lived. The army commander refused to send troops to protect soldiers' families and property, and white mobs ran wild.
Granger Collection.

THIS LITTLE BOY WOULD PERSIST IN HANDLING BOOKS ABOVE
HIS CAPACITY.

AND THIS WAS THE DISASTROUS RESULT.

Andrew Johnson Cartoon
Appearing in 1868 during President Andrew Johnson's impeachment trial, this cartoon includes
captions that read: "This little boy would persist in handling books above his capacity" and "And
this was the disastrous result." The cartoonist's portrait of Johnson being crushed by the Constitution refers to the president's flouting of the Tenure of Office Act, which caused Republicans to vote
for his impeachment. The cartoon's celebration of Johnson's destruction proved premature, however.
Granger Collection.

Despite its bold suffrage provision, the Military Reconstruction Act of 1867 disappointed those who advocated the confiscation and redistribution of southern plantations to ex-slaves. Thaddeus Stevens, who believed that at bottom reconstruction was an economic problem, agreed with the freedman who said, "Give us our own land and we take care of ourselves, but without land, the old masters can hire us or starve us, as they please." But most Republicans believed they had already provided blacks with what they needed: equal legal rights and the ballot. If blacks were to get forty acres, as some freedmen had in 1865 when Sherman distributed forty-acre lots, they would have to gain the land themselves.

Declaring that he would rather sever his right arm than sign such a formula for "anarchy and chaos," Andrew Johnson vetoed the Military Reconstruction Act. Congress overrode his veto the very same day, dramatizing the shift in power from the executive to the legislative branch of government. With the passage of the Reconstruction Acts of 1867, congressional reconstruction was virtually completed. Congress left whites owning most of the South's land but, in a departure that justified the term "radical reconstruction," had given black men the ballot. In 1867, the nation began an unprecedented experiment in interracial **democracy**—at least in the South, for Congress's plan did not touch the North. But before the spotlight swung away from Washington to the South, the president and Congress had one more scene to play.

Impeaching a President

Despite his defeats, Andrew Johnson had no intention of yielding control of reconstruction. In a dozen ways, he sabotaged Congress's will and encouraged southern whites to resist. He issued a flood of pardons to undermine efforts at political and economic change. He waged war against the Freedmen's Bureau by removing officers who sympathized too much with ex-slaves. And he replaced Union generals eager to enforce Congress's Reconstruction Acts with conservative men eager to defeat them. Johnson claimed that he was merely defending the "violated Constitution." At bottom, however, the president subverted congressional reconstruction to protect southern whites from what he considered the horrors of "Negro domination."

When Congress realized that overriding Johnson's vetoes did not ensure that it got its way, it looked for other ways to exert its will. According to the Constitution, the House of Representatives can impeach and the Senate can try any federal official for "treason, bribery, or other high crimes and misdemeanors." Radicals argued that Johnson's abuse of constitutional powers and his failure to fulfill constitutional obligations to enforce the law were impeachable offenses. Moderates interpreted the constitutional provision to mean violation of criminal statutes. As long as Johnson refrained from breaking the law, **impeachment** remained a faint hope.

Then, in August 1867, Johnson suspended Secretary of War Edwin M. Stanton from office. As required by the Tenure of Office Act, which demanded the approval of the Senate for the removal of any government official who had been appointed with Senate approval, the president requested the Senate to consent to the dismissal. When the Senate balked, Johnson removed Stanton anyway. "Is the President crazy, or only drunk?" asked a dumbfounded Republican moderate. "I'm afraid his doings will make us all favor impeachment."

News of Johnson's open defiance of the law convinced every Republican in the House to vote for a resolution impeaching the president. Supreme Court chief justice Salmon Chase presided over the Senate trial, which lasted from March until May 1868. Chase refused to allow Johnson's opponents to raise broad issues of misuse of power and forced them to argue their case exclusively on the narrow legal grounds of Johnson's removal of Stanton. Johnson's lawyers argued that the president had not committed a criminal offense, that the Tenure of Office Act was unconstitutional, and that in any case it did not apply to Stanton, who had been appointed by Lincoln. When the critical vote came, 35 senators voted guilty and 19 not guilty. The impeachment forces fell one vote short of the two-thirds needed to convict.

Although Johnson survived, he did not come through the ordeal unscathed. After his trial, he called a truce, and for the remaining ten months of his term, congressional reconstruction proceeded unhindered by presidential interference. Without interference from Johnson, Congress revisited the suffrage issue.

The Fifteenth Amendment and Women's Demands

In February 1869, Republicans passed the Fifteenth Amendment to the Constitution, which prohibited states from depriving any citizen of the right to vote because of "race, color, or previous condition of servitude." The Reconstruction Acts of 1867 already required black suffrage in

Major Reconstruction Legislation, 1865–1875

1865	
Thirteenth Amendment (ratified 1865)	Abolishes slavery.
1865 and 1866	
Freedmen's Bureau Acts	Establish the Freedmen's Bureau to distribute food and clothing to destitute Southerners and help freedmen with labor contracts and schooling.
Civil Rights Act of 1866	Affirms the rights of blacks to enjoy "full and equal benefit of all laws and proceedings for the security of person and property as is enjoyed by white citizens" and effectively requires the end of legal discrimination in state laws.
Fourteenth Amendment (ratified 1868)	Makes native-born blacks citizens and guarantees all citizens "equal protection of the laws." Threatens to reduce representatives of a state that denies suffrage to any of its male inhabitants.
1867	
Military Reconstruction Acts	Impose military rule in the South, establish rules for readmission of ex-Confederate states to the Union, and require those states to guarantee the vote to black men.
1869	
Fifteenth Amendment (ratified 1870)	Prohibits racial discrimination in voting rights in all states in the nation.
1875	
Civil Rights Act of 1875	Outlaws racial discrimination in transportation, public accommodations, and juries.

the South; the Fifteenth Amendment extended black voting nationwide. Partisan advantage played an important role in the amendment's passage. Gains by northern Democrats in the 1868 elections worried Republicans, and black voters now represented the balance of power in several northern states. By giving the ballot to northern blacks, Republicans could lessen their political vulnerability. As one Republican congressman observed, "Party expediency and exact justice coincide for once."

Some Republicans, however, found the final wording of the Fifteenth Amendment "lame and halting." Rather than absolutely guaranteeing the right to vote, the amendment merely prohibited exclusion on grounds of race. The distinction would prove to be significant. In time, inventive white Southerners would devise tests of literacy and property and other apparently nonracial measures that would effectively disfranchise blacks yet not violate the Fifteenth Amendment. But an amendment that fully guaranteed the right to vote courted defeat outside the South. Rising antiforeign sentiment—against the Chinese in California and European immigrants in the Northeast—caused states to resist giving up total control of suffrage requirements. (Because the vast majority of Native Americans became citizens only in 1924, the Fifteenth Amendment had little immediate impact on Indian voting.) In March 1870, after three-fourths of the states had ratified it, the Fifteenth Amendment became part of the Constitution. Republicans generally breathed a sigh of relief, confident that black suffrage was "the last great point that remained to be settled of the issues of the war."

Woman suffrage advocates, however, were sorely disappointed with the Fifteenth Amendment's failure to extend voting rights to women. Although women fought hard to include the word *sex* (as they had fought hard to keep the word *male* out of the Fourteenth Amendment), the amendment denied states the right to forbid suffrage only on the basis of race. Elizabeth Cady Stanton and Susan B. Anthony condemned the Republicans' "negro first" strategy and pointed out that women remained "the only class of citizens wholly unrepresented in the government." Black enfranchisement provoked racist statements from Stanton, who wondered aloud why ignorant black men should legislate for educated and cultured white women. Increasingly, activist

> Wendell Phillips concluded that the black man now held "sufficient shield in his own hands. . . . Whatever he suffers will be largely now, and in future, his own fault."

women concluded that woman "must not put her trust in man." The Fifteenth Amendment severed the early **feminist** movement from its abolitionist roots. Over the next several decades, women would establish an independent suffrage crusade that drew millions of women into political life.

Republicans took enough satisfaction in the Fifteenth Amendment to promptly scratch the "Negro question" from the agenda of national politics. Even that steadfast crusader for equality Wendell Phillips concluded that the black man now held "sufficient shield in his own hands. . . . Whatever he suffers will be largely now, and in future, his own fault." Northerners had no idea of the violent struggles that lay ahead.

> **REVIEW**   Why did Johnson urge the southern states to reject the Fourteenth Amendment?

The Struggle in the South

Northerners believed they had discharged their responsibilities with the Reconstruction Acts and the amendments to the Constitution, but Southerners knew that the battle had just begun. Black suffrage established the foundation for the rise of the Republican Party in the South. Gathering together outsiders and outcasts, southern Republicans won elections, wrote new state constitutions, and formed new state governments.

Challenging the established class for political control was dangerous business. Equally dangerous were the confrontations that took place on farms and plantations in the southern countryside, where blacks sought to give practical, everyday meaning to their newly won legal and political equality. Ex-masters had their own ideas about the social and economic arrangements that should replace slavery. Freedom remained contested territory, and Southerners fought pitched battles with one another to determine the contours of their new world.

Freedmen, Yankees, and Yeomen

African Americans made up the majority of southern Republicans. After gaining voting rights in 1867, nearly every eligible black man registered to vote. Almost all black men registered as Republicans, grateful to the party that had freed them and granted them the **franchise**. In Monroe,

Alabama, black men participating in their first political meeting pressed toward the speaker, crying "God bless you" and "Bless God for this." Black women, like white women, remained disfranchised but mobilized along with black men. In the 1868 presidential election, they bravely wore buttons supporting the Republican candidate, Ulysses S. Grant. Southern blacks did not have identical political priorities, but they united in their desire for education and equal treatment before the law.

Northern whites who made the South their home after the war were a second element of the South's Republican Party. Conservative white Southerners called them "carpetbaggers," men so poor that they could stuff all their earthly belongings in a single carpet-sided suitcase and swoop southward like buzzards to "fatten on our misfortunes." But most Northerners who moved south were restless, relatively well-educated young men who looked upon the South as they did the West—as a promising place to make a living. They expected that the South without slavery would prosper, and they wanted to be part of it. Northerners in the southern Republican Party consistently supported programs that encouraged vigorous economic development along the lines of the northern free-labor model.

Southern whites made up the third element of the South's Republican Party. Approximately one out of four white Southerners voted Republican. The other three condemned the one who did as a traitor to his region and his race and called him a "scalawag," a term for runty horses and low-down, good-for-nothing rascals. **Yeoman** farmers accounted for the majority of southern white Republicans. Some were Unionists who emerged from the war with bitter memories of Confederate persecution. Others were small farmers who wanted to end state governments' favoritism toward plantation owners. Yeomen usually supported initiatives for public schools and for expanding economic opportunity in the South.

The South's Republican Party, then, was made up of freedmen, Yankees, and yeomen—an improbable coalition. The mix of races, regions, and classes inevitably meant friction as each group maneuvered to define the party. But Reconstruction represents an extraordinary moment in American politics: Blacks and whites joined together in the Republican Party to pursue political change. Formally, of course, only men participated in politics—casting ballots and holding offices—but women also played a part in the political struggle by joining in parades and rallies, attending stump speeches, and even campaigning.

Reconstruction politics was not for cowards. Activity on behalf of Republicans in particular took courage. Most whites in the South condemned reconstruction politics as illegitimate and felt justified in doing whatever they could to stamp out Republicanism. Violence against blacks—the "white terror"—took brutal institutional form in 1866 with the formation in Tennessee of the Ku Klux Klan, a social club of Confederate veterans that quickly developed into a paramilitary organization supporting Democrats. The Klan went on a rampage of whipping, hanging, shooting, burning, and throat-cutting to defeat Republicans and restore white supremacy. (See "Historical Question," page 574.) Rapid demobilization of the Union army after the war left only twenty thousand troops to patrol the entire South, a vast territory. Without effective military protection, southern Republicans had to take care of themselves.

Republican Rule

In the fall of 1867, southern states held elections for delegates to state constitutional conventions, as required by the Reconstruction Acts. About 40 percent of the white electorate stayed home because they had been disfranchised or because they had decided to boycott politics. Republicans won three-fourths of the seats. About 15 percent of the Republican delegates to the conventions were Northerners who had moved south, 25 percent were African Americans, and 60 percent were white Southerners. As a British visitor observed, the delegate elections reflected "the mighty revolution that had taken place in America." But Democrats described the state conventions as zoos of "baboons, monkeys, mules . . . and other jackasses." In fact, the conventions brought together serious, purposeful men who hammered out the legal framework for a new order.

> Conservative white Southerners called them "carpetbaggers," men so poor that they could stuff all their earthly belongings in a single carpet-sided suitcase and swoop southward like buzzards to "fatten on our misfortunes."

The reconstruction constitutions introduced two broad categories of changes in the South: those that reduced aristocratic privilege and increased democratic equality and those that expanded the state's responsibility for the general welfare. In the first category, the constitutions adopted universal male suffrage, abolished property qualifications for holding office, and

What Did the Ku Klux Klan Really Want?

In the summer of 1866, six Confederate veterans in Pulaski, Tennessee, founded the Ku Klux Klan. Borrowing oaths and rituals from a college fraternity, the young men innocently sought fun and fellowship in a social club. But they quickly tired of playing pranks on one another and shifted to more serious matters. By the spring of 1868, when congressional reconstruction went into effect, new groups, or "dens," of the Ku Klux Klan had sprouted throughout the South.

According to former Confederate general and Georgia Democratic politician John B. Gordon, the Klan owed its popularity to the "instinct of self-preservation . . . the sense of insecurity and danger, particularly in those neighborhoods where the Negro population largely predominated." Everywhere whites looked, he said, they saw "great crime." Republican politicians organized ignorant freedmen and marched them to the polls, where they blighted honest government. Ex-slaves drove overseers from plantations and claimed the land for themselves. Black robbers and rapists made white women cower behind barred doors. It was necessary, Gordon declared, "in order to protect our families from outrage and preserve our own lives, to have something that we could regard as a brotherhood— a combination of the best men of the country, to act purely in self-defense." According to Gordon and other conservative white Southerners, Klansmen were good men who stepped forward to do their duty, men who

wanted nothing more than to guard their families and defend decent society from the assaults of degraded ex-slaves and a vindictive Republican Party.

Behind the Klan's high-minded and self-justifying rhetoric, however, lay another agenda. It was revealed in their actions, not their words. Klansmen embarked on a campaign to reverse history. Garbed in robes and hoods, they engaged in hit-and-run **guerrilla warfare** against free labor, civil equality, and political democracy. They aimed to terrorize their enemies— ex-slaves and white Republicans— into submission. As the South's chief terrorist organization between 1868 and 1871, the Klan whipped, burned, and shot in the name of white supremacy. Changes in four particular areas of southern life proved flash points for Klan violence: racial etiquette, education, labor, and politics.

The Klan punished those blacks and whites whom they deemed guilty of breaking the Old South's racial code. The Klan considered "impudence" a punishable offense. Asked to define "impudence" before a congressional investigating committee, one white opponent of the Klan responded: "Well, it is considered impudence for a negro not to be polite to a white man—not to pull off his hat and bow and scrape to a white man, as was done formerly." Klansmen whipped blacks for crimes that ranged from speaking disrespectfully and refusing to yield the sidewalk to raising a good crop and dressing well. Black women who "dress up and fix up like ladies"

risked a midnight visit from the Klan. The Ku Klux Klan sought to restore racial subordination in every aspect of private and public life.

Klansmen also took aim at black education. White men, especially those with little schooling, found the sight of blacks in classrooms hard to stomach. Schools were easy targets, and scores of them went up in flames. Teachers, male and female, were flogged, or worse. Klansmen drove northern-born teacher Alonzo B. Corliss from North Carolina for "teaching niggers and making them like white men." In Cross Plains, Alabama, the Klan hanged an Irish-born teacher along with four black men. But not just ill-educated whites opposed black education. Planters wanted ex-slaves back in the fields, not at desks. Each student meant one less laborer. In 1869, an Alabama newspaper reported the burning of a black school and observed that it should be "a warning for them to stick hereafter to 'de shovel and de hoe,' and let their dirty-backed primers go."

Planters turned to the Klan as part of their effort to preserve plantation agriculture and restore labor discipline. An Alabama white admitted that in his area, the Klan was "intended principally for the negroes who failed to work." Masked bands "punished Negroes whose landlords had complained of them." Sharecroppers who disputed their share at "settling up time" risked a visit from the night riders. Klansmen murdered a Georgia blacksmith who refused to do additional work for a white man until he was paid for a previous job. It was dangerous for freedmen to consider changing employers. "If we got out looking for some other place to go," an ex-slave from Texas remembered, "them KKK they would

Ku Klux Klan Rider in Tennessee about 1868 and Klan Banner

The white robes that we associate with the Ku Klux Klan are a twentieth-century phenomenon. During Reconstruction, Klansmen wore robes of various designs and colors. This robe's fancy trim and the man's elaborate hat make it highly unlikely that the rider sewed the costume himself. Women did not participate in midnight raids, but they often shared the Klan's reactionary vision and did what they could to help the cause. Hooded horses added another element to the Klan's terror. The Klansman holds a flag that looks very much like the satanic dragon on the colorful Klan banner shown here, which contains a Latin motto from Saint Augustine's definition of Catholic truth: "that which [has been believed] always, everywhere, by all." Among Klansmen, this motto was likely to refer to the truth of white supremacy.

Rider: Tennessee State Museum Collection; Banner: Chicago Historical Society.

tend to Mister negro good and plenty." In Marengo County, Alabama, when the Klan heard that some local blacks were planning to leave, "the disguised men went to them and told them if they undertook it they would be killed on their way." Whites had decided that they would not be "deprived of their labor."

Above all, the Klan terrorized Republican leaders and voters. Klansmen became the military arm of the Democratic Party. They drove blacks from the polls on election day and terrorized black officeholders. Klansmen gave Andrew Flowers, a black politician in Chattanooga, a brutal beating and told him that they "did not intend any nigger to hold office in the United States." Jack Dupree, president of the Republican Club in Monroe County, Mississippi, a man known to "speak his mind," had his throat cut and was disemboweled while his wife was forced to watch.

Between 1868 and 1871, political violence reached astounding levels. Arkansas experienced nearly three hundred political killings in the three months before the fall elections in 1868, including Little Rock's U.S. congressman, J. M. Hinds. Louisiana was even bloodier. Between the local elections in the spring of 1868 and the presidential election in the fall, Louisiana experienced more than one thousand killings. Political violence often proved effective. In Georgia, Republican presidential candidate Ulysses S. Grant received no votes at all in 1868 in eleven counties, despite black majorities. The Klan murdered three scalawag members of the Georgia legislature and drove ten others from their homes. As one Georgia Republican commented after a Klan attack: "We don't call them [D]emocrats, we call them southern murderers."

It proved hard to arrest Klansmen and harder still to convict them. "If a white man kills a colored man in any of the counties of this State," observed a Florida sheriff, "you cannot convict him." By 1871, the death toll had reached thousands. Federal intervention—in the Ku Klux Klan Acts of 1870 and 1871—signaled an end to much of the Klan's power but not to counterrevolutionary violence in the South. Other groups continued the terror.

575

Republican Rule Cartoon, California, 1867

This racist Democratic cartoon from California ridicules Republican support of black suffrage, and it links black voting with the enfranchisement of Chinese immigrants and Native Americans, topics of some urgency to westerners. Uncle Sam, on the left, admonishes George C. Gorham, Republican candidate for governor: "Young Man! Read the history of your Country, and learn that this ballot box was dedicated to the white race alone. The load you are carrying will sink you in perdition, where you belong." The black man, Chinese man, and Indian all speak in thick dialects that confirm white racial stereotypes. On the right, a man in a top hat, holding a monkey on a leash, calls out mockingly, "Say, Gorham! Put this Brother up."

Library of Congress.

Unionists that unless all former Confederates were banned from politics they would storm back and wreck reconstruction, no state constitution disfranchised ex-rebels wholesale.

Democrats, however, were blind to the limits of the Republican program. They thought they faced wild revolution. According to Democrats, Republican victories initiated "black and tan" (ex-slave and mulatto) governments across the South. But the claims of "Negro domination" had almost no validity. Although four out of five Republican voters were black men, more than four out of five Republican officeholders were white. Southerners sent fourteen black congressmen and two black senators to Washington, but only 6 percent of Southerners in Congress during Reconstruction were black (Figure 16.1). With the exception of South Carolina, where blacks briefly held a majority in one house of the legislature, no state experienced "Negro rule," despite black majorities in the populations of some states.

In almost every state, voters ratified the new constitutions and swept Republicans into power. When the former Confederate states ratified the Fourteenth Amendment, Congress readmitted them. Southern Republicans then turned to a staggering array of problems. Wartime destruction—burned cities, shattered bridges, broken levees—still littered the landscape. The South's

FIGURE 16.1   Southern Congressional Delegations, 1865–1877

The statistics contradict the myth of black domination of congressional representation during Reconstruction.

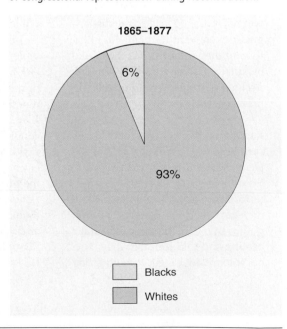

1865–1877

6%

93%

☐ Blacks
☐ Whites

made more offices elective and fewer appointed. In the second category, they enacted prison reform; made the state responsible for caring for orphans, the insane, and the deaf and mute; and exempted debtors' homes from seizure.

These forward-looking state constitutions provided blueprints for a new South but stopped short of the specific reforms advocated by some. Despite the wishes of virtually every former slave, no southern constitution confiscated and redistributed land. And despite the prediction of

share of the nation's wealth had fallen from 30 percent to only 12 percent. Manufacturing limped along at a fraction of prewar levels, agricultural production remained anemic, and the region's railroads lay devastated. Without the efforts of the Freedmen's Bureau, black and white Southerners would have starved. Making matters worse, racial harassment and reactionary violence dogged Southerners who sought reform. In this desperate context, Republicans struggled to breathe life into their new state governments.

Republican activity focused on three areas—education, civil rights, and economic development. Every state inaugurated a system of public education. Before the Civil War, whites had deliberately kept slaves illiterate, and planter-dominated governments rarely spent tax money to educate the children of yeomen. By 1875, half of Mississippi's and South Carolina's eligible children (the majority of whom were black) were attending school. Despite underfunding and dilapidated facilities, literacy rates rose sharply. Although public schools were racially segregated, education remained for many blacks a tangible, deeply satisfying benefit of freedom and Republican rule.

State legislatures also attacked racial discrimination and defended civil rights. Republicans especially resisted efforts to segregate blacks from whites in public transportation. Mississippi levied fines of up to $1,000 and three

Students at a Freedmen's School in Virginia, circa 1870s, and a One-Cent Primer

"The people are hungry and thirsty after knowledge," a former slave observed immediately after the Civil War. African American leader Booker T. Washington remembered "a whole race trying to go to school." The students at this Virginia school stand in front of their log-cabin classroom reading books, but more common were eight-page primers that cost a penny. These simple readers offered ex-slaves the elements of literacy. For people long forbidden to learn to read and write, literacy symbolized freedom. Literacy also allowed those who were deeply religious to experience the joy of reading the Bible for themselves and those who were merely practical to understand labor contracts and participate knowledgeably in politics.
Primer: Gladstone Collection; Students: Valentine Museum, Cook Collection.

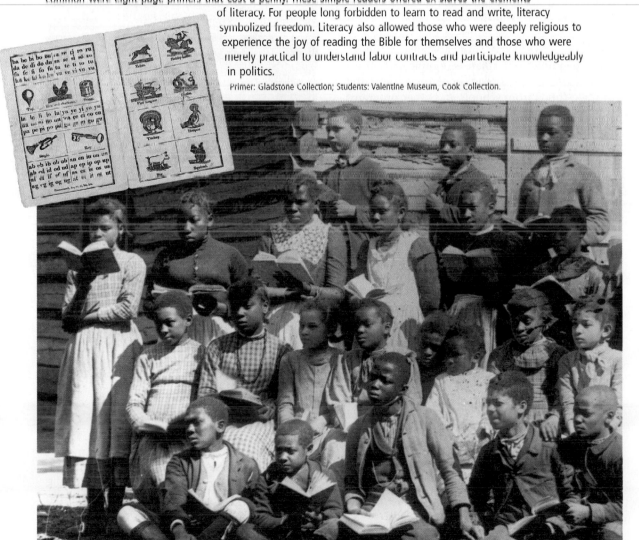

years in jail for railroads and steamboats that pushed blacks, regardless of their ability to pay, into "smoking cars" or to lower decks. Refined, well-off blacks took particular aim at hotels and theaters that denied "full and equal rights." An exasperated Mississippian complained: "Education amounts to nothing, good behavior counts for nothing, even money cannot buy for a colored man or woman decent treatment and the comforts that white people claim and can obtain." But passing color-blind laws was one thing; enforcing them was another. Despite the laws, segregation—later called **Jim Crow**—developed at white insistence and became a feature of southern life long before the end of the Reconstruction era.

Republican governments also launched ambitious programs of economic development. They envisioned a South of diversified agriculture, roaring factories, and booming towns. Republican legislatures chartered scores of banks and industrial companies, appropriated funds to fix ruined levees and drain swamps, and went on a railroad-building binge. These efforts fell far short of solving the South's economic troubles, however. Republican spending to stimulate economic growth also meant rising taxes and enormous debt that drained funds from schools and other programs.

The southern Republicans' record, then, was mixed. To their credit, the biracial party took up under trying circumstances an ambitious agenda to change the South. Money was scarce, the Democrats continued their harassment, and factionalism threatened the Republican Party from within. However, corruption infected Republican governments in the South. Public morality reached new lows everywhere in the nation after the Civil War, and the chaos and disruption of the postwar South proved fertile soil for bribery, fraud, and influence peddling. Despite problems and shortcomings, however, the Republican Party made headway in its efforts to purge the South of aristocratic privilege and racist oppression. Republican governments had less success in overthrowing the long-established white oppression of black farm laborers in the rural South.

White Landlords, Black Sharecroppers

In the countryside, clashes occurred daily between ex-slaves who wished to escape slave labor and ex-masters who wanted to reinstitute old ways. Except for having to put down the whip and pay subsistence wages, planters had not been required to offer many concessions to

Black Woman in Cotton Fields, Thomasville, Georgia
Few images of everyday black women during the Reconstruction era survive. This photograph was taken in 1895, but it nevertheless goes to the heart of the labor struggle after the Civil War. Before emancipation, black women worked in the fields; after emancipation, white landlords wanted them to continue working there. Freedom allowed some women to escape field labor, but not this Georgian, who probably worked to survive. The photograph reveals a strong person with a clear sense of who she is. Though worn to protect her head and body from the fierce heat, her intricately wrapped headdress dramatically expresses her individuality. Her bare feet also reveal something about her life.
Courtesy, Georgia Department of Archives and History, Atlanta, Georgia.

emancipation. They continued to believe that African Americans were inherently lazy and would not work without coercion. Whites moved quickly to restore the antebellum world of work gangs, white overseers, field labor for black women and children, clustered cabins, minimal personal freedom, and even whipping whenever they could get away with it.

Ex-slaves resisted every effort to turn back the clock. They argued that if any class could be described as "lazy," it was the planters, who, as one ex-slave noted, "lived in idleness all their lives on stolen labor." Land of their own would anchor their economic independence, they believed, and end planters' interference in their personal lives. They could then, for example, make their own decisions about whether women and children would labor in the fields. Indeed, within months after the war, perhaps one-third of black women abandoned field labor to work on chores in their own cabins just as poor white women did. With freedom to decide how to use family time, hundreds of thousands of black children enrolled in school. But landownership proved to be beyond the reach of most blacks once the federal government abandoned plans to redistribute Confederate property. Without land, ex-slaves had little choice but to work on plantations.

Although they were forced to return to the planters' fields, freedmen resisted efforts to restore slavelike conditions. In his South Carolina neighborhood, David Golightly Harris discovered that few freedmen were "willing to hire by the day, month or year." Instead of working for wages, "the negroes all seem disposed to rent land," which would increase their independence from whites. By rejecting wage labor, by striking, and by abandoning the most reactionary employers, blacks sought to force concessions. Out of this tug-of-war between white landlords and black laborers emerged a new system of southern agriculture.

Sharecropping was a compromise that offered both ex-masters and ex-slaves something but satisfied neither. Under the new system, planters divided their cotton plantations into small farms of twenty-five to thirty acres that freedmen rented, paying with a share of each year's crop, usually half. Sharecropping gave blacks more freedom than the system of wages and labor gangs and released them from the day-to-day supervision of whites. Black families abandoned the old slave quarters and scattered over plantations, building separate cabins for themselves on the patches of land they rented (Map 16.1, page 580). Black families now decided who would work, for how long, and how hard. Still, most blacks remained dependent on white landlords, who had the power to expel them at the end of each growing season. For planters, sharecropping offered a way to resume agricultural production, but it did not allow them to restore the old slave plantation.

Sharecropping introduced a new figure—the country merchant—into the agricultural equation. Landlords supplied sharecroppers with land, mules, seeds, and tools, but blacks also needed credit to obtain essential food and clothing before they harvested their crops. Thousands of small crossroads stores sprang up to offer credit. Under an arrangement called a crop lien, a merchant would advance goods to a sharecropper in exchange for a *lien*, or legal claim, on the farmer's future crop. Some merchants charged exorbitant rates of interest, as much as 60 percent, on the goods they sold. At the end of the growing season, after the landlord had taken half of the farmer's crop for rent, the merchant took most of the rest. Sometimes, the farmer's debt to the merchant exceeded the income he received from his remaining half of the crop, and the farmer would have no choice but to borrow more from the merchant and begin the cycle all over again.

An experiment at first, sharecropping spread quickly and soon dominated the cotton South. Lien merchants forced tenants to plant cotton, which was easy to sell, instead of food crops. The result was excessive production of cotton and falling cotton prices, developments that cost thousands of small white farmers their land and pushed them into the great army of sharecroppers. The new sharecropping system of agriculture took shape just as the political power of Republicans in the South began to buckle under Democratic pressure.

> **REVIEW** Why was the Republican Party in the South a coalition party?

Reconstruction Collapses

By 1870, after a decade of war and reconstruction, Northerners wanted to turn to their own affairs and put "the southern problem" behind them. Increasingly, practical, business-minded men came to the forefront of the Republican Party, replacing the band of reformers and idealists who had been prominent in the 1860s. While northern commitment to defend black freedom eroded, southern commitment to white supremacy intensified. Without northern protection, southern Republicans were no match for the Democrats' economic coercion, political corruption, and bloody violence. One

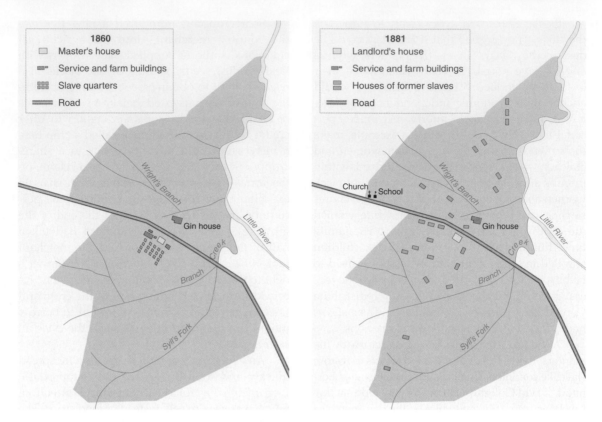

MAP 16.1   A Southern Plantation in 1860 and 1881

These maps of the Barrow plantation in Georgia illustrate some of the ways in which ex-slaves expressed their freedom. Freedmen and freedwomen deserted the clustered living quarters behind the master's house, scattered over the plantation, built family cabins, and farmed rented land. The former Barrow slaves also worked together to build a school and a church.

READING THE MAP: Compare the number and size of the slave quarters in 1860 with the homes of the former slaves in 1881. How do they differ? Which buildings were prominently located along the road in 1860, and which could be found along the road in 1881?

CONNECTIONS: How might the former master feel about the new configuration of buildings on the plantation in 1881? In what ways did the new system of sharecropping replicate the old system of plantation agriculture? In what ways was it different?

FOR MORE HELP ANALYZING THIS MAP, see the map activity for this chapter in the Online Study Guide at **bedfordstmartins.com/roark.**

---

by one, Republican state governments fell in the South. The election of 1876 both confirmed and completed the collapse of reconstruction.

Grant's Troubled Presidency

In 1868, the Republican Party's presidential nomination went to Ulysses S. Grant, the North's favorite general. Hero of the Civil War and a supporter of congressional reconstruction, Grant was the obvious choice. His Democratic opponent, Horatio Seymour of New York, ran on a platform that blasted congressional reconstruction as "a flagrant usurpation of power . . . unconstitu-

tional, revolutionary, and void." The Republicans answered by "waving the **bloody shirt**"— that is, they reminded voters that the Democrats were "the party of rebellion." During the campaign, the Ku Klux Klan erupted in a reign of terror, murdering hundreds of southern Republicans. Violence in the South cost Grant votes, but he gained a narrow 309,000-vote margin in the popular vote and a substantial victory (214 votes to 80) in the electoral college (Map 16.2).

Grant hoped to forge a policy that secured both justice for blacks and sectional reconciliation. But he

took office at a time when a majority of white Northerners had grown weary of the "Southern Question" and were increasingly willing to let southern whites manage their own affairs. Moreover, Grant had doubts about his preparation for the White House. "To go into the Presidency opens altogether a new field to me, in which there is to be a new strife to which I am not trained," he admitted. Indeed, Grant was not as good a president as he was a general. The talents he had demonstrated on the battlefield—decisiveness, clarity, and resolution—were less obvious in the White House. Able advisers might have helped, but he surrounded himself with fumbling kinfolk and old cronies from his army days. He also made a string of dubious appointments that led to a series of damaging scandals. Charges of corruption tainted his vice president, Schuyler Colfax, and brought down two of his cabinet officers. Grant's dogged loyalty to liars and cheats only compounded the damage. Though never personally implicated in any scandal, Grant was aggravatingly naive and blind to the rot that filled his administration. Congressman James A. Garfield declared: "His imperturbability is amazing. I am in doubt whether to call it greatness or stupidity."

In 1872, anti-Grant Republicans bolted and launched the Liberal Party. To clean up the graft and corruption, Liberals proposed ending the **spoils system**, by which victorious parties rewarded loyal workers with public office, and replacing it with a nonpartisan **civil service** com-

> "I BEG TO REPEAT THAT THESE FRAUDS ON THE GOVERNMENT SHALL BE PROBED TO THE VERY BOTTOM."

Grant and Scandal

This anti-Grant cartoon by Thomas Nast, the nation's most celebrated political cartoonist, shows the president falling headfirst into the barrel of fraud and corruption that tainted his administration. During Grant's eight years in the White House, many members of his administration failed him. Sometimes duped, sometimes merely loyal, Grant stubbornly defended wrongdoers, even to the point of perjuring himself to keep an aide out of jail. Library of Congress.

READING THE IMAGE: How does Thomas Nast portray President Grant's role in corruption? According to this cartoon, what caused the problems?
CONNECTIONS: How responsible was President Grant for the corruption that plagued his administration?

FOR MORE HELP ANALYZING THIS IMAGE, see the visual activity for this chapter in the Online Study Guide at bedfordstmartins.com/roark.

MAP 16.2 The Election of 1868

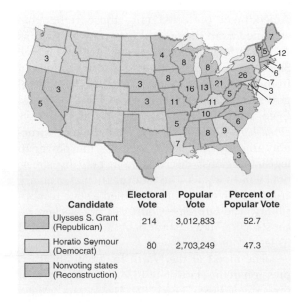

Candidate	Electoral Vote	Popular Vote	Percent of Popular Vote
Ulysses S. Grant (Republican)	214	3,012,833	52.7
Horatio Seymour (Democrat)	80	2,703,249	47.3
Nonvoting states (Reconstruction)			

mission that would oversee competitive examinations for appointment to office. Moreover, they demanded that the federal government remove its troops from the South and restore "home rule" (southern white control). Democrats liked the Liberals' southern policy and endorsed the Liberal presidential candidate, Horace Greeley, the longtime editor of the *New York Tribune*. However, the nation still felt enormous affection for the man who had saved the Union and reelected Grant with 56 percent of the popular vote.

Grant's ambitions for his administration extended beyond reconstruction, but not even foreign affairs could escape the problems of the

Grant's Proposed Annexation of Santo Domingo

South. The annexation of Santo Domingo in the Caribbean was Grant's greatest passion. He argued that the acquisition of this tropical land would permit the United States to expand its trade and also provide a new home for the South's blacks, who were so desperately harassed by the Klan. Aggressive foreign policy had not originated with the Grant administration. Lincoln's and Johnson's secretary of state, William H. Seward, had thwarted French efforts to set up a puppet empire under Maximilian in Mexico, and his purchase of Alaska ("Seward's Ice Box") from Russia in 1867 for only $7 million fired Grant's **imperialist** ambition. But in the end, Grant could not convince Congress to approve the treaty annexing Santo Domingo. The South preoccupied Congress and undermined Grant's initiatives.

Northern Resolve Withers

Although Grant genuinely wanted to see blacks' civil and political rights protected, he understood that most Northerners had grown weary of reconstruction. Average citizens wanted to shift their attention to other issues, especially after the nation slipped into a devastating economic depression in 1873. More than eighteen thousand businesses collapsed, leaving more than a million workers without jobs. Northern businessmen who wanted to invest in the South believed that recurrent federal intrusion was itself a major cause of instability in the region. Republican leaders began to question the wisdom of their party's alliance with the South's lower classes—its small farmers and sharecroppers. Grant's secretary of the interior, Jacob D. Cox of Ohio, proposed allying with the "thinking and influential native southerners . . . the intelligent, well-to-do, and controlling class."

Congress, too, wanted to leave reconstruction behind, but southern Republicans made that difficult. When the South's Republicans begged for federal protection from Klan violence, Congress enacted three laws in 1870 and 1871 that were intended to break the back of white terrorism. The severest of the three, the Ku Klux Klan Act (1871), made interference with voting rights a felony and authorized the use of the army to enforce it. Intrepid federal marshals arrested thousands of Klansmen, and the government came close to destroying the Klan but did not end terrorism against blacks. Congress also passed the Civil Rights Act of 1875, which boldly outlawed racial discrimination in transportation, public accommodations, and juries. But federal authorities never enforced the law aggressively, and segregated facilities remained the rule throughout the South.

By the early 1870s, the Republican Party had lost its principal spokesmen for African American rights to death or defeat at the polls. Others in Congress concluded that the quest for black equality was mistaken or hopelessly naive. In May 1872, Congress restored the right of officeholding to all but three hundred ex-rebels. In the opinion of many, traditional white leaders offered the best hope for honesty, order, and prosperity in the South.

Underlying the North's abandonment of reconstruction was unyielding racial prejudice. During the war, Northerners had learned to accept black freedom, but deep-seated prejudice prevented many from following freedom with equality. Even the actions they took on behalf of blacks often served partisan political advantage. Northerners generally supported Indiana senator Thomas A. Hendricks's harsh declaration that "this is a white man's Government, made by the white man for the white man."

The U.S. Supreme Court also did its part to undermine reconstruction. The Court issued a series of decisions that significantly weakened the federal government's ability to protect black Southerners under the Fourteenth and Fifteenth Amendments. In the *Slaughterhouse* cases (1873), the Court distinguished between national and state citizenship and ruled that the Fourteenth Amendment protected only those rights that stemmed from the federal government, such as voting in federal elections and interstate travel. Since the Court decided that most rights derived from the states, it sharply curtailed the federal government's authority to protect black citizens. Even more devastating, the *United States v. Cruikshank* ruling (1876) said that the reconstruction amendments gave Congress the power to legislate against discrimination only by states, not by individuals. The "suppression of ordinary crime," such as assault, remained a state responsibility. The Supreme Court did not declare reconstruction unconstitutional but undermined its legal foundation.

The mood of the North found political expression in the election of 1874, when for the first time in eighteen years the Democrats gained control of the House of Representatives. As one Republican observed, the people had grown tired of the "negro question, with all its complications, and the reconstruction of Southern States, with all its interminable embroilments." Reconstruction had come apart. The people were tired of it. Grant grew increasingly unwilling to enforce it. Congress gradually abandoned it. The Supreme Court busily denied the constitutionality of significant parts of it. Rather than defend reconstruction from its southern enemies, Northerners steadily backed away from the challenge. After the early 1870s, southern blacks faced the forces of reaction largely on their own.

White Supremacy Triumphs

Republican state and local governments in the South attracted more bitterness and hatred than any other political regimes in American history. In the eyes of the majority of whites, Republican rule meant intolerable insults: Black militiamen patrolled town streets, black laborers negotiated contracts with former masters, black maids stood up to former mistresses, black voters cast ballots, and black legislators such as James T. Rapier enacted laws. The northern retreat from reconstruction permitted southern Democrats to harness this white rage to politics. Taking the name "Redeemers," they promised to replace "bayonet rule" (some federal troops continued to be stationed in the South) with "home rule." They branded Republican governments a carnival of extravagance, waste, and fraud and promised that honest, thrifty Democrats would supplant the irresponsible tax-and-spend Republicans. Above all, Redeemers swore to save southern civilization from a descent into African "barbarism" and "Negro rule." As one man put it, "We must render this either a white man's government, or convert the land into a Negro man's cemetery."

Southern Democrats adopted a two-pronged racial strategy to

"White Man's Country"

White supremacy emerged as a central tenet of the Democratic Party before the Civil War, and Democrats kept up a vicious racist attack on Republicans throughout Reconstruction. This silk ribbon from the 1868 presidential campaign between Republican Ulysses S. Grant and his Democratic opponent, New York governor Horatio Seymour, openly declares the Democrats' racial goal. During the campaign, Democratic vice presidential nominee Francis P. Blair Jr. promised that a Seymour victory would restore "white people" to power by declaring the reconstruction governments in the South "null and void." The Democrats' promotion of white supremacy reached new levels of shrillness in the 1870s, when northern support for reconstruction began to waver. Collection of Janice L. and David J. Frent.

"Of Course He Wants to Vote the Democratic Ticket"

This Republican cartoon from the October 21, 1876, issue of *Harper's Weekly* comments sarcastically on the possibility of honest elections in the South. The caption reads, "You're free as air, ain't you? Say you are or I'll blow yer black head off." The cartoon demonstrates not only some Northerners' concern that violence would deliver the election to the Democrats but also the perception that white Southerners were crude, drunken, ignorant brutes.
Granger Collection.

READING THE IMAGE: What does the cartoon reveal about the cartoonist's political stance? How does the cartoonist demonstrate his view of white Southerners?

CONNECTIONS: Was the cartoonist's outrage about southern violence against blacks typical of white northern opinion in 1876?

FOR MORE HELP ANALYZING THIS IMAGE, see the visual activity for this chapter in the Online Study Guide at bedfordstmartins.com/roark.

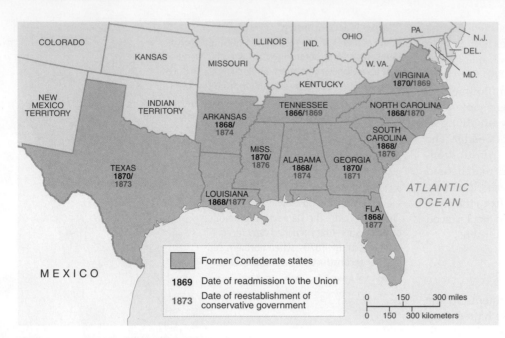

MAP 16.3   The Reconstruction of the South
Myth has it that Republican rule of the former Confederacy was not only harsh but long. In most states, however, conservative southern whites stormed back into power in months or just a few years. By the election of 1876, Republican governments could be found in only three states, and they soon fell.

READING THE MAP: List in chronological order the readmission of the former Confederate states to the Union. Which states reestablished conservative governments most quickly?
CONNECTIONS: What did the former Confederate states need to do in order to be readmitted to the Union? How did reestablished conservative governments react to reconstruction?

FOR MORE HELP ANALYZING THIS MAP, see the map activity for this chapter in the Online Study Guide at
bedfordstmartins.com/roark.

---

it on Republican financial policy. Government spending soared during reconstruction, and small farmers saw their tax burden skyrocket. "This is tax time," South Carolinian David Golightly Harris observed. "We are nearly all on our head about them. They are so high & so little money to pay with." Farmers without enough cash to pay their taxes began "selling every egg and chicken they can get." In 1871, Mississippi reported that one-seventh of the state's land—3.3 million acres—had been forfeited for nonpayment of taxes. The small farmers' economic distress had a racial dimension. Because few freedmen succeeded in acquiring land, they rarely paid taxes. In Georgia in 1874, blacks made up 45 percent of the population but paid only 2 percent of the taxes. From the perspective of a small white farmer, Republican rule meant that he was paying more taxes and paying them to aid blacks. Democrats asked whether it was not time for hard-pressed yeomen to join the white man's party.

If racial pride, social isolation, and Republican financial policies proved insufficient to drive yeomen from the Republican Party, Democrats turned to terrorism. "Night riders" targeted white Republicans as well as blacks for murder and assassination. "A dead Radical is very harmless," South Carolina Democratic leader Martin Gary told his followers. By the 1870s, only a handful of white Republicans remained.

The second prong of Democratic strategy aimed at the complete intimidation of black Republicans, especially local leaders. Emanuel Fortune, whom the Klan drove from Jackson County, Florida, declared: "The object of it is to kill out the leading men of the republican party . . . men who have taken a prominent stand." Violence expanded to all black voters and escalated to unprecedented levels. In 1873, a clash between black militiamen and gun-toting whites killed two white men and an estimated seventy black men in Louisiana. The whites slaughtered half of the black men after they sur-

overthrow Republican governments. First, they sought to polarize the parties around color. They went about gathering all the South's white voters into the Democratic Party, leaving the Republicans to depend on blacks. The "straight-out" appeal to whites promised great advantage because whites made up a majority of the population in every southern state except Mississippi, South Carolina, and Louisiana.

To dislodge whites from the Republican Party, Democrats fanned the flames of racial prejudice. A South Carolina Democrat crowed that his party appealed to the "proud Caucasian race, whose sovereignty on earth God has proclaimed." Ostracism also proved effective. Local newspapers published the names of whites who kept company with blacks. So complete was the ostracism that one of its victims said, "No white man can live in the South in the future and act with any other than the Democratic party unless he is willing and prepared to live a life of social isolation."

Democrats also exploited the severe economic plight of small white farmers by blaming

rendered. Although the federal government indicted more than one hundred of the white men, local juries failed to convict even one.

Even before adopting the all-out white supremacist tactics of the 1870s, Democrats had already taken control of the governments of Virginia, Tennessee, and North Carolina. The new campaign brought fresh gains. The Redeemers retook Georgia in 1871, Texas in 1873, and Arkansas and Alabama in 1874. Mississippi became a scene of open, unrelenting, and often savage intimidation of black voters and their few remaining white allies. As the state election approached in 1876, Governor Adelbert Ames appealed to Washington for federal troops to control the violence, only to hear from the attorney general that the "whole public are tired of these annual autumnal outbreaks in the South." Abandoned, Mississippi Republicans succumbed to the Democratic onslaught in the fall elections. By the election of 1876, only three Republican state governments—in Florida, Louisiana, and South Carolina—survived in the South (Map 16.3).

An Election and a Compromise

The centennial year of 1876 witnessed one of the most tumultuous elections in American history. Its chaos and confusion provided a fitting conclusion to the experiment known as reconstruction. The election took place in November, but not until March 2 of the following year did the nation know who would be inaugurated president on March 4. The Democrats nominated New York's governor, Samuel J. Tilden, who immediately targeted the corruption of the Grant administration and the despotism of Republican reconstruction. The Republicans put forward Rutherford B. Hayes, governor of Ohio. Privately, Hayes considered "bayonet rule" a mistake but concluded that waving the "bloody shirt"—reminding voters that the Democrats were the "party of rebellion"—remained the Republicans' best political strategy.

On election day, Tilden tallied 4,288,590 votes to Hayes's 4,036,000. But in the all-important electoral college, Tilden fell one vote short of the majority required for victory. The electoral votes of three states—South Carolina, Louisiana, and Florida, the only remaining Republican governments in the South—remained in doubt because both Republicans and Democrats in those states claimed victory. To win, Tilden needed only one of the nineteen contested votes. Hayes had to have all of them.

Congress had to decide who had actually won the elections in the three southern states and thus who would be president. The Constitution provided no guidance for this situation. Moreover, Democrats controlled the House, and Republicans controlled the Senate. Congress created a special electoral commission to arbitrate the disputed returns. All of the commissioners voted their party affiliation, giving every state to the Republican Hayes and putting him over the top in electoral votes (Map 16.4).

Some outraged Democrats vowed to resist Hayes's victory. Rumors flew of an impending coup and renewed civil war. But the impasse was broken when negotiations behind the scenes between Hayes's lieutenants and some moderate southern Democrats resulted in an informal understanding known as the Compromise of 1877. In exchange for a Democratic promise not to block Hayes's inauguration and to deal fairly with the freedmen, Hayes vowed to refrain from using the army to uphold the remaining Republican regimes in the South and to provide the South with substantial federal subsidies for internal improvements. Two days later, the nation celebrated Hayes's peaceful inauguration.

Stubborn Tilden supporters bemoaned the "stolen election" and damned "His Fraudulency," Rutherford B. Hayes. Old-guard radicals such as William Lloyd Garrison denounced Hayes's bargain as a "policy of compromise, of credulity, of weakness, of subserviency, of surrender." But the

MAP 16.4 The Election of 1876

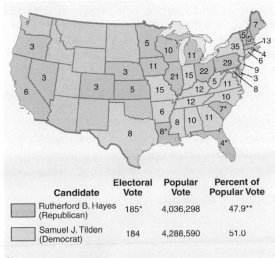

Candidate	Electoral Vote	Popular Vote	Percent of Popular Vote
Rutherford B. Hayes (Republican)	185*	4,036,298	47.9**
Samuel J. Tilden (Democrat)	184	4,288,590	51.0

*19 electoral votes were disputed.
**Percentages do not total 100 because some popular votes went to other parties.

"Reading Election Bulletin by Gaslight"
Throughout the nation in November 1876, eager citizens gathered on street corners at night to catch the latest news about the presidential election. When Democrats and Republicans disputed the returns, anxiety and anger mounted. With Samuel J. Tilden well ahead in the popular count, some Democrats began chanting "Tilden or War." Tilden received letters declaring that thousands of "well armed men" stood ready to march on Washington. In Columbia, Ohio, a bullet shattered a window in the home of Rutherford B. Hayes as his family sat down to dinner. Violent rhetoric and actions badly frightened a nation with fresh memories of a disastrous civil war, and for four long months, it was unclear whether the nation would peacefully inaugurate a new president.
Granger Collection.

nation as a whole celebrated, for the country had weathered a grave crisis. The last three Republican state governments in the South fell quickly once Hayes abandoned them and withdrew the U.S. army. Reconstruction came to an end.

> **REVIEW** How did the Supreme Court undermine the Fourteenth and Fifteenth Amendments?

Conclusion: "A Revolution But Half Accomplished"

In 1865, when General Carl Schurz visited the South, he discovered "a revolution but half accomplished." White Southerners resisted the passage from slavery to free labor, from white racial despotism to equal justice, and from white political **monopoly** to biracial democracy. The old elite wanted to get "things back as near to slavery as possible," Schurz reported, while African Americans such as James T. Rapier and some whites were eager to exploit the revolutionary implications of defeat and emancipation.

The northern-dominated Republican Congress pushed the revolution along. Although it refused to provide for blacks' economic welfare, Congress employed constitutional amendments to require ex-Confederates to accept legal equality and share political power with black men. Congress was not willing to extend such power to women. Conservative southern whites fought ferociously to recover their power and privilege. When Democrats regained control of politics, whites used both state power and private violence to wipe out many of the gains of Reconstruction, leading one observer to conclude that the North had won the war but the South had won the peace.

The Redeemer counterrevolution, however, did not mean a return to slavery. Northern victory in the Civil War ensured abolition, and ex-slaves gained the freedom to not be whipped or sold, to send their children to school, to worship in their own churches, and to work independently on their own rented farms. Even sharecropping, with all its hardships, provided more autonomy and economic welfare than bondage had. It was limited freedom, to be sure, but it was not slavery.

The Civil War and emancipation set in motion the most profound upheaval in the nation's history, and nothing whites did entirely erased its revolutionary impact. War destroyed the largest slave society in the New World. The world of masters and slaves succumbed to that of landlords and sharecroppers, a world in which old lines of racial dominance continued, though with greater freedom for blacks. War also gave birth to a modern nation-state. For the first time, sovereignty rested uncontested in the federal government, and Washington increased its role in national affairs. When the South returned to the Union, it did so as a junior partner. The victorious North now possessed the power to establish the nation's direction, and it set the nation's compass toward the expansion of industrial capitalism and the final conquest of the West.

Despite massive changes, the Civil War remained only a "half accomplished" revolution. By not fulfilling the promises the nation seemed to hold out to black Americans at war's end, Reconstruction represents a tragedy of enormous proportions. The failure to protect blacks and guarantee their rights had enduring consequences. Almost a century after Reconstruction, the nation would embark on what one observer called a "second reconstruction." The solid achievements of the Thirteenth, Fourteenth, and Fifteenth Amendments to the Constitution would provide a legal foundation for the renewed commitment. It is worth remembering, though, that it was only the failure of the first reconstruction that made the modern civil rights movement necessary.

Selected Bibliography

General Works

Eric Foner, *Reconstruction: America's Unfinished Revolution* (1988).

James M. McPherson, *Ordeal by Fire: The Civil War and Reconstruction* (3rd ed., 2000).

The Meaning of Freedom

Ira Berlin et al., eds., *Freedom: A Documentary History of Emancipation, 1861–1867*, 4 vols. to date (1982–).

Michael W. Fitzgerald, *The Union League Movement in the Deep South: Politics and Agricultural Change during Reconstruction* (1989).

John Hope Franklin and Loren Schweninger, *In Search of the Promised Land: A Slave Family in the Old South* (2006).

Leon F. Litwack, *Been in the Storm So Long: The Aftermath of Slavery* (1979).

Howard N. Rabinowitz, *Race Relations in the Urban South, 1865–1890* (1978).

Roger L. Ransom and Richard Sutch, *One Kind of Freedom: The Economic Consequences of Emancipation* (1977).

Loren Schweninger, *James T. Rapier and Reconstruction* (1978).

Clarence E. Walker, *A Rock in a Weary Land: The African Methodist Episcopal Church during the Civil War and Reconstruction* (1982).

The Politics of Reconstruction

Michael Les Benedict, *The Impeachment and Trial of Andrew Johnson* (1973).

Richard F. Bensel, *Yankee Leviathan: The Origins of Central State Authority in America, 1859–1877* (1990).

Ellen Carol DuBois, *Feminism and Suffrage: The Emergence of an Independent Women's Movement in America, 1848–1869* (1978).

Victor B. Howard, *Religion and the Radical Republican Movement, 1860–1870* (1990).

Heather Cox Richardson, *The Death of Reconstruction: Race, Labor, and Politics in the Post–Civil War North, 1865–1901* (2001).

Terry L. Seip, *The South Returns to Congress: Men, Economic Measures, and Intersectional Relationships, 1868–1879* (1983).

Brooks D. Simpson, *The Reconstruction Presidents* (1998).

Mark W. Summers, *The Era of Good Stealings* (1993).

C. Vann Woodward, *Reunion and Reaction: The Compromise of 1877 and the End of Reconstruction* (1951).

The Struggle in the South

James Alex Baggett, *The Scalawags: Southern Dissenters in the Civil War and Reconstruction* (2003).

Nancy D. Bercaw, *Gendered Freedoms: Race, Rights, and the Politics of Household in the Delta, 1861–1875* (2003).

Jane Turner Censer, *The Reconstruction of White Southern Womanhood, 1865–1895* (2003).

Paul A. Cimbala, *Under the Guardianship of the Nation: The Freedmen's Bureau and the Reconstruction of Georgia, 1865–1870* (1997).

Jane E. Dailey, *Before Jim Crow: The Politics of Race in Post-emancipation Virginia* (2000).

Laura F. Edwards, *Gendered Strife and Confusion: The Political Culture of Reconstruction* (1997).

Sarah E. Gardner, *Blood and Irony: Southern White Women's Narratives of the Civil War, 1861–1937* (2004).

Stephen Kantrowitz, *Ben Tillman and the Reconstruction of White Supremacy* (2000).

Robert C. Kenzer, *Kinship and Neighborhood in a Southern Community: Orange County, North Carolina, 1849–1881* (1987).

Scott Reynolds Nelson, *Iron Confederacies: Southern Railways, Klan Violence, and Reconstruction* (1999).

George C. Rable, *But There Was No Peace: The Role of Violence in the Politics of Reconstruction* (1984).

James L. Roark, *Masters without Slaves: Southern Planters in the Civil War and Reconstruction* (1977).

Hyman Rubin III, *South Carolina Scalawags* (2006).

Allen Trelease, *White Terror: The Ku Klux Klan Conspiracy and Southern Reconstruction* (1971).

Peter Wallenstein, *From Slave South to New South: Public Policy in Nineteenth-Century Georgia* (1987).

▶ FOR MORE BOOKS ABOUT TOPICS IN THIS CHAPTER, see the Online Bibliography at bedfordstmartins.com/roark.

▶ FOR ADDITIONAL FIRSTHAND ACCOUNTS OF THIS PERIOD, see Chapter 16 in Michael Johnson, ed., *Reading the American Past*, Fourth Edition.

▶ FOR WEB SITES, IMAGES, AND DOCUMENTS RELATED TO TOPICS AND PLACES IN THIS CHAPTER, visit bedfordstmartins.com/makehistory.

REVIEWING THE CHAPTER

Follow these steps to review and strengthen your understanding of the chapter.

STEP 1: *Study the* **Key Terms** *and* **Timeline** *to identify the significance of each item listed.*

STEP 2: *Answer the* **Review Questions**, *drawing on key terms and dates to support your answers.*

STEP 3: *Drawing on the Key Terms, Timeline, and Review Questions, answer the broader Making Connections questions.*

KEY TERMS

Who

James T. Rapier (p. 553)
Carl Schurz (p. 554)
Abraham Lincoln (p. 555)
Wendell Phillips (p. 555)
William Tecumseh Sherman (p. 557)
John Wilkes Booth (p. 561)
Andrew Johnson (p. 561)
Susan B. Anthony (p. 565)
Elizabeth Cady Stanton (p. 565)
Charles Sumner (p. 565)
Thaddeus Stevens (p. 568)
Edwin M. Stanton (p. 571)
Ulysses S. Grant (p. 573)
Horace Greeley (p. 581)
William H. Seward (p. 582)
Redeemers (p. 583)
night riders (p. 584)

Samuel J. Tilden (p. 585)
Rutherford B. Hayes (p. 585)

What

Proclamation of Amnesty and Reconstruction (p. 555)
Wade-Davis bill (p. 555)
suffrage (p. 556)
Confiscation Acts (p. 556)
Freedmen's Bureau (p. 557)
black codes (p. 562)
apprenticeship laws (p. 563)
Civil Rights Act of 1866 (p. 564)
radicals (p. 565)
Fourteenth Amendment (p. 565)
American Equal Rights Association (p. 565)
National Union Party (p. 568)
Memphis riots (p. 568)

Military Reconstruction Act (p. 569)
Reconstruction Acts of 1867 (p. 570)
impeachment (p. 571)
Tenure of Office Act (p. 571)
Fifteenth Amendment (p. 572)
carpetbagger (p. 573)
scalawag (p. 573)
Ku Klux Klan (p. 573)
sharecropping (p. 579)
country merchant (p. 579)
crop lien (p. 579)
waving the bloody shirt (p. 580)
Liberal Party (p. 581)
civil service commission (p. 581)
Ku Klux Klan Act (p. 582)
Civil Rights Act of 1875 (p. 582)
Slaughterhouse cases (p. 582)
United States v. Cruikshank (p. 582)
Compromise of 1877 (p. 585)

TIMELINE

1863 • Proclamation of Amnesty and Reconstruction.

  1864 • Wade-Davis bill.

    1865 • Freedmen's Bureau established.

    • President Abraham Lincoln shot; dies on April 15; succeeded by Andrew Johnson.
    • Black codes enacted.
    • Thirteenth Amendment becomes part of Constitution.

      1866 • Congress approves Fourteenth Amendment.
        • Civil Rights Act.
        • American Equal Rights Association founded.
        • Ku Klux Klan founded.

        1867 • Military Reconstruction Act.
          • Tenure of Office Act.

          1868 • Impeachment trial of President Johnson.
            • Republican Ulysses S. Grant elected president.

            1869 • Congress approves Fifteenth Amendment.

REVIEW QUESTIONS

1. Why did Congress object to Lincoln's wartime plan for reconstruction? (pp. 555–60)

2. How did the North respond to the passage of black codes in the southern states? (pp. 561–65)

3. Why did Johnson urge the southern states to reject the Fourteenth Amendment? (pp. 565–72)

4. Why was the Republican Party in the South a coalition party? (pp. 572–79)

5. How did the Supreme Court undermine the Fourteenth and Fifteenth Amendments? (pp. 579–86)

MAKING CONNECTIONS

1. Reconstruction succeeded in advancing black civil rights but failed to secure them over the long term. Why and how did the federal government retreat from defending African Americans' civil rights in the 1870s? In your answer, cite specific actions by Congress and the Supreme Court.

2. Why was distributing plantation land to former slaves such a controversial policy? In your answer, discuss why landownership was important to freedmen and why Congress rejected redistribution as a general policy.

3. At the end of the Civil War, it remained to be seen exactly how emancipation would transform the South. How did emancipation change political and labor organization in the region? In your answer, discuss how ex-slaves exercised their new freedoms and how white Southerners attempted to limit them.

4. The Republican Party shaped Reconstruction through its control of Congress and state legislatures in the South. How did the identification of the Republican Party with Reconstruction policy affect the party's political fortunes in the 1870s? In your answer, be sure to address developments on the federal and state levels.

▶ For practice quizzes, a customized study plan, and other study tools, see the Online Study Guide at bedfordstmartins.com/roark.

1871 • Ku Klux Klan Act.

 1872 • Liberal Party formed; calls for end of government corruption.
   • President Grant reelected.

  1873 • Economic depression sets in for remainder of decade.
    • *Slaughterhouse* cases.

   1874 • Democrats win majority in House of Representatives.

    1875 • Civil Rights Act.

     1876 • *United States v. Cruikshank.*

      1877 • Republican Rutherford B. Hayes assumes presidency; Reconstruction era ends.

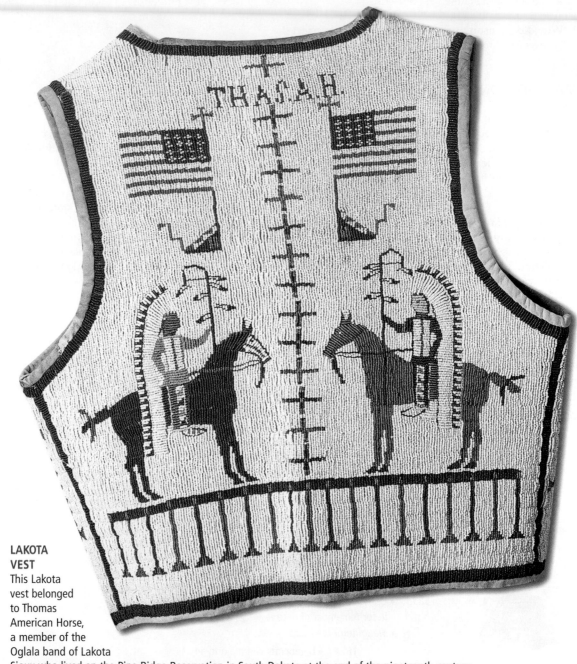

LAKOTA VEST
This Lakota vest belonged to Thomas American Horse, a member of the Oglala band of Lakota Sioux who lived on the Pine Ridge Reservation in South Dakota at the end of the nineteenth century. His initials are worked in beads across the shoulders. Made of tanned hide, with glass beads and tanned leather binding and lining, the vest shows how Native Americans adopted Euro-American articles of clothing and decorative motifs while employing materials that perpetuated native traditions. On the vest, two mounted Indians in feathered headdresses face each other under American flags. The American flag appeared frequently as a decorative motif in Indian bead art and testifies to some of the great changes taking place in the American West.

Private Collection, Photograph American Hurrah Archive, NYC.

Documents

For additional documents see the DocLinks feature at bedfordstmartins.com/roark.

THE DECLARATION OF INDEPENDENCE

In Congress, July 4, 1776,

THE UNANIMOUS DECLARATION OF THE
THIRTEEN UNITED STATES OF AMERICA

When in the course of human events, it becomes necessary for one people to dissolve the political bands which have connected them with another, and to assume, among the powers of the earth, the separate and equal station to which the laws of nature and of nature's God entitle them, a decent respect to the opinions of mankind requires that they should declare the causes which impel them to the separation.

We hold these truths to be self-evident, that all men are created equal; that they are endowed by their Creator with certain unalienable rights; that among these, are life, liberty, and the pursuit of happiness. That, to secure these rights, governments are instituted among men, deriving their just powers from the consent of the governed; that, whenever any form of government becomes destructive of these ends, it is the right of the people to alter or to abolish it, and to institute a new government, laying its foundation on such principles, and organizing its powers in such form, as to them shall seem most likely to effect their safety and happiness. Prudence, indeed, will dictate that governments long established, should not be changed for light and transient causes; and, accordingly, all experience hath shown, that mankind are more disposed to suffer, while evils are sufferable, than to right themselves by abolishing the forms to which they are accustomed. But, when a long train of abuses and usurpations, pursuing invariably the same object, evinces a design to reduce them under absolute despotism, it is their right, it is their duty, to throw off such government and to provide new guards for their future security. Such has been the patient sufferance of these colonies, and such is now the necessity which constrains them to alter their former systems of government. The history of the present King of Great Britain is a history of repeated injuries and usurpations, all having, in direct object, the establishment of an absolute tyranny over these States. To prove this, let facts be submitted to a candid world:

He has refused his assent to laws the most wholesome and necessary for the public good.

He has forbidden his governors to pass laws of immediate and pressing importance, unless suspended in their operation till his assent should be obtained; and, when so suspended, he has utterly neglected to attend to them.

He has refused to pass other laws for the accommodation of large districts of people, unless those people would relinquish the right of representation in the legislature; a right inestimable to them, and formidable to tyrants only.

He has called together legislative bodies at places unusual, uncomfortable, and distant from the depository of their public records, for the sole purpose of fatiguing them into compliance with his measures.

He has dissolved representative houses repeatedly for opposing, with manly firmness, his invasions on the rights of the people.

He has refused, for a long time after such dissolutions, to cause others to be elected; whereby the legislative powers, incapable of annihilation, have returned to the people at large for their exercise; the state remaining in the mean-time exposed to all the danger of invasion from without, and convulsions within.

He has endeavoured to prevent the population of these States; for that purpose, obstructing the laws for naturalization of foreigners, refusing to pass others to encourage their migration hither, and raising the conditions of new appropriations of lands.

He has obstructed the administration of justice, by refusing his assent to laws for establishing judiciary powers.

He has made judges dependent on his will alone, for the tenure of their offices, and the amount and payment of their salaries.

He has erected a multitude of new offices, and sent hither swarms of officers to harass our people, and eat out their substance.

He has kept among us, in times of peace, standing armies, without the consent of our legislature.

He has affected to render the military independent of, and superior to, the civil power.

He has combined, with others, to subject us to a jurisdiction foreign to our Constitution, and unacknowledged by our laws; giving his assent to their acts of pretended legislation:

For quartering large bodies of armed troops among us:

For protecting them by a mock trial, from punishment, for any murders which they should commit on the inhabitants of these States:

For cutting off our trade with all parts of the world:

For imposing taxes on us without our consent:

For depriving us, in many cases, of the benefit of trial by jury:

For transporting us beyond seas to be tried for pretended offences:

For abolishing the free system of English laws in a neighboring province, establishing therein an arbitrary government, and enlarging its boundaries, so as to render it at once an example and fit instrument for introducing the same absolute rule into these colonies:

For taking away our charters, abolishing our most valuable laws, and altering, fundamentally, the powers of our governments:

For suspending our own legislatures, and declaring themselves invested with power to legislate for us in all cases whatsoever.

He has abdicated government here, by declaring us out of his protection, and waging war against us.

He has plundered our seas, ravaged our coasts, burnt our towns, and destroyed the lives of our people.

He is, at this time, transporting large armies of foreign mercenaries to complete the works of death, desolation, and tyranny, already begun, with circumstances of cruelty and perfidy scarcely parelleled in the most barbarous ages, and totally unworthy the head of a civilized nation.

He has constrained our fellow citizens, taken captive on the high seas, to bear arms against their country, to become the executioners of their friends, and brethren, or to fall themselves by their hands.

He has excited domestic insurrections amongst us, and has endeavored to bring on the inhabitants of our frontiers, the merciless Indian savages, whose known rule of warfare is an undistinguished destruction of all ages, sexes, and conditions.

In every stage of these oppressions, we have petitioned for redress; in the most humble terms; our repeated petitions have been answered only by repeated injury. A prince, whose character is thus marked by every act which may define a tyrant, is unfit to be the ruler of a free people.

Nor have we been wanting in attention to our British brethren. We have warned them, from time to time, of attempts made by their legislature to extend an unwarrantable jurisdiction over us. We have reminded them of the circumstances of our emigration and settlement here. We have appealed to their native justice and magnanimity, and we have conjured them, by the ties of our common kindred, to disavow these usurpations, which would inevitably interrupt our connections and correspondence. They, too, have been deaf to the voice of justice and consanguinity. We must, therefore, acquiesce in the necessity which denounces our separation, and hold them as we hold the rest of mankind, enemies in war, in peace, friends.

We, therefore, the representatives of the United States of America, in general Congress assembled, appealing to the Supreme Judge of the world for the rectitude of our intentions, do, in the name, and by authority of the good people of these colonies, solemnly publish and declare, that these united colonies are, and of right ought to be, free and independent states: that they are absolved from all allegiance to the British Crown, and that all political connection between them and the state of Great Britain is, and ought to be, totally dissolved; and that, as free and independent states, they have full power to levy war, conclude peace, contract alliances, establish commerce, and to do all other acts and things which independent states may of right do. And, for the support of this declaration, with a firm reliance on the protection of Divine Providence, we mutually pledge to each other our lives, our fortunes, and our sacred honor.

The foregoing Declaration was, by order of Congress, engrossed, and signed by the following members:

JOHN HANCOCK

New Hampshire	New York
Josiah Bartlett	William Floyd
William Whipple	Phillip Livingston
Matthew Thornton	Francis Lewis
	Lewis Morris

Massachusetts Bay	New Jersey
Samuel Adams	Richard Stockton
John Adams	John Witherspoon
Robert Treat Paine	Francis Hopkinson
Elbridge Gerry	John Hart
	Abraham Clark

Rhode Island	Pennsylvania
Stephen Hopkins	Robert Morris
William Ellery	Benjamin Rush
	Benjamin Franklin
	John Morton
Connecticut	George Clymer
Roger Sherman	James Smith
Samuel Huntington	George Taylor
William Williams	James Wilson
Oliver Wolcott	George Ross

Delaware	North Carolina	Virginia	Georgia
Caesar Rodney	William Hooper	George Wythe	Button Gwinnett
George Read	Joseph Hewes	Richard Henry Lee	Lyman Hall
Thomas M'Kean	John Penn	Thomas Jefferson	George Walton
		Benjamin Harrison	
Maryland	**South Carolina**	Thomas Nelson, Jr.	
Samuel Chase	Edward Rutledge	Francis Lightfoot Lee	
William Paca	Thomas Heyward, Jr.	Carter Braxton	
Thomas Stone	Thomas Lynch, Jr.		
Charles Carroll,	Arthur Middleton		
of Carrollton			

Resolved, That copies of the Declaration be sent to the several assemblies, conventions, and committees, or councils of safety, and to the several commanding officers of the continental troops; that it be proclaimed in each of the United States, at the head of the army.

THE ARTICLES OF CONFEDERATION AND PERPETUAL UNION

Agreed to in Congress, November 15, 1777.
Ratified March 1781.

BETWEEN THE STATES OF NEW HAMPSHIRE, MASSACHU-
SETTS BAY, RHODE ISLAND AND PROVIDENCE PLANTA-
TIONS, CONNECTICUT, NEW YORK, NEW JERSEY, PENN-
SYLVANIA, DELAWARE, MARYLAND, VIRGINIA, NORTH
CAROLINA, SOUTH CAROLINA, GEORGIA.*

Article 1

The stile of this confederacy shall be "The United States of America."

Article 2

Each State retains its sovereignty, freedom and independence, and every power, jurisdiction, and right, which is not by this confederation expressly delegated to the United States, in Congress assembled.

Article 3

The said states hereby severally enter into a firm league of friendship with each other for their common defence, the security of their liberties and their mutual and general welfare; binding themselves to assist each other against all force offered to, or attacks made upon them, or any of them, on account of religion, sovereignty, trade, or any other pretence whatever.

*This copy of the final draft of the Articles of Confederation is taken from the *Journals,* 9:907–925, November 15, 1777.

Article 4

The better to secure and perpetuate mutual friendship and intercourse among the people of the different states in this union, the free inhabitants of each of these states, paupers, vagabonds, and fugitives from justice excepted, shall be entitled to all privileges and immunities of free citizens in the several states; and the people of each State shall have free ingress and regress to and from any other State, and shall enjoy therein all the privileges of trade and commerce, subject to the same duties, impositions, and restrictions, as the inhabitants thereof respectively; provided, that such restrictions shall not extend so far as to prevent the removal of property, imported into any State, to any other State of which the owner is an inhabitant; provided also, that no imposition, duties, or restriction, shall be laid by any State on the property of the United States, or either of them.

If any person guilty of, or charged with treason, felony, or other high misdemeanor in any State, shall flee from justice and be found in any of the United States, he shall, upon demand of the governor or executive power of the State from which he fled, be delivered up and removed to the State having jurisdiction of his offence.

Full faith and credit shall be given in each of these states to the records, acts, and judicial proceedings of the courts and magistrates of every other State.

Article 5

For the more convenient management of the general interests of the United States, delegates shall be annually appointed, in such manner as the legislature of each State shall direct, to meet in Congress, on the 1st Monday in November in every year, with a power reserved to each State to recall its delegates, or any of them, at any time within the year, and to send others in their stead for the remainder of the year.

No State shall be represented in Congress by less than two, nor by more than seven members, and no person shall be capable of being a delegate for more than three years in any term of six years; nor shall any person, being a delegate, be capable of holding any office under the United States, for which he, or any other for his benefit, receives any salary, fees, or emolument of any kind.

Each State shall maintain its own delegates in a meeting of the states, and while they act as members of the committee of the states.

In determining questions in the United States, in Congress assembled, each State shall have one vote.

Freedom of speech and debate in Congress shall not be impeached or questioned in any court or place out of Congress: and the members of Congress shall be protected in their persons from arrests and imprisonments, during the time of their going to and from, and attendance on Congress, except for treason, felony, or breach of the peace.

Article 6

No State, without the consent of the United States, in Congress assembled, shall send any embassy to, or receive any embassy from, or enter into any conference, agreement, alliance, or treaty with any king, prince, or state; nor shall any person, holding any office of profit or trust under the United States, or any of them, accept of any present, emolument, office or title, of any kind whatever, from any king, prince, or foreign state; nor shall the United States, in Congress assembled, or any of them, grant any title of nobility.

No two or more states shall enter into any treaty, confederation, or alliance, whatever, between them, without the consent of the United States, in Congress assembled, specifying accurately the purposes for which the same is to be entered into, and how long it shall continue.

No state shall lay any imposts or duties which may interfere with any stipulations in treaties entered into by the United States, in Congress assembled, with any king, prince, or state, in pursuance of any treaties already proposed by Congress to the courts of France and Spain.

No vessels of war shall be kept up in time of peace by any State, except such number only as shall be deemed necessary by the United States, in Congress assembled, for the defence of such State or its trade; nor shall any body of forces be kept up by any State, in time of peace, except such number only as, in the judgment of the United States, in Congress assembled, shall be deemed requisite to garrison the forts necessary for the defence of such State; but every State shall always keep up a well regulated and disciplined militia, sufficiently armed and accoutred, and shall provide, and constantly have ready for use, in public stores, a due number of field pieces and tents, and a proper quantity of arms, ammunition and camp equipage.

No State shall engage in any war without the consent of the United States, in Congress assembled, unless such State be actually invaded by enemies, or shall have received certain advice of a resolution being formed by some nation of Indians to invade such State, and the danger is so imminent as not to admit of a delay till the United States, in Congress assembled, can be consulted; nor shall any State grant commissions to any ships or vessels of war, nor letters of marque or reprisal, except it be after a declaration of war by the United States, in Congress assembled, and then only against the kingdom or state, and the subjects thereof, against which war has been so declared, and under such regulations as shall be established by the United States, in Congress assembled, unless such State be infested by pirates, in which case vessels of war may be fitted out for that occasion, and kept so long as the danger shall continue, or until the United States, in Congress assembled, shall determine otherwise.

Article 7

When land forces are raised by any State for the common defence, all officers of or under the rank of colonel, shall be appointed by the legislature of each State respectively, by whom such forces shall be raised, or in such manner as such State shall direct; and all vacancies shall be filled up by the State which first made the appointment.

Article 8

All charges of war and all other expences, that shall be incurred for the common defence or general welfare, and allowed by the United States, in Congress assembled, shall be defrayed out of a common treasury, which shall be supplied by the several states, in proportion to the value of all land within each State, granted to or surveyed for any person, as such land and the buildings and improvements thereon shall be estimated according to such mode as the United States, in Congress assembled, shall, from time to time, direct and appoint.

The taxes for paying that proportion shall be laid and levied by the authority and direction of the legislatures of the several states, within the time agreed upon by the United States, in Congress assembled.

Article 9

The United States, in Congress assembled, shall have the sole and exclusive right and power of determining on peace and war, except in the cases mentioned in the 6th article; of sending and receiving ambassadors; entering into treaties and alliances, provided that no treaty of commerce shall be made, whereby the legislative power of the respective states shall be restrained from imposing such imposts and duties on foreigners as their own people are subjected to, or from prohibiting the exportation or importation of any species of goods or commodities whatsoever; of establishing rules for deciding, in all cases, what captures on land or water shall be legal, and in what manner prizes, taken by land or naval forces in the service of the United States, shall be divided or appropriated; of granting letters of marque and reprisal in times of peace; appointing courts for the trial of piracies and felonies committed on the high seas, and establishing courts for receiving and determining, finally, appeals in all cases of captures, provided, that no member of Congress shall be appointed a judge of any of the said courts.

The United States, in Congress assembled, shall also be the last resort on appeal in all disputes and differences now subsisting, or that hereafter may arise between two or more states concerning boundary, jurisdiction or any other cause whatever; which authority shall always be exercised in the manner following: whenever the legislative or executive authority, or lawful agent of any State, in controversy with another, shall present a petition to Congress, stating the matter in question, and praying for a hearing, notice thereof shall be given, by order of Congress, to the legislative or executive authority of the other State in controversy, and a day assigned for the appearance of the parties by their lawful agents, who shall then be directed to appoint, by joint consent, commissioners or judges to constitute a court for hearing and determining the matter in question; but, if they cannot agree, Congress shall name three persons out of each of the United States, and from the list of such persons each party shall alternately strike out one, the petitioners beginning, until the number shall be reduced to thirteen; and from that number not less than seven, nor more than nine names, as Congress shall direct, shall, in the presence of Congress, be drawn out by lot; and the persons whose names shall be so drawn, or any five of them, shall be commissioners or judges to hear and finally determine the controversy, so always as a major part of the judges who shall hear the cause shall agree in the determination; and if either party shall neglect to attend at the day appointed, without shewing reasons which Congress shall judge sufficient, or, being present, shall refuse to strike, the Congress shall proceed to nominate three persons out of each State, and the secretary of Congress shall strike in behalf of such party absent or refusing; and the judgment and sentence of the court to be appointed, in the manner before prescribed, shall be final and conclusive; and if any of the parties shall refuse to submit to the authority of such court, or to appear or defend their claim or cause, the court shall nevertheless proceed to pronounce sentence or judgment, which shall, in like manner, be final and decisive, the judgment or sentence and other proceedings begin, in either case, transmitted to Congress, and lodged among the acts of Congress for the security of the parties concerned: provided, that every commissioner, before he sits in judgment, shall take an oath, to be administered by one of the judges of the supreme or superior court of the State where the cause shall be tried, "well and truly to hear and determine the matter in question, according to the best of his judgment, without favour, affection, or hope of reward:" provided, also, that no State shall be deprived of territory for the benefit of the United States.

All controversies concerning the private right of soil, claimed under different grants of two or more states, whose jurisdictions, as they may respect such lands and the states which passed such grants, are adjusted, the said grants, or either of them, being at the same time claimed to have originated antecedent to such settlement of jurisdiction, shall, on the petition of either party to the Congress of the United States, be finally determined, as near as may be, in the same manner as is before prescribed for deciding disputes respecting territorial jurisdiction between different states.

The United States, in Congress assembled, shall also have the sole and exclusive right and power of regulating the alloy and value of coin struck by their own authority, or by that of the respective states; fixing the standard of weights and measures throughout the United States; regulating the trade and managing all affairs with the Indians not members of any of the states; provided that the legislative right of any State within its own limits be not infringed or violated; establishing and regulating post offices from one State to another throughout all the United States, and exacting such postage on the papers passing through the same as may be requisite to defray the expences of the said office; appointing all officers of the land forces in the service of the United States, excepting regimental officers; appointing all the officers of the naval forces, and commissioning all officers whatever in the service of the United States; making rules for the government and regulation of the said land and naval forces, and directing their operations.

The United States, in Congress assembled, shall have authority to appoint a committee to sit in the recess of Congress, to be denominated "a Committee of the States," and to consist of one delegate from each State, and to appoint such other committees and civil officers as may be necessary for managing the general affairs of the United States, under their direction; to appoint one of their number to preside; provided that no person be allowed to serve in the office of president more than one year in any term of three years; to ascertain the necessary sums of money to be raised for the service of the United States, and to appropriate and apply the same for defraying the public expences; to borrow money or emit bills on the credit of the United States, transmitting, every half year, to the respective states, an account of the sums of money so borrowed or emitted; to build and equip a navy; to agree upon the number of land forces, and to make requisitions from each State for its quota, in proportion to the number of white inhabitants in such State; which requisitions shall be binding; and thereupon, the legislature of each State shall appoint the regimental officers, raise the men, and cloathe, arm, and equip them in a soldier-like manner, at the expence of the United States; and the officers and men so cloathed, armed, and equipped, shall march to the place appointed and within the time agreed on by the United States, in Congress assembled; but if the United States, in Congress assembled, shall, on consideration of circumstances, judge proper that any State should not raise men, or should raise a smaller number than its quota, and that any other State should raise a greater number of men than the quota thereof, such extra number shall be raised, officered, cloathed, armed, and equipped in the same manner as the quota of such State, unless the legislature of such State shall judge that such extra number cannot be safely spared out of the same, in which case they shall raise, officer, cloathe, arm, and equip as many of such extra number as they judge can be safely spared. And the officers and men so cloathed, armed, and equipped, shall march to the place appointed and within the time agreed on by the United States, in Congress assembled.

The United States, in Congress assembled, shall never engage in a war, nor grant letters of marque and reprisal in time of peace, nor enter into any treaties or alliances, nor coin money, nor regulate the value thereof, nor ascertain the sums and expences necessary for the defence and welfare of the United States, or any of them: nor emit bills, nor borrow money on the credit of the United States, nor appropriate money, nor agree upon the number of vessels of war to be built or purchased, or the number of land or sea forces to be raised, nor appoint a commander in chief of the army or navy, unless nine states assent to the same; nor shall a question on any other point, except for adjourning from day to day, be determined, unless by the votes of a majority of the United States, in Congress assembled.

The Congress of the United States shall have power to adjourn to any time within the year, and to any place within the United States, so that no period of adjournment be for a longer duration than the space of six months, and shall publish the journal of their proceedings monthly, except such parts thereof, relating to treaties, alliances or military operations, as, in their judgment, require secrecy; and the yeas and nays of the delegates of each State on any question shall be entered on the journal, when it is desired by any delegate; and the delegates of a State, or any of them, at his, or their request, shall be furnished with a transcript of the said journal, except such parts as are above excepted, to lay before the legislatures of the several states.

Article 10

The committee of the states, or any nine of them, shall be authorized to execute, in the recess of Congress, such of the powers of Congress as the United States, in Congress assembled, by the consent of nine states, shall, from time to time, think expedient to vest them with; provided, that no power be delegated to the said committee, for the exercise of which, by the articles of confederation, the voice of nine states, in the Congress of the United States assembled, is requisite.

Article 11

Canada acceding to this confederation, and joining in the measures of the United States, shall be admitted into and entitled to all the advantages of this union; but no other colony shall be admitted into the same, unless such admission be agreed to by nine states.

Article 12

All bills of credit emitted, monies borrowed and debts contracted by, or under the authority of Congress before the assembling of the United States, in pursuance of the present confederation, shall be deemed and considered as a charge against the United States, for payment and satisfaction whereof the said United States and the public faith are hereby solemnly pledged.

Article 13

Every State shall abide by the determinations of the United States, in Congress assembled, on all questions which, by this confederation, are submitted to them. And the articles of this confederation shall be inviolably observed by every State, and the union shall be perpetual; nor shall any alteration at any time hereafter be made in any of them, unless such alteration be agreed to in a Congress of the United States, and be afterwards confirmed by the legislatures of every State.

These articles shall be proposed to the legislatures of all the United States, to be considered, and if approved of by them, they are advised to authorize their delegates to ratify the same in the Congress of the United States; which being done, the same shall become conclusive.

THE CONSTITUTION OF THE UNITED STATES*

Agreed to by Philadelphia Convention, September 17, 1787. Implemented March 4, 1789.

Preamble

We the people of the United States, in order to form a more perfect union, establish justice, insure domestic tranquility, provide for the common defense, promote the general welfare, and secure the blessings of liberty to ourselves and our posterity, do ordain and establish this Constitution for the United States of America.

Article I

Section 1 All legislative powers herein granted shall be vested in a Congress of the United States, which shall consist of a Senate and a House of Representatives.

Section 2 The House of Representatives shall be composed of members chosen every second year by the people of the several States, and the electors in each State shall have the qualifications requisite for electors of the most numerous branch of the State Legislature.

No person shall be a Representative who shall not have attained to the age of twenty-five years, and been seven years a citizen of the United States, and who shall not, when elected, be an inhabitant of that State in which he shall be chosen.

Representatives and direct taxes shall be apportioned among the several States which may be included within this Union, according to their respective numbers, *which shall be determined by adding to the whole number of free persons, including those bound to service for a term of years and excluding Indians not taxed, three-fifths of all other persons.* The actual enumeration shall be made within three years after the first meeting of the Congress of the United States, and within every subsequent term of ten years, in such manner as they shall by law direct. The number of Representatives shall not exceed one for every thirty thousand, but each State shall have at least one Representative; *and until such enumeration shall be made, the State of New Hampshire shall be entitled to choose three, Massachusetts eight, Rhode Island and Providence Plantations one, Connecticut five, New York six, New Jersey four, Pennsylvania eight, Delaware one, Maryland six, Virginia ten, North Carolina five, South Carolina five, and Georgia three.*

When vacancies happen in the representation from any State, the Executive authority thereof shall issue writs of election to fill such vacancies.

The House of Representatives shall choose their Speaker and other officers; and shall have the sole power of impeachment.

Section 3 The Senate of the United States shall be composed of two Senators from each State, *chosen by the legislature thereof,* for six years; and each Senator shall have one vote.

Immediately after they shall be assembled in consequence of the first election, they shall be divided as equally as may be into three classes. The seats of the Senators of the first class shall be vacated at the expiration of the second year, of the second class at the expiration of the fourth year, and of the third class at the expiration of the sixth year, so that one-third may be chosen every second year; *and if vacancies happen by resignation or otherwise, during the recess of the legislature of any State, the Executive thereof may make temporary appointments until the next meeting of the legislature, which shall then fill such vacancies.*

No person shall be a Senator who shall not have attained to the age of thirty years, and been nine years a citizen of the United States, and who shall not, when elected, be an inhabitant of that State for which he shall be chosen.

The Vice-President of the United States shall be President of the Senate, but shall have no vote, unless they be equally divided.

The Senate shall choose their other officers, and also a President *pro tempore,* in the absence of the Vice-President, or when he shall exercise the office of President of the United States.

The Senate shall have the sole power to try all impeachments. When sitting for that purpose, they shall be on oath or affirmation. When the President of the United States is tried, the Chief Justice shall preside: and no person shall be convicted without the concurrence of two-thirds of the members present.

Judgment in cases of impeachment shall not extend further than to removal from the office, and disqualification to hold and enjoy any office of honor, trust or profit under the United States: but the party convicted shall nevertheless be liable and subject to indictment, trial, judgment and punishment, according to law.

Section 4 The times, places and manner of holding elections for Senators and Representatives shall be prescribed in each State by the legislature thereof; but the Congress may at any time by law make or alter such regulations, except as to the places of choosing Senators.

The Congress shall assemble at least once in every year, and such meeting *shall be on the first*

---

* Passages no longer in effect are in italic type.

Monday in December, unless they shall by law appoint a different day.

Section 5 Each house shall be the judge of the elections, returns and qualifications of its own members, and a majority of each shall constitute a quorum to do business; but a smaller number may adjourn from day to day, and may be authorized to compel the attendance of absent members, in such manner, and under such penalties, as each house may provide.

Each house may determine the rules of its proceedings, punish its members for disorderly behavior, and with the concurrence of two-thirds, expel a member.

Each house shall keep a journal of its proceedings, and from time to time publish the same, excepting such parts as may in their judgment require secrecy; and the yeas and nays of the members of either house on any question shall, at the desire of one-fifth of those present, be entered on the journal.

Neither house, during the session of Congress, shall, without the consent of the other, adjourn for more than three days, nor to any other place than that in which the two houses shall be sitting.

Section 6 The Senators and Representatives shall receive a compensation for their services, to be ascertained by law and paid out of the treasury of the United States. They shall in all cases except treason, felony and breach of the peace, be privileged from arrest during their attendance at the session of their respective houses, and in going to and returning from the same; and for any speech or debate in either house, they shall not be questioned in any other place.

No Senator or Representative shall, during the time for which he was elected, be appointed to any civil office under the authority of the United States, which shall have been created, or the emoluments whereof shall have been increased, during such time; and no person holding any office under the United States shall be a member of either house during his continuance in office.

Section 7 All bills for raising revenue shall originate in the House of Representatives; but the Senate may propose or concur with amendments as on other bills.

Every bill which shall have passed the House of Representatives and the Senate, shall, before it become a law, be presented to the President of the United States; if he approve he shall sign it, but if not he shall return it with objections to that house in which it shall have originated, who shall enter the objections at large on their journal, and proceed to reconsider it. If after such reconsideration two-thirds of that house shall agree to pass the bill, it shall be sent, together with the objections, to the other house, by which it shall likewise be reconsidered, and, if approved by two-thirds of that house,

it shall become a law. But in all such cases the votes of both houses shall be determined by yeas and nays, and the names of the persons voting for and against the bill shall be entered on the journal of each house respectively. If any bill shall not be returned by the President within ten days (Sundays excepted) after it shall have been presented to him, the same shall be a law, in like manner as if he had signed it, unless the Congress by their adjournment prevent its return, in which case it shall not be a law.

Every order, resolution, or vote to which the concurrence of the Senate and House of Representatives may be necessary (except on a question of adjournment) shall be presented to the President of the United States; and before the same shall take effect, shall be approved by him, or being disapproved by him, shall be repassed by two-thirds of the Senate and House of Representatives, according to the rules and limitations prescribed in the case of a bill.

Section 8 The Congress shall have power

To lay and collect taxes, duties, imposts, and excises, to pay the debts and provide for the common defense and general welfare of the United States; but all duties, imposts and excises shall be uniform throughout the United States;

To borrow money on the credit of the United States;

To regulate commerce with foreign nations, and among the several States, and with the Indian tribes;

To establish an uniform rule of naturalization, and uniform laws on the subject of bankruptcies throughout the United States;

To coin money, regulate the value thereof, and of foreign coin, and fix the standard of weights and measures;

To provide for the punishment of counterfeiting the securities and current coin of the United States;

To establish post offices and post roads;

To promote the progress of science and useful arts by securing for limited times to authors and inventors the exclusive right to their respective writings and discoveries;

To constitute tribunals inferior to the Supreme Court;

To define and punish piracies and felonies committed on the high seas and offences against the law of nations;

To declare war, grant letters of marque and reprisal, and make rules concerning captures on land and water;

To raise and support armies, but no appropriation of money to that use shall be for a longer term than two years;

To provide and maintain a navy;

To make rules for the government and regulation of the land and naval forces;

To provide for calling forth the militia to execute the laws of the Union, suppress insurrections and repel invasions;

To provide for organizing, arming, and disciplining the militia, and for governing such part of them as may be employed in the service of the United States, reserving to the States respectively the appointment of the officers, and the authority of training the militia according to the discipline prescribed by Congress;

To exercise exclusive legislation in all cases whatsoever, over such district (not exceeding ten miles square) as may, by cession of particular States, and the acceptance of Congress, become the seat of the government of the United States, and to exercise like authority over all places purchased by the consent of the legislature of the State, in which the same shall be, for erection of forts, magazines, arsenals, dock-yards, and other needful buildings;—and

To make all laws which shall be necessary and proper for carrying into execution the foregoing powers, and all other powers vested by this Constitution in the government of the United States, or in any department or officer thereof.

Section 9 *The migration or importation of such persons as any of the States now existing shall think proper to admit shall not be prohibited by the Congress prior to the year one thousand eight hundred and eight; but a tax or duty may be imposed on such importation, not exceeding ten dollars for each person.*

The privilege of the writ of habeas corpus shall not be suspended, unless when in cases of rebellion or invasion the public safety may require it.

No bill of attainder or ex post facto law shall be passed.

No capitation, or other direct, tax shall be laid, unless in proportion to the census or enumeration herein before directed to be taken.

No tax or duty shall be laid on articles exported from any State.

No preference shall be given by any regulation of commerce or revenue to the ports of one State over those of another; nor shall vessels bound to, or from, one State be obliged to enter, clear, or pay duties in another.

No money shall be drawn from the treasury, but in consequence of appropriations made by law; and a regular statement and account of the receipts and expenditures of all public money shall be published from time to time.

No title of nobility shall be granted by the United States: and no person holding any office of profit or trust under them, shall, without the consent of the Congress, accept of any present, emolument, office, or title, of any kind whatever, from any king, prince, or foreign state.

Section 10 No State shall enter into any treaty, alliance, or confederation; grant letters of marque and reprisal; coin money; emit bills of credit; make anything but gold and silver coin a tender in payment of debts; pass any bill of attainder, ex post facto law, or law impairing the obligation of contracts, or grant any title of nobility.

No State shall, without the consent of Congress, lay any imposts or duties on imports or exports, except what may be absolutely necessary for executing its inspection laws: and the net produce of all duties and imposts, laid by any State on imports or exports, shall be for the use of the treasury of the United States; and all such laws shall be subject to the revision and control of the Congress.

No State shall, without the consent of Congress, lay any duty of tonnage, keep troops, or ships of war in time of peace, enter into any agreement or compact with another State, or with a foreign power, or engage in war, unless actually invaded, or in such imminent danger as will not admit of delay.

Article II

Section 1 The executive power shall be vested in a President of the United States of America. He shall hold his office during the term of four years, and, together with the Vice-President, chosen for the same term, be elected as follows:

Each State shall appoint, in such manner as the legislature thereof may direct, a number of electors, equal to the whole number of Senators and Representatives to which the State may be entitled in the Congress; but no Senator or Representative, or person holding an office of trust or profit under the United States, shall be appointed an elector.

The electors shall meet in their respective States, and vote by ballot for two persons, of whom one at least shall not be an inhabitant of the same State with themselves. And they shall make a list of all the persons voted for, and of the number of votes for each; which list they shall sign and certify, and transmit sealed to the seat of government of the United States, directed to the President of the Senate. The President of the Senate shall, in the presence of the Senate and House of Representatives, open all the certificates, and the votes shall then be counted. The person having the greatest number of votes shall be the President, if such number be a majority of the whole number of electors appointed; and if there be more than one who have such majority, and have an equal number of votes, then the House of Representatives shall immediately choose by ballot one of them for President; and if no person have a majority, then from the five highest on the list said house shall in like manner choose the President. But in choosing the President the votes shall be taken by States, the representation from each State having one vote; a quorum for this purpose shall consist of a member or members from two-thirds of the States, and a majority of all the States shall be necessary to a choice. In every case, after the choice of the President, the person having the greatest number of votes of the electors shall be the Vice-President. But if there should remain two or more who have equal votes, the Senate shall choose from them by ballot the Vice-President.

The Congress may determine the time of choosing the electors, and the day on which they shall give their votes; which day shall be the same throughout the United States.

No person except a natural-born citizen, *or a citizen of the United States at the time of the adoption of this Constitution*, shall be eligible to the office of President; neither shall any person be eligible to that office who shall not have attained to the age of thirty-five years, and been fourteen years a resident within the United States.

In cases of the removal of the President from office or of his death, resignation, or inability to discharge the powers and duties of the said office, the same shall devolve on the Vice-President, and the Congress may by law provide for the case of removal, death, resignation, or inability, both of the President and Vice-President, declaring what officer shall then act as President, and such officer shall act accordingly, until the disability be removed, or a President shall be elected.

The President shall, at stated times, receive for his services a compensation, which shall neither be increased nor diminished during the period for which he shall have been elected, and he shall not receive within that period any other emolument from the United States, or any of them.

Before he enter on the execution of his office, he shall take the following oath or affirmation:—"I do solemnly swear (or affirm) that I will faithfully execute the office of the President of the United States, and will to the best of my ability preserve, protect and defend the Constitution of the United States."

Section 2   The President shall be commander in chief of the army and navy of the United States, and of the militia of the several States, when called into the actual service of the United States; he may require the opinion, in writing, of the principal officer in each of the executive departments, upon any subject relating to the duties of their respective offices, and he shall have power to grant reprieves and pardons for offenses against the United States, except in cases of impeachment.

He shall have power, by and with the advice and consent of the Senate, to make treaties, provided two-thirds of the Senators present concur; and he shall nominate, and by and with the advice and consent of the Senate, shall appoint ambassadors, other public ministers and consuls, judges of the Supreme Court, and all other officers of the United States, whose appointments are not herein otherwise provided for, and which shall be established by law: but Congress may by law vest the appointment of such inferior officers, as they think proper, in the President alone, in the courts of law, or in the heads of departments.

The President shall have power to fill up all vacancies that may happen during the recess of the Senate, by granting commissions which shall expire at the end of their next session.

Section 3   He shall from time to time give to the Congress information of the state of the Union, and recommend to their consideration such measures as he shall judge necessary and expedient; he may, on extraordinary occasions, convene both houses, or either of them, and in case of disagreement between them, with respect to the time of adjournment, he may adjourn them to such time as he shall think proper; he shall receive ambassadors and other public ministers; he shall take care that the laws be faithfully executed, and shall commission all the officers of the United States.

Section 4   The President, Vice-President and all civil officers of the United States shall be removed from office on impeachment for, and on conviction of, treason, bribery, or other high crimes and misdemeanors.

Article III

Section 1   The judicial power of the United States shall be vested in one Supreme Court, and in such inferior courts as the Congress may from time to time ordain and establish. The judges, both of the Supreme and inferior courts, shall hold their offices during good behavior, and shall, at stated times, receive for their services a compensation which shall not be diminished during their continuance in office.

Section 2   The judicial power shall extend to all cases, in law and equity, arising under this Constitution, the laws of the United States, and treaties made, or which shall be made, under their authority;—to all cases affecting ambassadors, other public ministers and consuls;—to all cases of admiralty and maritime jurisdiction;—to controversies to which the United States shall be a party;—to controversies between two or more States;—*between a State and citizens of another State;*—between citizens of different States;—between citizens of the same State claiming lands under grants of different States, and between a State, or the citizens thereof, and foreign states, citizens or subjects.

In all cases affecting ambassadors, other public ministers and consuls, and those in which a State shall be party, the Supreme Court shall have original jurisdiction. In all the other cases before mentioned, the Supreme Court shall have appellate jurisdiction, both as to law and fact, with such exceptions, and under such regulations, as the Congress shall make.

THE CONSTITUTION OF THE UNITED STATES

The trial of all crimes, except in cases of impeachment, shall be by jury; and such trial shall be held in the State where said crimes shall have been committed; but when not committed within any State, the trial shall be at such place or places as the Congress may by Law have directed.

Section 3 Treason against the United States shall consist only in levying war against them, or in adhering to their enemies, giving them aid and comfort. No person shall be convicted of treason unless on the testimony of two witnesses to the same overt act, or on confession in open court.

The Congress shall have power to declare the punishment of treason, but no attainder of treason shall work corruption of blood, or forfeiture except during the life of the person attainted.

Article IV

Section 1 Full faith and credit shall be given in each State to the public acts, records, and judicial proceedings of every other State. And the Congress may by general laws prescribe the manner in which such acts, records, and proceedings shall be proved, and the effect thereof.

Section 2 The citizens of each State shall be entitled to all privileges and immunities of citizens in the several States.

A person charged in any State with treason, felony, or other crime, who shall flee from justice, and be found in another State, shall on demand of the executive authority of the State from which he fled, be delivered up, to be removed to the State having jurisdiction of the crime.

No Person held to service or labor in one State, under the laws thereof, escaping into another, shall, in consequence of any law or regulation therein, be discharged from such service or labor, but shall be delivered up on claim of the party to whom such service or labor may be due.

Section 3 New States may be admitted by the Congress into this Union; but no new State shall be formed or erected within the jurisdiction of any other State; nor any State be formed by the junction of two or more States, or parts of States, without the consent of the legislatures of the States concerned as well as of the Congress.

The Congress shall have power to dispose of and make all needful rules and regulations respecting the territory or other property belonging to the United States; and nothing in this Constitution shall be so construed as to prejudice any claims of the United States, or of any particular State.

Section 4 The United States shall guarantee to every State in this Union a republican form of government, and shall protect each of them against invasion; and on application of the legislature, or of the executive (when the legislature cannot be convened), against domestic violence.

Article V

The Congress, whenever two-thirds of both houses shall deem it necessary, shall propose amendments to this Constitution, or, on the application of the legislatures of two-thirds of the several States, shall call a convention for proposing amendments, which, in either case, shall be valid to all intents and purposes, as part of this Constitution, when ratified by the legislatures of three-fourths of the several States, or by conventions in three-fourths thereof, as the one or the other mode of ratification may be proposed by the Congress; provided *that no amendments which may be made prior to the year one thousand eight hundred and eight shall in any manner affect the first and fourth clauses in the ninth section of the first article;* and that no State, without its consent, shall be deprived of its equal suffrage in the Senate.

Article VI

All debts contracted and engagements entered into, before the adoption of this Constitution, shall be as valid against the United States under this Constitution, as under the Confederation.

This Constitution, and the laws of the United States which shall be made in pursuance thereof; and all treaties made, or which shall be made, under the authority of the United States, shall be the supreme law of the land; and the judges in every State shall be bound thereby, anything in the Constitution or laws of any State to the contrary notwithstanding.

The Senators and Representatives before mentioned, and the members of the several State legislatures, and all executive and judicial officers, both of the United States and of the several States, shall be bound by oath or affirmation to support this Constitution; but no religious test shall ever be required as a qualification to any office or public trust under the United States.

Article VII

The ratification of the conventions of nine States shall be sufficient for the establishment of this Constitution between the States so ratifying the same.

Done in convention by the unanimous consent of the States present, the seventeenth day of September in the year of our Lord one thousand seven hundred and eighty-seven and of the Independence of the United States of America the twelfth. In witness whereof we have hereunto subscribed our names.

GEORGE WASHINGTON

PRESIDENT AND DEPUTY FROM VIRGINIA

New Hampshire
John Langdon
Nicholas Gilman

Massachusetts
Nathaniel Gorham
Rufus King

Connecticut
William Samuel
   Johnson
Roger Sherman

New York
Alexander Hamilton

New Jersey
William Livingston
David Brearley
William Paterson
Jonathan Dayton

Pennsylvania
Benjamin Franklin
Thomas Mifflin
Robert Morris
George Clymer
Thomas FitzSimons
Jared Ingersoll
James Wilson
Gouverneur Morris

Delaware
George Read
Gunning Bedford, Jr.
John Dickinson
Richard Bassett
Jacob Broom

Maryland
James McHenry
Daniel of St. Thomas
   Jenifer
Daniel Carroll

Virginia
John Blair
James Madison, Jr.

North Carolina
William Blount
Richard Dobbs Spaight
Hugh Williamson

South Carolina
John Rutledge
Charles Cotesworth
   Pinckney
Charles Pinckney
Pierce Butler

Georgia
William Few
Abraham Baldwin

AMENDMENTS TO THE CONSTITUTION WITH ANNOTATIONS
(including the six unratified amendments)

IN THEIR EFFORT TO GAIN Antifederalists' support for the Constitution, Federalists frequently pointed to the inclusion of Article 5, which provides an orderly method of amending the Constitution. In contrast, the Articles of Confederation, which were universally recognized as seriously flawed, offered no means of amendment. For their part, Antifederalists argued that the amendment process was so "intricate" that one might as easily roll "sixes an hundred times in succession" as change the Constitution.

The system for amendment laid out in the Constitution requires that two-thirds of both houses of Congress agree to a proposed amendment, which must then be ratified by three-quarters of the legislatures of the states. Alternatively, an amendment may be proposed by a convention called by the legislatures of two-thirds of the states. Since 1789, members of Congress have proposed thousands of amendments. Besides the seventeen amendments added since 1789, only the six "unratified" ones included here were approved by two-thirds of both houses and sent to the states for ratification.

Among the many amendments that never made it out of Congress have been proposals to declare dueling, divorce, and interracial marriage unconstitutional as well as proposals to establish a national university, to acknowledge the sovereignty of Jesus Christ, and to prohibit any person from possessing wealth in excess of $10 million.*

Among the issues facing Americans today that might lead to constitutional amendment are efforts to balance the federal budget, to limit the number of terms elected officials may serve, to limit access to or prohibit abortion, to establish English as the official language of the United States, and to prohibit flag burning. None of these proposed amendments has yet garnered enough support in Congress to be sent to the states for ratification.

Although the first ten amendments to the Constitution are commonly known as the Bill of Rights, only Amendments 1–8 actually provide guarantees of individual rights. Amendments 9 and 10 deal with the structure of power within the constitutional system. The Bill of Rights was promised to appease Antifederalists who refused to ratify the Constitution without guarantees of individual liberties and limitations to federal power. After studying more than two hundred amendments recommended by the ratifying conventions of the states, Federalist James Madison presented a list of seventeen to Congress, which used Madison's list as the foundation for the twelve amendments that were sent to the states for ratification. Ten of the twelve were adopted in 1791. The first on the list of twelve,

---

* Richard B. Bernstein, *Amending America* (New York: Times Books, 1993), 177–81.

known as the Reapportionment Amendment, was never adopted (see page A-15). The second proposed amendment was adopted in 1992 as Amendment 27 (see page A-24).

Amendment I

Congress shall make no law respecting an establishment of religion, or prohibiting the free exercise thereof; or abridging the freedom of speech, or of the press; or the right of the people peaceably to assemble, and to petition the government for a redress of grievances.

♦ ♦ ♦

The First Amendment is a potent symbol for many Americans. Most are well aware of their rights to free speech, freedom of the press, and freedom of religion and their rights to assemble and to petition, even if they cannot cite the exact words of this amendment.

The First Amendment guarantee of freedom of religion has two clauses: the "free exercise clause," which allows individuals to practice or not practice any religion, and the "establishment clause," which prevents the federal government from discriminating against or favoring any particular religion. This clause was designed to create what Thomas Jefferson referred to as "a wall of separation between church and state." In the 1960s, the Supreme Court ruled that the First Amendment prohibits prayer (see Engel v. Vitale, *online) and Bible reading in public schools.*

Although the rights to free speech and freedom of the press are established in the First Amendment, it was not until the twentieth century that the Supreme Court began to explore the full meaning of these guarantees. In 1919, the Court ruled in Schenck v. United States *(online) that the government could suppress free expression only where it could cite a "clear and present danger." In a decision that continues to raise controversies, the Court ruled in 1990, in* Texas v. Johnson, *that flag burning is a form of symbolic speech protected by the First Amendment.*

Amendment II

A well-regulated militia being necessary to the security of a free State, the right of the people to keep and bear arms shall not be infringed.

♦ ♦ ♦

Fear of a standing army under the control of a hostile government made the Second Amendment an important part of the Bill of Rights. Advocates of gun ownership claim that the amendment prevents the government from regulating firearms. Proponents of gun control argue that the amendment is designed only to protect the right of the states to maintain militia units.

In 1939, the Supreme Court ruled in United States v. Miller *that the Second Amendment did not protect the right of an individual to own a sawed-off shotgun, which*

it argued was not ordinary militia equipment. Since then, the Supreme Court has refused to hear Second Amendment cases, while lower courts have upheld firearms regulations. Several justices currently on the bench seem to favor a narrow interpretation of the Second Amendment, which would allow gun control legislation. The controversy over the impact of the Second Amendment on gun owners and gun control legislation will certainly continue.

Amendment III

No soldier shall, in time of peace, be quartered in any house without the consent of the owner, nor in time of war, but in a manner to be prescribed by law.

♦ ♦ ♦

The Third Amendment was extremely important to the framers of the Constitution, but today it is nearly forgotten. American colonists were especially outraged that they were forced to quarter British troops in the years before and during the American Revolution. The philosophy of the Third Amendment has been viewed by some justices and scholars as the foundation of the modern constitutional right to privacy. One example of this can be found in Justice William O. Douglas's opinion in Griswold v. Connecticut *(online).*

Amendment IV

The right of the people to be secure in their persons, houses, papers, and effects, against unreasonable searches and seizures, shall not be violated, and no warrants shall issue but upon probable cause, supported by oath or affirmation, and particularly describing the place to be searched, and the persons or things to be seized.

♦ ♦ ♦

In the years before the Revolution, the houses, barns, stores, and warehouses of American colonists were ransacked by British authorities under "writs of assistance" or general warrants. The British, thus empowered, searched for seditious material or smuggled goods that could then be used as evidence against colonists who were charged with a crime only after the items were found.

The first part of the Fourth Amendment protects citizens from "unreasonable" searches and seizures. The Supreme Court has interpreted this protection as well as the words search *and* seizure *in different ways at different times. At one time, the Court did not recognize electronic eavesdropping as a form of search and seizure, though it does today. At times, an "unreasonable" search has been almost any search carried out without a warrant, but in the two decades before 1969, the Court sometimes sanctioned warrantless searches that it considered reasonable based on "the total atmosphere of the case."*

The second part of the Fourth Amendment defines the procedure for issuing a search warrant and states the requirement of "probable cause," which is generally viewed as evidence indicating that a suspect has committed an offense.

The Fourth Amendment has been controversial because the Court has sometimes excluded evidence that has been seized in violation of constitutional standards. The justification is that excluding such evidence deters violations of the amendment, but doing so may allow a guilty person to escape punishment.

Amendment V

No person shall be held to answer for a capital, or otherwise infamous crime, unless on a presentment or indictment of a grand jury, except in cases arising in the land or naval forces, or in the militia, when in actual service in time of war or public danger; nor shall any person be subject for the same offence to be twice put in jeopardy of life or limb; nor shall be compelled in any criminal case to be a witness against himself, nor be deprived of life, liberty, or property, without due process of law; nor shall private property be taken for public use without just compensation.

◆◆◆

The Fifth Amendment protects people against government authority in the prosecution of criminal offenses. It prohibits the state, first, from charging a person with a serious crime without a grand jury hearing to decide whether there is sufficient evidence to support the charge and, second, from charging a person with the same crime twice. The best-known aspect of the Fifth Amendment is that it prevents a person from being "compelled . . . to be a witness against himself." The last clause, the "takings clause," limits the power of the government to seize property.

Although invoking the Fifth Amendment is popularly viewed as a confession of guilt, a person may be innocent yet still fear prosecution. For example, during the Red-baiting era of the late 1940s and 1950s, many people who had participated in legal activities that were associated with the Communist Party claimed the Fifth Amendment privilege rather than testify before the House Un-American Activities Committee because the mood of the times cast those activities in a negative light. Since "taking the Fifth" was viewed as an admission of guilt, those people often lost their jobs or became unemployable. (See chapter 26.) Nonetheless, the right to protect oneself against self-incrimination plays an important role in guarding against the collective power of the state.

Amendment VI

In all criminal prosecutions, the accused shall enjoy the right to a speedy and public trial, by an impartial jury of the State and district wherein the crime shall have been committed, which district shall have been previously ascertained by law, and to be informed of the nature and cause of the accusation; to be confronted with the witnesses against him; to have compulsory process for obtaining witnesses in his favor, and to have the assistance of counsel for his defence.

◆◆◆

The original Constitution put few limits on the government's power to investigate, prosecute, and punish crime. This process was of great concern to the early Americans, however, and of the twenty-eight rights specified in the first eight amendments, fifteen have to do with it. Seven rights are specified in the Sixth Amendment. These include the right to a speedy trial, a public trial, a jury trial, a notice of accusation, confrontation by opposing witnesses, testimony by favorable witnesses, and the assistance of counsel.

Although this amendment originally guaranteed these rights only in cases involving the federal government, the adoption of the Fourteenth Amendment began a process of applying the protections of the Bill of Rights to the states through court cases such as Gideon v. Wainwright *(online).*

Amendment VII

In suits at common law, where the value in controversy shall exceed twenty dollars, the right of trial by jury shall be preserved, and no fact tried by a jury shall be otherwise reexamined in any court of the United States, than according to the rules of the common law.

◆◆◆

This amendment guarantees people the same right to a trial by jury as was guaranteed by English common law in 1791. Under common law, in civil trials (those involving money damages) the role of the judge was to settle questions of law and that of the jury was to settle questions of fact. The amendment does not specify the size of the jury or its role in a trial, however. The Supreme Court has generally held that those issues be determined by English common law of 1791, which stated that a jury consists of twelve people, that a trial must be conducted before a judge who instructs the jury on the law and advises it on facts, and that a verdict must be unanimous.

Amendment VIII

Excessive bail shall not be required, nor excessive fines imposed, nor cruel and unusual punishments inflicted.

◆◆◆

The language used to guarantee the three rights in this amendment was inspired by the English Bill of Rights of

1689. The Supreme Court has not had a lot to say about "excessive fines." In recent years it has agreed that despite the provision against "excessive bail," persons who are believed to be dangerous to others can be held without bail even before they have been convicted.

Although opponents of the death penalty have not succeeded in using the Eighth Amendment to achieve the end of capital punishment, the clause regarding "cruel and unusual punishments" has been used to prohibit capital punishment in certain cases (see Furman v. Georgia, online) and to require improved conditions in prisons.

Amendment IX

The enumeration in the Constitution, of certain rights, shall not be construed to deny or disparage others retained by the people.

♦ ♦ ♦

Some Federalists feared that inclusion of the Bill of Rights in the Constitution would allow later generations of interpreters to claim that the people had surrendered any rights not specifically enumerated there. To guard against this, Madison added language that became the Ninth Amendment. Interest in this heretofore largely ignored amendment revived in 1965 when it was used in a concurring opinion in Griswold v. Connecticut (online). While Justice William O. Douglas called on the Third Amendment to support the right to privacy in deciding that case, Justice Arthur Goldberg, in the concurring opinion, argued that the right to privacy regarding contraception was an unenumerated right that was protected by the Ninth Amendment.

In 1980, the Court ruled that the right of the press to attend a public trial was protected by the Ninth Amendment. While some scholars argue that modern judges cannot identify the unenumerated rights that the framers were trying to protect, others argue that the Ninth Amendment should be read as providing a constitutional "presumption of liberty" that allows people to act in any way that does not violate the rights of others.

Amendment X

The powers not delegated to the United States by the Constitution, nor prohibited by it to the States, are reserved to the States respectively, or to the people.

♦ ♦ ♦

The Antifederalists were especially eager to see a "reserved powers clause" explicitly guaranteeing the states control over their internal affairs. Not surprisingly, the Tenth Amendment has been a frequent battleground in the struggle over states' rights and federal supremacy. Prior to the Civil War, the Democratic Republican Party and Jacksonian Democrats invoked the Tenth Amendment to prohibit the federal government from making decisions about whether people in individual states could own slaves. The Tenth Amendment was virtually suspended during Reconstruction following the Civil War. In 1883, however, the Supreme Court declared the Civil Rights Act of 1875 unconstitutional on the grounds that it violated the Tenth Amendment. Business interests also called on the amendment to block efforts at federal regulation.

The Court was inconsistent over the next several decades as it attempted to resolve the tension between the restrictions of the Tenth Amendment and the powers the Constitution granted to Congress to regulate interstate commerce and levy taxes. The Court upheld the Pure Food and Drug Act (1906), the Meat Inspection Acts (1906 and 1907), and the White Slave Traffic Act (1910), all of which affected the states, but struck down an act prohibiting interstate shipment of goods produced through child labor. Between 1934 and 1935, a number of New Deal programs created by Franklin D. Roosevelt were declared unconstitutional on the grounds that they violated the Tenth Amendment. (See chapter 24.) As Roosevelt appointees changed the composition of the Court, the Tenth Amendment was declared to have no substantive meaning. Generally, the amendment is held to protect the rights of states to regulate internal matters such as local government, education, commerce, labor, and business, as well as matters involving families such as marriage, divorce, and inheritance within the state.

Unratified Amendment

Reapportionment Amendment (proposed by Congress September 25, 1789, along with the Bill of Rights)

After the first enumeration required by the first article of the Constitution, there shall be one Representative for every thirty thousand, until the number shall amount to one hundred, after which the proportion shall be so regulated by Congress, that there shall be not less than one hundred Representatives, nor less than one Representative for every forty thousand persons, until the number of Representatives shall amount to two hundred; after which the proportion shall be so regulated by Congress, that there shall not be less than two hundred Representatives, nor more than one Representative for every fifty thousand persons.

♦ ♦ ♦

If the Reapportionment Amendment had passed and remained in effect, the House of Representatives today would have more than 5,000 members rather than 435.

Amendment XI
[Adopted 1798]

The judicial power of the United States shall not be construed to extend to any suit in law or equity, commenced or prosecuted against one of the United States by citizens of another State, or by citizens or subjects of any foreign state.

♦ ♦ ♦

In 1793, the Supreme Court ruled in favor of Alexander Chisholm, executor of the estate of a deceased South Carolina merchant. Chisholm was suing the state of Georgia because the merchant had never been paid for provisions he had supplied during the Revolution. Many regarded this Court decision as an error that violated the intent of the Constitution.

Antifederalists had long feared a federal court system with the power to overrule a state court. When the Constitution was being drafted, Federalists had assured worried Antifederalists that section 2 of Article 3, which allows federal courts to hear cases "between a State and citizens of another State," did not mean that the federal courts were authorized to hear suits against a state by citizens of another state or a foreign country. Antifederalists and many other Americans feared a powerful federal court system because they worried that it would become like the British courts of this period, which were accountable only to the monarch. Furthermore, Chisholm v. Georgia prompted a series of suits against state governments by creditors and suppliers who had made loans during the war.

In addition, state legislators and Congress feared that the shaky economies of the new states, as well as the country as a whole, would be destroyed, especially if loyalists who had fled to other countries sought reimbursement for land and property that had been seized. The day after the Supreme Court announced its decision, a resolution proposing the Eleventh Amendment, which overturned the decision in Chisholm v. Georgia, was introduced in the U.S. Senate.

Amendment XII

[Adopted 1804]

The electors shall meet in their respective States, and vote by ballot for President and Vice-President, one of whom, at least, shall not be an inhabitant of the same State with themselves; they shall name in their ballots the person voted for as President, and in distinct ballots the person voted for as Vice-President, and they shall make distinct lists of all persons voted for as President, and of all persons voted for as Vice-President, and of the number of votes for each, which lists they shall sign and certify, and transmit sealed to the seat of government of the United States, directed to the President of the Senate;—the President of the Senate shall, in the presence of the Senate and House of Representatives, open all the certificates and the votes shall then be counted;—the person having the greatest number of votes for President shall be the President, if such number be a majority of the whole number of electors appointed; and if no person have such majority, then from the persons having the highest numbers not exceeding three on the list of those voted for as President, the House of Representatives shall choose immediately, by ballot, the President. But in choosing the President, the votes shall be taken by States, the representation from each State having one vote; a quorum for this purpose shall consist of a member or members from two-thirds of the States, and a majority of all the States shall be necessary to a choice. And if the House of Representatives shall not choose a President whenever the right of choice shall devolve upon them, before *the fourth day of March* next following, then the Vice-President shall act as President, as in the case of the death or other constitutional disability of the President.

The person having the greatest number of votes as Vice-President shall be the Vice-President, if such number be a majority of the whole number of electors appointed; and if no person have a majority, then from the two highest numbers on the list the Senate shall choose the Vice-President; a quorum for the purpose shall consist of two-thirds of the whole number of Senators, and a majority of the whole number shall be necessary to a choice. But no person constitutionally ineligible to the office of President shall be eligible to that of Vice-President of the United States.

♦ ♦ ♦

The framers of the Constitution disliked political parties and assumed that none would ever form. Under the original system, electors chosen by the states would each vote for two candidates. The candidate who won the most votes would become president, while the person who won the second-highest number of votes would become vice president. Rivalries between Federalists and Antifederalists led to the formation of political parties, however, even before George Washington had left office. Though Washington was elected unanimously in 1789 and 1792, the elections of 1796 and 1800 were procedural disasters because of party maneuvering (see chapters 9 and 10). In 1796, Federalist John Adams was chosen as president, and his great rival, the Antifederalist Thomas Jefferson (whose party was called the Republican Party), became his vice president. In 1800, all the electors cast their two votes as one of two party blocs. Jefferson and his fellow Republican nominee, Aaron Burr, were tied with 73 votes each. The contest went to the House of Representatives, which finally elected Jefferson after 36 ballots. The Twelfth Amendment prevents these problems by requiring electors to vote separately for the president and vice president.

Unratified Amendment

Titles of Nobility Amendment (proposed by Congress May 1, 1810)

If any citizen of the United States shall accept, claim, receive or retain any title of nobility or honor or shall, without the consent of Congress, accept and retain any present, pension, office or emolument of any kind whatever, from any emperor, king, prince or foreign power, such person shall cease to be a citizen of the United States, and shall be incapable of holding any office of trust or profit under them or either of them.

◆ ◆ ◆

This amendment would have extended Article 1, section 9, clause 8 of the Constitution, which prevents the awarding of titles by the United States and the acceptance of such awards from foreign powers without congressional consent. Historians speculate that general nervousness about the power of the emperor Napoleon, who was at that time extending France's empire throughout Europe, may have prompted the proposal. Though it fell one vote short of ratification, Congress and the American people thought the proposal had been ratified, and it was included in many nineteenth-century editions of the Constitution.

The Civil War and Reconstruction Amendments (Thirteenth, Fourteenth, and Fifteenth Amendments)

In the four months between the election of Abraham Lincoln and his inauguration, more than 200 proposed constitutional amendments were presented to Congress as part of a desperate attempt to hold the rapidly dissolving Union together. Most of these were efforts to appease the southern states by protecting the right to own slaves or by disfranchising African Americans through constitutional amendment. None were able to win the votes required from Congress to send them to the states. The relatively innocuous Corwin Amendment seemed to be the only hope for preserving the Union by amending the Constitution.

The northern victors in the Civil War tried to restructure the Constitution just as the war had restructured the nation. Yet they were often divided in their goals. Some wanted to end slavery; others hoped for social and economic equality regardless of race; others hoped that extending the power of the ballot box to former slaves would help create a new political order. The debates over the Thirteenth, Fourteenth, and Fifteenth Amendments were bitter. Few of those who fought for these changes were satisfied with the amendments themselves; fewer still were satisfied with their interpretation. Although the amendments put an end to the legal status of

slavery, it took nearly a hundred years after the amendments' passage before most of the descendants of former slaves could begin to experience the economic, social, and political equality the amendments had been intended to provide.

Unratified Amendment

Corwin Amendment (proposed by Congress March 2, 1861)

No amendment shall be made to the Constitution which will authorize or give to Congress the power to abolish or interfere, within any State, with the domestic institutions thereof, including that of persons held to labor or service by the laws of said State.

◆ ◆ ◆

Following the election of Abraham Lincoln, Congress scrambled to try to prevent the secession of the slaveholding states. House member Thomas Corwin of Ohio proposed the "unamendable" amendment in the hope that by protecting slavery where it existed, Congress would keep the southern states in the Union. Lincoln indicated his support for the proposed amendment in his first inaugural address. Only Ohio and Maryland ratified the Corwin Amendment before it was forgotten.

Amendment XIII

[Adopted 1865]

Section 1   Neither slavery nor involuntary servitude, except as a punishment for crime whereof the party shall have been duly convicted, shall exist within the United States, or any place subject to their jurisdiction.

Section 2   Congress shall have power to enforce this article by appropriate legislation.

◆ ◆ ◆

Although President Lincoln had abolished slavery in the Confederacy with the Emancipation Proclamation of 1863, abolitionists wanted to rid the entire country of slavery. The Thirteenth Amendment did this in a clear and straightforward manner. In February 1865, when the proposal was approved by the House, the gallery of the House was newly opened to black Americans who had a chance at last to see their government at work. Passage of the proposal was greeted by wild cheers from the gallery as well as tears on the House floor, where congressional representatives openly embraced one another.

The problem of ratification remained, however. The Union position was that the Confederate states were part of the country of thirty-six states. Therefore, twenty-seven states were needed to ratify the amendment. When Kentucky and Delaware rejected it, backers realized that without approval from at least four former Confederate states, the amendment would fail. Lincoln's successor, President Andrew Johnson, made ratification of the Thirteenth Amendment a condition for southern states to rejoin the Union. Under those terms, all the former Confederate states except Mississippi accepted the Thirteenth Amendment, and by the end of 1865 the amendment had become part of the Constitution and slavery had been prohibited in the United States.

Amendment XIV

[Adopted 1868]

Section 1 All persons born or naturalized in the United States, and subject to the jurisdiction thereof, are citizens of the United States and of the State wherein they reside. No State shall make or enforce any law which shall abridge the privileges or immunities of citizens of the United States; nor shall any State deprive any person of life, liberty, or property, without due process of law; nor deny to any person within its jurisdiction the equal protection of the laws.

Section 2 Representatives shall be appointed among the several States according to their respective numbers, counting the whole number of persons in each State, excluding Indians not taxed. But when the right to vote at any election for the choice of Electors for President and Vice-President of the United States, Representatives in Congress, the executive and judicial officers of a State, or the members of the legislature thereof, is denied to any of the male inhabitants of such State, being twenty-one years of age and citizens of the United States, or in any way abridged, except for participation in rebellion, or other crime, the basis of representation therein shall be reduced in the proportion which the number of such male citizens shall bear to the whole number of male citizens twenty-one years of age in such State.

Section 3 No person shall be a Senator or Representative in Congress, or Elector of President and Vice-President, or hold any office, civil or military, under the United States, or under any State, who, having previously taken an oath, as a member of Congress, or as an officer of the United States, or as a member of any State legislature, or as an executive or judicial officer of any State, to support the Constitution of the United States, shall have engaged in insurrection or rebellion against the same, or given aid or comfort to the enemies thereof. Congress may, by a vote of two-thirds of each house, remove such disability.

Section 4 The validity of the public debt of the United States, authorized by law, including debts incurred for payment of pensions and bounties for services in suppressing insurrection or rebellion, shall not be questioned. But neither the United States nor any State shall assume or pay any debt or obligation incurred in aid of insurrection or rebellion against the United States, or any claim for the loss or emancipation of any slave; but all such debts, obligations, and claims shall be held illegal and void.

Section 5 The Congress shall have power to enforce, by appropriate legislation, the provisions of this article.

◆ ◆ ◆

Without Lincoln's leadership in the reconstruction of the nation following the Civil War, it soon became clear that the Thirteenth Amendment needed additional constitutional support. Less than a year after Lincoln's assassination, Andrew Johnson was ready to bring the former Confederate states back into the Union with few changes in their governments or politics. Anxious Republicans drafted the Fourteenth Amendment to prevent that from happening. The most important provisions of this complex amendment made all native-born or naturalized persons American citizens and prohibited states from abridging the "privileges or immunities" of citizens; depriving them of "life, liberty, or property, without due process of law"; and denying them "equal protection of the laws." In essence, it made all ex-slaves citizens and protected the rights of all citizens against violation by their own state governments.

As occurred in the case of the Thirteenth Amendment, former Confederate states were forced to ratify the amendment as a condition of representation in the House and the Senate. The intentions of the Fourteenth Amendment, and how those intentions should be enforced, have been the most debated point of constitutional history. The terms due process *and* equal protection *have been especially troublesome. Was the amendment designed to outlaw racial segregation? Or was the goal simply to prevent the leaders of the rebellious South from gaining political power?*

The framers of the Fourteenth Amendment hoped Article 2 would produce black voters who would increase the power of the Republican Party. The federal government, however, never used its power to punish states for denying blacks their right to vote. Although the Fourteenth Amendment had an immediate impact in giving black Americans citizenship, it did nothing to protect blacks from the vengeance of whites once Reconstruction ended. In the late nineteenth and early twentieth centuries, section 1 of the Fourteenth Amendment was often used to protect business interests and strike down laws protecting workers on the grounds that the rights of "persons," that is, corporations, were protected by "due process." More recently, the Fourteenth Amendment has been used to justify school desegregation and affirmative action programs, as well as to dismantle such programs.

Amendment XV

[Adopted 1870]

Section 1   The right of citizens of the United States to vote shall not be denied or abridged by the United States or by any State on account of race, color, or previous condition of servitude.

Section 2   The Congress shall have power to enforce this article by appropriate legislation.

♦ ♦ ♦

The Fifteenth Amendment was the last major piece of Reconstruction legislation. While earlier Reconstruction acts had already required black suffrage in the South, the Fifteenth Amendment extended black voting rights to the entire nation. Some Republicans felt morally obligated to do away with the double standard between North and South since many northern states had stubbornly refused to enfranchise blacks. Others believed that the freedman's ballot required the extra protection of a constitutional amendment to shield it from white counterattack. But partisan advantage also played an important role in the amendment's passage, since Republicans hoped that by giving the ballot to northern blacks, they could lessen their political vulnerability.

Many women's rights advocates had fought for the amendment. They had felt betrayed by the inclusion of the word male *in section 2 of the Fourteenth Amendment and were further angered when the proposed Fifteenth Amendment failed to prohibit denial of the right to vote on the grounds of sex as well as "race, color, or previous condition of servitude." In this amendment, for the first time, the federal government claimed the power to regulate the franchise, or vote. It was also the first time the Constitution placed limits on the power of the states to regulate access to the franchise. Although ratified in 1870, the amendment was not enforced until the twentieth century.*

The Progressive Amendments (Sixteenth–Nineteenth Amendments)

No amendments were added to the Constitution between the Civil War and the Progressive Era. America was changing, however, in fundamental ways. The rapid industrialization of the United States after the Civil War led to many social and economic problems. Hundreds of amendments were proposed, but none received enough support in Congress to be sent to the states. Some scholars believe that regional differences and rivalries were so strong during this period that it was almost impossible to gain a consensus on a constitutional amendment. During the Progressive Era, however, the Constitution was amended four times in seven years.

Amendment XVI

[Adopted 1913]

The Congress shall have power to lay and collect taxes on incomes, from whatever source derived, without apportionment among the several States, and without regard to any census or enumeration.

♦ ♦ ♦

Until passage of the Sixteenth Amendment, most of the money used to run the federal government came from customs duties and taxes on specific items, such as liquor. During the Civil War, the federal government taxed incomes as an emergency measure. Pressure to enact an income tax came from those who were concerned about the growing gap between rich and poor in the United States. The Populist Party began campaigning for a graduated income tax in 1892, and support continued to grow. By 1909, thirty-three proposed income tax amendments had been presented in Congress, but lobbying by corporate and other special interests had defeated them all. In June 1909, the growing pressure for an income tax, which had been endorsed by Presidents Roosevelt and Taft, finally pushed an amendment through the Senate. The required thirty-six states had ratified the amendment by February 1913.

Amendment XVII

[Adopted 1913]

Section 1   The Senate of the United States shall be composed of two Senators from each State, elected by the people thereof, for six years; and each Senator shall have one vote. The electors in each State shall have the qualifications requisite for electors of [voters for] the most numerous branch of the State legislatures.

Section 2   When vacancies happen in the representation of any State in the Senate, the executive authority of such State shall issue writs of election to fill such vacancies: Provided, that the Legislature of any State may empower the executive thereof to make temporary appointments until the people fill the vacancies by election as the Legislature may direct.

Section 3   This amendment shall not be so construed as to affect the election or term of any Senator chosen before it becomes valid as part of the Constitution.

♦ ♦ ♦

The framers of the Constitution saw the members of the House as the representatives of the people and the members of the Senate as the representatives of the states. Originally senators were to be chosen by the state legislators. According to reform advocates, however, the growth of private industry and transportation conglomerates during the Gilded Age had created a network of corruption in which wealth and power were exchanged for influence and votes in the Senate. Senator Nelson Aldrich, who represented Rhode Island in the late nineteenth and early twentieth centuries, for example, was known as "the senator from Standard Oil" because of his open support of special business interests.

Efforts to amend the Constitution to allow direct election of senators had begun in 1826, but since any proposal had to be approved by the Senate, reform seemed impossible. Progressives tried to gain influence in the Senate by instituting party caucuses and primary elections, which gave citizens the chance to express their choice of a senator who could then be officially elected by the state legislature. By 1910, fourteen of the country's thirty senators received popular votes through a state primary before the state legislature made its selection. Despairing of getting a proposal through the Senate, supporters of a direct-election amendment had begun in 1893 to seek a convention of representatives from two-thirds of the states to propose an amendment that could then be ratified. By 1905, thirty-one of forty-five states had endorsed such an amendment. Finally, in 1911, despite extraordinary opposition, a proposed amendment passed the Senate; by 1913, it had been ratified.

Amendment XVIII

[Adopted 1919; repealed 1933 by Amendment XXI]

Section 1   After one year from the ratification of this article the manufacture, sale, or transportation of intoxicating liquors within, the importation thereof into, or the exportation thereof from the United States and all territory subject to the jurisdiction thereof, for beverage purposes, is hereby prohibited.

Section 2   The Congress and the several States shall have concurrent power to enforce this article by appropriate legislation.

Section 3   This article shall be inoperative unless it shall have been ratified as an amendment to the Constitution by the legislatures of the several States, as provided by the Constitution, within seven years from the date of the submission thereof to the States by the Congress.

♦ ♦ ♦

The Prohibition Party, formed in 1869, began calling for a constitutional amendment to outlaw alcoholic beverages in 1872. A prohibition amendment was first proposed in the Senate in 1876 and was revived eighteen times before 1913. Between 1913 and 1919, another thirty-nine attempts were made to prohibit liquor in the United States through a constitutional amendment. Prohibition became a key element of the progressive agenda as reformers linked alcohol and

drunkenness to numerous social problems, including the corruption of immigrant voters. While opponents of such an amendment argued that it was undemocratic, supporters claimed that their efforts had widespread public support. The admission of twelve "dry" western states to the Union in the early twentieth century and the spirit of sacrifice during World War I laid the groundwork for passage and ratification of the Eighteenth Amendment in 1919. Opponents added a time limit to the amendment in the hope that they could thus block ratification, but this effort failed. (See also Amendment XXI.)

Amendment XIX

[Adopted 1920]

Section 1   The right of citizens of the United States to vote shall not be denied or abridged by the United States or by any State on account of sex.

Section 2   Congress shall have the power to enforce this article by appropriate legislation.

♦ ♦ ♦

Advocates of women's rights tried and failed to link woman suffrage to the Fourteenth and Fifteenth Amendments. Nonetheless, the effort for woman suffrage continued. Between 1878 and 1912, at least one and sometimes as many as four proposed amendments were introduced in Congress each year to grant women the right to vote. While over time women won very limited voting rights in some states, at both the state and federal levels opposition to an amendment for woman suffrage remained very strong. President Woodrow Wilson and other officials felt that the federal government should not interfere with the power of the states in this matter. Others worried that granting suffrage to women would encourage ethnic minorities to exercise their own right to vote. And many were concerned that giving women the vote would result in their abandoning traditional gender roles. In 1919, following a protracted and often bitter campaign of protest in which women went on hunger strikes and chained themselves to fences, an amendment was introduced with the backing of President Wilson. It narrowly passed the Senate (after efforts to limit the suffrage to white women failed) and was adopted in 1920 after Tennessee became the thirty-sixth state to ratify it.

Unratified Amendment

Child Labor Amendment (proposed by Congress June 2, 1924)

Section 1   The Congress shall have power to limit, regulate, and prohibit the labor of persons under eighteen years of age.

Section 2   The power of the several States is unimpaired by this article except that the operation of

AMENDMENTS TO THE CONSTITUTION WITH ANNOTATIONS

State laws shall be suspended to the extent necessary to give effect to legislation enacted by Congress.

♦♦♦

Throughout the late nineteenth and early twentieth centuries, alarm over the condition of child workers grew. Opponents of child labor argued that children worked in dangerous and unhealthy conditions, that they took jobs from adult workers, that they depressed wages in certain industries, and that states that allowed child labor had an economic advantage over those that did not. Defenders of child labor claimed that children provided needed income in many families, that working at a young age developed character, and that the effort to prohibit the practice constituted an invasion of family privacy.

In 1916, Congress passed a law that made it illegal to sell goods made by children through interstate commerce. The Supreme Court, however, ruled that the law violated the limits on the power of Congress to regulate interstate commerce. Congress then tried to penalize industries that used child labor by taxing such goods. This measure was also thrown out by the courts. In response, reformers set out to amend the Constitution. The proposed amendment was ratified by twenty-eight states, but by 1925, thirteen states had rejected it. Passage of the Fair Labor Standards Act in 1938, which was upheld by the Supreme Court in 1941, made the amendment irrelevant.

Amendment XX
[Adopted 1933]

Section 1   The terms of the President and Vice-President shall end at noon on the 20th day of January, and the terms of Senators and Representatives at noon on the 3rd day of January, of the years in which such terms would have ended if this article had not been ratified; and the terms of their successors shall then begin.

Section 2   The Congress shall assemble at least once in every year, and such meeting shall begin at noon on the 3rd day of January, unless they shall by law appoint a different day.

Section 3   If, at the time fixed for the beginning of the term of the President, the President-elect shall have died, the Vice-President-elect shall become President. If a President shall not have been chosen before the time fixed for the beginning of his term, or if the President-elect shall have failed to qualify, then the Vice-President-elect shall act as President until a President shall have qualified; and the Congress may by law provide for the case wherein neither a President-elect nor a Vice-President-elect shall have qualified, declaring who shall then act as President, or the manner in which one who is to act shall be selected, and such person shall act accordingly until a President or Vice-President shall have qualified.

Section 4   The Congress may by law provide for the case of the death of any of the persons from whom the House of Representatives may choose a President whenever the right of choice shall have devolved upon them, and for the case of the death of any of the persons from whom the Senate may choose a Vice-President whenever the right of choice shall have devolved upon them.

Section 5   Sections 1 and 2 shall take effect on the 15th day of October following the ratification of this article.

Section 6   This article shall be inoperative unless it shall have been ratified as an amendment to the Constitution by the Legislatures of three-fourths of the several States within seven years from the date of its submission.

♦♦♦

Until 1933, presidents took office on March 4. Since elections are held in early November and electoral votes are counted in mid-December, this meant that more than three months passed between the time a new president was elected and when he took office. Moving the inauguration to January shortened the transition period and allowed Congress to begin its term closer to the time of the president's inauguration. Although this seems like a minor change, an amendment was required because the Constitution specifies terms of office. This amendment also deals with questions of succession in the event that a president- or vice president-elect dies before assuming office. Section 3 also clarifies a method for resolving a deadlock in the electoral college.

Amendment XXI
[Adopted 1933]

Section 1   The eighteenth article of amendment to the Constitution of the United States is hereby repealed.

Section 2   The transportation or importation into any State, Territory, or Possession of the United States for delivery or use therein of intoxicating liquors, in violation of the laws thereof, is hereby prohibited.

Section 3   This article shall be inoperative unless it shall have been ratified as an amendment to the Constitution by conventions in the several States, as provided in the Constitution, within seven years from the date of the submission thereof to the States by the Congress.

♦♦♦

Widespread violation of the Volstead Act, the law enacted to enforce prohibition, made the United States a nation of lawbreakers. Prohibition caused more problems

than it solved by encouraging crime, bribery, and cor-
ruption. Further, a coalition of liquor and beer manufac-
turers, personal liberty advocates, and constitutional
scholars joined forces to challenge the amendment. By
1929, thirty proposed repeal amendments had been in-
troduced in Congress, and the Democratic Party made
repeal part of its platform in the 1932 presidential cam-
paign. The Twenty-first Amendment was proposed in
February 1933 and ratified less than a year later. The
failure of the effort to enforce prohibition through a con-
stitutional amendment has often been cited by oppo-
nents to subsequent efforts to shape public virtue and
private morality.

Amendment XXII

[Adopted 1951]

Section 1 No person shall be elected to the office
of the President more than twice, and no person
who has held the office of President, or acted as
President, for more than two years of a term to
which some other person was elected President
shall be elected to the office of President more than
once. But this article shall not apply to any person
holding the office of President when this Article
was proposed by the Congress, and shall not prevent any person who may be holding the office of
President, or acting as President, during the term
within which this Article becomes operative from
holding the office of President or acting as President during the remainder of such term.

Section 2 This article shall be inoperative unless it
shall have been ratified as an amendment to the
Constitution by the legislatures of three-fourths of
the several States within seven years from the date
of its submission to the States by the Congress.

◆◆◆

George Washington's refusal to seek a third term of of-
fice set a precedent that stood until 1912, when former
president Theodore Roosevelt sought, without success,
another term as an independent candidate. Democrat
Franklin Roosevelt was the only president to seek and
win a fourth term, though he did so amid great contro-
versy. Roosevelt died in April 1945, a few months after
the beginning of his fourth term. In 1946, Republicans
won control of the House and the Senate, and early in
1947 a proposal for an amendment to limit future presi-
dents to two four-year terms was offered to the states
for ratification. Democratic critics of the Twenty-
second Amendment charged that it was a partisan
posthumous jab at Roosevelt.
 Since the Twenty-second Amendment was
adopted, however, the only presidents who might have
been able to seek a third term, had it not existed, were
Republicans Dwight Eisenhower, Ronald Reagan, and
George W. Bush, and Democrat Bill Clinton. Since 1826,
Congress has entertained 160 proposed amendments to

limit the president to one six-year term. Such amend-
ments have been backed by fifteen presidents, including
Gerald Ford and Jimmy Carter.

Amendment XXIII

[Adopted 1961]

Section 1 The District constituting the seat of
Government of the United States shall appoint in
such manner as the Congress may direct: A number
of electors of President and Vice-President equal to
the whole number of Senators and Representatives
in Congress to which the District would be entitled
if it were a State, but in no event more than the least
populous State; they shall be in addition to those
appointed by the States, but they shall be considered for the purposes of the election of President
and Vice-President, to be electors appointed by a
State; and they shall meet in the District and perform such duties as provided by the twelfth article
of amendment.

Section 2 The Congress shall have the power to
enforce this article by appropriate legislation.

◆◆◆

When Washington, D.C., was established as a federal
district, no one expected that a significant number of
people would make it their permanent and primary
residence. A proposal to allow citizens of the district to
vote in presidential elections was approved by Congress
in June 1960 and was ratified on March 29, 1961.

Amendment XXIV

[Adopted 1964]

Section 1 The right of citizens of the United
States to vote in any primary or other election
for President or Vice-President, for electors for
President or Vice-President, or for Senator or
Representative in Congress, shall not be denied or
abridged by the United States or any State by reason of failure to pay any poll tax or other tax.

Section 2 The Congress shall have the power to
enforce this article by appropriate legislation.

◆◆◆

In the colonial and Revolutionary eras, financial in-
dependence was seen as necessary to political inde-
pendence, and the poll tax was used as a requirement
for voting. By the twentieth century, however, the
poll tax was used mostly to bar poor people, especially
southern blacks, from voting. While conservatives
complained that the amendment interfered with
states' rights, liberals thought that the amendment
did not go far enough because it barred the poll tax
only in national elections and not in state or local
elections. The amendment was ratified in 1964,

however, and two years later, the Supreme Court ruled that poll taxes in state and local elections also violated the equal protection clause of the Fourteenth Amendment.

Amendment XXV

[Adopted 1967]

Section 1   In case of the removal of the President from office or of his death or resignation, the Vice-President shall become President.

Section 2   Whenever there is a vacancy in the office of the Vice-President, the President shall nominate a Vice-President who shall take office upon confirmation by a majority vote of both Houses of Congress.

Section 3   Whenever the President transmits to the President pro tempore of the Senate and the Speaker of the House of Representatives his written declaration that he is unable to discharge the powers and duties of his office, and until he transmits to them a written declaration to the contrary, such powers and duties shall be discharged by the Vice-President as Acting President.

Section 4   Whenever the Vice-President and a majority of either the principal officers of the executive departments or of such other body as Congress may by law provide, transmit to the President pro tempore of the Senate and the Speaker of the House of Representatives their written declaration that the President is unable to discharge the powers and duties of his office, the Vice-President shall immediately assume the powers and duties of the office as Acting President.

Thereafter, when the President transmits to the President pro tempore of the Senate and the Speaker of the House of Representatives his written declaration that no inability exists, he shall resume the powers and duties of his office unless the Vice-President and a majority of either the principal officers of the executive department[s] or of such other body as Congress may by law provide, transmit within four days to the President pro tempore of the Senate and the Speaker of the House of Representatives their written declaration that the President is unable to discharge the powers and duties of his office. Thereupon Congress shall decide the issue, assembling within forty-eight hours for that purpose if not in session. If the Congress, within twenty-one days after receipt of the latter written declaration, or, if Congress is not in session, within twenty-one days after Congress is required to assemble, determines by two-thirds vote of both Houses that the President is unable to discharge the powers and duties of his office, the Vice-President shall continue to discharge the same as Acting President; otherwise, the President shall resume the powers and duties of his office.

◆ ◆ ◆

The framers of the Constitution established the office of vice president because someone was needed to preside over the Senate. The first president to die in office was William Henry Harrison, in 1841. Vice President John Tyler had himself sworn in as president, setting a precedent that was followed when seven later presidents died in office. The assassination of President James A. Garfield in 1881 posed a new problem, however. After he was shot, the president was incapacitated for two months before he died; he was unable to lead the country, while his vice president, Chester A. Arthur, was unable to assume leadership. Efforts to resolve questions of succession in the event of a presidential disability thus began with the death of Garfield.

In 1963, the assassination of President John F. Kennedy galvanized Congress to action. Vice President Lyndon Johnson was a chain smoker with a history of heart trouble. According to the 1947 Presidential Succession Act, the two men who stood in line to succeed him were the seventy-two-year-old Speaker of the House and the eighty-six-year-old president of the Senate. There were serious concerns that any of these men might become incapacitated while serving as chief executive. The first time the Twenty-fifth Amendment was used, however, was not in the case of presidential death or illness, but during the Watergate crisis. When Vice President Spiro T. Agnew was forced to resign following allegations of bribery and tax violations, President Richard M. Nixon appointed House Minority Leader Gerald R. Ford vice president. Ford became president following Nixon's resignation eight months later and named Nelson A. Rockefeller as his vice president. Thus, for more than two years, the two highest offices in the country were held by people who had not been elected to them.

Amendment XXVI

[Adopted 1971]

Section 1   The right of citizens of the United States, who are eighteen years of age or older, to vote shall not be denied or abridged by the United States or by any State on account of age.

Section 2   The Congress shall have power to enforce this article by appropriate legislation.

◆ ◆ ◆

Efforts to lower the voting age from twenty-one to eighteen began during World War II. Recognizing that those who were old enough to fight a war should have some say in the government policies that involved them in the war, Presidents Eisenhower, Johnson, and Nixon endorsed the idea. In 1970, the combined pressure of the antiwar movement and the demographic pressure of the baby boom generation led to a Voting Rights Act lowering the voting age in federal, state, and local elections.

In Oregon v. Mitchell (1970), the state of Oregon challenged the right of Congress to determine the age at which people could vote in state or local elections. The Supreme Court agreed with Oregon. Since the Voting Rights Act was ruled unconstitutional, the Constitution had to be amended to allow passage of a law that would lower the voting age. The amendment was ratified in a little more than three months, making it the most rapidly ratified amendment in U.S. history.

Unratified Amendment

Equal Rights Amendment (proposed by Congress March 22, 1972; seven-year deadline for ratification extended to June 30, 1982)

Section 1   Equality of rights under the law shall not be denied or abridged by the United States or by any State on account of sex.

Section 2   The Congress shall have the power to enforce, by appropriate legislation, the provisions of this article.

Section 3   This amendment shall take effect two years after the date of ratification.

◆ ◆ ◆

In 1923, soon after women had won the right to vote, Alice Paul, a leading activist in the woman suffrage movement, proposed an amendment requiring equal treatment of men and women. Opponents of the proposal argued that such an amendment would invalidate laws that protected women and would make women subject to the military draft. After the 1964 Civil Rights Act was adopted, protective workplace legislation was removed anyway.

The renewal of the women's movement, as a by-product of the civil rights and antiwar movements, led to a revival of the Equal Rights Amendment (ERA) in Congress. Disagreements over language held up congressional passage of the proposed amendment, but on March 22, 1972, the Senate approved the ERA by a vote of 84 to 8, and it was sent to the states. Six states ratified the amendment within two days, and by the middle of 1973 the amendment seemed well on its way to adoption, with thirty of the needed thirty-eight states having ratified it. In the mid-1970s, however, a powerful "Stop ERA" campaign developed. The campaign portrayed the ERA as a threat to "family values" and traditional relationships between men and women. Although thirty-five states ultimately ratified the ERA, five of those state legislatures voted to rescind ratification, and the amendment was never adopted.

Unratified Amendment

D.C. Statehood Amendment (proposed by Congress August 22, 1978)

Section 1   For purposes of representation in the Congress, election of the President and Vice-President, and article V of this Constitution, the District constituting the seat of government of the United States shall be treated as though it were a State.

Section 2   The exercise of the rights and powers conferred under this article shall be by the people of the District constituting the seat of government, and as shall be provided by Congress.

Section 3   The twenty-third article of amendment to the Constitution of the United States is hereby repealed.

Section 4   This article shall be inoperative, unless it shall have been ratified as an amendment to the Constitution by the legislatures of three-fourths of the several states within seven years from the date of its submission.

◆ ◆ ◆

The 1961 ratification of the Twenty-third Amendment, giving residents of the District of Columbia the right to vote for a president and vice president, inspired an effort to give residents of the district full voting rights. In 1966, President Lyndon Johnson appointed a mayor and city council; in 1971, D.C. residents were allowed to name a nonvoting delegate to the House; and in 1981, residents were allowed to elect the mayor and city council. Congress retained the right to overrule laws that might affect commuters, the height of federal buildings, and selection of judges and prosecutors. The district's nonvoting delegate to Congress, Walter Fauntroy, lobbied fiercely for a congressional amendment granting statehood to the district. In 1978, a proposed amendment was approved and sent to the states. A number of states quickly ratified the amendment, but, like the ERA, the D.C. Statehood Amendment ran into trouble. Opponents argued that section 2 created a separate category of "nominal" statehood. They argued that the federal district should be eliminated and that the territory should be reabsorbed into the state of Maryland. Although these theoretical arguments were strong, some scholars believe that racist attitudes toward the predominantly black population of the city was also a factor leading to the defeat of the amendment.

Amendment XXVII

[Adopted 1992]

No law, varying the compensation for the services of the Senators and Representatives, shall take effect, until an election of Representatives shall have intervened.

♦ ♦ ♦

While the Twenty-sixth Amendment was the most rapidly ratified amendment in U.S. history, the Twenty-seventh Amendment had the longest journey to ratification. First proposed by James Madison in 1789 as part of the package that included the Bill of Rights, this amendment had been ratified by only six states by 1791. In 1873, however, it was ratified by Ohio to protest a massive retroactive salary increase by the federal government. Unlike later proposed amend-ments, this one came with no time limit on ratification. In the early 1980s, Gregory D. Watson, a University of Texas economics major, discovered the "lost" amend-ment and began a single-handed campaign to get state legislators to introduce it for ratification. In 1983, it was accepted by Maine. In 1984, it passed the Colorado legislature. Ratifications trickled in slowly until May 1992, when Michigan and New Jersey became the thirty-eighth and thirty-ninth states, respectively, to ratify. This amendment prevents members of Congress from raising their own salaries without giving voters a chance to vote them out of office before they can benefit from the raises.

THE CONSTITUTION OF THE CONFEDERATE STATES OF AMERICA

In framing the Constitution of the Confederate States, the authors adopted, with numerous small but signifi-cant changes and additions, the language of the Con-stitution of the United States, and followed the same order of arrangement of articles and sections. The revi-sions that they made to the original Constitution are shown here. The parts stricken out are enclosed in brack-ets, and the new matter added in framing the Confed-erate Constitution is printed in italics.

Adopted March 11, 1861

WE, the People of the [United States] *Confederated States, each State acting in its sovereign and independent character,* in order to form a [more perfect Union] *permanent Federal government,* establish Justice, in-sure domestic Tranquillity [provide for the common defense, promote the general Welfare], and secure the Blessings of Liberty to ourselves and our Posterity, *invoking the favor and guidance of Almighty God,* do ordain and establish this Constitution for the [United] *Confederate* States of America.

Article I

Section I All legislative Powers herein [granted] *delegated,* shall be vested in a Congress of the [United] *Confederate* States, which shall consist of a Senate and House of Representatives.

Section II The House of Representatives shall be composed of Members chosen every second Year by the People of the several States, and the Electors in each State shall *be citizens of the Confederate States, and* have the Qualifications requisite for Electors of the most numerous Branch of the State Legislature; *but no person of foreign birth, and not a citizen of the Confederate States, shall be allowed to vote for any offi-cer, civil or political, State or federal.*

No Person shall be a Representative who shall not have attained to the Age of twenty-five Years, and [been seven Years a Citizen of the United] *be a citizen of the Confederate* States, and who shall not, when elected, be an Inhabitant of that State in which he shall be chosen.

Representatives and direct Taxes shall be ap-portioned among the several States which may be included within this [Union] *Confederacy,* according to their respective Numbers, which shall be deter-mined by adding to the whole Number of free Persons, including those bound to Service for a Term of Years, and excluding Indians not taxed, three-fifths of all [other Persons] *slaves.* The actual Enumeration shall be made within three Years after the first Meeting of the Congress of the [United] *Confederate* States, and within every subsequent Term of ten Years, in such Manner as they shall by Law direct. The Number of Representatives shall not exceed one for every [thirty] *fifty* Thousand, but each State shall have at Least one Representative; and until such enumeration shall be made, the State of [New Hampshire shall be entitled to choose three, Massachusetts eight, Rhode Island and Providence Plantations one, Connecticut five, New York six, New Jersey four, Pennsylvania eight, Delaware one, Maryland six, Virginia ten, North Carolina five, South Carolina five, and Georgia three] *South Carolina shall be entitled to choose six, the State of Georgia ten, the State of Alabama nine, the State of Florida two, the State of Mississippi seven, the State of Louisiana six, and the State of Texas six.*

When vacancies happen in the Representation from any State, the Executive Authority thereof shall issue Writs of Election to fill such Vacancies.

The House of Representatives shall choose their Speaker and other Officers; and shall have the sole Power of Impeachment; *except that any judicial or other federal officer resident and acting solely within the limits of any State, may be impeached by a vote of two-thirds of both branches of the Legislature thereof.*

Section III   The Senate of the [United] *Confederate* States shall be composed of two Senators from each State, chosen by the Legislature thereof, for six Years, *at the regular session next immediately preceding the commencement of the term of service;* and each Senator shall have one Vote.

Immediately after they shall be assembled in Consequence of the first Election, they shall be divided as equally as may be into three Classes. The Seats of the Senators of the first Class shall be vacated at the Expiration of the second Year, of the second Class at the Expiration of the fourth Year, and of the third Class at the Expiration of the sixth Year, so that one-third may be chosen every second Year; and if Vacancies happen by Resignation, or otherwise, during the Recess of the Legislature of any State, the Executive thereof may make temporary Appointments until the next Meeting of the Legislature, which shall then fill such Vacancies.

No Person shall be a Senator who shall not have attained to the Age of thirty Years, and [been nine Years a Citizen of the United] *be a citizen of the Confederate* States, and who shall not, when elected, be an Inhabitant of that State for which he shall be chosen.

The Vice President of the [United] *Confederate* States shall be President of the Senate, but shall have no Vote, unless they be equally divided.

The Senate shall choose their other Officers, and also a President *pro tempore,* in the Absence of the Vice President, or when he shall exercise the Office of President of the United States.

The Senate shall have the sole Power to try all Impeachments. When sitting for that Purpose, they shall be on Oath or Affirmation. When the President of the [United] *Confederate* States is tried, the Chief Justice shall preside: And no Person shall be convicted without the Concurrence of two-thirds of the Members present.

Judgment in Cases of Impeachment shall not extend further than to removal from Office, and Disqualification to hold and enjoy any Office of honour, Trust or Profit under the [United] *Confederate* States; but the Party convicted shall nevertheless be liable and subject to Indictment, Trial, Judgment and Punishment, according to Law.

Section IV   The Times, Places and Manner of holding Elections for Senators and Representatives, shall be prescribed in each State by the Legislature thereof, *subject to the provisions of this Constitution;* but the Congress may at any time by Law make or alter such Regulations, except as to the *times and* places of choosing Senators.

The Congress shall assemble at least once in every Year, and such Meeting shall be on the first Monday in December, unless they shall by Law appoint a different Day.

Section V   Each House shall be the Judge of the Elections, Returns and Qualifications of its own Members, and a Majority of each shall constitute a Quorum to do Business; but a smaller Number may adjourn from day to day, and may be authorized to compel the Attendance of absent Members, in such Manner, and under such Penalties as each House may provide.

Each House may determine the Rules of its Proceedings, punish its Members for disorderly Behaviour, and, with the Concurrence of two-thirds *of the whole number* expel a Member.

Each House shall keep a Journal of its Proceedings, and from time to time publish the same, excepting such Parts as may in their Judgment require Secrecy; and the Yeas and Nays of the Members of either House on any question shall, at the Desire of one-fifth of those Present, be entered on the Journal.

Neither House, during the Session of Congress, shall, without the Consent of the other, adjourn for more than three days, nor to any other Place than that in which the two Houses shall be sitting.

Section VI   The Senators and Representatives shall receive a Compensation for their Services, to be ascertained by Law, and paid out of the Treasury of the [United] *Confederate* States. They shall in all Cases, except Treason [Felony] and Breach of the Peace, be privileged from Arrest during their Attendance at the Session of their respective Houses, and in going to and returning from the same; and for any Speech or Debate in either House, they shall not be questioned in any other Place.

No Senator or Representative shall, during the Time for which he was elected, be appointed to any civil Office under the Authority of the [United] *Confederate* States, which shall have been created, or the Emoluments whereof shall have been increased during such time; and no Person holding any Office under the [United] *Confederate* States, shall be a Member of either House during his Continuance in Office. *But Congress may, by law, grant to the principal officers in each of the executive departments a seat upon the floor of either House, with the privilege of discussing any measures appertaining to his department.*

Section VII   All Bills for raising Revenue shall originate in the House of Representatives; but the Senate may propose or concur with Amendments as on other Bills.

Every Bill which shall have passed [the House of Representatives and the Senate] *both Houses,* shall, before it become a Law, be presented to the President of the [United] *Confederate* States; If he approve he shall sign it, but if not he shall return it, with his Objections to that House in which it shall have originated, who shall enter the Objections at

THE CONSTITUTION OF THE CONFEDERATE STATES OF AMERICA

large on their Journal, and proceed to reconsider it. If after such Reconsideration two-thirds of that House shall agree to pass the Bill, it shall be sent, together with the Objections, to the other House, by which it shall likewise be reconsidered, and if approved by two-thirds of that House, it shall become a Law. But in all *such* Cases the Votes of both Houses shall be determined by Yeas and Nays, and the Names of the Persons voting for and against the Bill shall be entered on the Journal of each House respectively. If any Bill shall not be returned by the President within ten Days (Sundays excepted) after it shall have been presented to him, the Same shall be a law, in like Manner as if he had signed it, unless the Congress by their Adjournment prevent its return, in which Case it shall not be a Law. *The President may approve any appropriation and disapprove any other appropriation in the same bill. In such case he shall, in signing the bill, designate the appropriation disapproved, and shall return a copy of such appropriation, with his objections, to the House in which the bill shall have originated; and the same proceedings shall then be had as in case of other bills disapproved by the President.*

Every Order, Resolution, or Vote to which the Concurrence of [the Senate and House of Representatives] *both Houses* may be necessary (except on a question of Adjournment), shall be presented to the President of the [United] *Confederate* States; and before the Same shall take Effect, shall be approved by him, or being disapproved by him, [shall] *may* be repassed by two-thirds of [the Senate and House of Representatives] *both Houses*, according to the Rules and Limitations prescribed in the Case of a Bill.

Section VIII   The Congress shall have Power

To lay and collect Taxes, Duties, Imposts and *Excises, for revenue necessary* to pay the Debts [and], provide for the common Defense [and general Welfare of the United States; but], *and carry on the government of the Confederate States; but no bounties shall be granted from the treasury, nor shall any duties, or taxes, or importation from foreign nations be laid to promote or foster any branch of industry; and* all Duties, Imposts and Excises shall be uniform throughout the [United] *Confederate* States;

To borrow Money on the credit of the [United] *Confederate* States;

To regulate Commerce with foreign Nations, and among the several States, and with the Indian Tribes; *but neither this, nor any other clause contained in this Constitution, shall ever be construed to delegate the power to Congress to appropriate money for any internal improvement intended to facilitate commerce; except for the purpose of furnishing lights, beacons, and buoys, and other aids to navigation upon the coasts, and the improvement of harbors, and the removing of obstructions in river navigation; in all such cases such duties shall be laid on the navigation facilitated thereby, as may be necessary to pay the costs and expenses thereof;*

To establish an uniform Rule of Naturalization, and uniform Laws on the subject of Bankruptcies throughout the [United] *Confederate* States; *but no law of Congress shall discharge any debt contracted before the passage of the same;*

To coin Money, regulate the Value thereof, and of foreign Coin, and fix the Standard of Weights and Measures;

To provide for the Punishment of counterfeiting the Securities and current Coin of the [United] *Confederate* States;

To establish Post Offices and post [Roads] *routes; but the expenses of the Postoffice Department, after the first day of March, in the year of our Lord eighteen hundred and sixty-three, shall be paid out of its own revenues;*

To promote the progress of Science and useful Arts, by securing for limited Times to Authors and Inventors the exclusive Right to their respective Writings and Discoveries;

To constitute Tribunals inferior to the supreme Court;

To define and punish Piracies and Felonies committed on the high Seas, and Offences against the Law of Nations;

To declare War, grant Letters of Marque and Reprisal, and make Rules concerning Captures on Land and Water;

To raise and support Armies, but no Appropriation of Money to that Use shall be for a longer Term than two Years;

To provide and maintain a Navy;

To make Rules for the Government and Regulation of the land and naval Forces;

To provide for calling forth the Militia to execute the Laws of the [Union] *Confederate States*, suppress Insurrections and repel Invasions;

To provide for organizing, arming, and disciplining the Militia and for governing such Part of them as may be employed in the Service of the [United] *Confederate* States, reserving to the States respectively, the Appointment of the Officers, and the Authority of training the Militia according to the Discipline prescribed by Congress;

To exercise exclusive Legislation in all Cases whatsoever, over such District (not exceeding ten Miles square) as may, by Cession of particular States, and the Acceptance of Congress, become the Seat of the Government of the [United] *Confederate* States, and to exercise like Authority over all Places purchased by the Consent of the Legislature of the State in which the Same shall be, for the Erection of Forts, Magazines, Arsenals, Dock Yards, and other needful Buildings;—And

To make all Laws which shall be necessary and proper for carrying into Execution the foregoing Powers, and all other Powers vested by this Constitution in the Government of the [United] *Confederate* States or in any Department or Officer thereof.

Section IX   [The Migration or Importation of such Persons as any of the States now existing shall think proper to admit, shall not be prohibited by the Congress prior to the Year one thousand eight hundred and eight, but a Tax or Duty may be imposed on such Importation, not exceeding ten dollars for each Person.] *The importation of negroes of the African race from any foreign country other than the slaveholding States or territories of the United States of America, is hereby forbidden; and Congress is required to pass such laws as shall effectually prevent the same. Congress shall also have power to prohibit the introduction of slaves from any State not a member of, or territory not belonging to, this Confederacy.*

The Privilege of the Writ of Habeas Corpus shall not be suspended, unless when in Cases of Rebellion or Invasion the public Safety may require it. No Bill of Attainder or ex post facto Law, *or law denying or impairing the right of property in negro slaves,* shall be passed.

No Capitation, or other direct, Tax shall be laid, unless in Proportion to the Census or Enumeration herein before directed to be taken.

No Tax or Duty shall be laid on Articles exported from any State, *except by a vote of two-thirds of both Houses.*

No Preference shall be given by any Regulation of Commerce or Revenue to the Ports of one State over those of another; nor shall Vessels bound to, or from, one State, be obliged to enter, clear, or pay Duties in another.

No Money shall be drawn from the Treasury, but in Consequence of Appropriations made by Law; and a regular Statement and Account of the Receipts and Expenditures of all public Money shall be published from time to time.

Congress shall appropriate no money from the Treasury except by a vote of two-thirds of both Houses, taken by yeas and nays, unless it be asked and estimated for by some one of the heads of departments and submitted to Congress by the President; or for the purpose of paying its own expenses and contingencies; or for the payment of claims against the Confederate States, the justice of which shall have been officially declared by a tribunal for the investigation of claims against the Government, which it is hereby made the duty of Congress to establish.

All bills appropriating money shall specify in Federal currency the exact amount of each appropriation and the purposes for which it is made; and Congress shall grant no extra compensation to any public contractor, officer, agent or servant, after such contract shall have been made or such service rendered.

No Title of Nobility shall be granted by the [United] *Confederate* States; and no Person holding any Office of Profit or Trust under them, shall, without the Consent of the Congress, accept of any present, Emolument, Office, or Title, of any kind whatever, from any King, Prince or foreign State.

[Here the framers of the Confederate Constitution insert the U.S. Bill of Rights.]

Congress shall make no law respecting an establishment of religion, or prohibiting the free exercise thereof; or abridging the freedom of speech, or of the press; or the right of the people peaceably to assemble, and to petition the Government for a redress of grievances.

A well-regulated Militia, being necessary to the security of a free State, the right of the people to keep and bear Arms shall not be infringed.

No Soldier shall, in time of peace, be quartered in any house, without the consent of the Owner, nor in time of war, but in a manner to be prescribed by law.

The right of the people to be secure in their persons, houses, papers, and effects, against unreasonable searches and seizures, shall not be violated, and no Warrants shall issue, but upon probable cause, supported by Oath or affirmation, and particularly describing the place to be searched, and the persons or things to be seized.

No person shall be held to answer for a capital, or otherwise infamous crime, unless on a presentment or indictment of a Grand Jury, except in cases arising in the land or naval forces, or in the Militia, when in actual service in time of War or public danger; nor shall any person be subject for the same offence to be twice put in jeopardy of life or limb; nor shall be compelled in any Criminal Case to be a witness against himself, nor be deprived of life, liberty or property without due process of law; nor shall private property be taken for public use, without just compensation.

In all criminal prosecutions, the accused shall enjoy the right to a speedy and public trial, by an impartial jury of the State and district wherein the crime shall have been committed, which district shall have been previously ascertained by law, and to be informed of the nature and cause of the accusation; to be confronted with the witnesses against him; to have Compulsory process for obtaining Witnesses in his favour, and to have the Assistance of Counsel for his defence.

In Suits at common law, where the value in controversy shall exceed twenty dollars, the right of trial by jury shall be preserved, and no fact tried by a jury shall be otherwise reexamined in any Court of the [United] *Confederate* States, than according to the rules of the common law.

Excessive bail shall not be required, nor excessive fines imposed, nor cruel and unusual punishments inflicted.

Every law or resolution having the force of law, shall relate to but one subject, and that shall be expressed in the title.

Section X   No State shall enter into any Treaty, Alliance, or Confederation; grant Letters of Marque and Reprisal; coin Money; [emit Bills of Credit;] make any Thing but gold and silver Coin a Tender in Payment of Debts; pass any Bill of Attainder, *or*

THE CONSTITUTION OF THE CONFEDERATE STATES OF AMERICA

ex post facto Law, or Law impairing the Obligation of Contracts, or grant any Title of Nobility.

No State shall, without the consent of the Congress, lay any Imposts or Duties on Imports or Exports, except what may be absolutely necessary for executing its inspection Laws: and the net Produce of all Duties and Imposts, laid by any State on Imports or Exports, shall be for the Use of the Treasury of the [United] *Confederate* States; and all such Laws shall be subject to the Revision and Control of the Congress.

No State shall, without the Consent of Congress, lay any Duty of Tonnage, *except on sea-going vessels, for the improvement of its rivers and harbors navigated by the said vessels; but such duties shall not conflict with any treaties of the Confederate States with foreign nations; and any surplus of revenue thus derived shall, after making such improvement, be paid into the common treasury; nor shall any State* keep Troops, or Ships of War in time of Peace, enter into any Agreement or Compact with another State, or with a foreign Power, or engage in War, unless actually invaded, or in such imminent Danger as will not admit of Delay. *But when any river divides or flows through two or more States, they may enter into compacts with each other to improve the navigation thereof.*

Article II

Section I [The executive Power shall be vested in a President of the United States of America. He shall hold his Office during the Term of four Years, and, together with the Vice President, chosen for the same Term, be elected, as follows:] *The executive power shall be vested in a President of the Confederate States of America. He and the Vice President shall hold their offices for the term of six years; but the President shall not be re-eligible. The President and Vice President shall be elected as follows:*

Each State shall appoint in such Manner as the Legislature thereof may direct, a Number of Electors, equal to the whole Number of Senators and Representatives to which the State may be entitled in the Congress; but no Senator or Representative, or Person holding an Office of Trust or Profit under the [United] *Confederate* States, shall be appointed an Elector.

The Electors shall meet in their respective States, and vote by ballot for President and Vice President, one of whom, at least, shall not be an inhabitant of the same State with themselves; they shall name in their ballots the person voted for as President, and in distinct ballots the person voted for as Vice President, and they shall make distinct lists of all persons voted for as President, and of all persons voted for as Vice President, and of the number of votes for each, which lists they shall sign and certify, and transmit sealed to the seat of the government of the [United] *Confederate* States, directed to the President of the Senate;—The President of the Senate shall, in the presence of the Senate and House of Representatives, open all the certificates and the votes shall then be counted;—The person having the greatest number of votes for President shall be the President, if such number be a majority of the whole number of Electors appointed; and if no person have such majority, then from the persons having the highest numbers not exceeding three on the list of those voted for as President, the House of Representatives shall choose immediately, by ballot, the President. But in choosing the President, the votes shall be taken by States, the representation from each State having one vote; a quorum for this purpose shall consist of a member or members from two-thirds of the States, and a majority of all the States shall be necessary to a choice. And if the House of Representatives shall not choose a President whenever the right of choice shall devolve upon them, before the fourth day of March next following, then the Vice President shall act as President, as in the case of the death or other constitutional disability of the President. The person having the greatest number of votes as Vice President shall be the Vice President, if such number be a majority of the whole number of Electors appointed, and if no person have a majority, then from the two highest numbers on the list the Senate shall choose the Vice President; a quorum for the purpose shall consist of two-thirds of the whole number of Senators, and a majority of the whole number shall be necessary to a choice. But no person constitutionally ineligible to the office of President shall be eligible to that of Vice President of the [United] *Confederate* States.

The Congress may determine the Time of choosing the Electors, and the Day on which they shall give their Votes; which Day shall be the same throughout the [United] *Confederate* States.

No Person except a natural-born Citizen [or a Citizen of the United States] *of the Confederate States, or a citizen thereof,* at the time of the Adoption of this Constitution, *or a citizen thereof born in the United States prior to the 20th of December, 1860,* shall be eligible to the Office of President; neither shall any Person be eligible to that Office who shall not have attained to the Age of thirty-five Years, and been fourteen Years a Resident within the [United States] *limits of the Confederate States, as they may exist at the time of his election.*

In Cases of the Removal of the President from Office, or of his Death, Resignation, or Inability to discharge the Powers and Duties of the said Office, the same shall devolve on the Vice President, and the Congress may by Law provide for the Case of Removal, Death, Resignation, or Inability, both of the President and Vice President, declaring what Officer shall then act as President, and such Officer shall act accordingly, until the Disability be removed, or a President shall be elected.

The President shall, at stated Times, receive for his Services, a Compensation, which shall neither be increased nor diminished during the Period for which he shall have been elected, and he shall not receive within that Period any other Emolument from the [United] *Confederate* States or any of them.

Before he enters on the Execution of his Office, he shall take the following Oath or Affirmation—"I do solemnly swear (or affirm) that I will faithfully execute the Office of President of the [United] *Confederate* States, and will to the best of my Ability, preserve, protect and defend the Constitution [of the United States] *thereof.*"

Section II   The President shall be Commander in Chief of the Army and Navy of the [United] *Confederate* States, and of the Militia of the several States, when called into the actual Service of the [United] *Confederate* States; he may require the Opinion, in writing, of the principal Officer in each of the executive Departments, upon any Subject relating to the Duties of their respective Offices, and he shall have Power to grant Reprieves and Pardons for Offenses against the [United] *Confederate* States, except in Cases of Impeachment.

He shall have Power, by and with the Advice and Consent of the Senate, to make Treaties, provided two-thirds of the Senators present concur; and he shall nominate, and by and with the Advice and Consent of the Senate, shall appoint Ambassadors, other public Ministers and Consuls, Judges of the supreme Court, and all other Officers of the [United] *Confederate* States, whose Appointments are not herein otherwise provided for, and which shall be established by Law: but the Congress may by Law vest the Appointment of such inferior Officers, as they think proper, in the President alone, in the Courts of Law, or in the Heads of Departments. *The principal officer in each of the executive departments, and all persons connected with the diplomatic service, may be removed from office at the pleasure of the President. All other civil officers of the executive department may be removed at any time by the President, or other appointing power, when their services are unnecessary, or for dishonesty, incapacity, inefficiency, misconduct, or neglect of duty; and when so removed, the removal shall be reported to the Senate, together with the reasons therefor.*

The President shall have Power to fill [up] all Vacancies that may happen during the Recess of the Senate, by granting Commissions which shall expire at the End of their next Session.

Section III   [He] *The President* shall from time to time give to the Congress Information of the State of the [Union] *Confederacy,* and recommend to their Consideration such Measures as he shall judge necessary and expedient; he may, on extraordinary Occasions, convene both Houses, or either of them, and in Case of Disagreement between them, with Respect to the Time of Adjournment, he may adjourn them to such Time as he shall think proper;

he shall receive Ambassadors and other public Ministers; he shall take Care that the Laws be faithfully executed, and shall Commission all the officers of the [United] *Confederate* States.

Section IV   The President, Vice President and all civil Officers of the [United] *Confederate* States, shall be removed from Office on Impeachment for, and Conviction of, Treason, Bribery, or other high Crimes and Misdemeanors.

Article III

Section I   The judicial Power of the [United] *Confederate* States shall be vested in one [supreme] *Superior* Court, and in such inferior Courts as the Congress may from time to time ordain and establish. The Judges, both of the supreme and inferior Courts, shall hold their Offices during good Behavior, and shall, at stated Times, receive for their Services a Compensation, which shall not be diminished during their Continuance in Office.

Section II   The judicial Power shall extend to all cases [in Law and Equity, arising under this Constitution], *arising under this Constitution, in law and equity,* the Laws of the [United] *Confederate* States, and Treaties made, or which shall be made, under their Authority;—to all Cases affecting Ambassadors, other public Ministers, and Consuls;—to all Cases of admiralty and maritime Jurisdiction;—to Controversies to which the [United] *Confederate* States shall be a Party;—to Controversies between two or more States;—between a State and Citizens of another State *where the State is plaintiff;—between* Citizens *claiming lands under grants* of different States,—[between Citizens of the same State claiming Lands under Grants of different States,] and between a State, or the Citizens thereof, and foreign States, Citizens or Subjects; *but no State shall be sued by a citizen or subject of any foreign State.*

In all Cases affecting Ambassadors, other public Ministers and Consuls, and those in which a State shall be Party, the supreme Court shall have original Jurisdiction. In all the other Cases before mentioned, the supreme Court shall have appellate Jurisdiction, both as to Law and Fact, with such Exceptions, and under such Regulations as the Congress shall make.

The Trial of all Crimes, except in Cases of Impeachment, shall be by Jury; and such Trial shall be held in the State where the said Crime[s] shall have been committed; but when not committed within any State, the Trial shall be at such Place or Places as the Congress may by Law have directed.

Section III   Treason against the [United] *Confederate* States shall consist only in levying War against them,

THE CONSTITUTION OF THE CONFEDERATE STATES OF AMERICA

or in adhering to their Enemies, giving them Aid and Comfort. No Person shall be convicted of Treason unless on the Testimony of two Witnesses to the same overt Act, or on Confession in open Court.

The Congress shall have Power to declare the Punishment of Treason, but no Attainder of Treason shall work Corruption of Blood, or Forfeiture except during the Life of the Person attainted.

Article IV

Section I Full Faith and Credit shall be given in each State to the public Acts, Records, and judicial Proceedings of every other State. And the Congress may by general Laws prescribe the Manner in which such Acts, Records and Proceedings shall be proved, and the Effect thereof.

Section II The Citizens of each State shall be entitled to all Privileges and Immunities of Citizens in the several States, *and shall have the right of transit and sojourn in any State of this Confederacy, with their slaves and other property; and the right of property in such slaves shall not be impaired.*

A Person charged in any State with Treason, Felony, or other Crime, who shall flee from Justice, and be found in another State, shall on Demand of the executive Authority of the State from which he fled, be delivered up, to be removed to the State having Jurisdiction of the Crime.

No *slave or* Person held to Service or Labor in [one State] *any State or Territory of the Confederate States* under the Laws thereof, escaping *or unlawfully carried* into another, shall, in Consequence of any Law or Regulation therein, be discharged from such Service or Labor, but shall be delivered up on Claim of the Party to whom such *slave belongs, or to whom such* Service or Labor may be due.

Section III [New States may be admitted by the Congress into this Union;] *Other States may be admitted into this Confederacy by a vote of two-thirds of the whole House of Representatives and two-thirds of the Senate, the Senate voting by States;* but no new State shall be formed or erected within the Jurisdiction of any other State; nor any State be formed by the Junction of two or more States, or Parts of States, without the Consent of the Legislatures of the States concerned as well as of the Congress.

The Congress shall have Power to dispose of and make all needful Rules and Regulations [respecting the Territory or other Property belonging to the United States; and nothing in this Constitution shall be so construed as to Prejudice any Claims of the United States, or of any particular State] *concerning the property of the Confederate States, including the lands thereof.*

The Confederate States may acquire new territory, and Congress shall have power to legislate and provide governments for the inhabitants of all territory belonging to the Confederate States lying without the limits of the several States, and may permit them, at such times and in such manner as it may by law provide, to form States to be admitted into the Confederacy. In all such territory the institution of negro slavery as it now exists in the Confederate States shall be recognized and protected by Congress and by the territorial government, and the inhabitants of the several Confederate States and territories shall have the right to take to such territory any slaves lawfully held by them in any of the States or Territories of the Confederate States.

[Section IV] The [United] *Confederate* States shall guarantee to every State [in this Union] *that now is, or hereafter may become, a member of this Confederacy,* a Republican Form of Government, and shall protect each of them against Invasion; and on Application of the Legislature, or of the Executive (when the Legislature [cannot be convened] *is not in session*) against domestic Violence.

Article V

[The Congress, whenever two-thirds of both Houses shall deem it necessary, shall propose Amendments to this Constitution, or on the Application of the Legislatures of two-thirds of the several States, shall call a Convention for proposing Amendments, which, in either Case, shall be valid to all Intents and Purposes, as Part of this Constitution, when ratified by the Legislatures of three-fourths of the several States, or by Conventions in three-fourths thereof, as the one or the other Mode of Ratification may be proposed by the Congress; Provided that no Amendment which may be made prior to the Year one thousand eight hundred and eight shall in any Manner affect the first and fourth Clauses in the Ninth Section of the first Article; and that no State, without its Consent, shall be deprived of its equal Suffrage in the Senate.]

Upon the demand of any three States, legally assembled in their several Conventions, the Congress shall summon a Convention of all the States, to take into consideration such amendments to the Constitution as the said States shall concur in suggesting at the time when the said demand is made; and should any of the proposed amendments to the Constitution be agreed on by the said Convention—voting by States—and the same be ratified by the Legislatures of two-thirds of the several States, or by Conventions in two-thirds thereof—as the one or the other mode of ratification may be proposed by the general Convention—they shall henceforward form a part of this Constitution. But no State shall, without its consent, be deprived of its equal representation in the Senate.

Article VI

The Government established by this Constitution is the successor of the Provisional Government of the

Confederate States of America, and all laws passed by the latter shall continue in force until the same shall be repealed or modified; and all the officers appointed by the same shall remain in office until their successors are appointed and qualified or the offices abolished.

All Debts contracted and Engagements entered into, before the Adoption of this Constitution, shall be as valid against the [United] *Confederate* States under this Constitution, as under the [Confederation] *Provisional Government.*

This Constitution and the Laws of the [United] *Confederate* States [which shall be] made in Pursuance thereof; and all Treaties made, or which shall be made, under the authority of the [United] *Confederate* States, shall be the supreme Law of the Land; and the Judges in every State shall be bound thereby, any Thing in the Constitution or Laws of any State to the Contrary notwithstanding.

The Senators and Representatives before mentioned, and the Members of the several State Legislatures, and all executive and judicial Officers, both of the [United] *Confederate* States and of the several States, shall be bound by Oath or Affirmation, to support this Constitution; but no religious Test shall ever be required as a Qualification to any Office or public Trust under the [United] *Confederate* States.

The enumeration in the Constitution, of certain rights, shall not be construed to deny or disparage others retained by the people *of the several States.*

The powers not delegated to the [United] *Confederate* States by the Constitution, nor prohibited by it to the States, are reserved to the States respectively, or to the people.

Article VII

The Ratification of the Conventions of [nine] *five* States shall be sufficient for the Establishment of this Constitution between the States so ratifying the same.

When five States shall have ratified this Constitution, in the manner before specified, the Congress under the Provisional Constitution shall prescribe the time for holding the election of President and Vice President; and for the meeting of the electoral college; and for counting the votes and inaugurating the President. They shall also prescribe the time for holding the first election of members of Congress under this Constitution, and the time for assembling the same. Until the assembling of such Congress, the Congress under the Provisional Constitution shall continue to exercise the legislative powers granted them, not extending beyond the time limited by the Constitution of the Provisional Government.

[Done in Convention by the Unanimous Consent of the States present, the Seventeenth Day of September in the Year of our Lord one thousand seven hundred and eighty-seven and of the Independence of the United States of America the Twelfth.] *Adopted unanimously March 11, 1861.*

Facts and Figures: Government, Economy, and Demographics

U.S. Politics and Government

PRESIDENTIAL ELECTIONS

Year	Candidates	Parties	Popular Vote	Percentage of Popular Vote	Electoral Vote	Percentage of Voter Participation
1789	**GEORGE WASHINGTON (Va.)***				69	
	John Adams				34	
	Others				35	
1792	**GEORGE WASHINGTON (Va.)**				132	
	John Adams				77	
	George Clinton				50	
	Others				5	
1796	**JOHN ADAMS (Mass.)**	Federalist			71	
	Thomas Jefferson	Democratic-Republican			68	
	Thomas Pinckney	Federalist			59	
	Aaron Burr	Dem.-Rep.			30	
	Others				48	
1800	**THOMAS JEFFERSON (Va.)**	Dem.-Rep.			73	
	Aaron Burr	Dem.-Rep.			73	
	John Adams	Federalist			65	
	C. C. Pinckney	Federalist			64	
	John Jay	Federalist			1	
1804	**THOMAS JEFFERSON (Va.)**	Dem.-Rep.			162	
	C. C. Pinckney	Federalist			14	
1808	**JAMES MADISON (Va.)**	Dem.-Rep.			122	
	C. C. Pinckney	Federalist			47	
	George Clinton	Dem.-Rep.			6	
1812	**JAMES MADISON (Va.)**	Dem.-Rep.			128	
	De Witt Clinton	Federalist			89	
1816	**JAMES MONROE (Va.)**	Dem.-Rep.			183	
	Rufus King	Federalist			34	
1820	**JAMES MONROE (Va.)**	Dem.-Rep.			231	
	John Quincy Adams	Dem.-Rep.			1	
1824	**JOHN Q. ADAMS (Mass.)**	Dem.-Rep.	108,740	30.5	84	26.9
	Andrew Jackson	Dem.-Rep.	153,544	43.1	99	
	William H. Crawford	Dem.-Rep.	46,618	13.1	41	
	Henry Clay	Dem.-Rep.	47,136	13.2	37	
1828	**ANDREW JACKSON (Tenn.)**	Democratic	647,286	56.0	178	57.6
	John Quincy Adams	National Republican	508,064	44.0	83	

*State of residence when elected president.

Year	Candidates	Parties	Popular Vote	Percentage of Popular Vote	Electoral Vote	Percentage of Voter Participation
1832	**ANDREW JACKSON (Tenn.)**	Democratic	687,502	55.0	219	55.4
	Henry Clay	National Republican	530,189	42.4	49	
	John Floyd	Independent			11	
	William Wirt	Anti-Mason	33,108	2.6	7	
1836	**MARTIN VAN BUREN (N.Y.)**	Democratic	765,483	50.9	170	57.8
	W. H. Harrison	Whig			73	
	Hugh L. White	Whig	739,795	49.1	26	
	Daniel Webster	Whig			14	
	W. P. Mangum	Independent			11	
1840	**WILLIAM H. HARRISON (Ohio)**	Whig	1,274,624	53.1	234	78.0
	Martin Van Buren	Democratic	1,127,781	46.9	60	
	J. G. Birney	Liberty	7,069		—	
1844	**JAMES K. POLK (Tenn.)**	Democratic	1,338,464	49.6	170	78.9
	Henry Clay	Whig	1,300,097	48.1	105	
	J. G. Birney	Liberty	62,300	2.3	—	
1848	**ZACHARY TAYLOR (La.)**	Whig	1,360,099	47.4	163	72.7
	Lewis Cass	Democratic	1,220,544	42.5	127	
	Martin Van Buren	Free-Soil	291,263	10.1	—	
1852	**FRANKLIN PIERCE (N.H.)**	Democratic	1,601,117	50.9	254	69.6
	Winfield Scott	Whig	1,385,453	44.1	42	
	John P. Hale	Free-Soil	155,825	5.0	—	
1856	**JAMES BUCHANAN (Pa.)**	Democratic	1,832,995	45.3	174	78.9
	John C. Frémont	Republican	1,339,932	33.1	114	
	Millard Fillmore	American	871,731	21.6	8	
1860	**ABRAHAM LINCOLN (Ill.)**	Republican	1,866,452	39.8	180	81.2
	Stephen A. Douglas	Democratic	1,375,157	29.4	12	
	John C. Breckinridge	Democratic	847,953	18.1	72	
	John Bell	Union	590,631	12.6	39	
1864	**ABRAHAM LINCOLN (Ill.)**	Republican	2,213,665	55.1	212	73.8
	George B. McClellan	Democratic	1,805,237	44.9	21	
1868	**ULYSSES S. GRANT (Ill.)**	Republican	3,012,833	52.7	214	78.1
	Horatio Seymour	Democratic	2,703,249	47.3	80	
1872	**ULYSSES S. GRANT (Ill.)**	Republican	3,597,132	55.6	286	71.3
	Horace Greeley	Democratic; Liberal Republican	2,834,125	43.9	66	
1876	**RUTHERFORD B. HAYES (Ohio)**	Republican	4,036,298	48.0	185	81.8
	Samuel J. Tilden	Democratic	4,288,590	51.0	184	
1880	**JAMES A. GARFIELD (Ohio)**	Republican	4,454,416	48.5	214	79.4
	Winfield S. Hancock	Democratic	4,444,952	48.1	155	
1884	**GROVER CLEVELAND (N.Y.)**	Democratic	4,874,986	48.5	219	77.5
	James G. Blaine	Republican	4,851,981	48.3	182	
1888	**BENJAMIN HARRISON (Ind.)**	Republican	5,439,853	47.9	233	79.3
	Grover Cleveland	Democratic	5,540,309	48.6	168	
1892	**GROVER CLEVELAND (N.Y.)**	Democratic	5,555,426	46.1	277	74.7
	Benjamin Harrison	Republican	5,182,690	43.0	145	
	James B. Weaver	People's	1,029,846	8.5	22	
1896	**WILLIAM McKINLEY (Ohio)**	Republican	7,104,779	51.1	271	79.3
	William J. Bryan	Democratic-People's	6,502,925	47.7	176	
1900	**WILLIAM McKINLEY (Ohio)**	Republican	7,207,923	51.7	292	73.2
	William J. Bryan	Dem.-Populist	6,358,133	45.5	155	
1904	**THEODORE ROOSEVELT (N.Y.)**	Republican	7,623,486	57.9	336	65.2
	Alton B. Parker	Democratic	5,077,911	37.6	140	
	Eugene V. Debs	Socialist	402,283	3.0	—	

U.S. POLITICS AND GOVERNMENT

Year	Candidates	Parties	Popular Vote	Percentage of Popular Vote	Electoral Vote	Percentage of Voter Participation
1908	**WILLIAM H. TAFT (Ohio)**	Republican	7,678,908	51.6	321	65.4
	William J. Bryan	Democratic	6,409,104	43.1	162	
	Eugene V. Debs	Socialist	420,793	2.8	—	
1912	**WOODROW WILSON (N.J.)**	Democratic	6,293,454	41.9	435	58.8
	Theodore Roosevelt	Progressive	4,119,538	27.4	88	
	William H. Taft	Republican	3,484,980	23.2	8	
	Eugene V. Debs	Socialist	900,672	6.1	—	
1916	**WOODROW WILSON (N.J.)**	Democratic	9,129,606	49.4	277	61.6
	Charles E. Hughes	Republican	8,538,221	46.2	254	
	A. L. Benson	Socialist	585,113	3.2	—	
1920	**WARREN G. HARDING (Ohio)**	Republican	16,143,407	60.5	404	49.2
	James M. Cox	Democratic	9,130,328	34.2	127	
	Eugene V. Debs	Socialist	919,799	3.4	—	
1924	**CALVIN COOLIDGE (Mass.)**	Republican	15,725,016	54.0	382	48.9
	John W. Davis	Democratic	8,386,503	28.8	136	
	Robert M. La Follette	Progressive	4,822,856	16.6	13	
1928	**HERBERT HOOVER (Calif.)**	Republican	21,391,381	57.4	444	56.9
	Alfred E. Smith	Democratic	15,016,443	40.3	87	
	Norman Thomas	Socialist	881,951	2.3	—	
	William Z. Foster	Communist	102,991	0.3	—	
1932	**FRANKLIN D. ROOSEVELT (N.Y.)**	Democratic	22,821,857	57.4	472	56.9
	Herbert Hoover	Republican	15,761,841	39.7	59	
	Norman Thomas	Socialist	881,951	2.2	—	
1936	**FRANKLIN D. ROOSEVELT (N.Y.)**	Democratic	27,751,597	60.8	523	61.0
	Alfred M. Landon	Republican	16,679,583	36.5	8	
	William Lemke	Union	882,479	1.9	—	
1940	**FRANKLIN D. ROOSEVELT (N.Y.)**	Democratic	27,244,160	54.8	449	62.5
	Wendell Willkie	Republican	22,305,198	44.8	82	
1944	**FRANKLIN D. ROOSEVELT (N.Y.)**	Democratic	25,602,504	53.5	432	55.9
	Thomas E. Dewey	Republican	22,006,285	46.0	99	
1948	**HARRY S. TRUMAN (Mo.)**	Democratic	24,105,695	49.5	303	53.0
	Thomas E. Dewey	Republican	21,969,170	45.1	189	
	J. Strom Thurmond	States'-Rights Democratic	1,169,021	2.4	38	
	Henry A. Wallace	Progressive	1,156,103	2.4	—	
1952	**DWIGHT D. EISENHOWER (N.Y.)**	Republican	33,936,252	55.1	442	63.3
	Adlai Stevenson	Democratic	27,314,992	44.4	89	
1956	**DWIGHT D. EISENHOWER (N.Y.)**	Republican	35,575,420	57.6	457	60.6
	Adlai Stevenson	Democratic	26,033,066	42.1	73	
	Other	—	—		1	
1960	**JOHN F. KENNEDY (Mass.)**	Democratic	34,227,096	49.9	303	62.8
	Richard M. Nixon	Republican	34,108,546	49.6	219	
	Other	—	—		15	
1964	**LYNDON B. JOHNSON (Texas)**	Democratic	43,126,506	61.1	486	61.7
	Barry M. Goldwater	Republican	27,176,799	38.5	52	
1968	**RICHARD M. NIXON (N.Y.)**	Republican	31,770,237	43.4	301	60.9
	Hubert H. Humphrey	Democratic	31,270,533	42.7	191	
	George Wallace	American Indep.	9,906,141	13.5	46	
1972	**RICHARD M. NIXON (N.Y.)**	Republican	47,169,911	60.7	520	55.2
	George S. McGovern	Democratic	29,170,383	37.5	17	
	Other	—	—		1	
1976	**JIMMY CARTER (Ga.)**	Democratic	40,830,763	50.0	297	53.5
	Gerald R. Ford	Republican	39,147,793	48.0	240	
	Other	—	1,575,459	2.1	—	

Year	Candidates	Parties	Popular Vote	Percentage of Popular Vote	Electoral Vote	Percentage of Voter Participation
1980	**RONALD REAGAN (Calif.)**	Republican	43,901,812	51.0	489	54.0
	Jimmy Carter	Democratic	35,483,820	41.0	49	
	John B. Anderson	Independent	5,719,722	7.0	—	
	Ed Clark	Libertarian	921,188	1.1	—	
1984	**RONALD REAGAN (Calif.)**	Republican	54,455,075	59.0	525	53.1
	Walter Mondale	Democratic	37,577,185	41.0	13	
1988	**GEORGE H. W. BUSH (Texas)**	Republican	47,946,422	54.0	426	50.2
	Michael S. Dukakis	Democratic	41,016,429	46.0	112	
1992	**WILLIAM J. CLINTON (Ark.)**	Democratic	44,908,254	43.0	370	55.9
	George H. W. Bush	Republican	39,102,282	38.0	168	
	H. Ross Perot	Independent	19,721,433	19.0	—	
1996	**WILLIAM J. CLINTON (Ark.)**	Democratic	47,401,185	49.2	379	49.0
	Robert Dole	Republican	39,197,469	40.7	159	
	H. Ross Perot	Independent	8,085,294	8.4	—	
2000	**GEORGE W. BUSH (Texas)**	Republican	50,456,062	47.8	271	51.2
	Al Gore	Democratic	50,996,862	48.4	267	
	Ralph Nader	Green Party	2,858,843	2.7	—	
	Patrick J. Buchanan	—	438,760	0.4	—	
2004	**GEORGE W. BUSH (Texas)**	Republican	61,872,711	50.7	286	60.3
	John F. Kerry	Democratic	58,894,584	48.3	252	
	Other	—	1,582,185	1.3	—	

PRESIDENTS, VICE PRESIDENTS, AND SECRETARIES OF STATE

The Washington Administration (1789–1797)

Vice President	John Adams	1789–1797
Secretary of State	Thomas Jefferson	1789–1793
	Edmund Randolph	1794–1795
	Timothy Pickering	1795–1797

The John Adams Administration (1797–1801)

Vice President	Thomas Jefferson	1797–1801
Secretary of State	Timothy Pickering	1797–1800
	John Marshall	1800–1801

The Jefferson Administration (1801–1809)

Vice President	Aaron Burr	1801–1805
	George Clinton	1805–1809
Secretary of State	James Madison	1801–1809

The Madison Administration (1809–1817)

Vice President	George Clinton	1809–1813
	Elbridge Gerry	1813–1817
Secretary of State	Robert Smith	1809–1811
	James Monroe	1811–1817

The Monroe Administration (1817–1825)

| Vice President | Daniel Tompkins | 1817–1825 |
| Secretary of State | John Quincy Adams | 1817–1825 |

The John Quincy Adams Administration (1825–1829)

| Vice President | John C. Calhoun | 1825–1829 |
| Secretary of State | Henry Clay | 1825–1829 |

The Jackson Administration (1829–1837)

Vice President	John C. Calhoun	1829–1833
	Martin Van Buren	1833–1837
Secretary of State	Martin Van Buren	1829–1831
	Edward Livingston	1831–1833
	Louis McLane	1833–1834
	John Forsyth	1834–1837

The Van Buren Administration (1837–1841)

| Vice President | Richard M. Johnson | 1837–1841 |
| Secretary of State | John Forsyth | 1837–1841 |

The William Harrison Administration (1841)

| Vice President | John Tyler | 1841 |
| Secretary of State | Daniel Webster | 1841 |

The Tyler Administration (1841–1845)

Vice President	None	
Secretary of State	Daniel Webster	1841–1843
	Hugh S. Legaré	1843
	Abel P. Upshur	1843–1844
	John C. Calhoun	1844–1845

U.S. POLITICS AND GOVERNMENT

The Polk Administration (1845–1849)

Vice President	George M. Dallas	1845–1849
Secretary of State	James Buchanan	1845–1849

The Taylor Administration (1849–1850)

Vice President	Millard Fillmore	1849–1850
Secretary of State	John M. Clayton	1849–1850

The Fillmore Administration (1850–1853)

Vice President	None	
Secretary of State	Daniel Webster	1850–1852
	Edward Everett	1852–1853

The Pierce Administration (1853–1857)

Vice President	William R. King	1853 1857
Secretary of State	William L. Marcy	1853–1857

The Buchanan Administration (1857–1861)

Vice President	John C. Breckinridge	1857–1861
Secretary of State	Lewis Cass	1857–1860
	Jeremiah S. Black	1860–1861

The Lincoln Administration (1861–1865)

Vice President	Hannibal Hamlin	1861–1865
	Andrew Johnson	1865
Secretary of State	William H. Seward	1861–1865

The Andrew Johnson Administration (1865–1869)

Vice President	None	
Secretary of State	William H. Seward	1865–1869

The Grant Administration (1869–1877)

Vice President	Schuyler Colfax	1869–1873
	Henry Wilson	1873–1877
Secretary of State	Elihu B. Washburne	1869
	Hamilton Fish	1869–1877

The Hayes Administration (1877–1881)

Vice President	William A. Wheeler	1877–1881
Secretary of State	William M. Evarts	1877–1881

The Garfield Administration (1881)

Vice President	Chester A. Arthur	1881
Secretary of State	James G. Blaine	1881

The Arthur Administration (1881–1885)

Vice President	None	
Secretary of State	F. T. Frelinghuysen	1881–1885

The Cleveland Administration (1885–1889)

Vice President	Thomas A. Hendricks	1885–1889
Secretary of State	Thomas F. Bayard	1885–1889

The Benjamin Harrison Administration (1889–1893)

Vice President	Levi P. Morton	1889–1893
Secretary of State	James G. Blaine	1889–1892
	John W. Foster	1892–1893

The Cleveland Administration (1893–1897)

Vice President	Adlai E. Stevenson	1893–1897
Secretary of State	Walter Q. Gresham	1893–1895
	Richard Olney	1895–1897

The McKinley Administration (1897–1901)

Vice President	Garret A. Hobart	1897–1901
	Theodore Roosevelt	1901
Secretary of State	John Sherman	1897–1898
	William R. Day	1898
	John Hay	1898–1901

The Theodore Roosevelt Administration (1901–1909)

Vice President	Charles Fairbanks	1905–1909
Secretary of State	John Hay	1901–1905
	Elihu Root	1905–1909
	Robert Bacon	1909

The Taft Administration (1909–1913)

Vice President	James S. Sherman	1909–1913
Secretary of State	Philander C. Knox	1909–1913

The Wilson Administration (1913–1921)

Vice President	Thomas R. Marshall	1913–1921
Secretary of State	William J. Bryan	1913–1915
	Robert Lansing	1915–1920
	Bainbridge Colby	1920–1921

The Harding Administration (1921–1923)

Vice President	Calvin Coolidge	1921–1923
Secretary of State	Charles E. Hughes	1921–1923

The Coolidge Administration (1923–1929)

Vice President	Charles G. Dawes	1925–1929
Secretary of State	Charles E. Hughes	1923–1925
	Frank B. Kellogg	1925–1929

The Hoover Administration (1929–1933)

Vice President	Charles Curtis	1929–1933
Secretary of State	Henry L. Stimson	1929–1933

The Franklin D. Roosevelt Administration (1933–1945)

Vice President	John Nance Garner	1933–1941
	Henry A. Wallace	1941–1945
	Harry S. Truman	1945
Secretary of State	Cordell Hull	1933–1944
	Edward R. Stettinius Jr.	1944–1945

The Truman Administration (1945–1953)

Vice President	Alben W. Barkley	1949–1953
Secretary of State	Edward R. Stettinius Jr.	1945
	James F. Byrnes	1945–1947
	George C. Marshall	1947–1949
	Dean G. Acheson	1949–1953

The Eisenhower Administration (1953–1961)

Vice President	Richard M. Nixon	1953–1961
Secretary of State	John Foster Dulles	1953–1959
	Christian A. Herter	1959–1961

The Kennedy Administration (1961–1963)

Vice President	Lyndon B. Johnson	1961–1963
Secretary of State	Dean Rusk	1961–1963

The Lyndon Johnson Administration (1963–1969)

Vice President	Hubert H. Humphrey	1965–1969
Secretary of State	Dean Rusk	1963–1969

The Nixon Administration (1969–1974)

Vice President	Spiro T. Agnew	1969–1973
	Gerald R. Ford	1973–1974
Secretary of State	William P. Rogers	1969–1973
	Henry A. Kissinger	1973–1974

The Ford Administration (1974–1977)

Vice President	Nelson A. Rockefeller	1974–1977
Secretary of State	Henry A. Kissinger	1974–1977

The Carter Administration (1977–1981)

Vice President	Walter F. Mondale	1977–1981
Secretary of State	Cyrus R. Vance	1977–1980
	Edmund Muskie	1980–1981

The Reagan Administration (1981–1989)

Vice President	George H. W. Bush	1981–1989
Secretary of State	Alexander M. Haig	1981–1982
	George P. Shultz	1982–1989

The George H. W. Bush Administration (1989–1993)

Vice President	J. Danforth Quayle	1989–1993
Secretary of State	James A. Baker III	1989–1992
	Lawrence S. Eagleburger	1992–1993

The Clinton Administration (1993–2001)

Vice President	Albert Gore	1993–2001
Secretary of State	Warren M. Christopher	1993–1997
	Madeleine K. Albright	1997–2001

The George W. Bush Administration (2001–)

Vice President	Richard Cheney	2001–
Secretary of State	Colin Powell	2001–2005
	Condoleezza Rice	2005–

ADMISSION OF STATES TO THE UNION

State	Date of Admission	State	Date of Admission
Delaware	December 7, 1787	Rhode Island	May 29, 1790
Pennsylvania	December 12, 1787	Vermont	March 4, 1791
New Jersey	December 18, 1787	Kentucky	June 1, 1792
Georgia	January 2, 1788	Tennessee	June 1, 1796
Connecticut	January 9, 1788	Ohio	March 1, 1803
Massachusetts	February 6, 1788	Louisiana	April 30, 1812
Maryland	April 28, 1788	Indiana	December 11, 1816
South Carolina	May 23, 1788	Mississippi	December 10, 1817
New Hampshire	June 21, 1788	Illinois	December 3, 1818
Virginia	June 25, 1788	Alabama	December 14, 1819
New York	July 26, 1788	Maine	March 15, 1820
North Carolina	November 21, 1789	Missouri	August 10, 1821

U.S. POLITICS AND GOVERNMENT

ADMISSION OF STATES TO THE UNION

State	Date of Admission	State	Date of Admission
Arkansas	June 15, 1836	Colorado	August 1, 1876
Michigan	January 16, 1837	North Dakota	November 2, 1889
Florida	March 3, 1845	South Dakota	November 2, 1889
Texas	December 29, 1845	Montana	November 8, 1889
Iowa	December 28, 1846	Washington	November 11, 1889
Wisconsin	May 29, 1848	Idaho	July 3, 1890
California	September 9, 1850	Wyoming	July 10, 1890
Minnesota	May 11, 1858	Utah	January 4, 1896
Oregon	February 14, 1859	Oklahoma	November 16, 1907
Kansas	January 29, 1861	New Mexico	January 6, 1912
West Virginia	June 19, 1863	Arizona	February 14, 1912
Nevada	October 31, 1864	Alaska	January 3, 1959
Nebraska	March 1, 1867	Hawaii	August 21, 1959

SUPREME COURT JUSTICES

Name	Service	Appointed by	Name	Service	Appointed by
John Jay*	1789–1795	Washington	Philip P. Barbour	1836–1841	Jackson
James Wilson	1789–1798	Washington	John Catron	1837–1865	Van Buren
John Blair	1789–1796	Washington	John McKinley	1837–1852	Van Buren
John Rutledge	1790–1791	Washington	Peter V. Daniel	1841–1860	Van Buren
William Cushing	1790–1810	Washington	Samuel Nelson	1845–1872	Tyler
James Iredell	1790–1799	Washington	Levi Woodbury	1845–1851	Polk
Thomas Johnson	1791–1793	Washington	Robert C. Grier	1846–1870	Polk
William Paterson	1793–1806	Washington	Benjamin R. Curtis	1851–1857	Fillmore
John Rutledge[†]	1795	Washington	John A. Campbell	1853–1861	Pierce
Samuel Chase	1796–1811	Washington	Nathan Clifford	1858–1881	Buchanan
Oliver Ellsworth	1796–1799	Washington	Noah H. Swayne	1862–1881	Lincoln
Bushrod Washington	1798–1829	J. Adams	Samuel F. Miller	1862–1890	Lincoln
			David Davis	1862–1877	Lincoln
Alfred Moore	1799–1804	J. Adams	Stephen J. Field	1863–1897	Lincoln
John Marshall	1801–1835	J. Adams	**Salmon P. Chase**	1864–1873	Lincoln
William Johnson	1804–1834	Jefferson	William Strong	1870–1880	Grant
Henry B. Livingston	1806–1823	Jefferson	Joseph P. Bradley	1870–1892	Grant
Thomas Todd	1807–1826	Jefferson	Ward Hunt	1873–1882	Grant
Gabriel Duval	1811–1836	Madison	**Morrison R. Waite**	1874–1888	Grant
Joseph Story	1811–1845	Madison	John M. Harlan	1877–1911	Hayes
Smith Thompson	1823–1843	Monroe	William B. Woods	1880–1887	Hayes
Robert Trimble	1826–1828	J. Q. Adams	Stanley Matthews	1881–1889	Garfield
John McLean	1829–1861	Jackson	Horace Gray	1882–1902	Arthur
Henry Baldwin	1830–1844	Jackson	Samuel Blatchford	1882–1893	Arthur
James M. Wayne	1835–1867	Jackson	Lucius Q. C. Lamar	1888–1893	Cleveland
Roger B. Taney	1836–1864	Jackson	**Melville W. Fuller**	1888–1910	Cleveland
			David J. Brewer	1889–1910	B. Harrison
			Henry B. Brown	1890–1906	B. Harrison
			George Shiras	1892–1903	B. Harrison
			Howell E. Jackson	1893–1895	B. Harrison

*Chief Justices appear in bold type.
[†]Acting Chief Justice; Senate refused to confirm appointment.

Name	Service	Appointed by	Name	Service	Appointed by
Edward D. White	1894–1910	Cleveland	Harold H. Burton	1945–1958	Truman
Rufus W. Peckham	1896–1909	Cleveland	**Frederick M. Vinson**	1946–1953	Truman
Joseph McKenna	1898–1925	McKinley	Tom C. Clark	1949–1967	Truman
Oliver W. Holmes	1902–1932	T. Roosevelt	Sherman Minton	1949–1956	Truman
William R. Day	1903–1922	T. Roosevelt	**Earl Warren**	1953–1969	Eisenhower
William H. Moody	1906–1910	T. Roosevelt	John Marshall Harlan	1955–1971	Eisenhower
Horace H. Lurton	1910–1914	Taft	William J. Brennan Jr.	1956–1990	Eisenhower
Charles E. Hughes	1910–1916	Taft	Charles E. Whittaker	1957–1962	Eisenhower
Willis Van Devanter	1910–1937	Taft	Potter Stewart	1958–1981	Eisenhower
Edward D. White	1910–1921	Taft	Byron R. White	1962–1993	Kennedy
Joseph R. Lamar	1911–1916	Taft	Arthur J. Goldberg	1962–1965	Kennedy
Mahlon Pitney	1912–1922	Taft	Abe Fortas	1965–1969	L. Johnson
James C. McReynolds	1914–1941	Wilson	Thurgood Marshall	1967–1991	L. Johnson
Louis D. Brandeis	1916–1939	Wilson	**Warren E. Burger**	1969–1986	Nixon
John H. Clarke	1916–1922	Wilson	Harry A. Blackmun	1970–1994	Nixon
William H. Taft	1921–1930	Harding	Lewis F. Powell Jr.	1972–1988	Nixon
George Sutherland	1922–1938	Harding	William H. Rehnquist	1972–1986	Nixon
Pierce Butler	1923–1939	Harding	John Paul Stevens	1975–	Ford
Edward T. Sanford	1923–1930	Harding	Sandra Day O'Connor	1981–2006	Reagan
Harlan F. Stone	1925–1941	Coolidge	**William H. Rehnquist**	1986–2005	Reagan
Charles E. Hughes	1930–1941	Hoover	Antonin Scalia	1986–	Reagan
Owen J. Roberts	1930–1945	Hoover	Anthony M. Kennedy	1988–	Reagan
Benjamin N. Cardozo	1932–1938	Hoover	David H. Souter	1990–	G. H. W. Bush
Hugo L. Black	1937–1971	F. Roosevelt			
Stanley F. Reed	1938–1957	F. Roosevelt	Clarence Thomas	1991–	G. H. W. Bush
Felix Frankfurter	1939–1962	F. Roosevelt			
William O. Douglas	1939–1975	F. Roosevelt	Ruth Bader Ginsburg	1993–	Clinton
Frank Murphy	1940–1949	F. Roosevelt	Stephen Breyer	1994–	Clinton
Harlan F. Stone	1941–1946	F. Roosevelt	**John G. Roberts Jr.**	2005–	G. W. Bush
James F. Byrnes	1941–1942	F. Roosevelt	Samuel Anthony Alito Jr.	2006–	G. W. Bush
Robert H. Jackson	1941–1954	F. Roosevelt			
Wiley B. Rutledge	1943–1949	F. Roosevelt			

SIGNIFICANT SUPREME COURT CASES

Marbury v. Madison (1803)

This case established the right of the Supreme Court to review the constitutionality of laws. The decision involved judicial appointments made during the last hours of the administration of President John Adams. Some commissions, including that of William Marbury, had not yet been delivered when President Thomas Jefferson took office. Infuriated by the last-minute nature of Adams's Federalist appointments, Jefferson refused to send the undelivered commissions out, and Marbury decided to sue. The Supreme Court, presided over by John Marshall, a Federalist who had assisted Adams in the judicial appointments, ruled that although

Marbury's commission was valid and the new president should have delivered it, the Court could not compel him to do so. The Court based its reasoning on a finding that the grounds of Marbury's suit, resting in the Judiciary Act of 1789, were in conflict with the Constitution.

For the first time, the Court had overturned a national law on the grounds that it was unconstitutional. John Marshall had quietly established the concept of judicial review: The Supreme Court had given itself the authority to nullify acts of the other branches of the federal government. Although the Constitution provides for judicial review, the Court had not exercised this power before and did not use it again until 1857. It seems likely that if the Court

SIGNIFICANT SUPREME COURT CASES

had waited until 1857 to use this power, it would have been difficult to establish.

McCulloch v. Maryland (1819)

In 1816, Congress authorized the creation of a national bank. To protect its own banks from competition with a branch of the national bank in Baltimore, the state legislature of Maryland placed a tax of 2 percent on all notes issued by any bank operating in Maryland that was not chartered by the state. McCulloch, cashier of the Baltimore branch of the Bank of the United States, was convicted for refusing to pay the tax. Under the leadership of Chief Justice John Marshall, the Court ruled that the federal government had the power to establish a bank, even though that specific authority was not mentioned in the Constitution.

Marshall maintained that the authority could be reasonably implied from Article 1, section 8, which gives Congress the power to make all laws that are necessary and proper to execute the enumerated powers. Marshall also held that Maryland could not tax the national bank because in a conflict between federal and state laws, the federal law must take precedence. Thus he established the principles of implied powers and federal supremacy, both of which set a precedent for subsequent expansion of federal power at the expense of the states.

Scott v. Sandford (1857)

Dred Scott was a slave who sued for his own and his family's freedom on the grounds that, with his master, he had traveled to and lived in free territory that did not allow slavery. When his case reached the Supreme Court, the justices saw an opportunity to settle once and for all the vexing question of slavery in the territories. The Court's decision in this case proved that it enjoyed no special immunity from the sectional and partisan passions of the time. Five of the nine justices were from the South and seven were Democrats.

Chief Justice Roger B. Taney hated Republicans and detested racial equality; his decision reflects those prejudices. He wrote an opinion not only declaring that Scott was still a slave but also claiming that the Constitution denied citizenship or rights to blacks, that Congress had no right to exclude slavery from the territories, and that the Missouri Compromise was unconstitutional. While southern Democrats gloated over this seven-to-two decision, sectional tensions were further inflamed, and the young Republican Party's claim that a hostile "slave power" was conspiring to destroy northern liberties was given further credence. The decision brought the nation closer to civil war and is generally regarded as the worst decision ever rendered by the Supreme Court.

Butchers' Benevolent Association of New Orleans v. Crescent City Livestock Landing and Slaughterhouse Co. (1873)

The *Slaughterhouse* cases, as the cases docketed under the *Butchers'* title were known, were the first legal test of the Fourteenth Amendment. To cut down on cases of cholera believed to be caused by contaminated water, the state of Louisiana prohibited the slaughter of livestock in New Orleans except in one slaughterhouse, effectively giving that slaughterhouse a monopoly. Other New Orleans butchers claimed that the state had deprived them of their occupation without due process of law, thus violating the Fourteenth Amendment.

In a five-to-four decision, the Court upheld the Louisiana law, declaring that the Fourteenth Amendment protected only the rights of federal citizenship, like voting in federal elections and interstate travel. The federal government thus was not obliged to protect basic civil rights from violation by state governments. This decision would have significant implications for African Americans and their struggle for civil rights in the twentieth century.

United States v. E. C. Knight Co. (1895)

Also known as the *Sugar Trust* case, this was among the first cases to reveal the weakness of the Sherman Antitrust Act in the hands of a pro-business Supreme Court. In 1895, American Sugar Refining Company purchased four other sugar producers, including the E. C. Knight Company, and thus took control of more than 98 percent of the sugar refining in the United States. In an effort to limit monopoly, the government brought suit against all five of the companies for violating the Sherman Antitrust Act, which outlawed trusts and other business combinations in restraint of trade. The Court dismissed the suit, however, arguing that the law applied only to commerce and not to manufacturing, defining the latter as a local concern and not part of the interstate commerce that the government could regulate.

Plessy v. Ferguson (1896)

African American Homer Plessy challenged a Louisiana law that required segregation on trains passing through the state. After ensuring that the railroad and the conductor knew that he was of mixed race (Plessy appeared to be white but under the racial code of Louisiana was classified as "colored" because he was one-eighth black), he refused to move to the "colored only" section of the coach. The Court ruled against Plessy by a vote of seven to one, declaring that "separate but equal" facilities were permissible according to section 1 of the Fourteenth Amendment, which calls upon the states to provide "equal protection of the laws" to anyone within their jurisdiction. Although the case was viewed as relatively insignificant at the time, it cast a long shadow over several decades.

Initially, the decision was viewed as a victory for segregationists, but in the 1900s and 1940s civil rights advocates referred to the doctrine of "separate but equal" in their efforts to end segregation. They argued that segregated institutions and accommodations were often *not* equal to those available to whites, and finally succeeded in overturning *Plessy* in *Brown v. Board of Education* in 1954 (see below).

Lochner v. New York (1905)

In this case, the Court ruled against a New York state law that prohibited employees from working in bakeries more than ten hours a day or sixty hours a week. The purpose of the law was to protect the health of workers, but the Court ruled that it was unconstitutional because it violated "freedom of contract" implicitly protected by the due process clause of the Fourteenth Amendment. Most of the justices believed strongly in a laissez-faire economic system that favored survival of the fittest. They felt that government protection of workers interfered with this system. In a dissenting opinion, Justice Oliver Wendell Holmes accused the majority of distorting the Constitution and of deciding the case on "an economic theory which a large part of the country does not entertain."

Muller v. Oregon (1908)

In 1905, Curt Muller, owner of a Portland, Oregon, laundry, demanded that one of his employees, Mrs. Elmer Gotcher, work more than the ten hours allowed as a maximum workday for women under Oregon law. Muller argued that the law violated his "freedom of contract" as established in prior Supreme Court decisions.

Progressive lawyer Louis D. Brandeis defended the Oregon law by arguing that a state could be justified in abridging freedom of contract when the health, safety, and welfare of workers was at issue. His innovative strategy drew on ninety-five pages of excerpts from factory and medical reports to substantiate his argument that there was a direct connection between long hours and the health of women and thus the health of the nation. In a unanimous decision, the Court upheld the Oregon law, but later generations of women fighting for equality would question the strategy of arguing that women's reproductive role entitled them to special treatment.

Schenck v. United States (1919)

During World War I, Charles Schenck and other members of the Socialist Party printed and mailed out flyers urging young men who were subject to the draft to oppose the war in Europe. In upholding the conviction of Schenck for publishing a pamphlet urging draft resistance, Justice Oliver Wendell Holmes established the "clear and present danger" test for freedom of speech. Such utterances as Schenck's during a time of national peril, Holmes wrote, could be considered the equivalent of shouting "Fire!" in a crowded theater. Congress had the right to protect the public against such an incitement to panic, the Court ruled in a unanimous decision. But the analogy was a false one. Schenck's pamphlet had little power to provoke a public firmly opposed to its message. Although Holmes later modified his position to state that the danger must relate to an immediate evil and a specific action, the "clear and present danger" test laid the groundwork for those who later sought to limit First Amendment freedoms.

Schechter Poultry Corp. v. United States (1935)

During the Great Depression, the National Industrial Recovery Act (NIRA), which was passed under President Franklin D. Roosevelt, established fair competition codes that were designed to help businesses. The Schechter brothers of New York City, who sold chickens, were convicted of violating the codes. The Supreme Court ruled that the NIRA unconstitutionally conferred legislative power on an administrative agency and overstepped the limits of federal power to regulate interstate commerce. The decision was a significant blow to the New Deal recovery program, demonstrating both historic American resistance to economic planning and the refusal of the business community to yield its autonomy unless it was forced to do so.

Brown v. Board of Education (1954)

In 1950, the families of eight Topeka, Kansas, children sued the Topeka Board of Education. The children were blacks who lived within walking distance of a whites-only school. The segregated school system required them to take a time-consuming, inconvenient, and dangerous route to get to a black school, and their parents argued that there was no reason their children should not be allowed to attend the nearest school. By the time the case reached the Supreme Court, it had been joined with similar cases regarding segregated schools in other states and the District of Columbia. A team of lawyers from the National Association for the Advancement of Colored People (NAACP),

SIGNIFICANT SUPREME COURT CASES

led by Thurgood Marshall (who would later be appointed to the Supreme Court), urged the Court to overturn the fifty-eight-year-old precedent established in *Plessy v. Ferguson*, which had enshrined "separate but equal" as the law of the land. A unanimous Court, led by Chief Justice Earl Warren, declared that "separate educational facilities are inherently unequal" and thus violate the Fourteenth Amendment. In 1955, the Court called for desegregation "with all deliberate speed" but established no deadline.

Roth v. United States (1957)

In 1957, New Yorker Samuel Roth was convicted of sending obscene materials through the mail in a case that ultimately reached the Supreme Court. With a six-to-three vote, the Court reaffirmed the historical view that obscenity is not protected by the First Amendment. Yet it broke new ground by declaring that a work could be judged obscene only if, "taken as a whole," it appealed to the "prurient interest" of "the average person."

Prior to this case, work could be judged obscene if portions were thought able to "deprave and corrupt" the most susceptible part of an audience (such as children). Thus, serious works of literature such as Theodore Dreiser's *An American Tragedy*, which was banned in Boston when first published, had received no protection. Although this decision continued to pose problems of definition, it did help to protect most works that attempt to convey ideas, even if those ideas have to do with sex, from the threat of obscenity laws.

Engel v. Vitale (1962)

In 1959, five parents with ten children in the New Hyde Park, New York, school system sued the school board. The parents argued that the so-called Regents' Prayer that public school students in New York recited at the start of every school day violated the doctrine of separation of church and state outlined in the First Amendment. In 1962, the Supreme Court voted six to one in favor of banning the Regents' Prayer.

The decision threw the religious community into an uproar. Many religious leaders expressed dismay and even shock; others welcomed the decision. Several efforts to introduce an amendment allowing school prayer have failed. Subsequent Supreme Court decisions have banned reading of the Bible in public schools. The Court has also declared mandatory flag saluting to be an infringement of religious and personal freedoms.

Gideon v. Wainwright (1963)

When Clarence Earl Gideon was tried for breaking into a poolroom, the state of Florida rejected his demand for a court-appointed lawyer as guaranteed by the Sixth Amendment. In 1963, the Court upheld his demand in a unanimous decision that established the obligation of states to provide attorneys for indigent defendants in felony cases. Prior to this decision, the right to an attorney had applied only to federal cases, not state cases. In its ruling in *Gideon v. Wainwright*, the Supreme Court applied the Sixth through the Fourteenth Amendments to the states. In 1972, the Supreme Court extended the right to legal representation to all cases, not just felony cases, in its decision in *Argersinger v. Hamlin*.

Griswold v. Connecticut (1965)

With a vote of seven to two, the Supreme Court reversed an "uncommonly silly law" (in the words of Justice Potter Stewart) that made it a crime for anyone in the state of Connecticut to use any drug, article, or instrument to prevent conception. *Griswold* became a landmark case because here, for the first time, the Court explicitly invested with full constitutional status "fundamental personal rights," such as the right to privacy, that were not expressly enumerated in the Bill of Rights. The majority opinion in the case held that the law infringed on the constitutionally protected right to privacy of married persons.

Although the Court had previously recognized fundamental rights not expressly enumerated in the Bill of Rights (such as the right to procreate in *Skinner v. Oklahoma* in 1942), *Griswold* was the first time the Court had justified, at length, the practice of investing such unenumerated rights with full constitutional status. Writing for the majority, Justice William O. Douglas explained that the First, Third, Fourth, Fifth, and Ninth Amendments imply "zones of privacy" that are the foundation for the general right to privacy affirmed in this case.

Miranda v. Arizona (1966)

In 1966, the Supreme Court, by a vote of five to four, upheld the case of Ernesto Miranda, who appealed a murder conviction on the grounds that police had gotten him to confess without giving him access to an attorney. The *Miranda* case was the culmination of the Court's efforts to find a meaningful way of determining whether police had used due process in extracting confessions from people accused of crimes. The *Miranda* decision upholds the Fifth Amendment protection against self-incrimination outside the courtroom and requires that suspects be given what came to be known as the "Miranda warning," which advises them of their right to remain silent and warns them that anything they say might be used against them in a court of law. Suspects must also be told that they have a right to counsel.

New York Times Co. v. United States (1971)

With a six-to-three vote, the Court upheld the right of the *New York Times* and the *Washington Post* to print materials from the so-called *Pentagon Papers*, a secret government study of U.S. policy in Vietnam, leaked by dissident Pentagon official Daniel Ellsberg. Since the papers revealed deception and secrecy in the conduct of the Vietnam War, the Nixon administration had quickly obtained a court injunction against their further publication, claiming that suppression was in the interests of national security. The Supreme Court's decision overturning the injunction strengthened the First Amendment protection of freedom of the press.

Furman v. Georgia (1972)

In this case, the Supreme Court ruled five to four that the death penalty for murder or rape violated the cruel and unusual punishment clause of the Eighth Amendment because the manner in which the death penalty was meted out was irregular, "arbitrary," and "cruel." In response, most states enacted new statutes that allow the death penalty to be imposed only after a postconviction hearing at which evidence must be presented to show that "aggravating" or "mitigating" circumstances were factors in the crime. If the postconviction hearing hands down a death sentence, the case is automatically reviewed by an appellate court.

In 1976, the Court ruled in *Gregg v. Georgia* that these statutes were not unconstitutional. In 1977, the Court ruled in *Coker v. Georgia* that the death penalty for rape was "disproportionate and excessive," thus allowing the death penalty only in murder cases. Between 1977 and 1991, some 150 people were executed in the United States. Public opinion polls indicate that about 70 percent of Americans favor the death penalty for murder. Capital punishment continues to generate controversy, however, as opponents argue that there is no evidence that the death penalty deters crime and that its use reflects racial and economic bias.

Roe v. Wade (1973)

In 1973, the Court found, by a vote of seven to two, that state laws restricting access to abortion violated a woman's right to privacy guaranteed by the due process clause of the Fourteenth Amendment. The decision was based on the cases of two women living in Texas and Georgia, both states with stringent antiabortion laws. Upholding the individual rights of both women and physicians, the Court ruled that the Constitution protects the right to abortion and that states cannot prohibit abortions in the early stages of pregnancy.

The decision stimulated great debate among legal scholars as well as the public. Critics argued that since abortion was never addressed in the Constitution, the Court could not claim that legislation violated fundamental values of the Constitution. They also argued that since abortion was a medical procedure with an acknowledged impact on a fetus, it was inappropriate to invoke the kind of "privacy" argument that was used in *Griswold v. Connecticut* (see page A-43), which was about contraception. Defenders suggested that the case should be argued as a case of gender discrimination, which did violate the equal protection clause of the Fourteenth Amendment. Others said that the right to privacy in sexual matters was indeed a fundamental right.

Regents of the University of California v. Bakke (1978)

When Allan Bakke, a white man, was not accepted by the University of California Medical School at Davis, he filed a lawsuit alleging that the admissions program, which set up different standards for test scores and grades for members of certain minority groups, violated the Civil Rights Act of 1964, which outlawed racial or ethnic preferences in programs supported by federal funds. Bakke further argued that the university's practice of setting aside spaces for minority applicants denied him equal protection as guaranteed by the Fourteenth Amendment. In a five-to-four decision, the Court ordered that Bakke be admitted to the medical school, yet it sanctioned affirmative action programs to attack the results of past discrimination as long as strict quotas or racial classifications were not involved.

Webster v. Reproductive Health Services (1989)

By a vote of five to four, the Court upheld several restrictions on the availability of abortions as imposed by Missouri state law. It upheld restrictions on the use of state property, including public hospitals, for abortions. It also upheld a provision requiring physicians to perform tests to determine the viability of a fetus that a doctor judged to be twenty weeks of age or older. Although the justices did not go so far as to overturn the decision in *Roe v. Wade* (see at left), the ruling galvanized interest groups on both sides of the abortion issue. Opponents of abortion pressured state legislatures to place greater restrictions on abortions; those who favored availability of abortion tried to mobilize public action by presenting the decision as a major threat to the right to choose abortion.

SIGNIFICANT SUPREME COURT CASES

Cipollone v. Liggett (1992)

In a seven-to-two decision, the Court ruled in favor of the family of Rose Cipollone, a woman who died of lung cancer after smoking for forty-two years. The Court rejected arguments that health warnings on cigarette packages protected tobacco manufacturers from personal injury suits filed by smokers who contract cancer and other serious illnesses.

Miller v. Johnson (1995)

In a five-to-four decision, the Supreme Court ruled that voting districts created to increase the voting power of racial minorities were unconstitutional. The decision threatens dozens of congressional, state, and local voting districts that were drawn to give minorities more representation as had been required by the Justice Department under the Voting Rights Act. If states are required to redraw voting districts, the number of black members of Congress could be sharply reduced.

Romer v. Evans (1996)

In a six-to-three decision, the Court struck down a Colorado amendment that forbade local governments from banning discrimination against homosexuals. Writing for the majority, Justice Anthony Kennedy said that forbidding communities from taking action to protect the rights of homosexuals and not of other groups unlawfully deprived gays and lesbians of opportunities that were available to others. Kennedy based the decision on the guarantee of equal protection under the law as provided by the Fourteenth Amendment.

Bush v. Palm Beach County Canvassing Board (2000)

In a bitterly argued five-to-four decision, the Court reversed the Florida Supreme Court's previous order for a hand recount of contested presidential election ballots in several counties of that battleground state, effectively securing the presidency for Texas Republican governor George W. Bush. The ruling ended a protracted legal dispute between presidential candidates Bush and Vice President Al Gore while inflaming public opinion. For the first time since 1888, a president who failed to win the popular vote took office. Critics charged that the Supreme Court had applied partisanship rather than objectivity to the case, pointing out that the decision went against this Court's customary interpretation of the Constitution to favor state over federal authority.

The American Economy

THESE FIVE "SNAPSHOTS" of the U.S. economy show significant changes over the past century and a half. In 1849, the agricultural sector was by far the largest contributor to the economy. By the turn of the century, with advances in technology and an abundance of cheap labor and raw materials, the country had experienced remarkable industrial expansion, and the manufacturing industries dominated. By 1950, the service sector had increased significantly, fueled by the consumerism of the 1920s and the post–World War II years, and the economy was becoming more diversified. Note that by 1990, the government's share in the economy had grown to more than 10 percent and activity in both the trade and manufacturing sectors had declined, partly as a result of competition from Western Europe and Asia. Manufacturing continued to decline, and by 2001 the service and finance, real estate, and insurance sectors had all grown steadily to eclipse it.

Main Sectors of the U.S. Economy: 1849, 1899, 1950, 1990, 2001

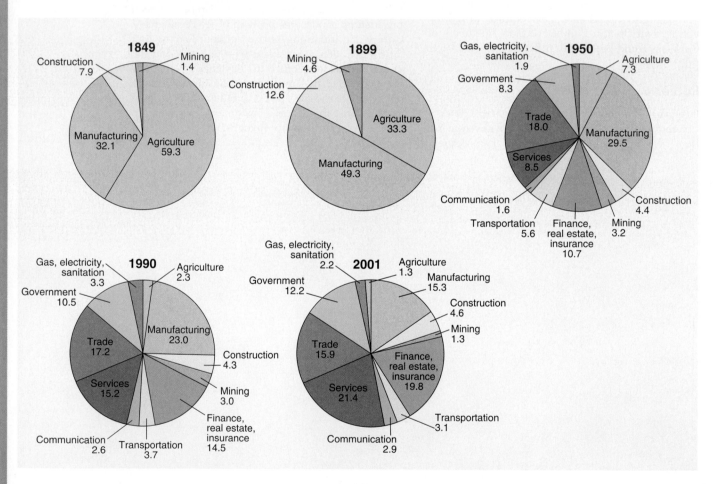

SOURCE: Data from *Historical Statistics of the United States, Colonial Times to 1970* (1975); *Statistical Abstract of the United States, 1998*; U.S. Bureau of Economic Analysis, *Industry Accounts Data, 2001*.

THE AMERICAN ECONOMY

FEDERAL SPENDING AND THE ECONOMY, 1790–2005

Year	Gross National Product (in billions)	Foreign Trade (in millions)		Federal Budget (in billions)	Federal Surplus/Deficit (in billions)	Federal Debt (in billions)
		Exports	Imports			
1790	NA	20	23	0.004	0.00015	0.076
1800	NA	71	91	0.011	0.0006	0.083
1810	NA	67	85	0.008	0.0012	0.053
1820	NA	70	74	0.018	−0.0004	0.091
1830	NA	74	71	0.015	0.100	0.049
1840	NA	132	107	0.024	−0.005	0.004
1850	NA	152	178	0.040	0.004	0.064
1860	NA	400	362	0.063	−0.01	0.065
1870	7.4	451	462	0.310	0.10	2.4
1880	11.2	853	761	0.268	0.07	2.1
1890	13.1	910	823	0.318	0.09	1.2
1900	18.7	1,499	930	0.521	0.05	1.2
1910	35.3	1,919	1,646	0.694	−0.02	1.1
1920	91.5	8,664	5,784	6.357	0.3	24.3
1930	90.4	4,013	3,500	3.320	0.7	16.3
1940	99.7	4,030	7,433	9.6	−2.7	43.0
1950	284.8	10,816	9,125	43.1	−2.2	257.4
1960	503.7	19,600	15,046	92.2	0.3	286.3
1970	977.1	42,700	40,189	195.6	−2.8	371.0
1980	2,631.7	220,600	244,871	590.9	−73.8	907.7
1990	5,832.2	393,600	495,300	1,253.2	−221.2	3,266.1
2000	9,848.0	1,070,054	1,445,438	1,788.8	236.4	5,701.9
2002	10,436.7	974,107	1,392,145	2,011.0	−157.8	6,255.4
2005	12,487.1	1,275,245	1,991,975	2,472.2	−423.2	7,905.3

SOURCE: Historical Statistics of the U.S., Colonial Times to 1970 (1975), Statistical Abstract of the U.S., 1998 (1996), Statistical Abstract of the U.S., 1999 (1999), and Statistical Abstract of the U.S., 2007 (2007).

A Demographic Profile of the United States and Its People

Population

FROM AN ESTIMATED 4,600 white inhabitants in 1630, the country's population grew to a total of more than 280 million in 2000. It is important to note that the U.S. census, first conducted in 1790 and the source of these figures, counted blacks, both free and slave, but did not include American Indians until 1860. The years 1790 to 1900 saw the most rapid population growth, with an average increase of 25 to 35 percent per decade. In addition to "natural" growth—birthrate exceeding death rate—immigration was also a factor in that rise, especially between 1840 and 1860, 1880 and 1890, and 1900 and 1910 (see table on page A-51). The twentieth century witnessed slower growth, partly a result of 1920s immigration restrictions and a decline in the birthrate, especially during the depression era and the 1960s and 1970s. The U.S. population is expected to reach almost 300 million by the year 2010.

POPULATION GROWTH, 1630–2000

Year	Population	Percent Increase	Year	Population	Percent Increase
1630	4,600	—	1820	9,638,453	33.1
1640	26,600	473.3	1830	12,866,020	33.5
1650	50,400	89.1	1840	17,069,453	32.7
1660	75,100	49.0	1850	23,191,876	35.9
1670	111,900	49.1	1860	31,443,321	35.6
1680	151,500	35.4	1870	39,818,449	26.6
1690	210,400	38.9	1880	50,155,783	26.0
1700	250,900	19.3	1890	62,947,714	25.5
1710	331,700	32.2	1900	75,994,575	20.7
1720	466,200	40.5	1910	91,972,266	21.0
1730	629,400	35.0	1920	105,710,620	14.9
1740	905,600	43.9	1930	122,775,046	16.1
1750	1,170,800	30.0	1940	131,669,275	7.2
1760	1,593,600	36.1	1950	150,697,361	14.5
1770	2,148,100	34.8	1960	179,323,175	19.0
1780	2,780,400	29.4	1970	203,302,031	13.4
1790	3,929,214	41.3	1980	226,542,199	11.4
1800	5,308,483	35.1	1990	248,718,302	9.8
1810	7,239,881	36.4	2000	281,422,509	13.1

SOURCE: *Historical Statistics of the U.S.* (1960), *Historical Statistics of the U.S., Colonial Times to 1970* (1975), *Statistical Abstract of the U.S., 1996* (1996), and *Statistical Abstract of the U.S., 2003* (2003).

A DEMOGRAPHIC PROFILE OF THE UNITED STATES AND ITS PEOPLE

Birthrate, 1820–2000

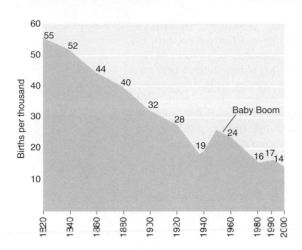

SOURCE: Data from *Historical Statistics of the U.S., Colonial Times to 1970* (1975) and *Statistical Abstract of the U.S., 2003* (2003).

Death Rate, 1900–2000

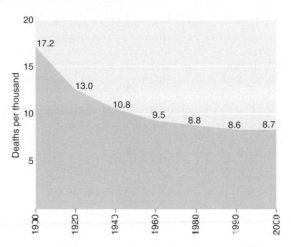

SOURCE: Data from *Historical Statistics of the U.S., Colonial Times to 1970* (1975) and *Statistical Abstract of the U.S., 2003* (2003).

Life Expectancy, 1900–2000

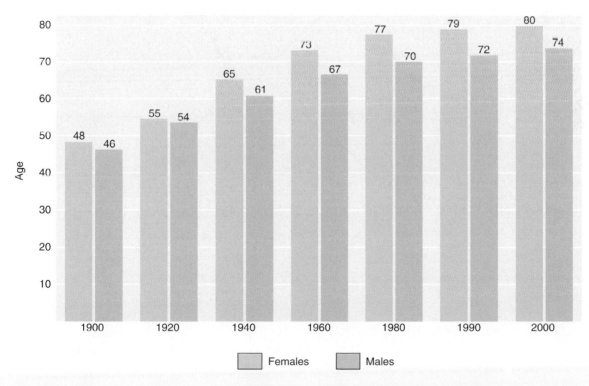

SOURCE: Data from *Historical Statistics of the U.S., Colonial Times to 1970* (1975) and *Statistical Abstract of the U.S., 2003* (2003).

MIGRATION AND IMMIGRATION

WE TEND TO ASSOCIATE INTERNAL MIGRATION with movement westward, yet equally significant has been the movement of the nation's population from the country to the city. In 1790, the first U.S. census recorded that approximately 95 percent of the population lived in rural areas. By 1990, that figure had fallen to less than 25 percent. The decline of the agricultural way of life, late-nineteenth-century industrialization, and immigration have all contributed to increased urbanization. A more recent trend has been the migration, especially since the 1970s, of people to the Sun Belt states of the South and West, lured by factors as various as economic opportunities in the defense and high-tech industries and good weather. This migration has swelled the size of cities like Houston, Dallas, Tucson, Phoenix, and San Diego, all of which in recent years ranked among the top ten most populous U.S. cities.

Rural and Urban Population, 1750–2000

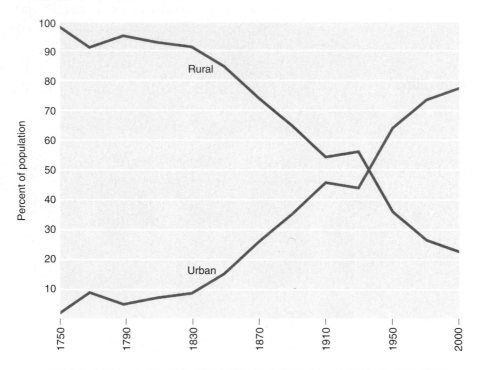

SOURCE: *Statistical Abstract of the U.S., 1991* (1991), *Statistical Abstract of the U.S., 2002* (2002).

MIGRATION AND IMMIGRATION

THE QUANTITY AND CHARACTER OF IMMIGRATION to the United States has varied greatly over time. During the first major influx, between 1840 and 1860, newcomers hailed primarily from northern and western Europe. From 1880 to 1915, when rates soared even more dramatically, the profile changed, with 80 percent of the "new immigration" coming from central, eastern, and southern Europe. Following World War I, strict quotas reduced the flow considerably. Note also the significant falloff during the years of the Great Depression and World War II. The sources of immigration during the last half century have changed significantly, with the majority of people coming from Latin America, the Caribbean, and Asia. The latest surge during the 1980s and 1990s brought more immigrants to the United States than in any decade except 1901–1910.

RATES OF IMMIGRATION, 1821–2005

Year	Number	Rate per Thousand of Total Resident Population
1821–1830	151,824	1.6
1831–1840	599,125	4.6
1841–1850	1,713,521	10.0
1851–1860	2,598,214	11.2
1861–1870	2,314,824	7.4
1871–1880	2,812,191	7.1
1881–1890	5,246,613	10.5
1891–1900	3,687,546	5.8
1901–1910	8,795,386	11.6
1911–1920	5,735,811	6.2
1921–1930	4,107,209	3.9
1931–1940	528,431	0.4
1941–1950	1,035,039	0.7
1951–1960	2,515,479	1.6
1961–1970	3,321,677	1.8
1971–1980	4,493,300	2.2
1981–1990	7,338,100	3.0
1991	1,827,167	7.2
1992	973,977	3.8
1993	904,292	3.5
1994	804,416	3.1
1995	720,461	2.7
1996	915,900	3.4
1997	798,378	2.9
1998	654,451	2.4
1999	646,568	2.3
2000	849,807	3.0
2001	1,064,318	3.7
2002	1,063,732	3.7
2003	704,000	2.4
2004	958,000	3.3
2005	1,122,000	3.8

SOURCE: *Historical Statistics of the U.S., Colonial Times to 1970* (1975), *2002 Yearbook of Immigration Statistics* (2002), and *Statistical Abstract of the U.S., 1996, 1999, 2003,* and *2005* (1996, 1999, 2003, 2005).

Major Trends in Immigration, 1820–2000

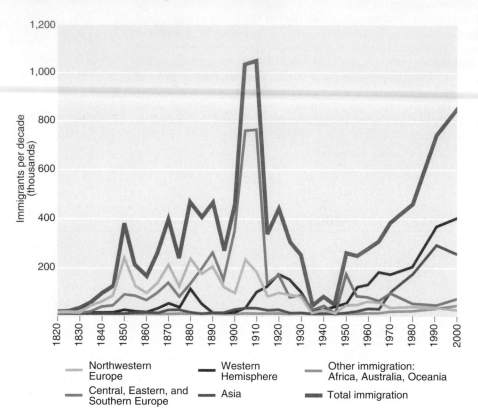

SOURCE: Data from *Historical Statistics of the U.S., Colonial Times to 1970* (1975), *Statistical Abstract of the U.S., 1999* (1999), and *Statistical Abstract of the U.S., 2003* (2003).

Research Resources in U.S. History

For help refining your research skills, finding what you need on the Web, and using it effectively, see "Online Research and Reference Aids" at bedfordstmartins.com/roark.

WHILE DOING RESEARCH IN HISTORY, you will use the library to track down primary and secondary sources and to answer questions that arise as you learn more about your topic. This appendix suggests helpful indexes, references, periodicals, and sources of primary documents. It also offers an overview of electronic resources available through the Internet. The materials listed here are not carried at all libraries, but they will give you an idea of the range of sources available. Remember, too, that librarians are an extremely helpful resource. They can direct you to useful materials throughout your research process.

Bibliographies and Indexes

American Historical Association Guide to Historical Literature. 3rd ed. New York: Oxford University Press, 1995. Offers 27,000 citations to important historical literature, arranged in forty-eight sections covering theory, international history, and regional history. An indispensable guide recently updated to include current trends in historical research.

American History and Life. Santa Barbara: ABC-Clio, 1964–. Covers publications of all sorts on U.S. and Canadian history and culture in a chronological/regional format, with abstracts and alphabetical indexes. Available in computerized format. The most complete ongoing bibliography for American history.

Freidel, Frank Burt. *Harvard Guide to American History*. Cambridge: Harvard University Press, Belknap Press, 1974. Provides citations to books and articles on American history published before 1970. The first volume is arranged topically, the second chronologically. Though it does not cover current scholarship, it is a classic and remains useful for tracing older publications.

Prucha, Francis Paul. *Handbook for Research in American History: A Guide to Bibliographies and Other Reference Works*. 2nd rev. ed. Lincoln: University of Nebraska Press, 1994. Introduces a variety of research tools, including electronic ones. A good source to consult when planning an in-depth research project.

General Overviews

Dictionary of American Biography. New York: Scribner's, 1928–1937, with supplements. Gives substantial biographies of prominent Americans in history.

Dictionary of American History. New York: Scribner's, 1976. An encyclopedia of terms, places, and concepts in U.S. history; other more specialized sets include the *Encyclopedia of North American Colonies* and the *Encyclopedia of the Confederacy*.

Encyclopedia of American Social History. New York: Scribner's, 1993. Surveys topics such as religion, class, gender, race, popular culture, regionalism, and everyday life from pre-Columbian to modern times.

Encyclopedia of the United States in the Twentieth Century. New York: Scribner's, 1996. An overview of American cultural, social, and intellectual history in articles arranged topically with useful bibliographies for further research.

Specialized Information

Black Women in America: An Historical Encyclopedia. Brooklyn: Carlson, 1993. A scholarly compilation of biographical and topical articles that constitute a definitive history of African American women.

Carruth, Gordon. *The Encyclopedia of American Facts and Dates*. 10th ed. New York: HarperCollins, 1997. Covers American history chronologically from 1986 to the present, offering information on treaties, battles, explorations, popular culture, philosophy, literature, and so on, mixing significant events with telling trivia. Tables allow for reviewing a year from a variety of angles. A thorough index helps pinpoint specific facts in time.

Cook, Chris. *Dictionary of Historical Terms*. 2nd ed. New York: Peter Bendrick, 1990. Covers a wide variety of terms—events, places, institutions, and topics—in history for all periods and places in a remarkably small package. A good place for quick identification of terms in the field.

Dictionary of Afro-American Slavery. New York: Greenwood, 1985. Surveys important people, events, and topics, with useful bibliographies; similar works include *Dictionary of the Vietnam War, Historical Dictionary of the New Deal,* and *Historical Dictionary of the Progressive Era.*

Knappman-Frost, Elizabeth. *The ABC-Clio Companion to Women's Progress in America.* Santa Barbara: ABC-Clio, 1994. Covers American women who were notable for their time as well as topics and organizations that have been significant in women's quest for equality. Each article is brief; there are a chronology and a bibliography at the back of the book.

United States Bureau of the Census. *Historical Statistics of the United States, Colonial Times to 1970.* Washington, D.C.: Government Printing Office, 1975. Offers vital statistics, economic figures, and social data for the United States. An index at the back helps locate tables by subject. For statistics since 1970, consult the annual *Statistical Abstract of the United States.*

Primary Resources

There are many routes to finding contemporary material for historical research. You may search your library catalog using the name of a prominent historical figure as an author; you may also find anthologies covering particular themes or periods in history. Consider also the following special materials for your research.

THE PRESS

American Periodical Series, 1741–1900. Ann Arbor: University Microfilms, 1946–1979. Microfilm collection of periodicals from the colonial period to 1900. An index identifies periodicals that focused on particular topics.

Herstory Microfilm Collection. Berkeley: Women's History Research Center, 1973. A microfilm collection of alternative feminist periodicals published between 1960 and 1980. Offers an interesting documentary history of the women's movement.

New York Times. New York: New York Times, 1851–. Many libraries have this newspaper on microfilm going back to its beginning in 1851. An index is available to locate specific dates and pages of news stories; it also provides detailed chronologies of events as they were reported in the news.

Readers' Guide to Periodical Literature. New York: Wilson, 1900–. This index to popular magazines started in 1900; an earlier index, *Poole's Index to Periodical Literature,* covers 1802–1906, though it does not provide such thorough indexing.

DIARIES, PAMPHLETS, BOOKS

The American Culture Series. Ann Arbor: University Microfilms, 1941–1974. A microfilm set, with a useful index, featuring books and pamphlets published between 1493 and 1875.

American Women's Diaries. New Canaan: Readex, 1984–. A collection of reproductions of women's diaries. There are different series for different regions of the country.

The March of America Facsimile Series. Ann Arbor: University Microfilms, 1966. A collection of more than ninety facsimiles of travel accounts to the New World published in English or English translation from the fifteenth through the nineteenth century.

Women in America from Colonial Times to the Twentieth Century. New York: Arno, 1974. A collection of reprints of dozens of books written by women describing women's lives and experiences in their own words.

GOVERNMENT DOCUMENTS

Congressional Record. Washington, D.C.: Government Printing Office, 1874–. Covers daily debates and proceedings of Congress. Earlier series were called *Debates and Proceedings in the Congress of the United States* and *The Congressional Globe.*

Foreign Relations of the United States. Washington, D.C.: Department of State, 1861–. A collection of documents from 1861, including diplomatic papers, correspondence, and memoranda, that provides a documentary record of U.S. foreign policy.

Public Papers of the Presidents. Washington, D.C.: Office of the Federal Register, 1957–. Includes major documents issued by the executive branch from the Hoover administration to the present.

Serial Set. Washington, D.C.: Government Printing Office, 1789–1969. A huge collection of congressional documents, available in many libraries on microfiche, with a useful index.

LOCAL HISTORY COLLECTIONS

State and county historical societies often house a wealth of historical documents; consider their resources when planning your research—you may find yourself working with material that no one else has analyzed before.

Internet Resources

The Internet is a useful place for scholars to communicate and publish information. Electronic discussion lists, electronic journals, and primary texts are among the resources available to historians. The following sources are good places to find historical information. You can also search the Web using any of a number of search engines. However, bear in

INTERNET RESOURCES

mind that there is no board of editors screening Internet sites for accuracy or usefulness. Be critical of all of your sources, particularly those found on the Internet. Note that when this book went to press, the sites listed below were active and maintained.

The American Civil War Homepage. <http://sunsite.utk.edu/civil-war/warweb.html> A comprehensive resource bank on the American Civil War. Maintained by George Hoemann of the University of Tennessee, the site contains letters, documents, photographs, information about battles, links to other sites, and regiment rosters.

American Memory: Historical Collections for the National Digital Library. <http://memory.loc.gov/ammem/index.html> A Web site that features digitized primary source materials from the Library of Congress, among them African American pamphlets, Civil War photographs, documents from the Constitutional Convention of 1774–1790, materials on woman suffrage, and oral histories.

Historical Text Archive. <http://historicaltextarchive.com/> One of the oldest and largest Internet archives of historical documents, articles, photographs, and more. Includes sections on Native American, African American, and U.S. history, in which can be found texts of the Declaration of Independence, the Constitution of Iroquois Nations, World War II surrender documents, and a great deal more.

Index of Native American Resources on the Internet. <http://www.hanksville.org/NAresources> A vast index of Native American resources organized by category. Within the history category, links are organized under subcategories: oral history, written history, geographical areas, timelines, and photographs and photographic archives. A central place to come in the search for information on Native American history.

Internet Resources for Students of Afro-American History and Culture. <http://www.libraries.rutgers.edu/rul/rr_gateway/research_guides/history/afrores.shtml> A good place to begin research on topics in African American history. The site is indexed and linked to a wide variety of sources, including primary documents, text collections, and archival sources on African American history. Individual documents such as slave narratives and petitions, and speeches by W. E. B. Du Bois and Martin Luther King Jr. are categorized by century.

Make History. <http://www.bedfordstmartins.com/makehistory> Comprising the content of five online libraries—Map Central, the Bedford Image Library, DocLinks, HistoryLinks, and PlaceLinks—Make History provides access to relevant digital content including maps, documents, and Web links. Searchable by keyword, topic, date, or specific chapter of *The American Promise.*

NativeWeb. <http://www.nativeweb.org> One of the best organized and most accessible sites available on Native American issues, *NativeWeb* combines an events calendar and message board with history, statistics, a list of news sources, archives, new and updated related sites each week, and documents.

Perry-Castañeda Library Map Collection. <http://www.lib.utexas.edu/maps/> The University of Texas at Austin library has put over seven hundred United States maps on the Web along with hundreds of other maps from around the world. The collection includes both historical and contemporary maps.

Smithsonian Institution. <http://www.si.edu> Organized by subject, such as military history or Hispanic/Latino American resources, this site offers selected links to sites hosted by Smithsonian museums and organizations. Content includes graphics of museum pieces and relevant textual information, book suggestions, maps, and links.

Supreme Court Collection. <http://www.law.cornell.edu/supct/> This database can be used to search for information on various Supreme Court cases. Although the site primarily covers cases that occurred after 1990, there is information on some earlier historic cases. The justices' opinions, as originally written, are also included.

United States Holocaust Memorial Museum. <http://www.ushmm.org> This site contains information about the Holocaust Museum in Washington, D.C., in particular and the Holocaust in general, and it lists links to related sites.

Women's History Resources. <http://www.mcps.k12.md.us/curriculum/socialstd/Women_Bookmarks.html> An extensive listing of women's history sources available on the Internet. The site indexes resources on subjects as diverse as woman suffrage, women in the workplace, and celebrated women writers. Some of the links are to equally vast indexes, providing an overwhelming wealth of information.

WWW-VL History Index. <http://vlib.iue.it/history/> A vast list of more than 1,700 links to sites of interest to historians, arranged by general topic and by continent and country. The United States history page includes links to online research tools as well as links arranged by topic and historical period.

GLOSSARY OF HISTORICAL VOCABULARY

A Note to Students: This list of terms is provided to help you with historical and economic vocabulary. Many of these terms refer to broad, enduring concepts that you may encounter not only in further studies of history but also when following current events. The terms appear in bold at their first use in each chapter. In the glossary, the page numbers of those chapter-by-chapter appearances are provided so you can look up the terms' uses in various periods and contexts. For definitions and discussions of words not included here, consult a dictionary and the book's index, which will point you to topics covered at greater length in the book.

antebellum A term that means "before a war" and commonly refers to the period prior to the Civil War. (pp. 412, 436, 537, 557)

antinomian A person who does not obey societal or religious laws. In colonial Massachusetts, Puritan authorities accused Anne Hutchinson of antinomianism because she believed that Christians could achieve salvation by faith alone. They further asserted, incorrectly, that Hutchinson also held the belief that it was not necessary to follow God's laws as set forth in the Bible. (p. 116)

archaeology A social science devoted to learning about people who lived in the past through the study of physical artifacts created by humans. Most but not all archaeological study focuses on the history of people who lived before the use of the written word. (pp. 3, 527)

Archaic A term applied to various hunting and gathering cultures that descended from Paleo-Indians. The term also refers to the period of time when these cultures dominated ancient America, roughly from 8000 BP to between 2000 and 1000 BP. (p. 11)

artifacts Material remains studied and used by archaeologists and historians to support their interpretations of human history. Examples of artifacts include bones, pots, baskets, jewelry, furniture, tools, clothing, and buildings. (p. 3)

artisan A term commonly used prior to 1900 to describe a skilled craftsman, such as a cabinetmaker. (pp. 56, 124, 141, 220, 273, 422, 440)

Bill of Rights The commonly used term for the first ten amendments to the U.S. Constitution. The Bill of Rights (the last of which was ratified in 1791) guarantees individual liberties and defines limitations to federal power. Many states made the promise of the prompt addition of a bill of rights a precondition for their ratification of the Constitution. (pp. 279, 289)

bloody shirt A refrain used by Republicans in the late nineteenth century to remind the voting public that the Democratic Party, dominated by the South, was largely responsible for the Civil War and that the Republican Party had led the victory to preserve the Union. Republicans urged their constituents to "vote the way you shot." (p. 580)

Calvinism The religious doctrine of which the primary tenet is that salvation is predestined by God. Founded by John Calvin of Geneva during the Protestant Reformation, Calvinism required its adherents to live according to a strict religious and moral code. The Puritans who settled in colonial New England were devout Calvinists. (p. 113) *See also* predestination.

checks and balances A system in which the executive, legislative, and judicial branches of the government curb each other's power. Checks and balances were written into the U.S. Constitution during the Constitutional Convention of 1787. (p. 282)

civil service The administrative service of a government. This term often applies to reforms following the passage of the Pendleton Act in 1883, which set qualifications for U.S. government jobs and sought to remove such jobs from political influence. (p. 581) *See also* spoils system.

colonization The process by which a country or society gains control over another, primarily through settlement. (pp. 40, 69, 108, 381, 528)

Columbian exchange The transatlantic exchange of goods, peoples, and ideas that began when Columbus arrived in the Caribbean in 1492, ending the age-old separation of the hemispheres. (p. 45)

conscription Compulsory military service. Americans were first subject to conscription during the Civil War. The Selective Service Act of 1940 marked the first peace-time use of conscription. (p. 531) *See also* draft.

conservatism A political and moral outlook dating back to Alexander Hamilton's belief in a strong central government resting on a solid banking foundation. Currently associated with the Republican Party, conservatism today places a high premium on military preparedness, free market economics, low taxes, and strong sexual morality. (pp. 501, 529, 563)

covenant An agreement or pact; in American history, this refers to a religious agreement. The Pilgrims used this term in the Mayflower Compact to refer to the agreement among themselves to establish a law-abiding community in which all members would work together for the common good. Later, New England Puritans used this term to refer to the agreement they made with God and each other to live according to God's will as revealed through Scripture. (pp. 104, 141) *See also* Halfway Covenant.

culture A term used here to connote what is commonly called "way of life." It refers not only to how a group of people supplied themselves with food and shelter but also to their family relationships, social groupings, religious ideas, and other features of their lives. (pp. 4, 41, 70, 103, 153, 309, 329, 358, 407, 436, 506, 535)

democracy A system of government in which the people have the power to rule, either directly or indirectly, through their elected representatives. Believing that direct democracy was dangerous, the framers of the Constitution created a government that gave direct voice to the people only in the House of Representatives and that placed a check on that voice in the Senate by offering unlimited six-year terms to senators, elected by the state legislatures to protect them from the whims of democratic majorities. The framers further curbed the perceived dangers of democracy by giving each of the three branches of government (legislative, executive, and judicial) the ability to check the power of the other two. (pp. 220, 255, 288, 340, 366, 466, 478, 515, 570) *See also* checks and balances.

disfranchisement The denial of suffrage to a group or individual through legal or other means. Beginning in 1890, southern progressives preached the disfranchisement of black voters as a "reform" of the electoral system. The most common means of eliminating black voters were poll taxes and literacy tests. (pp. 256, 346, 371, 493, 569)

draft (draftee) A system for selecting individuals for compulsory military service. A draftee is an individual selected through this process. (pp. 225, 529) *See also* conscription.

emancipation The act of freeing from slavery or bondage. The emancipation of American slaves, a goal shared by slaves and abolitionists alike, occurred with the passage of the Thirteenth Amendment in 1865. (pp. 259, 346, 381, 461, 511, 555)

English Reformation *See* Reformation.

Enlightenment An eighteenth-century philosophical movement that emphasized the use of reason to reevaluate previously accepted doctrines and traditions. (p. 162)

evangelicalism The trend in Protestant Christianity stressing salvation through conversion, repentance of sin, adherence to Scripture, and the importance of preaching over ritual. During the Second Great Awakening in the 1830s, evangelicals worshipped at camp meetings and religious revivals led by exuberant preachers. (pp. 358, 424, 458) *See also* Second Great Awakening.

feminism The belief that men and women have the inherent right to equal social, political, and economic opportunities. The suffrage movement and second-wave feminism of the 1960s and 1970s were the most visible

and successful manifestations of feminism, but feminist ideas were expressed in a variety of statements and movements as early as the late eighteenth century and continue to be expressed in the twenty-first. (pp. 292, 572)

franchise The right to vote. The franchise was gradually widened in the United States to include groups such as women and African Americans, who had no vote when the Constitution was ratified. (pp. 427, 572) *See also* suffrage.

free labor Work conducted free from constraint and in accordance with the laborer's personal inclinations and will. Prior to the Civil War, free labor became an ideal championed by Republicans (who were primarily Northerners) to articulate individuals' right to work how and where they wished and to accumulate property in their own name. The ideal of free labor lay at the heart of the North's argument that slavery should not be extended into the western territories. (pp. 384, 402, 440, 477, 556)

free soil The idea advanced in the 1840s that Congress should prohibit slavery within the western territories. "Free soil, free speech, free labor, and free men" became the rallying cry of the short-lived Free-Soil Party. (p. 477)

frontier A borderland area. In U.S. history, this refers to the borderland between the areas primarily inhabited by Europeans or their descendants and the areas solely inhabited by Native Americans. (pp. 40, 83, 117, 140, 176, 222, 333, 357, 407, 476)

gag rule A procedural rule invoked to prohibit discussion or debate on a particular subject in a legislative body. From 1836 to 1844, a series of gag rules prevented the House of Representatives from discussing the large number of antislavery petitions from abolitionist groups that flooded that chamber. (p. 386)

government bonds Promissory notes issued by a government in order to borrow money from members of the public. Such bonds are redeemable at a set future date. Bondholders earn interest on their investments. (p. 236)

Great Awakening The widespread movement of religious revitalization in the 1730s and 1740s that emphasized vital religious faith and personal choice. It was characterized by large, open-air meetings at which emotional sermons were given by itinerant preachers. (p. 162)

guerrilla warfare Fighting carried out by an irregular military force usually organized into small, highly mobile groups. Guerrilla combat was common in the Vietnam War and during the American Revolution. Guerrilla warfare is often effective against opponents who have greater material resources. (pp. 214, 496, 514, 574)

Halfway Covenant A Puritan compromise that allowed the unconverted children of the "visible saints" to become "halfway" members of the church and to baptize their own children even though they were not full members of the church themselves because they had not experienced full conversion. Massachusetts ministers accepted this compromise in 1662, but the compromise remained controversial throughout the seventeenth century. (p. 119)

hard currency (hard money)   Money coined directly from, or backed in full by, precious metals (particularly gold). (pp. 236, 264, 295, 365)

impeachment   The process by which formal charges of wrongdoing are brought against a president, a governor, or a federal judge. (p. 571)

imperialism   The system by which great powers gain control of overseas territories. The United States became an imperialist power by gaining control of Puerto Rico, Guam, the Philippines, and Cuba as a result of the Spanish-American War. (pp. 489, 582)

indentured servitude   A system that committed poor immigrants to four to seven years of labor in exchange for passage to the colonies and food and shelter after they arrived. An indenture is a type of contract. (pp. 70, 139)

Jim Crow   The system of racial segregation that developed in the post–Civil War South and extended well into the twentieth century; it replaced slavery as the chief instrument of white supremacy. Jim Crow laws segregated African Americans in public facilities such as trains and streetcars and denied them basic civil rights, including the right to vote. It was also at this time that the doctrine of "separate but equal" became institutionalized. (p. 578)

land grant   A gift of land from a government, usually intended to encourage settlement or development. The British government issued several land grants to encourage development in the American colonies. In the mid-nineteenth century, the U.S. government issued land grants to encourage railroad development and, through the passage of the Land-Grant College Act (also known as the Morrill Act) in 1862, set aside public land to support universities. (pp. 71, 120, 177, 223, 399, 489)

liberty   The condition of being free or enjoying freedom from control. This term also refers to the possession of certain social, political, or economic rights, such as the right to own and control property. Eighteenth-century American colonists invoked the principle to argue for strict limitations on government's ability to tax its subjects. (pp. 104, 176, 220, 255, 291, 327, 358, 428, 439, 492, 515, 561)

manifest destiny   A term coined by journalist John O'Sullivan in 1845 to express the popular nineteenth-century belief that the United States was destined to expand westward to the Pacific Ocean and had an irrefutable right and God-given responsibility to do so. This idea provided an ideological shield for westward expansion and masked the economic and political motivations of many of those who championed it. (pp. 408, 486)

mercantilism   A set of policies that regulated colonial commerce and manufacturing for the enrichment of the mother country. Mercantilist policies ensured that the American colonies in the mid-seventeenth century produced agricultural goods and raw materials to be shipped to Britain, where they would increase wealth in the mother country through reexportation or manufacture into finished goods that would then be sold to the colonies and elsewhere. (p. 90)

Middle Passage   The crossing of the Atlantic (as a slave destined for auction) in the hold of a slave ship in the eighteenth and nineteenth centuries. Conditions were unimaginably bad, and many slaves died during these voyages. (p. 153)

miscegenation   The sexual mixing of races. In slave states, despite the social stigma and legal restrictions on interracial sex, masters' almost unlimited power over their female slaves meant that liaisons inevitably occurred. Many states maintained laws against miscegenation into the 1950s. (p. 440)

monopoly   Exclusive control and domination by a single business entity over an entire industry through ownership, command of supply, or other means. Gilded Age businesses monopolized their industries quite profitably, often organizing holding companies and trusts to do so. (pp. 37, 360, 586)

Monroe Doctrine   President James Monroe's 1823 declaration that the Western Hemisphere was closed to any further colonization or interference by European powers. In exchange, Monroe pledged that the United States would not become involved in European struggles. Although Monroe could not back his policy with action, it was an important formulation of national goals. (p. 349)

nationalism   A strong feeling of devotion and loyalty toward one nation over others. Nationalism encourages the promotion of the nation's common culture, language, and customs. (pp. 337, 415, 535)

nativism   Bias against immigrants and in favor of native-born inhabitants. American nativists especially favor persons who come from white, Anglo-Saxon, Protestant lines over those from other racial, ethnic, and religious heritages. Nativists may include former immigrants who view new immigrants as incapable of assimilation. Many nativists, such as members of the Know-Nothing Party in the nineteenth century and the Ku Klux Klan through the contemporary period, voice anti-immigrant, anti-Catholic, and anti-Semitic sentiments. (p. 490)

New South   A vision of the South, promoted after the Civil War by Henry Grady, editor of the *Atlanta Constitution*, that urged the South to abandon its dependence on agriculture and use its cheap labor and natural resources to compete with northern industry. Many Southerners migrated from farms to cities in the late nineteenth century, and Northerners and foreigners invested a significant amount of capital in railroads, cotton and textiles, mining, lumber, iron, steel, and tobacco in the region. (p. 555)

nullification   The idea that states can disregard federal laws when those laws represent an overstepping of congressional powers. The controversial idea was first proposed by opponents of the Alien and Sedition Acts of 1798 and later by South Carolina politicians in 1828 as a response to the Tariff of Abominations. (pp. 312, 328, 373, 479)

paternalism   The idea that slavery was a set of reciprocal obligations between masters and slaves, with slaves providing labor and obedience and masters providing basic care and direction. The concept of paternalism denied that the slave system was brutal and exploitative. Although paternalism did provide some protection against the worst brutality, it did not guarantee decent living conditions, reasonable work, or freedom from physical punishment. (p. 449)

planters   Owners of large farms (or, more specifically, plantations) that were worked by twenty or more slaves. By 1860, planters had accrued a great deal of local, statewide, and national political power in the South despite the fact that they represented a minority of the white electorate. Planters' dominance of southern politics demonstrated both the power of tradition and stability among southern voters and the planters' success at convincing white voters that the slave system benefited all whites, even those without slaves. (pp. 77, 127, 153, 186, 215, 308, 334, 381, 443, 479, 516, 557)

popular sovereignty   The idea that government is subject to the will of the people. Before the Civil War, this was the idea that the residents of a territory should determine, through their legislatures, whether to allow slavery. (pp. 345, 478)

predestination   The idea that individual salvation or damnation is determined by God at, or just prior to, a person's birth. The concept of predestination invalidated the idea that salvation could be obtained through either faith or good works. (p. 113) *See also* Calvinism.

Protestantism   A powerful Christian reform movement that began in the sixteenth century with Martin Luther's critiques of the Roman Catholic Church. Over the centuries, Protestantism has taken many different forms, branching into numerous denominations with differing systems of worship. (pp. 62, 86, 106, 140, 200, 280, 340, 376, 407, 436, 490)

Protestant Reformation   *See* Reformation.

Puritanism   The ideas and religious principles held by dissenters from the Church of England, including the belief that the church needed to be purified by eliminating the elements of Catholicism from its practices. (pp. 87, 104, 140)

Reformation   The reform movement that began in 1517 with Martin Luther's critiques of the Roman Catholic Church, which led to the formation of Protestant Christian groups. The English Reformation began with Henry VIII's break with the Roman Catholic Church, which established the Protestant Church of England. Henry VIII's decision was politically motivated; he had no particular quarrel with Catholic theology and remained an orthodox Catholic in most matters of religious practice. (pp. 62, 105)

republicanism   The belief that the unworkable model of European-style monarchy should be replaced with a form of government in which supreme power resides in the hands of citizens with the right to vote and is exercised by a representative government answerable to this electorate. In Revolutionary-era America, republicanism became a social philosophy that embodied a sense of community and called individuals to act for the public good. (pp. 220, 252, 289, 323, 468)

Second Great Awakening   A popular religious revival that preached that salvation was available to anybody who chose to take it. The revival peaked in the 1830s, and its focus on social perfection inspired many of the reform movements of the Jacksonian era. (p. 375) *See also* evangelicalism.

separate spheres   A concept of gender relations that developed in the Jacksonian era and continued well into the twentieth century, holding that women's proper place was in the world of hearth and home (the private sphere) and men's was in the world of commerce and politics (the public sphere). The doctrine of separate spheres eroded slowly over the nineteenth and twentieth centuries as women became more and more involved in public activities. (p. 376)

spoils system   An arrangement in which party leaders reward party loyalists with government jobs. This slang term for *patronage* comes from the saying "To the victor go the spoils." Widespread government corruption during the Gilded Age spurred reformers to curb the spoils system through the passage of the Pendleton Act in 1883, which created the Civil Service Commission to award government jobs on the basis of merit. (p. 369) *See also* civil service.

state sovereignty   A state's autonomy or freedom from external control. The federal system adopted at the Constitutional Convention in 1787 struck a balance between state sovereignty and national control by creating a strong central government while leaving the states intact as political entities. The states remained in possession of many important powers on which the federal government cannot intrude. (p. 517)

states' rights   A strict interpretation of the Constitution that holds that federal power over the states is limited and that the states hold ultimate sovereignty. First expressed in 1798 through the passage of the Virginia and Kentucky Resolutions, which were based on the assumption that the states have the right to judge the constitutionality of federal laws, the states' rights philosophy became a cornerstone of the South's resistance to federal control of slavery. (pp. 274, 349, 373, 531, 562)

suffrage The right to vote. The term *suffrage* is most often associated with the efforts of American women to secure voting rights. (pp. 257, 376, 426, 468, 556) *See also* franchise.

temperance movement The reform movement to end drunkenness by urging people to abstain from the consumption of alcohol. Begun in the 1820s, this movement achieved its greatest political victory with the passage of a constitutional amendment in 1919 that prohibited the manufacture, sale, and transportation of alcohol. That amendment was repealed in 1933. (pp. 381, 424)

virtual representation The notion, propounded by the British Parliament in the eighteenth century, that the House of Commons represented all British subjects—wherever they lived and regardless of whether they had directly voted for their representatives. Prime Minister George Grenville used this idea to argue that the Stamp Act and other parliamentary taxes on British colonists did not constitute taxation without representation. The American colonists rejected this argument, insisting that political representatives derived authority only from explicit citizens' consent (indicated by elections), and that members of a distant government body were incapable of adequately representing their interests. (p. 187)

War Hawks Young Republicans elected to the U.S. Congress in the fall of 1810 who were eager for war with Britain in order to legitimize attacks on Indians, end impressment, and avenge foreign insults. (p. 334)

yeoman A farmer who owned a small plot of land that was sufficient to support a family and was tilled by family members and perhaps a few servants. (pp. 87, 156, 375, 463, 530, 573)

Spot Artifact Credits

p. 4 (Anasazi effigy) Jerry Jacka Photography; p. 21 (mica hand) Ohio Historical Society; p. 25 (dolls) Photo courtesy of the Oakland Museum, California; p. 40 (caravel) National Maritime Museum, London; p. 46 (knife) Photo by Michel Zabe/Banco Mexicano de Imágenes; p. 49 (toucan) Werner Forman/Art Resource, NY; p. 55 (crucifix) Courtesy of the Historical Archaeology Collections of the Florida Museum of Natural History; p. 74 (pot) Valentine Museum, Cook Collection; p. 87 (pipe) Niemeyer Nederlands Tabacologisch Musuem; p. 114 (die) Courtesy of Association for the Preservation of Virginia Antiquities; p. 118 (cradle) Wadsworth Atheneum, Hartford, Wallace Nutting Collection, Gift of J. Pierpont Morgan; p. 117 (barrel) Peabody Essex Museum, Salem, MA; p. 128 (bayonet) Pocumtuck Valley Memorial Association, Memorial Hall Museum; p. 141 (pitcher) Pocumtuck Valley Memorial Association, Memorial Hall Museum, Deerfield, MA; p. 150 (*Poor Richard's Almanack*) Courtesy, American Antiquarian Society; p. 156 (slave's doll) The Stagville Center, Division of Archives and History, North Carolina Department of Cultural Resources; p. 158 (mirror) Concord Museum; p. 187 (stamps) Courtesy of the Trustees of the British Library; p. 205 (pistols) Concord Museum; p. 205 (musket) Concord Museum; p. 218 (drum) Massachusetts Historical Society; p. 225 (red coat) Nichipor Collection/Picture Research Consultants & Archives; p. 236 (currency) Smithsonian Institution, Washington, D.C., Photo by Douglas Mudd; p. 237 (Howitzer) West Point Museum, United States Military Academy, West Point, N.Y.; p. 263 (penny note) Library of Congress; p. 275 (inkwell) Independence National Historic Park; p. 294 (cotton bales) Picture Research Consultants & Archives; p. 298 (coin) The American Numismatic Association; p. 305 (kettle) Ohio Historical Society;

p. 306 (shoes) Joël Garnier/Musée International de la Chaussure, Romans sur Isère, France; p. 329 (compass) Smithsonian Institution, Washington, D.C.; p. 336 (sword) National Museum of American History, Smithsonian Institution, Behring Center; p. 341 (McCoy's sampler) Chicago Historical Society; p. 351 (telescope) Thomas Jefferson Memorial Foundation, Inc.; p. 369 (spittoon) Courtesy, The Henry Francis du Pont Winterthur Museum; p. 375 (bank note) Miriam and Ira D. Wallach Division of Art, Prints and Photographs, The New York Public Library, Astor, Lenox and Tilden Foundations; p. 384 (printing press) Chicago Historical Society; p. 390 (miniature log cabin) National Museum of American History, Smithsonian Institution, Behring Center; p. 397 (plow) Courtesy Deere & Company; p. 399 (watch) Smithsonian Institution, Washington, D.C.; p. 410 (cooking pot) Oakland Museum of California; p. 414 (flag) The Center for American History, The University of Texas at Austin; p. 449 (shoes) Valentine Museum, Cook Collection; p. 457 (whip) Louisiana State Museum; p. 466 (fiddle) National Museum of American History, Smithsonian Institution, Washington, D.C.; p. 479 (ticket) Courtesy of the American Antiquarian Society; p. 485 (shackles) Private Collection; p. 496 (cane) Collection of McKissick Museum, University of South Carolina; p. 503 (revolver) Ohio Historical Society; p. 515 (flag) Smithsonian Institution, National Museum of American History, Behring Center; p. 518 (Confederate jacket) Smithsonian Institution, National Museum of American History, Behring Center; p. 523 (Union jacket) Smithsonian Institution, National Museum of American History, Behring Center; p. 537 (potholder) Chicago Historical Society; p. 560 (Bible) Anacostia Museum, Smithsonian Institution, Washington, D.C.; p. 571 (ticket) Collection of Janice L. and David J. Frent; p. 579 (plow) Courtesy Deere & Company; p. 580 (election artifact) Collection of Janice L. and David J. Frent.

A note about the index:

Names of individuals appear in boldface; biographical dates are included for major historical figures.

Letters in parentheses following pages refer to:

(i)   illustrations, including photographs and artifacts, as well as information in picture captions
(f)   figures, including charts and graphs
(m)   maps
(b)   boxed features (such as "Historical Question")
(t)   tables

Abenaki tribe, 22
Abolition of slavery
 American ideal and, 426–430, 427(i)
 leaders of movement for, 426, 427
 legal changes leading to, 259–262
 long-term results of, 548
 movement for, 381–385, 384(i)
 sending freed slaves to Liberia, 381,
  427, 428–429(b), 429(i)
 Thirteenth Amendment on, 562, 571(t),
  587
 transatlantic, 382–383(b)
 women in movement for, 383(b),
  384–385, 384(i), 427(i), 483, 493, 501
Academies, female, 341, 352, 379, 395,
  466
Acoma pueblo, 20, 61
Act of Supremacy (England), 105
AD, 6
Adams, Abigail (1744–1818), 229(i)
 on Alexander Hamilton, 288
 correspondence with husband, 215, 220
 influence on husband, 220–221, 229,
  229(i)
 interest in politics, 229, 326
 on sedition, 314(b)
 on women's rights, 256–257, 292(b)
Adams, Charles Francis, 479
Adams, Christopher, 86
Adams, John (1735–1826)
 appointments of, 327
 on Boston Tea Party, 198
 on breaking away from Britain, 215
 character and temperament of, 310,
  312(i)
 on City Tavern, 272(i)
 as diplomat, 231(b)
 in election of 1796, 310–311
 in First Continental Congress, 201
 as first vice president, 289, 290
 foreign policy of, 312–316
 on French Revolution, 307
 Hamilton and, 288, 310, 312, 313
 on higher education for women, 342(b)
 on importance of belonging to a fire
  club, 190(b)
 influence of wife on, 220–221, 229, 229(i)
 Jefferson and, 311
 loss of support for, 316
 presidency of, 310–316
 in Second Continental Congress, 215,
  222
 on voting rights, 257–258

 on wealthy merchants, 142
 XYZ affair and, 311–312
Adams, John Quincy (1767–1848), 350(i)
 character and temperament of, 349, 367
 in election of 1824, 345, 349, 350–351,
  350(i), 351(m), 357
 in election of 1828, 367–368, 368(i)
 presidency of, 351, 373
 as secretary of state, 348, 349
 tariff policy of, 373
Adams, Louisa Catherine, 349, 351
Adams, Samuel (1722–1803)
 on citizen disobedience, 270
 in First Continental Congress, 201
 orders to arrest, 191(b), 205(m)
 in resistance to British laws, 188, 189,
  194, 196, 197, 208
 in running of confederation
  government, 255
 in Second Continental Congress, 215
Adams-Onís Treaty (1819), 348
Adena culture, 21
Advice to American Women (Graves), 376
Advocate of Moral Reform (newspaper),
  381
Africa
 colonization of emancipated slaves
  in, 381
 cultures in, 153
 evolution in, 6
 exploration of, 39–40, 40(i)
 languages in, 153
 religion in, 162
 slave trade in, 137–138, 138(i)
African(s). *See also* Slavery
 European attitudes toward, 88–89(b),
  89(i), 90(i), 147
 musicians, 97(i), 156, 459(i)
 "New Negroes," 154–155, 156
 population of, 140(m), 142, 147,
  151–152, 437, 439(f), 461
 religion of, 97(i), 138
 in Spain, 40(i)
African Americans (blacks). *See also* Free
  blacks; Freedmen; Slavery
 in abolitionist movement, 426–430, 427(i)
 in American Revolution, 224–225
 black codes and, 562–564, 563(i)
 civil rights of, 554(i), 564–565
 in Civil War, 511–512, 512(i), 529–530,
  530(i), 531, 531(i), 532–533(b),
  533(i), 548
 in colonies, 97–98, 147–148, 196

 colonists' attitude toward, 147–148
 in Congress, 553, 576
 as cowboys, 3, 4(i)
 discrimination against, 402, 427, 530(i),
  562, 582
 education of, 340, 404(f), 427, 430, 462,
  557, 574(b), 577, 577(i), 579
 effect of Civil War on, 512, 535, 548
 effect of *Dred Scott* decision on, 498(t)
 effect of slavery on, 469–470
 emancipated, 260, 261(b), 381, 461,
  528–529, 555
 equality for, 554, 565, 568, 578, 582
 families of, 155, 156, 442(i), 457–458,
  462, 557, 558(b), 560(i)
 as free labor, 556–557
 intimidation of, 583(i), 584–585
 landownership and, 556(i), 557, 562,
  578–579
 leadership of, 427
 in Liberia, 381, 427, 428–429(b), 429(i)
 natural rights of, 499–500, 564–565
 in navy, 511–512, 512(i)
 "New Negroes," 154–155, 156
 pottery made by, 434(i)
 prejudice against, 427, 430, 532(b), 582,
  584
 quest for autonomy, 557–560, 560(i)
 during Reconstruction, 553–554,
  556–560, 560(i)
 religion of, 162, 435, 458–459, 462, 553,
  560, 561(i)
 as sharecroppers, 579, 586
 as slaveowners, 462
 voting rights of, 257, 258–259, 258(i),
  346, 427, 553, 554, 554(i), 556, 562,
  565, 569, 571–573, 583(i)
 women, 95, 97, 139, 153, 207, 207(i),
  261(i), 426, 430, 482, 573, 578(i), 579
Agawam Indians, 115
Agricultural settlements, 17–22, 18(i),
  18(m), 19(i), 20(i), 20(m)
Agriculture. *See also* Crop(s);
  Plantation(s)
 among ancient peoples, 17–20, 18(i), 19
 in California, 477(i)
 during Civil War, 537
 decline of, after Civil War, 548
 Department of, 537
 in early U.S., 294
 in England, 79(i)
 land policy and, 397–398, 398(i)
 in middle colonies, 147–151, 148(i), 149(i)

Agriculture (continued)
  of Native Americans, 17–20, 18(i), 19,
    22, 23, 24, 25, 75
  in New England colonies, 117, 141
  in Northwest Territory, 268(i)
  in Pennsylvania, 147–151, 148(i), 149(i)
  price of farmland, 148–149
  productivity of, 397
  sharecropping in, 579, 586
  tax-in-kind on, 534
  technological improvements and, 397
  in Virginia, 71(i), 73, 75, 77–78,
    80–81(b), 82(i), 86, 87–88, 465(i)
  yeomen farmers in. See Yeomen
    farmers
Air pollution, from steamboats, 361
Alabama
  African American voters in, 572–573
  during Reconstruction, 572–573,
    574–575(b), 585
  secession of, 505
Alabama (Confederate cruiser), 524
Alamo, 414
Alaska, 416, 582
Albany, New York, 130(b), 179, 237, 360,
  361
Albany Plan of Union, 175, 179
Albuquerque, New Mexico, 61
Alcohol, 305, 321, 380–381, 424
Alden, Emily Lucinda, 365(i)
Aleut language, 15(b)
Algiers, 330–331
Algonquian tribes, 22–23, 63(i), 68(i),
  69–75, 91, 178(m)
Alien and Sedition Acts (1798), 312, 373
Almy, Benjamin and Mary Gould,
  234(b)
Amalgamation (miscegenation), 440,
  442(i), 450, 455
Amendments to Constitution
  in Bill of Rights, 289, 290–291
  Fifteenth (ratified 1870), 571–572,
    571(t), 582, 587
  First, 371
  Fourteenth (ratified 1868), 565, 568,
    569, 571(t), 576, 582, 587
  Seventeenth, 501
  Thirteenth (ratified 1865), 562, 571(t),
    587
  Twelfth, 310, 323, 350
  Twentieth, 505
American Colonization Society, 381, 427,
  428(b)
American Equal Rights Association, 565
American ideal, 426–430, 427(i)
American Indians. See Native Americans
  (Indians)
American (Know-Nothing) Party, 490,
  490(t), 492, 492(i), 493
American Philosophical Society, 162
American Red Cross, 538
American Revolution (1775–1781),
  213–247
  British surrender at Yorktown,
    243–244, 244(i), 244(m)
  currency during, 218, 236
  divisions in families during,
    234–235(b)
  draftees in, 225
  early battles of, 204–206, 205(m), 215,
    218, 218(m), 219(i), 223
  financial instability and corruption
    during, 236

first year of (1775–1776), 222–236
  height of men in, 224(f)
  home front during, 228–236
  mercenaries in, 221, 223(i), 227, 227(i),
    228, 237
  Native Americans during, 214, 235(b),
    236–237, 239–240, 240(m), 246
  in North, 226(m), 236–238, 238(m)
  prisoners of war during, 230–231(b),
    231(i)
  slaves during, 206–207, 206(i), 208, 214,
    224–225, 244(i)
  Southern strategy in, 241–243, 242(m)
  traitors during, 233, 236, 242
  war debt from, 262–264, 287–288,
    295–296, 298, 300(b)
  in West, 239, 240(m)
American River, 421
American system, 349, 399
American Temperance Society,
  380–381
American Temperance Union, 381
Amerind language, 15(b)
Ames, Adelbert, 585
Amherst, Jeffery (1717–1797), 184(b),
  185(b)
Amherst College, 379
Amish, 146
Ampère, André, 402(b)
Anasazi culture, 18(m), 19–20, 24
Ancient America, 3–30
  agricultural settlements and chiefdoms
    in, 17–22, 18(i), 18(m), 19(i), 20(i),
    20(m)
  archaeology and history, 4–5
  Archaic hunters and gatherers in,
    11–17, 12(m), 13(i), 14–15(b), 15(i),
    16(i), 16(m)
  first Americans in, 5–10, 7(f), 8–9(b),
    14–15(b), 15(i)
  mound builders in, 20–22, 20(m)
  Paleo-Indian hunters in, 10–11, 10(i),
    11(i), 14(b)
  sports and games in, 19(i)
Anderson, "Bloody Bill," 522
Anderson, Robert, 510(i), 513–514
Andersonville Prison, 545(i)
Andros, Edmund (1637–1714), 128
Anglicans (Church of England), 86, 103,
  105, 108, 109, 114, 116, 124, 157,
  162, 234(b), 382(b)
Angola, 155
Animals, extinction of, 10–11, 12, 13. See
  also Livestock; names of specific
  animals
Annapolis, Maryland, 255, 271, 300(b)
Antebellum, 412, 436, 537
Anthony, Susan B. (1820–1906), 493,
  495(b), 565, 568(i), 572
Antietam, Battle of (1862), 519(m), 521,
  521(i), 523(t)
Antifederalists, 276, 277–278, 282
Antinomians, 116
Antislavery movement. See Abolition of
  slavery
Apache tribe, 24, 25, 412
Appeal . . . to the Coloured Citizens of the
  World, An (Walker), 381, 435
Appomattox (Virginia) Court House,
  surrender at (1865), 539(t), 546
Apprenticeship laws, 562–563
Arapaho tribe, 409
Arbella (Pilgrim ship), 108

Archaeology
  defined, 3
  history and, 4–5, 527(b)
Archaic hunters and gatherers, 11–17,
  12(m), 13(i), 15(i), 16(i), 16(m)
Arctic, Native American population in,
  23(m)
Arizona
  ancient cultures in, 18–19, 20
  Native Americans in, 486(i)
Arizona Colonization Company, 488(b)
Arkansas
  during Reconstruction, 585
  secession of, 514, 514(m)
Armies, private, 488–489(b), 489(i)
Arminianism, 116
Arms, right to bear, 290
Army of Northern Virginia, 520. See also
  Civil War; Confederacy
  (Confederate States of America)
Army of the Potomac, 519(m), 520–521,
  540–541. See also Civil War; Union
Arnold, Benedict (1741–1801), 225, 227,
  237, 242, 244
Articles of Confederation, 252–255. See
  also Confederation government
  acceptance of, 253–255
  defining the union, 253
  on diplomacy, 264
  on taxes, 253, 263, 264
  writing of Constitution and, 271, 273
Artifacts
  of ancient Native Americans, 2(i), 3–4,
    4(i), 11(i), 15(i)
  of Spanish conquest, 48(i)
Artificial limbs, 566–567(b), 567(i)
Artisans, 273. See also Crafts
  colonial, 56, 141, 220
  mestizo, 60
  on plantations, 448
  slaves as, 456–457, 457(i)
  Spanish, 56
  in West, 422
Ashley, Hannah and John, 260(b)
Asia
  Columbus's search for, 41, 41(m)
  immigrants from, 422–424, 423(i)
  literacy rates in, 404(f)
  Native American genetics and, 15(b)
Assimilation, 371
Assumption, 296, 298, 300(b)
Astrolabe, 38
Atahualpa (Incan emperor), 49
Atchison, David Rice, 496
Athapascan tribes, 25
Atlanta, Georgia, fall of (1864), 539(t),
  541(m), 544, 545
Atlantic Ocean
  sailor's life on, 144–145(b)
  slave trade on, 152(m). See also Slave
    trade
  trade on, 143(m). See also Trade and
    trading
Atlantic theater, of Civil War, 523–524
Attucks, Crispus (c. 1723–1770), 196
Augusta, Georgia, 241
Austin, Stephen F., 413
Avilés, Pedro Menéndez de (1519–1574),
  61
Ayllón, Lucas Vásquez de, 49
Aztec (Mexica) culture, 28–30, 28(i), 29(i),
  46–48, 50–51(b), 51(i), 53(i), 59(b),
  59(i), 63

Bache, Benjamin, 314(b)
Bacon, Nathaniel (1647–1676), 91, 92
Bacon's Laws (1676), 92
Bacon's Rebellion (1676), 87, 90–92, 97
Baker, Isaac Wallace, 423(i)
Baker, Samuel, 202(b)
Balboa, Vasco Núñez de (1475–1517), 44
Baltimore, Lord (c. 1580–1642), 87, 128
Baltimore, Maryland, 255, 300(b), 336
Baltimore and Ohio Railroad, 361
Bancroft, Hubert Howe, 423(b)
Bank(s) and banking
    during Civil War, 537
    in early U.S., 295, 298
    economy and, 365, 366, 375, 386–387
    Jackson's policy on, 356(i), 369,
        373–375, 374(i)
    law on, 537
    state-chartered, 365
Banknotes, 264, 365, 375
Bank of North America, 264
Bank of the United States
    first, 298, 365
    second, 365, 366, 369, 373–375, 390
Bankruptcy Act (1841), 389(b)
Baptists, 146(i), 162, 340, 379, 428(b), 458,
    466, 561(i)
*Baptizing on the South Branch of the
    Potomac near Franklin, Virginia*
    (painting), 467(i)
Barbados, 94–95, 95(m), 96, 97–98, 153
Barbary Wars (1801–1805), 330–331
Barley, Dave, 452(b)
Barnard, George N., 458
Barrow, Bennet H., 452–453(b)
Barton, Clara, 543(b)
Basket making, 11, 25, 41(i), 75
Battle(s). *See* War(s); *names of specific
    battles*
Battle of Savage's Station (painting),
    520(i)
Bayonet(s), 223(i)
"Bayonet rule," 583, 585
Bearden, Romare, 502(i)
Bear Flag Revolt (1846), 414
Beaufort, South Carolina, 556(i)
Beauregard, P. G. T., 527(b)
Beecher, Catharine, 341
Beecher, Lyman, 380
Beissel, Johann Conrad, 146(i)
Bell, John, 503, 504
Beloved (Morrison), 484(i)
Benton, Thomas Hart (1889–1975), 408,
    493
Beringia, 7, 7(m), 8, 11, 14(b)
Berkeley, William (1606–1677), 90, 90(i),
    91–92
Bernard, Francis (1712–1799), 188, 189,
    194, 196
Bethlehem, Pennsylvania, 149(i)
Bett, Mum (Elizabeth Freeman), 259,
    260–261(b), 261(i)
Bibb, Henry, 426
Bible, 113, 114, 116
Biddle, Nicholas (1786–1844), 374(i)
Bierstadt, Albert (1830–1902), 408(i)
Bight of Biafra, 155
Bill of Rights (federal), 289, 290–291
Bills of rights (state), 256, 258
Birney, James G., 415
Bishop, Bridget, 122(b)
Bishop Hill, Illinois, 398(i)
Bison, 4, 9, 12–13, 13(i), 24

Black(s), 88–89(b). *See also* African
    Americans (blacks); Free blacks;
    Freedmen
Black codes, 562–564, 563(i)
Black Death (bubonic plague), 37
Blackfoot tribe, 24, 24(m)
Black Hawk (Sauk and Fox Indian
    leader), 371, 410(i)
Black Hawk War (1832), 371, 517
Black markets, during American
    Revolution, 236
Blair, Francis P., 583(i)
Blasphemy laws, 280(b)
"Bleeding Kansas" (1850s), 496–497,
    496(i), 497(i), 506
"Bleeding Sumner," 497
Blockades, 511, 516, 523–524, 526–527(b),
    531
"Bloody shirt, waving the," 580, 585
Blue Jacket (Native American leader),
    304, 305
"Bluestocking," 342(b), 344
Boarding schools, 344(i)
Boats and ships
    caravels, 40, 41
    "coffin ships," 407
    dangers to, 61, 322, 323, 331
    French privateers, 311, 320(i), 330
    frigates, 320(i), 330–331, 356(i), 523
    ironclad warships, 523
    Pilgrim, 107
    prisoner ships, 230(b), 231(i)
    of Royal Navy, 197–198
    slave ships, 137, 153–154, 154(i),
        382(b), 383(i)
    Spanish Armada, 71
    steamboats, 359(m), 360–361,
        362–363(b), 363(i), 448(i)
    submarines, 524, 526–527(b), 527(i)
    warships, 164(f), 311, 330–331
Boleyn, Anne, 106
Bonaparte, Napoleon, 288, 323, 328
Bonds, government, 236
Book of Mormon, The, 411
Booms, economic, 365–366, 374–375,
    388(b), 537
Boonesborough, Kentucky, 239
Booth, John Wilkes, 547, 561
Boré, Étienne de, 443
Boston, Massachusetts
    economy in, 141, 142
    fire clubs in, 190(b), 191(i)
    military rule in, 196–197
    resistance to British laws in, 188–189,
        189(i), 190–191(b), 192, 193–197,
        197(i)
Boston Common, 141(i)
Boston Gazette, 160(b)
Boston Massacre (1770), 196–197, 197(i)
Boston News-Letter, 160(b)
Boston Port Act (1774), 199
Boston Tea Party, 198, 199(i)
Boudry, Nancy, 456
Bouquet, Henry, 185(i)
Bowdoin, James, 270, 271
Bowen, Ashley, 144–145(b), 145(i)
Bowie, James, 414
Bowl, silver, 270(i)
Bows and arrows, 13, 21, 25, 49(i), 73
Boycotts, 194, 196, 197, 198, 292(b)
Boyd, Maria Isabella ("Belle"), 535(i)
BP (years before the present), 6
Brackenridge, H. H., 308

Braddock, Edward (1695–1755), 180, 181,
    182
Bradford, William (1590–1657), 103, 107
Brady, Mathew (1823–1896), 480, 480(i),
    482–483(b), 483(i), 503(i), 521(i),
    546(i)
Branch, Jacob, 456
Brant, Joseph (Thayendanegea;
    1742–1807), 232, 233(i), 237, 239,
    246, 265, 333(i)
Brazil, 52, 94(i)
Brazos River, 413
Bread riots, 534
Breckinridge, John C. (1821–1875), 503,
    504
Bridge tolls (1796), 296(i)
Britain. *See* Great Britain
British West Indies, 308, 382(b)
Brook Farm (West Roxbury,
    Massachusetts), 424
Brooks, Preston, 496, 497
Brown, Charles Brockden, 293(i)
Brown, John (1800–1859), 476(i)
    aftermath of raid, 501–502, 502(i), 503,
        506
    death of, 501, 502(i)
    pikes of, 474(i)
    in raid on Harpers Ferry, 475–476,
        476(i), 501–502, 502(i), 503, 506
Brown, Joseph E., 531, 534
Brown, Samuel, 202(b)
Brown, William Wells, 427
Bubonic plague, 37
Buchanan, James (1791–1868), 493, 500,
    505
Bucktails, 367
Buena Vista, Mexico, 418, 419
Buffalo, New York, 388–389(b)
Buffalo hunting, 409, 410
Bull Run (Manassas)
    First Battle of (1861), 519–520, 519(m),
        523(t)
    Second Battle of (1862), 519(m), 521,
        523(t)
Bunker Hill, Battle of (1775), 218, 218(m),
    219(i), 223, 228
Bureau of Internal Revenue, 537
Bureau of Refugees, Freedmen, and
    Abandoned Lands, 557
Burgoyne, John (1722–1792), 218,
    236–238, 238(i)
Burial mounds, 20–22, 20(m), 25
Burnett, Peter W., 423(b)
Burns, Anthony, 483
Burnside, Ambrose (1824–1881), 521
Burr, Aaron (1756–1836), 252(i), 324(i)
    duel with Alexander Hamilton, 323,
        324–325(b)
    in election of 1796, 310
    in election of 1800, 323
    as vice president, 323, 324–325(b)
    on *A Vindication of the Rights of Woman,*
        292(b)
Busts, economic, 359, 366, 385, 386–390,
    387(i), 500
Bute, Earl of, 182, 186
Butler, Andrew P., 496
Butler, Benjamin F., 528
Butler, Pierce, 444(b)
Byles, Mather, 233

Cabot, John (1450–1498), 42–43
Cabral, Pedro Alvars, 43–44

Cabrillo, Juan Rodríguez, 49
Cadillac (French military leader), 268(i)
Cady, Elizabeth. *See* Stanton, Elizabeth Cady
Cahokia, 2(i), 21–22, 21(i)
Caldwell, John, 180(i)
Calhoun, John C. (1782–1850), 480(i)
    on annexation of Texas, 415
    in election of 1824, 349, 350
    in election of 1836, 386
    on Mexican-American War, 476
    as secretary of state, 415
    as secretary of war, 349
    on slavery, 415, 440(b), 478, 480, 498
    tariff of 1828 and, 369, 373
    as vice president, 350, 368, 385
    as War Hawk, 334
California
    acquisition of, 420, 420(m)
    agriculture in, 477(i)
    ancient animals in, 9(i)
    Archaic cultures in, 13, 16, 16(i), 16(m), 22
    Bear Flag Revolt (1846) in, 414
    Chinese immigrants in, 422–424, 423(i)
    gold rush (1849–1852) in, 394(i), 420–421, 422–423(b), 476, 522
    Mexican migration to, 414
    missionaries report on missions in, 168–169(b)
    Native Americans in, 23(f), 25, 168–169(b), 414, 423(b)
    settlement of, 166(f), 166(i), 414
    Spanish explorers in, 49
    statehood for, 479, 481
California Trail, 414
Calusa Indians, 49
Calvin, John (1509–1564), 113
Calvinism, 113
Cambridge (naval ship), 511
Cambridge University, 103
Camden (South Carolina), Battle of (1780), 241, 242(m)
Camels, origin of, 8–9
Campaign posters (1828), 368(i)
Camp chest, 219(i)
Camp followers, 223–224
Canada
    American Revolution in, 225, 226(m), 227, 236
    black loyalists in, 262(i)
    boundary with U.S., 363
    exploration of, 64
    French colonies in, 130–131(b), 131(i)
    Native Americans in, 130–131(b)
    plan to invade, 335
    in Seven Years' War, 176–177
    U.S. border with, 265
Canal(s), 359(m), 360(i), 361, 379, 530(i)
Cane Ridge revival meeting, 379, 466
Cannibalism, 25
Cannons, 237(i), 238
Canteen, 237(i)
Cape Fear River, 511
Cape of Good Hope, 40
Cape Verde, 40
Capital(s). *See also* Washington, D.C.
    early, 294, 300(b)
    final selection of, 300–301(b)
Caravel, 40, 41
Caribbean, French islands in, 181–182
Carmel, California, 166(i)
Carney, Kate, 454

Carolina colonies, 95–96, 95(m). *See also* North Carolina; South Carolina
Carpetbag, 552(i)
"Carpetbagger," 552(i), 573
Carter, James Earl (Jimmy), Jr. (1924–), in Liberia, 429(i)
Cartier, Jacques, 64, 130(b)
Carving, 17(i)
Cash crops, 443
Cass, Lewis (1782–1866), 478
Cast-iron, 338(b)
Catechism for Colored Persons (Jones), 459
Cathay Company, 64
Cathedral Forest (painting), 408(i)
Catherine of Aragon, 106
Catholic Church
    in California, 166–167, 166(i)
    in colonies, 87, 92–93, 98, 125, 128, 162, 200
    in England, 105
    English Reformation and, 105–106
    in Europe, 35–36, 62, 105
    immigrants in, 407
    in Mexico, 412
    in New France, 131(b), 162
    in New World, 53, 53(i), 58–59(b)
    in Pennsylvania, 125
    political parties and, 490
    predestination and, 113
    in Quebec, 200
    during Second Great Awakening, 379
Catlin, George (1796–1872), 333(i), 409, 410(i)
Cattle, 3
Cave paintings, 10(i)
Cayuga tribe, 23, 179, 232
Census, 297(f), 327
Central America, filibusters in, 488–489(b), 489(i)
Central Pacific Railroad, 422(b)
Ceremonies, among ancient cultures, 20, 20(i)
Cerro Gordo, Mexico, 419
Ceuta, Portuguese conquest of, 39
Chacoan culture, 19–20, 20(i)
Chaco Canyon, New Mexico, 19–20, 20(i)
Chairs, 112(i), 250(i)
Chamberlain, W. G., 411(i)
Chancellorsville, Battle of (1863), 539(t), 541(m)
Chaperones, 454
Chapultepec, Mexico, 419
Charles I, king of England (r. 1625–1649), 87, 105(t), 106, 108, 117, 127
Charles I, king of Spain (r. 1660–1685), 44, 62, 80(b)
Charles II, king of England (r. 1660–1685), 95, 105(t), 124, 127, 128
Charles V, Holy Roman Emperor (king of Spain as Charles I; r. 1516–1556), 62, 63–64
Charleston, South Carolina
    during American Revolution, 241, 242(m), 246
    in election of 1860, 503
    free blacks in, 461, 462
    harbor in, 151(i)
    nonimportation agreements in, 195
    in opening battle of Civil War, 510(i), 513–514, 513(i)
    plan for black settlement during Reconstruction, 557
    religion in, 162

    resistance to British laws in, 192
    on secession, 505
    slavery in, 260
Charleston City Gazette and Daily Advertiser, 307
Charlestown, Massachusetts, 218, 218(i)
Charles Towne, South Carolina, 96. *See also* Charleston, South Carolina
Charlottesville, Virginia, 243
Charter of Privileges, 125
Chase, Salmon P. (1808–1873), 480, 481, 517, 561, 571
Chattanooga, Battle of (1863), 539(t), 540, 541(m)
Checks and balances, 275, 282
Cherokee Indians, 127–128, 128(i), 165, 239, 371–372, 372(m), 522(i)
Chesapeake Bay, *Chesapeake* incident (1807) in, 331, 331(m)
Chesapeake Bay colony, 69–92, 72(m), 78(m)
    African Americans in, 95, 97
    agriculture in, 71(i), 73, 75, 77–78, 80–81(b), 82(i), 86, 87–88
    diseases in, 73, 74, 76, 83
    exports of, 159(f)
    food supplies in, 73
    founding of, 72
    government in, 76, 90–92
    indentured servants in, 70, 76(i), 78–79, 82–86, 87
    land grant for, 71
    laws in, 84–85(b), 89(b), 92
    Native Americans and, 69–70, 72–75, 91–92, 98
    political conflict in, 90–92
    population of, 76
    religion in, 84–85(b), 86–87, 98
    slavery in, 70, 77(i), 78, 84–85(b), 89(b), 92, 97–98
    society in, 87–90, 90(i)
    Spanish and, 72
    tobacco in, 70, 77–78, 80–81(b), 82(i), 86, 87, 90, 92, 97–98
    trading in, 159(f)
    women in, 76(i), 83, 86
Chesapeake incident (1807), 331, 331(m)
Chesnut, Mary Boykin, 455–456, 469
Cheyenne tribe, 24, 409
Chicago, Illinois, 486
Chickamauga, Battle of (1863), 539(t), 540, 541(m)
Chickasaw tribe, 24, 360, 371, 372, 522(i)
Chiefdoms, 20–21, 22
Child, Lydia Maria, 425, 501
Children
    with Continental Army, 223–224
    enslaved, 153, 155
    in Puritan colonies, 118–119, 119(i)
Chile, 14(b), 349
Chinese immigrants, in California gold rush, 422–424, 423(i)
Chippewa tribe, 22, 184(b)
Chivalry, 451, 454
Choctaw tribe, 24, 371, 372, 522(i)
"Christian guardianship" (paternalism), 448–450, 450(i)
Christianity. *See also* Catholic Church; Protestantism
    in Africa, 138
    African Americans and, 435, 441(b), 458–459, 560

in colonies, 84–85(b), 86–87, 92–93, 98, 102(i), 103–104, 105–120, 122–123(b), 124–125, 125(i), 132, 140, 158, 162–163
Constitution and, 280–281(b)
English Reformation and, 62, 105–106
European, 35–36, 50–51(b), 62, 73
immigrants and, 407
Mormons, 411–412
in New World, 53, 53(i), 58–59(b), 73
slaves and, 435, 441(b), 458–459
Chumash people, 16, 16(i)
Church, 561(i)
Church, John B., 325(i)
Church of England (Anglican), 86, 103, 105, 108, 109, 114, 116, 124, 157, 162, 234(b), 382(b)
Church of Jesus Christ of Latter-Day Saints (Mormons), 411
Churubusco, Battle of (1847), 419
Cibola, Seven Cities of, 49
Cigar case, 178(i)
Cities
  in 1860, 447(m)
  free blacks in, 462
  work of slaves in, 456–457
Citizens, defining, 256–258, 257(i)
Citoyenne, 292(b), 307(i)
City Tavern (Philadelphia, Pennsylvania), 272(i)
Civil rights, for African Americans, 554(i), 564–565
Civil Rights Act (1866), 564–565, 571(t)
Civil Rights Act (1875), 571(t), 582
Civil service, 369, 581
Civil War (1861–1865)
  African Americans in, 511–512, 512(i), 529–530, 530(i), 531, 531(i), 532–533(b), 533(i), 548
  artificial limbs for veterans of, 566–567(b), 567(i)
  Atlantic theater of, 523–524
  battles of. *See also names of specific battles*
    1861–1862, 510(i), 513–514, 513(i), 518–524, 519(m), 520(i), 521(i), 523(t)
    1863–1865, 539–544, 539(t), 540(i), 541(m)
  blockades in, 511, 516, 523–524, 526–527(b), 531
  combatants in, 515–518, 516(f), 517(i)
  costs of, 512, 517, 518, 520–521, 531, 542–543(b), 542(f), 543(i), 544, 546, 548
  cotton trade and, 444–445(b), 516, 524, 525(f)
  deaths in, 512, 517, 520–521, 542–543, 542(f), 543(i), 544, 544(i), 546, 548
  dissent during, 538–539
  draft in, 529–530, 531, 532(b), 534, 538–539
  eastern theater of, 518–521, 519(m), 520(i), 521(i)
  end of, 539(t), 546
  international diplomacy during, 524
  length of, 517
  mobilization for, 517–518, 517(i)
  Native Americans in, 522(i)
  opening battle of, 510(i), 513–514, 513(i)
  opposition to, 538–539
  politics during, 538–539
  resources of North and South in, 515–517, 516(f), 522, 536(i)

slavery and, 512, 515, 524–530, 531, 531(i), 548
states' rights in, 531, 534
turning point of, 540
western theater of, 522–523
women in, 534–536, 535(i), 537–538, 538(i), 543(b), 546, 548
Clappe, Louisa Knapp, 422(b)
Clark, George Rogers (1752–1818), 239, 240(m)
Clark, William (1770–1838), 329–330
Clarkson, Thomas, 382, 383(b)
Clay, Edward W., 442(i)
Clay, Henry (1777–1852)
  on annexation of Texas, 415, 415(i)
  on Bank of the United States, 374–375, 374(i)
  in election of 1824, 349, 350–351, 351(m)
  in election of 1828, 367, 368(i)
  in election of 1844, 415
  on expansion of slavery, 479–480
  family of, in Civil War, 515
  as "Great Pacificator," 479–480
  Missouri Compromise and, 347
  on tariffs, 373
  War of 1812 and, 334
Clay, Henry, Jr., 418
Clermont (steamboat), 360, 362(b)
Cleveland, Aaron, 202(b)
Cliff dwellings, 19–20
Climate changes, 10
Clinton, DeWitt, 335, 342(b)
Clinton, Henry (1738–1795), 218, 241, 242
Clocks, 286(i), 345(i)
Clothing
  of colonial women, 157(i), 214(i)
  Confederate flag dress, 564(i)
  of Continental Army, 212(i)
  of Dolley Madison, 332(i)
  eighteenth-century, 261(i)
  in 1832, 376(i)
  of English gentleman, 180(i)
  French Revolution and, 306–307, 307(i)
  Jefferson's simplicity in, 326, 326(i)
  made of homespun cloth, 195
  of Mexican warrior, 51(i)
  Native American, 180(i)
  of riflemen, 223(i)
  shoes, 361, 364–365, 365(i)
  as symbol system conveying status, 180(i)
  uniforms, 212(i), 417(i), 518(i), 523(i)
Clovis hunters, 8, 10, 11, 14–15(b), 15(i)
Clovis point, 10
Clovis spear straightener, 11(i)
Coal, 397
Cobb, Howell, 504
Cobb, Thomas R. R., 442
Cockade, tricolor, 306, 307(i)
Coercive Acts (1773), 199–200, 201, 204, 215
Coffee House (New York City), 298
"Coffin ships," 407
Cold Harbor, Battle of (1864), 539(t), 541(m), 544, 544(i)
Colfax, Schuyler, 581
College of William and Mary (Virginia), 436
Colleges and universities, 233(i), 251, 287, 436
  alcohol served at, 380
  women in, 342–343(b), 378(i), 379

Colleton, John, 95
Colombia, 349
Colonies, 126(m). *See also names of individual colonies*
  committees of correspondence in, 198, 200, 202(b)
  comparing areas of British, Spanish, and French colonies, 165(m)
  consumption in, 158, 158(i)
  economy of, 117–118, 139, 140–157, 158, 159(f)
  English empire and, 126–132
  exports of, 156, 158, 159(f)
  government in, 76, 90–92, 128–129, 132, 167–170, 200–201
  insurrections in (1774–1775), 204–207, 205(m), 206(i)
  political conflict in, 90–92
  population of, 118, 118(i), 138–139, 140, 140(m), 151
  religion in, 84–85(b), 86–87, 92–93, 98, 102(i), 103, 105–120, 122–123(b), 124–125, 132, 140, 158, 162–163, 163(i)
  resistance to British laws in, 187–193, 189(i), 190–191(b)
  royal, 76, 127, 130(b), 167–170
  slavery in. *See* Slavery
  society in, 87–90, 90(i), 156–157
  taxes on, 175, 186–187, 192–194, 197, 208
  women in, 76(i), 83, 86, 118, 119, 122–123(b), 139(i), 141(i)
Colonization
  English, 69, 76, 108, 132
  Lincoln on, 528
  Portuguese, 40
Colorado
  ancient cultures in, 19–20
  mining in, 522
Colored Orphan Asylum, 539
Columbian exchange, 45–46, 45(i)
Columbia Patriot (Mercy Otis Warren), 277
Columbia University, 287
Columbus, Christopher (1451–1506), 22, 34, 35–37, 36(i), 38, 41–42, 41(m), 44–45
Comanche tribe, 24, 409, 412
Commerce, in eighteenth century, 158
Commercial law, 365
Committees of correspondence, 198, 200, 202(b)
Committees of public safety, 207, 236, 251
Commodities trading, 366
Common Sense (Paine), 220, 221(i)
Communalism, 424–425, 425(i)
Communication
  in colonies, 198, 200, 202(b)
  through committees of correspondence, 198, 200, 202(b)
  by drum, 138
  through newspapers, 160–161(b), 161(i), 195, 203(b), 367, 381
  by telegraph, 399, 402–403(b), 403(i)
Compass, 38
Complex marriage, 425
Compromise of 1850, 481, 481(m), 485, 506
Compromise of 1877, 585
Comstock Lode, 476
Concord (Massachusetts), Battle of (1775), 204–206, 205(m), 208, 215

Conestoga Indians, 185(b)
Confederacy (Confederate States of America). *See also* Civil War
  claims Kentucky and Missouri, 514–515
  collapse of, 546–547, 547(i)
  deserters in, 534–535
  draft and, 529–530, 531, 532(b), 534
  European allies of, 516
  filibustering and, 489(b)
  hardships in, 534–535
  inflation in, 531
  mobilization of, 517–518, 517(i)
  Native American recruits in, 522(i)
  Ordnance Bureau of, 518
  secession and, 505, 513, 514–515, 514(m)
  slaves in Civil War, 531, 531(i)
  soldiers of, 531(i), 534(i)
  stake in slavery, 515
  states' rights in, 531, 534
  surrender of, 539(t), 546
  uniform of, 518(i)
Confederate flag dress, 564(i)
Confederation government (1781–1789), 252–255
  citizens of, 256–258, 257(i)
  Northwest Territory and, 265–269
  problems of, 262–271
  republicanism and, 255–256
  running of, 255
  Shays's Rebellion and, 269–271
  taxation and, 252, 253
  treaty with Native Americans, 264–265
  weakness of, 265
  western lands and, 252, 253–255, 254(m), 262
Confiscation Act (1861), 528, 556
Confiscation Act (1862), 529, 556
Congo, 155
Congregational Church, 162, 379, 385
Congress
  African Americans in, 553, 576
  on aliens, 312
  bank chartered by, 298
  Bill of Rights and, 289, 290–291
  Civil War legislation of, 537
  constitutional powers of, 275
  declares war on Great Britain (1812), 334–335
  in election of 1800, 323
  in election of 1876, 585
  in impeachment of Andrew Johnson, 565, 570–571, 570(i)
  on Jay Treaty, 308–309
  Matthew Lyon fight in, 313(i)
  Missouri Compromise and, 346–348, 348(m), 498
  prohibits trade with Britain and France, 333–334
  railroads and, 400, 486
  on removal of Indians, 371
  right to prohibit slavery, 498, 500, 503
  on sedition, 312–316
  selection of Washington, D.C., as capital, 300–301(b)
  on slavery, 382–383(b), 384
  taxes passed by, 299, 302, 373, 537
  on voting rights and property, 345
  on war with Mexico, 417
  on Wilmot Proviso, 478
  in XYZ affair, 311

Congressional Reconstruction, 555, 565–572
Connecticut
  boundaries of, 253
  Fundamental Orders of, 117
  ratification of Constitution by, 276–277, 276(m)
  slavery in, 259
Conquistadors, 46–51, 47(i), 47(m), 49(i), 50–51(b), 51(i), 52, 54. *See also* Exploration and conquest
Conscientious objector, 290
Conscription, 531. *See also* Draft (conscription)
Conservatives, 501, 563, 568, 571, 573
Constitution (frigate), 356(i)
Constitution, of states, 255–256, 258
Constitution, U.S.. *See* U.S. Constitution
Constitutional Convention (1787), 271–275
Constitutional Union Party, 503
Continental Army. *See also* American Revolution
  African Americans in, 224–225
  arming, 216–217(b)
  in Battle of Saratoga, 236–238, 238(m), 240
  canteen used by, 237(i)
  choosing commander of, 215
  creation of, 215
  discipline in, 218, 220
  draftees in, 225
  early battles of, 218, 218(m), 219(i), 223
  height of men in, 224(f)
  members at Constitutional Convention, 273
  recruits in, 213
  uniform of, 212(i)
  at Valley Forge, 238, 239
  women in, 213–214, 214(i), 223–224
Continental Association, 204
Continental Congress, 251–252. *See also* First Continental Congress; Second Continental Congress
Continental drift, 6, 6(m)
Contraband of war, 528–529
Cook, John F., 462(i)
Cookstoves, 338–339(b), 339(i)
Copper, 25, 75(i)
Corbin, Hannah, 257
Corey, Giles, 122(b)
Corinth, Mississippi, 519(m), 523
Corliss, Alonzo B., 574(b)
Corn (maize), 17, 18, 22, 24, 25, 45(i), 46, 71(i), 73, 75, 397, 465(i)
Cornplanter (Seneca leader), 264(i), 265
Cornstalk (Native American leader), 239
Cornwallis, Charles (1738–1805), 241, 242, 243–244
Coronado, Francisco Vásquez de (c. 1510–1554), 49, 49(i)
Corporations, and commercial law, 365
Corruption
  during American Revolution, 236
  in Grant administration, 581
Cortés, Hernán (1485–1547), 46–48, 47(i), 47(m), 50–51(b), 52, 58(b), 63, 419
Cortés Arrives in Tenochtitlán (painting), 47(i)
Costa Rica, 489(b)
Cotton, 578(i)
  Civil War and, 444–445(b), 516, 524, 525(f)

climate and, 437
economic bust and, 366
importance in South, 437, 438(m), 443–446, 516, 524, 525(f)
international need for, 294, 444–445(b), 516, 524, 525(f)
manufacturing and, 361–364, 361(m), 399
slavery and, 437, 438(m), 446, 446(i), 447–448
tariffs and, 373
trade in, 444–445(b), 446, 448(i), 525(f)
Cotton, John, 116
Cotton gin, 294, 403(b), 443, 444(b), 445(i)
Cotton kingdom, 437
Council Bluffs, Iowa, 401(i)
Counterblaste to Tobacco, A, 80(b)
"Country-born" slaves, 155
Country merchant, 579
Covenant, 104, 141
Covenant Chain, 179, 180(i)
Covenant of grace, 116
Covenant of works, 116
Coverture, 337, 346, 352
Cowboys, 3, 4(i)
Cowpens, Battle of (1781), 243
Cox, Jacob D., 582
Crabb, Henry A., 488(b)
Crafts. *See also* Artisans
  basket making, 11, 25, 41(i), 75
  beadwork, 68(i), 75(i)
  carving, 17(i)
  glassmaking, 75(i)
  jewelry making, 16(i)
  needlework, 141(i)
  pottery making, 17, 17(i), 25, 434(i)
  spinning and weaving, 26–27(b), 26(i), 27(i), 195–196, 195(i)
  woodworking, 16
Cragin, Mary, 425(i)
Crawford, William H. (1772–1834), 349, 350, 351, 351(m)
Credit, 366
Credit reporting industry, 389(b)
Creek tribe, 24, 165, 260, 335, 369, 371, 372, 437, 522(i)
Creek War (1813–1814), 335, 437
Creoles, 57
Creole slaves, 155
Crockett, David, 414
Cromwell, Oliver (1599–1658), 105(t), 117, 124
Crop(s)
  cash, 443
  corn (maize), 17, 18, 22, 24, 25, 45(i), 46, 71(i), 73, 75, 397, 465(i)
  cotton. *See* Cotton
  indigo, 152, 156, 157(i), 159(f), 241
  potatoes, 46
  rice, 96, 152, 154(i), 156, 159(f), 241, 443
  sugar, 94–95, 94(i), 96, 154(i), 158, 382(b), 443
  sunflowers, 17, 24
  tobacco. *See* Tobacco
  wheat, 147, 150, 294, 361, 366, 397, 399
Crop lien, 579
Crow tribe, 24
Cruikshank, United States v. (1876), 582
Cuba, 46
  in Adams-Onís Treaty, 348
  attempt to purchase, 486
  British siege of, 181, 182
  filibusters in, 488–489(b)

Cuffe, Paul and John, 258(i), 259
Culture(s). *See also* Education; Religion(s)
    African, 153
    African American, 155–156
    ancient, 2(i), 3–22, 12(m), 13(i),
        14–15(b), 15(i), 16(i), 16(m)
    manifest destiny and, 407
    Native American, 70, 103, 184(b), 329
    North vs. South, 506
    oral, 309
    of plain folk, 466
    shifts in, 375–385
    slaves and, 309, 437
    southern, 436–448, 535
    southwestern, 18–20, 18(m), 19(i), 20(i),
        22, 24(m)
    after War of 1812, 358
Cumberland River, 519(m), 522, 523
Cummings, Kate, 566(b)
Currency, 127(i)
    during American Revolution, 218, 236
    during confederation government,
        263–264
    paper money, 263–264, 275, 365, 390,
        518, 531, 537
Curtis, Benjamin R., 498
Curtis, Samuel R., 522

Da Gama, Vasco (c. 1460–1524), 40
Daguerre, Louis, 482(b)
Daguerreotypes, 482–483(b), 483(i)
Dallas, George M., 415(i)
Dalles, The, 25
Dance
    "General Burgoyne's Surrender," 238
    Native American, 63(i)
    plain folk and, 466
Darley, Felix O. C., 465(i)
Dartmouth College, 233(i)
Daughters of Liberty, 193, 195–196,
    292(b)
Davis, Addison, 365(i)
Davis, Henry Winter, 555
Davis, Jefferson (1808–1889)
    on balance of power between slave vs.
        free states, 479
    character and temperament of, 517
    Civil War strategy of, 516
    decision to take Fort Sumter, 513
    establishes Confederacy, 513, 531
    as military leader, 517
    as president of Confederacy, 505, 516,
        517, 522, 531, 535
    on slavery in territories, 503, 522
Davis, Paula Wright, 426
Dawes, William, 205, 205(m)
Dead Line, The (painting), 545(i)
Debt
    from American Revolution, 262–264,
        287–288, 295–296, 298, 300(b)
    national, 375
Debt consolidation, 296, 298, 300(b)
Decatur, Stephen, 330–331
"Declaration of Dependence, A,"
    232–233
Declaration of Independence, 221–222,
    256, 258
Declaration of Sentiments, 426
"Declaration on the Causes and
        Necessity of Taking Up Arms, A,"
    215
Declaratory Act (1766), 193
Deer, 16

Deere, John, 397
Deerfield Raid of 1704, 129(i)
Deism, 162
Delany, Martin R., 427
Delaware
    acceptance of Articles of Confederation
        and, 253, 254
    in American Revolution, 228
    colonies in, 78(m)
    ratification of Constitution by, 276–277,
        276(m)
    slavery in, 259
    Unionism in, 515
Delaware Indians, 125, 179, 180, 184(b),
    185(b), 185(i), 232, 239, 240(m), 265,
    268, 303, 305, 333
Delaware River, 124, 148, 149, 228
Democracy
    in churches, 340
    direct, 220, 255
    expansion of slavery and, 478
    Hamilton on, 288
    Jackson and, 366–369
    limits on, 275, 345–346
    republicanism vs., 275
    in South, 466, 467–468, 515
    spread of, 366–369
Democratic Party
    on annexation of Texas, 415
    in election of 1836, 386
    in election of 1856, 493
    in election of 1860, 503
    in election of 1864, 545
    in election of 1876, 585, 586(i)
    Jackson and, 369–375
    "peace" Democrats, 545
    realignment of, 490, 490(t)
    during Reconstruction, 563, 573, 574(b),
        575(b), 576, 576(i), 579, 582–585
    on slavery, 479
Democratic Republicans, 367
Denmark, warships of, 164(f)
Dennis, John Q. A., 558(b)
Depreciation, scale of, 263(i)
Depression
    of 1819, 366, 373
    of 1837, 385, 386–387, 387(i), 390
    of 1839, 385, 390
    of 1857, 500
Desks, 120(i), 174(t)
De Soto, Hernando (c. 1496–1542), 49
Detroit, Michigan, 268(i), 335
Devereux Station, Virginia, 517(i)
Dew, Thomas R., 436, 454
Dias, Bartolomeu, 40
Dibble, 18(i)
Dickinson, John (1732–1808), 193, 215,
    218, 220, 222
Dinwiddie, Robert, 177, 179
Disarmament, treaty with Great Britain
    (1817), 337
Discount rates, 365
Discrimination
    against African Americans, 402, 427,
        530(i), 562, 582
    against Hispanic Americans, 423(b)
    against immigrants, 402, 423(b)
    against women, 402, 426
Diseases
    during American Revolution, 218
    during California gold rush, 421
    during Civil War, 543(b), 545(i)
    colonists and, 73, 74, 76, 83

    in Europe, 37
    immigrants and, 147
    in Liberia, 428(b)
    in Mexican-American War, 419
    Native Americans and, 45(i), 46, 50(b),
        60, 64, 74, 109, 167, 185(b), 218, 414
    sailors and, 145(b)
    slaves and, 153, 154, 155, 207, 443
Disfranchisement, 256, 257, 346, 371, 427,
    493, 569, 573. *See also* Suffrage;
    Voting rights
Disqualification Act (1787), 271
Dissent, during Civil War, 538–539
District of Columbia, 481. *See also*
    Washington, D.C.
District schools, 340
Diversity, in eighteenth-century colonies,
    140(m), 142
Divorce, 338–339, 451
Dix, Dorothea, 537–538, 543(b)
Dominica (West Indian island), 137
Dominion of New England, 128
Doniphan, Alexander, 418(i)
Door, colonial, 129(i)
Douglas, Stephen A. (1813–1861)
    in Congress, 481, 487, 490
    in election of 1860, 504
    in Lincoln-Douglas debates, 500–501
    Mary Lincoln on, 396
    popular sovereignty and, 487, 490, 496
    on slavery in new territories, 486–487,
        490, 499
    support for Union, 514
Douglass, Frederick (1817–1895)
    autobiography of, 485
    on Civil War, 512, 532(b)
    during Reconstruction, 565
    on right of blacks to remain in U.S.,
        428(b)
    on slavery, 426–427, 427(i)
Dove, Samuel, 560(i)
Doyle, Mahala, 475
Draft (conscription)
    in American Revolution, 225
    in Civil War, 529–530, 531, 532(b), 534,
        535, 538–539
    exemptions from, 535
Draft riots (New York City, 1863), 539
Drake, Francis, 408
Dred Scott decision (1857), 496, 497–499,
    498(i), 500, 506
Dress, Confederate flag, 564(i)
Drinker, Elizabeth, 292(b)
Drum, 138
Dueling, 324–325(b), 450
Duke of York, 124
Dulany, Daniel, 187
Dun & Bradstreet, 389(b)
Dunmore, Lord (1732–1809), 206, 206(i)
Duplicating machine, 327(i)
Dupree, Jack, 575(b)
Dürer, Albrecht (1471–1528), 63–64
Durkee, John, 202(b)
Dutch. *See* Netherlands
Dutch East India Company, 120
Dutch Reformed Church, 121, 379
Dysentery, 543(b)

Eagle Hotel (Buffalo, New York),
    388–389(b), 389(i)
Earl, Ralph E. W., 358(i)
Eastern theater, of Civil War, 518–521,
    519(m), 520(i), 521(i)

Eastern Woodland cultures, 16–17, 17(i), 22
East India Company, 198
Eaton, William, 331
Economic policies, early, 294–299, 302
Economy
    agricultural productivity and, 397
    of antebellum South, 437, 438(m), 442–448, 443(m)
    banks and, 365, 366, 375
    booms and busts in, 359, 365–366, 374–375, 385, 386–390, 387(i), 388–389(b), 500, 537
    changes in 1840s and 1850s, 397–401
    during Civil War, 537
    commercial law and, 365
    of confederation, 263–264
    credit and, 366
    depression. *See* Depression
    economic inequality and, 405, 405(i)
    of English colonies, 139, 140–157, 158, 159(f), 194–196
    industrial evolution and, 397–401
    inflation and, 375, 518, 531, 538
    manufacturing and, 298–299, 361–365, 361(m), 364(i), 365(i), 398–399
    of middle colonies, 142–143, 146–151, 158, 159(f)
    of northern colonies, 117–118, 140–142, 141(i), 158, 159(f)
    railroads and, 399–401
    of southern colonies, 158, 159(f)
    transportation and, 359–361, 359(m), 360(i)
    after War of 1812, 358–366
    working women and, 361–364, 364(i), 378–379
Edenton, North Carolina, 194(i)
Education
    of African Americans, 340, 404(f), 427, 430, 462, 557, 574(b), 577, 577(i), 579
    of Chinese immigrants, 422(b)
    higher, 342(b), 378(i), 379. *See also* Colleges and universities
    Lincoln on, 403
    literacy rates and, 404(f)
    market economy and, 378–379
    of plain folk, 466
    universal, 403
    of women, 35, 291, 294, 340–344, 344(i), 352, 378–379, 378(i), 395, 454, 466
Edward VI, king of England (r. 1547–1553), 105(t), 106
Edwards, Jonathan (1703–1758), 162, 163
Effigies, 17(i), 25, 41(i)
Elections
    of 1796, 310–311
    of 1800, 322–323, 323(m)
    of 1804, 331
    of 1808, 331–332
    of 1812, 335
    of 1816, 344
    of 1820, 344
    of 1824, 349–351, 350(i), 351(m), 357
    of 1828, 357, 367–368, 368(i)
    of 1832, 357, 365
    of 1836, 385, 386
    of 1840, 390
    of 1844, 415
    of 1848, 479, 479(m)
    of 1852, 485
    of 1856, 493
    of 1860, 502–504

of 1864, 539, 544, 544(m), 545–546
of 1868, 553, 575(b), 580, 581(i)
of 1872, 553, 581
of 1876, 585–586, 585(m), 586(i)
participation in, 367. *See also* Voting rights
Electoral college, 275, 289, 335, 345, 350, 504, 585
Eliot, John, 109, 110–111(b)
Elizabeth I, queen of England (r. 1558–1603), 105(t), 106, 106(i)
Elliott, Aaron, 202(b)
Ellison, William, 462
Elocution, 341
El Paso, Texas, 93
Emancipation
    Civil War and, 526–527, 528–529, 555
    gradual, 259, 381
    law on, 259, 346, 381, 461
    Reconstruction and, 555
    of slaves, 260, 261(b), 381, 461, 528–529, 555
    of women, 426, 426(i)
Emancipation laws, 259, 346, 381, 461
Emancipation Proclamation (1863), 511, 512, 529, 558(b), 560
Embargo, 331, 333, 516, 524
Embargo Act (1807), 331
Emerson, John, 497
Emerson, Ralph Waldo (1803–1882), 424
Eminent domain, 365
Emma Willard School (New York), 343(b)
Emory, William, 486(i)
Empresario, 413
Encomendero, 53
Encomienda, 52–56, 98
England. *See also* Great Britain
    Civil War in, 105(t), 117
    conflicts with France, 129, 131(b), 176–185, 307–308, 323, 336
    exploration by, 42–43, 43(m), 64
    Glorious Revolution in, 128, 129
    immigrants from, 96(i)
    literacy rates in, 404(f)
    poverty in, 142
    religion in, 86, 87, 103, 105, 108, 109, 114, 116, 124, 157, 162, 164, 234(b), 382(b)
    trade with colonies, 127, 159(f), 194–196
    warships of, 164(f)
English Reformation, 62, 105–106
Enlightenment, 162
Entrepreneurs, 388–389(b)
Episcopalians, 379
Equality
    for African Americans, 554, 565, 568, 578, 582
    in American Revolution, 247
    in bills of rights, 256, 258
    in Declaration of Independence, 222, 256, 258
    economic, 405
    Fourteenth Amendment on, 565, 568, 569, 571(t), 576, 582, 587
    republican, 468
    slavery and, 258–259
Equiano, Olaudah (c. 1750–1797), 153, 153(i), 163
"Era of Good Feelings," 344–345
Erie Canal, 359(m), 360(i), 361, 379
Europe
    areas of influence in Seven Years' War, 178(m)

attitudes toward Africans and Native Americans in, 88–89(b), 89(i), 90(i), 147
in Civil War, 516, 524
Enlightenment in, 162
immigrants from, 95–96, 96(i), 143, 146, 146(i), 151, 406–407, 406(i), 408(i), 490, 492
intellectuals in, 44(i)
panic of 1819 in, 366
panic of 1837 in, 386–387
in sixteenth century, 52–65
slavery in, 40, 382–383(b)
smoking in, 45(i), 46, 70, 80–81(b), 81(i), 154(i), 156, 158, 366
trade in, 37–38, 38(m), 40
trade with colonies, 70–71, 142, 158, 159(f), 194–196
trade with U.S., 444–445(b), 516, 524
Evangelical faith, 358, 375–376, 379–380, 380(i), 385, 424, 428(b), 458, 466, 467(i)
Evans, Oliver, 362(b)
Everett, Sarah, 410
Evolution, 6
Excommunication, 117
Exhorting women, 340
Expansionism. *See* Imperialism; Manifest destiny; Westward movement
Exploration and conquest, 35–65
    of Africa, 39–40, 40(i)
    of Canada, 64
    Dutch, 43(m)
    English, 42–43, 43(m), 64
    French, 43(m), 64, 131(b)
    justification of, 54–55(b)
    Portuguese, 38(m), 39–40, 42, 52
    Spanish, 36–37, 36(i), 41–42, 41(m), 43(m), 44–51, 50–51(b)
Exports, colonial, 156, 158, 159(f)
Extinction, 10–11, 12, 13

Factories. *See* Manufacturing
Fallen Timbers, Battle of (1794), 304(m), 305, 321
Families
    African American, 155, 156, 442(i), 457–458, 462, 557, 558(b), 560(i)
    in American Revolution, 234–235(b)
    changes in, 376–378
    in Civil War, 534–535, 548
    economic panics and, 387(i)
    economic situation of, 405
    Mexican, 419(i)
    on plantations, 450(i)
    poor, 464–466, 469
    separate spheres in, 376–378
    slave, 155, 156, 442(i), 457–458
    in westward movement, 410, 411(i)
Family law, 337–340
Fan, lady's, 381(i)
Fandango (painting), 413(i)
Farming. *See* Agriculture
Farmland, price of, 148–149
Farragut, David, 526(b)
Fawkes, Guy, 190(b)
Federalist Papers, The, 278, 287, 290
Federalist Party
    attempt to reduce South's political power, 336–337
    beginnings of, 289, 310
    in election of 1800, 323, 323(m)
    on foreign policy, 311–316

at Hartford Convention, 336–337
ratification of Constitution and, 276–277, 282, 290
revival of, 331
on sedition, 314(b), 316
weakening of, 322, 336–337, 344–345
in XYZ affair, 311–312
Female Society of Lynn (Massachusetts), 364
Feme covert, 337, 346, 352
Feminism
early, 572
in France, 292(b)
Ferdinand, king of Spain (r. 1474–1504), 35–37, 36(i), 41, 42, 45(i), 54, 62
Fiddles, 459(i), 466, 466(i)
Fifteenth Amendment (ratified 1870), 571–572, 571(t), 582, 587
Figgins, J. D., 3, 13(i)
Figurehead, 356(i)
Filibusters (adventurers), 488–489(b), 489(i)
Fillmore, Millard (1800–1874), 481, 492(i), 493
Finney, Charles Grandison (1792–1875), 379–380, 380(i)
Fire, Native American use of, 25, 28
Firearms, 73, 75(i), 216–217(b), 217(i), 218, 219(i), 223(i), 518(i), 542(b)
Fire clubs (Boston), 190(b), 191(i)
Firestone Rubber Company, 429(b)
First Continental Congress (1774), 201, 204, 233
Fishing
among ancient cultures, 16
by Native Americans in 1490s, 22–23, 25
in New England colonies, 117, 142, 159(f)
Fitzhugh, George, 440, 451, 488(b)
Five Civilized Tribes, 522, 522(i)
Flags
Confederate flag dress, 564(i)
at Fort Sumter, 510(i), 513
"Southern Rights," 497(i)
Florentine Codex, 59(b), 59(i)
Florida
acquisition from Spain, 348–349
missionaries in, 92–93, 98
Native Americans in, 260, 369, 371
during Reconstruction, 575(b), 584, 585
search for escaped slaves in, 348–349
secession of, 505
Spanish explorers in, 49
Spanish outposts in, 60–61, 92–93
Flour, 149–150, 361
Flowers, Andrew, 575(b)
Floyd, John, 435
Floyd, Kitty, 252(i)
Folsom points, 3–4, 12–13, 13(i)
Food supplies, in Virginia colony, 73
Foote, Henry S., 480
Force Bill (1833), 373
Foreign Miners' Tax Law (1850), 422(b)
Foreign policy
of Adams administration, 312–316
expansionism, 407–408, 414–424, 430, 486
of Federalist Party, 311–316
of Grant administration, 582
imperialism, 489(b), 582
of Monroe administration, 348–349
Fort Dearborn, 335

Fort Detroit, 180(i), 184(b), 185(b), 239, 240(m)
Fort Donelson, Battle of (1862), 519(m), 523, 523(t)
Fort Duquesne, 177, 180, 181, 184(b)
Fort Greenville, 305
Fort Hamilton, 304
Fort Henry, Battle of (1862), 519(m), 523, 523(t)
Fort Jefferson, 304
Fort Laramie conference, 410
Fort Lee, New Jersey, 227(i), 228
Fort Lincoln, Virginia, 533(i)
Fort McIntosh, Treaty of (1785), 268
Fort Miami, 184(b), 305
Fort Michilimackinac, 184–185(b)
Fort Necessity, 177, 179
Fort Niagara, 180, 181, 185(b), 239, 265
Fort Ouiatenon, 184(b)
Fort Pickering, 569(i)
Fort Pitt, 184(b), 185(b), 240(m)
Fort Recovery, 305
Fort St. Joseph, 184(b)
Fort Sandusky, 184(b)
Fort Stanwix, 212(i), 237
Treaty of (1784), 264–265, 265(m), 302–303
Fort Sumter, Battle of (1861), 506, 510(i), 513–514, 513(i), 519(m), 523(t)
Fort Ticonderoga, 181, 237
Fortune, Emanuel, 584
Fort Vincennes, 239
Fort Washington, 227(i), 228, 230(b), 304
Fort Wayne, Treaty of (1809), 333
Forty-niners, 421, 423(b)
Fossils, in Southwest, 3, 9(i)
Fourier, Charles, 424–425
Fourierist phalanxes, 425
Fourteenth Amendment (ratified 1868), 565, 568, 569, 571(t), 576, 582, 587
France
during American Revolution, 221, 240–241, 244, 245(i), 246
areas of influence in Seven Years' War, 178(m)
claim to Louisiana Territory, 328
colony of. *See* New France
conflicts with Great Britain, 129, 131(b), 176–185, 307–308, 323, 336
Congress prohibits trade with, 333–334
exploration by, 43(m), 64, 131(b)
immigrants from, 312
Jefferson on, 288
literacy rates in, 404(f)
Native Americans and, 130–131(b), 165, 167(i), 178(m), 181, 182, 183
need for cotton in, 516
in Ohio Country, 177, 178(m)
Reign of Terror in, 308
religion in, 164
in Seven Years' War, 177–183, 184(b)
slavery in, 524
U.S. relations with, 307–308, 311–316, 333–334
warships of, 164(f)
in West Indies, 241
women's rights in, 292(b), 293(b)
in XYZ affair, 311–312
Franchise, 572
Franklin, Anne and Josiah, 140
Franklin, Benjamin (1706–1790)
Albany Plan of Union and, 179
background of, 140

on British, 182
on citizen disobedience, 270, 271
at Constitutional Convention, 273
as diplomat, 231(b)
division from loyalist son, 234–235(b)
as inventor, 338(b)
newspapers produced by, 150, 160(b)
Poor Richard's Almanack, 150, 150(i)
religion and, 162, 163
in Second Continental Congress, 215, 222
at signing of Constitution, 250(i)
at signing of Declaration of Independence, 222
slavery and, 147
on taxes, 187
work ethic and values of, 150–151, 150(i), 170
Franklin, James, 160(b)
Franklin, Virginia, 467(i)
Franklin, William, 234–235(b)
Franklin College (Georgia), 342(b)
Franklin stove, 338(b)
Fredericksburg, Battle of (1862), 519(m), 521, 523(t)
Free blacks. *See also* African Americans (blacks)
achievements of, 462
in cities, 462
freedom papers of, 461, 462(i)
population of, 461
restrictions on, 461
sending to Liberia, 381, 427, 428–429(b), 429(i)
Freedmen. *See also* African Americans (blacks)
black codes and, 562–564, 563(i)
church built by, 561(i)
education of, 577, 577(i)
land for, 556(i), 557, 562
during Reconstruction, 553–554, 556–557
as sharecroppers, 579, 586
voting rights of, 562, 565, 571–573
working on plantations, 579
Freedmen's Bureau, 557, 562, 564, 565, 568, 570, 571, 571(t), 577
Freedom
expressions of, 578(i), 580(m)
meaning of, 558–559(b)
privileges of, 97
Union and, 524–530
Freedom papers, 461, 462(i)
"Freeholder," 345, 346
Free labor, 402–407
economic inequality and, 405, 405(i)
immigrants, 405–407, 406(f), 406(i)
northern philosophy of, 440
during Reconstruction, 556–557
Republican Party on, 492
in West, 477
Free-labor ideal, 402–405
Free labor system, 384
Freeman, Elizabeth (Mum Bett), 259, 260–261(b), 261(i)
Freemen (Massachusetts Bay Company), 115
Freeport Doctrine, 500
Free soil, 477
Free-Soil Party, 479, 480, 481, 486, 490(t)
Free states, 346–348, 470, 476–481, 496–497, 497(i)
Frémont, Jessie Benton, 493, 493(i)

Frémont, John C. (1813–1890), 414, 493, 493(i)

French and Indian War. *See* Seven Years' (French and Indian) War

French Revolution (1792–1801), 306–308

Frigates, 320(i), 330–331, 356(i), 523

Frobisher, Martin, 64

Frontier, 40, 83, 117, 140, 176, 222, 357, 407, 412, 476. *See also* West

Fugitive Slave Act (1850), 481–484, 503, 506

Fuller, Margaret, 424

Fulton, Robert (1765–1815), 360, 362(b)

Fundamental Orders of Connecticut, 117

Furniture
  chairs, 112(i), 250(i)
  colonial, 112(i), 120(i), 174(i), 222(i)
  laptop writing desk, 222(i)
  map desk, 174(i)
  storage chest, 120(i)

Fur trade, 130–131(b), 131(i), 148, 165, 182, 184(b), 308, 408

Gabriel's Rebellion (1800), 323

Gadsden, James, 486

Gadsden Purchase (1853), 486, 486(m)

Gage, Thomas (1721–1787), 185(b), 199–201, 202(b), 204, 207, 218

Gag rule of 1836, 386

Gale, Benjamin, 202(b)

Gallery of Illustrious Americans, The (Brady), 483(b)

Galloway, Joseph, 201, 204

Games, 19(i)

Gansevoort, Peter, 212(i)

Garfield, James A. (1831–1881), 568, 581

Garner, Robert and Margaret, 484(i)

Garnet, Henry Highland, 427

Garrison, William Lloyd (1805–1879)
  abolitionist activities of, 382(i), 383(b), 384–385, 435, 442(i), 480
  on John Brown's raid, 501
  Liberator, 382(i), 384, 535
  on Rutherford Hayes's victory, 585
  women and, 385

Gary, Martin, 584

Gaspée (Royal Navy ship), 197–198

Gates, Horatio (c. 1728–1806), 237, 238(i), 241, 242(m)

Gathering Corn in Virginia (painting), 465(i)

Gender equality, 292–293(b), 294, 339, 376–378. *See also* Women

General Court, 115

Generall Historie of Virginia (Smith), 69

Geneva conventions, 231(b)

Gentilz, Theodore, 413(i)

Gentry, 156–157

Geographic revolution (fifteenth and sixteenth centuries), 42–43, 44

George III, king of England (r. 1760–1820), 182, 186, 186(i), 193, 197, 214, 220, 222, 230(b), 232

Georgetown, Maryland, 300(b)

Georgia
  agriculture in, 578(i), 580(m)
  during American Revolution, 241–242, 242(m)
  founding of, 152
  government of, 256
  on Missouri Compromise, 347
  Native Americans in, 260, 369, 371, 372(m), 373

politics in, 469

ratification of Constitution by, 276–277, 276(m)

during Reconstruction, 575(b), 584, 585

secession of, 505, 562

slavery in, 259–260, 449(f)

Spanish settlement in, 49

German immigrants, 143, 146, 146(i), 151, 406–407, 408(i), 490

German mercenaries, in American Revolution, 221, 223(i), 227, 227(i), 228, 237

Germany, literacy rates in, 404(f)

Gettysburg, Battle of (1863), 539(t), 540, 540(i), 541(m)

Ghent, Treaty of (1814), 336, 349

Gilbert, Humphrey, 64

Girdling, 77

Glaciers, 7

Glassmaking, 75(i)

Glorietta Pass, Battle of (1862), 519(m), 522, 523(i), 523(t)

Glorious Revolution, 128, 129

Go-aheadism, 388(b)

Gold, 39, 42, 48(i), 49, 54, 56, 56(f), 72, 98

Gold Coast, 155

Gold coins, 236, 264

Gold mining, 394(i), 405(i), 522

Gold nuggets, 394(i)

Gold rush, in California (1849–1852), 394(i), 420–421, 422–423(b), 476, 522

Goliad, massacre of (1836), 414

Gone to smash, 388(b)

Goode, John, 128

Gooding, James Henry, 532–533(b)

Gordon (slave), 453(i)

Gordon, John B., 574(b)

Gorgas, Josiah, 518

Gorham, George C., 576(i)

Gouges, Olympe de, 292(b), 293(b)

Gould, William, 511–512, 529, 548

Gourd fiddle, 459(i)

Government. *See also* Congress; President; Supreme Court
  checks and balances on branches of, 275, 282
  during Civil War, 537. *See also* Confederacy (Confederate States of America); Lincoln, Abraham; Union
  confederation. *See* Confederation government
  jobs in, 327–328
  of New England colonies, 128–129, 132, 167–170, 200–201
  under Puritans, 115–116
  under Quakers, 125
  republican, 220, 252
  state, 255–256. *See also* State(s); States' rights
  of Virginia colony, 76, 90–92, 167–170

Government bonds, 236

Gradual emancipation, 259, 381

Granada, 36

Grandees, 94–95

Grant, Ulysses S. (1822–1885)
  character and temperament of, 581, 581(i)
  in Civil War, 522–523, 539–544, 541(m), 544(i), 546
  in election of 1868, 553, 575(b), 580, 581(i)

presidency of, 580–582, 581(i), 582(i)

scandal in administration of, 581, 581(i)

Graves, Mrs. A. J., 376

Gray, Thomas R., 435

Great Awakening
  First, 162
  Second, 375–376, 379–380, 380(i), 390

Great Basin cultures, 13, 22

Great Britain. *See also* England
  abolition in, 381
  in American Revolution. *See* American Revolution
  areas of influence in Seven Years' War, 178(m)
  claim to Oregon Country, 407, 408
  colonies and, 126–132, 165–166, 165(m). *See also names of individual colonies*
  colonists' decision to break away from, 215, 218
  conflicts with France, 129, 131(b), 176–185, 307–308, 323, 336
  Congress prohibits trade with, 333–334
  impressment of U.S. sailors by, 331
  making peace with U.S., 245–246
  need for cotton in, 443, 444(b), 516, 524
  reasons for losing American Revolution, 246–247
  relations with U.S., 287, 288, 331, 333–335
  Revolutionary strategy of, 225
  in Seven Years' War, 176–185, 177(m), 178(m), 181(m)
  slavery in, 382–383(b), 524
  taxes on colonies, 175, 186–187, 192–194, 197, 208
  Texas and, 415
  trade with U.S., 333–334, 443, 444(b), 516, 524
  in War of 1812, 322, 333–337, 335(m), 336(i), 352

Great Compromise (1787), 274

Great Plains
  hunters on, 12–13
  Native Americans in, 22, 23(m), 24, 24(m)

Great Salt Lake, 411, 412

Greeley, Horace (1811–1872), 483(i), 518, 581

Greenbacks, 537. *See also* Paper money

Greene, Catherine and Nathanael, 444(b)

Greenville, Treaty of (1795), 305, 306(i), 308, 321, 334(m)

Grenville, George (1712–1770), 186, 186(i), 187, 189

Grimké, Angelina (1805–1879), 385

Grimké, Sarah (1792–1873), 293(b), 385

Griswold, Roger, 313(i)

Guadalupe Hidalgo, Treaty of (1848), 420

Guadeloupe, 181, 186

Guerrilla war
  during Civil War, 514, 522
  in Kansas, 496
  during Reconstruction, 574(b)
  in southern colonies, 214, 242–243, 243(i)

Gulf of Mexico, 131(b)

Habeas corpus, suspension of, 230(b)

Haires, Francis, 83

Haitian Revolution, 309–310, 309(m), 323, 554

Hakluyt, Richard, 71
Halfway Covenant, 119
Hamilton, Alexander (1755–1804), 288(i)
  background of, 251, 271, 287
  on banks and banking, 298
  character and temperament of, 287
  Constitution and, 271, 273, 278, 280(b),
    287
  death of, 323, 324–325(b)
  economic policies of, 288, 294–299, 302
  in election of 1796, 310
  in election of 1800, 323
  on Jay Treaty, 308
  Jefferson and, 287, 288, 296, 298, 323,
    326
  John Adams and, 288, 310, 312, 313
  Madison and, 251, 288, 296, 298, 300(b)
  on manufacturing, 298–299
  as secretary of the treasury, 287–288,
    290, 294–299, 302
  war debt and, 295–296, 298, 300(b)
  Washington and, 271, 287, 288, 289, 290
  whiskey tax and, 299, 302
Hammond, James H., 456, 478
Hancock, John (1737–1793), 141(i)
  in colonial resistance to British laws,
    188
  endorses Phillis Wheatley's book of
    poems, 207
  orders to arrest, 191(b), 205(m)
Handicrafts. See Crafts
Handkerchief, 136(i)
Hard money, 236, 264, 365, 390
Hardwick, Massachusetts, 258
Harmar, Josiah, 303–304
Harper, William, 440–441(b)
Harpers Ferry, Virginia, raid on (1859),
    474(i), 475–476
Harpoons, 17(i)
Harris, David Golightly, 579, 584
Harrison, William Henry (1773–1841)
  acquires Indian lands in Northwest
    Territory, 333, 334(m)
  death of, 415
  in election of 1836, 386
  in election of 1840, 390
  as territorial governor of Indiana, 321,
    322
  in War of 1812, 335
Hart, Emma, 342–343(b)
Hartford Convention (1814), 336–337
Hartford Seminary (Connecticut), 341
Havana, Cuba, 181, 182
Hayes, Rutherford B. (1822–1893),
    election of, 585–586, 586(i)
Headright, 78
Hemings, Sally, 266(i)
Hendrick (Native American leader), 179,
    180(i)
Hendricks, Thomas A., 582
Henry, king of Spain, 35
Henry VII, king of England
    (r. 1485–1509), 42
Henry VIII, king of England
    (r. 1509–1547), 105, 105(t), 106
Henry, Joseph, 402(b)
Henry, Patrick (1736–1799)
  committees of correspondence and, 198
  Constitution and, 273, 278
  in First Continental Congress, 201
  map desk of, 174(i)
  Virginia Resolves and, 174(i), 187–188
Henry Frank (steamboat), 448(i)

Henry the Navigator, prince of Portugal,
    39, 41
Herald in the Country, The (painting),
    499(i)
Heresy, 116–117
Hermitage, 449(i)
Herndon, William, 499
Herttell, Thomas, 494(b)
Hessian troops, 221, 223(i), 227, 227(i),
    228
Heyrick, Elizabeth, 383(b)
Hickory Clubs, 367
Hide painting, 167(i)
Higby, Richard, 86
Higginson, Thomas W., 533(i)
Hill, Aaron, 265
Hillbillies, 464–466
Hillman, Mary Daggett, 229
Hillsborough, Lord, 194
Hinds, J. M., 575(b)
Hispanic Americans
  discrimination against, 423(b)
  in Mexican borderlands, 412–414,
    413(i), 420
Hispaniola, 309–310, 309(m)
Hogeboom, Pieter, 260(b)
Hohokam culture, 18(m), 19, 19(i), 24
Holland. See Netherlands
Holmes, George F., 485
Holmes, Oliver Wendell, Jr. (1841–1935),
    566(b)
Home front, during American
    Revolution, 228–236
"Home rule," 583
Homespun cloth, 195
Homestead Act (1862), 537
Homo erectus, 6
Homo sapiens, 5, 6–7
Hone, Philip, 387
Honor, defending, 450
Hood, John B. (1831–1879), 546, 567(b)
Hooker, Thomas, 117
Hopewell culture, 21
Hopi culture, 20
Horses
  Native Americans and, 409
  in North America, 13, 409
  origin of, 8–9
Horseshoe Bend, Battle of (1814), 335
Housatonic (Union blockader), 526(b),
    527(b)
House(s)
  cliff dwellings, 19–20
  longhouses, 23
  pit houses, 19
  of poor planters, 91(i)
  pueblos, 18, 20, 20(i), 25
  of slaves, 449, 456–461, 457(i), 458(i),
    580(m)
House of Burgesses (Virginia), 76, 90, 92,
    174(i), 187, 198
House of Representatives. See also
    Congress
  African Americans in, 553
  in Constitution, 274, 277, 278
  on Jay Treaty, 308–309
  in presidential elections, 323, 349,
    350
Houston, Sam, 414
Howe, William (1729–1814), 218,
    227–228, 230(b), 236, 237, 238
Hudson, Carrie, 456
Hudson, Henry, 120

Hudson River, 121, 124, 130(b), 207, 213,
    227(i), 228, 236, 237, 242, 360, 361,
    362(b)
Hudson Valley (New York), 148, 148(i),
    232(m), 236, 300(b)
Huguenots, 162
Huitzilopochtli (war god), 29
Hull, John, 127(i)
Human sacrifice, 22, 25, 28(i), 29, 47
Hunchback (naval ship), 512(i)
Hunley (submarine), 526–527(b), 527(i)
Hunter, David, 528
Hunters and gatherers, 11–17, 12(m),
    13(i), 15(i), 16(i), 16(m), 25
Hunting
  ancient, 4, 7, 9, 10–13, 10(i), 11(i), 13(i),
    16, 17, 24
  in colonies, 71(i)
  by Native Americans, 22–23, 24, 25, 409
  of whales, 17(i), 159(f)
Huron tribe, 130(b), 131(b), 268
Hutchins, Thomas, 185(i)
Hutchinson, Anne (1591–1643), 116–117
Hutchinson, Thomas (1711–1780)
  destruction of house, 189
  as governor, 190(b), 196, 198, 207–208
  loyalty to Britain, 175–176, 176(i), 196,
    197, 229
  in Seven Years' War, 179
  on Stamp Tax, 187, 189
Hymnal, 146(i)

Illinois
  agriculture in, 395, 397, 398(i)
  during American Revolution, 244–245
  conflicts with Native Americans in,
    333, 371
  Mormons in, 412
  population growth in (1830–1860), 397
  on voting rights and property, 345–346
Immediate Not Gradual Abolition (Heyrick),
    383(b)
Immigrants
  Chinese, 422–424, 423(i)
  discrimination against, 402, 423(b)
  from Europe and Africa, 95–96, 96(f),
    143, 146, 146(i), 151, 406–407,
    406(i), 408(i), 490, 492
  free labor and, 405–407, 406(f), 406(i)
  German, 143, 146, 146(i), 151, 406–407,
    408(i), 490
  growth in number of (1820–1860), 405,
    406(f)
  as indentured servants, 70, 76(i),
    78–79, 82–86, 139, 147, 170
  Irish, 406, 406(i), 407, 490, 492
  laws on, 312
  in middle colonies, 142–143, 146–147
  in New England colonies, 109, 118
  as percentage of state populations
    (1860), 447(f)
  political parties and, 490
  population growth and, 139, 140(m)
  prejudice against, 406(i), 407, 572
  religions of, 146, 146(i), 407
  risks to, 146–147
  Scots-Irish, 146, 151
  in South, 447, 447(f)
  women, 407
Impartial Administration of Justice Act
    (1773), 199
Impeachment, of Andrew Johnson, 565,
    570–571, 570(i)

Imperialism, 489(b), 582
Impost, 263
Impressment
    in Civil War, 531
    of sailors by Great Britain, 322, 331, 336
Incan empire (Peru), 48–49
Incorporation, laws of, 365
Indentured servants, 70, 76(i), 78–79, 82–86, 84(b), 87, 139, 147, 170
Independence, Missouri, 412–413
Independence Hall (Philadelphia, Pennsylvania), 273(i)
India, 404(f), 445(b), 445(i)
Indian(s). *See* Native Americans (Indians)
Indiana
    conflicts with Native Americans in, 333, 334(m)
    population growth in (1830–1860), 397
    on voting rights and property, 346
Indian country, 302–303, 321–322
Indian Dialogues (Eliot), 110(b)
Indian Removal Act (1830), 371–372, 372(m)
Indian Territory, 304(m), 305(i)
Indigo, 152, 156, 157(i), 159(f), 241
Industrial evolution, 397–401
Industries. *See also* Manufacturing
    shoemaking, 361, 364–365, 365(i)
    textile, 361–364, 361(m), 364(i), 537
Inflation
    during Civil War, 518, 531, 538
    during Jackson administration, 375
Interesting Narrative (Equiano), 153, 153(i)
Internal Revenue Act (1863), 537
Intolerable Acts, 199–200
Inventions
    affordable clocks, 345(i)
    cotton gin, 294, 403(b), 443, 444(b), 445(i)
    inflatable rubberized bags, 396(i)
    patent for, 396(i)
    steamboat, 359(m), 360–361, 362–363(b), 363(i), 448(i)
    telegraph, 399, 402–403(b), 403(i)
Iowa
    population growth in (1830–1860), 397
    railroads in, 401(i)
Ireland, potato blight in, 407
Irisarri, Antonio Jose de, 489(b)
Irish immigrants, 406, 406(i), 407, 490, 492
Iron, 338(b)
Iron production, 399
Iroquoian confederation, 23, 232, 262
Iroquoian tribes
    in American Revolution, 236, 238(i), 240(m), 264–265
    French and, 130(b), 131(b), 165, 178(m)
    in fur trade, 130(b), 131(b), 148, 165
    treaty with (1784), 264–265
Iroquois League of Six Nations, 179, 264–265
Irrigation, 18, 19
Isabella, queen of Spain, 35–37, 36(i), 38, 41, 42, 45(i), 58(b), 62, 64
Isham, Edward, 464
Italy
    literacy rates in, 404(f)
    trade in, 37
Ivory saltcellar, 39(i)

Jackson, Andrew (1767–1845), 350(i), 356(i)
    on abuses of power, 365
    appointments of, 369
attempt to purchase California, 414
background of, 357, 450
banking policy of, 356(i), 369, 373–375, 374(i)
cabinet of, 369
character and temperament of, 357, 358, 367–368, 390
democratic agenda of, 368–369
Democratic Party and, 369–375
economy and, 387–390
in election of 1824, 349–350, 351, 351(m), 352, 357
in election of 1828, 357, 367–368, 368(i)
in election of 1832, 357, 365
farewell address of, 372
Indian policy of, 369–372, 370(i), 372(m)
invades Spanish Florida, 348
nickname of, 367
popularity of, 349–350, 356(i)
presidency of, 356(i), 357–358, 358(i), 368–375, 414
spread of democracy and, 366–369
tariff policy of, 373
use of veto by, 369, 374
in War of 1812, 335, 336, 348, 352, 357
Jackson, Rachel, 368
Jackson, Thomas J. ("Stonewall"; 1824–1863), 520, 535(i)
James I, king of England (r. 1603–1625), 71, 76, 80(b), 105(t), 106
James II, king of England (r. 1685–1688), 105(t), 128
James, W. T., 339(b)
Jamestown, Virginia, 69, 72–73, 72(m), 75(i), 76(i)
Japan, literacy rates in, 404(f)
Jay, John (1745–1829), 271, 278, 290, 308
Jayme, Father Luís, 168
Jay Treaty (1795), 308
Jefferson, Isaac, 457(i)
Jefferson, Thomas (1743–1826), 266(i), 326(i)
    acceptance of Articles of Confederation and, 254–255
    on banks and banking, 298
    Barbary Wars and, 330–331
    on beginning of American Revolution, 206
    committees of correspondence and, 198
    Declaration of Independence and, 222, 256
    as diplomat, 231(b), 326(i)
    in election of 1796, 310–311, 316
    in election of 1800, 323
    as first secretary of state, 290, 310
    on France, 288
    as governor of Virginia, 243
    Hamilton and, 287, 288, 296, 298, 300(b), 323, 326
    on higher education for women, 342(b)
    inaugural address of, 316
    John Adams and, 311
    laptop writing desk of, 222(i)
    letter writing by, 327(i)
    on liberty, 327
    Louisiana Purchase (1803) and, 322, 323, 328, 329(m), 352
    on Missouri Compromise, 347, 348
    Native Americans and, 322
    Northwest Territory and, 265, 267(m), 269
    presidency of, 311(i), 316, 320(i), 322–331
on public subsidies to private businesses, 299
religion and, 162, 280(b)
in Second Continental Congress, 215
simplicity in presidency of, 323, 326–327, 326(i)
slavery and, 157, 222, 265, 269, 309–310, 327, 449
as vice president, 311
western land ordinances and, 252
Whiskey Rebellion and, 302
on whiskey tax, 327
as widower, 266(i)
Jersey, HMS, 230(b), 231(i)
Jew(s)
    in colonies, 132
    Constitution and, 280–281(b), 281(i)
    persecution of, 36
Jewelry making, 16(i)
Jim Crow laws, 578
Jobs
    government, 327–328
    for women, 343(b), 344, 358, 361–365, 364(i), 377, 378–379, 537–538
John Brown Going to His Hanging (painting), 502(i)
John Brown's raid (Harpers Ferry, Virginia), 475–476, 501–502, 503, 506
Johnson, Andrew (1808–1875)
    assumes presidency, 547, 561
    background of, 561–562
    impeachment of, 565, 570–571, 570(i)
    on planters, 562
    presidency of, 561–565, 570–571, 570(i)
    on reconciliation between North and South, 562
    during Reconstruction, 561–564, 568, 570–571, 570(i)
    on slavery, 562
Johnson, Jane, 457
Johnson, William, 180, 183, 184(b), 185(b)
Johnson-Sirleaf, Ellen, 429(b)
Johnston, Albert Sidney, 523
Johnston, Joseph, 520
Jolliet, Louis, 131(b)
Jones, Charles Colcock, 459
Jones, Samuel, 202(b)
Jones, Timothy, 202(b)
Judicial review, 328
Judiciary Act (1789), 328
Judiciary Act (1801), 327
Justification by faith, 62

Kansas
    "Bleeding," 496–497, 496(i), 497(i), 506
    slavery in, 496–497, 496(i), 497(i), 500, 506
Kansas-Nebraska Act (1854), 485–487, 487(m), 492, 493, 496, 498, 499, 500
Kaskaskia, Illinois, 239
Kearny, Stephen Watts, 418
Kearsarge (Union ship), 524
Kendall, Mary, 454
Kennesaw Mountain, Battle of (1864), 539(t), 541(m), 544
Kentucky
    during American Revolution, 239, 244–245
    in Civil War, 514–515, 523
    evangelical revivals in, 379, 466
    Maysville Road project in, 369

removal of Indians in, 372
settlers in, 303, 328
Unionism in, 515
Kentucky Resolution (1798), 312, 373
Keokuk (Native American leader), 410(i)
Kill site, 14(b), 15(i)
King, Rufus, 344
King Cotton diplomacy, 524, 525(f)
King George, Grandy, 137, 138
King Philip (Metacomet; Native
    American leader), 110–111(b),
    127–128, 128(i)
King Philip's War (1675–1676), 127–128,
    128(i)
King's College, 287
Kingsley, Bathsheba, 163
King's Mountain, Battle of (1780), 243
King William's War (1689–1697), 129,
    131(b), 132
Kiowa tribe, 409, 412
Kiva (ceremonial room), 19, 20(i)
Know-Nothing Party, 490, 490(t), 492,
    492(i), 493
Knox, Henry (1750–1806), 290
Ku Klux Klan (KKK), 553, 573,
    574–575(b), 575(i), 580, 582, 584
Ku Klux Klan Acts of 1870 and 1871,
    575(b), 582

Labor code, 556–557
Labor force
    free. *See* Free labor
    strikes by, 363–364
    wages for, 361
    women in, 343(b), 344, 358, 361–365,
        364(i), 377, 378–379
Labor strikes, by New England women,
    363–364
Ladies Association, 229
*Lady's Magazine and Repository of
    Entertaining Knowledge,* 293(i)
Lafayette, Marquis de, 244(i), 343(b)
Lake Champlain, 178(m), 180
Lake Texcoco, 29
Lancaster, Pennsylvania, 255, 300(b)
Lancaster Turnpike (Pennsylvania), 294,
    294(m)
Land auctions, after Civil War, 556(i)
Land bridge, 7, 7(m), 14(b)
Land distribution, in New England
    colonies, 140–141
Land grant(s)
    during American Revolution, 223, 236
    by English king, 71, 126
    in middle colonies, 120
    in Nicaragua, 489(b)
    in Ohio Country, 177
    railroads and, 399–400
    to Virginia Company, 71
Land-Grant College (Morrill) Act (1863),
    537
Land ordinances, 252, 265–269, 266(m),
    267(m)
Land policy, and agriculture, 397–398, 398(i)
Languages
    African, 153
    of first Americans, 15(b)
    Latin, 58(b)
    in Mexico, 45(i), 46, 58(b), 59(b)
    Native American, 15(b), 46, 58(b),
        59(b), 73, 74(i)
    in New World, 46, 58(b), 59(b)
    Spanish, 45(i), 46, 58(b), 59(b)

Laptop writing desk, 222(i)
Las Casas, Bartolomé de, 55
Latin language, 58(b)
Law(s). *See also names of specific laws*
    apprenticeship, 562–563
    Bacon's, 92
    on banking, 537
    on bankruptcy, 389(b)
    banning importation of British goods,
        331
    British, 84–85(b), 89(b), 92, 175,
        186–200, 201, 204, 215
    on civil rights, 564–565, 571(t), 582
    commercial, 365
    on confiscation of slaves in
        Confederate military, 528, 529, 556
    on duties on molasses, 186–187, 193
    on emancipation, 259, 346, 381, 461
    on eminent domain, 365
    family, 337–340
    on federal use of force against states,
        373
    on French law in Quebec, 199, 200
    on fugitive slaves, 481–484, 503, 506
    governing servants and slaves,
        84–85(b), 89(b)
    on homesteading, 537
    of incorporation, 365
    Jim Crow, 578
    on judiciary, 327, 328
    on Ku Klux Klan, 575(b), 582
    on land grants, 537
    on legal tender, 537
    manumission, 259
    on marriage, 337
    on military reconstruction, 569–570,
        571(t)
    on negligence, 365
    on neutrality, 488(b)
    nonimportation, 331
    on paper money, 537
    prohibiting trade with Great Britain
        and France, 333–334
    on quartering British soldiers, 193
    on railroads, 537
    during Reconstruction, 570, 571–572,
        571(t), 573
    on religious issues, 280(b)
    on removal of Indians from Indian
        lands, 371–372, 372(m)
    right of states to nullify, 312–313, 373,
        479
    on Sabbath, 280(b), 281(b)
    on sedition, 312–316, 373
    on Shays's Rebellion dissidents, 271
    slave codes, 439
    on slavery in new territories, 485–487,
        487(m), 492, 493, 496–500, 506
    on taxes, 186, 187, 188, 188(i),
        190–191(b), 192, 192(i), 193–194,
        215, 299, 302, 327, 422(b), 537
    on tea, 198
    on tenure of office, 571
    Townshend Acts, 193–197
    on trade, 90, 92, 127, 156, 158, 186–187,
        331, 333–334
    on U.S. neutrality, 488(b)
    women and, 337–340
Law, Richard, 202(b)
Law of Baron and Feme, The, 337
Lawrence, Kansas, 496, 497(i)
League of Five Nations, 23
Lecompton constitution (Kansas), 500

Le Dru, Pierre, 322(i)
Lee, George Washington Curtis, 546(i)
Lee, Richard Henry (1732–1794), 192,
    198, 222, 257
Lee, Robert E. (1807–1870)
    in Civil War, 518, 520, 521, 540–541,
        541(m), 544, 546, 546(i)
    John Brown's raid and, 475
    surrender of (1865), 539(t), 546
Legal Tender Act (1862), 537
Leisler, Jacob, 128
L'Enfant, Pierre, 301(b)
Lenni Lenape Indians, 121(i), 125
Leopard (frigate), 331
Letters from a Farmer in Pennsylvania
    (Dickinson), 193, 215
Lewis, Meriwether (1774–1809), 327,
    329–330
Lewis and Clark expedition, 322,
    329–330, 329(m)
Lexington (steamboat), 363(b), 363(i)
Lexington (Massachusetts), Battle of
    (1775), 204–206, 205(m), 215
Liberal Party (1872), 581
Liberator (antislavery newspaper), 382(i),
    384, 535
Liberia, sending freed slaves to, 381, 427,
    428–429(b), 429(i)
Liberty
    in American Revolution, 247
    of blacks in Reconstruction, 561
    individual, 358, 365
    Jefferson's view of, 327
    property and, 192–193
    Roger Williams on, 104
    slavery and, 176, 206–207, 206(i), 208,
        220, 439, 492
    in state constitutions, 255
Liberty Party, 415
Liberty poles, 229
Liberty Tree (Boston), 190(b)
Lien, 579
Lien merchants, 579
Life expectancy, among ancient
    peoples, 17
Lincoln, Abraham (1809–1865)
    on African Americans as soldiers,
        532–533(b), 533(i)
    assassination of, 546–547, 561
    background of, 395–396, 396(i),
        401, 499
    at beginning of Civil War, 513, 514
    character and temperament of, 395,
        396, 499
    Civil War strategy of, 516, 517, 528(b)
    on divisions between North and South,
        476, 505, 506
    in election of 1860, 502–504, 503(i),
        504(i)
    in election of 1864, 539, 545–546
    Emancipation Proclamation of, 511,
        512, 529, 558(b), 560
    on free labor, 403, 407, 430
    in House of Representatives, 417
    on importance of Kentucky and
        Missouri, 515
    on importance of Union victory, 515
    inaugural address (1861) of, 506, 513
    inaugural address (1865) of, 555
    on John Brown's raid, 475–476,
        501–502
    in Lincoln-Douglas debates, 500–501
    as military leader, 517, 518–519, 520

Lincoln, Abraham (continued)
  on Polk, 417
  Proclamation of Amnesty and
    Reconstruction (1863), 555
  on Reconstruction, 555–556
  on resources of North, 536(i)
  on rights of African Americans,
    499–500
  on secession, 505, 506, 513
  slavery and, 457(i), 499–501, 525,
    528–529
  success of, 396, 405
  white supremacy and, 499
Lincoln, Mary Todd, 395, 396
Lincoln, Nancy, 395
Lincoln, Thomas, 395–396
Lincoln-Douglas debates, 500–501
Lipscomb, Smith and Sally, 464–466
Liquor, 305, 321, 380–381, 424
Literacy rates, 378, 404(f), 577
Literacy tests, 346
Little Turtle (Native American leader),
  304, 305
Livestock
  London market for, 79(i)
  of Native Americans, 25
  in New England colonies, 141, 142,
    159(f)
  transporting from Europe, 45(i), 46
  See also individual animals
Livingston, Robert R. (1746–1813), 328,
  362(b)
Lockport, New York, 360(i)
Lone Star Republic, 414
Longfellow, Henry Wadsworth
  (1807–1882), 485
Longhouses, 23
Long Island, Battle of (1776), 227
Lopez, Narciso, 488–489(b)
Los Angeles, California, in Mexican-
  American War, 418
Louisiana
  Civil War in, 519(m), 523
  during Reconstruction, 575(b), 584–585
  secession of, 505
  after Seven Years' War, 181(m)
  slavery in, 439, 452(b), 453(i), 476
Louisiana Purchase (1803), 322, 323, 328,
  329(m), 352, 398
Louis XIV, king of France, 130(b)
Louis XVI, king of France (1754–1793),
  308
Lovejoy, Elijah, 384
Lowell, Massachusetts, 361, 363, 365
Lower South, 513, 514
Loyalists (Tories), 221, 225, 228, 229,
  232–236, 232(m), 246, 262(i)
Luther, Martin (1483–1546), 62
Lutherans, 146, 146(i), 379
Lynn, Massachusetts, 364–365, 365(i)
Lyon, Mary, 379
Lyon, Matthew, 313(i), 315(b)

Machine tool industry, 399
Mackintosh, Ebenezer, 188, 189,
  190–191(b), 191(i)
Madison, Dolley (1768–1849), 332,
  332(i), 336, 337
Madison, James (1751–1836), 252(i)
  acceptance of Articles of Confederation
    and, 254–255
  background of, 251–252
  on banking, 298

Bill of Rights and, 290, 291
character and temperament of, 251
in confederation government, 255
on consolidation of war debt, 296, 298,
  300(b)
Constitution and, 250(i), 252(i), 271,
  273, 274, 275, 278, 280(b), 282
in elections, 256, 331–332, 335
Hamilton and, 251, 288, 296, 298,
  300(b)
on Jay Treaty, 308–309
in Jefferson's government, 327
presidency of, 331–337
on public subsidies to private
  businesses, 299
on religion, 280–281(b)
in Second Continental Congress,
  251–252
as secretary of state, 331
on taxes, 299
Virginia Resolution written by, 315(b)
in War of 1812, 333–335
Magellan, Ferdinand (c. 1480–1521), 44
Mahican tribe, 140
Mail service, 294, 537
Maine
  ban on liquor in, 381
  statehood for, 347, 348(m)
Maize (corn), 45(i), 46, 71(i), 73, 75, 397,
  465(i)
Malaria, 428(b), 443, 543(b)
Malinali (Tobascan girl), 46–47, 47(i)
Malvern Hill, Battle of (1862), 519(m),
  542(b)
Mammoths, 8, 9, 10, 10(i), 11, 15(i)
Manassas (Bull Run)
  First Battle of (1861), 519–520, 519(m),
    523(t)
  Second Battle of (1862), 519(m), 521,
    523(t)
Mandan Indians, 24, 329–330
Manhattan Island, 120, 121(i), 124, 228.
  See also New York City
Manifest destiny
  filibusters and, 488–489(b), 489(i)
  U.S. expansion and, 407–408, 415, 416,
    420, 430, 486
Manigault, Louis, 460(i)
Manning, William, 263
Manufacturing
  changes in, 398–399
  financing of, 365
  growth of jobs in, 397
  mechanization of, 399
  of shoes, 361, 364–365, 365(i)
  tariffs and, 399
  of textiles, 361–364, 361(m), 364(i), 537
  U.S. encouragement of, 298–299
  women in, 537
Manumission, 259
Map desk, 174(i)
Marblehead, Massachusetts, 144(b),
  145(i)
Marbury, William, 328
Marbury v. Madison (1803), 328
"March to the Sea" (Sherman, 1864),
  539(t), 541(m), 544
Marie Antoinette, queen of France, 308
Marina (Tobascan girl), 46–47, 47(i)
Marines, in Nicaragua, 489(b)
Marion, Francis ("Swamp Fox"), 243(i)
Marion Crossing the Pedee (painting),
  243(i)

Market revolution (1815–1840), 358–366
  banks and, 365
  booms and busts in, 359, 365–366,
    374–375, 385, 386–390, 387(i),
    388–389(b), 500, 537
  commercial law and, 365
  manufacturing and, 298–299, 361–364,
    361(m), 364(i), 365(i), 398–399
  transportation and, 359–361, 359(m),
    360(i)
  working women and, 361–364, 364(i),
    378–379
Marks, A. A., 567(i)
Marquette, Jacques, 131(b)
Marriage
  age of first marriage for women, 377(f)
  changes in, 376–378
  complex, 425
  importance of, 558(b)
  polygamy, 412
  separate spheres in, 376–378
  slave, 457–458
Marriage laws, 337
Marshall, James, 421, 422(b)
Marshall, John (Supreme Court justice;
  1755–1835), 325(b), 327–328, 371
Martha's Vineyard, Massachusetts, 229,
  258(i)
Martin, Anna, 233
Martineau, Harriet, 480(i)
Martinique, 181, 186
Mary I, queen of England (r. 1553–1558),
  105(t), 106
Mary II, queen of England (r. 1689–1694),
  105(t), 128
Maryland
  acceptance of Articles of Confederation
    and, 253, 254
  in Civil War, 521
  colonies in. See Chesapeake Bay colony
  loyalists in, during American
    Revolution, 221
  poor planter's house in, 91(i)
  ratification of Constitution by, 276–277,
    276(m)
  religion in, 87, 162
  slavery in, 207, 259, 459(i)
  Unionism in, 515
Mask, 2(i)
Mason, David, Joanna, and Abigail,
  119(i)
Mason, George, 258, 278
Mason, Priscilla, 292(b)
Mason-Dixon line, 436, 470, 493, 540
Massachusetts
  American Revolution in, 226(m)
  constitution of, 258, 260(b)
  insurrections in (1774–1775), 204–207,
    205(m), 206(i)
  Know-Nothing Party in, 492
  land claim of, 264–265
  manufacturing in, 361
  ratification of Constitution by, 276–277,
    276(m)
  Shays's Rebellion in, 261(b), 269–271, 302
  slavery in, 259, 260–261(b)
  on war with Mexico, 417
Massachusetts Bay Company, 108, 115
Massachusetts colony. See also Boston,
  Massachusetts
  founding of, 108–109, 112
  government of, 128–129, 132, 167–170,
    175, 199–200

religion in, 103–104, 105–120,
122–123(b)
seal of, 108(i)
towns in, 113
Massachusetts Government Act (1773),
199, 200, 202(b)
Mass markets, 158
Mathews, John, 456–457
Matrilineal rules of descent, 23
Maumee River, 305
Maverick, Elizabeth, 190(b)
Maverick, Samuel, 191(b)
Maxwell, Henry, 533(b)
Mayan culture, 45(i), 60
Mayflower (Pilgrim ship), 107
Mayflower Compact, 107
Maysville Road project (Kentucky), 369
McAlpin, Henry, 449(i)
McClellan, George B. (1826–1885)
in Civil War, 520, 521, 523(t), 543(i),
545, 555
in election of 1864, 545
McCormick, Cyrus (1809–1884), 397, 537
McCrea, Jane, 238(i)
McDowell, Irvin, 518–519, 520
McJunkin, George, 3, 4(i), 12, 13, 30
Meade, George G., 540
Meadowcroft (Pennsylvania), 14(b)
Measles, 45(i), 46, 50(b), 60
Mechanical reaper, 397, 537
Mechanization, of manufacturing, 399.
See also Technology
Mediterranean trade, 37–38, 38(m), 40
Meetinghouse, 115(i)
Melrose, Andrew, 401(i)
Melville, Herman, 212(i)
Memphis, Tennessee, 523(t), 569(i)
Mennonites, 146
Mercantilism, 90
Mercenaries, in American Revolution,
221, 223(i), 227, 227(i), 228, 237
Mercer, Frederick W., 453(i)
Méricourt, Théroigne de, 292(b)
Merrimack (frigate), 523, 523(t)
Merrimack River, 361
Mesa Verde, Colorado, 19
Mestizos (mixed races), 57, 57(i), 60
Metacomet (King Philip), 110(b),
127–128, 128(i)
Metcalf, Michael, 112(i)
Meteor impact on North America, 8, 8(m)
Methodist sects, 340, 379, 382(b), 428(b),
458, 466, 553
Mexica culture (Aztecs), 28–30, 28(i),
29(i), 46–48, 50–51(b), 51(i), 53(i),
59(b), 59(i), 63
Mexican-American War (1846–1848),
416–420, 416(m), 418(i), 476, 478(i),
516–517
Mexican borderlands, 412–414, 412(m),
413(i)
Mexican cession, 476, 477(m), 479
Mexican empire, 28–30
Mexico
ancient cultures in, 19, 19(i)
borders of, 412, 420, 420(m)
filibusters (adventurers) in, 488–489(b),
489(i)
human sacrifice in, 28(i), 29, 47
independence from Spain, 349, 412
lands in Southwest belonging to, 407,
412–414, 412(m), 413(i), 486(i)
language in, 45(i), 46, 58(b), 59(b)

Native Americans in, 28–30, 28(i),
29(i), 412
Spanish conquest of, 46–48, 47(i),
47(m), 50–51(b), 51(i)
spreading Christianity in, 58–59(b)
toll of Spanish conquest in, 60, 60(i)
U.S. relations with, 412–420
Mexico City, Mexico, 413, 416(m), 419
Miami tribe, 268, 303, 304, 305, 333
Michaud y Thomas, Julio, 418(i)
Michigan
conflicts with Native Americans in, 333
population growth in (1830–1860), 397
Middlebury College (Vermont), 342(b)
Middlebury Female Academy (Vermont),
342(b)
Middle colonies, 120(m), 126(m)
agriculture in, 147–151, 148(i), 149(i)
economy of, 142–143, 146–151, 158,
159(f)
founding of, 120–121, 124–125
immigrants in, 142–143, 146–147
Native Americans in, 120, 121(i)
population of, 118(i), 140(m), 142
religion in, 121, 124–125, 125(i),
132, 162
settlement of, 147–151
standard of living in, 150
trade and trading in, 149–150,
158, 159(f)
work ethic and values in, 150–151,
150(i)
Middle Passage, 153–154, 155, 156
Middling folk, 143
Midwest. *See also specific states*
immigrants in, 406–407
population growth in (1830–1860), 397
Migrations, to Western Hemisphere,
6–10, 7(f), 7(m), 8–9(b)
Military Reconstruction Act (1867),
569–570, 571(t)
Military service, during American
Revolution, 223–225. *See also*
Continental Army
Militia(s)
during American Revolution, 223–225,
237, 239
patriotism and, 320(i)
as peacetime defense, 327
right to bear arms and, 290
at Treaty of Fort Stanwix, 265
in War of 1812, 336
Militia Act (1862), 529
Mill, John Stuart, 524
Miller, Lewis, 446(i)
Milliken's Bend, Battle of, 530
Mimbres people, 19
Minavavana (Native American leader),
184(b)
Mingo Indians, 177, 179, 185(i), 265
Minguez, Father Juan, 167(i)
Minié, Claude, 518(i)
Minié balls, 518(i)
Mining
of coal, 397
of gold, 394(i), 405(i), 420–424, 522
of silver, 56, 61, 61(i), 522
Minuit, Peter, 120
Minutemen, 204, 205
Miscegenation (amalgamation), 440,
442(i), 450, 455
Mission(s), Spanish, 166(f), 166(i),
168–169(b), 414

Missionaries
in California, 168–169(b)
Evangelicals and, 379–380
Native Americans and, 53, 53(i), 54–55,
58–59(b), 92–93, 98, 131(b),
168–169(b), 370, 371
in New France, 131(b)
in New Spain, 53, 53(i), 54–55,
58–59(b), 92–93, 98
Mission Carmel, 166(i)
Mississippi
Civil War in, 519(m), 523
discrimination against African
Americans in, 562
during Reconstruction, 562, 564, 577,
584, 585
secession of, 505
on voting rights and property, 346
Mississippian cultures, 2(i), 20–22, 20(m)
Mississippi River, 360, 362(b), 522
Missouri
in Civil War, 514–515, 522
rights of slaves in, 497–498
statehood for, 346–348
Missouri Compromise (1820), 346–348,
348(m), 352, 476, 486, 498
Mobile, Alabama, 462
Mobilization, for Civil War, 517–518,
517(i)
Mogollon culture, 18(m), 19, 24
Mohawk River, 236, 264
Mohawk tribe, 23, 179, 232, 233(i), 236,
237, 246, 265
Mohawk Valley, 237, 239, 240(m)
Molasses Act (1733), 186
Molasses trade, 182, 193
Money
during American Revolution, 218, 236
banknotes as, 264, 365, 375
coins, 127(i), 298(i)
during confederation government,
263–264
hard, 236, 264, 365, 390
paper, 263–264, 275, 365, 390, 518,
531, 537
scale of depreciation of, 263(i)
Money supply, growth of, 359
Monitor (ironclad warship), 523, 523(t)
Moniz, Felipa, 41
Monk's Mound, 22
Monongahela, Battle of (1755), 180
Monopoly, 37
political, 586
for transport companies, 360
Monroe, Alabama, 572–573
Monroe, Elizabeth, 345, 349
Monroe, James (1758–1831)
American blacks in Liberia and, 428(b)
foreign policy of, 348–349
on Missouri Compromise, 347, 348
plot to kidnap, 323, 326
presidency of, 344–345, 348–349
Monroe Doctrine (1823), 348–349
Monrovia, Liberia, 428(b), 429(i)
Montecino, Antón, 54(b)
Monterey, California, 166
Monterrey, Mexico, 418
Monte Verde excavation (Chile), 14(b)
Montezuma (Mexica emperor), 47–48,
50(b), 59(i), 63
Montezuma, Isabel Tolosa Cortés, 61
Montgomery, Alabama, 505
Montgomery, Richard, 225, 227

Monticello, 310
Montreal, Canada, 181, 225, 226(m), 227
Moravians, 146
Mormon(s), 411–412
Mormon War (1857), 412
Morocco, 330–331
Morrill, Justin, 537
Morrill (Land-Grant College) Act (1863), 537
Morris, Robert (1734–1806), 251, 255, 263–264, 300–301(b)
Morris, Samuel, 482(b)
Morrison, Toni, 484(i)
Morristown, New Jersey, 228
Morse, Samuel F. B. (1791–1872), 399, 402–403(b)
Morse code, 402(b)
Moselle (steamboat), 363(b)
Mott, Lucretia, 383(b), 425
Mounds, burial, 20–22, 20(m), 25
Mount, William Sidney, 499(i)
Mount Holyoke Seminary (Massachusetts), 379
Mount Zion Baptist Church (San Antonio, Texas), 561(i)
Murray, Judith Sargent, 291, 291(i), 294, 341
Music, 97(i), 156, 459(i)
Muskets, 216–217(b), 217(i), 218, 219(i), 223(i), 518(i), 542(b)
Muskogean peoples, 23–24
Muslims, 39, 53

Na-Dené language, 15(b)
Nahuatl language, 45(i), 46, 58
Napoleon Bonaparte, 288, 323, 328
Naranjo, Domingo and Joseph, 167(i)
Narragansett Indians, 103
Narrative of the Life of Frederick Douglass, as Told by Himself (Douglass), 485
Narváez, Pánfilo de, 49
Nashville, Battle of (1864), 539(t), 541(m), 546
Nast, Thomas, 581(i)
Natchez tribe, 24
National Banking Act (1863), 537
Nationalism, 337, 535
National Negro Convention (Philadelphia, 1830), 381, 384
National Republicans, 367, 374, 386. *See also* Whig Party
National Road, 360
National Union Party, 568
Native Americans (Indians). *See also specific tribes*
　agriculture of, 17–20, 18(i), 19, 22, 23, 24, 25, 75
　in American Revolution, 214, 235(b), 236–237, 239–240, 240(m), 246
　ancient cultures, 2(i), 3–4, 11–22, 12(m), 13(i), 15(i), 16(i), 16(m)
　arrival in Western Hemisphere, 3, 5–8, 7(f), 7(m)
　artifacts of, 2(i), 3–4, 4(i), 11(i), 15(i)
　Asian genetic characteristics in, 15(b)
　assimilation of, 371
　in California gold rush, 422(b), 423(b)
　in Canada, 130–131(b)
　in Civil War, 522(i)
　in colonial New England, 103, 104, 107, 108, 109, 110–111(b), 115, 117, 127–128, 128(i), 140
　colonists' attitudes toward, 88(b), 89(b), 91, 128
　conflicts with
　　in colonies, 127–128, 128(i), 165, 175, 176–185
　　in Florida, 371
　　in Indiana, Illinois, and Michigan, 333, 333(i), 371
　　in Mississippi Territory, 335
　　in Ohio Country, 302–305, 304(m), 321–322
　　Pueblo revolt, 93
　　wars with U.S., 335, 371, 437, 517
　　in West, 93, 169(b), 407, 409–410
　crafts of, 11, 16, 16(i)
　dance of, 63(i)
　encomienda and, 52–56
　enslavement of, 96, 167
　European diseases and, 45(i), 46, 50(b), 60, 64, 74, 109, 167, 185(b), 218, 414
　in 1490s, 22–28, 23(f), 24(m), 25(i), 26–27(b), 26(i), 27(i)
　in fur trade, 130–131(b), 148
　Iroquois League of Six Nations, 179, 264–265
　languages of, 15(b), 46, 58(b), 59(b), 73, 74(i)
　Lewis and Clark expedition and, 329–330
　liquor and, 305, 321
　in Mexico, 412
　in middle colonies, 120, 121(i)
　in missions, 166–167, 168–169(b), 414
　in Northwest Territory, 268–269
　origins of, 6–10, 8–9(b)
　peace medals for, 370(i)
　policy of concentration of, 410
　population of, 22, 23(m)
　relations with British, 175–183, 180(i), 183(i), 184(b), 232, 236–237, 239, 246, 336, 352
　relations with French, 130–131(b), 165, 167(i), 178(m), 181, 182, 183
　religions of, 20, 22, 24, 25, 28(i), 29, 29(i), 58(b), 73, 92–93, 103, 110–111(b)
　relocation of, 369–372, 372(m)
　after Seven Years' War, 183, 183(i), 184–185(b)
　in Seven Years' War, 176–185
　Spanish explorers and, 37, 46–51, 47(i), 47(m), 49(i), 50–51(b), 51(i), 64
　steamboats and, 360
　trade with colonists, 73–74, 75, 75(i), 130–131(b), 148, 165
　Trail of Tears and, 372, 372(m)
　treatment in Spanish settlements, 52–56, 54–55(b), 61, 167
　treaty with confederation government, 264–265
　village of, 71(i)
　Virginia colonists and, 69–70, 72–75, 91–92, 98
　voting rights of, 572
　after War of 1812, 337, 352
　wars with U.S., 335, 371, 437, 517
　weaving of, 26–27(b), 26(i), 27(i)
　women, 18(i), 23, 57, 70, 70(i), 73, 75, 130(b), 168(b), 330, 370
Nativism, 490
Nat Turner's insurrection, 435–436, 436(i), 438
Natural increase, 139

Navajo tribe, 25
Navigation Acts (1650, 1651, 1660, and 1663), 90, 127, 156, 158, 164
Navigational aids, 38
Navy, 320(i), 349
　African Americans in, 511–512, 512(i)
　blockades by, 511, 516, 523–524, 526–527(b), 531
　in Civil War, 511–512, 523–524, 529
　submarines in, 524, 526–527(b), 527(i)
Nebraska
　naming of, 486
　slavery in, 486–487
Necklaces, 330(i), 370(i)
Needlework, 141(i)
Negligence, contributory, 365
Negro. *See* African Americans (blacks); Free blacks; Freedmen
"Negro rule," 553
Neolin (Native American leader), 184(b)
Netherlands
　colonies of, 78(m), 120–121, 121(i), 124
　exploration by, 43(m)
　height of men in, 224(f)
　involvement in fur trade, 130(b)
　warships of, 164(f)
Neutrality Act (1818), 488(b)
Neutrality Proclamation (1793), 308
Nevada
　Comstock Lode in, 476
　mining in, 522
Neville, John, 302
New Amsterdam, 78(m), 109
Newburgh, New York, 245
New England
　effect of Embargo Act (1807) in, 331
　manufacturing in, 399
　in War of 1812, 335, 335(m)
New England Anti-Slavery Society, 384
New England colonies, 109(m), 126(m)
　agriculture in, 117, 141
　American Revolution in, 226(m), 236–238
　British plan to isolate, 236–238
　economy of, 117–118, 140–142, 141(i), 158, 159(f)
　government of, 128–129, 132, 167–170, 199–201
　insurrections in (1774–1775), 204–207, 205(m), 206(i)
　land distribution in, 140–141
　Native Americans in, 103, 104, 107, 108, 109, 110–111(b), 115, 117, 127–128, 128(i), 140
　population of, 118, 118(i), 140, 140(m)
　religion in, 102(i), 103–104, 105–120, 122–123(b), 140, 162
　slavery in, 142
　society in, 112–120
　trade in, 117, 127, 141, 142, 158, 159(f)
　witch trials in, 119–120, 122–123(b)
New England Courant, 160(b)
New England Emigrant Aid Company, 496
Newfoundland, 37, 43, 64
New France, 165(m)
　fur trade in, 130–131(b), 131(i)
　Native Americans in, 130–131(b)
　Ohio Country as part of, 177, 178(m)
　tensions with New England colonies, 140, 176
New Hampshire, ratification of Constitution by, 276(m), 278
New Haven, Connecticut, 194

New Jersey
acceptance of Articles of Confederation and, 253, 254
colonial, 120, 120(m), 124
loyalists in, 236
ratification of Constitution by, 276–277, 276(m)
slavery in, 259
voting rights in, 257
women's rights in, 257, 292(b)
New Jersey Plan, 274
New Jerusalem, New York, 340
New Mexico
acquisition from Mexico, 418, 420, 420(m)
ancient cultures in, 18–20, 20(i)
boundary with Texas, 481
Civil War in, 522, 523(i)
missionaries in, 92–93, 98
Native American revolt in, 93
slavery in, 479, 481
Spanish outposts in, 61, 92–93
"New Negroes," 154–155, 156
New Netherland, 120–121, 121(i), 124
New Orleans, Louisiana
Battle of, 335(m), 336, 352, 357
Civil War in, 519(m), 523
free blacks in, 462
during Reconstruction, 568
shopping in, 451(i)
Spanish in, 328
steamboats in, 362(b), 448(i)
sugar mill in, 443
Newport, Rhode Island, 244, 281(i)
New South, 555. *See also* Reconstruction
New Spain, 52(m), 165(m)
borderlands of, 92–93, 167
mixed races (mestizos) in, 57, 57(i), 60
outposts of, 60–61, 92–93
religion in, 53, 53(i), 58–59(b), 92–93
in sixteenth century, 52–60
toll of Spanish conquest in, 60, 60(i)
treatment of Native Americans in, 52–56, 54–55(b), 132, 167
Newspapers, 161(i), 195, 203(b)
antislavery, 382(i), 384, 535
partisan, 367
technology and, 160–161(b), 367, 367(f)
in temperance movement, 381
New World, 34–65
Columbus in, 22, 34, 35–37, 36(i), 38, 41–42, 41(m), 44–45
conquistadors in, 46–51, 47(i), 47(m), 49(i), 50–51(b), 51(i), 52, 54
English in, 42–43, 43(m), 64
gold and silver in, 39, 42, 48(i), 49, 54, 56, 56(f), 61, 61(i), 62, 72, 98
languages in, 46, 58(b), 59(b)
New Spain in, 52–60, 52(i)
Portuguese in, 38(m), 39–40, 42, 52
religion in, 41–42, 47, 50(b), 51(b), 53, 53(i), 58–59(b), 73
sixteenth-century Europe and, 52–65
slavery in, 46–47, 56, 60
Spanish in, 36–37, 36(i), 41–42, 41(m), 43(m), 44–51, 47(i), 47(m), 48(i), 49(i), 50–51(b)
women in, 46–47, 57, 57(i), 61
New York
canals in, 361
colonial, 120, 120(m)
land claim of, 264–265
loyalists in, during American Revolution, 221, 225

New Netherland becomes, 124
ratification of Constitution by, 276(m), 278–279, 279(i)
representatives at Constitutional Convention, 273
slavery in, 259
on taxation, 264
in War of 1812, 336
New York City
during American Revolution, 245, 246, 255
banking in, 298
draft riots in (1863), 539
evangelical movement in, 379–380, 380(i)
nonimportation agreements in, 195
prisoners of war in, 230–231(b)
slaves in, 148, 260
traveling to and from by steamboat, 359(m), 360, 361
travel times from (1800), 295(m)
as U.S. capital, 294, 300(b)
New York Female Moral Reform Society, 381
New York Society of Pewterers, 279(i)
New York Suspending Act, 193–194
New-York Weekly Journal, 161(i)
Niagara (naval ship), 511
Nicaragua, filibusters in, 488–489(b), 489(i)
"Night riders," 584
Noble, T. S., 455(i)
Nonconsumption agreements, 194
Nonimportation agreements (1768–1770), 194–195
Nonimportation laws, 331
Non-Intercourse Act (1809), 334
Norfolk, Virginia, 523
Norsemen, 37
North. *See also* Civil War; Union
cities in 1860, 446, 447(m)
collapse of Reconstruction and, 582–583
on free labor, 440
on fugitive slave law, 482–484
geographical border with South, 436
immigrants in, 447, 447(f)
life in, during Civil War, 537–539, 538(i)
manufacturing in, 446, 447
tensions with South, 476–487, 502–506
view of dueling in, 325(b)
North, Frederick (1732–1792), 197, 198, 199, 204, 241
North Carolina
during American Revolution, 239, 243
founding of, 152
ratification of Constitution by, 276(m), 279
during Reconstruction, 585
secession of, 514, 514(m)
Secotan village in, 71(i)
slavery in, 207, 259
Northern colonies, 102–132, 109(m), 126(m)
economy of, 117–118, 140–142, 141(i), 158, 159(f)
land distribution in, 140–141
Native Americans in, 23(m), 103, 104, 107, 108, 109, 110–111(b), 115, 117, 127–128, 128(i), 140
population of, 118, 118(i), 140, 140(m)
religion in, 102(i), 103–104, 105–120, 122–123(b), 132, 140

slavery in, 142
trade in, 117, 127, 141, 142, 158
witch trials in, 119–120, 122–123(b)
Northup, Solomon, 485
Northwest cultures, 16, 22, 23(m), 25
Northwest Ordinance (1787), 269, 346, 476
Northwest Passage, 43, 64
Northwest Territory, 252
agriculture in, 268(i)
land ordinances and, 265–269, 266(m), 267(m)
Native Americans in, 268–269, 302–305, 304(m), 305(i), 333, 333(i), 334(m)
Ordinance of 1785 and, 266(m), 267
slavery in, 265, 269
"Note shaving," 388(b)
Nova Scotia, Canada, 262(i)
Noyes, John Humphrey, 425, 425(i)
Nullification
by states, 312–313, 373, 479
by Supreme Court, 328
Nursing, women in, 537–538

Oak Home Farm, San Joaquin County, California (painting), 477(i)
Oberlin College (Ohio), 378(i), 379
Ohio Company, 177, 183
Ohio Country
during American Revolution, 244–245
conflicts with Native Americans in, 185(b), 232, 302–305, 304(m), 321–322, 334(m)
French-British rivalry in, 177–179, 178(m), 185(b), 232
Ohio River, 303, 360
Ohio Valley, 176, 177, 177(m), 239, 265, 303
Ojibwa tribe, 130(b), 180, 184(b)
Old Calabar slave trade, 137–138
Olive Branch Petition (1775), 220
Oliver, Andrew, 188, 190(b)
Omnibus Bill (1850), 480–481
Oñate, Juan de (1550?–1630?), 61
Oneida community, 425, 425(i)
Oneida tribe, 23, 179, 180, 232, 235(b)
Onondaga tribe, 23, 179, 232
"On the Equality of the Sexes" (Murray), 294
Opechancanough (Native American leader), 75, 91
Oral culture, 309
Ordinance of 1784, 265, 267
Ordinance of 1785, 266(m), 267
Ordnance Bureau (Confederacy), 518
Oregon
settlement of, 408–410
statehood for, 415–416
Oregon Trail, 408–410, 409(m), 414
Oriskany, Battle of (1777), 237, 239
Ornamental arts, 341
O'Sullivan, John L., 408
Otis, Hannah, 141(i)
Oto Indians, 167
Ottawa tribe, 130(b), 180, 183, 184(b), 305
Overhiser, W. I., 477(i)
Overseer, 448, 452(b), 453(b), 463
Ozette culture, 17(i)

Pacific Coast cultures, 13, 16, 16(i), 16(m), 22, 25
Pacific Northwest cultures, 16, 22, 23(m), 25

Pacific Railroad Act (1862), 537
Paine, Thomas (1737–1809)
   Common Sense, 220, 221(i)
   as editor of *Pennsylvania Magazine,*
      219(i), 220
Palatine Germans, 237
Paleo-Indians, 10–11, 10(i), 11(i), 14(b)
Palmetto Guards, 497(i)
Panama, Isthmus of, 44
Pangaea, 6, 6(m)
Panic of 1819, 366, 373
Panic of 1837, 385, 386–387, 387(i), 390
Panic of 1839, 385, 390
Panic of 1857, 500
Paoli, Pasquale, 191(b)
Papago Indians, 486(i)
Paper money, 263–264, 275, 365, 390, 518,
   531, 537
Paris
   Treaty of 1763, 181, 182, 183,
      184(b), 328
   Treaty of 1783, 245–246, 264, 302, 321
Parker, Theodore, 480, 483
Parsons, Hugh and Mary, 123(b)
Parsons, Samuel H., 202(b)
Partible inheritance, 140
Partisanship, 316, 350, 367
Paternalism, 448–450, 450(i)
Patriotism, 320(i)
   during American Revolution, 228–229
   liberty and, 208
   of women, 195–196, 228–229
Pawnee tribe, 24, 167
Pawtucket, Rhode Island, 361
Paxton Boys, 185(b)
"Peace" Democrats, 545
Peace medal, 370(i)
Peale, Charles Willson (1741–1827), 252
Pea Ridge, Battle of (1862), 519(m),
   522, 523(t)
Peninsula campaign (1862), 520–521,
   521(i)
Peninsulares, 57
Penn, William (1644–1718), 120,
   124–125, 125(i)
Pennsylvania
   acceptance of Articles of Confederation
      and, 253, 254
   agriculture in, 147–151, 148(i), 149(i)
   canals in, 361
   colonial, 120, 120(m), 124–125, 125(i),
      150–151
   constitution of, 258
   first Americans in, 14(b)
   founding of, 120, 120(m)
   government of, 256
   immigrants in, 143, 146–147
   loyalists in, during American
      Revolution, 221
   Quakers in, 124–125, 150–151
   ratification of Constitution by, 276–277,
      276(m)
   slavery in, 259
   standard of living in, 150
   Whiskey Rebellion in, 294, 299, 302
Pennsylvania Dutch, 143
Pennsylvania Magazine, 219(i), 220
Pennsylvania Statehouse (Philadelphia,
   Pennsylvania), 273(i)
Penobscot tribe, 22
Pequot Indians, 127
Percy, George, 73
Perry, Oliver Hazard, 335

Peru, 48–49, 349
Petersburg, Virginia, fall of (1865), 539(t),
   541(m), 545, 546
Petersham, Massachusetts, 271
Philadelphia (warship), 330–331
Philadelphia, Pennsylvania
   British occupation during American
      Revolution, 238, 255
   City Tavern in, 272(i)
   colonial, 124–125, 150, 162
   First Continental Congress (1774) in,
      201, 204
   Independence Hall (Pennsylvania
      Statehouse) in, 273(i)
   National Negro Convention in,
      381, 384
   nonimportation agreements in, 195
   as U.S. capital, 294, 300–301(b)
   writing of Constitution in, 271–275
Philip, King (Metacomet), 110–111(b),
   127–128, 128(i)
Philip II, king of Spain (r. 1556–1598),
   62, 106
Philippines, 44
Phillips, Wendell, 382(i), 480, 555, 572
Photography, 482–483(b), 483(i)
Phyllis (slave woman), 139(i)
Pickering, Timothy, 310
Pickett, George E., 540
Pierce, Franklin, 485–486
Pike(s), 474(i)
Pike, James, 217(i)
Pilgrims, 107
Pinckney, Charles Cotesworth
   (1746–1825), 331–332
Pinckney, Eliza Lucas, 157(i)
Pinckney, Thomas (1750–1828), 310
Pioneer (submarine), 526(b)
Pioneers. *See* Westward movement
Pipes, 19(i), 45(i), 81, 87
Pippin, Horace, 502(i)
Pirates, 61, 323
Pistols, for dueling, 325(i)
Pit houses, 19
Pitt, William (1708–1778), 181, 182,
   184(b), 193
Pittsburgh, Pennsylvania, 177
Pizarro, Francisco (c. 1475–1541), 48–49
Plain folk, 462–466, 465(i), 469
Plains Indians, 409–410, 487
Plantation(s), 443(m), 448–461, 449(i),
   450(i), 463
   cotton, 437, 438(m), 443
   freedmen working on, 579, 580(m)
   planters on, 77, 153, 443, 448–449
   before and after Reconstruction, 580(m)
   rice, 96, 438(m), 443
   sharecropping on, 579, 586
   slave quarter on, 456–461, 457(i),
      458(i), 580(m)
   slavery on, 442–461
   sugar, 94–95, 94(i), 96, 241, 443
   tobacco, 82(i), 97–98, 438(m), 443
   women on, 450–451, 451(i), 454–455,
      454(i)
Plantation belt yeomen, 463
Planters
   "Christian guardianship" and,
      448–450, 450(i)
   exemption from draft, 535
   farmers vs., 443
   on free blacks, 461

   as masters of plantations, 448–449
   paternalism of, 448–450, 450(i)
   percent in southern legislatures, 468(t)
   plantation belt yeomen and, 463
   power of, 468–469
   President Johnson on, 562
   during Reconstruction, 557
   sharecropping and, 579, 586
   slave trade and, 153
Plows, 397
Plymouth colony, 103, 107
Pneumonia, 543(b)
Pocahontas (c. 1595–1617), 69–70,
   70(i), 98
Policy of concentration, 410
Political parties, 310–316. *See also* names
      of parties
   in antebellum South, 468
   beginnings of, 288–289, 310
   on foreign policy, 311–316
   geographic vs. national, 487
   immigrants and, 490
   importance in national elections, 368
   during Jackson administration, 366, 385
   partisanship in, 316
   realignment of, 487–495, 490(t)
   religion and, 490
   on slavery, 479, 506
Politics. *See also* Elections; *names of
      political parties*
   during Civil War, 538–539
   colonial, 90, 167–170
   democratic, 467–468
   of expansion, 414–416
   polarization of, 490–493, 492(i)
   popular, 367
   during Reconstruction, 573
   of slavery, 385–386, 466–469, 468(t)
   southern, 466–469
   women in, 220–221, 229, 229(i),
      332–333, 352, 371, 390, 396, 493, 573
Polk, James K. (1795–1849), 479
   in election of 1844, 415
   nationalism of, 415
   war with Mexico and, 414, 416–420
Polygamy, 412
Ponce de León, Juan, 49
Pontiac (Native American leader), 183,
   184(b)
Pontiac's Rebellion (1763), 183, 183(m),
   184(b), 185(i), 222
Pony Express mail service, 537
Poor Richard's Almanack (Franklin), 150,
   150(i)
Poor whites, 91(i), 464–466, 469
Popé (Native American leader), 93
Pope, John, 521
Pope's Day, 190(b)
Popular sovereignty, 345, 478, 490,
   496, 500
Population
   of African Americans, 95, 97, 142, 147,
      151–152, 437, 439(f), 443, 461
   census taking and, 297(i), 327
   of English colonies, 118, 118(i),
      138–139, 140, 140(m), 151
   in 1490s, 22, 23(m)
   of free blacks, 461
   growth of
      in Midwest (1830–1860), 397
      1770–1790, 303
      1790–1800, 295, 297(f)
   of slaves, 437, 439(f), 443

of middle colonies, 118(i), 140(m), 142
of New England colonies, 118, 118(i),
140, 140(m)
of southern colonies, 76, 118(i), 140(m),
151
of Virginia colony, 76, 140(m)
Port Hudson, Battle of, 530
Portolá, Gaspar de, 166
Portugal
exploration by, 38(m), 39–40, 42, 52
immigrants from, 96(i)
rejection of Columbus by, 36
Portulanos (sailing maps), 38
Potatoes, 46
Potawatomi tribe, 180, 305, 333
Potomac River, 300–301(b), 467(i)
Potosí, Bolivia, 61(i)
Pottawatomie, Kansas, 475
Pottery, 17, 17(i), 25, 434(i)
Pouch, Algonquian, 68(i)
Poverty
in England, 142
in middle colonies, 147–151
in New England colonies, 142
poor planter's house (Maryland), 91(i)
among southern whites, 464–466, 469
Powder Alarm of 1774, 200–204,
202–203(b)
Powder horn, 217(i)
Powell, Anne and William Dummer,
268(i)
Power loom, 364(i)
Powhatan (Native American leader;
1550?–1618), 68(i), 69–70, 71,
72–73, 72(m), 74–75, 74(i), 98
Prairie, 397
Predestination, 113
Prejudice. *See also* Racism (racial
prejudice and discrimination);
White supremacy
against African Americans, 427, 430,
532(b), 582, 584
against immigrants, 406(i), 407
Presbyterians, 162, 379
President. *See also names of presidents*
constitutional powers of, 275
inauguration of, 316, 505, 506, 513, 555
Presidential Reconstruction, 555–556,
561–565
Presidios, 166
Press, freedom of, 290
Preston, John Smith, 505
Preston, Thomas, 196, 199
Price of Blood, The (painting), 455
Princeton, New Jersey, 228, 255, 300(b)
Princeton University, 251
Printing, 36, 38, 102(i), 160–161(b), 160(i),
161(i), 367
Prisoners of war
during American Revolution,
230–231(b), 231(i)
during Civil War, 545(i)
held by Native Americans, 265
Privateers, 311, 320(i), 330
Procerberus, 8(b)
Proclamation of Amnesty and
Reconstruction (1863), 555
Proclamation of 1763, 183, 187, 239
Property
confiscation of, 233, 562
liberty and, 192–193
of loyalists, 233
slaves as, 439, 455(i), 528–529

voting rights and, 157, 256, 344,
345–346, 386
of women, 337, 340, 494–495(b)
Prophet, The (Tenskwatawa; Native
American leader), 321–322, 333,
333(i), 337
Prophetstown, 321–322, 333
Proprietors, 95–96
Prossor, Thomas, 323
Protestant Association, 128
Protestantism. *See also individual sects*
in colonies, 86–87, 98, 102(i), 103–104,
105–120, 140, 162–163, 200
Constitution and, 280–281(b)
evangelical, 358, 375–376, 379–380, 380(i),
385, 424, 428(b), 458, 466, 467(i)
among immigrants, 146, 146(i)
in Ireland, 407
political parties and, 490
Reformation and, 62, 105–106
slavery and, 436, 439–440, 441(b)
women and, 340, 341(i)
Protestant Reformation, 62, 105–106
Prussia, 231(b)
Public transportation, 359–360, 577–578
Pueblo, 18, 20, 20(i), 25
Pueblo Bonito, 20, 20(i)
Pueblo Indians, 93, 167(i)
Pueblo Revolt (1680), 93
Puritanism, 87, 102(i), 103, 104, 105–120
beliefs of, 113–114, 113(i), 114(i), 116
colonial economy and, 140
conformity and, 113–115
English Reformation and, 105–106
government under, 115–116
meetinghouse for, 115(i)
in settlement of New England,
107–109, 112, 132
splintering of, 116–117, 162
women and, 115, 116–117
Puritan Revolution, 105(t), 117, 164
Purses, abolitionist, 384(i)
Purvis, Robert, 498(i)
Putnam, Israel, 202(b)
Pynchon, William, 115

Quadrant, 38
Quakers (Society of Friends)
abolitionism of, 382(b), 383(b)
German immigrants and, 146, 150–151,
234(b), 340, 382(b), 383(b)
in New England colonies, 118, 119,
124–125, 146, 150–151, 234(b), 340,
382(b), 383(b)
in Pennsylvania, 124–125, 150–151
women, 340
Quantrill, William Clarke, 522
Quartering Act (1765), 193, 199–200
Quasi-War (1798–1799), 311–313, 316
Quebec, Canada, 131(b), 181
American Revolution in, 225, 226(m),
227, 236
Quebec Act (1773), 199, 200
Queen Anne's War (1702–1713), 143
Quetzalcoatl (Mexica god), 47
Quincy, Josiah, 196
Quitman, John A., 469, 488(b), 489(b)

Race relations
in Chesapeake colonies, 88–89(b), 97
in middle colonies, 147
in New Spain, 57, 57(i), 60
Racial segregation. *See* Segregation

Racism (racial prejudice and
discrimination). *See also* Ku Klux
Klan (KKK); White supremacy
antebellum, 147–148, 402, 427, 437, 470
in California, 422–423
in Civil War, 511–512, 512(i), 530(i),
532(b), 539
in colonies, 91, 147–148
among immigrants, 147–148
law on, 582
in Lincoln-Douglas debates, 501
in navy, 511–512, 512(i)
during Reconstruction, 553, 554, 562,
565, 568, 582, 584
Radical reconstruction, 568–570, 584
Railroads, 359(m), 361, 399–401, 401(i)
Chinese immigrants and, 422(b)
growth of, 399, 400(m)
land grants and, 399–400
manufacturing and, 399
ownership of, 399
transcontinental, 486, 537
Raleigh, Walter (1552?–1618), 64
Rammsay, Cato, 262(i)
Rancheros, 414, 423(b)
Ranchos, 414
Randall, A. B., 558(b)
Randolph, Edmund (1753–1813), 290,
450
Ranney, William T., 243(i)
Rapier, James T., 553–554, 554(i), 555,
583, 586
Rapier, John, 553
Rappahannock River, 521
Rathbun, Benjamin, 388, 389(b), 389(i)
Rathbun, Lyman, 388(b)
Ratification of the Constitution, 275–279,
276(m), 282, 290
Reaper, mechanical, 397, 537
Rebel(s). *See* Civil War; Confederacy
(Confederate States of America)
Rebellions, revolts, and uprisings
Bacon's Rebellion (1676), 87, 90–92, 97
Bear Flag Revolt (1846), 414
Gabriel's Rebellion (1800), 323
Native American revolts, 93, 169(b)
Nat Turner's insurrection, 435–436,
436(i), 438
in New England (1774–1775), 204–207,
205(m), 206(i)
Pontiac's Rebellion (1763), 183, 183(m),
184(b), 185(i), 222
Pueblo Revolt (1680), 93
Shays's Rebellion (1786–1787), 261(b),
269–271, 269(m), 270(i), 302
slave revolts, 155–156, 206–207, 206(i),
323, 326, 435–436, 436(i), 460–461,
554
Whiskey Rebellion (1794), 294, 299, 302
Reconquest, 35, 39, 51(b), 53
Reconstruction (1863–1877), 553–587,
584(m)
black codes during, 562–564, 563(i)
black suffrage in, 553, 554, 554(i), 556,
562, 565, 569, 572
"carpetbaggers" during, 552(i), 573
collapse of, 579–586, 584(m)
congressional, 555, 565–572
major legislation during, 571(t)
politics during, 573
presidential, 555–556, 561–565
radical, 568–570
second, 587

Reconstruction (continued)
  violence during, 568, 569(i), 573,
    574–575(b), 577, 579, 580, 582, 584
  wartime, 555–560, 556(i), 558–559(b),
    560(i)
Reconstruction Acts (1867), 570, 571–572,
  571(t), 573
Redcoats (British), 227. See also American
  Revolution; Great Britain
Red Cross, 538
Redeemers, 583, 585, 586
Redemptioners, 147, 170
Red Hawk (Native American leader), 239
Reed, Esther, 229
Reformation, 62, 105–106
Reign of Terror (France), 308
Religion(s). See also Catholic Church;
    Christianity; Protestantism
  in Africa, 97(i), 138
  of African Americans, 162, 435,
    458–459, 462, 553, 560, 561(i)
  of ancient people, 20, 22
  Constitution and, 280–281(b)
  controversies concerning, 117–120
  democratization of, 358
  European, 35–36, 50(b), 53(i), 62, 73
  evangelical, 358, 375–376, 379–380,
    380(i), 385, 424, 428(b), 458, 466,
    467(i)
  First Great Awakening, 162
  of immigrants, 146, 146(i), 407
  in middle colonies, 121, 124–125,
    125(i), 132, 162
  Mormons, 411–412
  Native American, 20, 22, 24, 25, 28(i),
    29, 29(i), 58(b), 73, 92–93, 103,
    110–111(b)
  in New England colonies, 102(i),
    103–104, 105–120, 122–123(b), 140,
    162
  in New World, 41–42, 47, 50(b), 51(b),
    53, 53(i), 58–59(b), 73
  political parties and, 490
  Second Great Awakening, 375–376,
    379–380, 380(i), 390
  slavery and, 162, 435, 439–440, 441(b),
    458–459
  in South, 84–85(b), 86–87, 92–93, 98,
    132, 162, 358, 375–376, 379–380,
    380(i), 385, 424, 428(b), 458, 466,
    467(i)
  in Spanish settlements, 53, 53(i),
    58–59(b), 92–93, 166, 166(i). See
    also Missionaries
Religious indifference, 162
Remond, Charles L., 498(i)
Rensselaer Polytechnic Institute, 342(b)
Repartimiento, 56
Report on Manufactures (1791), 298
Report on Public Credit (1790), 295
Republican(s), 310–316, 321–352
  beginnings of, 289, 310
  divisions in, 322, 367
  in election of 1800, 323, 323(m)
  on foreign policy, 311–316
  on sedition, 314(b), 315(b)
  after War of 1812, 337
  in XYZ affair, 311–312
Republican equality, 468
Republican government, 220, 252
Republicanism
  confederation government and, 255–256
  democracy vs., 275

Republican motherhood, 291, 291(i), 294
Republican Party
  Civil War legislation of, 537
  on Dred Scott decision, 498–499
  in election of 1856, 493
  in election of 1860, 502–504
  in election of 1864, 545
  in election of 1868, 553, 575(b), 580,
    581(i)
  in election of 1872, 553, 581
  in election of 1876, 585–586, 586(i)
  on free labor, 492
  Lincoln in, 499
  realignment of, 490(t), 492–493
  during Reconstruction, 562, 563, 564,
    565, 568, 572, 573, 574(b), 576–578,
    576(i), 579–580, 582, 583, 584,
    584(m)
  secession and, 505, 513
  women in, 492–493
Republic of Texas, 414–416
Requerimiento, 54–55(b)
Resaca de la Palma, Battle of (1846),
    416(m), 417
Revel, James, 83
Revenue Act (1764) (Sugar Act), 186, 193
Revenue Act (1767), 193–194
Revere, Paul (1735–1818), 197(i), 205,
    205(m)
Revivals, religious, 162–163, 379, 425, 466
Revolts. See Rebellions, revolts, and
    uprisings
Revolution(s)
  American. See American Revolution
  French, 306–308
  Haitian, 309–310, 309(m), 323, 554
Rhode Island
  acceptance of Articles of Confederation
    and, 253, 254
  during American Revolution, 244
  on Constitutional Convention, 273
  manufacturing in, 361
  ratification of Constitution by, 276(m),
    278–279
  religion in, 117
  slavery in, 142, 259
  on taxation, 264
Rice, 96, 152, 154(i), 156, 159(f), 241, 443
Richardson, Ebenezer, 196
Richmond, Virginia
  in Civil War, 519(m), 520, 521, 530, 531,
    534, 535
  fall of (1865), 539(t), 541(m), 546, 547(i)
Rifles, 216–217(b), 223(i), 518(i), 542(b)
Rights. See also Voting rights
  of African Americans, 499–500,
    564–565
  national Bill of, 289, 290–291
  of slaves, 497–498, 498(i)
  state bills of, 256, 258
  states' rights, 274, 349, 373, 531, 534,
    562
  of women, 115, 256–257, 291–294,
    293(i), 424, 425–426, 426(i), 554
Rights of Woman, The (de Gouges), 292(b)
Rio Grande, as border between Texas and
    Mexico, 416, 416(m), 420, 420(m)
Roads and trails
  California Trail, 414
  in early U.S., 294–295, 294(m)
  improvements after War of 1812, 359,
    359(m), 360
  National Road, 360

  in New England colonies, 141
  Oregon Trail, 408–410, 409(m), 414
  Santa Fe Trail, 412–413
  trails west, 408–410, 409(m)
Roanoke Colony, 64, 72
Robin John, Amboe, Ancona, and Little
    Ephraim, 137–138, 147, 153
Robinson, Solon, 448(i)
Rochambeau, Comte de, 244
Rockingham, Marquess of, 193
Rolfe, John (1585–1622), 70, 77, 88
Rolfe, Thomas, 70, 98
Roman Catholic Church. See Catholic
    Church
Romans, Bernard, 219(i)
Romney, George, 233(i)
Rose, Ernestine Potowsky, 494–495(b),
    495(i)
Rose, William, 494(b)
Rosecrans, William, 540
Ross, John (Cherokee chief), 371, 522(i)
Rowe, John, 191(b)
Royal charter, 107
Royal colony, 76, 127, 130(b), 167–170
"Royal fifth," 52
Rubber, 566(b)
Ruggles, Nathaniel, 202(b)
Ruggles, Timothy, 192
Runaway slaves, 460, 460(i), 481–485,
    484(i), 511, 512, 535
Rush, Benjamin, 291
Rush-Bagot disarmament treaty (1817),
    337
Russell, Martha, 483
Russia
  literacy rates in, 404(f)
  settlements of, 166
Russwurm, John, 428(b)

Sabbath breakers, 114(i)
Sabbath laws, 280(b), 281(b)
Saber-toothed cats, 9(i)
Sacajawea (Native American woman),
    330
"Sack of Lawrence" (Kansas), 496–497
Sacramento, Battle of, 418(i)
Safety, of steamboats, 360–361,
    362–363(b), 363(i)
Sager, Henry and Naomi, 411(i)
Sahagún, Bernardino de, 58–59(b)
Sahara Desert, 39
Sailors, 144–145(b), 145(i)
St. Augustine, Florida, 61
St. Clair, Arthur, 304, 305
St. Lawrence River, 64, 130(b), 148, 181
St. Leger, Barry, 237
St. Louis, Missouri, 2(i), 347(i)
St. Mary's City, Maryland, 91(i)
Salado culture, 29(i)
Salem, Massachusetts, 104, 119–120,
    122–123(b), 203(b), 216–217(b)
Saltcellar, 39(i)
Samoset (Wampanoag leader), 107
Sampson, Deborah, 213–214, 214(i), 245
Samuel, Rebecca, 280(b)
San Antonio, Texas, 413(i)
San Carlos Borroméo de Carmelo, 166
San Diego, California, 418
San Diego de Alcalá, California, 166,
    168–169
San Francisco, California, 421–423, 421(i)
San Jacinto, 414
San Joaquin County, California, 477(i)

San Miguel de Gualdape, 49
San Salvador, 41–42
Santa Anna, Antonio López de (1794–1876), 413–414, 418, 419
Santa Fe, New Mexico, 61, 418
Santa Fe Trail, 412–413
Santamaria, Juan, 489(b)
Santo Domingo, 309, 309(m), 582
Saratoga, Battle of (1777), 236–238, 238(m), 240
Savage's Station, Battle of (1862), 519(m), 520–521, 520(i), 523(t), 543(i)
Savannah, Georgia
　during American Revolution, 241, 246, 260
　fall of, during Civil War (1864), 539(t), 541(m), 546
"Scalawags," 573, 575(b)
Scale of depreciation, 263(i)
Scandinavia, literacy rates in, 404(f)
Schools. *See also* Education
　boarding, 344(i)
　district, 340
　for females, 340–344, 352, 379
　literacy rates and, 404(f)
　for nurses, 538
　public, 404, 466, 577, 577(i)
Schurz, Carl, 554, 586
Schuyler, Betsey, 287
Schuylkill Canal (Pennsylvania), 361
Schuylkill River, 149
Schwachheim, Carl, 3
Scots-Irish immigrants, 146, 151
Scott, Dred, 497–499, 498(i), 506
Scott, Winfield (1786–1866), 417(i), 419, 419(i), 485
Scriven, Abream, 458
Searches and seizures, in Bill of Rights, 290
"Seasoning," 155
Secession, 504–506, 513, 514–515, 514(m)
Second Bank of the United States, 365, 366, 369, 373–375, 390
Second Continental Congress (1775–1781), 215, 218
　during American Revolution, 225, 255
　Articles of Confederation and, 252–255
　assumes political and military authority, 215, 218
　attempts reconciliation with Britain, 215, 220
　currency of, 218, 236
　Declaration of Independence and, 221–222
　Madison in, 251–252
Second Great Awakening, 375–376, 379–380, 380(i), 390
Second Seminole War, 371
Secotan village (North Carolina), 71(i)
Sectionalism, 476, 481–487, 493
Sedgwick, Susan Ridley, 261(i)
Sedgwick, Theodore, 260(b)
Sedition Act (1798), 312–316, 373
Segregation
　Jim Crow laws and, 578
　in North, 427, 430
　in South, 578, 582
Self-control, 424, 430
Seminaries, female, 341, 342–343(b)
Seminole Indians, 260, 369, 371, 372, 522(i)
Seminole War (1836–1837), 371

Senate. *See also* Congress
　in Constitution, 278
　on Jay Treaty, 308
　on Wilmot Proviso, 478
Seneca Falls Declaration of Sentiments (1848), 426, 494(b)
Seneca tribe, 23, 179, 232, 237, 264(i), 265
Senegambia, 155
"Sentiments of an American Woman, The" (Reed), 229
Separate spheres, doctrine of, 376–378
Separatism, 107
Serra, Junípero (1713–1784), 166, 169(b)
Servants
　indentured, 70, 76(i), 78–79, 82–86, 87, 139, 147, 170
　runaway, 84
Settlement(s). *See also* Colonies; *names of individual settlements*
　agricultural, 17–22, 18(i), 18(m), 19(i), 20(i), 20(m)
　in Indian country, 302–303
　of Mexican borderlands, 412–414, 412(m)
　patterns of, 148(f)
　in West, 407–410, 409(m)
Seven Cities of Cibola, 49
Seven Days Battle (1862), 519(m), 520–521, 520(i), 523(t), 543(i)
Seventeenth Amendment, 501
Seventh-Day Baptists, 146(i)
Seven Years' (French and Indian) War (1754–1763), 165, 176–185
　causes of, 175, 176–179
　consequences of, 180–182
　European areas of influence in, 178(m)
　North America after, 181(m)
　summary of, 182
Seward, William H. (1801–1872), 480, 496, 503–504, 505, 517, 582
"Seward's Ice Box," 582
Seymour, Horatio, 580, 583(i)
Seymour, Jane, 106
Shako hat, 417(i)
Sharecropping, 579, 586
Shattuck, Job, 270(i)
Shaw, Nathaniel, 202(b)
Shawnee Indians, 179, 180, 180(i), 185(i), 232, 239, 240(m), 246, 265, 303, 304, 305, 321–322, 322(i), 333
Shays, Daniel, 270(i)
Shays's Rebellion (1786–1787), 261(b), 269–271, 269(m), 270(i), 302
Sheffield, Massachusetts, 260(b)
Sheffield, Robert, 231(i)
Sheldon, John, 129(i)
Shenandoah River, 149
Shenandoah Valley, sack of, 539(t), 541(m)
Shepard, William, 270(i)
Sheridan, Philip H. (1831–1888), 544
Sherman, William Tecumseh (1820–1891)
　in Civil War, 539(t), 541, 541(m), 544, 545, 546, 570
　plan for black settlement during Reconstruction, 557, 562
Shiloh, Battle of (1862), 519(m), 523, 523(t)
Ship(s). *See* Boats and ships
Shipbuilding, 141, 523
Shipping, and transportation improvements, 359–360, 361

Shirley, William, 180
Shoemaking, 361, 364–365, 365(i)
Shooting Star (Native American leader), 321
Shoshoni tribe, 330, 409
Shurtliff, Robert, 213
Siberia, 7, 14(b)
Sierra Nevada, gold rush in, 421
Silver, 56, 56(f), 61, 61(i), 62, 72, 98, 522
Silver coins, 236, 264
Singing plow, 397
Sioux tribe, 24, 409
Six Nations, Iroquois League of, 179, 264–265
Skipwith, Matilda, 429(b)
Skipwith, Peyton, 428–429(b)
Slater, Samuel, 361
Slaughterhouse cases (1873), 582
Slave codes, 439
Slave drivers, 457
Slaveholders, percent in southern legislatures, 468(t)
Slave revolts, 155–156, 206–207, 206(i), 323, 326, 435–436, 436(i), 459–461, 460(i), 554
Slavery, 435–470
　abolition of. *See* Abolition of slavery
　Africans in, 40(i), 60, 70, 78, 89(b), 94–95, 96(f), 97(i), 121(i), 137, 147, 151–155, 152(m)
　during American Revolution, 206–207, 206(i), 208, 214, 224–225, 244(i)
　in cities, 456–457
　Civil War and, 512, 515, 524–530, 531, 531(i), 548
　cost of, 147
　cotton and, 437, 438(m), 446, 446(i), 447–448
　culture and, 409, 437
　defense of, 436, 439–441
　diseases and, 153, 154, 155, 207, 443
　disintegration of, 535–536
　emancipated slaves, 260, 261(b), 381, 461, 528–529, 555. *See also* Freedmen
　Emancipation Proclamation and, 511, 512, 529, 558(b), 560
　end of, 548, 586
　equality and, 258–259
　in Europe, 40, 382–383(b)
　expansion of, 476–481, 477(m)
　families in, 155, 156, 442(i), 457–458
　growth of, 151–153, 152(t)
　legal changes to (1777–1804), 259–262, 259(m)
　Missouri Compromise and, 346–348, 348(m), 352, 476, 498
　Native Americans in, 96, 167
　in new territories, 269, 346–348, 348(m), 352, 476–481, 477(m), 496–500, 506
　in New World, 46–47, 56, 60
　in northern colonies, 142
　oral culture of, 309
　organizing against, 381–385, 384(i)
　paternalism in, 448–450, 450(i)
　on plantations, 442–461
　politics of, 385–386, 466–469, 468(t)
　population of slaves, 437, 439(f), 443
　pottery making and, 434(i)
　reinstitution of, 562–563, 563(i)
　religion and, 162, 435, 439–440, 441(b), 458–459

Slavery (continued)
   rights of slaves, 497–498, 498(i)
   runaway slaves and, 460, 460(i),
      481–485, 484(i), 511, 512, 535
   secession and, 504–506, 505(i), 513
   sending freed slaves to Liberia, 381,
      427, 428–429(b), 429(i)
   slave quarter and, 456–461, 457(i),
      458(i), 580(m)
   slaves as artisans, 456–457, 457(i)
   slaves as property, 439, 455(i), 528–529
   slaves suing for freedom, 260–261(b),
      261(i)
   spread of, in westward movement, 436,
      437, 438(m)
   taxes on, 469
   three-fifths clause of Constitution and,
      274, 327, 336
   trade and, 156–157
   voting rights and, 258–259, 258(i)
   in West Indies, 309, 382(b)
   whippings and, 449–450, 452–453(b),
      453(i)
   women in, 95, 97, 139, 153, 155, 207,
      207(i), 259, 260–261(b), 261(i), 426,
      430, 450, 450(i), 452(b), 456, 457,
      458
Slave ships, 137, 153–154, 154(i), 382(b),
   383(i)
Slave states, 346–348, 470, 476–481,
   496–497, 497(i)
Slave trade, 137–138, 151–155, 151(i),
   152(m), 152(t), 154(i), 274,
   382–383(b), 446(i), 455(i)
Sloths, 9
Smallpox, 45(i), 46, 50(b), 60, 185(b), 207,
   218, 228
Smith, Gerrit, 427(i)
Smith, John (1580?–1631), 69–70, 72(m),
   73, 74, 74(i), 77, 98
Smith, Joseph, Jr. (1805–1844), 411–412
Smith, William Thompson Russell,
   467(i)
Smithfield Market (London), 79(i)
Smoking
   in ancient cultures, 19(i)
   in Europe, 45(i), 46, 70, 80–81(b), 81(i),
      154(i), 156, 158, 366
   in New World, 45(i), 46, 77
   in southern colonies, 77. See also
      Tobacco
Smuggling, 182, 186–187, 198
Sneden, Robert Knox, 520(i), 545(i)
Snowshoes, colonial, 129(i)
Snuff, 81
Society
   in Chesapeake Bay colony, 87–90, 90(i)
   in New England colonies, 112–120
   in southern colonies, 156–157
Society for Effecting the Abolition of the
   Slave Trade, 382(b)
Society of Friends. See Quakers (Society
   of Friends)
Sons of Liberty, 188, 192, 193, 195, 196,
   197, 198
South. See also Confederacy (Confederate
      States of America)
   agriculture in, 437, 438(m), 442–448,
      443(m). See also Crop(s);
      Plantation(s)
   "carpetbaggers" in, 552(i), 573
   cities in 1860, 446, 447(m)
   climate of, 437

congressional delegations from, 576,
      576(f)
   culture of, 436–448, 535
   democracy in, 466, 467–468
   dueling in, 325(b), 450
   free blacks in, 461
   geographical border with North, 436
   growing distinctiveness of, 436–448
   honor in, 450
   immigrants in, 447, 447(f)
   importance of cotton in, 437, 438(m),
      443–446, 516, 524, 525(f)
   lack of diversification in, 447–448
   life in, during Civil War, 530–536,
      531(i), 534(i), 535(i)
   Lower, 513, 514
   manufacturing in, 446, 447, 456
   plain folk in, 462–466, 465(i), 469
   plantation economy of, 437, 438(m),
      442–448, 443(m)
   plantation life in, 448–456, 449(i),
      450(i), 453(i), 455(i). See also
      Plantation(s)
   political parties in, 468
   politics of slavery in, 466–469, 468(t)
   poor whites in, 464–466, 469
   Reconstruction in. See Reconstruction
   religion in, 84–85(b), 86–87, 92–93, 98,
      132, 162, 358, 375–376, 379–380,
      380(i), 385, 424, 428(b), 458, 466,
      467(i)
   Republican Party in, 562, 563, 564, 565,
      568, 572, 573, 574(b), 576–578, 576(i),
      579–580, 582, 583, 584, 584(m)
   resources of, 515–517, 516(f), 522
   secession of, 504–506, 505(i), 513,
      514–515, 514(m)
   slave codes in, 439
   slaveless whites in, 462–463
   slave revolts in, 155–156, 206–207,
      206(i), 323, 326, 435–436, 436(i),
      460–461
   slavery in. See Slavery
   tensions with North, 476–487, 502–506
   trade and, 516
   Upper, 513, 514–515
   voting rights in, 157, 345–346, 386, 468,
      553, 554, 554(i), 556, 562, 565, 569,
      571–572
   white supremacy in. See White
      supremacy
South America, and Monroe Doctrine,
   349
South Carolina
   African Americans in, 152
   during American Revolution, 241–242,
      242(m), 243
   discrimination against African
      Americans in, 562
   federal tariff policy and, 373
   loyalists in, during American
      Revolution, 221, 233
   politics in, 469
   poor whites in, 464–465, 469
   ratification of Constitution by, 276–277,
      276(m)
   during Reconstruction, 562, 565, 577,
      579, 585
   secession of, 505, 505(i), 562
   slavery in, 259–260, 434(i), 449, 456,
      457, 458, 458(i), 459, 460–461, 462
   voting rights in, 157
   yeomen farmers in, 463–464

Southeast cultures, population of, 23(m)
Southern colonies, 126(m). See also
      Chesapeake Bay colony; Virginia
      colony
   agriculture in, 70, 71(i), 73, 75, 77–78,
      80–81(b), 82(i), 86, 87–88
   economy of, 158, 159(f)
   government in, 76, 90–92, 167–170
   guerrilla warfare in, 214, 242–243,
      243(i)
   Native Americans in, 69–70, 72–75,
      91–92, 98
   political conflict in, 90–92
   population of, 118(i), 140(m), 151
   religion in, 84–85(b), 86–87, 92–93, 98,
      132, 162
   Revolutionary strategy in, 241–243,
      242(m)
   in seventeenth century, 69–98
   slavery in, 70, 77(i), 78, 84–85(b), 89(b),
      92, 94–98, 94(i), 151–157, 151(i),
      152(m), 154(i)
   tobacco in. See Tobacco
   trade with Europe in, 70–71, 158,
      159(f)
   trade with Native Americans in, 73–74,
      75, 75(i)
   women in, 76(i), 83, 86
"Southern Rights" flag, 497(i)
Southern strategy, 241–243
Southwest. See also names of states
   agriculture in, 17–18, 19
   cultures in, 18–20, 18(m), 19(i), 20(i),
      22, 24(m)
   fossils in, 3, 9(i)
   Mexican borderlands in, 407, 412–414,
      412(m), 413(i)
   Native Americans in, 23(m), 24–25,
      24(m), 486(i)
Spain
   acquisition of Florida from, 348–349
   areas of influence in Seven Years' War,
      178(m)
   claim to Louisiana Territory, 328
   conquest of Mexico, 46–48, 47(i), 47(m)
   exploration of New World by, 36–37,
      36(i), 41–42, 41(m), 43(m), 44–51,
      47(i), 47(m), 48(i), 49(i), 50–51(b)
   filibusters and, 488–489(b)
   immigrants from, 96(i)
   Mexican independence from, 349, 412
   monarchy in, 35, 36(i), 37
   religion in, 164
   settlements of. See New Spain
   in sixteenth century, 62–65
Spanish Armada, 71
Spanish sword, 34(i), 47, 48, 51(b),
   60(i), 93
Specie payment, 365
Speech, freedom of, 290, 538
Spinning, 195–196, 195(i)
Spinning mills, 361
Spoils system, 369, 581
Sports
   in Ancient America, 19(i)
   Native American, 184–185(b)
Spotsylvania Court House, Battle of
   (1864), 539(t), 541, 541(m)
Springfield, Illinois, 395, 396, 399, 499
Springfield, Massachusetts, 115
Squanto (Wampanoag leader), 107
Stability, of U.S., 289–294, 316
Stagecoach, 359, 360, 400

Stamp Act (1765), 187, 188, 188(i), 190–191(b), 192, 192(i), 193, 194, 215
Stamp Act Congress (1765), 192, 194
Standardized parts, 399
Standard of living, in middle colonies, 150
Stanton, Edwin M., 558(b), 571
Stanton, Elizabeth Cady (1815–1902), 343(b), 365(i), 425, 426, 494(b), 565, 572
State(s)
    acceptance of Articles of Confederation and, 253–255
    constitutions of, 255–256, 258
    federal use of force against, 373
    free, 346–348, 470, 476–481, 496–497, 497(i)
    right to nullify laws, 312–313, 373, 479
    slave, 346–348, 470, 476–481, 496–497, 497(i)
    sovereignty of, 255, 517
States' rights, 274, 349, 373, 531, 534, 562
Steamboats, 359(m), 360–361, 362–363(b), 363(i), 448(i)
Steam power, 397
Stephens, Alexander (1812–1883), 504, 505, 564
Stephens, Harry, 560(i)
Stevens, Elizabeth Alexander, 257(i)
Stevens, Thaddeus (1792–1868), 568–569, 570
Stewart, Maria, 384, 385
Stiles, Ezra, 203(b)
Stirrup, Spanish, 93, 93(i)
Stockbridge, Massachusetts, 260(b)
Stone tablet, 21(i)
Stono, South Carolina, 155–156
Storage chest, 120(i)
Stoves, 338–339(b), 339(i)
Stowe, Harriet Beecher (1811–1896), 341, 481, 484–485, 485(i)
Strait of Gibraltar, 39
Strikes. *See* Labor strikes
Stringfellow, Thornton, 441(b)
Strong, Bert, 452(b)
Stuart, Gilbert, 332(i)
Stuart, James E. B. ("Jeb"), 520
Stuyvesant, Peter, 121, 124
Submarines, 524, 526–527(b), 527(i)
Subsidies, to private businesses, 298–299
Suffrage. *See also* Voting rights
    African American, 553, 554, 554(i), 556, 562, 565, 569, 572
    qualifications for, 257, 344, 345, 386
    universal male, 344, 376, 468
    women's, 426, 493, 554
Sugar Act (Revenue Act of 1764), 186–187, 193
Sugar plantations, 94–95, 94(i), 96, 154(i), 158, 241, 443
Sullivan, John, 239
Sully, Thomas, 326(i)
Sumner, Charles (1811–1874), 415, 479, 496–497, 565, 568
Sunflowers, 17, 24
Supreme Court
    Dred Scott decision of, 496, 497–499, 498(i), 500, 506
    on impeachment of President Johnson, 571
    judicial review by, 328
    Marshall Court, 327–328, 371
    on Native American rights, 371

on personal liberty laws, 503
    on slave rights, 497–499, 498(i)
    undermines Reconstruction, 582, 583
Susquehanna River, 149
"Swamp Fox" (Francis Marion), 243(i)
Swords, 34(i), 47, 48, 51(b), 60(i), 73, 93
Synagogue, 281(i)

Tablet, Cahokia, 21(i)
Tainos, 41–42, 41(i)
Talcott, Samuel, 376(i)
Talleyrand-Périgord, Charles Maurice de (1754–1838), 311
Tallmadge, James, Jr., 346–347
Tanaghrisson (Native American leader), 177, 179
Taney, Roger B. (1777–1864), 497, 498, 503
Tapestry, 36(i)
Tarhe the Crane (Wyandot chief), 306(i)
Tariff(s), 90, 92, 186–187, 349, 369, 373, 399, 537
Tariff of Abominations (1828), 373
Tarring and feathering, 201(i), 233
Task system, 156
Taxes
    Articles of Confederation on, 253, 263, 264
    Civil War and, 518
    in colonies, 175, 186–187, 192–194, 197, 208
    confederation government and, 252, 253
    excise, 299, 302
    external vs. internal, 188
    laws on, 186, 187, 188, 188(i), 190–191(b), 192, 192(i), 193–194, 215, 299, 302, 327, 422(b), 537
    during Reconstruction, 584
    Shays's Rebellion against, 261(b), 269–271, 302
    on slaves, 469
    tax-in-kind, 534
    on trade (tariffs), 90, 92, 186–187, 349, 369, 373, 399, 537
    on whiskey, 299, 302, 327
Taylor, Charles, 429(b)
Taylor, Walter H., 546(i)
Taylor, Zachary (1784–1850)
    election of, 479
    in Mexican-American War, 416–417, 418
    presidency of, 479–481
Tea, tax on, 197–198, 199(i)
Tea Act (1773), 198
Tea Party (Boston, 1773), 198, 199(i)
Teapots, commemorative, 192(i)
Technology
    agricultural, 397
    artificial limbs, 566–567(b), 567(i)
    caravels, 40, 41
    clocks, 286(i), 345(i)
    compass, 38
    cookstoves, 338–339(b), 339(i)
    cotton gin, 294, 403(b), 443, 444(b), 445(i)
    daguerreotypes, 482–483(b), 483(i)
    in engineering canals, 360(i)
    inflatable rubberized bags, 396(i)
    irrigation, 18, 19
    Jefferson's duplicating machine, 327(i)
    mechanical reapers, 397, 537
    navigational aids, 38

newspapers and, 160–161(b), 367, 367(f)
    power looms, 364(i)
    printing, 36, 38, 102(i), 160–161(b), 160(i), 161(i), 367
    spinning mills, 361
    spinning wheel, 195(i)
    standardized parts, 399
    steamboats, 359(m), 360–361, 362–363(b), 363(i), 448(i)
    steel plow, 397
    submarines, 524, 526–527(b), 527(i)
    telegraph, 399, 402–403(b), 403(i)
    of weaving, 26–27(b), 195–196, 195(i), 364(i)
Tecumseh (Shawnee chief; 1768–1813), 321–322, 322(i), 333, 335, 337, 352
Tejano community, 412–414, 413(i), 420
Telegraph, 399, 402–403(b), 403(i)
Temperance movement, 380–381, 381(i), 424
Tennent, William, 162
Tennessee
    Civil War in, 522–523, 523(t)
    during Reconstruction, 563, 568, 569(i), 573, 574–575(b), 575(i), 585
    secession of, 514, 514(m)
    slave trade in, 446(i)
    statehood for, 357
Tennessee River, 519(m), 522, 523
Tenochtitlán (Mexico), 29, 47–48, 47(i), 47(m), 50(b). *See also* Mexico City, Mexico
Tenskwatawa (the Prophet; Native American leader), 321–322, 333, 333(i), 337
Tenure of Office Act (1867), 571
Terry, Eli, 345(i)
Testerian catechisms, 53(i)
Teton Sioux tribe, 24
Texas
    in Adams-Onís Treaty, 348
    border with Mexico, 416, 416(m), 420, 420(m)
    boundary with New Mexico, 481
    Hispanic community in, 413(i)
    as Lone Star Republic, 414–416
    during Reconstruction, 585
    secession of, 505
    settlement of, 413–414
    U.S. annexation of, 414–416, 415(i)
Texas Brigade (Confederacy), 534(i)
Texas War for Independence (1836), 414, 414(i)
Textile industry, 361–364, 361(m), 364(i), 537
Thames, Battle of (1813), 322, 335
Thanksgiving, 107
Thayendanegea (Joseph Brant; 1742–1807), 232, 233(i), 237, 239, 246, 265, 333(i)
Thirteenth Amendment (ratified 1865), 562, 571(t), 587
Thomasville, Georgia, 578(i)
Thompson, George, 382(i)
Thompson, John, 137
Thoreau, Henry David (1817–1862), 424
Three-fifths clause, 274, 327, 336
Tilden, Samuel J. (1814–1886), 585, 586(i)
Timber, in New England colonies, 117
Tippecanoe, Battle of (1811), 333, 334, 334(m)

Tlaxcala, 48, 50(b)
Tobacco
    British duties on, 90, 92
    as colonial export, 90, 92, 159(f), 366
    European market for, 45(i), 46, 70,
        80–81(b), 81(i), 154(i), 156, 158, 366
    as major cash crop, 443
    in New World, 17, 19(i), 46, 80–81(b)
    in panic of 1819, 366
    plantations, 82(i), 97–98
    slavery and, 154(i), 156
    in southern colonies, 77–78, 80(b), 87,
        97–98, 241
Tobacco cutter, 80(i)
Tobasco people, 46
Tocqueville, Alexis de (1805–1859), 437
Todd, Albert, 456
Todd, Anne, 252(i)
Toombs, Robert (1810–1885), 479, 502, 513
Tordesillas, Treaty of (1494), 42, 52,
    52(m), 71
Tories. See Loyalists (Tories)
Toronto, Canada, 335
Toussaint L'Ouverture, 309
Town meetings, 115
Townshend, Charles, 193
Townshend Acts, 193–197
Trade and trading
    of agricultural products, 294
    among ancient cultures, 16, 18
    colonial, 70–71, 73–74, 75, 75(i), 90, 92,
        127, 142, 143(m), 158, 159(f),
        194–196
    of commodities, 366
    of cotton, 444–445(b), 446, 448(i), 516,
        524, 525(f)
    English regulation of, 127, 194–196
    in Europe, 37–38, 38(m), 40
    between Europe and colonies, 70–71,
        142, 158, 159(f), 194–196
    between Europe and U.S., 444–445(b),
        516, 524
    fur, 130–131(b), 131(i), 148, 165, 182,
        184(b), 308, 408
    illegal, 182
    laws on, 90, 92, 127, 156, 158, 186–187,
        331, 333–334
    in middle colonies, 149–150, 158, 159(f)
    among Native Americans, 25
    with Native Americans, 73–74, 75,
        75(i), 130–131(b), 148, 165
    in New England colonies, 117, 127, 141,
        142, 158, 159(f)
    in New World, 45–46, 45(i), 73
    in slaves, 137–138, 151–157, 151(i),
        152(m), 152(t), 154(i), 274,
        382–383(b), 446(i), 455(i)
    smuggling and, 182, 186–187, 198
    taxes (tariffs) on, 90, 92, 186–187, 349,
        369, 373, 399
Trade goods, 75(i)
Trade routes, 38(m)
Trading posts, 40, 130(b)
Trail(s). See Roads and trails
Trail of Tears, 372, 372(m)
Traitors, 233, 236, 242
Transatlantic abolition, 382–383(b)
Transcendentalists, 424
Transcontinental railroad, 486, 537
Transportation. See also Roads and trails
    bridge tolls for, 296(i)
    improvements after War of 1812,
        359–361, 359(m)

public, 359–360, 577–578
    by railroad, 359(m), 361, 399–401,
        400(m), 401(i)
    by stagecoach, 359, 360, 400
    by steamboat, 359(m), 360–361,
        362–363(b), 363(i), 448(i)
    travel times from New York City
        (1800), 295(m)
    by wagon train, 409, 411
Transylvania University (Kentucky),
    342(b)
Travis, Joseph, 435
Travis, William B., 414
Treason, 325(b), 337, 515
Treasury system, 390
Tredegar Iron Works (Richmond,
    Virginia), 531
Trenton, New Jersey, 255, 300(b)
Tribute, 29, 59(i), 93, 330
Tripoli, 320(i), 330–331
Troy Female Seminary (New York), 341,
    342(b)
Trumbull, John (1756–1843), 288(i)
Trumbull, Lyman, 564
Truth, Sojourner, 426
Tubman, Harriet (1820?–1913), 430, 482
Tunis, 330–331
Turner, Nat (1800–1831), 435–436,
    436(i), 438
Turner, West, 457
Tuscarora tribe, 179, 232
Twelfth Amendment, 310, 323, 350
Twelve Years a Slave (Northup), 485
Twentieth Amendment, 505
Tyler, John (1790–1862), 415
Tyler, William, 90
Typhoid fever, 543(b)

Ulster County, New York, 207
Uncle Tom's Cabin (Stowe), 481, 484–485,
    485(i), 506
Underground railroad, 430, 483
Union. See also Civil War
    blockade by, 511, 516, 523–524,
        526–527(b), 531
    collapse of, 501–506
    draft and, 529–530, 532(b), 538–539
    freedom and, 524–530
    mobilization of, 517
    Native American recruits in, 522(i)
    resources of, 515, 516(f), 536(i)
    secession from, 505–506, 513, 514–515,
        514(m)
    uniform of, 523(i)
    victories of, 522–523, 539–541
Union Convention of Tennessee,
    558–559(b)
Unionism, vs. secession, 515
Unitarians, 379
U.S. Christian Commission, 538(i)
U.S. Constitution, 271–279. See also
        Amendments to Constitution
    Antifederalists on, 277–278, 282
    Bill of Rights in, 289, 290–291
    Federalists on, 276–277, 282, 290
    ratification of, 275–279, 276(m),
        282, 290
    religion and, 280–281(b)
    signing of, 250(i), 275
    on slavery, 274, 327, 336, 383(b)
    Virginia and New Jersey plans for, 274
    writing of, 271–275
U.S. Post Office, 294

U.S. Quartermaster Department, 542(b)
U.S. Sanitary Commission, 537, 538(i)
United States v. Cruikshank (1876), 582
Universal male suffrage, 344, 376, 468
Universities. See Colleges and
    universities
Upcountry yeomen, 463–464
Upper South, 513, 514–515
Uprisings. See Rebellions, revolts, and
    uprisings
Upton, Emory, 544(i)
Utah
    ancient cultures in, 19–20
    Mormon settlement in, 411, 412
    slavery in, 481
Utopian communities, 424–425, 425(i)

Vallejo, Mariano, 423(b)
Valley Forge, Pennsylvania, 238, 239
Van Bergen, Marten and Catarina, 148(i)
Van Buren, Martin (1782–1862), 372,
    385–390
    background of, 385–386
    economy and, 386–390, 387(i)
    in election of 1836, 385, 386
    in election of 1848, 479
    in Jackson administration, 385, 386
    Native Americans and, 372
    presidency of, 386–390, 387(i)
    on slavery, 385–386
Vanderlyn, John, 238(i), 324(i)
Van Dorn, Earl, 522
Veracruz, Mexico, 419
Vermont
    constitution of, 258
    male voting rights in, 345
Verrazano, Giovanni da (1485–1528), 64
Vesey, Denmark, 460–461, 462
Vesey conspiracy, 460–461
Vespucci, Amerigo (1454–1512), 43, 44
Veto, 369, 374
Vicksburg, siege of (1863), 539–540,
    539(t), 540(i), 541(m)
Vikings, 37
Vindication of the Rights of Woman, A
    (Wollstonecraft), 292(b)
Virginia
    bill of rights in, 256, 258
    boundaries of, 253
    canal in, 530(i)
    Civil War in, 519(m), 520–521, 521(i),
        540–541, 542(b)
    Civil War preparations in, 517(i)
    ratification of Constitution by, 276(m),
        278
    during Reconstruction, 585
    refugees from Haitian Revolution in,
        309
    secession of, 514, 514(m)
    shipbuilding in, 523
    slave revolts in, 435–436, 436(i)
    slavery in, 259, 435–436, 436(i), 457(i)
Virginia (frigate), 523, 523(t)
Virginia colony. See also Chesapeake Bay
        colony
    during American Revolution, 243
    government in, 76, 90–92, 167–170
    indentured servants in, 70, 76(i), 78–79,
        82–86
    Jamestown, 69, 72–73, 72(m), 75(i),
        76(i)
    laws in, 84–85(b), 89(b), 92
    political conflict in, 90–92

religion in, 84–85(b), 86–87, 98, 132
slavery in, 70, 77(i), 78, 84–85(b), 89(b),
    92, 97–98
society in, 87–90, 90(i), 156–157
tobacco in, 70, 77–78, 80–81(b), 82(i),
    86, 87, 90, 92, 97–98
voting rights in, 157
Virginia Company, 71, 72, 73, 74, 76, 77,
    78, 106
Virginia Convention, 251
Virginia Plan, 274
Virginia Resolution (1798), 312, 315(b),
    373
Virginia Resolves (1765), 174(i), 187–188,
    192, 273
Virtual representation, 187
"Visible saints," 113
Volta, Alessandro, 402(b)
Volunteers
    in Civil War, 537
    in war with Mexico, 417, 419(i)
Voting rights
    of African Americans, 257, 258–259,
        258(i), 346, 427, 553, 554, 554(i),
        556, 562, 565, 569, 571–573, 583(i)
    in Bill of Rights, 291
    literacy tests and, 346
    of Native Americans, 572
    in New England colonies, 129
    property qualifications for, 157, 256,
        344, 345–346, 386
    among Puritans, 115
    in South, 157, 345–346, 386, 468, 553,
        554, 554(i), 556, 562, 565, 569,
        571–572
    universal male suffrage, 344, 376, 468
    of women, 115, 256–257, 257(i), 340,
        346, 469, 554, 565, 568(i), 572

Wabash River, 304
Wade, Benjamin, 555
Wade-Davis bill (1864), 555
Wage labor, 361
Wagon trains, 409, 411
Waldseemüller, Martin, 44
Walker, David, 381, 435
Walker, Quok, 259
Walker, William, 489(b), 489(i)
"Walking Purchase" (1686), 148
Wallabout Bay (New York), 230(b)
Wampanoag Indians, 107, 127–128, 128(i)
Wampum (Native American currency),
    127(i)
War(s)
    among ancient cultures, 16
    Black Hawk (1832), 371, 517
    Civil. See Civil War
    Creek (1813–1814), 335, 437
    differing concepts of, 50(b)
    of 1812 (1812–1814), 322, 333–337,
        335(m), 336(i), 352
    guerrilla, 214, 242–243, 243(i), 496, 514,
        522, 574(b)
    King Philip's (1675–1676), 127–128,
        128(i)
    King William's (1689–1697), 129,
        131(b), 132
    Mexican-American (1846–1848),
        416–420, 416(m), 418(i), 476, 478(i),
        516–517
    Mormon (1857), 412
    national debt from, 262–264, 287–288,
        295–296, 298, 300(b)

with Native Americans, 127–128,
    128(i), 165, 175, 176–185, 335, 371,
    437, 517
Quasi-War (1798–1799), 311–313, 316
Queen Anne's (1702–1713), 143
Revolutionary. See American
    Revolution
Seven Years' (French and Indian)
    (1754–1763), 165, 175, 176–185
Texas War for Independence (1836),
    414, 414(i)
undeclared, 311–312
Yamasee War of 1715, 165
War bonds, in Civil War, 518
War club, 128(i)
Ward, Artemas, 215
War Hawks, 334–335, 337
Warren, Mercy Otis, 277
Warships
    in European navies, 164(f)
    U.S., 311, 330–331
Wartime Reconstruction, 555–560, 556(i),
    558–559(b), 560(i)
Washington, Augustine, 177
Washington, Booker T. (1856–1915),
    577(i)
Washington, D.C.
    burning of, 335–337, 336(i)
    established as capital, 300–301(b)
    plan for, 301(b), 301(m)
    role in national affairs, 586
    women in, 332–333, 332(i)
Washington, George (1732–1799)
    in American Revolution, 215, 218,
        219(i), 220, 223(i), 224, 227–228,
        227(i), 230(b), 231(b), 236, 237, 238,
        239, 244
    character and temperament of, 290
    clock, 286(i)
    at Constitutional Convention, 273
    on dress specifications for Continental
        Army, 212(i)
    farewell address of, 311(i)
    Federalist arguments of, 277
    in First Continental Congress, 201
    as first president, 289–290, 298, 302,
        303(i), 304, 305(i), 310, 311(i), 316,
        326
    on French Revolution, 308
    Hamilton and, 271, 287, 288, 289, 290
    journal of, 179(i)
    Neutrality Proclamation of (1793), 308
    proclamation protecting Indian
        Territory, 305(i)
    selection of capital by, 300–301(b)
    in Seven Years' War, 177, 179, 180,
        181
    on slavery, 155
    surrenders sword to Continental
        Congress, 289
    on whiskey tax, 302
Washington, Lawrence, 177
Washington, Martha (1731–1802), 262,
    326
Water travel, 359(m), 360–361. See also
    Boats and ships
"Waving the bloody shirt," 580, 585
Wayne, Anthony (1745–1796), 304–305,
    306(i)
Wealth
    in eighteenth century, 142
    in 1860s, 405
    in southern colonies, 97, 156–157

Weapons
    ancient, 3–4, 10, 11(i), 13, 13(i), 15(i), 21
    with bayonets, 223(i)
    bows and arrows, 13, 21, 25, 49(i), 73
    cannons, 237(i), 238
    of Continental Army, 216–217(b)
    dueling pistols, 325(i)
    of European explorers, 47, 48, 49, 49(i),
        50(b), 51(b), 60(i)
    firearms, 73, 75(i), 216–217(b), 217(i),
        218, 219(i), 223(i), 518(i), 542(b)
    harpoons, 17(i)
    muskets, 216–217(b), 217(i), 218, 219(i),
        223(i), 518(i), 542(b)
    pikes, 474(i)
    rifles, 216–217(b), 223(i), 518(i), 542(b)
    spears, 3–4, 12–13, 13(i), 15(i)
    swords, 34(i), 47, 48, 51(b), 60(i), 73, 93
    war clubs, 128(i)
Weathercock, 146(i)
Weaving, 26–27(b), 26(i), 27(i), 195–196,
    195(i)
Webster, Daniel (1782–1852), 374, 374(i),
    386, 480
Weld, Ezra Greenleaf, 427(i)
Wendell, Elizabeth Hunt, 139(i)
Werowance, 69
Wesley, Charles, 138
Wesley, John, 138
West. *See also names of specific states*
    American Revolution in, 239, 240(m)
    confederation government on lands in,
        252, 253–255, 254(m), 262
    conflicts with Native Americans in,
        302–305, 304(m), 306(i), 407,
        409–410
    expansion in, 414–424
    free labor in, 477
    land sales in, 375
    slavery in, 436, 437, 438(m), 476–478
    trails in, 408–410, 409(m)
Western Hemisphere. *See also* New World
    human habitation of, 7(f)
    migration to, 6–10, 7(f), 7(m), 8–9(b)
Western theater, Union victories in,
    522–523
West India Company, 120, 121, 124
West Indies, 95(m), 96(f), 241
    relations with U.S., 308
    sugar plantations in, 94–95, 96, 382(b)
    trade with New England colonies, 142,
        159(f)
Westmoreland Resolves, 192
West Point, New York, 242, 245
West Virginia, creation of, 515
Westward movement, 396, 407–414
    families in, 410, 411(i)
    manifest destiny and, 407–408, 415,
        416, 420, 430
    Mexican-American War and, 416–420,
        416(m), 418(i), 476, 478(i), 516–517
    in Mexican borderlands, 412–414,
        412(m), 413(i)
    Mormon exodus in, 411–412
    to Oregon, 408–410
    spread of slavery and, 436, 437, 438(m)
    trails west, 408–410, 409(m)
Whale hunting, 17(i), 159(f)
Wheat, 147, 150, 294, 361, 366, 397, 399
Wheatley, Phillis, 207, 207(i)
Wheelock, Eleazar, 233(i)
Whig Party
    on annexation of Texas, 415, 415(i)

Whig Party (continued)
  in bank war, 374
  in election of 1828, 368
  in election of 1836, 386
  in election of 1840, 390
  National Republicans become, 367, 386
  in panic of 1837, 387
  problems leading to demise of, 487,
    490, 490(t), 491(m), 493
  on slavery, 479
  on war with Mexico, 417
Whippings, 449–450, 452–453(b), 453(i)
Whiskey Rebellion (1794), 294, 299, 302
White, Hugh Lawson, 386
White, John, 63(i), 64, 71(i)
White Americans. See also Racism (racial
    prejudice and discrimination)
  abolitionist movement and, 381, 384,
    427
  Haitian Revolution and, 310
  poor, 91(i), 464–465, 469
  population in eighteenth century, 138,
    151–152
  as proportion of population (1860), 437
  southern, 437–442. See also
    Reconstruction; White supremacy;
    Yeomen farmers
    master-slave relationship on
      plantations, 448–450
    resistance to Reconstruction, 562–564
White Eyes (Native American leader), 239
Whitefield, George (1714–1770),
    162–163, 163(i)
White House, 332–333, 369
White supremacy. See also Ku Klux Klan
    (KKK)
  antebellum, 427, 430, 437, 470
  attempts to restore, 563, 573
  collapse of Reconstruction and,
    583–585
  in Confederacy, 515
  Democrats and, 583–585
  Lincoln and, 499
  during Reconstruction, 553, 554,
    574–575(b)
  slavery and, 147–148, 157, 424, 430,
    442, 515
  yeomen farmers, 463–464
"White terror," 573
Whitman, Marcus and Narcissa, 411(i)
Whitney, Eli (1765–1825), 294, 403(b),
    443, 444(b), 445(b), 445(i)
Whole Booke of Psalmes Faithfully Translated
    into English Metre, The, 102(i)
Wichita tribe, 409
Wigglesworth, Michael, 118
Wilberforce, William, 382(b)
Wilderness, Battle of (1864), 539(t), 541,
    541(m)
Wild Horse Arroyo, 3, 13(i)
Wilkinson, Eliza, 229
Wilkinson, Jemima, 340, 341(i)
Willard, Emma Hart, 341, 342–343(b)
Willard, John, 342(b)
William III (William of Orange),
    105(t), 128
Williams, Mary, 103
Williams, Nancy, 561
Williams, Roger (c. 1603–1683), 88(b),
    103–104, 116, 117, 132
Williamsburg, Virginia, 243
Wilmington, North Carolina, 533(b)

Wilmot, David (1814–1868), 476,
    477–478, 506
Wilmot Proviso (1846), 477–478, 480, 493
Winthrop, John (1606–1676), 103, 108,
    109, 112, 113, 116, 128, 132
Wisconsin
  population growth in (1830–1860), 397
  rights of slaves in, 497, 498
  statehood for, 479
Wisconsin glaciation, 7
Witch trials (Salem, Massachusetts),
    119–120, 122–123(b)
Wolfe, James, 181, 182
Wollstonecraft, Mary (1759–1797),
    292(b), 293(b), 337
Women
  in abolitionist movement, 383(b),
    384–385, 384(i), 427(i)
  African American, 95, 97, 139, 153, 207,
    207(i), 261(i), 426, 430, 482, 573,
    578(i), 579
  age of first marriage, 377(f)
  in American Revolution, 213–214,
    214(i), 223–224, 238(i), 245
  in California gold rush, 422(b)
  church governance and, 340, 341(i)
  in Civil War, 534–536, 535(i), 537–538,
    538(i), 543(b), 546, 548
  in colonies, 76(i), 83, 86, 118, 119,
    122–123(b), 139, 141(i), 157(i), 193,
    194–196, 194(i)
  cookstoves and, 338–339(b)
  discrimination against, 402, 426
  divorce and, 338–339, 451
  dueling and, 324–325(b)
  in early republic, 337–344
  education of, 35, 291, 294, 340–344,
    344(i), 352, 378–379, 378(i), 395,
    454, 466
  emancipation of, 426, 426(i)
  enslaved, 95, 97, 139, 153, 155, 207,
    207(i), 259, 260–261(b), 261(i), 426,
    430, 450, 450(i), 452(b), 456, 457,
    458
  evangelical revivals and, 379, 425
  exhorting, 340
  feminism and, 292(b), 572
  in fight to ratify Constitution, 277
  French Revolution and, 306–307, 307(i)
  immigrant, 407
  jobs for, 343(b), 344, 358, 361–365,
    364(i), 377, 378–379, 537–538
  Ku Klux Klan and, 575(i)
  law and, 337–340
  legal status of, 220
  on Lewis and Clark expedition, 330
  as loyalists, 233, 234(b)
  male attitude toward, 451
  Native American, 18(i), 23, 57, 70, 70(i),
    73, 75, 130(b), 168(b), 330, 370
  in New World, 46–47, 57, 57(i), 61
  in nursing, 537–538
  in Ohio conflict with Indians, 304
  patriotism of, 195–196, 228–229
  on plantations, 450–451, 451(i),
    454–455, 454(i)
  in politics, 220–221, 229, 229(i),
    332–333, 352, 371, 390, 396,
    493, 573
  in poor families, 464–466
  property of, 337, 340, 494–495(b)
  under Puritanism, 115, 116–117

  during Reconstruction, 554
  on removal of Indians from Indian
    lands, 371
  republican ideals for, 291, 291(i), 294
  in Republican Party, 492–493
  in resistance to British laws, 193,
    194–196, 194(i), 195(i)
  restrictions on, 454–456
  rights of, 115, 256–257, 291–294, 293(i),
    424, 425–426, 426(i), 554
  separate spheres of, 376–378
  on slavery, 383(b), 384–385, 384(i),
    427(i), 469, 483, 493, 501
  on small farms, 463–464
  spinning and weaving by, 26–27(b),
    195–196, 195(i)
  strikes by, 363–364
  in temperance movement, 381
  as utopians, 424, 425, 425(i)
  voting rights of, 115, 256–257, 257(i),
    340, 346, 469, 554, 565, 568(i), 572
  in westward movement, 410
Woodland cultures, 16–17, 17(i), 20–22,
    20(m), 22
Woodworking, 16
Worcester v. Georgia (1832), 371, 373
Workers. See also Immigrants; Labor force
  antebellum, 361–365
  artisans, 56, 60, 141, 220, 273, 422, 448,
    456–457, 457(i)
  colonial, 141, 147–151
  women, 343(b), 344, 358, 361–365,
    364(i), 377, 378–379
World Antislavery Convention (1840),
    383(b)
World Turn'd Upside Down, The, 113(i)
Worth, William, 419(i)
Writing
  by ancient cultures, 4–5, 5(i)
  defined, 5
  of Native Americans in 1490s, 25
Wyandot tribe, 306(i)

XYZ affair, 311–312

Yamasee War of 1715, 165
Yankees. See Union
Yankee traders, 142
Yellow fever, 443
Yeomen farmers
  in Civil War, 535
  defined, 87, 463
  idealism and, 465(i)
  Jackson administration and, 375
  plantation belt, 463
  during Reconstruction, 573
  taxes of, 469
  upcountry, 463–464
  wealthy farmers vs., 156–157
York, Pennsylvania, 255, 300(b)
Yorktown, Virginia
  Battle of (1781), 243–244, 244(i),
    244(m)
  Union Ordnance in, 536(i)
Young, Brigham, 412
Young, Lewis, 457
Yucatán Peninsula, 8, 8(m), 46

Zacatecas, Mexico, 61
Zemis (deities), 41(i), 42
Zenger, John Peter (1697–1746), 161(i)
Zuñi culture, 20, 49, 49(i)

ATLAS OF THE TERRITORIAL GROWTH OF THE UNITED STATES

THE ORIGINAL THIRTEEN COLONIES IN 1776   M-2

THE UNITED STATES IN 1783   M-3

THE UNITED STATES IN 1819   M-4

THE UNITED STATES IN 1853   M-6

THE CONTEMPORARY UNITED STATES   M-8

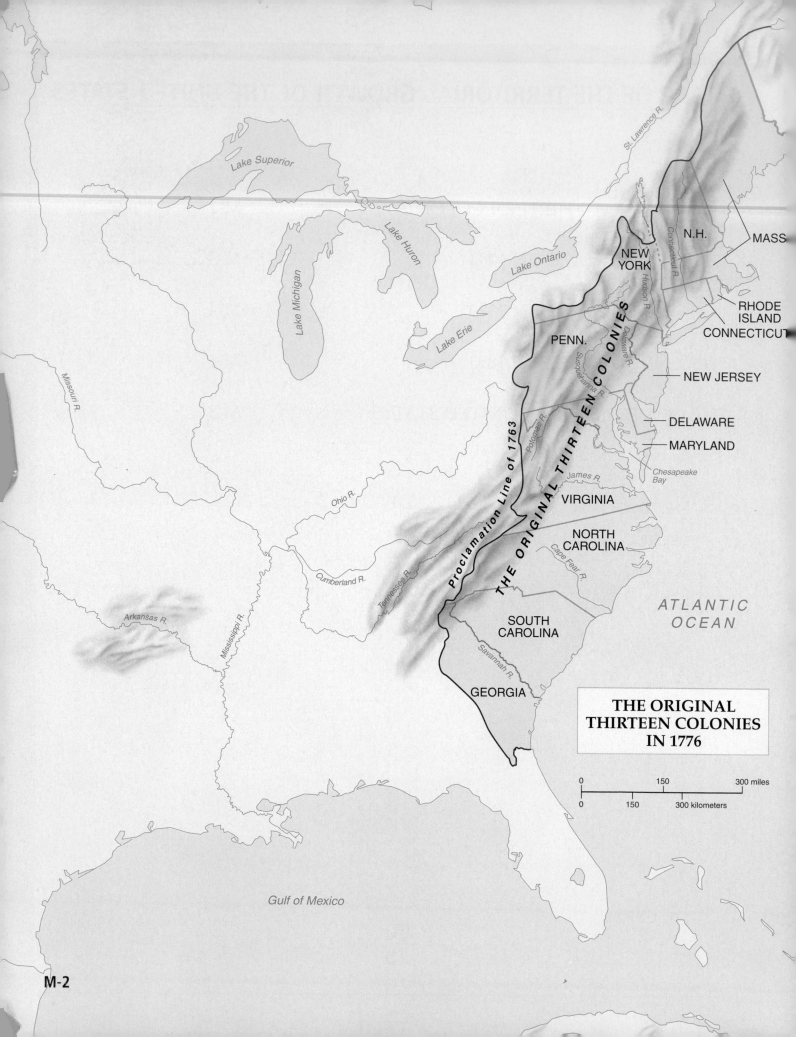

THE ORIGINAL THIRTEEN COLONIES

Lake Superior

Lake Huron

Lake Michigan

Lake Ontario

Lake Erie

St. Lawrence R.

Missouri R.

Ohio R.

Cumberland R.

Tennessee R.

Mississippi R.

Arkansas R.

Proclamation Line of 1763

Susquehanna R.

Delaware R.

Potomac R.

James R.

Hudson R.

Connecticut R.

Cape Fear R.

Savannah R.

Chesapeake Bay

N.H.

MASS

RHODE ISLAND

CONNECTICUT

NEW JERSEY

DELAWARE

MARYLAND

NEW YORK

PENN.

VIRGINIA

NORTH CAROLINA

SOUTH CAROLINA

GEORGIA

ATLANTIC OCEAN

Gulf of Mexico

THE ORIGINAL THIRTEEN COLONIES IN 1776

0   150   300 miles

0   150   300 kilometers

M-2

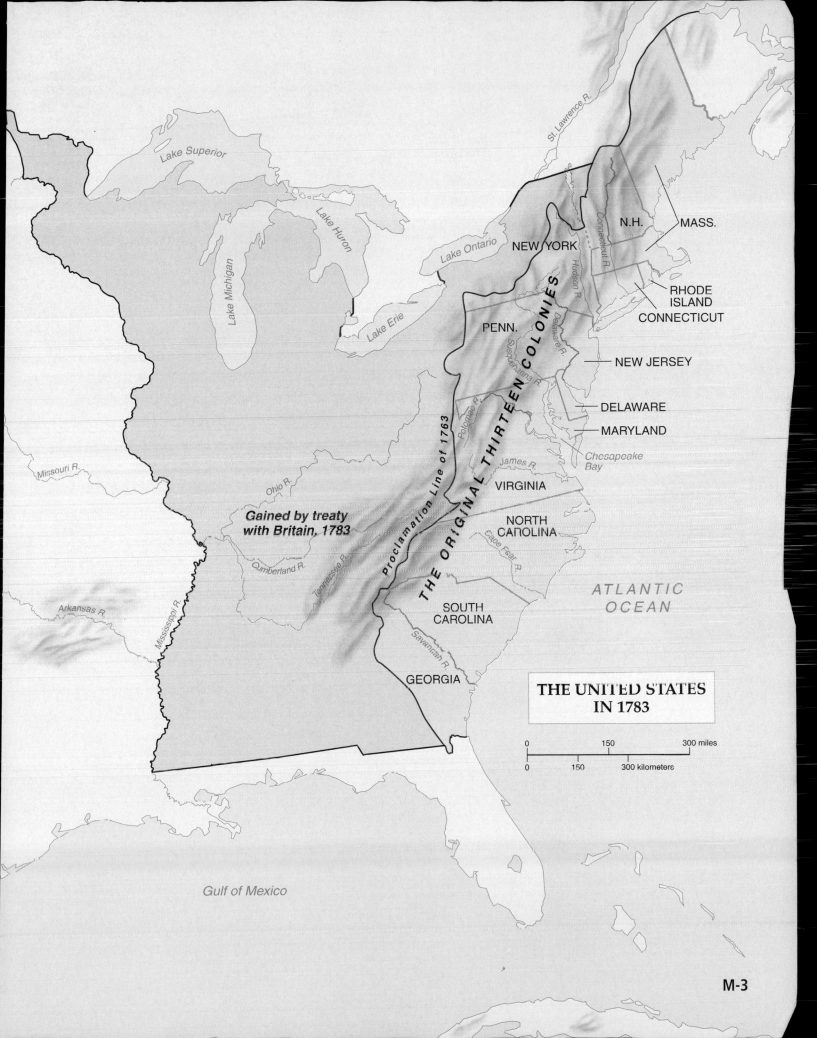

Lake Superior

Lake Michigan

Lake Huron

Lake Ontario

Lake Erie

St. Lawrence R.

Connecticut R.

N.H.

MASS.

NEW YORK

RHODE ISLAND

CONNECTICUT

Hudson R.

PENN.

Delaware R.

NEW JERSEY

Susquehanna R.

DELAWARE

MARYLAND

Potomac R.

THE ORIGINAL THIRTEEN COLONIES

Chesapeake Bay

Missouri R.

Ohio R.

James R.

VIRGINIA

Gained by treaty with Britain, 1783

Proclamation Line of 1763

NORTH CAROLINA

Cumberland R.

Tennessee R.

Cape Fear R.

ATLANTIC OCEAN

Arkansas R.

SOUTH CAROLINA

Mississippi R.

Savannah R.

GEORGIA

THE UNITED STATES IN 1783

0   150   300 miles

0   150   300 kilometers

Gulf of Mexico

M-3

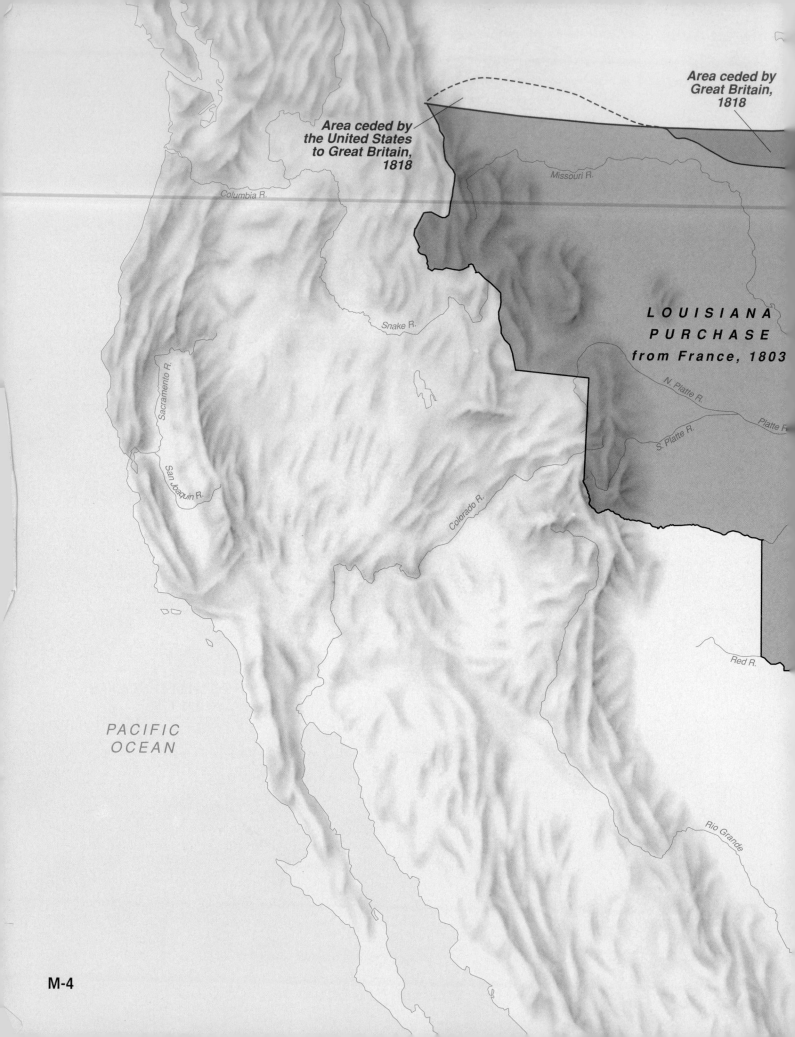

Area ceded by Great Britain, 1818

Area ceded by the United States to Great Britain, 1818

Missouri R.

Columbia R.

Snake R.

LOUISIANA PURCHASE from France, 1803

Sacramento R.

San Joaquin R.

N. Platte R.

S. Platte R.

Platte R.

Colorado R.

PACIFIC OCEAN

Red R.

Rio Grande

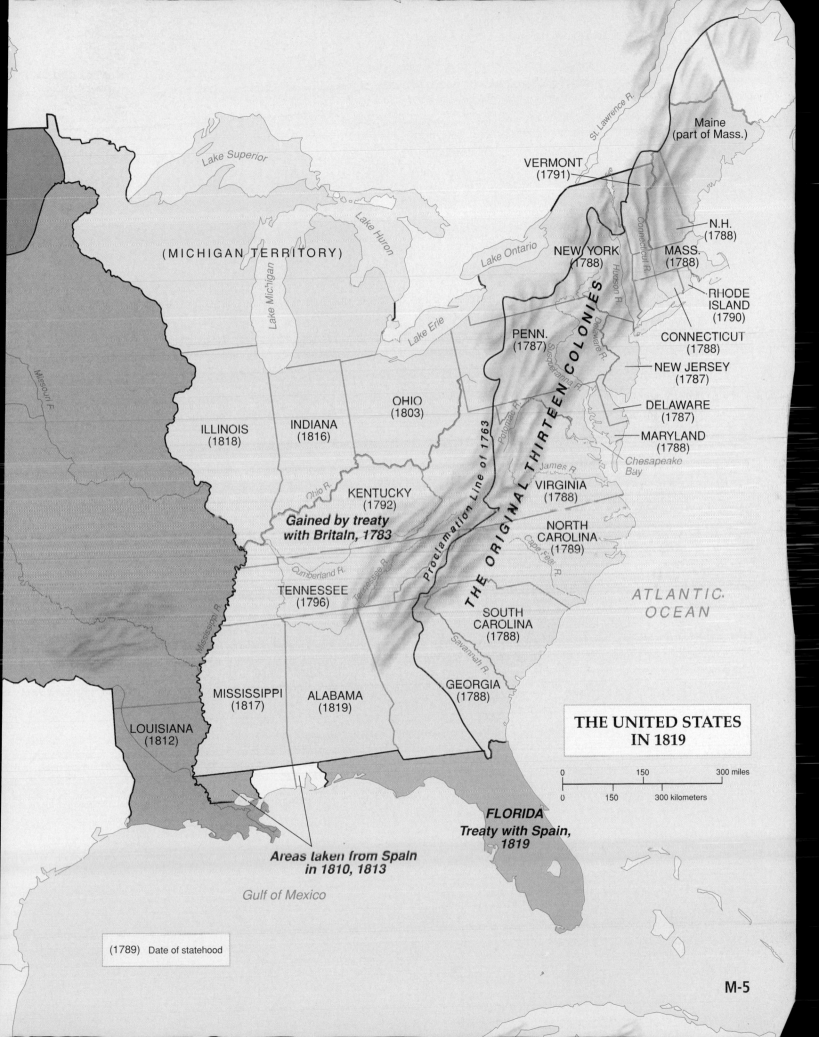

Maine
(part of Mass.)

St. Lawrence R.

VERMONT
(1791)

N.H.
(1788)

(MICHIGAN TERRITORY)

Lake Superior

Lake Huron

Lake Michigan

Lake Ontario

NEW YORK
(1788)

MASS.
(1788)

RHODE
ISLAND
(1790)

Lake Erie

PENN.
(1787)

CONNECTICUT
(1788)

NEW JERSEY
(1787)

THE ORIGINAL THIRTEEN COLONIES

OHIO
(1803)

DELAWARE
(1787)

MARYLAND
(1788)

Chesapeake
Bay

Missouri R.

ILLINOIS
(1818)

INDIANA
(1816)

Proclamation Line of 1763

Potomac R.

James R.

VIRGINIA
(1788)

Ohio R.

KENTUCKY
(1792)

**Gained by treaty
with Britain, 1783**

NORTH
CAROLINA
(1789)

Cape Fear R.

Cumberland R.

ATLANTIC
OCEAN

Tennessee R.

TENNESSEE
(1796)

Mississippi R.

SOUTH
CAROLINA
(1788)

MISSISSIPPI
(1817)

ALABAMA
(1819)

GEORGIA
(1788)

Savannah R.

**THE UNITED STATES
IN 1819**

LOUISIANA
(1812)

0   150   300 miles

0   150   300 kilometers

**Areas taken from Spain
in 1810, 1813**

**FLORIDA
Treaty with Spain,
1819**

Gulf of Mexico

(1789)   Date of statehood

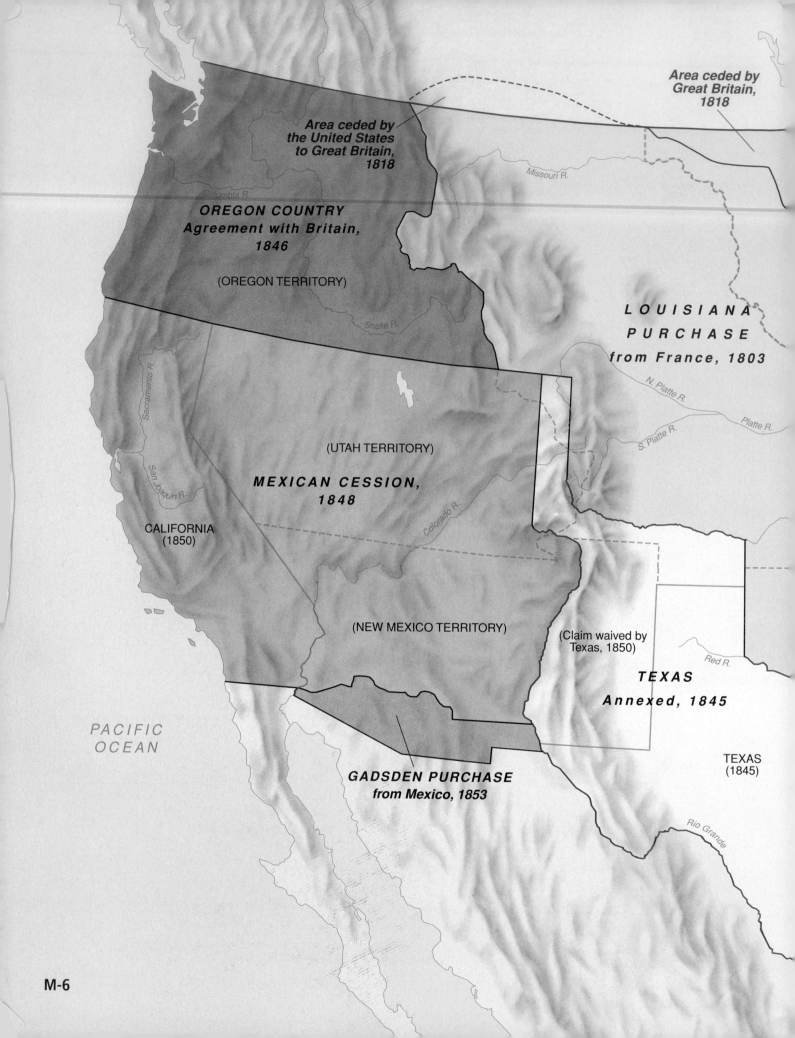

Area ceded by the United States to Great Britain, 1818

Area ceded by Great Britain, 1818

OREGON COUNTRY
Agreement with Britain, 1846

(OREGON TERRITORY)

LOUISIANA PURCHASE
from France, 1803

(UTAH TERRITORY)

MEXICAN CESSION, 1848

CALIFORNIA (1850)

(NEW MEXICO TERRITORY)

(Claim waived by Texas, 1850)

TEXAS
Annexed, 1845

TEXAS (1845)

PACIFIC OCEAN

GADSDEN PURCHASE
from Mexico, 1853

Columbia R.

Missouri R.

Sacramento R.

San Joaquin R.

Snake R.

Colorado R.

N. Platte R.

S. Platte R.

Platte R.

Red R.

Rio Grande

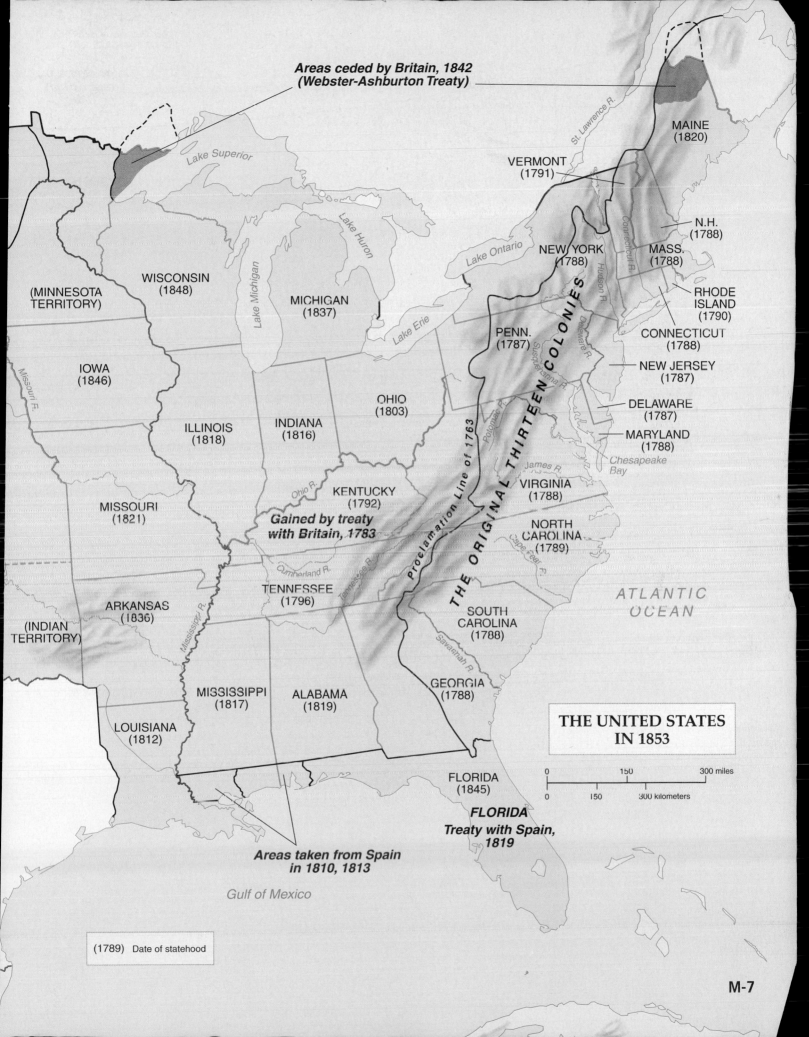

Areas ceded by Britain, 1842
(Webster-Ashburton Treaty)

MAINE
(1820)

VERMONT
(1791)

Lake Superior

N.H.
(1788)

St. Lawrence R.

(MINNESOTA
TERRITORY)

WISCONSIN
(1848)

Lake Huron

Lake Ontario

NEW YORK
(1788)

MASS.
(1788)

Connecticut R.

Lake Michigan

MICHIGAN
(1837)

RHODE
ISLAND
(1790)

Hudson R.

THE ORIGINAL THIRTEEN COLONIES

PENN.
(1787)

CONNECTICUT
(1788)

Lake Erie

IOWA
(1846)

Missouri R.

ILLINOIS
(1818)

INDIANA
(1816)

OHIO
(1803)

Susquehanna R.

NEW JERSEY
(1787)

Delaware R.

DELAWARE
(1787)

MARYLAND
(1788)

*Chesapeake
Bay*

Ohio R.

KENTUCKY
(1792)

Potomac R.

James R.

VIRGINIA
(1788)

Proclamation Line of 1763

MISSOURI
(1821)

Gained by treaty
with Britain, 1783

NORTH
CAROLINA
(1789)

Cumberland R.

Tennessee R.

ATLANTIC
OCEAN

ARKANSAS
(1836)

TENNESSEE
(1796)

Mississippi R.

SOUTH
CAROLINA
(1788)

Cape Fear R.

(INDIAN
TERRITORY)

Savannah R.

GEORGIA
(1788)

MISSISSIPPI
(1817)

ALABAMA
(1819)

THE UNITED STATES
IN 1853

LOUISIANA
(1812)

0   150   300 miles

0   150   300 kilometers

FLORIDA
(1845)

Areas taken from Spain
in 1810, 1813

FLORIDA
Treaty with Spain,
1819

Gulf of Mexico

(1789)   Date of statehood

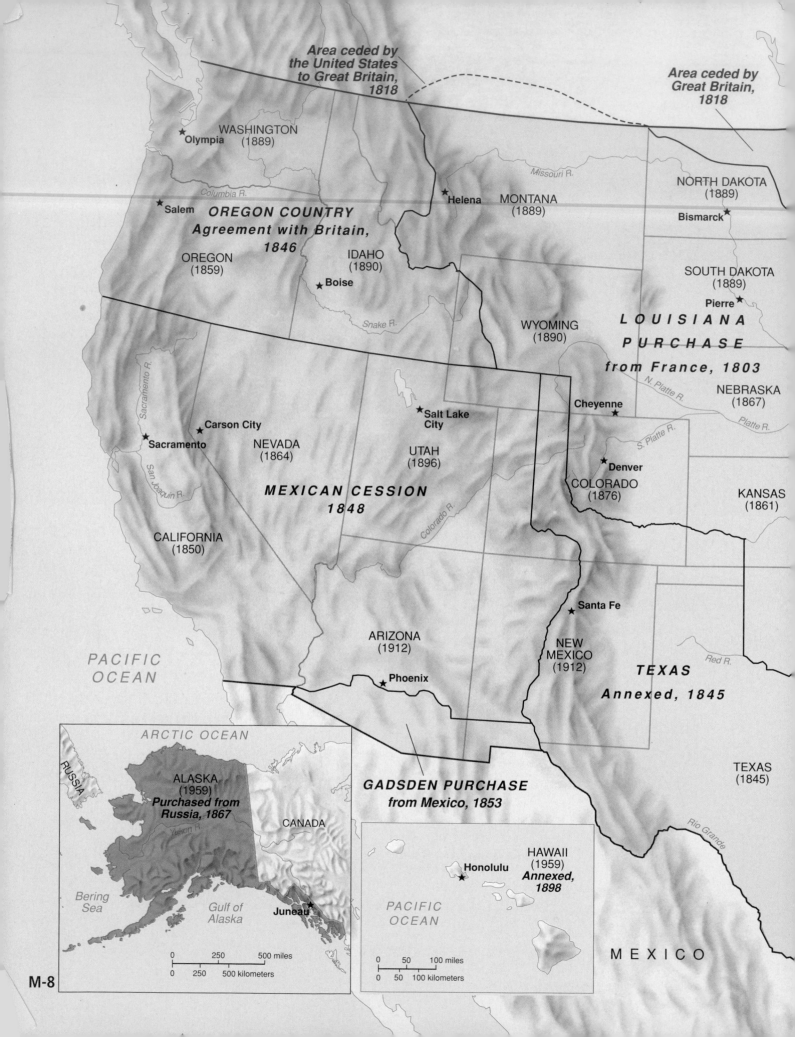

Area ceded by
the United States
to Great Britain,
1818

Area ceded by
Great Britain,
1818

★ Olympia
WASHINGTON
(1889)

Missouri R.

NORTH DAKOTA
(1889)

Columbia R.

★ Salem

OREGON COUNTRY
Agreement with Britain,
1846

★ Helena
MONTANA
(1889)

Bismarck ★

OREGON
(1859)

IDAHO
(1890)

★ Boise

Snake R.

WYOMING
(1890)

LOUISIANA

SOUTH DAKOTA
(1889)

★ Pierre

Sacramento R.

PURCHASE

from France, 1803

N. Platte R.

NEBRASKA
(1867)

Cheyenne
★

S. Platte R.

Platte R.

★ Salt Lake
City

★ Carson City

★ Sacramento

NEVADA
(1864)

UTAH
(1896)

★ Denver

COLORADO
(1876)

KANSAS
(1861)

San Joaquin R.

MEXICAN CESSION
1848

Colorado R.

CALIFORNIA
(1850)

PACIFIC
OCEAN

ARIZONA
(1912)

★ Santa Fe

NEW
MEXICO
(1912)

TEXAS
Annexed, 1845

Red R.

★ Phoenix

GADSDEN PURCHASE
from Mexico, 1853

TEXAS
(1845)

Rio Grande

MEXICO

ARCTIC OCEAN

RUSSIA

ALASKA
(1959)
Purchased from
Russia, 1867

CANADA

Yukon R.

*Bering
Sea*

*Gulf of
Alaska*

Juneau ★

HAWAII
(1959)
Annexed,
1898

★ Honolulu

PACIFIC
OCEAN

| 0 | 250 | 500 miles |
| 0 | 250 | 500 kilometers |

| 0 | 50 | 100 miles |
| 0 | 50 | 100 kilometers |

M-8

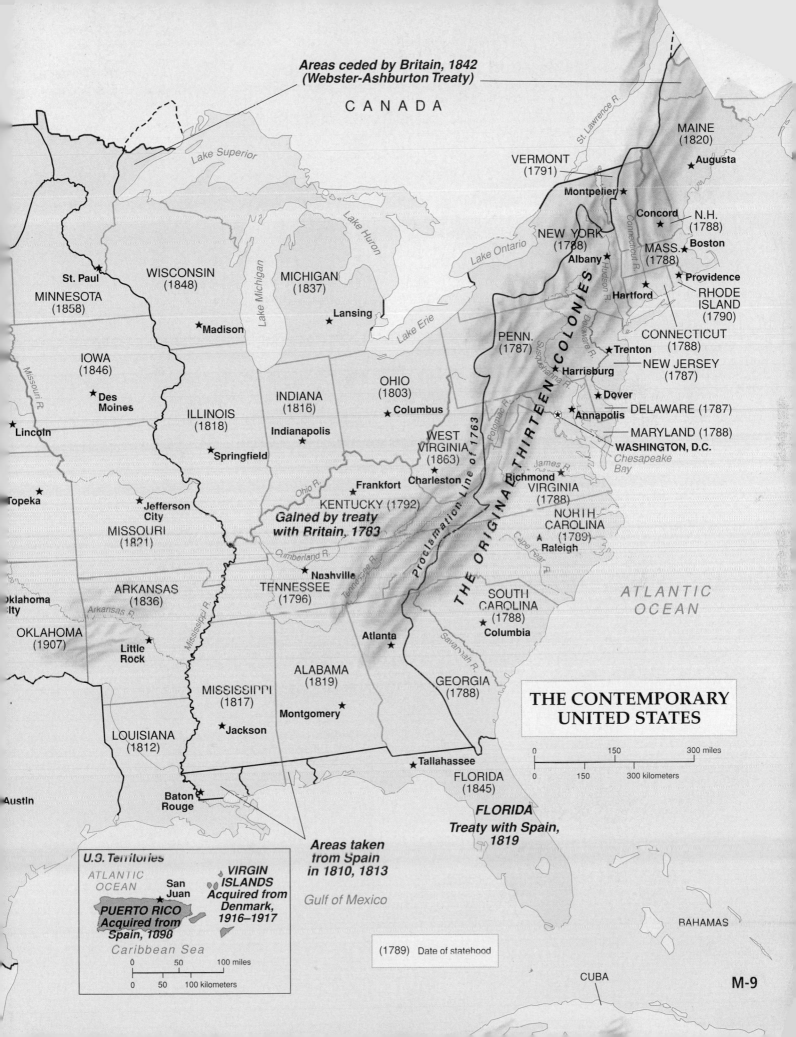

Areas ceded by Britain, 1842
(Webster-Ashburton Treaty)

C A N A D A

Lake Superior

Lake Huron

Lake Michigan

Lake Ontario

Lake Erie

MAINE
(1820)
★ Augusta

VERMONT
(1791)
★ Montpelier

NEW YORK
(1788)
★ Albany

Concord ★ **N.H.**
(1788)

MASS.
(1788)
★ Boston

★ Providence
Hartford **RHODE**
ISLAND
(1790)

CONNECTICUT
(1788)

★ St. Paul

MINNESOTA
(1858)

WISCONSIN
(1848)

MICHIGAN
(1837)
★ Lansing

★ Madison

PENN.
(1787)
★ Harrisburg

★ Trenton
NEW JERSEY
(1787)

★ Dover

IOWA
(1846)

★ Des
Moines

INDIANA
(1816)

OHIO
(1803)
★ Columbus

DELAWARE (1787)

Annapolis
MARYLAND (1788)
WASHINGTON, D.C.
Chesapeake
Bay

★ Lincoln

ILLINOIS
(1818)
★ Springfield

★ Indianapolis

WEST
VIRGINIA
(1863)

★ Richmond
VIRGINIA
(1788)

THE ORIGINAL THIRTEEN COLONIES

★ Topeka

MISSOURI
(1821)
★ Jefferson
City

★ Frankfort
Charleston
KENTUCKY (1792)
Gained by treaty
with Britain, 1783

Proclamation Line of 1763

NORTH
CAROLINA
(1789)
▲ Raleigh

★ Nashville
TENNESSEE
(1796)

Oklahoma
City

OKLAHOMA
(1907)

ARKANSAS
(1836)

★ Little
Rock

SOUTH
CAROLINA
(1788)
★ Columbia

ATLANTIC
OCEAN

★ Atlanta

ALABAMA
(1819)
★ Montgomery

GEORGIA
(1788)

THE CONTEMPORARY
UNITED STATES

MISSISSIPPI
(1817)
★ Jackson

LOUISIANA
(1812)

| 0 | 150 | 300 miles |
| 0 | 150 | 300 kilometers |

★ Baton
Rouge

★ Tallahassee

FLORIDA
(1845)

Austin

Areas taken
from Spain
in 1810, 1813

Gulf of Mexico

FLORIDA
Treaty with Spain,
1819

U.S. Territories

ATLANTIC
OCEAN

San
Juan

PUERTO RICO
Acquired from
Spain, 1898

VIRGIN
ISLANDS
Acquired from
Denmark,
1916–1917

Caribbean Sea

| 0 | 50 | 100 miles |
| 0 | 50 | 100 kilometers |

(1789)   Date of statehood

CUBA

BAHAMAS

M-9

Missouri R.
Mississippi R.
Arkansas R.
Ohio R.
Cumberland R.
Tennessee R.
Savannah R.
Cape Fear R.
James R.
Potomac R.
Susquehanna R.
Delaware R.
Hudson R.
Connecticut R.
St. Lawrence R.

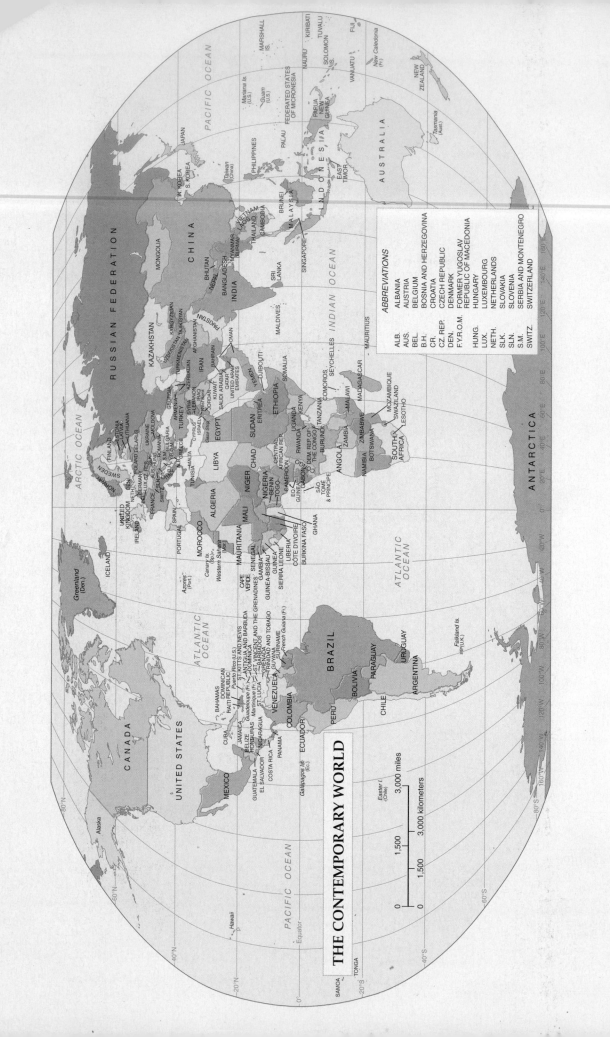

THE CONTEMPORARY WORLD